# The Cambridge Handbook of Bilingual Processing

How does a human acquire, comprehend, produce, and control multiple languages with just the power of one mind? What are the cognitive consequences of being a bilingual? These are just a few of the intriguing questions at the core of studying bilingualism from psycholinguistic and neurocognitive perspectives. Bringing together some of the world's leading experts in bilingualism, cognitive psychology, and language acquisition, *The Cambridge Handbook of Bilingual Processing* explores these questions by presenting a clear overview of current theories and findings in bilingual processing. This comprehensive handbook is organized around overarching thematic areas including theories and methodologies, acquisition and development, comprehension and representation, production, control, and the cognitive consequences of bilingualism. The handbook serves as an informative overview for researchers interested in cognitive bilingualism and the logic of theoretical and experimental approaches to language science. It also functions as an instrumental source of readings for anyone interested in bilingual processing.

JOHN W. SCHWIETER is an associate professor of Spanish and linguistics and Faculty of Arts Teaching Scholar at Wilfrid Laurier University in Waterloo, Ontario, Canada, where he is also the Director of the Psycholinguistics and Language Acquisition Laboratory. He is also a Visiting Professor of Applied Linguistics in the Centre for Applied Research and Outreach in Language Education at the University of Greenwich in London, England.

CAMBRIDGE HANDBOOKS IN LANGUAGE AND LINGUISTICS

Genuinely broad in scope, each handbook in this series provides a complete state-of-the-field overview of a major sub-discipline within language study and research. Grouped into broad thematic areas, the chapters in each volume encompass the most important issues and topics within each subject, offering a coherent picture of the latest theories and findings. Together, the volumes will build into an integrated overview of the discipline in its entirety.

## Published titles

*The Cambridge Handbook of Phonology*, edited by Paul de Lacy
*The Cambridge Handbook of Linguistic Code-switching*, edited by Barbara E. Bullock and Almeida Jacqueline Toribio
*The Cambridge Handbook of Child Language*, edited by Edith L. Bavin
*The Cambridge Handbook of Endangered Languages*, edited by Peter K. Austin and Julia Sallabank
*The Cambridge Handbook of Sociolinguistics*, edited by Rajend Mesthrie
*The Cambridge Handbook of Pragmatics*, edited by Keith Allan and Kasia M. Jaszczolt
*The Cambridge Handbook of Language Policy*, edited by Bernard Spolsky
*The Cambridge Handbook of Second Language Acquisition*, edited by Julia Herschensohn and Martha Young-Scholten
*The Cambridge Handbook of Biolinguistics*, edited by Cedric Boeckx and Kleanthes K. Grohmann
*The Cambridge Handbook of Generative Syntax*, edited by Marcel den Dikken
*The Cambridge Handbook of Communication Disorders*, edited by Louise Cummings
*The Cambridge Handbook of Stylistics*, edited by Stockwell and Whiteley
*The Cambridge Handbook of Linguistic Anthropology*, edited by Enfield, Kockelman and Sidnell
*The Cambridge Handbook of English Corpus Linguistics*, edited by Douglas Biber and Randi Reppen
*The Cambridge Handbook of Bilingual Processing*, edited by John W. Schwieter

## Further titles planned for the series

*The Cambridge Handbook of Morphology*, edited by Hippisley and Stump
*The Cambridge Handbook of Historical Syntax*, edited by Ledgeway and Roberts
*The Cambridge Handbook of Formal Semantics*, edited by Maria Aloni and Paul Dekker
*The Cambridge Handbook of English Historical Linguistics*, edited by Merja Kytö and Päivi Pahta
*The Cambridge Handbook of Linguistic Multicompetence*, edited by Li Wei and Vivian Cook
*The Cambridge Handbook of Child Language, Second Edition*, edited by Edith L. Bavin and Letitia Naigles
*The Cambridge Handbook of Areal Linguistics*, edited by Raymond Hickey
*The Cambridge Handbook of Linguistic Typology*, edited by Alexandra Aikhenvald and R. M. W. Dixon

# The Cambridge Handbook of Bilingual Processing

Edited by
**John W. Schwieter**

# CAMBRIDGE
UNIVERSITY PRESS

University Printing House, Cambridge CB2 8BS, United Kingdom

Cambridge University Press is part of the University of Cambridge.

It furthers the University's mission by disseminating knowledge in the pursuit of education, learning and research at the highest international levels of excellence.

www.cambridge.org
Information on this title: www.cambridge.org/9781107060586

© Cambridge University Press 2015

This publication is in copyright. Subject to statutory exception and to the provisions of relevant collective licensing agreements, no reproduction of any part may take place without the written permission of Cambridge University Press.

First published 2015

Printed in the United Kingdom by TJ International Ltd. Padstow Cornwall

*A catalogue record for this publication is available from the British Library*

*Library of Congress Cataloguing in Publication data*
The Cambridge handbook of bilingual processing / edited by John W. Schwieter.
    pages   cm. – (Cambridge handbooks in language and linguistics)
Includes bibliographical references and index.
ISBN 978-1-107-06058-6 (hardback)
1. Bilingualism – Handbooks, manuals, etc.  2. Education,
Bilingual – Handbooks, manuals, etc.  3. Language acquisition – Handbooks, manuals, etc.  4. Second language acquisition – Research.  5. Language and languages – Research.  I. Schwieter, John W., 1979– editor.
P115.2.C36   2015
404'.2083–dc23
2014048696

ISBN 978-1-107-06058-6 Hardback

Cambridge University Press has no responsibility for the persistence or accuracy of URLs for external or third-party internet websites referred to in this publication, and does not guarantee that any content on such websites is, or will remain, accurate or appropriate.

*In memory of our bilingual friend Simon Ratsamy, who was taken
far too early from
his friends and family. May he rest peacefully and always be
celebrated by those who loved him.*

# Contents

| | |
|---|---|
| List of figures | page x |
| List of tables | xii |
| Contributors | xiii |
| Acknowledgments | xvi |

**Part I**  Introduction  1
 1  Bilingual processing: a dynamic and rapidly changing field   *John W. Schwieter and Natasha Tokowicz*   3

**Part II**  Theories and methodologies  27
 2  Six decades of research on lexical presentation and processing in bilinguals   *Nan Jiang*   29
 3  Computational modeling of bilingual language acquisition and processing: conceptual and methodological considerations   *Ping Li and Xiaowei Zhao*   85
 4  Methods for studying adult bilingualism   *Michael Spivey and Cynthia Cardon*   108
 5  Methods for studying infant bilingualism   *Krista Byers-Heinlein*   133

**Part III**  Acquisition and development  155
 6  Becoming bilingual: are there different learning pathways?   *Núria Sebastián-Gallés*   157
 7  Phonology and morphology in lexical processing   *Kira Gor*   173
 8  Processing perspectives on instructed second language acquisition   *Bill VanPatten*   200
 9  Learning second language vocabulary: insights from laboratory studies   *Natasha Tokowicz and Tamar Degani*   216
 10  Second language constructions: usage-based acquisition and transfer   *Nick Ellis, Ute Römer, and Matthew O'Donnell*   234

11  Variability in bilingual processing: a dynamic
    approach   *Wander Lowie and Kees de Bot*                               255

**Part IV**   **Comprehension and representation**                         273
12  Conceptual representation in bilinguals: the role of language
    specificity and conceptual change   *Panos Athanasopoulos*             275
13  Emotion word processing within and between
    languages   *Jeanette Altarriba and Dana Basnight-Brown*                293
14  Orthographic processing in bilinguals   *Walter J. B. van Heuven
    and Emily L. Coderre*                                                   308
15  Bilingual lexical access during written sentence
    comprehension   *Ana Schwartz*                                         327
16  Cross-language interactions during bilingual sentence
    processing   *Paola Dussias, Amelia J. Dietrich, and Álvaro Villegas*  349

**Part V**   **Production**                                                367
17  Individual differences in second language speech
    production   *Judit Kormos*                                             369
18  Parallel language activation in bilinguals' word production
    and its modulating factors: a review and computer
    simulations   *Annette M. B. de Groot and Peter A. Starreveld*         389
19  Cross-language asymmetries in code-switching patterns:
    implications for bilingual language production   *Carol
    Myers-Scotton and Janice Jake*                                         416
20  Intra-sentential code-switching: cognitive and neural
    approaches   *Janet G. van Hell, Kaitlyn A. Litcofsky,
    and Caitlin Y. Ting*                                                   459

**Part VI**   **Control**                                                  483
21  Selection and control in bilingual comprehension and
    production   *Judith F. Kroll, Jason W. Gullifer, Rhonda McClain,
    Eleonora Rossi, and María Cruz Martín*                                 485
22  On the mechanism and scope of language control in bilingual
    speech production   *Cristina Baus, Francesca Branzi, and
    Albert Costa*                                                          508
23  Behavioral measures of language control: Production and
    comprehension   *Julia Festman and John W. Schwieter*                  527
24  Neural perspectives of language control   *Arturo Hernandez*           548

**Part VII**   **Consequences of bilingualism**                            569
25  Cognitive consequences of bilingualism: executive control and
    cognitive reserve   *Ellen Bialystok and Fergus Craik*                 571
26  Does bilingual exercise enhance cognitive fitness in traditional
    non-linguistic executive processing tasks?   *Matthew O. Hilchey,
    Jean Saint-Aubin, and Raymond M. Klein*                                586

27  Neural consequences of bilingualism for cortical and subcortical
    function   *Jennifer Krizman and Viorica Marian*            614
28  How bilingualism shapes the mental lexicon   *Gary Libben and
    Mira Goral*                                                 631
29  Losing a first language to a second language   *Eve Higby and
    Loraine Obler*                                              645
30  Moving beyond two languages: The effects of multilingualism on
    language processing and language learning   *Jared Linck, Erica
    Michael, Ewa Golonka, Alina Twist, and John W. Schwieter*   665

*References*                                                    695
*Index*                                                         829

# Figures

2.1 Lexical representation and processing in bilinguals: models and hypotheses    82
3.1 An illustration of (a) localist representation and (b) distributed representation    90
3.2 Three basic connectionist network architectures    92
3.3 A sketch of the DevLex-II Model (adapted from Zhao & Li, 2010)    102
3.4 Bilingual semantic representations as a function of age of acquisition    104
5.1 Growth in yearly citations from 1993–2012 of papers related to early life (infant, infancy, toddler, toddlerhood) and bilingualism (bilingual, bilingualism, dual language)    134
5.2 An illustration of different measures of vocabulary size in a hypothetical French–English bilingual infant    143
6.1 Illustration of the lack of clear separations between words in the speech signal    158
6.2 Four schematic developmental trajectories of phoneme perception in four groups of infants and contrasts    164
10.1 BNC verb type distribution for 'V across n' (left) and 'V of n' (right)    239
10.2 A semantic network for 'V across n' from the BNC using WordNet as a base. Node size is proportional to degree    240
10.3 Experiment 1 log10 verb generation frequency against log10 verb frequency in that VAC in the BNC for 'V of n'    242
10.4 L1 English and German, Spanish and Czech L2 English log10 verb generation frequency against log10 verb frequency in that VAC in the BNC for VACs 'V about n'    245
10.5 L1 English and German, Spanish and Czech L2 English log10 verb generation frequency against log10 verb frequency in that VAC in the BNC for VACs 'V between n'    246

| | | |
|---|---|---|
| 10.6 | L1 English and German, Spanish and Czech L2 English log10 verb generation frequency against log10 verb frequency in that VAC in the BNC for VACs 'V against n' | 247 |
| 10.7 | Correlations between learner and native speaker responses | 250 |
| 15.1 | The Bilingual Interactive Activation (BIA) Model (adapted from Dijkstra & van Heuven, 1998) | 331 |
| 15.2 | The Bilingual Interactive Activation Model revised (BIA+) (adapted from Dijkstra & van Heuven, 2002) | 332 |
| 18.1 | A model of picture naming in bilinguals (based on Costa et al., 2000) | 399 |
| 18.2 | The basic layout of the networks used in our simulations of the activation of a phonological node of a cognate (a) and a non-cognate (b) | 408 |
| 18.3 | A model of picture naming in bilinguals | 409 |
| 18.4 | Computer simulation results | 411 |
| 19.1 | Production model and the 4-M model of morpheme classification | 420 |
| 25.1 | Mean RT and standard error for facilitation and cost in the Stroop task | 574 |
| 26.1 | Group differences in inhibitory control and executive processing in children | 598 |
| 26.2 | Group differences in inhibitory control and executive processing in young adults | 604 |
| 26.3 | Discrepancy in interference effects as a function practice | 606 |
| 26.4 | Group differences in inhibitory control and executive processing in older adults | 607 |
| 26.5 | Discrepancy in interference effects as a function of task complexity | 609 |
| 27.1 | Schematic of the nuclei of the auditory and executive systems | 617 |
| 27.2 | Schematic of the nuclei of the auditory and executive systems | 622 |
| 27.3 | Bilinguals demonstrate unique relationships between auditory and executive systems | 629 |

# Tables

| | | |
|---|---|---|
| 5.1 | Best practice for characterizing language exposure in bilingual infants | 136 |
| 10.1 | Multiple regression summary statistics for the analyses of 131 L1 English respondents and 131 German, Spanish, and Czech L2 English respondents | 245 |
| 10.2 | 'V in n,' top-20 verbs in native speaker and learner responses | 251 |
| 12.1 | Summary of the degree to which each of the four main models discussed can accommodate language specificity, developmental aspects of bilingualism, and phenomena of conceptual change | 288 |
| 19.1 | Distribution of English nouns in Spanish-framed CPs (Milian corpus, 1995) | 439 |
| 19.2 | Italian-Swiss German asymmetry: mixed NPs vs. NP EL Islands (Perziosa-Di Quinzio, 1992, corpus) | 441 |
| 23.1 | Mean reaction times, standard deviations, accuracy rates, and costs in the language switching task, by language dominance and by group | 541 |
| 26.1 | Summary of the recent literature on bilingualism and non-linguistic executive function | 595 |
| 30.1 | Summary of implications for L3 course design and instruction | 692 |

# Contributors

Jeanette Altarriba, Department of Psychology, University at Albany, State University of New York
Panos Athanasopoulos, Department of Linguistics and English Language, Lancaster University
Dana Basnight-Brown, Department of Psychology, United States International University, East Africa
Cristina Baus, Center of Brain and Cognition, Universitat Pompeu Fabra/Université Aix-Marseille
Ellen Bialystok, Department of Psychology, York University/Rotman Research Institute at Baycrest
Francesca Branzi, Center of Brain and Cognition, Universitat Pompeu Fabra
Krista Byers-Heinlein, Department of Psychology, Concordia University
Cynthia Cardon, Department of Psychology, University of California, Merced
Emily L. Coderre, Department of Neurology, Johns Hopkins University School of Medicine
Albert Costa, Center of Brain and Cognition, Universitat Pompeu Fabra/Institució Catalana de Recerca i Estudis Avançats (ICREA)
Fergus Craik, Rotman Research Institute at Baycrest/Department of Psychology, University of Toronto
María Cruz Martín, Department of Psychology, Pennsylvania State University
Kees de Bot, Department of Applied Linguistics, University of Groningen
Annette M. B. de Groot, Department of Psychology, University of Amsterdam
Tamar Degani, Institute of Information Processing and Decision Making, University of Haifa
Amelia J. Dietrich, Department of Spanish, Italian, and Portuguese, Pennsylvania State University

Paola Dussias, Department of Spanish, Italian, and Portuguese, Pennsylvania State University

Nick Ellis, Department of Psychology, University of Michigan

Julia Festman, Research Group on Diversity and Inclusion, University of Potsdam

Ewa Golonka, Center for Advanced Study of Language, University of Maryland

Kira Gor, School of Languages, Literatures, and Cultures, University of Maryland

Mira Goral, Department of Speech–Language–Hearing Sciences, Lehman College, The City University of New York, New York

Jason W. Gullifer, Department of Psychology, Pennsylvania State University

Arturo Hernandez, Department of Psychology, University of Houston

Eve Higby, Program in Speech–Language–Hearing Sciences, University of New York Graduate Center, New York

Matthew O. Hilchey, Department of Psychology and Neuroscience, Dalhousie University

Janice Jake, Department of English, Midlands Technical College

Nan Jiang, School of Languages, Literatures, and Cultures, University of Maryland

Raymond M. Klein, Department of Psychology and Neuroscience, Dalhousie University

Judit Kormos, Department of Linguistics and English Language, Lancaster University

Jennifer Krizman, Department of Communication Sciences and Disorders, Northwestern University

Judith F. Kroll, Department of Psychology, Pennsylvania State University

Ping Li, Department of Psychology, Pennsylvania State University

Gary Libben, Office of the Vice-President: Research, Brock University

Jared Linck, Center for Advanced Study of Language, University of Maryland

Kaitlyn A. Litcofsky, Department of Psychology, Pennsylvania State University

Wander Lowie, Department of Applied Linguistics, University of Groningen

Rhonda McClain, Department of Psychology, Pennsylvania State University

Viorica Marian, Department of Communication Sciences and Disorders, Northwestern University

Erica Michael, Center for Advanced Study of Language, University of Maryland

Carol Myers-Scotton, Department of Linguistics and Languages, Michigan State University

Loraine Obler, Program in Speech-Language-Hearing Sciences, The City University of New York Graduate Center, New York

Matthew O'Donnell, Institute for Social Research/Communication Neuroscience Laboratory, University of Michigan

Ute Römer, Department of Applied Linguistics and ESL, Georgia State University

Eleonora Rossi, Department of Psychology, Pennsylvania State University

Jean Saint-Aubin, School of Psychology, Université de Moncton

Ana Schwartz, Department of Psychology, University of Texas at El Paso

John W. Schwieter, Psycholinguistics and Language Acquisition Laboratory, Department of Languages and Literatures, Wilfrid Laurier University/Centre for Applied Research and Outreach in Language Education, University of Greenwich

Núria Sebastián-Gallés, Center for Brain and Cognition and Department of Technology, Universitat Pompeu Fabra

Michael Spivey, Department of Cognitive and Information Sciences, University of California, Merced

Peter A. Starreveld, Department of Psychology, University of Amsterdam.

Caitlin Y. Ting, Department of Psychology, Pennsylvania State University

Natasha Tokowicz, Department of Psychology/Department of Linguistics/Learning Research and Development Center, University of Pittsburgh

Alina Twist, Center for Advanced Study of Language, University of Maryland

Janet G. van Hell, Department of Psychology, Pennsylvania State University

Walter J. B. van Heuven, School of Psychology, University of Nottingham

Bill VanPatten, Department of Romance and Classical Studies, Michigan State University

Álvaro Villegas, Department of Modern Languages and Literatures, University of Central Florida

Xiaowei Zhao, Department of Psychology, Emmanuel College

# Acknowledgments

I am lucky to have been supported by many people throughout the development of *The Cambridge Handbook of Bilingual Processing*. On a personal level, I am very fortunate to have the continuous support of Prof. J. Luis Jaimes-Domíguez and my wonderful parents, Herb and Melinda Schwieter. Professionally speaking, I am extremely thankful to several individuals at Cambridge University Press: to Helen Barton, Commissioning Editor, Linguistics, for having suggested this timely handbook idea and for her efficient assistance and support throughout this project; to Joanna Breeze, Senior Production Editor, Academic Books, for her professional and experienced guidance; to Sarah Green, Editor, Humanities and Social Sciences, for her promptness and resourcefulness; and to Martin Barr, copy-editor, for his meticulous and thorough copy-editing.

I am also very grateful to my two editorial assistants for their excellent work during the preparation of the manuscript: Dr. Aline Ferreira, associate director of the Psycholinguistics and Language Acquisition Research Laboratory and postdoctoral fellow in psychology at Wilfrid Laurier University and sessional instructor of Portuguese at the University of Toronto; and Gabrielle Klassen, my former undergraduate research assistant at Wilfrid Laurier University and a current Ph.D. candidate of Hispanic linguistics at the University of Toronto. I gratefully acknowledge that financial support to hire these two assistants was received from a grant partly funded by Wilfrid Laurier University operating funds and partly by a Social Sciences and Humanities Research Council of Canada Institutional Grant.

Needless to say, *The Cambridge Handbook of Bilingual Processing* would not exist had it not been for the dedication and hard work of individuals who contributed to its contents. I recall that one anonymous peer reviewer of this handbook proposal stated: "It would be difficult to put together a better line-up of authors. The vast majority of them are truly well known leaders in the field and I'm actually surprised that Schwieter was able to get them all on board." This statement still puts a smile on my face because

I too was pleasantly surprised and I continue to feel humbled that they graciously accepted my invitation to contribute to this project. They have helped me to build a comprehensive handbook which showcases prominent theories and findings regarding psycholinguistic and neurocognitive approaches to bilingualism and language acquisition which we feel is a much-needed addition to the field of Bilingual Processing.

Finally, I am extremely grateful to the scholars – both internal and external to this project – who accepted my invitation to serve as anonymous peer-reviewers of the chapters. It is without a doubt that their knowledge and expertise have strengthened the content of this handbook and its implications for future research. As such, I would like to extend my sincere thanks to the following researchers:

Jeanette Altarriba, University at Albany, State University of New York
Panos Athanasopoulos, Lancaster University
María Teresa Bajo, University of Granada
Joe Barcroft, Washington University in St. Louis
Cristina Baus, Universitat Pompeu Fabra
Alessandro Benati, University of Greenwich
Susan Bobb, Northwestern University
Agnes Bolonyai, North Carolina State University
Laura Bosch, Universitat de Barcelona
Amanda Brown, Syracuse University
Krista Byers-Heinlein, Concordia University
Emanuel Bylund, Stockholm University
Marco Calabria, Universitat Pompeu Fabra
Emily L. Coderre, Johns Hopkins University
Eva Commissaire, University of Strasbourg
Barbara Conboy, University of Redlands
Roberto de Almeida, Concordia University
Kees de Bot, University of Groningen
Annette M. B. de Groot, University of Amsterdam
Annick De Houwer, Universität Erfurt
Jean-Marc Dewaele, Birkbeck, University of London
Guosheng Ding, Beijing Normal University
Paola Dussias, Pennsylvania State University
Eileen Fancher, Florida State University
Corinne Fischer, St. Michael's Hospital/University of Toronto
Gabrielle Garbin, Universitat Jaume I
Monica Gonzalez-Marquez, Cornell University
Kira Gor, University of Maryland
Mira Goral, The City University of New York
Jonathan Grainger, Aix-Marseille University
Anna Hatzidaki, Universitat Pompeu Fabra
Roberto Heredia, Texas A&M International University

Arturo Hernandez, University of Houston
Eve Higby, The City University of New York Graduate Center
Noriko Hoshino, Kobe City University of Foreign Studies
Ludmila Isurin, Ohio State University
Scott Jarvis, Ohio University
Nan Jiang, University of Maryland
Jungna Kim, The City University of New York Graduate Center
Iring Koch, RWTH Aachen University
Gerrit Jan Kootstra, Radboud University Nijmegen
Raymond M. Klein, Dalhousie University
Judith F. Kroll, Pennsylvania State University
Wido La Heij, Universiteit Leiden
James Lee, University of New South Wales
Gary Libben, Brock University
Jared A. Linck, Center for Advanced Study of Language, University of Maryland
Gillian Lord, University of Florida
Wander Lowie, University of Groningen
Brian MacWhinney, Carnegie Mellon University
Katherine Mathis, Bates College
Silvina Montrul, University of Illinois at Urbana-Champaign
Loraine Obler, The City University of New York Graduate Center
Francisco Palermo, University of Missouri
Andrea Philipp, RWTH Aachen University
David Peeters, Max Planck Institute for Psycholinguistics
Gregory Poarch, York University
Anat Prior, University of Haifa
Mikel Santesteban, University of the Basque Country
Ana Schwartz, University of Texas at El Paso
Núria Sebastián-Gallés, Universitat Pompeu Fabra
Christine Shea, University of Iowa
Antonella Sorace, University of Edinburgh
Peter A. Starreveld, University of Amsterdam
Gretchen Sunderman, Florida State University
Arnaud Szmalec, Université Catholique de Louvain
Natasha Tokowicz, University of Pittsburgh
John Truscott, National Tsing Hua University
Jorge Valdes-Kroff, University of Florida
Janet van Hell, Pennsylvania State University
Walter J. B. van Heuven, University of Nottingham
Jungmee Yoon, The City University of New York Graduate Center

# Part I

# Introduction

# 1

# Bilingual processing
A dynamic and rapidly changing field

John W. Schwieter and Natasha Tokowicz

## 1.1 Introduction

How does a bilingual acquire, comprehend, produce, and control multiple languages in one mind? What are some of the cognitive and neurocognitive consequences of being a bilingual? These are just a few of the intriguing theoretical questions at the core of studying bilingualism from psycholinguistic and neurocognitive perspectives. For decades, researchers have been fascinated by how the human mind processes multiple languages. With intensified research efforts have come insightful inquiries, pioneering theories, and implications for future research. Perhaps an example of one of the earliest and most studied questions related to psycholinguistic perspectives of bilingualism is: whether humans have a separate or shared (whether fully or partially shared) system for the representation and cognitive processing of multiple languages (Kolers, 1963; McCormack, 1977; Weinreich, 1954). Although much progress has been made, this question will continue to be one of many topics of interest in this handbook.

It is clear that we can now argue that Bilingual Processing is an entire field of study on its own, yet there continue to be many unanswered questions and gaps that merit fine-tuning and special attention as in any growing research field. Indeed, there are several up-and-coming and innovative themes currently being debated in the field of Bilingual Processing, many of which will be discussed in this handbook. These issues have appeared and developed at rapid speeds in just the last couple of decades and new venues have been dedicated to them such as in handbooks and course books (de Groot, 2011; Grosjean & Li, 2013; Kroll, 1997; Kroll & de Groot, 2005), journals such as *Bilingualism: Language and Cognition* co-founded by editors Grosjean, Kroll, Meisel, and Muysken (1998), and a new book series Bilingual Processing and Acquisition founded by editor Schwieter (2014).

As the well-known fact that the majority of the world knows more than one language becomes stronger and more evident than ever and studies in Bilingual Processing continue to gain momentum, it is essential to capture the current state of a blossoming research field. *The Cambridge Handbook of Bilingual Processing* seeks to provide a unified home, unlike any other which showcases not only traditional and contemporary thematic areas within Bilingual Processing, but also topics that are reshaping what we know about the bilingual mind and are now considered prominent research areas. For instance, with the increase of research looking at language control processes in the last few decades, a section specifically dedicated to language control is featured in this handbook. While prior titles have explored language control within other thematic areas, it has become apparent that control is a vibrant area of investigation that cuts across multiple areas of bilingual processing (acquisition, comprehension, production, domain general control, etc.) and merits a complete section of its own. In all, this handbook offers a comprehensive overview of the key areas of study related to Bilingual Processing as identified and elaborated on by some of the leading scholarly authorities from around the world in the form of thematic chapters which together have been critiqued by over seventy international peer reviewers.

*The Cambridge Handbook of Bilingual Processing* is a comprehensive title which will take readers on a journey that begins with the origins of the field approximately sixty years ago and then explores current research trends and ends with thought-provoking implications and ideas for future research directions. During this exploration, the reader will be led through six parts that investigate areas including: theories and methodologies; acquisition and development; comprehension and representation; production; control; and the cognitive and neurocognitive consequences of bilingualism. The part on theories and methodologies introduces the reader to the history and development of the field of bilingual processing (Chapter 2) and also explores topics such as conceptual and methodological perspectives using computational models (Chapter 3), along with dialogues on the methods of studying Bilingual Processing among both adult (Chapter 4) and infant bilinguals (Chapter 5). The part on acquisition and development presents topics such as: whether there are different learning pathways in acquiring two languages from infancy (Chapter 6); phonology and morphology in lexical processing (Chapter 7); processing perspectives of second language (L2) instruction (Chapter 8); laboratory-based studies of L2 vocabulary learning (Chapter 9); transfer and usage-based theories of L2 acquisition (Chapter 10); and learner and language developmental variation from a dynamic approach (Chapter 11).

The part on comprehension explores topics such as language specificity, transfer, and conceptual change (Chapter 12); processing of emotion words (Chapter 13); processing implications of orthographic similarities between languages (Chapter 14); lexical access in sentence comprehension

(Chapter 15); and the role of the first language (L1) in the syntactic processing of the L2 and vice versa (Chapter 16). The part on production presents a dialogue on the individual characteristics that may cause variation in language production processes (Chapter 17); interpretations of parallel language activation and word production using computer simulations (Chapter 18); implications of naturally occurring code-switching on bilingual production models (Chapter 19); and cognitive and neurocognitive perspectives on intra-sentential code-switching (Chapter 20). The part on control is dedicated to a rather new area of inquiry in Bilingual Processing. In this part, the reader will find a set of chapters exploiting issues related to the cognitive control of two languages, including: language selection, activation, and control (Chapter 21); the mechanisms and scope of language control (Chapter 22); behavioral measures and other methodological issues in language control (Chapter 23); and neural perspectives of language control (Chapter 24).

The part on the consequences of bilingualism explores in depth the notion that bilingualism may incur cognitive benefits. In this handbook, we will refer to this as the bilingual advantage debate and the first three chapters of this part discuss topics such as cognitive reserve and executive control (Chapter 25); the potential explanatory power from bilingual social psychology perspectives (Chapter 26); and neural perspectives of brain plasticity (Chapter 27). The subsequent chapters review the effects of bilingualism on the mental lexicon (Chapter 28); factors influencing native language attrition (Chapter 29); and the effects of knowing more than two languages on language processing and learning (Chapter 30).

We have organized the sections below according to the six parts of the handbook to introduce the chapters and to highlight their importance along with their fit in the field at large.

## 1.2   Theories and methodologies

The section on theories and methodologies begins with a review of the research on bilingual language representation and processing in adults by Jiang that also includes a review of the relevant models that have been proposed over the decades. This review is then expanded upon in a chapter on the use of computational models to study bilingual processing and learning by Li and Zhao. Spivey and Cardon then shift the discussion to theories and methods of research on adult bilingualism, including some of the key issues studied in this area. Byers-Heinlein then does so in the context of infant bilingualism. Taken together, the chapters presented in this section describe the major methods and theories in bilingual processing from infants to adults, and emphasize the need for converging approaches to successfully answer questions about bilingual language learning and processing.

### 1.2.1 The development of bilingual representation and processing

In Chapter 2, Jiang reviews the research in the area of bilingual language representation and processing that has taken place during the past six decades, beginning with the 1950s. He reviews the early work on classifying types of bilingualism and assessing the degree of bilingualism. There is a discussion on issues of bilingual lexical organization and processing, including the key questions of whether bilingual language activation is fundamentally selective or non-selective. There is also a review of research on how bilinguals control access to the two languages. Throughout this chapter, Jiang provides an overview of the variety of methods that have been used to examine the relevant issues.

The chapter also includes an overview of the relevant models that have been proposed to explain the way that words are represented in the two languages, and how these representations are interconnected. The chapter concludes with a useful timeline demonstrating when the various models were introduced, providing the reader with a visual representation of the changes in the field.

### 1.2.2 Conceptual and methodological perspectives using computational models

Li and Zhao present in Chapter 3 an overview of computational models of bilingual language learning and processing. They emphasize the importance of modeling for advancing the field, and note that models force researchers to be explicit about the assumptions they are making. They further propose that computational models in particular may be especially helpful in dealing with complex interactions between multiple factors, which are common in bilingual processing and learning. Their review focuses on models from the connectionist (i.e., Parallel Distributed Processing) tradition, which emphasizes emergentism and dynamism as key features of the language system.

Li and Zhao describe some of the major distinctions between the various types of connectionist models, specifically whether the models use localist or distributed representations (e.g., as derived from co-occurrence metrics), and whether the learning mechanism employed is supervised or unsupervised. They review several specific models, including models informed by the interactive activation model of McClelland and Rumelhart (1981) including the Bilingual Interactive Activation (BIA) and BIA+ models, the Bilingual Single Network Model, and the Bilingual Simple Recurrent Network Model. Li and Zhao also include a useful overview of self-organizing maps models, which are a type of unsupervised model that uses topographic maps to organize input representations. This up-to-date review provides some recent models that make important and unique contributions to the literature, such as a model of recovery from bilingual aphasia (Kiranet et al., 2013) and a model that tests entrenchment as an alternative to the critical period hypothesis (Monner et al., 2013). The chapter concludes with a suggestion (see also Addyman and French, 2012) that user-friendly interfaces be offered to non-modelers to further advance the field.

### 1.2.3 Methodological considerations for adult bilinguals

Chapter 4 by Spivey and Cardon presents an overview of methods for the study of adult bilinguals. They emphasize the importance of generalizability to naturalistic contexts, ease of use in the field, and sampling richness. They describe a variety of methods in detail. In particular, they begin with methods that measure the end product of processing (e.g., an offline grammaticality judgment task), followed by methods that involve reaction time measurements (e.g., semantic priming). They also review the use of neuroimaging methods such as ERP and fMRI and discuss some of the advantages and pitfalls of using these methods. They conclude with a discussion of methods that involve many repeated measurements (e.g., eye tracking).

Spivey and Cardon emphasize the usefulness of these dense-sampling methods, noting that they allow for the examination of processing as it unfolds over a larger timescale than the single-trial time frame that is typically studied. As an example, they describe the use of time-series analysis for an unscripted conversation between individuals. Other similar methods use mouse tracking and eye tracking to gain insight into these processes. Spivey and Cardon advocate for the use of converging methods to provide a better-informed view of bilingual language processing and discuss the bilingual advantage as a particular area that has benefited from research from converging methodologies.

### 1.2.4 Methodological approaches for infant bilinguals

Chapter 5 by Byers-Heinlein presents an overview of the issues involved in the study of bilingual infant processing. The discussion includes a variety of factors involved in the definition of an infant as "bilingual," the role of length, timing, constancy, and context of exposure to two languages, and issues involved in stimulus selection for studies with bilingual infants. Furthermore, Byers-Heinlein presents an overview of the key methods used to study bilingual infants, including high-amplitude sucking, visual habituation, and preference paradigms. Several preference paradigms are described, including the anticipatory eye movement procedure, the switch procedure, and the intermodal preferential looking procedure.

This chapter also includes a review of the two brain-based methods that are used to study bilingual infants: ERPs and functional near infrared spectroscopy. These methods are noted to be useful in the study of bilingual infants because they do not necessarily require a response from the infant and can demonstrate whether bilingual and monolingual infants process information using similar brain structures and on a similar timescale. The chapter concludes with suggestions regarding the selection of stimuli for studies with infant bilinguals.

## 1.3 Acquisition and development

Part III on acquisition and development begins with a discussion on the learning pathways taken by bilingual and monolingual children by Sebastián-Gallés (Chapter 6). She emphasizes the need for bilingual children to separate their multiple language systems, and the possible cognitive benefits this may confer. Gor continues in this vein in Chapter 7 and discusses the interaction between the various levels of the language system and how phonological and lexical processing interact. This emphasis on the various levels of language is continued by VanPatten (Chapter 8) who argues that it is critical for pedagogical interventions to focus on processing so that the creation of form-meaning mappings through successful comprehension is achieved. Tokowicz and Degani (Chapter 9) proceed with a discussion of interventions, but focus instead on laboratory studies of adult second language vocabulary learning. They discuss the benefits of studying naïve learners in a controlled lab setting in addition to studying ongoing learning in more naturalistic contexts. Ellis, Römer, and O'Donnell (Chapter 10) use converging methodologies to examine learning of constructions in the L2 and demonstrate that the use of verb–argument constructions (VACs) is influenced not only by the usage of words in language but also by transfer from the learner's L1. Lowie and de Bot (Chapter 11) conclude Part III by discussing a newer framework for understanding the development of an L2, Dynamic System Theory (DST), drawing connections to emergentist views of language. This approach emphasizes the interactions of various dynamic subsystems rather than the fixed representations in other contemporary theories.

### 1.3.1 Learning pathways

In Chapter 6, Sebastián-Gallés reviews research on whether bilingual and monolingual infants and children follow similar or different learning pathways. The available evidence suggests that, by and large, there are not qualitative differences in pathways taken by bilingual and monolingual children. Instead, although bilingual and monolingual children share basic mechanisms, bilingual children must learn two repertoires of sounds and two language systems, which requires additional computation on their part. This additional computation allows them to separate these multiple systems and avoid interference between them, which bilingual children are able to accomplish without delays or confusion.

Sebastián-Gallés then links this idea to the research on bilingual advantages, and notes that the additional computation required by bilingual children may confer an advantage on them relative to monolingual children in terms of memory and/or inhibitory ability. These advantages may temper the purported disadvantage in terms of vocabulary size that may be due to the way that the number of words known is counted across languages, exposure differences between bilinguals and monolinguals, and socioeconomic differences between groups in previous studies. The chapter ends with a discussion of the importance of the under-studied topic of cross-language similarity because similarity at a variety of levels of language is likely to influence the learning trajectory.

### 1.3.2 Phonology and morphology in lexical processing

Gor begins Chapter 7 with an overview of phonology and morphology in lexical processing. There is a focus on words processed in isolation, asking how phonological learning and vocabulary learning interact. The chapter reviews four important models of native and non-native phonetic perception. In particular, two contrasting theoretical views of how auditory input is converted into lexical representations are presented: the episodic and abstractionist views. Ultimately, Gor argues for a hybrid abstractionist–episodic model that includes abstract representations that are attuned phonetically and remain flexible. She then presents evidence from a training study consistent with this view.

This follows with a review of the varying views on whether phonetic categorization precedes lexical representation or vice versa (the categories first and lexicon first positions) and argues that acquisition of phonemes and words proceeds in parallel and these processes bootstrap each other, leading to data that support both positions depending on a variety of factors. The chapter reviews evidence that orthography helps in the consolidation of phonological representations and in the role of allophonic variation in processing of phonetic contrasts in the L2. Gor concludes with evidence that bilinguals are able to process L2 morphology decompositionally but that the likelihood that this process will succeed depends on several factors including L2 proficiency and the frequency of the L2 word form.

### 1.3.3 Instruction based on processing perspectives

VanPatten in Chapter 8 articulates an argument for pedagogical interventions that take a processing perspective. In particular, he lays out a view of the nature of language as involving aspects of language that are innate and cannot be learned, aspects that are derived, and aspects that must be learned. What follows from this is that the problem for learners is to be able to process linguistic input, which is defined as successfully making form-meaning mappings in real time (i.e., correct sentence comprehension). Such processing instruction involves providing the learner with structured input, which is contrasted with noticing, which is said to affect attention to the input, rather than helping to foster form-meaning mappings per se.

The chapter includes a specific example of a processing-oriented pedagogical intervention called processing instruction. This example demonstrates the important features of this type of intervention, including beginning with referential structured input activities that have correct or incorrect answers, followed by affective structured input activities, which are more open-ended and allow for student creativity. Also, it is noted that learners are not tested on rules, but rather successful comprehension/meaningful processing is emphasized. The chapter concludes with a discussion on why this type of intervention aids the development of relevant mental representations.

### 1.3.4 L2 vocabulary learning: insights from laboratory-based studies

In Chapter 9, Tokowicz and Degani selectively review research on adult L2 vocabulary learning, specifically focusing on the research from laboratory-based studies. They argue that vocabulary is a foundational part of L2 learning and organize their review into three sections. They first focus on instructional/training factors in terms of whether what is manipulated is the input to the learner (e.g., spacing, grouping vs. randomization of materials, and training form vs. meaning aspects of the representations), or the action taken by the learner (the keyword mnemonic, generation of material, and practice testing). Following this, stimulus factors are discussed, including form overlap/familiarity, word concreteness, and translation ambiguity. Then, learner factors are outlined in terms of learner memory capacity and bilingualism vs. monolingualism.

They conclude with a discussion of the relationship between studying naïve vs. ongoing learners on a language and argue that this distinction can be thought of as a continuum rather than a dichotomy. They propose a three-step sequence beginning with a well-controlled lab study with naïve learners, followed by a similar study with actual learners, and finally a study in a less-constrained environment with ongoing learners.

### 1.3.5 Usage-based acquisition and transfer

Ellis, Römer, and O'Donnell present in Chapter 10 an analysis of verb–argument constructions (VACs). The data presented support the idea that these constructions are learned from usage, but also that there is transfer from the L1 in the case of L2 speakers. The chapter details a study that first examined corpus and natural language processing techniques to analyze the structure of use of VACs in English. This was followed by examining responses to sparse VAC frames generated by native speakers. Frequency, contingency, and prototypicality effects were described, emphasizing usage-based effects. Lastly, these constructions were given to speakers of English as an L2, and they showed similar effects across these three factors. The researchers conclude with an argument that L2 constructions demonstrate effects of the usage of both the L1 (transfer) and L2 (usage).

In addition to the presentation of this particular case, this chapter presents an overview of ways in which multiple converging methodologies can be combined. Furthermore, this chapter specifically provides one example of how corpus analyses can be used in concert with behaviorally collected data in a fruitful way to answer questions about L2 learning.

### 1.3.6 Variation in learners and development

In Chapter 11, Lowie and de Bot present an overview of a Dynamic System Theory (DST) approach to L2 development. DST emphasizes the role of variation across and within individuals, and proposes that language development arises from a set of systems interacting over time. This contrasts with a view of language that posits a role for fixed representations or rules. Furthermore, the authors discuss attractor states (states the system tends to travel toward) and repellor states (states the system tends to travel away from). These states are described from a mathematical perspective. This is followed by a discussion of variability studied at embedded time scales, and the utility of examining "pink noise," which is derived from an analysis that transforms the time dimension into a frequency dimension. This leads to a description of the emergentist view of language.

Lowie and de Bot conclude with three possible circumstances for the integration of a DST approach in the field of developmental psychology, namely that DST will not become integrated because the field is not ready for a paradigm shift, that DST will remain as subfield but will not perfuse the field, and that DST will become well integrated because we will reach a tipping point that will enable a shift.

## 1.4 Comprehension and representation

Part IV on comprehension and representation begins with a discussion of the degree to which words in two languages activate similar meanings, and the range of changes that can occur when an individual learns a new language. This raises an interesting set of questions about particular word and concept types by Athanasopoulos (Chapter 12) and is continued by

Altarriba and Basnight-Brown (Chapter 13) with their discussion on the processing of emotion words by bilinguals. They highlight the distinction between emotion words and non-emotion words, as well as the stronger processing of emotion words in L1 than L2. This discussion is followed by a review of research on orthographic processing in two languages by van Heuven and Coderre (Chapter 14). They review work suggesting that bilinguals whose languages do not share a script may be able to use language membership information as a cue in language processing. This issue is also raised by Schwartz (Chapter 15), who follows with a discussion on bilingual sentence processing and points to the importance of context for processing, highlighting models that incorporate context. Finally, Dussias, Dietrich, and Villegas (Chapter 16) discuss the role of several factors in bilingual sentence processing that are consistent with transfer both from L1 to L2 and from L2 to L1, and with the idea that the native language system is dynamic and open to change.

### 1.4.1 Language specificity, transfer, and conceptual change

In Chapter 12, Athanasopoulos presents an overview of research that examines the extent to which words in a bilingual's two languages access a common meaning. The chapter begins with a definition of concepts and then presents relevant research organized around several possible types of conceptual representation that were outlined by Pavlenko (1999) and in Jarvis and Pavlenko (2008). Specifically, these are: coexistence of two conceptual domains, L1 conceptual transfer, "internalization" of a new concept, a shift from L1 to L2 category boundaries, convergence of language-specific concepts, restructuring, and attrition of previously existing categories.

This chapter also includes a review of some of the dominant models of bilingual memory representation and describes how these cross-linguistic differences in meaning could be captured in these models. The chapter concludes with a description of the complex nature of bilingual conceptual representations and the challenges this poses for models.

### 1.4.2 Emotion words

Chapter 13 by Altarriba and Basnight-Brown presents an overview of research on emotion word processing in bilinguals. They begin with a definition of emotion words and specifically contrast these with emotionally laden words and other abstract words. They then present an overview of the factors that influence/interact with the processing of these words, including the context of learning, the age of acquisition, the word's valence, and L2 proficiency. Altarriba and Basnight-Brown then review evidence demonstrating that emotion words are processed differently than non-emotion words in terms of the timing of processing, and in terms of the brain and other physiological responses they elicit (e.g., as measured by skin conductance).

The chapter concludes with information about the application of research on emotion word processing to various domains. In particular, they discuss research on the appropriateness of marketing brands in multiple languages, given that the emotions elicited by words in the two languages differ. Similarly, Altarriba and Basnight-Brown review evidence that bilinguals make more emotionally influenced decisions when framed in L1, likely because of a closer emotional connection in that language. They also discuss the possibility that language choice can be useful in various ways in clinical settings, for example by using L2 to distance the person from emotional situations or by using L2 to bond with the individual at a deeper level.

### 1.4.3 Orthographic similarities between languages

In Chapter 14, van Heuven and Coderre present an overview of research on orthographic processing in bilinguals. They begin with a high-level overview of script differences and a discussion on the various orthographic effects that have been observed in monolingual contexts in a variety of languages and scripts. This research is drawn from studies employing both behavioral and cognitive neuroscientific approaches. They then describe relevant cross-language findings from bilingual populations in terms of processing, representation, and control. They conclude that most of the processing effects and networks of brain areas employed during processing are similar across languages and scripts, with some variations that may reflect the particular processing requirements of a given language (e.g., lateralization differences in reading Chinese and English).

The authors also present evidence that bilinguals whose languages do not share a script may be able to exploit these cues to speed processing, but not to completely eliminate cross-language interference. The chapter concludes with a discussion of bilingual word processing models. Van Heuven and Coderre note that many of the existing and most commonly cited models cannot easily be adapted to describe cross-script differences. They then present some models that are better able to describe processing in bilinguals whose languages do not share a script, by virtue of not specifically focusing on orthographic representations (e.g., the Bilingual Language Iterations Network for Comprehension of Speech model and self-organizing maps models), or by specifically feeding information from separate orthographic layers to a shared phonological network.

### 1.4.4 Lexical access in sentence comprehension

Schwartz begins Chapter 15 by situating the discussion on bilingual lexical access in sentence comprehension in the broader work on the role of sentence context in lexical access in general. She then reviews the research that has specifically focused on bilingual lexical access using single-word processing. This work generally supports the view that lexical access is fundamentally non-selective. This is followed by a description of the research that examined bilingual lexical access during sentence processing. Four specific factors are noted for modulating the relative non-selectivity of processing, namely the strength of contextual constraint, the amount and level of overlap of items across languages, the degree of mixing of the language context (e.g., "zooming in"), and individual differences in the bilingual.

Several models are discussed in relation to their ability to predict effects of these important factors, with particular emphasis placed on the Bilingual Re-Ordered Activation Model (B-RAM) and the Three-Factor Framework. Both of these models emphasize the role of context in processing and are related to the Monolingual Re-Ordered Access Model. These models differ in that the B-RAM focuses specifically on processing of words that are homonyms within a single target language, whereas the Three-Factor Framework emphasizes the processing of interlingual homographs. Throughout the chapter, Schwartz provides a useful overview of the relevant methods and their advantages and disadvantages.

### 1.4.5 Cross-linguistic interactions

In Chapter 16, Dussias, Dietrich, and Villegas present an overview of the bilingual sentence processing literature that speaks to the issues of transfer from the L1 to the L2 and the reverse. Their review emphasizes studies testing late sequential bilinguals who maintain regular use of both languages. Their discussion supports evidence of transfer in both directions, and that these effects are influenced by several factors. This is contrasted with the view that L2 learners engage in shallow processing.

The factors that Dussias, Dietrich, and Villegas emphasize are the degree of language mixing, the proficiency of the bilingual in L2, and exposure to the L2. Throughout the chapter, relevant theoretical debates are described, and an overview of relevant findings from both behavioral and electrophysiological studies is provided. They argue that the study of bilingual sentence processing is important not only for understanding bilingual processing in general, but also for explaining the dynamic nature of the native language system.

## 1.5 Production

We begin our exploration of work done in bilingual speech production in Part V with a discussion by Kormos who emphasizes how individual characteristics such as working memory capacity and attentional control, foreign language anxiety, and willingness to communicate in an L2 may lead to variation and serve as the basis for erroneous interpretations of bilingual speech production. Kormos' analysis is complemented in subsequent chapters by innovative ways that allow for a richer understanding of the processes and modeling of bilingual speech production investigating naturally occurring code-switching (Myers-Scotton and Jake, Chapter 19) and computer simulations (de Groot and Starreveld, Chapter 18). Van Hell, Litcofsky, and Ting (Chapter 20) conclude by bringing to light an emergent body of work that examines language switching within meaningful sentences. The researchers also advocate for an integration of linguistic, psycholinguistic, and neurocognitive approaches in studying cognitive and neural correlates of language switching. In all, Part V on production provides an overview of work done in bilingual speech production, discusses the methodological complexities involved, and offers ways that help to refine and improve future studies.

### 1.5.1 Individual characteristics leading to variation in production processes

Kormos in Chapter 17 provides a state-of-the-art work of the impact of individual characteristics on speech production processes from a psycholinguistic framework. The researcher offers a review of some of the most influential factors that have been postulated to explain bilingual production processes and after careful examination, argues that there are three particularly important factors to consider: working memory capacity and attentional control; foreign language anxiety; and willingness to communicate in L2 speech production.

In terms of individual differences in working memory capacity and attention control, Kormos notes that while previous research has generally suggested that differences in attention control affect the efficient functionality of speech production processes and the development of L2 speaking skills, results have been mixed for the effects of working memory capacity on the quality of speech production. The author also argues that L2 anxiety can increase these effects by potentially causing reduced working memory and decreased attentional control. No doubt related to L2 anxiety is one's willingness to communicate which can affect speech production due to its complex involvement of speech planning. This will determine how much and to what level of detail L2 learners say their utterances (more on the "costliness" of language switching and speech planning is discussed in Chapter 19 by Myers-Scotton and Jake). In all, Kormos' arguments suggest that affective individual characteristics potentially interact with cognitive factors and affect stages of speech production. She suggests a reconceptualization of research methodologies that will investigate the interaction of cognitive and affective factors.

### 1.5.2 Using computer simulations to explain parallel language activation

De Groot and Starreveld in Chapter 18 highlight the ways in which computer simulations can provide a clear and effective way of interpreting data in bilingual speech production studies. The researchers first review studies that suggest that sub-lexicons in the bilingual mind are activated in parallel during word comprehension, frequently known in the literature as support for language-non-selective lexical activation. They then review evidence that suggests that parallel activation is also apparent in word production but that a number of variables have a modulating effect on such activation.

Several individual differences such as relative language proficiency in both languages and methodological issues such as stimulus-set composition, stimulus repetition, sentence context, and sentence constraint, were identified as potentially nullifying the impact of the non-response language on the production of words in the response language. These claims were substantiated by computer simulations of results from studies using the picture-naming task. Some important observations came out of the computer simulations. First, there was support for the cognate effect, a common observation in a language-non-selective account to activation. Additionally, the computer simulations showed a reduction of this effect with increases in response-language proficiency and repeated picture naming. There was also an effect of language proficiency and sentence context on response-selection time. In all, de Groot and Starreveld's chapter argues for the notion that a null effect of the non-response language does not necessarily imply that it is deactivated and posits that the bilingual language system is profoundly language non-selective.

### 1.5.3 Implications of naturally occurring code-switching on production models

Myers-Scotton and Jake in Chapter 19 turn our attention to an analysis of naturally occurring code-switching data and how a more careful analysis of previous work can impact the development of bilingual speech production models. The authors review different types of data in mixed constituents in code-switching and offer insights as to how these differences are related to production costs.

Based on interpretations from Levelt's (1989) speech production model, the authors focus on three specific types of data: nonfinite verbs; determiner phrases; and conjunctions and subordinators. Their analysis suggests that different types of linguistic elements entail different production costs in bilingual speech production. In some instances, these costs are large enough to cause avoidance of the elements in question. From their extensive review, Myers-Scotton and Jake argue that there are differences at abstract structural levels between a bilingual's two languages and language-specific constructions that underlie his/her speech choices. Specifically, the researchers note that constructions which necessitate interaction with the formulator are more costly than those which do not. The chapter offers implications for models of bilingual speech production from a position that looks at bilingual language, and possibly language in general, as being structured at the abstract level.

### 1.5.4 Cognitive and neurocognitive perspectives on intra-sentential code-switching

Chapter 20 by van Hell, Litcofsky, and Ting reviews recent cognitive and neurocognitive studies on the correlates of language switching through a more naturally occurring speech situation, namely in intra-sentential code-switching (e.g., "I'll call you más tarde en el día [later in the day]" when a speaker switches from English to Spanish), an emergent area of research in bilingual speech production. Their chapter addresses issues of why code-switching occurs and how it proceeds in terms of the mechanisms that underlie its functionality. The authors also examine several linguistic factors that have been shown to affect the switch costs observed in intra-sentential code-switching.

Van Hell et al.'s conversation on the cognitive and neurocognitive underpinnings of language switching reveals the fairly consistent finding that it is more "costly" (in terms of the time it takes to respond) to switch into the dominant L1 compared to the weaker L2. These asymmetrical language switch costs have come from both behavioral and neurocognitive studies in which bilinguals switched between each of their languages in series of unrelated items (e.g., words, pictures, or digits). While there has been significantly less work done on within sentences, the situation thus far appears to be quite different: it is more "costly" to switch into the weaker L2 compared to the dominant L1. Van Hell et al.'s analysis suggests that the functional and neural processes involved in code-switching seem to be fundamentally different for switching between single unrelated items than for switching within a sentence. Building on the triggering hypothesis (Clyne, 1967, 2003), the researchers review studies which seek to determine linguistic factors that affect switch costs in intra-sentential code-switching and effectively demonstrate the fruitfulness of integrating linguistic, cognitive, and neurocognitive approaches into the study of intra-sentential code-switching.

## 1.6 Control

Van Hell et al. in Chapter 20 provide a springboard to transition to a closer examination of the control processes involved in bilingualism. As the authors have demonstrated, when there are two (or more) languages active in parallel, control mechanisms underpin switching between languages, whether this switching be between individual and unrelated words or within a meaningful sentence. Part VI on control seeks to hone in more closely on an area of inquiry which has grown large enough that we can now consider it a sub-area of Bilingual Processing. To begin this conversation, we first explore language selection, activation, and the interaction of language control with domain general cognitive processes in both speech comprehension and production studies (Kroll, Gullifer, McClain, Rossi, and Cruz Martín) and continue our dialogue through an analysis of the scope and mechanism underlying language control in bilinguals (Baus, Branzi, and Costa). Following this, Festman and Schwieter explore the complexities involved in measuring language control in behavioral studies of bilingual speech comprehension and production. Finally, Hernandez (Chapter 24) draws on neural foundations of domain general control to explore their interaction with language control.

### 1.6.1 Language selection, activation, and control

In Part VI, Kroll, Gullifer, McClain, Rossi, and Cruz Martín initiate the topic of control in both speech comprehension and production studies by exploring language selection, activation, and the interaction with domain general cognitive processes. The authors discuss evidence that alternatives in both languages are activated in parallel while bilinguals speak and understand language without constantly making errors due to massive intrusions from their language not currently being used. The researchers argue that there must be a language control mechanism which allows bilinguals to efficiently select the intended language. Kroll et al. additionally discuss these effects in terms of the cognitive benefits that seem to come with being a bilingual. It is indeed without a doubt that previous work has suggested that bilinguals, when compared to their monolingual counterparts, have a stronger ability to mitigate competition across competing responses including things such as switching between tasks and ignoring irrelevant information. Furthermore, brain networks in bilinguals are distinct to those of monolinguals in that bilinguals are able to engage control processes in more efficient manners (more on this issue will be discussed in Part VII on consequences of bilingualism).

Kroll et al.'s chapter makes it clear that "juggling" two languages in one mind produces a skill in other cognitive domains which involve similar types of competitive processing. The authors further analyze this argument by focusing on the processes that enable bilinguals to select the intended language in order to produce or comprehend speech. While their discussion supports parallel activation of both languages in which it is impossible to override language non-selectivity, their dialogue points to the possibility that these processes may differ for comprehension and production in terms of the nature of the information that is active and competing in both languages, the time over which inhibitory control will need to occur, and the scope of such control processes. The authors argue a need to relate bilingual processing more closely to its cognitive and neurocognitive consequences and to use bilingualism as a research tool which can be exploited to uncover foundational cognitive principles impossible to investigate in the monolingual realm.

### 1.6.2 Mechanisms and scope of language control

Baus, Branzi, and Costa in Chapter 22 explore how bilinguals are able to restrict their speech production to the selected language by subdividing this into two separate issues: one which looks at the mechanisms of language control; and one which discusses the scope of language control. In terms of the mechanisms of language control, the researchers provide support for the Inhibitory Control Model (Green, 1986, 1998), an enduring and pioneering model of language control which puts forth the basic notion that the unintended language is inhibited for efficient selection of words in the intended language. Baus et al. review evidence from language switching studies along with behavioral, neurophysiological, and neuroimaging paradigms by pointing out that the evidence in favor of the involvement of the inhibitory process as the mechanism for language control is more complex than originally anticipated.

In terms of the scope of language control which has received less attention than the mechanisms involved in language control, Baus et al. review evidence regarding the extent to which language control mechanisms are applied to specific lexical items or to the entire lexicon, a conversation commonly referred to as the local vs. global control debate. The researchers additionally discuss the functionality of language control and the potential modulating factor of context. They entertain the notion of flexibility and adaptability in language control and argue that the scope of the bilingual language control system is modulated by the demands of the particular situation in which the bilingual finds him/herself. Indeed, there are differences in speech production processes in situations in which a bilingual's two languages are continuously mixed (e.g., trial-by-trial language switching task) versus those in which the two languages are blocked (e.g., blocked naming task).

### 1.6.3 Behavioral measures of language control

In Chapter 23 Festman and Schwieter demonstrate the methodological complexities involved in language control in both comprehension and production studies. By focusing on processing costs as an indicator of language control, the authors distinguish two time-related types of language processing costs: language switch costs; and language mixing costs. Some of the behavioral measures reviewed in this chapter include production tasks such as: picture naming; digit naming; verbal fluency measure; and phrasal production; and comprehension tasks such as: reading aloud; self-paced reading; and categorization of animacy.

With respect to the production methodologies discussed, Festman and Schwieter illuminate trends in research findings that suggest that language proficiency is a modulating factor when it comes to the speed and accuracy of language production. Additionally, they take issue with studies that have employed mixed task blocks instead of single task blocks, a methodological characteristic which could limit researchers' ability to gather more information on language proficiency and processing by directly comparing participants' performance on one task (in the single task block) to performance of switching between two tasks (mixed task blocks). Under these comparative conditions, the costs (and benefits) associated with language switching and language mixing could be calculated, providing a more desirable and thorough examination of language control.

In terms of methodologies measuring language control in comprehension, which are scarcer than those in production, Festman and Schwieter once again note that such studies have so far been only exploratory in nature and require further fine-tuning. They argue that the role of language proficiency must not be ignored and that care must be taken to overestimate comprehension studies that are derived from the production literature, given that production studies are not easily replicated in language comprehension studies. In all, the chapter advocates the creation of innovative methodologies which systematically investigate behavioral perspectives of language control and it also brings to light the need for researching language control without ignoring task demands and language proficiency.

### 1.6.4 Neurological perspectives of language control

More recent studies have found fruitfulness in exploring language control from neural perspectives. Such is the topic of Chapter 24 by Hernandez who first discusses neural foundations of cognitive control in the non-verbal domain and then transitions to a conversation on how areas in the brain associated with *cognitive control* may be involved in *language control* in bilingualism. The researcher begins his analysis of cognitive control as a non-linguistic element that is essential to our everyday lives – such as in the simple task of switching lanes while driving – and discusses the relationship between executive control and cognitive development. By bringing to light new interpretations, Hernandez suggests that childhood and adolescent development is a time in which there is significant improvement in the utilization of cognitive control and executive function. Following this, Hernandez discusses recent work on the neural and behavioral nature of language control and demonstrates that there appear to be benefits to being a bilingual. These benefits emerge in cognitive control tasks even when such tasks involve little use of language.

Although in recent years a great amount of progress has been made investigating cognitive control and its implications for bilingualism and bilingual processing, Hernandez notes that discussions from what has become known as "the bilingual advantage" debate – which favors the idea that cognitive control may benefit from a lifetime of bilingualism – might be overshadowing a profound set of issues that may restrict the extendibility of these benefits. One such restriction is the case of bimodal bilinguals (individuals who use a spoken and a signed language) who appear to lack the "bilingual advantage" when compared to bilinguals who use two spoken languages. Two other clouding issues may lie within the research methodologies employed. Regarding the variables measured in experimental designs, few studies have made an attempt to integrate multiple variables into the same study in an attempt to uncover the possible differential effects on executive function. Indeed, executive function involves variables, both internal (i.e., genetic predispositions) and external (socioeconomic status, educational level, etc.). More about these variables is discussed in Hilchey, Saint-Aubin, and Klein's Chapter 26. Furthermore, because executive control (in both monolinguals and bilinguals) develops over time and well into adulthood, Hernandez argues that research methodologies must be improved by taking a non-static view of testing executive control.

## 1.7 Consequences of bilingualism

Hernandez's discussion on neural aspects of language control, along with some of the research reviewed in Kroll et al.'s chapter, touched on an ongoing dialogue related to the potential benefits that arise from being a bilingual which we will refer to in this handbook as the *bilingual advantage debate*. In Part VII the cognitive and neurocognitive consequences of bilingualism part of the handbook, the first three chapters dig deeper into the bilingual advantage debate. Bialystok and Craik provide evidence that bilingualism has the potential to maintain cognitive functioning and to safeguard against the normal decline of human mind and Hilchey, Saint-Aubin, and Klein discuss some shortcomings of subscribing to the notion that the driving factors of a bilingual advantage are purely cognitive in nature and suggest sociological factors may play a role. Krizman and Marian discuss the neural consequences of bilingualism by exploiting the plasticity of the brain and the modification of the neural architecture of the brain due to bilingualism, changes which lead to differences between bilinguals and monolinguals in language activation, comprehension, and learning. Moving away from the bilingual advantage debate,

Libben and Goral focus our attention on an exploration of the consequences of bilingualism on the mental lexicon and Higby and Obler discuss factors that may lead to losing an L1 to an L2. Finally, Part VII concludes with Linck, Michael, Golonka, Twist, and Schwieter's discussion on the effects of knowing more than two languages on processing and learning.

### 1.7.1 A bilingual advantage: cognitive reserve and executive control

Bialystok and Craik expand on some of their own pioneering work in Chapter 25. A hypothesis that is brought up on several occasions throughout this handbook (see Chapters 21, 24, 26, 27, 30) because of its timeliness and impact on the field of Bilingual Processing is the notion that bilingualism may lead to cognitive benefits. Bialystok and Craik review evidence supporting the idea that bilingualism contributes to cognitive reserve, a long-term benefit that helps to maintain cognitive functioning and to protect against the normal decline of the human mind that occurs with healthy aging. This evidence comes from studies which have consistently demonstrated that bilinguals compared to monolinguals have a superior ability of executive control, a term which encompasses an array of cognitive abilities involved in controlling attention, inhibiting distraction, and shifting between tasks. Although these effects have been documented among infants, children, younger adults, and older adults, Bialystok and Craik argue for studies which explore the interaction between language proficiency and the linguistic demands of tasks. By doing so, research may have a better insight as to whether the performance differences between monolinguals and bilinguals are due to cognitive processes or are influenced by proficiency level of the language(s) being tested.

The researchers' claim throughout the chapter, in addition to advocating for the idea that bilingualism leads to cognitive reserve, is that a promising approach to the intervention of dementia and other forms of cognitive dysfunction is by advocating bilingualism as a lifestyle that has been shown to contribute to cognitive reserve. In all, the chapter provides a state-of-the-art analysis of the benefits of bilingualism on executive control and on a larger scale, puts forth the idea that bilingualism has the potential to protect against cognitive function even in the context of a neurodegenerative disease. To continue the bilingual advantage debate, The next chapters take a dynamic look at the brain as a model of plasticity.

### 1.7.2 A bilingual advantage: potential explanatory power from a social psychology perspective

Hilchey, Saint-Aubin, and Klein in Chapter 26 provide alternative explanations for the variability in findings from studies investigating the bilingual advantage. After reviewing studies that suggest that bilingualism may lead to cognitive benefits, Hilchey et al. argue that the results are too inconsistent to fully support a central role of bilingualism in superior executive function and improved cognitive reserve. Their analysis suggests that most of the previous work done in this area has ignored sociological factors potentially related to bilingualism such as those mentioned in Chapter 24 by Hernandez.

The main goal of Hilchey et al.'s chapter is to explain divergent findings in the bilingual advantage debate by providing a contrastive view of Cognitive Bilingualism – namely through a sociological lens in which uncontrolled social factors representative of an individual's (social) bilingual experience may elucidate some variability and unexplained findings in previous work. Their arguments build on theories from Bilingual Social Psychology (Hakuta, Ferdman, and Diaz, 1985) which maintains that bilingualism has the ability to increase cognitive functions through social factors such as increasing socioeconomic status, widening cultural outlooks, and increasing social belonging within a speech community. Although Hilchey et al. do not deny the explanatory power of and significant impact of much of the work discussed in Bialystok and Craik's chapter, the researchers posit that there is a need and true potential for consideration of a bilingual social psychology perspective when asking questions such as the title of their chapter, "Does bilingual exercise enhance cognitive fitness in traditional non-linguistic executive processing tasks?"

### 1.7.3 A bilingual advantage: neural perspectives of brain plasticity

Building on Bialystok and Craik's arguments that bilingualism incurs cognitive advantages, Krizman and Marian in Chapter 27 focus more closely on neurological issues that support the bilingual advantage debate. The authors provide an overview of how electrophysiological and neuroimaging techniques have demonstrated interesting interactivity between the auditory and executive systems in bilinguals. Their focus is on how learning an additional language modifies the neural architecture of the bilingual brain and how these changes lead to differences between bilinguals and monolinguals in language activation, comprehension, and learning.

Krizman and Marian's analysis of neural consequences of bilingualism effectively demonstrates that a bilingual experience affects how the brain processes sound, understands speech, and controls attention. Their review shows that bilinguals have gained a rich auditory experience that has formulated the neural processes involved in language processing. This can be seen in several studies demonstrating brain plasticity and reorganization throughout the cortex and also in studies suggesting a fine-tuning of auditory subcortical structures potentially due to interactions between sensory and cognitive signaling. In all, Krizman and Marian argue that the bilingual brain is a model of neural plasticity and that experience with two languages can modify the auditory system and its interaction with executive control to facilitate effective language processing across two languages.

### 1.7.4 The effects of bilingualism on the mental lexicon

Libben and Goral shift our attention away from the bilingual advantage debate and toward a discussion on the effects of bilingualism on the developing mental lexicon in Chapter 28. In their chapter, Libben and Goral review prominent theories of lexical processing and their application to bilingualism and provide a compelling argument for the reconceptualization of the study of the mental lexicon in which monolingual perspectives can no longer be the norm, a reflection of the fact that the majority of the world's speakers know more than one language. At the core of this argument is the notion that bilingualism changes the mental lexicon from a monolingual to a bilingual functional configuration. Their hypotheses are primarily supported by an analysis of the consequences of differential morphological systems between the languages of a bilingual on the organization of the mental lexicon.

The authors argue that a re-evaluation of several assumptions that are currently accepted in theories and models of the bilingual mental lexicon must be carefully considered. These include: (1) the default lexical representation is a monomorphemic word; (2) the default mental lexicon is that of an adult educated monolingual; (3) a successful multilingual will build and maintain a mental lexicon for each language; and (4) the mental lexicon is a static knowledge store. Libben and Goral further acknowledge that the conceptualization of bilingual mental lexicon is on the verge of a major paradigm shift, one which will demonstrate a movement from adapting theories and models of the monolingual mental lexicon to accommodate and explain the bilingual mental lexicon to reconceptualizing the mental lexicon as a process capable of handling more than one language. Their chapter concludes by postulating a mental lexicon that is set up to comprise multiple languages as the default state.

### 1.7.5 Factors influencing native language attrition

Higby and Obler in Chapter 29 explore some of the variables that may lead to, as their title suggests, "losing a first language to a second language." Their chapter reviews a host of factors that potentially illuminate the complete or partial loss of an L1 including a discussion of the linguistic areas that are most vulnerable to attrition and how age of exposure to the L2 and amount of L1 input interact with these issues. Many of these factors are discussed in terms of models of L1 attrition through cross-linguistic interference or a weakening of L1 representations.

Higby and Obler's review covers quite a bit of ground ranging from cases in which L1 input has completely ceased abruptly (e.g., international adoptions) to those in which there is a subtle decline in the amount of native language input and this is replaced with increased interaction in an L2 (e.g., heritage language speakers and childhood immigration). The researchers also demonstrate that just as an L1 can be acquired and lost, it also can be recovered through, for example, hypnosis and re-exposure to the target language. After a closer examination, Higby and Obler note inconsistent findings based on a varied spectrum of substantiation and put forth several factors that could help to clarify previously explained findings. For instance, the researchers suggest that more studies are needed to investigate the role that attitudes toward the L1 and L2 play in L1 attrition. Other potentially modulating variables include cognitive and language-learning abilities which may determine the speed at and extent to which an L1 is lost, as we have seen from the wealth of support for individual differences in L2 acquisition. Neural perspectives may also illuminate the extent to which a language lost is either a "hidden language" (i.e., a language which is not lost, but merely "inaccessible") or a "forgotten language" (i.e., a language which is not accessible). The researchers also suggest that neurological methodologies coupled with examining cognitive abilities will provide more research precision that will increase our understanding of the biological and psychological foundations of language attrition.

## 1.7.6 Effects of more than two languages on processing and learning

If the majority of the world is bilingual and there is a growing number of speakers of more than two languages, it is a strong possibility that perhaps someday most of the world will be multilingual (in the sense that they know three or more languages). Linck, Michael, Golonka, Twist, and Schwieter in Chapter 30 report on a growing area of research involving the cognitive consequences of more than two languages in one mind. The researchers explore the additional complexities involved in language processing and learning among multilinguals while focusing attention on models of the bilingual lexicon and a discussion of cross-linguistic transfer.

After discussing several prominent models of bilingual language representation and processing, Linck et al. argue that models such as the Bilingual Interactive Activation (BIA+) model (Dijkstra, 2003) and the Revised Hierarchical Model (RHM) (Kroll & Stewart, 1994) are very amendable to the multilingual context and have the potential, if tested in the multilingual context, to generate new findings on the processing and cognitive interactions of multiple languages in one mind. The authors also review the Inhibitory Control Model (Green, 1986, 1998) and suggest that with certain theoretical alterations, the model has the potential to shed light on the types of cognitive control required for the successful cognitive management of multilingual languages. In their analysis of previous studies, Linck et al. acknowledge a need to disentangle the many factors that contribute to transfer (whether facilitative or negative) such as relative proficiency, age of acquisition, individual differences in cognitive control, objective and perceived similarities among languages, and task-specific variables. Finally, the researchers discuss ways in which the teaching of non-native languages could be enhanced to facilitate and encourage language learning beyond an L2.

## 1.8 Final remarks

There are a number of issues that can be briefly summarized as the reader begins his/her journey through *The Cambridge Handbook of Bilingual Processing*. First, there is a clear emphasis on the importance of using converging methodologies to answer important theoretical questions. Some researchers advocate specifically for the importance of rich datasets on a large timescale, whereas others emphasize the use of measurements of neural processing in addition to behavioral processing. Second, there is a need for the development of additional models in the field that can account for data in more of the research areas of interest. These models will help researchers to make clear, testable predictions. Finally, there is general agreement that the language processing system is dynamic and interactive, and that this interactivity creates many complexities. Interestingly, such complexity may be responsible for the purported bilingual advantages that are discussed in several of the chapters.

# Part II

# Theories and methodologies

# 2

# Six decades of research on lexical presentation and processing in bilinguals

Nan Jiang

## 2.1 Introduction

A bilingual speaker, by definition, has two linguistic systems. Many questions can be asked about the phenomenon of bilingualism. Two of them have been the focus of psycholinguistic study of bilingualism in the past six decades. The first is how the two lexical systems are represented in a bilingual speaker's mind. For example, are they stored in a single lexicon or two separate lexicons? If we assume they are connected in some way, at what level are they connected? Will such connections change as a bilingual speaker's length of residence in a second language (L2) or proficiency in L2 increases? How do age and manner of L2 acquisition affect such connections? These questions all have to do with lexical representation and organization among bilinguals, and may be collectively referred to as the bilingual representation issue. The other has to do with how the two lexical systems interact in language processing. Do the two languages compete with each other in speech production? If some competition is inevitable, how do bilinguals keep them functionally separate? Does switching between languages take extra time? These represent some of the questions related to bilingual processing.

In this chapter, I attempt to offer a historical sketch of the research on lexical representation and processing in bilinguals in the past six

---

I would like to express my gratitude to Judith F. Kroll for information about the 1981 New York symposium, to Jonathan Grainger and an anonymous reviewer for their comments on an earlier version of the paper, and to John W. Schwieter for his patience and assistance.

decades. Three caveats are in order. First, this review treats bilingual representation (or organization) and bilingual processing as two parallel lines of research. This is first for the convenience of exposition. It also reflects the fact that these two areas differ in research questions and often in methodology as well. The immediate focus of an individual study is usually on a specific representational or a processing question. However, this does not mean these two areas are not related. On the contrary, representational and processing issues are often two sides of the same coin. Early research on switch costs, a processing issue, for example, was partly motivated by the organizational issue of whether the two languages are stored together or separately. A switch cost was considered as evidence for the separate store hypothesis. A non-selective access view is often associated with the idea that the two languages share an integrated lexicon, as shown in the bilingual interactive activation model.

Second, a review such as this can be organized chronologically or by topic. A decision was made to organize the review chronologically by decade. This may help better show how the field as a whole has evolved over time, but this may also lead to some degree of redundancy and the loss of continuity in the discussion of how research on a specific topic progressed.

Finally, due to practical constraints, this review is very selective. For example, in the section on theoretical models proposed in the 1990s, only four models are discussed in relative detail. I have also intentionally excluded research from a neurolinguistic perspective. Research on the relationship between the brain and bilingualism began as early as behavioral research on the topic. There has been a surge of such research using ERP and fMRI methods in the past ten years. For example, language switching in bilinguals has been studied using both ERP and fMRI data (e.g., Jackson et al., 2001; Wang et al., 2007). But this review focuses on behavioral research. For those who are interested in neurolinguistic research on bilingualism, Albert and Obler (1978) and Vaid and Genesee (1980) offer very good reviews of research in the 1950s through 1970s, and Kroll et al. (2008) and van Heuven and Dijkstra (2010) are accessible reviews of more recent ERP and fMRI studies on bilingual processing.

Even for behavioral research, many important studies have to be left out. For example, recent studies on bilingual Stroop effects (e.g., Costa, Albareda, & Santesteban, 2008; Roelofs, 2010) are not included in the discussion of language selectivity. Choices also have to be made regarding which study to discuss in relative detail in order to illustrate how a research question is approached, how an idea is tested, or more generally, how a topic evolved over time. Psycholinguistic study of bilingualism is a fast-developing field where a vast amount of research has accumulated in six decades, as can be seen in the chapters of this handbook. This review samples some of this research to show what research questions have been explored and how.

## 2.2 Early research: 1950s to 1970s

Experimental psychometric study of bilinguals can at least be traced back to James McKeen Cattell's (1887) research on the association of ideas, in which he examined the amount of time bilinguals needed to name pictures in one's first language (L1), name pictures in L2, and to translate in both directions.[1] However, early bilingual research that had a lasting impact began in the 1950s. Psycholinguistic study of bilingualism emerged in the next three decades, slowly but steadily. It was slow compared to the scale of today's research output. However, it laid the foundation for subsequent research by helping define the research issues and experimenting with research methods. Most research in this period focused on one of the following four topics: classifying bilingualism, assessing degree of bilingualism and language dominance, examining lexical organization, and exploring bilingual processing.

### 2.2.1 Classifying bilingualism

All bilinguals are not identical in terms of how their lexical systems are organized. Weinreich (1954) was the first to recognize this and made an effort to differentiate three types of bilingualism. In Type A or the coordinative type, a word in one language and its translation in another, or the two "signifiers" in his term, have their own separate meanings, or "signified." In Type B, or the compound type, a translation pair forms a compound sign in the sense that they are linked to and express the same meaning or signified. In Type C, or the subordinative bilingualism, an L2 word is not directly linked to the signified but to its translation in the other language. It should be pointed out that by making such a three-way distinction, Weinreich did not imply that a bilingual speaker's entire linguistic systems had to be of one type. Instead, he explicitly suggested that "a person's or group's bilingualism need not be entirely of type A or B, since some signs of the languages may be compounded while others are not" (p. 10).

Ervin and Osgood (1954) made a similar but two-way distinction. A bilingual is said to have a compound language system when two linguistic systems are linked to the same "representational processes" or

---

[1] The researcher found that individuals needed 149–172 ms more to name pictures in a non-native language in comparison to naming in L1, and that translation from L2 to L1 took less time than the reverse. Both findings were well replicated in recent research, and the latter became important for the development of bilingual processing models in the 1990s.

meanings (without a further distinction between Type B and Type C in Weinreich's 1954 proposal). When the two languages have their own separate representational processes, it is referred to as a coordinate language system. They linked the two types of bilingualism to how a second language is learned. A compound system is developed when a second language is learned through its association with the first language, or when two languages are learned and used in the same context, e.g., the use of two languages interchangeably at home. In contrast, a coordinate system is developed when the two languages are learned and used in separate contexts, e.g., one in school and the other at home. Like Weinreich (1954), Ervin and Osgood recognized the likelihood of multiple types of connections in the same individual. They indicated that many factors, such as the type of feedback one gets, the person one is talking to, and the physical environment, may affect the extent to which the two languages interact in actual language use. Thus, "for any semantic area we would expect speakers of more than one language to distribute themselves along a continuum from a pure compound system to a pure coordinate system" (p. 141).

Weinreich's distinction of three types of bilingualism was a major contribution to bilingual research in that it differentiated lexical and conceptual levels of mental representation and specified how a bilingual's two lexical systems were linked with each other and with conceptual representations. However, this classification was not given due attention in bilingual research in the 1950s through 1980s. It was only mentioned mostly in passing in a small number of studies, such as Kolers (1963, 1966a), Macnamara (1967a), Paivio and Desrochers (1980), Mägiste (1984), Dalrymple-Alford (1985), and in a few studies by Lambert and his colleagues who attempted to validate the distinction. This neglect may have to do with the fact that Weinreich devoted less than two pages to this psychological discussion of bilingualism in a book of sociolinguistic study of bilingualism, but more importantly, I think, it was because Weinreich was way ahead of his time by making a distinction between lexical and conceptual levels of representation, when many others were quite vague in defining bilingual memory as a topic of research. It was rediscovered, e.g., by de Groot (1993), only when the field was ready for hierarchical models of bilingual representation in the 1990s.

### 2.2.2 Assessing degree of bilingualism and language dominance

Empirical study of bilingualism from a psychological perspective began with attempts to determine the degree of bilingualism and language dominance. A number of methods were developed for this purpose in the 1950s. Johnson (1953) assessed bilingual speakers' degree of bilingualism by comparing the number of words one was able to produce in each language in five minutes. Lambert (1955) was among the first to use reaction time (RT) data for the same purpose. He asked bilingual speakers to press a button as soon as they heard a direction, such as "left yellow," "right red," which corresponded to one of the eight buttons, four for each hand, each marked with one of four colors. Two results confirmed the usefulness of RT as a means of assessing language dominance: bilinguals responded faster to directions given in their dominant language, and as their experiences increased in the non-dominant language, the difference in RT between the two languages decreased. Lambert, Havelka, and Gardner (1959) developed an elaborate set of tests that included six measures as well as the RT measure developed in Lambert (1955). For example, in the word recognition threshold measure, words were presented to bilinguals with increasing duration until they were correctly identified. A word recognition threshold for the two languages, measured in RT, was then identified and served as a measure of a bilingual's proficiency in each language. Other measures included a word completion test, a word detection test, a word-naming test, a verbal response set test, and a translation test. When the participants' performance in the six tests was compared with measures of their RT in following directions in two languages, a significant correlation was found between all measures except for translation RT and the following-direction RT data. They concluded that "bilingualism is reflected in many aspects of linguistic behavior" (p. 82). Additionally, Ervin (1961) used picture-naming latencies in the two languages to determine language dominance. In a study intended to track second language development and changes in the degree of bilingualism, Mägiste (1979) adopted two encoding and two decoding tasks, the former being picture naming and digit naming, and the latter being following directions and reading words aloud.

It should be noted that these measures of language dominance were seldom used in determining language dominance of the participants in actual studies where it was a variable under consideration. Instead, language dominance was determined more often by means of self-rating or considering the participants' language learning history (e.g., Goodman et al., 1985; Grainger & Beauvillain, 1987; Macnamara, 1967a; Young & Navar, 1968).

### 2.2.3 Examining bilingual lexical organization

Early psychological study of bilingualism was closely related to ongoing research on human memory organization in the 1950s in both methodology and the formulation of research questions. Consequently, this research was not necessarily or always intended to understand how a bilingual's two lexical systems were organized in its early years. Instead, bilingual data were often used as a way to provide insights about the organization of memories in general. For example, Ervin's (1961) picture-naming and recall study was intended to examine "the effects on memory of varying the languages used in learning and recall" (p. 446). The two hypotheses that motivated much of the research in this period, *the shared hypothesis* and *the separate hypothesis* put forward by Kolers (1963), can be understood to refer to the organization of the two lexical systems, or the organization of memories and experiences in general. He seemed to have favored the latter, as shown in his concluding remarks of this word association study: "the data are interpreted to mean that experiences and memories of various kinds are not stored in common in some supra-linguistic form but are tagged and stored separately in the language S[ubjects] used to define the experience to himself" (p. 300). This focus on memory organization was also clear in his seminal free recall study (Kolers, 1965) that examined the effect on memory of language as a coding system as compared to color. To this end, words were presented in four conditions, in a single color, in mixed colors, in one language, and in mixed languages. Participants' recall rates were compared between the four conditions. Twice as many words were recalled in the mixed language condition than in the mixed color condition, which led the author to conclude that language was "a well-formed coding system" for memory organization. This vagueness in defining the target phenomenon under investigation, i.e., memory organization in general vs. lexical organization in particular, was prevalent in early bilingual research. At least by the time of Macnamara's (1967b) review of bilingual research, how the two lexical systems were organized had not become a central and explicitly stated issue, and few published studies had dealt specifically with lexical organization in bilinguals.

Two methods dominated early bilingual memory research: free recall and word association (examples of free recall studies: Dalrymple-Alford & Aamiry, 1969; Glanzer & Duarte, 1971; Kolers, 1965, 1966a; Lambert, Ignatow, & Krauthamer, 1968; Liepmann & Saegert, 1974; Lopez & Young, 1974; McCormack, Brown, & Ginis, 1979; McCormack & Novell, 1975; Nott & Lambert, 1968; Rose & Carroll, 1974; Saegert, Kazarian, & Young, 1973; Saegert, Obermeyer, & Kaszrian, 1973; Tulving & Colotla, 1970; Winograd, Cohen, & Barresi, 1976. Word association studies: Dalrymple-Alford & Aamiry, 1970; Kolers, 1963; Lambert & Moore, 1966; Taylor, 1971, 1976). In a free recall task, lists of words were presented to bilingual participants in at least two conditions, single language and mixed languages. Participants were asked to recall as many words as they could, and their performance between the two conditions were compared, so as to understand how memories or languages were organized. Other variables were often included to examine how these factors affected recall compared to language mixing. Examples of these variables were semantic relationship (unrelated vs. related or categorized words), concreteness (concrete vs. abstract words), frequency (the number of occurrences of a word on the list), number of languages involved (bilingual vs. trilingual), rate of presentation (fast vs. slow), and language dominance.

In a word association task, words in one language and their translations in another were presented as stimulus words, and a participant was asked to provide the first word coming to the mind either within the same language or in the other language. Bilingual organization can be inferred from the type of responses bilinguals produced while responding to different types of stimulus words across languages. For example, in responding to the English stimulus word *girl* and its Chinese translation *nuhai*, a Chinese–English bilingual speaker may produce *boy* and *nanhai* (boy), respectively. These are interlingual translation responses. Alternatively, he or she may produce *boy* in English but *qunzhi* (skirt) in Chinese. A high percentage of interlingual translation responses was considered evidence for the shared hypothesis, or a language-independent view of bilingual organization. Kolers (1963) found a low percentage of about 30 percent of such responses and consequently endorsed the separate or language-dependent hypothesis.

Both methods shared the characteristic of using individual words as stimuli. I suspect that because of this reason, somewhere along this line of research, a shift occurred away from general memory organization toward specifically focusing on lexical organization. This shift was already present in Macnamara (1967a) who was probably among the first to explicitly make a distinction between "how, functionally, two languages are separately stored and retrieved" and "the storage and retrieval of any sort of information" and focused his study on the former. In the 1970s, some researchers began to talk about the "organization of words," organization of languages, or bilinguals' lexical store (e.g., Caramazza & Brones, 1979; Liepmann & Saegert, 1974; Neufeld, 1976; Saegert, Obermeyer, & Kaszrian, 1973; Tulving & Colotla, 1970; Winograd, Cohen, & Barresi, 1976). The language-independent storage hypothesis and the language-dependent storage hypothesis were formulated to clearly mean the integrated vs. separate organization of a bilingual's two lexical systems (Liepmann & Saegert, 1974; Winograd, Cohen, & Barresi, 1976). The research question became "whether the two languages of the bilingual are stored independently or whether some system of shared, interdependent storage is used" (Saegert, Kazarian, & Young, 1973: 537). Lexical organization was clearly the focus of attention in a majority of studies in the late 1970s.

This shift can be best seen in the adoption of a task that is lexical in nature, i.e., the lexical decision task (LDT). Note that individuals' performance in free recall or word association tasks can be influenced by lexical, semantic, and episodic representations and memories. For example, a previously seen word can be correctly recalled because the word, i.e., the orthographic form, is remembered, because the concept is remembered, or both. In comparison, the LDT, in which a participant is asked to decide whether a letter string forms a word or not, is less susceptible to non-lexical factors. One only needs to search the lexical system in order to perform the task. Meyer and Ruddy (1974) and Caramazza and Brones (1979) were the pioneers in using the LDT for studying lexical organization in bilinguals. In the much cited Meyer and Ruddy study, for example, the purpose was explicitly stated as to "provide information about the organization of words from different languages in lexical memory." They adopted a double LDT in which two letter strings were presented simultaneously to participants who had to decide whether they were both words in either language. The word stimuli consisted of pairs of words that were related or unrelated in meaning and, for both related and unrelated pairs, the two words might be from the same or different languages. Thus, the study had a 2x2 factorial design with semantic relatedness (related vs. unrelated) and language paring (monolingual vs. bilingual pairs) as variables. The results showed that related pairs were responded to significantly faster than unrelated pairs, and this was true for both monolingual and bilingual pairs. It was also found that bilingual pairs produced longer reaction times (RTs) than monolingual pairs. By making a distinction between storage and operation, they interpreted these findings as suggesting that "words from different languages are stored in an 'integrated' memory structure, where the connections between locations of semantically associated words are equally direct within and across languages" while "retrieving stored words belonging to one language requires operations separate from those used to retrieve stored words belonging to another language."

A related development was the separation of lexical and conceptual representations. Such separation was already visible in Kolers (1966b), but was gaining more recognition in the mid 1970s, e.g., by scholars such as Liepmann and Saegert (1974), Winagrad, Cohen, and Barresi (1976), MacLeod (1976), and Paradis (1978). MacLeod was perhaps among the first to examine bilingual lexical organization explicitly and specifically based on a framework of separate lexical and conceptual representations. The issue under investigation was whether a word in one language and its translation in another had separate conceptual representations or shared the identical concept, an issue similar to the distinction of coordinate and compound bilingualisms made by Weinreich (1954) and Ervin and Osgood (1954), but seemed to have been raised independently by MacLeod, as there was no reference to these two studies in the paper. In one of the two experiments reported by MacLeod, the savings paradigm was used. The participants were asked to remember a list of twenty number–word pairs, such as *54-car*, until they showed perfect recall. Five weeks later, they were asked to recall the word in response to a number. For the items for which the participants failed to provide the correct words, a relearning session was given in which the word paired with the original number varied according to whether it was of the original meaning (OM) or of the original language (OL), thus creating four conditions: the same word (OL-OM), its translation (DL-OM), a word of different meaning but in the same language (OL-DM), and a word with different meaning in a different language (DL-DM). Previous savings studies showed that facilitation in relearning was found for the same word, its subordinates and superordinates, in comparison to unrelated words, but not for its antonyms, synonyms, or associates. In extending these findings to translation pairs, MacLeod reasoned that if a pair of translations share the identical meaning, there should be savings in the relearning session. If they did not share the same meaning and were thus more like synonyms, no savings should be observed. Thus, the presence or lack of savings should provide information about how translations were linked at the conceptual level. The results showed that translations also led to savings in relearning, thus supporting the view that translations shared the same concept.

It is appropriate in this context to point out that this examination of bilingual organization within a hierarchical model of mental representation already began in the 1950s. Inspired by the distinction of compound and coordinate bilingualisms, Lambert and associates conducted a series of studies testing the validity of this distinction (Jakobovits & Lambert, 1961; Lambert, Havelka, & Crosby, 1958; Lambert & Rawlings, 1969). Lambert, Havelka, and Crosby, for example, classified "balanced" English–French bilingual speakers into two groups based on a survey of their language learning background. The separate group learned the two languages in distinct contexts and the fused group learned the two languages in the same context. They asked the participants to complete a semantic differential test, a test developed by Osgood (1952) and used widely in the 1950s, in which they rated four English words, *house, drink, poor, me*, and their French translations along a number of semantic dimensions such as fast–slow, large–small. They reasoned that if a single semantic system was shared by the two languages in the fused bilinguals, they should show less differences in their semantic ratings while responding to the stimulus words in the two languages than separate bilinguals. Their results confirmed their prediction and thus the differentiation of two types of bilingualism based on learning contexts. In Lambert and Rawlings, English–French bilinguals were asked to identify a concept based on the lexical cues from both languages. Compound bilinguals were found to be more efficient in making use of mixed-language cues than coordinate bilinguals, further validating the distinction.

## 2.2.4 Exploring bilingual processing

On the lexical processing front, a noticeable development was the research on language switching and interference. In a language switching study, a participant was asked to perform a task involving stimuli from a single language or from two languages. A switch cost can be assessed by comparing the amount of time individuals take in performing the task in these two conditions. This line of research was motivated by two considerations. The first was the conceptualization of a language switch, initially proposed by Penfield and Roberts (1959), that was said to allow bilinguals to turn on or off a language so that their two languages could be kept separate functionally. The second was the debate on independent and interdependent bilingual lexical organization. Both language switching and interference results were believed to be able to shed light on the concept of a language switch and lexical organization. If a switch cost was observed, e.g., bilinguals taking longer to read 100 words taken from two languages (the mixed list) than 100 words from a single language (the unilingual list), one would argue that a language switch was involved and that switching on and off a language caused extra time. One may also use this finding as evidence in support of the idea that the two languages were represented separately and thus performing the reading task on a mixed list involved going between two lexical systems, thus resulting in extra processing time.

Kolers (1966b) reported the first study that provided empirical evidence for language switch costs. He tested bilinguals in three tasks: (1) to read passages for comprehension, (2) to read passages aloud, and (3) to read and then orally summarize passages. In the first two tasks, passages were presented in three different formats: in one language, in alternating languages between sentences, and in mixed languages both within and between sentences. In the third task, participants were asked to summarize the main ideas in one language, in alternating languages, and in mixed languages. The results showed that language mixing did not significantly affect bilinguals' comprehension rates. However, the participants were significantly slower in the reading-aloud task for the mixed condition than for the single- and alternating-language conditions. In the oral production task, they were also significantly slower in the mixed condition than in the other two, as shown by the number of words they produced in a minute. By dividing the increased time for the mixed condition and the number of switches occurred, Kolers was able to determine that in reading aloud, these bilinguals took an average of 300 ms to 500 ms for each switch of language, and in oral summary, each switch took 1,300 ms. He suggested that the difference in language switch cost between the two tasks was that switching language in oral production involved both switching itself and the decision to use a particular language. Thus, 300 ms to 500 ms was a good estimate of the time needed to switch between languages. The study was soon followed by Macnamara (1967a), Macnamara, Krauthammer, and Bolgar (1968), Macnamara and Kushnir (1971), and Caramazza, Yeni-Komshian, and Zurif (1974), Neufeld (1976), Wakefield et al. (1975), among others. Switch costs were confirmed in these studies and the findings were largely interpreted to support the separate representations of lexical systems and used to develop an enriched concept of language switch, e.g., the distinction between input switch and output switch by Macnamara (1967b; Macnamara, Krauthammer, and Bolgar (1968).

In a cross-language interference study, the focus was to determine whether performance in Language A would be affected by input in Language B. If bilinguals were able to turn on or off a language, as Penfield and Roberts (1959) suggested, performance in one language should not be affected by input in another as the latter should be turned off. The observation of between-language interference, on the other hand, would become a problem for the language switch idea. Another focus of such studies was to compare interference from stimuli from the same and different languages. A language-interdependent view of lexical organization would predict a similar amount of interference between within- and between-language distractors, as the two languages are represented in an integrated system. However, a language-independent model would predict stronger interference within languages than between languages.

The Stroop task was used in this interference research. In a classic Stroop color-naming task, a participant is asked to name the color of a color word that is presented in the same color it names (the congruent condition) or in a different color (the incongruent condition). For example, the word *blue* may be presented in blue or red color, thus creating a congruent and an incongruent item. A neutral condition is usually included where the target is a symbol, e.g., an asterisk or a non-color word. Automatic processing of language is assessed by comparing naming time in the incongruent condition and the neutral condition. Correctly naming the color red when the word *blue* is printed in red usually takes longer than naming the color of a symbol or non-color word because of the interference of the color word *blue*.

In a bilingual Stroop test, the stimuli were presented in either the same language as the response language or in a different language. The main interest of such studies lay in assessing whether a between-language Stroop effect could be observed and how it compared to within-language effect in magnitude. Among these studies was one reported by Preston and Lambert (1969) who formulated their research question as "does the activation of one language system make the other language system inoperative?" (p. 295). They presented color words in the incongruent conditions and used asterisks to create the neutral conditions. Furthermore, the participants were asked to respond in either Language A or Language B, and the words were presented in Language A or Language B in both response conditions, thus creating four conditions with the response and stimulus language being, AA, AB, BB, and BA. This design allowed them to determine if the non-response language was active by comparing performance in the cross-language conditions, AB and BA, and performance in the neutral conditions, and to compare the magnitude of within-language and between-language interferences by comparing AA and BA, and BB and

AB conditions. In all three experiments, significant between-language interference effects were observed and the size of the effect was similar to that of within-language interference, which provided early evidence for the activation of non-response language in bilingual research. Similar between-language Stroop interference effects were also observed in Dalrymple-Alford (1968) and Hamers and Lambert (1972) and were taken as evidence against the presence of an automatic language switch.[2]

In sum, a considerable amount of research was done in the 1950s through 1970s to study lexical organization and processing in bilinguals. It began by considering bilingual speakers as a unique opportunity for studying memory organization. The focus was then shifted in the 1970s to the issue of separate vs. integrated lexical stores, or the issue of "one or two lexicons" in Grosjean's (1982) words.[3] The results from the studies that employed different methods were often contradictory. For example, low percentage of interlingual translations in word association and a switch cost were interpreted as supporting a separate-store view and the function of a language switch, but cross-language interference was more consistent with an integrated lexicon and questioned the validity of a language switch. Research conducted in this period had drawbacks on both the theoretical and methodological fronts. Theoretically, many studies were done without a clear distinction between different levels of mental representations. As a result, there was a great deal of vagueness involved in what was being investigated, e.g., between the storage of information in general and the storage of words. This vagueness was also reflected methodologically in the employment of the free recall and word association tasks which, as mentioned earlier, were not effective in focusing observation on a specific level of mental representation.

## 2.3 The 1980s

At the beginning of the 1980s, hierarchical models of mental representation, e.g., focusing on the distinction of lexical and conceptual levels of representation, were gaining increasing recognition. In the spring of 1981, the Eastern Psychological Association organized a symposium in New York on concepts and their surface representations. The central theme of the symposium was a hierarchical model of mental representation where separate surface forms, i.e., pictures vs. words, or L1 words vs. L2 words,

---

[2] MacLeod (1991) considered Dalrymple-Alford (1968) as the beginning of bilingual Stroop study, but the first published bilingual Stroop study was actually Dalrymple-Alford and Budayr (1966). However, this study, along with a few others were not intended to explore the bilingual representation or processing issues. Instead, their focus was more on the mechanisms and factors involved in the Stroop effect itself. For example, Dalrymple-Alford and Budayr (1966) explored the role of list structure, and Dyer (1971) used bilinguals to explore the implicit speech explanation of the Stroop effect.

[3] The word "lexicon" was almost completely absent in the bilingual research literature prior to the 1980s, which may be another indication of a lack of a clear focus on lexical organization at the time.

are connected to a shared conceptual system. Five studies were presented at the symposium and then appeared in the first 1984 issue of *Journal of Verbal Learning & Verbal Behavior* (Kroll & Potter, 1984; Potter et al., 1984; Snodgrass, 1984; Scarborough, Gerard, & Cortese, 1984; Vanderwart, 1984). Among them were two bilingual studies, one by Potter et al. and the other by Scarborough, Gerard, and Cortese. The former was a direct empirical study of how a bilingual's two lexical systems are connected. It represented the beginning of research on bilingual organization carried out explicitly in a hierarchical framework. The latter produced influential findings in the integrated–separate lexicon and language selectivity debates.

Accompanying this development was a change in research methodology. Bilingual research had relied heavily on accuracy and response type data prior to the 1980s. The use of RT data was limited to the study of language dominance and degree of bilingualism (e.g., Lambert, 1955; Lambert, Havelka, & Gardner, 1959; Mägiste, 1979), and of language processing (e.g., Dalrymple-Alford & Budayr, 1966; Hamers & Lambert, 1972; Kolers, 1966b; Macnamara et al., 1968; Preston & Lambert, 1969). Compared to the large number of word association and free recall studies, they were a minority. The increasing availability of computers in research made it possible to examine bilingual performance in terms of response latencies with improved reliability and accuracy and in a wide range of tasks.

Thus, the exploration of bilingual lexical organization in a hierarchical model with RT data became the most significant development in the 1980s. Two specific research topics became the focus of a great deal of research: whether bilinguals have a single or two separate lexicons and whether the two lexical systems were linked directly at the lexical level or indirectly through the shared concepts. Additionally, the 1980s also witnessed an increase in research on language selectivity, which was built on earlier research on switch costs and cross-language interference, and the application of the dual-code theory to bilingualism.

### 2.3.1 An integrated lexicon or two separate lexicons

With the focus now on lexical organization, an immediate question was whether the two languages of a bilingual form an integrated mental lexicon or are represented separately as two independent lexicons? The cross-language priming paradigm figured prominently in this research. When the exposure to a word subsequently facilitates the recognition of the same word or another word, it is referred to as a priming effect. Cross-language priming occurs when the processing of a word in one language facilitates the recognition of a word in another. Some researchers reasoned that if words in two languages are stored in an integrated lexicon, it is more likely for them to interact and affect each other in lexical access. This interaction can be assessed through cross-language priming. The observation of a cross-language priming effect would be consistent with an integrated lexicon, and the lack of such effect would be indicative of separate representations.

Kirsner et al. (1980) reported the first cross-language priming study to my knowledge.[4] They tested Hindi–English bilinguals in a two-block priming experiment in which the participants were asked to perform a LDT in both blocks. The second block included three types of items: words that appeared in the first block, translations of words that appeared in the first block, and new items. This design allowed them to assess both a within-language priming effect by comparing repeated and new items, and a between-language priming effect by comparing translation and new items. Their results showed a reliable within-language priming effect, but no between-language priming was found, which led them to conclude that the two lexical systems were separate in mental representation.

The lack of between-language priming was replicated in several subsequent priming studies. Kirsner et al. (1984, Experiment 1) tested English–French bilinguals in the same design and obtained the same finding. Scarborough, Gerard, and Cortese (1984) tested Spanish–English bilinguals and found that performance in an LDT on English words in the second block was facilitated by earlier exposure to the same words, but not exposure to their Spanish translations in the first block. Cristoffanini, Kirsner, and Milech (1986) compared cognates and non-cognate translations, and found that only cognates showed a priming effect similar to within-language repetition priming. Gerard and Scarborough (1989) added another word type, homographs, words that shared the same spelling between Spanish and English, thus comparing three types of critical stimuli in their study: cognates, homographs, and non-cognate translations. In the same two-block design, only cognates and homographs benefited from exposure in the first block. Non-cognate translations did not. The findings from these studies reinforced the idea that the two lexical systems were represented separately.

## 2.3.2 Word association or concept mediation

If two lexical systems are represented separately, is there any connection between the two? And, if yes, how? Weinreich (1954) already outlined three possibilities. Meyer and Ruddy (1974) distinguish four different structures: the two languages are not connected (Type A), they are connected through translation equivalents only (Type B), not only translations but also all semantically related L1 and L2 words are interconnected (Type

---

[4] Kirsner et al. (1984) and many others considered Meyer and Ruddy's (1974) double lexical decision study a priming study, but the latter was very different in stimulus presentation from other priming studies in that the presentation of two words were simultaneous rather than serial. Meyer and Ruddy did not refer to their study as a priming study or the effect observed as a priming effect.

C), and L1 and L2 words have shared lexical entries (Type D). Until the early 1980s, little empirical research was available to determine how the two languages are connected except for MacLeod (1976).

Potter et al. (1984) put this issue to empirical test in an RT study. They distinguished two contrastive scenarios. One scenario, which they referred to as the word association hypothesis, was that words in a bilingual's two languages were linked directly at the lexical level through translation equivalents. No direct connections existed between L2 words and concepts. The other, which they referred to as the concept mediation hypothesis, was that words in both languages, along with pictures, are directly linked to shared concepts. No direct links existed between translation equivalents. In addition, they suggested a third possibility, referred to as the intermediate hypothesis, that L2 learners began by forming direct lexical connections between L1 and L2 words, and then as their proficiency increased, these direct lexical links were replaced by direct L2-concept connections. The first two hypotheses, which were similar to subordinate and compound bilingualisms in Weinreich's (1954) model, make different predictions about how quickly bilinguals can perform picture naming in L2 and translation from L1 to L2. According to the word association hypothesis, L1-L2 translation involves three cognitive steps: recognizing the L1 word → retrieving the L2 word through the direct L1-L2 link → articulating the L2 word. Picture naming in L2 has to go through five steps: recognizing the picture →activating the concept → retrieving the L1 word → retrieving the L2 word through the L1-L2 link → producing the L2 word. Thus, L1-L2 translation would take less time than L2 picture naming, assuming that the amount of time taken by each of these steps was comparable or was taken into consideration. The concept mediation hypothesis makes a different prediction. According to this hypothesis, L1-L2 translation involves four steps: L1 word recognition → concept activation → L2 word activation → L2 word articulation. L2 picture naming also goes through four steps: picture recognition → concept activation → L2 word activation → L2 word articulation. So the two tasks should take approximately the same amount of time. The intermediate hypothesis would predict that L1-L2 translation would be faster than L2 picture naming in less proficient bilinguals and the two tasks would take a similar amount of time among proficient bilinguals. Potter et al. compared proficient (Experiment 1) and less proficient (Experiment 2) bilingual speakers' performance in these two tasks and found that there was no significant difference in RT between the two tasks in either group. The findings were taken as support for the concept mediation hypothesis and as counterevidence for the word association hypothesis and the intermediate hypothesis.

Potter et al. (1984) inspired several follow-up studies, three of which dealt specifically with the intermediate hypothesis. Kroll and Curley (1988) divided their participants into two proficiency groups based on the number of years they had studied the L2 and compared their performance in L2 picture naming and L1–L2 translation. They found that those who had learned an L2 for less than two years performed L1–L2 translation faster than naming pictures in L2, but those with more experiences in an L2 showed similar RT in the two tasks. Similarly, arguing that the less proficient bilinguals in Potter et al. were probably proficient enough to have outgrown the word association stage, Chen and Leung (1989) tested adult proficient and beginning L2 learners with the same paradigm and found that while the proficient group showed no difference between the two tasks, the beginning group did perform L1–L2 translation faster than L2 picture naming, thus validating the intermediate hypothesis. They also found that child learners showed a very different pattern from that of adult learners in that they named pictures faster than translating. They attributed this finding to the use of objects and pictures in L2 learning by children. These findings led them to conclude, in their modified intermediate hypothesis, that "both L2 proficiency and age of acquisition (or learning strategy) are important determinants for the pattern of lexical processing in the nonnative language" (p. 324). This conclusion found further support in the results of a subsequent language learning study by Chen (1990).

In addition to comparing picture naming and translation, several other studies approached the same issue with a different method, i.e., cross-language priming. These priming studies differed from Kirsner et al. (1980) in both motivation and methodology. The underlying rationale of using the priming paradigm in this case was that if a word in one language and a semantically related word in another are linked through a shared conceptual system, cross-language priming should be observed. The early two-block priming studies failed to produce such priming because conceptual activation may be short-lived and thus the priming effect did not survive the long interval between the presentation of a word and its translation in the two-block priming studies. This speculation was first supported in Kirsner et al. (1984, Experiment 5) when they manipulated the interval between the two words (with 0, 2, or 32 words separating them) and found cross-language priming with 0 lag. Thus, these priming studies all adopted a single-block design in which a prime was immediately followed by a target and a participant only needed to respond to the target.

Schwanenflugel and Rey (1986) were among the first to adopt a single-block design. A prime was followed by a target with a stimulus onset asynchrony (SOA) of 300 ms (Experiment 1) and 100 ms (Experiment 2). The prime was a category name, e.g., *body*, or a neutral word, e.g., *ready*, and the target was a member of the category either in the same language as the prime, e.g., *hand*, or in the other language, in this case, Spanish, e.g., *mano*. The results from both experiments showed comparable priming effect on both within- and between-language prime–target pairs. These results provided further support for concept mediation.

Several more studies of a similar nature followed. In Frenck and Pynte (1987), category members such as *sparrow* served as targets for an LDT. They were either presented alone without a prime, or preceded by a category name (e.g., *bird*) as a prime in either language. The SOA was 250 ms. Again a similar amount of priming effect was found for both within- and between-language pairs. Chen and Ng (1989) compared between-language priming for translation pairs (*horse–ma*) and semantically related pairs (*cow–ma*) among Chinese–English bilinguals at an SOA of 300 ms, and found stronger priming for translation pairs. In Experiment 2, they also compared priming effects for semantically related word primes within language, semantically related word primes between language, and semantically related picture primes. These three types of primes produced similar amount of priming effect.

However, not all priming studies showed comparable within- and between-language priming effects. Grainger and Beauvillain (1988) differentiated two possible routes for intralingual associative priming effects, e.g., between *bread* and *butter* or *king* and *queen*, one at the conceptual level and the other at the lexical level. They argued that if associative priming was conceptual, then one should observe both intralingual and interlingual priming effects. If it were lexical, a possibility already raised by Kirsner et al. (1984), only intralingual priming should be found. In two experiments, they found interlingual associative priming in English–French bilinguals (*roi* (king) primed *queen*) at a long SOA of 750 ms, but not at a short SOA of 150 ms. But they found intralingual priming at both SOAs. They interpreted these findings as suggesting that associative priming was a result of lexical connections rather than conceptual mediation. Based on the absence of interlingual priming effect at a short SOA, they further argued that semantically related words in two languages are not connected at either the lexical or conceptual level. They attributed the interlingual effect at the long SOA to the application of certain predictive strategies, which required more time.

### 2.3.3 From language switching and interference to language selectivity

#### 2.3.3.1 Language switching studies

Research on language switch costs started by Kolers (1966b) continued in the 1980s. For example, Soares and Grosjean (1984) found that Portuguese–English bilinguals took longer to recognize English words presented within a Portuguese sentence than the same words presented in a purely English sentence. Timm (1983) analyzed natural code-switching talks and found code-switching did not cause extra time in speaking. Several studies showed that switch cost was a much more complicated phenomenon than previously known. In reading aloud monolingual and bilingual lists of words, for example, participants were found to show a switch cost when the words were not related (Dalrymple-Alford, 1985, Experiments 1 and 2), but not when stimuli were translations (Dalrymple-Alford, 1985, Experiment 3). In a similar reading-aloud study, but involving passages, Chan, Chau, and Hoosain (1983) found that there were switch costs for randomly switched passages, but not for naturally switched passages. Grainger and Beauvillian (1987) found a language alternation effect, i.e., a longer RT when a switch of language occurred between two items, but this effect disappeared if the items had language-specific orthography. In cases where a switch cost occurred, which was previously interpreted as evidence for the operation of a language switch, alternative explanations were often offered, such as semantic unrelatedness (Dalrymple-Alford, 1985), syntactic incongruency (Chan, Chau, & Hoosain, 1983), or search initiated in the incorrect lexicon (Grainger & Beauvillian, 1987).

New methods were also adopted to assess switch costs. Desrochers and Petrusic (1983) and Popiel (1987) adopted a semantic judgment task, in which a participant had to compare two objects or concepts (e.g., a mouse and a whale) along a given dimension (e.g., size) and make a timed decision, i.e., which was bigger, a mouse or a whale? The two words were presented either from a single language or from two languages to create a unilingual and a mixed-language condition. Neither study showed a difference between these two conditions, thus negating the switch concept. In Camarraza and Brones (1980), the participants were asked to decide whether an object belonged to a category, e.g., furniture. The object name and the category name were either from the same language or from two different languages. Little difference was found between the same-language and different-language conditions.

Priming studies provided additional but conflicting data about switch costs. In priming studies that consisted of both within-language and cross-language conditions, one may compare RT on targets that followed primes from the same or a different language to assess switch costs. In this regard, Schwanenflugel and Rey (1986) showed no difference between single- and mixed-language prime–target pairs when the prime was a neutral word. However, participants took longer in responding to targets that followed a cross-language prime in Grainger and Beauvillain (1988). Taken together, the findings about switch costs were far from consistent.

### 2.3.3.2 Cross-language interference studies

Earlier cross-language interference was examined by means of the bilingual Stroop effect. This research continued, but given the consistent observation of a between-language Stroop effect in previous studies, the focus was no longer on the language switching or interference issue per se. Instead, it was to examine what factors would affect the magnitude of the Stroop effect in bilinguals. To this end, Kiyak (1982) found greater intralingual interference than interlingual interference among English–Turkish bilinguals but comparable size of the interference effect among Turkish–English bilinguals in the two conditions. Based on the observation that the latter group showed higher level of familiarity with the second language, the author concluded that language proficiency affected the size of the Stroop effect. Similarly, Mägiste (1984, 1985) showed that language proficiency or dominance played an important role, with the dominant language producing more interference than the less dominant language. Smith and Kirsner (1982) and Chen and Ho (1986) both explored the role of orthography by examining Stroop interference among Chinese–English bilinguals. The former study found comparable interference between Chinese–English bilinguals and French–English bilinguals, thus rejecting the role of orthography, but the latter study produced more interference from Chinese, a logographic language.

A new interference paradigm was adopted in the place of the Stroop color naming task for investigating interlingual interference. Three studies, Ehri and Ryan (1980), Goodman et al. (1985), and Mägiste (1984, Experiment 1), all adopted a picture-naming task in which participants were asked to name pictures while trying to ignore the distractor words superimposed on the pictures. Guttentag et al. (1984) asked their participants to perform a categorization task, i.e., whether the target word (e.g., iron) represented a member of a given category (e.g., metal) while trying to ignore another word presented with the target. A manipulation shared by these studies was the use of intralingual and interlingual distractors. Thus, the distractor could be a word in the same language as the response language (in picture naming) or the target word (in categorization) or in a different language. This manipulation made it possible to determine whether words in a language irrelevant to the task would interfere with an individual's performance, and to compare the magnitudes of intralingual and interlingual interferences. If no interlingual interference was found, or if it was smaller than intralingual interference, one might argue that the task-irrelevant language was turned off or deactivated, thus validating the language switch concept. If the magnitude of interference was similar, it became difficult to uphold the idea of a mental switch. These studies all showed similar amount of interference in within- and cross-language conditions.

The findings of a lack of switch costs and the observation of comparable interference in within- and cross-language conditions were damaging evidence for the language switch concept. It is a fair assessment that there was a general sentiment against the concept of a language switch in the 1980s (e.g., Goodman et al., 1985; Guttentag, Haith, Goodman, & Hauch, 1984; Popiel, 1987). Along with this dissatisfaction with the language switch as a viable construct was the emergence of a new topic, that of language selectivity.

### 2.3.3.3 The emergence of the language selectivity topic

Underlying both the switch costs and cross-language interference issues is a more basic issue, i.e., whether bilinguals are able to selectively activate only one of their languages. If lexical access is always selective, i.e., one language at a time, one would expect a switch cost in terms of longer response latencies, as one has to turn on and off languages while responding to words from more than one language. However, if both languages can be activated at the same time, there is less reason to expect a switch cost. Additionally, if lexical access is selective, a bilingual's performance in a monolingual task should not be affected by stimuli simultaneously presented in another language. Any observation of cross-language interference would suggest that both languages are active. Thus, the shift toward the language selectivity issue represented a refocus on a more basic issue about bilingual processing.

Early indication of this shift can be seen in Altenberg and Cairns (1983) who contrasted two views regarding bilingual processing. The interaction hypothesis postulates that a bilingual speaker's two languages are both activated and interact with each other in language processing, and the independence hypothesis asserts that a bilingual speaker can selectively deactivate one of the two languages. These may be regarded as the predecessors of the subsequently better-known non-selective access hypothesis and the selective access hypothesis forwarded by Grainger (1993). They designed an ingenious study to test these two hypotheses. They tested English–German bilinguals in a monolingual English LDT. The critical stimuli included two types of nonwords. The first type did not follow phonotactic rules of either German or English (e.g., *tliep*), and the second type included nonwords that were phonotactically legal in German but not in English (e.g., *pflok*). They reasoned that if language processing in bilinguals was selective, these two types of nonwords should show no difference in RT, as they were both illegal in English. But if their German was also active while performing the English task, it would take longer to reject the second type of nonwords. The results showed that the participants indeed took longer to reject the second type of nonwords, thus suggesting that German phonotactic knowledge was also active in the monolingual English task.

Several other scholars also framed their studies around the language selectivity issue. In Scarborough, Gerard, and Cortese's (1984, Experiment 2) study, which was also presented at the 1981 symposium in New York, they included words in the other language known to the participants in a monolingual LDT. For example, in a monolingual English LDT, the participants were asked to treat Spanish words as nonwords. The rationale was that if lexical access is selective, the participants should be able to reject Spanish words as quickly as regular nonwords, but if both languages are active and affect participants' performance, they would take longer in rejecting Spanish words as nonwords than other nonwords. The results showed that the participants could reject words from the non-target language as quickly as other nonwords, thus, supporting a selective-access view.

Gerard and Scarbogrough (1989) explored the same issue with test materials of a different kind. They included noncognate homographs such as *red* (meaning *net* in Spanish) that were different in frequency in the two languages. In the case of *red*, for example, its English reading is much more frequent than its Spanish reading. They reasoned that if two languages were represented in a single integrated lexicon, or more relevant to the present context, if lexical access was non-selective, the RT on such words even in a monolingual LDT should be affected by the combined frequency of the homographs in both languages. However, if lexical access was selective, the RT should only reflect their frequency in the target language. Their results showed that it was the frequency in the target language, not the combined frequency in both languages, that determined the RT, thus leading them to conclude that "a bilingual's lexical memory is organized into separate lexicons, one for each language, and that a bilingual can selectively access a particular lexicon" (p. 312).

However, using similar test materials, Nas (1983) and Beauvillain and Grainger (1987) showed different results. Nas included Dutch words in a monolingual English LDT, and found that Dutch–English bilinguals took longer in rejecting these items than regular nonwords. Beauvillain and Grainger used English–French homographs similar to the ones used in Gerard and Scarbogrough (1989) but adopted a priming paradigm. They presented these homographs as primes and English words that were or were not related to the English meaning of the homograph as a target, e.g., *coin–money* for the related condition. The participants were asked to perform an LDT on the targets but were informed that the English targets were preceded by French words. They reasoned that if lexical access was selective, *coin* should not prime *money* as the participants were told to treat the prime as a French word. A priming effect found with such materials and task should be interpreted as an indication of non-selective access. They found reliable priming effects, which led them to conclude that "clearly, the results of these two experiments indicate that language-selective access does not operate in the processing of interlexical homographs" (p. 669).

Language selectivity remained an open issue for debate in the 1980s, with research evidence overwhelmingly in support of neither view, but this was about to change soon.

## 2.3.4 The dual-coding theory of bilingual representation

Another development in the 1980s was the application of the dual-coding theory (Paivio, 1971) to bilingual memory by Paivio and Desrochers (1980) and the subsequent empirical studies. Paivio and Desrochers proposed a three-system model of bilingual organization. The imagery system contained representational units, or *imagens* in their term, which had information about the physical attributes of events and things in some abstract and subconscious forms. There were then two verbal systems, one for each language, that contained the linguistic units of the language. These systems were functionally independent in the sense that "bilinguals can perceive, remember, and think about non-verbal objects and events without the intervention of either language system and, conversely, that they can behave or think verbally without constant intervention by the non-verbal system" (p. 390). At the same time, units in these systems are interconnected both within and across the systems. In the latter case, the two verbal systems were linked through translation equivalents, and concrete words in the two verbal systems were also linked to the related imagens in the imagery system. These interconnections allowed interactions between the systems.[5] The two principal tenets of the model, independence and interconnectedness, allowed it to accommodate findings that support both language-independent and language-interdependent memory organizations. But more importantly, it provides a principled explanation for the concreteness effect that emerged in several earlier studies. For example, in Kolers' (1963) word association study, there was a higher percentage of interlingual translation responses for concrete words than for abstract words.

Empirical test of the dual-coding theory among bilinguals already began before Paivio and Desrochers (1980) applied it to bilingualism. Winograd, Cohen, and Barresi (1976), for example, conducted a study in which bilinguals were asked to recognize (Experiment 1) or recall (Experiment 2) the words they were shown previously. They reasoned that if concrete words were represented in a language-independent image system, as the dual-coding theory suggested, and the abstract words are represented in a

---

[5] Several characteristics of such interconnections were specified. First, the connections between the two verbal systems were one-to-one through translations, while the connections within each system were one-to-many and "more varied." That is, the English word *dog* may be connected with words such as *cat, friend, bark* within the English verbal system, but is only connected with its translation equivalent in the other language. Second, the number and strength of cross-language connections varied individually among bilinguals due to language learning and use experiences. More language experiences lead to rich or stronger connections. Third, the connections between translations in the verbal systems and their related units in the imagery system were "partly shared and partly independent" in that a word in one language and its translation in another may or may not activate the same image. In other words, "referential overlap between languages is a matter of degree, that is, the translation equivalents do not necessarily have identical referential meanings" (Paivio & Desrochers, 1980: 391). Within this model, what was activated at a particular point in time was a result of the interaction between individual differences in language learning and using experiences among bilingual speakers on the one hand and "current stimulus situation" on the other, which involved factors such as the type of stimuli (e.g., verbal or nonverbal), the language involved, the task to be performed (e.g., description vs. translation).

language-dependent verbal system, it would be easier for bilinguals to correctly recognize or recall the exact words in the case of abstract words. The results showed otherwise, with better performance on concrete words than for abstract words.

Several more studies were reported in the 1980s that were specifically designed to test the bilingual dual-coding theory. Paivio and Lambert (1981) asked their participants to perform three tasks in each of the two experiments. In Experiment 1, the participants were asked to name pictures in English, translate French words into English, and copy English words. In Experiment 2, they were asked to sketch the images of the objects named by a set of English words, translate the English words into French, and copy the English words. We may refer to these three tasks in each experiment as the image task, the bilingual task, and the unilingual task. In both experiments, a surprise recall test was given in which the participants were asked to recall the target words presented to them earlier. They reasoned that, given the separation of these three systems, the task that involved two systems (i.e., the image and bilingual tasks) would produce better recall results than the unilingual task because the benefit of having two systems involved should be additive, but the repetition within the same system should be less additive. Between the image task and the bilingual task, they predicted that the former should lead to better recall as image traces led to better recall then verbal traces, as shown in previous research. The results were consistent with their prediction. Several other studies confirmed the superiority of image and bilingual tasks over unilingual tasks in recall tasks, or superior performance on concrete words than abstract words (Arnedt & Gentile, 1986; Paivio, Clark, & Lambert, 1988; Vaid, 1988).[6]

The 1980s may be perceived as a transitional period in bilingual research (see Grainger, 1987 for a similar assessment). It was a time when research questions became reoriented. On the representational side, the focus shifted more toward the issue of whether the two lexical systems are connected directly at the lexical level or indirectly at the conceptual level. On the processing side, the concept of a language switch was largely abandoned, and language selectivity became the new focus. It was also a time when new research methods and paradigms replaced the old. New tasks and paradigms that employed RT as primary data, such as picture naming, translation, picture–word interference, and cross-language priming, became increasingly important. The development of test materials also became more sophisticated, as can be seen in the use of cognates and homographs and in the consideration of phonotactic, orthographic, and frequency properties across languages. These changes set the stage for a fast-developing decade of the 1990s.

---

[6] See van Hell and de Groot (1998b) for counterevidence against the theory.

## 2.4 The 1990s

The 1990s witnessed a rapid growth in research on lexical representation and processing in bilinguals. Indicative of this growth was the publication of several volumes of state-of-the-art reviews (de Groot & Kroll, 1997; Harris, 1992; Schreuder & Weltens, 1993) which did not only showcase the progress made in the field but also provide in-depth and accessible treatments of various bilingual topics for students of bilingualism. This growth was also reflected in the introduction of two new journals, *Bilingualism: Language and Cognition* by Cambridge University Press in 1998, which deals specifically and exclusively with psychology of bilingualism, and the *International Journal of Bilingualism* by Sage Publications in 1997, which has a broader coverage. They offered new and exclusive forums for the dissemination of increasing psycholinguistic research of bilingualism which used to be scattered among studies dealing with psycholinguistic topics other than bilingualism in psychology journals. The ultimate indication of this rapid growth is the amount of research output produced, the level of theoretical sophistication shown, the diversity of research paradigms adopted, the new phenomena uncovered, and new questions raised about the psycholinguistics of bilingualism. Particularly noteworthy are the proposal for new models about lexical representation and processing in bilinguals and the research they motivated, and bilingual representation research explored through cross-language priming. Processing studies emerged toward the end of 1990s and will be discussed together with similar studies published in the 2000s.

### 2.4.1 Modeling bilingual lexical representation and processing

One of the most significant developments in bilingual research in the 1990s was the proposal for several models of bilingual lexical representation and processing. Among them, four received most attention. Dealing with lexical representation and organization are the distributed conceptual feature model by de Groot (1992b) and the revised hierarchical model by Kroll and Stewart (1994). Both represented a significant departure from the inherent assumption made in bilingual research in the 1980s, i.e., a bilingual's two lexical systems were linked in only one of two ways at a particular point in time, word association or concept mediation. Instead, they both recognize that multiple types of connections may be present simultaneously in a bilingual speaker. However, they differ in terms of what determines the specific patterns of connections. The other two, the bilingual interactive activation model proposed by Grainger and Dijsktra (1992) and Dijsktra and van Heuven (1998), and the inhibitory control model by Green (1986, 1998), concern themselves more with the issue of how the two languages interact in language processing.[7] All four models inspired a great deal of research in the 1990s.

### 2.4.1.1 The distributed conceptual feature model

The distributed conceptual feature (DCF) model proposed by de Groot (1992a, 1993) is based on three assumptions. The first is the separation of lexical and conceptual levels of representation, the second is that conceptual representation takes the form of distributed features, with a concept consisting of a varying number of semantic features, and the third is that a bilingual's two languages share the same conceptual system. On the basis of these assumptions, the connection between any pair of words, either within or across languages, can be seen in terms of the number of semantic features they share. The more features are shared between two words, the stronger the connection is between them. Furthermore, words can be connected both within and between languages as far as they are related in meaning. In the latter case, a translation pair are likely to share more semantic features and are thus better connected than two semantically related words across languages. A central claim of the model is that the number of semantic features shared by an interlingual pair of words differs among different types of words. Specifically, concrete words and cognates are believed to share more semantic features across languages than abstract words and noncogates. De Groot (1993) pointed out that such a model is more adequate for bilinguals who are either highly advanced in their L2 or learning their L2 in a natural setting than bilinguals who learned their L2 by associating L2 words with their L1 translations. In the latter case, lexical links may play a more important role.

The DCF model is able to explain a number of research findings. The interconnectedness among words from different languages through the shared semantic features offers an explanation for semantic priming effects across languages (e.g., Chen & Ng, 1989; Frenck & Pynte, 1987; Keatley et al., 1994), for example. More importantly, it offers an explanation for the word-type effect observed in a number of studies, which does not have a ready explanation in other models. The word-type effect refers to the finding that concrete words or cognates were found to be responded to faster or produce a stronger effect than abstract words or noncognates. For example, in a cross-language semantic priming study, Jin (1990) included both concrete and abstract words but found a reliable priming effect for concrete words only. In de Groot (1992b) and de Groot, Dannenburg, and van Hell (1994), bilinguals were found to be faster and/or more accurate in performing translation and translation recognition tasks on concrete words and cognates than on abstract words and

---

[7] For other bilingual processing models, see Grainger (1993) for the bilingual activation verification model, Grosjean (1997) for the bilingual model of lexical access, de Bot (1992) for the bilingual production model, and Poulisse and Bongaerts (1994) for their bilingual speech production model.

noncognates. De Groot and Nas (1991) found cross-language associative priming for cognates, but not for noncognates under the masked condition. Sánchez-Casas, Davis, and García-Albea (1992) found stronger cross-language priming effects and faster translation times for cognates than for noncognates. Concreteness and cognate effects were also found in bilinguals' word association performance in van Hell and de Groot (1998a).

An extension of the model, the distributed lexical/conceptual feature model (DLCF), was subsequently outlined in Kroll and de Groot (1997). As the name of the new version suggests, it has an added lexical component which is divided into two levels: lemmas and lexical features. At the lemma level, the two lexical systems are separate, but at the lexical feature level, words in both languages draw on a common repertoire of lexical features. This latter feature may potentially help explain orthography-based cross-language effects such as the neighborhood and homograph effects observed in van Heuven, Dijkstra, and Grainger (1998) and Dijkstra, van Jaarsveld, and Ten Brinke (1998).

### 2.4.1.2 The revised hierarchical model

Kroll and Stewart (1994) proposed a more elaborate model of bilingual lexical representation that also recognizes multiple types of connections in a bilingual speaker. Their revised hierarchical model (RHM) is based on two assumptions: a bilingual's two lexical systems are represented separately, and the two lexical systems share the same conceptual representations. The main ideas of the model can be summarized in the following statements. First, an L2 word and its L1 translation may be connected both directly at the lexical level and indirectly through the shared concept. Second, the strength of these lexical and conceptual connections varies in different directions. Specifically, L1-concept connections are stronger than L2-concept connections, and L2 → L1 lexical connections are stronger than L1 → L2 connections. A processing consequence of this claim is that bilinguals are more likely to rely on the direct and strong lexical links in performing backward translation (from L2 to L1) and use the conceptual route while performing forward translation. Third, L2-concept links become stronger and more involved in L2 processing as one's L2 proficiency increases.

Based on these ideas, the model makes three specific predictions about translation performance among bilinguals. First, backward translation should be faster than forward translation because the former relies on the direct and stronger lexical route and the latter on the conceptual route. Second, forward translation is more likely to be affected by any semantic or conceptual manipulation as it takes the conceptual route. Backward translation is less likely to be affected by such manipulation. This prediction may be extended to other paradigms such as cross-language priming. Third, as one's proficiency increases in L2, the effect of conceptual manipulation will become stronger in backward translation and other L2 processing tasks. The model inspired a great deal of research in which all three predictions were tested.

Kroll and Steward (1994) examined the effect of conceptual manipulation on forward and backward translation. Conceptual manipulation was achieved through the category interference effect. Words to be translated were categorized in one condition (e.g., furniture, clothing, fruit) and randomly selected in another. Based on previous research and confirmed by the result of Experiment 1, a categorized list of pictures would take longer to name than a random list which is referred to as the category interference effect, and this interference was believed to arise from competition at the conceptual level when words of the same category served as stimuli. English–Spanish bilingual participants were asked to perform a translation task in both directions with categorized and random lists of words. As predicted by the model, a category interference effect was found only in forward translation, and backward translation was significantly faster than forward translation. The conceptual involvement of L1–L2 translation, but not L2–L1 translation, was further supported in a study by Sholl, Sankaranarayanan, and Kroll (1995). They asked English–Spanish bilinguals to perform two tasks, picture naming followed by translation. Conceptual involvement in translation was assessed by examining whether picture naming, a task that required concept activation, would benefit subsequent translation in two directions. The results showed only forward translation benefited from picture naming. Additionally, backward translation was again found to be faster than forward translation for new items not involved in earlier picture naming.

Dufour and Kroll (1995) considered the role of proficiency in relation to the third prediction. English–French bilinguals of different L2 proficiencies were asked to perform a categorization task in which they decided whether a target word represented a member of the category shown earlier, a task that required conceptual activation. The category names and the targets were presented in the same language or different languages, thus creating four conditions for the positive responses. The RT data showed a response language effect among more proficient bilinguals in that they were faster in responding to L1 targets than L2 targets, but the language of the category names did not affect their performance, suggesting that they were able to access concepts equally effectively via L1 and L2. Less proficient bilinguals, however, did not show a category language effect, as predicted by the model. Instead, there was a language pairing effect in that the participants were faster when the category name and target words were in the same language than when they were not. The role of proficiency was also the focus of another study by Kroll and her colleagues (Talamas, Kroll, & Dufour, 1999). Bilinguals were asked to perform a translation recognition task deciding whether two words formed a translation pair. Critical stimuli were false translation pairs that were of two kinds. A form distractor was a pair with a member that was similar in spelling to the correct translation, and a meaning distractor was a pair with a word that was similar in meaning to the correct translation. They found that more proficient bilinguals were more affected by semantic distractors, responding to them much more slowly than to other non-translation pairs, while less proficient bilinguals were more affected by form distractors. These results were interpreted as showing more conceptual involvement in more proficient bilinguals, thus supporting the third prediction.

Additional supporting evidence in relation to the three claims made in the model was also shown in many other studies. For example, Keatley, Spinks, and de Gelder's (1994) cross-language priming data were consistent with the second prediction of the RHM. They found an asymmetrical cross-language priming effect in that associative priming occurred only from L1 to L2, and translation priming was stronger in L1–L2 direction than L2–L1 direction. The finding from de Groot and Hoeks (1995) that trilinguals showed a concreteness effect in L1–L2 translation but not in L1–L3 translation was also consistent with the general idea that proficiency affects level of conceptual involvement. Comparable latencies shown by proficient bilinguals in responding to pictures, L1 words, and L2 words in a drawing–writing task, reported by Amrhein and Sanchez (1997), was also consistent with the third prediction of the model.

Findings from other studies, however, were not in line with the predictions made by the model. Related to the first prediction, de Groot and Poot (1997) failed to replicate the translation asymmetry in favor of backward translation. Their participants were actually faster in performing forward translation than backward translation. Furthermore, Chen, Cheung, and Lau (1997) showed that the translation asymmetry had much to do with the fact that producing L1 words in backward translation was faster than producing L2 words in forward translation. When the difference in producing L1 and L2 words was taken into consideration, the asymmetry disappeared. Other findings were inconsistent with the second prediction. For example, de Groot and Poot (1997) found semantic involvement, in the form of an imageability effect, in translation in both directions. Concreteness effects was also found in both translation directions in de Groot, Dannenburg, and van Hell (1994). Conceptual mediation in both forward and backward translation was also found in La Heij et al. (1996), and more recently in the form of number distance priming effect in Duyck and Brysbaert (2004) and in Duyck et al. (2008). Some other findings were interpreted as showing conceptual involvement in L2 processing even in beginning L2 learners, for example, a Stroop effect in L2 among beginning learners in Altarriba and Mathis (1997)[8] and a category interference effect in both translation directions involving

---

[8] See Kroll and Tokowicz (2005) for alternative interpretations of the results in de Groot and Poot (1997), La Heij et al. (1996), and Altarriba and Mathis (1997).

newly learned items in Finkbeiner and Nicol (2003). See Brysbaert and Duyck (2010) and Kroll et al. (2010) for more about the model.

### 2.4.1.3 The bilingual interactive activation models

A bilingual interactive activation (BIA) model was first outlined by Grainger and Dijkstra (1992) and Grainger (1993) and then elaborated by Dijkstra and van Heuven (1998). The focus of the model centers on the selectivity issue and it endorses a non-selective-access view as well as an integrated lexicon. Four levels of representation are differentiated: feature, letter, word, and language node. As in other interactive activation models developed in the context of L1 word recognition, the BIA model contains concepts and mechanisms such as resting level, threshold level, parallel bottom-up activation, top-down feedback, and lateral inhibition (e.g., the recognition of a word would inhibit all other words). A word is recognized when its activation level reaches a threshold. Each word is associated with a resting level of activation which is determined by factors such as a bilingual's proficiency, a word's frequency, and recent use. What is unique about the BIA model is the presence of a language node that is connected to all words within a language. Thus, in an integrated bilingual lexicon, there are two language nodes, one for each language. An activated word would send activation to its corresponding language node which will send activation back to all words in that language and inhibition to words in the other language.

The non-selective access tenet of the model is reflected in the parallel activation from the letter level to the word level. The recognition of a letter would activate all words that contain that letter regardless of the language, with the exception of two languages that do not share the same script such as Chinese and English. Parallel activation makes selective access unlikely. This explains some non-selective-access findings such as the neighborhood effects observed in van Heuven, Dijkstra, and Grainger (1998). The conception of a language node, along with its ability to send top-down activation to words within a language and inhibition to words in another language, offers an explanation for findings such as switch costs (e.g., Grainger & Beauvillain, 1987; Von Studnitz & Green, 1997). When a word in Language B follows a word in Language A, for example, it would take longer to recognize the word because the language processor has to overcome the inhibition on words in Language B, including the target word, as a result of recognizing a word in Language A earlier. There would also be more competition from candidate words in Language A due to previous activation of its language node. A language node can also be pre-activated by linguistic and non-linguistic contexts, thus enhancing lexical access in the right language.

An expanded version of the model, the BIA+ model, was outlined by Dijkstra and van Heuven (2002). It retains the basic elements of the BIA model regarding lexical access process, such as parallel non-selective activation from letter level to the word level. It was also different from the BIA model in two major ways. First, a phonological system and a semantic system are added to the lexical system. In visual word recognition, they will be activated by related orthographic representations. This addition allows the model to accommodate findings showing the effect of phonological and semantic relatedness in bilingual word recognition. Second, a distinction is made between a word identification system and a task/decision system. The process of lexical access takes place within the word identification system, occurs early, and is automatic in the sense that it is not affected by the decision process or under an individual's control. A decision or response is made in the task/decision system. It typically occurs later, the specific decision is task specific (e.g., lexical decision vs. language decision), and its completion is usually dependent on what is going on in the word recognition system. That is, a decision is typically contingent on the word recognition process, even though word recognition is not the only factor affecting the decision process. Furthermore, the two systems are affected by different types of information. Linguistic context, including lexical, semantic, and syntactic information, is said to affect the function of the word identification system, and non-linguistic information such as task instructions and participant expectations is said to affect the task/decision system. Within this conception, much of what is done by the language node in the BIA model is moved to the decision system. For example, top-down suppression from the language node level to the word level in the BIA model is replaced with a change in decision criteria in the BIA+ model.

### 2.4.1.4 The inhibitory control model

The inhibitory control model (ICM) proposed by Green (1986, 1998) is concerned primarily with language control in bilingual production rather than visual word recognition. It is about the mechanisms involved in deciding which language or word to produce while performing a specific task. Within this model, there are four major components. The first is the conceptualizer which specifies the intended message to be communicated based on one's goal. The second is the supervisory attentional system (SAS) which makes decisions regarding which task to perform. The third is a set of language task schemas. Each language task, such as translation or picture naming, is said to have a task schema. It is a mental procedural blueprint specifying the procedural subcomponents necessary to complete a task. The fourth is the lexical–semantic system which contains lemmas and lexical forms of all words known to a person. The representation of a conceptual system is not explicitly spelled out in the model but can be assumed. For a bilingual speaker, all concepts and lemmas contain a language tag showing which language they belong to.

Language production begins with a goal, or an objective a person wants to achieve in a particular language-use situation. Based on the goal, the conceptualizer specifies the conceptual content to be activated and the SAS selects the right language task schema to be performed. Language and word selection occur at the lemma level through a checking procedure. Activated lemmas are checked with the activated concepts to make sure that it is the right lemma with the right language tag. The selection of a lemma triggers the inhibition of all lemmas with incorrect language tags. Such inhibition is reactive in the sense that it occurs after rather than prior to the selection of a lemma. Once a lemma is selected, the lexical form linked to the lemma is activated and produced. It is also suggested in the model that a stronger language takes more energy to suppress and thus more energy to bring back. This last point is particularly important in light of the findings from Meuter and Allport (1999) to be discussed later.

### 2.4.2 Cross-language priming studies

After its introduction to bilingual research in the 1980s and the initial observation of cross-language semantic priming effects (e.g., Frenck & Pynte, 1987; Schwanenflugel & Rey, 1986), the priming paradigm became a widely used method for studying bilingual representation. This cross-language priming research involved a variety of word types, such as concrete vs. abstract words and cognates vs. noncognates (e.g., de Groot & Nas, 1991; Jin, 1990), a variety of prime–target relationships such as translation pairs, associative or semantic pairs, phonologically or orthographically related pairs (e.g., Bijeljac-Babic, Biardeau, & Grainger, 1997; Brysbaert, Duck, & de Poel, 1999; de Groot & Nas, 1991; Keatley & De Gelder, 1992; Williams, 1994). It also involved the comparison of different tasks such as lexical decision and semantic categorization (e.g., Grainger & Frenck-Mestre, 1998; Sánchez-Casas, Davis, & García-Albea, 1992; Williams, 1996), the comparison of participants of different proficiencies (e.g., Williams, 1994), the comparison of different language pairs (e.g., Keatley, Spinks, & de Gelder, 1994), and the comparison of different prime durations (e.g., Altarriba, 1992; de Groot & Nas, 1991; Williams, 1994).

A significant methodological development was the emergence of the masked priming paradigm. Similar to the shift that occurred from a two-block design to a single-block design in priming studies in the 1980s, a methodological change also occurred in the 1990s where unmasked priming was gradually replaced by the masked priming procedure. In unmasked priming studies, the prime is usually presented long enough to be consciously visible to a participant, e.g., from 200 ms to 2,000 ms. This creates a problem. When both the prime and the target are visible and when they are related, e.g., either in the case of translation pairs or semantically related pairs, a participant may notice such a relationship and thus adopt certain strategies such as guessing. Priming effects observed under such circumstances are contaminated with nonautomatic processes. In a masked priming procedure, first adopted by Forster and Davis (1984), a prime is presented very briefly, e.g., 50 ms, and is sandwiched between a forward mask, e.g., a set of hash marks #########, and the target, such that it is no longer consciously visible to a participant. As a result, a participant is no longer aware of the presence of a prime, and consequently, of the relationship between the prime and the target, or the bilingual nature of the task. As shown by Forster and Davis, reliable priming effects can also be observed under this circumstance. De Groot and Nas (1991) were the first to adopt the masked priming paradigm in studying bilingual representation, and many more masked priming bilingual studies followed. The finding that cross-language priming effects were observed in unmasked priming condition but not observed in masked priming condition under some circumstances (e.g., noncognate associative priming in de Groot & Nas, 1991 and Williams, 1994) indicates that at least part of cross-language priming observed under unmasked condition reflected some strategic effects.

Cross-language priming studies produced a wealth of data. Some findings are summarized below.

### 2.4.2.1 The asymmetry in cross-language priming

One of the most consistent findings in cross-language priming studies was an asymmetry in cross-language priming. This asymmetry was displayed in two ways both within and across studies. First, priming effects were found in some studies only from the dominant language to the less dominant language, not the reverse. This is true for those studies that tested bilinguals in both priming directions. For example, Altarriba (1992) found translation priming effects from the dominant language to the less dominant language at a short stimulus onset asynchrony (SOA) of 200 ms. Keatley, Spinks, and de Gelder (1994) found priming effects only from L1 to L2 for associative prime–target pairs among Chinese–English and French–Dutch bilinguals. Where the masked priming paradigm was used, the same pattern was found. Gollan, Forster, and Frost (1997) found L1–L2 translation priming effects for both cognates and noncognates among Hebrew–English bilinguals, but not in the L2–L1 priming direction. Jiang (1999) found significant translation priming in the L1–L2 priming direction but L2–L1 priming was either weak or absent. Results from those studies that involved only one priming direction are also consistent with this pattern. For example, both de Groot and Nas (1991, Experiments 3 and 4) and Williams (1994) tested cross-language priming only in the L1–L2 direction and found significant priming effects for translation pairs. Participants in Sánchez-Casas, Davis, and García-Albea

(1992) were tested in the L2–L1 priming direction and showed no priming effects for non-cognate translation pairs (Experiment 1). Second, when priming effects were found in both priming directions, usually in unmasked studies, the magnitudes were usually larger in L1–L2 priming than in L2–L1 priming (e.g., Altarriba, 1992; Jin, 1990; Keatley, Spinks, & de Gelder, 1994). This asymmetry became a topic for investigation in several studies in the 2000s.

### 2.4.2.2 Cognate status, prime–target relation, and tasks in cross-language priming

Several factors were manipulated and examined in cross-language priming studies, and their effects can also be seen by comparing the results across studies. These factors were cognate status (cognates vs. noncognates), prime–target relation (translation pairs, semantic/associative pairs, form-related pairs), and experimental task (e.g., naming, lexical decision, semantic categorization). These factors were all found to have an impact on cross-language priming effects.

De Groot and Nas (1991) manipulated cognate status and prime–target relation, in addition to masking and priming direction. They found that under masked condition and in L1–L2 priming direction, translation priming effects were observed for both cognates and noncognates, but the size of the effect was larger for cognates than for noncognates. They also found associative priming for cognates, but not for noncognates. Sánchez-Casas, Davis, and García-Albea (1992) compared translation priming effects for cognates and noncognates in a semantic categorization task in which the participants were asked to decide if a target word belonged to the category shown earlier. The prime was masked and in the participants' L2 for most participants. The results showed a reliable masked L2–L1 translation priming for cognates only. Gollan, Forster and Frost (1997) tested Hebrew–English bilinguals on cognate and noncognate translation pairs and found reliable priming effects in the L1–L2 direction for both types of words, but the priming effect was stronger for cognates than for noncognates.

Williams (1994) compared three types of prime–target pairs in the L1–L2 priming direction under both masked and unmasked conditions. They were English–French word pairs with strong semantic relationship (e.g., *coin–argent/money*), with weak semantic relationship (e.g., *shoe–pied/foot*), and translation pairs. When the prime was masked, he found reliable priming effects for both translation pairs and pairs with strong semantic relationship, but not pairs with weak relationship. The latter type showed a priming effect when the prime was not masked.

Williams (1996) compared priming for different prime–target pairs in different tasks in order to explore the locus of the cross-language priming effect. He found that in a lexical task such as word naming, only prime–target pairs that had a strong associative relationship (i.e., they appeared together in language use) showed a priming effect, but semantically related pairs with a weak associative relationship did not. But the latter showed a reliable masked priming effect in the LDT, suggesting that it is the semantic relationship that underlies the masked cross-language priming effects when the LDT is adopted. Grainger and Frenck-Mestre (1998) also compared masked cross-language priming effects in two tasks, lexical decision and semantic categorization, the latter of which was similar to the one used by Sánchez-Casas, Davis, and García-Albea (1992), but focused on translation pairs. The bilingual participants who were highly proficient in L2 showed a reliable masked L2–L1 translation priming effect in the semantic categorization task but the effect was only marginally significant in the LDT. The findings provided further support for the idea that the cross-language effect observed in the masked condition is semantic in nature.

Contrary to the conclusion above is the finding of form-related cross-language priming observed in Bijeljac-Babic, Biardeau, and Grainger (1997) and in Brysbaert, Duyck, and de Poel (1999). The former study tested French–English bilinguals with both within- and between-language form-related prime–target pairs such as *less–loss* and *joie–join* under the masked condition. Compared to unrelated primes, both within- and between-language form-related primes showed an inhibitory effect on the targets. In the latter study, French monolingual and Dutch–French bilinguals were asked to identify a briefly presented target that was preceded by a masked prime. The prime was either within the same language as the target or from a different language, and it was either related to the target in form or unrelated. An example of a within-French and Dutch–French related prime–target pair was *fain–faim* and *wie–oui*, respectively. Both the monolingual and bilingual speakers showed improved performance in the higher probability of correct identification of the targets when they were preceded by a related prime, and in the case of bilinguals, the effect was reliable with both intralingual and interlingual primes.

Taken together, these findings suggest that semantic overlap may produce masked cross-language priming effects for noncognates. This is evident in the observation of masked cross-language priming effect for semantically related pairs in Williams (1994), of a stronger priming effect in a semantic task than in a lexical task in Grainger and Frenck-Mestre (1998), and of a stronger priming effect for translation pairs than for semantically related pairs in de Groot and Nas (1991) and Williams (1994). Form overlap may also result in a priming effect under a masked condition, as shown in Bijeljac-Babic, Biardeau, and Grainger (1997) and Brysbaert, Duyck, and de Poel (1999). This may help explain why cognates, that are related to each other both by meaning and form, tended to show stronger priming effects than noncognates (Gollan, Forster, & Frost, 1997; de Groot & Nas, 1991; Sánchez-Casas, Davis, & García-Albea, 1992).

## 2.5 The 2000s

If bilingual research was more about lexical organization than processing in the 1990s, the decade of the 2000s may be considered one of processing research. This research has mostly focused on two processing issues: language selectivity and switch costs, often in relation to the BIA model and ICM. But lexical organization was by no means forgotten, as can be seen in many cross-language priming studies.

### 2.5.1 Research on cross-language priming

The decade of the 2000s witnessed the publication of several dozens of cross-language priming studies. Many of these studies relate the observation of cross-language priming, or lack thereof, to the general issue of bilingual lexical organization, e.g., as a test of the RHM. Others used the priming paradigm to explore processing issues such as language selectivity. This section is more about priming studies related to lexical organization.

#### 2.5.1.1 Masked cross-language priming for noncognates: now you see it, now you don't

Since the publication of the first masked cross-language priming study by de Groot and Nas (1991), a great deal of progress has been made in understanding the phenomenon and what it can tell us about bilingual lexical organization. Just when we think we already know a great deal about this phenomenon, findings from some recent studies suggest that masked cross-language priming can be a far more complex phenomenon than we think. This complexity can be seen in the conflicting findings regarding when cross-language priming can be observed.

First, consider noncognate translation priming effects. Previous research showed that masked translation priming is less probable in the L2–L1 priming direction than in the L1–L2 direction (Gollan, Forster, & Frost, 1997; Jiang, 1999; Williams, 1994), and when L2–L1 priming does occur, it is more likely to occur in a semantic task than in a lexical task (e.g., Grainger & Frenck-Mestre, 1998). More recent studies replicated several of these findings. For example, Kim and Davis (2003) replicated noncognate translation priming effects in the L1–L2 direction in an LDT and SCT, Finkbeiner et al. (2004) obtained L2–L1 translation priming in an SCT but not in an LDT, Jiang and Forster (2001) replicated the asymmetry in translation priming in an LDT, and Voga and Grainger (2007) showed L1–L2 translation priming in an LDT.

However, findings from other recent studies seem to contradict these tendencies. First, several studies reported translation priming in both L1–L2 and L2–L1 directions in a masked LDT. Basnight-Brown and Altarriba

(2007) obtained comparable masked priming effects (33 ms and 24 ms) in two priming directions among Spanish–English bilinguals, Duyck and Warlop (2009), and Schoobaert et al. (2009) tested a group of unbalanced Dutch–French and balanced Dutch–English bilinguals, respectively, and reliable masked priming effects were found in both directions in both studies, and, finally, the Basque–Spanish bilinguals in Duñabeitia, Perea, and Carreiras (2010) also showed masked translation priming effects in both directions. In addition, a fifth study, reported by Duyck et al. (2008), also showed translation priming from L2 to L1 and from L2 to L3 in a translation task. Several methodological details should be noted, though, that may be relevant to these findings. First, the participants in both Basnight-Brown and Altarriba (2007) and Duñabeitia, Perea, and Carreiras (2010) were highly proficient in their L2. They learned the L2 at a young age and may be considered balanced bilinguals. Thus, they represented a different bilingual population from those involved in the studies that failed to observe an L2–L1 masked translation priming effect (e.g., Jiang & Forster, 2001; Kim & Davis, 2003). Second, there were some deviations in the presentation of the stimuli from the more widely used masking procedure in two of these studies. Basnight-Brown and Altarriba (2007) adopted a prime duration of 100 ms rather than a widely used shorter duration such as 50 ms. In Duyck and Warlop (2009), both the forward mask and the prime were presented for 56 ms each, which was different from a much longer mask duration, e.g., 500 ms, in other studies. A longer 100 ms prime duration and a reduced mask duration may lead to increased visibility of the prime. In both these studies, no information was provided regarding whether the participants were able to identify the primes.

Additionally, Davis et al. (2010) failed to obtain an L1–L2 masked non-cognate translation priming effect in an LDT among Spanish–English bilinguals. This is surprising considering the reliable L1–L2 translation priming in a LDT in many published studies. They cited de Groot and Nas (1991) and Grainger and Frenck-Mestre (1998) as showing the same pattern, but de Groot and Nas did obtain masked translation priming effects in the L1–L2 direction (but no masked semantic priming) and the priming direction was from L2 to L1 in Grainger and Frenck-Mestre. Recognizing that many studies that produced masked L1–L2 translation priming effects involved two languages of different scripts (e.g., Hebrew and English in Gollan, Forster, & Frost, 1997, Chinese and English in Jiang, 1999, Korean and English in Kim & Davis, 2003, and Greek and French in Voga & Grainger, 2007), they discussed a script explanation originally suggested by Gollan, Forster, and Frost (1997). It asserts that in the case of two languages sharing the same script, the processing of the prime may be delayed due to a lack of a clear orthographical cue to search the right lexicon. When two languages differ in script, the orthographic cues are available for efficient access of the prime in the right lexicon. While this explanation sounds plausible, it becomes problematic in the presence of masked translation priming effects observed among bilinguals whose two languages shared the same script, such as Dutch–English bilinguals in de Groot and Nas (1991) and Dutch–French bilinguals in Duyck and Warlop (2009).

Now consider masked semantic priming across languages. Cross-language semantic priming is equally, if not more, informative about bilingual lexical and conceptual organization. For example, it would provide stronger evidence than translation priming for a shared semantic system among bilinguals, as such priming is very unlikely to occur at the lexical level. This is more true for masked priming than unmasked priming, as the latter (e.g., Dong, Gui, & McWhinney, 2005; Silverberg & Samuel, 2004) can result from the involvement of processing strategies (Forster & Davis, 1984; de Groot & Nas, 1991). However, fewer studies have examined semantic priming under masked conditions. In the first masked priming study that considered semantically related prime–target pairs, de Groot and Nas (1991) did not find a reliable priming effect, in spite of the observation of such effect under unmasked conditions. In contrast, Williams (1994, 1996) observed reliable cross-language semantic priming effect under a masked condition for pairs high in semantic relatedness. Conflicting findings about cross-language semantic priming was again found in recent masked priming studies. Basnight-Brown and Altarriba (2007) found semantic priming from the dominant language to the less dominant language in an unmasked condition, but no such priming in either priming direction when a mask was used in combination with a 100-ms prime duration. Perea, Duñabeitia, and Carreiras (2008), however, found a cross-language semantic priming effect under a masked condition among highly proficient Basque–Spanish bilinguals and Spanish–Basque bilinguals, and the size of the effect was comparable to that of within-language semantic priming effects. Note that the participants in both studies were highly proficient in their L2. Both studies adopted the same mask (i.e., a set of hash marks) and the same mask duration of 500 ms, but the prime duration was 100 ms in Basnighjt-Brown and Altarriba (2007) and 47 ms in Perea, Duñabeitia, and Carreiras (2008). Thus, if anything, the presentation procedure in the former study would be more favorable for the observation of a priming effect because of the longer prime duration. Both studies made an effort to exclude cognates in their stimuli, and both used associative pairs of similar associative strength (47.6 percent in the former and 41.5 percent in the latter).[9] Finally, masked cross-language

---

[9] There was a difference between the two studies in the prime words used for the unrelated condition. In Basnight-Brown and Altarriba (2007), a separate set of words was selected to serve as primes for the unrelated condition. They were matched in lexical properties with the primes in the related condition. In the latter study, the same set of words was used for both the related and unrelated conditions. In Perea, Duñabeitia, and Carreiras (2008), a prime word was rematched with a target such that they were not semantically related. This meant that even though the prime and target were not related for a specific item in the unrelated condition, all primes were related to the targets across items. The impact of this practice in the present context is yet to be explored.

semantic priming was also found in both priming directions for concrete words, but not for abstract words among Dutch–English bilinguals in Schoobaert et al. (2009).

Conflicting findings about masked cross-language priming such as these do not necessarily invalidate what we already know about this phenomenon. For example, the asymmetry in translation priming continued to be replicated in some studies (e.g., Finkbeiner et al., 2004). What they do suggest is that many factors may affect the observation of cross-language priming in ways not known to us yet, such as the age at which an L2 is learned, as shown in the observation of L2–L1 translation among early balanced bilinguals in Duñabeitia, Perea, and Carreiras (2010). In light of these findings, discovering the factors that may impact the observation or absence of cross-language priming effects, and detailing the circumstances under which masked cross-language can be consistently observed or absent, e.g., through well-controlled replications, will be an important step to take in understanding masked cross-language priming and making use of this paradigm in the exploration of bilingual representation.

### 2.5.1.2 The components of masked translation priming for cognates

A review of cognate translation priming studies done in the 1990s already indicates that both semantic and form overlaps are responsible for the observed priming effects. Findings from several recent studies are consistent with this assessment. First, masked translation priming effects for cognates were found where no such effect was observed for noncognates (Davis et al., 2010), or they were much stronger than those for noncognates (Duñabeitia, Perea, & Carreiras, 2010). The role of form overlap was further confirmed in two studies. In Kim and Davis (2003), cognates behaved like homophones in that both types of items showed a priming effect in a naming task while translation pairs did not. In Bowers, Mimouni, and Arguin (2000), a two-block priming design was adopted in which participants were asked to read aloud visual stimuli or listen to and then repeat auditory stimuli in the first block which was followed by an LDT block. French–English bilinguals showed a cognate priming effect comparable to that for identical items, but only when the tasks were performed in the same modality. Furthermore, no similar cognate priming effect was found among Arabic–French bilinguals whose two languages share no orthographic overlap. Thus, they concluded that "orthography plays a critical role in cognate priming" (p. 1289). Finally, Voga and Grainger (2007) demonstrated the presence of both semantic and phonological components in the cognate translation priming by adding a phonological condition for comparison (Experiment 3). Thus, their stimuli included not only cognate and noncognate translations of the targets and unrelated words as primes, but also primes that were unrelated in meaning but were phonologically related to the target to the same extent as the cognates. The use of these phonological primes as baseline for comparison took away the advantage cognate translation used to enjoy because of the phonological overlap. The results showed that cognate translations produced a stronger priming effect than noncognate translation when they were compared to the unrelated primes, as shown in many other studies. However, when the phonological primes were used as baseline for comparison, cognate and noncognate translations showed a similar amount of priming.

### 2.5.1.3 Explaining the asymmetry in translation priming

In light of the asymmetry in translation priming observed in several studies, several others attempted to explore the cause of this asymmetry. The first such study was Jiang (1999). Three processing accounts of this asymmetry were tested. One was that the 50-ms prime duration was too brief for unbalanced bilinguals to access the prime. The second explanation tested was that the processing of the L2 prime might not be completed prior to the processing of the L1 target because of the longer processing time necessary for L2 primes and the short SOA. The third was the possibility that in the L1–L2 priming direction, bilinguals were more likely to work in a bilingual mode and could access the L1 prime, but in the L2–L1 priming direction, the L2 primes that were not consciously visible were less likely to be processed by unbalanced bilinguals. The three accounts were tested by providing more processing time for the L2 prime and by mixing L1- and L2-target items to promote the adoption of a bilingual mode, but no L2–L1 priming was observed under these conditions, in spite of the observation of a reliable L2–L2 repetition priming effect.

The asymmetry, specifically the lack of L2–L1 priming, was examined in Jiang and Forster (2001). They began with the question of why direct L2–L1 translation connections at the lexical level, the presence of which was recognized by the RHM and other researchers, failed to produce a reliable L2–L1 priming effect in an LDT. They hypothesized that the L2–L1 connections might be represented as part of an episodic system which was not accessible in a masked LDT in which the decision was made on the basis of the lexical system. To test this episodic L2 hypothesis, they switched the experimental task from lexical decision to episodic recognition. The participants were asked to remember a set of L1 words in the study phase. In the test phase, they were asked to decide whether a word presented to them was one of the words they were asked to remember earlier. The L1 target words were preceded by a masked prime that was either their L2 translations or unrelated L2 words. Significant priming effects were found in the L2–L1 direction in this task. This finding was replicated recently by Witzel and Forster (2012). An episodic L2 hypothesis was further supported in the latter study by the finding that a masked L2 repetition priming can be found for both "old" and "new" items in an episodic recognition task but only "old" items showed such effects in L1.

A further explanation of the asymmetry was offered in the sense model proposed by Finkbeiner et al. (2004). The sense model is based on two assumptions. First, semantic overlap underlies cross-language priming in a LDT. Second, L1 words are associated with a richer array of semantic senses and L2 words with significantly fewer. They reasoned that in the L1–L2 priming, an L1 translation prime should activate all the sense of an L2 target, thus facilitating its recognition. However, in the L2–L1 priming direction, an L2 prime may activate only part of the senses of its L1 translation, thus not necessarily resulting in a faster recognition. This idea is consistent with the finding that L2–L1 priming was often observed in a semantic task. They argued that in a semantic task, only a particular sense becomes relevant to decision making. This creates a situation where the L2 prime and its L1 translation target have a high degree of semantic overlap in the sense that is relevant to the task, which results in an L2–L1 priming effect. To specifically test this idea, they selected semantically related English word pairs such that one member has more semantic senses than the other, e.g., head–skull. If the sense model is correct, words with more senses would facilitate the recognition of a related word with fewer senses, but not the reverse. This is indeed what they found. The findings from Wang and Forster (2010) provided additional evidence consistent with the sense model by replicating the L2–L1 priming effects in a semantic task and ruling out some alternative explanations.

### 2.5.1.4 A comeback of the two-block priming paradigm

There seemed to be a comeback of the two-block priming paradigm in the 2000s. In a series of studies, Francis and her colleagues examined priming effects under different task, language pairing, and participant conditions. Francis, Augustini, and Sáenz (2003) found naming pictures in one language benefited picture naming in both the same language and in the other language, and translation and picture naming also produced comparable within- and between-language priming across tasks. They consider the results as indicating that bilinguals' performance in both tasks are concept medicated. In Francis and Gallard (2005), English–Spanish–French trilingual speakers were asked to translate in six directions (e.g., English–Spanish, Spanish–French, French–English) in the first block. In the second block, they performed translation from English to French and French to English. Translation in both directions was facilitated when the input and output words were involved in the first block, which was considered evidence for concept involvement in translation in both directions.[10] The other two studies, Francis and Sáenz (2007) and Francis et al. (2008) are immediately concerned with the components and duration of priming in picture naming in a transfer appropriate processing framework. But the

---

[10] It is not immediately clear how to rule out the possibility that the facilitation arose from repeated lexical access.

results were also interpreted to support conceptual involvement in translation and picture naming among bilinguals.

In another two-block priming study, Zeelenberg and Pecher (2003) focused on the long-term cross-language repetition effects. They suggested that the failure to obtain long-term cross-language priming in earlier research (e.g., Gerard & Scarborough, 1989; Kirsner et al., 1980) was due to the use of lexical tasks such as lexical decision. Based on the findings of some recent monolingual studies, they suspected that such effects could be observed if a task were adopted that required conceptual processing. To explore this idea, they tested Dutch–English bilinguals with a combination of tasks that might or might not require conceptual involvement. They might perform a conceptual task such as animacy or living/nonliving decision task in both the study and test blocks, a lexical task such as the LDT in both blocks, or a conceptual task in the study block and a lexical task in the test block. The test items might be words repeated in the same language across the two blocks or translation pairs. The results indicated that long-term cross-language repetition/translation priming effects could be observed only when a conceptual task was adopted in both blocks. The findings were interpreted as supporting shared conceptual representations by a bilingual's two languages. Li et al. (2009) replicated the study with the addition of a comparison between L2–L1 and L1–L2 priming directions and between participants of different L2 proficiencies. They found that a combination of conceptual and lexical tasks in the two blocks could produce priming in the L2–L1 direction (Experiment 3) but not in the L1–L2 direction for both proficient and less proficient bilinguals (Experiment 4).

### 2.5.2 Research on language selectivity

Since the late 1990s, a large number of studies have been published that explored the issue of whether bilinguals are able to selectively activate one of their languages. This research has considered lexical access in visual word recognition, auditory word recognition, and word production. A variety of research paradigms have been used such as cross-language priming, eye tracking, lexical decision, picture naming, and phoneme monitoring. The findings from most of these studies have been interpreted as supporting a non-selective-access view. However, to better assess these findings, it is desirable to make a distinction between a weak version and a strong version of the non-selective-access hypothesis.

#### 2.5.2.1 Weak and strong versions of the non-selective-access hypothesis

The weak version states that a bilingual speaker cannot ignore the language in the input or environment that is irrelevant to the task even while performing a monolingual task. If the input is available and perceived, it may have an effect on linguistic performance. Lexical access is non-selective in this version because a bilingual cannot selectively attend to only the language that is relevant to the task while ignoring the other language in the input or environment. The strong version asserts that a bilingual's two languages are always active to varying degrees such that his or her linguistic performance is affected by both languages even when both the task and the input/environment are monolingual.

To test either version of the non-selective-access hypothesis, it is not adequate to adopt a task that requires the activation of both languages, such as translation recognition, language decision (i.e., decide if the stimulus is a word in Language A or Language B), and general lexical decision (i.e., decide if a letter string is a word in either language). By requiring bilingual speakers to activate both languages, such tasks create a condition for non-selective results and deny selective access any chance to reveal itself.

To test the weak version of the hypothesis, it is common to ask bilingual speakers to perform a monolingual task while being exposed to both languages. The focus is on whether their performance in Language A is affected by the input in Language B. Cross-language effects obtained under such conditions are interpreted as supporting evidence for non-selective access. Examples of this approach are cross-language priming (e.g., Bijeljac-Babic, Biardeau, & Grainger, 1997; Duyck, 2005),[11] picture or word naming with distractor words in the nontarget language (e.g., Costa & Caramazza, 1999; Jared & Kroll, 2001), lexical decision with words in the nontarget language treated as nonwords (e.g., de Groot, Delmaar, & Lupker, 2000; Dijkstra, van Jaarsveld, & Ten Brinke, 1998). Most of these studies showed that the nontarget input affected the bilingual performance in a monolingual task, and the findings were taken as evidence for non-selective access in bilingual word recognition or production.

The weak version of the hypothesis is less interesting, though. For one thing, all these findings tell us is that what we see may affect what we do. When both languages are presented to the bilinguals, we would expect them to activate both languages. Furthermore, there has been a great deal of evidence, since as early as the 1960s, showing such cross-language effect, for example, in cross-language Stroop effects (Dalrymple-Alford, 1968; Hamers & Lambert, 1972; Preston & Lambert, 1969), in interlingual distractor effects in picture naming (Ehri & Ryan, 1980; Goodman et al., 1985; Mägiste, 1984) and semantic categorization (Guttentag et al., 1984). These early findings also suggest that while engaged in a monolingual

---

[11] Masking the prime does not change the fact that these primes are processed and activate the nontarget language and thus the bilingual nature of the stimuli.

task, a bilingual speaker cannot completely ignore or suppress the bottom-up activation of the task-irrelevant language.

### 2.5.2.2 Evidence for and against the strong version of the non-selective-access hypothesis

The more interesting issue is whether what we do not see will affect what we do. Or in the present context, will knowledge of Language B affect a bilingual's performance in Language A in a monolingual task and environment and with a set of monolingual stimuli? The strong version of the non-selective-access hypothesis holds a positive answer to this question. Research evidence, however, is far from being unequivocal.

Findings from several studies seem to support the hypothesis. One of them is reported by van Heuven, Dijkstra, and Grainger (1998). The study was built on the earlier monolingual research finding that word recognition was affected by the number of neighbors (words sharing all letters but one in the same position) words have, which is often referred to as the neighborhood density effect. The effect offers an excellent opportunity for exploring the selectivity issue. If the strong version of the non-selective-access hypothesis is correct, bilingual speakers' performance in a monolingual word recognition task on monolingual stimuli would be affected by the neighborhood size not only in the same language but also in the other languages. To test the idea, they selected Dutch and English words that had low or high neighborhood density in both Dutch and English, and assessed how within- and cross-language neighborhood density affected Dutch and English bilingual speakers' word recognition performance. In two experiments (Experiments 1 and 4) where both the task and the stimuli were monolingual, they found a cross-language neighborhood density effect. Bilingual speakers' word recognition performance in progressive demasking and lexical decision was affected not only by how many neighbors the target words had in the target language but also by the number of neighbors in the other language.

A series of studies reported by Marian and her colleagues also showed cross-language effects in a monolingual task and with monolingual stimuli in auditory word recognition (Kaushanskaya & Marian, 2007; Marian & Spivey, 2003a, 2003b; Spivey & Marian, 1999). They considered Russian–English bilinguals' eye movements while following auditory instructions in a monolingual condition. The participants were asked to use a mouse to move an object on a computer screen. The instructions were always given in one language. In addition to the target object, intralingual and interlingual distractors and control distractors were used. Intralingual distractors were pictures whose names in the input language overlapped in pronunciation with the name of the target object, and the interlingual distractors were pictures whose names in the non-input language were phonologically similar to the names of the target pictures. They reasoned that if the task-irrelevant language was also active in this monolingual task, the participants should look to the interlingual distractors as often as the intralingual distractors and both should be looked at more often than the control distractors whose names had no phonological overlap with that of the target pictures. This is what they found.

Finally, in a task that is more close to word production than word recognition, Colomé (2001) found evidence in favor of a non-selectivity view as well. She asked Catalan–Spanish bilinguals to perform a phoneme-monitoring task with picture stimuli. A positive response was expected if the Catalan name of a picture contained a target phoneme, e.g., /t/; otherwise, a negative response should be given. The critical stimuli were "no" items, i.e., pictures whose Catalan names did not contain the target phonemes. These pictures were divided into two conditions. In the control condition, the name of a picture in neither language contained the target phoneme. In the interlingual condition, the Spanish name of a picture had the target phoneme. The rationale for using this manipulation was that if Spanish was not active in performing a monolingual Catalan phoneme monitoring task, whether the Spanish names of the pictures had the target phoneme or not should not affect performance. However, if Spanish was active, the activation of the target phoneme in the Spanish name was likely to cause a delay in producing a negative response. Thus, a comparison of response latencies between the control and interlingual conditions provided an indication of whether Spanish was active in a monolingual Catalan phoneme-monitoring task. The results showed that bilinguals did respond to the interlingual items more slowly than control items, thus, confirming the activation of Spanish in the monolingual Catalan task. This finding was replicated in Korean–English bilinguals by Moon and Jiang (2012).

All three examples illustrate the involvement of a language irrelevant to the task in a monolingual task where the stimuli were also monolingual. These results provide reasonable evidence for the strong version of the non-selective-access hypothesis. They should be considered in any serious proposal of a selective-access hypothesis.

On the other hand, counterevidence exists for the non-selective-access view, as well. In Dijkstra, van Jaarsveld, and Brinke (1998), Dutch–English bilinguals were asked to perform a visual English LDT (Experiment 1). The critical stimuli included Dutch–English homographs (words with identical spellings but different meanings in the two languages, e.g., the English word *room* means "cream" in Dutch). These homographs were divided into four conditions according to their frequency in the two languages, i.e., HEHD (high in English and high in Dutch), HELD, LEHD, LELD. This manipulation allowed them to determine whether Dutch was active and affected bilinguals' performance in a monolingual English LDT. If Dutch was active, Dutch–English bilinguals' performance would be affected by the words' frequency in Dutch. For example, they should respond faster to items in the LEHD condition than those in the LELD condition. If Dutch was not active, no difference should be observed between these two conditions. Their results showed that English frequency affected the bilingual participants' performance, but Dutch frequency did not. Dutch frequency had an effect only after Dutch words were included in the stimuli (Experiment 2) or when the participants were asked to perform a general LDT considering both English and Dutch (Experiment 3).

In examining the issue in auditory word recognition, Ju and Luce (2004) adopted a design very similar to that of Spivey and Marian (1999). They examined how interlingual distractors would affect Spanish–English speakers' eye movement in a Spanish task. However, they manipulated the auditory stimuli such that the target Spanish words were either pronounced with Spanish-specific voice onset time or altered to have a more English-like voice onset time. They found that in performing the task in Spanish, the participants looked at English distractors more often than control distractors only with altered English-like stimuli. No such effect was found with unaltered Spanish stimuli.

Evidence for selective access is also available in production tasks. In a study reported by Jared and Kroll (2001), English–French bilinguals were asked to perform a monolingual English word-naming task. The critical stimuli included three types of words that differed in how the rhyme part (the vowel and following consonant) was pronounced. The "no enemy" condition contained words whose rhymes had consistent pronunciation in English, e.g., *bump* ("ump" is consistently pronounced as /ʌmp/ in English), the "English enemy" condition contained words whose rhyme is pronounced differently in different words in English, e.g., *bead* ("ead" is more often pronounced as /ed/ such as in *head* than /id/), and the "French enemy" condition contained English words whose rhyme part was pronounced consistently in English but was not consistent between English and French, e.g., *bait* ("ait" is consistently pronounced as /eit/ in English but pronounced as /ait/ in French). The rationale for this manipulation was that if French knowledge is not active, no difference would be expected between the "no enemy" condition and "French enemy" condition, as words in these two conditions all had consistent rhyme pronunciation in English. But if French was active and played a role, one would expect a slower RT on "French enemy" items than "no enemy" items, the former being more similar to "English enemy" items. The two different views about selectivity in lexical access differed in their predictions about naming latencies for the three conditions (< meaning faster than), i.e., selective view: "no enemy" = "French enemy" < "English enemy"; non-selective view: "no enemy" < "French enemy" = "English enemy." In Experiment 1, the participants performed an English naming task, a French naming task, and then an English naming task again. No French enemy effect was found in the first English task. It emerged only after the same participants performed the French task, i.e., in the third task. When French-dominant bilinguals were tested with the same set of stimuli (Experiment 4), the same pattern was found. Further evidence in support of a selective-access view in lexical production is available in studies reported by Costa and colleagues (Costa & Caramazza, 1999; Costa, Miozzo, & Caramazza, 1999).

What is common among these studies is that bilinguals seem to function in a selective-access mode unless they are required to activate both languages (such as the general LDT in Dijkstra, van Jaarsveld, and Ten Brinke, 1998 and the performance of the French task in Jared and Kroll, 2001), or they find themselves in a bilingual environment, such as the encounter of bilingual stimuli in Dijkstra, van Jaarsveld, and Ten Brinke (1998) or altered stimuli in Ju and Lucy (2004). For this reason, it is more appropriate to consider the findings as supporting a selective-access view.

A fair test of the strong version of the non-selective-access hypothesis should be done when data collection is done in a monolingual environment. This means, minimally, both the task and stimuli should be monolingual.[12] But it may also mean that anything that may affect a bilingual participant's language activation should be considered. This includes the physical setting. For example, testing Chinese–English bilingual speakers on the campus of an American university to determine if Chinese is involved in English processing is adequate, but not the other way around, because English is the language of the environment and thus is likely to be active even where the task and stimuli are monolingual. A review of studies that meet this "monolingual" requirement suggests that existing evidence is not overwhelmingly in support of any of the two opposing views on selectivity, in spite of a general sentiment in favor of a non-selective-access view among researchers. It is appropriate to note in this context that, like many other language processing phenomena, language selectivity may not be a black-or-white issue. Some intervening factors may affect how selective or non-selective lexical access is in bilinguals. The importance of one such factor, the relative proficiency of the two languages, has been well demonstrated. More proficient languages have been found to be more involved in the processing of less proficient languages than the reverse, as shown in Blumenfeld and Marian (2007), Jared and Kroll (2001), Marian and Spivey (2003b), and Schwartz and Kroll (2006). Thus, lexical access may be more selective in the processing of a dominant language while it is more non-selective in the case of a non-dominant or less proficient language.

### 2.5.2.3 Lexical access in sentence context

In addition to considering selectivity in isolated word recognition or production, several studies examined lexical access in sentence context. Using

---

[12] A tricky situation is the use of cognates and interlingual homographs. I am more inclined to consider the use of such words as violating the monolingual stimuli criterion, as it is very easy for these words to trigger the activation of the nontarget language.

a setup similar to that of Spivey and Marian (1999), Chambers and Cooke (2009) monitored bilingual speakers' eye movements while they listened to sentences. Visual stimuli included four objects, one being the target, a second being a homophonic interlingual competitor, plus two other objects. They also manipulated the degree of semantic constraint of the sentences used. A sentence was high in semantic constraints when a target was highly probable or predictable in that context. A low-constraint sentence could accommodate many possible words. They found that contextual constraints played a significant role in whether an increased fixation occurred for interlingual competitors in comparison to unrelated objects. Bilingual participants fixated on the interlingual competitor more often than unrelated objects only when sentences were semantically less constraining. When a competitor was semantically incongruent with a sentence, which occurred often when a sentence was high in semantic constraint, little interlingual activation was found.

Other studies approach the issue by comparing bilingual speakers' performance on cognates and their matched controls. A cognate advantage in terms of faster RTs is interpreted as evidence for the activation of the nontarget language and thus the non-selective-access hypothesis. Degree of semantic constraint of a sentence is also manipulated in these studies. Schwartz and Kroll (2006) was the first of such studies. They examined highly proficient and less proficient Spanish–English bilinguals' performance in a naming task in which they read aloud words that were embedded in high- or low-constraint sentences. They found a significant cognate effect in low-constraint sentences only, and this effect occurred in both groups of participants. They interpreted the results as showing that contextual constraints can serve to eliminate non-selective access, as shown in the lack of a cognate advantage in high-constraint sentences in both proficient and less proficient bilinguals.

Several other studies also examined the cognate effect in sentence context and the findings are largely consistent with those of Schwartz and Kroll (2006). Van Hell and de Groot (2008) asked Dutch–English bilinguals to perform a LDT (Experiment 1) and backward and forward translation (Experiments 2 and 3) on words that were embedded in high- and low-constraint sentences. A cognate effect was present in low-constraint sentences, but was either eliminated or significantly reduced in high-constraint sentences. A cognate effect was also observed in low-constraint sentences in Duyck et al. (2007) who did not use high-constraint sentences. Additionally, Libben and Titone (2009) and Titone et al. (2011) examined bilinguals' eye movements while they read sentences in their L2 and L1, respectively. They also found that non-selectivity interacted with sentence context in that cognate facilitation was greater for low-constraint sentences than for high-constraint sentences. The only study that showed a cognate effect in both low- and high-constraint sentences was one reported by Van Assche et al. (2011) who examined eye movements among Dutch–English bilinguals while they read English sentences.

Furthermore, three of these studies also included interlingual homographs to assess the activation of nontarget language, and the results were not as consistent as those with cognates. No homograph effect was observed in either groups of participants in Schwartz and Kroll (2006); Libben and Titone (2009) found a homograph inhibition effect for both low- and high-constraint sentences, and in Titone et al. (2011), a homograph effect was found only in one of the four measures, i.e., total reading time. These homograph results provided mixed evidence for a nonselective-access view.

### 2.5.3 Research on switch costs

Research on language switching emerged ever stronger in the late 1990s. If earlier research approached the topic from a broader perspective, involving language use in both comprehension and production and at the levels of words, sentences, and passages, research on the topic in the 2000s is better focused. On the theoretical front, most switching studies were intended to explore the locus and mechanism of switch costs. Methodologically, most studies considered the phenomenon at the word level with tasks such as lexical decision, e.g., Orfanidou and Sumner (2005), Thomas and Allport (2000) and naming, e.g., Meuter and Allport (1999), Costa and Santesteban (2004a). This practice is more advantageous as it allows the phenomenon to be examined in a better-controlled setting, and makes results more comparable across studies. Most switching studies have also focused on involuntary switching where the choice of language was not under a participant's control (see Gollan and Ferreira, 2009 for a study of voluntary switching).

#### 2.5.3.1 Discovering switch costs

A distinction can be made between mixing costs and switch costs in language switching studies. The former is computed by comparing participants' performance in a single-language and a mixed-language condition regardless of whether a switch occurred in the mixed condition. The latter is computed by comparing performances on trials that involve and do not involve a switch of language. Both mixing costs and switch costs were consistently found. For example, mixing costs were found by Hernandez and colleagues. They asked bilingual speakers to perform picture naming in a language-blocked condition and a language-mixed condition and a longer RT was found for the latter condition (e.g., Hernandez & Kohnert, 1999; Hernandez, Martinez, & Kohnert, 2000). The switch costs were replicated in many more studies. For example, bilinguals were slower in responding to switch trials than to non-switch trials in lexical decision

(Thomas & Allport, 2000; von Studnitz & Green, 1997), semantic classification (von Studnitz & Green, 2002), and naming (e.g., Costa & Santesteban, 2004a; Meuter & Allport, 1999).

In addition to confirming the switch costs, this line of research also produced some findings that may be counterintuitive and thus intriguing. The first is a switching advantage in RT observed in nonrepeated trials. Two types of switches may be involved in a language switching experiment. One is a switch between languages, and the other is a switch between response type (yes and no). Just like a distinction can be made between switch and non-switch trials in the former case, test items can also be divided, based on their response type, into repeated (yes–yes, no–no) and nonrepeated (yes–no, no–yes) trials. Most switching studies do not consider response-type sequence in data analysis, but in those that did, e.g., Thomas and Allport (2000) and von Studnitz and Green (2002b), bilinguals were found to respond faster to language switch trials than to non-switch trials when there was also a switch in response type. This switch advantage contrasts with a switch cost for repeated trials in these studies as well as widely reported switch costs in other studies. The same pattern was present in Experiment 2 of Finkbeiner et al. (2006). The picture-naming data in their Figure 4 showed a 12-ms language switching advantage for trials that involved a switch of task even though the difference was not statistically significant.

The second is an asymmetry in switch costs. Meuter and Allport (1999) were the first to report the asymmetry. In asking bilingual participants to name digits in the language indicated by the background color of the stimuli, they obtained two findings. The first was a switch cost: switch trials took longer than non-switch trials in both L1 and L2. The second was that the switch costs were greater for L1 than for L2. Compared to non-switch trials (L1–L1, or L2–L2), switching into L1 from L2 cost an average of 143 ms while switching into L2 from L1 cost 85 ms. This asymmetry was replicated in a number of subsequent studies (Campbell, 2005; Costa & Santesteban, 2004a; Finkbeiner et al., 2006; Philipp, Gade, & Koch, 2007) and thus is a quite consistent and robust phenomenon.

The third finding is an L2 advantage over L1 in RT in mixed language conditions. This is a language mixing effect rather than a language switching effect as faster RTs on L2 items were found for both switch and non-switch trials. Costa and Santesteban (2004a) reported the finding first. In their attempt to replicate the asymmetry in switch costs, they found that Spanish–Catalan bilinguals were faster in performing the picture-naming task in L2 than in L1 regardless of whether a switching was involved or not. The pattern occurred in all five experiments. In a subsequent study reported by Costa, Santesteban, and Ivanova (2006), the same advantage for a weaker language was replicated in the comparison of L1 and L2, and of L2 and L3 (Experiments 1 and 2). This L2 advantage is counterintuitive and in a sharp contrast with an L1 advantage when unbalanced bilinguals perform a task in two languages in separate blocks or sessions (e.g., Lee & Williams, 2001). An L2 advantage was present in Meuter and Allport (1999), but it only occurred in switch trials, supposedly due to a larger switch cost in L1. The L2 advantage in both switch and non-switch trials is certainly an interesting finding. It should be noted, though, that this finding was only reported from the Barcelona group. Findings from similar studies such as Finkbeiner et al. (2006) resembled that of Meuter and Allport, i.e., an L2 advantage for switch trials only. Additionally, the L2 advantage seemed to only appear where switch costs were symmetrical for the two languages. In the third and fourth experiments of Costa, Santesteban, and Ivanova, where an asymmetry in switch costs was observed, there was no advantage for the weaker language. Whether the two findings are related is yet to be explored.

#### 2.5.3.2 Explaining switch costs

Two controversies exist in the explanation of switch costs. One has to do with the locus of switch costs, i.e., whether switch costs occur inside or outside the lexicon, and the other has to do with the mechanism involved, specifically whether or not switch costs result from an inhibition of the task-irrelevant language or schema.

Green's (1998) inhibitory control model (ICM) represents a unified framework for answering both questions. It attributes switch costs to the inhibition of a language task schema and thus the costs occur outside the lexicon. The ICM postulates that each language task represents a separate schema and each language is also associated with a different task schema. For example, naming pictures in L1 and L2 involves two different task schemata even though the task is the "same." A change in language involves a change in task schema, just like a change in any other action. The model also asserts that the use of a task schema results in the inhibition of other schemata. In the context of lexical access, it means that the activation of a word results in the suppression of all words with a different language tag. Within this conception, "language switching may take time (1) because it involves a change in language schema for a given task, and (2) because any change of language involves overcoming the inhibition of the previous language tags" (p. 73). Thus, switch costs are a result of an inhibition process that occurs outside the lexicon. The model further asserts that a stronger language takes more energy to suppress and thus more energy to bring back.

Some data reported by Green and colleagues are considered to be consistent with the model. For example, in von Studnitz and Green (1997), switch costs were found to be reduced in a general LDT, as compared to those in a language-specific LDT. They suggest that in a general LDT, both language schemata need to remain active and thus there is less inhibition of one schema as a result of activating another. As a result, it takes less time to overcome the inhibition in comparison to a language-specific LDT. In von Studnitz and Green (2002b) where a semantic categorization task was adopted, the participants were found to show a switch cost in the first block of trials, not in the second block where translations of those items in the first block were used. Furthermore, there was an interaction between switch costs and response type in that a switch cost occurred for trials involving repeated responses only. They argued that if the switch costs had originated from the switch of lexicons, then a switch cost should have occurred in both blocks and for both repeated and nonrepeated trials. But they came short of a specific explanation regarding how an interaction between language switch costs and response type would "support the notion that costs arise in the course of mapping decisions onto responses" (p. 248). This interaction was also found in Orfanidou and Summer (2005) who tested Greek–English bilinguals in two lexical decision experiments. They also considered their results in accord with a task–schema explanation of language switch costs.

Additional support is also available in other studies. The idea that a stronger language takes more energy to suppress and thus more time to reactivate finds strong support in the asymmetry in switch costs (Costa & Santesteban, 2004a; Meuter & Allport, 1999). As the stronger L1 is more suppressed in L2 naming than the weaker L2 is in L1 naming, when a switch occurs from L2 to L1, it takes more energy to overcome the suppression and a longer RT to perform the task than the reverse. So a greater switch cost in L1 is exactly what the model predicts.

More recently, Philipp and Koch (2009) offered an impressive demonstration that switch costs were inhibition based. They asked German–English–French trilingual speakers to name digits. The critical manipulation was the sequence of languages, i.e., ABA vs. CBA, with each letter representing a language. In the ABA sequence, the task was performed in Language A first, then Language B, and then Language A again. In the CBA sequence, Language C was used first, followed by Language B and Language A. The crucial comparison was between the performance in Language A following AB and CB sequences. If language inhibition is involved, performing the naming task in Language A should take longer in the ABA sequence than in the CBA sequence even though both involve a BA switch. This is due to the inhibition of A while B is used in ABA trials (but not in CBA trials). If no inhibition is involved, these two sequences should show similar RTs. The results showed a faster RT in naming digits in Language A in the CBA sequences than in the ABA sequences, thus supporting the role of inhibition.[13]

---

[13] This explanation is based on the assumption that the activation of Language B would suppress the previously activated language, A in the ABA sequence, more than a language not activated previously, C in the CBA sequence. If the activation of B is believed to suppress all other known languages to the same extent, regardless of whether a language has been activated recently, the finding lends no support for the ICM. The ICM makes no specific assertion regarding this.

Some other researchers believe that switch costs occur within the lexicon and do not necessarily involve inhibition. A lexicon-based explanation of switch costs is already available in the preselective search hypothesis of Grainger and Beauvillian (1987) and in the bilingual processing models outlined in Grainger (1993). According to the preselective search hypothesis, for example, the language processor preselects a lexicon to initiate a search in word recognition on the basis of multiple factors, including which language the preceding word belongs to. When no switch is involved between two trials, the correct lexicon is always preselected. But when there is a switch in language, the language processor may incorrectly preselect the lexicon of the preceding item, thus causing a delay in word recognition. The switch costs can also be explained in the bilingual activation verification model by assuming that the verification may begin in the wrong lexicon in the case of a switch trial or, in the bilingual interactive activation model, by postulating an interference from the language of the preceding item (Grainger, 1993).

More recently, the role of inhibition or suppression was questioned by Finkbeiner et al. (2006) who argued that some switch costs observed in previous studies had to do with the characteristics of a particular set of materials used rather than with suppression. They demonstrated that under some circumstances, specifically when stimuli were named only in one language, and thus univalent, and embedded in stimuli that were named in two languages and thus bivalent, switch costs did not occur. They asked participants to name digits in L1 and L2 and name pictures only in L1. Test trials included sequences such as D1D1D1 (three digits all named in L1, referred to here as A sequence), D2D2D1 (B sequence, first two digits named in L2, the third in L1), D2D2D2 (C sequence), D1D1D2 (D sequence), D1D1D1P1 (E sequence, three digits plus a picture all named in L1), and D1D1D2P1 (F sequence). In this design, a switch cost for L1 in digit naming can be assessed by comparing participants' performance on the last stimulus in A and B sequences, a switch costs for L2 in digit naming by comparing C and D sequences, a switch cost for L1 picture naming by comparing E and F sequences. Note that digit naming was done in both L1 and L2 and thus was bivalent but picture naming was always done in L1 and thus was univalent. However, picture naming in Sequence F involved a switch of language, but not in Sequence E. If suppression is involved in language switching, one would expect a longer RT for picture naming in Sequence F than in Sequence E. But if switch costs interact with valence and only occur with bivalent stimuli, as the authors suggested, no switch costs should be expected. The results replicated an asymmetry in switch costs in digit naming, but more importantly, no switch costs for picture naming were present, thus rejecting the role of suppression in switch costs. To test the possibility that only the words involved in the task, not the whole language, were suppressed, they changed pictures into dot patterns so that numerical words had to be used in picture naming. The results showed the same pattern. They offered two alternative explanations for switch costs and the asymmetry: a response blocking account and a stimulus–response event encoding account.

Verhoef, Roelofs, and Chwilla (2009) also argued against an inhibition-based approach to explaining the asymmetry in switch costs. They suggested an alternative. Instead of attributing a larger switch cost for L1 to the need to overcome greater suppression in switching to L1, they argued that the great switch costs are due to a particularly fast RT in L1 repeat trials (i.e., L1-L1 sequences). They referred to this fast RT as L1-repeat benefit. According to their L1-repeat-benefit hypothesis, in unbalanced bilinguals, L2 processing faces interference from L1 regardless of whether a switch is involved. L1 faces interference from L2 only when L2 has just been used, i.e., at a switch trial. In this case, the previously activated L2 can compete with L1 for output. In an L1 repeat trial, however, L1 performance faces no interference from the weaker L2. On the contrary, it benefits from the preceding trial as it is in the same language. As a result, L1-repeat trials are particularly fast, which inflates the RT difference between switch and non-switch trials in L1. To test this hypothesis, they asked bilinguals to perform a picture-naming task and manipulated the interval between a cue (used to indicate which language to use) and a stimulus. It was either 500 ms or 1250 ms. They reasoned that if L1-repeat trials are already very fast, having more preparation time, i.e., at a longer cue–stimulus interval, this should minimally benefit L1-repeat trials. In contrast, longer preparation times may benefit other three types of trials. A comparison of RTs for the four types of trials, L2 switch (L1–L2), L2 repeat (L2–L2), L1 switch (L2-L1), and L1 repeat (L1-L1), at the two cue–stimulus intervals supported their prediction. The participants were faster at the longer interval in all conditions except for the L1-repeat trials.

The research on the three topics reviewed in this section, cross-language priming, language selectivity, and switch costs, seems to face different challenges. Consistent findings are yet to be obtained about the circumstances under which masked cross-language priming effects can be observed. Research findings regarding the selectivity issue are largely inconsistent as well. In both cases, more work is to be done to know more about the phenomena themselves. Both the switch costs and the asymmetry in switch costs, on the other hand, seem to be robust and well replicated effects. The challenge is to provide empirically tested explanations.

## 2.6 Looking forward

Six decades of research has produced a wealth of knowledge about lexical representation and processing in bilinguals. It has helped uncover many new phenomena of lexical representation and processing in bilinguals, and explore alternative explanations about them (see Figure 2.1 for some

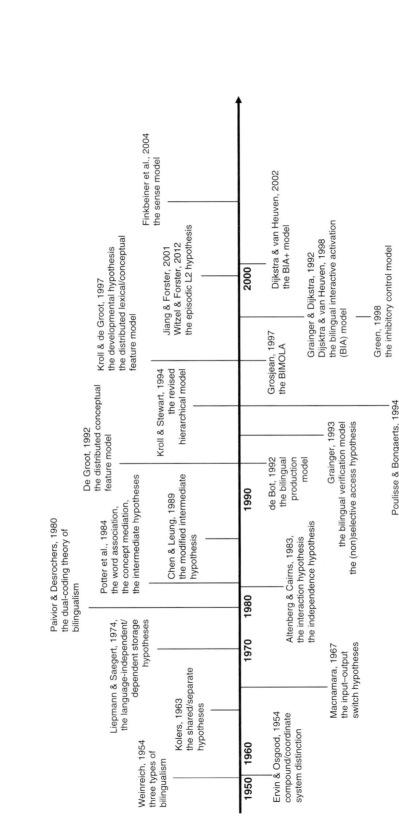

**Figure 2.1** Lexical representation and processing in bilinguals: models and hypotheses

of the models and hypotheses developed over the past six decades). At the same time, many questions remain. Some of these questions arise because of the inconsistency in current research findings, e.g., regarding cross-language priming and language selectivity. Other questions have to do with how to explain the phenomena. Existing explanations need to be empirically further tested, for example, in the case of the asymmetry in masked translation priming and the role of suppression in switch costs. New explanations may emerge and subsequently need to be verified. New phenomena about lexical access in bilinguals may be uncovered that require explanations as well. For example, some recent studies showed a larger frequency effect in L2 than in L1 (Duyck et al., 2008; Gollan et al., 2008). Another recently discovered phenomenon is that bilinguals seem to show a disadvantage in lexical access even in L1 in comparison to monolinguals (Gollan et al., 2005; Ivanova & Costa, 2008). These new findings call for explanations to be offered and empirically tested. Thus, many of the topics reviewed above will continue to inspire active research for many years to come.

Furthermore, most bilingual representation and processing research thus far has focused on the lexical level. It is a fair and equally important question to ask whether bilinguals' linguistic knowledge also interacts at other levels and how. In this regard, there has already been some research on whether syntactic knowledge is shared or separate in bilinguals, as expressed in the shared-syntax account and the separate-syntax account in Hartsuiker, Pickering, and Veltkamp (2004). These studies examined whether exposure to a particular sentence structure, e.g., double object dative structure (*I gave John many books*) in one language would result in the subsequent more frequent use of the same structure in the other language. This cross-language syntactic priming effect has been explored using dative structures and relative clauses in tasks such as sentence recall (Meijer & Fox Tree, 2003; Shin & Christianson, 2009), picture description (Bernolet, Hartsuiker, & Pickering, 2007; Hartsuiker, Pickering, & Veltkamp, 2004; Loebell & Bock, 2003; Schoonbaert, Hartsuiker, & Pickering, 2007), and sentence completion (Desmet & Declercq, 2006; Kantola & van Gompel 2011; Salamoura & Williams, 2007). The finding was quite consistent across these studies: a cross-language syntactic priming effect was reliably found, and it is often as strong as the within-language effect. The only inconsistency is regarding the role of word order between languages. In Loebell and Bock (2003) and Bernolet, Hartsuiker, and Pickering (2007), cross-language syntactic priming was found only when the two languages shared the same word order on the target structure. But Shin and Christianson (2009) found a cross-language syntactic priming effect where two languages had different word orders, i.e., dative structures in Korean and English. I expect to see more research on this topic, e.g., to explore the role of word order in cross-language syntactic priming and to test alternative explanations of this effect, such as the implicit-learning account offered by Loebell and Bock (2003) and the lemma-based account endorsed by Meijer and Fox Tree (2003) and Hartsuiker, Pickering, and Veltkamp (2004). See Hartsuiker and Pickering (2008) for a review of the findings and how they relate to different explanations.

The interaction of linguistic knowledge among bilinguals can be explored even from a broader perspective or at a more abstract level. Languages differ in how they categorize and lexicalize the physical world. For a quick example, the same object may be called a bowl in one language but a dish in another. This is believed to have an impact on how individuals view the world (Lucy, 1992; Slobin, 1996; Whorf, 1956) or on individuals' "habitual thought and behavior" in Sapir's words (Spier, Hallowell, & Newman, 1941). If this is true at least to some extent, we then have to ask how bilingual speakers handle their two different systems of categorization for the same physical world. Do bilinguals keep them separate? Or do they converge and form a single system that is different to each individual language? There is already some evidence showing that a bilingual speaker may gradually adopt a way of categorizing objects or concepts in a way specific to their L2 in L2 processing, e.g., in the categorization of objects (Athanasopoulos & Kasai, 2008; Cook et al., 2006; Malt & Sloman, 2003), in the categorization of colors (Athanasopoulos, 2009), and in the conceptualization of events (Bylund, 2009). It would be interesting to explore in future research whether such shifting only occurs temporarily in L2 processing, or whether it represents a more permanent change at the conceptual level that may affect language processing in both languages. The latter possibility is indicated by a converged pattern of categorization among balanced bilinguals that is different from that of either monolingual group (Ameel et al., 2005). Progress in this area will certainly elevate bilingual representation and processing research to a new level.

# 3 Computational modeling of bilingual language acquisition and processing

Conceptual and methodological considerations

*Ping Li and Xiaowei Zhao*

## 3.1 Introduction

In recent years research in bilingual language acquisition and processing has become increasingly important in formulating and testing mainstream theories of language and cognition. Traditional behavioral methods continue to play an important role, but new methods including neuroimaging and computational methods have also helped investigators to tackle complex theoretical and practical issues involving multiple languages. Computational models offer particular advantages in dealing with complex interactions between variables that are often intertwined in natural language learning situations, because modelers can systematically bring target variables under tight experimental control to test theoretically relevant hypotheses (McClelland, 2009). Modeling is particularly useful when we consider the many types of interactions that occur in the bilingual situation, including interactions between variables that modulate the acquisition, representation, and processing of multiple languages such as age of acquisition and levels of proficiency.

Computational modeling has played a vital role in understanding human cognitive and linguistic behaviors. Although modeling offers clear advantages in its flexibility and systematic control of variables, at the same time it poses some significant challenges to researchers. Specifically, it requires efforts on the part of the researcher to conduct algorithmic and representational implementations. It also requires the modeler to be very explicit about assumptions of their hypotheses, as they must specify, algorithmically, the very basic concepts in a model (e.g., such as "similarity," "adjacency," or "association" defined in quantitative and numerical terms).[1] In cognitive science and related fields, computational models based on algorithmic implementations have been very influential (see examples in Elman et al., 1996; MacWhinney, 2010). By contrast, while a number of computational models of bilingualism have been developed (see Grosjean & Li, 2013; Thomas & van Heuven, 2005, for reviews), the progress here has been slow, especially compared with advances in computational modeling in the monolingual context.

A wide variety of computational models has been implemented for language studies in the past decade, but a specific class of computational models has proved to be particularly useful for the understanding of the bilingual mind. This is the class of models that is inspired by connectionism, Parallel Distributed Processing (PDP), or artificial neural networks. In this chapter, we will discuss how connectionist models have been applied to the study of bilingual language acquisition and processing. Connectionist models have in the last twenty-five years provided an important theoretical framework as well as a computational tool for linguistics and cognitive science in general. Connectionist researchers hold that human cognition and behavior can be captured by a system that consists of large networks of interactive processing units operating simultaneously. Language as a hallmark of human behavior has received in-depth treatment since the beginning of connectionist research. However, researchers have only recently begun to explore the significance and implications of these models in bilingual acquisition and processing (see a recent special issue on computational modeling of bilingualism edited by Li, 2013).

In what follows, we will provide discussions of conceptual and methodological issues in connectionist modeling, and attempt to give an integrative review on how connectionist models can be used effectively to study bilingualism and second language acquisition. We will first introduce the basic philosophy of connectionist networks, and then provide some important methodological considerations for constructing a successful model of bilingual learning. We will review existing bilingual connectionist models, and demonstrate some general principles used in these models. We finally examine one specific model in detail, and end with a discussion of the challenges that face computationally minded bilingualism researchers.

## 3.2 Connectionist networks: basic concepts

Although some basic ideas of connectionism can be traced back to the 1940s (see Gardner, 1987 for a historic tour), connectionist perspectives in

---

[1] In some cases, of course, this means that the researcher may have to make assumptions based on the best knowledge or evidence available when the constructs themselves are unclear. On the other hand, the modeling of slippery constructs or concepts may also help us understand what they really mean (see Li & MacWhinney, 1996, for an example).

the study of human cognition and language became popularized only in the mid 1980s when research in connectionism promised it as a powerful theoretical framework for understanding the emergence of human thoughts in the brain. In 1986, Rumelhart, McClelland, and the PDP Research Group developed the Parallel Distributed Processing (PDP) framework, and published two volumes that contained descriptions of the PDP theories and models, new algorithmic designs, and applications of PDP to the study of language, memory, and learning. The two volumes quickly attracted widespread attention and brought PDP and connectionism under the spotlight. Given the relevance of connectionist networks as computational models for bilingual studies, we will first discuss the basic philosophy of connectionism below.

Connectionism emphasizes 'brain-style computation' (Rumelhart, 1989), in that information processing in connectionist networks is considered a process that simulates information processing in the real brain, albeit in a simplified form. Unlike digital computers, the human brain relies on parallel processing, involving simultaneous activities in a massive network of billions of neurons and trillions of synaptic connections between neurons. The speed of individual neurons in transmitting signals in terms of rate of firing is not very fast compared to modern digital computers (milliseconds rather than nanoseconds), but parallel computation allows for fast and effective human information processing. Because of parallel computation, the brain represents external information as patterns of neural activity rather than random collections of neuronal firing. These patterns emerging from joint actions of multiple neurons are well coordinated both spatially (i.e., which neurons become active) and temporally (i.e., when neurons become active). Such patterns of neural activity, unlike coded computer programs, dynamically change in response to external stimuli and to the learning individual's specific experiences.

With these considerations of brain features for computing (rather than digital serial computing), researchers build connectionist networks as artificial neural networks with two fundamental components: simple processing elements (*units, nodes*, or *artificial neurons*), and connections among these processing elements (hence the term 'connectionist networks' or 'connectionism'). Like real neurons, a node receives input from other nodes. The input signals are accumulated and further transformed via a mathematical function (e.g., a sigmoid function) to determine the activation value of the node. A given connectionist network can have varying numbers of nodes, many of which are connected so that activations can spread from node to node via the corresponding connections, either within the same level or across levels. Like real synapses, the connections can have different levels of strength (*weights*), which can be adjusted according to learning algorithms as discussed below, thereby modulating the amount of activation by which a source node can influence a target node. In this way, the network can develop unique combinations of weights and activation patterns of nodes in representing different input patterns from the learning environment.

Unlike traditional computer programs that are dedicated to specific tasks and are fixed *a priori*, the weights and activation patterns in most connectionist networks are allowed to continuously adapt during learning. It is these adaptive changes that make connectionist networks rather than computer programs as interesting models of human behavior. The ability of the human brain to derive the 'optimal' set of synaptic connections for problem solving in a complex learning environment is the basis of neural information processing that has inspired connectionist theories of learning, memory, and language. Each individual neuron in the brain (or a node in the model) is not very powerful, but a simultaneously activated neural network makes human cognition possible and makes connectionist models powerful in simulating human cognition.

There are two basic concepts underlying connectionist networks. A key idea is *emergentism*, which indicates that thoughts (e.g., percepts, concepts, semantics) emerge from parallel interactions among the computing neurons in our brain. Another key feature of connectionist networks is its "dynamic" feature, which indicates the "non-static" status of a network, in that the network's internal representation dynamically changes in response to the complexity and the demands of the learning environment. Extending these two ideas into linguistics, connectionist linguistic models often embrace the philosophy that static linguistic representations (e.g., words, concepts, grammatical structures) are emergent properties, and can be dynamically acquired from the input environment (e.g., the speech data received by the learner).

## 3.3 Connectionist simulations: methodological issues

To conduct a connectionist simulation, as in conducting any other experiments, one needs a well-established testable hypothesis, a carefully designed experimental framework (network structure), a well-controlled setting of variables, and eventually a clear explanation of the simulation outcome. Although connectionist networks have been a valuable tool for mining useful information from large amounts of data in certain areas (e.g., data mining in marketing), in cognitive and linguistic studies researchers cannot simply feed a large amount of language data into a model and expect that some useful patterns will come out of the model. A clear research goal is the key to a successful connectionist network simulation. Usually modelers should carefully first select certain linguistic phenomena found in empirical studies, identifying the issues or debates, identifying the key variables under investigation, and then by simulating them, researchers can support or build alternative explanations for certain theories. In the following, we will focus on some methodological issues when conducting connectionist modeling that may be particularly relevant to the study of bilingualism.

### 3.3.1 Linguistic representations

A critical issue facing all connectionist language researchers is how to accurately represent various linguistic features (e.g., phonology, morphology, semantics) in their models. Christiansen and Chater (2001) argued that "input representativeness" is crucial for computational modeling of language (see a similar argument in Jacquet & French, 2002). This issue may be even more important for studies of bilingualism and second language acquisition, as cross-language overlap or similarity of two languages can have significant implications for patterns of bilingual processing, representation, and acquisition (see Li, 2015, for a recent discussion of behavioral and neurolinguistic evidence).

In connectionist models, a crude way to represent lexical entries is to use the so-called 'localist' representation, according to which a single, unitary processing unit in the network randomly picked by the modeler is assigned a numerical value to represent a linguistic item (e.g., the meaning, sound, or other linguistic property of a word). In this fashion, the activation of a node can be unambiguously associated with a linguistic property of a unique word that the node is supposed to represent, and the strength of the activation can be taken as the indicator of how well the property is represented (Plunkett & Elman, 1997).

A different way, championed by the PDP models in general, is to represent lexical entries as distributed representations, according to which a given lexical item is represented by multiple nodes and their weighted connections, as a distributed pattern of activation of relevant microfeatures. This contrasts with a localist representation, in which a word, for example, may be represented by only one unit. The distributed representation requires the assembly of multiple units corresponding to multiple semantic features for representing the semantic concept of a word, and is more useful for simulating realistic language learning. Figure 3.1 demonstrates the difference between localist and distributed representations with an example in representing the concepts of words.

Which of the two representation methods should we use for simulating bilingual learning? Because of the one-to-one mapping between linguistic entities and units, the localist representation has the simplicity and efficiency for modeling. Localist representations have been successfully used in simulating several important cognitive/ linguistic phenomena within the connectionist framework (see a review in Bowers, 2002). A well-known computational model in bilingualism, the original BIA model (Dijkstra & van Heuven, 1998), was a localist model. However, in simulating bilingual learning and processing, the similarities and differences between two

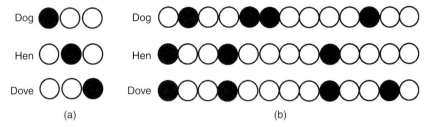

**Figure 3.1** An illustration of (a) localist representation and (b) distributed representation. In (a) each of the three concepts is uniquely represented by the activation of a unit in the input; while in (b) each concept is represented by a distributed pattern of activation across all the 13 units in the input. Similar concepts have similar activation patterns (e.g., *hen* and *dove*)

languages are often important factors under consideration and could be part of the research goals. The localist one-node-one-entity representations cannot effectively capture the similarities and differences and therefore lack linguistic and psychological reality (Jacquet & French, 2002). For example, one cannot easily simulate similarity-based semantic priming effects with a localist representation, given that semantic similarities among concepts are not explicitly encoded in the representation patterns when concepts have randomly assigned values in the model (although the modeler can manually assign different connection strengths between the representations). In these situations, the researcher will need to consider the distributed representations and build models that can more accurately simulate language acquisition in monolingual and bilingual contexts. Below we discuss a few methods for generating distributed semantic and phonological representations.

### 3.3.2 Generating semantic and phonological representations

Methods for generating distributed semantic representations of words can be roughly classified into two groups. First, the feature-based approach involves the representation of a word's meaning by a vector, and each dimension of this vector represents a possible descriptive feature/attribute of the concept. For example, the representations of *dove* and *hen* are very similar except one dimension representing the flying feature (refer back to Figure 3.1 for a demonstration; also see Ritter & Kohonen, 1989, for a detailed representation of sixteen animals based on thirteen attributes). In this type of representation, empirical data are often used to help generate the features describing the meaning of words (see Li & MacWhinney, 1996; McRae et al., 2005 for examples). Second, the corpus-based approach derives meanings of words through co-occurrence statistics from large-scale language or speech corpora. The underlying hypothesis is that if two words have similar meanings or belong to similar lexical categories they would often occur in similar contexts (e.g., *table* and *chair*). Some of the corpus-based methods rely on calculating the word–word co-occurrence frequencies (e.g., Burgess & Lund, 1997; Jones & MewHort, 2007; Li, Farkas, & MacWhinney, 2004), while others rely on calculating the co-occurrence matrix of target words with their surrounding context (e.g., Landau & Dumais, 1997). The resulting representation in each of these methods can be thought of as points in a high-dimensional hyperspace, and the number of dimensions in the vector's representation usually increases as the corpus size increases. Zhao, Li, and Kohonen (2011) recently developed the Contextual Self-Organizing Map, a software package that can derive corpus-based semantic representations based on word co-occurrences in multiple languages, and the method has been shown to capture unique linguistic features of different languages (Zhao, Doyle-Smith, & Li, 2011).

Methods for generating phonological representations of words are many, but recent development favors the approach that codes a word's pronunciation on a slot-based representation while taking into consideration the articulatory features of phonemes in the word. In particular, the phonology of a word is encoded in term of a template with a fixed set of slots; each phoneme of the word is assigned to a different slot, depending on which syllable it belongs to and in which position it appears in the syllable, such as onset, nucleus, or coda. Li and MacWhinney (2002) provided a method for automatically generating distributed phonological representations for English words, which can also be extended to other languages such as Chinese (Zhao & Li, 2009).

Unlike the above methods that attempt to capture realistic semantic or phonological features of the language, some connectionist linguistic models use artificially generated features to represent words or other linguistic properties in the training data. For example, in a model of early word learning by Mayor and Plunkett (2010), the authors used artificially generated random dot matrices to represent the visual objects and their acoustic labels (see similar representations in the BSN and BSRN models, discussed in the section on models). The artificially generated representations may also take the form of localist representation. For example Servan-Schreiber, Cleeremans, and McClelland (1991) trained a Simple Recurrent Network (Elman, 1990; see discussion below) in which each word was assigned a unique node in the input pattern. Although patterns from artificial languages are easy to construct and can greatly streamline the modeling process, regardless of whether they are distributed or localist, it raises the issue of whether results from such models can make direct contact with the statistical properties of natural linguistic input to which the learner or language user is exposed.

### 3.3.3 Learning algorithms and network architecture

Different connectionist networks use different algorithms to adjust weights to achieve learning. These algorithms can be classified roughly

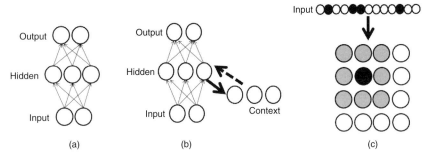

**Figure 3.2** Three basic connectionist network architectures. (a) a multilayer network trained by backpropagation; (b) a Simple Recurrent Network with a context layer, which keeps a copy of the hidden unit activations at a prior point in time; and (c) a self-organizing map with 16 units: the black node indicates the Best Matching Unit (BMU) corresponding to the input and the gray nodes are the BMU's neighbors

into two groups: *supervised* and *unsupervised* learning. A typical connectionist network with supervised learning consists of three layers of nodes: input layer, hidden layer, and output layer (see Figure 3.2a). The input layer receives information from input patterns (e.g., representations of alphabetic features), the output layer provides output patterns produced by the network (e.g., classifications of alphabets according to shapes), and the hidden layer forms the network's internal representations as a result of the network's learning to map input to output (e.g., the visual similarities between 'O' and 'Q'). The most widely used supervised learning algorithm in psychological and cognitive studies is "backpropagation" (Rumelhart, Hinton, & Williams, 1986): each time the network learns an input-to-output mapping, the discrepancy (or error, $\delta$) between the actual output (produced by the network based on the current connection weights) and the desired output (provided by the researcher) is calculated, and the error is propagated back to the network (sometimes through a couple of layers of units) so that the relevant connection weights can be changed relative to the amount of error (represented as the so-called Delta rule: $\Delta\omega = \eta^*\delta$, where $\Delta\omega$ indicates change of weight, $\eta$ the rate of learning, and $\delta$ the error).[2] Continuous weight adjustments according to the Delta rule lead the network to fine-tune its connection weights in response to regularities in the input–output relationships. At the end of learning, the network derives a set of weight values that allows it to take on any pattern in the input and produce the desired pattern in the output.

An important connectionist model for language based on supervised learning is the Simple Recurrent Network (SRN; Elman, 1990). A typical SRN combines the classic three-layer backpropagation learning with a recurrent layer of context units (see Figure 3.2b). During the training of an SRN, temporally extended sequences of input patterns (e.g., a sequence

---

[2] Practically, new parameters could be added into the equation to facilitate learning in the network (e.g., a "Momentum" parameter).

of words within a sentence) are sent to the network, and the goal/target of the network is to predict the upcoming items in the sequences (i.e., predicting the next word given the current word input in the sentence). A novel aspect of the SRN model is its use of context units, which keep a copy of the hidden-unit activations at a prior point in time, and then provide this copy along with the new input to the current stage of learning (hence "recurrent" connections). This method enables connectionist networks to effectively capture the temporal order of information, since the context units serve as a dynamic memory buffer for the system. Given that language unfolds in time, the SRN therefore provides a simple but powerful mechanism for identifying structural constraints in continuous streams of linguistic input.

In contrast to supervised learning models, unsupervised learning models use no explicit error signal at the output level to adjust the weights. There have been several different types of unsupervised learning algorithms developed (see Hinton & Sejnowski, 1999). Among them, a popular type is the self-organizing map (SOM) (Kohonen, 2001), upon which we will focus here (for further technical details, see Li, Farkas, & MacWhinney, 2004; Li, Zhao, & MacWhinney, 2007).

The SOM usually consists of a two-dimensional topographic map for the organization of input representations, where each node is a unit on the map that receives input via the input-to-map connections (see Figure 3.2c). At each training step of SOM, an input pattern (e.g., the phonological or semantic information of a word) is randomly picked out and presented to the network, which activates many units on the map, initially randomly. The SOM algorithm starts out by identifying all the incoming connection weights to each and every unit on the map, and for each unit, compares the combination of weights (called the "weight vector") with the combination of values in the input pattern (the "input vector"). If the unit's weight vector and the input vector are similar or identical by chance, the unit will receive the highest activation and is declared the "winner" (the best matching unit, BMU). Once a unit becomes highly active for a given input, its weight vector and that of units in its neighborhood are adjusted,[3] such that they become more similar to the input and hence will respond to the same or similar inputs more strongly the next time. This process continues until all the input patterns elicit specific response units in the map. As a result of this self-organizing process, the statistical structure implicit in the input is captured by the topographic structure of the SOM and can be visualized on a 2-D map as meaningful clusters. This topographic structure is a salient feature of SOM-based models since several areas in the cortex (e.g., the primary motor and somatosensory areas) are

---

[3] In the standard SOM algorithm, the size of the neighborhood of a BMU is set to decrease as learning progresses but some variations have been developed, such as the self-adjusted neighborhood function introduced in DevLex-II model (see Li et al., 2007).

known to form topographic maps, which means that nearby locations in the brain represent adjacent areas on the body when stimulated.

Unsupervised learning may also be realized in the brain, as captured by Hebbian learning (Hebb, 1949). Hebbian learning is a neutrally inspired and biologically plausible mechanism, which essentially simulates the principle that "neurons that fire together wire together." The Hebbian learning rule can be expressed simply as $\Delta w_{kl} = \beta \cdot \alpha_k \cdot \alpha_l$, where $\beta$ is a constant learning rate, and $\Delta w_{kl}$ refers to change of weights from input $k$ to $l$ and $\alpha_k$ and $\alpha_l$ the associated activations of neurons $k$ and $l$. The equation indicates that the connection strengths between neurons $k$ and $l$ will be increased as a function of their concurrent activities. Although Hebbian learning is not part of the SOM model, different self-organizing maps can be linked via adaptive connections trained by the Hebbian learning rule to simulate complex cognitive or linguistic behaviors (see further discussion in the models section).

Although supervised and unsupervised learning networks are two mostly widely used types in connectionist linguistic simulations, there are also other connectionist network structures, such as "hybrid" models that combine both supervised and unsupervised learning methods, and models that have adjustable structures or involve dynamic unit growth (e.g., the cascade-correction network of Shultz, 2003; the DevLex model of Li et al., 2004; the constructivist neural network of Ruh & Westermann, 2009a). Researchers should carefully choose an appropriate network structure based on their specific research questions. For example, if the researcher is interested in semantic representation and organization, a SOM-based architecture might be highly appropriate and relevant, but if the researcher is interested in simulating the processing of temporally ordered components (e.g., syntax), a network with a portion resembling the SRN structure might be a better candidate.

## 3.3.4 Selection of parameters for modeling

Regardless of the type of model architecture a researcher uses, every model will involve a set of "parameters" that need to be considered and set up. Among them, there are research variables whose effects on the network's output are of interest to the researchers. A benefit of computational modeling is that researchers can easily bring a research variable under tight experimental control by systematically manipulating different levels of the variable and see the effects while holding other variables constant. For example, in studies of second language acquisition, a researcher can try a model with L1 (first language) data first and then introduce the L2 (second language) data to the model at different stages during the training, so as to simulate effects of ages of L2 acquisition (early vs. late L2; see more discussion in the next section). In this way, we can investigate the outcome caused by the use of different levels of a specific research variable, which may be difficult to manipulate in the natural environment (e.g., one cannot have the same individual at both an early and late learning stage, as can be done in the model).

Other than the research variables, there are also some "free parameters" in a model that often need to be adjusted by the modelers. For example, how large should the size of the network be to adequately learn the target aspect of the second language? What value should be assigned to the learning rate? For an SOM model, how many nodes should be included initially in the neighborhood of a BMU before training? Decisions need to be made by the researchers in advance on such practical questions before a simulation is run. Often, there are no correct answers to these questions as each model involves a different degree of complexity and different input-to-output relationships (i.e., task difficulty), and the researcher needs to use experience based on previous models and conventional wisdom in setting up appropriate values for the free parameters (see Haykin, 1999). One caution here is that the researcher should avoid introducing too many free parameters in a simulation project. Although more free parameters usually means better fitting of the model to the target data, it may compromise the external validity of the network in relating to the phenomena being simulated. As in empirical studies, findings from overly tight controlled experiments with too many variables under consideration may not generalize to other situations.

Once the training of a network is completed, it is crucial for the researcher to evaluate the performance of the network and see if it has successfully simulated the empirical patterns. Importantly, researchers need an "operational definition" of the network's performance. A common approach is to analyze the activation pattern of the output layer of a network. For example, considering a three-layer backpropagation network trained to learn the meaning-to-sound association of words (e.g., in simulating the lexical production), the researcher can calculate the error level of the network corresponding to an input pattern (e.g., matching to the semantic features of a word). If the corresponding error is below a certain threshold (i.e., the output is quite similar to the target – the correct sound of the word), one can operationally define that the network has learned to correctly produce the word. As behavioral studies, the percentage of the total correctly associated meaning-to-sound pairs can be used to evaluate the overall performance of the network in producing words. As in any experimental studies, multiple trials and multiple simulation run with different random initial weights should be used in a connectionist simulation. Variability should be expected on the results across the trials and runs, and the significance of the results should be tested with appropriate statistical analyses. Another common approach is to analyze the "internal representation" of the network, as reflected in the weights or the activation patterns of the hidden layer. Some techniques have been used for the purpose of analyzing a connectionist network's internal representation, such as cluster analysis, principal component analysis, Hinton diagram, and the U-matrix for SOM models (see Kohonen, 2001; Plunkett & Elman, 1997). In the next section, we will show how both approaches in model analyses are applied to connectionist models of bilingualism.

## 3.4 Connectionist models of bilingualism

In this section we will briefly review a few key connectionist models of bilingualism. For a more detailed review of earlier models, see Thomas and van Heuven (2005). For more recent models, see articles in a recent special issue on computational modeling of bilingualism edited by Li (2013). For a more complete bibliography with annotations, see Li and Zhao (2012).

### 3.4.1 Earlier models

One of the best-known computational models of bilingualism is the Bilingual Interactive Activation (BIA) model of Dijkstra and van Heuven (1998). The BIA model is a localist model based on the Interactive Activation (IA) model of McClelland and Rumelhart (1981). In the original IA model, there are three levels of nodes: (1) features of a letter such as curves, straight lines, or crossbars; (2) individual letters; and (3) words. Information at all three levels can interact with each other during word recognition, in both "bottom-up" (features to letters to words) and "top-down" (words to letters to features) fashions. Within levels, nodes compete for activation (thus inhibiting each other); across levels, nodes either inhibit or excite each other. These inhibitory and excitatory connections give rise to the appropriate activation of patterns that capture the word recognition process. Incorporating these design features into the study of bilingualism, the BIA model consists of four levels of nodes: features, letters, words, and languages. BIA uses the same parameters to regulate interactions within and across levels as in the IA model. What is special to the BIA model, apart from modeling two different lexicons, are the language nodes (e.g., one for English and one for Dutch). Language nodes in BIA function as an important mechanism for the selection or inhibition of words in one or the other language. BIA argues for and implements the language-independent access hypothesis, according to which words from different languages are simultaneously activated during word recognition.

The BIA model was later expanded as the BIA+ model (Dijkstra & van Heuven, 2002), in which non-linguistic properties such as decision and task schemas were added to the original BIA model to account for a variety of empirical patterns. Although the BIA models have found a great deal of empirical evidence in bilingual processing, they do not incorporate dynamic learning mechanisms to allow for the effects of developmental changes because they were designed to capture proficient bilingual speakers' mental representation. This was partly due to the design characteristics of the original IA model, which preceded the PDP models that developed learning algorithms, and partly due to the fact that earlier models were more interested in modeling the end state of bilingualism rather than developmental changes. Developmental issues such as effects of age of acquisition (AoA) and relative proficiency over time did attract the attention of several other connectionist models that have incorporated learning mechanisms, as discussed below.

Thomas (1997) used a Bilingual Single Network (BSN) model to learn the orthography-to-semantics mapping in visual word recognition. The BSN used a standard three-layer network with the backpropagation algorithm to transform a word's orthography (input) to a word's semantic representation (output) through the network's internal representation (hidden units). The model was trained on vocabulary sets from two simplified artificial languages (L1 and L2), and the network was exposed to both L1 and L2 material, either in a balanced condition (equal amount of training) or unbalanced condition (L1 trained three times as often as L2). The orthography and the meaning of these pseudo words were represented in a distributed (rather than localist) fashion (though artificially generated). Their language membership was also explicitly marked in both the input and output layer of the network. After learning, the network's internal representation (the activation pattern of the hidden units) of each pseudo word was analyzed by a statistical technique called Principal Component Analysis (PCA). This analysis indicated that under both conditions, the network was able to develop distinct internal representations for L1 vs. L2, although in the unbalanced condition the L2 words were less clearly represented as compared with those in the balanced condition. The BSN model demonstrated that connectionist models are able to account for both language independence and language interaction within a single network.

Incorporating sentence-level input, French (1998) tested a Bilingual SRN (BSRN) model also trained on artificially generated sentences of the N–V–N structure in two artificial languages (Language Alpha and Beta). The network was exposed to bilingual input as in Thomas (1997), but with the two artificial languages intermixed at the sentence rather than the word level, and with the input having a certain probability of switching from one to the other language. In addition, no explicit language membership marker was included in the model (i.e., no "language nodes" as in the BIA model). The model adopted the architecture of Simple Recurrent Network (Elman, 1990), and as in the SRN model, the task was to predict the next word given the current word input in the sentence. Learning in the SRN, as discussed earlier, leads to the emergence of distinct linguistic representations as a result of the network's analysis of the context in which the current word occurs among the continuously unfolding input. French tested his network under two scales: a small-scale dataset with twelve localist-represented pseudo words per language and a large-scale dataset with 768 distributed-represented pseudo words per language. Simulations with the BSRN model under both conditions showed that distinct patterns of the two languages emerged after training: words from the two languages became separated in the network's internal representations (the hidden-nodes activations) as analyzed by PCA. The model provided support to the hypothesis that the bilingual input environment itself (mixed bilingual sentences in this case) is a sufficient condition for the development of a distinct mental representation of each language, without invoking separate processing or storage mechanisms for the different languages.

The BSN and BSRN models were based on supervised learning algorithms. To explore unsupervised learning for bilingual processing, Li and Farkas (2002) proposed a self-organizing model of bilingual processing (SOMBIP), in which training data derived from actual linguistic corpora were used for the model. The SOMBIP was based on the SOM architecture discussed above. Through Hebbian learning, the model connects two SOM maps: one trained on phonological representations and the other on semantic representations. The phonological representations of words were based on articulatory features of phonemes (using the PatPho software of Li & MacWhinney, 2002), whereas the semantic representations were derived from the extraction of co-occurrence statistics in child-directed, bilingual, parental speech. Chinese and English were the two target languages, and the activation patterns (the distribution of BMUs corresponding to the words) on the two SOMs were analyzed. Simulation results from SOMBIP indicated that the simultaneous learning of Chinese and English led to distinct lexical representations for the two languages, as well as structured semantic and phonological representations within each language. Consistent with the general patterns of BSN and BSRN, these results suggest that natural bilingual input contains sufficient information for the learner to differentiate the two languages. An interesting aspect is that SOMBIP provides a different way to assess proficiency. By having the network exposed to fewer sentences in L2, the model simulates a novice learner having limited linguistic experience, and this differs from a predetermined, more artificial training schedule in simulating learner differences (e.g., BSN's balanced versus unbalanced training schedule in which L1 was trained three times as often as L2 for the latter). This more natural way of modeling proficiency, interestingly, yielded comparable results to those from the unbalanced BSN: the 'novice' network's representation of the L2 was more compressed and less clearly delineated, compared to the 'proficient' network.

The SOMBIP model later evolved into the DevLex (Developmental Lexicon) models in an attempt to provide a more general mechanistic account for both monolingual and bilingual learning and processing (Li, Farkas, & MacWhinney 2004; Li, Zhao, & MacWhinney, 2007; Zhao & Li,

2010). Before we discuss the DevLex model, we will provide a short summary of several recent connectionist models of bilingualism.[4]

## 3.4.2 Recent models

In recent years there has been a growing interest in using computational models, specifically connectionist models, to study bilingual language acquisition and processing. Monner et al. (2013) developed a connectionist model in an effort to address a long-standing issue in bilingual language acquisition: to what extent is the learning of a second language influenced by the entrenchment of one's first language? This question is related to the so-called critical period, which has traditionally been attributed to a biologically determined timetable. Recent studies, however, have argued against the original account put forth by Lenneberg (1967) that there is a biologically based critical period for language acquisition due to brain lateralization; instead, the evidence points in favor of cognitive and linguistic mechanisms underlying the age of acquisition effects seen with L1 and L2 acquisition. For example, Johnson and Newport (1989) suggested that language learning in childhood carries certain cognitive advantages precisely because of children's limited memory and cognitive resources (the "less is more" hypothesis; see also Elman, 1993). Monner and colleagues tested the "less is more" hypothesis using a connectionist model that learns the gender assignment and agreement in Spanish and French. A significant contribution of their model is that it not only tests a theoretical hypothesis, but also illustrates that computational models can flexibly bring important variables under systematic control, variables that are otherwise confounded in natural learning settings, as we have discussed earlier under methodological considerations. For example, in Monner et al.'s network, increase of working memory is simulated by the use of new cell assemblies in the model, whereas L1 entrenchment is simulated by training of the network with variable-length exposure to L1 before the onset of L2 (see more discussion below on this in the DevLex-II model). In this way, the modeling results allow us to dissociate effects due to age of L2 onset and those due to capacity of memory, thereby specifying individual and joint contributions of these two variables. The authors concluded that their model supported the "less is more" hypothesis while at the same time showing an L1 entrenchment effect as a function of L2 onset time. This example illustrates the important role that modeling can play in bilingualism research, as discussed earlier, given that in human learning the two variables (age and memory) are naturally confounded.

Cuppini, Magosso, and Ursino (2013) built a connectionist model to tackle the relationship between the degree of L2 proficiency and the

---

[4] The reader is encouraged to read the details of these studies in a recent special issue in *Bilingualism: Language and Cognition*, edited by Li (2013).

interaction between L1 and L2 lexical semantic representations. In the last decade there has been growing evidence that bilingual speakers may recruit the same brain areas to handle both L1 and L2 (for a review, see Abutalebi, 2008), although the degree of involvement of these areas may be different depending on the level of L2 proficiency. Cuppini and colleagues' model has a distinct lexical representation for each language but a common conceptual representation for the two languages, and training in the model shows different strengths of connection between the L1 and L2 lexical systems as a function of different L2 proficiency: as it becomes more proficient in the L2, the model is able to make direct connections between L2 lexical form and conceptual knowledge, not relying heavily on the connections between L1 and L2 lexical form representations. These patterns are consistent with Green's (2003) convergence hypothesis, according to which increased L2 proficiency will lead to neurocognitive convergence with regard to the way bilinguals represent and process the two languages. The model also aspires to connect with neuroscience and neuroimaging data through simulations with neutrally plausible mechanisms such as Hebbian learning and long-term potentiation, which is another unique feature of the model (see general discussion on bridging modeling and neuroimaging data).

Shook and Marian (2013) developed the Bilingual Language Interaction Network for Comprehension of Speech, or the BLINCS model. In contrast to the BIA or BIA+ models that have been used to account for visual word recognition, the BLINCS model is designed to examine spoken word comprehension. A previous computational model of spoken word recognition, the BIMOLA model (Bilingual Model of Lexical Access, Lewy & Grosjean, 2008), involves the use of the original IA model mechanisms and localist representations, as in the BIA models. The unique features of the BLINCS model are at least two: first, its incorporation of both classic connectionist learning algorithms and unsupervised self-organizing maps (SOM), and second, the use of bidirectional excitatory and inhibitory connections within and across different levels of processing. The first feature provides the model with a means to represent the detailed linguistic and phonological properties while at the same time adapt to cognitive demands in real-time processing, whereas the second feature allows the model to capture lexical interactions within and across languages. The BLINCS model is a significant step forward from the SOMBIP model (Li & Farkas, 2002) in that it simulates bilingual lexical activation as it unfolds in time; even though the SOMBIP model was also motivated by considering issues of learning and representation and bidirectional cross-language interactions, it did not have the detailed learning and representation mechanisms as in BLINCS. The BLINCS model has successfully accounted for cross-language co-activation, effects of cognate facilitation, and audiovisual integration in speech comprehension. Moreover, the model allows researchers to simulate interactions of two separate lexicons without requiring a global language-identification system (in contrast to the BIA+ model).

Filippi, Karaminis, and Thomas (2014) presented a connectionist model of language switching in bilingual production. This work provided a good example for integrating empirical experimentation and connectionist modeling. Their results were based on simulations of behavioral experiments in which Italian–English adult bilinguals were asked to name visually presented words in the two languages (and their language switch costs were measured). Their models were based on previous connectionist network architectures (e.g., Cohen, Dunbar, & McClelland, 1990; Seidenberg & McClelland, 1989). The results from both their modeling and experimentation demonstrated a pattern of asymmetry: bilinguals showed a greater cost in reaction time when naming involved switching from their less fluent language to their dominant language than switching in the reverse direction (see Meuter & Allport, 1999, for empirical evidence). The authors argued that this switching asymmetry arises from the competition between the bilingual's two languages during production and the resolution of this competition. Note that such asymmetries arose not as a function of the explicit manipulation of weights in the model (as some earlier models may do); rather, they emerged from the model's processing of different characteristics of the input language (e.g., with or without switch trials and in which direction the switching occurs).

While a large number of connectionist models of language acquisition have used unsupervised learning, specifically the SOM architecture (see Li & Zhao, 2012, for a bibliography), only a handful of bilingual models have used SOM (including the SOMBIP and BLINCS discussed above). Kiran, Grasemann, Sandberg, and Miikkulainen (2013) presented a SOM-based model to simulate patterns of bilingual language recovery in aphasic patients following treatment. Their model, DISLEX, had been previously applied to simulate aphasia and bilingual lexical representation (Miikkulainen, 1997; Miikkulainen & Kiran, 2009). In Kiran et al. (2013), the model is applied to simulate behavioral patterns on a case-by-case basis for each of the seventeen patients who underwent treatment following injury. The model's close match with real behavioral data from individual patients is a testimony that computational models, when properly constructed, can closely reflect realistic linguistic processes (in addition to other advantages of modeling discussed in this Introduction). Their model incorporated important variables underlying patterns of bilingual behavior, including the patient's language history with regard to age of L1 and L2 acquisition, proficiency, and the dominance of the treatment language. More impressive is their model's ability to predict the efficacy of rehabilitation in each of the bilingual patient's languages. In reality, each bilingual patient underwent rehabilitation treatment for only one of their languages (English or Spanish) due to empirical constraints, but Kiran et al.'s model was trained for recovery in both languages following the lesion, thus showing considerable advantage and flexibility of the model as compared with examination of the actual patient. Finally, in empirical

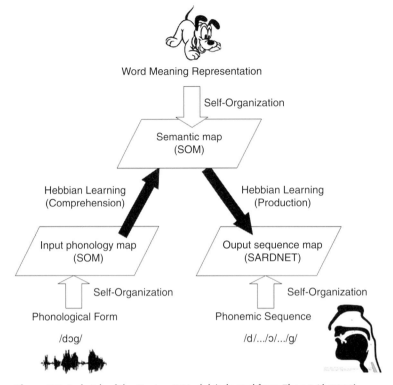

**Figure 3.3** A sketch of the DevLex-II Model (adapted from Zhao & Li, 2010)

studies the researcher works with the injured patient and cannot go back to study the patient's pre-lesion condition, whereas in computational modeling the researcher can examine the intact model, lesion it, and then track the performance of the same model before and after lesion, as was well done by Kiran and colleagues in their model.

### 3.4.3 DevLex-II model

In what follows we will discuss the DevLex-II model of bilingual processing so as to illustrate the theoretical and methodological issues discussed above. DevLex-II uses the basic structure of multiple SOMs connected via Hebbian learning. The architecture of the model is illustrated in Figure 3.3 (see Li, Zhao, & MacWhinney, 2007 for further technical details). The model includes three basic levels for the representation and organization of linguistic information: phonological content, semantic content, and the articulatory output sequence of the lexicon. The core of the model is a SOM that handles lexical–semantic representation. This SOM is connected to two other SOMs, one for input (auditory) phonology, and another for articulatory sequences of output phonology. Upon training of the network, the semantic representation, input phonology, and output phonemic sequence of a word are simultaneously presented to the network. This process can be analogous to that of a child hearing a word and performing analyses of its semantic, phonological, and phonemic information.

In DevLex-II, the associative connections between maps are trained via the Hebbian learning rule. As training progresses, the weights of the associative connections between the frequently and concurrently activated nodes on two maps will become increasingly stronger. After the cross-map connections are stabilized, the activation of a word form can evoke the activation of a word meaning via form-to-meaning links, so as to model word comprehension. Similarly, the activation of a word meaning can trigger the activation of an output sequence via meaning-to-sequence links, to model word production.

To capture realistic linguistic data, DevLex-II used as our simulation material the real Chinese and English lexicons based on the MacArthur-Bates Communicative Development Inventories (the CDI; Dale & Fenson, 1996). The model was trained on a total of 1,000 words, with 500 words from the CDI Toddler list of each language. Input to the model was coded as vector representations of the phonemic, phonological, or semantic information of words. As in SOMBIP, the PatPho software was used to generate the sound patterns of words based on articulatory features of English and Chinese (Li & MacWhinney, 2002; Zhao & Li, 2009). For semantic representations, two types of information were used: (1) the co-occurrence probabilities of words computed from the parental input in the Child Language Data Exchange System (CHILDES) database (MacWhinney, 2000); this was done by WCD, a special recurrent neural network that learns the lexical co-occurrence constraints of words (see Li et al., 2004 for details); (2) the semantic features based on computational thesauruses available for each of the two languages (WordNet, see Miller, 1990, and HowNet, see www.keenage.com). The two types of information above were then combined to form each word's semantic vector.

One important theoretical issue we wanted to study was the impact of age of acquisition (AoA) on L1 and L2 representations in our model. Much of the current debate about the nature of L2 learning and how it differs from L1 learning stems from the "critical period" hypothesis, and Monner et al.'s (2013) model provided useful insights in this regard, as discussed above. DevLex-II simulated two learning scenarios in our model: early L2 learning, and late L2 learning. In early L2 learning, the onset time of L2 input to the model was slightly delayed relative to that of L1 input (e.g., L2 learning occurs when 1/5 of the L1 vocabulary has been learned), and in late L2 learning the onset time of L2 input was significantly delayed relative to that of L1 (e.g., L2 learning occurs when 4/5 of the L1 vocabulary has been learned). By systematically manipulating the relative timing of L1 versus L2 input, the model should yield results to identify the impact that L1 has on L2 lexical representation and organization.

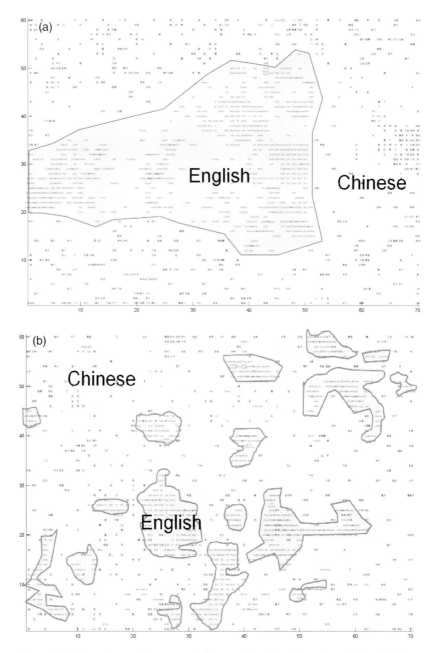

**Figure 3.4** Bilingual semantic representations as a function of age of acquisition. Dark areas correspond to L2 (English) words. (a): early L2 learning; (b) late L2 learning

Analyses of the network's activation pattern on the semantic map and phonological map, as shown in Figure 3.4, indicate how the BMUs of the words from the two languages are distributed differently across the two learning conditions on the semantic map. The results indicate that AoA plays a major role in modulating the overall representational structure of L2 (see Figure 3.4): in early L2 learning, the network could organize the L2 lexical structure well (as assessed through measures of lexical space and accuracy in form-meaning mapping), though not as well as in the simultaneous learning situation as shown in the SOMBIP model (Li & Farkas, 2002), whereas in late L2 learning, the network was unable to establish an independent lexical space for the L2. In particular, if L2 onset occurs at a time when the L1 has been consolidated, as in late L2 learning, the learned structure in L1 will constrain what can be learned, as the network becomes more committed to L1. Therefore, as shown in Figure 3.4, the L2 structure (b) is distinctly more fragmented as a whole compared to the L1, more compressed within each L2 space, and had fuzzier representations.[5] Such representational structures could also have implications for accounting for L2 learners' difficulty in efficient and effective lexical access and retrieval, as well as how effectively they can learn new words across different stages. Our modeling results also indicated more rapid learning for the early rather than the late learning situation, suggesting that representation and learning go hand in hand in connectionist models (see Zhao & Li, 2010). These findings also provide new evidence for the perspective on critical period in terms of the changing plasticity, L1 entrenchment, and L1–L2 competition (see Li, 2009).

Zhao and Li (2013) further showed that DevLex-II can integrate learning and processing, as demonstrated also by other models (e.g., Shook & Marian, 2013). DevLex-II was extended to simulate the effects of age of acquisition on cross-language semantic priming. The model incorporated additional mechanisms such as spreading activation and was able to demonstrate a number of classic effects of priming that have been reported in the empirical literature, including effects of priming direction (stronger priming from L1 to L2 than from L2 to L1) and types of priming (stronger priming for translation equivalents than semantic related word pairs across the two languages). The simulations suggest that bilingual representation is the result of a high dynamic learning process, and enriched (vs. less enriched) semantic representations from different learning stages and context could significant impact processing behavior such as in semantic priming.

## 3.5 Future directions

In the previous sections, we have demonstrated the utility of connectionist network models for bilinguals' language learning and processing. At this point it should become clear that computational models, especially connectionist models, have much to offer to the understanding of the

---

[5] Similar results were obtained when English was trained as the L1 and Chinese the L2.

bilingual mind. Through modeling we can systematically identify the interactive effects of multiple languages in terms of L2 onset time (e.g., early vs. late), L2 input frequency (e.g., high vs. low), amount of L1 versus L2 input, order of L1 versus L2 learning, and how the effects impact both the learning trajectory and the learning outcome. In particular, mechanisms of competition, organization, and plasticity in the development and processing of two linguistic systems can be systematically investigated as a function of variables that are inherent in the learning process, such as those discussed in previous models, including AoA, proficiency, dominance, and individual difference in cognitive capacity. As such, computational models can serve as an important tool to deepen our understanding of the processes and mechanisms involved in the acquisition and processing of multiple linguistic systems.

McClelland (2009) provided a good discussion of the role that computational modeling plays in cognitive science in general. Yermolayeva and Rakison (2013) also had a comprehensive review and discussion of the contributions of and challenges for connectionist modeling of developmental changes. Implementation of computational models forces the researcher to be very explicit about their hypotheses, predictions, materials, and testing procedures, and at the same time offers the flexibility in parameter selection and reliability of testing that are not often found in empirical studies. Indeed, the potential of a bilingual computational model lies in its ability to identify gaps in experimental designs, and in systematic manipulation of variables such as age of acquisition, cognitive capacity, and proficiency, variables that may be naturally confounded in experimental or learning situations.

Computationally minded bilingual researchers are also faced with several significant challenges. One is how we can bridge computational modeling results with a variety of other behavioral, neuropsychological, and neuroimaging findings. Current computational models suggest the need for greater integration of computational results with behavioral results and neuroimaging findings, and the need for increased ability of the model to make predictions in light of non-convergent data. For example, Kiran et al. (2013), as discussed earlier, provided an example in this regard, in which the investigators constructed a model to simulate neuropsychological patterns of each of the seventeen bilingual patients following traumatic brain injury and subsequent treatment.

A second, more general, challenge that lies ahead is how we can develop models that make predictions in light of the simulations and empirical data. In some cases, the empirical data have not yet been obtained, or cannot be obtained (e.g., as in the case of brain injury, one cannot go back to pre-lesion conditions), and this is the occasion where modeling results will be extremely helpful. Not only should computational modeling verify existing patterns of behavior on another platform, it should also inform theories of bilingualism by making distinct predictions under different hypotheses or conditions. In so doing, computational modeling will provide a new forum for generating novel ideas, inspiring new experiments, and helping formulate new theories. For example, simulation results based on the DevLex-II model showed that cross-language priming effects decrease as a function of stimulus onset asynchrony (SOA, Zhao & Li, 2013). Many studies of semantic priming in the monolingual context have indicated the effects of SOA, but not many such studies exist in the bilingual context (see Schoonbaert et al., 2009 for an exception in this domain). The simulation findings can therefore serve to inspire future empirical studies in this direction.

A third challenge is how computational models of bilingualism, especially of the type discussed in this chapter, can move beyond the lexical level. Most of the work in the current literature, as reviewed here, has focused on the bilingual lexicon, perhaps for the obvious reason that words and concepts are more manageable in terms of their explicit representations in the model (see Introduction on the 'explicitness' requirement for computational models). However, there is ample empirical data on cross-language interaction in word order, morphosyntax, and even discourse level, and researchers will wonder how computational models or connectionist models may contribute to the understanding of mechanisms of bilingual language acquisition and processing in these domains other than the lexicon. This will prove to be a major challenge in the years to come.

Finally, computationally minded researchers should follow a recent call by Addyman and French (2012) to make an effort to provide user-friendly interfaces and tools to non-modelers, so that many more students of bilingualism can test computational models without fearing the technical hurdles posed by programming languages, source codes, and simulating environments. Some initial efforts have been made elsewhere in this regard. For example, Ruh and Westermann (2009b) introduced Oxlearn, a MatLab-based connectionist network simulator, which can build multilayered feedforward networks, including the simple recurrent network. A more comprehensive and research-oriented neural network simulator is "Emergent," which includes an online manual from http://grey.colorado.edu/emergent. PDPTool is another Matlab-based neural network simulator that serves as the accompanying teaching tool for the new PDP handbook by McClelland (2014). However, many of these tools were not designed for bilingual studies, and were not equally easy to understand or to use, and therefore further efforts are required of both the modeler and the user.

# 4
# Methods for studying adult bilingualism

Michael Spivey and Cynthia Cardon

## 4.1 Introduction

As awareness of multilingualism all over world has increased, it is not a surprise that there has been an increased focus on research investigating bilingualism. In the fields of cognitive science, psycholinguistics, and neuroscience, researchers have studied the processes of the bilingual mind to better understand how a bilingual manages two or more language systems, and how these language systems interact, and what consequences bilingualism has for other cognitive processes. In this chapter, we describe a variety of experimental methods used to explore the mechanisms of bilingual language processing. We place emphasis here on experimental methods, rather than qualitative and observational methods, because they are ideal for scientifically testing the theories that exist – many of which were originally developed and proposed via more qualitative research methods. A detailed treatment of more observational methods in bilingualism research can be found in Wei and Moyer (2008).

The experimental methods we describe in this chapter each have their strengths and weaknesses, and can often complement one another. For example, whereas some methods provide fine-grain temporal or spatial resolution for observing the real-time cognitive and linguistic processes involved in comprehending a sentence as it is delivered, those methods tend to be less flexible and less portable, and can sometimes infringe on the ecological validity of the language use situation. By contrast, low-tech methods that are flexible and portable (and thus readily used in an ecologically valid non-laboratory environment) will tend to focus on the endpoint result of a linguistic event, and not on the ongoing processes during a linguistic event – thus providing somewhat less insight into the real-time cognitive mechanisms involved. Rather than ruling out certain methods because of their weaknesses, we encourage the use of multiple methods to triangulate on the phenomena at hand. Nonetheless, we do place special focus in this chapter on the dual strengths of what we call "dense-sampling methods" in the study of bilingual language processing. Certain dense-sampling methods can often allow both a moment-by-moment record of the ongoing processing of linguistic input and also a greater degree of ecological validity than is often availed by other laboratory methods.

This chapter will briefly describe a wide range of experimental methods that provide a variety of perspectives into the processes of bilingual language comprehension, production, and learning. There are many ways that one could structure this list of methods, and we have chosen to structure it in such a way that two compensatory continua of strengths can be compared: (a) ecological validity in the circumstances of language use; and (b) real-time sampling of ongoing linguistic processes. Our treatment starts with offline methods that tend to allow for more ecological validity but little real-time measurement and move toward methods that provide more real-time measurements and perhaps less ecological validity. However, the last set of methods that we discuss are called "dense-sampling" methods, because they sample multiple measurements of a single cognitive process densely over time. In certain circumstances, these dense-sampling methods can actually achieve both goals of maintaining ecological validity and obtaining real-time measurements of ongoing linguistic processing. The chapter ends with a concrete example of how the integration of multiple methodologies has elucidated the field's understanding of the cognitive advantages and disadvantages of having two languages coexist in one mind. The lesson here is that every methodology for measuring a phenomenon has its inherent assumptions, its strengths, and its weaknesses. We try to identify those, with the goal of encouraging researchers to use a multitude of methods when possible, in an attempt to leave behind the problematic assumptions of any one methodology and to triangulate multiple perspectives on the phenomena at hand.

## 4.2  Proficiency levels in bilingualism

Before getting started, it is important to discuss certain methodological criteria with the goal of establishing a universal understanding of the goals and outcomes of the research being conducted in the area of bilingual language processing. Grosjean (1998) points out that central to the difficulties in bilingual research are the variability in concepts and definitions. De Houwer (1998) recommends that researchers should refrain from using challenged or debated terminology, and be wary of terms that are too general which can be used to describe too many different types of bilingual behavior. Here we address the concept of "proficient," definitions of "dominant" and "balanced" as it applies to levels of language proficiency, and the terms "early" and "late" in reference to the age of onset at which a bilingual begins to learn a second language. Selection of bilingual participants in experimental designs is not an easy task, especially when understanding that the language proficiency of the participant is crucial for the task. In bilingual research, a measure of proficiency of the bilinguals' languages is necessary to obtain an accurate measure of performance (Marian, Blumenfeld, & Kaushanskaya, 2007), and to say that a participant is "proficient" in a language is not reliable without an established "baseline for cross-linguistic comparison" (De Houwer, 1998: 258) for all languages. Related to the proficiency conundrum is the question of language dominance. Petersen (1988) and De Houwer (1988) define "dominant" language as the language in which a bilingual is most proficient. The difficulties that arise in terms of determining dominance is that in order to gauge the level of dominance in a bilingual, their "proficiency" in each language must be determined, but without a baseline for comparison in proficiency (see also Festman & Schwieter, Chapter 23), dominance may be difficult to define. In current research, bilinguals that perform each language equally well are considered "balanced" bilinguals (Butler & Hakuta, 2004; Grosjean, 1982). Because language processing and representation can be affected by many factors such as age of acquisition (Genesee et al., 1978; Grosjean, 1998; Lambert, 1981), language history, and proficiency (Grosjean, 1998), established measures should be considered to reduce variation in the "balanced" bilingual designation. Two other terms often seen in current bilingualism literature are "early" or "late" learner bilinguals. Genesee et al. (1978) describes "early" bilinguals as those who learn both languages simultaneously from birth, and "late" bilinguals as those who become bilingual at school age or later on. When age of acquisition is an important consideration in a study, Genesee et al. (1978) suggests that using "early" and "late" would be a more accurate description of the bilingual participants. Describing bilinguals as "early" or "late" also implies differences in processing, as age of acquisition may affect how a bilingual's two linguistic systems interact (Butler & Hakuta, 2004; Genesee et al., 1978). This discussion by no means suggests the aforementioned points will remedy all, but by keeping track of the proficiency levels of one's experimental participants, many pitfalls in experimental design and data interpretation can be avoided.

## 4.3 Offline methods

There is a range of traditional offline methods that have been used in bilingualism research. These offline experimental paradigms do not record the ongoing real-time processes of language comprehension or production in bilinguals. Instead, they record the end result of language comprehension or production in bilinguals. Therefore, these methods do not allow one to measure the temporal dynamics of language processing as it is happening, however they are helpful in providing insight into what the final product of comprehension is for a sentence or vignette. Moreover, since they do not require electronic equipment, they tend to be quite portable methods that can be taken into the field and into participants' homes when necessary, allowing for some degree of ecological validity in the circumstances in which the linguistic phenomena are being tested.

For example, grammaticality judgments have been used as a measure of what types of sentence structures are perceived as acceptable exemplars from the grammar and which ones are not. When reading a sentence such as (1) or (2), one can use his/her own intuitions about whether the sentence is grammatically acceptable or not. If the sentence is considered ungrammatical, the convention is to place an asterisk before it.

(1) It was the painting that the artist who scolded the critic admired.

(2) *It was the painting that the artist who scolded the critic who admired.

For bilingual research, the grammaticality judgment task has been useful for assessing adult's and children's proficiency with a second language (Bialystok, 2001; McDonald, 2006). Certain complex syntactic structures that may be processed correctly by a native speaker will instead be treated as ungrammatical by a less proficient speaker of that language. However, treating a given sentence as categorically grammatical or ungrammatical may be an oversimplification of how language is processed, even by native speakers. There has been a temptation in linguistics to imagine that a grammaticality judgment reflects direct access to one's "linguistic competence," wherein formal syntactic rules determine whether a given sentence belongs to the grammar or not. And the fact that, during natural conversation, people routinely comprehend and produce ungrammatical sentences is often attributed to "linguistic performance," which is treated as a separate process that is prone to statistical noise and imperfection. However, the fact is that making a judgment about the grammaticality of a sentence is an artificial and unusual task that a person performs, and thus it may not provide as direct an access to linguistic competence as some have assumed. This meta-linguistic aspect of the task, where a participant is thinking about how their mind is processing language, rather than simply processing language in an "auto-pilot" fashion the way they normally do, poses some concern for treating this task as though it were an ecologically valid measurement of linguistic processing. And it may not be that sentences are sensibly categorized into discretely grammatical and discretely ungrammatical. For example, when Bard, Robertson, and Sorace (1996) adapted a magnitude estimation task (borrowed from psychophysics) for use in grammaticality judgments, they found a very systematic pattern of gradation in degrees of grammaticality among a range of sentences, and this pattern was quite consistent across participants. Therefore, if the grammaticality judgment task is measuring linguistic competence, then that competence must not be composed of formal syntactic rules that force a given sentence to either be wholly grammatical or wholly ungrammatical. Alternatively, if it is merely measuring behavioral linguistic performance, then there may be no accepted method at all for testing the existence of an abstract formal linguistic competence.

Another traditional offline method that has provided some insight into bilingual language processing is feature-listing tasks. In this method, a participant is presented with a concept, such as "bird," and asked to provide a list of features or properties that first come to mind when thinking about that concept (Rosch & Mervis, 1975a). As with grammaticality judgment tasks, one should be careful about treating this deliberative meta-cognitive task as providing some kind of direct unadulterated access to the concept itself. Nonetheless, the task does provide useful data regarding people's impressions about what is important about a given concept. For example, Boroditsky, Schmidt, and Phillips (2003) asked a group of German–English bilinguals and a group of Spanish–English bilinguals to generate three English adjectives for each of a set of concepts (such as "key" and "bridge") that have opposite grammatical gender in Spanish and in German. For example, in Spanish the word for key is "la llave," with the feminine determiner "la," whereas in German, the word for key is "der Schlüssel," with the masculine determiner "der." It should be noted that nouns that have neutral gender in German were not used in the study. As evidence that the arbitrary grammatical gender for that word in their native language may have influenced their semantic representation of the concept, for the stimulus "key," German–English bilinguals listed features such as hard, heavy, and jagged, whereas Spanish–English bilinguals listed features such as golden, intricate, and lovely. This observation provides some interesting support for a weak version of the Whorfian hypothesis of linguistic relativity, in which different language subsystems in a single bilingual speaker may train that person's conceptual representations to take on even some of the arbitrary features inherent in the language.

More often than not, we experience language in meaningful sentences rather than in the form of a single, unattached adjective or noun. In language research, sentence completion tasks offer a useful methodology to explore how the knowledge of multiple languages influences sentence processing. In this research design, participants are given a variety of sentence fragments to complete with either a word or a phrase (either written or spoken). Researchers using this method to study sentence processing are able to gain a better understanding of bilingual lexical processing in a sentence context. Sentence completion tasks are also convenient methods for norming one's stimuli in advance for later use in a real-time methodology.

In psycholinguistics, the sentence completion task has been an easy and informative method for use with monolingual populations. Some examples include studies on syntactic priming (Pickering & Branigan, 1998; Scheepers, 2003), research with aphasics in support of training to produce past tense verb morphology (Weinrich, Boser, & McCall, 1999), and exploration of subject–verb agreement errors (Eberhard, 1999). Although somewhat less prevalent in bilingual research, there is considerable promise in using this method. For example, Desmet and Declercq (2006) used sentence completion tasks to find evidence for cross-linguistic priming of relative clause attachments in Dutch–English bilinguals. Nicol and Greth (2003) used sentence completion tasks to provide more evidence for interactions between L1 and L2, with English–Spanish bilinguals who had near-advanced proficiency with Spanish. Although native Spanish speakers exhibit semantic influences in their patterns of subject–verb number agreement errors (Vigliocco, Butterworth, & Garrett, 1996) whereas native English speakers tend not to (Bock & Miller, 1991), Nicol and Greth found that their English–Spanish bilinguals exhibited the same pattern of subject–verb number agreement errors in their L2 as in their L1.

Like sentence completion tasks, behavioral methods such as the act-out task have been used to investigate relative clause attachments, syntax, and sentence comprehension (Gentner & Toupin, 1986; Kemper, 1986; Kidd & Bavin, 2002). A study using an act-out task requires the participant to act out the events depicted in a spoken or written sentence by using dolls, figurines, or some type of physical object. The ability to perform the actions correctly is interpreted as the participant's understanding of the constructions being presented (Kidd & Bavin, 2002). Customarily, this methodology has been used widely in studies of monolingual children with focus on acquisition and development of various grammatical structures (Gentner & Toupin, 1986; Kidd & Bavin, 2002), or with aphasic patients (Postman, 2004). However, Martohardjono et al. (2005) used the act-out task to demonstrate similar developmental trends in L1 and L2 performance among Spanish–English kindergarteners.

Some of the advantages of using act-out tasks in language research are that they are inexpensive, easy to administer, and they can be done almost anywhere with minimal equipment and preparation. Unfortunately, like feature lists, the act-out task operates on the assumption that each concept being used should be easily recognizable in the target language because they are defined by a specific set of characteristics that each person understands. Even for monolinguals, there is a lot open to individual interpretation in terms of the sentences and words being used. For bilinguals, knowledge from the first language informs meaning of words in the second language (Meyer, 2000), which could mean that people from different cultures may construct different meanings for the same concept, which could result in varying interpretations of sentences.

Another frequently used offline experimental method is the free recall memory task, where a list of words is presented and then after a period of time the participant is prompted to freely report as many items from the list as possible. Interestingly, even when a mixed-language memorization list discordantly intermixes different semantic categories across the two languages, bilinguals are still able to store in memory the groups of semantically clustered items that were delivered in different languages (Lambert, Ignatow, & Krauthamer, 1968). Lambert et al. interpreted this result as evidence that the two language systems in a bilingual play a cooperative role in how input gets organized for memory. Related to this method is the recognition memory task, in which a list of words is presented and then after a period of time the participant is prompted with candidate items that may or may not have been on the list, and she reports which ones are recognized from the original list. Kintsch (1970) replicated Lambert et al.'s basic finding with bilingual list memory, using a recognition memory task, and concluded that bilinguals can alternately organize their memory along language-specific cues or along general semantic cues. And a similar kind of result was found by Marian and Neisser (2000) for memories elicited in an autobiographical recall task. They found that while eliciting memories from their Russian–English bilinguals with certain key words, such as "birthday," "summer," and "doctor," the language in which they presented those words influenced what age of memory they came up with. Those same words in Russian tended to elicit autobiographical memories from a time when they mostly spoke Russian: their early childhood. Whereas when the elicitation words were in English (their second language), the memories elicited were more recent.

In addition to using individual word stimuli to elicit autobiographical memories, one can use individual word stimuli to elicit individual words. In the word association task, as used in bilingual research (Kolers, 1963), participants are instructed to respond to a single word stimulus with the first word that comes to mind. If they are in a same-language condition, their response should be in the same language but should not be the same word as the stimulus word. If they are in a different-language condition, their response should be in their other language but should not be a translation of the stimulus word. Similar to the findings with autobiographical memory (Marian & Neisser, 2000), the pattern of responses in this task led Kolers to conclude that bilinguals store their memories and word associations in ways that are partly language specific. Importantly, this task can be converted into an RT method by recording the latency of the participants response with a microphone switch (van Hell & de Groot, 1998a).

In general, this array of offline experimental methods benefits from being easy to set up, and can therefore be used in ecological valid environments of natural language use, especially with rare bilingual populations in hard-to-reach locales. However, as these methods focus almost exclusively on the final output of a language processing event, they do not provide a detailed window into the internal cognitive and linguistic mechanisms that carry out the process of language comprehension or production.

## 4.4 Neuroimaging methods

Neuroimaging methods provide an opportunity to peek inside the internal workings of a bilingual brain when it is processing one or more of its languages. However, these methods tend to be rather expensive and do not easily lend themselves to mobility and ecological validity. Although the delivery of linguistic input can take place with little or no metalinguistic processing, lending these methods a modicum of ecological validity, they generally require the participant to be immobile to prevent artifacts in the signal of neural activity, which takes away from their ecological validity. Some technologies sacrifice spatial resolution of brain areas in order to obtain fine-grain temporal resolution of the neural activity signal (e.g., EEG), while others sacrifice temporal resolution of the signal in order to obtain fine-grain spatial resolution of brain areas (e.g., fMRI). And one methodology (e.g., MEG) balances these two goals. All of these methods, however, have a tendency to rely – at least somewhat – on the assumption that certain brain regions function as domain-specific modules devoted to various subcomponents of the language processing system (see Hernandez, Chapter 24).

Methods such as electroencephalography (EEG), and the Event-Related Potential (ERP) analysis of the signal, have been utilized to improve our understanding of bilingual cognition. In this method, a scalp EEG is used, which records the brain's electrical activity by way of surface electrodes that are placed on the participant's head.

The benefits of using the EEG are that it is non-invasive, equipment is relatively inexpensive as compared to most other neuroimaging techniques, and EEG does not entail using excessively bulky equipment, which allows for some degree of transportability for access to a greater range of participants. Another benefit of this methodology is EEG's fine-grain temporal resolution, in milliseconds rather than seconds (Kroll et al., 2008), which is not available with functional magnetic resonance imaging (fMRI). Also with ERPs, researchers are able to look at ongoing moments of real-time processing rather than just the end reaction or result. Upon visual delivery of a target word in a sentence, the EEG waveform can have a characteristic (positive or negative) deflection – after averaging over many trials and many participants – that can be seen 100, 400, or even 600 milliseconds later. For example, a negative deflection in the waveform 400 ms after delivery of a critical word in a sentence (the so called N400) is often indicative of a semantic anomaly in the sentence

(Kutas & Hillyard, 1980). By contrast, a positive deflection in the waveform 600 ms after delivery of a critical word in a sentence (the so called P600) is often indicative of a syntactic anomaly in the sentence (Osterhout & Holcomb, 1992). And it can also be elicited by an anomalous note in the structure of a musical melody (Patel, 1998). Alongside this advantage in temporal resolution is the disadvantage that EEG and ERPs have poor spatial resolution, which can make data analysis challenging in that results would require an extensive amount of interpretation to determine exactly which brain areas are activated.

Although behavioral methods in bilingual research have been successful in increasing our understanding of bilingual cognition, questions still arise in terms of the underlying activity in areas of the cortex that may be involved in bilingual language processing. For this reason, EEG and ERPs are a very effective tool to use in combination with behavioral measures, especially because with EEG no additional responses are required beyond what is needed for the chosen behavioral task (Kroll et al., 2008). Recent research by Christoffels, Firk, and Schiller (2007) combined a picture-naming task with ERP to investigate language control and phonological activation of the non-response language in unbalanced German (L1)–Dutch (L2) bilinguals. ERPs and naming latencies were examined and they found cognate facilitation effects for L1 and L2 in mixed and blocked language conditions. Other research investigated language-switch costs in terms of response-switching to evaluate executive control in bilinguals (Jackson et al., 2001). Native English speakers who could name digits 1–8 in French, German, Spanish, Mandarin, or Urdu performed a digit-naming task while switching between their two languages. EEG and high-density ERPs were recorded. Jackson et al. (2001) found that the combined recorded ERPs and behavioral data suggested that L1 is more inhibited when accessing L2, than vice versa. EEGs have also been used in conjunction with a delayed naming task to study reading of Chinese–English bilinguals (Liu & Perfetti, 2003). ERPs were recorded while participants were asked to produce a word in either Chinese or English in response to a given stimulus. Liu and Perfetti report findings that suggest Chinese and English reading include some shared processes.

The literature discussed here has suggested that EEG and ERP methodologies may help to reveal aspects of bilingual language processing that behavioral measures alone may not. The ability to detect stages in processing in terms of millisecond measures is invaluable when studying processes such as language selection in bilinguals, and also in determining the cortical areas involved in bilingual language processing.

Functional magnetic resonance imaging (fMRI) has much coarser temporal resolution than EEG, typically having to average the data over a full second or more. However, the spatial resolution of fMRI is much finer grained than what can be achieved with EEG, thus allowing for quite specific spatial localization of brain region activation. For this reason, it is often desirable to combine results from EEG and fMRI when developing neurological models of language processing. Both EEG and fMRI require laboratory infrastructure and extensive training of multiple research team members. While an EEG facility can be expensive in the range of tens or hundreds of thousands of dollars, an fMRI facility is typically in the range of several million dollars to set up and maintain.

By detecting volume differences in oxygenated blood versus deoxygenated blood, fMRI can identify precise brain regions whose neural activation patterns have increased and therefore are drawing more blood flow (to feed the metabolic processes of those neural structures). Importantly, there is a delay time of at least a few seconds for this blood flow, depending on the vasculature in that brain region. For this reason, precise temporal resolution for knowing what part of a sentence elicited an increase in neural activation in a particular brain area is not typically possible with fMRI. However, averaged activation patterns over the course of overall language use can provide a very detailed map of what brain regions were generally active. For example, Kim et al. (1997) used fMRI to find that early and late bilinguals exhibit the same regions of activation in temporal-lobe language areas (e.g., Wernicke's area) for processing their L1 and L2, whereas late bilinguals alone exhibit separate non-overlapping regions of activation in frontal-lobe language areas (i.e., Broca's area) for processing their L1 and their L2.

Magnetoencephalography (MEG) provides something of a balance between the fine spatial resolution of fMRI and the fine temporal resolution of EEG. With millisecond timing, MEG records the fluctuation of magnetic fields that are produced by the synchronous firing of large groups of neurons, much like EEG. However, by using a large array of extremely sensitive magnetometers, MEG is able to obtain much finer spatial resolution than EEG – though still not as fine grained as that of fMRI. Whereas EEG can typically localize activation patterns to entire lobes, such as frontal, parietal, temporal or occipital, MEG can localize activity to particular cortical regions such as primary auditory cortex, or differentiate between primary motor and premotor cortices. Still finer spatial resolution requires fMRI, which can identify sub-regions of activity in those cortical functional areas. Like EEG and fMRI, extensive training and laboratory infrastructure are required for this methodology, and the cost for MEG is in the same general range as fMRI.

Bialystok et al. (2005) used MEG to explore the neural correlates of bilinguals' superior performance in cognitive control tasks. In a variety of bilinguals from various language backgrounds, performance on Simon tasks (which require the participant to inhibit certain automatized responses in order to produce the correct response) is significantly better than that of monolinguals (for a review, see Bialystok, 2001). By recording MEG data from bilinguals and monolinguals while they performed Simon tasks, Bialystok et al. (2005) found that on trials where monolinguals were performing well on the task, it was bilateral middle frontal brain regions that were most active. By contrast, on trials where bilinguals were performing well, it was mostly left hemisphere language-related areas that were active. Based on these results, they suggested that the learning and management of two languages leads to substantial changes in the neural circuitry that implements cognitive control for bilinguals, compared to that of monolinguals.

Clearly, these neuroimaging methods provide a great deal of information about the mechanisms and processes that carry out bilingual language processing. That said, the theoretical interpretation of the data should be conducted with great care. Even separate from the ecological validity concern about whether a person who is immobilized while having linguistic input delivered to them is really processing language in a natural way, there are concerns about how to interpret the neural activation patterns observed. In previous decades, many neuroimaging studies relied heavily on the assumption that there are anatomically separate brain regions that are specialized for the various component processes that linguists have postulated for language processing (e.g., modules for phonology, morphology, syntax, semantics, etc.). However, more recent examination of the evidence in the cognitive neuroscience of language suggests that the constellation of neuroimaging results in the field is not consistent with the idea that each component process is carried out by a separate brain region, or even by a separate network of brain regions. Rather, based on co-activation graphs, it appears that the functional units that are associated with the different component processes in language and in cognition may be different patterns of cooperation between brain areas (Anderson, Brumbaugh, & Suben, 2010); and those different patterns of cooperation may be what give rise to semantic processes in one situation and to syntactic processes in another. Due to the limitations on how to interpret neuroimaging data, de Bot (2008) has suggested that neuroimaging methods have yet to fulfill their promise to the field of bilingualism. Therefore, the clear lesson here is that for all the wealth of information provided by neuroimaging studies of bilingual language processing, they still should not be used in a vacuum. The best scientific progress will be achieved by combining these methods with others.

## 4.5 Reaction time methods

Perhaps the most commonly used experimental methods in bilingualism research fall into a general class of what we will loosely refer to as RT methods. These methods tend to fall in between the extremes of offline methods (that aim for ease of use at the cost of mechanistic insight) and neuroimaging methods (that aim for mechanistic insight at the cost of ecological validity). In fact, some offline methods have been converted into speeded-response versions that place them in this rough category of RT methods. For example, when people make speeded grammaticality judgments, with response deadlines at 300, 550, or 800 milliseconds, this speed–accuracy tradeoff method provides intriguing insight into the time course of the gradual accumulation of syntactic and semantic information (McElree & Griffith, 1995). Similarly, speeded spoken sentence completions, with response deadlines at 300, 600, or 900 milliseconds, can reveal the early ambivalence between syntactic structures to choose from in completing the sentence (see Spivey, 2007: ch. 7). Although these methods have not yet been applied to bilingual research, they could be of significant use. Note, however, that both of these speeded–response methods are somewhat difficult for participants to carry out, and they clearly involve intensive meta-linguistic processing, which makes them less ecologically valid than some other methods.

Two of the most frequently used RT methods in bilingualism research are the word-naming task and the lexical decision task (deciding whether a string of letters is a word or nonword). Word naming is perhaps closely related to the reading aloud that we occasionally do in ecologically valid natural language-use environments, whereas the lexical decision task clearly recruits a fair amount of meta-linguistic processing. Fast RTs in these tasks are interpreted as evidence for an easily activated lexical representation. Slower RTs in these tasks are often interpreted as evidence for some form of interference in the activation process of the relevant lexical representation, or competition from other lexical representations. For example, Jared and Kroll (2001) had English–French bilinguals simply name words presented on a computer screen, and recorded as the RT the latency between the onset of the word on the screen and the onset of their speech into the microphone. Critical English words in these experiments had portions of French words embedded in them, such as the English word bait, which has orthographic similarity with the French words, *lait* and *fait*. Naming times for these words were a few dozen milliseconds slower than frequency-matched words that did not have words in French that had similar orthography.

Lexical decision times show similar results. De Groot, Delmaar, and Lupker (2000) had Dutch–English bilinguals perform an English-specific lexical decision task (with Dutch words as foils) and a Dutch-specific lexical decision task (with English words as foils). In both cases, words that happened to be interlingual homographs, such as glad (which means slippery, in Dutch) elicited RTs that were a couple dozen milliseconds slower than control words, suggesting that interlingual homographs activate both lexical representations in the two lexicons and there is some response competition between the two. These results were interpreted as evidence that when bilinguals read words, the orthographic input is mapped non-selectively onto both lexicons – even when the task requires only one lexicon to be used. While these methods are more portable than eyetracking reading, in that they can be brought anywhere that a laptop can go, they involve a somewhat unnatural task, forcing the participant to respond to isolated words and even requiring an unusual judgment about whether a string of letters is a word or not. The somewhat meta-cognitive aspects of the lexical decision task have caused some to suggest that it may tap post-lexical processes rather than lexical activation processes themselves (West & Stanovich, 1982).

Progressive demasking (Grainger & Segui, 1990) is another way to measure the activation of a lexical representation, which may provide an earlier index of the actual time course of activation of the lexical representation more directly than with the lexical decision task. In progressive demasking, a stimulus mask is quickly alternated with the word stimulus, and gradually the duration of the flickering mask is decreased while the duration of the flickering word stimulus is increased. This process stretches out the time course of the word recognition event, allowing the button-press RT to more easily take place during word recognition rather than after it. Van Heuven, Dijkstra, and Grainger (1998) employed this technique to show that when Dutch–English bilinguals responded to Dutch words that had more orthographic neighbors from English, they showed slower RTs, and vice versa for English words. As with the other methods, these results were interpreted as evidence that a bilingual's two lexicons are both taking up orthographic input even while processing monolingual written word stimuli.

Picture–word interference tasks have also been used in bilingual research to explore the potential for competition between lexical representations in a bilingual's two lexicons. In this paradigm, a line drawing of an object is presented on the computer screen, and the participant is instructed to name that object as quickly as possible. However, embedded in the line drawing is a written word that will often interfere with processing and elicit slower RTs. Ehri and Ryan (1980) first demonstrated that written words from one language do in fact interfere with naming of an object in a bilingual's other language – suggesting that activation of a lexical representation for speech production may involve activation of both of a bilingual's lexicons. However, just as with the lexical decision task, there have been concerns that RTs in the picture–word interference task may reflect post-lexical processes rather than purely lexical activation effects (La Heij & Van den Hof, 1995). Therefore, Kaushanskaya and Marian (2007) augmented the method with eyetracking to obtain measures of processing that precede the button-press response. With the object to be named in one quadrant of the screen and the irrelevant written word (in a different language) in another quadrant of the screen, eye movement measures were able to show that linguistic information from the nontarget language draws participants' attention even before the object naming takes place. Russian–English bilinguals naming objects in English were more visually distracted by written words when they were Russian than when they were English. As before, these results are consistent with the claim that lexical access in bilinguals is non-selective. While processing in one language, bilinguals do not appear to be able to summarily deactivate the irrelevant language.

A significant proportion of this co-activation across the two language subsystems may be due to cognates (full and partial ones) spreading activation to one another. Multiple different methods have shown that cognates exhibit cross-language priming and non-cognates do not. Cross-language priming is a sort of meta-methodology in this context, in which a briefly presented word from one language can prime (or speed the recognition of) the next presented word from the bilingual's other language. The actual task that the participant performs on that second-presented word can be a lexical decision or various other types of responses. Priming from L1 to L2 is sometimes stronger than priming from L2 to L1 (Keatley, Spinks, & de Gelder, 1994). Using a lexical decision task, de Groot and Nas (1991) reported faster-than-control RTs for *rico* in Spanish when primed by *rich* in English (cognate translations), and same-as-control RTs for *pato* in Spanish primed by "duck" in English (non-cognate translations). Then Sánchez-Casas, Davis, and García-Albea (1992) found that same finding with a translation task. They presented a brief masked prime word (such as "duck") for 60 milliseconds, followed immediately by an all-capital-letter target word (such as *PATO*) which the participant was to translate into English (in this case, by saying "duck"). The RT with which one can generate the translation of the target word is treated as an indication of how readily the lexical representation for the target word can spread its activation to the translation-equivalent lexical representation in the other language. As with the lexical decision task, Sanchez-Cases et al.'s cued translation task found that, due to the shared orthography, cognates exhibit priming whereas non-cognates do not.

In addition to producing a translation in the translation task, one can also measure the speed of recognizing a translation, in the translation recognition task. By presenting simultaneously on the computer screen a word from L1 and a word from L2, and asking the participant to determine whether these two words are translations of one another or not, RTs again provide an index of how readily the associated lexical representations in a bilingual's two language subsystems can spread their activation to one another. De Groot and Comijs (1995) found that the translation recognition task produces generally similar results to the translation task, with a few exceptions. For example, coincidental orthographic similarity between non-translation pairs can cause slower and less accurate responses when compared to control conditions.

Orthographic similarity also plays a role in the bilingual variant of the Stroop task (Preston & Lambert, 1969). When naming the color of the ink for a string of letters, reactions times are significantly longer if the string of letters happens to form a different color name (Stroop, 1935). This response competition (between the name for the color of ink and the name for the string of letters) is called Stroop interference. In the bilingual variant of the Stroop task, this Stroop interference persists across languages, especially when the orthography and phonology are similar for the names of that color in the two languages. For example, when an English–German bilingual sees the word "braun" (German for "brown") in red ink, and their task is to name the color of the ink in English, they are supposed to respond with the word "red." But their response times are noticeably slower than a control condition with simple asterisks. This cross-language Stroop interference is interpreted as follows: The sequence of letters activates the lexical representation for "braun" in their German language subsystem, and since the orthography and phonology are similar, this activation then readily spreads to the lexical representation for "brown" in their English lexicon and this lexical representation competes with the lexical representation for "red" during the language production process, thus slowing it down. When the translation-equivalent color words across the two languages do not share substantial orthography or phonology (such as "yellow" in English, and "gelb" in German), the cross-language Stroop interference is noticeably reduced, because the activation spreads less readily from one language subsystem to the other in this case (Preston & Lambert, 1969).

These various RT tasks, that present a sequence of unrelated words in isolation, provide useful insight into the cognitive processes involved in bilingual language processing, but many of them involve somewhat unusual tasks that are significantly different from our typical everyday language use. One step toward making RT tasks like these somewhat more ecologically valid is to not present unrelated words in isolation but instead present a sequence of words that form a sentence. This can be done in a rapid serial visual presentation task, where the words are presented individually in the center of the screen one after another (Altarriba & Soltano, 1996). Or this can be done with a self-paced reading task, in which each button press slides a moving window that reveals one word at a time in the sentence. Self-paced reading tasks provide a useful method that allows the experimenter to measure how long it takes a person to read various portions of a sentence, which can be used to interpret comprehension of the sentence in the designated language. Typically, in this methodology, the sentence is presented on the screen with Xs replacing all the letters. Then, with each button-press, one of the words is converted from Xs into its letters. The participant then reads that word, and presses the button again to get the next word, while the previous word reverts back to Xs. Not only are self-paced reading tasks relatively easy to implement, but this online methodology also allows researchers to measure a participant's reading time at any location in the sentence, word by word (or in some cases, phrase by phrase), which allows for a better understanding of any difficulties that occur in sentence processing (Marinis, 2010).

A number of bilingual language studies have used self-paced reading to explore the effects of L1 syntactic knowledge on the processing of L2 sentences (Jiang, 2004; Marinis et al., 2005; Papadopoulou & Clahsen, 2003). For example, self-paced reading experiments have been used to investigate ESL Chinese–English speakers' sensitivity to the plural morpheme when used in a sentence (Jiang), to examine attachment preferences for relative clauses of bilingual Greek speakers of various backgrounds (Papadopoulou & Clahsen, 2003), and to look at second language English learners' processing of sentences with long-distance wh-dependencies (Marinis al., 2005).

There are some clear advantages to using a self-paced reading task, some of which include minimal cost to implement, suitable for populations with normal or corrected vision and developed literacy skills, and it is an easy way to measure online language processes. On the other hand, although self-paced reading tasks allow researchers to measure the point in a sentence where a participant experiences difficulties, it still requires a somewhat less than ecologically valid finger-press method for determining how long the reader spends on each word. Self-paced reading tasks may illustrate differences in parsing for bilingual speakers, but unfortunately, they can leave much open to interpretation in terms of illustrating the cognitive mechanisms responsible for differences in processing. A more informative approach may be to use this type of research paradigm in tandem with eyetracking and neuroimaging techniques for a more fine-grained analysis of sentence processing.

In contrast to reading a sequence of words as input in self-paced reading, the verbal fluency task involves the participant generating a sequence of words as output. The participant is given a category, such as "types of clothing" or words that start with "fa," and in a short period of time, such as 60 seconds, they must generate in spoken form as many exemplars from that category as they can. Curiously, monolinguals routinely perform better than bilinguals on this task (Gollan, Montoya, & Werner, 2002). It has been hypothesized that the reason for this is that a bilingual's two language systems exert interference on one another while they both compete to generate responses (Sandoval et al., 2010). Sandoval et al. examined the temporal dynamics of the sequence of words that bilinguals and monolinguals produce, finding that high frequency words are generated first and lower frequency words are generated later. Time-series analysis is becoming an important component of how contemporary research programs statistically analyze sequential data. For example, in a verbal fluency task with monolinguals, Rhodes and Turvey (2007) found that the heavy tailed statistical distribution of intervals between generated words exhibits the same Lévy distribution as does the pattern of distances traveled by a wide variety of foraging animals. That is, the statistical pattern that describes the distances traveled by various birds, fish, and squirrels foraging from food cache to food cache is the same statistical pattern that describes a human "foraging" through their own mental state space from one retrieved word to the next.

As we bring this RT methods section to a close, it is worth taking a bird's-eye view on these kinds of tasks. Delivering a series of words that form a sentence, or eliciting a series of words as spoken output, are important ways to stretch the cognitive act out in time so that multiple measures can be made during its time course. Taking multiple measurements during the time course of a cognitive act is the best way to uncover the mechanisms that underlie that cognitive act. In fact, if one conceptualizes an hour-long session of linguistic button-press RTs as a kind of overall cognitive performance during that time period, one can treat it as a single cognitive act from which hundreds of measurements were made. The resulting time series of RTs can then be analyzed for long-term correlations in its variance over time. When these long-term correlations are found – sometimes referred to as pink noise or 1/f scaling of variance – it can be interpreted as evidence for self-organization in the cognitive system producing that behavior (Kello, 2013; Van Orden, Holden, & Turvey, 2003). This self-organization, and its 1/f scaling signature, arises not from systems that are composed of separate modules that solve their domain-specific tasks and then exert minimal interaction to combine their results, but instead from systems in which the interactions among the subsystems are doing more cognitive work than the individual subsystems are doing on their own (much like Anderson et al.'s, 2010, patterns of cooperation between brain areas). Importantly, this time-series analysis approach to RT data holds promise for bilingualism research as well (see Lowie & de Bot, Chapter 11).

## 4.6 Dense-sampling methods

Like time-series analysis in particular, a broader, more inclusive set of dense-sampling methods in general are becoming important new tools for the tool belt of psycholinguists. These methods are just beginning to take hold in psycholinguistics overall, and in bilingualism research specifically. Rather than treating an experimental session as though it is comprised of individual unrelated trials, from each of which only one data point is collected, dense-sampling methods record multiple measurements in sequence during the time course of a single linguistic act. That linguistic act could be an entire conversation, or the reading of a single sentence, or the comprehension of a single spoken word. By examining the time course of accrual for different sources of linguistic information, and the timing of their interactions, during a linguistic act, psycholinguists can develop a more detailed understanding of the cognitive architecture of the mechanisms involved in bilingual language processing, and their dynamics.

For example, during unscripted conversation between two people, a variety of time-series analysis methods can be used to uncover patterns of coordination between the two people. When postural sway is measured via a pressure-sensitive force plate under each participant while they stand and converse, their co-creation of the discourse leads to recurrent shared patterns in their respective postural sway (Shockley, Santana, & Fowler, 2003). Using recurrence quantification analysis (RQA), which records cyclic patterns in the phase space of the time series, Shockley et al. were able to detect the motoric coordination into which two bodies settle during a shared conversation. Dale and Spivey (2005) developed a categorical version of RQA that allowed them to track the recurrent patterns of linguistic structures used by child and caregiver in the CHILDES corpus. In those data, sometimes the caregiver could be seen to lead the child in their coordinated language use, and sometimes the child led the caregiver. Even brain activity measured by EEG exhibits correlated patterns between interlocutors. When Kuhlen, Allefeld, and Haynes (2012) recorded the continuous time series of EEG – instead of carving the signal up into N400s and P600s from individual experimental trials – they found that the brain activity of a listener exhibits significant correlations with content-specific patterns of brain activity in the speaker. In addition to coordinated postural sway, coordinated word choice, and coordinated brain activity patterns, participants engaging in a conversation about a shared scene of images also exhibit recurrent patterns of eye movements to those images (Richardson, Dale, & Kirkham, 2007). Interestingly, better coordination among the two people's eye-movement patterns results in better comprehension and memory of the content of the spoken conversation (Richardson & Dale, 2005).

Like many real-time measures of ongoing language processing, eyetracking requires sophisticated electronic equipment and laboratory apparatus that usually rules out the possibility of taking the method out into the field or into people's homes (however, new goggles-based versions are being developed for this kind of portability). Although tracking eye movements to objects on a table, or pictures on a computer screen, can often be done with a remote eyetracker or a lightweight headband-mounted eyetracker, allowing relatively free movement of the head and trunk, eyetracking of reading generally requires reduced mobility. In order to track a reader's eye movements with fine enough accuracy to know which word is being fixated at any given point in time, or perhaps even what part of the word, the participant's head usually needs to be stabilized at least with a chinrest. Typical measures from eyetracking are regressive eye movements, where a reader moves their eyes back to a previously read portion in order to reread it, and slowed reading times on particular words. When a sentence becomes difficult to understand, due perhaps to it having been syntactically parsed incorrectly in the beginning, regressive eye movements are common (Frazier & Rayner, 1982). The reading times are often divided up into total reading times (which sum the durations of all fixations on a given word), "first-pass" reading times (which sum the durations of only the fixations on a word that precede any regressive eye movements), "first-fixation" reading times (which only count the duration of the first fixation on a given word), and other more fine-detailed types of fixation patterns (for a detailed review, see Rayner 1998). The more immediate measures of reading time, such as first-pass and first-fixation durations, are often treated as indices of early stages of reading comprehension, and may reflect syntactic and lexical processes that have undergone somewhat less contextual integration.

For example, to explore mixed-language reading processes, Altarriba et al. (1996) tracked the eye movements of Spanish–English bilinguals while they read code-switching sentences that were in English but contained one Spanish word near the end. When the first half of the English sentence was strongly contextually constraining, and the code-switched word was a rare low-frequency word, such as *basura* (garbage), first-fixation times on that critical word were fast due to the conceptual features primed by the contextual constraint. By contrast, when the critical word was high-frequency, such as *dinero* (money), it appeared that not only conceptual features were being primed but even lexical features of the expected English word, money, were being primed, because first-fixation times were slower than usual on this critical Spanish word.

By using cognates instead of code-switching, Duyck et al. (2007) were able to explore the degree to which this lexical priming was indeed language specific. With Dutch–English bilinguals, they found that when a contextually constraining unilingual English sentence contains a non-identical cognate, such as "Luke went to the supermarket and bought an apple," where the Dutch cognate is appel, there was no facilitation due to the lexical–featural overlap between the two critical words. By contrast, with identical cognates such as "The other children laughed at Mike's fat lip," cognate facilitation was observed as faster first-fixation durations on that critical word. Thus, even though the contextual constraint of the sentence should have primed only the English lexical features of the critical word lip, it appeared that additional facilitation may have been obtained from activation of those lexical features in the Dutch linguistic subsystem as well. These results were interpreted as evidence that, in bilinguals reading cognates, lexical activation is language independent, such that the orthographic input activates lexical representations in both languages (see also van Hell & Dijkstra, 2002).

Headband-mounted eyetracking methodologies have enabled researchers to study spoken language processing in bilinguals in a way that combines both visual contexts and spoken linguistic input (Spivey & Marian, 1999; Tanenhaus et al., 1995). By tracking the center of the pupil and the corneal reflection, headband-mounted eyetracking devices record a person's eye movements and allow for a measure of attention at the timescale of hundreds of milliseconds (Magnuson et al., 1999), while providing insight to the cognitive mechanisms at play during real-time spoken language comprehension in a natural interactive environment – rather than holding the head motionless and reading isolated sentences on a computer screen in a dark room. An advantage of using this paradigm is that participants do not need to make specific decisions about the information that is being presented to them because eye movements are tracked while they spontaneously and naturally respond to spoken language (see Richardson, Dale, & Spivey, 2007, for a detailed review of this particular experimental technique). Unfortunately, as mentioned previously, eyetracking methodologies do require the use of expensive, sophisticated equipment that tends to limit transport and access to the use of this paradigm.

One easier and less expensive alternative to eyetracking is computer mouse-tracking (Spivey, Grosjean, & Knoblich, 2005). In much the same way that participants' eyes can be diverted to an object that has phonological similarity in one language or another, their reaching movements with the computer mouse can also veer toward a competitor object on the screen before settling on the correct object. For example, Bartolotti and Marian (2012) showed a close correspondence between the eyetracking results and the mouse-tracking results for monolinguals and bilinguals performing a task with a newly learned artificial language.

Eyetracking studies in spoken language processing with bilinguals have produced evidence for joint activation of both languages (Ju & Luce, 2004; Marian & Spivey, 2003a, 2003b; Spivey & Marian, 1999; Weber & Cutler, 2004). Research with Russian–English bilinguals found that, compared to the control condition baseline, bilinguals fixated more on phonologically similar interlingual distractors while following simple spoken instructions (Spivey & Marian, 1999). For example, when instructed to "pick up the marker," Russian–English bilinguals would often briefly look at a stamp (*marka* in Russian) before finally fixating the felt pen marker and picking it up. This result was interpreted as indicating that a bilingual's two language subsystems are both simultaneously uptaking phonological input phoneme by phoneme, even during monolingual language processing.

A key benefit of this headband-mounted eyetracking technique is that one can measure the equivalent of cross-language priming (as is done with RT tasks) without imposing a meta-linguistic task (such as lexical decision) and without even presenting any stimuli from the bilinguals' other language. Even when a bilingual is placed in a "monolingual mode" (Grosjean, 1998) with their L2, due to an entirely monolingual environment, the eye-movement data still show competition from interlingual distractors in L1 (Marian & Spivey, 2003b). However, the reverse is less robust. When a Russian–English bilingual is in a monolingual L1 mode, due to the research assistant speaking native Russian, the consent form being in Russian, and Russian music playing in the background, interlingual distractors from L2 do not exert much competition. For example, when instructed to "*Poloji marku nije krestika*" ("put the stamp below the cross," in Russian), these Russian–English bilinguals rarely look at the felt pen marker.

Eyetracking research by Ju and Luce (2004) investigated Spanish–English bilinguals' sensitivity to acoustic–phonetic differences between their languages during spoken language processing. Other research investigating lexical competition in Dutch–English bilinguals found when listening to spoken English, Dutch listeners fixated more on distractor pictures with names that had similar-sounding vowels to the vowels of the target picture name and also on distractor pictures with phonologically similar names to targets (Weber & Cutler, 2004).

Eyetracking during spoken language processing has provided useful insight into how bilingual speakers experience and naturally process the words of the languages they speak, but alone this paradigm is unable to provide complete information about the cognitive mechanisms at work during language comprehension. A more comprehensive picture can be seen by combining different methods. Marian, Spivey, and Hirsch (2003) used eyetracking and fMRI methodologies together to explore bilingual processing of phonetic and lexical information, and to determine brain structures associated with the processing of L1 and L2 in bilinguals. Results from those eyetracking experiments replicated the evidence for parallel activation of both languages in bilinguals, and the fMRI results showed similar cortical activation for both L1 and L2, but found differences in the volume of activation and locus of activation, with L2 being greater than L1 in late bilinguals. Combining both methodologies enables researchers to not only observe the behavioral aspect of bilingual cognition, but also determine the cortical areas involved in bilingual language processing. Future directions for eyetracking of spoken language processing would benefit from also incorporating computational models to better understand the mechanisms that operate in the bilingual mind (e.g., Li & Farkas, 2002; van Heuven et al., 1998).

## 4.7 Discussion

In this chapter, we have reviewed a variety of experimental methods in bilingual language processing research. Some of these methods have the advantage of being portable and inexpensive, such as offline measures. But they also have their disadvantages, in that they typically record only the final product of a language comprehension event, not its internal processes. We reviewed some neuroimaging methods that provide varying degrees of spatial resolution and temporal resolution in detecting neural correlates of language processing in bilinguals. These methods provide an unprecedented view inside the neural processes of bilingual language processing, but are clearly not portable to take into distant locales where special bilingual populations might be found, can be prohibitively expensive for some research programs, and can sometimes involve problematic assumptions in their theoretical interpretation. In order to understand the perceptual and cognitive mechanisms of a mental process, it is often helpful to measure intermediate points during the time course of the process itself. RT methods take us a step in that direction, by providing measures of the latency of processing times for various linguistic events. However, dense-sampling methods (e.g., time-series analysis, eyetracking, computer-mouse tracking) provide multiple measurements during the time course of the linguistic event in progress, not just the latency of its completion. Moreover, dense-sampling methods generally do not interrupt the participant's natural processing of the linguistic information with a meta-linguistic query in order to obtain their measurement. RT methods and dense-sampling methods typically involve some amount of laboratory infrastructure, are less portable, and somewhat more expensive than the more traditional offline methods. Due to the compensatory strengths and weaknesses of these various methods, no one method has any sovereign superiority over any other. The best advice is to be eclectic and collaborate with different colleagues who have expertise in all of them.

We briefly describe here a case study of an important issue in bilingualism that benefited greatly from converging evidence from multiple different experimental methodologies. While some observational reports in bilingualism research have suggested that the bilingual brain enjoys cognitive advantages compared to the monolingual brain, other observational reports have suggested that the bilingual brain suffers disadvantages compared to monolingual counterparts. Clearly, this issue has worldwide impact for understanding cultural trends, implementing governmental policy, and developing educational policy – and therefore it deserves careful scientific attention. By bringing together a variety of experimental methods to analyze different aspects of how bilingualism affects cognition and language, the field as a whole is producing evidence that certain aspects of a bilingual's mind are improved and other aspects can exhibit some interference.

Careful multi-methodology research on bilingualism is crucial so that we can understand what benefits and drawbacks (if any) are entailed from being bilingual. Studies comparing bilinguals to monolinguals investigate to what degree bilinguals' cognitive and linguistic abilities vary from those who know only one language. Are there advantages or disadvantages to knowing more than one language? What intrinsic mechanisms account for differences in linguistic processing between monolinguals and bilinguals? Also, what methodologies are most successful at determining the cognitive abilities and underlying processes that are unique to a person that speaks more than one language?

Several studies have emerged that show cognitive advantages for people who speak more than one language. Evidence from several studies on bilingual children have demonstrated a bilingual advantage in various cognitive and linguistic tasks (Ben-Zeev, 1977; Bialystok, 1999; Bialystok, Majumder, & Martin, 2003; Cummins, 1978). Early research by Ben-Zeev found that bilingual Hebrew–English-speaking children displayed greater cognitive flexibility in terms of syntactic rule usage and more advanced problem-solving skills as compared to monolingual children. Studies have also shown that bilingual children exhibit greater metalinguistic awareness, which may be due to their knowledge of more than one language, and the ability to assign multiple words from different languages to the same concept (Adesope et al., 2010; Bialystok et al., 2003; Cummins, 1978). In addition to increased problem-solving skills and greater metalinguistic awareness, Bialystok found that bilingual children displayed greater attentional control during difficult problem-solving tasks than their monolingual counterparts in a non-verbal card sort task. Further support for advantages in cognitive function of bilingual speakers has also been found in studies on bilingual adults (Bialystok et al., 2004; Bialystok, Craik, & Luk, 2008). Similar to Bialystok's findings on bilingual children, Bialystok et al. (2004) and Bialystok et al. (2008) reported that older adult bilinguals exhibited greater attentional control than their monolingual counterparts.

In contrast to studies that have reported cognitive advantages in bilingual speakers, results from a number of experiments have shown subtle deficits when comparing monolinguals to bilinguals on tasks that activate lexical knowledge or lexical retrieval (Bialystok et al., 2008; Gollan et al., 2005; Ransdell, & Fischler, 1987; Scarborough, Gerard, & Cortese, 1984; Soares & Grosjean, 1984). As found with the verbal fluency task above (Gollan et al., 2002), research investigating lexical retrieval has found that bilinguals have slower response times than monolinguals in mixed language tasks where their second language is the target language (Scarborough et al., 1984). Soares and Grosjean (1984) also reported bilinguals' slower reading times for mixed language, or code-switched, sentences than monolinguals in a phoneme triggered lexical decision task. Further support for a bilingual disadvantage in lexical retrieval comes from a study conducted by Ransdell and Fischler (1987), in which bilinguals were much slower than monolinguals in identifying words in a lexical decision task, and also research by Bialystok et al. (2008) confirmed similar evidence of deficits in lexical access in bilinguals using a modified Boston naming task. In a recent study, Gollan et al. (2005) observed that a bilingual's deficit in lexical access is not limited to reading or word identification. Under the assumption that picture naming required lexical knowledge of the target language, in a picture-naming task, Gollan et al. (2005) reported that bilinguals made more mistakes, and were much slower than their monolingual counterparts when naming pictures in their dominant language.

The aforementioned studies support a bilingual disadvantage in lexical access, but controversy exists in terms of the cause of this disadvantage. At one end of the debate, some argue that both languages are organized in two separate lexicons, and are accessed independently of each other (MacNamara & Kushnir, 1971; Scarborough et al., 1984; Soares & Grosjean, 1984). Both Scarborough et al. (1984) and Soares and Grosjean (1984) attribute bilinguals' slower response to having to scan both mental lexicons for each language individually in order to obtain a correct response. In contrast to the "separate-lexicon model" (Gerard & Scarborough, 1989), other research argues for joint parallel activation of both languages (Bijeljac-Babic, Biardeau, & Grainger, 1997; Green, 1986; Marian & Spivey, 2003a; Spivey, & Marian, 1999), and slowed responses may be due to competition between multiple related lexical representations across the two language subsystems.

This brief case study communicates the diversity of findings in the field of bilingualism on this issue. Rather than concluding that the being bilingual is somehow summarily good for you, or bad for you, the results from multiple different methodologies converge to indicate that while lexical processing in bilinguals may be slowed down by a few dozen milliseconds, measures of cognitive flexibility and cognitive control appear to show improvement when compared to monolinguals.

## 4.8 Conclusion

In an ideal approach to science, we tend to think that theories are developed first and then experimental methodologies are designed to test those theories. And that may in fact be how the first iteration usually starts. However, when the results of the experiments do not quite fit the data, the natural reaction is to modify the theory and then see how well it predicts new results from subtle modifications in the now "tried and tested" methodology. In this cyclic iterative process of predict-from-theory and then test-with-method and then modify-the-theory, there can be a worrisome tendency to continue using the same experimental method again and again – oblivious to the fact that while every methodology has its strengths, it also has its weaknesses. In this chapter, we have briefly outlined some of the strengths and weaknesses of a wide range of experimental methodologies in bilingual language processing research. Some of the key weaknesses are in the theoretical assumptions that are inherent in the methods. If one exclusively uses a methodology that does not have finegrain temporal resolution of the ongoing linguistic process, such as offline measures or fMRI, there can be a tendency to see little importance in the temporal dynamics of what the mind does when each new word of a sentence comes into the system every few hundred milliseconds, with a different syntactic category, different semantic influences, a different phonological sequence. In the development of a theory of language, those temporal dynamics are ignored at your peril. But by the same token, if one exclusively uses measures that are laboratory bound and provide only indirect insight into the neural mechanisms involved, such as eyetracking for example, then one may tend to see little importance in special hard-to-reach bilingual populations or in natural ecologically valid real-world circumstances or in identifying the network of neural subsystems that subserves language processing in bilinguals. In the development of a theory of bilingualism, those special populations, that ecological validity, and those neural subsystems are, likewise, ignored at your peril.

In this way, the actual practice of science stands in stark contrast to the ideal approach to science, in that the experimental method that one uses can have a surprisingly powerful effect on the kinds of theories one entertains. As they say, when the only tool you know how to use is a hammer, everything starts to look like a nail. Rather than adhering to only one, or a couple of, experimental methodologies in one's research program, and thus thinking only in terms of the theoretical assumptions inherent in that particular set of methods, we encourage bilingualism researchers to apply a range of disparate experimental methods to test their theory's predictions so that they may triangulate on the most robust account of the phenomena at hand. There are so many ways to scientifically measure a phenomenon. There are so many ways to scientifically measure bilingual language processing. Limiting oneself to only a few would be shame.

# 5
# Methods for studying infant bilingualism

Krista Byers-Heinlein

## 5.1 Introduction

Bilingual infants are one of the most fascinating but also one of the most difficult groups of bilinguals to study. Infancy research is methodologically challenging due to infants' very limited behavioral repertoire. Infants cannot be asked to follow instructions, fill out questionnaires, or complete hundreds of trials. Thus methods for studying bilingual adults (see Jiang, Chaper 2) would fail miserably if applied to infants. Instead, researchers working with bilingual infants must use specialized methods that capitalize on their spontaneous behaviors and automatic brain responses.

For nearly one hundred years (Ronjat, 1913), bilingual language acquisition was studied by observing infants' early productions (De Houwer, 1998). More recently, beginning with Bosch and Sebastián-Gallés (1997), researchers have used experimental methods to understand language acquisition in bilingual infants. The use of these experimental methods, in conjunction with longstanding parental report techniques, have corresponded with an explosion of interest in infant bilingualism (see Figure 5.1 for a yearly citation count of papers on early bilingualism).

This chapter will introduce methods and measures used in research with bilingual infants below the age of 2 years. These methods overlap considerably with techniques used to study language acquisition in monolinguals (Blom & Unsworth, 2010; Hoff, 2012). Yet, research with bilingual infants presents additional challenges. This chapter will explore how infant research methods are applied to bilinguals, and how the results arising from such studies can be interpreted (see also

---

This work was supported by grants from the Natural Sciences and Engineering Council of Canada, and the Fonds de recherche du Québec-Société et culture. I would like to thank Chelsea da Estrela and Alexandra Polonia for their assistance with manuscript preparation.

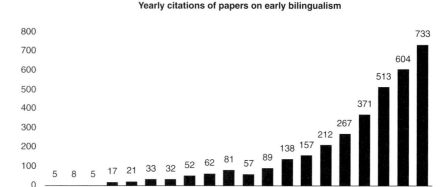

**Figure 5.1** Growth in yearly citations from 1993–2012 of papers related to early life (infant, infancy, toddler, toddlerhood) and bilingualism (bilingual, bilingualism, dual language). Retrieved from the Web of Science database (Thomson Reuters)

Curtin, Byers-Heinlein, & Werker, 2011; and Sebastián-Gallés, Chapter 6 for theoretical overviews). The focus here will be on parental report and experimental techniques (see De Houwer, 1998 for a discussion of case-study and diary methods). The chapter will begin with a discussion of how language background and vocabulary size can be assessed in bilingual infants using parental report. Next, behavioral and brain-based methods for testing young bilinguals will be described using current examples from the infant bilingualism literature.

## 5.2 Who is bilingual? Assessing language background

At first blush, the term "bilingual infant" can seem puzzling. Adult bilinguals can be defined as individuals who use two or more languages in their everyday lives (Grosjean, 1989), or those "using or able to use two languages especially with equal fluency" (*Collins English Dictionary*). Yet infants typically produce little speech, so such definitions do not clearly apply to them. Instead, the term "bilingual" or "monolingual" in infancy typically refers to infants' language exposure, rather than their language use or proficiency (De Houwer, 1990). Assigning infants to monolingual and bilingual groups for purposes of comparison is a common approach in experimental studies of early bilingualism. Yet, characterizing infants' language exposure, and determining how this information should be used to map infants into "bilingual" and "monolingual" categories, is a challenging problem that will be explored in this section.

Even when infants can be reasonably described as "monolingual" or "bilingual," comparisons of these groups can be problematic. Although infants do not decide for themselves whether to grow up monolingual or bilingual, bilingualism is not randomly assigned. Depending on the population, bilingualism can co-vary with numerous factors. One of the most important of these is socioeconomic status (SES). Bilingual families can be of systematically higher or lower SES than monolinguals living in the same community (Morton & Harper, 2009). Bilingual children also tend to be raised by bilingual parents, who may provide different types of input (i.e., accented speech, language mixing) than monolingual parents (Bosch & Ramon-Casas, 2011; Byers-Heinlein, 2013). In some cases, differences between monolingual and bilingual infants will be due to these SES or input differences, rather than the fact of acquiring two languages per se (Byers-Heinlein & Fennell, 2014). Researchers in the field of early bilingualism must be careful before causation is attributed to bilingualism itself, rather than to other factors. In some cases, the interaction between bilingualism and such factors may be of particular interest.

Nevertheless, researchers interested in early bilingualism still must assess language background to identify the population of interest. Most researchers rely on various forms of parental report to assess infants' language exposure, although to date no published studies have compared the validity of different measures. An obvious way to measure infants' language exposure is to simply ask parents for their best one-off guess, for example the percentage of time or hours per week that their infant is exposed to different languages. However, this simplistic approach can often lead to inaccurate estimates, as parents do not always consider all aspects of their child's life, and sometimes report what they wish their child heard rather than what the child actually hears. Instead, many researchers use detailed parent questionnaires, which assess multiple facets of the child's life and language history (De Houwer & Bornstein, 2003 for a diary-based method; see also Place & Hoff, 2010). A particularly effective approach is to use a structured or semi-structured interview, as many bilingual infants' language backgrounds are complex (Hoff & Luz Rumiche, 2012). A skilled interviewer can elicit information that might be missed or misrepresented in a pen-and-paper questionnaire.

As an example, one popular language background questionnaire for infants was developed by Bosch & Sebastián-Gallés (2001). The questionnaire is administered in an interview format, and has three sections. In the first section, the interviewer asks parents about the family's language background, including the native language of each of the parents, and the language that each parent speaks to the infant. In the second section, the interviewer walks the parent through a "day in the life" of the infant, quantifying the number of waking hours the infant is exposed to each language from different caregivers. Exposure from media such as radio and television is excluded (Weisleder & Fernald, 2011). If exposure changes on different days of the week, or has varied over the course of the child's life (e.g., upon entry to daycare), each component is noted separately. This information is used to compute a weighted average of the number of hours

**Table 5.1** *Best practice for characterizing language exposure in bilingual infants*

1. Use a detailed parent interview rather than relying on a one-off parental estimate.
2. Ask about input from all individuals who interact with the infant, including parents, other family members, and childcare providers.
3. Exclude indirect exposure such as television.
4. Assess continuity of exposure by asking about travel and changes in caregiving arrangements.
5. Consider both cumulative and current exposure in assessing language exposure.
6. Use a-priori and consistent definitions for "bilingual" groups, specifying requirements for onset of exposure and amount of exposure.

per week the child is exposed to each language, from which an overall percentage is computed. Finally, once the parent has completed this second section and thus reflected in detail on the infant's exposure, in the third section the researcher asks the parent to provide a global estimate of the percentage of time that the child hears each language. The percentages from section 2 and section 3 are compared. If the two are widely discrepant, the researcher consults with the parents to identify the source of the difference.

Once accurate information has been gathered about an infant's language background and exposure, researchers must decide whether or not an infant should be included as part of a "bilingual" group in a particular study. This decision is anything but straightforward, and depends on a myriad of factors including the onset of exposure (when the exposure began), the amount of exposure (how much exposure there is to each language), continuity of exposure (whether exposure has changed over time), contexts of exposure (how exposure is provided by different caregivers), and the particular languages of exposure (whether the particular language matters is important). Best practices for assessing bilingual infants' language exposure are summarized in Table 5.1. Researchers will need to consider each of these factors, discussed in turn below, in defining the inclusion criteria for their particular study. Depending on the nature of and theoretical motivation for a study, some or all of these factors might be important.

### 5.2.1 Onset of exposure

Bilingual infants can vary as to when exposure to their two languages began. Exposure to two languages from birth implies acquiring two systems concurrently, while exposure to a second language sometime after birth implies acquiring a new language in the context of a first language that has been partially acquired (De Houwer, 1990; Sebastián-Gallés, Bosch, & Pons, 2008; Werker, 2012; Werker & Byers-Heinlein, 2008).

Simultaneous bilinguals are the most frequently studied group of bilingual infants. Infants are considered simultaneous bilinguals if they have consistently encountered two languages from their caregivers on a daily basis, within the first few days or weeks of life (see also De Houwer, 1995, for use of the term bilingual first language acquisition). One study of newborn infants also considered prenatal bilingual exposure, i.e., whether the mother spoke one or two languages during pregnancy (Byers-Heinlein, Burns, & Werker, 2010). Although no research has directly addressed whether very early exposure has lasting developmental consequences, it is generally considered unlikely, and thus prenatal exposure is not usually assessed in studies of older infants.

Depending on the goals and theoretical motivations of the study, not all studies of bilingual infants have been limited to simultaneous bilinguals. For example, some studies have included infants whose first exposure to both languages occurred no later than age 6 months (e.g., Conboy & Thal, 2006), while others have used a mixed group whose exposure to their second language began sometime between birth and ten months of age (e.g., Petitto et al., 2011). Still other studies have explicitly looked at early second language learners, for example infants whose exposure to their second language began at daycare (Von Holzen & Mani, 2012).

Currently, there is little, if any, research on the impact of different onsets of exposure during the infancy period, but it is a strong possibility that simultaneous and early sequential bilinguals develop differently in at least some respects. Researchers working with bilingual infants should consider the age of onset of exposure to each language, as well as the months of experience the infant has had with each language. While more stringent inclusion criteria for onset and/or length of exposure will make participant recruitment more difficult, researchers should strongly consider how study results might be affected by combining groups of infants that vary in this respect. In groups that vary widely, it may be informative to include age of onset of exposure and/or length of exposure as an independent variable in statistical analyses. However, given the small samples typical of infancy research, potential effects will often be masked by other sources of variability. The necessity of controlling for different aspects of exposure will be determined by the particular research question being addressed.

### 5.2.2 Amount of exposure

The amount of exposure that children receive to their languages is a key determinant of whether they will grow up to be fluently bilingual (Pearson, 2008). This is therefore one of the most important, but also most challenging to measure, variables in determining whether an infant should be considered bilingual in the context of an experimental group. The most common quantification of amount of exposure is the percentage of time infants are exposed to each language (but see also studies that have used a Likert scale such as Garcia-Sierra et al., 2011; Shafer, Yu, & Datta, 2011). As discussed above, the use of a detailed parental interview is an effective way to accurately estimate relative language exposure. A limitation of this approach is that it does not capture absolute exposure to each language. For example, given two different babies with 30 percent exposure to Spanish, one baby with talkative parents might hear four hours/day in Spanish, while another baby hears two hours. Emerging technologies such as digital voice recorders and sophisticated computer algorithms that parse and automatically categorize speech might soon facilitate the measurement of both absolute and relative exposure to each language (e.g., Weisleider & Fernald, 2013).

A perfectly balanced bilingual would be exposed to each language half of the time, but in practice this type of exposure is extremely uncommon. Typically, studies of bilingual infants set an inclusion criterion for the minimum percentage of time children should be exposed to each language. However, these minimums have varied widely in the literature: 40% (Bosch & Sebastián-Gallés, 1997), 35% (Bosch & Sebastián-Gallés, 2001), 30% (Fennell, Byers-Heinlein, & Werker, 2007; Singh & Foong, 2012; Sundara, Polka, & Molnar, 2008), 25% (Byers-Heinlein & Werker, 2009; Gervain & Werker, 2013), 20% (Ramon-Casas et al., 2009), and 10% (Hoff et al., 2012; Place & Hoff, 2010). Thus, studies of bilingual infants have varied from being extremely conservative in their definition of "bilingual" to being extremely inclusive, and there is thus far no consensus in the field about what minimum is reasonable.

One consequence is that the minimums in some studies of "bilingual" infants overlap with the maximums of second language exposure for "monolingual" infants in other studies. For example, some studies of monolingual infants have included infants with up to 20% (Fennell & Werker, 2003; Poulin-Dubois et al., 2011) or even 25% (Bosch et al., 2013) exposure to another language. In multicultural, multilingual areas, almost all infants are likely to have at least some exposure to another language, and it may be nearly impossible to recruit monolingual infants with strict exposure to a single language.

The crux of the problem is that language exposure ranges continuously (i.e., percentages can range from 0 to 100), but "monolingual" and "bilingual" describe discrete groups of infants. It is currently not known whether infants' underlying language abilities and development operate in a continuous or a discrete way relative to language exposure. Should children with small amounts of exposure to a second language be considered bilingual, or is that small amount of input disregarded by the system (Byers-Heinlein & Fennell, 2014)? Several studies have suggested that even small amounts of exposure to a second language can result in learning (Bijeljac-Babic et al., 2009; Conboy & Kuhl, 2011; Kuhl, Tsao, & Liu, 2003). Further, results from other studies have suggested that functions describing development relative to exposure might be discontinuous (Pearson, Fernández, & Oller, 1995; Thordardottir, 2011), in that there may be qualitative differences between more and less balanced bilinguals. However, the robustness and nature of these potential differences are not well understood.

A consequence for researchers wishing to use the terms "monolingual" and "bilingual" is that they must decide whether infants in their study should be exhaustively categorized into these two groups. Some researchers take a conservative approach. For example, researchers might consider infants to be bilingual if they hear at least 25% of each of two languages, and monolingual if they hear a single language at least 90% of the time. Thus, a child hearing 85% English and 15% French might not meet inclusion criterion for either group (see also Hoff & Luz Rumiche, 2012). Because a complete and precise assessment of infants' language background is usually unfeasible before infants arrive in the lab, this will likely mean that some data might be collected but excluded because infants do not fit into either the monolingual or the bilingual group. Another approach would be to test infants with a wide range of exposure, and analyze data using percent exposure as a continuous variable, rather than defining discrete monolingual and bilingual groups. However, thus far, there is little published research with bilingual infants that has taken this approach.

A related challenge is how studies should handle infants exposed to more than two languages: trilingual and multilingual infants (see also Quay, 2001). Sometimes these infants are grouped together with bilinguals as long as they meet the inclusion criterion (i.e., an infant exposed to 40% English, 40% French, and 20% Spanish might be included in a bilingual group as there is at least 25% exposure to two languages). However, other studies exclude infants with more than a fixed amount (say 10%) of exposure to a third language. There has been very little experimental research with groups of tri- or multilingual infants; however at least one study has found systematic differences between bilinguals and trilinguals (Byers-Heinlein & Werker, 2009), suggesting that in some cases combining data from bilinguals and multilinguals might obscure important variation.

### 5.2.3 Continuity of exposure

Infants' exposure to different languages often changes over time, for example due to changing caregiving arrangements. Thus, even among seemingly straightforward populations such as simultaneous bilinguals, researchers need to consider the continuity of their language exposure. For example, imagine a 12-month-old infant who was initially exposed to two languages in a balanced proportion (50/50), but whose exposure to one language increased dramatically upon entering daycare at age 6 months (90/10). In this scenario, the infant's average exposure (70/30) might meet study inclusion criteria, but current exposure (90/10) might not. Studies with older children have suggested that both current as well as cumulative exposure play a role in bilingual development (Unsworth, 2013). Where practically feasible and theoretically important, study inclusion criteria should consider past, current, as well as cumulative exposure to each language. However, it should be noted that past and cumulative exposure are particularly difficult to assess accurately.

### 5.2.4 Contexts of exposure

Bilingual infants also vary in how they encounter their two languages. The one-person-one-language environment is often considered to be typical and/or optimal for bilingual infants (Barron-Hauwaert, 2004). However, research with large representative samples has suggested most bilingual infants have at least some exposure to bilingual adults (De Houwer, 2007; Döpke, 1998), and even parents who intend to use a one-person-one-language approach do sometimes use both languages with their bilingual children (Goodz, 1989). Variables such as whether speech is provided by a native speaker (Place & Hoff, 2010), the relationship between parental and community languages (De Houwer, 2007), how much bilingual parents mix their languages (Byers-Heinlein, 2013), and which of the two languages is spoken by the mother (Ramon-Casas et al., 2009; Sebastián-Gallés & Bosch, 2002) have all been shown to influence bilingual development. Infants may also differ on other experiential variables, for example their exposure to television. In a recent study with bilingual infants and toddlers, low-quality television viewing was associated with reduced vocabulary size (Hudon, Fennell, & Hoftyzer, 2013).

### 5.2.5 Languages of exposure

Studies with bilingual infants vary widely in the particular language being learned by the infants, and to date, very few studies have been replicated across groups of bilingual infants learning different language pairs. In some cases, experimental studies have used samples of bilingual infants all acquiring the same two languages. This is crucial for studies in which infants are tested in both languages (e.g., Bosch & Sebastián-Gallés, 2001), or when the comparative properties of these languages are theoretically interesting (e.g., Bosch & Sebastián-Gallés, 2003). However, other studies have used heterogeneous samples, grouping together bilingual infants who share one language, but vary on their other language (e.g., Bijeljac-Babic et al., 2012; Byers-Heinlein & Werker, 2009; Houston-Price, Caloghiris, & Raviglione, 2010; Liu & Kager, 2013). This is typically done in areas where the recruitment of a homogeneous sample is unfeasible, or when heterogeneous samples are interpretable from a theoretical perspective.

The choice of whether to study a homogeneous or a heterogeneous bilingual group will depend on the research question, research design, stimuli, and on the types of bilingual infants available in the local population. The use of a heterogeneous sample will typically speed recruitment efforts by making inclusion criteria less stringent, but can make interpretation of study results more difficult. Few studies have directly compared infants from different language backgrounds, making it hard to predict when infants learning different language pairs might differ from each other. However, one study tested a group of heterogeneous (English–other) and two groups of homogeneous bilinguals (English–Chinese, English–French) on the same task with identical stimuli (Fennell et al., 2007). The three bilingual groups showed similar results, suggesting that at least in some cases, testing heterogeneous groups of bilinguals is an appropriate approach. At the same time, the use of heterogeneous groups without comparison to homogeneous groups has the potential to mask underlying variability across infants learning different language pairs. Further, when it is important to gain a complete picture of bilingual children's language functioning, testing in both languages is essential (Bedore & Peña, 2008; Kohnert, 2010; Paradis, Genesee, & Crago, 2010).

## 5.3 Assessing vocabulary size in bilingual infants

Infant language researchers are often interested in how performance on experimental tasks relates to infants' developing vocabulary knowledge. The most common way to measure infants' vocabularies is with a standardized instrument called the MacArthur–Bates Communicative Development Inventory (CDI) (Fenson et al., 1993; 2007), although several other studies of bilingual infants have used different instruments (e.g., Junker & Stockman, 2002; Patterson, 2000; 2004; Poulin-Dubois et al., 2012). The CDI comprises two scales, the Words and Gestures scale (used from 8–18 months) and the Words and Sentences scale (used from 16–30 months).

A key part of the CDI is the vocabulary checklist. From a pre-set list of words, parents indicate the words their child understands/says (Words and Gestures) or says (Words and Sentences). Other aspects of the CDI assess early communicative gestures, symbol use, and emerging grammar; some studies of bilinguals have investigated correlations among these different parts of the CDI (Conboy & Thal, 2006; Hoff et al., 2012; Hurtado et al., 2013; Marchman, Martinez-Sussmann, & Dale, 2004).

The CDI has been adapted for dozens of languages, from Basque to Icelandic to Brazilian Sign Language (CDI Advisory Board). These adaptations are not simply translations, but take into account language and culture-specific differences. Each of these adaptations is independently normed, to account for variability in how different languages are acquired.

How can the CDI be used with bilingual infants, whose knowledge spans two languages? One popular method, particularly for homogeneous bilingual populations, is to administer two forms of the CDI, one in each of the child's languages (for a discussion see Pearson, 1998; Pearson, Fernández, & Oller, 1993). Sometimes the same reporter completes each form, while other times different reporters complete each form, depending on who is the most familiar with the child's knowledge in each language. Other approaches have multiple reporters fill out each form (De Houwer, Bornstein, & Putnick, 2013), although it is difficult to compare across children with different numbers of reporters. Research suggests that the use of two CDIs with bilingual infants is a valid measure of their vocabularies (Marchman & Martinez-Sussmann, 2002).

When heterogeneous groups of bilinguals are studied, assessing vocabulary is less straightforward, as in this case different infants are acquiring different language pairs. One approach is to use different pairs of CDIs for each infant, depending on the languages they are learning. However, as many languages do not yet have an adaptation of the CDI, another approach is to use a single adaptation of the CDI to assess both languages. For example, in one study, parents were asked to use the same form to indicate whether their child knew a particular word in English or its translation in the other language (Houston-Price et al., 2010). However, this approach may reduce the validity of the measurement, as parents have to translate on the fly, and no adaptations are made for cultural and language-specific factors. A final approach for heterogeneous groups is to use only one CDI, for example the CDI measuring knowledge in the language of testing (e.g., Byers-Heinlein & Werker, 2009). However, this approach can only partially quantify the language knowledge of bilingual infants and toddlers (Pearson, 1998), which may be useful in some cases (e.g., investigating links between vocabulary knowledge in the language of testing and performance) but not in others (e.g., comparing monolinguals and bilinguals on overall language development).

Monolinguals' CDI vocabulary can be described by a single number for their comprehension and/or production vocabularies, and this can be compared to age- and gender-specific norms. There are currently no bilingual CDI norms. One reason is that the quantification of bilinguals' vocabulary size is complicated. The vocabularies of bilingual infants and toddlers can be measured in either language, thus a French–English bilingual has both a French and an English vocabulary size. Vocabulary size in a single language is typically smaller than a same-aged monolingual's vocabulary size (e.g., Hoff et al., 2012). Some researchers have argued that it is

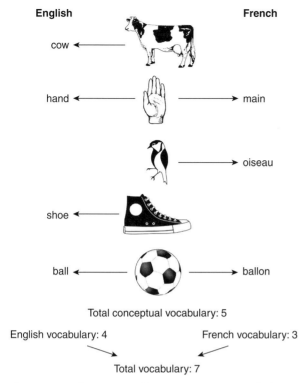

**Figure 5.2** An illustration of different measures of vocabulary size in a hypothetical French–English bilingual infant. Note: English vocabulary counts the English words known by the infant. French vocabulary counts the French words known by the infant. Total vocabulary sums the English and French words known by the infant. Total conceptual vocabulary counts the total number of concepts lexicalized by the infant, which is equivalent to the total vocabulary minus the number of words whose meanings are captured by its translation equivalent.

necessary to measure bilingual infants' vocabulary knowledge across both of their languages to gain a complete picture of language competence (Core et al., 2013; Patterson, 2004; Pearson, 1998; Pearson et al., 1993). One way to do this is to simply sum the words known across the two languages (except any words that might be identical in the two languages), which yields a measure called total vocabulary size (Core et al., 2013).

A second way to measure a bilingual child's vocabulary knowledge is to count the concepts for which a child has a word, rather than all the words the child knows. This is called total conceptual vocabulary size. Total conceptual vocabulary size is different from the total vocabulary size, because bilinguals tend to know translation equivalents (cross-language synonyms; David & Wei, 2008; De Houwer, Bornstein, & De Coster, 2006; Pearson et al., 1995; Poulin-Dubois et al., 2012; Sheng, Lu, & Kan, 2011; Umbel et al., 1992). Figure 5.2 provides an illustration of single-language vocabulary, total vocabulary, and total conceptual vocabulary measurement in a hypothetical infant. It is not yet well understood how each of these vocabulary measures might differently relate to performance in experimental tasks. Researchers are recommended to look at relations of performance to each of these measures.

## 5.4 Behavioral methods for testing speech discrimination and preference

Behavioral research methods are experimental approaches that rely on infants' well-understood tendencies to direct their attention to certain types of stimuli (Colombo & Mitchell, 2009). An important application of these methods is in investigating infants' discrimination of and preference for different types of speech and language stimuli. As discussed below, behavioral techniques using sucking and looking-time measures have provided considerable insight into bilingual infants' nascent language knowledge.

### 5.4.1 High-amplitude sucking procedures

High-amplitude sucking is a behavioral research technique that can be used with infants in the first few months of life (Jusczyk, 1985). This method capitalizes on infants' natural sucking reflex. Infants are trained that every time they produce a strong or "high-amplitude" suck they will hear a sound played from an adjacent speaker. Thus their sucking is taken as an index of their interest in different sounds. Variants of this technique can be used to test very young infants' discrimination of and preference for different types of language stimuli. Looking-based discrimination and preference procedures will be discussed in the next section.

One high-amplitude sucking study investigated language discrimination in newborns whose mothers were either monolingual English speakers or bilingual English–Filipino speakers (Byers-Heinlein et al., 2010). Because fetal hearing is well developed in the last trimester, and the mother's voice in the womb is quite loud, these infants had several months of prenatal bilingual exposure. Infants were tested within a few days of birth at a maternity hospital. Infants were seated in a baby bath chair in their bassinet, and offered a sterilized pacifier. This was connected to a pressure transducer and computer that measured infants' sucking. There were two phases of the study: the habituation phase and the test phase. During the habituation phase, infants were played a sentence every time they produced a high-amplitude suck. Infants either heard all English sentences or all Filipino sentences during habituation. After their sucking declined to a predetermined level, indicating habituation (roughly equivalent to boredom), they were tested with either new sentences in the same language or new sentences in the other language. Both monolingual and bilingual newborns increased sucking only to the sentences in the other language, suggesting that they discriminated English and Tagalog.

Research with a preference variant of the high-amplitude sucking procedure has also demonstrated that, while prenatal bilingualism does not alter early discrimination abilities (thought to be driven by experience-independent sensitivity to languages' rhythmicity), it does alter newborns' language preferences (thought to be driven by familiarity engendered by in-utero exposure). Infants were played alternating minutes of English and Filipino sentences. Bilingual newborns showed equal interest in both of their native languages, sucking similarly during both minute types, while monolinguals preferred their single native language, sucking more during English minutes (Byers-Heinlein et al., 2010).

To date, these are the only published studies of bilingual infants that have used the high-amplitude sucking paradigm. One likely reason is that there are considerable challenges associated with implementing this method. Newborn infants spend most of their time sleeping, and thus many infants recruited for high-amplitude sucking studies never begin the procedure, fall asleep, or start crying partway through the study, yielding high attrition rates. Second, there are no commercially available systems on the market, so equipment for this procedure must be custom-built. As a consequence, this technique has recently lost popularity. Instead, it is increasingly common for brain-based methods such as event-related potentials (Teinonen et al., 2009), and near-infrared spectroscopy (Gervain et al., 2011; Lloyd-Fox, Blasi, & Elwell, 2010) to be used in studies of newborn infants. Neuroimaging methods will be discussed in greater detail in a later section.

### 5.4.2 Visual habituation procedures

As infants become older, looking-time procedures become an age-appropriate and popular experimental method for studying language acquisition. By age 4 months, infants begin to have reasonable head and neck control, and they will visually orient toward a stimulus that interests them. Importantly for language researchers, infants will also orient to a visual stimulus when an accompanying auditory stimulus interests them.

Visual habituation procedures, so-called because infants' visual fixations are measured, are often used to assess infants' discrimination abilities. Infants are tested seated on their parents' lap in a soundproof testing room. Similar to habituation procedures using high-amplitude sucking, there are two main phases in this type of study: the habituation phase and the test phase. During the habituation phase, infants are presented with a repeated type of auditory stimulus, for example a particular syllable type. At the same time, their looking to an unrelated visual stimulus (e.g., a checkerboard pattern presented on a television monitor) is measured. Over time infants habituate, decreasing their looking time to the visual stimulus, implying that they have learned about and become bored with the stimuli. During the test phase, a new type of auditory stimulus is presented in an experimental condition, and the old type of stimulus is presented in a control condition (either within or between subjects). If infants can discriminate between the two types of stimuli, they are expected to look more to the changed (experimental) stimulus than to the unchanged (control) stimulus (for a discussion about implementing infant habituation procedures see Fennell, 2012). Habituation procedures have been used to test a wealth of abilities in bilinguals, from the discrimination of different phonetic categories (e.g., Sundara & Scutellaro, 2011), to the discrimination of languages spoken by silent talking faces (e.g., Sebastián-Gallés et al., 2012; Weikum et al., 2007).

For example, Sundara, Polka, and Molnar (2008) tested bilingual infants' discrimination of the French and English pronunciations of the /d/ sound. During habituation, infants saw a checkerboard on a television screen, while they heard one pronunciation of the syllable /da/, for example the French pronunciation. Infants' looking at the monitor was recorded online by an experimenter through a closed-circuit camera. Habituation continued until infants' looking to the television declined below 50 percent of the looking time for the longest three consecutive trials. At test, infants heard two types of trials. On control trials, infants heard the same type of /d/ sound as in habituation (e.g., the French pronunciation), while on experimental trials they heard the other /d/ sound (e.g., English pronunciation). Results showed that bilingual 10–12-month-olds looked longer when they heard the new stimulus type than when they heard the old stimulus type. This demonstrated that bilingual infants could discriminate English and French pronunciations of /d/.

In an innovative variant of this procedure, bilingual infants were tested on their ability to make phonetic distinctions in each of their languages. Burns et al. (2007) noted that across French and English, there are intermediate sounds that are perceived as /p/ in French and /b/ in English. In their study, infants were habituated to this intermediate sound, and then tested on their response to new syllables that were unequivocally English /p/s and unequivocally French /b/s. The results showed that young bilinguals discriminated both contrasts at 10–12 months of age, while same-aged monolinguals only discriminated the contrast that was meaningful in their own language.

### 5.4.3 Preference procedures

Rather than using habituation to test infants' discrimination abilities, another approach is to use a preference procedure. The logic of preference procedures is that if infants prefer one stimulus to another, then they can necessarily discriminate the two. Thus, preference procedures not only reveal what infants inherently like to listen to, but also provide an index of discrimination. Preference techniques have been fruitful for understanding bilingual infants' preference for their native languages over unfamiliar languages (Bosch & Sebastián-Gallés, 2001), their nascent phonotactic (Sebastián-Gallés & Bosch, 2002) and phonetic knowledge (Bosch & Sebastián-Gallés, 2003; Sebastián-Gallés & Bosch, 2009), and their ability to recognize familiar word forms (Vihman et al., 2007).

The head-turn preference procedure is one popular paradigm (Fernald, 1985; Kemler Nelson et al., 1995). Infants sit on their parent's lap in a three-sided booth fitted with light bulbs (screens in more recent implementations) located in front of and to each side of the infant. Most studies begin with a familiarization phase where infants are exposed to a certain type of speech stimulus or speech stream. Unlike in habituation studies, the duration of familiarization is fixed. After familiarization, infants move to the test phase, where two different types of auditory test stimuli are presented. Each test trial begins with a side light bulb blinking. Once infants initiate a head turn of 30 degrees or more, a test stimulus starts playing from a speaker hidden near the bulb, and continues until the infant looks away for at least 2 seconds or until the trial times out (e.g., 30 seconds). Infants' looking time is taken as a measure of their interest in the sound. Different trials are presented on different sides, although there is no contingency between side and stimulus type. Infants show their discrimination of the two types of test stimuli if they look longer during one type of trial than during the other.

In a recent study, Gervain and Werker (2013) used the head-turn preference procedure to examine links between prosody (i.e., rhythm, stress, and intonation) and word order in bilingual 7-month-olds. Across the world's languages, there are systematic relationships between a language's prosody and its word order. For this reason, a language's prosody can provide infants with information about how to correctly segment the speech stream. Gervain and Werker's study tested whether bilingual infants learning languages with different word orders could use prosodic information as a cue for segmentation.

During a familiarization phase, infants heard a 4-minute-long speech stream. Importantly, without prosodic information the speech stream was ambiguous in terms of how it should be segmented, but prosodic information was included in the speech stream designed to cue infants to parse the stream in a particular way. After familiarization, infants heard eight test trials of words with no prosodic information. Bilingual infants looked longer on test trials (i.e., showed surprise) when words were grouped inconsistently with the familiarization stream's prosody than where they were grouped consistently, suggesting they had parsed the original stream accurately. Further, bilingual infants were flexible across the two types of prosodic patterns heard in each of their languages.

However, monolingual infants only succeeded when they heard a familiarization stream consistent with their native language.

Rather than measuring total looking time, other studies have measured the time that it takes for infants to orient toward different types of stimuli, known as orientation latency. For example, Bosch and Sebastián-Gallés (1997) implemented a visual orientation latency measure to test whether Spanish–Catalan bilingual infants discriminated their maternal language from an unfamiliar language. Infants were seated in a small testing room, facing a computer monitor and two loudspeakers covered with a picture of a woman's face. Each trial started with colorful images presented on the central monitor to draw the infants' attention. Next, infants heard sentences from either their maternal or an unfamiliar language play from one of the side loudspeakers. Videos were coded offline to measure how long it took infants to look toward the loudspeaker on each trial. The authors predicted that infants would orient more quickly to a familiar stimulus over an unfamiliar stimulus. Indeed, monolingual infants did orient more quickly to their native language than to the unfamiliar language. Surprisingly, bilingual infants showed the opposite pattern, orienting more *slowly* to one of their native languages than to the unfamiliar language. This difference in orientation latency still demonstrated infants' discrimination of the two languages, however the direction of the difference was unexpected. One tentative explanation was that bilingual infants tried to ascertain which of their two languages was being spoken before orienting toward the familiar stimulus.

The above study provides a good illustration of how interpreting the results of preference studies can be more difficult than interpreting the results of habituation studies. In habituation studies, infants are expected to dishabituate to a novel stimulus, as infants have been exposed to the first stimulus precisely to the point of losing interest in it (the definition of habituation). That is, if they are truly habituated, infants should always show greater interest in a novel than in a familiar stimulus. In preference procedures, infants can display either a novelty preference (longer/faster looking at novel test trials) *or* a familiarity preference (longer/faster looking at familiar test trials). The direction of preference depends on the complexity of the stimulus, the amount of familiarization, and the developmental level of the infant (Hunter & Ames, 1988). Thus any difference in looking at the two trial types is taken as evidence for discrimination, even though it is difficult to predict the direction of the difference a priori. Null results (equal interest in two test trial types) are particularly hard to interpret, as a lack of preference does not necessarily imply a lack of discrimination.

### 5.4.4 Anticipatory eye movement procedures

Anticipatory eye movement procedures are a recently developed measure of discrimination in infancy (McMurray & Aslin, 2004). In such procedures, infants learn to associate an auditory stimulus type with a visual reinforcer. Typically, two different types of auditory stimuli are paired contingently with the left and right sides of a visual display. If infants can anticipate where the visual reward will appear after hearing only the auditory stimulus, this implies both that they can discriminate the two types of stimuli, and that they can learn the associated rule.

For example, Albareda-Castellot, Pons, and Sebastián-Gallés (2011) tested Spanish–Catalan bilingual infants' discrimination of a vowel contrast that exists only in Catalan, /e/-/ɛ/. Infants saw an Elmo cartoon loom on the screen, then disappear behind a t-shaped occluder. When infants heard the nonsense word *dedi*, Elmo reappeared on the right side of the occluder. When infants heard the nonsense word *dɛdi*, Elmo reappeared on the left side of the occluder. The side of association was counterbalanced across infants. Researchers coded whether infants' eye movements correctly anticipated the side of the cartoon's reappearance, which could only be done successfully if infants discriminated the /e/-/ɛ/ sound. Bilinguals were successful in this procedure, anticipating the visual reward at above-chance levels. The results of this study raise the possibility that anticipatory eye movements might be particularly sensitive for bilingual infants, as in a previous study using familiarization-preference bilinguals had not demonstrated discrimination of this contrast (Bosch & Sebastián-Gallés, 2003).

In a different variant of anticipatory looking, bilingual infants' ability to inhibit an anticipatory response has been used to investigate cognitive advantages of bilinguals relative to monolinguals. Kovács & Mehler (2009) taught 7-month-old infants that an auditory cue would predict the appearance of a visual reinforcer on one side of the screen. Once infants had learned the rule, they switched the side of appearance of the reward. Thus, infants who had been trained to look to the right side to see the reward now had to inhibit this response and look to the left. Both monolingual and bilingual infants were able to learn the first rule, but bilinguals showed an advantage when the rule was switched. This was taken as evidence that bilingualism confers enhanced inhibitory control even in infancy.

## 5.5 Behavioral methods for testing word recognition and word learning in older infants

### 5.5.1 The Switch procedure

The Switch procedure was developed by Werker et al. (1998) as a habituation-based method for studying infant word learning in the lab. In a habituation phase, infants repeatedly encounter two word-object pairings: word A – object A, word B – object B. Once infants have habituated (i.e., looking to the stimuli has declined), they proceed to the test phase. There are two types of test trials: a Same trial that presents a familiar pairing (e.g., word A-object

A), and a Switch trial that presents a novel pairing (e.g., word A-object B). A key aspect of this design is that on both the Same and the Switch trial, the auditory stimulus and the visual stimulus are familiar, but on the Switch trial the pairing itself is novel. If infants have successfully learned the association between the object and the word, they are expected to look longer on the Switch trial than on the Same trial.

As an illustration, Fennell and colleagues (2007) used the Switch task to test bilingual infants' ability to learn the minimal pair *bih* and *dih*. On half of habituation trials, infants heard the word *bih* paired with a novel crown-shaped object, and on the other half infants heard the word *dih* paired with a novel molecule-shaped object. At test, infants saw two trials in a counterbalanced order. On the Same trial, infants saw one of the previously habituated pairings, either *bih*-crown or *dih*-molecule. On the Switch trial, infants saw a novel pairing, either *bih*-molecule, or *dih*-crown. Twenty-month-old bilingual infants succeeded on this task, but 14- and 17-month-old bilinguals did not. As other research has shown that bilingual infants can learn a word–object pairing at 14 months if the words are dissimilar sounding (Byers-Heinlein, Fennell, & Werker, 2013), this implies that minimal pair word learning can be a challenge for young bilinguals, just as it is for monolinguals (Stager & Werker, 1997). Other studies which have varied properties of the auditory stimuli have shown that in some cases bilinguals succeed in minimal pair word learning at the same age as monolinguals (Fennell & Byers-Heinlein, 2014; Mattock, Polka, Rvachew, & Krehm, 2010).

### 5.5.2 Intermodal preferential looking procedure

The intermodal preferential looking procedure is commonly used to test infants' comprehension of words and sentences (Golinkoff et al., 1987; Golinkoff et al., 2013). In this paradigm, infants' fixations to two side-by-side pictures (a target and a distractor) are measured as they hear a word or sentence referring to the target. If infants look at the target more than the distractor (often measured relative to a silent baseline), this indicates comprehension. Intermodal preferential looking tasks have been used with bilingual infants as young as 17 months (Byers-Heinlein & Werker, 2009; Houston-Price et al., 2010), although recent methodological advances with monolinguals suggest that variants of the task can show word knowledge as young as 6 months (Bergelson & Swingley, 2012, 2013).

In one variant, Ramon-Casas and colleagues (2009) used the intermodal preferential looking procedure to investigate how Catalan–Spanish bilingual toddlers categorize vowels in familiar words. Toddlers heard words that were either correctly pronounced or mispronounced. Critically, the mispronunciations involved a vowel contrast (/e/ – /ɛ/) that is meaningful in Catalan but not in Spanish. Catalan monolingual infants easily detected the mispronunciation, spending more time looking at the labeled object when the word was correctly pronounced than when it was mispronounced. However, bilingual toddlers, particularly those who were Spanish dominant, failed to detect the mispronunciation. One reason might be that Spanish and Catalan have many cognates, words that are similar-sounding across the two languages (e.g., Catalan *abella* and Spanish *abeja,* both meaning bee). Subsequent research has suggested that young bilinguals' insensitivity to mispronunciations might be specific to cognate words (Ramon-Casas & Bosch, 2010).

Another implementation of the intermodal preferential looking paradigm has investigated how bilingual infants respond to novel, unknown words. Monolingual infants and children show a mutual exclusivity heuristic, whereby they disambiguate an unfamiliar word by expecting it to refer to an unfamiliar picture rather than a familiar picture (Halberda, 2003; Markman & Wachtel, 1988). Using a method devised by Halberda (2003), Byers-Heinlein and Werker (2009) investigated whether bilinguals and trilinguals show disambiguation from the same age as monolinguals. Infants were shown pairs of pictures on an eye-tracking monitor. Some pairs were familiar (ball–car) and some pairs contained a novel object (shoe–phototube). During a silent baseline, infants' overall tendency to look at each object was measured. On familiar label trials, infants heard a sentence labeling a familiar object, e.g., "Where is the car?," and on disambiguation trials, infants heard a sentence labeling a novel object, e.g., "Where is the nil?" The dependent variable was the proportion of time that infants spent looking at the labeled picture. Monolingual, bilingual, and trilingual infants looked at the target significantly above baseline on familiar label trials. However, on disambiguation trials, only monolinguals looked at the novel object significantly above chance, with bilinguals showing a marginally significant looking at the novel object, and trilingual performing at chance. Subsequent studies have used a similar method to replicate and extend this basic finding that bilingual infants are less likely to show disambiguation than monolinguals (Byers-Heinlein & Werker, 2013; Houston-Price et al., 2010).

A third recent application of the preferential looking method is in priming studies (Arias-Trejo & Plunkett, 2009 for priming with monolingual infants; see Styles & Plunkett, 2009). In such studies, infants hear a prime sentence such as "I like the dog," and then a related target word, e.g., "cat," or an unrelated target, e.g., "cookie." Infants' task is to look toward the referent of the target, which appears on the screen paired with the distractor (e.g., a cat and a truck). Evidence for priming is found if infants look longer at the target object on trials with a related prime as compared to trials with an unrelated prime. Using this paradigm with Mandarin–English bilingual toddlers, Singh (2013) varied both the relation of the target and prime (e.g., related vs. unrelated words), the language of the target and the prime (English and Mandarin), and consequently the language match between prime and target (e.g., same-language vs. different language). Within and cross-language priming was observed only when the prime was in the dominant language. In another study, Von Holzen and Mani (2012) tested phonological priming through translation in German learners exposed to English at daycare. A priming effect was found both when prime–target pairs were phonologically related (e.g., English *slide* and German *kleid)*, and when the translation of the prime was phonologically related to the target (e.g., *leg* primed *stein* because the German word for *leg* is *bein)*.

## 5.6 Procedures using brain-based measures

While most experimental research to date with bilingual infants has used the behavioral techniques discussed above, a handful of studies has used brain-based measures. These techniques can provide information that is complementary to behavioral methods. For example, only brain-based measures can help identify the neural correlates of language processing and acquisition. Thus, such studies can explore whether monolinguals and bilinguals use the same versus different brain systems to perform the same task. Further, some brain-based techniques (e.g., event related potentials) can reveal temporally precise information about in-the-moment processing that is often unavailable in behavioral paradigms. Finally, because these techniques do not require an overt behavioral response, they can be particularly useful for very young infants such as newborns. There are currently two brain-based techniques, which will be discussed further below, which have been used with young bilinguals: event related potentials (ERPs), and functional near-infrared spectroscopy (fNIRS). Two other neuroimaging techniques have been used with monolingual infants but not yet with bilinguals: functional magnetoencephalography (fMEG) (Cheour et al., 2004) and functional magnetic resonance imaging (fMRI; Dehaene-Lambertz, Dehaene, & Hertz-Pannier, 2002).

In ERP studies, infants wear a flexible cap of electrodes, which record electrical activity on the scalp. Various sound stimuli are played to infants, time-locked brain responses are recorded, and infants' brain responses to different types of stimuli are compared. For example, Conboy and Mills (2006) examined bilingual infants' brain responses to dominant and non-dominant language words that were either known or unknown to the infant. Infants showed more mature patterns of ERPs to words in the dominant language (see also Vihman et al., 2007, for related work), demonstrating an important role for experience in how the developing brain responds to language. Several other studies have used ERPs to examine bilingual infants' discrimination of speech sounds (Garcia-Sierra et al., 2011; Shafer et al., 2011; Shafer, Yu, & Garrido-Nag, 2012). Other studies with bilingual infants have correlated ERP responses with complementary measures such as pupil dilation (Kuipers & Thierry, 2013; but see Sebastián-Gallés, 2013).

fNIRS is an emerging technology for understanding infant language processing and cognition (Gervain et al., 2011). In fNIRS, infants are fitted with an array of light emitters and detectors that are placed on the scalp. Light is shone through the skull to the cortex of the brain. Because oxygenated and deoxygenated hemoglobin have different patterns of oxygen absorption and refraction, the light that returns to the detectors provides an index of how much oxygen is present in a given area of the brain. Only one study to date including bilingual infants has used this technology (Petitto et al., 2011), but this approach is likely to become increasingly common in the study of bilingual newborns and young infants.

## 5.7 Considerations in choosing stimuli for experimental studies

A crucial issue in the design of experimental studies with bilingual infants is stimulus choice. Researchers studying bilingual infants face many of the same issues in stimulus choice as those who study monolingual infants. For example, they must consider factors such as salience of different stimuli, whether to use infant-directed or adult-directed speech, and infants' likely knowledge of words used in a study. Further, they must consider issues faced by adult bilingualism researchers, such as word frequency and cognate status.

Additionally, in studies of bilingual infants, researchers must decide which language infants should be tested in. One possibility if a homogeneous sample is used is to test infants in both of their native languages. However, due to infants' limited attention spans, order effects, and the need for direct comparisons with monolingual groups, this approach can be challenging. Another possibility is to choose a single language of testing. For heterogeneous samples, this will be the language that is common across infants. For homogeneous samples, the choice is trickier. Researchers can test all infants in their dominant language, test all infants in the same language, or test infants in a randomly assigned language. The choice will depend on the research question, and the availability and comparability of stimuli in different languages.

Even when stimuli are presented in a single language, there is evidence that different results can be obtained if stimuli are produced in a "monolingual" vs. a "bilingual" manner. For example, as mentioned in the discussion of the Switch task, two studies using nearly identical methods tested bilingual infants' ability to learn minimal pair words. In one study, bilinguals succeeded at 17 months (Mattock et al., 2010), while in the other infants did not succeed until 20 months (Fennell et al., 2007). Why were the results divergent? A key difference between the studies was the manner in which the stimuli were produced. In the former study (Mattock et al., 2010), words were produced by a bilingual speaker, and their phonetic values were intermediate between the two languages. In the latter study (Fennell et al., 2007), a monolingual speaker produced the stimuli in a monolingual manner. These very subtle differences are thought to have affected infants' performance on the task, indicating that young children might learn words better when productions closely match their language environment (Fennell & Byers-Heinlein, 2014; Werker, Byers-Heinlein, & Fennell, 2009).

## 5.8 Conclusions

Bilingual infants provide a fascinating window into the earliest roots of bilingualism, but they can be a challenging population to study. Over the past twenty years, research with young bilinguals has grown exponentially due in part to the application of experimental methods, in conjunction with parental-report techniques, to bilingual infants. These methods complement numerous other approaches toward understanding early bilingualism such as diary studies (e.g., De Houwer, 1995), analyses of speech corpora from young bilinguals (for a comprehensive list of available bilingual corpora, see MacWhinney, n.d.; for information on corpus-based research methods, see Corrigan, 2012; MacWhinney, 2000), and new methods for automated analysis of continuous recordings (e.g., Naigles, 2012; Weisleder & Fernald, 2013). Beyond the methods described here, emerging technologies and methodological innovations are likely to add to the toolkit of infant bilingualism researchers in coming years.

# Part III

# Acquisition and development

# 6

# Becoming bilingual

Are there different learning pathways?

Núria Sebastián-Gallés

## 6.1 Introduction

When children are born, they face several laborious tasks that need to be addressed in the first years of life. One of the most challenging tasks is that of learning their parents' language(s). As adults learning a foreign language can attest, this is not easy. The sound wave "looks" like the representation in Figure 6.1, with no clear boundaries between words or sentences, etc., and thus the infant must discover where they are, what they mean, how they are organized into sentences, etc. Although the way infants are addressed (Infant Directed Speech) facilitates the task by providing additional cues, such as a slower speech rate and an exaggerated intonation, parsing the speech signal is not trivial.

But humans are equipped with an amazing brain and within a few months, infants already start spotting some words. There is evidence that by the sixth month of life infants are able to identify several nouns, but only when uttered by a familiar speaker (Bergelson & Swingley, 2012). Though being able to spot some words is far from knowing a language, it reflects the successful computation of complex structures and the discovery of relevant language-specific regularities in the speech signal. To be able to learn their language, infants need to learn at least its grammar (in a broad sense, including phonology, morphology, syntax and semantics) and its vocabulary.

Many infants are born in environments where more than one language is spoken. One may think that this means learning two language systems: two phonologies, two vocabularies, two sets of syntactic rules, etc. In fact, as discussed below, bilingual and multilingual infants have to do more than just learn two language systems. I will enumerate only a few of these additional tasks entailed by bilingualism: learning how to separate the two languages (at least in some cases, as discussed below), keeping track

**Figure 6.1** Illustration of the lack of clear separations between words in the speech signal. As it can be seen in the sentence *"El abuelo estaba agotado y se sentó a descansar"* ("The grandfather was exhausted and sat for a rest"), generally there is no pause between spoken words. Infants must track the underlying patterns and regularities to learn the environmental language.

of language specific information, learning how to use them, and avoiding interference between them. In this chapter, I will focus on studies that have used an experimental approach to investigate the simultaneous acquisition of more than one language. In particular, I will concentrate on the first years of life, as they represent a particularly challenging phase in the process of becoming a proficient language user (of one or more languages).

The present chapter is organized in three sections. In the first section, I will present evidence from what we know about the learning of two language systems in infancy. In the second section, I will focus on what else bilingual infants have to learn and do. In the final section, I will conclude and comment on what is not known and what we need to know. The chapter does not intend to provide an exhaustive review of the existing literature, but rather to point to different issues relevant to understanding the differences (and similarities) between early monolingual and bilingual language acquisition.

Before moving further, however, a few comments contextualizing this field of research are due.

## 6.2 Two preliminary comments

My first comment refers to the definition of what constitutes a bilingual infant (or individual). Bilingualism comes in many different forms; an individual may become bilingual because different languages are spoken in the family (as in the case of multilingual homes), because different languages are spoken in the society (as in the case of multilingual societies), because the language spoken at home is different from the one of the society (as occurs in the case of immigrant families), and there are many other situations. Also, the amount of exposure and the timing of the exposure vary from individual to individual, even if we restrict it to the case of very early bilinguals. Children may be raised as monolinguals, but when they go to daycare, they start to be exposed to a new language, as in the case of some immigrant families, or in the case of generally affluent families who decide to send their children to an international school, for instance. An important consequence of this heterogeneity is the variation it induces when classifying participants for a particular study. This is a challenging issue and it is essential for bilingual research, for progress to be made in the field. In Chapter 5, Byers-Heinlein presents an overview of the different situations and specificities under which variation in the input may occur (and she makes interesting remarks about how this information should be taken into consideration when investigating bilingualism).

The second comment refers to the issue of sample sizes and replicability of studies. The experimental study of bilingualism (as opposed to observational single-case studies) requires the recruitment of a relatively high number of participants distributed in homogeneous groups (usually in the range of 16 to 24 individuals in each experimental group). As said before, finding homogeneous groups is very difficult, and usually only possible in the case of multilingual societies (again Byers-Heinlein presents these problems clearly in Chapter 5). The number of laboratories currently focused on carrying out experimental research on early language learning in bilingual infants is quite limited (there are a few more that sporadically may run one study with bilingual populations), and the number of published studies is also relatively small. This reduced number of studies implies a reduced number of language pairs for which data is available. On top of this, the experimental study of infant bilingualism is very new, counting on fewer than twenty years of experience. Therefore, the empirical evidence we have now is patchy: few research questions have been addressed, and often the evidence comes from different laboratories, testing different bilingual situations and populations and often differing in methodologies. These facts make comparisons of studies complicated. Quite often, the available evidence for a particular phenomenon comes from a single study from a single laboratory. It is with these limitations in mind that the rest of this chapter has to be read.

Still, surprisingly, a patchy and incomplete, yet consistent picture emerges.

## 6.3 Learning two language systems

Learning two languages involves learning two systems of rules (or frames, depending on the theoretical perspective): phonological, morphological, and syntactic, and two vocabularies, among other types of language-related knowledge. Available experimental evidence about early bilingual development mostly investigates the acquisition of the phonological system and the onset of word learning and comprehension.

### 6.3.1 Learning two phonological systems

Previous studies have described a common developmental trajectory for most phonemes across all languages in the world, in monolingual infants. The pioneering studies of Janet Werker and Patricia Kuhl established that during the first months of life (monolingual) infants are able to perceive phoneme contrasts, even if not present in their environment and not produced or perceived by their parents (see for reviews, Kuhl, 2009; Werker & Gervain, 2013). In the second half of the first year of life, infants show evidence of tuning to the phoneme repertoire of their maternal language by decreasing their capacity to perceive non-native phonemes and by increasing their capacity to perceive native phonemes. Other studies also show that this pattern is modulated by different factors. Particularly relevant is the observation that the amount of exposure to a particular phoneme influences the speed with which a contrast is established (Anderson, Morgan, & White, 2003).

As mentioned above (see also Chapter 5 by Byers-Heinlein), there is a large variability in the amount of exposure bilingual infants receive to each of their languages, ranging from 80–90 percent of their input to, logically, 10–20 percent. However, when considered globally, bilingual infants (regardless of the specific unbalance) are less exposed to each of their languages than monolingual ones (this statement does not refer to individual cases, but to group averages; obviously, a monolingual infant raised by very silent parents may receive less input than a bilingual infant raised by very talkative parents). If establishing the phoneme repertoire is influenced by the amount of exposure, and bilingual infants have less exposure to each of their languages than monolingual ones, then it might be the case that bilingual infants are delayed in this domain, at least for language-specific phonemes or phones. At present it is unknown how bilingual infants process speech sounds that may be allophones in one language and phonemes in the other, such as the English phoneme /ð/, first sound in words such as "this" and the Spanish allophone /ð/, as in the second consonant of the word "dado," *dice* in English.

First studies exploring the development of phoneme categories in bilingual infants showed an unexpected U-shape pattern of sensitivities to *native* contrasts (pairs of phonemes that belong to the native language of the listener, for instance, /r-l/ would be a native contrast for English listeners, but a non-native for Japanese listeners). In a series of studies, Bosch & Sebastián-Gallés (2003) explored the discriminability of vowels in Catalan-Spanish monolingual and bilingual infants of different ages (see also Sebastián-Gallés & Bosch, 2009). Catalan and Spanish are two Romance languages; relevant to the present goals is the fact that these two languages differ in their vowel inventory. Spanish has five vowels, while Catalan has eight vowels. Crucially, Spanish has one mid-front vowel (/e/) falling roughly in between the two Catalan mid front vowels. Previous research has shown that native Spanish-speaking adults, even with a lifelong exposure to Catalan, experience major difficulties in perceiving the Catalan mid-front vowel contrast (Bosch, Costa, & Sebastián-Gallés, 2000; Pallier, Bosch, & Sebastián-Gallés, 1997; Sebastián-Gallés et al., Diaz, 2006; Sebastián-Gallés & Soto-Faraco, 1999) in accordance with models of non-native phoneme perception (Best, 1995; Flege, 1995). The results of the Bosch, Costa, & Sebastián-Gallés (2000) studies showed that at 4–5 months of age, all infants, regardless of the previous language exposure history, could discriminate native and non-native vowel contrasts, as predicted. At 8 months of age, infants growing in a monolingual environment only discriminated the phoneme contrasts of their native language, also replicating previous studies about perceptual narrowing of the phoneme space to the native language in the second half of the first year of life. However, at 8 months of age, bilingual infants failed to show a discriminatory behavior for contrasts existing in just one of their languages (the Catalan-specific /e/–/ɛ/, Bosch, Costa, & Sebastián-Gallés, 2000) or even for contrasts present in both languages (the common /o/–/u/ contrast, Sebastián-Gallés & Bosch, 2009). The fact that when tested with an acoustically distant vowel contrast (such as /e/–/u/, Sebastián-Gallés & Bosch) bilingual 8-month-olds showed discrimination, ruled out the possibility that bilingual infants were not responding in general. Discrimination by bilingual infants was observed again at 12 months of age. The pattern was interpreted as a "delay" and different explanations were put forward to account for it. They generally focused on the possibility of an influence of the specific distributional properties of the phonemes across both languages. In particular, it was suggested that the high frequency of the Spanish vowel /e/, together with the low frequency of the two mid-front Catalan vowels would create a unimodal distribution making discriminability difficult (Bosch & Sebastián-Gallés). However, an explanation in terms of distributional properties of the two phoneme systems fails to account for the similar U-shape results obtained for the /o/–/u/ contrast, as this occurs in both languages. Also, it has been suggested that this U-shape pattern may be related to the lack of discriminability between the two languages of the bilinguals during the first months of life. Sundara and Scutellaro (2011) suggested that because Catalan and Spanish cannot be distinguished before 4–5 months of age (studies about language discrimination are presented in section "Is there anything else?" further below), bilinguals would conflate the phoneme repertoires of the two languages during a certain time window (see section 6.4.1 for a description of studies on language differentiation). In fact, other studies looking at how the phoneme repertoire is established in the first year of life have reported equivalent discrimination patterns for native contrasts in monolinguals and French–English bilinguals (Burns et al., 2007; Sundara, Polka, & Molnar, 2008; Sundara & Scutellaro, 2011), i.e., two languages that, based on previous language discrimination abilities in newborns, infants should already discriminate at birth (Nazzi et al., 1998; Mehler et al., 1988).

Sebastián-Gallés and Bosch (2009) suggested that different factors converge to induce the reported U-shape pattern. First, Bosch & Sebastián-Gallés (2003) and Sebastián-Gallés and Bosch used a familiarization procedure that had not been employed in other studies testing phoneme perception in infants. Second, similarity at the lexical level (because of historical reasons, Catalan and Spanish have more similar words, such as "hombre"$_{SP}$ and "home"$_{CAT}$ than French and English, as in "homme"$_{FR}$ and "man"$_{EN}$) made the studied phoneme contrasts not salient for this population. Let's examine each of these effects in turn.

In the familiarization procedure used by these authors infants were exposed to tokens from one of the two categories during a familiarization period. Then, once the familiarization criterion was reached (in these studies, it was accumulating two minutes of attentive exposure), new tokens were presented (test phase). Those tokens could belong to the same category as in the familiarization phase ("same" tokens), or they could be from a "different" category. Longer looking times for different tokens as compared to same tokens at the test phase would be a sign of differentiating between the two categories. A crucial difference when compared to other studies is that the criterion used for the familiarization phase was not a habituation criterion (diminishing looking times per trial by a fixed percentage), but an accumulation of total looking times. It may well be the case that infants in the Bosch and Sebastián-Gallés (2003) and Sebastián-Gallés and Bosch (2009) studies were not habituated and thus showed reduced attentional responses.

In any case, this methodological difference by itself might not be enough to account for the observed results and it might just contribute to the lack of responsiveness showed by the 8-month-old bilinguals. Second, the overlap at the lexical level, together with an increased variability in the input bilingual infants receive, could also account for their lack of response when tokens from a different category were presented. The lexicon of bilingual individuals often contains words that have overlapping phonological representations, such as the French and English words "table." The typologically closer the two languages of a bilingual are, the more cognates their mental lexicons consist of. In the case of Spanish and Catalan infants, this overlap may be higher than 50 percent, while for French and English it may be around 30 percent. Crucially, cognates sound similar, but very rarely the same, thus, for French–English bilingual infants, the phonetic realizations of "table" would be [tabl] and [teɪbl] (in French and English, respectively). As for the case of Catalan and Spanish, many cognates involve a change in the vowels, as in the case of "chocolate," [tʃokolate] in Spanish and [ʃukulatə] in Catalan. Additionally, as Ramon-Casas et al. (2009) pointed out, the fact that in many bilingual homes, as parents tend to use only one language to communicate between them, at least one of the parents is speaking a non-native language, most likely mispronouncing some words because they are speaking with a foreign accent (see Bosch & Ramon-Casas, 2011, for specific evidence concerning Spanish–Catalan bilinguals). In this context, a category change in the "change" trials might have not been salient enough to trigger bilinguals' attention. Thus, it may well be the case that monolingual and bilingual infants show equivalent sensitivities, and that the procedure used was not the most appropriate to test them. These hypotheses were confirmed by the study of Albareda-Castellot, Pons, and Sebastián-Gallés (2011). These authors used the same stimuli employed by Bosch and Sebastián-Gallés (2003) but tested 8-month-old monolingual and bilingual infants using an anticipatory looking procedure. In this procedure, a visual object disappeared and reappeared in one of two spatial locations, contingent to each phoneme category. Infants had to learn where the visual object would reappear. In this case, bilinguals matched monolinguals.

A few studies have gathered ERPs of the developmental course of phoneme perception in Spanish–English bilingual infants (Garcia-Sierra et al., 2011; Shafer, Yu, & Datta, 2011; Shafer, Yu, & Garrido-Nag, 2012). Taken together, these studies show patterns of performance that the authors interpret as an indication of a delay in bilinguals. The data from these studies are difficult to interpret because the monolinguals and bilinguals came from different ethnic and socioeconomic backgrounds. Contrary to most of the behavioral studies reviewed above, where infants came from bilingual societies (such as the Montreal or Barcelona areas) where the two languages enjoy a social status and populations are ethnically homogeneous, data from ERP studies were obtained in the USA (greater New York area in Shafer et al., 2011; Shafer et al., 2012, and California in Garcia-Sierra et al., 2011) with bilinguals coming from families with Hispanic origins (the articles provided no information about the origin of the monolingual families). As Morton and Harper (2007) indicated (see also Chapter 5 in this handbook), differences between monolinguals and bilinguals often correlate with differences in socioeconomic status and ethnicity (though see for a reply Bialystok, 2009c). Crucially, such differences go hand in hand with differences in attention-related measures, disfavoring individuals from Caucasian origins and monolingual participants. Indeed, Mezzacappa (2004) provided evidence indicating that Hispanic children show less distraction on measures of executive attention than Caucasian children. Given the ethnic and social origins of the infants tested in the electrophysiological studies available so far, it might be the case that the observed differences between the monolingual and bilingual infants in these studies could also reflect the effect of other variables only, or on top

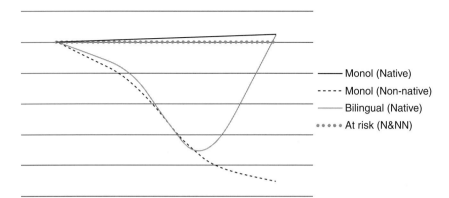

**Figure 6.2** Four schematic developmental trajectories of phoneme perception in four groups of infants and contrasts. In black, monolingual infants (solid (——): native; dashed (------): non-native). In solid gray, Spanish–Catalan bilingual infants (results from Bosch & Sebastián-Gallés, 2003 and Sebastián-Gallés & Bosch, 2009). In dotted gray, infants at risk of language delay, both native and non-native contrasts (Kuhl et al., 2005).

of bilingualism. Therefore, further research is needed before solid conclusions can be drawn from studies using these kinds of techniques.

All in all, although it is possible for bilinguals to experience a "delay" in establishing their phoneme repertoire, at present this possibility lacks empirical support. In particular, any explanation in terms of a "delay" of the U-shape pattern observed in the studies analyzing Spanish–Catalan bilinguals is at odds with what is known from the study of infants showing delays in language acquisition. Indeed, different studies seem to suggest that infants showing a delay in language learning in general, and in particular in establishing the phoneme categories, are characterized by a protracted period of sensitivity to non-native sounds when compared to normally developing infants (Kuhl, 2010; Kuhl et al., 2005; Tsao, Liu, & Kuhl, 2004; Weikum et al., 2012). Figure 6.2 depicts a schematic representation of the existing data from different developmental trajectories in monolingual, bilingual and infants at risk of language delays. As it can be clearly seen, the trajectory of Spanish–Catalan bilingual infants for native contrasts follows neither the pattern of monolinguals, nor the one of infants at risk.

Finally, although most of the studies addressing the learning of two phonological systems have focused on the acquisition of the phoneme repertoires, it is worth mentioning another study that explored other phonological domains. Sebastián-Gallés and Bosch (2002) studied how phonotactic information was learned by monolingual and bilingual infants exposed to Spanish and/or Catalan. In this study, the authors compared the preference for Catalan legal and illegal final word consonant clusters in 10-month-old infants, varying in their degree of exposure to Catalan and Spanish. Because Spanish does not license consonant clusters at the end of words (except for some loanwords), monolingual Spanish infants were expected to show no preference for one type of cluster over the other. On the contrary, Catalan monolingual infants were expected to prefer listening to stimuli conforming to the phonology of their native language. The results of the monolingual infants fully confirmed the expected pattern of results. Interestingly, bilingual infants showed a significant effect of amount of exposure to Catalan. Bilinguals were split into two groups, depending on the amount of exposure they had to each language (Catalan-dominant bilinguals listened on average to this language 60 percent of the time, and Spanish-dominant bilinguals listened to Catalan 40 percent of the time, on average). The group of Spanish-dominant 10-month-olds showed an intermediate pattern of preference between the two monolingual groups. Interestingly, the Catalan-dominant group showed the same pattern as the Catalan monolingual group. These results indicate a non-linear relationship between amount of exposure and the learning of phonotactics. As in many learning scenarios, acquisition reaches asymptote values. Accordingly, in spite of the fact that Catalan-dominant bilinguals received on average 35 percent less input in that language than Catalan monolingual infants, at 10 months of age they showed equivalent sensitivity to quite subtle final word phonological information.

### 6.3.2 Learning two vocabularies

Vocabulary learning is without any doubt the domain where we have most evidence about early bilingual language acquisition (see Chapter 5 in this handbook; Core et al., 2013; Hoff et al., 2012). Two facts have favored the boost of studies in this domain. First, the existence of standardized inventories in a large number of languages (in particular the MacArthur–Bates Communicative Development Inventory) has facilitated the task of researchers interested in the development of bilingual vocabulary research. Additionally, the administration of such tools is relatively simple, not requiring complex laboratory settings. The second factor has been the reliability of estimates of number of words children know at a certain age, as a good predictor of posterior language performance. Taken together, these studies agree in that while there is no difference in the total number of words monolingual and bilingual infants know, bilinguals know fewer words than monolinguals do in each of their languages (Core et al., 2013; Hoff et al., 2012). Whether this pattern can be considered a delay or not often depends more on political implications than on scientific ones. Further discussion about these measures can be found in Chapter 5 in this handbook.

Experimental studies on bilingual infants' word learning also point in the direction of common mechanisms between monolinguals and bilinguals. Janet Werker and colleagues reported first a different pattern of responses between monolinguals and bilinguals in associating objects and labels using a Switch paradigm. In this paradigm, infants (toddlers) are successively presented with two (unknown) objects and a corresponding label. Then in the test phase the objects may be presented with the same label as in the familiarization phase (match condition) or with another label (switch condition). If infants can learn the association between label and object, they should show a different pattern of looking times between the two conditions. As in the phoneme learning studies just presented, the first studies showed contrasting effects between monolingual and bilingual infants. Indeed, 17-month-old monolingual infants succeeded in this task, but bilinguals did not until 20 months of age (Fennell, Byers-Heinlein, & Werker, 2007). However, other studies showed that methodological issues might be at the origin of the reported delay. In the Fennell et al. study, the auditory stimuli constituted minimal pairs (bih–dih). Additionally, the stimuli were realizations that, although not prototypical, they were acceptable exemplars for adult native listeners of French and English (phonemes /b/ and /d/ are realized in French and English in different ways). In this way, the authors were able to use the same materials with all the populations tested (monolingual French, monolingual English and French–English bilinguals). Mattock et al. (2010) showed equivalent learning abilities in monolinguals and bilinguals using minimal pairs, provided the phonemes were uttered in a language-specific way. More recently, Byers-Heinlein, Fennell, and Werker (2014) have shown that bilinguals succeed at the same age as monolinguals provided the stimuli are dissimilar sounding (converging evidence on the hindering effects of label similarity when testing bilingual infants and toddlers has also been reported in word-recognition tasks, Ramon-Casas & Bosch, 2010; Ramon-Casas et al., 2009). These results suggest that monolingual and bilingual infants share basic mechanisms involved in word learning. However, bilingual infants are particularly sensitive to language-specific cues.

In summary, it would be misleading to assume that the learning and processing of new words in bilinguals is equivalent to what happens in monolinguals, except for it being multiplied by two (as bilinguals need to learn two vocabularies). As François Grosjean rightly pointed out some time ago, the bilingual is not two monolinguals in one person (Grosjean, 1989). As we will see further below, handling two lexicons involves additional computations.

## 6.4   Is there anything else?

So far we have described the challenges that bilingual infants must face when learning two languages instead of one in those domains where just "more work" seems to be needed (learning two phoneme repertoires, two lexicons). But even if not considering issues related to potential interactions between the representations of the two languages of a bilingual (such as the allophone issue described above, or the fact that the bilingual's lexicons include cognates, false friends, etc.) there are still bilingual-specific computations, described below.

### 6.4.1 Noticing that there is more than one system

To properly learn two different languages, a mandatory first step is to notice the existence of the two "speech objects." Just a few studies have tackled this fundamental issue; nevertheless, in spite of the fact that stimuli, populations, and methods differ significantly, the results converge: exposure to two languages does not "confuse" bilinguals. However, do monolinguals and bilinguals discriminate languages in an equivalent way?

Only three studies compared monolinguals and bilinguals in their capacity to distinguish the sound of one language from another. Byers-Heinlein, Burns, and Werker (2010) observed that monolingual newborn infants exposed to Tagalog (a language spoken in the Philippines and typologically very different from English) and newborn infants exposed to English and Tagalog before birth had no difficulties in noticing that the two languages sounded different. These authors compared monolingual and bilingual newborns in two different tasks. They first compared patterns of language preference. It is well known that newborns prefer to listen to their maternal language (Mehler et al., 1988; Moon, Cooper, & Fifer, 1993). When presented with English and Tagalog sentences, monolingual English newborns preferred listening to English, and bilingual English–Tagalog newborns showed no preference for one language over the other. This result may be interpreted as either showing equivalent preference for the maternal language(s) or as showing an inability to differentiate between languages. A second experiment, using a habituation procedure, showed that both monolingual and bilingual newborns had no difficulties in distinguishing one language from the other. The capacity to distinguish typologically (and rhythmically) different languages at birth is an ability that we share with other animals (Ramus et al., 2000; Toro, Trobalon, & Sebastián-Gallés, 2003).

Two studies by Bosch and Sebastián-Gallés (1997, 2001) explored the capacity of 4–5-month-old Catalan–Spanish monolingual and bilingual infants to distinguish these two languages. Although there is no direct published evidence, previous studies have reported that newborns are not able to detect differences between typologically (rhythmically) similar languages, such as Dutch and English or Italian and Spanish (Nazzi, Bertoncini, & Mehler, 1998). Given the similarities between Spanish and Catalan, it is likely that newborn infants cannot notice the difference in how they sound. Bosch and Sebastián-Gallés (2001) reported that both monolinguals and bilinguals at 4–5 months of age had no difficulties in discriminating them. Nazzi and colleagues, who investigated the language discrimination capacities of monolingual infants exposed to English and tested in different Germanic languages, provided converging evidence also showing that similar languages can be discriminated around this age (Nazzi, Jusczyk, & Johnson, 2000). Thus, the evidence of early language discrimination capacities of speech sounds shows no delays and no evidence of confusion in bilinguals.

Two additional studies have explored the early capacity of monolingual and bilingual infants to discriminate languages. These studies did not expose infants to speech sounds, but to talking faces only (there were no sounds provided during the entire experiment). Weikum et al. (2007) explored the developmental trajectory of (monolingual) infants in their capacity to discriminate French from English in silent video clips of three French–English bilinguals reciting the *Little Prince* story. These authors observed that 4- and 6-month-old French or English monolingual infants discriminated French from English. However, this discrimination capacity disappeared at 8 months of age. In contrast, when French–English bilinguals were tested at 8 months of age, they still showed a discriminatory capacity. The authors interpreted these results within the perceptual narrowing framework. Indeed, the observed decline would parallel previous findings in the phoneme or face discrimination (Kelly et al., 2007; Werker et al., 1981), showing changes in perceptual capacities as a function of experience. However, more recently the same authors have challenged whether this is the unique underlying cause (Sebastián-Gallés et al., 2012). These authors tested 8-month-old Catalan and Spanish monolingual and bilingual infants with the same materials as Weikum et al. The results of the Catalan and Spanish infants were strikingly similar to the French–English ones: monolingual 8-month-old infants failed to discriminate between silent talking French and English faces, while 8-month-old bilingual infants, regardless of their lack of previous exposure to the test languages, showed discrimination behaviors. The authors extended the initial explanation of the contrasting discrimination patterns between monolinguals and bilinguals by including the need for additional computations in order to separate (and track) two languages, a computation that, as said, bilingual infants must perform, to properly acquire their two languages. These additional computations would be responsible for this boost in bilingual infants' attentional competences.

### 6.4.2 Enhanced cognitive capacities

For many years, bilingualism was associated with hindered cognitive development. Bilingualism was thought to "confuse" infants, making even harder the already difficult tasks of language learning and of making sense of the world. However, in recent years, we have witnessed a change of balance in favor of the opposite point of view. A recent hot research topic in bilingual research is how bilingual input may enhance some general cognitive capacities (for reviews, see Bialystok, Craik, & Luk, 2012; Hernandez et al., 2013). There are a vast number of studies showing that bilinguals outperform monolinguals in a wide variety of attention-related tasks, from infancy to aging populations. The origin of such advantage has been attributed to bilinguals' increased need to select, inhibit, and monitor their speech in language production tasks. Several studies have shown that when speaking, bilinguals activate their two lexicons in parallel. That is, when having to name an apple, a French–Spanish bilingual activates the French word *pomme* and the Spanish word *manzana* (the respective translations of the English word "apple"), even if the context is fully monolingual. In other words, bilinguals activate their lexicons in a non-selective and parallel way (Colomé, 2001; Costa, Caramazza, & Sebastián-Gallés, 2000; Poulisse & Bongaerts, 1994). This extended activation requires the involvement of additional attentional resources, when compared to monolinguals, to ensure the selection of the contextually (linguistically) adequate word. Different studies have reported behavioral and electrophysiological evidence consistent with the proposed model of parallel activation of the two lexicons, even in bilingual toddlers, who possess limited vocabularies (Kuipers & Thierry, 2013; Von Holzen & Mani, 2012).

Yet, the above explanation involving the bilinguals' constant need to inhibit the non-target language when they speak was challenged by the results of a study by Kovács and Mehler (2009). These authors compared monolingual and bilingual 7-month-olds in their capacity to inhibit a previously learned response. In this experiment infants learned first to orient their gaze to one spatial location in response to a previous cue. After nine trials in one spatial location, the test phase followed, during which the spatial location was shifted. While there were no differences between monolingual and bilingual infants in their capacity to learn the first location, only bilinguals managed to shift their gaze to the new spatial location in the second phase. The authors considered that their results supported the idea of enhanced inhibitory skills in preverbal infants. The theoretical consequences of these results are considerable, given that the differences between monolingual and bilingual infants could not be attributed to an increased need to inhibit a lexicon (in the case of bilinguals) in language production tasks. Along the same lines of enhanced cognitive functioning in very young bilinguals, other studies have reported a cognitive advantage for bilingual toddlers in the domain of memory processing. In particular, Brito and Barr (2012) showed that bilinguals outperform monolinguals in some memory tasks as well. These authors tested 18-month-old monolingual and bilingual toddlers in a delayed-imitation task. Children first saw the experimenter performing a sequence of movements playing with a mitten. Then children were allowed to play with a new mitten. The results showed that bilingual children were better at generalizing (repeating) actions previously seen when compared to monolinguals, therefore suggesting an enhancement of memory capacities in bilingual toddlers.

## 6.5 Is there a different learning pathway?

Bilinguals are equipped with the same cognitive resources as monolinguals, which allow them to learn languages and to achieve a fully functioning and adaptive cognitive processing. Monolingual and bilingual infants face the same fundamental challenges. In this sense, it is not surprising that most of the linguistic and cognitive development is equivalent in both populations. There is no evidence to suggest that the fundamental milestones in language development are swapped, significantly delayed or absent in bilinguals when compared to monolinguals. However, bilingualism poses additional challenges that infants must face and these specific challenges lead to a series of adaptations.

There are two fundamental differences between monolinguals and bilinguals that may result in significant differences between the two populations. The first one is the total amount of input infants receive in the language(s) they are exposed to. To the best of my knowledge there is no evidence indicating that bilingual parents are more talkative than monolingual ones. If the total amount of language input is equivalent between monolinguals and bilinguals, then by necessity, bilingual infants are, on average, less exposed to each of their languages. There is a vast literature showing effects of the amount of exposure on different levels of the language system, in monolinguals and in bilinguals (Hoff et al., 2012). We have mentioned above some studies relevant for the case of bilingually exposed infants. Indeed, there is evidence showing effects of the amount of exposure on the learning of phonotactics (Sebastián-Gallés & Bosch, 2002). Also, there is significant evidence showing that bilingual children have reduced vocabularies in each of their languages. This reduction in vocabulary size often raises concerns in parents, and also in educators. Vocabulary size is a good predictor of later academic achievement. Indeed, if children know fewer words, they will have more difficulty learning in school. Just considering statistical values, bilingualism should be considered a risk factor for poor academic performance in the USA (Federal Interagency Forum on Child and Family Statistics, 2002; Hoff et al., 2012). However, it is likely that not bilingualism in itself, but other associated factors – in particular lower SES in bilingual populations – are responsible for low performance in bilinguals. While not denying the importance of vocabulary knowledge, in particular for reading and writing, one should wonder why academic failure is not higher in multilingual societies, or why some parents are willing to pay a lot of money to send their kids to private international schools, where some subjects are taught in a second language. So, the relationship between vocabulary size, language development, reading, writing, and academic success is far more complex than it seems to be.

The second fundamental difference between monolinguals and bilinguals is directly related to the prima facie trivial fact that bilinguals have to learn two languages and monolinguals just one. In the preceding sections, I have discussed the impact of either the need for separating two languages, or the impact of the amount of exposure on language learning. As said at the beginning of this chapter, our current knowledge of early bilingual language acquisition is very patchy and incomplete. The difficulties associated with finding homogeneous groups of infants (see also Chapter 5 in this handbook) severely restrict advancement in this field. This has led to a generalized neglect of the impact of the similarity between the languages bilinguals have to learn (with a few exceptions). It is obvious an individual learning Spanish and Catalan (as said, two Romance languages from the Indo-European family) faces different challenges from somebody learning Spanish and Basque (Basque is an isolated language, not belonging to the Indo-European family). Typological distance is a good proxy for estimating language distance (typological distance reflects how closely two languages relate historically, thus, German and Dutch are typologically very close, while German and Spanish are typologically less close, but still closely related; German and Hungarian are typologically more distant than German and Spanish). Although this is undoubtedly the case, similarities and differences must be established at different levels and considered in the context of specific research targets. For instance, if the focus is on phonology (and on vowel learning in particular), Catalan and Spanish are quite different, while Basque (a non-Indo-European and very different from Romance languages) and Spanish share the same vowel space. Just to make things more complicated, because the different language dimensions are not acquired and processed independently, it is important to note how language similarity/difference scales over time. Let us consider the following: it is well known that from the sixth month of life, infants start to show language-specific consonant perception (earlier for vowels); their capacity to perceive nonnative sounds clearly declines (and the perception of native ones sharpens, see for reviews Kuhl, 2010; Werker, Byers-Heinlein, & Fennell, 2009). At the same time, as said, there is clear evidence that by 6 months of age infants have already succeeded in learning a few words, and that before the end of the first year of life they will have learned a sizeable number of words. Not surprisingly then, early language development must involve some kind of cross-talk between lexical and segmental (phoneme) representations. Because phonemes represent the minimal contrastive speech unit involving a change of word meaning, phonemes only make sense if a lexicon exists (whether phonemes or words are established first is still under debate, see Bergelson and Swingley, 2012, for instance). Let's consider then the distinct scenarios resulting from the various types of language differences in bilinguals. Typologically close languages (such as Spanish and Italian or Dutch and German) have more cognate words than typologically more distant ones (cognate words, by definition share the same etymological origin). Cognates, such as the word "television" in many different languages, share a lot of phonological information. How does the relative number of cognate words in the lexicons of infants exposed to typologically similar or dissimilar languages impact the establishment of phoneme categories? How do similarities in fundamental phonological properties (such as vowel inventory, or the existence of lexical tones in just one of the languages, to mention only two of the potential properties) impact lexical acquisition? Analogous arguments can be made with respect to syntax. Although typologically close languages share fundamental syntactic properties, relevant differences may also be observed between closely related pairs of languages. For instance, some Romance languages such as Italian, Spanish, Catalan, Portuguese are pro-drop (or null subject) languages (sentential subjects may not be uttered in some contexts), while in French the pronunciation of subjects is mandatory in all instances. Another fundamental syntactic property is word order. There is evidence that 7-month-old infants raised in bilingual environments, where the two languages possess different word orders (such as English and Japanese) are able to make use of different prosodic cues (duration and pitch), together with distributional information, to establish the word order of the different languages (Gervain & Werker, 2013). However, typologically close languages such as German and English may also differ in word order. Germanic languages comply with what is called verb–second word order. English is the only exception, as it follows a quite strict SVO word order (a sentence like "Before school play the kids football in the park" would be correct in German). Thus, similarities and dissimilarities at different levels may show a multifaceted pattern of interactions. How the different types of knowledge and computations interact in the process of early bilingualism remains an open question.

## 6.6 Conclusion

To conclude, our current knowledge of how infants exposed to bilingual environments manage to learn the two languages (or more in the case of multilingual environments) is still incomplete. Nonetheless, from this fragmentary picture two major conclusions can be drawn. First, monolinguals and bilinguals follow the same learning pathways: fundamental milestones are acquired in the same sequence in both populations. Second, bilingual (and multilingual) learning imposes additional computations that result in specific adaptations. Importantly, some of these adaptations – such as the non-selective parallel activation of lexical entries, considered distinctive features of adult bilingual processing – can already be observed early in life.

# 7

# Phonology and morphology in lexical processing

Kira Gor

## 7.1 Introduction

Imagine a non-native listener of English with some English vocabulary internalized, struggling with ambiguous auditory input. Was it *road* or *load*? Broadly speaking, there are several possible scenarios. First, the word may not be stored in the mental lexicon of a second language (L2) learner, and the learner decides, "I don't know this word." This is a quite common, but the least interesting case. Second, the learner may be hesitant about which word was pronounced because it contained a phonological contrast that made it difficult to tell which of the two similarly sounding words it was, *still* or *steal*, *rip* or *reap*, or maybe *lip* or *leap*? Third, L2 learners quite often misidentify one word as another that sounds similar, but not identical, even in the case when no problematic phonological contrasts are involved. *Whisper* and *whisker*, which one belongs to a kitten? And fourth, L2 learners need to decide whether a word is mono- or polymorphemic and decompose morphologically complex words into constituent morphemes in order to process morphosyntactic information: was it *guessed* or *guest*, *patients* or *patience*? Here, the morphological analysis prompted by sentence structure will achieve two goals: access of the lexical entry and interpretation of the information contained in the inflection, past-tense *-ed* marker in *guessed* and plural *-s* marker in *patients*. This chapter will review recent findings and discuss new directions in research addressing two major interfaces in L2 acquisition and processing, those of phonology and lexical access and morphology and lexical access. It will focus on lexical access of words presented in isolation and will leave the growing body of research on lexical access in a sentence, as well as the study of word boundary effects and assimilation across word boundaries in phrases, outside its scope due to space limitations.

## 7.2 Phonological aspects of L2 lexical access

### 7.2.1 Models of L2 phonetic categorization

Recent years have seen several developments in research devoted to the acquisition and processing of L2 phonology: a long-awaited realization that most research on L2 perception had been dealing with categorization of phones that have no connection to their linguistic function. First, the function of phonemes, abstract linguistic units, is to serve as building blocks of morphemes and words, as they are represented in the mental lexicon. Accordingly, researchers have turned to the phoneme as opposed to a theoretically neuter phone, which is made possible only by focusing on the interface of phonology and the lexicon, as opposed to meaningless segments and sequences. Second, there has been a renewed interest in the phonology–phonetics interface and the study of the interactions of bottom-up and top-down processing. Third, in addition to looking at phonological processing in L2 learners differing in proficiency, age of acquisition, amount of L2 input received, and other biographical non-linguistic variables in order to recreate the developmental learning curve, recent studies report highly controlled vocabulary learning experiments to gain direct insights into how phonological learning and vocabulary learning interact in a bootstrapping fashion. And fourth, this new interest in phonology in lexical access and lexical learning explores the dimension of the phonology–lexicon interface that is extremely important for L2 processing: phonological representations of words and lexical competition, and the impact of unfaithful phonological representations of words on L2 lexical access.

Until recently, theories of L2 phonological acquisition were not overly concerned with how the interaction of bottom-up phonetic and top-down lexical processing leads to the formation of abstract phonological categories, and rather took this interaction for granted. In this sense, they were precursors of the new paradigm in research on phonological categorization in L2 lexical access. This section will review four such theories, all of which explore native and nonnative phonetic categories. The Native Language Magnet (NLM) (Kuhl & Iverson, 1995) model of native (L1) and L2 perception focuses on the properties of the phonetic space in the vicinity of, and at a distance from, the prototype and the perceptual warping phenomenon. According to NLM, the prototype acts as a perceptual magnet attracting the sounds that are close in the perceptual space so that the listener categorizes them as the prototype. This is true of L2 sounds being "caught" in the space of the L1 prototype. The prototype is assumed to be a functional L1 sound unit, and its phonetic properties and the space – usually, the F1/F2 vowel space – seem to refer to the main allophone. NLM has found support with the prototypes of the American English /i/ and /e/, and Swedish /y/. Thus, NLM shows nonlinearities in the perceptual space that underlies the categorization of new phones based on their acoustic properties and remains agnostic with regard to the phonological status of the phones. Moreover, the NLM model is primarily concerned with early infant perception, before lexical learning and the establishment of phonological categories.

The Speech Learning Model (SLM) (Flege, 1995) aims to account for age-related constraints on the ability to produce L2 vowels and consonants in a native-like fashion. It is concerned with the acquisition of phonetic categories rather than phonological contrasts. SLM states that acquisition of the sound shape of L2 proceeds by establishing perceptual similarity between the positional allophones rather than L1 and L2 phonemes themselves. It is based on (dis)similarity of perceptually linked L1 and L2 sounds, diaphones, with the status of the L2 phone in L2 acquisition depending on the phonetic characteristics of the relevant positional allophones of L1 and L2 rather than the more abstract phonemic level (p. 239). Accordingly, phonological parsing of L2 lexical units remains outside the scope of the model.

The Perceptual Assimilation Model (PAM) (Best, 1995) explores the consequences of perceived similarity between L1 and L2 phones with the phonetic space organized based on articulatory gestures. It finds its origins in Articulatory Phonology, and in this respect, stands apart from the other purely perceptually based models. In its original version, PAM was intended for the situation of the initial cross-linguistic contact and focused on naïve listeners. It is not concerned with how the perceptual space is directly mapped onto the phones, since the model accepts and treats the outcome of such complex categorization process as a given.

PAM has been extended to the situation of L2 acquisition in its PAM-L2 version (Best & Tyler, 2007) that addresses the consequences of exposure to L2. The articulatory–phonetic interface remains the mechanism driving L1 and L2 linguistic perception, though the emphasis has shifted to the developmental aspects of the model.

PAM-L2 was the first to state explicitly that the phonological level is central to the perception of speech by L2 learners. Naïve learners at their first contact with L2 cannot possibly be dealing with L2 phonemes, the units supporting lexical representations and lexical access in a language completely unknown to them. While cross-linguistic research on phonetic categorization of new sounds establishes a much-needed baseline, it is uninformative about phonemic categorization; hence the need for research aiming at the phonological level of L2 closely connected to lexical acquisition.

The most recent model of L2 phonological perception by Escudero, the Second Language Linguistic Perception Model, or L2LP (Escudero, 2005; Mayr & Escudero, 2010), combines elements of two models, PAM and SLM. L2LP assumes the full copying stage at the first encounter of the learner with the new phonological system, when the L1 phonological system is copied, and the duplicate is used by the learner to handle the new L2 sounds. After this copying stage, the perceptual development in L2 follows one of the two scenarios. Under the New Scenario, listeners either create a new L2 category or split the category existing in L1 to correspond to two categories in L2. Under the Similar Scenario, listeners reuse the existing L1 categories. They may still need to shift the L1 perceptual boundary to the L2 setting. L2LP places emphasis on individual variation in perceptual learning and connects the acquisitional trajectory to learners' L1 accent that includes regional, social, and idiosyncratic features. The features of the L1 accent define the initial categorization pattern of L2 sounds as a new category, a split, or an existing category.

In summary, the models of L2 sound acquisition briefly reviewed above all focus on perception and explore the notion of the phonological sieve introduced by Polivanov in the 1930s and the mechanisms underlying perceptual equivalence of L1 and L2 phones (Polivanov, 1931). Together, they address the lower end of phonological processing, i.e., the creation of L2 phonetic categories that constitute the perceptual basis for abstract phonemes. The studies carried out in support of each of the models use sound segments that are not meaningful lexical units in L2. This is often done for methodological reasons: lexically driven factors, such as word frequency, can create response biases. At the same time, this has generated a situation when research in support of the models targeting L2 phonological perception,[1] in fact, explores lower-level phonetic processing outside of lexical access. At the same time, these earlier models and the empirical studies supporting them have set the ground for the new research direction. Indeed, phonetic categorization is the foundation for the development of phonological contrasts.

### 7.2.2  L2 phonological contrasts in lexical access

A new interest in the role of phonology in lexical access and acquisition is evolving in two directions (Darcy et al., 2012; Escudero, Hayes-Harb, & Mitterer, 2008). The first direction is a continuation of the 'phonological sieve' tradition, in other words, the research supporting the models of phonetic categorization of L2 sounds. However, the major difference is that the focus now is on the mechanisms at work at the phonetic–lexical interface. This type of investigation is done in two ways: by exploring the influence of L2 difficulties with phonological contrasts on lexical access of existing and familiar words, or by staging a learning experiment when

---

[1] This chapter consistently makes a distinction between phonetic perception that deals with phonetic features and contrasts, and phonological perception that targets phonemes, minimal linguistic units potentially associated with meaning. Phonemes are language specific and are the building blocks for morphemes and words. While phonetic perception can be observed in naïve listeners, phonological perception can only be observed in L2 learners who are familiar with some words in their L2.

L2 learners learn new vocabulary with manipulated phonological properties in highly controlled experimental conditions (Escudero et al., 2008).

The second direction concerns itself with a different challenge presented by L2 lexical acquisition and access, namely, the ability to represent, store, and retrieve a lexical entry as a sequence of phonemes associated with a meaning(s) (see Eulitz & Lahiri, 2004). When L2 learners integrate L2 words into their mental lexicon, these words do not have strong phonological representations, which results in weak and uncertain mappings among similarly sounding words and their meanings (Cook, 2012). For example, *lisp* and *limp,* which differ only by one phoneme, may be weakly linked to their respective meanings, and as a result, an L2 learner may be unsure which phonological form corresponds to which meaning.

An L2 learner hears new words of a second language and needs to store them in the mental lexicon, access them, and retrieve them. In order to accomplish this task, L2 learners (and L1 speakers as well) need to convert auditory input into lexical representations. There are two extreme points of view on how this is done.[2] The first, the episodic model, assumes a direct mapping of the acoustic signal onto the lexical representation. Thus, there is an acoustically rich trace of all the encounters with the word associated with its lexical representation stored in the mental lexicon (Bybee, 2001; Goldinger, 1998; Pierrehumbert, 2001). According to this approach, no abstract phonological level of representation is needed. Conversely, according to the abstractionist approach, acoustic input is processed pre-lexically and converted into phonological representations associated with lexical representations. Thus, all the detailed phonetic information is removed at the abstract phonological stage (Norris, McQueen, & Cutler, 2000). We will follow the position expressed in a hybrid abstractionist–episodic model that claims that pre-lexical phonological representations are abstract, and at the same time flexible and phonetically attuned. This position is explored in an L1 training study involving Dutch [f]-final and [s]-final words and words with a manipulated word-final consonant that could be interpreted as either [f] or [s] (McQueen, Cutler, & Norris, 2006). In the training stage, participants, L1 speakers of Dutch, who performed a lexical decision task (LDT), were biased to interpret the ambiguous word-final consonant as [f] or [s] depending on the word itself and the other words on the list. They were subsequently tested in a cross-modal priming LDT on new words with the same word-final ambiguous and unambiguous consonants. The biases developed in lexical access during the training stage were carried over to new lexical items, which excludes a mechanism purely based on episodic representations and requires an abstract phonological level that is associated with perceptual retuning. The study

---

[2] According to a recent proposal, learning phonological categories is a single-stage process that does not make use of the lexicon (Dillon, Dunbar, & Idsardi, 2013). The model uses acoustic data on Inuktitut in simulations.

interprets the demonstrated perceptual retuning as an analogy of adjustments made in listening to idiosyncratic pronunciations of different talkers (including accented nonnative speech). However, it also provides evidence that acoustic/phonetic information in auditorily perceived words is processed by skilled listeners in a "linguistic mode." Phonetic cues are associated with allophones of the same phoneme or with different phonemes, as appropriate, based on an implicit system of language-specific rules that work at the phonetics–phonology interface. We will return to allophonic variation in a subsection below.

### 7.2.3 L2 phonetic categorization and lexical representation: what comes first?

Given that L2 learners may experience problems at several levels involved in the phonological encoding of L2 words, it comes as no surprise that there is no equivalence between their performance on lower-level phonetic categorization tasks and higher-level processing of phonological contrasts in lexical access. However, different studies do not agree on the direction of the difficulties. Darcy and colleagues refer to these two opposite points of view as the 'categories first' and 'lexicon first' positions (Darcy et al., 2012).

The more plausible and widely accepted view is the 'categories first' view: that learners need to establish robust phonetic L2 categories before creating lexical representations (Darcy et al., 2012). A series of studies on Spanish–Catalan bilinguals explicitly formulated and explored this view (for a review, see Sebastián-Gallés & Díaz, 2012). The 'categories first' position draws on the understanding of speech perception as a hierarchically organized set of processes (e.g., Poeppel, Idsardi, & van Wassenhove, 2008) starting with lower-level acoustic input that is analyzed to derive phonetic features, then going on to convert the output of the phonetic analysis into phonological representations, and finally, matching the sequence of phonemes with a lexical representation. If this hierarchical structure is translated into the degree of difficulty in L2 phonological perception, then the higher the processing level, the less successful L2 learners are expected to be. This pattern seems to emerge from the studies conducted and reviewed by Sebastián-Gallés and Díaz that used tasks ranging from lower-level categorization to lexical decision and quantified the percent of Spanish-dominant bilinguals who handled the Catalan /e/–/ɛ/ phonological contrast within the range of native speakers. In the identification task with a continuum of seven synthesized vowels in an earlier study, 60 percent of Spanish-dominant bilinguals fell within the range of Catalan native speakers (Pallier, Bosch, & Sebastián-Gallés, 1997). In the 'matching-gating' task, 25 percent of Spanish–Catalan bilinguals matched the native performance (Sebastián-Gallés & Soto-Faraco, 1999). In this modification of the gating task, participants listened to minimal pairs of nonwords differing by the Catalan /e/–/ɛ/ contrast and presented multiple times, in short increments, or 'gates'. They chose from these two alternatives of nonword stimuli from the first gate. Their performance was assessed based on the length of the nonword (the number of gates) required for a correct decision. Finally, only 18 percent of Spanish–Catalan bilinguals performed within the native range in a LDT when judging Catalan nonwords created by switching the /e/ or /ɛ/ vowels (Sebastián-Gallés, Echeverria, & Bosch, 2005). Note that, strictly speaking, the 'matching-gating' task and LDT employed in the two above-mentioned studies posed different problems for the bilinguals. The 'matching-gating' task challenges listeners to categorize the segment based on incomplete phonetic information. It expects expert listeners to make efficient use of the properties of the short auditory segment that define or predict the vowel quality. In the LDT with nonwords created by switching the /e/ or /ɛ/ vowels, the task of the listener is to detect the mismatch in phonetic quality.

Additionally, in the often-cited medium range priming study by Pallier and colleagues (Pallier, Colomé, & Sebastián-Gallés, 2001) that used identity pairs and minimal pairs of words differing by the vowel, /e/ or /ɛ/, Spanish-dominant bilinguals, but not Catalan-dominant bilinguals, showed spurious facilitation priming effects for minimal pairs because Spanish does not have the Catalan /e/–/ɛ/ distinction. Facilitation in Spanish-dominant bilinguals was interpreted as the result of treating the members of the minimal pair as homophones. Thus, the sequence emerging from these studies is the lack of a phonetic distinction leading to the inability to differentiate lexical representations for two separate lexical items.

Studies that show that correct L2 lexical encoding can be achieved even in the absence of robust L2 phonological discrimination support the alternative 'lexicon first' view (Cutler, Weber, & Otake, 2006; Escudero et al., 2008; Weber & Cutler, 2004). Any asymmetrical biases in the lexical encoding of problematic L2 phonological contrasts, as opposed to their complete neutralization, are taken as evidence against the idea that homophonous L2 lexical entries correspond to the lack of differentiation of the phonological contrasts (as done in Pallier et al., 2001). In an eye-tracking study, L1 Dutch speakers had to click on pictures corresponding to auditorily presented L2 English words with the critical condition involving the English contrast between the /æ/ and /ɛ/ phonemes in the first syllable, as in *panda* and *pencil* absent in Dutch (Weber & Cutler, 2004). There was a clear bias in the pattern of fixations, so that 'panda' activated 'pencil,' but not the other way round. This asymmetry was problematic for the homophony-based account found in the Pallier and colleagues (2001) study and required additional explanation. The asymmetry reported in the Weber and Cutler (2004) study could be due to the fact that the Dutch phoneme /e/ may be perceptually closer to the English /ɛ/ than /æ/, and therefore the Dutch L1 category serves as the perceptual anchor. However, the phonetic categorization task conducted on the same vowel contrast showed no bias in the categorization of these two English vowels by Dutch L1 listeners (Cutler et al., 2004).

The findings by Hayes-Harb and Masuda (2008) represent a somewhat different case. Following a training session, their English learners of L2 Japanese were able to reliably match the pictures with the nonword 'brand names' that they were given during the training. The targeted contrast was Japanese phonological geminates, /tt/ vs. /t/, absent in English. At the same time, they failed to produce the contrast in picture naming. This discrepancy should be interpreted as a manifestation of the asymmetry between L2 perception and production rather than an argument in favor of the lexical encoding of Japanese geminates in the absence of robust phonetic categorization. Also, the auditory templates for the L2 words used in the training session could serve as episodic representations rather than phonological. This effect could be similar to having robust L2 lexical representations for highly frequent words, without being able to handle all the phonetic cues to the phonemes constituting the word in all the phonetic environments occurring in other words.

A recent study reported an asymmetry in the relationship between categorization and lexical representation of a phonological contrast. The study compared the outcomes of two tasks, lower-level phonetic processing in an AXB discrimination task that used consonant–vowel–consonant (CVC) nonwords, and a lexical decision task (LDT) that used real and nonce words with the same contrasts in a repetition priming design (Darcy et al., 2012). Two groups of American learners of French, at the intermediate and advanced levels, were tested on two sets of front/back rounded vowel contrasts, high /y/ – /u/ and mid /œ/ – /ɔ/, notoriously difficult for English-speaking learners of French.[3] The study calls the obtained results "a curious anomaly for standard assumptions according to which the development of new categories is a necessary prerequisite for lexical contrast" (p. 28), since although it displays a pattern of dissociation between the outcomes of two tasks for the two contrasts in question, the direction is flipped between the tasks. Indeed, the advanced learners had robust lexical representations for the lexical items testing all the contrasts in LDT; however, they showed persistent errors in the AXB task testing phonetic categorization. Intermediate L2 French learners showed spurious homophony for the /y/-/u/ contrast, but not the /œ/-/ɔ/ contrast in the repetition priming LDT; however, they observed the opposite hierarchy of difficulty for these contrasts in AXB, with the average error rate of 37 percent for the /œ/-/ɔ/ contrast, and only 15 percent for the /y/-/u/ contrast. The similarity in the results of AXB task

---

[3] The study tests its own novel approach, 'direct mapping from acoustics to phonology' (DMAP), that explores the application of phonological theory to L2 lexical encoding of difficult phonological contrasts. The proposed model will largely remain outside the scope of this review.

for both groups with a significant difference in the LDT task, points to a dissociation between phonetic categorization and lexical encoding instead of a causal relationship between them. The authors argue that the frequency of the lexical items used in the materials, their familiarity, or their orthographic and acoustic properties, did not cause the observed asymmetries. A possibility still remains that the lexical items were integrated into the mental lexicons of L2 participants to different degrees, given that the frequencies were balanced across the high/mid pairs, but not within the front/back pairs, which is crucial for avoiding lexical biases. If, hypothetically, the /œ/ items had higher frequency than the /ɔ/ items, this could explain their more robust lexical representation. Similarly, the average familiarity score was 61 percent for the /y/–/u/ pair and 85 percent for the /œ/–/ɔ/ pair (p. 22), which points to the possibility that the items in the mid condition were subjectively more familiar to the participants. These two factors taken together could account for better lexical entrenchment of the words with the mid front rounded /œ/ than those with the high /y/. Differences in the level of entrenchment could signify more or less robust phonological representations of the lexical items (Diependaele et al., 2013).[4] Given that there were only five words representing each vowel, lexical biases could be significant. On the other hand, an important outcome of the study is the fact that the intermediate group's categorization in AXB was affected by the allophonic variation; they were more accurate in the labial context for both contrasts.

The study by Darcy and colleagues (2012) suggests that dissociations in categorization and lexical representation are in fact possible and to be expected since lexical items are more or less entrenched in L2 mental lexicons dependent on the level of L2 proficiency, while at the same time different contextual and positional allophones of L2 phonemes may present different perceptual difficulties according to the hierarchy of difficulty. This ultimately means that while the 'categories first' position corresponds better to the hierarchical view of linguistic processing, both positions may find support in the experimental data precisely because phonological and lexical acquisition proceed in parallel in a bootstrapping fashion, both in L1 and L2. Depending on whether the study uses more or less frequent lexical items, and the positional allophones occurring in the stimuli happen to be more or less perceptually salient, the outcomes of a particular study may favor either the 'categories first' or the 'lexicon first' view. The issue of allophonic variation as it pertains to lexical access will be addressed below.

---

[4] The lexical quality hypothesis developed by Perfetti for reading, but also adaptable for listening "claims that variation in the quality of word representations has consequences for reading skill, including comprehension. High lexical quality includes well-specified and partly redundant representations of form (orthography and phonology) and flexible representations of meaning, allowing for rapid and reliable meaning retrieval. Low-quality representations lead to specific word-related problems in comprehension" (Perfetti, 2007: 357).

### 7.2.4 Orthography in L2 auditory lexical access

The possible influence of both L1 and L2 orthography on the coding of lexical representations in L2 has received attention in recent years as well (Cutler et al., 2006; Escudero et al., 2008; Escudero & Wanrooij, 2010; Hayes-Harb, Nicol, & Barker, 2010; Ota et al., 2009; Showalter & Hayes-Harb, 2013; Veivo & Järvikivi, 2013; Weber & Cutler, 2004).[5] Orthography is treated as the code used in visual access of lexical representations, but also as explicit information that raises metalinguistic awareness (Escudero et al., 2008). Its supporting role in learning new phonological features is tested not only for conventional grapheme–phoneme correspondences, but also for the tone marks in the learning of Mandarin lexical tones by English L1 speakers with no prior knowledge of Mandarin (Showalter & Hayes-Harb, 2013).

The study by Weber and Cutler (2004) discussed above suggested the possibility of an orthography-based explanation for the observed bias in their eye-tracking experiment. It is possible that the different orthographic coding of the members of the contrast in English with letters *a* and *e* supports the differentiation of the two phonemes, with the letters mapping onto different phonemes in Dutch. However, the /æ/ phoneme as in *panda* is orthographically coded as a low back vowel in Dutch, which is inconsistent with its phonetic nature, being a low front vowel in English. Another eye-tracking study with Japanese learners of English and the notoriously difficult /r/-/l/ consonantal contrast was designed to test the two alternative explanations of asymmetric mapping of the contrast to L2 lexical representations (Cutler et al., 2006). The obtained bias was in the direction of the preference for the /l/-initial targets over the /r/-initial ones, so that instructions to click on a picture of a *rocket* induced fixations on the picture of a *locker*, but not the other way round. This asymmetry speaks in favor of the role of phonetic proximity between the Japanese corresponding phoneme /ɾ/ and the English /l/, and not in favor of the orthographically based explanation, with the Japanese romanji spelling system using the letter *r* for such segments. Note that both studies consider the possible influence of L1 orthography on the biases in L2 lexical representations, and not the L2 graphic–phonological correspondences that could serve as metalinguistic perceptual anchors in the process of lexical encoding of new words.

A learning study was designed to directly address the role of L2 orthography in encoding L2 lexical representations as opposed to discussing it post hoc, as was done in the studies discussed above (Escudero et al., 2008). L1 speakers of Dutch learned nonword names of non-objects in English, their L2, and were later tested on picture–word matching using eye-tracking. The words contained the /ɛ/ – /æ/ contrast confusable for

---

[5] See the special issue 53(3) of *Language and Speech*, 2010, devoted to the relation between orthography and phonology from a psycholinguistic and SLA perspective.

Dutch speakers. Crucially, two groups of participants received different input in the training session, one group only auditory names of non-objects, and the other both auditory and visual spellings. Accordingly, only the first group trained solely on the auditory input showed a symmetrical pattern of confusions with fixations on pictures representing both phonemes in response to both. The second group that received additional orthographic input was biased to look at both /ɛ/-word and /æ/-word pictures in response to /æ/-words, but only to /ɛ/-word pictures in response to /ɛ/-words. Given that the vowel letters 'a' and 'e' chosen to represent the contrast orthographically are the same that are used by the English spelling system, the study demonstrates the role of orthography in shaping (and biasing) lexical representations with confusable L2 phonemes.

Thus, orthography contributes to consolidating L2 phonological representations if it is consistent with the expected phonetic–orthographic mappings. When the phoneme–grapheme mappings are inconsistent with the orthographic system of L1 or L2, orthography cannot help to consolidate the new lexical representations (e.g., the letter 'a' is expected to correspond to a back, and not front English vowel based on Dutch orthography). Remarkably, phonological confusions in L2 also lead to orthographic confusions and spurious homonymy, as was shown in a visual study using the /r/ – /l/ contrast in a semantic relatedness task with Japanese learners of English (Ota et al., 2009). The participants judged the semantic relatedness of the pairs such as LOCK/HARD and ROCK/KEY to be higher than that of the controls. Thus, lexical representations of the minimal pairs of words differing by a difficult L2 phonological contrast are not well separated in the mental lexicon. As we will see below, this fuzziness of L2 lexical representations may go beyond the confusable L2 phonological contrasts and lead to uncertainty about any potentially confusable word segments, as in word neighborhoods.

### 7.2.5 Allophonic variation

The previous sections have discussed the processing of nonnative phonetic input with the goal of forming easily retrievable lexical representations of L2 words. This process is hypothesized to hinge on the development of L2 phonological representations that serve as the coding units for lexical representations. The difficulties experienced by L2 learners have to do with the need to attune the phonetic categories to L2 input and to reassemble the distinctive features into new L2 feature matrices corresponding to the phonological system of L2 (see Darcy et al., 2012). In doing so, they will need to overcome the categorization routines deployed in L1. As the study by Darcy and colleagues shows, there is a certain dissociation between the establishment of robust L2 phonetic categories and lexical representations.

At the lexical representations' end, the level of entrenchment depends on word frequency in the input and its familiarity.[6] At the phonetic categorization end, perceptual correlates of different allophones of the same phoneme, that depend on the phonetic environment (adjacent sounds) and phonetic position (e.g., position in the word, or in relation to lexical stress), have different perceptual salience. Therefore, in order to establish robust phonological units (phonemes), the learner needs to develop phonetic correlates of the unit that are connected to the unit through a system of allophonic variation rules. Perceptual salience is often defined by universal constraints on production and perception, e.g., articulatory weakening of the word coda may lead to final consonant devoicing in some languages.

Allophonic variation has been documented in studies focusing on phonetic categorization (Darcy et al., 2012; Levy, 2009; Lukyanchenko & Gor, 2011; Shea & Curtin, 2010). Levy (2009) reported the influence of the consonantal context on perceptual assimilation of French vowels by naïve American listeners and American learners of French. The study by Darcy and colleagues (2012) observed a perceptual facilitation in the categorization of French front rounded vowels when the labial context was conducive to a better discrimination of the front/back rounded vowel contrast.

Lukyanchenko and Gor (2011) explored a phonological contrast that is heavily functionally loaded in the Russian consonantal system, and is present in a large set of consonant allophones. Their study investigated the acquisition of the distinctive feature (DF) of softness (opposed to hardness) in Russian consonants by early (heritage) and late L2 learners, native speakers of American English. It demonstrated that the DF of softness that has different articulatory and acoustic correlates for different consonants depending on their place of articulation, is acquired not "all or nothing," but rather in piecemeal fashion, with contextual and positional allophones acquired in a sequence determined by their robustness in terms of containing interpretable acoustic information. While native speakers are able to interpret subtle phonetic cues to the hard/soft feature and perform at ceiling, L2 learners seem to be able to handle only the more salient phonetic cues.

Shea and Curtin have reported a gradually developing L2 ability in intermediate learners of Spanish, L1 English speakers, to connect the allophones of voiced consonants in Spanish with the position in relation to word onset and stress, and to link stops to stressed word onsets and approximants to unstressed word-medial position (Shea & Curtin, 2010). Their finding supports the idea that native speakers develop the ability to pay attention to the relevant perceptual information in the acoustic wave

---

[6] Note that both a more detailed and a more global Gestalt lexical representation are the possible outcomes of greater entrenchment.

and ignore the irrelevant information, an ability lacking in L2 learners who are not attuned to the L2 phonetic contrast.[7]

These studies show how the differences in the strength of perceptual cues in contextual and positional allophones affect L2 processing of phonological contrasts, while native speakers are performing at ceiling. They stop short of addressing the issue of lexical representations, since they work with nonword materials; however, they demonstrate that at the low end of the phonetics–phonology interface, the robustness of a phonological representation depends on the robustness of perceptual cues to all its contextual and positional allophones. The differences in the strength of perceptual cues provide a reasonable explanation for the "anomaly or paradox" of the findings of Darcy and colleagues (2012). Lexical representations for very high-frequency lexical items may be more robust than the representation of the phoneme itself, when it gets to all its possible perceptual correlates in different allophones.

### 7.2.6 Individual variation and L2 proficiency

The variation observed in individual acquisitional paths has received increasing attention in the context of L2 phonological coding of lexical representations (Diaz et al., 2012; Mayr & Escudero, 2010; Sebastián-Gallés & Díaz, 2012). Since L2 linguistic performance is typically characterized as highly variable, both within and across individual learners, the data on individual variability in L2 phonology fit well with general L2 acquisitional patterns and present no exception to variation witnessed in other domains. The L2LP model (Escudero, 2005; Mayr & Escudero, 2010), as discussed above, states that L2 phonological perception is strongly influenced by the L1 accent, which includes the regional, social, and individual features of the L2 learner. The claim about individual variation in L2 perceptual patterns was confirmed by a study of German vowel perception in L1 English listeners (Mayr & Escudero, 2010).

In a study by Díaz and colleagues, L2 learners, late Dutch–English bilinguals, have shown more individual variation in lower-level phonetic categorization than higher-level phonological identification and especially in lexical decision performance in processing the difficult /æ/ – /ɛ/ contrast (Díaz et al., 2012). Sebastián-Gallés and Díaz (2012) review several behavioral and neurolinguistic studies that additionally point to a crucial relationship between L1 and L2 perception capacities, a dimension often overlooked in L2 perceptual studies.

---

[7] This chapter advocates the position that the information about the adjacent phonetic segments and the position of the segments in the word and the sentence is relevant, and needs to be part of the phonological representation of the word. However, according to a more restrictive view, only the information supporting the contrastive features is represented in the brain (see Eulitz et al., 2004).

While some aspects of individual variation are more idiosyncratic and involve L1 and L2 regional dialects in contact, others are more systematic in that they reflect a general developmental trend associated with the differences in L2 proficiency (Darcy et al., 2012; Lukyanchenko & Gor, 2011; Shea & Curtin, 2010; Veivo & Järvikivi, 2013). As predicted, the studies that compare late L2 learners at different proficiency levels document a developmental tendency in phonetic categorization of nonnative L2 phones. The improvement evidenced in perceptual performance is shown to depend on increased efficiency in the processing of the less salient perceptual cues in the most difficult allophones (Lukyanchenko & Gor, 2011), and allophonic distributions determined by the phonetic position, both in perception and production (Shea & Curtin, 2010). One can expect that the level of entrenchment of lexical representations will also depend on its frequency in the input, and ultimately, on the amount of exposure and the L2 proficiency level, given the findings on the fuzziness of lexical representations discussed below.

### 7.2.7 Phonological encoding of L2 lexical representations

This section will review the studies focusing on phonological encoding in L2 lexical access. They seek to explain the mechanisms of lexical activation leading to spurious priming effects involving minimal pairs of L2 words, as well as words and nonwords (Broersma, 2009; Broersma & Cutler, 2008). This line of inquiry leads to a more puzzling and less researched aspect of nonnative lexical access, when the form–meaning mappings of the lexical entries that have similar phonological representations are insufficiently robust, which leads to spurious effects in L2 lexical access (Cook, 2012; Gor, Cook, & Jackson, 2010).

A series of cross-modal priming studies has demonstrated facilitation in L2, but not L1 participants (Broersma, 2009; Broersma & Cutler, 2008). Dutch learners of English showed facilitation for near-words that constituted minimal pairs with real words and differed by the voicing of the final consonant, as in *groof–GROOVE* (Broersma & Cutler, 2008), a phenomenon that the authors called "phantom word activation." In another cross-modal experiment, *flash* primed FLESH and *robe* primed ROPE in some Dutch learners, but caused inhibition in other Dutch learners and native speakers of English, following the predictions based on the perceptual problems with the /æ/ – /ɛ/ contrast and the final consonant voicing contrast in Dutch L2 learners of English (Broersma, 2009). The proposed explanation is spurious activation of the lexical representations of phonological neighbors when the phonological contrast is not robust in L2 learners. In other words, the prime *flash* activates *flash* and also its neighbor *flesh*, and in L2 learners, the absence of competition among the activated neighbors produces facilitation. Also left open is the possibility that the lack of the phonological contrast that differentiates the two words leads to the creation of two homophones that do not compete with each other in the absence of any disambiguating context.

The phenomenon of facilitation in L2 phonological priming was confirmed in an auditory priming experiment involving Russian words with an initial three-phoneme overlap as in /vrak/ *enemy* – /vratʃ/ *doctor*, and American learners of Russian as participants. While native Russian controls showed the expected inhibition, L2 learners showed facilitation (Gor, Cook, & Jackson, 2010). A study that proposed the Second Language Lexical Access Model (SLLAM) tested the hypothesis that L2 learners have fuzzy lexical representations due to underspecified phonological encoding of the word forms, resulting in less than robust form–meaning mappings (Cook, 2012). This hypothesized feature of L2 lexical representations leads to two consequences predicted by the author. First, in a phonological priming experiment, L2 listeners show pre-lexical facilitation because they are not ready to commit themselves to the selection of one competitor, and the cohort neighborhood activated by the prime facilitates access to the target. Second, a pseudo-semantic priming experiment was designed to explore the puzzling finding of L2 phonological facilitation in the absence of phonological difficulty (Cook, 2012). It used the following logic: if L2 learners do not have robust phonological representations of lexical entries, they may be uncertain about the form–meaning mappings of the words that they confuse. As a result, a semantically unrelated target could be interpreted as its neighbor that is semantically related to the prime. If this is the case, L2 learners should show the priming effects for such unrelated trials with potentially phonologically confusable targets, while native speakers would ignore any neighbors in a pseudo-semantic priming task. In the experiment, the word pair *корова–молоко* /karova/ – /malako/, Eng. 'cow'–'milk' is presented in the true semantic condition, while the pair *корова–молоток* /karova/ – /malatok/, Eng. 'cow'–'hammer,' with /malatok/ 'hammer' phonologically confusable with /malako/ 'milk,' is presented instead of a true semantically related pair in the pseudo-semantic condition. The participants, American learners of Russian at two proficiency levels, intermediate and advanced, as well as a control group of Russian native speakers heard only one pair depending on the presentation list. Neither NSs of Russian nor intermediate L2 learners were sensitive to pseudo-semantic primes. However, advanced L2 learners showed inhibition in the pseudo-semantic condition for high-frequency items. This effect is attributed to underspecification of phonological representations of words that leads to the competition with the semantically congruent phonologically confusable word (when *milk* is expected after *cow, hammer* is accessed more slowly). Thus, phonological encoding of L2 lexical representations may be unfaithful even in the absence of a perceptually difficult phoneme.

### 7.2.8 Summary

This section on the processing of L2 phonology has reviewed the models, theories, and empirical research focusing on both sides of the phonetics–phonology interface and the interaction of bottom-up and top-down processing. L2 phonological categories emerge in a bootstrapping fashion through perceptual training and vocabulary learning. In late L2 phonological acquisition, learners need to learn how to handle several auditory processing stages in order to efficiently encode, store, and access lexical units. These stages include auditory processing that is largely unaffected by the specific language or languages in contact, but also phonetic cue extraction that is language specific, association of phonetic cues with phonetic allophones through the rules that make adjustments for the phonetic position and context, encoding of the auditory input as a sequence of phonemes, and access of the lexical representation(s) that match the phonological sequence. All these stages are not linearly sequenced, but rather overlap, or are activated in a parallel or cascaded manner (and also affected by top-down processing depending on the use of the semantic cues, sentence context, and beyond, etc.). On the phonetic side of the interface, L2 phonetic cue extraction plays a crucial role. On the phonological side of the interface, lexical frequency and ultimately the role of L2 input determine the robustness of L2 phonological representations of lexical units containing the contrast. The important consequence is that phonology in L2 lexical access can 'break' at any stage, and thus L2 learner faces multiple challenges, with a failure at each level having consequences for other levels. Thus, for example, if one is confused about the phonological make-up of a stored word, one risks retrieving its phonological neighbor instead. However, if one does not have a robust system of rules for handling the cues for phonetic allophones, one can erroneously misinterpret a phonetic segment as an allophone of a different phoneme, which may lead to the same outcome – retrieval of an incorrect word.

## 7.3 Processing of L2 morphology

Efficient phonological encoding discussed above is a crucial part of creating robust form-meaning mappings that L2 learners need for word storage and retrieval from the mental lexicon. However, words may have complex internal structure, i.e., comprise two or more morphemes, minimal linguistic units carrying lexical or grammatical meaning. The main issue in research on morphological aspects of L2 lexical access is whether L2 learners decompose morphologically complex words or if they retrieve them as whole words, by relying only on phonological form–meaning mappings. While this issue concerns inflectional and derivational morphology alike, there are indications in the literature that L2 learners master English inflection before derivation (e.g., Gardner, 2007), and it is still an open question whether the sequence remains the same for languages with a rich inflectional system and many inflectional morphemes (and their exponents, or surface phonological forms) to be internalized. Inflectional and derivational morphology have distinct linguistic functions; inflection subserves morphosyntax, e.g., the English *-ed* morpheme signals that the verb is in the past tense, and derivation contributes to the creation of new words by adding derivational morphemes and often changing the word class, e.g., adding the morpheme *-er* with the general meaning 'doer of the action named by the verb' to the verb *read* creates the noun *read-er*. It is believed that both inflection and derivation are processed by the same decompositional mechanisms (see Diependaele et al., 2011). At the same time, functional magnetic resonance imaging (fMRI) evidence on brain localization of auditory processing of inflection and derivation indicates that in English, inflection is indeed processed by the left-lateralized decompositional system, while derivation is processed by a widely distributed bilateral system that is also involved in the processing of monomorphemic words (Bozic et al., 2010). A combined electroencephalography (EEG) and magnetoencephalography (MEG) study of Finnish inflection and derivation using an acceptability judgment task came to similar conclusions, that while inflected words are processed by decomposition, derived words may be initially processed as whole words as well as through constituents (Leminen et al., 2011). One possibility is that complex derived words are stored in the mental lexicon both as whole words and constituents, while inflected words may or may not have whole-word representations at the lemma level depending on their surface frequency, and the complexity and productivity of the inflectional pattern. Another possibility is that decomposition of derived words has implications for lexical processing more than syntactic processing. From a linguistic standpoint, inflectional and especially derivational morphemes are involved in word-internal syntax (Marantz, 2013). The following subsections discuss research on L2 inflection and derivation separately, while acknowledging that both create potentially decomposable morphologically complex words.

### 7.3.1 Processing of L2 derived words

The processing of derivation in lexical access has been studied in masked priming experiments when the prime is visually presented for a very short time, around 50 ms, after a mask (often, a line of hash marks), and then immediately followed by a visual target. The effects observed in L1 speakers point to more than one underlying processing mechanism involved in early visual processing of derivational morphology (for a review, see Diependaele et al., 2011). Native speakers of English are sensitive to morphological structure in both transparent (e.g., *singer*–SING) and opaque (*department*–DEPART) derivations, and even pseudo-derived words, such as *corner-CORN* (Rastle & Davis, 2008). Such early automatic morpho-orthographic decomposition appeared to be blind to semantic properties or the actual morphological structure, with *corner* facilitating responses to *CORN*, as long as the word contained a phonological segment corresponding to an existent derivational suffix. However, the situation is complicated by a graded facilitatory effect observed in English speakers, with a greater facilitation for semantically transparent (*viewer*–VIEW) than opaque (*department*–DEPART) derivations (Diependaele et al., 2011). This graded effect suggests that native speakers are sensitive to semantic properties of derived words very early on in the time course of lexical access. Both effects can be accommodated within the cascaded approach with morpho-orthographic and morpho-semantic processing starting early and overlapping in time.

The predictions regarding the differences between L1 and L2 processing of derivational morphology in lexical access tasks, such as the masked priming task, range from the position that the L1 and L2 mechanisms are different, albeit less so than the ones responsible for inflection (Clahsen et al., 2010; Kirici & Clahsen, 2012), to the claim that they are the same (Diependaele et al., 2011). Diependaele and colleagues (2011) replicated the findings on the significant graded effect of transparent and opaque derivation in a masked priming study comparing two groups of L2 learners of English with Dutch and Spanish as L1 with native speakers of English. They confirmed that L2 learners relied both on early morpho-orthographic decomposition (hence the masked priming effects) and that the magnitude of facilitation was mediated by semantic transparency (hence the gradedness of the effect). The two L2 groups had similar, though not identical learning profiles, including self-assessed measures of proficiency. The results were taken as support of the same processing strategies in L2 and L1 speakers, and the reality of early morpho-semantic transparency effects.

Early morpho-orthographic effects were likewise demonstrated in a masked priming study involving a group of advanced L2 learners of English with L1 Spanish, and a group of balanced early Basque–Spanish bilinguals (Duñabeitia et al., 2013). The main focus of the study was to establish that morpho-orthographic decomposition did not crucially depend on the translation of the prime in the mixed-language condition when the prime and the target belonged to different languages. This was done by carefully manipulating the cognate status and the adjusted Levenshtein distance (the degree of orthographic overlap) between the prime and the target. The study does not report significant differences between the unbalanced (L2) and balanced (bilingual) groups. Given that the "weaker" Spanish–English group included highly proficient English learners, both groups could have been at ceiling in their L2.

A different pattern of results was reported in a study of English deadjectival nominalizations using the suffixes *-ness* and *-ity* in a series of LDT and masked priming experiments with native speakers and L2 learners of English, whose L1 was Chinese and German (Clahsen et al., 2010; Silva & Clahsen, 2008). The English L1 participants showed full priming, but two groups of L2 learners only partial priming for the derived words. The weakening of the priming effect in L2 participants was taken as evidence in support of Ullman's (2001, 2012) declarative/procedural model, according to which combinatorial structure affects L2 processing less. Remarkably, there was no significant difference between the two learner groups despite the fact that Chinese is an inflectionally poor language and has ideographic script, while German is typologically close to English, both being Germanic languages.

Diependaele and colleagues (2011) compared the two datasets, their own and the one from the Silva and Clahsen study (2008), to identify the loci of the differences. Several possibilities emerge, including differences in L2 proficiency, with the participants in Silva and Clahsen (2008) having lower proficiency than those in their study. Other potential reasons include the differences in L1 background, a limited set of only two derivational suffixes, and few items per condition in the study by Silva and Clahsen (2008). Given that the study of Silva and Clahsen (2008) reports partial priming for derived words, and not complete absence of priming, and also given some of their methodological choices listed above (i.e., their participants are not highly proficient L2 learners, and they include Chinese L1 speakers), it appears that a strong non-decompositional account for L2 does not find conclusive experimental support. Conversely, the studies by Diependaele and colleagues (2011), and Duñabeitia and colleagues (2013) show robust decomposition of semantically transparent derivations and a graded effect depending on semantic transparency with highly proficient L2 learners. These two datasets suggest a developmental tendency whereby L2 learners gradually learn to quickly and efficiently decompose words with derivational affixes. In other words, L2 learners do not rely on a categorically different processing mechanism of whole-word lexical access as postulated by the declarative/procedural model (Ullman, 2001, 2012), but gradually develop sensitivity to morphological structure of derived words. A somewhat different pattern of results was observed in a masked priming study in L2 Turkish, an agglutinative language that extensively uses affixes, comparing the facilitation patterns for inflection and derivation (Kirici & Clahsen, 2013). While L1 speakers of Turkish showed facilitation both for inflection and derivation, L2 learners showed facilitation only for derivation, but not for inflection. These results led the authors to conclude that the differences in L1 and L2 processing of morphologically complex words are subtle rather than superficial or obvious. Overall, the reviewed studies converge on the fact that L2 learners decompose derived words in lexical access, albeit showing less facilitation than native speakers.

### 7.3.2 Do L2 learners decompose inflected words?

Similar to the debates surrounding morphological decomposition in a native language that started with English regular and irregular past-tense inflection, the research on L2 morphological processing initially focused on English past-tense verbs and later turned to morphologically rich languages with a developed inflectional paradigm (see Gor, 2010). L2 decomposition of inflectional morphology has generated two opposite points of view (for a review, see Gor & Jackson, 2013). According to the non-decompositional account, L2 learners do not decompose inflected words, but instead store and retrieve whole-word representations (Babcock et al., 2012; Clahsen & Felser, 2006; Clahsen et al., 2010; Ullman, 2001, 2012). Proponents of this view see the developmental trajectory in L2 acquisition of inflection as the initial reliance on whole-word storage that persists and only gives way to decomposition at advanced proficiency levels. With regard to the impact of regularity on L2 morphological decomposition, this view supports the dual-system approach and claims that while native speakers decompose regularly inflected words and store irregularly inflected ones, L2 learners store both types of words. From English as a native language, the agenda soon expanded to include a range of typologically different languages as L1 and L2 in nonnative and early bilingual populations.

The studies supporting the non-decompositional view of L2 inflectional morphology use a range of tasks, including oral and written verb generation, auditory and visual lexical decision tasks, priming experiments with a visual, auditory, and cross-modal presentation, and short to medium lag, and masked priming. Data collected include behavioral measures, accuracy and response latencies, as well as positron emission tomography (PET), fMRI, MEG, and EEG neural data. This short review mainly focuses on reaction time data. In a masked priming study, Polish learners and native speakers of German showed similar partial priming for German irregular -*n* inflected past participles, while the groups differed on regularly inflected -*t* participles serving as primes for first-person singular targets. Native speakers were fully primed by regular participles, but L2 learners were not primed (Clahsen et al., 2010; Neubauer & Clahsen, 2009).[8] The authors interpreted these findings within the shallow-structure hypothesis postulating that L2 learners rely on whole-word access and do not decompose inflected words (Clahsen & Felser, 2006); however, it is unclear what mechanism drives selective L2 sensitivity to morphological similarity between primes and targets in irregular, but not regular inflection. Indeed, in keeping with the logic of the regular/irregular morphological processing distinction, one would expect decomposition of irregular word forms to be more effortful than that of regular forms. A partial replication of the study using the same materials, but

---

[8] See Smolka and colleagues (2007) for a critical analysis of the methodological issues in the study.

only the regular verb condition, and two presentation procedures, with one including a 200-ms blank between the masked prime and the target, obtained no priming in L1 Arabic speakers, L2 learners of English (Clahsen et al., 2013).

Two studies demonstrated frequency effects in the generation of both irregular and regular English past-tense verbs (Babcock et al., 2012), and Spanish present-tense verbs (Bowden et al., 2010). The dependent variable was reaction times in a production task.[9] These findings were interpreted as support for the declarative/procedural model predicting the reliance on whole-word storage for both regular and irregular verbs in L2 learners. While the frequency effects in L2 regular and irregular verb generation are well documented, their interpretation as the proof of the lack of decomposition in L2 learners is less straightforward. The studies by Babcock and colleagues (2012) and Bowden and colleagues (2010) interpret the observed surface frequency effects as proof of whole-word storage; however, according to Baayen and colleagues, surface frequency effects are indicative of decomposition, and not whole-word storage (see Baayen, Wurm, & Aycock, 2007 for a detailed argumentation and experimental support of this interpretation). Additionally, since surface frequency often correlates with stem frequency, the frequency effects in verb generation could be driven by stem frequency, which is traditionally associated with decomposition, as well (Gor & Jackson, 2013). Indeed, a greater effect of frequency on L2 lexical processing is well established (Diependaele, Lemhöfer, & Brysbaert, 2013). These methodological limitations open to reasonable doubt the interpretation of the findings based on the effect of surface frequency as straightforward evidence for the lack of decomposition in L2.

The opposite, decompositional account has been gaining more ground with experimental support from studies of Swedish and Russian as L2. According to the decompositional account, L2 learners of morphologically complex languages, but also English, decompose inflected words in lexical access (Basnight-Brown et al., 2007; Gor & Cook, 2010; Gor & Jackson, 2013; Portin et al., 2008; Portin, Lehtonen, & Laine, 2007). This does not imply that there are no differences in L1 and L2 morphological processing; indeed, depending on their proficiency level, L2 learners may not be very efficient at decomposition. They are also notoriously slower than native speakers on all reaction time tasks involving lexical decisions or some form of lexical access. On the other hand, it is unlikely that they can rely on whole-word storage instead of decomposition, because they do not benefit from sufficient input and practice to internalize all the inflected forms in the paradigm of a given lexical entry, especially in inflectionally rich languages. Memory constraints can also play a role in

---

[9] Since the reaction times measured in a production experiment also include the interpretation of the initial word form, these data speak both to the decomposition costs involved in the processing of the presented stimulus word and the composition costs involved in the generation of the required word form. This negatively affects the interpretability of RTs in production.

L2 learners if they store multiple forms of the same lexeme. An additional argument in favor of L2 decomposition is the need to interpret the grammatical information contained in the inflection for successful speech processing that makes decomposition of inflected words obligatory, even if it is done post-lexically. The developmental trajectory, beyond the initial chunk learning in novice L2 learners, is hypothesized to go from decomposition to whole-word representation of inflected words, with the high-frequency ones stored first. Crucially, this view interprets regularity as a continuum rather than a categorical parameter, and accordingly, places emphasis on the role of complex allomorphy in the efficiency of L2 decomposition (Basnight-Brown et al., 2007; Feldman et al., 2010; Gor & Cook, 2010; Gor & Jackson, 2013).

The decompositional account is supported by the research on decompositional costs incurred by L2 learners of Swedish when accessing Swedish polymorphemic words matched on a number of criteria, such as length and frequency, with monomorphemic words (Portin et al., 2007; Portin et al., 2008). According to the studies, L2 learners gradually develop whole-word representations of polymorphemic words, by starting with high-frequency polymorphemic words and later adding lower-frequency ones. These studies demonstrate the role of the L1 background, with Chinese L1 speakers lagging behind Hungarian L1 speakers in developing whole-word representations (Portin et al., 2008). Given that Chinese lacks inflectional and derivational morphology, a reduced sensitivity of Chinese L1 speakers to Swedish polymorphemic words is to be expected. Indeed, a study that investigates visual word recognition of L2 Finnish inflected nouns with transparent and semitransparent morphophonology, confirms the role of L1 and typological distance between L1 and L2. Russian has a rich inflectional system, while Chinese does not make extensive use of inflectional morphology, and accordingly, the response pattern (RTs) of L1 Russian participants was similar to that of Finnish native speakers and different from Chinese L1 speakers (Vainio, Pajunen, & Huönä, 2013).

Two studies of facilitation in masked and cross-modal priming experiments targeting English past-tense regular and irregular verbs highlight the role of form similarity in visual morphological decomposition (Basnight-Brown et al., 2007; Feldman et al., 2010). The first study compared the RTs to regular, irregular nested (drawn–DRAW) and irregular stem-change verbs (*ran*–RUN) in L1 speakers of English, Serbian, and Chinese (Basnight-Brown et al., 2007). Crucially, the two nonnative groups were matched for proficiency. While in English speakers there were comparable priming effects for regular and irregular nested verbs, and a reduced priming effect for irregular stem-change verbs, there was no facilitation in either L2 group for irregular stem-change verbs. At the same time, Serbian participants showed facilitation for regular and irregular nested verbs, while Chinese participants showed facilitation for regular verbs only, which again supports their reduced sensitivity to morphological structure. Thus, the study demonstrates that English regularly inflected verbs are decomposed by L2 learners regardless of the language background, while irregular verbs elicit a graded priming effect in L1 and L2 speakers. Depending on the degree of form overlap and L1 background, irregular verbs may or may not produce the priming effects in L2.[10]

The second study (Feldman et al., 2010) used regular, and length-preserved (*fell*–FALL) and length-change (*taught*–TEACH) irregular verbs in a masked and cross-modal priming tasks. Both native English speakers and L1 Serbian learners of English produced the strongest priming effects for regular verbs. English L1 speakers also showed facilitation for irregular length-preserved verbs, while L1 Serbian speakers showed no difference between irregular verbs and their orthographically matched controls (*fill*–FELL). Another finding important for the understanding of L2 lexical storage and access is the lack of inhibition in the orthographic control condition in L2 learners, with significant inhibition in L1 speakers. This effect seems to point in the same direction as the data on the lack of inhibition in phonological priming reported for L2 learners of Russian (Gor et al., 2010), namely their inefficiency in L2 form processing that possibly leads to fuzzy or unfaithful L2 lexical representations.

An auditory priming study explored the graded effect of regularity treated as complexity and productivity in stem allomorphy in Russian first-person singular non-past tense primes with infinitive targets and its interaction with L2 proficiency (Gor & Jackson, 2013). Three groups of L2 Russian learners, native speakers of American English, with highly controlled proficiency levels, advanced, advanced high, and superior on the standardized test, the oral proficiency interview (OPI), and a group of Russian native speakers participated in the study. The critical conditions used three types of verbs ranging in the degree of regularity – regular, semi-regular, and irregular – balanced in lemma and surface frequency across the verb types. While robust facilitation was observed in native speakers of Russian for all three verb types at all frequency ranges, in L2 learners it was observed only for high-frequency verbs. Low-frequency verbs produced an interaction of the degree of regularity with proficiency level. Priming effects were present for regular verbs at all three proficiency levels, semi-regular verbs at two higher levels, and irregular verbs only at the highest level. The study concludes that L2 learners rely on decomposition rather than whole-word storage and access of inflected words with simple and productive stem allomorphy. With increasing L2 proficiency, they gradually learn to efficiently access complex stem allomorphs in unproductive inflected forms of low-frequency words, and thus expand the range of complex words that they decompose in lexical access.

---

[10] Note that the masked priming effects have been shown for stem-change verbs such as *fell*–FALL for native speakers of English (Crepaldi et al., 2010).

### 7.3.3 The inflectional paradigm in L2 processing

A new agenda emerging in L1 and L2 studies of morphological processing is the role of the inflectional paradigm in lexical access of inflected word forms. This line of research has started with the nominal paradigm in Serbian, a Slavic language with a Latin-based system of cases (Milin, et al., 2009). The information–theoretical approach applied to the Serbian paradigm has generated a measure, relative inflectional entropy, that positively correlates with reaction times (RTs) and error rates in a visual LDT. The calculations are based on the understanding that it is the deviation of the distribution of the frequencies of inflectional exponents (inflections that have the same surface form and belong to a particular paradigm) in the inflectional paradigm of a particular word from the similar distribution established for the whole inflectional class to which the word belongs that increases response latencies in word recognition. The greater the difference between the two measures of entropy, or the relative entropy, the longer latencies are to be expected. It should be noted, however, that the predictive power of this measure is weaker than that of surface frequency of the inflected word. This measure has been shown to work for single-word presentations in a LDT, and it is to be expected that it will be competing with expectancies based on phrase or sentence context when it is available.

The role of the inflectional paradigm in the processing cost incurred by L1 and L2 Russian listeners was evaluated in an auditory LDT that used Russian nouns in the nominative singular (the citation form) and the genitive (oblique) case matched in surface and lemma frequency, and in length (Gor & Lukyanchenko, 2013). Crucially, nouns in the masculine paradigm have zero overt inflections in the nominative (and also in the accusative if they are inanimate), and the inflection -*a* in the genitive singular. Conversely, feminine nouns have the inflection -*a* in the nominative and a zero (-ø) overt inflection in the genitive plural. The exponent frequency is comparable for all four exponents within each inflectional class (-*a* and -ø, each in the masculine and feminine paradigms). Such a design made it possible to evaluate the processing costs and to test three predictions about the speed of access for each of the four critical conditions, $zavod\text{-}ø_{MascSgNOM}$, $zavod\text{-}a_{MascSgGEN}$ (*factory*), $bumag\text{-}a_{FemSgNOM}$, and $bumag\text{-}ø_{FemPlGEN}$ (*paper*). Based on the decomposition costs, the overt -*a* inflection should incur an additional decomposition cost, regardless of the case. Based on case (exponent) frequency, *bumag-a* should be processed slower than *zavod-ø*, and both faster than the oblique forms. Based on case hierarchy, the nouns in the nominative case should be processed faster than the nouns in the genitive. The results obtained for L1 support the prediction based on case hierarchy, with the nouns in the nominative processed at the same speed, regardless of their inflection, overt or zero, and faster than the nouns in the genitive. Crucially, the noun *bumag-ø*$_\text{FemPlGEN}$ showed a processing cost in L1 comparable to *zavod-a*$_\text{MascSgGEN}$. However, intermediate to advanced L2 learners did not incur a processing cost for the zero-inflected *bumag-ø* while they did so for *zavod-a*$_\text{MascSgGEN}$. These results are taken as evidence of decomposition both in L1 and L2, and document the role of the case status (the nominative is represented as whole word at the lemma level), and case frequencies. However, L2 learners did not incur the decomposition cost in processing zero-inflected oblique nouns that were observed in L1 participants. Results of the study suggest that L2 learners decompose inflected words in lexical access and use the stem to access the word's lexical meaning. Similarly to L1 speakers, L2 learners process the grammatical information encoded in the inflection. However, unlike L1 speakers, lower-proficiency L2 learners are less concerned with the outcomes of recomposition and may ignore the rechecking stage altogether under specific conditions. In this sense, they are more focused on the lexical meaning expressed by the stem than on the integration of the stem and the morphosyntactic information contained in the inflection.

### 7.3.4 Summary

Do L2 learners decompose morphologically complex words? The general answer is 'yes,' as it is for L1 speakers, however, it requires a set of qualifications:

- This pertains to L2 learners beyond the beginner level of proficiency, at which they tend to memorize words and phrases as unanalyzed chunks.
- Even L2 learners may have whole-word representations for high-frequency inflected words, and will use the direct access route.
- In the case when both decompositional and whole-word access routes are available to the L2 learner, the choice of the route will depend on the task.[11]
- There is an interaction between L2 proficiency and complexity and productivity in stem allomorphy. The higher the L2 proficiency, the more efficient the decomposition of words with complex allomorphy.
- Decomposition of derived words is driven by semantic transparency, as in L1.
- L2 morphological decomposition is often effortful and may be unsuccessful.

---

[11] In processing natural input, the choice of the route will likely be influenced by the linguistic structure, in which the word is embedded. For example, case agreement in a sentence will call for decomposition and morphosyntactic interpretation of inflections, even if it is done postlexically, after the lexical meaning of the word is accessed. In psycholinguistic experiments, priming may be conducive to decomposition while LDT may be conducive to whole-word retrieval. The composition of nonwords (whether the violation is in the stem, the inflection or in their illegal combination) will also influence the access route (Taft, 2004).

Do L2 learners rely on the same mechanisms as L1 speakers in lexical access of morphologically complex words? Here, the answer 'yes' needs even more qualifications. It depends on what evidence will be considered as supporting qualitative differences (since quantitatively, L2 learners are obviously slower and have smaller mental lexicons, with lower subjective lexical frequencies compared to L1 speakers). It crucially depends on L2 proficiency level, since L2 learners need time to understand the morphological structure of L2 and then practice to become efficient at using L2 morphology in native-like ways. Reliance on the same processing mechanisms and successful processing are not the same thing.

## 7.4 Future directions: L2 phonology and morphology in lexical access

The domain of L2 phonology in lexical access has seen a new interest in the phonology/lexicon interface, both with regard to perceptually difficult L2 contrasts embedded in L2 words, and the phonological encoding of words with robust contrasts, but unfaithful lexical representations and fuzzy form-to-meaning mappings. A promising direction is word-learning experiments that introduce new vocabulary with highly controlled phonological properties (Escudero et al., 2008). These experiments obviate the problems of existing vocabulary items that are often impossible to match on phonological parameters, and have different familiarity for L2 learners. The use of highly controlled materials in vocabulary learning holds a promise in distinguishing the levels of processing difficulty encountered by L2 learners – be it phonetic categorization, attending to allophonic rules, or developing robust lexical representations with the phonological form clearly spelled out.

Researchers examining the phonological structure of L2 lexical entries and the organization of L2 mental lexicon have begun to explore an L2-specific effect, namely the lack of inhibition (observed in L1), or even facilitation in phonological priming and pseudo-semantic priming (Gor et al., 2010; Cook, 2012), and the lack of inhibition in the orthographic condition in cross-modal priming (Feldman et al., 2010). These effects are indications that L2 form representations are fuzzy, which leads to less than robust form-meaning mappings, and to confusion and lack of competition among phonologically similar L2 lexical entries. The effects are in agreement with the weaker lexical entrenchment account in L2 (Diependaele et al., 2013). Future research will elucidate the nature of the mechanisms underlying the reported form priming (phonological and orthographic). It is possible that fuzzy form–meaning mappings lead to a certain L2 processing mode when the L2 learners 'procrastinate' at early stages of lexical access and do not move on to the final selection.

In L2 morphological processing, research is focusing on issues of morphological decomposition, and the linguistic conditions, such as the complexity and productivity of stem allomorphy in inflection or semantic transparency in derivation, that promote or impede morphological decomposition in L2 learners. Dual-route models of morphological processing proposed for L1 have been supported by neurological evidence (Bozic et al., 2010; de Diego Balaguer et al., 2006).[12] In L2 learners, the issue is how much they rely on morphological decomposition, as opposed to whole-word storage and access under different conditions, and depending on their L2 proficiency level.

The role of expectancies in L2 lexical access of inflected words is explored in research on the influence of the inflectional paradigm on access speed, with reaction times supposedly indicative of decomposition costs in single word recognition. Indeed, in L1, expectancies based on the frequency of the particular inflected noun form within its inflectional paradigm interact with the expectancies based on the frequency of its case in the whole inflectional class of nouns. The degree of deviance in frequency of the actual noun form from the predictions based on the inflectional class has been quantified in the measure of relative entropy that positively correlates with the RTs in word recognition Milin et al. (2009). It is an open question how and when L2 learners develop a native-like system of expectancies for inflected word forms that are part of productive paradigms.

Finally, there is a possibility that L2 learners decompose inflected words to access their lexical meaning, and that the recomposition and rechecking stage necessary for the efficient processing of morphosyntactic information is less automatized. As in phonological aspects of L2 lexical access, L2 learners may tend to concentrate on earlier stages of lexical retrieval that ensures lemma access, and be less concerned about the processing of morphosyntactic information that becomes available when the stem and inflection are reintegrated in the whole word. In speech processing beyond the single word level, this morphosyntactic information is integrated with the sentence context, and it will be for future studies to explore the interaction of expectancy driven by the context and the mechanisms of morphological decomposition in lexical access.

---

[12] According to an fMRI study of silent generation of regular and irregular Spanish-inflected verbs (de Diego Balaguer et al., 2006), regular and irregular verb inflection involves overlapping brain areas responsible for morphological decomposition, and also separate non-overlapping areas for regular and irregular verbs. The findings are interpreted as shared processing of regular and irregular verb inflections, with additional reliance on reactivation of the same stem in regular verb generation, as opposed to lexical search and retrieval of the additional stem for irregular verbs.

# 8
# Processing perspectives on instructed second language acquisition

Bill VanPatten

## 8.1 Processing perspectives on instructed SLA

A central concern of instructed SLA is whether pedagogical intervention affects the acquisition of formal properties of language (e.g., Long, 1990). There are two questions underlying this concern. The first is this: how does the researcher conceptualize "formal properties"? That is, how does the researcher conceptualize the nature of language? Embedded in this question is the issue of underlying *mental representation*. In this chapter, I will argue that a good deal of instructed SLA fails to clearly articulate what it means by language and thus what it means by formal properties. I will suggest an alternative account, based on VanPatten and Rothman (2014), which takes a generative perspective on the nature of language and identifies three sets of formal properties: those given by UG, those derived from UG, and those that are language specific.

The second question underlying the central concern of instructed SLA is this: how does the researcher conceptualize acquisition? Embedded in this question is the nature of *underlying processes*. Thus, research on instructed SLA ought to specify the particular processes involved in acquisition that a pedagogical intervention attempts to affect; however, as in the case of the nature of language and mental representation, this aspect of instructed SLA is often unspecified. In this chapter, I will outline why it makes sense to approach instructed SLA as a processing problem, showing how the critical step in acquisition that pedagogical interventions might help is in how learners turn linguistic data from the input into useable materials for the internal mechanisms that build language over time.

I am thankful to Justin White, John W. Schwieter, and the reviewers for comments and suggestions on the first draft of this chapter. I am also thankful to Jason Rothman and Megan Smith for various discussions we have had over the last several years about some of the ideas contained in this chapter.

The outcome of this discussion is an argument for what I call POPIs: processing oriented pedagogical interventions. I will illustrate this with one particular approach called processing instruction.

## 8.2 The nature of language and mental representation

Distinct from skill, mental representation refers to the underlying linguistic system we typically call "language."[1] This system is implicit and largely abstract. It is implicit in that, although laypersons may know they have a linguistic system in their heads, they normally cannot articulate its contents; and if they try, they may very well come up with a description that is non-linguistic in nature (examples will follow later). It is abstract in that what is often described by a "rule" is not a rule at all, but the surface result of an interaction of underlying features of language (again, examples to follow). As the reader may guess, I am taking a generative perspective on language in this chapter. This perspective leads me to posit that the underlying mental representation for language consists of three types of linguistic elements: (1) those that cannot be learned; (2) those that aren't learned but are derived; (3) those that are learned. I will take each in turn.[2]

However, before doing so, I should be clear on what I mean by "learn" and "learned." I take learning in its classic sense; that is, learning is the result of the extraction of data from the environment that are used to build a cognitive structure in the mind/brain. In this sense, what is learned is directly linked or traceable to features in the environment. Innate constructs are not learned.

### 8.2.1 Aspects of language that cannot be learned

Aspects of language that cannot be learned are those contained in Universal Grammar (UG). These include abstract features available to all languages (e.g., case, tense and finiteness), basic syntactic operations (e.g., move/merge, agree), and constraints imposed on all human languages (e.g., phrase structure, the Extended Projection Principle (EPP), and the Overt Pronoun Constraint (OPC)).[3] The reason that these aspects of language need not be learned is that they are "there from the start." The language learner has access to them and they become relevant or not depending on the language learned (although some, like phrase structure, apply to all languages). For example, Spanish selects for tense/finiteness, as does English. Spanish has agree operations that work on both verbs and nominals,

---

[1] For a full discussion on the distinction between mental representation and skill, see VanPatten (2013).
[2] This section is based largely on discussion in VanPatten and Rothman (2014). The reader is referred to that publication for more detail. I thank my co-author Jason Rothman for allowing me to include these ideas here.
[3] One reviewer commented that "Chinese is assumed not to have Tense." Actually, Chinese is assumed not to instantiate tense as a feature, but it is still available as such a feature in UG. The reader should not confuse what is available in UG with what is instantiated in a given language.

English does not (at least, not to the same degree). Because Spanish is a null-subject language, it must obey the OPC, while English does not (see, Montalbetti, 1984). I illustrate the OPC in (1) and (2), where 2(a) is a translation of 1(a) and 1(b), and 2(b) is a rough translation of 1(c) and 1(d).

(1) a. Cada estudiante$_i$ dice que pro$_{i/j}$ es muy listo.
  b. Cada estudiante$_i$ dice que él*$_{i/j}$ es muy listo.
  c. El estudiante$_i$ dice que pro$_{i/j}$ es muy listo.
  d. El estudiante$_i$ dice que él $_{i/j}$ es muy listo.

(2) a. Each student says he $_{i/j}$ is very smart.
  b. The student says he $_{i/j}$ is very smart.

In the sentences under (1), *él* (he) cannot be co-indexed with *cada estudiante* (each student) although it can with *el estudiante* (the student); compare (1b) with (1d). *Pro*, however, is free to link with either antecedent. In the English examples in (2), we see no constraints on what *he* can take as an antecedent in the same types of situations. As a constraint relevant to null-subject languages, the OPC prohibits co-reference between embedded overt subject pronouns and quantified subjects (e.g., *no student, not a single student, each student*) or *wh*-subjects (e.g., *which student*) in a matrix clause. This restriction applies only to null-subject languages; hence the differences between (1) and (2) above. The OPC is not learned as part of acquiring a null-subject language; it is part of UG and becomes relevant once the learner's grammar is determined to be null subject. There is nothing in the input that says, "This is the OPC. Learn it." (For some discussion, see Pérez-Leroux & Glass, 1999.)

Aspects of language contained in UG, then, are not acquired or learned in the classic sense. As the learner interacts with linguistic data, features may or may not be selected from UG (but only those sanctioned by UG can be selected – learners' grammars cannot make up new features that don't exist), and as the learner interacts with linguistic data, constraints on language may or may not be relevant depending on the language of exposure. Again, these universal aspects of language basically "lie in wait" from the get-go and are not picked up from input data.

### 8.2.2 Aspects of language that are derived

Derived aspects of language have been referred to in the past as "parameters" and "parametric variations." I call these "derived" because in current generative theory (i.e., minimalism), parameters are not claimed to be part of UG but are consequences of language based on the properties of UG. A clear example involves the nature of subjects. UG requires that languages have subjects – the basic idea of the Extended Projection Principle (EPP); but UG does not specify what must be a subject. Two types of subject pronouns fall out of this requirement. One has phonetic content (overt subjects) and one is phonetically empty (null subjects). Languages, then, may have null subjects or they may not. So, the universal aspect of language in question is the EPP and the parametric variation is null subject/non-null subject language. While both Spanish and English obey the EPP, Spanish is null subject while English is not. Null-subjectness means that Spanish freely licenses null subjects in basic sentences[4] but English does not, as exemplified in (3) and (4). It should be noted that *pro* indicates a null subject and (4) is the translation of (3).

(3) ¿Dónde está María? *pro* Salió hace rato.

(4) Where's Mary? *\*pro* Left a little while ago.

Such derivations/parameters may have other consequences. One such consequence is that overt subject pronouns must have an antecedent; null subjects do not require an antecedent. In Spanish, the result is that not only are null subjects freely permitted, they are required in sentences in which there is no antecedent (i.e., overt pronouns are barred in sentences where the subject pronoun does not have an antecedent). These are weather expressions, time expressions, existential expressions, and others, as illustrated in (5) through (9).

(5) weather: Está lloviendo/*Ello está lloviendo. 'It's raining.'[5]

(6) time: Es la una/*Ello es la una. 'It's one o'clock.'

(7) existential statements: Hay café./*Allí hay café. 'There's coffee.' (Note that *allí* is unacceptable for 'there' if it's meant as a subject.)

(8) impersonal statements: *Es imposible que así te portes.*/*Ello es imposible que así te portes.* 'It's impossible that you behave this way.'

(9) unidentified subjects: Me robaron./*Ellos me robaron. 'They robbed me/I was robbed.' (Here the idea is that the perpetrators are not known.)

In addition, languages that license null subjects must have some way to recuperate the information from phonetically empty subject pronouns; that is, information related to person and number. This can be achieved in one of two ways; through discourse/pragmatics (as in Japanese), or through verbal inflections as in Spanish. In a language like Spanish, then, there is a tight relationship between null subjects and rich verbal morphology for indicating person–number. Indeed, Spanish has unique endings for all person–number combinations in the present tense indicative and engages in syncretism in only a handful of cases (i.e., first- and third-person singular in the subjunctive and in the imperfect). For example, 'I drink' *tomo*, 'you drink' *tomas*, 'he/she drinks' *toma*, 'we drink' *tomamos*, 'you all drink' *tomáis*, 'they drink' *toman*.[6]

---

[4] By "freely license" I mean that syntactically the sentences are fine. There may be pragmatic or discourse constraints. I will touch on this in the section on aspects of language that must be learned.

[5] Some dialects of Spanish, most notably isolated to the Dominican Republican, may be in transition from null subject to non-null subject. See Toribio (2000).

[6] To be sure, Latin American dialects use *toma* for both 'you drink' formal and 'he drinks.' This is not syncretism in its traditional sense. Rather, this is a historical derivative from the colonial era when *vuestra merced* 'your majesty' morphed into *usted*. In short, *usted* actually is a third-person pronoun used to refer to a second person.

To be clear, parametric variation has sometimes been claimed to be "triggered" by input data.[7] This claim means that something in the input data causes the internal system to be null subject or non-null subject in nature, for example. In the case of null-subject languages, the clear "trigger" would be sentences such as *¿Tomas vodka?* 'Do you drink vodka?" and *Está lloviendo* 'It's raining.' Such sentences force the positing of *pro* early on in development, especially during parsing where the theta grid of a verb needs to be satisfied (e.g., Pritchett, 1992). But even though something in the input may push parametric variation, the consequences of parametric variation, such as those noted in sentences (5)–(9), fall out of the establishment of null-subjectness, and thus don't have to be learned. To be sure, they may be verified by input data, but the idea here is that once null-subjectness is established, the learner doesn't have to encounter all null-subject sentence types in order for the grammar to "know" that overt subjects are referential and subjects without antecedents must be null.

### 8.2.3 Aspects of language that must be learned

Aspects of language that must be learned are the surface morpho-phonological instantiations of underlying properties; in short, lexical items and morphological inflections and variations.[8] Thus, while UG specifies that languages must have subjects, it does not tell a language what the morpho-phonological shape of an overt pronoun must be. So, English has *he* as a third-person singular pronoun, Spanish has *él*, and Turkish has *o* (the latter two being overt pronouns, as both Spanish and Turkish are null-subject languages). Also, because there is a link between null-subjectness and verbal morphology in a language like Spanish, learners must acquire the language-specific endings of verbs for person and number. In a language like Japanese, learners would have to acquire the discourse constraints.[9]

Because the examples used so far focus on null and overt subjects, I add here that there are other properties of the language that must be learned from exposure. One is anaphoric interpretation where ambiguity exists. In Spanish, learners must also acquire the discourse/pragmatic functions of subject pronouns, linked to concepts such as topic continuity/discontinuity and various types of focus. For example, in the following exchange, both (11a) and (11b) are grammatical, but the latter sounds pragmatically odd:

---

[7] I use the term "triggers" here understanding that current theory has moved away from this conceptualization, especially given that at least some parametric variations emerge more gradually than others. For discussion, see Yang and Roeper (2011).

[8] Some linguists restrict the use of morpho-phonological units to mean unbound functionally related elements such as clitics, particles, and articles. I have broadened the meaning to include not just these elements but lexical items and inflections as well.

[9] This holds only if one analyzes Japanese as being null subject. One could argue that Japanese is a topic drop language, in which subject and topic are often conflated.

(10) ¿Qué pasó con Rafael? 'What happened to Rafael?'

(11a) Perdió el campeonato. 'He lost the championship.'

(11b) Él perdió el campeonato. 'He lost the championship.'

Sentence (11b) is odd as an answer to (10) because there is no topic shift from question to answer; in short, there is no need to specify the subject. Overt subject pronouns are preferred when there is a topic or focus shift. Related to this situation is how speakers prefer to resolve ambiguity in sentence interpretation where a null subject has two antecedent choices. In (12a) and (12b), when asked 'Who came back from Europe?' the speaker of Spanish prefers to have the null subject of the subordinate clause take the Spec,IP (subject) of the main clause as its antecedent, whereas the overt subject pronoun is free to take either the subject or non-subject of the main clause as its antecedent (e.g., Carminati, 2002; Keating, VanPatten, & Jegerski, 2011).

(12a) Juan vio a Roberto después que regresó de Europa.
'John saw Robert after he came back from Europe.'

(12b) Juan vio a Roberto después que él regresó de Europa.
'John saw Robert after he came back from Europe.'

Again, it is not a question of which of the two sentences is grammatical (both are), nor a question of whether or not the OPC (see above) is operative here (it isn't relevant to the sentence). Instead, the question is one of discourse/pragmatic *preference* among native speakers of Spanish. Most monolingual children learning Spanish as a first language do not arrive at adult-like use of null and overt subject pronouns until well into school, normally somewhere around the age of 14 (Shin & Cairns, 2009). This finding suggests that something like subject pronoun distribution and interpretation in Spanish must be learned from the input and that this takes considerable time (assuming, of course, interaction and feedback about interpretation that would naturally occur during communication).

### 8.2.4 Interim summary

What I have argued so far is that there are three aspects of language related to whether or not they have to be learned from the input. They are the following, with illustrations from Spanish.

- Aspects that cannot be learned: the Extended Projection Principle, the Overt Pronoun Constraint.
- Aspects that are derived: the null-subject parameter and its consequences.
- Aspects that must be learned: the particular overt subject pronouns of Spanish, person–number morphology for verbs, distribution of null and overt subject pronouns related to topic shift and focus.

## 8.3 The acquisition problem

We are now in a position to ask ourselves what the acquisition problem is for learners. First I will articulate a consequence from the previous discussion: learners do not acquire rules from the input. Rules, as commonly conceived, don't exist. Instead, what appears as a sentence in a language like English or Spanish is the surface manifestation of underlying features and lexical items that interact under constraints provided by the grammar. For example, learners don't learn a rule such as "the verb agrees with the subject." Instead, learners' grammars instantiate the feature of agreement (provided by UG), which in turn requires a particular phrase (AgrP) projected into the syntax. The features of this phrase must be satisfied every time a complete sentence is made. Satisfaction is achieved by move, in which a lexical item containing the feature in question moves to that phrase to get the feature checked. In this case, it is a verb with the corresponding features. The verb raises out of the VP and lands in AgrP, and the features get checked. Thus, it is not the case that verbs agree with their subjects, but that AgrP needs something to occupy its space in the sentence for the sentence to be "good." This does not mean that the verb stays in AgrP, but we are focused here solely on the relationship between verbs and AgrP.[10] This also does not mean that "verbs must agree with subjects" is not a good characterization from the outside; but in this and most cases, such an "outside rule" is a far cry from what exists in the mental representation. Finally, out of all this it is clear that learners do not acquire something like the OPC or the consequences of null subjectness, or that verbs move from the VP to a position higher up in the sentence. These are all things that "happen" during development. So, just what is the acquisition problem, then? The claim made in VanPatten and Rothman (2014) is this:

> Learners do not acquire rules from the input. Instead, learners process surface morpho-phonological units (e.g., lexical form, morphological form) and internalize these units along with underlying features or specifications. These units interact with information provided by UG and the language making mechanisms of the human language faculty such that anything that resembles rules (from an outside perspective) evolves over time. (p. 25)[11]

Aside from casting suspicion on the status of "rules" in applied linguistics research (e.g., VanPatten & Rothman, 2014), this claim entails two other issues. The first is that a good deal of acquisition happens outside of

---

[10] For more specific accounts of V movement and its relationship to verbal inflections, see Alexiadou and Anagnostopoulou (1998), Bobaljik (2004), Biberauer and Roberts (2010), among others.

[11] Ignored for purpose of discussion are phonological processing and other steps (i.e., linking to conceptual structure). For detailed discussion of all the modules of processing and how they provide input to each other, see Carroll (2001) as well as Truscott and Sharwood Smith (2004).

awareness. Although it is not the point of this chapter to enter into a discussion of the explicit/implicit learning debate, the perspective on language and acquisition taken here suggests that much of the implicit mental representation that develop in learners' minds/brains is implicit because it is learned without awareness. This should be clear from the discussion regarding aspects of language that cannot be learned and those that are derived and not learned.

A second issue is that pedagogical interventions that focus on conscious rule learning or conscious form learning miss the mark. If actual learning from the environment involves the processing of morpho-phonological units in the input, then memorization and practice of things such as verb forms do not directly aid acquisition (and probably do not aid their acquisition indirectly either). For instructional efforts to be efficacious in the acquisition of surface properties of language, those efforts must consider the nature of input processing and how instructional efforts might affect such processing. This is the focus of the next section, but before continuing it is important to recall what the term processing means: the linking of form and meaning and meaning and form. In the quote from VanPatten and Rothman (2014) above, "underlying features or specifications" include meaning. I will emphasize and clarify processing as the discussion continues.

## 8.4 Processing-oriented pedagogical interventions

Processing-oriented pedagogical interventions (POPIs)[12] are those that take the perspective that the first step (but not the only one) in developing a grammar involves the processing of input data from the environment. Once again, by processing I mean that some internal mechanism isolates a morpho-phonological unit and attaches both a meaning and a function to it; in short, form and meaning are linked both at the local level (e.g., the word/form) and the sentence level. In the speech stream ¿Tomasmartinisconvodka? ('Doyoudrinkvodkamartinis?'), the learner must isolate units of meaning so that sentential meaning can be constructed. We will focus on the verb for right now: *tomas*. Somehow, the learner must isolate *tomas* and link it with these features: <'drink'> <+V> <-N> <+present> <-past> <2nd person> <sing>.[13] In doing this, the learner is not creating a rule that says -s is second-person singular. Instead, the learner is processing and internalizing a lexical item that bundles all of the features/specifications just listed. This lexical item, if robustly represented enough in the grammar, can enter into syntactic computations as described in the previous section.

---

[12] I have been asked about how to pronounce this acronym, and I suggest POE-peeh.
[13] In natural speech stream processing, this would be done using a combination of prosody, context, and any relevant prior knowledge. (To be sure, ignored here is the phonological encoding of the lexical unit.)

With this in mind, then, "learning verb forms" in a language like Spanish cannot be equated with memorizing and practicing verb forms, but instead with processing, storing, and retrieving morpho-phonological units with particular bundles of features. Instruction, then, if it is to be useful for the development of mental representation, must be processing oriented.

But what might a POPI look like? This question entails another: what does input processing look like? I will present one model here because it is the model I am most familiar with and with which I am most associated. However, it is consistent with other models (e.g., acquisition by processing; see Truscott & Sharwood Smith, 2004). The presentation will be necessarily sketchy, given the space limitations, but should be sufficient to launch a discussion of the nature of intervention.

### 8.4.1 A sketch of input processing

During acts of communication, learners are driven to get meaning from the input. For various reasons, this places a premium on lexical items, particularly content lexical items such as verbs, nouns, adjectives, and so on. In this model, then, learners first approach the processing problem of new L2 input by searching for lexical items by whatever means they have: prosody, pausing, words appearing in isolation, repetition of sound sequences across and within sentences, previous knowledge, and of course, the context in which sentences are uttered.[14] In addition, if at the same time learners are acquiring reading skills (assuming a literate language), print information may help isolate word boundaries. So, we might have a principle of early-stage processing that goes something like this:

*Primacy of Content Words Principle.* Learners tend to process content lexical items as primary cues to meaning.

At this stage, even if learners "notice" things that aren't content words (e.g., articles, particles), what they actually process are lexical items. Again, it is important to underscore what we mean by processing: the linking of form to meaning and vice versa. To go back to a previous sentence, *Doyoudrinkvodkamartinis?*, it is possible that learners isolate both *do, you,* and *drink,* for example. However, in the earliest stages, it is likely that only *you* and *drink* get processed; that is, get linked with meaning and any underlying features. The functional dummy auxiliary *do* may simply get dumped after processing because it has not been linked to anything. In the early stages, functional aspects of language will get processed only if they are the sole purveyors of a particular meaning. A corollary of the above principle might be something like this:

---

[14] Not all languages are aural/oral, but processing issues are the same regardless of language learned.

*Preference for Meaning and Non-redundancy Principle.* Learners tend to process non-redundant meaningful items before those that are not redundant or not meaningful.

Under this scenario, things like case marking – which encodes meaning when it comes to active canonical sentences – may not get processed early on if learners are exposed to canonical SVO and SOV sentences. The case marking is redundant with word order (see First-noun Principle below). For this reason, learners generally misinterpret passive sentences in early and intermediate stages of learning, even if there is correspondence structurally between passives in the L1 and the L2 (e.g., Ervin-Tripp, 1974). Because redundant functional items require linking with (usually) content words, then such items will not get processed until the lexicon is sufficiently built up. This aspect of processing is captured by something like the following principle:

*Lexical Preference Principle.* For learners to process redundant meaningful functional items, they must first have robust representations for the items with which the functional items are linked.

The above principles refer to what I call "local processing": processing at the word level. They of course affect a wide array of functional items in languages. Turning now to sentence-level issues, a basic aspect of processing is determining who does what to whom. Research has led to the following principle:

*The First-noun Principle* (FNP). Learners tend to process the first noun or pronoun of the sentence as the agent/subject.[15]

For rigid word order languages like English, the FNP is not problematic for most active sentences, but does cause a problem in interpreting passives (e.g., Uludag & VanPatten, 2012). And there is substantial literature on how this processing problem affects the processing of case marking in languages like German and Russian (e.g., VanPatten et al., 2013), differential object marking in Spanish (VanPatten & Cadierno, 1993), non-canonical sentences in which scrambling is allowed (e.g., VanPatten, 1984; VanPatten et al., 2013). In addition, it conflates with local processing principles in the acquisition of verbal inflections for person-number (i.e., learners rely on word order to determine sentential subjects and not verbal inflections).

Once more, I have been necessarily brief here and certainly not complete in portraying input processing and processing as part of acquisition

---

[15] Two issues deserve mention here. First, is that recent research on VS orders in Spanish do not always invite a first-noun "reading" by L2 learners whereas OVS and VSO orders do. Thus, there may have to be two noun-phrases for there to be a strong first-noun bias in interpreting L2 sentences (see, for example, Tight, 2012). The second issue is whether or not the principle is universal or restricted to L1 speakers with non-flexible word orders like English. For discussion on why the first-noun principle is probably universal, see VanPatten (2014).

(see also Truscott & Sharwood Smith, 2004, in which a larger and compatible framework is presented, as well as the discussion in VanPatten, 2009, in which differing perspectives on processing converge on a similar POPI). But with the above sketch in mind, we can see that an effective POPI for aiding the acquisition of grammar would be one that pushes along processing in some way, specifically, by forcing the processing of elements that would otherwise not be processed or processed incorrectly. I will take a classic example with the FNP, first presented in VanPatten and Cadierno (1993).

As noted above, the FNP has negative consequences for object-first sentences (i.e., learners mistake objects for subjects). Languages like Spanish are not strictly subject–verb–object (SVO), with OV and OVS being frequent word orders, and the FNP may lead to erroneous sentence interpretation. For example, *gustar*-like structures are misinterpreted as are any object pronoun-first constructions. In *gustar*-like (to please) constructions, word order has been grammaticalized as indirect object–verb–subject as in *A Juan le gusta María* (lit: To John$_{DAT}$ is pleasing Mary$_{NOM}$). Learners tend to misinterpret *Juan* as the subject, 'John likes Mary' when the verb does not mean *to like*. In the same vein, learners misinterpret simple OVS sentences in which the object is a clitic direct object, such as Lo ve María (lit: Him$_{ACC}$ sees Mary$_{NOM}$). In this case, learners misinterpret the clitic pronoun as a subject and equate lo (him) with 'he,' that is, 'He sees Mary.' Learners also misinterpret simple reflexives such as *Se levanta* (lit: Himself$_{REFL}$ raises, 'He gets up') and tag the pronoun *se* as some kind of subject pronoun meaning 'he.' The result is problems in the acquisition of the Spanish pronoun system and a processing system with a rather strict reliance on word order as the principal means to comprehend sentences.

### 8.4.2 Processing instruction as a POPI

One particular POPI has been developed to address this problem: processing instruction (PI). In PI, learners receive activities that manipulate input such that the learners are forced to abandon the strategies embodied in the various principles of the model of input processing. This manipulated input is referred to as structured input. Referential structured input activities within PI usually begin with a string of activities structured so as to have right or wrong answers. We can illustrate with PI and the First-noun principle as it affects the processing of clitic object pronouns in Spanish – but the same PI activities can be used to inform work on case marking in languages like German and Russian. Learners hear a mixture of SVO/SOV, OVS, OV sentences in which both the subject and object are capable of performing the action (e.g., a boy looking for a girl or a girl looking for a boy). They are asked to select between two pictures in order to indicate they have correctly processed and comprehended the sentence. Such activities are designed to force the learners' internal processors to abandon a strict reliance on the FNP. For Spanish clitic object pronouns, then, this means correctly processing something like *lo* in *Lo ve María* as an accusative pronoun meaning 'him' and interpreting the sentence as 'Mary sees him' and not incorrectly as 'He sees Mary.' Research has demonstrated that learners begin correctly processing OVS sentences with clitic object pronouns after exposure to between thirteen and eighteen items. These items include a mixture of SOV and OVS sentences but with the latter being a majority (for specifics, see Fernández, 2008; VanPatten et al., 2013). Affective structured input activities follow referential activities and are those that do not have right or wrong answers, but instead allow learners to offer opinions, indicate something about themselves, and so on. The purpose, again, of PI activities is to push learners away from the FNP (in the present case) and to correctly process both OV(S) and SOV sentences. At no point during PI activities are learners required to produce the target structure, although they may produce isolated words or short phrases that do not contain the structure. (For detailed information on PI and structured input activities, see Farley, 2005; Lee & VanPatten, 1995, 2003; Wong, 2004.)

In Cadierno (1995), we see the first attempt to use PI to address a local processing issue: correct temporal reference assignment. In that study, Cadierno used the Lexical Preference Principle to inform her PI. Based on the idea that learners use lexical items to make temporal reference assignments, and are thus able to ignore verbal inflections for tense for some time, she constructed PI in which learners could not rely on lexical items such as adverbials of time to assign general temporal reference to sentences. A basic referential activity in her study had learners hearing adverbial-less sentences (e.g., *John attends class, Mary talked on the phone*) and then selecting words that matched the sentence (e.g., *yesterday* vs. *everyday* vs. *tomorrow*). The study was conducted in Spanish but I present the examples in English for the reader's ease. The underlying motivation in this study was to push learners away from relying on adverbials and instead relying on verbal cues as indicators of temporal reference.

### 8.4.3 Some fundamental issues in processing instruction as a POPI

Note that unlike other pedagogical interventions, PI is not concerned with rule learning but with correct sentence interpretation. Learners are not tested on rules but on sentence comprehension and/or form–meaning links. Although my focus here is on PI, my claim is that most POPIs would contain an assessment related to processing and not rule learning.

To be clear, it is worth adding here that input-based pedagogical interventions such as text enhancement, dictogloss, input floods, and others are not POPIs. Many of these are predicated on the idea of "noticing." Noticing is a construct that seems to have some elasticity, or at least has evolved since its original conception (e.g., Schmidt, 1990, 2001).[16] What I think is fair to say is that noticing is not synonymous with processing. Noticing entails some level of awareness (which can vary from definition to definition of the term) while processing does not. What is more, noticing requires only that a particular datum be, well, noticed; there is no part of the definition that says that a morpho-phonological unit is linked to meaning. However, a definition of processing requires that linguistic data are linked to meaning during real-time processing. In short, one can notice something in the input, but not process it (see VanPatten, 2004, for a full discussion). Finally, noticing has never been meant to apply beyond the word level. That is, to my knowledge, there is no noticing that is related to syntactic computation of sentences. It is also worth adding here that although PI is input oriented, it cannot be reduced to being a "comprehension-based" intervention, because many comprehension-based interventions are precisely those that are predicated on noticing (e.g., text enhancement, input flood). I raise these issues here because there has been and continues to be confusion in the literature with just what input processing is and what the intent of PI is. Such confusion can be seen in the work by Han and Peverly (2007), Salaberry (1997), DeKeyser and Sokalski (1996), and others. I also raise these issues because there have been some misguided attempts to refute the underlying claims of PI and the results of dozens of studies on it, largely because the interventions developed in those attempts fall far short of being PI or any kind of POPI (e.g., Allen, 2000; Erlam, 2003; Qin, 2008).

In actuality, PI has yielded consistent and robust findings in a variety of contexts and languages, with various factors manipulated to examine intervening effects. Some of the related studies are well known, some are not and/or are very recent. I will list a few here.[17]

- The foundational studies: VanPatten and Cadierno (1993), Cadierno (1995).
- The role of explicit information and explicit feedback: VanPatten and Oikennon (1996), Fernández (2008), Henry, Culman, and VanPatten (2009), VanPatten et al. (2013), Sanz and Morgan-Short (2004), White and DeMil (2013a)
- The use of different assessment measures/transfer of training: VanPatten and Sanz (1995), Sanz and Morgan-Short (2004), VanPatten and Uludag (2011), White and DeMil (2013a)
- The role of aptitude/individual differences: VanPatten et al. (2013), Lee and Benati (2013)

---

[16] It is not within the scope of this chapter to address the controversial nature of noticing. For some discussion, see Truscott (1998).
[17] There are some fifty-plus studies of PI to date, focusing on the factors noted in this chapter as well as a few others. It is one of the most researched interventions in instructed SLA.

- PI and discourse level effects: Wong (2010), Benati and Lee (2010)
- Secondary effects: Benati and Lee (2008), White and DeMil (2013b)
- Long-term effects: VanPatten and Fernández (2004)
- Comparative studies with other interventions: VanPatten and Cadierno (1993), Cadierno (1995), Benati (2001, 2005), VanPatten et al. (2009), Uludag and VanPatten (2012), VanPatten, Farmer, and Clardy (2009), Comer and deBenedette (2010), White (2013), and many others.

I draw the reader's attention to the last group of studies, the comparative studies. In these, PI is compared to some other intervention (e.g., traditional instruction, dictogloss, meaning-based output). What is interesting about these studies is that PI almost always yields superior results on measures of interpretation/processing. On measures of output manipulation, PI yields similar results to other interventions, and sometimes greater results. At no time is there ever a non-effect for PI. The same cannot be said of non-POPIs such as text enhancement, dictogloss, and input floods, which yield mixed findings at best (e.g., Wong, 2005). I also draw the reader's attention to the sole study that found long-term effects for PI: nine months after the initial intervention (VanPatten & Fernández, 2004). No other research on pedagogical interventions has found long-term effects after a single period of intervention. That PI (and probably any kind of solidly motivated POPI) yields consistently positive results suggests that a focus on processing is well motivated. And this motivation is traced back to an articulated account of acquisition: (1) understanding the *what* of representation; (2) understanding how that representation comes about; and (3) understanding the nature of processing as one of the factors contributing to the development of representation. To drive the point home, because PI is not concerned with the learning of rules but instead with the correct processing of morpho-phonological units in the input, it is more appropriately grounded in theory and research than interventions that are grounded in concepts such as noticing and rule learning.

To remind the reader, I have focused on PI in this section largely because it is well articulated and widely researched. This does not mean that there cannot be other POPIs predicated on other models of processing; we just haven't seen them yet.

## 8.4.4 Back to mental representation

At this juncture, it is appropriate to return to mental representation for a moment and ask how something like PI (or any true POPI) would aid in its development. Given that the emphasis in PI is on correct sentence processing and the linking of meaning and form, then what does this have to do with underlying abstract representation? To illustrate, let's take a concrete example from Spanish and the processing of clitic object pronouns in something like the VanPatten and Cadierno foundational study.

Languages are parameterized regarding certain functional features related to clitic object pronouns. This parameterization revolves around the abstract features contained in a clitic and its forced movement to satisfy certain agree relationships in a tensed clause (for one of the most influential accounts of clitic object pronouns in Romance languages, and the analysis adopted here, see Uriagareka, 1995). Without getting into the technical details, languages either have a phrase denoted AgrOP within the TP (tense phrase) or they do not. AgrOP contains a bundle of features that must be satisfied. Spanish is one such language with AgrOP. At the same time, these languages also have a functional projection (FP) contained somewhere in the CP (comp phrase) above the TP. Clitics contain features that these phrases attract for satisfaction (e.g., D [determiner] features). For the parameter to be instantiated in a language like Spanish, learners have to process clitic object pronouns as clitic object pronouns and not subject pronouns or something else. This means they must be linked to a meaning related to theme or patient of the verb. For example, when *lo* is correctly processed, it minimally must be tagged with the following meaning-based as well as functional features: <3rd person> <sing> <accusative> <anaphor>; that is accusative 'him.' This information is delivered to the internal mechanisms and because of the features contained in UG and information regarding placement in the sentence (i.e., a position above VP), AgrOP is initially projected and parameterization is begun. Note that unless learners actually process clitic object pronouns for what they are in terms of meaning, then parameterization of underlying features and syntactic operations in a language like Spanish can be delayed. As the work on input processing has shown, learners may not do this for some time. Processing instruction, then, provides a mechanism that induces correct processing of clitic object pronouns so that needed information can make its way to the internal language-making architecture. From this discussion, it should be even clearer why interventions predicated on noticing are not as consistently successful as something like PI; if critical information is denied to the internal mechanisms responsible for language, then development doesn't happen – at least development of representation. It could be the case that noticing and other interventions affect explicit or meta-linguistic knowledge, but these knowledge types are neither equivalent to underlying representation nor particularly useful for its development (for some discussion, see Truscott, 1998; Truscott & Sharwood Smith, 2011).

## 8.5 Conclusion

In this chapter, I have made a number of major claims and reviewed research to support them. Those claims include the following:

- Language acquisition involves both the acquisition of mental representation of language and skill (i.e., the use of language in communicative settings). Focusing on representation, I outlined a generative perspective useful for informing ideas about the product of acquisition. A major result of this perspective is the jettison of rule-learning as a construct in adult SLA.
- A major problem confronting the learner, then, is the processing of morpho-phonological units in the input. Processing is defined here as the linking of meaning and form during real-time comprehension.
- Processing is not the same as noticing: the latter does not by definition entail the linking of form with meaning, nor the processing of sentences.
- Because input processing is the first step in getting data to build a linguistic system, I outlined the reasons for POPIs – processing-oriented pedagogical interventions.
- I reviewed one POPI – processing instruction – and briefly reviewed the research related to it. My claim is that the success and consistent findings of PI research is related to its well-articulated framework for understanding early-stage input processing. By focusing on processing (as opposed to noticing and as opposed to any product/knowledge gained), PI is better motivated as an intervention compared to such things as text enhancement and input floods.

As stated previously, PI receives a good deal of research and scholarly attention because it is currently the only established POPI. To be sure, it is predicated on one particular model of input processing. The question becomes whether other models exist or to what extent other POPIs can be developed. In VanPatten (2009), I compared the model of input processing underlying PI to two other approaches. However, in the end I determined that all three would converge on a very similar pedagogical intervention – namely, PI. A more encompassing model of acquisition by processing is offered in Truscott and Sharwood Smith (2004), but a close scrutiny of that model suggests that PI is compatible with any pedagogical suggestions one could derive from that model. Indeed, Sharwood Smith (personal communication), has suggested that according to the acquisition by processing framework, PI is the pedagogical intervention that makes the most sense. Nonetheless, other POPIs may arise as other models emerge. Alternatively, other models may provide alternative principles to input processing that replace the model sketched in this chapter, yet the intervention derived from such models may resemble PI in important ways. As long as the focus of POPIs is on pushing learners to make form-meaning connections and to correctly process the meaning of sentences, we will likely see similarity among such interventions.

# 9

# Learning second language vocabulary
Insights from laboratory studies

Natasha Tokowicz and Tamar Degani

## 9.1 Introduction

Adult second language (L2) learners face a unique challenge when they begin to learn an L2 because they already have a well-formed set of concepts and first language (L1) labels for the majority of those concepts. In this chapter, we selectively review the laboratory training literature on the factors that influence adult L2 vocabulary learning, emphasizing (1) instructional/training factors, (2) stimulus factors, and (3) learner factors. Many important and foundational classroom vocabulary learning studies have also been conducted. The goal of this review is to explore the insights gained from laboratory studies that can be transferred to actual learning contexts.

Vocabulary is a foundational aspect of language (e.g., Beck, Mckeown, & Kucan, 2002; de Groot, 2011; Folse, 2004; Juffs, 2009). The goal of directed vocabulary instruction is to provide the learner with a foundation of words that they can use to express thoughts, to understand what they hear and read, and to learn additional aspects of the target language. These goals will only be accomplished if the L2 learner learns strong representations of new word forms, and builds strong connections between the new vocabulary words and their meanings. Furthermore, the learner must be able to access that information rapidly, as it is needed in communicative settings. Therefore, within the psycholinguistic study of vocabulary learning, an emphasis has been placed on the effectiveness of various training methods to help establish strong form-to-meaning connections. In this area of research, there is a general divide between two theoretical frameworks. The first framework posits that initially, adult L2 learners have difficulty linking L2 words with meaning, and instead mediate processing of L2 words through the L1 (e.g., the Revised Hierarchical Model, Kroll & Stewart, 1994). By contrast, other frameworks posit that learners either never experience this mediation phase, or that it ends rather quickly, and therefore L2 words are rapidly linked with meaning (e.g., Altarriba & Mathis, 1997; Brysbaert & Duyck, 2010; de Groot, 1992b; de Groot, Dannenburg, & van Hell, 1994). Regardless of one's particular theoretical perspective, it is still the case that some methodologies will be more successful than others in leading to a strong connection between L2 words and their meanings. Note that there are other general divisions within this literature that could be considered (e.g., input vs. output-focused tasks; incidental vs. intentional vocabulary learning); we focus on the divide that is most prominent in the study of adult L2 learning from a cognitive psychology perspective.

## 9.2 Instructional/training factors

Several methods of instructing vocabulary take advantage of general memory and learning phenomena. These can be divided broadly into manipulations of the material that is presented to the learner during training, and of the learners' actions on the training material.

### 9.2.1 Input to the learner

#### 9.2.1.1 Spacing of presentations

A key finding that has emerged as a stable contributor to successful learning is being exposed to the material in a spaced rather than massed fashion, with larger gaps between presentations leading to stronger gains in learning (for recent reviews, see Benjamin & Tullis, 2010; Dunlosky et al., 2013). For example, Pavlik and Anderson (2005) taught native English speakers a set of Japanese–English word pairs. Manipulating the time interval between different practice sessions, they found that forgetting was slower under spaced than massed practice conditions. Thus, while keeping total study time constant, it is beneficial for learners to space out presentation and practice of the material to improve learning. Longer lags should be favored, but the ideal lag in between practice episodes is complex to determine, and depends on the desired retention interval (see Cepeda et al., 2008). (See Bahrick et al. (1993), and Bahrick & Phelps (1987) for investigations of retention of foreign language vocabulary for more than one year.)

#### 9.2.1.2 Grouping of presentation

In textbooks and online language learning environments, foreign vocabulary is often taught in semantic groupings (e.g., all the fruits together, all the vegetables, etc.), presumably to facilitate conversation about a specific topic, and perhaps to emphasize meaning. However, semantic categorization leads to the repeated activation of concepts that overlap in their semantic features, and can therefore lead to interference (e.g., Kroll & Stewart, 1994). Such interference may reduce learners' ability to appropriately map precise meanings to new vocabulary words. Note that this criticism does not hold for thematic groupings in which the words are related but are not necessarily from the same semantic category, as described below.

To directly test the impact of semantic grouping on foreign vocabulary learning, Tinkham (1993) taught native English speakers relatively small sets of English word-alien vocabulary (three and six pairs per condition in Experiments 1 and 2, respectively). These word pairs were taught using a semantically associated condition (i.e., "shirt," "jacket," "sweater"), and a semantically unassociated condition (i.e., "rain," "car," "frog"). The primary learning measure was the time it took participants to reach 100 percent accuracy in each condition, which was lower in the unassociated than the semantically associated condition. A similar finding was observed by Finkbeiner and Nicol (2003), who taught native English speakers "alien" vocabulary in semantically organized or randomized lists using pictures during training. In their study, translation latencies for correct responses were slower for participants who learned the words in semantically organized lists than for participants who learned the words in randomly ordered lists; no accuracy differences were observed. Thus, despite the communicative goals that may be achieved by providing learners with a particular set of vocabulary, the findings from these studies suggest that grouping semantically related words together leads to worse learning of the vocabulary items (see also Waring, 1997). The most likely mechanism is interference between the alternative translations – when multiple related concepts are activated, they compete with each other (e.g., Kroll & Stewart, 1994).

As mentioned above, thematic groupings in which the words are not all drawn from the same semantic category, do not overlap in features, and vary in part of speech, can assist learning. Using a design similar to that of Tinkham (1993), Tinkham (1997) taught native English speakers relatively small sets of English word-alien vocabulary under a thematically associated condition (i.e., "beach," "sunny," "swim"), and a thematically unassociated condition. Again, the primary learning measure was the time it took participants to reach 100 percent accuracy in each condition, which was lower in the thematically associated condition. This finding is consistent with the idea that it is not association per se that is problematic for learning, but rather semantic overlap in particular.

Tseng et al. (in revision) used a similar manipulation to Tinkham (1997) with a larger set of stimuli and a more extensive training paradigm. They taught native English speakers a set of 96 Arabic words in eight sessions across four weeks. They manipulated whether the words were presented in thematic groupings or a random order. Similar to the learning rate results of Tinkham, accuracy rates were higher in the thematic grouping condition as compared with the random grouping condition. Thus, this alternative grouping method enhances rather than detracts from learning, likely because it strengthens interconnections among the learned vocabulary, thereby enhancing the resonance of the L2 system (e.g., MacWhinney, 2005). Given the available evidence that semantic groupings are worse than random groupings and that thematic groupings are better than random groupings, thematic grouping should be favored over semantic groupings.

### 9.2.1.3 Training different aspects of the word

In contrast to many paired-associate word learning paradigms, in which participants are familiar with the two representations and are required only to learn the new mapping between them, foreign-vocabulary learners need not only to learn the *mapping* between the new word's form and its meaning, and/or its L1 translation (which may be ambiguous, as discussed in section 9.4), but also the form representation itself. Sommers and Barcroft (2013) found an interesting dissociation between memory for known L1 words and learning of novel L2 word forms. Specifically, they found that presentation of the to-be-retained item along with multiple pictures of the object (referent token variability) led to better retention when learning was in the L1, in accordance with the 'level of processing' hypothesis by which deeper, more semantically oriented processing leads to better learning (e.g., Craik & Tulving, 1975). Critically, however, when the to-be-retained item was an L2 word, such picture variability led to worse learning than presentation of the word with a single consistent picture. The authors suggested that at the early stages of learning a new word, it is important that the learner focus on word form (among other things), and that variability in the pictures takes away from the resources needed to focus on form (see the Type of Processing-Resource Allocation (TOPRA) Model, e.g., Barcroft, 2002). This is in contrast to variability in form-related characteristics (e.g., talker characteristics, speaking rate), which have been shown to improve learning of novel L2 word forms (Barcroft & Sommers, 2005; Sommers & Barcroft, 2007).

There is also evidence to suggest that form-related and meaning-related factors may operate in parallel to improve foreign language vocabulary learning. As described above, Tseng et al. (in revision) taught native English speakers Arabic words and included a meaning-focused thematic organization manipulation, which led to higher accuracy. In addition, they included a manipulation intended to increase the quality of form representations. Specifically, the words were trained in their phonological form along with transliterations, to provide additional orthographic representations. When asked to produce the Arabic words, in either free recall or

English to Arabic translation production, accuracy was higher in the transliteration condition as compared with the no transliteration condition, even though oral production was emphasized during testing. And, this effect increased over time. The effect of their form and meaning-focused manipulations did not interact, so the highest accuracy was observed in the thematic organization transliterations condition. Thus, it is relevant to consider both meaning- and form-related aspects during foreign vocabulary learning.

Notably, not all learners can benefit to the same extent from form-related and meaning-related emphasis during learning. For example, Kaushanskaya and Marian (2009a) demonstrated that monolingual speakers had more difficulty learning foreign words in a bimodal training condition (hearing and seeing an orthographic form) than in a unimodal (hearing an orthographic form) training condition. The authors attributed the difficulty to the need to map a novel phonological form to an already known orthography (i.e., that of English), which creates competition. Interestingly, English–Spanish bilinguals who are more experienced with such competing mappings, because both English phonology and Spanish phonology map onto the same orthographic code, were as efficient in learning under bimodal and unimodal conditions. Note that in the Tseng et al. (under review) study there was no need to map competing phonology to known orthography, because unique letter combinations were used to differentiate English from Arabic phonology (e.g., the illegal English letter string <Dh> was used to denote the Arabic phoneme [dˤ] which does not exist in English). In Kaushanskaya and Marian's study, testing was focused on meaning, rather than form, and thus only L2 to L1 translation production and recognition were used. It remains to be examined whether the difficulty associated with bimodal presentation persists when L2 words are to be produced, as in Tseng et al.'s study.

It is thus clear that focusing on different aspects of form and meaning during learning are likely to influence L2 word learning differently for learners with different resources, and for stimuli with different characteristics. In many cases, the to-be-learned form-representation also entails novel sub-lexical information when the phonology of the languages is different (e.g., Kaushanskaya & Marian, 2009b). When participants are familiar with the meaning of the novel word, L2 word learning is more difficult when the phonology of the novel word is composed of unknown sub-lexical phonological units as opposed to familiar phonology (Kaushanskaya, Yoo, & Van Hecke, 2013). Notably, these effects of phonological familiarity also suggest that as learners become more proficient in the L2, and familiar with the L2 phonology, word learning should become less difficult. We return to this issue in section 9.5.2.

### 9.2.1.4 Training with pictures vs. words

In addition to some of the previously reviewed studies that emphasized meaning during training, another method researchers have used to emphasize meaning is training with pictures rather than words. Kroll, Michael, and Sankaranarayanan (1998) examined learning of Dutch vocabulary by native English speakers who were naïve with respect to Dutch. They compared learning with pictures vs. words, and showed a general advantage for picture training (Experiment 1). In a unique manipulation, Kroll et al. (Experiment 2) presented half of the pictures during study and test in a noncanonical (i.e., unusual) orientation, reasoning that this might provide an unusual cue to the Dutch translation. In support of this conjecture, for concepts that were rated as familiar, Dutch words that were associated with pictures in noncanonical orientations were responded to more quickly in picture-naming and translation tests than Dutch words that were associated with pictures in canonical orientations; the opposite pattern was found for unfamiliar concepts. Thus, pictures presented in a non-canonical orientation led to a more effective connection between novel words and their meanings. The fact that this effect did not hold for unfamiliar concepts suggests that the non-canonical orientation may make resolution of the object identity difficult.

Despite these findings, there are inconsistent effects of picture training for learning foreign language vocabulary. Carpenter and Olson (2012) examined the potential reasons for a lack of superiority for learning foreign words (Swahili words) with pictures as opposed to L1 translations (e.g., Lotto & de Groot, 1998), despite a consistent picture superiority effect found in memory research. Carpenter and Olson show that this paradox is rooted in the overconfidence of learners. Because pictures are perceived as easier to process, learners are overconfident that they will remember the L2 word better when paired with a picture (although this is not actually the case). However, when overconfidence is reduced by practice retrieving the words (or a simple warning), learning with pictures is in fact superior to learning with L1 translations.

Lotto and de Groot (1998) also found a disadvantage for learning foreign language vocabulary paired with pictures relative to learning these words paired with L1 translations. Lotto and de Groot suggest that the inconsistent findings with respect to picture vs. word vocabulary training may be due to the nature of the learners tested in various studies. In particular, they suggest that individuals with prior experience with a foreign language learn better from rote learning with word pairs (e.g., van Hell & Candia Mahn, 1997, as described below), whereas novice learners (i.e., monolinguals) may benefit from more visual or interactive learning (e.g., Kroll et al., 1998). This highlights, again, the need to take learner characteristics into account when selecting appropriate training methods (e.g., Kaushanskaya & Marian, 2009a).

### 9.2.2 Activity of the learner

We now focus on experimental manipulations of the actions taken by the learner during training, rather than on variations in the input to the learning during training.

#### 9.2.2.1 The keyword mnemonic

A method of L2 vocabulary instruction that varies the actions taken by the learner is the keyword mnemonic. In this method, a keyword is to be created for each L1–L2 vocabulary pairing. In particular, the keyword should be an L1 word that is similar to and will serve as a memory cue for the (beginning of the) L2 word. The participant first forms an association between the L1 translation and the keyword. For the English–Spanish translation pair "clown–payaso," "pie" serves as an effective keyword. Then, the learner is to imagine the keyword and the L1 translation/word meaning interacting, so in this case the learner could envision a clown with a pie in his face. In a classic test of the keyword mnemonic, Atkinson and Raugh (1975) compared native English speaking learners' acquisition of Russian vocabulary using the keyword method vs. an unconstrained training condition and observed a learning advantage for the keyword method. A number of additional studies have demonstrated that the keyword mnemonic is an effective method of language learning (see review in de Groot, 2011).

However, some investigations have not shown this advantage (e.g., see Barcroft, Sommers, & Sunderman, 2011). In one such study, van Hell and Candia Mahn (1997) compared the keyword method to rote learning in an investigation with native English speakers who were not proficient in another language, and native Dutch speakers who had extensive experience with foreign languages. Both populations were naïve learners of the target language (Dutch for the native English speakers, Spanish for the native Dutch speakers). They found that rote learning led to better memory for the experienced language learners, whereas the inexperienced language learners showed no difference in accuracy for the two learning methods (but longer latencies in the keyword condition). Although the keyword mnemonic is sometimes found to be an effective method of learning L2 vocabulary, it is difficult to develop the materials and may not be effective for all vocabulary items, particularly items that do not refer to imageable concepts, or that do not overlap enough with L1 phonology for an adequate keyword to be found, and is therefore of limited value (see evaluation in Dunlosky et al., 2013).

#### 9.2.2.2 The generation effect

Another general memory mechanism that can be exploited in L2 vocabulary training is the "generation effect" by which material generated by the learner is remembered better than material that is not generated by the learner (e.g., Slamecka & Graf, 1978; see Bertsch et al., 2007, for a meta-analysis). In one relevant study, Gollub and Healy (1987) presented learners with a list of English (L1) words to remember. The learners in the critical condition were instructed to generate a sentence for the target words, and then assess the difficulty associated with producing the sentence. Participants in a yoked condition were instructed to evaluate the usage of the target word in the sentences generated by other learners and assess the difficulty associated with producing the sentence. Participants in the critical generation condition remembered significantly more words than participants in the yoked evaluate condition.

Tokowicz and Jarbo (2009, in revision; see also Eddington, Martin, & Tokowicz, 2012) applied the generation effect to native English speakers who were naïve learners of Dutch vocabulary. In their study, learners in the generate condition created L1 sentences and inserted the L2 words into them. For example, for the Dutch word for lightening (bliksem), one learner generated the sentence: "Last night I heard thunder and saw bliksem." Learners in this condition remembered significantly more words than learners in a yoked condition in which participants evaluated the sentences, and in an alternative condition in which participants repeated pairs of translations. Thus, the generation effect applies to learning in a variety of contexts, and it can be used to improve L2 vocabulary learning as well as retention. This method has several advantages over other training methods. Specifically, it does not require the advance creation of any additional materials – learners generate the study material themselves, so it is not a difficult method to implement. Furthermore, it can be used with any type of word stimuli (concrete or abstract words, cognates or noncognates, etc.), and theoretically can be used with learners of any skill level, although it has not yet been tested with more advanced learners.

### 9.2.2.3 Practice testing

In their extensive review of effective learning techniques, Dunlosky et al. (2013) highlight the efficacy of practice testing (also known as retrieval practice or the "testing effect") for learning (see also Roediger & Butler, 2011). Such practice testing effects have been demonstrated across a wide range of learning materials, test formats, and learner ages. Directly relevant to foreign-vocabulary learning, several studies have demonstrated that practice testing improves learning of L2 words. For instance, Karpicke and Roediger (2008) had participants learn a list of forty Swahili–English word pairs, and then tested them in an L2 to L1 backward translation task (i.e., asked participants to provide the English translation of each Swahili word). Critically, the authors manipulated what happened once an item was correctly produced on this initial test. Specifically, they contrasted a training manipulation in which a correctly produced item was studied and tested repeatedly, with ones in which such an item was dropped from further study, from further testing, or from both. The results clearly show that repeated learning of a correctly produced item was associated with no benefit for long-term retention, as measured by a delayed test one week following learning. In contrast, repeated testing produced a substantial benefit, with repeatedly tested items recalled at .80 recall rate, as compared to about .36 for items dropped from further testing.

Kang, Gollan, and Pashler (2013) recently contrasted the efficacy of practice testing in comparison to oral rehearsal, or imitation, during learning. Participants heard forty Hebrew nouns while a picture of the object was presented visually on the screen. Following this initial presentation, training continued in one of two conditions. In the imitation-vocal rehearsal condition, participants heard the word while the picture was presented visually, and were asked to repeat the word out loud. In the practice testing condition, they were given the picture and asked to attempt to produce the Hebrew word before the correct pronunciation was given to them. Although participants in both conditions were presented with both an auditory record of the word and a picture of the object, and time spent learning was identical, a clear dissociation was evident in performance. Whereas retrieval of the L2 word was more accurate under the imitation training condition during the training itself, it was more accurate under the practice testing condition (in both production and recognition) at the end of the training (and 48 hours later). Practice testing is thus a highly useful technique for foreign vocabulary learning.

Moreover, Potts and Shanks (2012) showed that practice testing can provide immunization against interference. In their study, participants learned 20 English–Swahili word pairs to criteria, and a day later learned 20 Finnish translations for the same 20 English words. Results showed that learning of this second list led to substantial interference in recall of the Swahili words, but dramatically less so when a cued–recall test preceded learning of the Finnish translations. Thus, practice testing immediately prior to learning of competing materials substantially protects against interference.

Despite the strong and stable effect of testing on learning, students do not necessarily engage in such practice testing activities during training, and are rarely aware that such activities are likely to lead to better performance (Dunlosky et al., 2013; Karpicke, Butler, & Roediger, 2009; Karpicke & Roediger, 2008). Interestingly, practice testing may also serve to reduce participants' overconfidence, and thus allow them to benefit more from training (see Carpenter & Olson, 2012).

These studies suggest that incorporating tests during training of foreign-vocabulary items is a highly efficient technique to improve long-term retention of these items. When learning associations between known representations, it seems to be the case that the testing effect is strengthened when the practice testing activities require learners to generate a response (i.e., recall vs. recognition; Carpenter & DeLosh, 2006), but it remains to be examined if this holds for foreign vocabulary learning. In addition, the extent to which learners' characteristics modulate the effect awaits further study (Dunlosky et al., 2013; Tse & Pu, 2012).

To summarize, in terms of the input given to the foreign language vocabulary learner, spaced practice is better than massed practice, with the best interval being determined by several factors, including the desired retention interval. Research suggests that thematic groupings of words (with varying parts of speech but a common theme) lead to learning that is superior to that in randomized groupings, which, in turn, is better than learning of semantically organized groupings (with overlap in meaning and part of speech). These studies also suggest that early in vocabulary learning, it is helpful to allow the learner to focus on form, and it may also be useful to provide an added orthographic representation (e.g., in the form of transliteration). Past research also shows that picture training in canonical and non-canonical orientations is less reliably helpful, and likely depends on stimulus familiarity and learner characteristics. With respect to the activity of the learner, the keyword method is sometimes useful but there are some limits to the generalizability of this method and finding. Generation of material and practice testing during training are also beneficial for learning. We now turn to the stimulus factors that influence vocabulary learning.

## 9.3 Stimulus factors

Because foreign vocabulary learning is in part a task of learning new mappings of form-to-meaning, it is not surprising that form-related and meaning-related aspects of the stimulus are extremely influential on the trajectory of learning. With respect to meaning, it has now been consistently shown that concrete words are easier to learn than abstract words (de Groot, 2006; for a recent review, see de Groot & van den Brink, 2010; de Groot & van Hell, 2005). This finding is explained by the greater overlap in semantic features for concrete vs. abstract words that are assumed to exist between L1 and L2 (van Hell & de Groot, 1998a), or by inherent differences between concrete and abstract concepts (see de Groot, 2011, for a summary). With respect to form, there is evidence to suggest that cognates, which are translation equivalents that overlap substantially in phonology and sometimes orthography between the two languages, enjoy an advantage in learning (e.g., de Groot & Keijzer, 2000; Lotto & de Groot, 1998), such that they are learned faster and retained better than non-cognates. Conversely, false-cognates, which overlap in form but not in meaning between the two languages (e.g., the Spanish word "pan" means bread), have been consistently shown to interfere with bilingual processing, but their learning trajectory deserves further research (see Laufer, 1989, for discussion of such deceptive transparencies in word learning). Thus, it is clear that aspects of form and meaning of the to-be-learned words are relevant to consider. Interestingly, because learners are to incorporate L2 words into an existing lexicon with L1 items, the mapping between L1 and L2 translations is also relevant to how these words are learned. We turn to this issue next.

## 9.4 Translation ambiguity

In many cases, a given word in one language maps onto more than one translation in another language. Such "translation ambiguity" is prevalent (as measured normatively in word lists; e.g., Prior, MacWhinney, & Kroll, 2007; Tokowicz et al., 2002; Tseng, Chang, & Tokowicz, 2014), and it has been shown to hinder proficient bilinguals' performance in translation production (e.g., Prior, Kroll, & MacWhinney, 2013; Tokowicz & Kroll, 2007) and translation recognition tasks (Boada et al., 2013; Eddington & Tokowicz, 2013; Laxén & Lavaur, 2010; Prior et al., 2013; for recent reviews see Tokowicz, 2014; Tokowicz & Degani, 2010). We have recently demonstrated that such ambiguity in the mapping between the two languages is also detrimental to word learning (Degani & Tokowicz, 2010a). Native English participants were taught a set of English–Dutch translation pairs, half of which were translation ambiguous in that they had two translations in Dutch.

Translation-ambiguous words elicited lower accuracy scores on both translation production and translation recognition tasks compared to translation-unambiguous words, both immediately after learning and following a two-week delay. Based on these findings, Degani and Tokowicz (2010a) concluded that one-to-many mappings create difficulty in learning, and avoiding such ambiguous mappings may assist learners. In an extension of that work, we tested whether particular instructional methods can alleviate the translation-ambiguity disadvantage in learning (Degani, Tseng, & Tokowicz, forthcoming). We reasoned that if participants' attention is somehow drawn to the indirect mapping of the translation early on, they may be able to overcome the interference and reduced strength associated with such mapping ambiguity. To test this, we compared a condition in which the two alternative translations of a given translation-ambiguous item were presented one after the other, on consecutive trials (i.e., "together condition"), with a condition in which one translation was presented on the first study session, and the other was withheld until the second study session two days later (i.e., "separate condition"). Results from tests administered one and three weeks after initial learning revealed again a translation-ambiguity disadvantage in translation production and recognition, and further demonstrated that accuracy was higher when the two alternative translations were presented together. Thus, teaching both alternatives together, from the beginning, produces substantial improvements during learning as compared with the more common approach of withholding one of the alternative translations until a later time (later classes, semesters, or sessions).

In many cases, translation ambiguity manifests itself in the opposite direction, such that two L1 words map onto a shared translation in another language (Degani, Prior, & Tokowicz, 2011; Degani & Tokowicz, 2013). When asked to learn such shared-translation labels, participants do better when the two L1 words are related in meaning than when they are unrelated in meaning (see review in Tokowicz, 2014). Thus, again, if learners are able to avoid the one-to-many mapping issue by linking the shared translation to a single meaning that encompasses both L1 words, learning performance is improved.

To summarize, the findings of studies on stimulus factors demonstrate that the mapping between the two languages in terms of form (i.e., cognates) has a strong impact on learning and processing. The greater the overlap, the easier learning will be. In terms of the learning of abstract vs. concrete concepts, there is fairly consistent evidence that concrete words are learned more easily than abstract words, although the precise mechanism of this advantage is still debated. Finally, the mapping across translation pairs affects learning, such that more direct mappings are associated with better learning.

## 9.5 Learner factors

### 9.5.1 Learner memory capacity

Learners come to the task of learning foreign vocabulary with different abilities and experiences. Domain-general abilities such as phonological short-term memory and working memory have been studied as potential factors that influence the learning process. Martin and Ellis (2012) found that phonological short-term memory, as measured by nonword repetition and nonword recognition tasks, as well as working memory, as measured with a listening span task, were positively correlated with auditory learning of words and grammar of an artificial language. Similarly, Kaushanskaya (2012) showed that monolingual speakers with higher phonological short-term memory, as measured by the digit span and nonword repetition tasks, outperformed monolinguals with lower phonological short-term memory when learning phonologically unfamiliar (but not familiar) words. The lack of an effect for phonologically familiar word forms was explained by the possibility of relying more on long-term phonological storage in this condition. Interestingly, that same study found an advantage for bilingual speakers over monolingual speakers in learning foreign vocabulary that could not be reduced to differences in phonological short-term memory. We turn to this in the following section.

### 9.5.2 Bilingualism vs. monolingualism

As mentioned earlier, different learners may bring different resources and experiences with them to the task of L2 vocabulary learning. One such important resource is the amount of prior experience in learning foreign languages. As previously mentioned, van Hell and Candia Mahn (1997) found that native Dutch speakers who had taken English, French, or German classes, were better at learning novel Spanish vocabulary than learners without such foreign language experience (native English speakers learning Dutch). Experienced language learners bring with them more relevant prior knowledge, and they may be able to capitalize on such knowledge when faced with similar learning tasks (e.g., the Matthew Effect, by which the 'rich get richer'; see also Pulido, 2003). In support of this finding, Kaushanskaya et al. (2013) recently showed that participants who were better at learning unfamiliar phonological labels for familiar objects were those with increased exposure to L2.

Such effects of expertise are important to consider not only between individuals but also within individuals. Experienced learners bring with them more experience in learning new words, more stable knowledge of the sub-lexical phonological and orthographic aspects of the foreign language, and a more elaborate network of semantic connections within the L2. Even within the realm of vocabulary (ignoring the scaffolding that syntactic knowledge offers), advanced students may be substantially different than novice learners. The ideal training procedure for such learners and their learning trajectory is likely to differ in important ways. We return to this issue below.

Interestingly, the advantage for experienced L2 learners may not be the sole result of their direct experience in classroom learning of L2 vocabulary. Rather, other aspects related to their language background and their being bilingual, may contribute to the observed effect. To examine whether bilingualism rather than experience with classroom L2 learning benefits L2 vocabulary learning, Kaushanskaya and Marian (2009b) had participants learn a set of forty-eight novel words including phonologically unfamiliar sounds. Critically, one-third of the participants were early bilinguals of English and Mandarin, one-third were early bilinguals of English and Spanish, and one-third were functionally monolingual English speakers. On both immediate and delayed (one week) testing of L2 to L1 production and recognition accuracy, both bilingual groups outperformed the monolingual group. The authors proposed that this benefit may be rooted in more efficient phonological encoding, memory storage and/or retrieval processes of bilinguals as compared to monolinguals. In a related study, Kaushanskaya and Marian (2009a) demonstrated that early

English–Spanish bilinguals outperformed monolinguals in learning phonologically unfamiliar L2 words, and as mentioned above, their advantage was especially pronounced when words were trained bimodally.

In addition, the advantage of bilinguals over monolinguals in learning phonologically unfamiliar novel words may be the result of increased executive function abilities for bilinguals over monolinguals (for a review, see Chapter 25 in this handbook; Bialystok, Craik, & Luk, 2012), or some other domain-general difference between the groups. As mentioned, Kaushanskaya (2012) examined learning of phonologically familiar and unfamiliar novel words by bilinguals and monolinguals, taking into account potential differences in phonological short-term memory. She reasoned that if the bilingual advantage in word learning is tied to their superior phonological short-term memory, then the bilingual advantage should be stronger for phonologically unfamiliar words, for which the learner cannot rely as much on stored long-term phonological representations. The results revealed, however, that the bilingual advantage was comparable in learning both phonologically familiar and unfamiliar words. Furthermore, although bilinguals generally outperformed monolinguals on phonological short-term memory tasks (digit span and nonword repetition tasks), this difference alone could not explain the bilingual advantage because bilinguals learned better than a subset of monolinguals who were matched to them on these phonological-short-term memory measures. Thus, although efficient phonological abilities on the part of bilingual speakers may contribute to their advantage, there likely exist other sources for the bilingual advantage in word learning.

An alternative, though not mutually exclusive, explanation for the bilingual advantage in word learning is rooted in meaning rather than form-related processes. Specifically, Kaushanskaya and Rechtzigel (2012) showed that the bilingual advantage in word learning depends on the concreteness level of the to-be-learned words. When asked to learn phonologically familiar novel words, English–Spanish bilinguals produced more correct responses on an L2 to L1 production test compared to monolingual English speakers, but only when the new words referred to concrete concepts. Learning new labels for abstract concepts did not vary across the two language background groups. This semantic modulation of the bilingual advantage led the authors to suggest that the advantage stems from more resonance and co-activation within the bilingual semantic lexicon.

Processing differences, rather than learning differences, may also contribute to the bilingual advantage in word learning. In an eye and mouse tracking experiment, Bartolotti and Marian (2012) showed that bilinguals are better than monolinguals at managing cross-language interference, and suggested that this ability contributes to the bilingual advantage in retrieving newly acquired words. Participants learned a set of novel words to criterion, and were later tested on their ability to retrieve the meanings of these items using a visual-world paradigm. Upon hearing the new word, they were to decide if one of two objects presented on the screen matched the item's meaning. On critical trials, one of these objects was a distractor whose English name overlapped phonologically with the newly acquired item. Bilinguals were better than monolinguals at managing this cross-language interference in that their eye movements and mouse trajectories were less influenced by the presence of the distractor, despite comparable performance during the learning phase. Similarly, Bogulski and Kroll (in preparation) showed that the bilingual advantage in word learning is restricted to bilinguals who are learning the foreign language via their L1, and suggested that the bilingual advantage in word learning is linked to increased inhibitory abilities.

To summarize, there is growing evidence to suggest that bilingual speakers outperform monolinguals in word learning (Bartolotti & Marian, 2012; Bogulski & Kroll, in preparation; Kaushanskaya, 2012; Kaushanskaya & Marian, 2009a, 2009b; Kaushanskaya & Rechtzigel, 2012; Kaushanskaya et al., 2013; van Hell & Candia Mahn, 1997). This advantage could not be explained solely on the basis of direct experience with similar learning situations (i.e., their experience with classroom word learning, Kaushanskaya & Marian, 2009a, 2009b). Instead, it appears that other factors that differentiate bilingual from monolingual speakers contribute to the finding. Superior phonological short-term memory is insufficient to explain the effect (Kaushanskaya, 2012), and more complex factors need to be explored. Reliance on meaning (Kaushanskaya & Rechtzigel, 2012), experience with mapping competing phonology onto known orthography (Kaushanskaya & Marian, 2009a), superior inhibition ability (Bogulski & Kroll), and superior managing of cross-language interference during retrieval (Bartolotti & Marian, 2012) have been suggested to date. Future studies are needed to shed light on the mechanism(s) of this fascinating bilingual advantage.

## 9.6 Insights gained and considerations for future studies

Up to now, we have described the instructional/training, stimulus, and learner factors that may influence vocabulary learning. In addition to the insights gained from reviewing these issues, several broader themes emerge that should be considered in future research.

### 9.6.1 Testing ongoing vs. naïve learners

One important issue is the extent to which findings from laboratory studies obtained with naïve learners (who were not studying the language prior to the experiment) can be generalized to ongoing learners of a language. Some advantages of conducting laboratory studies are that there is a larger amount of experimental control over the manipulated variables and that more sensitive measures can be used (e.g., reaction time measures that are harder to get reliably with non-specialized equipment, event-related brain potentials, eye-tracking measures, etc.). However, some studies take a combined approach and conduct lab experiments with classroom learners (e.g., Liu, Perfetti, & Wang, 2006). This method has the advantages of a lab study, with the characteristics of ongoing learners. What is lost is that the starting point of the learners likely varies and is a bit more difficult to assess.

We suggest that it is useful to think of naïve learners who participate in laboratory studies and ongoing language learners as falling along a continuum of several dimensions, such as prior knowledge of the language, time to consolidate and practice, and potentially (though not necessarily) motivation. There is no reason to assume that these two populations are two distinct classes of learners, because basic memory and learning mechanisms in operation should be similar in all learners (see comparisons between ongoing and naïve learners in Dunlosky et al., 2013; but see Neisser's, 1984, arguments about learner schemas). Instead, it is useful to consider the generalizability of findings obtained from a specific context to other learning contexts, while taking into account the variability in learners' characteristics. The literature on paired associate learning (within L1) or other L1 training (e.g., of rare vocabulary; Balass, Nelson, & Perfetti, 2010; Nelson, Balass, & Perfetti, 2005), can be useful in assessing effectiveness for learners with more advanced knowledge.

We propose that the best path forward is to use a three-step sequence, in which researchers first try a training manipulation in a controlled environment with naïve learners, then try the same manipulation with ongoing learners (with necessary adjustments for differences in proficiency), and then try the manipulation in an actual classroom or other (e.g., online) learning environment. Such convergence is useful in highlighting the factors that are highly useful for vocabulary learning (Dunlosky et al., 2013). Even when instructional method and stimulus characteristics are held constant, it is critical to take into account throughout the entire process, learners' memory capacity (especially when phonology of the to-be-learned language differs from that of the L1), multilingualism and experience in L2 learning, and prior knowledge of the to-be-learned language.

A related issue is that the studies we reviewed varied in whether they used a natural or artificial language. The advantages for using an artificial language are that learners will definitely have no prior exposure to the target items, and that the stimuli can be manipulated along some important dimensions more easily (e.g., cognate overlap). However, it is unclear how learners treat these artificial words. Specifically, we do not know whether they treat them as new L1 labels for existing concepts (e.g., synonyms) or instead like new labels in a new language. Note that even adults resist learning new labels to existing concepts ("mutual exclusivity"; e.g., Au & Glusman, 1990; Davidson & Tell, 2005; Degani & Tokowicz, 2010a), although this mechanism appears to operate more strongly in monolinguals than bilinguals (Davidson & Tell, 2005). Thus, although there is no a priori reason to assume that using a natural vs. artificial language will affect the learning process, to our knowledge, this has yet to be demonstrated empirically.

### 9.6.2 Testing following a delay

We also note that a variety of recent studies emphasize the importance of testing learners following a delay of several days. In particular, research has shown that words become integrated into the lexicon following sleep (e.g., Dumay & Gaskell, 2007), allowing competition between representations to emerge (see also Gaskell & Dumay, 2003, but see Lindsay & Gaskell, 2013, for evidence that sleep is not necessary for integration to occur). In one study, sleep was directly shown to improve retention of German vocabulary by native English-speaking high school students, especially when sleep followed closely after learning (Gais, Lucas, & Born, 2006). Therefore, when testing learners after training, a delay should be implemented.

### 9.6.3 Building strong form-to-meaning connections

Returning to one of the key aspects of directed vocabulary instruction – namely, to help the learner build strong connections between the new vocabulary words and their meanings – we note that different instructional methods can influence not only the effectiveness of forming these representations and connections, but also the nature of these representations. For example, some methods may more strongly encourage meaning activation during training (e.g., picture training, generation, keyword mnemonic, thematic organization), whereas others, such as word-translation training may encourage more of a form-related focus. Thus, it is important that the goal of learning be kept in mind and that tests appropriate to the goal be used. For example, some tests focus on recognition rather than recall of material, and even within the set of recall tasks, some are thought to more reliably assess semantic processing (e.g., categorization manipulations in Kroll & Stewart, 1994). It is also critical to keep in mind that what leads to the most effective learning initially may not lead to the most effective retention longer term (Schmidt & Bjork, 1992), and therefore appropriate delayed tests should be used.

## 9.7 Conclusions

In summary, we have provided a selective overview of some of the key findings of laboratory experiments on foreign language vocabulary learning. Some of the effective training methods we reviewed are spacing, practice testing, thematic grouping, and generation. Some of these methods are more difficult than others to implement with ongoing learners. We also note that it is important to pay attention to learner characteristics because such factors can interact with learner and stimulus characteristics (see van Hell & Candia Mahn, 1997, for interactions of instruction method and learner characteristics; Kaushanskaya & Yoo, 2011, for interactions of instruction method and stimulus characteristics; Kaushanskaya & Rechtzigel, 2012, for interactions of stimulus and learner characteristics).

Finally, we refer the interested reader to several useful reviews. In particular, de Groot (2012) contrasts vocabulary learning in monolingual and bilingual children, and in de Groot (2011: ch. 3), the researcher summarizes much of the recent research on foreign language vocabulary learning, emphasizing the keyword method, learning in context, and methods of assessing vocabulary knowledge. Dunlosky et al. (2013) present a summary of several learning techniques, emphasizing generalization to ongoing learners and whether the methods are of high value. And, Pashler et al. (2007) similarly make recommendations based on relevant research for organizing instruction and study to improve student learning. The goal of these reviews and others like them is to encourage the use of attested training methods with ongoing learners to improve learning and retention.

# 10

# Second language constructions

Usage-based acquisition and transfer

Nick Ellis, Ute Römer, and Matthew O'Donnell

## 10.1 Constructing a second language

Cognitive linguistic theories of construction grammar posit that language comprises many thousands of constructions – form–meaning mappings, conventionalized in the speech community, and entrenched as language knowledge in the learner's mind (Goldberg, 1995; Robinson & Ellis, 2008a; Trousdale & Hoffmann, 2013). Usage-based approaches to language acquisition hold that schematic constructions emerge as prototypes from the conspiracy of memories of particular exemplars that language users have experienced. This chapter investigates second language (L2) processing of abstract verb–argument constructions (VACs) and its sensitivity to the statistics of usage in terms of verb exemplar type-token frequency distribution, VAC–verb contingency, and VAC–verb semantic prototypicality.

Second language and first language (L1) learners alike share the goal of understanding language and how it works. Since they achieve this based upon their experience of language usage, there are many commonalities between L1 and L2 acquisition (L2A) that can be understood from corpus analyses of input and from cognitive–linguistic and psycholinguistic analyses of construction acquisition following associative and cognitive principles of learning and categorization. Usage-based approaches, cognitive linguistics, and corpus linguistics are thus increasingly influential in L2A research too (Collins & Ellis, 2009; Ellis, 1998, 2003; Ellis & Cadierno, 2009; Robinson & Ellis, 2008a). However, because they have previously devoted considerable resources to the estimation of the characteristics of another language – the native tongue in which they have considerable fluency – L2 learners' computations and inductions are often affected by transfer, with L1-tuned expectations and selective attention (Ellis, 2006b; Ellis & Sagarra, 2011) blinding the acquisition system to aspects of the L2 sample. Learned attention biases their estimation from naturalistic usage and produces a distinctive attainment that is characteristic of L2A from speakers of different L1s (Ellis, 2007; Ellis & Sagarra, 2011). L2A is thus different from L1A in that it involves processes of construction and *re*construction. These are the issues explored here.

The organization of the chapter is as follows. Section 10.2 presents a psychological analysis of the effects of form, function, frequency, and contingency that are common to both L1 and L2 construction learning following statistical learning processes which relate input and learner cognition. Section 10.3 analyzes these factors in the statistics of a representative sample of VAC usage – the British National Corpus, a 100-million-word corpus of English (BNC, 2007). Section 10.4 tests the psycholinguistic reality of VACs in terms of the effects of VAC form, function, and contingency on the processing of VACs by native speakers of English. Respondents generated the first verb that came to mind that would fill the V slot in sparse VAC frames such as 'he __ across the ...,' 'it __ of the ...,' etc. For each VAC, we compared the results from such experiments with the corpus analyses of verb selection preferences described in section 10.3 to show independent contributions of (1) verb frequency in the VAC, (2) VAC–verb contingency, and (3) verb prototypicality in terms of centrality within the VAC semantic network. The fact that native-speaker VACs implicitly represent the statistics of language usage implies that they are learned from usage. Section 10.5 investigates the nature of these constructions in German, Spanish, and Czech advanced learners of English as a second language. When participants from these first-language backgrounds performed the same tasks, their responses were again sensitive to type-token frequency distribution, VAC–verb contingency, and semantic structure, confirming that they too acquired these constructions from English usage. Section 10.6 shows, however, that there are differences in the representation of these VACs in L2 speakers that result from L1 → L2 transfer or "learned attention." These were particularly apparent in L1 speakers of typologically distinct verb-framed Spanish as opposed to German and Czech which, like English, are satellite framed. It considers how learned attention affects learners' sensitivity to different aspects of the linguistic form of constructions.

## 10.2 Form, function, and frequency in L1 and L2 learning of constructions

Our experience of language allows us to converge upon similar interpretations of novel utterances like "the ball mandools across the ground" and "the teacher spugged the boy the book." You know that *mandool* is a verb of motion and have some idea of how mandooling works – its action semantics. You know that *spugging* involves some sort of gifting, that the teacher is the donor, the boy the recipient, and that the book is the transferred object. How is this possible, given that you have never heard these verbs before? There is a close relationship between the types of verb that typically appear within constructions, hence their meaning as a whole is inducible from the lexical items experienced within them. So your reading of "the ball mandools across the ground" is driven by an abstract 'V *across* noun' VAC which has inherited its schematic meaning from all of the relevant examples you have heard, and your interpretation of *mandool* emerges from the echoes of the verbs that occupy this VAC – words like *come, walk, move, . . ., scud, skitter,* and *flit*.

The specific claim under test in this chapter is that a VAC inherits its schematic meaning from the constituency of all of the verb exemplars experienced within it, weighted according to the frequency of their experience and the reliability of their association to that construction (their contingency), and their degree of prototypicality in the semantics of the VAC.

### 10.2.1 Frequency

Psycholinguistic research demonstrates language processing to be sensitive to usage frequency across many language representations: phonology and phonotactics, reading, spelling, lexis, morphosyntax, formulaic language, language comprehension, grammaticality, sentence production, and syntax (Ellis, 2002). That language users are sensitive to the input frequencies of constructions entails that they must have registered their occurrence in processing, and these frequency effects are thus compelling evidence for usage-based models of language acquisition. Is there evidence that language users have knowledge of the verb type-token distributions within VACs? Goldberg et al. (2004) showed that the verb types which children used in a VAC broadly follow the same relative frequencies as the verb types they experienced in their input. Ellis and Ferreira-Junior (2009b) investigated effects upon naturalistic second language acquisition of type-token distributions in the islands comprising the linguistic form of three schematic English VACs (VL verb locative, VOL verb object locative, VOO ditransitive) sampled from approximately 25,000 sentences of interaction between native English and adult non-native speakers in the European Science Foundation (ESF) corpus (Dietrich, Klein, & Noyau, 1995; Perdue, 1993). They showed that (1) the frequency profile of the verbs in each family follows a Zipfian profile (Zipf, 1935) whereby the highest frequency types account for the most linguistic tokens. Zipf's law states that in human language, the frequency of words decreases as a power function of their rank. They also showed that (2) learners first acquire the most frequent, prototypical and generic exemplar (e.g., *put* in VOL, *give* in VOO, etc.), and that (3) the rank order of verb types in the learner constructions was very similar to that in native-speaker usage: for the VL construction, frequency of lemma use by learner was correlated with the frequency of lemma use in comparable native language input ($r = 0.97$); for VOL the correlation was 0.89, for VOO 0.93.

### 10.2.2 Contingency

Psychological research into associative learning has long recognized that while input frequency is important, more so is contingency of mapping. Consider how, in the learning of the category of birds, while eyes and wings are equally frequently experienced features in the exemplars, it is wings which are distinctive in differentiating birds from other animals. Wings are important features to learning the category of birds because they are reliably associated with class membership, eyes are neither. Some verbs are closely tied to a particular VAC (for example, *give* is highly indicative of the ditransitive construction, whereas *leave*, although it can form a ditransitive, is more often associated with other constructions such as the simple transitive or intransitive). The higher the contingency between a cue and an outcome, the more readily an association between them can be learned (Shanks, 1995), so constructions with more faithful verb members are more transparent and thus should be more readily acquired (Ellis, 2006a). In their study of L2 acquisition, Ellis and Ferreira-Junior (2009b) used a variety of metrics to show that VAC acquisition is determined by the contingency of form–function mapping: the one-way dependency statistic ΔP (Allan, 1980) that is commonly used in the associative learning literature (Shanks, 1995), as well as collostructional analysis measures current in corpus linguistics (Gries & Stefanowitsch, 2004; Stefanowitsch & Gries, 2003), both predicted effects of form–function contingency upon L2 VAC acquisition.

### 10.2.3 Prototypicality of meaning

Categories have graded structure, with some members being better exemplars than others. In the prototype theory of concepts (Rosch et al., 1976; Rosch & Mervis, 1975b), the prototype as an idealized central description is the best example of the category, appropriately summarizing the most representative attributes of a category. As the typical instance of a category, it serves as the benchmark against which surrounding, less representative instances are classified – people more quickly classify as *birds* sparrows (or other average sized, average colored, average beaked, average featured specimens) than they do birds with less common features or feature combinations like geese or albatrosses. Prototypes are judged faster and more accurately, even if they themselves have never been seen before – someone who has never seen a sparrow, yet who has experienced the rest of the run of the avian mill, will still be fast and accurate in judging it to be a bird

(Posner & Keele, 1970). The greater the token frequency of an exemplar, the more it contributes to defining the category, and the greater the likelihood it will be considered the prototype. The best way to teach a concept is to show an example of it. So the best way to introduce a category is to show a prototypical example. Ellis and Ferreira-Junior (2009a) show that the verbs that second language learners first used in particular VACs are prototypical and generic in function (*go* for VL, *put* for VOL, and *give* for VOO). The same has been shown for child language acquisition, where a small group of semantically general verbs, often referred to as *light verbs* (e.g., *go, do, make, come*) are learned early (Clark, 1978; Ninio, 1999; Pinker, 1989). Ninio argues that, because most of their semantics consist of some schematic notion of transitivity with the addition of a minimum specific element, they are semantically suitable, salient, and frequent; hence, learners start transitive word combinations with these generic verbs. Thereafter, as Clark describes, "many uses of these verbs are replaced, as children get older, by more specific terms. General purpose verbs, of course, continue to be used but become proportionately less frequent as children acquire more words for specific categories of actions" (p. 53).

If these are the factors in learners' experience of language usage that drive the emergence of schematic VACs, then the first step is to assess these factors in VAC usage. The second is to demonstrate their effects on VAC processing. We do this, like Rosch and Mervis (1975b), by simply asking respondents to generate exemplars of categories, in this case the verbs that come to mind when they see schematic VAC frames such as 'he __ across the . . .,' 'it __ of the . . .,' etc.

## 10.3 Analyzing the statistics of VAC usage

Ellis and O'Donnell (2011, 2012) investigated the type-token distributions of twenty VACs such as 'V(erb) *across* n(oun phrase)' in a 100-million-word corpus of English usage. The other prepositions sampled were *about, after, against, among, around, as, at, between, for, in, into, like, of, off, over, through, towards, under*, and *with*.

They searched a dependency-parsed version of the British National Corpus (BNC, 2007) for specific VACs previously identified in the Grammar Patterns volume resulting from the Collins Birmingham University International Language (COBUILD) corpus-based dictionary project (Francis, Hunston, & Manning, 1996). The details of the linguistic analyses, as well as subsequently modified search specifications in order to improve precision and recall, are described in Römer, O'Donnell, and Ellis (2013). The steps were, for each VAC, such as the pattern 'V *across* n':

1. Generate a list of verb types that occupy each construction (e.g., *come, walk, run, ..., scud*).
2. Produce a frequency ranked type-token profile for these verbs (e.g., *come* 628, *walk* ... 243, ... *spread* 96, ... *scurry* 13, ... *float* 9, ...), and determine whether this is Zipfian. Zipfian distributions exhibit a characteristic long tail in a plot of rank against frequency. Zipf's law, like other power–law distributions, is most easily observed when plotted on doubly logarithmic axes, where the relationship between log (rank order) and log (frequency) is linear. The advised method to do this is via the (complementary) cumulative distribution (Adamic, 2002; Adamic & Huberman, 2002). We generated logarithmic plots and linear regressions to examine the extent of this trend using logarithmic binning of frequency against log cumulative frequency. The binning allows us to select and illustrate an example verb type from each frequency band. Illustrative plots for 'V *across* n' and for 'V *of* n' can be seen in Figure 10.1.
3. Because some verbs are faithful to one construction while others are more promiscuous, calculate measures of contingency which reflect the statistical association between verb and VAC. We adopted various measures of contingency in usage, including ΔP (Ellis & Ferreira-Junior, 2009b): the association of *give* to the ditransitive (ΔP Word → Construction) is 0.025, that for *leave* is 0.001, the association of the ditransitive to *give* (ΔP Construction → Word) is *give* 0.314, that for *leave* is 0.003.

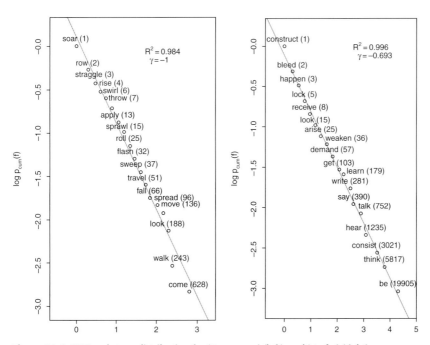

**Figure 10.1** BNC verb type distribution for 'V *across* n' (left) and 'V *of* n' (right)

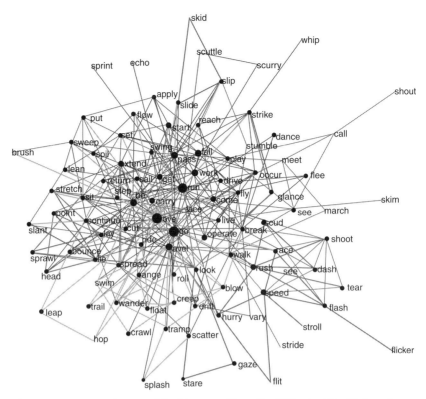

**Figure 10.2** A semantic network for 'V *across* n' from the BNC using WordNet as a base. Node size is proportional to degree

4. Using WordNet, a distribution-free semantic database based upon psycholinguistic theory which has been in development since 1985 (Miller, 2009), measure the semantic similarity of the meanings of the verbs occupying each construction and apply networks science, graph-based algorithms (de Nooy, Mrvar, & Batagelj, 2010) to build semantic networks in which the nodes represent verb types and the edges of strong semantic similarity for each VAC. Standard measures of network density, average clustering, degree centrality, transitivity, etc. are then used to assess the cohesion of these semantic networks. We also apply algorithms for the detection of communities within the networks representing different semantic sets (Clauset, Newman, & Moore, 2004; Danon et al., 2005). The network for 'V *across* n' is shown as an example in Figure 10.2. The network is fairly dense. The hubs, shown here as larger nodes, are those that are most connected, i.e., have the highest degree. They are *go, move, run*, and *travel* – the prototypical 'V *across* n' senses. However, there are also subcommunities, for example one relating to vision including *look, stare, gaze, face*, another speeded movement: *run, shoot, scud, race, rush*, etc., and another emphasizing flat contact: *lay, lie, sprawl*, etc. Note that both degree and

centrality in the network are unrelated to token frequency in the corpus; they simply reflect verb type connectivity within the network. Betweenness centrality is a measure of a node's centrality in a network equal to the number of shortest paths from all vertices to all others that pass through that node (McDonough & De Vleeschauwer, 2012). In semantic networks, central nodes are those which are prototypical of the network as a whole.

This research demonstrated: (1) The frequency distribution for the types occupying the verb island of each VAC is Zipfian, with the most frequent verb taking the lion's share of the distribution. (2) The most frequent verb in each VAC is prototypical of that construction's functional interpretation, albeit generic in its action semantics. (3) VACs are selective in their verb form family occupancy: individual verbs select particular constructions; particular constructions select particular verbs; there is high contingency between verb types and constructions. (4) VACs are coherent in their semantics. Psychology theory relating to the statistical learning of categories suggests that these are the factors which make concepts robustly learnable. Ellis and O'Donnell (2011, 2012) conclude, therefore, that these are the mechanisms which make linguistic constructions robustly learnable too, and that they are learned by similar means.

## 10.4 L1 sensitivity to VAC structure

Ellis, O'Donnell, and Römer (2014a) used free association and verbal fluency tasks to investigate verb–argument constructions (VACs) and the ways in which their processing is sensitive to statistical patterns of usage (verb type-token frequency distribution, VAC–verb contingency, VAC–verb semantic prototypicality). In one experiment (Experiment 1), 285 native speakers of English (mostly students enrolled at a large mid-western research university) generated the first word that came to mind to fill the V slot in 40 sparse VAC frames such as 'he __ across the . . .,' 'it __ of the . . .,' etc. In a second experiment (Experiment 2), 40 English speakers generated as many verbs that fit each frame as they could think of in a minute. For each VAC, we compared the results from the experiments with the corpus analyses of verb selection preferences in 100 million words of usage and with the semantic network structure of the verbs in these VACs as described in section 10.3.

For illustration of the kind of responses generated, we plot the lemmatized verb types for each VAC generated in Experiment 1 in the space defined by log token generation frequency against log token frequency in that VAC in the BNC. The plot for 'V *of* n' is shown in Figure 10.3 for detailed study. Items appear on the graph if the lemma

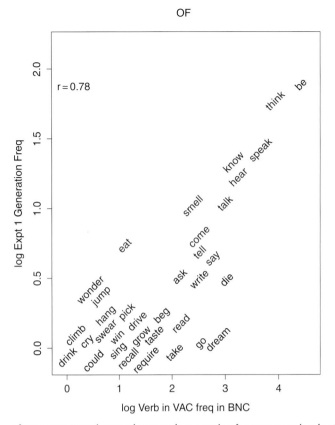

**Figure 10.3** Experiment 1 log10 verb generation frequency against log10 verb frequency in that VAC in the BNC for 'V of n'.

both appears as a response in the generation task for that VAC and it also appears in the BNC. It can be seen that generation frequency follows verb frequency in that VAC in the BNC with a correlation of $r = 0.78$. After the copula *be*, cognition verbs (*think* and *know*) are the most frequent types, followed by communication verbs (*speak, say, talk, ask*), and also perception verbs (*smell, hear*). Thus the semantic sets of the VAC frame in usage (of the sort shown in Figure 10.2) are all sampled in the free association task, and the sampling follows the frequencies of usage.

For both experiments, the frequencies of verb types generated for each VAC were affected by three factors:

1. Entrenchment – verb token frequencies in those VACs in usage experience.
2. Contingency – how faithful verbs are to particular VACs in usage experience.

3. Semantic prototypicality – the centrality of the verb meaning in the semantic network of the VAC in usage experience.

Multiple regression analyses showed that these factors make significant independent contributions. For example, the analysis of the Experiment 1 ('first word that came to mind') responses, including cases where the verb appeared in the generations for that VAC and in the BNC in that VAC, explained 30 percent of the variance of the responses, with relative importance determination showing that the major predictor was ΔPconstruction →word (0.45) followed by BNC verb frequency in that VAC (0.29), followed by verb betweenness centrality in the semantic network for VAC usage in the BNC (0.26). How might these factors affect processing in the generation fluency task?

1. Effects of frequency of usage upon language learning, entrenchment, and subsequent fluency of linguistic processing are well documented and understood in terms of Hebbian learning (Bybee, 2010; Bybee & Hopper, 2001; Ellis, 2002; MacWhinney, 2001).
2. Effects of contingency of association are also standard fare in the psychology of learning (Rescorla & Wagner, 1972; Shanks, 1995), in the psychology of language learning (Ellis, 2006a, 2006b; MacWhinney, 1987a; MacWhinney, Bates, & Kliegl, 1984), and in the particular case of English VAC acquisition (Ellis & Ferreira-Junior, 2009a, 2009b; Ellis & Larsen-Freeman, 2009) and of German L2 English learners' verb-specific knowledge of VACs as demonstrated in priming experiments (Gries & Wulff, 2005, 2009).
3. We interpret the effects of semantic prototypicality in terms of the spreading activation theory of semantic memory (Anderson, 1983). The prototype has two advantages: The first is a frequency factor. We have already described how in usage, the greater the token frequency of an exemplar, the more it contributes to defining the category, and the greater the likelihood it will be considered the prototype (Rosch et al., 1976; Rosch & Mervis, 1975b). Thus it is the response that is most associated with the VAC in its own right. But beyond that, it gets the network centrality advantage. When any response is made, it spreads activation and reminds other members in the set. The prototype is most connected at the center of the network and, like Rome, all roads lead to it. Thus it receives the most spreading activation. Likewise in social networks, individuals with high betweenness centrality are key agents in navigating the network – they mediate communication between most other individuals.

These findings promote a usage-based view of L1A, with L1 VAC processing involving rich associations, tuned by verb type and token frequencies and their contingencies of usage, which interface syntax, lexis, and semantics.

## 10.5 Similarities: L2 speakers' sensitivity to the statistics of usage

What about L2A? Ellis, O'Donnell, and Römer (2014b) investigated how similar or different the mental representations of common VACs are between native speakers and learners of English and whether there are observable effects of the learners' first language. They had 131 advanced English language learners of three different first language backgrounds (German, Czech, and Spanish) complete the same type of free association task as in Experiment 1 described in section 10.4. The L1 German, L1 Czech, and L1 Spanish learners were students enrolled at research universities in Germany, the Czech Republic, and Spain. The mean number of years of English instruction was 10.04 years for German, 11.37 for Czech, and 12.68 for Spanish. The responses made by these groups of L2 learners were compared with each other and with those of a random subset of 131 L1 English speakers from Experiment 1. Illustrative plots of the responses for the VACs 'V *about* n,' 'V *between* n,' and 'V *against* n' against frequencies of the verbs in that VAC in the BNC are shown in Figures 10.4, 10.5, and 10.6 where it can be seen that the advanced L2 English speakers generated a similar set of verb types for these VACs with similar token frequencies.

As with the native speaker data, in order to assess the degree to which these patterns hold across the VACs and the degree to which each causal variable makes an independent contribution, for each L1 we stacked the generation data for the different VACs into a combined dataset, including cases where the verb appeared in the generations for that VAC and in the BNC in that VAC. We then used this dataset to perform a multiple regression of generation frequency against BNC verb frequency in that VAC, ΔPcw, and verb betweenness centrality in that VAC usage in the BNC. All three independent variables were entered into the regression. The resultant coefficients are summarized in Table 10.1, showing the results for each L2 against those for English L1 participants.

Recall that for the 285 English L1 responses, the multiple regression explained 30 percent of the variance, with the relative importance of the predictors being ΔPcw (0.45), BNC verb frequency in that VAC (0.29), verb betweenness centrality in the semantic network for VAC usage in the BNC (0.26). The data here for the random 131 English subset showed a very similar pattern: $R^2$=31 percent, relative importances ΔPcw (0.40), BNC verb in VAC frequency (0.29), verb betweenness centrality (0.31) with each of these factors making significant independent contributions. Table 10.1 shows that the L2 data pattern in a very similar fashion. For each language, each of the three independent variables make significant independent contributions.

**Table 10.1** *Multiple regression summary statistics for the analyses of 131 L1 English respondents and 131 German, Spanish, and Czech L2 English respondents*

| | | b | | | Relative importance | | |
|---|---|---|---|---|---|---|---|
| Group | R sq | Frequency | Contingency | Prototypicality | Frequency | Contingency | Prototypicality |
| English | 0.31 | .07** | 0.39*** | 0.30*** | 0.29 | 0.40 | 0.31 |
| German | 0.34 | .06** | 0.48*** | 0.29*** | 0.28 | 0.47 | 0.25 |
| Spanish | 0.44 | .06** | 0.60*** | 0.23*** | 0.29 | 0.53 | 0.17 |
| Czech | 0.33 | .08** | 0.54*** | 0.17*** | 0.31 | 0.56 | 0.14 |

Significance levels: *** < .0001
                ** < 0.001
                * < 0.05

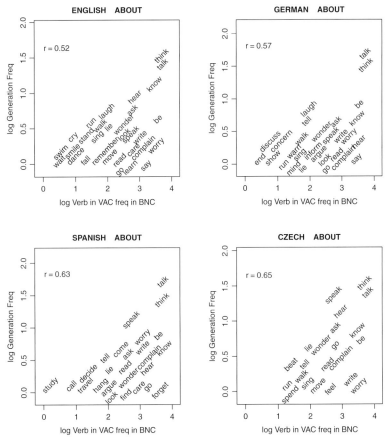

**Figure 10.4** L1 English and German, Spanish and Czech L2 English log10 verb generation frequency against log10 verb frequency in that VAC in the BNC for VACs 'V about n'.

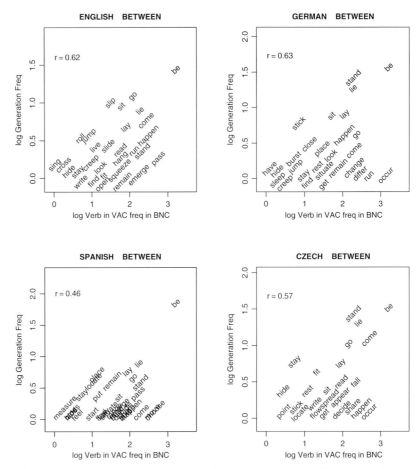

**Figure 10.5** L1 English and German, Spanish and Czech L2 English log10 verb generation frequency against log10 verb frequency in that VAC in the BNC for VACs 'V between n'.

Thus we conclude that for L1 speakers and advanced L2 speakers alike, the frequencies of verb types generated for VACs is affected by three factors:

1. Entrenchment – verb token frequencies in those VACs in usage experience.
2. Contingency – how faithful verbs are to particular VACs in usage experience.
3. Semantic prototypicality – the centrality of the verb meaning in the semantic network of the VAC in usage experience.

We take this as evidence for common processes of construction learning from usage in L1A and L2A.

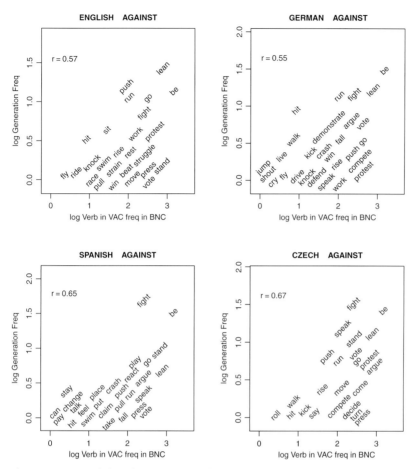

**Figure 10.6** L1 English and German, Spanish and Czech L2 English log10 verb generation frequency against log10 verb frequency in that VAC in the BNC for VACs 'V *against* n'.

## 10.6 Differences: L1 transfer effects upon L2 speakers' VAC usage

Cognitive linguistics (Croft & Cruise, 2004; Langacker, 1987, 2000; Robinson & Ellis, 2008a; Taylor, 2002) provides detailed qualitative analyses of the ways in which language is grounded in our experience and our physical embodiment which represents the world in a very particular way. Constructions are conventionalized linguistic means for presenting different interpretations or construals of an event. They structure concepts and direct attention to aspects of experience through the options specific languages make available to speakers (Talmy, 2000a, 2000b). The different degrees of salience or prominence of elements involved in situations that we wish to describe affect the selection of subject, object, adverbials, and other clause arrangements. In language comprehension, abstract linguistic constructions (like simple locatives, datives, and passives) serve as a "zoom lens" for the listener, guiding their attention to a particular perspective on a scene while backgrounding other aspects (Croft, 2001; Croft & Cruise, 2004; Langacker, 1987, 1999; Taylor, 2002). Language has an extensive system that assigns different degrees of salience to the parts of an expression, reference, or context. Talmy (2000a, 2000b) analyses how the Attentional System of Language includes some fifty basic factors, its "building blocks." Each factor involves a particular linguistic mechanism that increases or decreases attention on a certain type of linguistic entity. Learning a language involves the learning of these various attention-directing mechanisms of language, and this, in turn, rests upon L1 learners' developing attentional systems and L2 learners' attentional biases.

Languages lead their speakers to experience different 'thinking for speaking' and thus to construe experience in different ways (Slobin, 1996). Cross-linguistic research shows how different languages lead speakers to prioritize different aspects of events in narrative discourse (Berman & Slobin, 1994). Because languages achieve these attention-directing outcomes in different ways, learning another language involves learning how to construe the world like natives of the L2, i.e., learning alternative ways of thinking for speaking (Brown & Gullberg, 2008, 2010; Cadierno, 2008) or learning to 'rethink for speaking' (Robinson & Ellis, 2008b). Transfer theories such as the Contrastive Analysis Hypothesis (Gass & Selinker, 1983; James, 1980; Lado, 1957, 1964) hold that L2 learning can be easier where languages use these attention-directing devices in the same way, and more difficult when they use them differently. To the extent that the constructions in L2 are similar to those of L1, L1 constructions can serve as the basis for the L2 constructions, but, because even similar constructions across languages differ in detail, the acquisition of the L2 pattern in all its detail is hindered by the L1 pattern (Cadierno, 2008; Odlin, 1989, 2008; Robinson & Ellis, 2008a).

There is good reason to expect that there will be L1 effects upon VAC acquisition. Languages differ in the ways in which verb phrases express motion events. According to Talmy (2000),

> The world's languages generally seem to divide into a two-category typology on the basis of the characteristic pattern in which the conceptual structure of the macro-event is mapped onto syntactic structure. To characterize it initially in broad strokes, the typology consists of whether the core schema is expressed by the main verb or by the satellite. (p. 221)

The "core schema" here refers to the "framing event," i.e., the expression of the path of motion. Talmy (2000) goes on to say that "[l]anguages that characteristically map the core schema into the verb will be said to have a **framing verb** and to be **verb-framed** languages" and that "languages that characteristically map the core schema onto the satellite will be said to have a **framing satellite** and to be **satellite-framed** languages"

(p. 222; emphasis in original). Included in the former group are Romance and Semitic languages, Japanese, and Tamil. Languages in the latter group include Germanic, Slavic, and Finno-Ugric languages, and Chinese. This means that a Germanic language such as English often uses a combination of verb plus particle (*go into, jump over*) where a Romance language like Spanish uses a single form (*entrar, saltar*).

While verb-framed languages express the path of motion in the main verb and are "path-incorporating" (Talmy, 1985) or "path-type" languages (Mani & Pustejovski, 2012), satellite-framed languages are "manner-incorporating" or "manner-type" languages in which manner is expressed in the main verb (e.g., English *run, stroll*). According to Slobin (2003: 162), "English speakers get manner for free." They commonly use manner verbs in the expression of motion events and have more lexical items available to do so than speakers of satellite-framed languages like Spanish. The Spanish motion verb *saltar*, for example, has a range of English translation equivalents including *jump* (*over, up*), *leap, climb, skip, spurt*, and *hop*. Manner of motion is a "highly saturated" semantic space in satellite-framed languages (Slobin, 2003: 163). In verb-framed languages, manner of motion is less commonly expressed. It is "an adjunct – an optional addition to a clause that is already complete" (Slobin, 2003: 162), such as a participial form (e.g., Spanish *entró corriendo*, "enter running"). We therefore assume "manner of motion" to be a less entrenched, less salient concept in the minds of speakers whose L1 is verb framed. The concept is less easily codable and requires additional effort to express.

Römer, O'Donnell, and Ellis (2014) therefore expected to find speakers of satellite-framed languages (here English, German, and Czech)[1] to produce more verbs that express specific manners of motion in the verb generation tasks. Conversely, we expected speakers of a verb-framed language (here Spanish) to produce specific manner of motion verbs less frequently and instead respond with more general motion verbs such as *go, come*, or *move*. All groups of speakers were asked to produce verbs in response to VAC frames that encode a path of motion, with the path expressed by a satellite (a particle or preposition). We therefore also expected that learners whose L1 is satellite-framed (and hence typologically similar to English) might find it easier to respond to the survey prompts and produce more target-like verbs (verbs that correlate more closely with those produced by L1 English speakers) than speakers whose L1 is verb framed.

---

[1] Whereas Slavic languages are generally considered satellite framed (Slobin, 2003, 2006), Gehrke (2008) cautions that Czech is "neither straightforwardly verb-framed nor straightforwardly satellite-framed" (p. 203) and that, while motion and manner are included in the verb (as is typically the case for a satellite-framed language), paths of motion may be mapped onto the verb and/or a directional preposition. To give one example, Czech offers three ways of expressing jump over: *skočit přes* ('jump over'), *přeskočit přes* ('overjump over'), and *přeskočit* ('overjump'). Czech hence appears to be a less prototypical satellite-framed language than English or German.

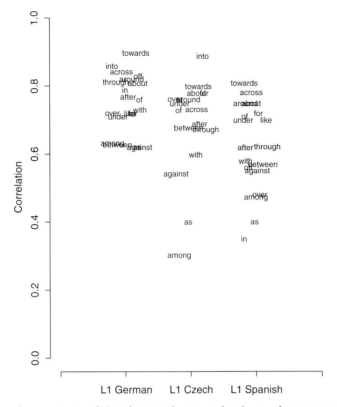

**Figure 10.7** Correlations between learner and native speaker response

In order to investigate these hypotheses, we compared lists based on the learner responses with lists based on English native speaker responses: L1 German vs. English, L1 Czech vs. English, and L1 Spanish vs. English. We plotted L2 responses against L1 responses (rather than BNC usage as in sections 10.4 and 10.5), and the effects of transfer became apparent in the residuals. Figure 10.7 provides a visual representation of these bilingual correlations for each VAC, with data points represented by prepositions. The possible range of values is 0 to 1. The closer the value is to 1, the stronger the correlation between the responses. Based on the language typology issues, our hypothesis is that Spanish learners will find it harder to produce verbs that correlate closely with those produced by native English speakers than German and Czech learners.

Across the 57 datasets (19 VACs times three learner groups), correlations range from 0.3 ('V *among* n,' L1 Czech) to 0.9 ('V *towards* n,' L1 German). As Figure 10.7 indicates, L1 German vs. English correlations are much more homogeneous across VACs (0.62 to 0.9) than L1 Spanish vs. English and (even more so) L1 Czech vs. English correlations (0.35 to 0.81 and 0.3 to 0.89 respectively). For L1 German, we also observe a higher average correlation of 0.75 than for L1 Czech (0.68) and L1 Spanish (0.62). Overall then, the

**Table 10.2** 'V in n,' top-20 verbs in native speaker and learner responses

| Rank | Native speakers | | German learners | | Czech learners | | Spanish learners | |
|---|---|---|---|---|---|---|---|---|
| 1  | BE    | 19 | BE          | 27 | BE          | 33 | BE      | 53 |
| 2  | SIT   | 15 | SIT         | 11 | LIVE        | 10 | LIVE    | 9  |
| 3  | JUMP  | 10 | LIVE        | 8  | STAND       | 7  | STAY    | 8  |
| 4  | WALK  | 8  | GO          | 8  | SIT         | 7  | PLAY    | 4  |
| 5  | GO    | 7  | WALK        | 8  | WAIT        | 6  | SLEEP   | 3  |
| 6  | LOOK  | 6  | HIDE        | 5  | WORK        | 5  | HIDE    | 3  |
| 7  | FALL  | 6  | STAND       | 5  | COME        | 5  | COME    | 3  |
| 8  | COME  | 4  | LOOK        | 4  | SLEEP       | 4  | STAND   | 3  |
| 9  | LIVE  | 4  | SLEEP       | 3  | STAY        | 4  | PUT     | 3  |
| 10 | SING  | 3  | COME        | 3  | PARTICIPATE | 3  | WORK    | 2  |
| 11 | RUN   | 3  | FALL        | 3  | FALL        | 3  | TRAVEL  | 2  |
| 12 | STAND | 3  | STAY        | 3  | LIE         | 3  | ENTER   | 2  |
| 13 | SWIM  | 3  | WORK        | 2  | LOOK        | 3  | ARRIVE  | 2  |
| 14 | HIDE  | 3  | PARTICIPATE | 2  | GO          | 3  | GET     | 2  |
| 15 | SLEEP | 3  | STUDY       | 2  | WALK        | 3  | FILL    | 2  |
| 16 | SLIDE | 2  | WAIT        | 2  | HIDE        | 2  | REMAIN  | 2  |
| 17 | DRAW  | 2  | BITE        | 2  | SWIM        | 2  | GO      | 2  |
| 18 | LIE   | 2  | SEARCH      | 2  | PUT         | 2  | EAT     | 2  |
| 19 | READ  | 2  | RUN         | 2  | JUMP        | 2  | INVOLVE | 1  |
| 20 | BLOW  | 2  | JUMP        | 2  | RELAX       | 1  | STUDY   | 1  |

German learner responses most closely and the Spanish learner responses least closely match the native speaker responses, with the Czech learner responses falling somewhere between these two groups (see our note above on Czech's status as a less clear-cut exemplar of a satellite-framed language). It appears that, at least with respect to a large number of VACs, Spanish learners' form–meaning mappings are less in line with native-speaker peers than those of German or Czech learners. This is particularly true for the VACs 'V *against* n,' 'V *among* n,' 'V *as* n,' 'V *between* n,' 'V *in* n,' 'V *off* n,' 'V *over* n,' and 'V *with* n'. These quantitative analyses confirm our hypothesis that Spanish learners find it harder than German and Czech learners to produce verbs that correlate closely with those produced by native English speakers.

A qualitative analysis of 'V *in* n' provides a detailed example. Correlations are high for German (0.79), slightly above average for Czech (0.69), and low for Spanish (0.35). We hence expect strong overlap in terms of verb preferences between native speaker and German and Czech learner responses. We expect the verb choices of Spanish learners to be rather different from those of native speakers and from those of their German and Czech peers. Table 10.2 shows lemmatized lists of the 20 most frequent verbs produced by the four groups of survey participants in response to the prompts 'he ___ in the … ' and 'it ___ in the … '. The native speaker responses in the left-hand column serve as a reference point for comparisons with the German, Czech, and Spanish learner responses. Verbs are italicized in a learner list if they also appear in the native speaker list.

It is generally the case that learners have stronger associations with verbs that are common in general language use. Hasselgren (1994) describes how in an L2 we "regularly clutch for the words we feel safe with: our 'lexical teddy bears'" (p. 237) and shows how even advanced L2 learners often overuse high frequency basic words rather than risking making a word selection error going for a less frequent but more appropriate term.

In addition to this general effect, we observe more overlap between native speaker and German (13 verbs) and native speaker and Czech (14 verbs) top-20 lists than between native speaker and Spanish lists (7 verbs). These shared verbs do, however, occupy different ranks across lists and/or have quite different token frequencies. Although shared among the top 20, verbs that express static meanings (including BE, LIVE, STAY, and STAND) are more often produced by German and Czech learners than by native speakers. Several of the motion verbs produced by native speakers (GO, WALK, COME) have the same or similar frequencies in the German and (though to a lesser extent) Czech lists. Other motion verbs produced by native speakers (SLIDE, BLOW, DRAW, JUMP, SWIM) are absent from or less common in the German and Czech learner responses.

The Spanish learner responses are different from both the native speaker and the German/Czech learner responses. Over 40 percent of Spanish survey participants (53 of 131) respond to the 'V *in* n' prompt with forms of the most frequent, semantically bleached verb BE. They share their preference for LIVE and STAY with the German and Czech groups but largely avoid motion verbs. WALK, FALL, and JUMP are absent from the Spanish list while COME and GO are rare. Such differences between native speaker and Spanish learner responses are consistent with our hypotheses relating to language typology and thinking-for-speaking. 'V *in* n' is one of many VACs in our set in which a path of motion is expressed by a 'satellite' (here the preposition *in*). The verb-framed language Spanish tends to encode this path in the verb and the manner of motion in an adjunct, so *walk in* is realized as *entrar caminando* (enter walking). It is hence not surprising that our Spanish learners do not (or very rarely) produce verbs such as WALK, GO, FALL, or JUMP in response to the 'V *in* n' prompt.

## 10.7 Conclusions

This work is framed within cognitive linguistic theories of construction grammar which hold that language comprises many thousands of constructions as form–meaning mappings, conventionalized in the speech community, and entrenched as language knowledge in the learner's mind. Usage-based approaches to language acquisition believe that schematic constructions emerge as prototypes from the conspiracy of memories of particular exemplars that language users have experienced. Psychological analyses of the learning of constructions as form–meaning pairs is informed by the literature on the associative learning of cue-outcome contingencies where the usual determinants include: factors relating to the form such as type and token frequency; factors relating to the interpretation such as prototypicality and generality of meaning, and factors relating to the contingency of form and function. These various psycholinguistic factors conspire in the acquisition and use of any linguistic construction. Constructionist accounts of language acquisition thus involve the distributional analysis of the language stream and the parallel analysis of contingent perceptual activity, with abstract constructions being learned from the conspiracy of concrete exemplars of usage following statistical learning mechanisms (Christiansen & Chater, 2001; Rebuschat & Williams, 2012) relating input and learner cognition.

We explored these assumptions for VACs, first by using corpus and NLP techniques to investigate the latent structures of their usage in language. This research demonstrated: (1) the frequency distribution for the types occupying the verb island of each VAC is Zipfian, with the most frequent verb taking the lion's share of the distribution. (2) The most frequent verb in each VAC is prototypical of that construction's functional interpretation, albeit generic in its action semantics. (3) VACs are selective in their verb form family occupancy: individual verbs select particular constructions; particular constructions select particular verbs; there is high contingency between verb types and constructions. (4) VACs are coherent in their semantics.

Next we investigated native speakers' processing of VACs and demonstrated that the frequencies of verb types generated for each VAC were affected by the three factors of frequency, contingency, and prototypicality. These findings promoted a usage-based view of L1A, with L1 VAC processing involving rich associations, tuned by verb type and token frequencies and their contingencies of usage, which interface syntax, lexis, and semantics.

We did the same for L2 constructions. When German, Czech, and Spanish L1 advanced learners of English as an L2 were given the same tasks, their processing too showed independent effects of frequency, contingency, and prototypicality. So L2A depends upon learners' experience of language usage and upon what they can make of it. Language learners, L1 and L2, both share the goal of understanding language and how it works. Since they achieve this based upon their experience of language usage, there are many commonalities between first and second language acquisition that can be understood from corpus analyses of input and cognitive-linguistic and psycholinguistic analyses of construction acquisition following associative and cognitive principles of learning and categorization (Collins & Ellis, 2009; Robinson & Ellis, 2008b).

Yet L2 learners are distinguished from infant L1 acquirers by the fact that they have previously devoted considerable resources to the estimation of the characteristics of another language – the native tongue in which they have considerable fluency. As Slobin (1993) notes, "[f]or the child, the construction of the grammar and the construction of semantic/pragmatic concepts go hand-in-hand. For the adult, construction of the grammar often requires a revision of semantic/pragmatic concepts, along with what may well be a more difficult task of perceptual identification of the relevant morphological elements" (p. 242). Since they are using the same apparatus to survey their L2 too, their inductions are often affected by transfer, with L1-tuned expectations and selective attention (Ellis, 2006b) blinding the computational system to aspects of L2 form and meaning, thus rendering biased estimates from naturalistic usage. As we explored these factors in L2 learners of different L1 typologies, we found that learners whose L1 is satellite framed (and hence typologically similar to English) find it easier to produce more target-like verbs (verbs that correlate more closely with those produced by L1 English speakers) than speakers whose L1 is verb framed. L2 learning from usage shows additional influences of L1 transfer. Second language constructions thus demonstrate effects of L2 and L1 usage.

# 11

# Variability in bilingual processing
## A dynamic approach

*Wander Lowie and Kees de Bot*

## 11.1 Introduction

In Chapter 2 of this handbook, Jiang's historical overview of research on bilingual representation and processing shows how research on bilingual processing gradually moved over time from a "verbal learning and verbal behavior" approach to an approach based on models with different layers of processing. With ever more sophisticated experimental techniques and refinements of such models, 'words' became 'representations' and the old distinction between storage and processing evaporated. Still, some issues remained unchanged over those sixty years. One is the tendency to generalize from specific groups, more often than not psychology students, to 'the bilingual.' In this generalization, individual differences were not seen as relevant for theory building. The other issue is even though the terminology 'words' changed into 'representations,' they were and still are seen as stored symbols that are stable over time. In fact, the whole idea of the widely used priming paradigm is based on the principle that the representation of a word remains the same, in spite of the different degrees of activation it may have. In this contribution we argue for a new approach that does take into account individual differences in processing and that starts from the idea that essentially nothing in the brain is static, but that everything is constantly changing. This is done within the framework of Dynamic System Theory (DST). While a DST perspective on cognition has been around for quite some time in cognitive science (Port & van Gelder, 1995), it was not until recently that this perspective became more widely embraced in the field of applied linguistics. An article written by Larsen-Freeman acted as the impetus for the stirring of the field's original interest in a dynamic perspective (Larsen-Freeman, 1997), but it has only been in the last five years that DST (or complexity theory) has gained ground in applied linguistics, as evidenced by a wealth of publications (de Bot, Lowie, & Verspoor, 2007; Dörnyei, 2013; Larsen-Freeman & Cameron, 2008; Lowie & Verspoor 2015; Segalowitz, 2010). Initially, the application of DST to language development was limited to a metaphorical interpretation, but now the mathematical toolbox of DST applications to cognition is rapidly growing. And although this toolbox is yet to be implemented in full for Second Language Development (SLD), many studies have now used analytic methods based on DST to explore their data.

Since DST is essentially about change over time, analyses from a DST perspective focus on long-term patterns of variability and change in the data. Using the foundation of DST research developed by van Geert (2008) and colleagues, tools have been developed to investigate "wobbles, humps, and sudden jumps" in variability patterns (van Dijk & van Geert, 2007). Subsequently, modeling techniques have been deployed to corroborate these observations on variability (Caspi & Lowie, 2013; Chan, 2013; Chan, Lowie, & de Bot, forthcoming). Recently, analyses of variability in second language use have been extended to nonlinear spectral analyses and dispersion analyses of response time measurements (Lowie, Plat, & de Bot, 2014). This could lead to another potential breakthrough in second language research by enabling the investigation of the organization of language systems based on the analysis of variability patterns in real-time data. In this chapter we will focus on the role of variability in second language development within the framework of DST.

Besides variability, another crucial characteristic of applications of this theory is that it is about individuals. Starting from the initial conditions and shaped by iterations based on the complex interaction of internal and external variables over time, including motivation, aptitude, age-related factors, and exposure, the language system of each and every individual language user is essentially different. Consequently, in addition to inter-learner variability, intra-learner variation is of crucial importance in understanding the dynamic developmental process. Moreover, the relationship between variables affecting this developmental process may be nonlinear and therefore unpredictable. For instance, the impact of a certain amount and quality of language exposure may be unpredictably related to achievement, as achievement dynamically interacts with attitude, motivation, learning behaviors, and an infinite number of individual characteristics. And just as it is impossible to unscramble eggs, it may be a fruitless operation to try to single out the influence of any of these variables on the developmental process using a single factor analysis based on group means. In spite of all we have learned about the 'grand sweep' of second language development and bilingualism from traditional group studies, these studies have mostly focused on the product of learning and use, rather than on the process. Instead, a DST approach focuses on the process of development and real-time language use by individuals. This means a move away from single-factor group studies that try to show the unique contribution of a specific factor.

Finally, since DST is about change over time and about the dynamic interconnectedness of subsystems like aspects of the first language and aspects of the second language, another crucial characteristic of DST approaches is the focus on development at different timescales (see de Bot, 2012). Each subsystem has its own typical developmental timescale. In addition, the timescales interact, which makes the classic distinction between long-term 'acquisition' and short-term 'processing' problematic.

In this chapter we will discuss between-learner variation and within-learner variability from a DST perspective, and discuss how variability and variation are manifestations of the nature of the second language system. We will relate this to how the extensive sociolinguistic literature and research on variation has increasingly demonstrated a more dynamic approach, although not situated within a complex dynamic systems framework. Subsequently, we will focus on variability in longitudinal studies on two timescales: months/years and milliseconds, and discuss what this variability can tell us about the principles of development and about the organization of the second language system. More generally, we will discuss the implications of these observations for research in applied linguistics, and discuss ways in which research in our field should alter its focus to incorporate the dynamic nature of language systems.

## 11.2 DST and second language development

In several of the articles and books mentioned in the previous section a full description is given of why language can be seen as a dynamic system and second language development as a dynamic process. The main focus is on in these publications are the interconnectedness of subsystems, the dependence on initial conditions, the dynamic nonlinear interaction between variables, the role of variability, and the non-modularity of the cognitive (and therefore the linguistic) system. If there is one characteristic of the dynamic systems approach to human cognition that strikingly deviates from traditional views, it is the assumption that the human mind does not sequentially operate on input and output of dichotomous modules. Instead, cognition must be seen as the continuous process of the dynamic interaction of embedded systems. In this view of cognition, the mind is not seen as the central executive organism that controls the body, but an integral subsystem that is strongly embedded in other subsystems. Human cognition, then, is a continuous interaction of all of the relevant subsystems, like the nervous system, the body, and the environment. Or, as Port and van Gelder (1995) put it, "the cognitive system does not interact with the body and the external world by means of symbolic and periodic inputs; rather, inner and outer processes are *coupled*, so that both sets of processes are continually influencing each other" (p. 13). Since the coupling of embedded subsystems takes place over time, this implies that the central construct of dynamic systems is *time*.

It is in this dynamic framework that we are trying to understand second language development and bilingual language processing. This dynamic approach is different from traditional models in a number of ways. Traditional approach models assume that language processing is carried out by a number of autonomous cognitive modules like phonology, syntax and lexis, in the first and second language, each of which may or may not "interact" in an input–output fashion. These models also assume that language processing is incremental, and they implicitly take on the notion that language processing involves operations on invariant and abstract representations. Even current models that are based on activation principles implicitly assume the existence of declarative linguistic knowledge. Because of these underlying assumptions, isolated elements (phonemes, words, sentences) are studied without taking the larger linguistic and social context they are part of into account (see de Bot, 2010).

Conversely, in a dynamic framework, language processing in the bilingual mind is seen as an integral part of cognition. The crucial assumption of the continuity of mind as opposed to the modularity of mind is one of the essential differences between dynamic models and traditional models (see also Spivey, 2007). In dynamic models, there is no room for strict assumptions about modularity and sequential interaction of modules when accounting for the way in which the bilingual individual acquires, comprehends, produces, and controls multiple languages. Instead, a dynamic system consists of coupled and embedded subsystems that do not interact in a predetermined manner or direction. Consequently, in a DST framework there are no (linguistic) rules that operate on stored, declarative mental content, but only stimuli that operate on mental states. The interaction of subsystems over time is responsible for the self-organization of the system. If we want to make sense of second language development from a dynamic systems point of view, we will have to observe and describe the continuous change over time of all related aspects of cognition.

The focus of this chapter is on variation and variability, and is especially concerned with their effects on the developmental pattern. As argued above, variability results from the myriad of coupled variables over time. If we take a simple activity like a language learner giving a short oral presentation, a host of variables will play a role, such as the level of proficiency in the second language, time pressure, self-confidence, difficulty of the topic, amount of preparation, and the interaction with the audience. Other, more remote factors such as global health, food, ambient temperature, and noise from the street may also play a role. Just as it is impossible to predict the weather at the square meter and minute scale, it is impossible to predict the variability in the performance of the task by this learner. She may be well prepared, and knowledgeable about the topic, but due to time pressure she becomes nervous which affects her disposition and her mood. She may also be worried about a personal relationship, or the fact that her bike has a flat tire. None of these factors will be continuously influential; they will come in waves and affect each other. It could be argued that, again like the weather, we can retroactively explain some aspects of the variability ("I can understand that her performance was worse when holes were being drilled in through the ceiling"), but listing the impact of the constitutive parts of the setting and system will not lead to a full description of the patterns of variability.

## 11.3 Sociolinguistic approaches to variation in SLD

Variation between individuals has been studied extensively in sociolinguistics (Preston, 1996; Tarone, 1988, 2007). And in spite of a minority of linguists who study language outside the context of use, it has long been argued that language processing cannot be detached from the sociolinguistic context in which it takes place (Larsen-Freeman, 1985). Sociolinguistic studies involving language change and language interaction are therefore relevant for the study of language processing.

In what has been labeled the first wave of sociolinguistic studies, the work of Labov has been pre-eminent. His well-known studies on variation in Martha's Vineyard (Labov, 1963) and New York City (Labov, 1966, 1972) focused on often dichotomous choices between two variants, and how factors like age, gender, social class, and setting determined this choice. However, this approach has essentially been one in which the variation was explained as a function of the interaction of these factors. In this, the factors were seen as stable rather than dynamic and variability was largely looked at within the group rather than at the individual level (Llamas, 2011). A typical design of a first wave study on social or regional variation would include age, gender, or level of education as the independent variable. As it became increasingly clear that single variable studies could only explain a small portion of the variation, second wave studies on variation took a multi-factor and multivariate approach in which the impact of a number of factors and their interaction on a number of linguistic aspects was tested. Most of these studies focused on attempting to explain the outcomes of a process without taking a time dimension into account, and as such failed to acknowledge the dynamics of the process. In the third wave of variationist studies this pattern changed. While the large categories of gender and socioeconomic status (SES) remain effective in explaining variation, the studies in the third wave pointed out that speakers were not defined by these categories but that they used the categories partly to position themselves in a social setting. The focus shifted from group tendencies to the choices and behavior of individuals, and in particular identity formation and agency. With that change, the approach became more qualitative in nature, compared to the uniquely quantitative approaches from the first and second wave. As Regan (2013) shows in her overview of variation studies on SLA, the combination of quantitative and qualitative data is becoming the new standard. Changes in linguistic choices are related to lifespan events. The third wave was also characterized by a move toward a more ethnographic approach and a move away from essentialist variables like gender and socioeconomic status. Fixed, categorical variables like age and gender were replaced by more gradual variables and were layered. Also, age can never be a causal factor. Being 18 years of age is by itself meaningless; age becomes relevant through other factors, like the option to get a driver's license, buy alcohol, or being able to rent or buy a house. The same is true for age-related factors in the field of applied linguistics (Singleton, 2005). As such, the factor is not age itself but age-related cognitive changes.

Variation is one of the hallmarks of SLD. Learners show variation within and between themselves in all possible ways. There is also an active community of SLD researchers that tries to explain variation in SLD from a sociolinguistic perspective, using the methodology of that branch of linguistics. But the relationship between sociolinguists and SLD researchers is far from easy. Preston (1996: 20) lists a number of reasons why this relationship is so complex:

1. The apparent reluctance or inability of variationists to advance plausible psycholinguistic models.
2. The mistaken understanding of sociolinguistic aims as sociological, social psychological, and anthropological (including ethnomethodological) ones.
3. Misunderstandings of concepts, findings, and research tools developed in variation linguistics.
4. The recent relative hegemony of the generative program in SLA research.

Subsequently, as the overview of research from 1997 till 2007 on sociolinguistic approaches to SLA conducted by Tarone (2007) shows, not that much has improved. While the overwhelming influence of psycholinguistics on SLD research clearly has been replaced by a more social one, little has been done to improve the relationship between the two. Tarone refers to Preston's (1996, 2002) psycholinguistic Model of variation, which is (very) loosely built upon Levelt's (1989) Speaking model (and bilingual variations of it). Preston's model is not particularly a cutting edge model in terms of psycholinguistic ideas. It assumes the existence of separate grammars for separate languages (other parts of the system are not discussed, so it must be assumed that the lexical and phonological systems are somehow part of the grammar). This flies against the findings in psycholinguistic research from the last decade that the language system is essentially unitary with languages partly overlapping and sharing components rather than forming strictly separate modules. Part of the proposed model is a "Sociocultural selection device" that selects the language to be used in a given situation. In the original Levelt model (1989), there was a component that contained information about the conversational setting, including factors like formality of the situation, conversational partners, and, according to most researchers in this area, the selection of a language. The communicative intention that is the starting point for an utterance includes the choice of the linguistic forms to be used and therefore the choice of language. The strong focus on linguistic forms arises from the relative hegemony of the generative program, which is also pervasive in Preston's own writing and thinking. The multilingual model he opts for in the end is the one proposed by Towell and Hawkins (1994). This model deviates at crucial points from the Levelt model and its derivatives in clinging to uncompromising generative assumptions like the primacy of universal grammar and the first language as the main point of departure.

For the crucial interaction between psycholinguistically oriented SLD researchers and sociolinguistically oriented ones to be fruitful, some awareness of the basic assumptions and relevant recent developments on both sides are essential. Claiming that the sociolinguistic approach to SLD should be seen as the best model for the whole process, as Tarone (2007) seems to argue, is equally ill-founded as claiming, like Long used to do in his publications from the 1980s and 1990s (e.g., Long 1990), that everything in language acquisition comes down to cognitive processes and that therefore theories and models of SLD should be considered psycholinguistic in nature.

Although the DST approach to language development and language use is relatively new, the focus on societal dynamics by including a time dimension was already part of Labov's (1963) Martha's Vineyard study, even though that aspect did not draw a lot of attention at the time. He demonstrated that the choice of varieties was not essentially fixed, but varying with changes in the social setting. The way the fishermen spoke appeared to be influenced by the influx of outsiders (mainlanders who came to the island for their holidays and tried to sound like the locals), and their linguistic behavior began to alter as a result of this. "Labov's account, therefore, locates the meaning of linguistic variation not in abstract social categories of class and sex, but within concrete forms of social participation and engagement located in the context of wider social interaction" (Llamas, 2011: 505).

The view on variation has changed significantly in sociolinguistics. As Llamas (2011) claims: "The messy variation, which is everywhere in language use, is not simply noise, but it signals, in minute ways, who we are, how we feel and how we respond to the world around us" (p. 512). Thus in the more recent sociolinguistic approaches, change over time and interaction between variables over time have been taken into account, giving it an implicit dynamic perspective.

While sociolinguistically oriented studies of variation differ with respect to their basic orientation from more psycholinguistically oriented studies, they do share a number of assumptions. The most important one is that variation is meaningful and reflects underlying social and psychological processes. The second is that language changes over time, both at the group level and at the individual level. The third is that most variables that affect language change interact over time. As Regan (2013: 285) argues: "It is generally accepted in this research that individuals are shaped by the structures within which they operate just as they themselves shape these structures." A final shared assumption is that change and development take place at different but interacting timescales. Some linguistic changes take place over centuries, but there are also many changes that happen within months or years, like the spread of *like* as a discourse marker (Schweinberger, 2011). Vernaculars like local street languages are all about change: a word may be in vogue one day, only to be replaced by another word within weeks. It is this sort of linguistic shift that means it is necessary to examine data not only over large timescales, but also over shorter periods of time to examine the minutiae of the dynamic development present in the data. Therefore, in the second part of this contribution we will present data on variation in the psycholinguistic domain and on the time scale of milliseconds.

It may be time to renegotiate the link between sociolinguistic and psycholinguistic approaches to variation in SLD, and overcome the differences as sketched by Preston (1996, 2002). The view that language is a dynamic system and language acquisition and change are dynamic processes is evidenced in much of the work in the third wave of sociolinguistic studies, even though they were not labeled as such. Accepting that many variables are interactive and do not point in one direction only but are shaped and altered by other variables means that the research methodology has to be adapted too. For the psycholinguistic side this is gradually taking place, as we will try to demonstrate in the second part of this contribution.

## 11.4  Variability, timescales, and attractors

In a DST approach to second language acquisition, variability within individuals over time has been used as an important source of information about the trajectory of the individual's cognitive development and about the degree of automatization of cognitive processing. Intra-individual variability may be the result of interacting variables, but it may also cause or affect change itself. Systems do not change over time in a linear way, as there are more stable phases (attractor states) and less stable phases, which can be seen as the transitions between attractor states. During these transition phases the system is more sensitive to specific input, which coincides with a higher degree of variability. It could even be argued that variability allows the system to change. The variability unties the system as a whole, making change possible. If we consider any type of evolution, including the evolution of language, it is obvious that without variability no change can take place.

From this it logically follows that DST approaches highly value variability in cognitive development, as variability discloses aspects of the system's process of self-organization and reveals the very nature of the system. Self-organization of a system is best understood as resulting from the abstract coupling of embedded subsystems. Each subsystem changes over time as a function of the characteristics of that subsystem and its interaction with other subsystems, and each subsystem has its own typical timescale of development. If we regard each of the system's embedded subsystems as one dimension changing over time, the emerging picture is that of a multidimensional state space that is continuously in motion. Even when the system as a whole may seem to remain stable for some time, it is very likely that at least some of the subsystems are changing. Spivey (2007) emphasizes that this change does not take place in discrete steps, but is a truly continuous process:

> If, at the spatial scale of neurons and behaviour, time is truly continuous, that is, not decomposable into discrete quanta, then changes in a system's state (or even its units' states) over time must also be continuous. Thus, claiming that a system was in a particular 'state' X, at a particular point in time, really boils down to saying that the *average* of the system's states during that period of time was X. (p. 30)

The system's characteristics of change are often described in terms of attractor states and repellors. Attractor states are the areas of the system's state space that the system tends to travel toward, while repellors are those areas the systems tends to stay away from or move away from. The multidimensional state space is therefore also often referred to as an "attractor landscape" (e.g., Spivey, 2007). However, each subsystem is not only characterized by a multitude of attractors and repellors, but also by its own typical timescale. Therefore, what counts as an attractor state is defined by the timescale of the observation of the system. What appears to be an attractor on one timescale may show variation and instability on other timescales. If we look at the famous example for a point attractor of the ball in the bowl, it seems as if the ball comes to a standstill at the lowest point of the bowl. It is in an attractor state on timescales of minutes and hours. But on a timescale with finer granularity, at the millisecond scale, it will show small movements due to changes in the environment, like temperature, wind, humidity, and so on. At that timescale there may also be attractor states or repellors, due to unevenness of the surface of the bowl and the ball. On a much larger, less granular scale there may be changes as well over timespans of years and decades. The bowl and the ball will change slightly, and there may be long cycles of variation in gravity, or the surface the bowl is standing on may change – to mention just a few options. So essentially real point attractors do not exist, as the relative stability of a state depends on the timescale that is used.

Attractors can also be looked at from a mathematical perspective. A simple, yet powerful dynamic interaction is described by the logistic function, $x_{t+1} = r^*x_t(1 - x_t)$. This equation describes the state of a variable at a certain moment in time ($x_{t+1}$) as a function of the same variable at the previous point in time ($x_t$), as affected by the growth rate of the variable ($r$) and the maximum growth that is possible under the given conditions ($1-x_t$). The equation shows that there are points in the state phase that the system will pass through frequently, while there are other points where it will never go. In other words, attractors are defined by the characteristics of the system that result from the interaction between subsystems and the iterative cycles the system goes through. From that perspective, contrary to what their name seems to imply, attractors are not 'magnets' shaping this state space of a system. And even though the state of a system seems to be an effect of the attractor, it remains unclear whether such a change is *caused* by the attractor. Attractors do not attract, they simply are. Moreover, as Spivey (2007) argues, most of the time systems are traveling between attractor states rather than staying in attractor states, because systems do not actually move from one attractor to the other, but only approach them temporarily:

> Perhaps the relevant neural networks in the brain only need to approach an attractor basin in their state space closely enough so that it is unambiguously the most coherent of the partially active population codes, and then that attractor's associated motor actions and anticipated perceptions go on to carry out their own activation processes ... The image is one in which the neural system continuously traverses intermediate regions of its state phase and occasionally briefly brushes up near an attractor basin just long enough to bring that attractor's associated percepts and actions into prominence. The emphasis in on the journey, not the destinations. (p. 23)

This again emphasizes the crucial importance of variability in the study of cognition as a dynamic system. Evidently, 'the journey' is different for every individual, even though there may be similar paths between individuals. Ultimately we want to try to understand every piece of information in an individual's behavior as it happens over time. The variability found in learners' behavior may be different at different timescales, reflecting the journey between attractor states before the current stage. Variability on a particular timescale is the result of the interaction of variables, also at other timescales, but that same interaction affects variability on both higher and lower timescales as well.

Consequently, whether or not we manage to capture meaningful intra-individual variability in our observations largely depends on the timescale at which we measure. Meaningful variability signals development that can take place at timescales ranging from the lifespan to milliseconds (de Bot, 2012). Therefore, variability at a timescale of decades, years, months, and weeks can all be revealing for the overall developmental process and the dynamic relationship between cognitive subsystems.

## 11.5 Studies of second language development on longer timescales

The study of intra-individual variability shows that variability is not random noise blurring the true effect, but contains relevant information about the developmental process. An analogy can be made with learning to ride a bicycle. Initially, novice bikers heavily sway and may occasionally fall, but with increased practice the variability in the direction decreases and is reduced to miniscule corrections, just enough to cycle (roughly) straight ahead. When the difficulty of the task is increased, e.g., riding a bicycle without having your hands on the handlebar, or riding on a very rough surface, the variability increases again until that next stage is mastered. An interesting observation is that when initial learning is supported by training wheels, the learning process is considerably delayed. The reason is that the training wheels take away the natural variability that is necessary for learning to take place. This shows that learning a complex task is a holistic experience that cannot be compartmentalized.

An increasing number of studies have applied insights about the meaningfulness of intra-individual variability to second language development. In an important study of first language development (van Dijk, 2003; van Dijk & van Geert, 2002) a number of tools and measures were introduced to analyze non-linear intra-individual variability over time. Many of these are techniques to visualize and interpret developmental trajectories, like min–max graphs, moving averages and moving correlations. Later these techniques were fine-tuned to measure the significance or meaningfulness of an observed pattern over time (see Verspoor, Lowie, & de Bot, 2010), mostly by using Monte-Carlo analyses. In addition, studies of second language development have tested which measures of complexity, accuracy, and fluency are most appropriate for use in long-range longitudinal studies. For instance, in a study of L2 writing development of a single case over a period of three years, Verspoor, Lowie, and van Dijk (2008) report on the dynamic competition between lexical creativity (operationalized as type-token ratio) and syntactic complexity (operationalized as finite verb ratio). Although the overall correlation between these measures was low, the dynamic analyses showed clear periods in which there was a positive correlation, pointing to support between these variables, and periods in which there was a negative correlation, pointing to competition, depending on the developmental stage of the participant. Many studies that followed revealed interesting dynamic relationships that cannot be found in traditional, means-based analyses. In a longitudinal variability study, Spoelman and Verspoor (2010) show the coexistence of a developmental connection between word complexity and sentence complexity and the lack of a developmental connection between complexity and accuracy in their data. The strong developmental association between lexical and syntactic knowledge seems to point toward ambiguous boundaries between these subsystems (also see the discussion about representations below).

Studies of developmental variability have not been limited to the domain of lexical and syntactic knowledge. Variability over time has also been studied in the field of phonology, and has also revealed interesting characteristics of the process of acquisition. In a longitudinal study of vowel development in English learners of Dutch, Lowie (under review) demonstrates that the production of the Dutch front rounded vowel /y/ strongly fluctuates between the two L1 (English) alternatives, the unrounded front vowel /i/ and the rounded back vowel /u/. The emerging pattern of variability over time within a single participant revealed stages of development that coincided with an increased amount of variability. This variability occurred at many different timescales, from seconds to weeks. He also shows that the productions in a shadowing task do not act as a precursor for more spontaneous production, and that target-like productions are realized in spontaneous production before repetition.

A next important step in investigating dynamic relationships based on variability in L2 data is to apply dynamic modeling techniques to test and corroborate the observed relationships (Lowie et al., 2011). Simulating data can give us insight into the changing relationships between variables either by fitting a model to the data and "reading" the relationships, or by creating a model based on theoretical expectations and comparing that to the observations. Caspi (2010) and Caspi and Lowie (2013) investigated the dynamic relationship between four different levels of L2 vocabulary knowledge by fitting a logistic growth model to the data of four language learners. Using this approach, they were able to track the complex relationship between more receptive and more productive levels of vocabulary knowledge. The generally observed gap between receptive and productive knowledge was confirmed, but there was a clear, although variable, interaction between these knowledge types, showing that in spite of the gap the different vocabulary levels were interconnected.

While at times they showed patterns of competition due to limitation of resources, there were also periods of unidirectional or mutual support.

Studies of intra-individual variability at longer timescales of language development have revealed many aspects of the developmental process. Variability is not just a meaningful by-product of development, but can be considered as the major driving force behind the developmental process. In addition to these long-term observations using dynamic research techniques, recent studies in language processing have focused on the variability at the millisecond level in online processing. Also, at this level variability can be regarded as the driving force of cognition and, it is argued, "contains the dynamical signature of purposive behaviour" (van Orden, Holden, & Turvey, 2003: 331).

## 11.6 Variability and self-organized criticality

The dimensions of variability studied at embedded timescales have been compared to the fractal dimensions in measuring the length of the British coastline (e.g., Holden, 2002). The argument presented here is that the length of the coastline is not fixed, but is determined by the dimensions of the yardstick. If the coastline is measured on a mile scale, it will be considerably shorter than when it is measured at the scale of feet, and shorter again when inches are used. The increasingly larger length resulting from the use of smaller yardsticks is principally infinite. And although these patterns are not as regular as purely mathematical fractal dimensions ('Mandelbrot'), these increasing lengths result from the nested, self-similar structure of the coastline representing a power-scaling relation or fractal (Holden, 2002: 53). Power-scaling relations are generally observed in many naturally occurring phenomena (like trees and broccoli), in naturally occurring patterns of change over time (like the development of crystals from minerals), but also in aspects of foreign language learning. Waninge, Dörnyei, and de Bot (forthcoming) present an example of such a power–scale relation by considering the degree to which motivation is embedded in classroom learning. Similar patterns of variation were found for motivation at the time scale of minutes and of days/weeks. In the physical world, power–scale relations are not observed when the state of a system is a robust equilibrium. They do occur when there is an equilibrium that is close to a critical state and they are habitually observed in phase transitions, like the change from a solid state to a liquid state of a substance. The decay of the fluctuations in phase transitions tends to show a clear power–scale relation.

A common representation of power-scaling is to convert the time dimension to a frequency dimension by transforming the time series of observations into a spectrum using a Fourier transform. The power–law decay of the time-based correlation then becomes a power–law decay of the frequency (f) resulting from that analysis, which is then referred to as 1/f noise (or 'pink noise'). A very interesting example of 1/f noise is the dynamic system of a sand pile (Bak, 1996). Adding grains of sand to the pile, one by one and in a random place, will initially lead to a little activity in the pile that can be seen as a miniscule avalanche. When more grains are added, more and more avalanches occur, resulting in major phase transitions. Bak noted that the variability in the size of the avalanches over time shows the proportions of a power relation (1/f noise). The interesting observation is that with each grain of sand that is added from outside the system (a perturbation), the system organizes itself toward its critical state. This is why Bak referred to this phenomenon as self-organized criticality (SOC). De Bot, Broersma, and Isurin (2009) used the concept of SOC to explain patterns of code-switching. They demonstrate that code-switching can be triggered by linguistic elements that show some resemblance between the two languages focused on. Just as a single grain of sand can cause an avalanche, a single word or sound can make the system switch completely from one language to another.

Since SOC typically results in variability patterns that resemble 1/f noise, it can inversely be assumed that whenever 1/f noise is found, this is evidence of self-organization of a dynamical system around its critical state. For instance, when 1/f noise is found in a person's heart rate (Pagani et al., 1986), this is taken as evidence of SOC in the body and the brain. Contrary to what might be expected, 1/f noise in heart rate is a characteristic of a healthy cardiovascular system, while the power relation breaks down for subjects at high risk of sudden death (Peng et al., 1995). The functional explanation is that by being around its critical state, the system is able to respond to perturbations quickly and accurately. The same finding is reported in studies investigating motor behavior. For instance, spectral analyses of data from physiological studies on the dynamics of hand movement in repeated reaching show clear patterns of 1/f noise (Diniz et al., 2011), indicating processes of self-organized criticality.

Similar to the automated functions in body and brain and human physiology, 1/f noise is also found in human cognition. Analogous to conclusions based on findings from the physical domain, it could therefore be assumed that SOC is an important organizing principle of human cognition (Kello et al., 2007). The pervasive existence of 1/f noise in behavior and cognition leads to another important conclusion. When variability displays power–law relations, this implies that subsystems must indeed be coordinated or coupled and that motor behavior is not controlled by modules or components. Van Orden et al. (2003) make a strong claim for viewing both human behavior and human cognition in terms of interaction-dominant dynamics rather than component-dominant behavior:

> Either additivity so far is too shy to show itself and remains to be teased out of data or it is simply the wrong assumption. We claim it is the wrong

assumption. There are no encapsulated components. Ordinary things that people do – perceiving, remembering, discussing, imagining, touching, walking – have been misconstrued as components of which they are composed (Van Orden & Kloos, 2003). History finds psychology courting once again the psychologists' fallacy – the products of psychological processes have been mistaken for the processes themselves (Fitch & Turvey, 1978; James, 1890/1950; Turvey et al., 1980). (p. 337)

Although there is some discussion about the validity of the interpretation of observed 1/f noise as SOC and interaction-dominant dynamics (see, for instance, Waegemaekers. Farrell, & Ratcliff, 2005), the evidence for interaction-dominant dynamics in human cognition is rather strong (Ihlen & Vereijken, 2010). That this interpretation is also viable for language processing is indicated in recent work by Waegemaekers (2013). In an experiment on production (picture naming) and perception (a picture–word matching task in two languages), she shows that her findings fit better into an interaction-dominant perspective than into the component-dominant approaches to language production and perception that form the basis of all current models of bilingual lexical processing. Wagemakers' evidence builds on earlier studies showing that language can be seen as an integral part of cognition, manifested by 1/f noise in language production. Van Orden et al. (2003) show that variability in the time series of a naming task, in which the naming of a random selection of English words from a computer screen was timed, clearly displays 1/f noise. They too interpret this as evidence of SOC in language production. In another experiment, Kello et al. (2008) asked participants to repeat the word "bucket" 1,000 times. The fluctuations across acoustic measurements of the repetitions again show clear 1/f scaling relations.

The increasing evidence for SOC in language processing calls for a dynamic continuous perspective on processing in which subsystems at all levels are interconnected and in which language processing is contextualized. The nature of processing is revealed by patterns of variability rather than by differences in means. This is not entirely new. In an earlier study that focused on variability in a single case study, Segalowitz, Watson, and Segalowitz (1995) introduced the coefficient of variance (CV) to reflect "the blend of underlying mechanisms" (p. 124), which represents the balance between automatic and controlled processes. SOC provides a further step toward our understanding of this blend of underlying processing mechanisms.

## 11.7 (In)stability of representations and languages as entities

Recent research has shown that we may need to reconceptualize our views of what constitutes a language. In the structuralist tradition, languages were seen as systems of rules that were consistent and could be described with ever more advanced tools and paradigms. A language could be defined as a unique set of specific rules and elements. Languages may share some elements but each language is its own fixed and unique set. Speakers of that language are assumed to be highly similar with largely overlapping sets.

An alternative view on what constitutes a language has been developed by researchers working from an emergentist perspective. "The term 'emergentism' emphasizes the progressive nature of the process of both short-term language processing and long-term language development, namely that qualitatively new and more complex representations can emerge on the basis of knowing its simpler component parts" (Behrens, 2009: 40). The most outspoken representative of the emergentist movement is probably Paul Hopper. An often quoted statement comes from his 1998 article:

> There is no natural fixed structure to language. Rather, speakers borrow heavily from their previous experiences of communication in similar circumstances, on similar topics, and with similar interlocutors. Systematicity, in this view, is an illusion produced by the partial settling or sedimentation of frequently used forms into temporary subsystems. (pp. 157–158)

This implies that there are no separate languages but only communicative discourses. If we accept this position, we will need to rethink what languages are, both in terms of development and cognitive processing.

Hopper (1998) argues that the idea that we acquire a language that then represents a fixed set in our mind is wrong:

> This means that the task of "learning a language" must be reconceived. Learning a language is not a question of acquiring grammatical structure but of expanding a repertoire of communicative contexts. Consequently, there is no date or age at which the learning of language can be said to be complete. New contexts, and new occasions of negotiation of meaning, occur constantly. A language is not a circumscribed object but a loose confederation of available and overlapping social experiences … That what adults know, and what children learn, is not an abstract system of units with meanings and rules for combining them, but are integrated normative modes of interactive behavior and the accompanying social use of corporeal signs such as words and gestures, to which concepts like language and grammar are almost entirely secondary. (pp. 171–172)

This perspective on language and linguistic elements is supported by recent research that looked at the stability of lexical representations (de Bot & Lowie, 2010). The data from a simple word-naming task in L1 and L2 show that when the exact same sequence of items is used repeatedly using the same participant, there are low correlations between latencies on the same items over time, even within the same day. So a word that was reacted to fast in the morning may have a much longer latency in the afternoon, or next day or month. The fixed order in which the items were presented also allowed for the interpretation of possible priming effects using time-series analyses. However, also these effects were different in each run of the experiment. Rather than being stable representations over time, 'words in the mind' may therefore be seen as fairly unstable and highly influenced by the context in which they are used or the pattern they are part of. In a follow-up experiment, a condition was added to both ensure semantic processing and avoid shallow naming (Plat, Lowie, & de Bot, under review). However, forced semantic processing did not lead to more consistency of the response latencies of items over time: this finding substantiates the important implication of a DST approach to linguistic processing that we referred to earlier in this chapter. There is no room for linguistic rules that operate on stored, declarative mental content, but there are only internal and external stimuli that operate on mental states.

As Spivey (2007: 30) argues, a dynamic perspective entails a view on representations that inherently includes a time dimension:

> If, for the purposes of analyzing physical processes at the molar scale, time is best described as continuous and unhesitating, then it is perhaps difficult to imagine that the time-dependent trajectories of the mind, through the brain's state space, could be any different ... What this means is that there is no point in time during which the mind is not changing. There is simply no such thing as a static internal representation, as required by the computer metaphor of the mind.

## 11.8 Future developments

The dynamic turn in cognitive science and developmental psychology will take time, and the same is probably true for the field of applied linguistics. Van Geert (2011: 277) sketches three scenarios for the impact of DST on developmental psychology:

- The pessimistic stance is that such a paradigm shift will not occur, primarily because the forces that act against paradigm shifts in developmental psychology – if not in all scientific disciplines – are now too strong to allow for paradigm shifts.
- The less pessimistic prediction is that [DST] will not diffuse into developmental psychology as a whole, as I would hope, but will survive as yet another subdivision in developmental psychology...
- The optimistic prediction is that, in line with DST itself, the growing number of currently rather isolated islands of [DST] applications in the world will finally form a critical mass, leading to a tipping point phenomenon ... or a velvet evolution.

Taking a DST position with respect to language processing and language development has far-reaching consequences for theorizing and types of data needed. Depending on the timescale a researcher is interested in, data will have to be gathered that allow us to trace the development of a system on different dimensions. We may be interested in changes in articulation in an intensive language course, but also in such changes in a non-instructed learning situation. So the articulatory changes will be measured at the millisecond level, but the developmental span may be of one or two weeks vs. a couple of years.

As we have tried to argue in this contribution, an important issue is the relationship between group data and individual data. Group studies will continue to be valuable, since they point to the general direction groups and individuals are likely to take, even if the group data do not reflect the pattern each individual will follow. However, to come to a better understanding of the process of language use and language development over time, it is inevitable that we study time series. The density and the duration of the time series will have to depend on the timescale of the entity we are interested in. Doing research based on DST principles and applying the analytical toolbox of DST calls for a specific type of data. In order to find fractal characteristics in individuals' behavior on different timescales, large numbers of data points are essential. In some of the experiments mentioned above, more than 1,000 reaction times had to be gathered. For many aspects of language use such numbers are simply unfeasible. For instance, for the study of sociolinguistic variation spontaneous speech data are useful, but these will never generate the large number of data points required for the analysis. This means that other approaches may be needed. Experiments with eye movement and cued reading may be useful for certain aspects of language processing and use.

A final relevant issue is whether we can explain the differences and similarities between individuals in SLD as possible outcomes of the same mechanisms. In the present contribution, the focus has been on the variability between and within individuals, but the question of why they are so similar in many respects is equally interesting. This question is likely to dominate the research agenda in a DST approach to SLD in the years to come.

# Part IV

# Comprehension and representation

# 12

# Conceptual representation in bilinguals

The role of language specificity and conceptual change

Panos Athanasopoulos

## 12.1 Introduction: on the meaning of meaning and concepts

In a discussion of conceptual representation, it is useful to begin by defining what the current chapter takes conceptual representation, and concepts, to mean. Evidence from the field of cognitive neuroscience has challenged the long-held assumption that language is a separate module from other cognitive processes by showing that lexical and grammatical subsystems are connected with each other and with non-verbal cognitive systems (Pulvermüller, 2003). Under this view, conceptual representations are distributed neuronal networks reciprocally linking lexical and grammatical categories to their visual, action, olfactory, somatosensory, etc. attributes (Kiefer & Pulvermüller, 2012). In other words, concepts in the human brain are organized in terms of distributed representations, where conceptual representation in memory entails linked sensory (visual, aural, olfactory, etc.), action, and linguistic–semantic knowledge. For example, color words like "green" unconsciously, automatically, and concurrently stimulate vision and language areas of the brain (Siok et al., 2009); production and comprehension of verbs like "kick," "lick," and "run," and nouns such as "cinnamon" and "coffee" stimulate the expected language areas of the brain, but the former set of words also show word-specific somatotopic activation of the sensorimotor cortex (Pulvermüller, 2005), while the latter stimulate olfactory brain areas (Pulvermüller & Fadiga, 2010).

This evidence of multi-modal distributed representation inevitably has consequences for how the notions of 'concepts' and 'meaning' are operationalized. If meaning refers only to linguistic meaning (i.e., to a word's formal semantic features and its relationship to other words only), then clearly one cannot assume that linguistic–semantic representation is the same thing as conceptual representation (Paradis, 1997; Pavlenko, 1999). However, if meaning is used in a broader sense to include linguistic meaning as well as non-linguistic experiential representation, then it can be conceived of as a synonymous term to concepts. It is this broader definition of meaning and concepts that the current chapter assumes throughout. That is, concepts refer to multi-modal representations that include linguistic, extra-linguistic, and non-linguistic knowledge.

Non-linguistic experiential elements may account for universals in conceptual representation constrained by basic physiological mechanisms of perception in humans. At the same time, because of the multi-modal, distributed nature of conceptual representation, it follows that such representation is open to individual differences to a considerable extent (de Groot, 2000). Many individual differences probably pertain to an individual's biographical characteristics as these may shape and influence interactions with the experienced world. One such biographical characteristic may be the particular language(s) that one is exposed to from birth, and, in the case of multilingualism, additional languages learned thereafter. The reason why linguistic experience is such a prime candidate to account for some specificity in conceptual representation is because languages vary greatly in how they lexically and grammatically describe the world and assign prominence to certain perceptual distinctions therein.

The coexistence of universal and language/culture-specific conceptual units of representation may seem like a contradiction in terms at first glance. However it is robustly supported by empirical evidence. For example, a neurophysiological investigation shows that Greek and English speakers are perceptually aware of luminance differences in blue and green, but at the same time there is increased brain activation in Greek speakers for blue rather than green contrasts (Thierry et al., 2009), because Greek has two basic terms denoting two different categorical degrees of lightness to refer to the blue area of color space (Androulaki et al., 2006). Similarly, to give an example from the grammatical domain, both Japanese and English speakers are aware of the ontological distinction between objects and substances, but English speakers are more prone than Japanese speakers to categorize objects based on their common shape properties, because English has (but Japanese lacks) an obligatory grammatical number-marking system (Imai & Gentner, 1997; Imai & Mazuka, 2003). Shape is a perceptual marker of individuation, and individuation is a prerequisite for applying grammatical marking appropriately (Lucy, 1992).

The examples above are discussed in more detail below, but it is important to note at this stage that empirical evidence such as the above comes from cross-cultural approaches that have their roots in Whorfian (Whorf,

1956) and neo-Whorfian (Levinson, 1996; Lucy, 1997; Roberson, Davies, & Davidoff, 2000; Slobin, 2003) enquiry into the relationship between language and cognitive processing. Such approaches aim to study higher level, linguistically mediated cognitive processes, such as working and long-term memory, and categorical perception, utilizing tasks such as semantic categorization, visual search, oddball detection, free-sorting and grouping. The main advantage of these tasks is that they allow the researcher to establish a connection between words/grammatical constructions and their real-world referents. This is crucial for unraveling the constituent elements of conceptual representations, given that those representations are assumed to be multi-modal in nature, combining verbal and non-verbal elements. Thus, studies employing such methodological approaches reveal that concepts across languages and cultures are for the most part partially (instead of completely) equivalent, with various degrees of equivalence on a continuum of near-equivalence to minimal equivalence (for a review, see Jarvis & Pavlenko, 2008).

In some cases, words in one language may not have a conceptual equivalent in the other language. This phenomenon is often demonstrated in studies showing effects of conceptual non-equivalence on translation latency and lexical priming (Finkbeiner et al., 2004; Tokowicz & Kroll, 2007). One area of research where conceptual non-equivalence has been repeatedly demonstrated is the domain of emotion concepts. Indeed, Pavlenko (2009) demonstrates that the Russian emotion word *perezhivat* is conceptually distributed to several notions, such as "to suffer, to worry, to experience things keenly," while the Greek word *stenahoria* may entail several different states of being, such as "discomfort," "sadness," and "suffocation" (Panayiotou, 2004, cited in Pavlenko, 2009). But even in the domain of concrete concepts, notions such as 'color' (in the sense that the word is used in the Western world to refer to distinct physical properties of hue and luminance) may be entirely absent from certain languages and cultures, who may conceptualize that category as 'texture' (such that they 'feel' rather than 'see' colors) (Levinson, 2001).

Understanding the cross-cultural differences and similarities between concepts provides the first step to hypothesis-building on the relationship between these concepts in the mind of the bilingual person. Adopting the cross-cultural methods mentioned above provides a methodological blueprint upon which to begin to put some of these hypotheses to the test. In what follows, I present the main theoretical postulates of the possible nature of conceptual representations in bilinguals and draw upon recent empirical evidence to bear on the validity and operational reality of each. I then examine the extent to which these possible states of representation in bilingual memory can be accounted for by past and current models of bilingual conceptual representation.

## 12.2 Bilingual concepts

Pavlenko (1999, see also Pavlenko, 2005a; Jarvis & Pavlenko, 2008) proposed seven possible outcomes for conceptual representation in bilinguals whose languages exhibit contrasting conceptual representations:

1. conceptual coexistence;
2. L1 conceptual transfer;
3. internalization of new conceptual representations;
4. conceptual shift;
5. conceptual convergence;
6. conceptual restructuring (or reverse transfer); and
7. conceptual attrition.

All of these outcomes come under the umbrella of conceptual change, which refers to the interaction of language-specific concepts in the mind of the bilingual person. Below I describe, drawing on recent empirical evidence, each of these outcomes.

### 12.2.1 Coexistence of language-specific conceptual representations

This outcome entails coexistence of distinct L1 and L2 conceptual representations that are accessed separately. This state of affairs could present itself in bilinguals who use, or who have learnt their languages in different contexts. For example, depending on their living circumstances, bilinguals may use one language at home and another in a professional setting, or in formal education. For sequential bilinguals, the first language is typically learned at home naturalistically, while subsequent languages may have been learned at school, or in a different country in the case of migration, naturalistically, formally, or via a mixture of both. Empirical evidence for coexistence of conceptual domains comes from studies that vary the experimental context in their research designs. For example, Barner, Inagaki, & Li (2009) asked English monolinguals, and two groups of Mandarin–English bilinguals, one group tested in Mandarin and one group tested in English, to extend the novel name of a target object to a shape alternative (that had the same shape but made from a different material from the target) or a material alternative (made from the same material but with a different shape from the target). Mandarin, like Japanese, is a non-obligatory plural marking language, so the authors reasoned that speakers of English would be more prone than speakers of Mandarin to extend the novel name of an object on the basis of shape rather than material (see previous discussion on the studies by Imai and colleagues). Results showed that when the bilinguals were tested in English, their performance was near identical to that of English monolinguals in extending by shape significantly more than the bilinguals tested in Mandarin. There was no comparable group of monolingual Mandarin speakers, but these differences as a function of language of task instruction strongly suggest coexistence of a Mandarin-like and an English-like conceptual representation of objects and individuation in the bilingual mind.

Another demonstration of conceptual coexistence, this time taking into account age of onset of bilingualism, is provided by Kersten and associates' study of motion events in English and Spanish monolinguals, and Spanish–English bilinguals (Kersten et al., 2010). When describing motion events, speakers of English are prone to use verbs that denote the manner of motion (e.g., 'The boy ran out of the building'), while speakers of Spanish tend to denote motion outside of the main verb by using for example adverbials (e.g., "*El niño salió del edificio corriendo*," "The boy exited the building running"). Based on this cross-linguistic difference, the authors hypothesized that in a non-verbal training task, speakers of English would learn to sort novel, inanimate moving objects on the basis of manner of motion quicker and more accurately than Spanish monolinguals. Their results confirmed their hypotheses, and additionally showed that when Spanish–English bilinguals were tested in a Spanish-speaking context, their non-verbal behavior was more like that of Spanish monolinguals, whereas when they were tested in an English-speaking context, their non-verbal behavior was more like that of English monolinguals. This pattern, however, was qualified by an age of onset of bilingualism effect. Specifically, later bilinguals showed a greater contextual variation effect, while early bilinguals performed similarly in the two language contexts. This suggests differential conceptual representation as a function of age of onset. Early bilinguals display a merged or convergent system, combining elements from both the L1 and L2 in a shared representation, while late bilinguals seem to access distinct conceptual representations.

## 12.2.2 Conceptual transfer from the L1

This outcome entails that L1-based concepts underlie both the L1 and the L2 linguistic systems. That is, L2 words and grammatical constructions are anchored on the already established L1-based conceptual system. This state of the conceptual system is most apparent in foreign language learners and L2 users who have not reached advanced levels of proficiency in their L2. For example, Athanasopoulos (2006) hypothesized on the basis of the demonstrated differences in grammatical number marking between English and Japanese (Imai & Gentner, 1997) that monolingual speakers of English would attend more to changes in the number of countable objects than monolingual speakers of Japanese in a picture similarity judgment task. The results confirmed this prediction, and furthermore showed that Japanese speakers who knew English at an intermediate level behaved similarly to Japanese monolinguals, despite the fact that these bilinguals were tested in an English-speaking context with instructions in English. However, once bilinguals had reached an advanced level of proficiency in English, their categorization behavior resembled that of English monolinguals. This developmental pattern, from L1 conceptual transfer to conceptual internalization of the L2-specific sensitivity to number differences in countable objects, although observed cross-sectionally, demonstrates the dynamic nature of bilingual conceptual representation, with conceptual changes occurring as a function of increased L2 proficiency.

In a study looking at the effects of grammatical gender while having to make decisions about the semantic relationships between objects, Boutonnet, Athanasopoulos, & Thierry (2012) presented Spanish–English bilinguals and native speakers of English with triplets of pictures in an all-in-English context while measuring event-related brain potentials (ERPs). Participants were asked to indicate by means of a button press when the third picture of a triplet belonged to the same or different semantic category as the first two. Unbeknown to the participants, the gender of the third picture name in Spanish was the same as that of the preceding two pictures in half of the trials, and different from the preceding two pictures in the other half of the trials. Behavioral results showed that semantic categorization in bilinguals was almost identical to that of English monolinguals, suggesting that bilinguals have a shared representation for these objects. No measurable effect of gender (in)consistency in bilinguals was found. In contrast, ERPs (a measure of brain activity with extremely accurate temporal indices of on-line behavior) revealed not only the expected semantic priming effect in both groups, but also a different brainwave pattern, modulated by gender inconsistency in Spanish–English bilinguals, exclusively. These results show that these bilinguals spontaneously and unconsciously access grammatical gender in their L1, even though on the surface they perform like native speakers of their L2. This pattern of results is a demonstration of L1 conceptual transfer, because clearly these bilinguals are influenced by their L1 when making semantic decisions about objects in their L2.

In a study of placement descriptions in the speech and gestures of Dutch and German foreign language learners of L2 French, Gullberg (2011) found that both L2 groups produced target-like spoken L2 French with respect to the semantic categories under scrutiny, suggesting shift of conceptualization patterns as a function of L2 acquisition. However, when Gullberg (2011) examined the accompanying gesture behavior of the learners, she found that both L2 groups displayed L1-like gesture behavior when speaking in the L2, showing evidence of L1 conceptual transfer. At the same time, many learners displayed both L1 and L2 gesture patterns within the same utterance, indicative of conceptual convergence, in addition to L1 conceptual transfer. This finding not only suggests multi-modal levels of representation, but also different types of conceptual representation operating within the same bilingual individual.

### 12.2.3 Internalization of a new concept is a typical trait of human communication in general

We borrow a word from another language that may more accurately and more economically convey a certain state of affairs or a referent in the real world for which no concept or word exist in our native language. Typical examples in English are words like "baklava," "schadenfreude," and "ombudsman." In the case of bilingualism, conceptually driven lexical borrowing is a common phenomenon, especially in immigrant bilinguals who often use L2 words when speaking L1 to refer to abstract and concrete concepts specific to the L2 language and culture (Pavlenko, 1999). Conceptual internalization has been documented experimentally by Athanasopoulos and Kasai (2008) who tested the saliency of common shape as a basis of categorization in English–Japanese bilinguals and monolinguals of either language. Athanasopoulos and Kasai (2008) asked participants to match a novel artificial computerized object to one of two alternates, differing in shape or color from the target. The researchers used artificial stimuli because previous studies using real objects (e.g., Lucy, 1992; Imai & Gentner, 1997: 5 and 9) had been criticized on the grounds that the objects are covertly verbalized with count and mass nouns and therefore differences in categorization behavior are not indicative of differences in conceptualization. The focus on shape alone versus a category irrelevant to number marking (such as color) aimed to test differences in conceptualization of the perceptual property that previous studies claimed to radically differ between populations (i.e., shape). Results showed that native speakers of English and advanced Japanese users of L2 English selected the shape alternate significantly more often than native speakers of Japanese and intermediate users of L2 English. Crucially, the study statistically correlated bilinguals' shape preferences with their linguistic marking of plurals on a picture description task. The correlation was significant: successful application of plural marking was related to degree of shape preference.

Recent studies demonstrate that a language's grammatical gender system can influence conceptual representation of objects, as indexed by the voice attribution task where participants are asked to assign a male or female voice to pictured objects (Kurinski & Sera, 2011). Results from Kurinski and Sera indicated that native speakers of English (a language with no grammatical gender on common nouns) who were learning Spanish (a language with an obligatory grammatical gender system on all nouns) began assigning male and female voices to objects consistent with their grammatical gender in Spanish after 20 weeks of instruction, showing concept internalization even at very early stages of L2 learning.

However, data from a comparable group of more advanced English–Spanish bilinguals revealed that their Spanish-congruent voice attribution patterns did not resemble those of Spanish monolinguals, but were in-between monolingual peers of either language. Thus, even though internalization was apparent early in development, the outcome of this process was only partial instead of complete.

### 12.2.4 Shift from an L1 to an L2 conceptual representation entails that L1 concepts have become fully congruent with the L2 and can be reflected as a shift in category prototypes or boundaries

For example, Athanasopoulos (2009) showed shift of the native Greek prototype for the color category "ble" (dark blue) to the English monolingual prototype for blue in Greek advanced L2 English users. At the same time, these bilinguals shifted the light blue (ghalazio) prototype away from the English blue prototype, thus maintaining the physical distance in luminance between the two native prototypes. This then is another case of a conceptual process taking place concurrently with another conceptual process, in this case transfer of the perceptual distance of the two L1 prototypes.

Brown and Gullberg's (2008) findings on gesture and description of motion in Japanese second language learners of English also constitute evidence of conceptual shift. Brown and Gullberg (2008) found that although the learners' motion event descriptions in Japanese did not deviate from monolingual L1 patterns, interestingly the researchers found a shift toward the second language gesture pattern (when speaking in the L1) even in bilinguals who had never lived in an English-speaking country before. This pattern of results suggests that language experience alone is sufficient to trigger changes in conceptual representation. The learners' representation of motion had changed as a result of additional language learning, but this change was not visible in their speech, only in their gesture.

### 12.2.5 Convergence of language-specific concepts

This pattern entails a unitary system that is an amalgamation of the L1 and the L2 conceptual representations. While such a system shares elements from the two languages, the resulting concepts are distinct from both L1 and L2 specific concepts. In the case of the early bilinguals in the study by Kersten et al. (2010) described earlier, this convergence manifested itself in that manner-based categorization was in-between that of English and Spanish monolinguals, regardless of whether the bilinguals were tested in Spanish or English.

Perhaps the most comprehensive demonstration of the conceptual convergence process comes from a study by Ameel et al. (2005). The researchers asked adult balanced simultaneous bilinguals of Dutch and French to name and provide typicality judgments of 73 photographs of storage containers (such as bottles and jars) and 67 photographs of cups and dishes, in both of their languages. Their category boundaries and prototypes were compared to those of monolingual speakers of Dutch and French. The results showed that while the monolinguals displayed language-specific naming patterns with different category boundaries for the different classes of objects, the bilinguals converged toward a common pattern, regardless of which language they were using, suggesting merged representations sharing elements from both languages. The researchers concluded that "through the mutual influence of the languages, the category boundaries in the two languages move towards one another and hence diverge from the boundaries drawn by the native speakers" (p. 79).

### 12.2.6 Reverse transfer (restructuring)

During this process, new elements from the L2 are incorporated into previously existing L1-based concepts. The result of this process could be convergence or complete shift (see above for examples). Brown and Gullberg (2010) studied verbal descriptions and gesture behavior on motion events, in adult native speakers of Japanese (a path language) learning English (a manner language, see the earlier description of the Kersten et al. 2010 study which relied on a similar linguistic distinction) and in monolingual Japanese and English speakers. The results showed an effect of the L2 on the L1 even at intermediate stages of English proficiency in the bilinguals. L2 learners used in their L1 a mixed strategy for path lexicalization (a typically Japanese presence of path verbs mixed with a high use of path adverbials, more typical of English). Brown and Gullberg (2008) report dissociations in surface production and gesture behavior in Japanese and English monolinguals and L2 users. When Japanese speakers mention manner of motion in speech, they are most likely to also gesture about manner. However, when English speakers mention manner in speech, they often gesture only about the path of motion. Japanese L2 English users were significantly more likely to talk about manner and gesture about path in their L1 Japanese than were monolingual Japanese speakers, thus displaying English-like conceptualization in their L1 gesture behavior.

Pavlenko and Malt (2011) found L2 influence on L1 performance in their study of Russian–English bilinguals' naming and categorization patterns of drinking containers. The researchers found that this reverse transfer was modulated by the age of arrival in the L2 context. Early bilinguals showed the greatest degree of L2 influence. A small round styrofoam container typically called *piala* by Russian monolinguals and late bilinguals, was called *chashka* by early bilinguals, in line with the English typical name "cup." The data showed further over-extension of the *chashka* category in line with the referents of the English word 'cup' to include containers that fell under different categories in the naming patterns of Russian monolinguals and late bilinguals.

Bylund and Athanasopoulos (2014) report conceptual restructuring in native speakers of IsiXhosa who are multilingual in a number of languages. Previous research showed that speakers of grammatical aspect languages like English attend less to the endpoint (goal) of events than speakers of non-aspect languages like Swedish in a non-verbal categorization task involving working memory (Athanasopoulos & Bylund, 2013). IsiXhosa being a non-aspect language, Athanasopoulos and Bylund investigated how the knowledge and use of additional languages with grammatical aspect might influence cognition of endpoint-oriented motion events in these functional multilinguals. Results from a triads-matching task where participants had to match videos based on whether an endpoint had been reached or not, showed that multilinguals who often used aspect languages and had greater exposure to English (an aspect language) in primary education were less prone to relying on endpoints when making their categorization decisions, even when they were given task instructions in their native IsiXhosa.

### 12.2.7 Attrition of previously existing concepts

Attrition may occur in cases where conceptual distinctions relevant for the L1 are not instantiated, or are instantiated differently, in the L2. Prolonged exposure to the L2-speaking environment has been shown to bring about such conceptual attrition in the domain of color perception. Based on the fact that Greek has two basic terms for the blue area of the color spectrum (see earlier sections), Athanasopoulos et al. (2010) asked bilingual Greek–English speakers and monolingual speakers of English to perform an odd-ball detection task. Participants were instructed to press a button when they saw a square shape stimulus among a stream of circles. The stimuli also differed in color and luminance (light blue–dark blue, light green–dark green), however, the participants were not instructed to attend to these differences. Instead, the participants' brain electrical activity was monitored while they were exposed to these series of stimuli, focusing specifically on neural correlates of the unattended change in luminance. Results showed that in native speakers of English the visual mismatch negativity (an index of automatic pre-attentive change detection) was the same for light and dark blue and light and dark green contrasts. Bilinguals who had stayed in the L2-speaking environment between 5 and 12 months displayed more sensitivity to the light/dark blue contrast than bilinguals who had lived in the L2-speaking environment between 1.5 and 5 years, as evidenced by a larger visual mismatch negativity for light/dark blue contrasts relative to light/dark green contrasts in the former group. The latter group's brain activity for light/dark blue contrasts began approximating that of English monolinguals. In other words, these long-stay bilinguals were on the way to losing their native color contrast, even though on the surface they were well aware of the semantic difference between their native color terms.

## 12.3 Modeling bilingual conceptual representation

As we have seen in the previous section, the recent empirical investigations of bilingual conceptual representation have revealed that such representation is dynamic and flexible, entailing a number of processes and outcomes. Such processes may operate at different levels of behavior and representation, at different stages and degrees of bilingual experience, concurrently and diachronically, without mutual exclusivity. We now turn to consider psycholinguistic models of bilingual conceptual representation, and examine the degree to which concept specificity is or can be accommodated in each.

The organization of bilingual conceptual store has featured in models of bilingualism as soon as systematic enquiry into this research domain began. Thus, Weinreich (1954) proposed that in the case of compound bilinguals (who learn the two languages in the same context simultaneously) words in the bilingual lexicon may share the same conceptual representation. Coordinate bilinguals (who learn their languages in separate environments) have two separate conceptual representations for each word. Subordinate bilinguals (who learn their L2 after their L1 often in a different learning context) link L2 words to their conceptual representations by first translating them to the L1. The compound–coordinate distinction receives support in current investigations, as in for example Kersten et al.'s (2010) study that found shared merged concepts for simultaneous bilinguals, but coexistence of separate representations in coordinate bilinguals. Weinreich's model also included a developmental component, such that subordinate bilingualism may be more prevalent at early stages of L2 acquisition, but with increased L2 expertise subordinate bilingualism comes to gradually be replaced by coordinate bilingualism in the individual. This anticipates the phenomenon of L1 conceptual transfer, although the outcome of this process may not only be coordinate conceptual structure, but also compound, as the phenomena of reverse transfer and convergence suggest. Weinreich's postulation nonetheless allowed for different types of structures to coexist (transitorily or more permanently) in bilingual conceptual organization, thus recognizing the dynamic nature of bilingual development and memory representations. The distinctions that Weinreich proposed took into account the learning trajectory of languages in the bilingual person, and anticipated much of the empirical research and theorizing that later models of bilingualism would engage in. Weinreich also seemed to recognize that some degree of conceptual (non)equivalence between languages exists, as attested in his postulation of coordinate bilingualism. Subsequent enquiries (Kroll & Stewart, 1994; Potter et al., 1984) however, tended to focus predominantly on conceptual access and inter-lingual connections in the lexicon (i.e., how fast individuals were in mapping words to concepts and in translating from one language to the other) without examining the nature and identity of the representation of concepts per se.

One the most prominent models of bilingual memory, the revised hierarchical model (RHM) (Kroll & Stewart, 1994), assumes that different words from the two languages map onto a single, shared conceptual representation. Under this assumption, the task of the bilingual, once a concept is activated, is to select between two alternative lexical items (a word and its translation equivalent in the other language). The main feature of the RHM is its explanatory power in terms of bilingual conceptual development. The model assumes that in the early stages of L2 acquisition, L2 words are connected to their L1 translation equivalents rather than directly to their corresponding concepts. Therefore, beginner or intermediate learners access the conceptual store in the L2 via translation to the L1. As L2 proficiency increases, more advanced learners strengthen connections between L2 words and their conceptual representations without going through the L1 translation route.

The postulation that links between words and concepts can vary in strength over time (as a function of proficiency and language use, e.g., Kroll & Tokowicz, 2005) provides the tools to accommodate phenomena of conceptual change such as internalization and attrition, at least as regards conceptual access. However, while these patterns of conceptual access have been empirically corroborated in the psycholinguistic laboratory by means of reaction time experiments, and can account for a number of translation phenomena, the nature of the conceptual representations themselves in the model remains elusive. One could infer looking at the developmental pattern the model assumes that such development would entail near-perfect conceptual equivalence between the bilingual's languages. However, this is rarely the case as we have seen in the previous section. Another assumption one could make is that L2 words map onto L1-specific concepts, since to map onto concepts they need to be translated to the L1. This appears to be a more plausible hypothesis, since this is the well-documented phenomenon of L1 conceptual transfer. But this developmental stage usually concerns bilinguals, or L2 users, at early stages of acquisition and L2 proficiency. If, as the model assumes, L2 linguistic forms gradually become independent of their L1 translation equivalents (however imperfectly they conceptually correspond across languages), and map directly onto the conceptual store, we cannot know, at least from the assumptions the model makes, what this conceptual store actually contains. Kroll and colleagues assumed more recently (e.g., Sunderman & Kroll, 2006) that bilinguals even at lower proficiency levels might have direct access to concepts via L2 (thus without accessing translation equivalents), but even this modification to the original RHM does not reveal the nature of the representations per se in its proposed conceptual store. One possibility of course would be that L2 words continue to map onto L1-specific concepts (without the translation route now), but as a number of studies has shown, L1 conceptual transfer is only one of the possible states of bilingual conceptual representation. The model does not account for most conceptual change phenomena in bilinguals such as shift, convergence, restructuring, etc. (see Brysbaert & Duyck, 2010 for a comprehensive critique of the RHM, as well as the reply by Kroll et al., 2010). (Table 12.1 provides a synthesis of the degree to which each of the four main models discussed above can accommodate language specificity, developmental aspects of bilingualism, and phenomena of conceptual change.)

The distributed conceptual feature model (DFM) (de Groot, 1992b; 1993; van Hell & de Groot, 1998) offers a more nuanced account of conceptual representation in general, and of cross-linguistic differences in concepts in particular. The model assumes that representations of concrete words are mostly shared between languages, while abstract words display greater cultural and linguistic specificity and therefore are likely candidates for distinct or at least not fully shared representations in bilingual memory. The model also assumes a distributed representation of meaning, where a number of more basic conceptual units make up a word's meaning. This not only resonates with current theoretical assumptions derived from neuroscience approaches (see Pulvermüller, 2003), but it also provides the model with a theoretical advantage in accounting for partial (non) equivalence of concepts across languages. Words in the bilingual lexicon may share a number of basic conceptual units: the more they share, the closer they are in meaning; the less they share, the more language specific their meaning is. Because of the distributed nature of representation in the model, conceptual (non)equivalence can be conceived as a continuum rather than as separate stores (a store of shared concepts, a store of L1-specific concepts, and a store of L2-specific concepts). This kind of modeling allows far greater flexibility with regard to conceptual change, reflects the dynamic nature of conceptual representation, and in fact can accommodate many phenomena relating to conceptual change in the course of bilingual development. For example, lexicalization of motion events in Spanish–English bilinguals in Kersten et al.'s (2010) study maps onto more shared than distinct L1 and L2 conceptual units when the languages have been learned simultaneously, but to more distinct and less shared conceptual units in sequential bilinguals, accommodating the phenomena of convergence and coexistence.

One of the drawbacks of the model is the assumption that words with concrete referents map onto shared representations. However, as has been empirically demonstrated time and again, even concrete words display

**Table 12.1** Summary of the degree to which each of the four main models discussed can accommodate language specificity, developmental aspects of bilingualism, and phenomena of conceptual change

|  | Language specificity | Bilingual development | Coexistence | Transfer | Internalization | Conceptual change | | | | |
|---|---|---|---|---|---|---|---|---|---|---|
|  |  |  |  |  |  | Shift | Convergence | Restructuring | Attrition |
| RHM | Yes | Yes |  |  | Partially |  |  |  | Partially |
| DFM | Yes |  | Yes | Yes | Yes | Yes | Yes |  | Yes |
| SAM | Yes | Yes | Yes | Yes | Yes | Yes |  | Yes | Yes |
| MHM | Yes | Yes | Yes | Yes | Yes | Yes | Yes | Partially | Yes |

large cross-linguistic variation in their conceptual denotations (Ameel et al., 2005; Pavlenko & Malt, 2011). In addition, unlike the RHM, the DFM lacks a developmental component, thus not accounting for a basic characteristic of bilingual conceptual system, namely its dynamic, ever-changing nature as a function of increasing proficiency, context of acquisition, etc. Despite these drawbacks, the model remains appealing as it can easily accommodate most of the different possible states of the identity of bilingual concepts, and assumptions about development can readily be inferred and applied onto the model based on the conceptual patterns empirically observed in the previous section. For example, one can imagine that the native blue terms in Greek gradually come to share more basic conceptual units with the English word 'blue' and less with the original L1 categories, accounting for phenomena of conceptual attrition and restructuring reported earlier (Athanasopoulos et al., 2010). Indeed, the DFM provides the fundamental mechanisms behind such conceptual change, and as such laid a solid foundation for the next two models under consideration.

The shared distributed asymmetrical model (SAM) (Dong, Gui, & MacWhinney, 2005) also assumes smaller distributed conceptual elements making up a word's conceptual representation, like the DFM. It explicitly takes into account cultural and linguistic specificity of concepts, and assumes that the L1 and L2 lexicons share some conceptual elements, but at the same time they may also map to L1-specific and L2-specific elements. Unlike the DFM, the model assumes that the basic conceptual elements that make up a word's conceptual representation are separated into L1-specific elements, L2-specific elements, and common elements. A distinguishing characteristic of the model is that it takes into account the dynamics of change and restructuring in the bilingual conceptual store and representation, in adding the developmental component that the DFM lacked. Thus like the RHM, the model predicts that at early stages of L2 development the connections between L2 words and their conceptual representations are weaker than the connections between L1 words and their conceptual representations, and that initially L2 words may map onto the L1 conceptual representations. With increasing L2 proficiency, L2 word connections to L1 concepts gradually weaken, and L2 word connections to L2 concepts gradually strengthen. These assumptions of the model neatly accommodate the phenomena of L1 conceptual transfer, conceptual coexistence, and many other phenomena of conceptual change such as shift and attrition. However, there remains some vagueness with regard to how exactly conceptual change takes place in bilingual memory: if conceptual units are separated into language-specific stores, then how does reverse transfer, and L1–L2 convergence take place? One may assume that once these processes are in operation, the original conceptual units then become part of the common elements store in the model. However, the nature of common elements in the model is not clearly specified with regard to these possibilities. In other words, it is not clear whether common elements refer to shared meanings (i.e., conceptual equivalence in the languages of the monolinguals), or merged concepts (i.e., convergence in the mind of the bilingual). In other words, the model offers a succinct account of the developmental nature of bilingual memory representations in the context of language-specific and shared concepts, but it is not specific enough in defining the nature of the representations once conceptual change begins to take place in the developmental process. Such further nuance is provided by the next model under consideration.

The modified hierarchical model (MHM) (Pavlenko, 2009) postulates conceptual representations that may be shared (fully or partially), or be completely language specific. In this respect, the MHM, like the SAM, succinctly captures the linguistic and cultural specificity of concepts. However the MHM goes a step further: it specifies two different types of shared representations. One type relates to concepts that are more or less shared between the two languages of the monolinguals. In this case, all the bilingual has to do is map the newly learned word to a pre-existing conceptual category. The other type relates to shared representations that come about as a result of conceptual change. These representations typically involve merged (or converged) concepts sharing elements from the L1 and L2, where the resulting concept is an amalgamation of the two original concepts, and the degree of restructuring differs in the individual as a function of their specific bilingual characteristics (AoA, proficiency, context, etc.). The model thus provides a coherent theoretical basis for the very common convergence phenomena attested in the bilingual processing literature. At the same time the model adopts SAM's postulation of concepts that are separated into language-specific stores. This leaves the mechanism of reverse transfer or restructuring unaccounted for. If concepts are stored in unique language-specific components, then it is not clear from the model how L1 representations can be influenced by L2 representations, or indeed whether the affected L1 concept remains in the L1-specific store, whether it moves to the common merged store, or whether the original L1 concept remains intact, and an entirely new concept is created merging elements from the L1 and the L2. It appears that both the SAM and the MHM, because of their operationalization of language specificity as unique language-specific stores, lack the degree of flexibility for conceptual change afforded by the DFM, which operationalizes language specificity as part of the overall variability that characterizes human conceptual representation.

Nevertheless, the MHM is able to theoretically account for mixed patterns of representation, by assuming that conceptual representations need not be one type of representational format, which is also a basic tenet of the DFM. Under this assumption, several states among the possibilities described in the previous section may coexist in the same conceptual system at the same time. For example, Athanasopoulos and Kasai (2008) found that Japanese intermediate L2 users of English made significantly less shape-based categorizations than advanced learners and English monolinguals. The intermediate learners displayed L1 conceptual transfer, while the advanced learners displayed concept internalization. At the same time, all participant groups, regardless of language background, made shape-based categorizations significantly above chance level. That is, shape was a salient categorization feature for all participants. It was the relative degree of this salience that differed across groups. This pattern conforms to the postulation of coexistence of universal and language-specific constraints on categorization (Imai & Mazuka, 2003), but additionally demonstrates that bilinguals must have some shared conceptual units in their representation of objects, alongside some language-specific ones, neatly conforming to multi-modal distributed models of representation. The study of Ameel et al. (2005) also shows shared representation of objects in bilinguals, but in this case such representations are really convergent systems, combining L1 and L2 conceptual units into a single category. In addition, in a free-sorting task Ameel et al. (2005) did not find any cross-linguistic differences among monolinguals (or bilinguals): all groups freely sorted objects based on their common perceptual properties, regardless of language background. In this case, bilinguals display shared representations, but these are common to the two languages of the monolinguals. This overall mixed pattern of shared representation (a linguistically informed convergent representation alongside a non-linguistic one common to all speakers) is again entirely in line with the theoretical postulates of the DFM and the MHM. Finally, the MHM retains the RHM's developmental components, and holds that relationships between words and concepts, as well as relationships between language-specific concepts are subject to constant change over time as a function of a number of experiential factors such as proficiency development and acculturation. While this model has yet to be tested in a comprehensive empirical investigation, its theoretical nuance regarding the two types of shared representations allows us to interpret findings such as those described above that were not readily captured in previous models.

## 12.4 Conclusion

Empirical evidence on bilingual conceptual representations highlights three major points. First, the representational formats described in 12.2 are not mutually exclusive; more than one may be observed simultaneously in the mind of the bilingual person, depending on the conceptual category under investigation and the biographical characteristics of the bilingual individual. Second, the non-mutual exclusivity of these outcomes is not only synchronous, but also diachronic. That is, a bilingual may experience a series of different conceptual states at different points in their development, depending on several factors such as language proficiency, socialization/acculturation, age of onset of bilingualism, frequency of language use, etc. Third, the cross-cultural methodological approaches combining verbal and non-verbal tasks, as well as co-verbal behaviors like gesture, and implicit measures such as ERPs, provide substantial insight into the different levels of processing and representations in the bilingual mind, highlighting the multi-modal nature of representation. This empirically justifies earlier claims that assumptions made about bilingual concepts based on evidence exclusively from verbal tasks that focus on individual words may present a partial and ultimately erroneous picture of underlying conceptual representation in bilinguals (Pavlenko, 1999).

Synthesizing features from existing models of bilingual memory against the current empirical evidence leads to the conclusion that the most coherent account of bilingual conceptual representation combines three fundamental assumptions. The first one is the distributed, multi-modal nature of representation, a cornerstone of the DFM and subsequently also incorporated into the SAM and the MHM. The second one concerns cross-linguistic and cross-cultural variation of concepts, a central feature of the SAM and the MHM. The third one makes assumptions about the development of concepts, and the emergent links between those concepts and their linguistic instantiations, as pioneered in the RHM and further developed in the SAM and the MHM.

These advances in our knowledge of conceptual structure and representation in the bilingual mind suggest that the organization of the bilingual conceptual system is far more complicated than has traditionally been assumed. It is no longer tenable to take as a given that languages are equivalent at the conceptual level and the task of the bilingual, once a concept is activated, is to select one of two translation equivalents. The majority of words that may seem like translation equivalents across languages do not have exactly the same conceptual representation, even when they refer to concrete entities, and there is now a substantial body of evidence from cross-cultural investigations of bilingual cognition that shows systematic cross-linguistic variation in conceptual representation, not only of individual words, but of grammatical constructions as well. Learning and using an additional language entails creating and accessing a new conceptual system, alongside the acquisition of surface lexical and grammatical forms. As such, the development of conceptual proficiency in a new language, and the resulting process of conceptual change need to be afforded a much more prominent role in any future model of the cognitive architecture of bilingualism, and of the processes underpinning multilingual language acquisition and use.

# 13

# Emotion word processing within and between languages

Jeanette Altarriba and Dana Basnight-Brown

## 13.1 Introduction

While much has been written regarding the mental representation of concrete and abstract concepts, less is known about how the mind represents, stores, and processes emotional language both within and between languages (see e.g., Altarriba & Bauer, 2004). Words that label emotions (e.g., *happy, sad, scared*) and words that have an emotional component, so-called emotion-laden words (e.g., *butterfly, cancer, blood*), are currently being explored in terms of how they are encoded, stored, and retrieved in the course of language learning. What is new and novel in this area of investigation is the understanding of how these sets of words are represented in more than one language in a bilingual speaker particularly as a function of the origin of languages, the functional, pragmatic, and contextual environment in which the languages are being used, and the mode of acquisition of these words (e.g., Caldwell-Harris et al., 2011). Important applications of the study of emotional language run the gamut from the understanding of how emotional words may be accessed and strategically used in settings that range from mental health and counseling (e.g., Santiago-Rivera & Altarriba, 2002), to the questioning of bilingual eyewitnesses and interviewees in a variety of settings (see e.g., work on bilingual false memory effects in Bauer et al., 2009). Empirical and applied research from language and memory perspectives will be discussed within a framework that highlights the characteristics and mechanics of emotional stimuli, and their relation to models and theories of word representation in general.

## 13.2 Why examine emotion word processing?

As has been indicated in a recent review of the study of mood and emotion as published via the *American Journal of Psychology* (Altarriba, 2012), the field has long been interested in the ways in which individuals display emotions toward others, portray emotional states themselves, and categorize the types of emotions (positive or negative; highly arousing or less so) that are demonstrated across cultures and across peoples. In fact, Daniel Goleman in his classic work, *Emotional Intelligence*, published in 1995, indicated that mental health and well-being rests on our ability to detect emotional states in others and label those emotions, as well as the ability to label emotions in ourselves. It is our ability to detect when an individual is happy, sad, or frightened that allows us to navigate the series of social and behavioral scripts that will allow us to aptly communicate with other individuals and provide the kinds of responses that will positively enhance that communication. Additionally, when one acquires another language, there could be situations in which emotion is communicated differentially in each language, and the knowledge of both languages becomes essential in fully understanding a bilingual's state of mind (Heredia & Altarriba, 2001).

Altarriba (2003), in fact, indicated that words that express emotion in a bilingual's native language may be more closely tied to that language, as compared to a second language, due to the fact that the first learning encounter with the word also occurred in a specific context. Learning the term for anger or disgust in one's first language, for example, co-occurs with having experienced the accompanying feelings for those words within that language. Thus, a physiological association to those words develops such that the memory for those words is coded not only by the language in which they were learned, but also by the level of physiological arousal that was experienced when those words were first learned. This richness of encoding is what typically leads to the notion that a native or first language may be viewed as more "emotional" than a bilingual's second language. Thus, *context* is often a mediator for the strength or intensity of an emotion, and unlike words for concrete objects, for example, a certain level of arousal is also experienced within the context in which emotional language is learned (Altarriba, 2008). As Pavlenko (2012) has also suggested, this context effect is most likely responsible for the increased automaticity and heightened physiological arousal that one has when processing emotional stimuli in the first language (L1).

## 13.3 Emotion word processing within a language

Emotional stimuli have long been found to actually be better remembered than non-emotional stimuli (see e.g., Doerksen & Shimamura, 2001). Doerksen and Shimamura found that individuals were better able to remember a color (blue or yellow) that had been associated to a given word when that word was emotional in nature. Thus, emotional information can effectively code a stimulus word, so much so, that it is then subsequently more accurately recalled. Likewise, Sutton and Altarriba

(2011) found that participants were better able to recall the location of a letter probe if it appeared in place of a negative emotion word as compared to a neutral word (see also Kousta, Vinson, & Vigliocco, 2009). That is, the valence and arousal components of emotion words help to code memory for the sources of words as well as for the spatial locations in which those words appeared. Thus, the influence of emotion words is quite powerful and helps not only to direct attention but to enhance a memory for related information, as well (see similar results as reported by Kensinger & Corkin, 2003).

Interestingly, it is the negative emotion words that seem to moderate findings across a variety of tasks and effects more strongly than positive or neutral stimuli (see e.g., Larsen, 2008). While it appears that negative words have a strong influence on memory and memory enhancement, Larsen, Mercer, Balota, and Strube (2008) reported that negative words can also slow down timed responses to those words, if they are also moderately arousing.

In contrast, across several different tasks, positive words seem to afford the same kind of responses as neutral words, in many cases (Hunt & Ellis, 1994). The literature on emotional Stroop effects within languages has provided ample data and support for the attentional capture effects of emotional stimuli prompting participants to produce slower color naming times for emotion words presented in different colors, as compared to neutral words (e.g., the word "sad" presented in red ink vs. the word "table" presented in red ink; see e.g., McKenna, 1986; McKenna & Sharma, 2004). When lexical characteristics are controlled across lists of neutral and negative words, color naming times are typically slower for the negative words (Larsen, Mercer, & Balota, 2006; but see Schacht & Sommer, 2009, who reported that positive and negative verbs were processed more quickly than neutral verbs, in a lexical decision task). In terms of semantic priming effects (i.e., the finding that reaction time to a word like "doctor" is facilitated when preceded by the word "nurse"), it has been reported that negative word stimuli slow down response times to the point where the facilitation is diminished and the advantages of having been first "primed" by a semantically related item are no longer evident in reaction time data (see e.g., Rossell & Nobre, 2004). Altarriba and Bauer (2004) also demonstrated that while abstract words serve to prime or speed up responses to subsequently presented emotion words that are semantically related, the reverse is not the case. That is, reading the word "busy" speeds up responses to the word "preoccupied," however, seeing the word "rage" does not automatically produce facilitation in responding to "violence." Thus, processing of an emotion word first does not seem to accord facilitation in responding to a related abstract word. The authors theorize that emotion words, having many more associated words than abstract words in memory, actually "share" the activation they produce when first accessed and processed across a whole host of "paths" in memory. Thus, any one word that then follows may be recognized but not to the extent it would have been, had it not been one of many words that had been mentally associated to the emotion prime word.

A recent direction of research regarding the representation of emotion words within language has focused on tip-of-the-tongue (TOT) states and the influence of emotion on promoting these difficult word-finding states in specific paradigms (see Schwartz, 2010). Schwartz prompted participants with emotion-related questions such as "What is the term for ritual suicide in Japan?" and compared response states to questions that were more neutral in nature (e.g., "What is the capital of Denmark?"). In cases where a target word was not readily retrieved, TOT states were reported more frequently in the emotion condition as compared to the neutral condition. The author states that the arousing nature of the emotionally related question served to interrupt the ability of participants to access the correct word though they had a sense that the reporting of the word was imminent. This "blocking" effect was much more pronounced for words that followed emotional questions vs. neutral questions. Just why negative emotion words serve to at once heighten arousal and awareness, capturing attention, and often impairing performance at the same time, is not precisely known. Perhaps a closer look at the characteristics that define and delimit different word types will offer some insight onto the ways in which negative emotion words, in particular, moderate language and memory performance.

### 13.3.1 Differences between concrete, abstract, and emotion words

More recently, a growing body of research has focused on the distinction between different word types and the influence of those word types on tasks such as lexical decision, word rating, memory recall, and word priming (see Altarriba & Bauer, 2004; Bleasdale, 1987; Tse & Altarriba, 2009). In a series of papers, Altarriba and colleagues set out to distinguish across the three word types above – concrete, abstract, and emotion – in terms of their lexical characteristics and their overall effects on a variety of distinct tasks (Altarriba & Basnight-Brown, 2012; Altarriba & Bauer, 2004; Altarriba, Bauer, & Benvenuto, 1999). Tasks such as these are performed by participants on sets of words that have been matched in terms of their length, frequency, and other characteristics known to moderate language processing. For example, in terms of word ratings, while concrete words were found to be higher in concreteness as compared to abstract and emotion words, emotion words were found to be more imageable than abstract words. It is likely that emotion words that can often be used to describe a facial expression can more easily yield an image than say abstract words such as "myth" or "fact." It was also reported that emotion words can more easily be recalled as compared to matched sets of abstract or concrete words, likely due to their arousal and valence components.

Interestingly, Altarriba and Basnight-Brown (2012) reported that when these three word types are acquired in a second language by an emerging bilingual (e.g., native English speakers acquiring vocabulary words in Spanish), there is a gradient in terms of their acquisition such that newly learned emotion words vs. non-emotion words produced faster color naming times, longer recognition times, and higher error rates in recognition. The authors point out that since the emotion words were acquired within the context of an experiment and not in a context in which the emotion itself was highly experienced (as is the case in the native language in emotional contexts), these words tend to elicit fewer of the components of arousal that would have accumulated overtime, using the words in multiple ways across a variety of situations. Therefore, these items are actually attention-getting because they are emotions (i.e., and as a result, affect behavior to some degree depending on the task). However, the impact of their negative valence has not accumulated to the point of negatively impacting behavior, at this early stage of learning. Lastly, an additional factor to consider in the processing of different word types emerged when Bauer and Altarriba (2008) reported that females rated concrete words as more emotional than males – a new finding which indicates that emotion word ratings can also be moderated by individual differences across participants.

While some researchers argue that abstract words can also have powerful, moderating effects if they are emotional in nature (Kousta et al., 2011; Vigliocco et al., 2013), it is important to note that earlier work actually combined abstract and emotion words into one, solid category without separating out emotionally valenced stimuli from more neutral stimuli within that category. As described earlier, much is currently known regarding how emotional stimuli differ from abstract stimuli even when numerous characteristics have been controlled for (e.g., frequency, length, naming time, valence, arousal, etc.). Emotion words simply carry components that moderate behaviors above and beyond any notion of "abstractness" that may characterize them, as shown in the various works cited above.

### 13.3.2 Differences between emotion and emotion-laden words

In addition to distinguishing emotion words from abstract (and concrete) words, a growing body of literature has focused on distinguishing between individual emotion word types within and between languages. Altarriba (2006) provided an overview of the study of emotion words (e.g., *happy, sad*) as compared to emotion-laden words (e.g., *prisoner, death*). Note that in the first instance, emotion words describe an actual emotional state or a feeling. In the case of emotion-laden words, the emotional component or sensation is mediated via an association that has been made between the word and a given feeling. These are "mediated" effects. So, for example, for some individuals the word "clown" elicits a positive response that might elicit memories of carnivals, parades, and happy occasions. For other individuals, this word might elicit negative feelings, as they may have encountered a clown that was particularly frightening or who perhaps made an unexpected gesture or movement that served to mediate a negative response that then became associated to this word. One does not feel "clown" but one has a feeling as a result of accessing the word and activating different memory traces that are coded along with the word. Altarriba and Basnight-Brown (2011) asked participants to respond to words on the basis of their valence (positive or negative) or on the basis of their color (blue or green) via a key press. Words were either emotion words or emotion-laden words, and bilingual participants viewed those words in both English and in Spanish. During the task, the participants pressed one of two keys to denote whether a word presented in white ink was positive or negative, and on other trials they pressed one of two keys to denote whether the word was presented in blue or green ink. When the correct response key for the valence of the word (e.g., pressing the POSITIVE key for a positive emotion word), matched the *same* response key as the correct color of that word presented later (e.g., pressing the same key on the keyboard to denote that the word was BLUE) – the trial was considered a "congruent" case (as both the response for the valence of the white word and the response for the ink color of the word, on a later trial, matched). Faster responses when the response keys were matched (referred to as a congruency effect), as opposed to a mixed set of responses, results in a finding known as the Affective Simon Effect (see also de Houwer & Eelen, 1998, for specific examples with monolingual populations). In Altarriba and Basnight-Brown's study (2011), the interesting result was that this congruency effect elicited faster responses for both positive and negative items in the emotion-laden condition, while the same results only occurred for emotion words that were negative. Bilinguals showed similar effects across each of their languages. Thus, emotion words moderate the Affective Simon Task much more than do emotion-laden words that often, in fact, perform more like neutral words, in many cases. It appears that emotion words – those that directly label an emotional state – tend to influence responses much more readily than emotion-laden words in both the dominant and the subordinate language of a bilingual (see also Pavlenko, 2008, for a related discussion).

In a different task, Knickerbocker and Altarriba (2013) presented participants with a series of short word lists in which an emotion word or an emotion-laden word was repeated among a list of symbol strings (e.g., *******). These lists were shown quite quickly, and participants were asked to recall the words in the order in which they had been presented. The result is typically termed "repetition blindness" or RB, as quite often, participants fail to report the second occurrence of the word when the words are repeated, as compared to an unrepeated control.

When emotion words are repeated, participants display larger RB effects as compared to emotion-laden words or neutral words. That is, the first instance of the emotion words tends to "capture attention," so much so that it becomes difficult for the participant to encode the second occurrence as a separate, discrete, repetition. Again, even when emotion and emotion-laden words are controlled across a variety of categories and characteristics, the emotion words tend to exert a stronger influence on encoding, storage, and retrieval as compared to emotion-laden or neutral words. Results such as these call for researchers to use caution when creating stimulus lists so as not to mix words unsystematically within conditions – words that could exert varying influences on performance and ultimately affect the observed outcomes of a study.

## 13.4 Emotion word processing across languages

### 13.4.1 Behavioral measures of emotion processing

In the past decade, the study of emotion word processing has been extended to bilingual populations, in an effort to determine whether emotional stimuli are represented in memory in a similar way for each language. The study of emotional stimuli across languages has focused on lower-level cognitive behavioral processes (e.g., Emotion Stroop tasks, Simon tasks), biological responses (e.g., skin conductance responses, ERPs, etc.), as well as higher order, semantic processes that affect the memory system (e.g., priming tasks, memory recall, autobiographical memory, etc.). Given the specific interest from some researchers to determine whether emotion words are *automatically* processed differently in the L1 versus the L2, the Emotion Stroop task, which was introduced previously, was used in several cross-language studies. In one of the first studies to use this popular cognitive task to explore underlying emotion representation, Sutton et al. (2007) investigated emotional Stroop effects in Spanish–English bilinguals. Response latencies to negative and neutral color words that appeared in both languages revealed significant interference effects (i.e., slower response times to emotion words) in both the L1 and L2 – replicating the pattern observed in monolingual studies. However, of specific interest in the bilingual case, was the observation that the size of the interference effects did not differ across language, which indicates that emotion words are capable of capturing attention in both of a bilingual's two languages (i.e., at least for early bilinguals who are highly proficient in both languages). In a second demonstration of emotional Stroop in bilinguals, emotion word processing was tested in Finnish–English bilinguals, who also exhibited high levels of proficiency in their two languages (Eilola, Havelka, & Sharma, 2007). Eilola et al. (2007), like Sutton et al. (2007), observed significant interference effects in both the L1 and L2. Other studies that have used priming paradigms to explore the automaticity of emotion word processing have also reported similar effects in the L1 and L2 (Altarriba & Canary, 2004; Degner, Doycheva, & Wentura, 2012), replicating those observed in other behavioral tasks.

Recent data from late Thai–English bilinguals, who did not show the same degree of interference in their two languages (Winskel, 2013), further support the key role that proficiency plays in Emotion Stroop performance. However, it is important to note that differences in methodology might be responsible for this observation, as an analysis of the emotion stimuli used in the study by Winskel showed a mix of emotional and emotion-laden items. Furthermore, differences also arose for the neutral words, where items belonging to that condition did not all belong to the same category, as they have in several other studies (see Sutton et al., 2007, for a discussion on this issue).

### 13.4.2 Physiological measures of emotion processing

Some of the first studies to explore physiological measures of emotional influence used skin conductance responses (SCRs) specifically because it is known that

> the autonomic nervous system responds to signs of threat by preparing systems of the body to take action. Part of the overall physical response to danger is sweating of the palms and fingertips, signals that can be quantified by measuring the transient increase in skin's electrical conductivity. (Harris, Gleason, & Ayçiçeği, 2005: 259)

Early studies that used this technique revealed stronger SCRs when processing words in the bilingual's L1, as compared to the L2, suggesting that the emotional representation of a word in the L1 (or dominant language) exerts a stronger biological response (Harris, 2004; Harris, Ayçiçeği, & Gleason, 2003; Harris et al., 2005; Simcox et al., 2012). Furthermore, comparisons across the different types of emotional stimuli examined, revealed that responses to reprimands (e.g., "Don't do that!" or "Shame on you!") were strongest in the L1. This is not surprising given that the environment in which these words were learned, most likely provided a specific context that enhanced the encoding and retrieval processes of that specific type of emotional material. As seen in much of the bilingual literature using various research paradigms, results from these initial studies also suggest that proficiency and age of acquisition (AoA) affect the strength of the physiological response in each language. As Harris (2004) suggested, SCR scores may be higher in the L1 for lower proficiency bilinguals, but the same (in the L1 and L2) for those with greater proficiency in both languages. In a similar vein, AoA, which is often correlated with proficiency, was naturally found to be influential as well, in that weaker physiological responses in the L2 only appeared when that language was learned after the age of 7 (Harris et al., 2005).

Like much of the phenomena observed within the psycholinguistic domain, reported interactions between additional variables, some of which are specific to emotional stimuli, continue to complicate the picture that emerges with regard to emotion processing in a bilingual context. For example, the strength of SCRs elicited appears to depend on the modality in which the emotional stimuli are presented. Harris et al. (2003) reported that for Turkish–English bilinguals, stronger SCRs were observed in the L1 for words presented auditorily, as compared to visually. In contrast, items presented in the L2, showed no modality differences. In addition, a recent study that examined *both* physiological (e.g., ERP data) and behavioral responses to positive and negative stimuli emphasized the role of valence during processing. Wu and Thierry (2012) had Chinese–English bilinguals participate in a translation-priming task, where valence was manipulated (i.e., stimuli consisted of positive, negative, and neutral items). Results from the ERP data revealed that both the L1 and L2 appeared active when the bilinguals read positive and neutral English (L2) words; however, when they read negative words in the L2, translations in Chinese (L1) did not appear to be automatically activated (i.e., which suggests that the physiological response is not only language dependent, but valence dependent as well). Although this finding is interesting because this study is one of the first to explore the processing of emotion with ERP and translation *simultaneously*, it is important to note that the participants in this study were all adolescent bilinguals; therefore, it would be interesting to see if this interaction between valence and priming holds for those who learned their L2 at an earlier age.

Another recent study that has shed light on the complexity of the processing of emotion in bilingual speakers, focused on the differences that emerge between data collected at a physiological level, and those obtained from a more conscious level of processing. Caldwell-Harris et al. (2011) collected SCRs from Mandarin–English bilinguals, as they listened to emotional phrases in both of their languages. Interestingly, for those with high levels of proficiency in both languages, SCR data showed stronger responses for English endearments, despite the fact that the bilinguals rated those phrases similarly in both languages. Although this finding may seem to contradict previous studies, an interview portion of the study revealed that many of these bilinguals indicated English as being their more emotional language. As the authors explained, "respondents associated English with the cultural permission to freely speak about emotional topics" (p. 331). Based on these findings, Caldwell-Harris et al.'s study stresses the important role that culture (i.e., or more specifically the culture that coincides with a particular language) plays in the emotional development of one acquiring that language (see also Dewaele, 2008). Lastly, this new finding once again stresses the complex nature of emotion, by revealing that self-reports and interviews regarding how a bilingual consciously perceives their two languages should be used in conjunction with other physiological and behavioral measures, in an effort to explain why data from the two may reveal similar or dissimilar patterns.

Further support that behavioral and physiological data may produce patterns that differ, appeared in a study where the degree of interference in a Stroop task, in addition to SCR data, was examined in both native and non-native speakers of English. Specifically, in the Emotion Stroop task, Eilola and Havelka (2011) observed similar interference effects in both native and non-native speakers (for negative and taboo words). However, the SCR data revealed stronger responses to negative and taboo words (as compared to positive and neutral words), only for the native speakers of English. Therefore, similar behavioral data for the two groups, but stronger SCRs for native speakers (as compared to those processing the negative emotional items in their L2), underscores that discrepancies can arise from tasks that can be found to measure different levels of processing.

### 13.4.3 Semantic and autobiographical measures of emotion processing

As mentioned, the influence of emotional content on higher order cognitive processes that affect both the semantic and autobiographical memory systems have also been examined empirically. For example, Anooshian and Hertel (1994) had Spanish–English bilinguals rate emotion and neutral words on several linguistic and semantic factors (i.e., ease of pronunciation, emotionality, etc.). Later, they unexpectedly gave the bilinguals a recall test. The results revealed that in the L1, emotion words were remembered better than neutral words, whereas in the L2, no difference emerged between word types. Although this finding was one of the first of its kind to show the effect that emotional content has on the bilingual memory system, several authors have suggested that one must be cautious when interpreting this finding, as an analysis of the stimuli used in the study revealed that 70 percent of the emotional items were of a positive valence. Therefore, in an attempt to make up for this shortcoming, Ayçiçeği and Harris (2004) studied bilingual memory for words that were either positive (e.g., friend, love), negative (e.g., anger, cancer), taboo items (e.g., raped, whore), and reprimands (e.g., Shame on you!; Stop that!). Furthermore, they also manipulated the type of memory test given, by using a recall vs. recognition test as a between-subjects manipulation in their design. Results from both of the memory tests revealed that in the L2, more emotion words were accurately recalled, as compared to neutral items. Interestingly, in the L1, only the taboo words showed this same advantage. However, it is important to mention that the emotion words used in this study were a mix of emotional and emotion-laden items, an issue which was discussed earlier and which can produce differing results.

Due to the fact that many of the previously published studies within this area have focused on bilingual populations who were living in an environment where their L2 was the majority language, Ayçiçeği-Dinn and Caldwell-Harris (2009) conducted a study where they examined memory for emotional content in bilinguals who were residing in the country where their L1 was spoken. In their study, bilinguals were presented with positive, negative, and neutral words, and for each item, were asked to complete either a shallow processing task (e.g., "How many letters contain a closed circle?") or a deep processing task (e.g., "Translate the word into the other language, or provide associates to the item presented"). Replicating what has been observed in previous studies, the results indicated greater recall for emotional items across all tasks. However, further analysis also revealed that positive items resulted in slightly better memory across languages, but that taboo words and reprimands appeared to be the driving force behind this "emotion memory effect" (see also Ferré et al., 2010). Finally, although this finding is promising since it was designed to compare the results of shallow versus deep encoding processes, it is important to point out once again, that the positive and negative emotional words used within this study were also a mix of emotional and emotion-laden items.

Other studies designed to explore the interaction between emotional content and the human memory system have focused on the effect of emotional arousal (or strength) on autobiographical memories. Studies that have employed the use of ratings, personal narratives, and interview sessions, have suggested that emotion words are encoded and expressed more deeply in a bilingual's L1, as compared to their L2 (Dewaele, 2004, 2010; Dewaele & Pavlenko, 2002; Pavlenko, 2005b). For example, Dewaele (2008) reported that the phrase "I love you" was perceived with more emotional weight (i.e., felt strongest in) the bilingual's first language. In a similar vein, Pavlenko and Driagina (2007) observed that bilinguals use fewer emotion words during L2 discourse, as compared to L1 discourse. Furthermore, retrieval of autobiographical memories was shown to be dependent on the language and context present during encoding (e.g., known as the *Language Dependent Memory Hypothesis*). Specifically, bilinguals appear to access more autobiographical memories, and produce memories that have stronger emotional intensity, when the language of "questioning" (i.e., interview language or cue word) matches that used when the event they are discussing occurred (Marian & Kaushanskaya, 2004; Marian & Neisser, 2000).

When discussing research that has used these methods (e.g., interviews, narratives, ratings of "emotionality" of a phrase, etc.) to explore language use, the role of culture and its effect on emotional expression cannot be ignored. For example, research conducted on Korean–English bilinguals, who immigrated to an English-speaking country during adolescence, reported that they were more likely to use swear words in the L2 (English) (Kim & Starks, 2008). Many of these participants explained that they had learned these words by watching TV, and that either they did not know these words in Korean, or that they did not use them because their parents would not approve. Interestingly, most of these bilinguals did express a preference for expressing emotion in their L1, with the exception of anger, which, when felt, resulted in increased L2 use. Some explained that this was a way of distancing themselves from the emotion, an important aspect of bilingual language use, which will be addressed further in the section that follows. Finally, in a provocative study which shows the strong influence that cultural norms and attitudes can have on emotional expression, Panayiotou (2004) interviewed individuals who were fluent in both Greek and English, and asked them to express their emotions about a brief synopsis given about a fictional man Andy (in English)/Andreas (in Greek). The wording of both situations was identical, except that one was read in Greek and the other in English (one month apart). The character was described as a man who worked too much, and as a result, did not have enough time to visit his widowed mother, or to spend with his girlfriend. Interestingly, when describing the individual in this scenario, the participants seemed to have more concern for Andreas (when the situation was presented in Greek and they were interviewed in Greek), and more disapproval for Andy (the character in the English situation). As Panayiotou (2004) describes, one bilingual reported feeling "frustrated and disapproval because his [Andy's] priorities are wrong," another felt that Andy was "purely selfish," while those describing Andreas, felt that "he needed to work, maybe because of his mom, and because he was getting married" (p. 130). Basically, these results reveal that the same story or character description can be interpreted in a completely different manner, where different emotions are aroused or expressed, simply based on the language being used at the time, and the cultural expectations that go along with that language.

Overall, these studies that have focused on emotion processing in bilinguals reveal that the manner and context in which emotional stimuli are encoded in memory have the ability to affect later retrieval – in the degree of accuracy, number of details, and degree of emotion felt. Importantly, these findings also show that knowing and using a second language, influences the way one perceives events, which has an impact on the general cognitive system. Finally, the studies that have stressed the importance of cultural constraints on bilingual emotional expression also reveal the importance of examining specific emotions individually, rather than generalizing that all emotions behave in a similar manner (as demonstrated by results from Kim & Starks, 2008). In the section that follows, the role of bilingual emotion expression in more applied settings will be explored, specifically the role of bilingualism in advertising, decision-making, and clinical psychology settings.

## 13.5 Emotion word processing in applied contexts

Although much of the cognitive and psycholinguistic research on emotion processing in bilinguals has focused on the underlying memory representation of emotion in each language, the practical implications for such findings have a great impact on several different areas of applied research. For example, knowing two or more languages, and the specific way in which emotion is activated in each of those languages, has been shown to affect the manner in which individuals are influenced by advertising and marketing slogans, the decisions that are made in various situations, and the way that clients express themselves in clinical settings. Specifically, it has been reported that advertising slogans presented in the L1 are viewed as being more emotional than those that appear in the L2 (Puntoni, Langhe, & van Osselaer, 2009). Further García et al. (2013) recently revealed that mixed language advertisements, which are common in many places of the world where bilingual populations exist, tend to be "rejected when they challenge the identity of the brand" (p. 90). For example, in their study, Spanish–English bilinguals reported that mixed language or English language slogans for a Mexican brand beverage "Jarritos," left a feeling that the slogan was a violation of the brand (due to the language used). These bilinguals felt that Spanish should be used exclusively when marketing this product, in order to elicit a more genuine and convincing emotional response. In addition, a recent, and provocative line of research has focused on whether bilinguals make the same decisions in a foreign language as they would in their native language (Keysar, Hayakawa, & An, 2012). When participants were presented with a series of classic scenarios, where the options were each framed differently, the results revealed that people were willing to take more risks in a foreign language, as they relied more on systematic processes when making a decision in that language. In contrast, decision-making biases were greater in the L1 (i.e., individuals were less objective or rational when making decisions in that language, and relied more on emotion), since emotional responses and reactions could not be as easily separated when making a decision in that language (Keysar et al., 2012; see also Pavlenko, 2012). However, it is important to note that the bilinguals who participated in these experiments were adolescent bilinguals; therefore, it would be interesting to see how the results compared to those who learned two languages simultaneously, as decision-making differences across languages may not exist.

Finally, a series of studies aimed at exploring the important role of language and emotional expression in clinical settings, have revealed several findings that are extremely useful to those working in those environments, as well as shedding additional light on how bilinguals know and use two languages to express emotion. Some of the original research conducted in this area revealed that during therapy sessions, bilinguals will often switch into their L2, if they want to distance themselves emotionally from an event, as they often described this language as being the emotionally distant language (Altarriba & Santiago-Rivera, 1994; Dewaele & Costa, 2013; Santiago-Rivera & Altarriba, 2002). Furthermore, this unique way of using language, to distance oneself per se, has also been supported by Bond and Lai (1986), who reported that bilinguals found it easier to discuss more sensitive or embarrassing topics in the L2. The applied aspects of these findings are of great importance, as they suggest that the use of bilingual approaches in a clinical or counseling setting could help the bilingual be able to express themselves more naturally, to remember more facts about certain events, and to discuss certain topics differently, as compared to therapy that was conducted only in one language.

Although most research conducted in a clinical domain has focused on the clients in these situations and the manner in which they use language to express emotion, one study explored the linguistic strategies used by therapists during sessions. It was discovered that switching to the client's L1 helped the clinician to form stronger bonds with the client, and that it also allowed the client to understand certain aspects of the situation more clearly (Santiago-Rivera et al., 2009). One therapist even noted that "it was easier for one of her clients to talk about a threatening situation because it felt less intense when recounting the experience in that language [English, the L2]" (p. 440). In summary, the role of bilingualism and the manner in which emotion is expressed in these specific settings is something that must be considered when one is examining mental status and assessing clients (see Martinovic & Altarriba, 2012, for guidelines and a discussion on suggested training for clinicians and counselors). Overall, the results from these studies that explore applied situations in life, are far reaching, novel in their approach, and promising in that they provide other ways of thinking about the importance of emotional expression in a bilingual context.

## 13.6 Conclusions and future directions

In summary, studies that compare emotional vs. non-emotional stimuli have produced findings that argue for distinguishing between these word types and considering emotional stimuli as a distinct group of words that moderate a whole host of cognitive paradigms and effects. The preceding review indicates that positively valenced and negatively valenced words do not affect behavior in the same way, and that effects such as emotional Stroop effects, for example, are more highly affected by negative stimuli than by positive or neutral stimuli. Language proficiency also seems to matter more than Age of Acquisition (AoA) per se, as regardless of when a word is acquired, if its frequency or familiarity are driven by its repeated occurrences across a variety of contexts, it appears to be easier to access and retrieve from memory than a less commonly used word.

Additionally, many of the recent studies of emotion word representation within and across languages have started to combine behavioral (Stroop, priming, etc.) and physiological data (SCRs, ERPs) signifying a strong trend in this area of investigation and an overall protocol that should be considered in future studies. Interestingly, many of these studies are reporting a different pattern in their data, based on what one might call "levels of processing" – that is, whether one considers late vs. early; biologically mediated responses vs. more conscious semantic responding, and the like. These works also have implications for future work in the realm of social cognition. For example, Matsumoto, Anguas-Wong, and Martinez (2008) reported that Spanish–English bilinguals judge emotions differently (in faces), depending on the language they use when making the judgments. Thus, future work might be focused on examining how linguistic knowledge, particularly for a bilingual speaker, can moderate the perceptions of emotion leading to perhaps different behavioral outcomes (as well as physiological responses), as a result. Recent brain imaging studies have found that perhaps personality variables, dispositional affect, and genotype might all moderate the neural bases of emotion processes in the brain affecting emotion memory and perception (Hamann & Canli, 2004). Thus, an analysis that combines both behavioral and biological investigations may shed more light onto the complex interplay between emotion, language, and behavior.

In general, it is the case that science still has not uncovered exactly how humans store and mentally represent emotions. One can discuss the ways in which facial expressions denote emotions, the labels one gives emotions, a value for their intensity, but the question remains – how are emotional states coded in the brain and what are the patterns of neural connections that make up those states? Future research directions should include a combination of both behavioral and neural approaches to understanding how emotions are closely tied to language and to culture and the ways in which emotional knowledge and emotional language develop across the lifespan in both monolingual and bilingual speakers. Is emotion more closely tied to the native or first language? What are the exceptions to this notion? Are those exceptions based on age of acquisition, mode of acquisition, linguistic variability across languages, or other variables? The mechanisms by which emotions are coded in the brain require further investigation and an overall approach that spans across methodologies to provide a comprehensive explanation of the complexity of human emotion.

# 14

# Orthographic processing in bilinguals

Walter J. B. van Heuven and Emily L. Coderre

## 14.1 Introduction

The ability to speak more than one language is what distinguishes bilinguals from monolinguals. However, many bilinguals are also biliterate, which means that they can read and write in more than one language. Whereas spoken (or signed) language has evolved in every human culture on earth and is acquired by children relatively effortlessly, reading and writing are not inherent human skills. Learning to read and write takes years of practice and problems like dyslexia often persist into adulthood. The writing systems[1] that exist in the world differ in many ways (for an overview see Cook & Bassetti, 2005; Daniels & Bright, 1996; DeFrancis, 1989), for example in terms of whether they are meaning-based or sound-based, the script[2] used (e.g., Arabic, Hanzi, or Roman), their smallest unit (e.g., stroke, radical, letter, syllable, or character), and the rules for using the script (i.e., orthography, e.g., English or German). Biliteracy introduces a further level of complexity because the writing system of a bilingual's two languages can be similar (e.g., both alphabetic as for English–French bilinguals) or different (e.g., logographic and alphabetic as for Chinese–English bilinguals or syllabic and alphabetic as for Japanese–English bilinguals). Thus, writing systems of biliterate bilinguals (from this point referred to as bilinguals) can be a combination of alphabetic (e.g., Arabic, Cyrillic, Greek, Hebrew, Korean, Roman), syllabic (e.g., Japanese), and logographic (e.g., Chinese) languages.

---

[1] The term "writing system" refers to the genre of a language's symbolic system. For example, in alphabetic writing systems like English, each symbol represents a letter; in syllabic writing systems, such as Japanese kana, each symbol represents a syllable; and in logographic writing systems like Chinese, each symbol represents an entire word or concept.

[2] *Script* refers to the specific symbols within a written language: for example, Japanese has two scripts: the syllabic kana and the logographic kanji.

All writing systems involve different smaller orthographic units that map onto other language representations, such as larger orthographic (sub-lexical) units, phonemes, morphemes, and lexical representations. Furthermore, the degree of complexity of these orthographic units varies. For example, most Chinese characters are made up of radicals, subcomponents of the entire character, which can provide information about the pronunciation of the character (phonetic radical, e.g., 平 in 评) and the meaning of the character (semantic radical, e.g., 讠 in 评) (DeFrancis, 1989). Languages that use the Roman script such as English, French, and Italian also differ in terms of the transparency or orthographic depth of the mappings between the spelling and sounds of words (Katz & Frost, 1992). The regularity of spelling-to-sound mappings determines the strategies that readers use for orthographic processing (Lallier et al., 2013; Ziegler & Goswami, 2005): opaque or deep orthographies (e.g., English) encourage whole-word lexical processing, whereas transparent or shallow orthographies (e.g., Italian) encourage sub-lexical decoding strategies.

In this chapter we focus on the orthographic processing aspects of word recognition in bilinguals, with specific focus on how similarities and differences between the orthography of their languages influence visual word recognition. We first review behavioral and neural correlates of monolingual orthographic processing in different languages to establish the orthographic processing characteristics relevant for bilinguals. We then discuss the case of bilingualism, concentrating on cross-linguistic influences in same-script and different-script bilinguals. Next, we discuss models of bilingual orthographic processing, and end by highlighting outstanding questions in the field and offering suggestions for future research.

## 14.2 Orthographic processing in different languages

In order to successfully recognize written words, visual input has to be mapped onto corresponding representations in the mental lexicon. The visual word recognition system involves perceptual processes that map visual information (i.e., features) onto abstract symbols (e.g., letters or characters; for reviews see Dehaene et al., 2005; Grainger, Rey, & Dufau, 2008), and subsequent language processes that map these representations onto word representations in the mental lexicon.

A number of experimental tasks have been used in the literature to study orthographic processing such as lexical decision, which requires participants to judge whether letter strings are legal words or not. These tasks have often been combined with the masked priming technique (for a discussion of masked priming see Grainger, 2008; Kinoshita & Lupker, 2003). The masked priming paradigm usually involves the presentation of a mask (e.g., row of hash marks) for about 500 ms followed by the brief presentation of a prime letter string presented in lower case (e.g., nonword or word) that is then replaced by a target word presented in upper case. Unlike an unmasked priming paradigm, the prime is presented very briefly (< 60 ms) so that participants are unaware of the prime. The unconscious perception of the masked prime is thought to affect the recognition process of the subsequently presented target. An unrelated prime provides a baseline reaction time for a lexical decision on the target word; a priming effect occurs when the reaction time is reduced due to various orthographic, morphological, or semantic similarities of the prime with the target word.

One of the key questions in the visual word recognition literature has been to what extent target word recognition is influenced by words that are visually similar to the target word. Visually similar words have originally been defined as words with the same length that differ only by one letter (e.g., WORD and WORK). Such words, referred to in the literature as substitution neighbors, have been found to influence the recognition process of the target word (e.g., Carreiras, Perea, & Grainger, 1997; Grainger, 1992; Perea & Pollatsek, 1998; for reviews see Andrews, 1997; Perea & Rosa, 2000). Deletion and addition neighbors (e.g., HAT and THAT, PLANET and PLANE respectively) have also been found to influence target word recognition (e.g., Bowers, Davis, & Hanley, 2005) as well as the twenty closest Levenshtein neighbors (OLD20, see Yarkoni, Bolata, & Yap, 2008). Levenshtein neighbors have a distance value that is based on the Levenshtein metric, which refers to the minimum number of insertions, deletions, and substitutions to transform the neighbor into the target word.

The effects of orthographic neighbors on target word recognition have also been found in other scripts, such as the logographic script of Chinese (Hong & Yelland, 1997; Huang et al., 2006; Tsai et al., 2006; Zhao, Li, & Bi, 2012). In this script, the neighborhood of compound words has been defined as the number of compound words that share a character with the target compound word (e.g., Huang et al., 2006; Tsai et al., 2006), whereas for single characters the neighborhood has been defined in terms of the number of characters that share the same radical (e.g., Li et al., 2011; Zhao et al., 2012) or strokes (e.g., Hong & Yelland, 1997).

In order to distinguish between similarly written words it is important to identify individual letters and characters, and to code the position of letters and characters within the words. For example, whereas substitution neighbors such as BLOCK and CLOCK differ in terms of their first letters, transposition neighbors such as ACT and CAT can only be distinguished in terms of the position at which the letters appear. Just as substitution, addition, and deletion neighbors, transposition neighbors have also been found to influence target word recognition (e.g., Acha & Perea, 2008; Andrews, 1996; Chambers, 1979). The visual word recognition system must therefore also have a letter position coding system. Although some research has suggested that this position coding system works for any kind of visual object (García-Orza, Perea, & Muñoz, 2010), other data suggest that it is letter specific (Massol et al., 2013).

There have been a number of theoretical proposals of how letter positions can be coded (see Grainger, 2008; Grainger & van Heuven, 2003; and below) and there is an ongoing debate about which of these proposals can account best for the data in the literature (e.g., Grainger, 2008; Norris, 2013). Most studies investigating position coding have focused on alphabetic languages. However, position coding is also relevant in other writing systems. For example, the data from Su et al. (2012) provides evidence for position specific coding of radicals in Chinese character recognition. Furthermore, masked priming studies have found transposition priming (e.g., *salior–SAILOR*; e.g., Perea & Lupker, 2003) and relative position priming effects (e.g., *blcoy–BALCONY*; e.g., Grainger et al., 2006), which indicates that letter position coding needs to be flexible to account for these effects. Importantly, whereas most of orthographic priming effects have been reported in alphabetic languages (e.g., Dutch, English, French, Spanish), they have also been reported in non-alphabetic languages such as Japanese Kana (e.g., Perea, Nakatani, & van Leeuwen, 2011), Korean (e.g., Lee & Taft, 2011) and Chinese (e.g., Hong & Yelland, 1997; Huang et al., 2006), which suggests that this aspect of orthographic processing is universal.

In the next sections we briefly discuss evidence of the neural correlates of orthographic processing in terms of the time course, using event-related potentials (ERPs), and the localization, using functional magnetic resonance imaging (fMRI), of orthographic processes.

### 14.2.1 Time course of orthographic processing

Monolingual language studies using electroencephalography (EEG) have identified a series of ERPs reflecting specific steps throughout the time course of linguistic processing (Grainger & Holcomb, 2009; Sereno, Rayner, & Posner, 1998). The most salient ERP components with regard to word recognition, which will be reviewed below, are those sensitive to featural overlap (N/P150), orthographic/phonological (sub-lexical) overlap (N250), whole-word overlap (N320), and form–meaning overlap (N400) between primes and targets.

The first component elicited during word recognition is a positive peak at approximately 100 ms after stimulus presentation, referred to as the P1. This is believed to reflect perceptual and attentional processes (e.g., Luck et al., 1990; Mangun et al., 1998), although some have reported linguistic influences at the P1 component (Segalowitz & Zheng, 2009; Sereno et al., 1998).

Following the P1 is a negative peak at approximately 170 ms, known as the N1 or N170. An N170 is elicited for a range of visual stimuli, such as faces, objects, and words (Bentin et al., 1996; Rossion et al., 2003;

Rousselet, Macé, & Fabre-Thorpe, 2004; Tanaka & Curran, 2001). This component is sensitive to expertise, showing a larger negative amplitude or longer latency for familiar stimuli than for control stimuli or unfamiliar objects (e.g., Bentin et al., 1996; Boehm, Dering, & Thierry, 2011; Itier, Latinus, & Taylor, 2006; Maurer, Rossion, & McCandliss, 2008; Tanaka & Curran, 2001). For example, in bird experts, Tanaka and Curran (2001) demonstrated a larger N170 amplitude when viewing pictures of birds compared to pictures of dogs. The N170 is therefore not specific to linguistic stimuli. However, given that most adult readers are experts in visual word recognition, it is language sensitive: the N170 shows enhanced negative amplitudes to orthographically legal strings (words, pseudowords) compared to non-orthographically legal stimuli (consonant strings, symbols) (Appelbaum et al., 2009; Bentin et al., 1999; Hauk et al., 2009; Maurer et al., 2005; Wong et al., 2005). This "N170 effect" (i.e., the amplitude difference between word and symbol stimuli, at or around the N170 peak) is usually larger over the left hemisphere than the right (Appelbaum et al., 2009; Bentin et al., 1996, 1999; Grossi et al., 2010; Hauk & Pulvermüller, 2004; Maurer et al., 2005; Rossion et al., 2003; Sereno et al., 1998). This word vs. symbol string N170 effect is believed to reflect orthographic processes that are dependent on language experience (Appelbaum et al., 2009; Bentin et al., 1999; Grossi et al., 2010; Maurer et al., 2005; Ruz & Nobre, 2008). For example, adults show a typical N170 distinction between letters and symbol strings, but pre-literate children do not (Maurer et al., 2005), suggesting that the N170 effect to words requires extensive reading experience. The very early occurrence of this language-sensitive component indicates that low-level orthographic processing occurs early in the time course of linguistic processing.

The time window from 100–200 ms has also been identified by Rey et al. (2009) as reflecting the transition from visual feature analysis to letter identification. In their study they found that ERPs for letters and pseudoletters significantly deviated from each other at 145 ms. Using a mask priming paradigm, Petit et al. (2006) investigated the time course of processes involved in letter perception. They demonstrated that sub-lexical orthographic processing proceeds in series of hierarchical steps with effects of visual similarity occurring first (120–180 ms), followed by effects of case-specific letter identity (180–220 ms), and then effects of case-independent letter identity (220–300 ms).

The N250, a negativity occurring approximately 250 ms after stimulus presentation, is commonly elicited in masked priming paradigms. This component is sensitive to orthographic overlap of primes and targets, showing increasing negativity with decreasing letter overlap (Holcomb & Grainger, 2006). It is also sensitive to semantic transparency, showing increasing N250 amplitude with increasing semantic similarity of prime–target pairs (Morris et al., 2007). Similarly, an N250 component is often reported in the translation priming literature in bilinguals (in which a prime is the translation equivalent of the target), and is particularly sensitive to priming from the second language (L2) to the first language (L1) (Schoonbaert et al., 2011). The N250 is thus sensitive to both morphological structure and semantic transparency of prime–target pairs.

A later component known as the N320 has been associated with phonology (Bentin et al., 1999; Simon et al., 2004). This component was elicited only by pronounceable words and pseudowords but not by unpronounceable, orthographically illegal consonant strings in a rhyming decision task (Bentin et al., 1999), suggesting a role in grapheme-to-phoneme conversion. Similarly, Simon et al. (2004) reported that this component was elicited by strings of consonants and pseudowords but not for false fonts. Therefore the N320 seems to be sensitive to the lexical/phonological properties of a stimulus.

Finally, the N400 component has been found to be sensitive to the number of substitution neighbors (neighborhood density) of words and pseudowords. Holcomb, Grainger, & O'Rourke (2002) observed that words and pseudowords with a large number of substitution neighbors generated a larger N400 than words and pseudowords with a small number of substitution neighbors in both lexical decision and go/no-go semantic categorization tasks. Furthermore, earlier effects of neighborhood density were also found from 150–350 ms, but only in the go/no-go semantic categorization task. The N400 neighborhood effects have been replicated in a number of other studies (e.g., Huang et al., 2006; Vergara-Martinez & Swaab, 2012). For example, Vergara-Martinez and Swaab (2012) reported also N400 (260–500 ms) effects of orthographic neighborhood defined by OLD20 (Yarkoni et al., 2008) in a go/no-go semantic categorization task.

### 14.2.2 Effects of script on ERP components

Most of the research described above was performed on languages using a Roman script. However, an important question is whether the temporal characteristics and/or amplitude of the ERP components mentioned above are modulated by specificities of the script and/or of the writing system. The N170 is reported across different languages, including Chinese (Lin et al., 2011), French and Arabic (Simon et al., 2006, 2007), and Hebrew (Bar-Kochva, 2011). However, language-specific script differences have been reported at the N170. For example, Bar-Kochva (2011) investigated the two scripts of Hebrew, which have different orthographic depths, reporting that the shallow Hebrew script generated a larger N170 than the deep orthographic script. Simon et al. (2006) reported that N170 amplitudes were less negative for Arabic compared to French. They also reported differences in laterality such that French elicited a more left-lateralized N170 whereas Arabic elicited a bilateral component. Laterality effects at the N170 may also be affected by proficiency. For example (Maurer, Zevin, & McCandliss, 2008) found less left-lateralization in the less-proficient or less-familiar language for Japanese–English speakers. On the other hand, Proverbio, Čok, & Zani (2002) reported a left-lateralized N170 for Slovenian but not for Italian in Italian–Slovenian bilinguals. Nevertheless, it seems that the left-lateralization of the N170 is not specific to the writing system, whereas the amplitude of this component is sensitive to script differences. Interestingly, while script has been shown to modulate N170 amplitude, no differences have been reported in the latency of the effect: the N170 effect occurs at similar latencies across languages regardless of other linguistic differences (e.g., in Chinese: Lin et al., 2011; Yum, Holcomb, & Grainger, 2011; in French and Arabic: Simon et al., 2006, 2007; in Hebrew: Bar-Kochva, 2011). This suggests that orthographic processing occurs at a relatively similar time course for all languages.

Script differences at later ERP components of the linguistic processing timeline are less widely reported, although Simon et al. (2006) report differences at the N320 grapheme-to-phoneme conversion component. In their comparison of French and Arabic, an N320 was present for French but not for Arabic, indicating a heavier reliance on spelling-to-sound conversion in the more regular French orthography. Therefore, differences have been reported between orthographies at early ERP components reflecting lexical processing. However, there are few studies that explicitly address differences between languages, so a full exploration of the influences of orthography on the timing and magnitude of these ERP components is still needed.

One recent study by Okana, Grainger, and Holcomb (2013) investigated within-language script differences using ERP. They investigated within- and cross-script repetition priming effects in Japanese using the syllabary scripts hiragana and katakana (hiragana is used for native words, whereas katakana is generally used for specific circumstances such as words imported from other languages). Their data revealed that repetition priming modulated the same ERP components as reported with alphabetic scripts (see Grainger & Holcomb, 2009). Within-script repetition modulated the N/P150, whereas both within- and between-script repetition modulated the N250 and N400 ERP components, although somewhat delayed. The authors concluded that these findings suggest that the neurocognitive processes involved in visual word recognition are similar across languages and writing systems.

### 14.2.3 Localization of orthographic processing

Whereas EEG studies primarily concern the timing of linguistic processes, fMRI is employed to address the spatial representations of language in the brain. In monolinguals, the various facets of language activate a widespread fronto-temporal network of brain areas (e.g., Binder et al., 1997; Ferstl et al., 2008; Gitelman et al., 2005; Richardson et al., 2011). There is extensive overlap in the functional specificity of these regions: in a conjunction analysis, Gitelman et al. (2005) identified a neural network commonly involved in orthographic, phonological, and semantic processing (in English) which included the left inferior frontal gyrus (LIFG), middle frontal gyrus (MFG), insula, precentral sulcus, and supplementary motor area (SMA). Although sensitive to language, these brain areas are not exclusively dedicated to reading; all regions involved are also active in other tasks and perform more domain-general functions (Vogel et al., 2013).

However, one area commonly reported in neuroimaging studies of word recognition is the visual word form area (VWFA), localized in the left fusiform gyrus. This region is sensitive to the processing of letter strings (words and pseudowords) compared to non-orthographic symbols, and is thought to integrate the letters of a word together into a "visual word form" while being relatively insensitive to other perceptual variations such as font, case, and size (e.g., Cohen et al., 2000; McCandliss, Cohen, & Dehaene, 2003). The VWFA does not distinguish between words with semantic similarity (Braet, Wagemans, & Op de Beeck, 2011), suggesting it is involved in low-level visual discrimination of words rather than higher-level lexical and semantic access.

### 14.2.4 Impact of writing systems on language organization in the brain

Language organization in the brain is to some extent influenced by writing system (e.g., Bick, Goelman, & Frost, 2011; Bolger, Perfetti, & Schneider, 2005; Coderre et al., 2008; Nelson et al., 2009; Perfetti et al., 2007; Sakurai et al., 2000; Tan et al., 2001; Tan et al., 2005). Even within alphabetic languages, the orthographic depth of a language can influence its representations. For example, Paulesu et al. (2000) reported that native readers of Italian, a shallow language, recruited left superior temporal regions involved in print-to-sound mapping when reading Italian; in contrast, native readers of English, a relatively more opaque language, recruited inferior frontal areas involved in word retrieval and holistic word processing when reading English. Workman et al. (2000) showed that Welsh involved more left-hemisphere processing than English in native speakers of each language. They hypothesized that the shallower script in Welsh led to a greater reliance on phonology, driven by the left hemisphere, than on ideographic processing of words, driven by the right.

Comparisons of the differences in processing for alphabetic and logographic writing systems have in general indicated a large network of overlapping regions (Bolger et al., 2005; Tan et al., 2005) such as the left superior temporal gyrus, left inferior frontal gyrus, and left occipitotemporal region. However, disparities are present: for example, Bolger et al. (2005) reported differences between writing systems in the posterior superior temporal gyrus, left anterior dorsal frontal region, and right occipitotemporal cortex. They attributed these disparities to processing differences in phonological coding, the integration of phonology and orthography, and orthographic coding, respectively.

In a recent study, Kawabata Duncan et al. (2014) compared the neural response and functional connectivity in response to kanji or kana words, two scripts used in the Japanese language: kanji is logographic while kana is syllabic. They reported similar areas of activation for both scripts, but differences in the connectivity between regions. Kanji showed more interhemispheric connectivity than kana, specifically in connections between the right and left ventral occipitotemporal cortex; this was interpreted as a greater need to integrate the more spatially and visually complex kanji stimuli in the right hemisphere with language processing regions in the left. Furthermore, the strength of this connectivity was modulated by proficiency in reading kanji, suggesting increased efficiency of information transfer with higher proficiency. In contrast, kana showed stronger connectivity from the pars opercularis in the frontal cortex to the supramarginal gyrus in the parietal cortex, which may indicate a greater need for phonological assembly in this syllabic script.

The VWFA has also been shown to be consistently activated by both alphabetic and logographic writing systems (Bolger et al., 2005; Dehaene & Cohen, 2011; Liu et al., 2008; Perfetti, Liu, & Tan, 2005). However, while English typically activates the left fusiform gyrus, Chinese has been shown to activate the bilateral fusiform gyri (Bolger et al., 2005; Tan et al., 2005), a finding which has been attributed to the more complex visual, spatial, and orthographic processing in Chinese. In contrast, in a comparison of orthographic, phonological, and semantic processing in Chinese, Wu, Ho, and Chen (2012) reported bilateral activation for phonological and semantic processing but only left-lateralized activation for orthographic processing. Therefore the more complex nature of orthographic processing in logographic languages like Chinese is still poorly understood, but seems to affect the neural organization of language processing.

## 14.3 Orthographic processing in bilinguals

Given the complexities of language processing in monolinguals, the situation of bilingualism becomes a fascinating case and raises many interesting questions regarding the processing and representation of multiple languages in the brain. Especially when a second language is acquired early in life and mastered to a high degree of proficiency, bilingualism confers significant effects on cognitive processing (e.g., Bialystok et al., 2009). This section explores the effects of bilingualism on orthographic processing, with specific focus on the impact of language similarity and script. Furthermore, we discuss whether bilinguals can utilize script differences between their languages to manage their languages.

### 14.3.1 Bilingual lexical organization and access in same-script and different-script bilinguals

One important issue in early bilingualism research concerned the organization of, and access to, the bilinguals' languages. For example, bilingual aphasics sometimes lose only one of their languages while the other is kept intact (for a review, see Lorenzen & Murray, 2008), which would suggest separate language representations. However, an overwhelming number of studies now support the view that word recognition involves non-selective access to an integrated lexicon (for reviews see Dijkstra, 2005; Dijkstra & van Heuven, 2002). Evidence for this view comes from, for example, studies with bilinguals that manipulate the number of substitution neighbors of target words within and between languages (e.g., Grossi et al., 2012; Midgley et al., 2008; van Heuven, Dijkstra, & Grainger, 1998). For example, van Heuven et al. (1998) reported behavioral effects of both within- and between-language neighbors in Dutch–English bilinguals, and Midgley et al. (2008) reported N400 modulations of cross-language neighborhood density in L1 and L2 target words with French–English bilinguals (see also Grossi et al., 2012, with proficient Welsh–English bilinguals).

Further evidence comes from studies using interlingual homographs (i.e., words from two or more languages with same spelling but a different meaning, e.g., RAMP meaning "disaster" in Dutch) to assess cross-linguistic influences in alphabetic scripts (e.g., Dijkstra, van Jaarsveld, & Ten Brinke, 1998; Kerkhofs et al., 2006; van Heuven et al., 2008). For example, van Heuven et al. (2008), using fMRI with an English lexical decision task, found that compared to control words that only occur in English, interlingual homographs elicited in Dutch–English bilinguals enhanced activation in the dorsal anterior cingulate and the inferior frontal cortex, areas involved in managing conflicting information. This suggests parallel activation of both languages in the bilingual brain despite a monolingual context.

Finally, a large number of studies have investigated cross-linguistic interactions and the organization of the bilingual lexicon using cognates. Cognates are words that have the same meaning in two or more languages and also share a similar or identical spelling and/or pronunciation. Thus, whereas interlingual homographs can only exist between languages written in the same script, cognates can exist in languages with either the same or different scripts. Same-script cognates can have complete (e.g., WINTER in Dutch and English) or partly overlapping spelling (e.g., BANAAN in Dutch and BANANA in English), whereas different-script cognates have identical or very similar pronunciations (e.g., the word SYSTEM in English and システム /shisutemu/ in Japanese). In bilinguals with languages using the same script, the general finding is that cognates are recognized faster than non-cognate words (e.g., Dijkstra, Grainger, & van Heuven, 1999; Peeters, Dijkstra, & Grainger, 2013; van Hell & Dijkstra, 2002). ERP studies have found that the N400 component in particular is sensitive to both the cognate (e.g., Peeters et al., 2013) and homograph (e.g, Kerkhofs et al., 2006) status of words. Importantly, the amount of orthographic and/or phonological similarity of the cognate words determines the size of the cognate effect (Dijkstra et al., 2010), raising interesting questions for bilinguals who use two very different languages.

Cognate effects have also been found in different-script bilinguals using lexical decision and picture naming (e.g., Japanese–English: Allen & Conklin, 2013; Hoshino & Kroll, 2008). Although cognate effects are found in both same- and different-script language pairs, it is unclear whether general language similarity modulates these effects, as there are so far no studies, as far as we know, that systematically have compared cognate effects between different language pairs.

Cross-script cognates have also been used in masked translation priming studies. The general finding is that L1 translation primes facilitate L2 cognate recognition relative to unrelated L1 primes (e.g., Gollan, Forster, & Frost, 1997; Voga & Grainger, 2007). Masked priming studies using non-cognates have also demonstrated cross-language masked translation priming effects in same-script and different-script bilinguals (for an overview see Schoonbaert et al., 2009).

Cross-script interactions have also been observed through automatic unconscious translation in a purely L2 context. Thierry and Wu (2007) asked Chinese–English bilinguals to judge whether a pair of English words were semantically related. Interestingly, half of the items comprised pairs of English words for which their Chinese translations (compound words) shared the same characters. For example, the English words "train" and "ham" are not related, but their Chinese translations, 火车 and 火腿, respectively, share the character 火. The data revealed that the N400 was modulated by this hidden character repetition effect, indicating that bilinguals automatically translated the English words into their native language. In a similar design, Zhang, van Heuven, and Conklin (2011) used a masked priming paradigm with Chinese–English bilinguals and found a Chinese morpheme priming effect in a purely English lexical decision task: the masked prime EAST (东) primed a lexical decision on the word THING (东西) because the Chinese translations of these words shared a morpheme. Therefore the presence of cross-linguistic effects in both same-script and different-script bilinguals indicates the highly integrated and interactive nature of their language systems.

Cross-linguistic influences also affect the neural representations of language in the brain. As mentioned earlier, in monolinguals, alphabetic languages generally activate left-lateralized regions of the language network, whereas logographic languages show a more bilateral distribution. This may be related to the left hemisphere's better ability to manage phonological information, whereas the right is better suited for ideographic processing (Bolger et al., 2005; Perfetti et al., 2007; Siok et al., 2009; Tan et al., 2001). These language-specific orthographic properties can affect language representation during development. For example, research has shown that native speakers of a logographic writing system who are learning an alphabetic language (such as Chinese speakers learning English) activate bilateral language networks for reading both Chinese and English (Cao et al., 2013; Nelson et al., 2009; Perfetti et al., 2007). This is interpreted as an *assimilation* strategy: they use the language networks already in place to process the new language and essentially "try to read English as if it were Chinese" (Perfetti et al., 2007: 136). In contrast, in native speakers of an alphabetic language learning a logographic language (e.g., English speakers learning Chinese), reading English elicited a left-lateralized pattern of language processing, whereas reading Chinese activated a bilateral pattern. This was interpreted as an *accommodation* strategy, such that the typical structures are used to process the native language but additional neural structures not usually used for alphabetic languages are recruited for processing the more spatial logographic language.

Relatively little work has been done on the issue of assimilation and accommodation, and it may be that the balance of assimilation and accommodation in L2 reading depends on the nature of the spelling-to-sound mappings between languages. Cao et al. (2013) proposed that because Chinese is a more complex language system, with arbitrary mappings between orthography and phonology, it can handle the relatively simpler English system. In contrast, English has semi-regular mappings between orthography and phonology, so adapting to a more complex system like Chinese requires the recruitment of additional resources. However, evidence for assimilation and accommodation has also been reported for Hindi–English bilinguals (Das et al., 2011), suggesting that even subtle differences in orthographic depth can affect the neural organization of an L2. Additional factors such as age of acquisition (AoA) and proficiency in the second language may also play a role: higher proficiency in an alphabetic L2 has been associated with greater assimilation and less accommodation (Cao et al., 2013), while late bilinguals showed greater accommodation compared to early bilinguals who demonstrated native-like patterns of lateralization in both their languages (Das et al., 2011). Nevertheless, it seems apparent that cross-linguistic influences between a bilingual's languages can also affect neural organization and processing.

A large number of studies have investigated the localization of L1 and L2 in the bilingual brain, with some reporting separated brain regions and others reporting overlapping brain regions. For example, the VWFA has been associated with orthographic word processing in various scripts and languages in monolinguals (see above), and a recent study concluded that this region is also engaged in processing of Chinese and Korean in Chinese–Korean bilinguals (Bai et al., 2011). Meta-analyses of studies investigating the localisation of the bilingual's languages have concluded that the L1 and L2 brain activations overlap (e.g., Indefrey, 2006; Stowe & Sabourin, 2005). However, language proficiency is an important factor when considering the spatial extent of brain activation when processing the L2, with more extensive activation (both wider activation of similar regions as the L1 and recruitment of additional regions) for a less-proficient language (e.g., Chee et al., 2001; Hasegawa, Carpenter, & Just, 2002; Meschyan & Hernandez, 2006; Rüschemeyer, Zysset, & Friederici, 2006; Vingerhoets et al., 2003), indicating more processing effort.

Related to the issue of the localisation of L1 and L2 in the bilingual brain is the question of language laterality, which has also been debated extensively in the literature. For example, Workman et al. (2000) showed that Welsh involved more left-hemisphere processing than English in native speakers of each language. However, Paradis (2002) has argued that "All of the experimental studies of the past 25 years combined and the meta-analyses of their findings have not advanced our knowledge of the lateralization of language in bilingual speakers one bit." Thus, whether different writing systems in bilinguals impact laterality is far from clear.

Finally, several EEG studies have investigated the time course of second language processing. Many studies have reported delays in early (Liu & Perfetti, 2003) and late (Proverbio, Adorni, & Zani, 2009) ERP components of orthographic processing in L2 relative to L1. Proverbio et al. (2009) observed in a letter detection task with highly proficient trilinguals that the latency of lexicality effect (difference between words and pseudowords) occurred in the N1 (160–180 ms) for L1, the N2 (260–320 ms) for L2, and in the N3 (320–380 ms) window for L3. Several studies have also reported that the N400 latency for L2/L3 is delayed relative to L1 (e.g., Aparicio et al., 2012; Ardal et al., 1990) although some have failed to find a N400 delay (e.g., Lehtonen et al., 2012). These temporal delays in L2 may be related to reduced proficiency or age-of-acquisition differences with L1 (for further discussion see Coderre, 2012).

### 14.3.2 Language control in same-script and different-script bilinguals

An interesting question is whether bilinguals are able to avoid cross-language interactions by suppressing non-target language representations. Whereas language control is obviously needed for bilinguals when speaking in one of their languages (e.g., Green, 1998), it is less clear whether this occurs in language comprehension. Although some early studies (e.g., Rodriguez-Fornells et al., 2002) suggested that bilinguals are able to control their languages, there are a huge number of studies that found that bilinguals are unable to suppress non-target language representations (for reviews see, Dijkstra & van Heuven, 2002; van Heuven & Dijkstra, 2010). For example, van Heuven et al.'s (2008) study with Dutch–English bilinguals involved interlingual homographs embedded in a list of English words and pseudowords. Bilinguals were instructed to focus only on deciding whether letter strings were correct English words or not (English lexical decision task). The data revealed behavioral interference effects and brain activation in regions associated with conflict processing. As the bilinguals in this study were not informed about the presence of interlingual homographs, they may not have utilized potential suppression mechanisms. However, a study with Welsh–English bilinguals (Martin et al., 2009) that explicitly instructed bilinguals to ignore one of their languages still found evidence of cross-linguistic interference, suggesting that knowledge of the presence of interlingual homographs is unlikely to affect the ability to suppress the non-target language.

One possibility is that different-script bilinguals are better able to use script cues during word processing to avoid cross-script/language interactions. However, different-script bilinguals also seem to be susceptible to cross-linguistic interference. Strong evidence for different-script bilinguals' inability to suppress the activation of written words comes from bilingual Stroop tasks. For example, van Heuven et al. (2011) tested three groups of trilinguals on a color-naming Stroop task: German–English–Dutch (all alphabetic writing systems), Chinese–English–Malay (Chinese logographic; English and Malay alphabetic), and Chinese–English–Uighur (Chinese and Uighur logographic; English alphabetic). The results revealed both within- and between-language Stroop interference effects. Stroop interference was reduced for different-script trilinguals compared to same-script trilinguals. However, Stroop interference was still significant for different-script trilinguals, which suggests that these trilinguals were unable to utilize script characteristics successfully to avoid interference.

Script characteristics could, however, still potentially be used to speed up task performance. Evidence for this comes from studies that investigated the impact of language-specific bigrams (Vaid & Frenck-Mester, 2002) and language-specific letters and bigrams (van Kesteren, Dijkstra, & de Smedt, 2012). Vaid and Frenck-Mestre (2002) reported that language decisions of French–English bilinguals were faster for L2 words that contained high frequency bigrams in L2 only (e.g., SNOW) than for L2 words with high bigram frequencies in L1 and L2 (e.g., BLIND). Furthermore, van Kesteren et al. (2012) reported that Norwegian–English bilinguals were able to utilize the sub-lexical orthographic characteristics of letters and bigrams to facilitate their lexical and language decisions. Overall, these findings suggest that whereas bilinguals can utilize script characteristics to speed up responses, they are unable to suppress the activation of non-target language representations to avoid cross-language interactions, even when these are marked by script. In the next section we discuss models of bilingual orthographic processing and their ability to account for data discussed above.

## 14.4 Models of bilingual orthographic processing

In the last fifty years, many models of orthographic processing have been developed. The focus and level of detail of these models vary enormously. Furthermore, relatively few have been implemented computationally. One of the most influential computational models of orthographic processing is McClelland and Rumelhart's (1981) *Interactive activation* (IA) model. This localist connectionist model consists of three *Interactive* layers of visual letter features, letters, and word nodes. Although the model was originally developed to account for context effects in letter perception (simulating the word superiority effect, i.e., easier detection of letters in words than nonwords), the model has been extended and successfully used to account for orthographic neighborhood and priming effects in monolingual word recognition (e.g., Grainger & Jacobs, 1996). The focus of many other monolingual models proposed around the same time was less on orthographic processing and more on phonological processes (reading aloud), impaired word reading and/or semantic processing and their developmental patterns (e.g., Coltheart et al., 2001; Harm & Seidenberg, 1999; Plaut et al., 1996).

One of the key aspects of the IA model is the slot-based letter coding system (the letter B at position 1, O at position 2, O at position 3, and K at position 4, for the word BOOK). This coding scheme has limitations because it lacks flexibility to account for transposition neighbors and transposition priming effect, and relative position priming effects discussed earlier. A number of alternative monolingual models have been proposed to allow for more flexibility in the letter coding (e.g., open-bigrams, spatial coding, etc., see Grainger & van Heuven, 2003; Frost, 2012; Norris, 2013). All of the above models focus on the processing of alphabetic languages. There have also been a number of models proposed in the literature to account for data on Chinese word processing (e.g., Taft & Zhu, 1997; Perfetti et al., 2005) but computational non-alphabetic models focusing on other languages have been very limited.

The models discussed so far are all monolingual models of word processing. The first computational model of bilingual orthographic processing was the *Bilingual Interactive Activation* (BIA) model (Dijkstra & van Heuven, 1998; van Heuven et al., 1998). This computational model was based on the IA model and is an implementation of a system that assumes non-selective lexical access to an integrated lexicon. Therefore, the lexical level of the model contains words from the two languages. An input letter string can activate word candidates of both languages in parallel and these word candidates can influence each other's activations. Unique to the BIA model are language nodes that are activated by words of the language that they represent at the lexical level. Language nodes can also influence the activation level of words in the other language. The BIA model was successful in simulating within- and between-language neighborhood effects (Dijkstra & van Heuven, 1998; van Heuven et al., 1998).

The successor of the BIA model, the *Bilingual Interactive Activation+* (BIA+) model (Dijkstra & van Heuven, 2002) extended the BIA model with phonological and semantic representations as part of a word identification system and a task/decision system. In the word identification system of the BIA+ model, orthographic inputs activate associated phonological and semantic representations, as well as associated language nodes, which act as tags specifying a word's language membership. These language nodes receive activation from lexical representations, just as in the BIA model. However, unlike the BIA model, the BIA+ model assumes that the language nodes cannot influence the activation level of words at the word level. The task/decision system of the BIA+ model uses the information about activated representations in the word identification system to make a decision based on the specific task requirements. Importantly, the task/decision system cannot influence the activation levels of representation in the word identification system in accordance with the previously discussed evidence that bilinguals are unable to suppress the non-target language (for reviews see, Dijkstra & van Heuven, 2002; van Heuven & Dijkstra, 2010).

The assumptions of BIA+ are compatible with behavioral data (Dijkstra & van Heuven, 2002) and neuroimaging data (van Heuven & Dijkstra, 2010). For example, the assumption of a temporal delay of L2 representations is compatible with the delay observed in ERP components associated with orthographic processing (e.g., Liu & Perfetti, 2003; Proverbio et al., 2009). Furthermore, the components and architecture of BIA+ word identification system are similar to those of the *Bi-modal Interactive–Activation Model* (BIAM) of monolingual word recognition (Grainger & Holcomb, 2009), in which units (e.g., V-features, O-units, O-words) have been mapped onto temporal electrophysiological markers of visual word recognition (e.g., N250, N400). Therefore, BIA+'s word identification system is also compatible with the temporal dynamics in L1 word recognition. A first implementation of the BIA+ model in a computer program (e.g., the Semantic, Orthographic, and Phonological Interactive Activation (SOPHIA) model, van Heuven & Dijkstra, 2003; van Heuven, 2005) showed that it is able to successfully simulate interlingual homograph effects and cross-linguistic phonological effects.

The BIA and BIA+ models are limited to simulating cross-linguistic effects in bilinguals with alphabetic languages. Furthermore, the model's letter coding system in the present implementations is slot based and therefore unable to account, for example, for transposition and relative position priming effects, and the impact of cross-linguistic orthographic similarity on the size of the cognate effect (Dijkstra et al., 2010). It is clear that the orthographic route of BIA+ requires a more sophisticated approach, for example, based on the dual-route proposal by Grainger and Ziegler (2011), in which position specific letters detectors activate coarse-grained (e.g., open-bigrams) as well as fine-grained (e.g., graphemes) orthographic representations, which both subsequently activate whole-word representations. Furthermore, to account for script markedness effects in bilingual word recognition (discussed earlier), the model should also link specific visual features to language membership (see van Kesteren et al., 2012 for a proposal).

A number of other theoretical and computational models of bilingual language processing have been proposed in the literature (for a review, see Thomas & van Heuven, 2005). However, the goal and focus of most of these models (e.g., Green, 1996, 1998; Li & Farkas, 2002; Kroll & Stewart, 1994; Shook & Marian, 2013; Yang, Shu, McCandliss, & Zevin, 2013; Zhao & Li, 2013) has not been on orthographic processing. For example, the revised hierarchical model (Kroll & Stewart, 1994) is a theoretical model that contains only lexical and semantic connections and focuses on translation and picture-naming tasks. The BLINCS model (Shook & Marian, 2013) is a computational model of speech perception that can account for cross-linguistic interactions during speech perception. The model of Zhao and Li (2013) is a self-organizing neural network that was developed to simulate translation and semantic priming in Chinese–English bilinguals. Although this last model is one of the few that focus on different-script bilinguals, the model does not include orthographic representations and only focuses on learning the mapping of input onto output phonology through a semantic map.

Another recent model, developed by Yang et al. (2013), also focuses on Chinese–English bilinguals. This model was developed to address the question whether it is possible to simulate with a bilingual model the different development reading disabilities (i.e., developmental dyslexia) observed in native Chinese and English readers. Importantly, the architecture of the bilingual model was similar to the architecture of Yang et al.'s Chinese and English monolingual models. It consists of two separate orthographic layers, one specific for English and one for Chinese, which have feed-forward connections to a single phonological attractor network that is similar to Harm and Seidenberg's (1999) model. Furthermore, the network has a single semantic layer that is also connected to the phonological attractor network. The structure of this semantic layer is based on the one used by Plaut (1997) and was included to resolve ambiguous spelling-to-sound mappings. The training of Yang et al.'s model consisted of a combination of listening training, involving only the phonological attractor network, and reading training that involved the whole model. Importantly, to simulate simultaneous bilingualism, a word of either language had an equal chance of being trained on each trial. After training, the model was tested using a set of Chinese and English words that differed in the regularity and consistency of their spelling-to-sound mappings, and normal reading as well as two types of developmental dyslexia were simulated. Interestingly, the pattern of results for the bilingual model trained with Chinese and English words was similar to results for the two monolingual models. Thus, this indicates that through statistical learning a reading skill can be acquired in two completely different writing systems and that different developmental difficulties in each of these writing systems emerge as a consequence of learning the mappings between spelling, sound, and meaning in a single architecture.

Yang et al.'s (2013) bilingual model focuses on mapping orthography onto phonology in two different writing systems. However, it is unclear what kind of naming errors the model produces and the impact of simulating different types of bilinguals (e.g., late unbalanced bilinguals) through various training schemes. Although Yang et al.'s model does include Chinese and English orthographic representations, it is unclear whether it is possible to simulate lexical decision latencies and masked priming effects, such as translation priming (e.g., Chen & Ng, 1989; Jiang & Forster, 2001) and homophone priming (e.g., Zhou et al., 2010).

## 14.5 Future directions and outstanding questions

From the studies discussed in this chapter it is clear that there are still a large number of outstanding questions about bilingual orthographic processing. For example, whereas there is a large amount of data about orthographic similarity effects in monolinguals (e.g., transposition effects, relative position priming) it is unclear whether these also occur in the second language and what the impact is of proficiency. Also, the generalizability of the impact of cross-language orthographic similarity on cognate processing could be investigated in trilinguals with a different-script L1. Furthermore, it is important to systematically investigate whether the ERP components associated with orthographic processing in alphabetic languages are present at the same latencies and magnitudes in non-alphabetic scripts and in bilinguals' first and second languages. In particular, more research is needed to investigate the impact of script on later ERP components and the ability to utilize script in cognitive processing.

The work from Yang et al. (2013) suggests that a universal model of reading is possible; their work is compatible with Frost's (2012) universal model for orthographic processing in all writing systems. A truly universal model should also be able to account for cross-script and cross-language interactions in bilinguals. As Li (2013) indicated, Yang et al.'s (2013) simulation results contrast with the assumption of assimilation and accommodation strategies (Perfetti et al., 2007), which assumes different neurocognitive architectures for Chinese and English. However, Yang et al. simulated simultaneous bilingualism, whereas the assimilation and accommodation strategies are based on late L2 learners. Thus, further simulation work is needed, in particular testing the impact of simulating different types of bilinguals (e.g., late bilinguals).

The number of models in the literature that focus on bilingual orthographic processing is very limited. Existing implemented bilingual models need flexible letter coding schemes to account for a wider range of data on cross-language orthographic interactions. Furthermore, future computational modeling work should focus on a wider range of different-script bilinguals, as most work so far has focused on Chinese–English bilinguals.

# 15

# Bilingual lexical access during written sentence comprehension

Ana Schwartz

## 15.1 Introduction

Since the cognitive revolution of the 1960s, research on lexical access has served as an elegant way for studying key questions regarding the modularity of mind. For example, there has been a long-standing debate regarding whether the bottom-up processes of word recognition are directly influenced by the top-down processes of sentence comprehension (e.g., Onifer & Swinney, 1981; Swinney, 1979). Take as an example the homograph *cabinet* in the following sentence: "The president decided to replace the entire *cabinet* by the end of the year." Although the more common meaning of "cabinet" is something that serves as storage, the previous sentential context biases the alternative meaning. If bottom-up processes of lexical access are encapsulated from top-down processes, then the more frequent meaning of *cabinet* will be accessed first, irrespective of message-level information provided by the previous sentence context. As a consequence, selection of the less-common meaning should take more time. If, on the other hand, top-down processing can interact directly with bottom-up processes of lexical access, then the previous context should allow the weaker meaning to be more strongly activated – reducing the time needed to select it.

Finding a limited role of context would suggest that conceptual processes are kept separate from the bottom-up lexical level information of word identification. On the other hand, finding that contextual information significantly alters the activated set of lexical candidates, would suggest an interactive system in which conceptual-level computations directly affect the bottom-up computations of lexical access. Existing research does make clear that: (1) lexical access of a given word involves the simultaneous activation of multiple lexical representations (e.g., automatic, spreading activation of the various meanings of a homonym like *cabinet*) (Gottlob et al., 1999; Pexman & Lupker, 1999; Rodd, Gaskell, & Marslen Wilson, 2002); and (2) that information from sentence context does, *at some point*, influence selection of the target lexical candidate, whether it be prior to or only after initial lexical access of a word is completed (Duffy, Kambe, & Rayner, 2001; Tabossi, 1988; Tabossi & Zardon, 1993; Tabossi, Colombo, & Job, 1987; Vu, Kellas & Paul, 1998; Vu et al., 2000). Unfortunately, there are mixed findings and interpretations regarding whether influences from context genuinely occur before the completion of initial lexical access (supporting interactivity) or occur only once access is complete (supporting modularity). Consequently, there is no single, agreed-upon answer to the question of modularity versus interactivity of sentence processing.

There are at least three factors that modulate the influence of sentence context on processes of lexical access. These are: (1) the degree of semantic bias provided by the preceding context for the target word or a specific meaning of a homonym (Duffy, Henderson, & Morris, 1989; Duffy et al., 2001; Tabossi, 1988; Tabossi & Johnson-Laird, 1980); (2) the relative frequency of the target meaning relative to competitors (Duffy et al., 2001; Rayner, Pacht, & Duffy, 1994; Sereno, O'Donnell, & Rayner, 2006); and (3) individual differences in the reading skill of the comprehender (Gernsbacher & Faust, 1991, 1995; Gernsbacher & St John, 2001). Evidence supporting selective access of a target meaning is most likely to be observed if the preceding context strongly biases that meaning, if that meaning is of higher frequency than its competitors and if the reader possesses the cognitive skill to efficiently select the meaning among competitors. If the target meaning is of a lower frequency than competing entries, as in the case of a low-frequency meaning of a homonym (e.g., the "government" meaning of *cabinet* in English), then it seems that selective access of that meaning and bypassing the dominant competing meaning is extremely unlikely, if not impossible (e.g., Binder & Rayner, 1998). In that case there will be evidence for competition between the target and competing meanings. How much additional time is needed to select that meaning will vary according to the degree of sentential bias and individual differences in reading skill.

A critical limitation of the body of work reviewed above is that, with few exceptions, the focus is on monolingual processing. This is a problem, not only because it might not generalize to a significant portion of the world's population that is proficient in more than one language, but also because it leaves an incomplete examination of the different types of linguistic cues the mind can potentially exploit when comprehending language. For example, perhaps language membership cues (such as distinct orthographic and phonological patterns) limit spreading activation of lexical competitors to just one language. A few, early single-word recognition studies sought to determine if parallel activation of lexical candidates extended across languages for bilingual speakers (Gerard & Scarborough,

1989; Scarborough, Gerard, & Cortese, 1984). It was hypothesized that language membership could provide a cognitive cue during access such that only candidates from the language of processing are activated. This hypothesis was coined the "language selective hypothesis" while the opposite possibility, that activation spreads across languages, was termed the "language non-selective hypothesis." The general strategy for testing these alternative hypotheses was to have bilingual speakers complete a word recognition task, such as lexical decision or word naming. In a lexical decision task a string of letters is presented to the participant (e.g., *cart* or *blart*), and the task is to decide as quickly and accurately as possible whether that string forms an actual word (e.g., *cart* => "yes"; *blart* => "no"). On critical trials, the stimulus word shares some degree of lexical form overlap with the non-target language, such as cognates, which share form and meaning (e.g., *piano* in English and Spanish), interlingual homographs, which share identical or near-identical orthography (e.g., *pan* in Spanish means "bread") and homophones, which share similar phonology (e.g., *sol* in Spanish is pronounced rather like *soul* in English). Results from these initial studies suggested that in fact a word's language membership limited activation to that language, supporting the language selective hypothesis. For example, in one study, lexical decision performance on English–Spanish interlingual homographs, did not differ across monolinguals and English–Spanish bilinguals (Gerard & Scarborough, 1989).

However, starting in the late 1980s and going through the early 2000s, there was a substantial increase in the number of studies investigating bilingual lexical processing. This first generation of studies relied mostly on single-word processing paradigms such as the lexical decision task (described above) and word naming. The underlying assumption is that, variations in the latency and accuracy to identify a word, either by making a lexical decision or naming it out loud, is a function of the number and type of lexical candidates that were co-activated. Thus, if a to-be-identified word has highly similar orthography and semantics (such as a cognate word), co-activation of these convergent representations will reduce time to identify and increase accuracy. Investigators can also add various permutations to the lexical decision and naming tasks. For example, in primed lexical decision a word stimulus can be presented briefly to the participant before onset of the target.

One issue with lexical decision and naming tasks is they can arguably be performed without fully accessing the semantic representation of a word. That is, one can make a "word" decision based solely on orthographic features. Similarly, one could feasibly read out loud a word by solely engaging orthographic to phonological representations. Thus, researchers have also used tasks that require semantic processing such as word translation and translation recognition. In the former task, words from one language are presented one by one and the participant translates them, typically out loud. In the latter task pairs of words (one from each language) are presented and the participant decides if the two are translation equivalents or not, typically through a key press. These single-word paradigms have yielded strong evidence that both of a bilingual's languages are in fact dually activated in a language non-selective way (Bijeljac-Babic, Biardeau, & Grainger, 1997; Brysbaert, van Dyck, & van de Poel, 1999; Dijkstra, van Jaarsveld, & Ten Brinke, 1998; Dijkstra, Grainger, & van Heuven, 1999; Jared & Kroll, 2001; Jared & Szucs, 2002; Lemhöfer & Dijkstra, 2004; Lemhöfer, Dijkstra, & Michel, 2004; van Heuven, Dijkstra, Grainger, & Schriefers, 2001). Specifically, numerous studies have shown facilitated access of cognate words relative to noncognates across a striking variety of tasks (Dijkstra & van Hell, 2003; Dijkstra et al., 2010; Gollan, Forster, & Frost, 1997; Lemhöfer & Dijkstra, 2004; Lemhöfer et al., 2004; van Hell & Dijkstra, 2002). Furthermore, these cognate effects have been observed to persist across languages with different scripts (Gollan et al., 1997), irrespective of participants' expectations to see words from the other language and even when the words are cognates with an L3 (Dijkstra & van Hell, 2003; Lemhöfer et al., 2004; van Hell & Dijkstra, 2002). There is also evidence that, during lexical access, bilinguals non-selectively activate sub-lexical units such as word–body cohorts (van Heuven et al., 2001) and spelling–sound correspondences (Brysbaert et al., 1999; Jared & Kroll, 2001; Jared & Szucs, 2002).

Although persistent effects of language non-selectivity demonstrate that bilingual lexical access is language non-selective in nature, studies have also shown that the degree to which the effects of this non-selectivity are in fact observed depends on what aspects of lexical form are shared across languages as well as the extent to which the task demands require full specification of those forms (Dijkstra et al., 1999; Dijkstra et al., 2010; Grainger & Beauvillain, 1987; Schwartz, Kroll, & Diaz, 2007). For example, cognate facilitation has been eliminated (Schwartz et al., 2007) and even reversed to inhibition (Dijkstra et al., 2010) when corresponding phonological/orthographic forms of the cognate translations were more distinct. Also, unlike the frequently observed effects of cognate facilitation, effects of interlingual homograph status on word identification performance are quite mixed. In some cases no effects are observed, in others the effects may be inhibitory or facilitative, depending on task demands, the relative frequency of its meanings, and the composition of the stimulus list set in which they are embedded (Beauvillain & Grainger, 1987; Dijkstra et al., 2000; Dijkstra, Timmermans, & Schriefers, 2000; Gerard & Scarborough, 1989; Lemhöfer & Dijkstra, 2004; Von Studnitz & Green, 2002). This difference in consistency of cognate versus interlingual homograph effects suggests that overlap in semantics may be crucial for producing strong effects of non-selectivity. In terms of task demands, effects of co-activated phonology or spelling–sound correspondences are more likely to be observed in a word naming, which requires specification of a word's phonological form (Jared, 2002; Jared & Szucs, 2002; Schwartz et al., 2007).

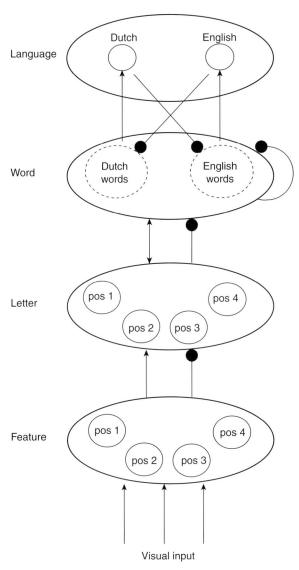

**Figure 15.1** The Bilingual Interactive Activation (BIA) Model (adapted from Dijkstra & van Heuven, 1998)

To account for these non-selective findings, a model of the bilingual lexicon was proposed, the Bilingual Interactive Activation (BIA) model (Dijkstra & van Heuven, 1998). This model was an extension of the existing Interactive Activation model (McClelland & Rumelhart, 1981) and included a language node level in addition to feature, letter and word levels (see Figure 15.1). It used a localist, connectionist architecture and focused only on orthographic from (it was later revised as the BIA+, described later and shown in Figure 15.2). A critical assumption of the model was that bilingual lexical access involves bottom-up activation of lexical representations

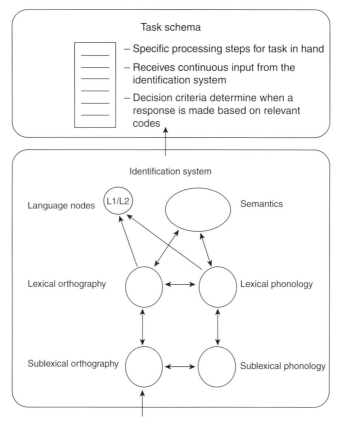

**Figure 15.2** The Bilingual Interactive Activation Model revised (BIA+) (adapted from Dijkstra & van Heuven, 2002)

across languages which are stored in an integrated lexicon. Thus, lexical representations across languages are represented within an interconnected network through which activation flows, which can be either excitatory or inhibitory in nature. The language nodes were connected to and collected activation from localist word representations from their respective language. This in turn allowed the language nodes to exert top-down inhibition to word representations in the competing language. As such, the language nodes could act as language filters, gradually suppressing the competing language as a function of their own collected activation. It was assumed that the language nodes' relative activation levels could be influenced by factors both within the lexicon as well as outside the lexicon, such as processing occurring at the level of task-related decision making.

## 15.2 Bilingual lexical access in sentence context: methods

The initial set of studies on bilingual lexical access demonstrating language non-selectivity, reviewed above, focused on single word identification. More recently researchers have turned their attention to whether information from a context, such as a sentence, can be recruited to constrain parallel activation of the non-target language. Thus, lexical decision and word-naming paradigms were extended so that the critical, to-be-identified or named word was inserted in a sentence. A common way of doing this is through Serial Visual Presentation (SVP) in which a sentence is presented, one word at a time, usually at a fixed pace until the critical word is reached. When the critical word is presented, the participant makes a response (names it or presses a key) before the next word is shown. Another option is the Moving Window paradigm. In this paradigm, the entire sentence frame is presented at once, but each word is initially masked. For each key press, one word at a time is un-masked, and the previous word is masked again. In this way, only one word at a time is available for processing.

Another method is eye-tracking. Eye-tracking provides a continuous record of the location and duration of eye fixations (when the eyes are still) as well as the speed and trajectory of saccades (when the eyes are moving to the next fixation). Psycholinguists interested in processes of lexical access and sentence comprehension first identify critical regions within a sentence stimulus. They then extract different measures that either tap into processes occurring prior to lexical access or after access is complete. Some of the most commonly used measures are First Fixation Duration (FFD), Gaze Duration (GD), and Total Reading Time (TRT). FFD is the duration, in milliseconds, of the first fixation made in the target region (typically a word). GD is the sum of the durations of all fixations made in that region before moving forward in the sentence. Both of these measures are assumed to tap into processes prior to the completion of lexical access. TRT is the sum of all fixations made, and is assumed to reflect processing occurring after the word has been lexically accessed, such as sentence-integration processes (for a review, see Rayner, 1997). Because the eye-movement record provides a continuous measure of processing, it allows for a finer-grained analysis of cross-language influences on processing as they unfold across time. This allows researchers to identify the specific stages of reading that are affected (or unaffected) by cross-language activation.

## 15.3 Bilingual lexical access in sentence context: models

Although previous research with monolinguals had clearly demonstrated that exhaustive activation of homonym meanings persist in sentence context, bilinguals have at their disposal language membership as a potential cue that might allow activation to flow more selectively than for a monolingual. This review will focus on integrating available research on bilingual lexical access in sentence context to three models: the BIA+ (Dijkstra & van Heuven, 2002), the Three-Factor Framework (Degani &

Tokowicz, 2010b), and the Bilingual Re-Ordered Activation Model (B-RAM) (Arêas da Luz Fontes, & Schwartz, 2010, 2011; Arêas da Luz Fontes, Yeh, & Schwartz, 2010; Schwartz, Yeh, & Shaw, 2008).

The BIA+ is an extension of the BIA described earlier. It is based on distributed representations of orthographic, phonological and semantic units across languages that exist in a single, integrated lexicon (see Dijkstra & van Heuven, 2002 for a complete description). The key difference between the two models is the operation of "language nodes" and assumptions regarding what factors can directly constrain non-selective spreading activation within the lexicon. In the earlier BIA the language nodes could act as language filters, gradually suppressing the competing language as a function of their own collected activation. Critically, it was assumed that the language nodes' relative activation levels could be influenced by factors both within the lexicon as well as outside the lexicon, such as processing occurring at the level of task-related decision making. In the BIA+, the functioning of the language nodes fundamentally changed and the factors that could influence them were restricted to those arising from within the lexicon. More specifically, the language nodes could no longer act as language filters, rather they became representational tags, indicating the language membership of a word. Also, in the BIA+, the lexicon is further encapsulated from a task decision-making system. As a consequence, factors relating to differences in task demands, the language mode of the experimental situation or a participants' expectations regarding what languages will be processed no longer can directly affect the initial activation of lexical entries within the lexicon. Instead, such influences operate after lexical access has been completed. What is most critical for the following review of bilingual lexical access in sentence context is the assumption of the BIA+ that a linguistic context, such as the lexical and syntactic cues provided by a sentence, can in fact directly impact activation within the lexicon. As stated by the authors, "In fact, such linguistic context information may exert serious constraints on the degree of language selective access that may be observed" (Dijkstra & van Heuven, 2002: 187).

Whereas the BIA+ model is a computational model of bilingual lexical access in general (both in and out of context), the Three-Factor Framework and B-RAM are theoretical models that were formulated specifically for bilingual access in sentence context. Both models were largely inspired by and intended to be bilingual extensions of the monolingual Re-Ordered Access Model of within-language homonym disambiguation (RAM) (Duffy, Morris, & Rayner, 1988; Rayner et al., 1994). According to the RAM, how quickly a specific, target meaning of a homonym (e.g., *spring*) is accessed will depend on two factors, the relative frequency of that meaning and the preceding, contextual bias. In the absence of a strong, contextual bias, the order in which the multiple meanings of a homonym are activated will be dictated by relative frequency. Thus, the more frequent (dominant) meaning of *spring* (the season) will be accessed before the lesser frequent meanings (e.g., the coil meaning). Some homonyms have meanings of similar frequency (called "balanced homonyms"). In that case, both meanings will compete for selection, and this will delay initial processing times of that homonym. The presence of a biasing context can reorder the frequency-dictated order of activation. If the context biases the lower frequency (subordinate) meaning of a homograph (e.g., "The toy could not be fixed because it was missing a spring") that meaning is activated early enough to compete directly with the default-activated dominant meaning. This competition will slow down processing time. The opposite pattern is observed for balanced homonyms; a biasing context favoring one meaning over the other allows that meaning to be activated in an earlier time-frame, bypassing competition.

Both the Three-Factor Framework and B-RAM propose adding a third, influential factor that is unique to bilingual processing, namely, the existence of another language. The difference between the two models is in their specific focus. The Three-Factor Framework focuses on how language membership of the words in a sentence context influences lexical access of words that are interlingual homographs. For example, *pan* is an interlingual homograph across English and Spanish, referring to "bread" in the latter language. The Three-Factor Framework proposes that how quickly the target meaning is accessed is influenced by (1) the relative frequency of that meaning, (2) the semantic context of the preceding sentence, and (3) the language context of the preceding sentence. The model takes into consideration that the relative frequency of a specific meaning of an inter-lingual homograph will be influenced by both objective, language-absolute differences in usage as well as subjective, proficiency-dependent differences in exposure (Degani & Tokowicz, 2010b). For example, *pan* is a relatively high frequency word in both English and Spanish. It is also a word that is likely to be part of the lexicon of even a lower-proficiency bilingual. In the absence of any context at all, there will be strong competition between the two meanings. In the presence of a sentence context that does not semantically favor one meaning over the other (e.g., "She brought me the pan") language membership of the sentence can boost the English-specific meaning. In the presence of sentence that provides semantic constraints in addition to language membership (e.g., "She fried the egg in a pan"), the English-specific meaning will be accessed even earlier, perhaps allowing for a complete bypass of competition from the Spanish meaning.

The B-RAM focuses on the processing of words that are homonyms *within the target language* and how cross-language lexical activation dynamics further influence the ordering in which competing meanings will be activated. Specifically, it proposes that when the to-be-selected meaning maps on to a similar lexical form across a bilingual's languages, co--activation of these representations accelerates the time-frame in which that meaning is activated and available for selection. For example, the English word *arms* is a homonym for which one meaning is far less frequent than the other (i.e., the "weapons" meaning). Yet, that low frequency meaning maps on to two, highly similar orthographic representations for a speaker of English and Spanish (*armas* shares the "weapons" meaning). The assumption is that this lexical form overlap accelerates activation of the corresponding meaning, allowing it to potentially bypass competition from the dominant meaning. As a consequence, selection of a subordinate meaning that is also a cognate with the non-target language, will be facilitated relative to selection of a non-cognate, subordinate meaning.

## 15.4 Bilingual lexical access in sentence context: general effects

Early studies on bilingual lexical access in sentence context suggest that the presence of a sentence context alone does not allow for language-selective access of a target word. Three separate studies using SVP with different bilingual populations found evidence for persistent language non-selective activation in sentence context. For example, when cognates were embedded in sentence contexts that did not strongly bias the cognate (e.g., "They walked in and saw the *piano* in the corner of the room"), facilitated responding relative to noncognates was observed. These facilitative effects were observed in SVP methods using three different modes of responding: word naming (Schwartz & Kroll, 2006), lexical decision (Duyck et al., 2007; van Hell & de Groot, 2008), and translation (Duyck, Assche, Drieghe, & Hartsuiker, 2007; Schwartz & Kroll, 2006; van Hell & de Groot, 2008). In one of these studies, the magnitude of the observed cognate facilitation in low-constraint context did not differ from that observed in a single-word experiment (Duyck et al., 2007). Also, the persistent effects of non-selectivity were observed for highly proficient (van Hell & de Groot, 2008), intermediate proficiency bilinguals responding in a weaker L2 (Schwartz & Kroll, 2006, Experiment 2), as well as for bilinguals responding in an L2 in which they had become dominant (Schwartz & Kroll, 2006, Experiment 1).

Findings from eye-tracking studies have mostly converged in finding non-selective access in sentence context, demonstrating effects of cognate facilitation (Duyck et al., 2007; Libben & Titone, 2009; Pivneva et al., 2014; Titone et al., 2011; Van Assche et al., 2011) and interlingual homograph inhibition (Libben & Titone, 2009) when target words were embedded in low constraint sentences in the L2 as well as in the L1 (Van Assche et al., 2009). Also, these non-selective effects have been observed in both early and later measures of processing, indicating that, in neutral sentence contexts, sentence comprehension involves the parallel activation of the non-target language throughout initial access and into integration. The conclusion from these studies is that the mere presence of a sentence and language cues it may provide are not sufficient to allow lexical activation to flow selectively within a single language. This supports the BIA+'s assumption of language nodes functioning as representational tags rather than as filters that can collect activation and suppress the competing language as originally proposed in the BIA.

However, a recent study suggests that, even a semantically low constraint sentence context can provide syntactic cues that allow activation to flow selectively within a language (Bultena, Dijkstra, & van Hell, 2014). Unlike the studies cited earlier, word class of target words was systematically manipulated. Through the use of eye-tracking the authors presented highly proficient Dutch–English bilinguals with English low-constraint sentences. In addition to cognate status, the word class (noun versus verb) of the target word was manipulated. Cognate facilitation effects were observed for nouns, but not verbs. The interpretation is that verb processing engages syntactic information that is more language-specific than the processing of nouns. This finding provides support for the Three-Factor Framework's assumption that language context of a sentence (in this case the syntactic cues that it provides) can in fact influence which representation of a language-ambiguous word is accessed more readily.

What about when the sentence context provides semantic information that strongly biases the meaning of the upcoming target? Does the message-level information provided by top-down processing of sentence comprehension directly influence the bottom-up language non-selective activation of bilingual lexical access? There have been a few studies in which the predictability of the upcoming, target word (also referred to as the semantic constraint of the sentence) was manipulated. In these studies the general pattern has been an attenuation or elimination of cognate facilitation and interlingual homograph inhibition effects in high-constraint sentences (Libben & Titone, 2009; Pivneva et al., 2014; Schwartz & Kroll, 2006; van Hell & de Groot, 2008). In two studies using SVP, effects of cognate facilitation on naming (Schwartz & Kroll, 2006) and lexical decision (van Hell & de Groot, 2008) performance observed in low-constraint sentences, were completely eliminated in high-constraint sentences. However, it should be noted that in both of these cases, the dependent measures were based on a single response. In studies using eye-movement monitoring, effects were not completely eliminated but rather limited to earlier aspects of the eye-movement record tapping into pre-lexical access processes (Libben & Titone 2009; Pivneva et al., 2014; Titone et al., 2011). More specifically, first fixation and gaze durations were shorter for cognates than non-cognates, but no difference was observed in total reading times. Together the findings from both single response and eye-tracking studies suggest that, even when rich semantic information is provided, the bilingual lexicon operates in a fundamentally non-selective way although the extent and longevity of this interactivity can be modulated.

Although the four studies discussed above all found attenuating effects of high semantic constraint on effects of language non-selectivity, in some cases this influence was qualified by other factors, and some studies have failed to observe any effects of contextual constraint at all (Van Assche et al., 2011). A synthesis of the major findings across studies suggests that whether semantic information from sentence context constrains language non-selectivity at all depends critically on: (1) the nature of the lexical form overlap of the critical word (e.g., sharing strictly form or a combination of form and meaning); (2) the language context both within and beyond a single sentence; and (3) individual differences in proficiency and in working memory/executive control processing. Each of these factors will be reviewed separately.

## 15.5 Moderating effects of lexical overlap

Whether effects of language non-selectivity are observed in sentence context depends critically on the degree and type of lexical overlap that the critical word shares with the non-target language. Specifically, the magnitude and consistency of cross-language activation effects are attenuated with decreasing overlap in orthography, morphology, and semantics. For example, cognate facilitation effects are modulated by the corresponding orthographic overlap between the cognate translations. In three separate studies, Van Assche, Duyck, and colleagues inserted cognates of differing orthographic overlap into sentence contexts and presented these to highly proficient Dutch–English bilinguals (Duyck et al., 2007; Van Assche et al, 2009a, 2011). In the first study, orthographic overlap was kept as a dichotomous variable identical or non-identical (Duyck et al., 2007). In that study they observed stronger cognate facilitation for identical relative to non-identical cognates in both lexical decision/SVP and eye-tracking experiments. In a third, eye-tracking experiment cognate facilitation effects were observed throughout all measures of the eye-movement record tapping into both pre-lexical access and post-lexical access for identical cognates only. In two later studies orthographic overlap was analyzed as a continuous measure (Van Assche et al., 2009a, 2011). The magnitude of cognate facilitation increased significantly as a function of increases in form overlap when bilinguals were reading in their L2, English, as well as their L1, Dutch.

Further evidence of the modulating role of lexical form overlap comes from studies examining processing of cognates with differing morphology across languages in sentence context. In one study, Dutch–English cognate verbs were placed in neutral sentence contexts in either the present or simple past tense ("The girls learn/learned a lot in their new school") (Van Assche, Duyck, & Brysbaert, 2013). In Dutch the various verb tenses are marked by language specific morphology that does not exist in English. For example, the infinitive form of Dutch verbs end in *-en* as in "*learnen*." The eye-movement data from highly proficient Dutch–English bilinguals showed no evidence of cognate facilitation in early, pre-lexical access measures. Instead, a facilitative effect was only observed in go-past times (the sum of all fixations made on a target word before moving rightward in the text but it includes regressive eye movements launched from the target to earlier portions of the sentence). The authors interpret this pattern as reflecting a lack of facilitation of co-activated forms, since the verb's translations had distinct orthography, coupled with facilitated post-lexical access processing of semantically integrating cognate versus noncognate verbs. In another study Danish–English bilinguals read authentic texts (magazine passages) (Balling, 2013). The author observed facilitation in the processing of morphologically simple cognates (reduced gaze duration and total reading time) but inhibition for cognates that were morphologically complex, providing convergent evidence that the distinct orthography of morphological units compete during lexical access.

Effects of context are also moderated by the semantic overlap of critical words. When words share meaning across languages, as is the case for cognates, effects of non-selectivity are more likely to be observed than when they do not, as is the case for interlingual homographs. For example, Schwartz and Kroll (2006) did not observe any evidence of interlingual homograph interference on naming performance in a SVP paradigm (Experiment 1). Similarly, in an eye-tracking study, Titone and others only observed homograph inhibition in total reading time, while cognate facilitation was observed across several measures including first fixation and total reading time (Titone et al., 2011). In fact, in two studies demonstrating language selective processing, the critical stimuli were interlingual homographs (Baten, Hofman, & Loeys, 2011; Elston-Güttler, Gunter, & Kotz, 2005). The issue of how cross-language activation in sentence context is moderated by semantic overlap was directly addressed in a study by Schwartz and Arêas da luz Fontes (2008). They tested the hypothesis that the presence of a sentence context modifies the type of lexical candidate that is most strongly activated from the non-target language. Specifically, since sentence comprehension is a semantically driven task, they hypothesized that the set of activated word candidates would be semantically related to target words. Across two experiments, highly proficient Spanish–English bilinguals performed a semantic verification task in which prime words were presented in isolation or at the end of a sentence. On critical trials, the prime and target words shared a mediated relationship through the non-target language, Spanish. In Experiment 1, the prime–target pairs were based on a form-mediated relationship such that the target word (e.g., *BOAT*) was the translation of a Spanish word (e.g., *barco*) that shared only lexical form with the prime word (e.g., *bark*). Thus an example prime target pair would be *bark–BOAT*, presented either in isolation or at the end of a sentence (e.g., "The dog began to *bark*. BOAT").

In Experiment 2, the same pairs were used but the order was reversed (e.g., *boat – BARK* in isolation, or in sentence context: "The sailor rowed the boat." BARK) so that now the relationship was mediated through semantics (*boat* translates into *barco* which is similar in form to the target, *BARK*). As predicted, form-mediated inhibitory priming (e.g., *bark* [barco] priming "BOAT") was only observed when the primes were presented in isolation. In sentence context only targets that had a semantically mediated relationship to the primes (e.g., *boat* [barco] priming "BARK") showed inhibitory priming.

The differences in semantic overlap between cognate translations and interlingual homographs may cause them to be represented in qualitatively different ways in the bilingual lexicon. It has been proposed that form-identical cognates have a single representation (Dijkstra et al., 2010). Because of this Jouravlev and Jared (2014) have made the argument that examining the processing of interlingual homographs provides a more stringent test of language non-selectivity than testing cognates. To push the envelope of non-selectivity even further, they tested whether effects of interlingual homograph status would be observed across languages that have a different script, namely English and Russian. Because these two languages share a handful of letters (M, K, O, P, T), there are in fact homographs between them (e.g., *pot* in Russian means "mouth"), providing the ideal linguistic combination for examining if non-selectivity persists even when sentences have language-unique orthography. They presented native speakers of Russian, who were immersed in an English-speaking environment but still rated higher dominance in Russian, with all-English sentences that biased the Russian meaning of the interlingual homograph. Thus, the English specific meaning of the homograph did not make sense in the context (e.g., "The doctor asked Tom to open his *pot* widely"). They recorded and compared the Event Related Potentials (ERPs) to three types of words: (1) the target interlingual homographs; (2) a control word that shared no form overlap across languages and also did not fit the semantics of the sentence (e.g., *net*); and (3), the translation of the interlingual homograph, which did in fact fit the meaning of the sentence (e.g., *mouth*). The authors focused their analyses on the N400 ERP component, which reflects detection of semantic anomalies. This is a negative spike that peaks between 300 and 500 milliseconds. The amplitude of this component increases as a function of the difficulty in processing and integrating the anomaly. Remarkably, the N400 generated by the bilingual readers to the interlingual homographs did not differ from that generated by the English translations which did in fact fit the sentence. Thus, the bilinguals did not find it harder to integrate the non-target reading of the homograph into the sentence than the language-unique control. This finding is compatible with the present interpretation that activation of shared semantics is key in boosting effects of cross-language activation. Recall that the sentences biased the meaning of the non-target reading of the interlingual homographs. This demonstrates that even when reading a language with a different script, semantic information from the sentence feeds activation to words matching those activated semantic features across languages.

There have been a few studies examining how effects of cross-language activation in context may differ for words that have an intermediate degree of semantic overlap. These are words that are intra-language homonyms, and thus lack a simple one-to-one mapping between lexical form and meaning either within or across languages. As such, they cannot be classified as either interlingual homographs or cognates, but rather a blend of the two (Arêas da Luz Fontes et al., 2010; Arêas da Luz Fontes & Schwartz, 2011; Elston-Güttler, Paulmann, & Kotz, 2005; Schwartz et al., 2008). For example, the English homonym *novel* can mean either a book that one reads or something that is new. The "book" meaning is a cognate with "*novela*" in Spanish, whereas the other meaning is a homograph meaning, not being shared with Spanish. The studies reported next examined processing of these items within semantically constraining contexts, in which one particular meaning of the homonym is favored. All three studies converge in finding effects of cross-language non-selectivity on the activation of homonym meanings from the non-target language, even though the semantic constraints of the sentence strongly bias one meaning. In one such study German–English bilinguals performed an English, primed lexical decision in which the prime and target words were both translations of a German homonym (e.g., *kiefer* in German means both "pine" and "jaw"), but had no semantic relationship in the target language, English (Elston-Güttler, Paulmann, & Kotz, 2005). For the low-proficiency participants only, there was significant priming between these English translations of German homonym meanings, in both reaction time and ERP measures. Specifically, reaction times were slowed relative to unrelated trials. Also, there were significant modulations of the ERP N200 component, which is indicative of processing at the orthographic level and tends to be less negative when items are orthographically similar. In this bilingual study, the component was more negative for related trials, reflecting inhibited processing. These effects are particularly striking given the constraints of the sentence contexts as well as the fact that the English prime and targets had no direct relationship in English itself.

In a set of related studies, Schwartz and colleagues sought to test the major assumptions of the B-RAM, described earlier, by examining bilingual processing of intra-language homonyms (Arêas da Luz Fontes et al., 2010; Arêas da Luz Fontes & Schwartz, 2011; Schwartz et al., 2008). The overarching goal was to examine the role that non-selective bilingual lexical activation might play in either facilitating or inhibiting homonym meanings for which one meaning was a cognate. The general procedure across these studies consisted of presenting bilinguals with all-English sentences in which the subordinate meaning of English homonyms (i.e., lower frequency like the "not to eat" meaning of *fast*) is the target meaning. Since monolingual research clearly demonstrates that access to subordinate meanings typically involves competition from the dominant meaning (Duffy, Morris, & Rayner, 1988; Duffy et al., 2001; Rayner & Duffy, 1986), they wanted to know whether the magnitude of this competition would be influenced by cross-language activation of cognate meanings. That is, would selection of the subordinate meaning of *novel* be influenced by co-activation of the dominant, cognate meaning? In two studies highly proficient Spanish–English bilinguals, who were L2 dominant in reading, read all-English sentences ending in a homonym prime that either had a cognate meaning with Spanish (e.g., *novel*) or no cognate status (e.g., *fast*). The sentence context biased the subordinate meaning of the up-coming homonym (e.g., "Her ideas were always interesting and *novel*"). On critical trials the follow-up target word was related to the contextually irrelevant dominant meaning (e.g., BOOK). The bilinguals showed longer latencies and increased error rates in rejecting target words that were related to the dominant meaning of the homonym primes. However, more critically, the magnitude of this inhibition was significantly greater when rejecting cognate, dominant meanings (e.g., rejecting BOOK after seeing *novel*) relative to non-cognate meanings (e.g., rejecting SPEED after seeing *fast*).

Having observed an increased cost in processing when the competing, dominant meaning of a homonym was also a cognate (e.g., the "book" meaning of *novel/novela*), the authors examined whether cross-language activation would facilitate access to the subordinate meaning of an English homonym (e.g., the "ethnicity" meaning of *race*) when it was also a cognate meaning with Spanish (e.g., *raza* in Spanish) (Arêas da Luz Fontes et al., 2010). For this purpose cognate homonyms for which only the subordinate meaning was shared (e.g., *raza* in Spanish shares the "ethnicity" meaning of "race") were placed at the end of sentence contexts biasing the dominant meaning (e.g., "He trained for months before entering the *race*"). On critical trials the follow-up target was related to the contextually irrelevant and weaker subordinate meaning; the task was to respond "yes" if the target was related to *any* meaning of the homonym prime (e.g., respond "yes" to ETHNICITY because it is a meaning of *race*). When the subordinate meaning of the homonym was also a cognate, bilinguals' ability to correctly accept the target as being related to the homonym prime was facilitated relative to non-cognate meanings. Thus, these studies together demonstrate that access to homonym meanings for bilinguals involves activation dynamics across both of their languages, which can either facilitate or slow down performance depending on the convergence between form and meaning.

The modulating effects of overlap in lexical form and semantics are particularly relevant to the BIA+ since it is a model of the bilingual lexicon (whereas the Three Factor Framework and B-RAM are theoretical frameworks of homonym-meaning activation in sentence context).

Recall that this model assumes an integrated bilingual lexicon in which activation flows non-selectively across languages. Within this model the key factor determining the relative activation of a lexical candidate is how similar it is to the input string. Thus, competing words across languages with differing orthographic, phonological, semantic codes will be less strongly activated than those with more complete overlap. In terms of the observed attenuation of facilitation for morphologically complex cognates, the BIA+ contains sub-lexical orthographic units within the integrated bilingual lexicon that feed and receive activation from matching lexical units. The competition resulting from different morphological units of cognates slows down access, which can either nullify or reverse facilitation.

What about the differences in the consistency of observed effects of interlingual homograph versus cognate status? According to the BIA+, identical cognates share one single representation, unlike interlingual homographs, which have two, separate representations. As a consequence, speeded processing of identical cognates is the result of the pooled, subjective frequency of exposure, they are functionally higher-frequency words. However, non-identical cognates do not share a single representation; as a consequence any distinction in lexical form can slow access. Even non-identical cognates are more likely to be affected by cross-language activation than interlingual homographs in sentence context because they share semantics. Sentence comprehension requires processing of semantic codes and that is why shared or non-shared semantics has a fundamental influence on the probability that effects of cross-language activation will be observed on performance.

Both the Three-Factor Framework and B-RAM focus specifically on the processing of cross-language homonyms that have either partial semantic overlap (e.g., *novel/novela* sharing only one meaning) or no semantic overlap (e.g., interlingual homographs). The evidence that competition from interlingual homographs is reduced in sentence context supports the Three-Factor Framework's assumption that language and semantic information provided by a sentence context alters the relative activation of the competing meaning. The evidence that cognate meanings of within-language homonyms (e.g., "book" meaning of *novel/novela* and "ethnicity" meaning of *race/raza*) can either hurt or help performance depending on whether they are the target meanings, supports the B-RAM's assumption that activation of intra-lingual homograph meanings is influenced by language non-selectivity.

## 15.6 Moderating effects of language intermixing

Some studies have found that the linguistic environment beyond the local sentence context influences the degree of non-selectivity observed. In one study, both behavioral and neural indices of processing were affected by viewing a film before the task in either the target, L2 (English) or in the non-target, L1 (German) (Elston-Güttler, Paulmann, & Kotz, 2005). In that experiment, proficient bilinguals read all L2 sentences and performed a lexical decision on follow-up, target words. On critical trials, the sentences ended in a German–English interlingual homograph and the target was the translation of the German meaning (e.g., *gift*, POISON). Effects of homograph status on performance and on the ERP signal (N400 component) were observed only for participants who had first viewed the German film, and only during the first block of trials. Otherwise, processing appeared language selective. The authors interpreted this as demonstrating the ability for bilingual lexical processing to gradually "zoom in" to the target language when there are sufficient linguistic cues.

Like Elston-Güttler and others, Baten, Hofman, and Loeys (2011) observed an attenuation of cross-language activation in the latter half of the experiment. In that study, highly proficient, Dutch–English bilinguals read low-constraint sentences ending in interlingual homographs whose translations were either of the same or different syntactic category. Lexical decision performance was facilitated for the homographs sharing syntactic class, but the magnitude was significantly reduced by the second half of trials.

In an eye-tracking study Titone and colleagues (Titone et al., 2011) found that effects of the weaker language on the more dominant L1 are greater after reading a block of L1 sentences. Specifically, when the experiment was L1 pure, cognate facilitation effects were reliably observed only in total reading times, and only for bilinguals whose L2 age of acquisition was earlier. When the experiment included the L2 block, cognate facilitation was observed in gaze duration and less dependent on age of acquisition.

Since the moderating effects observed in these studies were all due to linguistic features of the context beyond a single sentence, they can be accommodated by the BIA+. This model allows for more language selective processing because lexical representations within a language are assumed to receive excitatory activation from each other, allowing for higher levels of resting activation. The key distinction is that such moderating effects are not due to participant expectations regarding what languages they may encounter, as this would occur outside of the encapsulated lexicon and only affect processing after initial word access has been complete.

These results can also be easily accommodated within the Three Factor Framework. This framework assumes that the activation level of an interlingual homograph meaning can be directly affected by the surrounding language context (Degani & Tokowicz, 2010b). The B-RAM does not make any assumptions about the impact of language context in its present form.

## 15.7 Moderating effects of individual differences of the reader

Several individual differences pertaining to the bilingual reader have been found to moderate the effects of sentence context on observed language non-selectivity. One set of individual differences pertains to the bilingualism of the reader, reviewed first, and the other class of influences pertains to cognitive-general differences in working memory capacity and executive control, reviewed second. Similar to research on lexical access of individual words, the research using sentence context shows that the magnitude of effects of non-selectivity depends on bilinguals' relative dominance in the competing versus target language. When the target language is the weaker language, greater proficiency in that language is linked to decreased effects of cross-language activation; when processing is in the dominant language, greater proficiency in the non-target language is associated with greater effects of non-selectivity. For studies examining processing in the weaker language, there is a consistent pattern of observing greater effects of cross-language activation when proficiency in that language is more limited (Elston-Güttler, Paulman, and Kotz, 2005; Libben & Titone, 2009; Schwartz & Kroll, 2006). For example, Schwartz and Kroll recruited from two different populations of highly proficient Spanish–English bilinguals. One group (Experiment 1) was immersed in a border community in which both languages were used throughout the day and across academic and personal contexts. Also, although this group acquired English later than Spanish, the age of acquisition was still quite young (about 7 years of age) and most of their formal education was in that language. In fact, that group had become L2 dominant in English. The second group (Experiment 2) was immersed in the environment of their L1, Spanish (Valencia, Spain), in which they were also more dominant. Their usage of English was restricted to academic contexts and travel. Whereas the performance of both groups reflected reliable cognate facilitation effects that were reduced in high constraint sentences, only the group in Spain showed inhibitory effects of interlingual homograph status, which was not at all reduced by the presence of semantically constraining sentences. Similarly, the reader will recall that in the study by Elston-Güttler, Paulman, and Kotz (2005), it was only the intermediate English proficiency group whose reaction time performance and ERPs reflected consisted inhibition from German homonym meanings when making English lexical decisions, irrespective of the presence of a biasing sentence context.

However, in two separate eye-tracking studies of French–English bilinguals reading in their weaker L2, proficiency in the L2 did not moderate effects of interlingual homograph status (Libben & Titone,

2009; Pivneva et al., 2014). There are two, non-mutually exclusive reasons for the divergence in this pattern. First, the participants in those studies may have had greater reading proficiency in the L2 and/or a more limited range relative to the participants of Experiment 2 in Schwartz and Kroll (2006) and those of Elston-Güttler, Paulman, and Kotz (2005), since participants in both of those cases were not immersed in an English-speaking environment. Second, effects of interlingual homograph status in sentence context are less reliably observed overall, being moderated by other factors such as proficiency. Consistent with this latter interpretation, L2 proficiency in both of the eye-tracking studies with French–English bilinguals (Libben & Titone, 2009; Pivneva et al., 2014) did in fact moderate cognate facilitation effects, with greater cognate benefits being observed for those who either had slower reading rates in their L2 or later L2 acquisition. Pivneva et al. point out that the greater cognate facilitation observed at lower proficiency levels may in fact be due to lower functional frequency of L2 words, since the cognate facilitation in that group is largely driven by longer processing times of L2 noncognates.

What about when bilinguals are reading sentences in a dominant L1? Perhaps greater automaticity in L1 lexical access is speeded enough to prevent effects of cross-language activation from being manifest in performance. However, available evidence suggests that a complete elimination of effects is unlikely. First, in one study, in which highly proficient Dutch–English bilinguals read low-constraint sentences exclusively in their L1, consistent cognate benefits in processing time were observed across aspects of the eye-movement record tapping into pre-lexical and post-lexical processing (Van Assche et al., 2009).

However, another eye-tracking study of L1 sentence comprehension which included both high and low constraint sentences, paints a more complicated picture (Titone et al., 2011). When reading low-constraint sentences, English–French bilinguals total reading times were reduced for cognates. When reading high constraint sentences, reduced reading times for cognates was again observed, but only for those bilinguals who had acquired the L2 earlier. In a second experiment, which included French, filler sentences, effects of cognate status were observed across low- and high-constraint sentences and were not susceptible to effects of sentence constraint. Thus, whether cross-language activation of a weaker L2 will influence processing in a more dominant L1 will vary as a function of L2 proficiency and semantic information provided by the sentence. When L2 proficiency is greater and there is less semantic bias provided, effects in the L1 will tend to be greater.

A couple of recent studies have demonstrated that individual differences in working memory also affect the interactions between sentence context and language non-selectivity. For example, in one of the studies examining processing of L2 homonym meanings (Arêas da luz Fontes & Schwartz,

2011) only bilinguals with relatively low verbal working memory, measured through digit span, showed greater inhibitory effects of competing cognate meanings relative to noncognate meanings. The accuracy of bilinguals with higher digit spans was not affected by cognate status, thus they were equally efficient in suppressing competing meanings that existed across and within languages.

In one of the most thorough investigations of the influence of working memory, Pivneva et al. (2014) created a composite score of domain-general working memory for French–English bilinguals reading in their L2 while their eye-movements were tracked. They also obtained objective measures of L2 proficiency and in their analyses examined the differential impact these two classes of individual differences have on whether sentence context constrains effects of either cognate facilitation or interlingual homograph inhibition. The major finding from that study is that greater executive control was associated with reduced interlingual homograph interference in low-constraint sentences as well as greater reductions in processing time in high-constraint sentences. Importantly, the modulating role of executive control on interlingual homograph processing was observed in both early eye-movement measures (gaze duration) and late measures (total reading time), suggesting that general working memory had a direct impact on activation within the lexicon, as well as later post-lexical integration.

All three models highlighted in this review can accommodate the moderating effects of language proficiency and dominance on the degree of cross-language activation observed. Within the Three-Factor Framework and B-RAM, individual differences are expressed through different levels of sensitivity to the three factors of frequency, semantic context and language context. In the BIA+ proficiency differences are expressed in differing levels of resting activation of representations across languages.

Because it is a computational model, the BIA+ makes specific assumptions about the differing influences of language proficiency versus cognitive-general, working-memory capacity. Variation in verbal working memory can be accommodated by assuming greater verbal span allows for faster activation of potential lexical candidates. The findings of Pivneva et al. (2014) have important implications for this model. Recall, that this model makes an explicit distinction made between linguistic influences operating within the lexicon, and extra-linguistic factors operating outside the lexicon. However, finding effects of nonverbal, domain-general working memory is harder for the model in its present form. The findings from Pivneva et al. suggest that such extra-linguistic variability might in fact directly affect processing within the bilingual lexicon, especially since the moderating effects were observed in eye-movement measures reflecting pre-lexical processing (i.e., gaze duration).

## 15.8 Conclusion and future directions

The studies in this review make clear that the bilingual lexicon is fundamentally non-selective, but certain factors, such as meaningful context, can push activation to flow in a more targeted way within a specific language. What remains to be done is a fuller specification of the key factors that allow for more efficient, selective-like activation within a target language. Future studies should examine the precise moderating role that individual differences in verbal ability and non-linguistic working memory play. The reviewed studies suggest individual cognitive differences may impose significant constraints on what sources of contextual constraint can be exploited by the reader. The influence of these individual differences is likely to depend on the degree of contextual constraint provided by the sentence. There are other aspects of sentence comprehension, such as anaphoric referencing, that remain unexplored and that are likely to be affected by activated lexical information from the non-target language.

# 16

# Cross-language interactions during bilingual sentence processing

Paola Dussias, Amelia J. Dietrich, and Álvaro Villegas

## 16.1 Introduction

The field's view of how bilinguals process sentences in their two languages has experienced seismic shifts in the past two decades. It was once thought that transfer of processing routines from the first language (L1) was a feature of second language (L2) performance that characterized even the most highly proficient second language learners. There are, indeed, many studies showing that reliance on processing routines from the first language affect the computation of syntactic structure in the second language, and numerous studies have demonstrated that linguistic information from the dominant L1 constrains second language processing. Studies subsumed under the framework of the Competition Model (e.g., MacWhinney, 1987b; MacWhinney & Bates, 1989), for example, have examined language pairs that differ in the way forms map onto semantic functions in order to determine whether second language speakers are able to learn the mappings and weights specific to the second language. Many findings have shown that they do not (e.g., Gass, 1987; Harrington, 1987; Heilenman & McDonald, 1993; Hernandez, Bates, & Avila, 1994; Liu, Bates, & Li, 1992; McDonald, 1987; McDonald & Heilenman, 1991; Sasaki, 1994; Wulfeck et al., 1986), although a few studies also began to point to

The writing of this chapter was supported in part by NIH Grant R21 HD071758-01A1, NSF Grants BCS-0955090, and OISE-0968369 to P.E. Dussias and by NSF Graduate Fellowship DGE1255832 to A. J. Dietrich. Any opinions, findings, and conclusions or recommendations expressed in this material are those of the authors and do not necessarily reflect the views of the National Science Foundation.

proficiency in the second language as a significant modulating factor (e.g., Su, 2001).

In subsequent work, attention has shifted to other aspects of syntactic processing, most notably those involving the assignment of structural relationships between phrases in a sentence (e.g., Dussias, 2001, 2003; Felser et al., 2003; Fernández, 2003; Frenck-Mestre, 1999, 2002; Papadopoulou & Clahsen, 2003; Witzel, Witzel, & Nicol, 2012); the use of lexically encoded syntactic information (e.g., Dietrich, 2014; Dussias & Cramer Scaltz, 2008; Frenck-Mestre & Pynte, 1997; Lee, Lu, & Garnsey, 2013); gap processing and *wh*-processing (e.g., Dussias & Piñar, 2010; Jackson, 2008; Juffs & Harrington, 1996; Pliatsikas & Marinis, 2013; Williams, 2006; Williams, Möbius, & Kim, 2001); and sensitivity to morpho-syntactic information not instantiated in the first language such as gender-, number- and case-marking as well as the processing of multiple concord (e.g., Foucart & Frenck-Mestre, 2011, 2012; Gillon-Dowens et al., 2010; Guillelmon & Grosjean, 2001; Hopp, 2006, 2010, 2013; Jackson & Dussias, 2009; Jackson, Dussias, & Hristova, 2012; Jiang, 2004, 2007; Sabourin & Stowe 2008).

The results of these studies have had a profound influence on what we know about the cues and mechanisms that bilinguals use to process sentences in their two languages. First, they have challenged the existence of fundamental differences between native (L1) and non-native (L2) processing in sequential bilinguals (Clahsen & Felser, 2006) and suggest that proficiency in the L2 (Kotz, 2009), speed of lexical access (Hopp, 2012, 2013), and cognitive and computational resources (Hopp, 2010; McDonald, 2006) rather than age of acquisition per se may be more important in determining processing similarities between native and non-native speakers. Second, evidence from behavioral and electrophysiological studies investigating the time course of language processing provides evidence that even subtle aspects of the second language may be acquired by adult second language learners (e.g., Foucart & Frenck-Mestre, 2011, 2012; Gillon-Dowens et al., 2010; Pliatsikas & Marinis, 2013; Witzel et al., 2012). This argues against the view that there are hard constraints that distinguish non-native from native processing. Finally, emerging findings suggest that not only can the L1 affect L2 processing (e.g., Hatzidaki, Branigan, & Pickering, 2011; Kotz, 2009; Morales et al., under review; Weber & Paris, 2004) but that the L2 can come to affect processing in the native language (e.g., Dussias, Perrotti, & Brown, 2013; Dussias & Sagarra, 2007; Valdés Kroff, 2012). This points toward a system that is far more open and dynamic than previously thought (Hernandez, Li, & MacWhinney, 2005).

In this chapter, we review the research examining the interactions between bilinguals' two languages during the process of making structural decisions about the words they read or hear. We discuss research examining this question from the perspective of the role of the first language in the syntactic processing of the second language, and also examine cross-language interactions in the opposite direction (from the second language to the first language) in adult, sequential bilinguals who actively use their two languages in their daily lives and who value maintenance of the first language. We also discuss work on processing mixed language, a uniquely bilingual behavior. Understanding how people process language mixing, such as code-switching, has important implications for models of language processing. It also provides us with useful insights into how two languages are organized in the bilingual brain and how bilinguals negotiate language switching or alternating while challenging existing assumptions about the plasticity of cognitive and neural representations of language. Our aim is to show that research on sentence processing in second language speakers has the potential to lead to significant advancements in the conceptualization of the mind with two languages and in current views about the permeability of the first language system.

## 16.2 Effects of the first language on syntactic processing in the second language

One fact about L2 sentence comprehension is that non-native speakers approach the task of L2 sentence processing with a fully developed processing system from the L1. Given this, many past studies have asked how the presence of particular linguistic features in the first language might impact syntactic processing in the second language. As we will see, claims about the pervasiveness of L1 transfer effects during L2 processing may have been premature; factors such as proficiency in the L2, structural similarities/dissimilarities between the L1 and the L2, and whether the bilingual is immersed in an L1- or L2-dominant environment at the time of testing have a bearing on whether highly proficient L2 learners show patterns of processing that strongly resemble native-speaker sentence processing (e.g., Dietrich, 2014; Dussias et al., 2013; Foucart & Frenck-Mestre, 2011; Hoover & Dwivedi, 1998; Hopp, 2013; Jackson & Dussias, 2009; Pliatsikas & Marinis, 2013; Witzel et al., 2012).

The logic in these studies has been to examine syntactic structures that differ in obvious ways between the L1 and the L2 to test whether syntactic properties of the native language partly account for L2 processing outcomes. One candidate that has been extensively studied in the literature is the processing of empty categories ($e$). To illustrate, languages differ on whether *wh*-words such as *who, what*, or *which* 'move' overtly from their theta-marked position to another position in the sentence during question formation. English (1) and Spanish are examples of languages with overt *wh*-movement, e.g.:

(1) Q: What$^i$ are you doing $e_i$?
    A: I am doing something$_i$.

Chinese (2) and Japanese are languages without overt *wh*-movement:

(2) Q: *Ni zai zuo shenmo?*
    'you at do what'

Many findings in the monolingual sentence processing literature (e.g., Clifton & Frazier, 1989; Gibson & Warren, 2004; Love & Swinney, 1996) provide evidence that when a *wh*-word (a *filler*) is displaced from its canonical position to another position in the sentence (e.g., during question formation), it leaves behind an empty syntactic category (called a *gap* in the *wh*-movement work). One important task during native language sentence processing is to identify the correct gap site, given that gaps have no overt phonological manifestation. Because native speakers of languages with overt *wh*-movement show evidence of gap processing (e.g., Gibson, 1998; Gordon, Hendrick, & Johnson, 2004; van Dyke & McElree, 2006; Warren & Gibson, 2002), one question has been whether speakers of languages without overt *wh*-movement also show evidence of identifying gaps during L2 processing. Findings across many studies show remarkably similar reading patterns for L2 speakers with and without overt *wh*-movement (e.g., Juffs, 2005; Juffs & Harrington, 1995, 1996; Marinis, Roberts, Felser, & Clahsen, 2005; Pliatsikas & Marinis, 2013; Williams et al., 2001). Juffs (2005), for example, reported that although native speakers of Spanish reading English *wh*-sentences were reliably better than native Chinese speakers at providing grammaticality judgments (at rates similar to those of native speakers, likely due to the presence of *wh*-movement in Spanish), both groups of learners demonstrated similar processing patterns, as indicated by reading times, when reading object extractions (e.g., 'Who$_i$ does the nurse know the doctor saw $e_i$ in his office?') and subject extractions (e.g., 'Who$_i$ does the nurse know $e_i$ saw the patient at the hospital?'), suggesting only a weak effect of the L1 on L2 syntactic processing. Lack of L1 transfer effects has also been reported when non-native speakers engage in processing empty categories associated with other syntactic elements not instantiated in the L1 (Hoover & Dwivedi, 1998), the processing of preverbal clitics in French by L1 English speakers), suggesting that the absence of L1 effects when L2 speakers process empty categories is not modulated by the nature of the empty category per se.

Weak evidence for L1-to-L2 transfer effects also comes from studies that have considered whether syntactic information encoded in verbs affects structural decisions during L2 processing. The question in these studies has been whether subcategorization information and probabilistic sentence-structural preferences of individual verbs in the first language constrain parsing decisions in the second language. To see how this might happen, consider the case of the temporarily ambiguous noun phrase (NP) 'the kids' in (1) (adapted from Garnsey et al., 1997):

(3) The resident warned the kids ...

The temporary ambiguity arises because the sentence fragment could continue in a variety of ways. For instance, "the kids" could function as the direct object of 'warned' as in "The resident warned the kids when she saw them throwing rocks," but it could also function as the subject of a subordinate clause (e.g., "The resident warned the kids did not respect others' property"). A general observation in this type of work is that participants make initial commitments to the interpretation that is more consistent with the syntactic frame in which the verb is most likely to occur, called its *verb bias* (Trueswell, Tanenhaus, & Kello, 1993; Wilson & Garnsey, 2009). In English, 'warn' is twice as likely to be followed by a direct object than by a sentence complement (Garnsey et al., 1997); participants use this information to anticipate the presence of an upcoming direct object and assign this interpretation to the ambiguous NP (Garnsey et al., 1997; Wilson & Garnsey, 2009). Unlike English, Spanish 'warn' (*advertir*) is normally followed by a sentence complement (Dussias et al., 2010). Given this, one critical question is whether L2 readers use verbal information from the first language to resolve syntactic ambiguity in the second language. Studies with proficient learners from different L1 backgrounds demonstrate sensitivity to L2-specific verb information when the lexical constraints of the verbs conflict in the two languages (e.g., Dietrich, 2014; Dussias & Cramer, 2006; Dussias & Cramer-Scaltz, 2008; Frenck-Mestre & Pynte, 1997). There is also evidence that when the L1 does not encourage the use of lexically encoded verbal information such as verb bias to anticipate an upcoming verbal complement (e.g., in verb final languages like Korean), if proficiency in the L2 is high enough, speakers access verbal information specific to the L2 to generate predictions about an upcoming sentence structure (Lee et al., 2013).

Evidence for L1 transfer effects that are modulated by proficiency in the second language are not restricted to cases in which verbal information is employed to resolve syntactic ambiguity. Studies examining structural relationships between phrases also reveal a range of findings. The linguistic context examined in these studies involves two noun phrases separated by a (non-theta assigning) preposition, as in "Peter called the daughter of the man who lived in Paris." Here, the relative clause "who lived in Paris" can *attach* to the syntactically higher noun 'daughter' ("the daughter lived in Paris") or to the lower noun 'man' ("the man lived in Paris"). The explanation of what leads to the decision to attach the relative clause high or low is a matter of debate in the literature. Some accounts explain it in terms of universal discourse-based principles that interact with language-specific rules (Frazier & Clifton, 1996), whereas other explanations are based on the application of structure-based parsing strategies (e.g., Gibson et al., 1996). The relevant finding for our purposes is that speakers of languages that strongly favor one interpretation over the other have sometimes not shown any preference for high or low attachment when reading in their L2 (e.g., Felser et al., 2003; Papadopoulou & Clahsen, 2003; for a review, see

Clahsen & Felser, 2006). Other studies report evidence for L1-to-L2 transfer at low levels of proficiency (Frenck-Mestre, 1999) but convergence on target attachment preferences at higher levels of proficiency (Dussias, 2001; Frenck-Mestre, 2002). To illustrate, Frenck-Mestre (1999) examined the processing of this construction in less proficient learners of French – a language in which high attachment is the preferred attachment site – by considering whether the general attachment preferences in the L1 and the L2 were congruent or incongruent. In the congruent case (i.e., L1 Spanish–L2 French), learners showed a preference for high attachment. In the incongruent case (i.e., L1 English–L2 French), the trend was toward low attachment ambiguity resolution. That is, the L2 readers only followed the target language's general attachment preference when it was congruent with the general preference in their L1. Frenck-Mestre attributed this pattern of results to the influence of the native language on L2 processing. A subsequent study (Frenck-Mestre, 2002), however, found that English–French learners who had been immersed in the L2 environment for an average of five years resolved the ambiguity in favor of high attachment, the same pattern found in the French monolingual group. This suggests that proficiency and immersion experience in the L2 modulated the degree to which L2 learners were guided by phrase structure-based parsing principles of the type that are evidenced during L1 processing (see also Witzel et al., 2012).

More recently, evidence from experiments using Event-Related Potentials (ERPs) to investigate the neural basis of bilingual sentence processing support findings reported in behavioral studies that L1-to-L2 transfer effects do not always occur where one expects to see them (see also Slabakova, 2013 for a related argument concerning L2 knowledge of the syntax–discourse interface). Given that most of this work comes from studies examining the processing of grammatical gender, we will discuss some of this evidence below.

In some languages of the world, the pervasiveness of grammatical gender is evident in almost every phrase, playing a crucial role in the coherence of the sentence as a whole (Corbett, 2005; Friederici & Jacobsen, 1999). In other languages, grammatical gender is largely missing. This contrast raises interesting questions about the representation and function of gender during second language processing. A robust finding in monolingual studies of grammatical gender processing (e.g., Bates et al., 1996; Colé & Segui, 1994; Dahan et al., 2000; Lew-Williams & Fernald, 2007; van Berkum, 1996) is that the recognition of a target noun is affected by grammatical gender information provided by a prenominal modifier. When the gender of an article or adjective is congruent with the gender of the following noun, recognition of the noun is enhanced relative to a neutral baseline; when it is incongruent, recognition of the noun is slowed down.

In one study recording electrophysiological responses of the brain (ERPs), Sabourin and Stowe (2008) reported a P600 – generally elicited by grammatical errors or syntactic anomalies – response during the processing of grammatical gender agreement violations in the L2 only when the gender system of the L2 (Dutch) was very similar to that of the L1 (German). When the two systems were dissimilar (as was the case with Romance speakers proficient in Dutch), there was no evidence of a P600 effect in the L2, although the presence of frontal negativity suggested that these L2 speakers were indeed sensitive to the ungrammaticality despite their lack of a P600 effect. From these results, Sabourin and Stowe concluded that the mere presence of grammatical gender in the L1 does not lead to the recruitment of the same type of neurological areas to process gender violations, and that the specific degree of syntactic and lexical similarity between the L1 and the L2 plays an important role. Other recent ERP evidence, however, suggests that under conditions in which the gender agreement system of the L1 has little in common with that of the L2 (e.g., Foucart & Frenck-Mestre, 2011) or even when the grammatical features in question are entirely absent in the L1 (e.g., Foucart & Frenck-Mestre, 2012; Gillon-Dowens et al., 2010, 2011), L2 speakers with enough proficiency in the L2 show some of the same signature effects associated with native-speaker detection of gender and number-agreement anomalies.

A recent study by Foucart and Frenck-Mestre (2012) illustrates this. The authors compared native speakers of French to second language learners of French (L1 English) while processing noun–adjective gender agreement violations that were embedded in two types of constructions: preverbal adjective constructions (e.g., "*De nos jours, les anciennes montres sont rares*"/ Nowadays, old watches are rare) which are allowable in both English and French (but are less canonical in French), and post-verbal adjective constructions, which are allowable only in French (e.g., "*Depuis une semaine, les chaises vertes sont dans le jardin*," Since last week the chairs green are in the garden; examples taken from Foucart & Frenck-Mestre, 2012). The goal was to examine whether and how differences in L1 grammars might influence the processing of adjectival phrases. For post-nominal adjective constructions, the L1 English learners of French showed P600 effects just like native speakers of French, indicating that they were using gender information on the first constituent (i.e., the noun) to predict the agreement morphology on the second constituent (i.e., the adjective). Relevant to our discussion of L1-to-L2 transfer effects are the results for the prenominal adjective violations, which elicited a P600 effect in the French native speakers but an N400 effect in the L2 learners. This is striking because a transfer account would predict that when word order is the same for both English and French, neural responses of the L2 learners should resemble those of L1 speakers. However, they differed from native French speakers, suggesting that the less canonical prenominal adjective word order in French is acquired later by the L2 learners, despite it being the canonical word order in their L1.

Together, the findings provide important evidence that L1 speakers of a language without grammatical gender can show electrophysiological correlates during the processing of L2 gender agreement violations that are qualitatively similar to those of native speakers, and also weaken a strong version of the L1-to-L2 transfer account (for additional supporting evidence on gender and number processing see Frenck-Mestre et al., 2009; Gillon-Dowens et al., 2011; for evidence from an artificial language paradigm see Morgan-Short et al., 2010; but see Chen et al., 2007; and Guo et al., 2009 for incongruent findings).

## 16.2.2 Alternatives to L1 transfer

### 16.2.1.1 Shallow processing

Ultimately, if transfer effects from the L1 to the L2 do not entirely explain differences in sentence processing behavior between native and L2 speakers, a more adequate account is needed that can capture the range of findings. According to a proposal by Clahsen and Felser (2006), non-native speakers are like native speakers in every other respect, except when it comes to processing that is guided by structure-driven parsing principles. Their Shallow Structure Hypothesis postulates that adult online L2 parsing processes are solely guided by lexical–semantic, thematic role and plausibility information. This contrasts with processes that subserve sentence processing in the native language which, according to some accounts, are based initially on syntactic or grammatical information alone and are driven by a limited number of phrase-structure based, least-effort locality principles (Frazier, 1990; Frazier & Clifton, 1996; Gibson et al., 1996; for an alternative view, see Gennari & MacDonald, 2009; MacDonald, 1994; MacDonald & Seidenberg, 2006). According to this view, native and non-native speakers are fundamentally different when it comes to processing; whereas native speakers generate highly detailed syntactic representations that contain hierarchical phrase structure and abstract elements, the product of non-native processing has little abstract syntactic detail. The classic evidence in favor of shallow processing in L2 speakers comes primarily from work on the resolution of syntactically ambiguous relative clauses and from the processing of long-distance filler–gap dependencies. To illustrate, we will briefly discuss this evidence as well as some recent claims to the contrary.

As we mentioned earlier, when L2 learners parse ambiguous relative clause constructions for which no lexical–semantic information is available to guide the parsing process, some learners do not show any preference for one attachment site over the other. This was the case for the native speakers of high attaching languages such as German, Spanish, and

Russian tested in Papadopoulou and Clahsen (2003; see also Felser et al., 2003). When these speakers read temporarily ambiguous relative clauses in their L2 Greek, e.g.:

(4) A man called the student$_{MASC}$ of the teacher$_{FEM}$ who was disappointed$_{MASC}$ by the new educational system,

they showed no particular commitment to high or low attachment, suggesting that in the absence of lexical cues, they were not able to apply structure-based principles (in this case, grammatical gender agreement) that have been argued to guide the decision process. A prediction that follows from this is that if the structure includes lexical–semantic information that can guide parsing decisions, these same speakers should now show clear attachment preferences. And this is precisely what happened. When the case-assigning preposition 'of' in the example above was replaced with the semantically contentful preposition 'with' (creating a local thematic domain that favored n–2 attachment), L2 speakers consistently showed a preference for low attachment.

A second piece of critical evidence in favor of fundamental processing differences between native and non-native processing comes from the work on gap processing. In a study by Marinis et al. (2005), speakers of language backgrounds that either allowed (German, Greek) or did not allow (Chinese, Japanese) *wh*-movement, read sentences like (5):

(5) The nurse who$_i$ the doctor argued $e_i$ that the rude patient had angered $e_i$ is refusing to work late.

In this type of structure, there is a long-distance dependency between the filler "who" and its subcategorizing verb "angered." Past reading time evidence has shown that when native speakers of English process structures of this kind, they posit multiple gaps (signaled by "e" in the example) to break the long-distance dependency into smaller chunks, thereby facilitating the parsing process (Gibson & Warren, 2004). Marinis et al. (2005) reported that L2 speakers of languages with and without overt *wh*-movement alike did not make use of intermediate gaps purported to facilitate filler integration with the subcategorizing verb and argued that the syntactic representations that second language learners construct while processing input in their L2 are syntactically less detailed than those computed by adult L1 speakers.

Recent studies, however, have disputed the presumed inability of L2 speakers to rely on abstract syntactic information when processing their second language. Witzel, Witzel, and Nicol (2012) demonstrated that at high levels of L2 proficiency, L2 speakers reading different configurations of temporarily ambiguous structures show attachment preferences that are independent of lexically driven biases. Admittedly, their finding could be amenable to a shallow structure account. One reason is that comprehenders greatly favor local modification (Kimball, 1973), which predicts that processing adjacent constituents such as syntactically ambiguous relative clauses or adverb phrases should not cause major difficulties. More compelling evidence would come from examining the kinds of long-distance dependencies that are expected to be most problematic for L2 learners. Pliatsikas and Marinis (2013) provided this type of evidence. They compared reading times of immersed and non-immersed L2 speakers matched on measures of L2 proficiency while they read sentences involving the very same structures tested in Marinis et al. (2005) on non-immersed learners only. Remarkably, only the learners with extensive immersion experience in the L2 environment showed evidence of native-like processing of the intermediate gaps. This finding provides crucial evidence that proficiency and immersion experience in the L2 can lead to native-like abstract syntactic processing and pose a challenge for the view that there are hard constraints on late L2 processing.

### 16.2.1.2 Prediction during sentence processing

A competing account to explain differences in L1 and L2 processing comes from the work of Kaan and colleagues (e.g., Kaan, 2014; Kaan, Dallas, & Wijnen, 2010). The proposal ascribes a central role to the ability of language users to predict how language will unfold. Concurrent linguistic and non-linguistic contexts or inputs, which are derived from learning via experience with language and with real-world events, drive the predictive process (Altmann & Mirković, 2009).

The idea that prediction is a key mechanism underlying adult sentence comprehension is not new. Much of the work in the monolingual sentence processing literature has been aimed at explaining how humans comprehend language so quickly and with little apparent effort. According to one view (e.g., Altmann, 1998; Altmann, Garnham, & Dennis, 1992), the adult comprehension system is able to do this because it exploits multiple sources of information to generate predictions for what may come next in an input string. We mentioned earlier that monolingual English readers experience a processing advantage when presented with sentences in which a verbal complement is congruent with their expectations about a verb's preferred continuation (e.g., Trueswell, Tanenhaus, & Kello, 1993; Wilson & Garnsey, 2009). This is an example of how prediction helps guide the comprehension system. Another one comes from the work on grammatical gender processing. Lew-Williams and Fernald (2007) showed that Spanish-speaking listeners anticipate a forthcoming noun on the basis of the linguistic and visual information available to them. In Spanish, as in many other gendered languages in the world, nouns must agree in grammatical gender with their modifiers. In the sentence '*La canción es bonita*' (The$_{FEM}$ song$_{FEM}$ is pretty$_{FEM}$), the form of the determiner is '*la*' and of the adjective is '*bonita*' because '*canción*' is a feminine noun. Lew-Williams and Fernald wondered whether speakers used their knowledge of gender agreement in Spanish to facilitate processing. In their study, native Spanish-speaking children and adults were presented with visual scenes showing same gender objects (e.g., *galleta*$_{FEM}$/cookie and *pelota*$_{FEM}$/ball) or different gender objects (*galleta*$_{FEM}$ and *zapato*$_{MASC}$/shoe). Participants were asked to view the visual scene and to follow instructions that were played through a speaker (e.g., *encuentra la pelota*/find the ball). The main finding was that shortly after the article (e.g., *la* in the example above) was available in the auditory input but before the onset of the target noun was heard, participants directed reliably more and longer fixations to the appropriate object in the picture (i.e., *pelota*) than to the inappropriate object, demonstrating that they had anticipated what they would hear next. There is now growing evidence demonstrating that different types of information, including referential context (e.g., Spivey et al., 2002), verb bias (e.g., Trueswell, Tanenhaus, & Kello, 1993), plausibility (e.g., Garnsey et al., 1997), and prosody (e.g., Snedeker & Yuan, 2008), are used by native readers and listeners to generate syntactic expectations that allow them to constrain how incoming strings of words will be processed. In fact, a substantial number of recent findings have demonstrated that this type of prediction-based processing is a key component of efficient interpretation of language as it unfolds over time.

The predictive sentence processing account proposed by Kaan (2014) to explain L2 comprehension assumes that the same factors that drive individual differences in the ability of native speakers to engage in prediction account for the differences observed between L1 and L2 processing. Unlike the Shallow Structure Hypothesis, then, in Kaan's account there are no inherent or fundamental differences between native and non-native processing. Rather, a host of factors can give rise to differences in the anticipatory ability of native and non-native speakers. These include differences between native and non-native speakers' knowledge bases, which are graded representations that emerge from experience with language tokens (MacDonald, 2013) and with real-world events (Altmann & Mirković, 2009), competing information from the first and the second language, quality of the lexical representation, cognitive resources and control, and task demands. Put in another way, differences between native and non-native speakers are not rooted in the predictive mechanisms per se, but in what drives the mechanisms (e.g., Martin et al., 2013).

Although there is still much research to be conducted to better understand the factors that underlie purported differences in predictive sentence processing between native and L2 speakers, the account is promising in that it can adequately explain past research highlighting differences between L2 and native syntactic processing, in particular the absence of ELAN (early left anterior negativity, an effect associated with phrase–structure rule violations) effects in electrophysiological studies (Hahne, 2001; Hahne & Friederici, 2001), delayed filler–gap effects (Dallas, 2008), lack of anticipatory gender effects (Dussias et al., 2013; Grüter,

Lew-Williams, & Fernald, 2012; Hopp, 2013; Lew-Williams & Fernald, 2010), and absence of intermediate trace effects in processing of *wh*-movement by intermediate-level L2 learners (Marinis et al., 2005; see Kaan et al., 2010).

## 16.3 Effects of the second language on syntactic processing in the first language

To date, most research on sentence processing in L2 speakers has examined the role that the native language plays in making structural decisions during processing of the second language. Few studies have examined cross-linguistic interactions in the opposite direction, from the second language to the first language. An important insight from the work reviewed above is that prolonged naturalistic exposure can have profound effects on how a second language is processed, reversing parsing strategies that result from transfer of L1 information (Frenck-Mestre, 2002) or causing shifts in L2 processing strategies from lexically driven to structurally driven (Pliatsikas & Marinis, 2013). Given this, an important aspect of the comparison between L2 and L1 speaker performance is to consider how immersion experience might affect L1 processing. Work examining this question shows a great deal of permeability across language boundaries at different levels. For example, in immersion contexts, L2 speakers experience reduced access to the first language (Linck, Kroll, & Sunderman, 2009), and extensive contact with a second language can affect both L1 naming performance of common objects (Malt & Sloman, 2003) and L1 phonology (e.g., Flege, 1987; Flege & Eefting, 1987).

These findings confirm that a bilingual is not two monolinguals in one brain (Grosjean, 1989); the seemingly stable L1 system is open to influence once individuals become proficient in the L2 (e.g., Gollan et al., 2008; Ivanova & Costa, 2008; Runnqvist et al., 2013). Given this scenario, one might expect that experience in a second language environment should also produce changes on syntactic processing in the native language. Examining how knowledge of a second language impacts first language sentence processing in speakers who actively use their two languages has important implications for existing assumptions about the permeability of the language system. From a theoretical standpoint, finding that exposure to the L2 affects syntactic processing in the L1 would provide strong support for experience-based models of sentence parsing (e.g., MacDonald & Thornton, 2009), given the assumption within these models that frequency-based exposure is crucial to parsing.

Dussias and Sagarra (2007) documented changes to the L1 processing system in a study that investigated the effect that intense contact with English had on attachment preferences in Spanish, the participants' first language. L1 Spanish speakers proficient in English, who had lived in an L2 environment for an extended period of time, and functionally monolingual Spanish speakers were tested. Participants read syntactically ambiguous relative clause constructions of the type discussed earlier (4). Whereas the Spanish monolinguals showed the conventional bias for high attachment reported in the literature (e.g., Carreiras & Clifton, 1993; Dussias, 2003), the immersed Spanish–English speakers showed a consistent preference for low attachment when reading sentences in Spanish (their first language), suggesting that the parsing routines recruited to process the L2 had had an impact on the processing of the L1.

One might wonder whether immersion in the L2 can come to affect any aspect of L1 sentence processing or whether some structures are more susceptible to intense exposure to a second language. Given that syntactic structures differ along many dimensions, it is possible that different L1 structures are differentially affected by immersion in the second language. Effects of naturalistic exposure may become evident in the processing of, say, relative clause ambiguity resolution, but may be harder to obtain when information is encoded lexically and has syntactic consequences. To test this, Valdés Kroff (2012) examined whether intense contact with Spanish–English code-switched speech (defined below) had consequences in the processing of grammatical gender in Spanish. Grammatical gender is interesting in that it is a lexically specified feature of nouns that triggers syntactic agreement with other function and open-class elements, such as determiners and adjectives.

In many bilingual communities, speakers regularly switch from one language to another, often several times in a single utterance. This phenomenon is called 'code-switching.' The ability to engage in fluent code-switching is a hallmark of high proficiency in two languages (Miccio, Scheffner-Hammer, & Rodríguez, 2009), as successful and fluent code-switching requires a high degree of knowledge of and sensitivity to the grammatical constraints of both languages. In the production literature of Spanish–English code-switches, one widely attestable pattern is that when a code-switch occurs within a noun phrase composed of a determiner and a noun, the determiner overwhelmingly surfaces in Spanish and the noun in English, e.g., "*el* building" and not "the *edificio*." Researchers have also documented a production asymmetry in grammatical gender assignment in these mixed noun phrases. The Spanish masculine article '*el*' (the) surfaces with English nouns regardless of the grammatical gender of their translation equivalents, for example, '*el* juice' [Spanish *jugo*, masculine], '*el* cookie' [Spanish *galleta*, feminine]. By contrast, mixed noun phrases involving the Spanish feminine article '*la*' are rare and occur in restricted environments, such that only English nouns whose Spanish translation equivalents are feminine surface with '*la*' in code-switching (e.g., '*la* cookie' but not * '*la* juice'; Jake, Myers-Scotton, & Gross, 2002; Otheguy & Lapidus, 2003; Poplack, 1980). These production distributions in Spanish–English code-switching stand in marked contrast to monolingual Spanish, where the grammatical gender of a noun and its accompanying article must obligatorily match, and where masculine and feminine nouns are evenly distributed (Eddington, 2002; Otheguy & Lapidus, 2003).

As we mentioned above, Valdés Kroff (2012) investigated whether L1 Spanish-L2 English speakers who had been immersed in a code-switching environment used grammatical gender information encoded in Spanish articles anticipatorily, as Lew-Williams and Fernald (2007) showed with monolingual speakers of Spanish. Given the asymmetry observed in production data, it seemed plausible that the gender-marking of articles would facilitate to a lesser extent the processing of code-switched speech. To investigate this, the eye movements of Spanish–English bilinguals were recorded. The design was similar to the one in Lew-Williams and Fernald (2007), except that two pictures which represented objects whose nouns were either of the same or different grammatical genders were presented while they also listened to code-switched sentences (i.e., *Hay un niño que está mirando el* candy/There is a boy looking at the candy). Words were spoken with a Spanish article that either matched the gender of the word's Spanish translation equivalent (e.g., *el* candy$_{MASC}$ [Spanish "caramelo," masculine) or didn't match (target: *el* candle$_{FEM}$ [Spanish "vela," feminine). A control group of monolingual speakers listened to sentences entirely in Spanish. Participants were asked to listen to each sentence and to click on a named object. Where the grammatical gender of the Spanish names for each of the pictures was different between the two pictures, the gender information in the article was informative. In that condition, monolingual Spanish speakers showed the expected anticipatory effect on masculine and feminine different-gender trials. Results for the L2 speakers revealed an anticipatory effect, but only on different-gender trials where the auditory stimulus was feminine. Where the auditory stimuli was masculine in different-gender trials, participants did not launch anticipatory looks but rather waited to hear the target noun, meaning that they did not use masculine articles as cues to anticipatory processing. Because the masculine article is overwhelmingly more common in Spanish–English code-switching but not so in monolingual Spanish, these group differences suggest that how grammatical cues are exploited in mixed language processing is driven by experience with the statistical patterns attested in actual communicative contexts. Critically, it also reveals the key role that linguistic exposure has on language comprehension processes.

## 16.4 Processing mixed language

An important insight from the monolingual psycholinguistic work on sentence comprehension is that individuals make strikingly similar structural choices as they interpret the sentences that they read. For example, experimental studies using a variety of techniques have shown that readers preferentially interpret the noun phrase "the players" in the sentence fragment 'The coach warned the players … ' as the direct object of 'warned,' even though 'the players' can plausibly function as the subject of an ensuing clause (e.g., 'The coach warned the players were getting tired'). The pervasiveness of these choices during language comprehension has been taken as evidence for the application of a small number of hardwired structure-based parsing principles that guide the comprehension system (see, for example, Frazier, 1979, 1987; Frazier & Rayner, 1982; Pearlmutter & Gibson, 2001). In contrast to these so-called *structure-based* models of processing, *experienced-based* accounts challenge the existence of parsing principles as a key component of the architecture of the comprehension system and argue, instead, that the preferences observed during sentence comprehension reflect speakers' knowledge about statistical regularities in their environment. Accordingly, readers' structural decisions during sentence comprehension do not arise because of inherent biases in the comprehension system; instead, they are derived from exposure to statistical regularities in language (e.g., Bybee, 2002; Gahl & Garnsey, 2004; Garnsey et al., 1997; Gennari & MacDonald, 2009; Jurafsky, 1996; Jurafsky et al., 2001; MacDonald & Seidenberg, 2006; MacDonald & Thornton, 2009; Trueswell & Tanenhaus, 1994; Trueswell et al.,1993; Wilson & Garnsey, 2009).

In support of this claim, many past studies have shown that comprehension difficulty is influenced by the match between syntactic structure and the frequency with which verbs appear in that structure (e.g., Spivey-Knowlton & Sedivy, 1995; Tanenhaus & Trueswell, 1995; Trueswell & Kim, 1998). For example, a transitive verb like "worry," which is most often used by speakers with a sentential complement, causes less comprehension difficulty when followed by a sentence complement (e.g., "The bus driver worried the passengers might complain to his manager") than by a noun-phrase complement (e.g., "The bus driver worried the passengers because he drove very quickly") (examples taken from Wilson & Garnsey, 2009).

Until now, the evidence in favor of experience-based models of processing has come primarily from studies with monolingual speakers, and predominantly from studies with monolingual English speakers (e.g., Gennari & MacDonald, 2009; Treiman et al., 2003). In recent years, the recognition that more individuals are bilingual than monolingual has led to an explosion of studies investigating the way in which bilinguals manage the presence of two languages in a single mind. Within the bilingual literature, the study of code-switching has provided a unique lens through which the link between production and comprehension can be studied. We illustrate this using Spanish–English code-switching involving two types of auxiliary phrases because of their distribution in written and oral naturalistic code-switching corpora.

Switches involving the Spanish auxiliary '*estar*' (be) and an English present participle ('*los profesores están* developing a new course'/The teachers are developing a new course) occur with the same frequency as switches at the auxiliary ('*los profesores* are developing a new course'). However, switches involving the Spanish auxiliary '*haber*' (have) and an English past participle ('*los profesores han* developed a new course'/The teachers have developed a new course) are less frequent compared to switches at the auxiliary ('*los profesores* have developed a new course') (Pfaff, 1979; Poplack, 1980). Crucially, differences in the distributional probabilities of these code-switches reflect differences in syntactic probabilities and not differences in meaning biases. That is, although the progressive and perfect forms inherently convey different temporal meanings, whether a code-switch is produced at the verb phrase boundary (i.e., at the auxiliary) or at the participle verb (i.e., immediately following the auxiliary) does not change the meaning of the utterance. In other words, '*Los profesores están* developing a new course' means exactly the same thing as '*los profesores* are developing a new course.' This is an important point when examining the predictions of models arguing that frequency of exposure to certain constructions is a major factor guiding sentence comprehension (e.g., Jurafsky, 1996; MacDonald & Seidenberg, 2006). Because the two variants (e.g., '*está developing*' and 'are developing') do not differ in meaning, findings that show frequency effects in comprehension can be more readily attributed to particular distributional patterns in code-switched speech than to the meaning conveyed by the structures themselves (see Newmeyer, 2006). By using code-switching data, then, it is possible to disentangle probabilities from meaning in a way that cannot be easily done by examining monolingual speech.

In a study testing whether code-switching patterns in production influence ease of comprehension, Guzzardo Tamargo (2012) recorded the eye movements of Spanish–English code-switchers while participants read sentences on a computer screen. The experimental stimuli comprised four versions of the same sentence, corresponding to four experimental conditions. Conditions 1 and 2 were code-switched conditions with the progressive structure. In Condition 1, the switch occurred at the auxiliary ('*El director confirmó que los actores* are rehearsing for the movie'/The director confirmed that the actors are rehearsing for the movie) and in Condition 2 the switch occurred at the English present participle ('*El director confirmó que los actores están* rehearsing for the movie'/The director confirmed that the actors are rehearsing for the movie). Conditions 3 and 4 were analogous to Conditions 1 and 2, but involved the perfect structure ('*El director confirmó que los actores* have rehearsed for the movie'/The director confirmed that the actors have rehearsed for the movie, and '*El director confirmó que los actores han* rehearsed for the movie'/The director confirmed that the actors have rehearsed for the movie, respectively). Results showed that participants took longer to read the critical region (the verbal participle) in

Condition 4 compared to Condition 3, but that switches in Conditions 2 did not incur more costs than switches in Condition 1. The findings are congenial with models of language processing (e.g., the Production–Distribution–Comprehension model of Gennari & MacDonald, 2009) in which linguistic experience plays a crucial role in the way language is processed. Importantly, they also demonstrate that the representation and processes with processing two languages are not fundamentally different from those employed by monolingual speakers.

## 16.5 Concluding remarks

The framing question underlying the studies discussed in this chapter is to what extent L2 processing is qualitatively similar or different from L1 processing. In addressing this question, we have discussed a number of variables that affect reading processing among L2 learners. Some of these variables are linguistic in nature in that they are concerned with the specific sources of linguistic information that L2 learners access and use during L2 sentence comprehension. Others have to do with how learners' characteristics, such as proficiency and type of linguistic experience, interact with linguistic aspects of the input in producing a parsing outcome. Here, we have reviewed an approach that employs sentence processing research in speakers of more than one language as a tool to uncover basic aspects of human cognition. This approach takes advantage of the existence of two languages in a single mind and of the varying linguistic experiences across different types of L1–L2 speakers to empirically test the constraints of human cognition. What is promising about this line of work is that it has led researchers to uncover a property of human cognition that is not obvious when studying speakers of one language alone. What is clear from the work we have discussed is that the comprehension system in bilinguals and, by extension monolinguals, is remarkably flexible, adapting dynamically to language experience. As might be expected, the presence of the entrenched native language system has consequences for how sentences in the L2 are processed. Finally, what is surprising is that knowledge of and exposure to a second language can have profound consequences for the purportedly stable native-language system.

# Part V

# Production

# 17

# Individual differences in second language speech production

Judit Kormos

## 17.1 Introduction

Individuals differ with regard to their ability to speak at length, with ease, even in their first language (Fillmore, 1979), and research in the field of second language (L2) speech production has also long been concerned with the question of why students show such great variation in the attainment of speaking skills in another language. The individual factors that influence language learning have also been widely researched in the past thirty years in the field of second language acquisition (for a recent overview see Dewaele, 2012). The variables in which language learners as well as bi- and multilingual language users differ are generally subdivided into affective, cognitive and personality-related individual differences (Gardner, 1985). With some overlaps, motivation, language learning anxiety and self-confidence are generally listed among affective factors, whereas personality-related differences comprise a number of traits, such as openness to experience, conscientiousness, extraversion, agreeableness, and emotional stability (Costa & McCrae, 1992). The cognitive factors that are held to be important predictors of success in language learning and bi- and multilingual attainment are intelligence (Skehan, 1986), foreign language aptitude (Carroll, 1981; Carroll & Sapon, 1959), working memory capacity and phonological short-term memory capacity (for an overview see Juffs & Harrington, 2011).

For a long time in the field of second language acquisition, cognitive, affective, and personality-related differences were regarded as traits that remain stable both during the language learning process and across a wide variety of language learning activities and language use contexts. This view, however, has been challenged by dynamic approaches to second language acquisition which argue that learner internal factors dynamically interact with the features and characteristics of the learner's external communicative, social, and instructional context (Larsen-Freeman & Cameron, 2008). Dynamic approaches also highlight that individual difference factors that were previously postulated to be separable into cognitive, affective and personality-related variables interact with each other (Dörnyei, 2010). For example, students' actual cognitive ability impacts on their view of themselves as learners, and these self-efficacy beliefs might enter into dynamic interaction with language learning motivation, the willingness to communicate, and language use anxiety (Csizér et al., 2010).

In this chapter I will review the most important individual difference factors that can explain variation in bi- and multilingual speech production processes and outcomes, describe the existing research in this area and outline new directions for future studies. The chapter will start with a brief overview of second language speech production, with a particular focus on the role of attention. As will be apparent in the discussion below, attention is the key link between individual difference variables and the cognitive processes of speech production. I will then explore the role of cognitive factors that are responsible for individual differences in attention control, and research investigations into the relationship between spoken performance and working and phonological short-term memory will be presented. The importance of working memory capacity limitations in regulating attention during the speaking process and its interaction with task complexity factors will also be discussed. Next, I will focus on two relevant individual difference variables that are generally characterized as belonging to the affective domain: namely foreign language anxiety (FLA) and willingness to communicate (WTC). I will show how L2 speakers' affective characteristics interact with the cognitive processes of speaking and attention control. FLA will be shown to have a pervasive effect on all levels of speech production by interfering with the attentional resource pools available for speaking, as well as with learners' capacity to attend to their own output and thereby notice gaps in their L2 knowledge. It will be argued that WTC also affects L2 speech production processes and opportunities to learn through speaking. The chapter concludes by suggesting new directions for research into the interaction of individual learner variables on the one hand, and speaking and second language acquisition processes on the other.

## 17.2 An overview of the role of attention in L2 speech production

Speech production is traditionally assumed to consist of four important processes: (1) *conceptualization*, i.e., planning what one wants to say; (2) *formulation*, which includes the grammatical, lexical and phonological encoding of the message; (3) *articulation*, in other words the production of speech sounds; and (4) *self-monitoring*, which involves checking the correctness and appropriateness of the output produced (Levelt, 1989, 1999). There seems to be agreement in the field of L1 production that, in speaking, conceptualization, formulation, and articulation follow each other, in this order, and that because certain formulation and most articulation processes are automatic, parallel processing of already processed parts of the message might be possible (Levelt, 1989, 1999), which makes L1 speech generally smooth and fast. The speech production system is assumed to consist first of hierarchical processing levels (conceptualization, formulation, articulation), between which information is transmitted by means of activation spreading, and second of knowledge stores, such as the lexicon and conceptual memory store, within which activation can also spread from one item to related items. Decisions are made on the basis of the activation levels of so-called *nodes* that represent various units, such as concepts, word forms, phonemes, etc.

Although a number of differences exist between first and second language speech production, the basic psycholinguistic mechanisms involved in speech production seem to be very similar (for a discussion of this issue see Kormos, 2006). As in Levelt's (1989, 1999) model, L2 speech production is also assumed to consist of four phases: conceptualization, linguistic formulation, articulation, and monitoring. It is postulated that similarly to L1 speech processing, L2 speech production can also work incrementally, i.e., a fragment of a module's characteristic input can trigger encoding procedures within the module. This also entails that for learners above a certain level of proficiency, parallel processing is theoretically possible. However, as long as an encoding process requires conscious attentional control, encoding can only work serially.

Monolingual and bilingual speech production differ in a variety of ways (for an overview see Kormos, 2006), and one of the most significant differences concerns the fact that producing L2 speech is considerably more demanding on attentional resources than speaking in one's first language. In L1 speech production, two important processes are subject to conscious attentional control: conceptualization and monitoring. Linguistic encoding and articulation mechanisms are mostly automatic and do not require conscious attention (Levelt, 1989), with the exception of L1 lexical selection and retrieval processes that necessitate certain levels of consciousness and can be prone to interference effects (Ferreira & Pashler, 2002). Attention plays a key role in planning one's message, both conceptually and linguistically, and in checking whether one has encoded the intended message appropriately and accurately, hence planning and monitoring processes might interfere with each other (Horton & Keysar, 1996; Levelt, 1983). High conceptual demands on monolingual speakers might cause interference with monitoring processes, and consequently certain errors might not be noticed either before or after articulation (Levelt, 1983).

The role of attention in L2 speech processing role is even more complex than in monolingual speech. For an L2 speaker, not only do conceptual planning and monitoring require attentional control but, depending on the level of proficiency, L2 users display varying degrees of automaticity in linguistic encoding. In L2 speech production this might require a conscious search mechanism to retrieve the appropriate lemma matching the activated concept and to perform the ensuing syntactic, morphological, phonological and articulatory encoding procedures (for a detailed discussion of L2 speech production procedures see Kormos, 2006). Speaking is an online activity that takes place under time constraints; hence L2 speakers often need to balance fluency with the complexity and grammatical accuracy of their message (Kormos, 2011; Robinson, 2001, 2005; Skehan & Foster, 2001). This explains why there are trade-off effects in accuracy and fluency if the cognitive demands of a given task are high. If conceptualizing the message requires particular attention on the part of the speaker, fewer resources will be available for lexical, syntactic and phonological encoding as well as for monitoring, which might result in errors in the student's output and in reduced fluency.

## 17.3 Working memory and second language speech production

### 17.3.1 The construct of working memory

Attention control, which is a key feature of L2 speech production is inherently linked to working memory, and hence, it is important to describe the construct of working memory and its constituents. The most widely accepted conceptualization of short-term memory today is the working memory model developed by Baddeley and Hitch (1974; Baddeley, 1986). The working memory model proposed by Baddeley (2003) comprises a multi-component memory system consisting of the central executive, which coordinates two modality-specific subsystems, the phonological loop and the visuo-spatial sketchpad. Later, a fourth component was added to the model – the episodic buffer; this uses multidimensional coding, integrates information to form episodes, and is in communication with long-term memory (Baddeley, 2000). The visuo-spatial sketchpad works with visual and spatial information, while the phonological loop is specialized for the manipulation and retention of speech.

The central executive has several functions, including attentional control, directing the flow of information through the system and planning (Gathercole, 1999). Although the central executive is conceptualized somewhat differently in Baddeley's (1996) work, it shows great degrees of similarity with central executive functions, which play a key role in attention control (for a review, see Miyake et al., 2000). First, the central executive functions regulate how individuals shift attention between the tasks they need to carry out in parallel or consecutively (Monsell, 1996), which is called the shifting function of attention. Second, the updating and monitoring function of attention control helps people select, revise, and review information which is relevant to successful completion of the task (Morris & Jones, 1990). Finally, the central executive functions also include inhibitory mechanisms that hinder automatic responses when they are not relevant or useful to a particular task. Although it is debated whether central executive functions constitute parts of working memory, in this chapter I will draw on Unsworth and Spiller's (2010) work, which has convincingly demonstrated that attention control is an important component of working memory. As I will also argue below, the functions of attention control are particularly relevant in understanding the role of individual differences in L2 speech production.

Another widely researched component of working memory is the phonological loop. This subsystem consists of a phonological store, which holds information for a few seconds, and an articulatory rehearsal process, which refreshes decaying information, among other functions. The rehearsal process is analogous to sub-vocal speech and takes place in real time, resulting in a limited span of immediate memory.

An additional important issue to consider with regard to the conceptualization of working memory is the relationship between working memory and long-term memory. According to Baddeley and Loggie (1999), working memory is a processing module which is separate from, but interacts with, long-term memory, whereas other researchers perceive working memory as the relevant activated component of long-term memory (e.g., Cowan, 1995, 1999; Engle et al., 1999). Although these two standpoints differ greatly, they both agree that long-term memory representations, in other words previous knowledge and expertise, play an important role in the mental operations carried out in working memory.

### 17.3.2 Working memory and speech production processes

On a theoretical level it is easy to see that individual differences in working memory capacity can influence L2 speech production in a number of ways. First, as shown above, a large number of L2 speech production processes require conscious attentional control. Therefore, the availability of attentional resources might affect the speed and accuracy with which bilingual speakers retrieve L2 words from their lexicon, encode syntactic structures, and give their message a phonological form. Second, speech production requires keeping pieces of the message that have already been processed in short-term memory while further speech encoding mechanisms are at work. Consequently, it can be assumed that individual differences in phonological short-term memory span might also affect the efficiency of speech production mechanisms. Third, speech production, particularly in the L2, is a complex process in which various sub-processes need to be orchestrated and function either incrementally or in parallel. In turn, individual differences in attention control are also expected to be apparent in the speed and accuracy of L2 speech.

A number of studies have been carried out to investigate the link between working memory capacity and second language speech production. In one line of studies that I will review first, working memory scores were related to various measures of bilingual speakers' output. Interestingly, a considerable number of these studies found no, or only a very weak, relationship between working memory tests and L2 spoken performance. In one of the first such projects, Mota (1995) replicated Daneman's (1991) research originally conducted with L1 speakers, in which significant associations were found between working memory and spoken fluency. Following Daneman's design, Mota administered a speaking and reading span test to Brazilian learners of English in both their L1 and L2. The speaking test involved producing well-formed sentences from subsets of words that were previously presented to the participants and that progressively increased in length. The reading span test required that the participants read a series of sentences and remember and recall the last word of the sentence. The number of sentences increased incrementally until the participants could not accurately reproduce the words any more. Mota also asked the learners to describe a picture for 90 seconds and to read sentences aloud. Her study operationalized fluency as the number of words produced during the 90 seconds of the oral task performance and as reading speed in the reading task. The results revealed that the speaking span test scores in L2 English, but not in L1 Portuguese, correlated significantly with the fluency measures of the speaking task, and that the reading span scores in both languages were significantly related to fluency in the reading task. A number of aspects of this study make it difficult to draw conclusions with regard to the nature of the link between working memory capacity and L2 speech production. On the one hand, the use of the speaking and reading span task in L2 seems to conflate working memory capacity with L2 proficiency (McLaughlin & Heredia, 1996; van den Noort, Bosch, & Hugdahl, 2006). On the other hand, reading aloud a passage only involves the speech production processes of phonological encoding, articulation and monitoring, which makes the findings more relevant for the field of L2 reading rather than speech production. Furthermore, the study only involved sixteen advanced level participants which makes the findings difficult to generalize.

In a follow-up study with eleven intermediate and advanced Brazilian learners of English, Fortkamp (1999) administered a wider range of oral tasks – a personal narrative and picture description – and used a number of different measures of fluency, including speech rate and the frequency of filled and unfilled pauses and hesitations. Her working memory measures were a test of speaking span and operation word span, both of which were conducted in the students' L2. In the operation span task participants were asked to solve a series of mathematical problems and memorize the word presented after each problem. The series increased in length and operation span was calculated as the length of the set for which all the words were correctly recalled. Fortkamp's correlational analyses did not reveal any significant links between working memory test scores and oral fluency measures. Although the sample size in this study was probably too small, the lack of association with working memory tests that were administered in L2 and fluency was surprising. Fortkamp argues that not finding a significant relationship in her study might be due to the fact that the tests used for assessing working memory capacity were not tapping into cognitive abilities that are directly relevant to L2 speech production.

Mizera (2006) used three types of tests, two of which, the speaking span and operation span tasks can be considered tests of working memory, and which were conducted in the participants' L1. The third task, a nonword repetition test, which aimed to assess phonological short-term memory, involved the use of words in Arabic, a language unknown to the students. The participants, who were 44 L2 learners of Spanish in the United States, performed three oral tasks: a cartoon description, a word translation, and an imitation task, in which they not only had to reproduce sentences they previously listened to but also to correct any errors they noticed. His study only found weak correlations between the speaking span task and word-naming speed and accuracy in the imitation task. None of the measures of fluency for the cartoon description task correlated significantly with any of the working memory and phonological short-term memory test scores. He argues that the lack of a relationship between working memory capacity and spoken performance measures may be due to the fact that other personality-related factors and language learning aptitude override the influence of working memory.

Gilabert and Muñoz (2010) set out to establish what role working memory plays in oral task performance at different levels of language proficiency. Their participants were 59 Catalan learners of English who were selected from a larger pool of students based on their scores on the Oxford Placement Test. They assessed working memory with a reading span test in the students' L1 (Spanish and Catalan depending on students' reported L1) and oral language ability with a film retelling task. For the whole sample they found significant but weak correlations between speech rate and lexical variety and the reading span score, whereas for the high proficiency participants, reading span scores correlated strongly only with lexical variety. No relationship between any of the oral performance measures and working memory scores emerged in the lower proficiency group.

In a more recent study, Kormos and Trebits (2012) investigated the question of how language learners' working memory capacity relates to the quality of their spoken output. Their study involved 44 Hungarian learners of English, in their late teens, who were at an intermediate to upper-intermediate level of proficiency. They administered a backward digit span test in the students' L1 and two narrative tasks. The oral tasks differed with regard to whether the students had to plan the content of the narrative. In one of the tasks, the content was a series of pictures depicting a story, whereas in the other task the students had to plan their own narrative based on unrelated picture prompts.

Their results indicated that working memory capacity was not significantly associated with most measures of the students' output in these narrative tasks. Similar to Fortkamp (1999), Mizera (2006), and Gilabert and Muñoz (2010), they found no link between fluency as assessed by speech rate and working memory test scores. However, participants with a high backward digit span scores produced longer clauses in the cartoon description task than students with a low backward digit span. This suggests that higher working memory capacity might be beneficial and help students to produce more complex sentences. However, in the case of another measure of syntactic complexity, the ratio of subordinate clauses, they found that students with a high backward digit span performed similarly to students with a low backward digit span and that those learners who used subordinate clauses the most frequently were the ones with an average backward digit span. The mean values for the ratios of error-free relative clauses, error-free verbs and past-tense verbs, as well as for lexical variation, showed a similar pattern: students with the lowest and highest backward digit spans seemed to be achieving the lowest mean values, and learners in the middle range of backward digit span the highest ones. They argued that there might not be a linear relationship between working memory capacity and narrative performance in narrative tasks. They hypothesized that too low working memory capacity might prevent learners from allocating their attentional resources efficiently to the different stages in speech production. They also noted that very high working memory capacity might be detrimental to speech production as learners may try to pay attention to too many aspects of performance at the same time, which results in lower lexical variety, accuracy and less frequent use of complex structures such as relative clauses in certain tasks.

In the studies described so far, working memory capacity was found to be only weakly, if at all, associated with spoken performance. Nevertheless, there exists research which attests that phonological short-term memory might play an important role in L2 speech production. O'Brien et al. (2006) conducted a study in which they correlated a number of measures of oral narrative performance with scores on a nonword recognition test which required participants to decide whether a sequence of nonwords was same or different. For their participants, who were English L1 learners of Spanish, phonological short-term capacity seemed to be an important predictor of a number of features of oral performance, including productive vocabulary use, narrative ability, accuracy in the use of free grammatical morphemes and the use of subordinate clauses. When they subdivided the students into low and high Spanish proficiency groups, their results indicated that phonological short-term memory was not related to any aspects of oral performance in the case of the low-proficiency group, whereas for the high-proficiency group nonword recognition scores correlated with the oral narrative ability measure.

Kormos and Sáfár's (2008) research investigated the relationship between test scores that students received for their performance in an oral language proficiency exam and two cognitive tests in the participants' L1: a nonword repetition test, aimed to assess phonological short-term memory capacity, and a backward digit span test, which was intended to serve as a working memory test. The students were Hungarian learners of English in an intensive language learning setting and were assessed after one year of training. Similar to O'Brien et al.'s (2006) study, in the case of students who started from beginner level no relationship was found between phonological short-term memory capacity and proficiency scores. For those students, however, who were at a pre-intermediate level at the start of their studies, a significant correlation emerged between nonword repetition test scores and fluency, lexical variety and appropriateness ratings of their performance. The backward digit span results and the overall oral speaking test scores, as well as the marks for grammatical accuracy and lexical variety and appropriateness, also correlated significantly for this group of learners. Kormos and Sáfár (2008) argued that phonological short-term memory and general working memory capacity, as assessed by the backward digit span task, might play a differential role in spoken performance. From their results, they concluded that the ability to hold verbal material in short-term memory might be a less important predictor of L2 spoken performance than the ability to carry out complex operations in working memory. Their study also highlighted that working memory capacity might play a differential role at various stages of L2 learning and in L2 competence.

To summarize, there seems to be conflicting evidence for the role of working memory in L2 speech production when researchers have investigated the associations between various working memory tests and spoken output despite the theoretical arguments that highlight the possible relevance of this cognitive factor in L2 processing. Several reasons might explain this discrepancy. One issue to consider is that all studies have used either complex working memory tests, such as backward digit span and reading and operation span, which tap both storage and processing functions, or tests of phonological short-term memory capacity, such as a nonword repetition or recognition test. From the discussion of speaking processes, however, it becomes apparent that as attention control might be a key factor contributing to the efficiency and accuracy of L2 speech production, specific tests that aim to assess the various functions of the central executive independently of storage capacity might be more relevant (e.g., Miyake et al., 2000).

Such tests have been recently used in identifying high-aptitude language learners and were proven to contribute differently to L2 reading and listening attainment from phonological short-memory tests such as nonword repetition tasks that measure storage functions (Linck et al., 2013).

Another reason for the somewhat contradictory findings might be that all the studies use spoken output measures to draw inferences about the link between working memory and L2 speech production. Nonetheless, the quality of speech L2 users produce is only partly determined by the adequate functioning of speech processing mechanisms. Students' underlying knowledge and acquired skills also contribute significantly to L2 speech fluency and the accuracy and complexity of output. Therefore, in this way, it is not possible to separate the effect of working memory on processing from its role in determining what knowledge representation and skills L2 users bring to the spoken task. It is also conceivable that individuals might have different preferences toward allocating their attention in speech production and that L2 speakers might make conscious decisions to pay heed to accuracy over fluency (see e.g., Kormos, 1999; Mizera, 2006). Furthermore, other factors, such as the level of anxiety experienced in speaking, might overshadow the effect of working memory on L2 speech production (see below).

Another issue to consider is that the characteristics of the spoken tasks students need to perform interact with working memory capacity. As pointed out earlier, oral communication tasks might make different demands on various speech production processes. In many of the tasks used in the studies reviewed, participants were not required to engage in detailed conceptual planning as the content that they had to produce was determined by the prompts they received. In this way students' attentional resources might not need to compete between conceptualization on the one hand and formulation and monitoring on the other (Skehan, 2009). Therefore working memory limitations might have played a smaller role when performing these tasks. Interestingly, the only available study on this issue, by Niwa (2000), does not support this assumption. In her unpublished dissertation, Niwa found that in a task that placed higher reasoning demands on participants, those with higher working memory scores spoke less fluently. She explained her findings by arguing that students with high working memory capacity made a greater effort to meet the reasoning and linguistic demands of the more complex task, which negatively affected their fluency. Niwa's findings also indicate that students with different working memory capacity might have different agendas and priorities in task performance and thus allocate their attentional resources differently when faced with various types of tasks.

### 17.3.3 Working memory and the development of speech production

The role of working memory capacity in the development of speaking skills seems to be stronger than in attainment, which is demonstrated by O'Brien et al.'s (2006) study already described above. In this study they did not only correlate oral performance measures with nonword repetition scores at particular points in time but were also interested in finding out how phonological short-term memory capacity can explain gains in spoken performance during one academic term. Their results revealed that for the whole sample of participants, nonword repetition scores correlated significantly with improvements in narrative ability, the use of free morphemes, and subordination. In the case of the low proficiency group in their sample, very strong correlation was found between narrative ability gains and nonword repetition test scores, and weak correlation between free morphemes and phonological short-term memory. In the case of the higher proficiency group, nonword recognition test scores and gains in the correct use of function words and the frequency of subordinate clauses were found to be related. They argued that at lower levels of proficiency, phonological short-term memory is implicated in lexical and grammatical development, which was assessed by the narrative ability variable. They also pointed out that high ability learners who already have a good command over L2 syntactic structures need to rely less on phonological short-term memory in their learning processes. The findings with regard to the association between phonological short-term memory and the correct use of function words were explained by hypothesizing that advanced learners might have more attention available for processing semantically more redundant and less salient grammatical morphemes such as function words and inflections in the input they receive. Phonological short-term memory capacity was also found to influence development of the use of subordinate clauses which are acquired at later stages of second language acquisition.

Speaking in another language also provides opportunities for learning. As pointed out by Swain's (1993, 1995) Output Hypothesis, engagement in communicative tasks can be beneficial for second language acquisition in four different ways. First, they create practice opportunities, and as such develop the automaticity of linguistic encoding processes. When L2 learners produce spoken output they might also test their hypotheses about how particular linguistic constructions can be used and can gain feedback on whether their hypotheses are correct by observing to what extent their interlocutors understand their message and by receiving explicit feedback on their output. In relation to this, they can also reflect on these hypotheses and feedback, which is termed the metalinguistic function of output. Finally, learners might also notice gaps in their knowledge as they speak, especially when they realize that they lack the necessary L2 knowledge to express their intended meaning. If we consider these four possible ways of learning through speaking, it becomes apparent that, with the exception of the automatizing function of output, all require highly conscious language processing and sustained and focused attention. Speaking in another language is taxing on attentional resources and requires a high level of attentional control, which might seriously limit how much students can learn through engaging in spoken interaction. Consequently, individual differences in working memory capacity and attention control might play a significant role in how L2 learners can exploit learning opportunities in oral communication. Recent research by Mackey and Sachs (2012) seems to support this assumption, as they showed that students with high working memory scores benefited more from form-focused feedback in the context of oral communication tasks than students with a shorter working memory span (for similar research findings see also Mackey et al., 2002).

## 17.4 Foreign language anxiety and second language speech production

Anxiety is one of the affective individual difference factors which is intricately linked to working memory and has an important effect on L2 speech production processes. Anxiety can be defined as "the subjective feeling of tension, apprehension, nervousness, and worry associated with an arousal of the autonomic nervous system" (Spielberger, 1983: 1), and it is one of the most important affective factors than can influence learning processes and performance in any cognitive domain. Anxiety can be both a general personality trait or arise in response to particular situations. The role of anxiety in second and foreign language learning is particularly relevant because communicating in another language may often invoke feelings of uncertainty and perceptions of a threat to one's self-esteem and self-concept (Horwitz, Horwitz, & Cope, 1986). It was this feature of second language communication that led Horwitz et al. (1986) to argue for the existence of a type of situation-specific anxiety, which they termed foreign language anxiety (FLA). FLA was shown to be distinct from general trait anxiety and other situation-specific anxieties such as test anxiety (for a summary, see Horwitz, 2000).

FLA was found to be negatively related to achievement in second language learning, although the strength of association between scales measuring FLA and grades and test scores has been found to vary from weak to moderate in most studies (Horwitz, 2000). A negative relationship between FLA and attainment in other language skills, including speaking, writing, and tests of grammatical ability, was also found (see e.g., Gardner & MacIntyre, 1993). Correlational studies, however, cannot provide evidence for causation which made Sparks and Ganschow (1991) reverse the question of whether FLA impacts negatively on achievement and argue that FLA is the result of foreign language learning difficulties caused by underlying L1 processing problems. Their Linguistic Coding Differences Hypothesis has been widely debated and both MacIntyre (1995) and Horwitz (2000) have highlighted the fact that it is not only L2 learners with learning difficulties that experience anxiety in foreign language learning.

One of the skills on which FLA might have the largest effect is speaking. As mentioned earlier, oral communication in another language, especially if one has limited L2 proficiency and little preparation time to plan the message, can be particularly anxiety-provoking. This led researchers to propose speaking-related sub-constructs for FLA: communication apprehension (Horwitz et al., 1986) and second language speaking anxiety (Woodrow, 2006). Research evidence provides support for the role of anxiety in spoken performance, although the strength of association between anxiety and spoken performance measures did not emerge as strongly as expected. Phillips (1992) found a moderately strong correlation between oral test scores and anxiety measures, whereas Woodrow's (2006) and Cheng, Horwitz and Schallert's (1999) research indicates only a weak link between the two.

There might be several reasons why many studies report only moderate strength of association between anxiety and spoken performance despite students' detailed accounts of how seriously anxiety might impede oral communication (see Price, 1991). One of these is that global assessments of speaking performance might not yield insights into the differential effect of anxiety on the fluency, accuracy and complexity of students' spoken output. Another potential explanation is that most studies assessed anxiety as a unitary construct using a composite anxiety scale. MacIntyre and Gardner's (1994) study is an exception to this and yields important insights into how anxiety might influence speaking processes. Their research is based on Eysenck's (1992) cognitive interference theory, which argues that anxiety exerts a negative effect on performance by interfering with cognitive processes. Eysenck (1992) claimed that worry, which is the cognitive component of anxiety, induces fear of negative evaluation and failure as well as excessive concern about one's ability. These self-related thoughts draw away attention from task-related cognitive activities and result in interference during task performance. MacIntyre and Gardner (1994) also drew on Tobias' (1986) model of anxiety when they argued that anxiety affects second language learning processes at three stages: processing input, carrying out the cognitive operations involved in turning input into knowledge representations, and producing L2 output. Their results indicated that judgments of L2 fluency, syntactic complexity, and accentedness were moderately or strongly related to input, processing, and output anxiety measures.

In order to gain a better understanding of how FLA can influence L2 speech production, it is important to consider more recent theories of the cognitive effects of anxiety. Processing Efficiency Theory from Eysenck and Calvo (1992) is relevant to this discussion for a number of reasons. First, it can explain why the link between FLA and output measures of spoken performance might not be as straightforward as previously assumed. Eysenck and Calvo point out that increased anxiety does not always result in diminished performance because anxious individuals might invest more effort into completing the task due to fear of failure or negative evaluation. Therefore one needs to consider processing efficiency, hence the name of the theory, which consists of the effort and time spent on performing the task and not just effectiveness, i.e., the accuracy of performance. The inclusion of this motivational component in their model of anxiety might explain why a number of studies found only weak correlation between speaking test scores and overall evaluations of spoken performance and anxiety. It also highlights that other individual difference variables, such as motivation, goals and intended effort and investment in language learning, interact with FLA (see also below).

Eysenck and Calvo's (1992) Processing Efficiency Theory also elucidates how anxiety affects attentional processes and poses demands on working memory resources, which in turn impact on L2 speech production. This theory makes specific predictions about which components of working memory will be affected by anxiety. They argue that because self-related cognition, in other words, worry, interferes mostly with the phonological loop and functioning of the central executive, tasks that require keeping verbal material in short-term memory and sustained and focused attention will be most prone to anxiety effects. Empirical evidence largely supports these predictions (e.g., Calvo & Eysenck, 1996). In a later extension of the theory they further specified that it is the inhibition and switching functions of attention that are most likely to be influenced by anxiety (Eysenck et al., 2007). As shown in the previous section all the speech production processes that require conscious control are reliant on working memory limitations, and consequently they can be negatively affected by anxiety. We can hypothesize that L2 users with high levels of anxiety might find it more effortful to retrieve words from their mental lexicon and encode syntactic structures in the L2. They might also experience difficulties in inhibiting the activation of L1 items and constructions due to problems of attentional control caused by worry. Orchestration of the speech production processes of conceptualization, formulation, and monitoring might also be more demanding in cases where anxiety interferes with working memory and attentional resources. As indicated by the findings in MacIntyre and Gardner's (1994) study, these problems might manifest in inaccurate and/or slow performance, and in the avoidance of complex topics and linguistic constructions.

Processing Efficiency Theory is also useful when considering the effect of FLA on how L2 users exploit the learning opportunities provided by oral communication and the act of speaking itself. As explained above, spoken interaction might offer various possibilities for learners to expand their knowledge of the L2 through reflection on their output and the feedback they receive from interlocutors. Nevertheless, I have argued that limitations on working memory and attentional capacity often make it challenging for L2 learners to attend to their own speech production processes, manage the interaction, and process and integrate feedback into their language system all at the same time. These limitations on speaking and learning simultaneously might be particularly relevant in the case of students who experience anxiety when communicating in the L2. Sheen's (2008) study, in which she compared the uptake from recasts on article usage in a spoken narrative delivered in front of a whole class in the case of low- and high-anxiety learners, provides empirical support for this. Her results clearly indicate that the low-anxiety group learned more from the feedback they received during their performance than the high anxiety group, as demonstrated by improved post-test performance. Students with low levels of anxiety also modified their output more efficiently following a recast than those with high anxiety. Kim and Tracy-Ventura's (2011) study also led to similar findings. In their research they investigated how foreign language anxiety impacts on students' improvement in past-tense morphology after a treatment session which consisted of four communicative tasks involving learner–learner interaction. The results indicated that students with low anxiety scored significantly higher on both post-tasks than high-anxiety participants, although it should be noted that the effect of anxiety was found to be small.

Finally, Eysenck and Calvo's (1992) theory is helpful in accounting for the interaction of task characteristics and anxiety effects. They argued that the higher cognitive demands a particular task poses, the more substantial will be the effect of anxiety on task performance. In the field of second language acquisition, Robinson's (2001, 2005) Cognition Hypothesis also postulates that individual learner differences will exert greater influence on spoken task performance if tasks are cognitively more complex. Robinson (2007) tested this assumption by administering to 42 Japanese learners of English, three interactive oral communication tasks and MacIntyre and Gardner's (1994) Input, Output and Processing Anxiety Questionnaire. His results indicated that only output and processing anxiety were significantly related to oral performance measures. Output anxiety showed some correlation with syntactic complexity as measured by the number of clauses per C-unit (a single independent clause plus any subordinate clause and non-clause structures attached or embedded in it), and that the strength of the relationship increased as tasks became more complex. In the case of processing anxiety, the findings did not support his hypothesis, as the accuracy of performance only correlated with this anxiety measure for simple and medium-complexity tasks, and with syntactic complexity for the medium-complexity task. Robinson's research suggests that although in interactive oral communication anxiety might also play a role, the anxiety felt concerning producing output in the L2 seems to have a more substantial effect on the linguistic quality of students' output. The results with regard to output anxiety also reveal that anxiety and the characteristics of spoken tasks interact and might jointly influence the efficiency of speech production.

## 17.5 Willingness to communicate and L2 speech production

Willingness to communicate (WTC), i.e., "the probability of speaking when free to do so" (MacIntyre, 2007: 564), is another important factor that affects L2 speech production processes. MacIntyre et al. (1998) established a pyramid model for WTC that describes the various sources of influence on L2 learners' decision to engage in communicative interaction in the target language. At the bottom of the pyramid they placed the social and individual context, which includes the inter-group climate, i.e., the social relations between the L1 and L2 speaking communities, as well as the personality of the learner. In the next layer one can find the affective–cognitive context, which they see as consisting of inter-group attitudes, the social situation and the student's communicative competence. The following level represents the motivational properties of the speaker, such as interpersonal motivation, intergroup motivation, and L2 self-confidence. Nearer the top of the pyramid come the situational antecedents of WTC that comprise the desire to communicate with a specific person and the state of communicative self-confidence. These two factors are seen to directly influence WTC, which in turn predicts L2 communicative behavior.

From the description of the pyramid model of WTC it is apparent that both individual difference factors, such as foreign language anxiety and language learning motivation, as well as social context play an important role in influencing L2 communication. In this respect, WTC is an important bridge between the social context in which interaction takes place and the cognitive processes that underpin communication. WTC is also strongly influenced by two important individual difference factors: communication apprehension, which is a component of foreign language anxiety (Baker & MacIntyre, 2000), and motivation (MacIntyre et al., 1998). Thus it also serves as a useful construct to help us understand how trait-like individual learner characteristics influence volitional choices made in particular contexts and how these choices then affect speech production (MacIntyre, 2007).

In a recent study by MacIntyre and Legatto (2011), they investigated momentary changes in WTC in a series of speaking tasks and found that willingness to communicate was strongly interrelated with the ease of speech production. Their results indicated that particularly in cases when students had difficulties retrieving task-relevant vocabulary items from their lexicon, WTC deteriorated. This finding provides strong support for the close link between the affective system of L2 speakers and cognitive processing. Their study also revealed that when L2 speakers' emotional state is affected before engaging in a communicative event or task, given the choice, learners often avoid communication. If, however, affective disturbances occur during communication, "they seem to generate coping attempts" (MacIntyre & Legatto, 2011: 166) such as the use of various strategies to reduce their anxiety levels.

The link between WTC and spoken performance is under-researched. While there is evidence that L2 speakers with higher WTC engage in communicative interaction using the target language more frequently (Dörnyei & Kormos, 2000; Yashima, Zenuk-Nishide, & Shimizu, 2004) and therefore create more opportunities for themselves to produce output, practice and negotiate meaning (MacIntyre, 2003), we know relatively little about how WTC affects the quality of L2 learners' speech. Kormos and Dörnyei (2004) investigated how various motivational characteristics, self-confidence and FLA were related to a number of linguistic measures of performance on an interactive oral argumentative task. Overall their findings revealed that WTC predicted how many turns students would produce during task performance but had no significant links to the accuracy, syntactic complexity, or lexical variety of the participants' output. They argued that motivational variables such as task attitude, students' general course-related attitude, and WTC might account for whether and to what extent students engage with the task, but they might play a less important role in determining the quality of language produced.

Although there is little research evidence to date that WTC impacts on speech production, on a theoretical level WTC may potentially be an important factor in L2 speech encoding mechanisms. In order to understand the potential impact of WTC, it is useful to consider Dörnyei's (2003) task motivation system. In this model, learners engage in three mechanisms: task execution, appraisal, and action control. Task execution involves learning behaviors that support engagement with the task, in which the efficient allocation of attention and the appropriate assessment of the requirements of the task, in terms of conceptualization, linguistic formulation, and monitoring, are particularly relevant in the case of L2 speech production. "Appraisal refers to the learner's continuous processing of the multitude of stimuli coming from the environment and of the progress made toward the action outcome, comparing actual performances with predicted ones or with ones that alternative action sequences would offer" (Dörnyei & Tseng, 2009: 119), which in the case of L2 speech is mainly done in the monitoring and conceptualization phases. "Action control processes denote self-regulatory mechanisms that are called into force in order to enhance, scaffold, or protect learning-specific action." As shown by MacIntyre and Legatto (2011),

WTC is an important factor in predicting whether students will in fact engage in task execution and how they appraise their performance and enhance its quality through action control mechanisms.

## 17.6 Conclusions and directions for future research

In this chapter I have discussed the role of three important individual difference factors, working memory capacity, foreign language anxiety, and willingness to communicate in L2 speech production. I argued that working memory capacity and individual differences in attention control are important theoretical constructs in understanding individual differences in the efficiency of the functioning of speech production processes and in explaining the development of L2 speaking skills. Research findings to date, however, are contradictory with regard to the effect of working memory capacity on the quality of speech L2 users produce. The chapter highlighted the need for the application of cognitive tests that assess attention control independently of storage capacity in the study of L2 speech production. It would also be necessary to investigate working memory and attention control effects in interaction with the characteristics of the cognitive demands of speaking tasks. This would help us gain more detailed insights into how these cognitive factors influence various stages of speech production.

The chapter also considered the role of foreign language anxiety in L2 speech production. I pointed out that the most important effect of anxiety can be seen in the interaction with reduced working memory capacity and in decreased attentional control. Therefore, foreign language anxiety can have an important influence on the efficient functioning of speech production processes and can also interfere with the cognitive learning processes that might take place when learners engage in oral communication.

I have also shown that WTC is influenced by the social context of the interaction and is closely related to both motivation and foreign language anxiety. It was pointed out that WTC can be seen as both a relatively stable trait-like individual difference factor that can predict how likely a bilingual is to engage in interaction and as a state variable that fluctuates during speech production. WTC has important consequences for the number of opportunities L2 speakers use the target language and for how often and successfully they create opportunities for themselves to learn through speaking. WTC can also affect processes in speech production as it can determine how much L2 learners will say and how detailed and complex the information they attempt to convey will be.

As is apparent in this chapter, affective individual characteristics may interact with cognitive factors, and they can be hypothesized to separately and jointly affect the planning, formulation, articulation, and monitoring stages of speech production. These individual differences may also exert influence on how L2 speakers process feedback, the extent to which they notice gaps in their knowledge, the aspects of the target language they pay attention to and, consequently, how they exploit the learning opportunities provided by communicative interactions. In order to support these hypotheses, however, future research would be necessary that investigates the interplay of cognitive and affective factors in L2 speech production.

As this chapter reveals, there is more need for research on the role of individual differences in L2 speech production and to investigate how students learn through speaking. Many of the existing studies, especially with regard to cognitive factors and foreign language anxiety, are quantitative in nature and mainly use correlational designs, which makes it difficult to gain deeper insights into possible causal relationships between speaking and learning processes and individual variables. On the one hand, in the quantitative research paradigm, there is more need for studies that experimentally manipulate certain variables, such as anxiety or a willingness to communicate. Future experimental research could also focus on the role of cognitive and affective factors in various sub-processes of speech production, such as lexical and syntactic encoding and monitoring.

On the other hand, it is also important to investigate the role of individual difference factors using qualitative methods, such as think-aloud and retrospective interviews, either in combination with quantitative methods or as a single method. Rich information and interesting insights could be gained by comparing the speaking processes of learners with different cognitive and affective profiles and by analyzing how they exploit the learning opportunities provided by speaking activities. Studies that employ an idiodynamic approach and explore longitudinal changes in feelings, attitudes, motivation, and their interaction with cognitive processing (see MacIntyre & Legatto, 2011) can also yield new insights into how individual learner characteristics can dynamically interact with speech production processes.

Finally, it should be mentioned that the role of individual differences can vary in different types of spoken tasks. For example, Robinson (2001) argues that individual learner variables may have a stronger effect on task performance in cognitively complex tasks, in which learners have to divide their attentional resources between content planning and linguistic encoding, than in cognitively simple tasks. Learners with different individual profiles may also vary in the extent to which they exploit the potential of cognitively complex tasks that demand syntactically and lexically more varied and complex language use (Robinson, 2001). Another important aspect of task and individual difference interactions is that students with different learning profiles vary in how they interact with learning tasks and benefit from different types of instruction. This so-called aptitude treatment interaction, which is well documented in academic learning (for a review, see Ackerman, 2003), has clear implications both for teaching speaking and for highlighting the importance of research into the role of individual differences variables in speech production and L2 acquisition.

# 18

# Parallel language activation in bilinguals' word production and its modulating factors

A review and computer simulations

Annette M. B. de Groot and Peter A. Starreveld

## 18.1 Introduction

Witnessing fluent bilinguals holding a conversation can give the distinct impression that the language currently not in use does not interfere with the selected language, as if it is fully at rest, deactivated. Still, this common observation does not square with a substantial body of empirical evidence that suggests otherwise. In this chapter we will review this evidence. We will first show that during word recognition in bilinguals lexical elements in both sub-lexicons are activated in parallel, in other words, that bilingual word recognition involves language-non-selective lexical activation. From then we will focus on our main topic, bilingual word production, considering the results obtained with three versions of the picture-naming task: the picture–word interference task, simple picture naming, and phoneme monitoring. Meanwhile a number of variables that modulate the influence of activation in the other language will be identified: relative proficiency in the two languages, stimulus-set composition, stimulus repetition, sentence context, and sentence constraint.

A final section presents simple computer simulations of the main findings obtained in studies that used the simple picture-naming task. One of the simulated results is the cognate effect, the common marker of language-non-selective activation in these studies. Other simulated results are the reduction of the cognate effect with repeated picture naming and with increases in response-language proficiency, and the effect of language proficiency and sentence context on response-selection time. The most important message emerging from these simulations is that the absence of a measurable influence of the non-response language can still be fully compatible with the claim that the bilingual language system is profoundly language non-selective.

## 18.2 Recognizing single words

There is quite a bit of evidence to suggest that the presentation of a printed or spoken word to a bilingual results in the activation of representation units in both sub-lexicons. Most of this evidence has been gathered in studies in which the stimulus words were presented visually and in isolation, that is, not embedded in a larger linguistic unit such as a sentence or a paragraph. In the majority of these studies one of two special types of stimulus words were used, namely, stimulus words that share a resemblance with one particular word in the other language (interlexical homographs and cognates), or stimulus words that vary with respect to their numbers of neighbors (intralexical or interlexical). An interlexical homograph is a written word that has two totally different meanings in a bilingual's two languages. For instance, for a Dutch–English bilingual *brand* is an interlexical homograph (it means 'fire' in Dutch). A cognate is a word that not only shares meaning with its translation in the other language but also all, or a large part, of its form (e.g., for a French–English bilingual the two components of the translation pair *table–table* are cognates). Finally, intralexical neighbors are words from the same language that have totally different meanings but very similar, though not identical, word forms (e.g., English *band* and *bank*) whereas interlexical neighbors are words from two different languages that have different meanings but very similar forms (e.g., Dutch *rook*, 'smoke,' and English *book*).

### 18.2.1 Recognition of printed words

Earlier monolingual studies have shown that the time it takes speakers of just one language to recognize a printed word depends on the number of its neighbors, obviously all intralexical in this case (e.g., Andrews, 1989; Grainger, 1990). This finding suggests that the presentation of a word not only activates its own representation in the mental lexicon but also those of its neighbors and that all activated representations compete with one another during the recognition process. Bilingual studies have built on this finding by posing the question whether the set of activated representations includes interlexical neighbors as well, thus providing an indication that word recognition in bilinguals is language non-selective. These studies suggest that this is indeed the case (e.g., Bijeljac-Babic, Biardeau, & Grainger, 1997; Grainger & Dijkstra, 1992; van Heuven, Dijkstra, & Grainger, 1998).

Because, like interlexical neighbors, interlexical homographs and cognates share form between a bilingual's two languages, presenting the latter two types of words should also cause parallel activation in both sublexicons. To be able to infer the occurrence of parallel activation, recognition time for interlexical homographs is compared with the time it takes to recognize control words, that is, words that are not interlexical homographs but are matched to the latter on preferably all other stimulus aspects that are known to affect recognition time (e.g., length and frequency of use). Similarly, recognition times for cognates and matched control words are compared, the control stimuli in this case being non-cognates. Quite a few studies have shown an interlexical homograph effect, that is, a difference in recognition time between interlexical homographs and control words (e.g., de Groot, Delmaar, & Lupker, 2000; Dijkstra, Grainger, & van Heuven, 1999; Dijkstra, van Jaarsveld, & Ten Brinke, 1998; Jared & Szucs, 2002; von Studnitz & Green, 2002). This effect is attributed to co-activation of the homographs' representations in the non-target lexicon. Von Studnitz and Green furthermore found that the interlexical–homograph effect gets smaller over the course of the experiment, suggesting that task practice can modulate the effect.

Similarly, a number of studies have obtained a cognate effect, a difference in recognition time for cognates and non-cognates (e.g., van Hell & Dijkstra, 2002; Schwartz, Kroll, & Diaz, 2007). Interestingly, a cognate effect has also been obtained in a visual-word-recognition study that tested bilinguals speaking Hebrew and English, two languages that use completely different alphabets (Gollan, Forster, & Frost, 1997). The cognates used in this study were thus phonological cognates, translation equivalents that share sound between a bilingual's two languages. This finding suggests that bilingual visual-word recognition not only involves the parallel activation of orthographic representations in the two sublexicons, but that activated orthographic representations immediately send on their activation to phonological representations and that they do so in a language-non-selective way. Studies using other experimental techniques have provided converging evidence to support this claim (e.g., Duyck, 2005; Jared & Kroll, 2001; Nas, 1983; van Leerdam, Bosman, & de Groot, 2009). Accordingly, computational models of visual-word recognition in bilinguals (BIA+, Dijkstra & van Heuven, 2002; SOPHIA, van Heuven & Dijkstra, 2001, as summarized in Thomas & van Heuven, 2005) contain both orthographic and phonological memory units and assume activation to spread between these two types of units, both within and across languages.

### 18.2.2 Recognition of spoken words

That the bilingual word-recognition system operates in a language-non-selective manner is also supported by studies in which the recognition of spoken rather than written words was examined. Most of these have used the visual-world paradigm (e.g., Blumenfeld & Marian, 2007; Marian & Spivey, 2003a, 2003b; Weber & Cutler, 2004): Participants are presented with aural instructions to (mentally) carry out specific actions related to a display of objects on a computer screen while their eye movements are registered. Russian–English bilinguals may for instance hear the instruction *put the marker below the cross*. In addition to a marker, a couple of filler objects, and a cross sign in the middle of the display, the display may show an object, the *competitor*, with a name in Russian that shares phonology with the target object's English name (e.g., a stamp, called *marka* in Russian). The critical finding is that the competitor is looked at significantly more often than the filler objects (with names that do not resemble the target object's name). Earlier monolingual studies had already shown that participants more often look at objects with a name similar to the target object's name in the same language (e.g., to a candy when the target object is a candle) than to objects with completely different names (Tanenhaus, Spivey-Knowlton, Eberhard, & Sedivy, 1995). Bilingual participants show this same within-language effect (e.g., Marian & Spivey, 2003b). The combined results suggest that, just as written words, spoken words activate similarly sounding words in both the target- and the non-target language. However, while some of these studies have demonstrated the cross-language effect with both the native language (L1) and the second language (L2) as the target language (Marian & Spivey, 2003a; Spivey & Marian, 1999), in other studies it was only obtained when L2, the weaker language of the two, was the target language (Blumenfeld & Marian, 2007; Marian & Spivey, 2003b; Weber & Cutler, 2004). This suggests that language-non-selective bilingual word recognition might only hold for L2 or that it holds for both languages but that there are limits to *the effects of* language-non-selective bilingual word recognition.

## 18.3 Recognizing words in context

Unlike in the studies discussed above, during natural language comprehension words typically occur in meaningful sentences and discourse. Therefore, to properly evaluate the claim that bilingual word recognition involves the parallel activation of elements in both sub-lexicons, the above evidence in support of language-non-selective word recognition must be augmented by similar evidence from studies where the critical words are presented in veridical linguistic contexts. A number of these have been conducted. In most of them sentence contexts were used, both these contexts and the target words were presented visually, and cognate effects and/or interlexical homograph effects were used as the markers of language-non-selective activation (see Chambers & Cooke, 2009, for a related study that examines how bilinguals recognize spoken words in sentence context).

The dependent variables were reaction times, ERPs, eye-fixation measures, and combinations of these. These studies have produced mixed results. Cognate effects still showed up when the critical words were preceded by low-constraint sentence contexts, that is, sentence contexts that do not severely constrain the set of possible target words (e.g., *Across from the supermarket stood an old* tree *which was home to a lot of birds*, with *tree* as target word), especially when the experiment was conducted in L2, the weaker language (Duyck, Van Assche, Drieghe, & Hartsuiker, 2007; Libben & Titone, 2009; Schwartz & Kroll, 2006; Titone et al., 2011; Van Assche et al., 2011; van Hell & de Groot, 2008). When low-constraint sentences were used and the experiment was run in dominant L1 the effect is less clear-cut but has also been obtained (Titone et al., 2011; Van Assche et al., 2009). When high-constraint sentences were used (e.g., *The bird sat in the branches of the highest* tree *because cats could not reach him there*, again with *tree* as target word) often no cognate effect occurred (but see Van Assche et al., 2011).

Contrary to the cognate effects, homograph effects were generally absent (Elston-Güttler, Gunter, & Kotz, 2005; Schwartz & Arêas Da Luz Fontes, 2008; Schwartz & Kroll, 2006; Titone et al., 2011; but see Libben & Titone, 2009), although during the first part of Elston-Güttler et al.'s experiment, but not the second, such an effect *did* show up when before presenting the experimental sentences the activation level of the non-target language was boosted by showing a film fragment narrated in the non-target language. The finding that under these circumstances the effect is present at first but then disappears suggests again (see also von Studnitz & Green, 2002) that length of practice in the experimental task modulates the influence of the non-target language.

In conclusion, the joint findings from the bilingual word-recognition studies indicate that the presentation of a word, printed or spoken, to a bilingual induces parallel activation in both sub-lexicons, but they also point out that (the effect of) this phenomenon is modulated by three factors: relative proficiency in L1 and L2, stimulus type (cognates vs. interlexical homographs), and degree of sentence constraint. In addition, it appears that task practice can reduce or annihilate (the effect of) co-activation in the non-target language.

## 18.4 Producing single words

The evidence provided above that word recognition involves language-non-selective activation in the bilingual lexicon does not necessarily imply that the same holds for word production. Word recognition in fluent language users is an automatic process, and if a bilingual is fluent in both languages, word recognition will come about automatically in both languages. In other words, word recognition in fluent bilinguals will automatically activate representations in both sub-lexicons. As we claimed before (Starreveld, de Groot, Rossmark, & van Hell, 2014), for this reason evidence of language-non-selective lexical activation as obtained in word-recognition studies is in fact rather trivial. On the other hand, word production is a controlled, attention-demanding process. It is therefore conceivable that bilingual speakers can choose to focus attention exclusively on the sub-lexicon of the language they intend to speak, only activating representations in this sub-lexicon (see also Costa & Santesteban, 2004b).

Nevertheless, there is evidence to suggest that also during bilingual word production elements in the non-response (non-target) language get activated. This evidence has primarily been gathered in experiments that exploited one or another version of the task that is most frequently used in research on word production, both monolingual and bilingual: the picture-naming task. A crucial assumption underlying the use of this task in studying word production is that after the completion of the first stage of the picture-naming process, the computation of the visual percept, picture naming (invoked by an external stimulus) and word production (invoked by internal thought processes) involve the same processing stages: the activation of the appropriate concept, the selection of the target word from the mental lexicon, phonological encoding, phonetic encoding, and articulation (e.g., Levelt et al., 1998). Word-production research usually focuses on the first three of these five stages and the corresponding representations in the mental lexicon: the conceptual/semantic, lexical, and phonological representations, respectively.

### 18.4.1 The picture–word interference task

In one version of the picture-naming task, the picture–word interference task, each picture is accompanied by a spoken or printed distracter that shares a specific relation with the pictured entity (or its name) or is unrelated to it. Monolingual experiments in which this task version was used (e.g., Schriefers, Meyer, & Levelt, 1990; Starreveld & La Heij, 1995) have shown that, at specific intervals between the presentation of the picture and the distracter, semantic distracters (that share a semantic relation with the pictured object; e.g., a picture of a cat accompanied by the distracter word *dog*) slow down picture naming as compared with unrelated distracters (e.g., *mug*) whereas phonological distracters (sharing a phonological relation with the picture's name; e.g., a picture of a cat accompanied by the distracter word *cap*) speed up naming, again as compared with an unrelated distracter word. These two effects are known as the semantic-interference effect and the phonological-facilitation effect, respectively.

In explanation of the semantic-interference effect, models of monolingual word production hold the assumption that, following the activation of a conceptual representation (or, simply, concept) upon the presentation of a picture, not only the lexical representation associated with this concept (e.g., the cat concept) becomes activated next, but also those associated with semantically related concepts (e.g., the concepts for dog and tiger). Depending upon the type of word-production model that is adopted, with distributed or localist conceptual representations (see de Groot, 2011: 132–135 and 230–231, for details), these non-targeted lexical representations receive their activation directly from the concept activated by the picture, or indirectly, via a process whereby activation spreads within a semantic network from the concept activated by the picture to semantically related concepts. The latter then transmit activation to the corresponding lexical representations.

All activated lexical representations compete with one another during lexical selection, a process that, if all goes well, results in selecting the lexical representation associated with the target. The other activated but non-lexical representations interfere with the selection process. The more highly they are activated the more interference they will cause and the longer lexical selection and, thus, responding will take. Both semantic and unrelated distracters will activate their corresponding lexical representations, through the automatic bottom-up word-recognition process elicited by the distracter. Consequently, the lexical representations of both types of distracters will act as competitors during lexical selection and delay the response. However, as described above, the lexical representation associated with a semantic distracter will receive additional, top-down, activation from the conceptual representation activated by the picture. The high level of activation resulting from these two sources combined will have the effect that the lexical representations of semantic distracters are stronger competitors than the lexical representations of unrelated distracters. This is assumed to be the reason why picture naming takes longer when the picture is paired with a semantic distracter than when it is paired with an unrelated distracter.

A phonological distracter (e.g., the word *cap* accompanying a picture of a cat) will also initiate a bottom-up recognition process during which the corresponding lexical representation will be activated, but the level of activation in this representation is not increased further by the top-down activation process incited by the picture. But why, if both phonological and unrelated distracters give rise to bottom-up but no top-down activation from conceptual representations, does the phonological-facilitation effect occur at all? The reason is that a phonological distracter, but not an unrelated distracter, pre-activates part of the presented picture's phonological representation (the /ca/ part), thus facilitating phonological encoding of the picture's name.

Starreveld and La Heij (1996) implemented the assumptions underlying both explanations mentioned above in a connectionist model. Simulated word-production latencies indeed showed semantic effects, phonological effects, and the interactions of those effects (see also Roelofs, 1992, for a related neural network model that produced semantic effects), indicating that the assumptions are computationally plausible. Because in models of word production (and word recognition) memory representations are usually called nodes, we will henceforth use the terms representations and nodes interchangeably.

### 18.4.1.1 Bilingual studies

While monolingual picture-word interference studies have shown that an activated concept excites the lexical representations of a set of semantically related words, bilingual studies have used this methodology to see whether the set of activated lexical representations also includes the one for the concept's name in the non-response language (i.e., its translation; Costa et al., 2003; Hermans et al., 1998). To be able to detect parallel activation in the non-response language, in addition to the semantic, phonological, and unrelated distracters used in the monolingual studies, one further critical type of distracter word was included in these studies: distracters that were phonologically related to the picture's name in the non-response language. For instance, for a Dutch–English bilingual asked to name pictures in English and presented with a picture of a frog, the word *kitchen* would be a *phonological-translation distracter* (a frog is called *kikker* in Dutch). If the activated frog concept activates the lexical nodes for both *frog* and *kikker*, the combined activation converging on the *kikker* node from the activated concept on the one hand and the phonological-translation distracter *kitchen* on the other hand will turn this node into a strong competitor for the *frog* response and delay it, again as compared with a condition with unrelated distracters. This interference effect has indeed been observed during L2 picture naming, both in unbalanced bilinguals (Hermans et al., 1998) and in proficient bilinguals (Costa et al., 2003). The effect was particularly robust when the distracters were words in the non-response language (which in both studies was the participants' L1) and when at the same time relatively many of the distracters were related to the picture's name (Hermans et al., 1998, Experiment 2; Costa et al., 2003, Experiment 1). When the distracters were words from the response language L2 (Hermans et al., Experiment 1; see the above example) or when the proportion of related to unrelated distracters was reduced by the inclusion of unrelated filler trials (Costa et al., 2003, Experiment 2), the effect was less robust, only showing up when the interval between the presentation of picture and distracter was relatively long.

Perusal of the reports of the original studies shows that the use of the picture-word interference task produces complex and not seldom equivocal data patterns. As pointed out by various researchers (e.g., Kroll, Sumutka, & Schwartz, 2005; Starreveld, 2000), this is probably due to the simultaneous presentation of two stimuli, the picture and the distracter, each of them triggering a separate process (of encoding and decoding, respectively) and the two unfolding in opposite directions. An effect of a distracter can only be observed if the top-down activation triggered by the picture and the bottom-up activation elicited by the distracter meet, and are measured, at a moment that both activation streams have had a chance to build up to a sufficiently strong level to be detected at all and neither of the two has decayed below some critical minimal level. Due to the sequential nature of the different stages involved in word production and word recognition, different types of distracters exert their effect at different intervals between the presentation of picture and distracter. For instance, to detect an effect of an aurally presented phonological distracter, a relatively long interval between the presentation of, first, the picture and, next, the distracter is required. This is because otherwise the processing of non-overlapping phonological representations of a spoken distracter might overwrite the processing of the overlapping representations completely, thus preventing the occurrence of the phonological effect (see Starreveld, 2000, for details). Therefore, the absence of a phonological-translation effect with some picture-distracter intervals can per se be perfectly consistent with a language-non-selective account of bilingual word production and even be predicted.

But what, given the complexity of the paradigm, may also happen is that one predicts a phonological-translation effect to occur at a particular picture-distracter interval and yet obtains a null-effect, not because the word-production process is in fact language-selective but because of inaccurate assumptions about the exact intersection point between the top-down and bottom-up streams of activation and the choice of picture-distracter interval based on these incorrect assumptions. Imagine, for instance, two bilingual studies in which the stimuli are presented with exactly the same interval between picture and phonological-translation distracter, that both ask for responses in the participants' L2, but that test participants with different levels of L2 proficiency. Even if, in actual fact, language-non-selective word production would hold for both participant groups, one of the groups might show a response pattern suggesting language-selective word production (equally long naming times for trials with phonological-translation distracters on the one hand and unrelated distracters on the other hand), because the chosen picture–word interval caused the two activation streams to miss each other.

Given the equivocal data patterns that picture–word interference studies may produce, converging evidence for language-(non)selective bilingual word production from other tasks is desirable. Other reasons why additional evidence is needed are the findings, mentioned above, that phonological-translation effects occurred most reliably when L2 was the response language and the distracters were L1 words, or when a relatively large proportion of related to unrelated picture-distracter pairs was used. The first of these two findings suggests that the effect might at least partly be due to the subjects being put in a bilingual mode by the presence of both languages during task performance (e.g., Grosjean, 1998), the non-response language of the distracters keeping this language activated as well. As pointed out by Costa et al. (2003), the second finding suggests that, when presented with a large proportion of related picture-distracter pairs, the participants may notice the relationships between picture names and distracters and develop a response strategy that deviates from the instruction, common in these experiments, to ignore the distracter words. Conscious attention to the distracter words may, again, have the effect of putting the participants in a bilingual mode.

### 18.4.2 Simple picture naming

In fact, additional evidence that word production in bilinguals involves the simultaneous activation of representations in both sub-lexicons already exists. Most of it has been gathered in studies that employed the simplest possible version of the picture-naming task, in which each picture is presented alone, unaccompanied by a distracter, and has to be named out loud (e.g., Christoffels, de Groot, & Kroll, 2006; Costa, Caramazza, & Sebastián-Gallés, 2000; Hoshino & Kroll, 2007; Starreveld et al., 2014). Crucially, in these studies the picture names were either cognates or non-cognates in the participants' two languages. Costa and colleagues, who were the first to use this paradigm in a Catalan–Spanish study, argued that the occurrence of a cognate effect, shorter naming times for pictures with cognate names than for those with non-cognate names, indexes parallel activation in the bilingual word-production system. What is more, they reasoned that it would indicate that language-non-selective activation holds for both main stages of word production following concept activation: the activation of the lexical representations and, next, the phonological representations. Figure 18.1 illustrates (with a Dutch–English example taken from Starreveld et al., 2014) Costa et al.'s view of what happens when bilinguals name pictures with cognate and non-cognate names and the underlying assumptions about the structure of the word-production system, containing three levels of representations.

After visual processing, the picture first activates the corresponding semantic representation or concept, which consists of a set of nodes in a semantic representational level that is shared between the two languages. The activated semantic nodes propagate activation forward to the associated lexical nodes in both languages and the latter send on activation to a level that stores sub-lexical phonological nodes. Like the level of semantic representations, the level containing the sub-lexical nodes is shared between the two languages. Consequently (most of) the sub-lexical nodes

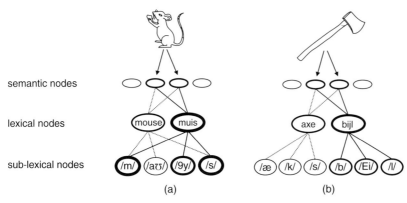

**Figure 18.1** A model of picture naming in bilinguals (based on Costa et al., 2000). Note: All connections shown in the model are bidirectional; thicker ellipses represent more activation. Panels a and b illustrate the activation of the memory representations of the (English–Dutch) cognate pair *mouse–muis* and the non-cognate pair *axe–bijl* when the picture is named in Dutch and activation has just reached the sub-lexical nodes. Subsequently, the lexical node of the cognate *muis* will receive more feedback from the sub-lexical layer to the lexical layer than the lexical node of the non-cognate 'bijl.' As a result, with the continued spread of activation through the network, the complete set of sub-lexical nodes representing a cognate will receive more activation than the one representing a non-cognate.

that represent cognate names accumulate activation from two previously activated lexical nodes (Figure 18.1a), whereas those representing non-cognate names receive activation from one lexical node only (Figure 18.1b). Furthermore, the cognates' lexical nodes receive more activation than those of non-cognates due to feedback from the phonological level back to the lexical level. Because the lexical nodes continue to feed activation forward to the sub-lexical nodes, the differential activation in the lexical nodes for cognates and non-cognates caused by this feedback also results in a relatively high level of activation in the sub-lexical nodes representing cognates. The differential activation in the sub-lexical nodes for cognates and non-cognates resulting from these feed-forward and feed-backward activation processes results in faster naming for cognates.

The cognate effect has shown up with both dominant L1 and weaker L2 as response languages, though it was generally larger in the latter case (Christoffels et al., 2006; Costa et al., 2000; Poarch & van Hell, 2012; Starreveld et al., 2014). In other words, relative language proficiency in the two languages modulates the non-response language's influence on producing words in the target language, just like it has been shown to influence the non-response language's role in word recognition (e.g., Marian & Spivey, 2003b; Weber & Cutler, 2004). The different magnitude of the cognate effect in the participants' two languages is attributed to a difference in the strength of the connections between the conceptual, lexical, and sub-lexical phonological nodes in the two language-subsystems, both the links between the conceptual and lexical nodes and those between the lexical and sub-lexical nodes being stronger for dominant L1 than for L2 (Costa et al., 2000; Starreveld et al., 2014; weaker and stronger links are represented by dotted and solid lines, respectively, in Figure 18.1). Stronger links transmit more activation than weaker links. Consequently, when dominant L1 is the response language the targeted sub-lexical nodes receive less activation from the lexical node in the non-response language than when weaker L2 is the response language. Stated differently, cognate naming in weaker L2 benefits more from activation in stronger L1 than vice versa.

Although only fleetingly alluded to in a footnote, Starreveld at al. (2014) found that picture-naming repetition also modulates the cognate effect in word production. The cognate effect gradually became smaller over four presentation series that all included the same set of pictures to name. When the pictures had to be named in L2 English, the participants' weaker language, the effect was 151 ms, 113 ms, 90 ms, and 65 ms in Series 1, 2, 3, and 4, respectively, and significant in all cases. When the pictures were named in L1 Dutch, the cognate effect was 35 ms, 15 ms, 1 ms, and 7 ms in Series 1, 2, 3, and 4, respectively, and only significant in Series 1 and 2. Correlated with the cognate effect, naming time decreased considerably in the successive presentation series: overall naming time was 924 ms, 798 ms, 750 ms, and 728 ms, respectively, when the pictures were named in weaker English, and 737 ms, 653 ms, 638 ms, and 635 ms, respectively, when they were named in dominant Dutch.

The correlation between naming speed and the size of the cognate effect, as shown in Starreveld et al.'s study for both the effects of relative language proficiency and stimulus repetition, appears to be a general phenomenon (see below for two further demonstrations). Importantly, we believe that the null-effects obtained when the pictures were named in dominant Dutch and the participants had already named the stimuli a couple of times before do not point at language-selective processing, because how could the bilingual word-production system have evolved from one operating in a language-non-selective manner (the system illustrated in Figure 18.1) to a language-selective system during just one half hour or so? An alternative interpretation of these null-effects, which we consider to be more likely, is that stimulus repetition brings about temporary changes in components of the word-production system, for instance, in the strength of the connections between the memory nodes and/or the baseline level of activation in the memory nodes that are exploited during naming. These temporary changes may then influence both the size of the cognate effect and naming time. Similarly, it is unlikely that the smaller vs. larger cognate effects associated with naming in the stronger and weaker language, respectively, indicate that word production is language-non-selective in both cases but less so with naming in the stronger language. Given the word-production system shown in Figure 18.1, the activation pattern that follows picture presentation is *always* language non-selective. However, *the effect of* the activation of the non-response language, as manifested in the size of the cognate effect, varies with, for instance, the strength of the connections between the various types of nodes and the associated difference in activation transmission across these connections.

We are aware of the drastic theoretical consequences of these claims because if even a zero cognate-effect is not regarded as an unequivocal marker of language-selective word production, what is? Nonetheless, simple computer simulations to be presented later demonstrate how, indeed, varying parameters such as the connection strength of the links between nodes and the nodes' activation level affect both the magnitude of the cognate effect and naming time. But before presenting these data we will provide evidence of parallel language activation in bilinguals' word production as obtained in studies using one further version of the picture-naming task, starting that section by expressing a concern, hitherto ignored, related to using the cognate effect as a marker of language-non-selective activation. In addition, a couple of studies that examined word production in sentence context will also be discussed first.

### 18.4.3 Phoneme monitoring

As described above, the relatively fast naming for pictures with cognate names as observed in the simple picture-naming task is attributed to activation converging on the sub-lexical phonological nodes from two sources: the concept's lexical nodes in both languages. In other words, the effect is explained in terms of the simultaneous activation of two lexical nodes that benefits cognates but not non-cognates while, implicitly, the representation structures are assumed not to differ between cognates and non-cognates. Yet, it is disputed whether this implicit assumption is a legitimate one. In fact, indications that the representations of cognates and non-cognates differ from one another have been gathered in more than an occasional study and the authors of these studies have suggested a number of possible representational differences between the two types of words. For instance, a pair of cognates may share a morphological representation in memory whereas a pair of non-cognates does not (Sánchez-Casas & García-Albea, 2005), or cognate pairs may share a larger part of their meaning representations than pairs of non-cognates do (van Hell & de Groot, 1998). If such representational differences indeed exist, instead of a process of parallel activation that affects cognates and non-cognates differently, these might somehow underlie the cognate effect in picture naming.

Given the concerns raised earlier regarding the picture-word interference task and the present concern about the use of cognates in the simple picture-naming task, additional evidence for parallel activation in bilinguals' word production is desirable. In a study with fluent Catalan–Spanish bilinguals as participants, Colomé (2001) introduced a clever new version of the picture-naming task by which the problems associated with the use of the other task versions can be circumvented: it does not require the use of cognate stimuli, nor the use of distracters that, if they involve words from the non-response language, may put the participants in a bilingual mode. In this study each picture was accompanied by a phoneme (more precisely, by a letter that represented this phoneme) and the participant had to indicate, by pushing one of two response keys, whether or not that phoneme occurred in the picture's Catalan name, Catalan being the participants' L1. All pictures in the experimental stimuli had non-cognate names and care was taken that the participants had no reason to suspect that their bilingualism was being tested so that deliberate activation of the non-response language was unlikely. (Unfortunately though, some pictures in a set of filler stimuli had cognate names; we will return to this point below.)

To detect co-activation in the non-response language that might nevertheless occur, in addition to stimuli inviting a "yes" response (e.g., a picture of a chair, *cadira* in Catalan, accompanied by the letter *c*), two types of stimuli requiring a *no* response were presented, labeled *no-translation* and *no-unrelated* stimuli here. The phoneme that accompanied the picture in a no-translation stimulus did not occur in the picture's Catalan name but was the first phoneme of its Spanish name (e.g., the same picture of a chair but now paired with *s*, a chair being called *silla* in Spanish). Finally, the phoneme in a no-unrelated stimulus occurred in neither the picture's Catalan name nor in its Spanish name (e.g., the same picture again but now paired with a totally unrelated letter, for example, the letter *m*).

To perform this *phoneme-monitoring* task, a participant must first tacitly generate the picture's name and then monitor the internally generated name for the presence of the specified phoneme. Longer response times for no-translation stimuli than for no-unrelated stimuli (the *no-translation effect*) serve as the marker of parallel activation in both sub-lexicons during word production, on the assumption that co-activation of the picture's name in the non-response language is particularly harmful for the former of these two types of no-trials. One reason might be that, given parallel activation in both sub-lexicons, the phoneme presented in a no-translation stimulus and occurring as part of the co-activated memory units in the non-response language, would create a tendency in the participants toward the *yes*-response; overcoming this tendency would consume additional processing time. Alternatively, and again given parallel activation in both sub-lexicons, the incongruence between a tendency to respond *yes* on the one hand (because the picture's name in the non-response language contains the specified phoneme) and a simultaneous tendency to respond *no* (because the picture's name in the response language does not contain this phoneme) causes the delay in the no-translation condition (note that the no-unrelated condition produces two congruent *no*-response tendencies).

In three experiments, in which different intervals between the presentation of picture and phoneme were used, Colomé (2001) found that the no-translation stimuli indeed took longer to respond to than the no-unrelated stimuli. The magnitude of this effect varied between 41 ms and 55 ms over the three experiments. The overall response times for the two types of no-trials varied between 952 ms and 1132 ms across the three experiments. The longer response times for the phoneme-monitoring task in comparison with the times required for simple picture naming (cf. the response times provided above for the latter task) plausibly reflect the relative complexity of the phoneme-monitoring task, which requires tacit naming, keeping both the generated name and the phoneme available in working memory, conscious monitoring of the internally generated name for the presence of the phoneme, converting the outcome of this matching process into a *yes* or *no* response and, finally, response execution.

Several studies have followed up on Colomé's (2001) study. In a Dutch–English study testing unbalanced bilinguals in their weaker L2, Hermans et al. (2011) wondered whether the set of filler materials that Colomé used in her study might have contained pictures with cognate names in Catalan and Spanish and, if so, how this might have affected the results. After personal communication with Colomé had confirmed that, indeed, there were a few pictures with cognate names among her filler materials, Hermans et al. examined the influence of the proportion of pictures with cognate names among the filler materials on the no-translation effect. As in Colomé's study, the pictures used in the experimental stimuli all had non-cognate names.

In a first experiment in which the pictures in the filler stimuli, also 24 in all, all had non-cognate names, no no-translation effect occurred. In a second experiment in which pictures in the filler stimuli all had cognate names (so that, overall, 50% of the pictures had cognate names and the remaining 50% had non-cognate names) a significant no-translation effect was obtained: Responding took 37 ms longer in the no-translation condition than in the no-unrelated condition. Interestingly, in a third experiment wherein only 25% of the filler stimuli had pictures with cognate names (so that, overall, 87.5% non-cognate pictures and 12.5% cognate pictures were used) a statistically equally large (and numerically even larger) no-translation effect of 53 ms was obtained. The authors concluded that, depending on the composition of the stimulus set, "the bilingual language production system … can operate in different language activation states" (Hermans et al., 2011: 1696) or, in other words, that "language activation in bilinguals' speech production is dynamic" (the article's title). Furthermore, from the fact that the experiment with only 12.5% cognate pictures produced the same data pattern as Colomé's (2001) study, despite the fact that the two studies tested different types of bilinguals (fluent, early bilinguals vs. unbalanced, late bilinguals), Hermans and colleagues concluded that their findings appear to be "impervious to variations in language learning history and proficiency" (p. 1702).

Hermans et al.'s (2011) results are consistent with studies on visual word recognition that have shown the inclusion of words from the other language to influence the response patterns (e.g., de Groot et al., 2000; Dijkstra et al., 1998; von Studnitz & Green, 2002) and with the earlier indication that in the picture-word interference studies with L2 as the response language and L1 distracter words (Costa et al., 2003; Hermans et al., 1998, Experiment 2) the distracters may have put the participants in a bilingual mode. The present results add the important suggestion that for this effect to occur the words from the non-response language do not have to be present in the form of an external stimulus but that it suffices if they are internally generated. Apparently, if a cognate name instead of a non-cognate name is generated on only a small proportion of trials, this (or, perhaps, noticing this) boosts the activation of the non-response language and a no-translation effect ensues.

While the conclusion that bilingual speech production is dynamic is thus substantiated by other studies, Hermans et al.'s (2011) suggestion that the data are resistant to variations in language learning history and proficiency is nuanced by de Groot, Starreveld, and Geambaçu (in preparation). We drew our participants from the same population as Hermans et al. did, but unlike them we asked one group of participants to respond in their weaker L2 English while for a second group dominant L1 Dutch was the response language. The same picture set was used in both language conditions. Despite a vigorous attempt to only have pictures with non-cognate names as stimuli, it could not be prevented that the names of 6 out of the 22 filler pictures (13.6% of the total stimulus set) embedded a (non-identical) cognate as part of a polysyllabic word (e.g., *seahorse–zeepaardje*, *sea* and *zee* being cognates). (The set of 520 pictures from which we selected our stimuli did not contain any more pictures that met all our selection constraints.)

When L2 English was the response language, we observed a no-translation effect of 50 ms in a first presentation series and a statistically equally large effect of 38 ms in a second series in which all stimuli were presented a second time. These effects are comparable in size to those in Colomé (2001) and in Hermans et al.'s (2011) two experiments that included cognate pictures among the filler materials. However, despite the fact that the same picture materials, including the embedded-cognate filler stimuli, were used in both language conditions, on neither of the two presentation rounds was a no-translation effect obtained when dominant Dutch was the response language. In other words, the presence of cognate stimuli is no guarantee that the effect occurs. To be absolutely sure that this null-effect was real, we selected a further group of participants from the same population and repeated the experiment with dominant Dutch as response language. Again, both presentation rounds showed a null-effect. It thus appears that relative language proficiency modulates the critical effect in the phoneme-monitoring task, just like it modulates the cognate effect in simple picture naming and the markers of parallel activation in bilingual word recognition.

Rodriguez-Fornells et al. (2005) used a modified version of the phoneme-monitoring task that, like the original task, requires phonological encoding and mental inspection of the pictures' names. These researchers asked Spanish–German bilinguals and monolingual German speakers to push a response button if the picture's name in the response language started with a vowel and to not respond if it started with a consonant, or vice versa, using behavioral measures, ERPs and fMRI data as dependent variables. Crucially, in a *coincidence* condition, the pictures' names started with a vowel or a consonant in both of the bilinguals' two languages (e.g., *asno–Esel*, 'donkey'; *vela–Kerze*, 'candle'), whereas in a *non-coincidence* condition the pictures' names started with a consonant in one language and with a vowel in the other (e.g., *embudo–Trichter*, 'funnel'). All response measures showed an effect of the coincidence manipulation for the bilinguals, but not for the monolinguals. For instance, only the bilinguals made fewer errors in the coincidence condition than in the non-coincidence condition and only the bilinguals showed a different ERP pattern for these two conditions. These results point, again, at parallel phonological encoding in both languages, the activation in the non-response language affecting the response differently in the coincidence and non-coincidence conditions. For example, the opposite response tendencies incited by the pictures' names in both languages when one starts with a vowel and the other with a consonant likely led to the relatively large number of errors in the non-coincidence condition. Interestingly, the fMRI data revealed that the bilingual participants exploited brain areas that are also used to control behavior in non-verbal tasks, probably in order to cope with the interference caused by activation of the non-response language. These results accord with those of studies on bilingual language control as examined by means of the language-switching paradigm (e.g., Abutalebi et al., 2008; Hernandez & Meschyan, 2006).

## 18.5 Producing words in context

Just like language comprehension normally involves the recognition of words presented in a larger linguistic context, during normal speech production words are spoken in the context of larger linguistic utterances (and non-linguistic sources of information, ignored here). This larger linguistic context may modulate the influence of the non-response language in word production, as it does in word recognition. To examine this possibility, Starreveld et al. (2014) and de Groot et al. (in preparation) not only studied picture naming out of context (as discussed above), but also included experiments wherein the pictures to name were preceded by a sentence fragment presented visually, word by word. In Starreveld et al. both high-constraint and low-constraint sentence fragments were used (see section 18.3) whereas de Groot et al. only presented low-constraint sentence fragments. As described before, in Starreveld et al. the participants named the pictures aloud and the cognate effect served as marker of parallel activation whereas de Groot et al. used the phoneme-monitoring task, involving tacit naming, and parallel activation was indexed by the no-translation effect. The two studies tested participants from the same population: late Dutch–English bilinguals with a relatively high level of L2 English but clearly dominant in L1 Dutch. In these subjects the dominance of Dutch over English is more obvious for production than for comprehension, presumably because they use English actively less often than passively.

Recall that Starreveld et al. (2014) obtained a cognate effect when the pictures were named out of context, both with L1 Dutch and L2 English as response language, though the effect was substantially larger in the latter case (Dutch: 35 ms; English: 151 ms). Furthermore, in both language conditions the cognate effect decreased with picture repetition and in the Dutch condition it was annihilated after the first two presentation rounds (see section 18.4.2). In out-of-context phoneme monitoring (de Groot et al., in preparation; see section 18.4.3), we observed a no-translation effect when English was the response language and this effect was (statistically) equally large in two subsequent presentation rounds (50 ms and 38 ms). When Dutch was the response language no no-translation effect occurred.

When in Starreveld et al.'s (2014) study the pictures were preceded by low-constraint sentence fragments, cognate effects still turned up in both language conditions. The size of these effects (17 ms in Condition Dutch; 44 ms in Condition English) was comparable to the effect of 35 ms observed in the Dutch out-of-context condition (the statistical analysis showed no difference between these three effects), but the effects were substantially smaller than the 151 ms effect obtained in the English out-of-context condition. Interestingly, response times were considerably shorter when the pictures were preceded by context (704 ms overall) than when presented alone (830 ms overall). When the pictures were preceded by high-constraint sentence fragments, response time reduced even further to 464 ms and 613 ms overall with Dutch and English as response language, respectively. A cognate effect (of 28 ms) now still turned up when the pictures were named in English, but not when Dutch was the response language. This general pattern of results once again illustrates the close relation between the size of the cognate effect and naming speed. In section 18.4.2 we demonstrated this relation to hold for the effects of picture repetition and relative language proficiency. Furthermore, our finding that degree of sentence constraint modulates the cognate effect agrees with, and extends, a similar result from studies on bilingual word recognition in context (see section 18.3).

Finally, in de Groot et al. (in preparation) we obtained an equally large (39 ms) no-translation effect in both language conditions during phoneme monitoring in context. Unlike in Starreveld et al. (2014), in this study no clear relation between the size of the critical effect, here the no-translation effect, and response time was observed.

To summarize, the joint set of studies on bilingual word production reviewed above indicates that the production of single words involves the parallel activation of representations in both sub-lexicons but that several factors modify the influence that the activated representations in the non-target language's sub-lexicon exert on performance. First, like in the studies on bilingual word recognition reviewed in the first part of this chapter, relative language proficiency in L1 and L2 turns out to be one of the relevant factors. This variable affects the response pattern both in simple out-of-context picture naming and in out-of-context phoneme monitoring, the cognate effect in simple picture naming being smaller in L1 than in L2 and the no-translation effect in phoneme monitoring only occurring in L2. Second, the influence of the other language depends on the composition of the stimulus set, as is shown from the effect of having pictures with cognate names among the stimulus materials in out-of-context phoneme monitoring. Third, stimulus repetition is a relevant factor, as is indicated by the reduction of the cognate effect in successive presentations of the same pictures in the out-of-context simple-picture-naming studies. Interestingly, in out-of-context phoneme monitoring the no-translation effect was not reduced by stimulus repetition. Fourth, the in-context overt-picture-naming study (but not the phoneme-monitoring study) revealed that sentence context tempers the influence of the non-target language, in particular during word production in the weaker language. This can be concluded from the substantial reduction of the cognate effect when the picture was preceded by a sentence fragment and named in L2. Fifth, the type of sentence context has been identified as a relevant variable, as can be concluded from the fact that no cognate effect occurred when the picture was preceded by a high-constraint sentence fragment and named in dominant L1.

In the next section we will redeem our earlier promise to show by means of simple computer simulations that variations in the strength of the connections between nodes in the bilingual lexicon and in the nodes' activation levels can, in principle, account for fluctuations in the size of the cognate effect in picture naming despite the fact that the system always operates in a language-non-selective manner. In this section we will not only simulate the cognate effect in picture naming itself, but also how it is modulated by relative language proficiency, picture repetition, and sentence context.

## 18.6 Computer simulations

### 18.6.1 Models and assumptions

In order to show that our theoretical interpretations of the effect of relative language proficiency, sentence context, the cognate effect, and the modifying effect of picture repetition on the size of the cognate effect are computationally realistic, we performed a number of computer simulations. To keep the simulations as insightful as possible, we kept them as simple as possible. We simulated the time course of activation of only one of the phonological output nodes of both a cognate and of a non-cognate under various conditions.

We used two simple models that both consisted of two layers. The output layer of both models contained only one output node. For each simulation the time course of activation of this node is reported below. For the simulations involving the output node of a cognate, the input layer contained two nodes, one representing the lexical node in the target language (T) and the other representing the lexical node in the non-target language (nT, see Figure 18.2a). For the simulations involving the output node of a non-cognate, the input layer contained just one node, representing the lexical node in the target language (T, see Figure 18.2b). The resulting implemented

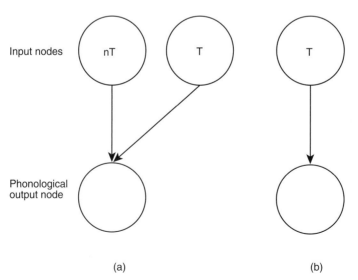

**Figure 18.2** The basic layout of the networks used in our simulations of the activation of a phonological node of a cognate (a) and a non-cognate (b). T = target language; nT = non-target language

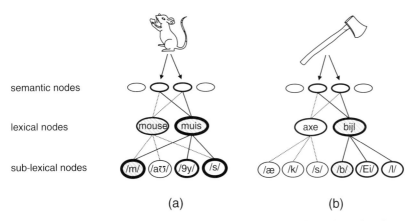

**Figure 18.3** A model of picture naming in bilinguals. The nodes indicated with ellipses correspond to the nodes of the implemented models depicted in Figure 18.2

models correspond to the patterned light gray nodes of the model depicted in Figure 18.3.

Two assumptions were made to keep processing within the models simple. First, we kept the activation level of the input nodes constant during each simulation. A slow accrual of activation of these nodes, which would reflect lexical activation processes better than a constant activation level, would just decrease the speed of activation accrual at the output layer but would not change the general behavior of the model. Second, connections were assumed to be one-way only, from the input nodes to the output nodes. In the model depicted in Figure 18.3 (see also Figure 18.1), connections are reciprocal, so our present implemented models are simplified versions of that model.

All connections in our models had strengths, expressed as weights, referred to with parameter $w$. At the start of the simulation, input activation ($A_{input}$) was applied to the input nodes and activation was propagated through the network in successive steps, called iterations. An iteration can be conceived of as a time step and any number of iterations can directly be linked to processing time by multiplying the iteration number with a constant. For example, if it is assumed that one iteration takes 4 ms, an effect of 10 iterations corresponds to a 40 ms effect in RT data.

At each iteration, an activation function was applied to calculate the activation of the output node. In order to simulate the spreading activation process, we used a basic activation function that calculates the amount of activation that reached the output node at each iteration by just multiplying the activation of each input node with the weight of the connection between that input node and the output node. We added the resulting amounts of activation, both within an iteration and between iterations. These calculations were performed by the repeated use of formula (1) in which $i$ is the iteration number, $j$ is an index that identifies the input nodes, $n$ is the number of input nodes (two for the simulation of an output node of a cognate, one for the simulation of an output node of a non-cognate), and $w_j$ is the weight connecting input node $j$ to the output node. In all simulations it was assumed that selection of the output node occurred when its activation level reached a critical threshold of 100 activation units.

$$A_{output}(i+1) = A_{output}(i) + \sum_{j=1}^{n} A_{input}(j) * w_j \qquad (1)$$

### 18.6.2 Simulations of the effects of relative language proficiency and sentence context on selection times

Using these very basic assumptions, we first simulated the effect of relative language proficiency in L1 and L2 on the selection times of a non-cognate output node (the corresponding model is depicted in Figure 18.2b). If it is assumed that language proficiency involves different weights between nodes in the language system, changing the weights should affect processing time. In our simulations, we set the input activation to 1 and kept it constant. For the simulation of a high level of language proficiency (as in L1), we set the weight between the input and output node to 3. For the simulation of a lower level of language proficiency (as in L2), we (arbitrarily) set the weight between the input and output node to 2. The results of the simulations showed that the threshold of 100 activation units was reached in 34 and 50 iterations, respectively, for the simulation of picture naming in dominant L1 and in weaker L2 (Figure 18.4a, dotted and solid line, respectively), an effect of 16 iterations. Note that the size of the effect is linearly related to the strength of the weights, so the model can simulate any effect size by adjusting the strength of the weights. Therefore, the fit of the model to actual data is trivial, but we note that the model naturally accounts for the effects of relative language proficiency on selection times in terms of weight differences.

Next, we simulated the effect of a low-constraint sentence context on the selection times of a non-cognate output node. If it is assumed that a sentence context increases the amount of activation in the corresponding language sub-system (e.g., Starreveld et al., 2014), an increase of the input activation in the model should mimic the effects of sentence context we obtained empirically.

Interestingly, models of the kind we used here exhibit the feature that any effect of a change in the strength of the weights can also be obtained by keeping the weights constant, but changing the amount of input activation to the model. This can easily be understood by realizing that

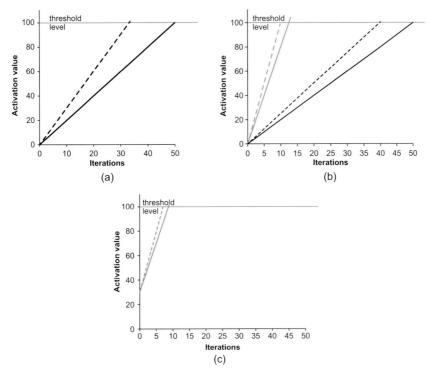

**Figure 18.4** Computer simulation results. Panel (a) shows the results of a simulation of the influence of language proficiency and sentence context; panel (b) shows the results of a simulation of a regular cognate effect and the results of a simulation of the influence of repeated picture naming on the size of the cognate effect when it is assumed that repetition only involves the increase of the weights between input nodes and output nodes; panel (c) shows the results of a simulation of the influence of repeated picture naming on the size of the cognate effect when it is assumed that repetition involves both an increase of the weights between input nodes and output nodes and an increase in the resting level of activation of the output nodes. See the text for further explanation

the amount of activation that reaches a node at each time step is the result of a multiplication of weights and activations. To increase or decrease the result of the multiplication, both the strength of the weights or the amount of activation can be adjusted. This feature explains why we can use the same figure to show the results of the simulation of sentence context (to be described next) as we used for the simulation of relative language proficiency in L1 and L2.

In our simulation of the effects of sentence context, we used the same model as in the previous simulation. We first simulated the time course of activation of the output node of a non-cognate for the situation in which pictures were named in isolation. In this simulation, we set the activation of the input node T to 2 activation units. In order to reflect our assumption that adding a sentence context results in the increase of activation in the corresponding language sub-system, we simulated the effect of a sentence context by increasing the amount of activation of the input node T. We (arbitrarily) set the activation of the input node T to 3 activation units for the simulation of picture naming in context. In both simulations, of picture naming with and without sentence context, the weight between the input and output nodes was set to 1 and was kept constant. The results showed that the threshold of 100 activation units was reached in 50 and 34 iterations for the simulation of picture naming in isolation and in context, respectively (Figure 18.4a, solid and dotted line, respectively), an effect of 16 iterations.

In conclusion, the model is able to simulate that picture naming in a sentence context is faster than picture naming in isolation. These results were caused by additional activation in the appropriate language sub-system induced by a sentence context. Note that the size of the effect is linearly related to the amount of input, so the model can simulate any effect size by adjusting the amount of input activation. Therefore, the fit of the model to actual data is trivial, but the numerical demonstration that adding activation to the appropriate language sub-system can indeed cause a decrease of selection time is not. The simulation results concerning both relative language proficiency and sentence context are a natural consequence of the models' processing assumptions.

### 18.6.3 Simulations of cognate effects and the modulating effect of picture repetition

Our next step was to simulate a cognate effect. To that end we first simulated the activation accrual of a non-cognate output node (the corresponding model is depicted in Figure 18.2b) by setting the activation of the input node T to 2 activation units and the weight between the input node and the output node to 1. Using these parameters, the selection threshold was reached in 50 iterations (Figure 18.4b, black solid line). Next we simulated the activation accrual of a cognate output node (the corresponding model is depicted in Figure 18.2a) by using identical parameters for the T node, but, in addition, we set the activation of the input node nT to 1 and its weight to the output node to 0.5. Using these parameters, the selection threshold was reached in 40 iterations (Figure 18.4b, black dotted line). Thus, these simple models simulated a cognate effect of 10 iterations, demonstrating that additional activation from the non-target language that reaches a phonological output node from the target language can indeed cause a decrease of selection time.

In our third pair of simulations, we simulated the effect of picture-naming repetition on the response times, using the same two models. In order to explain the shorter response times with each repeated presentation of a picture, we assumed earlier in this chapter that the weights of the links connecting lexical nodes to phonological nodes get stronger with each presentation. As an example of this principle, the weights in the present simulations were multiplied by the number of presentations. So, at the fourth presentation, the weights between the T nodes and the output nodes was set to 1 * 4 = 4 and the weight between the nT node and the output node was set to 0.5 * 4 = 2. All other parameters were kept identical to those in the previous cognate simulations. Using these parameters, the selection thresholds for non-cognate and cognate output nodes were reached in 13 (Figure 18.4b, gray solid line) and 10 (Figure 18.4b, gray dotted line) iterations, respectively (effect size = 3). Thus, the simulations show a clear decrease of the size of the cognate effect as a result of picture-naming repetition (from 10 to 3 iterations for the first and fourth presentation, respectively). The models naturally account for this decrease in terms of an increase in the strengths of weights.

In the previous simulation, it was assumed that repetition only affected the strengths of the model's weights. However, we argued earlier in this chapter that it is reasonable to assume that also the resting level activation of the output nodes is affected by repetition. Therefore, in our fourth pair of simulations, we used the exact same parameters as in the previous simulations, but added 10 units of activation to the resting level of the output nodes after each repetition. Therefore, at the start of the fourth repetition, the resting level activation of the output nodes was set to 30 units. Using these parameters, the selection threshold for non-cognates and cognates was reached in 9 (Figure 18.4c, solid line) and 7 iterations (Figure 18.4c, dotted line), respectively (effect size = 2). Thus, when in addition to an increase in the strength of the weights we also assumed an increase in the resting level activation of the output nodes due to repetition, the simulated cognate effect reduced even further, from 3 iterations (see above) to 2 iterations.

### 18.6.4 Simulations of cognate effects and the modulating effect of relative language proficiency

If it is assumed that proficiency in a language is reflected, among other things, in the strength of the links between the lexical nodes and the sub-lexical nodes, the results of the simulations of the effect of picture repetition on the size of the cognate effect can also be used to computationally show that an increase in language proficiency causes a decrease of the cognate effect (a finding that has often been reported, see section 18.4.2, which shows larger cognate effects in weaker L2 than in stronger L1). The reason is that we simulated the effect of repetition by increasing the weights in our models. If it is assumed that an increase in proficiency also causes an increase in those weights, these simulations thus also show the influence of relative language proficiency on the size of the cognate effect. In that case, Figure 18.4b should be read as showing the results of the simulation of a bilingual naming pictures in L1 (gray lines) and in L2 (black lines). For both types of line color, the solid lines portray non-cognate output-node activation and the dotted lines portray cognate output-node activation. The cognate effect for naming in L1 is much smaller (3 iterations) than the one for naming in L2 (10 iterations). Note that our simulated models will produce a less severe reduction of the cognate effect if smaller increases of the weights are used than the multiplication by 4 that we chose for this particular simulation.

### 18.6.5 Implications of the simulations

The results of the simulations of the cognate effects clearly show that a cognate effect of 10 iterations obtained in a simulation of picture naming during the first presentation might reduce to a very small cognate effect of only 3 or 2 iterations in a simulation of picture naming during the fourth presentation. In real experiments, such a small cognate effect might be very hard to detect. Therefore, these simulations suggest that the fact that we failed to find a cognate effect when the pictures were named for the third and fourth time in the stronger language (L1 Dutch) need not indicate that the language system was language-selective at that time. Instead, the simulations show that the size of a cognate effect caused by an intrinsically non-selective bilingual language system might have been too small to be detected.

On a broader level, the simulations suggest that the absence of any marker of language non-selectivity in RT data does not necessarily imply selectivity in the language system. For example, when a marker of language non-selectivity (e.g., a cognate effect) is obtained in L2 whereas it is not obtained in L1, it might be argued that strong connections within the L1 language sub-system and/or strong activation of the L1 language sub-system could have reduced the marker to an undetectable size, despite the fact that the bilingual language system in itself is fundamentally language non-selective.

## 18.7 Conclusion

In an early study on language switching in bilinguals, Macnamara, Krauthammer, and Bolgar (1968) likened the bilingual's linguistic performance to that of a musician "who observes the notation for key at the beginning of a piece of music and then forgets about it though in his playing he performs the actions appropriate to the key." They continued noting that: "Similarly, the bilingual once started in one language can forget about which language he is speaking and yet obey the rules of that language" (p. 213). These authors thus suggest that initially choosing the language to use requires effort but that subsequently staying in the chosen language does not; in other words, that the non-selected language does not interfere with the language in use. The empirical data and the computer simulations presented in this chapter suggest that this observation at least holds true for fluent bilinguals involved in authentic monolingual discourse. We have seen that, even in experiments that do not truthfully mimic real discourse, the influence of the non-target language is modest if the participants' stronger language serves as the target language. Furthermore, it was found that sentence context and stimulus repetition mitigate the influence of the other language. In veridical discourse word production is not only supported by sentence context but also by the wider linguistic context and by extra-linguistic contextual information. In addition, in realistic discourse specific words (those central to the discourse's topic) are likely to be repeated. These ingredients of rich contextual information, repeated word use, and speaker fluency may combine into a solid firewall against an influence of the other language in discourse. Importantly though, this conclusion does not imply that under these circumstances the language not in use is deactivated, because our computer simulations have shown it need not be. These simulations furthermore indicated that immunity from activation in the language not in use likely emerges from simple structural and processing features of the bilingual word-production system, such as (temporarily) strong connections between specific representations in the word-production system and a high level of activation in these representations.

# 19

# Cross-language asymmetries in code-switching patterns

Implications for bilingual language production

Carol Myers-Scotton and Janice Jake

## 19.1 Introduction

Many readers of this chapter are familiar with the writings of those researchers who study conversational or discourse structure and who are interested in the variation that naturally occurring code-switching (CS) can exhibit. They study CS because switching from one language to another may give a speaker's turn certain socio-pragmatic effects that monolingual speech cannot easily provide (see Auer, 1998; Gardner-Chloros, 2009; Gumperz, 1982; Myers-Scotton, 1993b). That is, speakers capitalize on the socio-psychological associations that the language of the switch brings with it. The psycholinguists who study bilingualism and who construct language production models are interested in some of the same variations that CS offers, but for another reason. They address this question: how are certain distributions of the participating languages in CS likely evidence for well-grounded models of language production? In this chapter, we offer explanations of cross-language asymmetries in three different construction types, suggesting the analysis offers a partial answer to this question.

### 19.1.1 Why study code-switching in particular?

Any linguistic structure that develops in interaction between bilinguals and presumably between their cognitive systems may provide clues as to the nature of language processing. But CS is special for several reasons. First, CS is not a phenomenon that depends on showing the effects of bilingualism over time, as do such other contact phenomena, such as lexical borrowing or cross-language convergence. That is, naturally occurring CS is 'in the moment' regarding interactions between the cognitive systems (Grosjeau, 1989). Speakers have often reported that they are often not even aware their conversational turns include CS. Second, even though CS seems to be unplanned and unconscious, its drag on the language production system seems surprisingly low. That is, most CS researchers agree that switching, whether for a single word or for a full phrase, usually appears to be seamless. For example, CS is rarely marked by hesitations or pauses. So CS is something of a puzzle.

Because of its distinctiveness, CS increasingly seems to interest psycholinguists who study bilingualism. However, the type of CS studied here is not the same as the language switching that psycholinguists have often studied and sometimes may even call code switching if the data are cross-linguistic. Such studies often involve timing in the directed switching of single lexical elements (see Myers-Scotton & Jake, 2014, for some comparisons between psycholinguistic 'language switching' and what linguists call CS). Because naturally occurring CS typically occurs in informal interactions among friends or family, it unfortunately does not seem very amenable to study in the laboratory. Some eye-tracking experiments show limited promise of replicating the contexts in which natural CS appears (e.g., Dussias & Sagarra, 2007).

### 19.1.2 Overview of the chapter

In this chapter, we study CS within a cost–benefit framework. We use the term 'costs' somewhat metaphorically to refer to the likely effects of the complex grammatical procedures at abstract levels of production that are involved in accessing certain grammatical elements in some languages in order to build the constructions which satisfy the speaker's communicative intentions. Thus, 'winners' in the competition between the languages participating in CS may depend on the relative costs of how certain constructions are built cross-linguistically. That is, complexities are equated with costs. Relative cross-linguistic complexities are features of lexical elements, or the grammatical structures in which the elements occur.

Our studies show that at least in CS, grammatical complexity is costly. The evidence that grammatical complexity is costly is that the critical element in the construction under study comes from the language with the less complex procedures. That is, the language of less complexity in CS is selected more frequently to build the critical element in a selected construction. In the case of some constructions (e.g., complementizers), one of the participating languages is always the choice (i.e., it is categorical) for the critical element for some languages. Our usage of costs may include, but goes beyond, the costs that are associated in psycholinguistics with the time that elapses when the experimental subject performs a task; psycholinguists refer to such lapsed time as "response time" (RT). Psycholinguists use RT largely to measure fluency differences in performing different tasks involving lexical items, sometimes cross-linguistically (see Meuter & Allport, 1999).

Thus, we argue that the more frequent patterns that we study here are the ones that occur in CS because they avoid costs as they are characterized here. That is, our overall point is that a major characteristic of CS is that certain structures occur because they avoid cost. It is true that the distribution of the participating languages in CS ultimately may depend on various factors, but for the elements studied here, the language with the less complex production procedures is the one that appears in the critical slot. That is, at least in CS, what is less costly is less complex. We support this claim with empirical data involving three CS construction types. Examples below illustrate the constructions we consider. We suggest that our results can inform models of language production in a general sense, or at least offer a new perspective on parts of bilingual processing.

As a preliminary, we assume the validity of the basic asymmetry between the participating languages that the Matrix Language Frame (MLF) model presupposes: one language is called the Matrix Language (ML) and the other language(s) are called Embedded Languages (EL). The ML is the source of the abstract grammatical frame of the CS clause; the role of the EL is limited largely to supplying content elements and peripheral monolingual (EL) phrases (see Myers-Scotton, 1993a [1997], 2002a; Myers-Scotton & Jake, 2009). Our unit of analysis is the clause, or CP, the projection of complementizer, or COMP.

### 19.1.3 The type of data studied

The three CS constructions we discuss are:

- Nonfinite EL verbs that occur with ML inflections in a clause with an ML frame, with examples from various language pairs (example 1).
- Determiner + Noun structures (or DPs, determiner phrases) in Spanish–English in which Spanish determiners are most frequent (example 2).
- Morphemes signaling connections between clauses – subordinators, complementizers, and conjunctions – and their distribution across the participating languages from representative datasets, with extended examples from Spanish–English and Palestinian Arabic–English CS as well as Quechua–Spanish contact data (example 3).

The following examples illustrate the corpora. In example (1) an English verb ("punish") receives Swahili verbal inflections that show co-indexing for subject and object. Example (2) shows the typical pattern for mixed nominal constituents when Spanish is the ML. An English noun appears with a determiner from Spanish. Example (3) illustrates a subordinator from Arabic, *li?anha,* introducing an otherwise monolingual English clause.

1. Swahili–English CS (Myers-Scotton, 2013)
   (two women discussing stoppages of the urban water supply)
   Hawa watu wa-na-tu-**punish** sana.   Ha-wa-ju-i sisi ni binadamu.
   CL2DET people CL2-NONPST-1PL.         NEG-CL2-know-NEG we are people.
   OBJ-punish a lot
   Ha-tu-wez-i           **survive** bila maji.
   NEG-1PL-can-NEG       survive without water

   'These people punish us a lot. They don't think that we are people. We can't survive without water.'

2. Spanish–English (Milian, 1995 corpus)
   Ah,         ahí     tiene         que     ver      mucho el **peer pressure**
   Exclamation there   have.PRES.3S  that.COMP see.INF much DET.M.S peer pressure
   'Oh, it is that there is very much peer pressure.'

3. Palestinian Arabic–English (Okasha, 1999: 112)
   Lamma raaħat libnaan **she got a lot of attention**       li?anha **she was natural**
   When go.PERF.3F Lebanon she got a lot of attention because.3F she was natural
   'When she went to Lebanon she got a lot of attention because she was natural.'

In the following sections, as already indicated, we discuss these three construction types in terms of a cost–benefit analysis that is based on our understanding of 'costs' in CS corpora. Of course, we assume that CS itself must have a cost. For the language production system to produce well-formed CS structures at all must involve some stress. Not only are these CS structures made up of two or more languages, but they must maintain the grammaticality of the clause according to the ML requirements. Still, that CS happens at all implies that the cost of activating and presumably inhibiting production of elements from one language in favor of those from another is low.

## 19.1.4 Language production model

The discussion and analysis in this chapter of CS assumes a language production model based on that of Levelt (1989). In brief, speakers' intentions at a pre-linguistic conceptual level activate semantic/pragmatic feature bundles that express what the speakers wish to communicate. These bundles activate lemmas in the Mental Lexicon. (See Figure 19.1.) The lemmas underlying what we call content morphemes (e.g., nouns and verbs) are directly elected and they, in turn, can indirectly elect what we call 'early' system morphemes (e.g., 'definiteness' in determiners, plural markers, satellites in verbs). At this level, certain phrases are ready to be assembled by the formulator. Content morphemes send directions to the formulator for building more complex grammatical structures and producing shallow and surface linguistic constituents. These procedures require the structurally assigned system morphemes that are critical in building syntactic

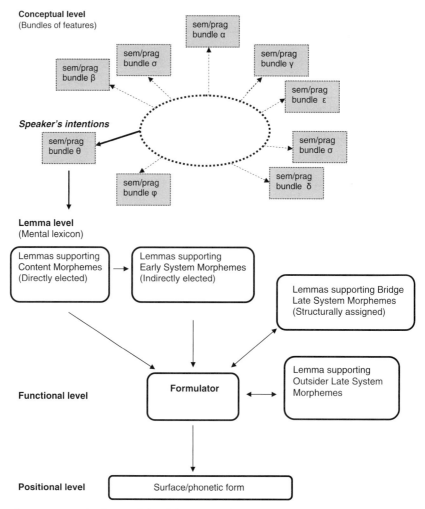

**Figure 19.1** Production model and the 4-M model of morpheme classification

structure. These morphemes are called 'late' system morphemes under the 4-M model. The model and these morphemes are discussed further below when they are relevant to the analyses.

### 19.1.5 The Matrix Language Frame model

In addition to assuming such a production model, which is detailed in Figure 19.1 and somewhat more below, we frame the discussion of the costs of bilingual production within several additional models. First is the Matrix Language Frame (MLF) model, mentioned above where we need to distinguish participating languages as the ML and EL. The MLF model has three defining features.

First, it assumes that within each bilingual clause that contains CS one of the participating languages provides the abstract grammatical frame

(Myers-Scotton, 1993a, 2002a). The unit of analysis is the bilingual clause (the CP, or projection of complementizer). A bilingual clause of course includes morphemes from two or more languages. It also includes some sort of main verb, typically a finite verb, and content morphemes that are in grammatical relationships with the verb.

Second, the model designates the ways to identify the ML. These ways are contained in two principles, which in effect are testable hypotheses; they identify the frame-building language as the Matrix Language (ML). The more critical principle is the System Morpheme Principle, which states that all instances of one type of morpheme, now called the 'outsider' system morpheme must come from only one of the participating languages, the ML. This morpheme type will be discussed more extensively below; in brief, it includes morphemes that co-index relations within a clause (e.g., subject–verb agreement). We hypothesize that these 'outsider' morphemes are only salient at the level of the formulator because they entail more structural congruence checking than early system morphemes. We develop this point later. In this instance, 'salience' means that these morphemes become active at this level when the procedures in the formulator assign them to building structure.

Third, the model differentiates content morphemes from system morphemes: content morphemes assign or receive thematic roles, but system morphemes do not. An EL may supply any morpheme type that is not an outsider late system morpheme, although those EL morphemes which are called at the conceptual level to realize the speaker's intentions are most frequent. That is, content morphemes are most frequent, followed by early system morphemes. A second type of system morpheme, 'bridge' system morphemes, also sends directions to the formulator, but only to combine constituents into larger structures. Bridge system morphemes very rarely come from the EL. However, in some cases, bridge system morphemes from the EL may be perceptually more salient than those from the ML. Moreover, the complexity of directions sent to the formulator by bridge system morphemes plays a role in either promoting or inhibiting the CS involving bridges. The examples of EL bridge system morphemes examined in this chapter involve CS at the boundaries of clauses as opposed to CS within clauses.

## 19.1.6 The Uniform Structure Principle

The nature of the grammatical frame detailed by the MLF model is elaborated by another principle and two other models that are especially relevant to the constructions discussed in sections 19.3 through 19.6. All three have application to language in general, not just CS.

The Uniform Structure Principle (USP) states simply that a given constituent type in any language has a uniform abstract structure and this structure must be observed whenever the constituent appears. This principle may seem too obvious to mention, but it is only obvious in monolingual speech. In CS, without the principle, either or both languages could supply the grammatical frame for clauses. Within a discourse or even an extended utterance, the language of this frame can change, and sometimes does, from one clause to another, but that is another matter.

The USP is important to CS because it specifies that in bilingual speech the structures of the ML are always preferred (Myers-Scotton, 2002a: 8). It will become clear, when the constructions we discuss are elaborated, that the USP is behind the finding that morphemes and phrases within a clause or connecting clauses structured by the ML are more frequent even when the possibility of other structures exists. In fact, it is possible to argue that the USP makes the seamless nature of CS possible because of its preference for the ML. Still, there is always a tension in CS because of the costs of complex structures and sometimes, as we will show in regard to nonfinite verbs in section 19.3 and various clause connecting elements in section 19.6, an EL element is possible or even preferred.

### 19.1.7 The 4-M model

The 4-M model adds precision to the MLF model's discussion of morpheme type, but it is a model of morpheme classification in general, not CS. (Jake & Myers-Scotton, 2009; Myers-Scotton & Jake, 2009). The 4-M model details four types of morpheme. It is tied to the production model outlined above through the Differential Access Hypothesis (Myers-Scotton, 2005b). This hypothesis states that the different abstract properties that the four morpheme types have under the 4-M model determine how speakers activate the lemmas underlying the surface form of morphemes. Late system morphemes are not called until the level of the formulator.

The model differentiates morpheme types by their roles in syntactic structures in the same sense that traditional models of morphology do. For example, content morphemes that are nouns or pronouns occur in argument positions, such as subject and object, and receive thematic roles such as agent or patient. Also, early system morphemes do not occur independently of their content morpheme heads (e.g., 'plural' is an early system morpheme, as are derivational morphemes, including satellites in phrasal verbs (Myers-Scotton & Jake, 2009). The descriptors 'early' and 'late' are not intended literally; we have nothing to say about activation times or sequences.

But the most far-reaching distinction the 4-M model makes is the distinction at abstract levels between conceptually activated morphemes (content morphemes and early system morphemes) and structurally assigned morphemes (the two types of late system morphemes, bridges and outsiders). As we have already indicated, late system morphemes are only available in the production process at the level of the formulator. Late system morphemes also contrast with content morphemes and early system morphemes in that they convey little meaning; again, their role is structure building. Bilingual constituents in naturally occurring CS provide evidence that only one language, the ML, provides the one type of morpheme detailed by the System Morpheme Principle discussed above. That is, outsider system morphemes come only from the ML.

Because content and early system morphemes satisfy the speaker's intentions regarding the semantic–pragmatic message to be communicated, they are necessarily at least initially activated at the level of lexical–conceptual structure and are available in the mental lexicon for building certain structures.

The distinctions between levels of activation are especially relevant in sections 19.4 and 19.5 which deal with mixed Determiner + noun phrases (DP, or determiner phrases) and section 19.6 on CS involving clausal connectors – subordinators, complementizers, and conjunctions. In CS, it becomes clear that morphemes and constituents from a language including any procedure that adds the potential cost of assigning late system morphemes at the level of the formulator are avoided when the other language involved doesn't call for this procedure and is therefore preferred. An earlier study (Myers-Scotton & Jake, 2001) supports the utility of the 4-M model beyond CS because it shows how the model can explain other distributions, such as those found in Broca's aphasia and second language acquisition (see also Myers-Scotton & Jake, 2000a, 2000b; Wei, 2000).

### 19.1.8 The Abstract Level model

One more model, the Abstract Level model, is relevant to the discussion in this chapter. It is relevant to the discussion in section 19.6 when CS involving Quechua–Spanish is discussed in regard to the role of Spanish subordinators and conjunctions. The reason is that the Abstract Level model views lexical elements as showing some flexibility regarding the realization of their abstract structures. Under the model, there are three levels of abstract lexical structure: lexical–conceptual structure (generally semantic/pragmatic information), predicate–argument structure (syntactic structure), and the level of morphological realization patterns (surface language-specific morphosyntactic patterns).

The model presupposes that all levels need not be equally salient in all instances of structure building. More important, it indicates that, especially in situations of unusual or long-term language contact, the three levels of abstract structure in an element from one language can be split and recombined with levels from another language. For example, the conceptual meaning contributed by a morpheme from one language may lead to grammatical change at the level of predicate–argument structure or morphological realization patterns. Thus, the model is relevant to the emergence of what are called mixed languages and also in creole development. This 'splitting and recombining' characterizes a variety of Quechua–Spanish CS referred to as Media Lengua (Jake & Myers-Scotton, 2009; Muysken, 1997).

### 19.1.9 Plan of discussion

The discussion in this chapter assumes knowledge of all of the models and the Uniform Structure Principle including the Differential Access Hypothesis mentioned above. They underlie the following sections that aim to support generalizations about how the role of the EL in CS is restricted (or not) in ways that are related to psycholinguistic cost that is evident in complexity in grammatical procedures. The CS literature in general and analyses in the following sections support the claim that only one language at a time can serve as the ML in a bilingual clause. Clauses that include 'portmanteau' morphemes may present a problem because they include an element or phrase (sometimes the VP) which is doubled, with one entry from each language. However, such structures seem to be rare and they resist comprehensive analysis that competes with the MLF model (Chan, 2009). Myers-Scotton (1993a) addresses one type of morpheme doubling and proposes an analysis in which one form from one language, usually the EL, is accessed in the production process at the conceptual level and the doubling morpheme, usually from the ML, is accessed later in production, often at the level of the formulator. This is further discussed in Myers-Scotton and Jake (2000a). Backus (1996: 340, 344) also discusses "double marking" and "ragged switches" in Turkish–Dutch CS. Backus (1996) suggests these are at least partly related to the discontinuous dependencies created by typologically distinct VP structures as well as performance factors, noting in one instance "the speaker seems to be caught off guard … and 'forgets' that he was speaking the other language" (350).

## 19.2 Types of morphemes

The cornerstone of the MLF model is that asymmetry characterizes the participation of languages in CS. This asymmetry is obvious in the main provisions of the model: first, the language identified as the ML always supplies the abstract grammatical frame to the bilingual clause. Second, morphological realization patterns in the clause come from the ML. Third, morpheme order and those system morphemes (i.e., functional elements) that co-index relationships within the clause come from the ML. Clearly, the other participating language, the EL, is left with a very restricted role. Still, the EL plays a very visible role in that it often supplies a number of lexical elements in the bilingual clause. That is, many of the morphemes that are called content morphemes under the 4-M model come from the EL.

### 19.2.1 Characterizing content morphemes

Content morphemes are identified in several ways. First, as noted above, the MLF model places these morphemes in the content category if they assign or receive theta roles (Myers-Scotton, 1993a). In further identifying what the MLF model calls content morphemes, we follow Bock and Levelt (1994) in characterizing content morphemes as "directly elected by the speaker's intentions" in contrast to the other morphemes that Bock and Levelt refer to as "indirectly elected" by their heads. That is, they are not forms that add semantic/pragmatic information to their heads and they occur only with their heads. Finally, as already indicated, the 4-M model adds another way to distinguish content morphemes. At the abstract level content morphemes, along with 'early' system morphemes, are identified as conceptually activated. They contrast at this level with the other two types of system morphemes that are referred to as structurally assigned. In all these cases, the generalization that covers all content morphemes is that carrying messages of content is their main function. That is, they carry the semantic/pragmatic information that conveys the speaker's intentions.

Most of the EL content morphemes in the bilingual clause are nouns. We refer to these EL nouns as 'free' in the sense that they don't need special checking with the abstract frame of the clause; the only checking they undergo is against the speaker's intentions. This means checking procedures (checking for congruence) are only salient for nouns at the lexical–conceptual level of the Abstract Level model. In addition to nouns, there are other content morphemes and, while they also convey meanings, they may undergo checking at other levels, as will become clear below.

### 19.2.2 System morphemes

Morphemes that are not content morphemes are considered system morphemes under the 4-M model (see Myers-Scotton, 2002a: 70–72, on why the designation, "system morpheme" is preferred over other terms used in the linguistic literature.) There are three types of system morphemes. Like nouns, 'early' system morphemes convey content, but, as noted above, early system morphemes are considered to be indirectly elected by their heads, not directly elected. They are called early because they become salient along with their heads at the level of the Mental Lexicon in the production model we follow. Early system morphemes never occur on their own but always with their head elements, such as nouns. Examples of early system morphemes are plural markings and satellite prepositions in phrasal verbs.

The other two types of morphemes are called late system morphemes; they are called *late* because they are not salient until the level of the formulator in our production model. There are two types of late system morphemes, bridges and outsiders. Bridges join together two constituents, such as two NPs (*destruction of the army, friend of the family*). While bridges may be the same lexical category as content morphemes, such as a thematic-role assigning preposition, they do not assign specific thematic roles, but only specify head–complement relations within and among parts of more complex constituents. For example, *army* can be interpreted as agent or patient in *the destruction of the* army. The speaker's and addressee's real-world knowledge determines this. Bridges that join together two clauses will be considered in section 19.6. Outsiders are so named because they occur as surface forms in constituents outside the linguistic element that calls them. For example, in many languages that have case, it is assigned by verbs, but is also realized in other elements in the clause, such as nouns or determiners.

### 19.2.3 Nouns and their 'cost'

Because the checking of nouns at abstract levels is limited to seeing that the noun selected meets the speaker's intentions about meaning, speakers who only insert nouns into phrases framed by the ML can engage in CS even with limited knowledge of the EL. Of course they must select nouns that carry thematic roles (e.g., actor, patient) that are congruent with slots projected by the ML at the levels of predicate–argument structure and of morphological realization patterns.

Still, in this chapter we take a production point of view to CS that includes a cost–benefit analysis and so we consider nouns in those terms. Put simply, the cost of selecting EL nouns is low because the extent of checking for congruence they undergo is low – only with speakers' intentions. Examples (4) through (6) illustrate some of the diversity and frequency of how EL nouns occur in CS clauses with structurally diverse ML and EL pairs. In various ways, they show how EL nouns 'fit into' the plan of the ML frame.

Example (4) shows two English words (English is the EL) in a clause framed by Xhosa, the ML. Note that compound nouns, such as *crime rate* in English are rare, if they occur at all in Xhosa–English CS. Rather, NP + of + NP constructions with an ML bridge system morpheme are preferred, as in this example. In example (5) there is a compound noun from Norwegian in a Turkish frame. Türker (2005) suggests that "bilingual speakers apparently reanalyze Norwegian compound nouns according to Turkish conventions for nominal compounds before affixing the Turkish compound marker (CM). Norwegian compound nouns receive the Turkish CM just as Standard Turkish equivalents would" (p. 470).

4. Xhosa–English CS (Myers-Scotton, 2004 corpus)
   **i-rate**      y-e           **crime**      i-nyuk-ile
   CL9-rate   CL9-ASSOC   crime      CL9-go up-PERF
   '[the] rate of crime is high.'

5. Turkish–Norwegian CS (Türker, 2005: 471)
   Hala-m-lar **saftflaske**-si-ne         yağ-i      dol-dur-muş
   aunt-POSS.1S-PL juice bottle-CM-DAT oil-ACC   fill-CAUS-PPART
   'My aunt and others have filled the fruit juice bottle with olive oil.'

In example (6), there are two examples of EL nouns in what are called EL islands. Such islands are defined as well-formed phrases in the EL whose structure shows dependency relations. *Un faux geste* is such an island, an NP entirely in French. The other EL island, *les problèmes*, is also a well-formed NP, but it occurs as an internal EL island because its head element is a preposition (*d*) from Arabic.

6. Moroccan Arabic–French (Ziamari, 2008: 131)
   **Un faux geste**       yqder         ydir         bezzaf d **les problèmes**
   INDEF.M false gesture can.3P.IMPERF do.3P.IMPERF a.lot of DEF.PL problems
   'A false gesture can make a lot of problems.'

## 19.3 EL verbs in a cost–benefit analysis

Although verbs also count as content morphemes under the 4-M model, they are quite a different story from nouns, and for that matter, from other content morphemes. Of course, as indicated above, they differ from nouns in regard to theta roles in that nouns receive thematic roles and verbs assign them. From the standpoint of grammatical structure, verbs are more critical; the entire verb phrase carries information about predicate–argument structure.

Thus, if an EL finite verb were elected by a speaker's intentions at the lexical–conceptual level to convey a desired meaning, it still would have to be checked for congruence with the ML frame at the other two levels of Abstract lexical structure under the abstract Level model, as EL nouns do. EL verbs are less frequent in CS by far than EL nouns. However, the difference in frequency has received little comment in the literature (but see Myers-Scotton & Jake, 2014). Little potential explanation at an abstract level was even attempted, except to note that all EL elements would undergo congruence checking (see Myers-Scotton, 1993a; Myers-Scotton & Jake, 1995, for this view). For a revised view, see Myers-Scotton & Jake (2014).

### 19.3.1 How much do EL verbs cost?

However, now that we are looking for an explanation for naturally occurring CS patterns in a cost–benefit analysis, we look in a different way at the EL verbs which actually do occur from just noting that they are not as frequent as nouns. First, for the first time we evaluate the scarcity of EL verbs against the ease of CS production that has already been mentioned. We suggest that the psycholinguistic cost of syntactic checking for congruence that would have to be done for finite EL verbs in relation to the ML frame is not consonant with the ease and speed of CS. For this reason, we argue here that the EL verbs that do occur in finite verb slots in the ML VP frame are not EL finite verbs, but EL nonfinite verbs because they show less complexity in their participation in the grammatical structure.

### 19.3.2 'Do' verb constructions

Next, this leads us to look at the data on those EL verbs that do occur in CS. In fact, it is only when they occur in 'do' verb constructions that EL verbs are frequent. They occur across many diverse datasets around the world. This construction includes an ML verb for 'do,' or a similar meaning, and it is this verb that receives ML inflections for ML markers for Tense–Mood–Aspect (TMA) and other required ML verbal affixes. Note, however, that the speaker's intended meaning is carried by a nonfinite verb, an infinitive, that occurs in the predicate. In example (7) from Turkish–Dutch CS, *yap-* is the verb for 'do' and in example (8) from Chichewa–English CS, *-chita* is the 'do' verb.

7. Turkish–Dutch (Backus, 1992: 83)
   bu bir sürü **taal**-lar-i          **beheers-en**     yap-iyor-ken
   he a range language-PL-ACC   control-INF       do-PROG-while
   'while he knows a lot of languages ...'

8. Chichewa–English (Simango, 1995 ms., cited in Myers-Scotton, 2002b: 216)
   a-ma-ngo-chit-a     **think about**    ku-ma-umbuz-a       a-nthu
   3.S-HAB-just do-FV  think about       INF-HAB-beat.up-FV  CL2-person
   'He just thinks about beating up people.' [quarreling brother to parent about sibling]

An EL verb has a role in these constructions, but it is only to carry critical semantic/pragmatic meanings. Furthermore, it is a nonfinite EL verb that fills this function, typically an infinitive. That is, the EL verb in a "do construction" has none of the shallow syntactic characteristics of a finite verb; it does not occur in the appropriate slot for verbs that will be inflected with ML affixes. Because they are clearly not finite verbs and occur as objects of the "do" verb, some researchers have accounted for the EL verbs in these constructions as functioning as nouns (see Backus, 1996, for an overview on verbs in CS).

## 19.3.3 EL verbs in finite verb slots

Except in these "do" verb constructions, EL verbs have an unusual distribution in CS corpora. In some corpora they hardly occur at all, but in certain corpora they are very frequent. These frequently occurring EL verbs appear in the appropriate slot for finite verbs in the ML frame. We refer to this as the finite verb slot in the discussion that follows. That is, they receive the appropriate ML inflections for TMA markers and also for co-indexing of subjects and objects. In fact, they can also appear with ML derivational affixes. In example (9) from Xhosa–English CS, the English verb "deserve" receives Xhosa prefixes co-indexing both the subject and the object, as well as a prefix and a suffix, both marking 'negative.'

9. Xhosa–English (Myers-Scotton, 2004, Pretoria corpus)
   ... **but** eziny'izo-nto             a-ba-zi-**deserve**-i
   ... but other CL10-thing         NEG-3PL-CL10.OBJ-deserve-NEG
   '... but other things, they do not deserve them.'

## 19.3.4 Evidence indicating EL verbs are nonfinite

One question raised by examples such as (9) is whether the EL verb in the ML finite verb slot is a finite verb. We argue that it is a nonfinite verb, an unmarked form of the infinitive, similar to verbs that occur in "do" constructions. We present evidence below for this position.

First, there are examples of EL verbs where the nonfinite–finite identity is not clear. This is especially the case when English is the EL because English finite verbs and some infinitive verbs, those not preceded by *to*, can have the same surface realization. That is, even in monolingual English, not all instances of the English infinitive occur with the morpheme *to* that definitively marks the verb as an infinitive (compare *Let him go* with *He wants to go*). Consider the English verb *confirm* in example (10). It is not overtly marked by English as a nonfinite or a finite form. However, one can argue it is a nonfinite verb on the basis of its limited contribution of EL structure to the clause. The clause asks a question as to whether a certain action has been completed. Here, the Swahili TMA marker in the verb complex, *-me-*, has an aspectual meaning of non-completed action. For non-completed action, in monolingual English, the verb form would receive a suffix (i.e., *confirm-ed* as in *Have you confirmed that ...*). That no English *-ed* occurs certainly implies that the verb is nonfinite, not a finite verb.

10. Swahili–English CS (Myers-Scotton, 2013, Nairobi corpus)
    u-me-**confirm**      kama kesho       tu-na-end-a       **job**?
    2S-NON-PAST-confirm    COMP tomorrow   1PL-PROG-go-FV    work
    'Have you confirmed that tomorrow we will go to [that] job?'

However, another example (11) from Swahili–English makes it even clearer that the English verb is not a finite form. Here, the 'completed action' meaning of the verb is conveyed by the past tense Swahili *-li-* marker. But the really telling evidence that the English verb is an infinitive is that if the English verb were a finite form, it would have to appear as *chose* not *choose*. We suggest that the same argument can be made for all instances of EL verbs from English: they are nonfinite forms in CS even though they occur in finite slots.

11. Swahili–English (Myers-Scotton, 1988, Nairobi corpus)
    Wengi       wa-li-chuku-a           kazi  hii kuwa     **dirty and bad for health.**
    many   3PL-PST-take-FV    work CL0.DEM COP dirty and bad for health
    Lakini a-li-**choose to risk his life to do this work**.
    But 3S.PST- choose to risk his life to do this work.

    'Many [people] take this work that is dirty and bad for [one's] health. But he chose to risk his life to do this work.'

### 19.3.5 French as the EL and nonfinite verbs

A first look at French as an EL leaves some uncertainty about the finite quality of French verbs in CS. French is the EL in a number of CS pairs; here we discuss French as the EL with African languages in former francophone colonial areas.

12. Bukavu Swahili–French (Goyvaerts & Zembele, 1992: 72)
    Kweli? Ndjo mana u-li-**esquiver** ile **question**?
    Really COP reason 2S-PST-avoid CL9-DEM question
    'Really? Is that [the] reason you avoided that question?'

Example (12) comes from Bukavu in the Eastern part of the Democratic Republic of the Congo (DRC). Goyvaerts & Zembele (1992) write *esquiver* as if it were an infinitive, but it is difficult to tell in spoken French whether an infinitive or certain finite forms are intended if the verb comes from the *-er* conjugation. This is the conjugation with the most numerous verbs. However, another example from written material, this time from Moroccan Arabic–French CS, also suggests that French verbs so written are infinitives. However, other researchers on Moroccan Arabic–French CS do not necessarily report that they find such examples (see Ziamari, 2007).

13. Moroccan Arabic–French (Bentahila & Davies, 1983, cited in Backus, 1996: 215
    Tajbqa j-**confronter ces idées**
    'He keeps confronting his ideas'

### 19.3.6 Clearer evidence of French nonfinite verbs in finite slots

Still, when the French verb from the *-re* conjugation or the *-ir* conjugation is selected, its status as an infinitive is on solid footing. Thus, the following

CS example from a different part of the Democratic Republic of the Congo makes the status of the French verb very clear: it is an infinitive. The verb *rendre* receives a subject prefix from Chiluba (*ba-*) that co-indexes it as subject elsewhere in the discourse, as well as several suffixes (*-ang-* 'habitual' and *-ana* 'reciprocal' plus 'final vowel.')

14. Chiluba–French (Kamwangamalu, 1994: 75)
    ba-vwa ba-**rendre**-angana      **visites** ya bungi **quand elle etait ici**
    3PL-AUX.PAST 3PL-give-RECIP.HAB  visit.PL ASSOC many when she was here
    'they used to visit each other a lot when she was here' (i.e., "visits of many")

In addition to those French EL verbs in Bantu languages, such as example (14) above, in some West African CS corpora, the French verb is also clearly a nonfinite verb. Note that these West African examples come from a language that is typologically very different than the Bantu language examples just given. Researchers report they transcribe French verbs from the *-er* conjugation as *-er* and therefore seem to indicate it is the infinitive that occurs (personal communication, Amuzu, 2011), but stronger evidence is provided when the verb comes from the *-oir* conjugation; it appears in full infinitive form in a finite slot. The West African languages examined in this chapter are analytic languages in which co-indexing markers (i.e., for subject) and TMA markers are typically clitics, not affixes as they would be in the Bantu languages referred to above, which are agglutinative languages.

15. Ewe–French (Amuzu, 2011, Ewe contact corpus)
    Wo mu **concevoir** be nuḍe ts ela te s'**accompagner**
    3PL NEG.POT imagine that something too 3PL.PROSP.accompany
    'They don't imagine that something else can accompany it.'

Elsewhere there are other CS corpora where EL infinitives appear in finite verb slots. In North Africa and specifically in Moroccan Arabic–Spanish CS, a Spanish infinitive receives Arabic inflections, as in example (14).

16. Moroccan Arabic–Spanish (Vincente & Ziamari, 2008: 462)
    Kā yəm ȋ y**trbajaru** küli yawm f-əs-**sentro**
    'ils vont travailler chaque jour au centre-ville.'
    ['They go to work every day in the city center.']

## 19.3.7 Acholi–English CS: another nonfinite EL form

Finally, another language pair, Acholi–English in Uganda, provides confirming data for the argument that when EL verbs occur inflected by the ML, they are nonfinite verbs (Myers-Scotton, 2005a). Acholi, a Western Nilotic language, marks aspect on all verbs in finite positions, so an

English bare infinitive is not as good a match as another nonfinite form, the present participle. In this corpus, all English EL verbs are verb + *ing*, and are inflected with other Acholi TMA markers, as in (17), in which *i-**boarding taxi*** occurs. Note that the English present participle functions as a finite verb, not as a present participle; English present participles occur in other CS language pairs, such as Spanish–English, but functioning as participles.

17. Acholi–English (Myers-Scotton, 2005b: 12)
    **chances** me   **accident**   pol ka i-**boarding taxi**
    Chances ASSOC accident many if 2s-boarding taxi
    '[The] chances of [an] accident [are] many if you board [a] taxi.'

### 19.3.8 The motivation for nonfinite verbs

It is true that we have exemplified nonfinite verbs in finite verb slots for relatively few CS corpora, although we predict in any CS corpus where either French or English is the EL and there are EL verbs in the finite verb slot, these are also examples of nonfinite verbs. We suggest that it may be that they exist in other corpora with other EL languages, but have just not been identified.

The examples above support the argument that when EL verbs occur in CS in the slot for a finite verb, they are nonfinite verbs, not finite ones. We note again that EL verbs, in general, are not frequent in CS corpora. When they have verbs in their bilingual clauses, they are only ML finite verbs.

A reason why EL verbs are relatively infrequent in most datasets may be that speakers in many communities have negative attitudes about CS. It is often referred to as 'broken language.' Even calling CS 'mixed' is somewhat negative because that term implies lack of discernable structure. Some researchers have noticed that speakers who recognize that they engage in switching are often overtly concerned that they do not corrupt their L1, which many times is the ML (personal communication, Smith, 2014, regarding Spanish–English CS in the USA).

But is there also concern about the EL? This is the language that does not supply many verbs. It may be that speakers' attitudes toward the EL are not so personal, but attitudes still make them conscious of their linguistic choices. That is, speakers may feel 'personal pride' toward their L1, but restrained by linguistic prescriptivism in regard to at least certain ELs. That is, if the EL is often a language of high social prestige because it is associated with education, sources of power, and high status in general, speakers may feel that 'corrupting' its grammar reflects badly on their own public status. And of course English and French are languages that generally have high social prestige in the communities that our examples come from, and they are often EL languages in CS corpora. Further, it may be that verbs are somehow considered 'more part of the grammar' than nouns (because of the critical role of verbs in predicate–argument structure in the clause) and therefore they receive more prescriptive attention.

It would be interesting to see how psycholinguists contrast production and attitudes toward nouns and verbs in bilingual contexts. Unfortunately, there is little or nothing in the literature on this subject. Instead, the emphasis by psycholinguists has been in contrasting RT across languages in various experimental procedures, but dealing only with one lexical category at a time. Usually concrete nouns have been studied.

Further, we admit that there is surface ambiguity as to the nature of all EL verbs that do occur. However, that said, we argue that the context and details around the ambiguity point to resolving it in favor of recognizing that *all* EL verbs in the VP slot for a finite verb, in fact, are nonfinite verbs.

However, speakers of many CS language pairs seem to prefer the "do" verb construction with the EL nonfinite verb in the predicate. This is a more conservative strategy from the standpoint of the implications of the role of nonfinite verbs in CS because in such constructions the nonfinite verb is simply in the same slot that could hold an EL noun or an ML verb in some constructions. Also, the use of "do" verbs in such constructions has a long history in many communities, such as those where Turkish languages are spoken.

The analysis of nonfinite EL verbs offered here does explain the structures that occur in CS corpora. It covers both nonfinite verbs appearing in finite verb slots (usually infinitives) and those bare nonfinite forms in the "do" constructions (again, usually infinitives).

The question remains: how do these nonfinite verbs reduce the cost of engaging in CS? Both strategies have their advantages. "Do" verb constructions are very transparent; because their structure is largely at the surface level, this may mean some more abstract and complex production costs are avoided. Certainly, the fact that they are so omnipresent across the world indicates that speakers find them attractive for encoding their communicative intentions. That is, while do they require quite a bit of structure (i.e., adding to the "do" verb itself any ML verbal affixes required as well as adding the EL infinitive), these constructions do not add abstract levels of grammatical complexity or require that additional directions be sent to the formulator regarding late system morphemes. The EL verb in its indirectly elected infinitive form is activated at the conceptual level to realize speaker intentions. That is, their cost is low.

In contrast to 'do' constructions, nonfinite verbs in ML finite slots avoid production costs in a different way. They have special advantages at a more abstract level. In line with the argument laid out in the introduction, there is less cost when complexity is avoided. When EL nonfinite verbs appear in ML finite verb slots, they do not add complexity beyond receiving ML verbal inflections. So in what ways are EL nonfinite verbs less costly than

EL finite ones? The answer is that if EL finite verbs were selected, they would have to undergo at the very least competition with ML finite verbs and they would have to be checked for congruence with the ML frame regarding directions for the predicate–argument structure that they intrinsically can direct. The cost advantage with nonfinite verbs is that they do not control or contribute any elements to the bilingual clause's grammatical structure. That is, they are less complex because they only meet congruence requirements at the level of the lexical–conceptual structure; that is, the only requirement that they must satisfy is meeting the speaker's intentions regarding semantic/pragmatic content. This means that CS mixed constituents bypass the additional congruence checking that finite verbs would require. This partly explains why their selection makes producing the entire clause simpler, and therefore possibly faster (see Myers-Scotton & Jake, 2014 for more on the psycholinguistic advantages that nonfinite verbs in finite verb slots offer).

In sum, EL nonfinite verbs carry desired meanings. While the ML must still send directions to the formulator for relevant TMA affixes and co-indexing, the EL does not impinge on the ML's grammatical roles. In addition, both constructions, nonfinite verbs in ML finite slots and 'do constructions,' offer a bonus: they avoid introducing the type of EL elements that can indicate grammatical dependency relations and thus avoid the cost of complexities which could include procedures at the level of the formulator.

## 19.4 Nouns and determiners: determiner phrases (DPs)

This section of the chapter presents quantitative evidence from a CS corpus (Spanish–English) that suggests a reason why when mixed DET + noun constituents occur in CS, their production is seemingly effortless, with little cost. Determiner phrases with determiners from Spanish dominate, as the quantitative analysis below shows. Whether Spanish or English is the ML, the MLF model (the model we follow for CS structures) places no restrictions on the language of determiners in determiner phrases that have elements from both the CS languages. The following examples from the corpus studied illustrate the most frequent pattern, Det + N or N-bar: *el* **freezer** or *un* **good job**. For reasons that will become clear, the production process in accessing Spanish determiners is more transparent than that for English determiners. Because English determiners have less salience at the lexical–conceptual level, they have a higher cost. Spanish also dominates, of course, because it is the ML (see the Uniform Structure Principle) but that principle is not categorical.

The section includes two arguments about abstract structure in linguistic elements and clause structure: first, we hypothesize that not all abstract levels of lexical structure are equally available when determiners that convey definiteness are being built. A second hypothesis, which the data support, at least indirectly, is that not all bilingual elements achieve saliency at the same level in a language production model. The assumptions of both the Abstract Level model regarding abstract levels in lexical entries and the Differential Access Hypothesis are relevant to these arguments. Data analyzed in this section imply these arguments, but they also support the MLF model for CS and the Uniform Structure Principle that figure throughout the arguments of this chapter.

### 19.4.1 An asymmetry in Spanish–English DPs

The main CS corpus studied consists of Spanish–English CS, where it becomes clear that Spanish is the Matrix Language (ML) and English is the Embedded Language (EL), according to the MLF model. The distribution to be explained is the preponderance of NPs with a determiner from Spanish and a noun/noun bar from English. That is, examples such as **el driveway** or **un baby shower** are the most frequent structure with English nouns in such mixed constituents.

Note that other patterns do occur, showing more English. For example, there are a few monolingual English DPs in the corpus (e.g., **the first one**, or **the old work**) but the point is that they are not mixed constituents (including two languages). However, even such EL islands as these are very infrequent. Recall EL islands are well-formed phrases entirely in the EL in a clause for which another language, Spanish in this corpus, is the ML. There are no examples at all of mixed DPs with an English determiner + a Spanish noun (e.g.* **the** *puertas,* 'the doors'). Also, in other corpora, examples such as *I visited the hacienda),* which is a mixed constituent with an English determiner and a Spanish noun do occur. But one can argue that such nouns as this are likely borrowings into English. More important, the ML of this clause is English, not Spanish, so a determiner in English, the ML, is not a surprise.

The data from the Spanish–English corpus support three theoretical claims; additional data from Italian–Swiss German CS reinforce the overall argument. First, the strength of the ML across the bilingual clause in CS, not just in specific mixed constituents, becomes obvious in actual CS corpora. That is, the strength of Spanish as the ML shows that not just one constituent, such as the verbal complex as some have argued, identifies the ML (e.g., Klavans, 1985). The corpus also supports the Uniform Structure Principle because the strength of the ML as uniformly supplying abstract structure underlying the morphosyntax is apparent across the clause. That is, not just DPs with material from both languages support the ML and the Universal Structure Principle; for example, mixed PPs also show a similar distribution involving Spanish and English. There are more headed by Spanish than by English.

Second, quantitative evidence (N = 63 mixed DPs) support a notion that depends on the Abstract Level model discussed previously in this chapter. As indicated, this model presupposes abstract lexical structure as present at three levels of abstraction that underlie what ultimately become lexical elements: lexical–conceptual structure, predicate–argument structure, and morphological realization patterns. Recall that lexical–conceptual structure has to do with speakers' intentions regarding the meanings that they wish to communicate. Predicate–argument structure refers to syntactic structure and how thematic relations between lexical elements are realized. Morphological realization patterns refer to elements on the surface level. In the language production model we envision, all three abstract levels are present in the semantic/pragmatic feature bundles that are activated by a speaker's intentions to communicate ideas. These bundles underlie lemmas in the Mental Lexicon that underlie surface level morphemes. But under the Abstract Level model, an important assumption is that not all levels of abstraction need be equally salient, and not equally critical, when these lemmas are initially activated at the level of the Mental Lexicon. Below, we will argue that the feature of 'gender' in Spanish is activated at the level of lexical–conceptual structure. Because Spanish has the feature of early activation of grammatical gender, the stage is set for determiners to come from Spanish, not from English, which does not have grammatical gender or any other feature that can assure early activation of an English determiner in competition with Spanish.

Third, the claim of the Differential Access Hypothesis is that not all linguistic elements that are present in the Mental Lexicon are salient, and thus prominent, at the same abstract level when larger constituents are assembled in language production. That is, the hypothesis refers not to levels of abstraction of the Abstract Level model, but to specific lemma entries supporting actual lexical elements. The Differential Access Hypothesis assumes that some elements only become fully available at all abstract levels in our language production model at the level of the formulator. These elements are available only when they are called to provide morphosyntactic structure for the larger clause. The 4-M model refers to them as late outsider system morphemes; these are the morphemes covered by the System Morpheme Principle in the MLF model.

Earlier in this chapter, we referred to the central abstract distinction that the 4-M model makes among morpheme types: conceptually activated vs. structurally assigned. Content morphemes and the early system morphemes that content morphemes elect are activated conceptually by speakers' intentions regarding the messages of semantics and pragmatics they wish to convey. In contrast, the two types of late system morphemes, bridges and outsiders, are structurally assigned. They are important, not to convey meaning, but either to build larger grammatical structures beyond basic phrases (bridges join together phrases or fuller constituents) or to make that structure more transparent (outsiders co-index relationships between elements in the clause).

The specific claim that we will support is regarding the feature 'definiteness' in Spanish–English determiners in mixed DPs. The claim depends on both the Abstract Level model and the Differential Access Hypothesis. It is this: not all of the abstract features that refer to 'definitiveness' in surface level determiners are available at the same abstract level of production in all languages. Spanish and English differ in this regard.

### 19.4.2 The role of *phi*-features in determiners

*Phi*-features are abstract features of person, number, and gender. All nouns and pronouns have some of these features (person, number, and gender if they have grammatical gender). *Phi*-features are important to this discussion at least for two reasons. First, Spanish and English nouns have determiners that can convey 'definiteness,' but encoding this feature is not possible in English at the same abstract level as is available in Spanish. We argue that 'definiteness' is activated 'early' in Spanish, along with the *phi*-feature gender, at the level of lexical–conceptual structure when Spanish nouns indirectly elect early system morpheme determiners. Recall that it is at this level that speakers' intentions regarding the meanings that they wish to communicate become activated. Second, grammatical *phi*-features, including gender, are salient at all levels in Spanish because it employs these features to enable nouns be linked to other elements in a clause. For example in Spanish, in *me gusta la manzana* 'I like the apple' (me-OBJ like-3.S the.3.F apple.F) person and number *phi*-features link the subject *la manzana* to the verb *gusta*. In other languages, the *phi*-feature of gender has different roles. Class markers in various languages can be considered realizations of this *phi*-feature (e.g., the Bantu languages; see Henderson, 2006).

In pro-drop languages, such as Spanish, the presence of agreement features makes it possible to 'drop' pronominal subjects because a subject is 'recoverable' (when the clause is interpreted) because strong *phi*-features make the identity of the subject clear; this is another way of saying, 'strong grammatical agreement licenses null subjects.' It is *phi*-features that make the referent of the null subject recoverable, as in an example such as "*no tienen las* manzanas," "[they] don't have the apples" (no have-PRES.3PL DEF.F.PL apple.F.PL). Danon (2011) discusses recent proposals in the distribution of *phi*-features within the noun phrase (DP), and suggests that some *phi*-features are most relevant for satisfying DP internal agreement, e.g., gender, while other features are required at the clause level.

Even though grammatical gender may be the *phi*-feature that is critical in the realization of DPs in Spanish and other languages, this feature is not always visible on the noun itself. It only becomes visible on elements that have a dependency relation with the noun, including the DP. For example, in Spanish, the abstract *phi*-features underlying gender in nouns are mapped onto the surface realizations of articles and adjectives that occur with nouns; that is, articles and adjectives in their surface realizations are marked for gender, even when the gender of the noun is not overtly marked on the surface. So, for example, in the phrase, *la llave* 'the key,' the determiner shows the gender (feminine), but the noun does not.

Many linguists have studied whether the gender (masculine or feminine) of a Spanish noun is maintained when its EL counterpart appears in CS (see Poplack & Meechan, 1998; Jake, Myers-Scotton, & Gross, 2002). In general, the finding is that masculine is the default gender in CS. That is, if the ML counterpart is feminine in monolingual Spanish, it is likely to be masculine in mixed constituents in CS (see Otheguy & Lapidus, 2003, who argue convincingly that having masculine as a default is an "adaptive simplification" in this case). However, the specification of masculine or feminine gender is not relevant to our argument; the critical issue is just that gender is a grammatical *phi*-feature in Spanish and it is available at the level of lexical–conceptual structure for mixed DPs.

What is important in this discussion is our claim that, cross-linguistically, *phi*-features are not necessarily salient at the same abstract level. To repeat, in Spanish, they have to be activated at the level of lexical–conceptual structure because it is necessary for them to be available to indirectly elect determiners specified for *phi*-features and to map semantic/pragmatic meaning onto the level of predicate–argument structure (at the level of the Mental Lexicon in the production model we follow). This 'early' mapping election is necessary for Spanish because it has a number of syntactic structures that link nouns to other lexical elements and this link is made through *phi*-features, which includes gender.

As already indicated, English nouns have *phi*-features, too, but they are not realized on determiners. But English does not have grammatical gender, nor does it have syntactic structures that depend on making 'visible' the *phi*-feature of gender at the level of the mental lexicon. Therefore, in English, *phi*-features only become salient at the level of the formulator. English requires little of *phi*-features, but the features of person and number are needed at the formulator because it is here that structurally assigned agreement (AGR) needs to be specified, as in <u>the woman play-s tennis well</u>. In CS between Spanish and English, only Spanish determiners are available at the level of the Mental Lexicon, unless pragmatics or a significant collocation adds saliency to a full English NP. This is because it is only Spanish whose *phi*-features are salient when any DP is being constructed to encode 'definiteness.'

### 19.4.3 Quantified evidence favors Spanish determiners

In reference to NPs, Spanish determiners dominate in the corpus of 67 turns with English nominal elements in the bilingual clauses that we

**Table 19.1** *Distribution of English nouns in Spanish-framed CPs (Milian corpus, 1995)*

| English nouns in Spanish-framed clauses: Construction types | Tokens |
|---|---|
| **Mixed NPs:** Spanish DET + English N/N-BAR | 63/67 (94%) |
| [Spanish DET + English N/N-BAR] | [54/63 (86%)] |
| [Ø DET + English N/N-BAR] | [9/63 (14%)] |
| **NP EL Islands:** English DET + English N/N-BAR | 4/67 (6%) |
| **Total NPs with English N/N-BAR** | 67 (100%) |

studied (see Table 19.1; Milian, 1995). Of this total, English nouns or N-bars occur with determiners in 63, or 94%, of the clauses. The statistic of most interest to us is 54/63. That is, 86% of the examples in which an English N/N-Bar occurs in a Spanish-framed clause consist of an English noun with a Spanish determiner (i.e., in a mixed DP). Nine other examples are English nouns without determiners (9/63 or 14%). English NP EL islands (entirely in English, the EL) are 6% of the entire corpus (4/67). And, as suggested above, these NPs are pragmatically salient, contrastive as in *the first one,* or *the old work.*

Examples (18) through (20) illustrate the mixed DPs, with Spanish determiners from the Milian (1995) corpus. Note that the determiners carry the *phi*-features of number and gender, as well as definiteness. Jake, Myers-Scotton, and Gross (2002) discuss similar data from another corpus (Blazquez-Domingo, 1998).

18. Spanish–English (Milian, 1995, unpublished corpus)
    No, la **potato** de anoche,         **you** acabaste con ella
    DET.3.F.S. potato ASSOC night, you finish.2S.PST with it.F
    'No, the potato from last night, you finished it.'

19. yo he cometido un **error**
    1S.NOM have.1S.PRES make.PART INDEF.M error
    'I have made a mistake.'

20. ... viene mi         familia     para los **holidays**,
    ... come.3S 1S.POSS family.F     for DEF.3.M.PL holiday.PL
    y yo me compré este **stereo**
    and 1S 1S.OBJ buy-1S-PST DEM.M.S stereo
    'my family is coming for the holidays, and I bought myself this stereo.'

Because Spanish *phi*-features are activated at the level of lexical–conceptual structure, they are available when DPs are activated. English grammatical *phi*-features, which include person and number, but not gender, only become salient when needed to encode structurally assigned agreement (AGR) at the level of the formulator, that is, outside of the maximal projection of the NP. This differential activation means that English determiners are less available in encoding 'definiteness' than Spanish ones – because of the Spanish requirement that *phi*-features be active at the level of constructing full DPs at the lexical–conceptual level and for mapping lexical conceptual structure onto predicate-argument structures involving DPs. But, as already indicated, in Spanish, more than the DP is at stake in a bilingual clause. To say that a language 'has' pro-drop means that in a given clause, the pronoun that would mark the main verb's subject can be dropped. *Phi*-features are also relevant to the interpretation of clitic pronouns that receive their surface realizations because of the same *phi*-features on the nouns that they co-index. Also, because of pro-drop, all Spanish NPs, even null pronominals, must be 'visible' at all levels of structure, especially predicate–argument structure, not just at the surface level, because pro-drop reflects speaker intentions that originate at an abstract level (i.e., as part of predicate–argument structure).

Although Spanish is the ML of the corpus studied here, if the speaker's intentions are to produce full DPs in English, then of course both the determiner and the noun can come from English. But unless there is pragmatic emphasis on the language-tag of the noun as English, the prediction is that a Spanish–English corpus will have few such EL (English) islands. Example (21) illustrates a contrastive DP in English, as is clear from the final clause, whose ML has switched to English.

21. Spanish–English CS (Milian, 1995, unpublished corpus)
    El que          tiene          Brinca es          **the old work**.
    DET.M COMP      have.3S.PRES   Brinca COP.3S.PRES the old work.
    El que estábamos usando        ayer por la noche, **that's the new work**.
    3S.M COMP COP.1PL.PST use.GER  yesterday for the.F night.F that's the new work
    'The one that Brinca has is the old work; the one we were using last night, that's the new work.'

## 19.5 Italian–Swiss German DPs

Another set of data also shows how asymmetry, when certain elements are available, characterizes mixed DPs in CS (see Myers-Scotton & Jake, 2001). These data come from Italian–Swiss German CS (Perziosa-Di Quinzio, 1992). Of most interest is the relative robustness of Italian over German, especially in DPs. We argue that differences in the complexity of building structures makes a difference as it does in Spanish–English DPs. That is, the language that does not first have to check procedures involving the formulator having to do with agreement before building the underlying structure of the DP is the language incurring less cost and in which DPs are more robust.

### 19.5.1 An asymmetry in DP constructions

Again, our analysis employs the MLF model's distinction between the Matrix Language (ML) and the Embedded Language (EL) in discussing the data. The ML supplies the grammatical frame of the bilingual clause. In this corpus, the ML switches; sometimes it is Italian and sometimes it is Swiss German. When Italian is the ML in the corpus German nouns occur 13 times. Most German nouns occur in mixed DPs with Italian determiners (9/13, or 69%); see example (22). There are only 4 German EL islands (31%); see example (23). In contrast, when Swiss German is the ML, Italian nouns occur 32 times. Swiss German provides the determiners with Italian nouns on only 4 DPs (4/32, or 12.5%). See example (24). In this corpus, Italian nouns are more likely to occur in NP EL islands (28/32, or in 87.5%) when Swiss German is the ML of the clause; that is these islands are entirely in Italian. See example (25). This kind of asymmetry – in which NP EL islands occur much more frequently when Swiss German, and not Italian, is the ML – has been reported in other Italian–Swiss German corpora (see Table 19.2; Schmid, 2005).

22. Italian ML, mixed NP: Italian DET + Swiss German N (N=9/13, 69%)
    E' sempre buono avere <u>una</u> **Uusbildig** [INDEF.F.S education.F]
    'It's always good to have <u>some education</u>.' [professional training]

23. Italian ML, Swiss German NP EL island: (N=4/13, 31%)
    ... **susch     die       anderä in America** bevevano
    ... otherwise the.PL other.PL in America drink.3PL.IMPERF
    tutti il vino            col chiaccio
    all.PL the.M wine.M      with/the.M.SG. ice
    'otherwise the others in America drink all the wine with ice'

24. Swiss German ML, mixed NP: German DET + Italian N (N=4/32, 12.5%)
    Hei, verzell ämol was isch gsii mit em **maiale**
    hey tell.IMP once what be.3SG be.PASTPART with the.M.DAT pig
    'Hey, tell [us] again what happened with <u>the pig</u>.'

25. Swiss German ML, Italian NP EL Island (N=28/32, 87.5%)
    Vo mir       uus gseeh,     **gli Americani**      sind ächli Banausä
    from me.DAT out see.PASTPART the.M.PL Americans.M.PL be.3PL a bit
    ignorant.PL
    'From my point of view, <u>[the] Americans</u> are ignorant.'

**Table 19.2** *Italian–Swiss German asymmetry: mixed NPs vs. NP EL islands (Perziosa-Di Quinzio, 1992, corpus)*

| ML | Mixed NP | NP EL island |
|---|---|---|
| Italian | 9/13 (69%) | 4/13 (31%) |
|  | (Italian Det+German N/N-bar) | (Full German NPs) |
| Swiss German | 4/32 (12.5%) | 28/32 (87.5%) |
|  | (German Det+Italian N/N-bar) | (Full Italian NPs) |

The asymmetry in distribution in mixed NPs and NP EL Islands is easily explained if the level in the language production model at which German determiners become available is considered. Of course the role of the ML vs. the EL also plays a part. But we suggest that German determiners are always only available at the level of the formulator in language production. In contrast, Italian determiners are available at the level of the Mental Lexicon.

In both languages, *phi*-features include grammatical gender: Italian nouns are masculine or feminine; German nouns are masculine, feminine, or neuter. This means that definiteness and the *phi*-features of person, number, and gender of determiners in both Italian and Swiss German are present at the lemma level (Mental Lexicon), when directly elected nouns indirectly elect determiners to realize speaker intentions. But the actual *form* of determiners realizing *phi*-features of German depends on case assignment. That is, in German, case features on determiners cannot be "spelled out" until structural and lexical information *outside the NP that includes determiners* is available. This information is only available when German verbs and prepositions assign case to determiners. And, according to the Differential Access Hypothesis, this information about case, an outsider late system morpheme, occurs only when larger constituents are assembled at the level of the formulator.

Thus, we hypothesize that if Italian features to encode a determiner are available, Italian is more likely to supply the determiner than is the German counterpart. With Italian determiners, there are fewer directions to the formulator and less congruence checking between NPs and the larger constituent that governs them. Italian DPs do not have overt case, a feature that is not available until the formulator. This means psycholinguistic costs are less for Italian determiners, which do not have to involve the formulator to realize their *phi*-features. When German is the ML, it can build DPs with German determiners and Italian nouns, but German determiners involve congruence checking at the formulator where case is available. Thus, German DPs are 'costly.' Further, we can assume the speaker wishes to make available the Italian nouns that convey his/her intentions. This can be done through building Italian EL islands rather than 'waiting for' mixed DPs with German determiners. Thus, Italian EL islands are the main type of CS in this corpus when German is the ML. This leads to the observed distribution regarding mixed DPs, many with Italian determiners, few with German ones.

### 19.5.2 A unified explanation for bilingual DPs

Note that the same general production model can account for the observed asymmetries in Spanish–English CS and Italian–Swiss German CS.

Projecting Spanish and Italian determiners is not very costly; but in both German and English, the grammar does not refer to *phi*-features until the level of the formulator and this is what adds complexity to the production process and therefore a cost. In English, *phi*-features are not relevant until the formulator sends directions that ensure matching between the *phi*-features that have to do with agreement in the NP and larger constituents, as in subject–verb agreement or reflexive pronouns. This involves procedures at the formulator. In German, having to determine case assignment prior to realization of determiners makes it even more costly for German to supply determiners in mixed DPs. This analysis provides a unified explanation for what occurs in CS. It also makes predictions for other language pairs based on the relative roles of *phi*-features and agreement and case-assignment procedures in the ML and EL. Based on the level at which the elements that underlie mixed DPs are salient and available in production, we can predict that the language where 'definiteness' first is available and whose structure building does not involve the formulator is the more likely candidate for supplying determiners to the DP.

This comprehensive approach employing the notion of ML contrasts with MacSwan's (2000) reliance on *phi*-features alone to determine which language supplies determiners in DPs in Spanish–English CS (see Jake, Myers-Scotton, & Gross, 2002). His assumptions would result in three unsupported, and conflicting, predictions for the Italian–Swiss German data from the Perziosa-Di Quinzio (1992) corpus we examined. First, his prediction would be German should provide more determiners than Italian with German nouns because not only does German have the same number of *phi*-features as Italian, but it also has case. Instead, there are even more Italian EL islands; recall 28/32, or 87.5%, when Swiss German is the ML. Second, there should be German determiners with Italian nouns or N-bars, but instead, there are very few (4/32, or 12.5%) in this corpus. Even when German is the ML, projecting determiners is costly. Finally, there also should be many full German NPs (EL islands) when Italian is the ML (similar to the many Italian NP (EL) islands when German is the ML) but, as noted, this is not the case; only 4/13, or 31%, of German NPs occur with German determiners (as German EL islands) when Italian is the ML.

Simply put, an analysis such as in MacSwan (2000) overpredicts German determiners and full German NPs at the expense of Italian, regardless of ML. It does not happen. Instead, analyses of NPs in bilingual clauses must take into account how morphemes realizing *phi*-features become salient at different levels of production and interact with directions from the formulator building larger constituents in the ML. Because Italian can project determiners without sending additional directions to the formulator, it costs less for full NPs in Italian to occur in German-framed clauses.

Moreover, it is essentially free for Italian to supply the determiners for German nouns when it is the ML.

In sum, this section of the chapter has suggested that there is flexibility across *languages* in the extent to which predicate–argument structure becomes salient along with lexical–conceptual structure. This is in line with the Abstract Level model and is evident in the distribution of Spanish–English DPs. Perhaps even more important is the claim of the Differential Access Hypothesis that all morphemes are not salient at the level of the Mental Lexicon. Instead, late system morphemes, especially outsiders, are not available in either English (in the Spanish–English corpus) or Swiss German (Italian–Swiss German corpus) until their form is spelled out when case and subject–verb agreement are structurally assigned at the level of the formulator. Yes, their slot is conceptually activated at the lexical-conceptual level, but it is only at the formulator that predicate–argument structures are mapped on to surface level morphological realization patterns, and this is what makes *phi*-features in German and English structurally salient.

## 19.6 Code-switching between clauses

The analysis of language production exemplified throughout this chapter makes predictions regarding relative costs of producing certain morpheme types from one language, the EL, within the grammatical frame of another, the ML. We now examine how the principles of our analysis make predictions for the connectors that occur between clauses in CS.

Subordinators, complementizers, and conjunctions allow one clause to be connected with another. Of particular interest is the language of the elements connecting clauses and the ML of the clauses they connect. Sometimes the connector comes from the EL, and not the language of the clause it introduces. Further, there are asymmetries in terms of when an EL connector can introduce a clause in the ML. We examine the production costs of several types of connected clauses and show how more complex structures are disfavored and less complex structures are favored.

CS involving two types of subordination, adverbial subordinators and sentential complementizers, such as English "that" and Spanish *que,* are considered first. For ease of discussion, we refer to adverbial subordinators as simply subordinators and sentential complementizers as simply complementizers. After discussing some examples of CS involving conjunctions, CS involving two typologically different languages is considered, Ecuadorian Quichua and Spanish. CS between clauses involving this language pair provides evidence for how complexity impacts outcomes in CS and may even promote structures of the EL, Spanish in this case, at the expense of the ML, Quichua.

## 19.6.1 Adverbial subordinators

Adverbial subordinators add optional thematic structure to the matrix clause like other optional thematic adjuncts; for example, *before* and *after* clauses provide optional thematic roles such as *place* and *time*. Similarly, *because* clauses add *reason* or *purpose* thematic information. While these subordinate clauses are not part of the theta-grid of the matrix clause, they expand its thematic structure much like optional adjunct prepositional phrases; the subordinators themselves clarify the thematic role added. In some languages, subordinators are directly elected content morphemes. As such, they can and do come from the EL as well as the ML.

Subordinators contribute thematic structure in two ways. First, as noted above, adverbial subordinators, such as *because,* spell out the thematic role (e.g., reason or cause) a subordinate clause has in the higher clause and make clear how the clause fits into the thematic structure of the matrix clause. Second, many elements that mark clause boundaries also convey added meaning because they indicate how conceptual information is tied to the larger context of an utterance and point to the more complete meaning. Wilson and Sperber (1993, 2012) and other relevance theory analysts (see, e.g., Blakemore, 2002), refer to this added meaning as procedural knowledge. They suggest that specific words provide evidence for the addressee in understanding the speaker's meaning; such words point to a concept involved in the meaning the speaker is trying to convey.

Of interest to clause boundaries are words, acting as pointers, that tell how the parts of an utterance are to be related and that such pointers can result in a clustering effect of the word with other non-verbal pointers, including prosody, intonation, as well as other overt discourse particles. As such, they provide added meaning at the pragmatic level. We make the assumption that elements such as subordinators that connect clauses often function as pragmatic pointers. Thus, subordinators are relevant to the thematic structure of an utterance because they add optional thematic structure in a conceptual sense, and they add pragmatic or procedural meaning to how the parts of an utterance are connected and how the utterance is connected to the speaker's intentions and the larger real-world, or pragmatic, experience of the interlocutors. In this way, adverbial subordinators add to and direct the inferencing process for the addressee.

According to the 4-M model of morpheme classification, subordinators in many languages are content morphemes because they assign thematic roles. Thus, we predict that in many language pairs, a subordinator can introduce a clause entirely in the other language. See examples (26) and (27) from Pfaff (1979), which we discuss elsewhere (Jake & Myers-Scotton, 2009). In (26) *porque* introduces a clause entirely in English; in (27), *because* introduces a clause in Spanish. Jake and Myers-Scotton (2009) also discuss examples of Haitian Creole–English CS and Xhosa–English CS that illustrate that either language can provide an adverbial subordinator that introduces a subordinate clause in the other language.

26. Spanish–English (Pfaff, 1979: 312)
    trabajé            menos porque **then I didn't know some of his business**
    work.PRET.1S       less because       then I didn't know some of his business
    'I worked less because then I didn't know some of his business.'

27. Spanish–English (Pfaff, 1979: 312)
    **Como** here you can because **viven todos juntos**
    'Like here you can because (they) live altogether.'

In terms of our argument that the cost of switching can be overridden when the benefits of the switch outweigh the cost, the case of adverbials is instructive. In the language pairs noted above, the addition of an optional thematic role, together with the extra pragmatic meaning added by the overt connection encoded by a subordinator, contributes to the benefits of switching. At the same time, switching only involves morphemes that are activated by the speaker's intentions at the conceptual level. That is, the activated content morphemes do not send directions to the formulator that activate other morphemes relevant to their realization at the functional level. In terms of the production model, there is little cost.

However, the benefits of switching a subordinator do not always outweigh the costs because of the complexity of the relationship between some subordinators and the clause they introduce. This, as predicted, depends on the languages involved in CS. Consider Arabic–English CS. Although Arabic subordinators are directly elected by speakers' intentions at the conceptual level, they are inflected with outsider late system morphemes agreeing with the lower clause subject. That is, agreement morphemes identifying the subject of the subordinate clause occur as suffixes on subordinators. Such late system morphemes add complexity to subordination in Arabic because the realization of Arabic subordinators requires additional directions to be sent to the formulator.

In examples (28) and (29), Arabic subordinators introduce English subordinate clauses. In both cases, the Arabic subordinator is suffixed with morphology identifying the lower clause subject. In example (29), an Arabic pronoun *hummi* 'they' also occurs under COMP. Elsewhere Myers-Scotton, Jake, and Okasha (1996) have discussed pronoun doubling, as in (29), in Arabic–English CS: the English pronoun is in argument position within the IP clause and the Arabic pronoun is topicalized under COMP.

28. Palestinian Arabic–English (Okasha, 1999: 112)
    Lamma raaḥat libnaan **she got a lot of attention**    liʔanha **she was natural**
    When go.PERF.3 F Lebanon she got a lot of attention because.3 F she was natural
    'when she went to Lebanon she got a lot of attention because she was natural.'

29. Palestinian Arabic–English (Okasha, 1999: 98)
    **I envy them** li?anhum hummi **they don't care**
    I envy them because.3P they don't care
    'I envy them because they don't care.'

While Arabic subordinators can introduce English clauses, English subordinators do not introduce Arabic-framed clauses. Both Eid (1992) and Okasha (1999) note this asymmetry. They report no instances of an English adverbial subordinator, nor of a sentential complementizer, introducing an Arabic-framed clause. The overt agreement on Arabic subordinators li?anha and li?anhum illustrates Arabic subordinators are more complex. However, they are well-formed constituents composed of a content morpheme and a late system morpheme, called by directions the subordinator sends to the formulator. This suggests that the asymmetry, i.e., the absence of English subordinators introducing Arabic-framed clauses, lies elsewhere, not in the complexity of the Arabic subordinator itself.

Arabic, unlike English, is a null-subject language; its extensive verbal agreement morphemes match the strong *phi*-features of person, number, and gender. In contrast, as noted above in the section on Spanish–English DPs, English *phi*-features are weak and consequently, they do not license null pronouns. Subjects of English finite clauses are always realized at the functional and surface levels. In Arabic, there appears to be another aspect to this parametric, or typological, difference from English. There is further checking of the *phi*-features of a subject with the subordinator in COMP. This adds complexity to the relationship between Arabic elements in COMP and lower clause subjects, complexity in terms of an added *phi*-feature checking operation that is absent in English.

However, the fact that seemingly more simple English subordinators like *because* do not occur with Arabic-framed clauses suggests the complexity in checking is based on the *phi*-features of Arabic subject–verb agreement within the IP clause trying to check outside of the maximal projection, and not vice versa. As noted above, in terms of the cost of switching between a subordinator and the grammatical frame of a clause, Arabic subordinators should not be especially costly. This is because they are EL islands and because the affix on the subordinator is based on procedural meaning, which indexes a nominal of an utterance in a specific discourse and pragmatic context. In contrast, the checking of verb agreement *phi*-features is syntactic; the *phi*-features of the subject must match those of the verb.

The asymmetry in Arabic–English CS involving subordinators provides evidence for the distinction between pragmatic indexing and grammatical checking. When Arabic is the ML of the clause, there is apparently an added complexity; the strong *phi*-features within the clause check *phi*-features of elements under COMP as well as elements within the clause. In this way, the

ML, Arabic, sets the grammatical frame of the entire CP, not just the IP subordinate clause introduced by the subordinator. This means there are no mixed CPs in which an English EL subordinator occurs with an Arabic ML clause. Checking at the level of the formulator outside of the IP is too costly.

In contrast, when English is the ML of the clause, weak *phi*-features in the clause do not look up, or outside of, the clause, and consequently, speaker intentions at the conceptual level and procedural knowledge permit construction of a well-formed Arabic EL constituent under COMP composed of the directly elected subordinator and the late system morphemes indexing the subject of the English-framed clause. In terms of the formulator, checking within the clause and within the COMP is less costly than checking features across the entire CP.

### 19.6.2 Sentential complementizers

Conventional wisdom is that sentential complementizers like *that* do not add additional semantic and pragmatic information to realize a speaker's intentions. However, as noted above in the discussion of subordinators, recent proposals within relevance theory suggest elements overtly marking boundaries play a role in creating meaning because they point to larger constituents. We assume sentential complementizers mark a more complex structure for ease of processing by the addressee. In this sense, sentential complementizers are like subordinators. However, they are also different from subordinations because, under the 4-M model, *that*-type complementizers are bridge system morphemes because they do not assign additional thematic roles. Nevertheless, complementizers do introduce arguments, primarily themes, at the clause level. Examples (30)–(31) illustrate that a Spanish complementizer can introduce an English clause and an English complementizer can introduce a Spanish clause.

30. Spanish–English (Pfaff, 1979: 314)
    'It goes without saying I think **que** [that] along with the picketing we are doing a boycott.'

31. Spanish–English (Pfaff, 1979: 312)
    They sell so much of it that **lo están sacando y** many people ...
    'The sell so much of it that they're taking it out and many people ... '

Even though the System Morpheme Principle of the MLF model does not block EL bridge complementizers in CS, the Uniform Structure Principle preferences ML structure-providing options in CS. In terms of structure, the function of complementizers is to build larger structures through subordination of one clause to another. However, they contribute procedural meaning as acting as overt indicators of this more complex structure.

Because speakers' intentions do not call bridge system morphemes at the conceptual level, and because they are called when the matrix clause sends directions to the formulator, the prediction is that most bridge complementizers will come from the same language as the complement clause. This prediction is borne out by Pfaff's (1979) data, as well as data from other Spanish–English corpora, such as Milian (1995); the language of the complementizer is more frequently the language of the complement clause.

However, as illustrated by examples (30) and (31) above, EL complementizers do occur. Although a complementizer such as *que* is a bridge, as a marker of procedural meaning, it can add other meaning within a discourse. Linguists working with naturally occurring CS data have pointed out that complementizers such as *que* often add social meaning. As such, this benefit can outweigh the cost of a switch between the language of Complementizer and the ML of the subordinate clause, For example (30) above illustrates what Pfaff (1979: 314) refers to as a solidarity marking function of Spanish discourse including complementizer "function words" in Spanish–English CS in the USA.

The case of Spanish–English CS illustrates how the cost of calling a bridge system morpheme in the EL can be offset by the benefit of drawing attention to a complex structure or marking solidarity. However, what happens in CS regarding complementizers is predicted to vary depending on the language pair. Languages mark sentential complements in various ways; a nominalization strategy is considered later in section 19.6.4. Further, languages have different types of restrictions on complementizers, and this can lead to asymmetries in their distributions in CS. For example, in English, most bridge complementizers are optional. In other languages, such complementizers are always required. This is the case for Arabic. Elsewhere we have discussed this difference between CS in subordinate clauses in Chichewa–English CS: Chichewi *kuti* 'that' can introduce an English-framed clause, but English *that* cannot introduce a Chichewa-framed clause (Jake & Myers-Scotton, 2009). Such distributional constraints may make it more complex to call a complementizer in a language different from the ML of the complement clause.

As was the case with Arabic subordinators discussed above, Arabic complementizers are co-indexed with the subject of the complement clause; see examples (32)–(34). The complementizer agrees with the *phi*-features of the lower clause subject, whether the ML of the complement clause is Arabic (see the bilingual clause in (32), or English, as in (33) and (34)). And, as was the case with subordinators, there is an asymmetry: English complementizers do not introduce Arabic-framed complement clauses.

32. Palestinian Arabic–English (Okasha, 1999: 72)
    ma ba9ti?id         ?inni-k **worried** bas ?inti **curious**
    no HAB.IMPF.think.1s    that-2F worried but you curious
    'I don't think that [you are] worried, but you [are] curious.'

33. Palestinian Arabic–English (Okasha, 1999: 71)
    kaan          el-**doctor**    yišuk                    ?innu **it is not reliable**
    PERF.3M.BE    the-doctor       IMPERF.3M.doubt that.3M  it is not reliable
    '[he] was, the doctor, doubting that it was not reliable.'

34. Palestinian Arabic–English (Okasha,1998: 71)
    Mneeh      ?inn-ek **you are doing something you like**
    good       that-2M you are doing something you like
    '[it is] good that you are doing something you like.'

The same explanation for this asymmetry in distribution of subordinators can be advanced for complementizers. The *phi*-features of the subject of an Arabic subordinate clause looks for *phi*-features on the complementizer in COMP. The form of Arabic sentential complementizers is determined by procedural indexing instead of syntactic checking. Although the Arabic complementizer is affixed with late system morphemes, the entire construction occurs under COMP, as a constituent entirely realized in Arabic. As EL islands, they are well-formed constituents. The absence of English complementizers introducing Arabic-framed clauses receives a parallel explanation as well. If Arabic is the ML, it continues to direct *phi*-feature checking under the entire CP of the clause, not just the IP of the clause, and this syntactic checking can only be satisfied if the features within the IP also match the features under COMP. However, English complementizers lack such features, so the cost is too great.

### 19.6.3 Conjunctions

In the CS literature analyzing naturally occurring bilingual conversations, there are many examples of conjunctions from one language introducing a clause from another. Under the 4-M model, conjunctions are conceptually activated content morphemes that provide information for the addressee to use in interpreting the larger meaning of an utterance. As such, unless there are language-specific directions sent to the formulator which make the occurrence of a conjunction more complex, a conjunction from one language should be able to introduce a clause in another if the additional meaning is sufficient to compensate for the cost of the conjunction being in a language different from the ML of its conjuncts. This prediction is at least partly confirmed, as illustrated by the analysis of conjunctions in Bantu languages–English CS and Spanish–English CS in Jake and Myers-Scotton (2009). In example (35), a Spanish conjunction *pero* 'but' introduces a clause in English. There should be little cost to this switching, and in fact, if the speaker's intention is to maintain the bilingual mode, insertion of a conjunction that is a directly elected content morpheme from another language may promote switching.

35. Spanish–English (Pfaff, 1979: 312)
    No voy      tanto como   iba     pero    **I still believe in it, you know**
    'I don't go as much as   I went  but     I still believe in it, you know.'

A priori, a speaker's intentions should determine the choice of language of a conjunction at the conceptual level, regardless of the ML of the following clause. However, the ML may be preferred, especially in certain social settings. In Spanish–English CS, Spanish conjunctions can freely introduce English clauses. However, English conjunctions rarely introduce Spanish clauses, reflecting, as Pfaff (1979: 313) notes, "the tendency (not constraint)" that such forms "be realized in Spanish even in predominately English sentences." An exception to this tendency is the more frequently occurring *so*. Lipski (2005: 12) presents a largely social explanation: "English – the ... language of evaluation, criticism, and correction – is used to set off ... or highlight discourse ... in Spanish." Other linguists have suggested that *so* is a discourse marker that has been borrowed into varieties of Spanish spoken in the USA.

36. Spanish–English (Lipski, 2005: 11)
    Siempre me ha      gustado estudiar
    [always me have.3s please.PASTPART study-INF
    **so** creo           que eso     me va a ayudar
    so believe.1s.PRES that that.3s.N me go.3s.PRES to help.INF
    'I have always enjoyed studying so I believe that it is going to help me.'

In Arabic–English CS, Arabic can provide a conjunction before an English clause, as shown in (37). In example (38), an Arabic conjunction occurs between two English clauses. In (38), an Arabic topic pronoun hiyyi ('her') occurs as well. In fact, in Okasha's (1999) Generation I data, Arabic conjunctions introduce English clauses more frequently than they introduce Arabic-framed clauses. For example, the conjunctions *bas* 'but' and *laakin* 'however,' occur 25 times introducing an English clause out of 40 total occurrences.

37. Palestinian Arabic–English (Okasha, 1999)
    ?ana      bat9ala? bilbait **bas I can move from this house**
    I HAB.IMPF.1s.attach to.the.house but I can move from this house.
    'I get attached to the house but I can move from this house.'

38. Arabic-English (Okasha, 1999: 119)
    they had a wedding in Canada **wa hiyyi** she had a wedding for herself and her family in Egypt ...
    'they had a wedding in Canada and she, she had a wedding for herself and her family in Egypt ... '

In theory, an English conjunction should be able to occur with an Arabic ML clause because English conjunctions are directly elected content morphemes and there do not appear to be added ML conditions that would disfavor switching. However, Okasha (1999) reports in her

Arabic–English data, only Arabic supplies the conjunction. In her data, in all instances where the language of the conjunction is different from the language of the following clause, only English clauses are introduced by Arabic conjunctions. Eid (1992: 55) also reports this asymmetry in her Arabic–English CS data; she concludes "that switching ... is restricted after the conjunction if the conjunction is English." However, in other Arabic CS datasets, there is no such asymmetry and some switching of an EL conjunction before an Arabic clause is reported. For example, Redouane (2005) notes that French conjunctions before Arabic-framed clauses occur in the speech of Moroccan Arabic–French speakers, although the switches are not frequent. Redouane notes that these results are similar to those reported in Bentahila and Davies (1983).

39. Moroccan Arabic-French CS (Redouane, 2005: 1928).
    ila bʁiti nduːz ʕlik **et** nmshiw **ensemble**
    'if you want me to pass by you and we go together.'

The examples considered above illustrate how the cost of switching the conjunction between clauses can be overridden when the conjunction conveys social or pragmatic functions; conjunctions can contribute information regarding the speaker's attitudes and affiliations in a particular bilingual context. Use of Arabic or Spanish conjunctions mark speaker identification with the minority language in a largely English-speaking context. Similarly, French conjunctions signal different affiliations in a Moroccan Arabic–French CS context.

In terms of production costs, because conjunctions are content morphemes in many languages, there should be little cost when an EL conjunction occurs before a clause framed in a different language. However, election of many EL conjunctions is less likely than other content morphemes because they contribute less thematic information to a clause. Still, some conjunctions are also discourse markers signaling contrast or consequence as well as conjunction or disjunction, as is the case of *so* in Spanish–English CS. This added discourse meaning provides a benefit in switching conjunctions, especially in contexts where the ML–EL relationship among clauses in specific utterances contrasts with cultural identity and language dominance. In such situations, EL discourse markers may signal solidarity among minority-group members. Apparently such benefits outweigh the cost of switching in Arabic–English CS in the USA, where Arabic conjunctions dominate.

### 19.6.4 Subordinators and conjunctions in Quichua–Spanish CS

To conclude this section, we note that morphemes connecting clauses can be elected in different ways. Thus far, we have considered subordinators and conjunctions that are content morphemes, although some may send directions to the formulator to realize additional, late system morphemes, such as Arabic subordinators. We have also considered independently occurring bridge *that*-type sentential complementizers. Again, in Arabic, these complementizers send directions to the formulator to realize additional morphemes. One CS language pair in which there are typological, parametric differences between the languages is Quechua–Spanish. For example, in the Quechua language family, the verbs of subordinate clauses, both adverbial clauses and sentential complements, are nominalized and subordination is indicated by an indirectly elected affix. However, the form and distribution of such affixes depend on additional directions sent to the formulator by other elements within the clause. Thus, while they are conceptually salient, their form is only available at the functional level.

Elsewhere we have discussed how lack of congruence regarding subordinators and conjunctions in Ecuadorian Quichua and Spanish promotes Spanish subordinators and complementizers in CS (Jake & Myers-Scotton, 2009). The influence of Spanish on Quichua structure in CS has led to contact varieties referred to as Media Lengua (Muysken, 1997). We have noted that in Quichua–Spanish CS, many Spanish subordinators, complementizers, and conjunctions occur. We have argued that such forms are conceptually and structurally salient, especially in contrast to the ML, Quichua. These forms are clause-initial in Spanish, but occur in final position in Quichua, an SOV postpositional language. Further, Spanish subordination does not alter the grammatical structure of clauses; in Quichua, sentential complements and adverbial subordinate clauses are nominalized. The verb no longer agrees with the subject and instead occurs with an aspect-encoding nominalizing suffix. Thus, subordination in Quichua involves more complexity in terms of directions sent to the formulator. In Quichua, there is checking for finiteness and other grammatical features between the subordinate clause and its matrix clause. Thus, the small cost of activating an EL content morpheme at the conceptual level in Spanish is offset by a reduction in checking in the ML. The prediction is that such Spanish morphemes will occur in Quichua–Spanish CS; this prediction is borne out, as is illustrated below.

In Quichua, subordinators are essentially case postpositions expressing the thematic role of the subordinate clause. The postpositions are not realized until directions to the formulator have specified other information, such as aspect; see monolingual example in (40) in which the ablative case -*manda* is suffixed onto the nominalized verb.

40. Monolingual Imbabura Quichua (Jake & Myers-Scotton, 2009: 236)
    cai tucu-shca-mi           cai amaru   ri-shca-manda ...
    this happen-FAR.PAST-VAL   this snake go-PAST.NOM-ABLA ...
    'this was happening because the snake went ...'

While the suffix -*manda* is directly elected to further realize the speaker's intentions, its occurrence depends on other directions being sent to the formulator that inhibit late outsider system morphemes, i.e., finite verb agreement. In Spanish, however, subordinators are salient at the conceptual level and are directly elected content morphemes, occurring in discourse prominent initial position. Their form does not depend on directions sent to the formulator activating other morphemes or inhibiting any morphemes. Thus, Spanish subordinators are less costly in terms of production. They are content morphemes whose realization depends only on information available at the lexical conceptual level. See (41) in which Spanish *porque* introduces a subordinate clause with Quichua as the ML.

41. Imbabura Quichua–Spanish Chaupi-Lengua (Jake & Myers-Scotton, 2009: 236)
    cai **sucedi**-ju-shca     **porque** cai **culebra**     ri-shca ...
    this happen-PROG-FAR.PAST  because this snake   go-PAST.NOM ...
    'this was happening because the snake went ...'

Like subordinators, in monolingual Quichua, conjunctions are suffixes and are affixed after the verb. While Quichua conjunctions may be salient at the conceptual level, their form is not available until the verbal complex is constructed, that is, after directions have been sent to the formulator regarding tense, aspect, and agreement. While the conjunction itself is not a late system morpheme, its form depends on late system morphemes, and as such its inherent cost is higher than the cost of Spanish conjunctions, which are directly elected content morphemes that are simply inserted before a sentential conjunct. In (42), for example, the coordinator is the suffix -*pash* after the finite verb, inflected for a third-person subject. Compare (42) with (43), in which Spanish *y* occurs in place of the suffix -*pash*. The insertion of clause-initial Spanish subordinators and conjunctions has additional consequences for the structure of Quichua–Spanish CS. In (43), for example, the subject occurs after the verb, as might be expected in a Spanish intransitive clause, and would not occur in monolingual SOV Quichua clauses.

42. Monolingual Imbabura Quichua: (Jake & Myers-Scotton, 2009: 237)
    picha runa-ta-ca       yali-y       ri-rca-pash-mi
    five people-ACC-TOP    pass-NOM     go-3s.PAST-ALSO/CONJ-VAL
    'and more than five people went ...'

43. Imbabura Quichua–Spanish (Jake & Myers-Scotton, 2009: 237)
    **y** ri-rca **más de** pichag       **persona-s**-cuna ...
    and go-FIN.PASt more than five       people-PL-PL ...
    'and more than five people went ...'

A final example from Quichua–Spanish CS may illustrate a commonality between the high frequency of Spanish subordinators in Quichua–Spanish

CS and the asymmetry of subordinators in Arabic–English CS. Recall that Arabic clauses are not introduced by English subordinators and complementizers and that Arabic subordinators and complementizers agree with the lower clause subject. This agreement reflects an inherent complexity of Arabic clauses – a requirement to check for agreement in the entire CP, including elements in COMP, not just the IP clause introduced by the subordinator or complementizer. The cost of checking between the subordinate clause and COMP is avoided if the complementizer clause is framed in English. Moreover, if an English subordinator or subordinator introduced an Arabic clause, checking between the lower clause and elements in COMP would have to be inhibited, also an added cost.

Similarly, one type of inherent complexity in Quechua languages seems to promote occurrence of Spanish subordinators in Quichua–Spanish CS. In Quechua languages, the verbs of purpose clauses and co-temporaneous adverbials are marked for co-reference and switch reference with their matrix clause subjects. If the subject of the subordinate clause is the same as the subject of the matrix clause, one suffix occurs; if the subject is different, another suffix occurs. However, in Ecuadorian Quichua–Spanish CS, Quichua verbs are unmarked for co-/switch-reference when introduced by a Spanish subordinator. See (44) below in which *como que* 'as/when' introduces a Quichua-framed clause. In a monolingual Quichua clause, *-jpi* 'while, switch-reference form' would be suffixed to the verb, as in (45). In example (44), the Quichua verb in the clause introduced by the Spanish subordinator is finite. Thus, a more complex ML procedure, inhibition of agreement dependent on checking subject co-indexing, is avoided and a simpler structure results.

44. Quichua–Spanish CS (Jake, 2001)
    **y más o menos a las 4** chishi-pi-mi        ricu.shca **y** oya-shca
    and more or less at [the] 4 afternoon.loc-val see-pst and hear-pst
    **como que** tamia.grí.n
    how that rain-INCHOA-3SG
    'and at more or less four in the afternoon [she] saw and heard [something], as it starts to rain.'

45. Quichua–Spanish with expected switch-reference morphology:
    . . . ricu.shca **y** oya-shca        tamia-grí-jpi-ca
    . . . see-pst and hear-pst        rain-inchoa-ing.sw.ref-top
    '[she] saw and heard [something] as it started to rain.'

In terms of cost, direct election of Spanish subordinators in constructions like (44) reduces the need for suspending one kind of *phi*-feature checking – that of subject–verb agreement in Quichua subordinate clauses – and the addition of another kind of *phi*-feature checking – the checking of features between matrix and subordinate clause subjects. Further, the directly elected subordinator introducing the subordinate clause does not interact with the independently directed subject–verb agreement of main clauses in Quichua. Overall, this canonical checking is simpler than a doubling of checking procedures; moreover, the clause-initial discourse emphatic properties of Spanish subordinators further promote switching and presumably pay for its cost.

Examples from Ecuadorian Quichua–Spanish CS illustrate one possible consequence of switching an EL subordinator or conjunction. In this case, the Spanish EL morphemes are directly elected, while the ML morphemes depend on activation of other late system morphemes for their form. In brief, Spanish structure is creeping into Quichua in the bilingual mode because the psycholinguistic cost of signaling relations between clauses using Spanish is a bargain in terms of processing costs; they do not depend on additional directions sent to the formulator. Moreover, clause-initial Spanish subordinators and conjunctions are more salient as discourse markers, pointers to procedural knowledge used to connect the utterance to real-world meaning. The restructuring observed in Quichua–Spanish CS further illustrates one cost of CS that cannot be ignored – the need to preserve a coherent grammatical frame for every clause. In the case of Ecuadorian Quichua–Spanish CS, the benefit of switching is paid for by an alternate grammatical structure in Quichua.

## 19.7 Conclusion

When the speech of bilinguals contains intrasentential code-switching, this conveys at least two messages to linguists. First, what these speakers want to say is better conveyed in part by employing two languages. Second, the linguistic elements they use in one language vs. the other depend partly on the relative costs of switching. The ML will dominate in the key structure-building in any bilingual clause, but not necessarily in more peripheral constructions.

In this chapter we go behind surface-level asymmetries in the distribution of either particular lexical elements or the participating languages themselves in certain constructions in bilingual clauses from naturally occurring CS. Altogether, we examine three categories of asymmetry. First, we suggest that while ML finite verbs occur in CS, the EL verbs that occur are nonfinite verbs. We argue that EL nonfinite verbs carry less cost than EL finite verbs because nonfinite verbs undergo congruence checking only at the lexical–conceptual level of abstract lexical structure to ensure they satisfy the speaker's intentions. In this regard, they contrast with EL finite verbs that intrinsically carry directions for EL predicate–argument structure. Such verbs would add complexity because of the congruence checking with ML material that they would call for. Although the System Morpheme Principle ensures outsider late system morphemes from the EL cannot occur, other directions to the formulator are also too costly. These include mapping thematic roles onto argument structure. Thus, nonfinite verbs are streamlined; they cost little to appear either in finite verb slots or as predicates of the 'do' verb in the 'do construction.'

Second, we consider determiners in mixed Determiner Phrases (DPs) and also of EL islands in CS involving two language pairs, Spanish–English and Italian–Swiss German. We point to quantitative evidence that there is an asymmetry regarding the language of determiners in these bilingual DPs that favors Spanish and Italian respectively. This asymmetry is related to differences in the languages regarding the abstract levels at which their *phi*-features that underlie determiners are available. Because the *phi*-feature of gender is available at the lexical conceptual level in both Spanish and Italian, these languages frequently supply the determiners for the bilingual DPs in CS. The feature of 'definiteness' is available in both English and Swiss German at the lexical–conceptual level, but these languages must also check agreement features at the level of the formulator. Thus, the structures they project for determiners are more complex than those for Spanish and Italian. In CS, the less complex structure is preferred because its production is less costly. Therefore, determiners from Spanish and Italian win out more often in the bilingual CPs we study. That is, they can make 'definiteness' in determiners available with less cost than languages that require interaction with the formulator (English and Swiss German respectively). Also, selection of determiners depends on which language is the ML, reflecting a basic asymmetry in bilingual clauses identified by the MLF model. To put it briefly, constructions relying on some structure building at the level of predicate–argument structure (involving the formulator) involve more complexity and therefore are less frequent in CS. Grammatical constructions that rely on activation only at the lexical–conceptual level involve less complex procedures and promote less cost and therefore are more likely in CS.

Third, we consider CS patterns that include elements connecting one clause with another, exemplifying the discussion with CS involving various language pairs, especially Spanish–English, Arabic–English, and Ecuadorian Quichua–Spanish. In some language pairs, adverbial subordinators, sentential complementizers, and conjunctions from either language should occur because they are content morphemes, but language specific features can impact the relative cost of switching. Sometimes complexity can promote EL connectors introducing clauses with a different ML. The unequal status of subordinators and conjunctions in typologically different languages, as in Quichua–Spanish CS, also plays a role in determining complexity of structures connecting clauses, and this impacts CS between clauses.

Overall, then, our analysis points to differences at abstract structural levels between the languages and language-specific constructions that underlie speakers' choices. In turn, we relate these differences to the production costs that preference choosing one language or one structure over another. In summary, we can make this generalization: constructions that require interaction with the formulator are more costly. Such constructions usually involve content morphemes that send directions to the formulator to activate late system morphemes. These late system morphemes are critical to building larger grammatical constituents (bridges do this) or in making relationships more transparent by co-indexing them in various ways (outsiders do this). In CS, the cost of complexity is not a problem if it is ML procedures that are involved with assigning late system morphemes to the formulator. What are avoided as costly are EL procedures that would involve late system morphemes, especially outsider late system morphemes that are involved with co-indexing. EL constructions sometimes do override the dominance of the ML in certain mixed constituents and the Uniform Structure Principle but this only happens if the EL elements have limited complexity. They can do this when elements, such as nonfinite verbs or subordinators or EL islands, do not compete with core argument structure supplied by the ML.

Overall, the abstract level at which an EL element is available is important in predicting whether it will appear in CS. In turn, complexity and its ensuing cost figure in the same equation.

# 20

# Intra-sentential code-switching

Cognitive and neural approaches

Janet G. van Hell, Kaitlyn A. Litcofsky, and Caitlin Y. Ting

## 20.1 Introduction

A unique feature of bilingual speech is that bilinguals often produce utterances that switch between languages, such as "*I ate huevos esta mañana*" "I ate [eggs this morning]." This switching between languages, or code-switching, has been shown to occur in various natural discourse situations. Listeners who overhear bilinguals switching back and forth between languages are often impressed by this seemingly effortless switching between the two languages. Code-switching in a natural discourse situation is one of the few forms of language behavior that overtly reflect that bilinguals have both languages active to some extent, and that they are able to dynamically use one language in some utterances and both languages in others. This merging of two different languages into a coherent utterance not only reveals the flexibility of language processing, but also signifies a highly skilled cognitive control.

The scientific study of code-switching is, therefore, an excellent test bed to examine the cognitive and neural correlates of cross-language interaction in comprehension and production, and the cognitive control mechanisms involved in this process. There is a long tradition of research on code-switching in the field of linguistics that studies the structural properties of code-switching, typically on the basis of linguistic corpora (for reviews, see Bullock & Toribio, 2009; Isurin, Winford, & de Bot, 2009). These corpus-based studies have yielded valuable theories on structural aspects of code-switching (some of which will be discussed below), but largely remained silent on the psychological and neural underpinnings.

On the other hand, cognitive and neurocognitive studies examining switching between languages have mainly focused on the processing of a series of single, unrelated items (e.g., unrelated words, digits, or pictures)

The writing of this chapter was supported by NSF Grants BCS-0955090 and OISE-0968369.

rather than switching between languages in a meaningful utterance (e.g., a sentence). In these studies bilinguals are presented with isolated items that switch between languages across trials (in comprehension tasks) or bilinguals must change the language of their response across non-switch and switch trials (in production tasks); for reviews, see Bobb and Wodniecka (2013) and Abutalebi and Green (2008). As will be discussed in the next section, these studies show that switching between languages incurs a measurable processing cost that is often asymmetric, i.e., larger when switching from the second language (L2) into the first language (L1) than vice versa.

An emergent body of studies seeks to examine the cognitive and neural correlates of language switching in more naturally occurring situations: switching within meaningful sentences, i.e., intra-sentential code-switching. In this chapter we will review in particular cognitive and neurocognitive studies on intra-sentential code-switching (for studies on inter-sentential code-switching, see e.g., Gullifer, Kroll, & Dussias, 2013; Ibáñez, Macizo, & Bajo, 2010). We will also discuss studies that address the question of *why* code-switching occurs and what the cognitive and neural mechanisms are that drive bilinguals to switch into the other language. We will finally review studies that investigated the cognitive underpinnings of a corpus-based linguistic theory of code-switching, namely the triggering theory originally proposed by Clyne (e.g., 1967, 2003). Together these studies attest to the value of integrating linguistic, psycholinguistic, and neurocognitive approaches to gain more insight into the neural and cognitive mechanisms of intra-sentential code-switching in comprehension and production, and into cross-language interaction processes in sentence comprehension and production more generally.

Psycholinguistic and neurocognitive studies often focus on externally induced switches, i.e., non-spontaneous language switches where bilinguals switch languages prompted by an external cue or respond to an externally generated switch (for exceptions, see Broersma, 2011; Gollan & Ferreira, 2009; Kootstra, van Hell, & Dijkstra, 2010). Corpus studies, on the other hand, reflect internally generated switches in natural discourse. Both externally induced switches and internally generated switches enable researchers to address different questions related to language switching that in concert will advance our understanding of one of the most fascinating instances of cross-language interaction (for an excellent discussion see Gullberg, Indefrey, & Muysken, 2009).

Before reviewing the literature on intra-sentential code-switching, we will first briefly discuss empirical studies and theoretical perspectives on language switching in the production and comprehension of unrelated items presented in isolation, on which the current psychological and neurocognitive models of language switching and cognitive control are predominantly based (see Green & Abutalebi, 2013).

## 20.2 Language switch costs when switching between single stimuli

In a seminal language-switching study, Meuter and Allport (1999) asked bilinguals to name a series of single digits alternating between their first language (L1) and second language (L2). The digits were presented one at a time against a colored background, and the color cued the response language (either L1 or L2). Language switches could occur from L1 into L2, or vice versa, and were unpredictable. The bilinguals were either L1 or L2 speakers of English, and spoke one of five other languages (French, German, Italian, Portuguese, or Spanish). The results showed that naming latencies on the switched trials (in which the response language changed from that used in the previous trial) were slower than on the non-switched trials. Interestingly, the language switch costs (defined as the latency difference between the switched and non-switched trials) were asymmetrical: switch costs were larger when switching from the weaker language, L2, into the dominant language, L1, than when switching from the dominant L1 into the weaker L2.

Since the publication of Meuter and Allport's study, numerous studies examined language-switching effects in the naming of single items in unbalanced bilinguals and multilinguals, using behavioral (e.g., Costa, Santesteban, & Ivanova, 2006; Jiang & Forster, 2001; Linck, Schwieter, & Sunderman, 2012; Philipp, Gade, & Koch, 2007; Schwieter & Sunderman, 2008) and neurocognitive (e.g., Christoffels, Firk & Schiller, 2007; Jackson et al., 2001; Verhoef, Roelofs, & Chwilla, 2009) techniques. These studies overwhelmingly report switch costs (which parallels basic findings in the more general task-switching literature; for a review, see Kiesel et al., 2010). Moreover, most studies replicated the finding that switching is most costly when switching from the weaker L2 into the dominant L1 (for more details, see reviews of behavioral (Bobb & Wodniecka, 2013) and neurocognitive (van Hell & Witteman, 2009) studies).

Studies examining the reading of language-switched versus non-switched series of words have also observed switch costs. In contrast to the naming studies, however, the effects in the reading studies are less conclusive with respect to the asymmetry in switch costs: some studies observed that switch costs are not modulated by switch direction (Jackson et al., 2004, ERP data; Macizo, Bajo, & Paolieri, 2012), or are asymmetrical, with larger costs when switching from L2 into L1 (Chauncey, Grainger, & Holcomb, 2008 (N400); Litcofsky et al., 2009), or when switching from L1 into L2 (Alvarez, Holcomb, & Grainger, 2003; Chauncey, Grainger, & Holcomb, 2008 (N250); Jackson et al., 2004, behavioral data).

For example, Jackson et al. (2004) had native English speakers with French, German, or Spanish as their L2 perform a parity judgment task on number words. Bilinguals were presented with a series of single number words in L1 or L2, and had to decide whether the number word was odd or even by pressing one of two buttons. Behaviorally, an asymmetric switch cost was found where it was harder to switch into L1 than L2, but ERP data did not yield clear switching effects in the components typically associated with language switching (including the N2, N400, and Late Positive Complex (LPC)). Later ERP studies measured switching of visually presented words (Alvarez et al., 2003; Chauncey et al., 2008; Litcofsky et al., 2009). In the switching condition, Alvarez et al. (2003) presented native English speakers who were beginning learners of Spanish with single words in L1 or L2 (in mixed lists) that on the previous trial were preceded by its translation (e.g., perro–dog). Using a go/no-go semantic categorization task, where participants were instructed to only press a button when the word referred to a body part, they observed that language switches resulted in a slightly larger N400 when switching into L1, but stronger later effects when switching into L2. In contrast to Alvarez et al. (2003), Chauncey et al. (2008) used unrelated prime-target pairs, and the targets were preceded by masked primes (i.e., briefly presented primes). Testing moderately proficient bilinguals, Chauncey et al. (2008) observed a larger N400 for switch as compared to non-switch trials when switching into L1, but a larger N250 modulation when switching into L2. Finally, in a mixed-language lexical decision task where English–French bilinguals were presented with a series of L1 English words, L2 French words, and nonwords, and had to decide if the item was a word in either of their languages, Litcofsky et al. (2009) observed a larger N400 switch cost when switching into L1 as compared to non-switch trials, but no N400 modulation when switching into the L2. These ERP comprehension studies show variation in the response to language switching that may depend on the nature of the task (priming vs. lexical decision) and proficiency of the bilinguals (beginning learner, moderately proficient, or immersed learner).

The evidence discussed so far is based on externally induced switches, as is typical in the aforementioned language-switching studies. Switch costs have also been observed in the absence of experiment-induced cues, when switching was under the voluntary control of the bilingual in a picture-naming task (Gollan & Ferreira, 2009). The observation that both voluntary (internally generated) switching and forced (externally induced) switching of isolated items are associated with measurable switch costs is important. As will be discussed below, forced single-item switching engages cognitive processes related to language control and inhibition. Voluntary single-item switching, on the other hand, bears more similarity to spontaneous code-switching in natural discourse.

Finally, under certain conditions, language switch costs have been found to be similar in both switching directions. Specifically, switch costs tend to be symmetrical when bilingual speakers are about equally proficient in L1 and L2 (e.g., Costa & Santesteban, 2004a; Costa et al., 2006; Meuter & Allport, 1999). Symmetrical switch costs have also been found in unbalanced bilinguals when given a pre-language cue that provided sufficient time to prepare for the subsequent naming response, which could be a language switch or not (Verhoef, Roelofs, & Chwilla, 2009).

The dominant account to explain language switch costs is based on the Inhibitory Control model (Green, 1998); alternative explanations distinguish between endogenous and exogenous attentional control (Verhoef et al., 2009), or emphasize differential language activation rather than inhibition (e.g., La Heij, 2005), the speed of response availability (Finkbeiner et al., 2006), or the persisting activation of L2 rather than the persisting inhibition of L1 (e.g., Phillip et al., 2007). The Inhibitory Control model proposes that for successful performance in one language, bilinguals employ a general cognitive mechanism, inhibitory control, to actively inhibit their other language. The model states that language task schemas, part of a general language control system that is external to the bilingual lexico-semantic system, control language actions. These language task schemas either activate or inhibit lemmas in the lexico-semantic system that are tagged for language-specific information. For example, when a bilingual speaks or reads in the weaker L2, the L2 task schema has to suppress the L1 task schema and inhibit the L1 lemmas in the lexico-semantic system. When a speaker switches into the other language, the task schema that is currently active has to be suppressed and the previously inhibited task schema needs to be reactivated, and this results in a language switch cost (see for a related account in terms of Task Set Inertia, Meuter & Allport, 1999). The Inhibitory Control model predicts that switching into the L1 would yield larger switch costs than switching into the L2, because the dominant language L1 needs to be inhibited more strongly during L2 processing than the weaker L2 needs to be during L1 processing. So when the switch goes from L2 to L1, the L1 has been strongly suppressed and thus requires more time to be reactivated than in the case of switching from L1 to L2. Indeed, the above review of isolated item switching studies indicated that most studies testing bilinguals who were more proficient in their L1 than in L2 found that switching into L1 was more costly than switching into L2. The Inhibitory Control model would further predict that when bilingual speakers are equally proficient in the two languages, the inhibition of one language is not more effortful than the inhibition of the other language. Instead, switch costs should be similar in the two switching directions, which has indeed been observed (e.g., Costa & Santesteban, 2004a; Meuter & Allport, 1999).

In sum, the language switching studies that examined the switching between a series of single, unrelated items (words, digits, pictures) overwhelmingly show that switching is associated with a measurable cost, observed in both behavioral and neurocognitive measures. Moreover, of the studies that examined switching in both directions, the large majority shows that switching from the L2 into the L1 is more costly than vice versa. Most studies explain these findings in terms of inhibitory control: switching into L1 is more costly because it is more effortful to suppress L1 during L2 processing.

A critical question the single-item switching studies raise is which insights they provide into the switching between languages within a meaningful utterance, like a sentence. The cognitive and neural mechanisms underlying successful switching between single, unrelated items pertain to the control and inhibition of languages, and keeping languages apart. Intra-sentential code-switching, on the other hand, requires the integration of two languages to form a semantically and syntactically coherent utterance. Does keeping two languages apart, as needed in single-item switching, lead to different switching patterns than integrating two languages, as needed in intra-sentential code-switching? For example, are switch costs, and the observation that switching into the L1 is more costly than switching into the L2, specific to single-item switching tasks, or are similar switch costs (and asymmetries in switch costs) associated with intra-sentential code-switching? In the next section, we will review behavioral and neurocognitive studies that examined intra-sentential switching.

## 20.3 Switch costs in intra-sentential code-switching

Psycholinguistic and neurocognitive studies on intra-sentential code-switching show that, in general, switching languages within a sentence takes time and is more effortful relative to processing single-language sentences, in line with costs observed in switching between single, unrelated items. In an early study, Altarriba et al. (1996) compared the silent reading of mixed language sentences (e.g., "He wanted to deposit all of his *dinero* at the credit union") with single language sentences (e.g., "He wanted to deposit all of his money at the credit union") in Spanish–English bilinguals, using eye-tracking technology. The sentences were always presented in the L2 English, and the switched target word was in L1 Spanish. The eye movement data showed that first fixation times were longer on switched words than on non-switched words. In a second experiment, the sentence contexts were presented visually word by word, and bilinguals were asked to name the target presented in uppercase letters. In line with the eye-tracking data, switched words took longer to name than non-switched words. This pattern of intra-sentential switch costs parallels basic findings in the unrelated, single-item language-switching literature discussed above.

The next question is which cognitive or neural mechanisms drive these intra-sentential switch costs, and one way to gain more insight into this question is to examine which factors modulate switch costs. In other words, is intra-sentential code-switching less effortful in some bilingual speakers than in others, or less costly in specific linguistic situations? In the remainder of this chapter we will review intra-sentential code-switching studies that examined these issues in comprehension or production, using behavioral and neurocognitive techniques. We will also review experimental studies that studied the modulation of switch costs to test selected theories of code-switching that were developed in linguistics and based on corpus data. We will conclude the chapter with a review of neuroimaging studies exploring brain areas that subserve language switching.

In a groundbreaking study, Moreno, Federmeier, and Kutas (2002) used ERPs to compare intra-sentential language switches with within-language lexical switches as English–Spanish bilinguals read for comprehension. They sought to examine whether language switches incur a cost at the lexical level of word recognition and lexical–semantic processing, or whether switches were essentially unexpected events at the level that affect later decision-making stages (see Thomas & Allport, 2000) rather than at the lexico-semantic level. Moreno et al. argued that if language switching incurs a cost at the level of lexical access and semantic integration, language-switched words should elicit an increased N400 response (the ERP component that indexes lexical–semantic integration, Kutas & Federmeier, 2000). On the other hand, if bilinguals perceive a language switch as an unexpected event and a change in form rather than meaning, language-switched words should evoke an enhanced late positivity (LPC, an ERP component indexing sentence-level integration (Kaan et al., 2000)), re-analysis (e.g., Friederici, 1995), or restructuring (Kolk & Chwilla, 2007), or the processing of unexpected or improbable events (e.g., Coulson, King, & Kutas, 1998; McCallum, Farmer, & Pocock, 1984). Highly proficient English–Spanish bilinguals read sentences in L1 English, while ERPs were recorded where the sentence-final word was either a code-switch into L2 (e.g., "Each night the campers built a *fuego* [fire]"), a lexical switch (e.g., "Each night the campers built a *blaze*"), or no switch (e.g., "Each night the campers built a *fire*"). The sentences were either regular sentences (as the previous example) or highly constraining idioms (e.g., "Out of sight, out of [*mente* (code-switch), *brain* (lexical switch), *mind* (no switch)]"). Lexical switches resulted in an N400 in both regular and idiomatic sentences. Code-switches resulted in an N400 in the regular sentences, but not in the highly constrained idioms; the N400 effect in the regular sentences had a left, frontally skewed distribution, which is not a typical N400 distribution. Finally, a switch-related modulation was observed in the LPC, in both regular sentences and highly constrained idioms. Subsequent regression analyses to examine the influence of L2 proficiency on these switches showed that higher L2 Spanish proficiency was associated with earlier peak latency and smaller amplitude of the LPC to code-switches, whereas individuals who were L1 English-dominant showed greater N400 amplitudes and earlier onsets for within-language switches. These findings suggest that code-switched words are processed differently from within-language lexical switches. Moreno et al. (2002) interpret the absence of an unequivocal N400 modulation in code-switched versus non-switched sentences to imply that switch costs do not incur a cost in the lexical–semantic integration of the switched word into the sentence. Rather, bilinguals may treat a code-switch as an unexpected event at a non-linguistic level. This would support the idea that language switch costs arise from outside the bilingual lexico-semantic system, and originate from competition between task schemas that coordinate the output of the lexico-semantic system with the response task. Finally, the finding that bilinguals with higher proficiency in L2 showed an earlier peak latency and a smaller amplitude of the LPC suggests that these more proficient bilinguals noticed the language switch earlier and experienced the switch as less unexpected.

Proverbio, Leoni, and Zani (2004) examined the neural correlates of intra-sentential code-switching in eight Italian–English simultaneous interpreters, a unique population of highly proficient individuals who use and switch between their languages as part of their job. These interpreters read incomplete sentence frames, which began in either L1 or L2 (e.g., "Global market is facing serious"), and were followed by a sentence-final word about 3200 ms later that was either a code-switch into the other language (here: "problemi") or a word in the same language that could be semantically congruent or incongruent with the sentence frame. The interpreters were instructed to read the sentences and target words, and decide whether the final word was a sensible completion of the sentence. The different sentence-target conditions were presented in separate blocks, so the language switches were completely predictable. A group of eight Italian monolinguals also read the Italian versions of the semantically congruous and incongruous sentences, and showed an N400 effect. Interpreters showed a similar N400 to the incongruity that was larger in code-switched sentences than non-switched sentences. No switch-related modulation of the LPC was observed. With respect to language-switching directions, the N400 was larger when switching from the dominant L1 into the weaker L2 than when switching from L2 into L1. The behavioral data also showed that switching into the weaker L2 was more costly. Interestingly, this switching asymmetry in meaningful sentences is in the opposite direction as the switching asymmetry typically observed in the single, unrelated item switching studies.

The Moreno et al. (2002) and Proverbio et al. (2004) studies show that intra-sentential code-switching incurs a processing cost in the form of a modulation of the N400 and LPC (Moreno et al., 2002), or the N400 only

(Proverbio et al., 2004). So even when bilinguals could fully predict the occurrence of a language switch, as in Proverbio et al., a switch-related modulation of the N400 was observed. However, because of substantial differences in the experimental methodology between these two sentential code-switching studies (e.g., predictability of code-switches, sentence presentation, instructions, type of bilinguals), it is difficult to compare these results. Nonetheless, these two studies do indicate that the N400 and LPC are critical ERP components that are associated with comprehending code-switched words embedded in meaningful sentences.

These early studies are not without some methodological concerns. First, both studies used both cognates (i.e., words that have a similar orthography, phonology, and meaning across languages, like "problemi"–problems) and non-cognates as critical target words, but it remains unclear whether this factor was explicitly controlled. Given the large literature showing that cognates and non-cognates are processed differently in both comprehension and production (for a review, see van Hell & Tanner, 2012), it is possible that the effects of intra-sentential code-switching are confounded with bottom-up lexical effects related to cross-language activation. Specifically, using a cued picture-naming switching task in German–English bilinguals, Declerck, Koch, and Philipp (2012) found that switching between German and English yielded smaller costs when the items were pictures of cognates or when they were digits (which included many cognates) compared to non-cognate pictures. This suggests that the co-activation of the cognates' phonology across two languages reduces the switch costs associated with cognate items.

Second, Proverbio et al. (2004) examined the effect of code-switching in the context of semantically anomalous sentences, which may have confined their effects to the N400 component. Third, Proverbio et al. (2004) presented the sentences in such a way that may have distorted natural processing. Namely, the sentence (minus the final word) was presented in its entirety for 1800 ms (and an inter stimulus interval (ISI) between 1400–1500 ms), followed by the critical final word for 250 ms. The singling out of the critical word may have brought extra attention to the code-switch, in addition to encouraging the use of strategic behavior as opposed to natural reading.

Fourth, in Proverbio et al. the code-switched sentences and the non-switched sentences were presented in blocked lists (and the code-switched sentences were also blocked by switching direction) and thus predictable, whereas in Moreno et al. the switched and non-switched sentences were presented in mixed blocks and thus unpredictable. As the LPC is associated with the processing of unexpected or improbable events (e.g., Coulson et al., 1998; McCallum et al., 1984), variations in mere predictability incurred by blocked vs. mixed presentations may have resulted in an absence of an LPC in Proverbio et al. (2004) and the presence of an LPC modulation in Moreno et al. (2002).

Finally, in both studies the code-switches always appeared as the sentence-final word, and processing of the sentence-final word is possibly confounded with sentence-general wrap-up processes. The LPC component is highly similar to the P600 component, and the P600 has been associated with sentence-level integration and re-analysis (e.g., Friederici, 1995; Kaan et al., 2000) or restructuring related to monitoring and executive control (e.g., Kolk & Chwilla, 2007). Brain activity associated with code-switched words when presented as final-sentence words may not only reflect language switching per se, but also processes related to sentence reanalysis, reintegration, and restructuring. This may also explain why the highly proficient interpreters tested in Proverbio et al. (2004) did not show an LPC, but the less proficient bilinguals tested in Moreno et al. (2002) did: integrating and reanalyzing language-switched sentences may be less effortful for interpreters as they are professionally trained to switch between languages. As will be discussed below, two recent intra-sentential code-switching studies disentangled L2 proficiency and bilinguals' frequency of code-switching in everyday life.

Building upon Moreno et al. (2002) and Proverbio et al. (2004), Van der Meij et al. (2011) investigated the influence of L2 proficiency on intra-sentential code-switching using ERPs, while addressing some of the methodological concerns of the earlier studies. Their bilinguals were native Spanish speakers who had learned their L2 English at school, and were divided into higher and lower proficiency speakers (mean score self-reported speaking, listening, and reading skills high proficiency speakers: 7.9; mean score low proficiency speakers: 6.0; scale from 1 (almost none) to 10 (native speaker). The Spanish–English bilinguals read sentences in L2 English that either contained a (one-word) code-switched sentence-medial adjective or a non-switched control word. The adjectives were all non-cognates, and the sentences were presented in mixed lists. Sentences were only presented in L2 English and the switched word was always in L1 Spanish. Both higher and lower proficiency bilinguals showed an enhanced N400 and LPC (both larger in the high proficiency group) to code-switched words. Additionally, both groups showed an early negativity that may be related to orthographic processing (left occipital N250) and a lasting frontal positivity that may be the onset of the LPC. In the higher proficiency bilinguals, the switch-modulated N400 effect extended to left anterior electrodes, suggestive of a LAN, as has also been observed by Moreno et al. (2002). The Van der Meij et al. (2011) study shows that switching of words midway in the sentence incurs switch-related modulations of both the N400 and the LPC, in line with Moreno et al. (2002), indicating that code-switched words elicit both lexico-semantic integration costs, as well as more sentence-level updating and reanalysis costs. Though neither study examined code-switching in both language-switching directions, together they suggest that switch-related biphasic

N400-LPC responses can occur when switching from L1 into L2 (Moreno et al., 2002) and when switching from L2 into L1 (Van der Meij et al., 2011).

Litcofsky and van Hell (in revision; Litcofsky, 2013) examined intra-sentential code-switching in both language-switching directions in Spanish–English bilinguals, in a behavioral study (self-paced reading; Experiment 1) and ERP studies (Experiments 2 and 3). The bilinguals tested in Experiments 1 and 2 were habitual code-switchers, and reported to frequently code-switch in their everyday life. They were living in an L2 English environment (USA), and a series of subjective and objective proficiency measures (including the Boston Naming task, a lexical decision task, a self-paced sentence reading task, and self-rated proficiency, all in both languages) indicated that they were nearly equally proficient in their two languages. The bilinguals read sentences that began in Spanish or English and could contain a sentence-medial, full code-switch into the other language (e.g., "Each year, the shopkeeper makes his own *juguetes para los niños pequeños*") or not ("Each year, the shopkeeper makes his own toys for the young children"). The sentences were presented in mixed lists, so the code-switches were unpredictable, and all words prior to the code-switch and the first code-switched word were non-cognates. The behavioral self-paced reading study showed that the first code-switched word and the three subsequent words, as compared to non-switched words, were read more slowly, but that this switch cost only appeared when switching from the dominant into the weaker language, not vice versa. The ERP study, testing a new group of bilinguals from the same population, corroborated the behavioral findings. The ERPs revealed a late positivity (LPC) in response to code-switched words, but only when switching from the dominant into the weaker language, and not vice versa. No switch-related modulation of the N400 was observed.

To examine to what extent the absence of a switch-related N400 was related to the high proficiency level of these bilinguals, a new group of Spanish–English bilinguals was tested (Experiment 3) who were less proficient in their L2 (mean self-reported proficiency, out of 10, in speaking, listening, and reading ranged from 7.5–8.7); these ratings are comparable to the high proficiency Spanish–English bilinguals tested in Van der Meij et al. (2011). All Spanish–English bilinguals were immersed in their L1 (they all lived in Spain), and similar to the participants tested by Van der Meij et al. (2011), they did not code-switch regularly in their everyday life. If code-switching incurs a cost at the level of lexical access and semantic integration (as indexed by the N400), these lower proficiency bilinguals may show a switch-related N400 modulation (as in the Van der Meij et al. study). The ERP data yielded no switch-related N400 effect. As in the ERP and behavioral experiments with the highly proficient bilinguals, these lower proficiency bilinguals' ERPs showed a late positivity (LPC) in response to the code-switched words, but only when the bilinguals switched from the dominant into the weaker language, and not vice versa. The observation that switching from the dominant language into the weaker language incurs larger behavioral and neural switch costs is thus consistent, and was observed both in highly proficient habitual code-switchers immersed in L2 and moderately proficient non-habitual code-switchers immersed in L1.

In conclusion, the emergent literature on the cognitive and neural correlates of intra-sentential code-switching is far from being conclusive, but together these first studies suggest some first patterns. The major ERP components that are associated with intra-sentential code-switching are the N400 (indexing switch costs related to lexico-semantic access and integration) and the LPC (indexing switch costs associated with sentence level integration and reanalysis, the processing of unexpected task-related events, and restructuring processes related to executive control and monitoring). Assuming that particularly low proficient bilinguals or non-habitual code-switchers would experience more lexical-level integration difficulties (as indexed by the N400) than highly proficient bilinguals or habitual code-switchers, one would expect a switch-related modulation of the N400 to be more pronounced in the former than in the latter. However, the currently available evidence does not justify this assumption, as switch-related N400 effects have been found in bilinguals with different L2 proficiency levels, ranging from moderately proficient L2 classroom learners (Van der Meij et al., 2011) to highly proficient professional interpreters (Proverbio et al., 2004).

With the exception of Proverbio et al. (2004), all studies observed switch-related LPC effects. Although in Moreno et al. (2002) the switch-related LPC on the sentence-final word was possibly confounded with sentence wrap-up effects, the mid-sentence code-switching studies (Van der Meij et al., 2011; Litcofsky & van Hell, in revision) confirm that these LPC effects reflect true code-switching processes that appear related to sentence-level integration and reanalysis, and were observed in moderately and highly proficient bilinguals and in habitual and non-habitual code-switchers. The absence of the LPC effect in Proverbio et al. (2004) is likely due to the fact that in this study switched sentences and non-switched sentences were presented in blocks, and code-switches were thus predictable, whereas in the remaining studies presentation of switched and non-switched sentences was mixed and code-switches were unpredictable. Variations in the predictability of code-switches impact code-switch costs, as has also been observed in the single, unrelated item language switching literature (for a review, see Bobb & Wodniecka, 2013).

Finally, those studies that tested switching in both directions (Litcofsky & van Hell, in revision; Proverbio et al., 2004), using both behavioral and ERP techniques, consistently found asymmetrical switch costs such that switching from the dominant L1 to the weaker L2 incurs higher switch costs than switching from the weaker L2 to the dominant L1, in the behavioral, as well as in the ERP data. This asymmetry is in the direction opposite to the asymmetry observed in the single, unrelated item switching literature where switching into L1 has been found to be more costly. The latter finding is typically explained by the mechanism of inhibitory control stating that switching into L1 is more costly because it is more effortful to suppress L1 during L2 processing than the L2 during L1 processing. The currently available evidence on intra-sentential code-switching suggests that inhibitory control is not the cognitive mechanism underlying switching words within a meaningful sentence. Rather, when processing a meaningful sentence, bilinguals seek to integrate individual words into a coherent semantic and syntactic structure. This higher-order integration of lexical items is fundamentally different from processing a series of isolated and unrelated items. When processing words in language-switched sentences, bilinguals do not rely on response inhibition in every single trial (as in processing a series of single, unrelated items). Rather, they may continuously adjust the level of activation of their L1 and L2 to optimize task performance by reducing the level of activation of L1 in order to facilitate language comprehension or production in L2, or vice versa.[1] The fact that the pattern of behavioral and ERP techniques affects intra-sentential code-switching was similar for habitual and non-habitual code-switchers suggests that this dynamic adjustment of activating L1 and L2 is more related to language proficiency rather than code-switching experience per se.

The intra-sentential code-switching studies reviewed above yield important information about the temporal unfolding of neural events associated with the different subprocesses of code-switching, and the locus of the code-switch costs. In the next section, we will discuss studies that sought to unravel the linguistic and cognitive mechanisms underlying code-switching by translating descriptive linguistic theories, often based on linguistic corpora, into predictive hypotheses that are tested in controlled experiments using psycholinguistic research techniques. We will discuss tests of one of these linguistic theories in more detail: the triggering theory.

## 20.4 Triggering and intra-sentential code-switching

The triggering hypothesis was first proposed by Clyne (e.g., 1967, 2003) who noted in his study on the language use of German, Dutch, Hungarian,

---

[1] On the basis of the currently available evidence we cannot rule out the alternative explanation that the larger switching costs into L2 in intra-sentential code-switching only occur in comprehension (i.e., reading), but not in production. Even though a similar asymmetry was found in intra-sentential code-switching when bilinguals were asked to perform a shadowing task that also includes a production component (Bultena, Dijkstra, & Van Hell, 2015; this study will be discussed later), in both reading and shadowing the linguistic input is externally induced and not controlled by the participant, so non-target language inhibition may be of less importance than is possibly the case in the production of code-switched sentences. Future research comparing the comprehension and production of code-switched sentences may shed more light on this issue.

Italian, Spanish, Croatian, and Vietnamese immigrants in Australia that code-switches tend to occur when a sentence contains one or more cognates (like "tennis" in the example below). Clyne proposed that cognates, but also proper nouns and homographs, can function as triggers that facilitate a switch to the other language. For example, the Croatian–English cognate "tennis" triggered a switch to English, in "Imam puno zadaca I sutra mi igramo *tennis*... that's about all" ("I have a lot of assignments and tomorrow we are playing *tennis*... that's about all"; Hlavac, 2000, as cited in Clyne 2003: 164). On the basis of his corpus research, Clyne (1967) further distinguished three triggering loci: sequential facilitation, where the code-switch takes place after the trigger, anticipational facilitation, where the code-switch takes place before the trigger, and a combination of these two, where the code-switch is surrounded by two trigger words. The mechanism of triggering nicely aligns with the ubiquitous finding that cognates co-activate a bilingual's two languages, which then facilitate a switch to the other language, although at the time Clyne (1967) first proposed the triggering theory, empirical evidence on lexical processing of cognates and the parallel activation of bilinguals' two languages was basically non-existent.

Clyne's work was based on examples of triggered code-switches in his corpus. Broersma and de Bot (2006) were the first to statistically test the triggering hypothesis in their corpus study. They analyzed several conversations in which three Moroccan Arabic-Dutch bilinguals code-switched, and coded both the code-switches and the cognates in each sentence. The results showed that code-switches were indeed more likely to occur after a cognate, especially if the cognate and the code-switch were in the same clause. They therefore proposed the adjusted triggering hypothesis, which states that a cognate can function as a trigger for a code-switch if both occur in the same clause. The adjusted triggering hypothesis integrates lexical triggering with bilingual language production models, and states that triggering occurs at the lemma level. The selection of the lemma of a trigger word, for example a cognate in Language X, activates not only words in Language X, but also words in Language Y. This leads to an increase in the activation level of Language Y, which makes it more likely that the speaker will select lemmas from Language Y in the course of the utterance.

Subsequent analyses of natural speech corpora of Dutch immigrants in New Zealand and Australia (Broersma, 2009; Broersma et al., 2009) and of Russian immigrants in the USA (Broersma et al., 2009) corroborated the earlier findings that code-switches occur more frequently in clauses containing a cognate than in clauses not containing a cognate, even in typologically related languages like Dutch and English which contain a high proportion of cognates. Broersma et al. (2009) also observed that interlingual homophones (words in two languages that share phonology but not meaning) sometimes served as triggers.

These corpus studies provide important quantitative evidence for the co-occurrence of trigger words and code-switches, but in order to gain more insight into the processing mechanisms underlying triggered code-switching, these off-line counts need to be validated by experimental research that allows for specific manipulations of critical variables and a more systematic control of potentially modulating factors (cf. Gullberg, Indefrey, & Muysken, 2009). Kootstra (2012) and Kootstra, van Hell, and Dijkstra (in revision) examined the triggering hypothesis in a mimicked discourse situation in the lab, using the confederate-scripted priming technique. In this technique, two participants perform a task, but (unbeknownst to the 'true' participant) one of them is actually a confederate who is instructed by the experimenter and whose language behavior is scripted, in this case to produce code-switched or non-switched (one language) sentences. Dutch–English bilingual 'true' participants interacted with the Dutch–English bilingual confederate, and described pictured events to each other (e.g., a picture of a hunter putting a rose on a chair). The patient object in the picture was a cognate (e.g., rose–roos), a false friend (e.g., rock–rok [skirt]), or a non-cognate control word that did not overlap in form or meaning across languages (e.g., bike–fiets). The confederate was scripted to code-switch, directly after the critical patient trigger (i.e., the cognate or false friend) or non-trigger (non-cognate control word), in half of the picture descriptions (e.g., "De jager legt de roos on the chair" ['The hunter puts the rose on the chair']), and the other half were not code-switched. After the true participant had selected the correct picture from one of two pictures on the screen (which was the cover task), the true participant described the next pictured event on the screen (e.g., a grandma putting a baby on a chair). The patient objects in the participants' pictures were cognates, false friends, or non-cognate control words, as in the confederate's pictures. Participants were free to use Dutch or English in their description, and were not forced to code-switch.

The critical question was whether participants would code-switch more often in their picture description when their picture contained a lexical trigger (cognate or false friend) relative to a non-trigger, and to what extent the participants' likelihood to code-switch was influenced by the confederate's switched or non-switched utterance in the previous trial. It appeared that participants switched more often when their picture contained a cognate or a false friend than when it contained a non-trigger control word, but this effect only emerged when the confederate had switched in the previous trial. This finding indicates that lexical triggering of code-switches only occurs when there is already a high tendency to code-switch in a discourse situation (here when the interlocutor has just code-switched). This qualifies the lexical triggering hypothesis and suggests that lexical triggering in free code-switching in language production is not a basic psychological mechanism that is impervious to contextual information, but is restricted to those discourse situations in which code-switching is quite frequent.

In another study, using the structural priming technique, noun cognate lexical triggers were found to boost the priming of code-switches (Kootstra, van Hell, & Dijkstra, 2012). Dutch–English bilinguals were asked to repeat a code-switched prime sentence that started in L1 Dutch and switched into L2 English (e.g., De jongen gooit een bal to the butcher [The boy throws a ball to the butcher]), and subsequently describe a target picture (e.g., of a boy throwing a ball to a diver) by means of a sentence that switched from L1 Dutch to L2 English. The object noun in the prime sentence (here: ball) was either a cognate or a non-cognate and was repeated or not repeated in the target sentence. Two groups of Dutch–English bilinguals were tested: a group of highly proficient bilinguals and a group of moderately proficient bilinguals. Analyses of the switch location in the target sentence showed that bilinguals were more likely to switch at the same position as in the prime sentence when the noun object was a cognate and when it was repeated across prime sentence and target picture. These cognate triggering and lexical repetition effects were more pronounced in the highly proficient bilinguals than in the moderately proficient bilinguals. This study shows that cognate lexical triggers enhance the likelihood that the switch location in a spoken sentence aligns with the switch-location in a previously encountered utterance, and thus provides converging evidence that cognate (noun) triggers can affect code-switching.

Further evidence for the impact of cognate triggering on the production of switches comes from a picture-naming study in which Dutch–English bilinguals had to name a series of pictures that were preceded by a phonologically similar cognate (e.g., sock–sok) or a non-cognate picture (Broersma, 2011). The crucial items were the pictures following the cognate and non-cognate pictures. Bilinguals were either required to switch from L1 into L2 or vice versa (as indicated by a color cue; Experiment 1) or were free to switch as long as they switched about half the time (Experiment 2). Bilinguals switched faster after cognates than after non-cognates in the cued condition (in both switching directions), and switched more often after cognates than after non-cognates in the free switching condition (but only when switching from L1 into L2).

The experimental studies discussed so far used nouns as cognate triggers. Two recent studies using verb cognate triggers suggest that triggering effects are restricted to nouns, at least in languages in which cognate verbs rarely fully share orthography and phonology. Using a shadowing task, Bultena, Dijkstra, and van Hell (2015) examined whether verb cognates could modulate switch costs. Dutch–English bilinguals were presented with code-switched sentences that started in L1 Dutch and switched into L2 English, or vice versa. The code-switch was preceded by a verb cognate (e.g., De ervaren schilders schetsen the flowers from a distance

[The experienced painters <u>sketch</u> the flowers from a distance]) or a verb non-cognate (e.g., De ervaren schilders <u>tekenen</u> the flowers from a distance [The experienced painters <u>draw</u> the flowers from a distance]). As soon as bilinguals heard the beginning of the sentence, they were asked to reproduce the incoming signal and repeat ("shadow") what they heard as quickly and as accurately as possible. The shadowing task allows for the measurement of the delay between word onset in the original recording and the participant's reproduction of the word. Shadowing latencies showed that switching from L1 into L2 was more costly than switching from L2 into L1, thereby replicating the ERP studies by Proverbio et al. (2004) and Litcofsky & van Hell (in revision). However, the switch costs were not modulated by the preceding verb cognate, indicating that shadowing a verb cognate trigger did not facilitate the shadowing of the subsequent code-switch. Such an absence of a verb triggering effect was observed in both switching directions, and in the two syntactic structures that were tested in the study (i.e., word order that is shared (SVO) or not shared (XVSO) across Dutch and English).

These findings were paralleled in a follow-up study (Bultena, Dijkstra, & van Hell, forthcoming), using the self-paced reading variant of the moving window paradigm (Just, Carpenter, & Woolley, 1982). Two new groups of Dutch–English bilinguals who varied in L2 proficiency were visually presented with code-switched sentences (i.e., the above SVO sentence materials). The self-paced reading times showed a switch cost for switching from L1 into L2, but not vice versa; the switch costs into L2 were smaller as L2 proficiency increased. Importantly, reading a verb cognate trigger directly preceding the code-switch did not modulate the switch cost.

In his original writing, Clyne had observed that triggers do not necessarily have to be lexical, and noted that if the context was a typical, for example, Australian context, speakers were more likely to switch into the language of this context, here English. In the example described below, a German native speaker who worked in an Australian setting was asked about his occupation, and Clyne argued that this work situation triggered a switch into English. "*Well*, wir müssen zuerst sagen, was wir sind von Beruf und für sich und was *what we are doing daily, more or less is that right?*" [*Well*, we first have to say what our occupation is and what] *what we are doing daily, more or less is that right?*]; Clyne (1967: 90). In a series of three experiments, van Hell, Sánchez-Casas, & Ting (in preparation) studied whether switch costs are modulated when preceded by a socio-contextual cue. Participants first read a sentence containing a socio-contextual cue that was either congruent with the language of the code-switch (e.g., "Women in *Valencia* are incredibly stylish. Their *cabello* [hair] is always cut fashionably") or not congruent with the language of the code-switch (e.g., "Women in *Chicago* are incredibly stylish. Their *cabello* is always cut fashionably"). Three groups of Spanish–English bilinguals participated: highly proficient Spanish–English bilinguals tested in Central

Pennsylvania (habitual code-switchers immersed in their second language), highly proficient Spanish–English bilinguals tested in El Paso, close to the US–Mexican border (habitual code-switchers living in an environment where both languages are spoken), and moderately proficient Spanish–English bilinguals tested in Spain (non-habitual code-switchers immersed in their first language; this population is similar to the Dutch–English bilinguals tested in a similar study by Witteman and van Hell (2008), as discussed in van Hell and Witteman, 2009). It appeared that code-switches were read faster when preceded by a congruent socio-contextual cue than by a non-congruent cue, but this effect was most pronounced in the highly proficient Spanish–English bilinguals tested in El Paso, who were habitual code-switchers immersed specifically in a context where both languages were used. This suggests that socio-contextually congruent cues can facilitate the comprehension of code-switched sentences, and that this effect seems particularly strong in habitual code-switchers who live in a bilingual environment.

In conclusion, although the quantitative analyses of corpus studies suggest that lexical triggers co-occur with code-switches in a wide variety of situations involving different types of bilingual speakers, the experimental studies indicate that lexical triggering per se is not a basic cognitive mechanism that facilitates or leads to code-switching in all circumstances. Rather, in a language production situation where bilinguals were free to code-switch (or not), cognates or false friends only triggered a code-switch to the other language when the speaker's discourse partner had just code-switched (Kootstra et al., in revision; Kootstra, 2012), suggesting that lexical triggering is restricted to discourse situations in which code-switching occurs frequently. Importantly, this discourse situation may mimic the contextual situation in which linguistic corpora are collected, suggesting that quantitative analyses of code-switches in corpora may reflect code-switching behavior in specific discourse situations, but do not necessarily provide a window onto the cognitive underpinnings of code-switching in speakers or listeners/readers.

Furthermore, the available evidence suggests that lexical triggering effects are restricted to nouns (both cognates and false friends), and that the cognate verbs do not facilitate a code-switch to the other language, at least not in languages where cognate verbs rarely fully share orthography and phonology.

## 20.5 Brain areas subserving language switching

In addition to behavioral and electrophysiological investigations of language switching, in recent years neuroimaging has been used to examine the neural substrates underlying language switching. In the large majority of these studies bilinguals have been presented with a series of unrelated, isolated items (for a review, see Luk et al., 2012). Although very few studies examined the switching of words embedded in a meaningful linguistic context, combining the outcomes of these studies with the isolated item switching studies may yield some first insights into the neural mechanisms underlying switching.

Mariën et al. (2005) sought to identify the neural correlates of language switching and language mixing by examining the correlates of pathological language switching and pathological language mixing. Pathological language switching is defined as uncontrolled switching between multiple languages within the course of the same sentence, whereas pathological language mixing is defined as uncontrolled switching of languages across sentences. EM was a 10-year-old English–Dutch bilingual who suffered from two strokes, resulting in vascular-acquired aphasia in both English and Dutch. Mariën and colleagues reported computerized tomography, magnetic resonance imaging, and single-photon emission computed tomography data from EM. While damage was observed to the left frontal cortex, left temporo-parietal areas, left caudate nucleus, and left thalamus, both the pathological switching and mixing subsided upon reperfusion of the left frontal cortex and left caudate nucleus. This pattern of behavior supports the neuroanatomical device response Fabbro et al. (1997) proposed for controlling language selection, which involves a number of brain regions otherwise associated with general cognition and executive control. Specifically, it appears that the proposed articulatory anterior cortical-subcortical loop is also involved in the selection of items from the target language via inhibition of items from the non-target language.

Adrover-Roig et al. (2011) reported the clinical and neuroimaging data from a bilingual individual with aphasia. JZ was a 53-year-old Basque–Spanish bilingual who suffered from a hematoma in the left basal ganglia. Like EM in Mariën et al. (2005), JZ acquired bilingual aphasia following the trauma. However, JZ's aphasia impacted his languages to different degrees. JZ's first language, Basque, was more impaired than his second language, Spanish. By administering a series of neuropsychological tests, Adrover-Roig and colleagues observed asymmetry in both production and translation. In particular, the Bilingual Aphasia Test (BAT) (Paradis & Libben, 1987) revealed deficits in first language production, but intact production in his second language. Deficits were also found when JZ was asked to translate from his second language into his first language. In the Trail Making Task (TMT) (Reitan, 1958), JZ was asked to connect together a series of randomly distributed twenty-five circles containing numbers and letters using paper and pencil. The TMT is considered an indicator of executive functioning processes, such as attentional awareness and visual scanning, and is often used to measure the severity of brain damage. JZ's poor performance on the TMT led researchers to believe that while poor first language lexical access could explain his asymmetric translation performance on the BAT, JZ's translation pattern could also be the result of a more domain general switching impairment where bilingual aphasia presents as part of a larger impairment that encompasses linguistic and non-linguistic aspects of executive control.

Recent neuroimaging techniques have allowed researchers to investigate language switching in non-clinical populations. Abutalebi et al. (2007) used functional magnetic resonance imaging (fMRI) to study the neural correlates of language switching in Italian–French bilinguals who had greater exposure to French (because they lived in a French community in Switzerland). Participants passively listened to four stories in the scanner that contained unpredictable language switches from Italian to French or vice versa. Two of the stories contained regular switches, which occurred at the start of noun and verb phrases (e.g., "Il picolo principe *qui m'a posé beaucoup de questions*" ['The little prince who has asked me a lot of questions']), and two of the stories contained irregular switches, which occurred within noun and verb phrases (e.g., "Il picolo *prince était* …" ['The little prince was …']). The order of the stories was randomized among participants. The neuroimaging data showed that for regular switches into L1 Italian, the language of less exposure, there was increased activity across the left hemisphere, including the prefrontal, parietal, and temporal cortex, as well as in the anterior cingulate cortex, basal ganglia, and thalamus. Neural activity in the right hemisphere was observed in the prefrontal and temporal cortex, as well as the putamen. A similar pattern of activation was found for regular switches into L2 French, but the activation was notably less extensive. For irregular switches into Italian, the neuroimaging data showed heightened activation in the left inferior frontal gyrus, left parietal lobule, right inferior and middle frontal gyri, and right insula. Again, a similar pattern of activation was found for irregular switches into French.

Regular and irregular switches yielded different patterns of neural activation. Generally, regular switches resulted in activation of regions associated with lexical processing, including the inferior frontal gyrus – pars orbitalis (BA47). On the other hand, irregular switches resulted in activation of regions associated with phonological and syntactic processing, such as the opercular portion of Broca's area and the left inferior parietal area. Abutalebi et al. (2007) interpreted the differences in neural recruitment as evidence for regular switches being treated like translation equivalents, or lexical alternatives, and irregular switches being treated like violations that require phonological and/or statistical analysis for successful comprehension.

Conjunction analyses on the neuroimaging data revealed a difference in neural activation by switch direction in the regular switches. Regular switches into L1 Italian as compared to L2 French activated the left caudate nucleus, the right supramarginal gyrus, and bilaterally, the anterior cingulate cortex and posterior cingulate cortex. Regular switches into L2 French as compared to L1 Italian activated the left superior parietal lobule, left anterior superior temporal gyrus, and the right temporal pole. Conjunction analyses also revealed a difference in neural activation by switch direction for irregular switches. Irregular switches into L1 Italian as compared to L2 French activated the left caudate head and the bilateral anterior cingulate cortex. Activation was also found in the left insula, left superior temporal gyrus, and right middle temporal gyrus. Irregular switches into L2 French as compared to L1 Italian activated the left superior frontal gyrus, left inferior parietal lobule, left precuneus, and the right precentral gyrus.

These results show that language switching recruits a large network of bilateral prefrontal and temporal associative regions with a dissociation in recruitment between switch types. The set of areas activated by irregular switching are the brain regions typically recruited by syntactic and phonological processing, whereas the set of areas activated for regular switching are brain regions associated with lexical processing. Interestingly, switching into Italian, the native language which is also the language of less exposure, required brain areas typically associated with executive control and cognition. The researchers interpreted these findings as neural evidence of a switch cost in which the less-exposed language requires activation of cognitive control mechanisms and correlates in order for it to be activated successfully in a dominant-to-weak language switch.

Abutalebi and Green (2008) proposed a neurocognitive model of bilingual language switching, based on previous neuroimaging studies involving language switching and translation (see also Abutalebi & Green, 2007). The model consists of five brain regions: left dorsolateral prefrontal cortex, anterior cingulate cortex (ACC), caudate nucleus (a subcortical structure belonging to the basal ganglia), and bilateral supramarginal gyri. Abutalebi and Green posited that each of the brain areas in this subcortical–cortical network contribute distinct and complementary functions to negotiate the cognitive demands needed to successfully manage a bilingual's two languages during language switching. More specifically, the prefrontal cortex (involved in executive functions, response selection and inhibition, decision making, and working memory) works together with the ACC (involved in the detection of response conflict) and the basal ganglia for response inhibition, in particular, the inhibition of non-target language interference. According to their model, the ACC signals potential response conflict to the prefrontal cortex, and the prefrontal cortex biases against incorrect language selection. A more anterior part of the ACC withholds a response to the current language and the more posterior part of the ACC initiates a response to the relevant language. Abutalebi and Green further suggest that, in cases of unpredictable language switches, the left posterior parietal cortex may bias language selection away from the previous language and the right parietal cortex may bias language selection toward the current language. Parietal activity appears to be absent in cases of predictable and expected language switches.

Finally, Abutalebi and Green propose that the basal ganglia subserves language planning through a circuitry of left basal ganglia and left prefrontal cortex and/or works with the supplementary motor area (SMA) to inhibit a prepotent response.

A few years later, Luk et al. (2012) conducted a meta-analysis in order to evaluate Abutalebi and Green's (2008) bilingual subcortical–cortical network control network, using the Activation Likelihood Estimation (ALE) method (Eickhoff et al., 2009; Turkeltaub et al., 2002). They aimed to identify which neural regions show common activity in response to the cognitive control demands involved in bilingual language switching. The meta-analysis included ten studies that had employed either fMRI or positron emission tomography and a combined sample of 106 bilinguals. All but one study (Abutalebi et al., 2007) employed a single item switching task, where the switched items were not embedded in a meaningful linguistic context. Ten distinct neural clusters were identified that were largely left lateralized and frontal. Among these clusters were the bilateral caudate and the left prefrontal regions. While there was no significant engagement of the anterior cingulate cortex or the supramarginal gyri (unlike in Abutalebi and Green's model), the finding remains overall consistent with the argument that there is a frontal-subcortical circuit involved in language switching (Fabbro et al., 1997; Green & Abutalebi, 2008; see Green & Abutalebi, 2013, for a proposed set of neural correlates that underlie eight control processes in bilingual speech production). It also aligns with research reporting bilingual patients with aphasia who had lesions in subcortical brain regions and exhibited pathological language switching (Adrover-Roig et al., 2011; Mariën et al., 2005). As noted, these neural models are largely based on neuroimaging studies using single item switching tasks, but the proposed subcortical–cortical network provides a valuable basis for future neuroimaging studies examining code-switched utterances embedded in a meaningful linguistic context such as sentences.

## 20.6 Concluding remarks

Intra-sentential code-switching is a hallmark of bilingual language processing, but we are only beginning to understand the intricate cognitive and neural mechanisms that underlie this seemingly effortless skill. The emergent body of research on intra-sentential code-switching shows that switching languages within a sentence is typically associated with a measurable behavioral and neural cost, just like switching between a series of single, unrelated items. A notable difference between these two types of language switching pertains to the observed asymmetry in switch costs. Studies on intra-sentential code-switching in two directions consistently found that switching is more effortful when switching from the dominant

L1 into the weaker L2 than vice versa. In contrast, single unrelated item switching is typically more effortful when switching from the weaker L2 into the dominant L1 than vice versa. These opposite asymmetries suggest that the basic mechanism underlying language switching differs in these tasks. A dominant explanation for single unrelated item switching, based on inhibitory control, is that switching into L1 is more costly because the more dominant L1 requires more inhibition when processing L2 items, and overcoming L1 inhibition when switching back to L1 is more effortful. Such item-based inhibitory control may not pertain to intra-sentential code-switching, as bilinguals need to integrate lexical items into a coherent syntactic and semantic structure when producing or comprehending a language-switched sentence. To optimize sentence-level performance, they need to navigate the levels of L1 and L2 activation by dynamically adjusting the level of L1 activation when processing in L2, and vice versa. Clearly, more empirical research is needed to specify the functional and neural mechanisms, but it seems clear that language switching within a meaningful sentence differs fundamentally from switching between single unrelated items (and possibly from switching between full sentences, e.g., Ibáñez et al., 2010).

Furthermore, current models on the subcortical–cortical circuitry engaged in language switching are largely based on single unrelated item switching studies, and little is known about the neural substrates of intra-sentential code-switching. Given that the switching asymmetry in intra-sentential code-switching differs from single unrelated items switching, future research on the neural substrates of intra-sentential code-switching should systematically examine both switching directions.

In an attempt to bridge linguistic and (neuro)cognitive theories on switching between languages, recent studies 'translated' linguistic theories on code-switching into experimentally testable hypotheses using psycholinguistic techniques; these studies include tests of grammatical constraints on code-switching (Guzzardo Tamargo & Dussias, 2013; Hatzidaki, Branigan, & Pickering, 2011; Kootstra et al., 2010), including Poplack's (1980) equivalence constraint hypothesis. In this chapter, we reviewed experimental studies that tested the psychological validity of the triggering hypothesis, originally developed on the basis of linguistic corpus research. Quantitative analyses of off-line data drawn from linguistic corpora show that lexical triggers co-occur with code-switches in a wide variety of bilinguals, but the available experimental studies that tested the triggering hypothesis in systematically controlled environments show that triggering facilitates intra-sentential code-switches only in specific circumstances. For example, lexical triggering appears to facilitate code-switching in discourse situations with two speakers who code-switch frequently (mimicking the typical contextual situation in which linguistic corpora of code-switches are collected), and in habitual code-switchers. In addition, cognates, false friends, and socio-contextual cues that are nouns or pronouns can trigger a switch to the other language, but verb cognates do not appear to serve this function. Clearly, more research is needed to further specify the linguistic and contextual specifics of the triggering mechanism in code-switching. Such future research, like the experimental studies testing the triggering hypothesis discussed in this chapter, will contribute to a further strengthening of the link between linguistic, psycholinguistic, and neurocognitive approaches to the study of intrasentential code-switching.

# Part VI

## Control

# 21

# Selection and control in bilingual comprehension and production

Judith F. Kroll, Jason W. Gullifer, Rhonda McClain, Eleonora Rossi, and María Cruz Martín

## 21.1 Introduction

Two observations about bilingualism have dominated the recent literature. One is the discovery that the bilingual's two languages are continuously active, even when the task and context require that only one language be used. The co-activation of the bilingual's two languages has been observed in the simplest of tasks, when naming words (e.g., Schwartz, Kroll, & Diaz, 2007), naming pictures (e.g., Costa et al., 2000), and recognizing spoken words (e.g., Marian & Spivey, 2003b). But it has also been shown to persist when these tasks are placed in sentence context (e.g., Libben & Titone, 2009) and when features of the two languages are markedly different, as in the case of two languages that utilize different written scripts (e.g., Hoshino & Kroll, 2008) or when one language is written and the other language is signed (e.g., Morford et al., 2011). The observation that it is not simple for adult bilinguals to exploit cross-language differences that might serve to separate the two languages makes the problem of language selection complex. It suggests that there is a high level of cross-language activation and potential competition when the intended language is selected. The fact that some groups of bilinguals code switch, changing language while in the midst of an utterance, provides additional support for the claim that the parallel activation of the two languages is not an obstacle, but a feature that can be exploited.

The second observation is that experience in using two or more languages has consequences not only for language processing itself but also

The writing of this chapter was supported in part by NIH Grant HD053146 and NSF Grants BCS-0955090 and OISE-0968369 to J. F. Kroll, by NSF Grant BCS-1226471 to J. F. Kroll, R. McClain, and E. Rossi, and by NSF Grant BCS-1251896 to J. F. Kroll and J. W. Gullifer.

for cognition and the brain. Bilinguals, at all points across the lifespan, have been shown to differ from monolinguals in their ability to negotiate competition across alternative responses, to switch from one task to another, and to ignore irrelevant information (e.g., Bialystok, Craik, & Luk, 2012). Critically, the brain networks that enable cognitive control are different in bilinguals and monolinguals, with evidence that bilinguals are able to engage control mechanisms more efficiently than their monolingual peers (e.g., Abutalebi et al., 2012; Gold et al., 2013). What is notable in these studies of cognitive control is that the tasks that have been used to assess cognitive performance and brain activation are themselves not language tasks. Rather, they are non-verbal cognitive tasks that induce conflict (e.g., Stroop tasks, flanker tasks, the Simon task).[1]

The initial interpretation of these two set of observations was that they are related. Bilinguals must negotiate the stream of competition across their two languages and experience in doing so creates expertise in the realm of cognitive control. Indeed, we have used the metaphor of the juggler to describe the situation that bilinguals face (e.g., Kroll et al., 2012). Learning to juggle two languages is hypothesized to produce skill in other cognitive domains in which similar types of competitive processes are manifest. But what aspect of linguistic athleticism produces these changes in cognition and the brain? Bilinguals do many different things with language and it is not at all clear that all or even most of them necessarily have any sort of direct correspondence with the observed cognitive and neural consequences.

Brain imaging studies show that the bilingual's two languages share the same neural tissue (e.g., Abutalebi, Cappa, & Perani, 2005). When there are differences in patterns of brain activation for the first (L1) and second (L2) languages, they are likely to reflect the level of proficiency or skill associated with the two languages, with the L2 more likely to require additional cognitive control (e.g., Abutalebi & Green, 2007). The requirement to engage control mechanisms in using the L2 and in regulating the activity of the L1 seems likely to be the source of the observed consequences of bilingualism. At the same time, there is no accepted model to date of how language processes differentially recruit cognitive resources to enable fluent performance and to produce domain-general consequences.

In the recent literature, there is a set of proposals that begins to address the broader issues of how bilingual experience shapes the neural networks that support language and its cognitive consequences (e.g., Baum & Titone, 2014; Green & Abutalebi, 2013; Kroll & Bialystok, 2013). In the present chapter we focus more narrowly on the processes that enable bilinguals to select the intended language when they read text, listen to spoken

---

[1] There are a few recent papers that attempt to catch the cognitive consequences of language processing as it takes place online (e.g., Blumenfeld & Marian, 2011; Martín, Macizo, & Bajo, 2010; Wu & Thierry, 2013). We discuss this work later in the chapter.

language, or plan speech in one language or the other. We return at the end of our discussion to consider how mechanisms of selection, which, as we will show, may differ for comprehension and production, may hold a clue to better understanding the cognitive consequences of multiple language use. Our review and analysis considers evidence primarily from lexical comprehension and production because that is where there has been the greatest number of studies and where these processes can be compared systematically. There is a valid and important question to be asked about how the claims about lexical processing might be extended to the comprehension and production of phrases, sentences, and discourse, but that question is beyond the scope of the present chapter.

As we noted at the onset, there is compelling evidence in all domains that bilinguals activate both languages in comprehension and in production. Curiously, there has been little direct comparison of the evidence in comprehension and production. Cross-language co-activation may be resolved quite differently in comprehension than in production because the intended language may not always be explicitly selected in comprehension. In language production, selection is forced by the fact that, at least for unimodal bilinguals who speak each of the two languages, there is only one output channel, making it is physically impossible for a bilingual to produce both languages at the same time. In contrast, in comprehension, it may not be a requirement to resolve co-activation fully. In this sense, language selection may not be necessary, or necessary to the same degree, during language comprehension. The goal of our chapter is to begin to compare these language processes as means to identify the scope of the control mechanisms that are engaged when bilinguals use each language alone or both languages together in mixed language contexts.

## 21.2  Bilingual comprehension

The evidence for parallel activation during language comprehension comes primarily from processing effects involving words with cross-language overlap, or words that are ambiguous between two languages, such as cognates and interlingual homographs (for a review, see Dijkstra, 2005). Cognates – translations which share both lexical form and meaning – often exhibit facilitated processing compared to lexically matched non-cognate control words due to the overlap at all levels (orthography, phonology, and semantics). In contrast, homographs are words that share lexical form but not meaning. To illustrate, the word "hotel" is a cognate in Dutch and English, with virtually the same form and meaning in both languages. In contrast, the word "room" means cream for your coffee in Dutch and is pronounced differently in the two languages. Homographs, also called false friends, often exhibit slower processing compared to lexically matched controls, but depending on the context in which they are presented, they can exhibit facilitated processing (e.g., Dijkstra, Van Jaarsveld, & Ten Brinke, 1998; Lemhöfer & Dijkstra, 2004). Presumably, homographs facilitate processing at the levels of lexical form, but the conflicting semantics create competition that produces interference. The form of the resulting homograph effect will then depend on the extent to which task demands require different levels of processing. Theoretically, the facilitation observed in cognate and homograph processing is presumed to stem from heightened activation levels, a decreased threshold for activation, increased functional frequency, common lexical storage, or a combination of these factors (e.g., Dijkstra, 2005). Regardless of the exact locus of the facilitation, all accounts attribute the effects of cross-language interaction to the overlap of lexical codes. Cognate and homograph effects can occur only for speakers of two or more languages and not for monolingual speakers of any language alone; they are considered the hallmark of language co-activation or non-selectivity. Models like the Bilingual Interaction Activation Model (BIA+) proposed by Dijkstra and van Heuven (2002), assume that bottom-up processes govern the earliest stages of word recognition, increasing the activation of all form-related codes regardless of the language that is actually presented.

Perhaps the most straightforward way to investigate language selection during comprehension is to ask whether bilinguals exploit cues to selectively attend to the language in use. If language cues enable selection to occur in advance or to reduce cross-language activation that is in process, then bilinguals should be able to function as monolinguals. That is, the presence of cross-language ambiguity should have little consequence for processing. For example, a Chinese–English bilingual reading text in English, knows immediately that the text is not in Chinese and, in theory, should be able to shut down the activation of phonology or meaning that is shared across the two languages. Likewise, the context in which a bilingual is processing spoken or written information should provide higher level cues to better enable the selection of the intended language. The evidence, overall, provides surprisingly little support for the notion that bilinguals can utilize cues of this sort to select the intended language in advance. The situation is counterintuitive given the great number of potential language cues. But there are also some differences in the evidence for the comprehension of written text vs. spoken language and we consider below how the modality of language processing may affect language selection.

### 21.2.1 The search for cues: modulating non-selectivity in comprehension

A logical approach in the search for language selection in comprehension is to determine whether there are cues in the input or in the context of language use that can modulate markers of language co-activation. If a cue is successful in reducing the influence of the unintended language or enhancing the activation of the intended language, then the presence of that cue should eliminate cognate and homograph effects. Language cues can fall into at least two different categories, although these categories may not be mutually exclusive. The first category consists of factors that function as a cue because they exploit cross-language differences. The Chinese–English reader encountering text in English is an example because of the difference in written script between Chinese and English. One need not be bilingual to know that the English text is not Chinese, but the question here is whether the bilingual can use that information to guide processing. The second category includes cues that capitalize on higher order contextual or linguistic information that may provide a pointer to the upcoming language. If bilinguals can exploit the presence of contextual cues, then processing text or listening to speech in one language alone should provide sufficient information to restrict processing to that language. As we will show, although there are some examples of language selectivity (e.g., Ju & Luce, 2004), more of the evidence demonstrates that bilinguals have difficulty in using this information to restrict processing (e.g., Van Assche et al., 2009).

### 21.2.2 Can bilinguals exploit language-specific features?

Examples of cross-language differences abound during language comprehension. One difference that should theoretically influence selection in word recognition includes the distinct lexical form of words in each language. While cognates and homographs share lexical form across the two languages, they also exhibit subtle differences in their degree of form overlap. The phonology of the bilingual's two languages is never identical and the orthography can overlap to varying degrees. In the case of different-script bilinguals, there may be phonological overlap between cognates or homographs but no overlap in the orthography. In the case of bimodal bilingualism, where one language is written or spoken and the other signed (e.g., American Sign Language and English), the two languages are structurally distinct. Yet in each case, there is evidence that readers activate information, including the translation equivalent, in one language when reading the other (e.g., Morford et al., 2011; Thierry & Wu, 2007). Although the magnitude of cognate and homograph effects in languages that share orthographic and phonological codes appears to be modulated by the degree of overlap (e.g., Dijkstra, Grainger, & van Heuven, 1999; Schwartz, Diaz, & Kroll, 2007), in language pairings that do not share lexical form, distinct cross-language features do not function as a cue to enable language selective processing, at least when information is presented in written form.

The evidence on spoken word recognition is more mixed with respect to cue sensitivity than the evidence on visual word recognition. Some studies have reported a pattern that is consistent with the language non-selectivity revealed in visual word recognition. Lagrou, Hartsuiker, and Duyck (2011) compared the performance of Dutch–English bilinguals on an auditory lexical decision task in which they had to decide whether spoken tokens were real words in one language alone. The tokens included Dutch–English homophones, words that sound similar but that have different meanings in the two languages. The cue that was introduced was the accentedness of the speaker's voice, with either a native English or native Dutch speaker producing the tokens to be judged. Lagrou et al. found that bilinguals were indeed sensitive to the presence of accentedness overall, but the accentedness of the spoken words did not affect the magnitude of the homophone effect. Bilinguals were slower to judge homophones than control words regardless of whether the accentedness of the spoken voice provided a cue to the language spoken. The overall sensitivity to accentedness suggests that they were not deaf to the cue – they indeed processed it. But they did not use it selectively to interpret the input as coming from one language alone.

Other studies of spoken word recognition have used the visual world paradigm (Allopenna, Magnuson, & Tanenhaus, 1998) to examine cross-language effects. In the visual world paradigm, participants see a real or computer-generated grid of objects in front of them while they hear a spoken word. Their task is to point to or click on the object that is named by the spoken word. The critical manipulation is whether among the objects in the visual display, there is another object whose name is phonologically similar to the target object (e.g., *candy–candle*). Eye movements are tracked while the task is performed and the basic finding is that listeners fixate longer on objects whose names are phonological competitors with the target name. Marian and Spivey (2003b) reported that there is an effect of phonological competitors not only within languages, but also between languages when bilinguals perform the task in one of their two languages. Like other word recognition results in the visual domain, these cross-language effects are typically larger and more robust when performing the task in the L2, but the fact that they are observed when performing the task in one language alone reveals the fundamental non-selectivity of word recognition.

Subsequent studies using the visual world paradigm have shown that subtle phonetic differences can alter the selectivity of the system. For example, Ju and Luce (2004) found that language-specific differences in voice onset time (VOT) changed the degree to which participants fixated on cross-language homophone distractors. When Spanish words were pronounced with a Spanish VOT, English competitor items were not fixated on any more than compared to control words. In contrast, when Spanish words were pronounced with English VOTs, English distractors were then considered by the participants as evidenced by an increase in the number of fixations compared to controls. This finding suggests that Spanish phonetic differences may have allowed the participants to selectively access Spanish without influence from English (see also Weber & Cutler, 2004). On the surface, the selectivity imposed by the presence of language-specific cues to the phonology in the visual world task would seem to be at odds with the lexical decision results of Lagrou et al. (2011), although the recognition tasks performed in each case are somewhat different. This leaves open the possibility that some types of cues may allow for selective access but it is not yet clear under what circumstances or over what time course.

In addition to orthographic and phonological ambiguity, language ambiguous words such as homographs or homophones frequently differ in their grammatical properties within each language. It appears that bilinguals may be able to capitalize on these differences in word class to exploit them as a language cue. Sunderman and Kroll (2006) found that lexical form interference could be eliminated in a translation recognition task (i.e., decide whether two words are translations of one another) when the two words differed in their grammatical class. When two words were not translation equivalents but the translation of one resembled the other (e.g., *hombre* (man)–*hambre* (hunger) in Spanish) there was interference only when the grammatical class of the two words matched. Likewise, Baten, Hofman, and Loeys (2011) showed that word class modulated the degree of language co-activation in a lexical decision task. They found a facilitatory homograph effect in lexical decision only when the meaning of the homograph shared grammatical class with its translation. In each of these examples, it is not clear whether the locus of selection occurs early or late in processing. According to models such as the BIA+ (Dijkstra & van Heuven, 2002), the earliest stages of bilingual word recognition should be data driven and higher-order cues, such as grammatical class, should only influence selection processes at a relatively late point in processing. In future research it will be critical to use methods such as eye tracking and event-related potentials (ERPs) that permit a sensitive analysis of the early time course of processing to answer this question. However, like the VOT results in the visual world studies, the report of a pattern of processing that is influenced by grammatical class also suggests that bilinguals may be able to exploit cues to language status under some circumstances.

### 21.2.3 Can bilinguals use context to guide language-specific lexical access?

Words do not typically appear in isolation, they are embedded within multiple contexts: in sentences, in text, and in extended discourse. Much of the research on language selection in bilingual word recognition has focused on how different contexts of use (particularly list composition and sentential context) might influence non-selectivity. Cognate facilitation seems to be relatively robust in the face of different language contexts (e.g., Dijkstra et al., 1998). Dijkstra et al. showed that cognate effects were present in an isolated lexical decision task regardless of the specific list composition, whether the lists contained words all in one language, or whether the list contained other-language distractor words. This was among the first studies to suggest that top-down contextual information was not utilized by bilinguals to control activation of the two languages.

With an isolated presentation, it is perhaps not surprising that both languages will be activated, especially for words with a high degree of cross-language overlap, such as cognates. In theory, isolated presentation heightens the ambiguity of language membership of a word. A Spanish–English bilingual who sees the cognate word "bus" presented alone would not know whether to activate Spanish or English, unless it were possible to utilize top-down information about the language membership of other words in the list. However, everyday language use includes many discourse and sentential features that go beyond list composition and that might function as language cues. A question then is whether a richer linguistic context, such as a sentence context, might provide bilinguals with information to predict the language of the upcoming words.

Quite surprisingly, even for words embedded in unilingual sentences, there is overwhelming evidence that bilinguals activate both language representations (e.g., Libben & Titone, 2009; Schwartz & Kroll, 2006; van Hell & de Groot, 2008). Duyck et al. (2007) showed that when Dutch–English bilinguals read English sentences naturalistically cognate words were fixated on for less time compared to matched control words. This pattern of fixation differences originated during very early measures of reading time and persisted until later measures, suggesting that both languages were activated throughout the entire time course of processing, despite the presence of a coherent sentence context all in one language. When bilinguals recognize words within sentences, cognate and homograph effects are still present. In visual word recognition within sentence context, eye movements have been used to track lexical co-activation throughout the entire time course of recognition (e.g., Libben & Titone, 2009). Data indicate that both languages are activated from the initial stages of word recognition that track orthographic encoding and lexical access, and they remain active until later stages that include semantic integration. This suggests that the presence of a coherent sentence context by itself does not cause lexical access to become language selective. Indeed, a few studies have shown that these cross-language effects can be observed even when bilinguals are reading in the native language alone (e.g., Van Assche et al., 2009). The only exception to language non-selectivity has been reported in the presence of sentences that are highly semantically constrained, with highly constrained contexts reducing or eliminating language non-selectivity (e.g., Libben & Titone, 2009; Schwartz & Kroll, 2006; van Hell & de Groot, 2008; but see Van Assche et al., 2010).

Another potential cue is in the context of usage. Socio-contextual situations which require only one language might allow bilinguals to selectively access that language whereas situations in which two languages are required might show evidence of co-activation. This finding would be consistent with Grosjean's (2001) language mode hypothesis, the idea that the activity of the bilingual's two languages varies along a continuum from monolingual mode, with one language used primarily, to bilingual mode, where both languages are actively used. More recently, Green and Abutalebi (2013) have extended this hypothesis into the Adaptive Control Hypothesis stating that the context in which bilinguals acquire and speak their second language may fundamentally determine how language selection proceeds. Hence, different language contexts (e.g., unilingual context vs. code-switching context) are proposed to lead to distinct patterns of language selection and to place differential demands on the cognitive and neural processes that support each language. Surprisingly, research on word recognition in isolation and in sentence context suggests that context plays less of a role in initial language selection than might be expected. For example, Gullifer, Kroll, and Dussias (2013) showed that cognate effects were present and of the same magnitude for words recognized within sentences regardless of whether the language of the sentence context was consistent within the experiment or whether the language of the sentence context switched every two sentences. The magnitude of the cognate effect for cognate translations embedded within the sentence did not depend on whether the previous sentence was in the same or in a different language and there was virtually no switch cost to process target cognates in sentence contexts that had changed language from those that had not.

In comparison to cognates, homographs appear to be more sensitive to the language context. After sufficient experience with a unimodal context in an experiment, bilinguals show effects of "zooming in" to the intended language. Following sufficient exposure to the language of the sentence context, homograph effects are diminished or eliminated (e.g., Elston-Güttler, Gunter, & Kotz, 2005). Likewise, in research on isolated word recognition, the magnitude of homograph effects are more closely related with aspects of list composition. Homograph effects are greatest, for example, when other language distractor items are included in the list of words for a unilingual lexical decision task (Dijkstra et al., 1998). It may be the case that homographs simply offer a more sensitive measure of relative activation levels of each language and the control mechanisms that regulate those activation levels compared to cognates. In a dynamic system that is under the control of executive function mechanisms and must take into account the context of language usage the contrast in sensitivity to context makes sense. Parallel activation of cognates is almost always beneficial to processing providing a facilitatory effect, where the parallel activation of homographs imposes a conflict that is only occasionally beneficial to processing in the face of conflict in meaning across languages. Hence, for homographs, bilinguals who are particularly skilled in control of both languages may be able to regulate the inhibition of competitors that are detrimental to fluent processing. By comparison, the resonance created by the convergence across lexical codes for cognates may be driven more directly by bottom-up processes that are immune to the influence of control mechanisms (for additional evidence on access in sentence context, see Titone et al., 2011).

The persistence of language non-selectivity, even in the presence of rich context, is counterintuitive and puzzling. Indeed, the evidence reviewed earlier, suggesting that there are no switch costs in lexical access when the entire sentence context switches back and forth, is surprising. But what happens when words switch from one language to the other? Language switching has been used as a means to understand the nature of the selection mechanism. Lexical switch costs have been documented in a number of word recognition studies (e.g., Thomas & Allport, 2000). Typically a switch cost is observed, with longer response times on trials following a language switch than following a same-language trial. That result is notable because the persistent activity of the two languages that we have documented might have led to a prediction of no switch costs if the bilingual is always in a functionally mixed language context. Critically, Thomas and Allport found effects of language-specific orthography but no modulation of those effects in the switch and no-switch conditions, suggesting that language selection affects late stages of processing in word recognition. As we will see in reviewing the evidence on bilingual production, the pattern of switch costs in comprehension stands in contrast to the one reported for production. While the explicit mechanism of language selection during comprehension is yet to be unequivocally identified, there is emerging research elucidating the link between a bilingual's capacity for inhibitory control and language selection and co-activation during comprehension. We turn to that evidence next.

### 21.2.4 How do bilinguals control selection processes in comprehension?

The fact that cross-language activation is observed even when bilinguals are required to only use one of their languages raises the question about how they select the language they need according to the context. Much of the recent research on bilingual language processing has focused on understanding the control mechanisms that allow them to overcome the negative influence of activating their two languages, and importantly, how the consequences of this parallel activation impact domain-general cognitive processes.

Two important remarks are relevant for language selection: first, given that language co-activation occurs, the presence of between-language competition introduces the need for a control mechanism that regulates the activation of the non-target language in order to correctly select the intended one; second, the non-selective activation of the two languages may give rise to differences in lexical access and the degree of between-language competition that depend on several factors that influence bilingual processing (Green & Abutalebi, 2013). For example, lexical selection may vary depending on the locus of cross-language activation, and so cross-language interference and the control effects may occur at different levels of language processing (Kroll, Bobb, & Wodniecka, 2006). Considering this, it is important to note that the consequences of the cross-language activation might be not the same for comprehension and production. Production is a conceptually driven process, in which the concept of a given word is activated before the word form and phonological properties of possible target words are available (e.g., Levelt, 1989). Comprehension, as we have documented in the studies we have reviewed above, is a bottom-up process, in which the orthography and phonology drive later conceptual access (e.g., Dijkstra & van Heuven, 2002). The implication of these fundamental differences between production and comprehension is that the locus and the control mechanisms for lexical selection may differ across both domains.

While there is no agreement about the nature of the control mechanisms that enable language selection, a recent body of evidence suggests the presence of inhibitory processes (for a review, see Kroll et al., 2008). Although most of the empirical evidence supporting inhibitory processes in bilingual processing comes from the language production domain (Costa & Santesteban, 2004a; Meuter & Allport, 1999) recent studies also demonstrate the involvement of inhibitory processes in bilingual language comprehension (Macizo, Martín, & Bajo, 2010).

As reviewed in the earlier section on language non-selectivity, most of the studies on cross-language interactions have used the general strategy of examining words that share lexical, orthographic, or phonological properties in two languages (e.g., false friends or homographs, cognates, and homophones). So, for example, in visual and spoken word recognition, competition may arise among lexical neighbors with either similar orthography or phonology. Following this strategy, Martín, Macizo, and Bajo (2010) investigated the role of the control processes involved in language selection using a paradigm that allows observing the cross-language activation and how it is resolved. They asked Spanish–English bilinguals to perform semantic relatedness judgments on English word pairs. On the critical trials, interlingual homographs were presented among the word pairs (e.g., the word "*pie*" means foot in Spanish and dessert *pie* in English). On the following trial, the word pair included the English translation of the Spanish meaning of the homograph. Bilinguals were slower to judge word pairs that contained a homograph (e.g., *pie*–*toe*). Critically, after responding to homographs, bilinguals slowed their responses when its Spanish meaning became relevant in the subsequent trial as compared to a control word pair (e.g., *foot–hand*). The interference effect found in the first trial was taken as an index of cross-language activation. Given the interference effect stemming from the parallel activation of the two homograph meanings, the bilinguals appeared to resolve the interference by suppressing the non-target and competing homograph meaning in order to select the appropriate one.

Martín et al. (2010) focused on the interval between the time in which interference was produced and the presentation of the irrelevant homograph meaning as a means to map out the time course of resolving inhibition. They found that the inhibitory effects were relatively short lived since they were observed in a time interval between 500 ms and 750 ms. After an interval of 750 ms, they seem to have recovered from inhibition. These findings indicate that inhibitory control processes are involved in the resolution of cross-language competition in comprehension, and this inhibition has transient effects. A critical point is that overcoming inhibition may take time and it can impose a cost in bilinguals' performance. The effects we have described were observed when bilinguals processed words, out of context, and under artificial experimental conditions. Bilinguals rarely use their two languages in this manner. In future work it will be important to ask whether these time-constrained processes are manifest when bilinguals comprehend language in higher-level context and, if so, whether context modulates the presence and time course of language selection.

Converging support for the idea that there is a brief period of inhibitory control that can be caught on the fly in comprehension has been reported by Blumenfeld and Marian (2011). They developed a variant of the visual world paradigm that has been used extensively as a means to investigate spoken word recognition. On a first trial, native English-speaking bilinguals and monolinguals were presented with a display in which they had to identify a word in English, the L1 for both groups. Their eyes were tracked while they performed the identification task. One of the pictures displayed on the first trial had a name that was a phonological competitor to the target English word that was spoken. Blumenfeld and Marian reported that both bilinguals and monolinguals experienced within-language competition on the first trial, revealed in the eye movement record, with somewhat longer fixations on the phonological competitor than on the control pictures. Critically, on a subsequent trial, the same grid was presented but without pictures of objects. Instead, in one of the four corners of the grid, an asterisk appeared and the participant was asked to click on the asterisk. They found an inhibitory pattern for the monolinguals on the second trial when the asterisk appeared in the position on the grid that had previously held the phonological competitor. Blumenfeld and Marian argued that the bilinguals had apparently resolved the inhibition by the time of the second trial, whereas the monolinguals had not.

They suggest that bilinguals are more efficient at resolving cross-language competition online, a result that is congenial with the findings of brain imaging studies that show that bilinguals produce less activation than monolinguals in brain areas such as the anterior cingulate cortex (ACC) that are implicated in the resolution of competition in non-linguistic tasks. Without a fine-grained analysis of the time course of processing, it is difficult to compare the Blumenfeld and Marian results directly to those of Martín et al. (2010), and of course the tasks are quite different, spoken word recognition in one case and a semantic relatedness judgment in the other. However, in both studies there is evidence that suggests that bilinguals cannot turn off the initial bottom-up processes that produce competition in comprehension. Rather, they learn to modulate its consequences in the moments afterwards. Each of these studies also suggests that the processing of inhibiting competitors is one that extends over a relatively brief time-span in comprehension. As we will see, this will stand in contrast to the findings in production, where inhibitory processes may include longer-lasting consequences for performance.

## 21.3 Bilingual production

Like the evidence on comprehension, studies of bilingual speech planning show that information about both languages is active, at least momentarily, when bilinguals plan to speak even a single word in one language alone (e.g., Costa, 2005; Hanulovà, Davidson, & Indefrey, 2011; Kroll et al., 2006). The parallel activation of two languages occurs for speakers who are highly proficient in both languages as well as for those who are still learning the L2. A focus in the most recent research in bilingual language processing is to understand what mechanisms allow bilinguals to negotiate language activation and, once proficient, to make few language errors (e.g., Gollan, Sandoval, & Salmon, 2011). Although bilinguals normally make few errors of language, the importance of a control mechanism has also been recognized in cases of aphasia where bilingual speakers who suffered neurological damage cannot properly control language selection, leading to pathological language mixing (Abutalebi & Green, 2008).

### 21.3.1 Two views of bilingual speech planning

A number of different mechanisms have been hypothesized to allow bilinguals to constrain selection to the intended language during speech planning (for a recent detailed review, see Kroll & Gollan, 2014). Findings also generally indicate that parallel activation can have multiple consequences, making the locus of language selection in production variable rather than fixed (e.g., Kroll et al., 2006), and dependent on a range of factors including the context of the language to be spoken (e.g., language immersion and the language profile of interlocutors), proficiency in the L2, and the demands of speaking associated with the particular production task to be performed. One alternative proposes that selection is language specific (e.g., Costa, Miozzo, & Caramazza, 1999; Finkbeiner et al., 2006; Finkbeiner, Gollan, & Caramazza, 2006). On this view, there may be activation of words within the language not in use but the activation of those words does not make them candidates for selection. This first hypothesis would require that bilinguals have a mechanism in place that allows them to use cues to enable them to select the language as efficiently as possible, a solution that we have called the "mental firewall" (e.g., Kroll et al., 2012).

Like the research on bilingual comprehension, external cues may be related to linguistic features of the two languages (e.g., phonological or lexical cues) but also to features of the context in which the two languages were acquired and are used. However, studies of language production that have examined the role of language cues, such as cross-language script differences, have failed to provide evidence that bilinguals can easily exploit the available cues (Hoshino & Kroll, 2008). Similarly, typological differences that should provide a clear means to categorize the two languages do not appear to function effectively as cues. For example, production studies in hearing bimodal bilinguals who speak one language and sign the other, have also shown that there are cross-language influences even when production engages different articulatory systems (e.g., Emmorey et al., 2008). It is possible, however, that script and typological differences are subtle in the sense that activation of information pertaining to script or typology does not occur in response to a trigger in the immediate environment. Cues may only become effective as a consequence of the bilingual's lifetime experience, with collective past experiences likely to be stored in memory (Jared, Poh, & Paivio, 2013), but not accessible in the moments leading up to speech unless there is an additional contextual trigger (e.g., Zhang et al., 2013). In this sense, the evidence on production would seem to mirror the results we have reviewed for comprehension. In each case, there appears to be activation of alternatives related to both the target language and the language not in use. For production, however, this observation is quite counterintuitive, because unlike comprehension, production is initiated by a top-down process that first engages ideas and then maps them to their respective linguistic forms. Logically, it would seem possible to identify the intended language at an early stage of speech planning.

If the logic of the language selective view is straightforward, providing a clear explanation of how selectivity is accomplished is not. By a language-selective account, there would have to be a means for sending greater activation to the intended language and the studies to date seem to suggest quite clearly that the intention to plan speech in one language alone is insufficient to restrict activation to that language (but see La Heij, 2005, for a defense of the selective position).

The alternative view is that all activated candidates compete for selection.[2] Superficially, this view would seem to align with the models of word recognition like BIA+ that account for non-selectivity in comprehension by assuming that bottom-up activation spreads to form-related words in both languages. But it is important to remember that the top-down planning of speech means that the codes that are first activated are related in meaning rather than form with the ideas to be communicated. Those meanings may subsequently activate word forms, including translation equivalents and phonological relatives (e.g., Colomé & Miozzo, 2010; Hoshino & Kroll, 2008; Hoshino & Thierry, 2011), but the sequence of processing differs in comprehension and production. Although the initiation of speech planning begins at a conceptual level, the evidence suggests that cross-language activation reaches all the way to the phonology and even beyond, to the execution of speech that is manifest in the acoustic representation of the spoken utterance, to the point where the unintended word may literally be on the tip of the bilingual's tongue (e.g., Gollan & Goldrick, 2012).

### 21.3.2 Evidence on language switching and language mixing

Studies of language production often adopt a logic similar to the one applied to word recognition so that bilingual speakers are asked to produce language ambiguous words, such as cognates. In production, unlike comprehension, the cognate word is not actually present, so showing that there is facilitation in naming a picture whose translation is a cognate in the language not to be spoken provides evidence for cascading activation all the way to the phonology of the alternative (e.g., Costa et al., 2000; Hoshino & Kroll, 2008).

In comprehension, the effects of cross-language ambiguity are perhaps the most compelling in revealing the architecture of the system because language ambiguous forms affect the earliest stages of recognition. In production, the evidence for language non-selectivity has relied more on the consequences of language switching and/or mixing. The logic is simple. If bilinguals can plan speech in one language alone, as if they were monolingual speakers, then a cost should be observed when there is uncertainty about the language to be spoken or when the languages switch from one utterance to the next. For production, this logic affects the earliest stages of planning, potentially revealing the most basic features of the architecture that underlie speech, unlike cognate facilitation effects that necessarily reflect later processing once speech planning has already been initiated.

---

[2] A third alternative is the frequency lag or weaker links hypothesis that has been proposed by Gollan and colleagues (e.g., Gollan et al., 2008) to account for the relatively lower frequency of use of each language in bilinguals relative to monolinguals. See Kroll and Gollan (2014) for a discussion of how this alternative contrasts with the competition for selection hypothesis.

### 21.3.3 Costs of language switching and mixing

When bilinguals are forced to switch from one language to the other in a naming task (e.g., name pictures or digits) there is a cost to processing, with longer naming latencies following switch than no-switch trials (e.g., Meuter & Allport, 1999). In language switching tasks, a picture or number is presented with a cue signaling in which language the stimulus is to be named. The finding that there is a cost to naming, following a language switch, might be interpreted as support for a language selective model of bilingual production. However, Meuter and Allport and many subsequent studies have reported that there is a curious asymmetry in switch costs, with larger costs when switching from the L2 into the L1 than the reverse. The greater switch cost into the L1 was initially taken as support for the claims of the Inhibitory Control (IC) model (Green, 1998) which suggested that production of the L2 requires inhibition of the L1 and that subsequent production of L1 then reflects the spillover of that inhibitory process. It is beyond the scope of the present chapter to provide a comprehensive review of the switch cost asymmetries and there are other many discussions of how these asymmetries might be interpreted (e.g., Bobb & Wodniecka, 2013; Gollan & Ferreira, 2009; Schwieter & Sunderman, 2008). For present purposes, the critical observation is that there are switch costs and that sometimes the more dominant L1 reveals those costs more clearly than the less dominant L2.

A similar differential pattern has been reported for language mixing (e.g., Kroll et al., 2000). When the language of production is uncertain, the L1 suffers a cost and that cost can be observed to the point where even highly L1-dominant bilinguals are slower to speak the L1 than the L2 and where the consequences of mixing can be observed not only in behavior but also in the earliest time course of planning revealed using ERPs and in brain imaging patterns using fMRI (e.g., Christoffels, Firk, & Schiller, 2007; Guo et al., 2011). Kroll et al. (2000) found that Dutch–English speakers were slower to produce the Dutch names of pictures when faced with the requirement to produce picture names in English unpredictably, relative to blocked trials in which they produced words in one language only. Critically, the time for the same speakers to produce English L2 names of pictures was unaffected by whether picture naming was blocked or mixed, suggesting that the L1 is active during speech planning in the L2, regardless of whether there is a requirement to make it active.

A language switching study that has generated a great deal of discussion was reported by Costa and Santesteban (2004a). They compared the language switching performance of balanced and highly proficiency Spanish–Catalan bilinguals with less proficient speakers for whom there was clear dominance in the L1. For the L1-dominant speakers, they replicated the switch cost asymmetry reported by Meuter and Allport (1999) but for the balanced and high proficiency speakers, the switch costs were symmetric for the two languages. The different pattern for the two speaker groups was initially interpreted as meaning that inhibitory control is required for those who are less proficient but once high proficiency is achieved, there is no longer a need for inhibition. Essentially the idea was that once the two languages are equal sparring partners, they can be engaged without differential regulation. However, another result in the Costa and Santesteban study betrays that interpretation. Although there was indeed a difference in the symmetry of the switch costs for the different types of bilingual speakers, there was also evidence that even for the high proficiency and balanced bilinguals, under the conditions of language mixing that are required by the switching paradigm, the L1 was produced more slowly than the L2. The fact that these two sources of evidence on switching and mixing produce different results can be understood if we assume that in production there may be multiple components of inhibitory control (for a discussion of these issues in the domain of translation and interpretation, see de Groot & Christoffels, 2006). The recent research on bilingual production has focused on this issue as a means to understand how language selection might be achieved.

### 21.3.4 Components of inhibitory control in production

The forced switching that is imposed by the language switching paradigm requires that bilinguals speak words in each of the two languages in a sequence that is highly unnatural. Although one might argue that all decontextualized lexical performance is unnatural to some degree, bilinguals often switch between two languages after speaking one language for a period of time. Another approach to investigating selection in production was taken by Misra et al. (2012). The idea was to enable bilinguals to speak one language alone, the way that they might more naturally, and then to impose a switch of language across blocks. If the switch costs that have been documented in forced trial-to-trial switching reflect a process that is imposed by the artificial nature of the task, then within a few trials, bilinguals should recover from the switch. Misra et al. asked relatively proficient Chinese–English bilinguals to name pictures in blocks of trials in either L1 (Chinese) or L2 (English). The manipulation was only whether naming was performed first in the L1 and then in the L2 or in the reverse order. The pictures to be named in each language were identical, with the prediction of priming on the second presentation of a picture relative to the first. Misra et al. recorded ERPs while the pictures were named and also behavioral measures of response time and accuracy. They found that when pictures were named in the L2 following the L1, the hypothesized priming was observed. ERPs were less negative on the second naming of a picture than the first, suggesting that there was facilitation in processing. In contrast, an inhibitory pattern was observed when the L1 followed the L2. Not only was there not a pattern consistent with priming, but there was a larger n-2 component and greater negativity for the L1 following the L2, consistent with the presence of inhibition for the L1. Beyond the different patterns as a function of language naming order, the most surprising result was that the inhibitory pattern in L1 following L2 was maintained over the course of two blocks of L1 naming. These bilinguals had ample opportunity to recover from any momentary inhibition imposed by speaking the L2 but many trials later were still showing the consequences (and see Phillip, Gade, & Koch, 2007, and Philipp & Koch, 2009, for evidence from the n-2 repetition paradigm that supports a similar inhibitory account). The use of the same pictures across languages in the Misra et al. study did not permit an assessment of the scope of inhibition but the pattern suggests that there is inhibition that is extended in time. As noted earlier, there may be multiple components of inhibitory control. Local inhibition may operate over specific words or conceptual categories and may extend for brief periods of time. Global inhibition may engage an entire language and last for a relatively long time.

Guo et al. (2011) used fMRI to track the patterns of brain activation when bilinguals name in extended blocks as they did in the Misra et al. (2012) study. The design in the Guo et al. study was identical to the blocked picture-naming procedure in Misra et al. except that following the blocked picture-naming trials, Chinese–English bilinguals named pictures in a mixed language block. Critically, different patterns of brain activation were found when comparing the blocked and mixed naming trials (hypothesized to reflect local inhibition) and the spillover effect of naming in different block orders (hypothesized to reflect global inhibition). The dorsal anterior cingulate cortex (ACC) and the supplementary motor area (SMA) appeared to play important roles in local inhibition, while the dorsal left frontal gyrus and parietal cortex appeared to be important for global inhibition.

In recent studies, each of these observations has been replicated in behavioral studies that used different tasks and different language pairings. For example, Van Assche, Duyck, and Gollan (2013) compared performance on a verbal letter fluency task as a function of the order of the language blocks (L1 or L2 first), the type of speaker (Dutch–English or Chinese–English), and whether the letter cues were the same or different across languages. They replicated the block order effect reported by Misra et al. (2012) in that letter fluency was reduced for the dominant language when it followed the less dominant language. The groups differed, however, in that only the Chinese–English bilinguals, but not the Dutch–English bilinguals, showed these effects globally, regardless of whether the letter cues were repeated or not. The pattern of results suggests that all bilinguals, regardless of their proficiency, show evidence of inhibitory processing, but that proficiency may determine the scope of inhibition.

Martín, Bajo, and Kroll (2013) reported a study that compared the behavioral performance of relatively proficient Chinese–English bilinguals when they named pictures in blocked or mixed language trials. The innovation in this study was to add a concurrent updating task that required speakers to listen to a continuous series of tones and to press a key whenever three equal tones appear consecutively. The logic here was to determine whether the addition of a dual task would selectively disrupt inhibitory processing. The results showed that the updating task eliminated the block order effect. When bilinguals named pictures in L1 following L2 while they were performing the dual task, there was no apparent inhibition of the L1. In contrast, a robust effect of language mixing was observed regardless of whether bilinguals were performing the updating task or not. Although bilinguals were slower to name pictures overall when performing the concurrent updating task than not, the result of interest was that the disruptive effects were differential for the two hypothesized components of inhibitory control.

The findings on bilingual production converge on the conclusion that bilinguals, regardless of their proficiency, inhibit the L1 to enable speech planning in the L2. The clue first present in the Costa and Santesteban (2004a) language switching data, that there might be more than one component of inhibitory control, has been supported by the recent studies that were designed to examine this issue explicitly. It remains to be determined how not only language proficiency and dominance, but also the context of language use, may modulate each of these components. Green and Abutalebi (2013) argue that the neural networks that support bilingual language processes are necessarily tuned differently in response to the requirement to engage these processes differentially. So a bilingual who is a habitual code switcher and living in an environment in which code switching is prevalent, may engage inhibitory mechanisms differently than a bilingual who uses each of his or her two languages in separate environments. Likewise, individuals who are immersed in an L2 environment may adjust the need for endogenous control. Linck, Kroll, and Sunderman (2009) showed that university students studying abroad for a semester produced reduced output in their L1 in a category fluency task relative to classroom learners but their L1 performance rebounded upon their return home (and see Baus, Costa, & Carreiras, 2013, and Levy et al., 2007, for a related laboratory version of language immersion). Critically, what these new data on language production show is that inhibitory control processes are engaged by the most proficient bilinguals as well as by L2 learners. It remains to be seen which of these processes are ephemeral, producing short-term effects that are modulated by context and language usage, and which of them depend on characteristics of the bilinguals themselves and the linguistic structure associated with the bilingual language pairings (see Lev-Ari & Peperkamp, 2013, for a recent discussion of this issue for how individual differences in inhibitory control may modulate the effects of the L2 on L1 phonetics).

## 21.4 Language selection in comprehension vs. production

The research we have reviewed in this chapter demonstrates that language selection is not a simple nor unitary mechanism. Bilinguals develop the means to negotiate persistent cross-language activation and to resolve the resulting competition in ways that reflect the demands that are selective in comprehension and production. In comprehension, there appear to be short-lived inhibitory processes whereas in production there may be control processes that require different types of inhibition and that sometimes extend over relatively long periods of time. There is a great deal that remains to be investigated, including the implications of the selection mechanisms in comprehension and production for domain-general cognitive performance and the way that these language processes, in and of themselves, may change and adapt in different circumstances.

Green and Abutalebi (2013) argue there may be particular language skills and contexts that determine how the neural networks that support language change with experience. A topic that we haven't mentioned in our review but that draws on both comprehension and production in unique ways is translation and simultaneous interpretation. In a sense, skilled translation is a special form of extreme bilingualism. For interpreters, in particular, there are time pressures that render the task of using both languages quite differently than ordinary bilingualism. Although the basic research program on these issues is relatively new, the picture that emerges suggests that these skills sometimes modulate basic mechanisms of language processing and sometimes do not. For example, in a study examining lexical processing in sentence context, Ibáñez, Macizo, and Bajo (2010) reported that translators were less likely to engage inhibitory mechanisms. That finding makes sense, from the perspective that the goal for translators is to activate the other language continually, but demonstrating that it affects their performance even when they are not actively translating suggests that the nature of their language experience has consequences that extend beyond specific tasks. Likewise, Christoffels, de Groot, and Kroll (2006) showed that although interpreters have exceptional memory skills, a finding that in and of itself is difficult to interpret with respect to cause and effect, their performance in basic lexical production tasks like those we have reviewed in this chapter, is similar to other high proficiency bilinguals. In this instance, their cognitive abilities did not appear to modulate language processing.[3]

---

[3] In the literature on translation and simultaneous interpretation there is often discussion about the contribution of possible self-selection factors. Only particular people seek training in these skills and it is not clear whether the observed cognitive advantages reflect individual differences that led them to seek training or the consequences of the training itself. Likewise, in a context such as the Netherlands, where virtually all university-educated individuals are multilingual, it is not clear whether the absence of differences on basic language processing tasks for interpreters and ordinary bilinguals means that there is no consequence of having these skills for language processing or whether the bilinguals to

The findings of the studies reported above suggest that the performance of professional translators and interpreters might not differ from other bilinguals while performing different production tasks but, at the same time, they show differences in the use of cognitive control in bilingual processing. In line with this source of evidence, a recent study shows that translators show a similar pattern of performance in comprehension tasks as that reported for language production. Martín et al. (under review) tested a group of professional translators using the same procedure as Macizo et al. (2010). The translators performed a semantic relatedness task in their L2 (i.e., English) on word pairs including interlingual homographs or control matched words (see the description of the paradigm in the section about selection processes in comprehension in this chapter). They found that the translators were similar to the control bilingual group, showing longer latencies in response to the word pairs containing homographs. Given that they showed the interference effect in this kind of trial, it would be expected that after responding to homographs the translators would also perform similarly to the control bilinguals by showing an inhibitory effect in the subsequent trial as a sign of the suppression of the non-target and competing homograph meaning. However, unlike the bilingual control group, the translators did not show the inhibitory effect as a result of solving cross-language competition. This results show nicely how a specific bilingual context can shape the experience in the usage of control processes involved in language processing. In the practice of their profession, a translator rarely speaks. The input for a translator comes mainly from the comprehension domain and the output is elaborated in written production. Although they do not have the temporal pressure as interpreters do, they are required to change from one language to another constantly. It is not strange then, that when they are required to work only in one language, they perform as other bilinguals do. However, the particular experience they have changing between languages shows that the interplay between comprehension and production shapes the way in which they use cognitive control mechanisms and it is reflected in a differential performance solving cross-language competition (Green & Abutalebi, 2013). A question for future research will be to determine the scope of the consequences of particular types of bilingual language experience in both comprehension and production for altering the manner in which cross-language competition is negotiated.

One implication of the research that we have discussed is that bilinguals and monolinguals might be understood to be processing language under very different task demands and those differences might be expected to have consequences not only for language, but also for

whom the interpreters were compared also use their languages in a unique environment that masks the contribution of other factors.

cognition and brain function. Recent imaging studies (e.g., Parker Jones et al., 2012) have reported differences in patterns of brain activation for bilinguals and monolinguals even when they perform the same tasks in their L1 only. Because the neural support for language processing is shared across the bilingual's two languages (e.g., Abutalebi et al., 2005) and because the networks of control that are associated with them change with language experience (e.g., Abutalebi et al., 2012; Gold et al., 2013), it may not be surprising that differences between monolinguals and bilinguals emerge even when they perform the same tasks only in the native language.

The characterization we have provided of selection and control in bilingual comprehension and production might allow a reader to come to the mistaken conclusion that these processes are independent of one another. To the contrary, we assume that they are tightly linked (e.g., MacDonald, 2013). One context in which it is possible to begin to identify the way in which performance in production provides a cue to comprehension comes from studies of code switching behavior. Studies have begun to ask whether the few markers of disfluency that occur in the context of code switches are informative about the locus of planning and control in code switching mode. Hlavac (2011) found that Croatian–English speakers tended to produce few hesitation and monitoring phenomena (e.g., hesitations, pauses, verbal fillers) overall in code switched speech (around 2 percent of the total utterances contained these phenomena). He also found that a significantly greater proportion of verbal fillers preceded than followed a code switch. More importantly, when hesitation and monitoring phenomena occurred, they were found more often in the context of code switched words that do not contain the phonology or morphological patterns of the base language. The Hlavac results suggest that presence of disfluencies may not be the result of retrieval difficulties during code switches, but instead may serve to allow the speaker to signal an upcoming switch to the listener.

The pattern of code switching behavior reported by Hlavac can be understood within the framework of the Adaptive Control Hypothesis (Green & Abutalebi, 2013). The description of the highly proficient group of Croatian–English speakers sampled for his study suggests that this group may have adapted to a language context in which dense code switching is the norm. The Adaptive Control Hypothesis predicts that these bilinguals have developed a strategy that allows the speaker to opportunistically exploit co-activation of two languages, rather than having them in competition. It is our interpretation that the use of integrated word forms in code switched speech is one sign that cooperative co-activation of L1 and L2 exists. Code switching may therefore provide a model, and a uniquely bilingual model, for evaluating the way in which comprehension is tuned to production.

## 21.5 Conclusions

In this chapter we reviewed the basic evidence for language non-selectivity at the lexical level in bilingual comprehension and production. At a general level, the findings in the two domains are similar. There is parallel activation of the bilingual's two languages in both comprehension and in planning for production and it is difficult, if not impossible, for bilinguals to easily exploit available cues to the language in use to override language non-selectivity. At a more detailed level, comprehension and production differ in some important respects, including the nature of the information that is active and competing across languages, the scope of inhibitory processes, and the time course over which inhibition occurs. There is a call now to relate language processing more closely to its cognitive and neural consequences and to identify the causal basis of these experiential changes (e.g., Baum & Titone, 2014; Green & Abutalebi, 2013; Kroll & Bialystok, 2013). The research findings we have discussed provide an initial basis to pursue this question, paying closer attention to what it is that bilinguals are doing with language when they speak and understand one another. Like other proposals, our analysis of differences in comprehension and production suggests that the situation is more complex than we understood it to be. But it also shows that using bilingualism as a tool demonstrates the way that juggling two languages in one mind and brain may reveal more about foundational principles than we could ever know by studying monolingual speakers alone.

# 22

# On the mechanism and scope of language control in bilingual speech production

Cristina Baus, Francesca Branzi, and Albert Costa

## 22.1 Introduction

The issue of how bilingual speakers manage to control their two languages in the course of speech production is central to the study of bilingualism. The fact that bilingual speakers have a situation of cross-language "synonymy" and that the decision of speaking in one language does not suffice to turn off the other prompts two questions: how the selection of the various linguistic representations in the desired language is achieved and how interference from the non-desired language is avoided.

The problem of how bilinguals control their two languages (referred to as "bilingual language control," bLC) is present at all levels of linguistic representation, lexical, syntactic and phonological.[1] In this chapter, we will focus on the lexical level, for which each concept has two potential words that map onto it and, in particular, on how speakers manage to focus their lexicalization process (i.e., word selection) on those lexical representations belonging to the response language. We address the reader to other chapters in this handbook to find a detailed description of the bLC mechanisms that might operate at other levels of representation (e.g., syntactic).

---

This research was supported by one grant from the Spanish government, PSI2011-23033, one grant from the Catalan government, SGR2009-152, and one European grant, FP7/2007–2013, Cooperation grant agreement n. 613465-AThEME. C. Baus is supported by a post-doctoral fellowship of the Marie Curve Actions (FP7-PEOPLE 204–2016, REA agreement n. 623845). F. Branzi is supported by a pre-doctoral fellowship from the Spanish government (FPU-2009–2013).

[1] Models of speech production agree that in the course of speaking, information flows through the different levels of processing: semantic, syntactic, lexical and phonological (e.g., Caramazza, 1997; Dell, 1986; Levelt et al., 1999). A more detailed sketch on how bilingual language production is achieved can be found in Chapter 18 of this handbook.

The chapter is structured in two main sections. In the first, we review the current evidence on the nature of the cognitive mechanisms involved in bLC and more specifically on the involvement of the inhibitory process during bilingual language production. We do so by paying special attention to the evidence coming from the language switching paradigm, findings from behavioral, electrophysiological, and neuroimaging studies. We argue that the evidence in favor of such a mechanism is more mixed than is usually acknowledged. In the second section of the chapter, we turn to two aspects of the scope of the bilingual language control mechanisms. First, we review the evidence on whether such bLC mechanisms act on specific lexical items or rather involve control over the whole lexicon (the so-called "local" vs. "global" control). Second, we describe the (scarce) evidence regarding how the bLC system works in the different contexts in which bilinguals might be engaged: those contexts in which the two languages are continuously mixed (e.g., trial-by-trial language switching task) and those contexts in which the two languages are blocked (e.g., blocked naming task). This comparison is informative about the flexibility of the bLC system in adapting to the demands of different bilingual situations (Green & Abutalebi, 2013).

## 22.2 On the involvement of the inhibitory processes during bLC

The various proposals of bLC functioning can be divided into two groups regarding the extent to which competition is proposed between the two languages at the lexical level. According to some models, lexical selection in bilinguals proceeds basically in the same way as in monolinguals. These models propose that given that the decision of which language to use is already set at the conceptual level, this should be enough for the lexical selection mechanism to focus only on the representations of the desired language (Costa & Caramazza, 1999; Costa, Miozzo, & Caramazza, 1999; Finkbeiner, Gollan, & Caramazza, 2006; La Heij, 2005). However, this is not to say that these models do not differ in the extent to which the non-response language is activated. In contrast with these models, other researchers have advocated for a model in which, not only are the two lexical systems activated during the course of bilingual language production, but also that such systems enter into competition (e.g., de Bot, 1992; Green, 1986, 1998; Hermans et al., 1998; Lee & Williams, 2001; Poulisse & Bongaerts, 1994). This competition is then resolved by an inhibitory mechanism that suppresses the activation of the lexical items belonging to the non-response language. Within this view, the Inhibitory Control Model (ICM) (Green, 1998) has been the one receiving more experimental attention (e.g., Levy et al., 2007; Linck, Kroll, & Sunderman, 2009; Misra et al., 2012; Philipp, Gade, & Koch, 2007). The basic assumption of this model is that language is considered an instantiation of motor action, and therefore those processes underlying language control are recruited from those of action control. Similarly, the same neural circuits are considered to underlie bLC and more general cognitive control (Abutalebi & Green, 2007). This is important because as we will see most of the experimental paradigms on bLC have been borrowed from those employed to explore domain-general cognitive control (e.g., language switching paradigm). Before critically reviewing the most relevant evidence claimed to support the involvement of inhibitory processes and evidence problematic for this view, let us first describe the basic tenets of the ICM (Green, 1998).

## 22.2.1 The Inhibitory Control Model: main assumptions

The ICM (Green, 1998) assumes that the two languages of a bilingual become activated during the process of lexicalization, and that such activation leads to lexical competition. To avoid potentially massive cross-language competition, an inhibitory mechanism operates over the lexical representations of the non-target language (see also Abutalebi et al., 2008). As a result, the activation of these representations is hampered, reducing potential cross-language interference and allowing for the successful selection of lexical items from the intended language. For example, if the intention of an English–Spanish bilingual is to name a picture in the L1 (e.g., "dog"), the language schemas will inhibit the activation of all those lemmas with an incorrect language tag. In our example "*perro*" will be inhibited in addition to all the semantically related words in Spanish ("*gato*," "*zorro*").

This view also posits two important assumptions regarding the functioning of the inhibitory control system. First, the amount of inhibition applied to a given language depends on the strength with which its representations are activated to begin with. Hence, when trying to speak in a weak language (i.e., the L2), the inhibition applied to the dominant language (i.e., the L1) is higher than vice versa. This assumption comes from the reactive nature of the inhibitory system, in the sense that it only acts after the lexical representations of the non-target language have been activated. Second, the activation of previously inhibited representations takes time. That is, overcoming inhibition requires time, and indeed the higher the inhibition exerted the more time is needed to overcome its after-effects.

The large majority of experimental evidence regarding the presence of inhibitory processes in bLC comes from the pattern of results observed in the language switching paradigm. Despite differences between the specific instantiations of this paradigm, they all involve speakers using their two languages, and hence facilitate the ability to test the after-effects of using one language on the subsequent use of the other language. Given the concrete and detailed assumptions of the ICM regarding such after-effects, the language switching task provides the ideal ground to test them.

## 22.2.2 Experimental evidence from language switching: the switch cost

The first and most-used instantiation of the language switching paradigm is the trial-by-trial language switching task (for a review, see, Bobb & Wodniecka, 2013), a task borrowed from the domain-general task switching literature (e.g., Allport, Styles, & Hsieh, 1994; Jersild, 1927; Monsell, 2003). Indeed, as mentioned above, most of the studies using this paradigm assume some sort of relationship between the bLC mechanisms and those involved in domain-general control processes (e.g., Meuter & Allport, 1999). In the trial-by-trial language switching task, participants are required to name pictures in their two languages. The language in which a given picture is supposed to be named is signaled by a cue (e.g., color), which varies from trial to trial. If a given picture is named in the same language as the one used in the preceding trial, this trial is considered a repeat trial. In contrast, if a given picture is named in a different language, this trial is considered a switch trial. The basic finding in this context is the slower naming latencies for switch than repeat trials: the so-called "switch cost."[2] This cost is found in switching paradigms that do not involve linguistic processes (Martin et al., 2011; Meiran, 1996; Monsell, 2003; Schneider & Anderson, 2010). Indeed, one of the interpretations of this switch cost, but by no means the only one, is that it originates from the inhibitory control applied to the non-response task; an interpretation consistent with the main tenet of the ICM.

Perhaps the most frequently cited evidence regarding the inhibitory nature of the bLC is the presence of asymmetrical switch costs in speech production (Costa & Santesteban, 2004a; Costa, Santesteban, & Ivanova, 2006; Jackson et al., 2001; Linck, Schwieter, & Sunderman, 2012; Macizo, Bajo, & Paolieri, 2012; Meuter & Allport, 1999; Philipp, Gade, & Koch, 2007; Schwieter & Sunderman, 2008; Wang et al., 2007). This effect refers to the observation that switching from the weak to the dominant language is more costly than vice versa. This effect finds a ready explanation in the ICM because the model assumes that the amount of inhibitory control applied to a given language is proportional to its strength; that is, the stronger the language, the more the inhibition needs to be applied. Hence, the dominant language would be more inhibited than the non-dominant language as a result of the imbalance in their strengths (level of activation). As a consequence, language reactivation becomes harder for

---

[2] In the task switching literature the "switch cost" has been also called the "n-1 shift cost" (e.g., Philipp & Koch, 2006). However, "switch cost" and "n-1 shift cost" refer to the same effect, which is calculated by subtracting response times of repeat trials from those of switch trials.

the dominant language (due to the stronger inhibition) leading to the observed asymmetrical switch cost.

Further studies have produced results consistent with this interpretation, showing that when asked to switch between two languages of similar strength, the asymmetrical switch cost disappears, presumably because the same amount of inhibitory process is applied to the two languages, leading to a symmetrical switch cost between the two languages (Calabria et al., 2012; Costa & Santesteban, 2004a; Costa, Santesteban, & Ivanova, 2006; Gollan & Ferreira, 2009; Schwieter & Sunderman, 2008).

Hence, the evidence reported up to this point is consistent with the tenets of the ICM and can even be taken as support for the inhibitory account. However, other results appear to be problematic. For instance, it has been reported that switching between the dominant and non-dominant languages does not always lead to asymmetrical switch costs as predicted by the ICM. Indeed, when high-proficient bilinguals switch between their L1 and a much weaker L3, symmetrical rather than asymmetrical switch costs are observed (Costa et al., 2004, 2006). Although these results are problematic for the ICM, Costa and Santesteban (2004a) argued that they might reflect differences in the control mechanisms put in play by high-proficient and low-proficient bilinguals, since inhibitory control is engaged more in the latter type of speaker. Therefore, bilinguals with higher levels of proficiency in their two languages would have developed specific language selection mechanisms that do not rely on inhibition, and, allow them to successfully select the intended language regardless of the strength between the languages required for production (Costa, Santesteban, & Ivanova, 2006; Schwieter & Sunderman, 2008, 2009; but see Costa et al., 2006, for contrasting findings, with an asymmetrical switch cost for high-proficient bilinguals when a very weak language was involved, L4 or a new learned language, along with the dominant language).

There are however other results that are more difficult to reconcile with the ICM.[3] For instance, Christoffels, Firk, and Schiller (2007) found symmetrical switch costs with low-proficient bilinguals (see also Prior & Gollan, 2011). They tried to accommodate this observation by appealing to the fact that these bilinguals switch between languages frequently on an everyday basis. While this may be the case, at the very least these results reveal that it is not only the level of proficiency of the two languages that determines the asymmetry or symmetry of the switch costs. Consistent with this view, and rather problematic for the ICM, is the study of Verhoef et al. (2009) in which the same bilingual participants showed asymmetrical and symmetrical costs in slightly different versions of the language switching paradigm. Indeed, when the language cue was

---

[3] Challenging also the ICM, Runnqvist, Strijkers, Alario, & Costa (2012) showed no trace of inhibition when bilinguals were asked to switch between languages in the cumulative semantic interference (CSI) paradigm.

presented very close in time to the target picture (500 ms), asymmetrical switch costs were present, and when the cue and the picture were separated by a longer interval (1,250 ms), the switch costs turned out to be symmetrical (see also Verhoef, Roelofs, & Chwilla, 2010). The authors acknowledged the problematic nature of this result for the inhibitory control interpretation of asymmetrical switch costs, and provided an alternative explanation that dispensed with this assumption.

Along the same lines, Finkbeiner et al. (2006) report a striking observation of asymmetrical switch costs and a lack of switch costs for the same participants in the very same language-switch session. In their experiment, participants named digits in either the dominant or the non-dominant language according to the language cue. Furthermore, the experiment also included some pictures that had to be named only in the dominant language interspersed between the digit trials. Responses for the digits revealed an asymmetrical switch cost, switching being more difficult for the dominant language. Conversely, there was no switch cost for picture naming. That is, picture naming in the dominant language was not affected by the language in which the previous digit was named (the same or not). The authors claimed that the pattern of switch costs depended on whether the items used in the experiment needed to be named in the two languages (bivalent stimulus) or not (univalent stimulus). Although, at present the origin of the switch cost is still not clear, these observations pose some challenges to the ICM.

Together, the studies that have addressed the presence of asymmetrical/symmetrical switch costs related to language proficiency reveal a complex pattern of results that is occasionally in accord with the ICM and in other instances is not. Clearly, further studies are needed to pay special attention to how what seem to be irrelevant experimental details modulate the pattern of language-switch costs. In this respect, a close inspection of the large literature on domain-general task switching will be of great help (e.g., Koch et al., 2010).

We turn now to review the studies that have explored the electrophysiological correlates of the language-switch costs and how they support the existence of inhibitory processes in bLC. The critical ERP component in this respect is a negative deflection in switch trials. That is, switch trials elicit an enhanced negativity (N200)[4] as compared to repeat trials. In the context of domain-general task switching this component has often been interpreted as revealing inhibitory processes, although other interpretations have also been advanced. In the linguistic context, Jackson et al. (2001) found that switch trials elicited an increased N200 relative to repeat trials. Interestingly, this N200 modulation associated

---

[4] The N200 ERP modulation appears somewhat delayed in the language experiments (see, i.e., Christoffels et al., 2007; Branzi et al., 2014; Misra et al., 2012). Importantly, regardless of its latency, both negativities are considered to reflect the same control processes.

with language switching was only present when switching to the non-dominant language (see also Verhoef et al., 2010). Such asymmetry was interpreted as revealing that the L1 must be strongly inhibited when accessing lexical representations in the L2. Note here, that the asymmetrical patterns in behavioral and ERP measures mirror each other, an issue that, according to the authors, is consistent with the workings of the inhibitory system. Unfortunately, subsequent (and, to a certain extent, comparable) studies have failed to report consistent results.

In the study of Christoffels et al. (2007) described above, the modulation of the N200 behaved rather differently. First, the modulation was only present for the dominant language (unlike in Jackson et al.'s (2001) results). Second, and perhaps more problematically, the enhanced negativity was present for the repeat trials, rather than for the switch trials as in Jackson et al. In spite of the explanation offered by the authors regarding the experimental differences between the two studies (i.e., the predictability of the switch trials), it is nevertheless difficult to reconcile their results.

Finally, Verhoef et al. (2009) obtained a quite different pattern of results compared with the above-mentioned studies. Recall that in this study there were two conditions regarding the interval between the language cue and the target picture. In the short interval condition, asymmetrical behavioral switch costs were observed; however, the ERPs did not show any modulation of the N200 associated with switching (see also Martin et al., 2013). Hence, to the extent that the N200 indexes inhibitory processes, one could claim that asymmetrical switch costs can be present without any trace of inhibition. In the long interval condition, in addition to symmetrical switch costs (despite the fact that the participants were relatively low-proficient bilinguals), surprisingly, there were also N200 modulations of the same magnitude in the two languages.

In sum, the evidence from the electrophysiological studies has not helped to elucidate how the asymmetries/symmetries in the language switching task should be interpreted. However, what seems clear is that more caution should be exercised when interpreting the N200 modulation as an unequivocal index of inhibition in bilingual speech production. Again, the task-switching literature and the different interpretations of what the N200 component indexes, can help us in this regard (e.g., Barcelo, 2003; Martin, Barcelo, Hernandez, & Costa, 2011).

When considering the evidence from neuroimaging data focusing on bLC, at a more theoretical level, the relation between bLC and more domain-general control is relatively clear. Thus, similar brain areas are considered to underlie language switching and task-switching (Abutalebi & Green, 2007, 2008; see also Luk et al., 2012, for a meta-analysis of brain areas involved in language switching), and as such they are constituted by a brain network involving prefrontal areas, left inferior and superior parietal cortices, the anterior cingulate cortex (ACC), and the caudate nucleus. However, once again a complex picture arises when comparing the experimental evidence across studies. Wang et al. (2007) tested a group of late Chinese–English bilinguals in the language switching paradigm. Together with the behavioral asymmetrical switch cost, which was larger when switching to the dominant language than to the non-dominant language, the authors observed that only switches to the non-dominant language activated the left ACC and pre-SMA. Similar to the ERP switch cost, the switch effect observed at the neural level (in the non-dominant language) mirrored the one observed at the behavioral level (in the dominant language). The asymmetrical neural switch cost was interpreted as a result of the increased executive processes recruited to allow successful production in the L2 while avoiding competition from the L1, an explanation clearly in line with the inhibitory account. Further studies have also associated the asymmetrical activation of the ACC and the pre-SMA to the inhibition applied to the dominant language when processing the less dominant language (e.g., van Heuven et al., 2008), at least for low proficient bilinguals. If the asymmetrical involvement of the ACC/pre-SMA in the language switching paradigm is the result of bilinguals having to inhibit their dominant language, a clear prediction can be drawn for those bilinguals with two dominant languages: symmetrical switch cost patterns at the behavioral level should be accompanied by a similar activation of the ACC/pre-SMA regardless of the direction of the language switch. However, this is certainly not the case. In a recent study, Garbin et al. (2011) tested a group of early and high-proficient bilinguals and found that switches from the dominant to the non-dominant language activated the left caudate whereas the reverse switches activated the SMA/ACC. That is, the same areas considered to underlie the switches to the non-dominant language were now observed for switches to the dominant language. As suggested by Garbin et al., it is difficult to understand neuro-imaging results when making hypotheses uniquely derived from the behavioral pattern of the switch cost. Accordingly, it is possible that the involvement of different neural substrates in language switching does not correspond directly to the magnitude of the behavioral switch cost. It is also questionable whether the described brain areas should be taken as a direct index of inhibition. Indeed, the workings of those areas have been described for different executive control functions (including inhibition) and therefore, the same brain activations could be explained by embracing alternative proposals of bLC. For instance, in the model of bLC proposed by Abutalebi and Green (2007), activations of the prefrontal cortex are considered to index both response selection and response inhibition processes (in addition to other functions). Then, activations of brain areas in the prefrontal cortex could be taken as an index of inhibition of the unintended language to avoid competition but also as an index of word selection processes specific to the intended language of the bilingual (Costa et al., 1999; Finkbeiner et al., 2006).

Considering the aforementioned evidence, it becomes apparent that we do not have a consistent picture of switch costs or their origin. Whether or not language-switch costs are affected by language dominance appears to depend on many variables, such as the degree of proficiency in the two languages (Costa & Santesteban, 2004a), the degree of language switching experience (Christoffels, Firk, & Schiller, 2007), specific details of the task switching such as preparation time (Verhoef, Roelofs, & Chwilla, 2009), the bivalent nature of the stimuli (Finkbeiner, Gollan, & Caramazza, 2006), and switching predictability (Jackson et al., 2001). Hence, we believe that the present evidence is too varied to be considered as coherent support for the involvement of inhibitory control processes in bLC. However, this is not to say that inhibitory mechanisms are not involved at all in bLC. This is certainly an open question.

### 22.2.2.1 Experimental evidence from language switching: the n-2 repetition cost

Further evidence for the role of inhibitory control in bilingual language production comes from the so-called n-2 repetition cost. This effect refers to the extra cost associated with switching into a task that has been recently performed, as compared to switching into one that has not (e.g., Mayr & Keele, 2000). For example, in paradigms where participants have to switch between three different tasks (e.g., A, B, C), there can be two types of switch trials: (1) trials that require to switch into a previously encountered task (ABA); (2) trials that require to switch into the other task (CBA). Interestingly, responses are slower for the former type of trials, leading to the n-2 repetition cost. This cost has often been taken as an index of the after-effects of inhibition. That is, retrieving task A in AB**A** involves reactivating a task that was previously inhibited while performing task B. Such inhibition is not supposed to be present (or to a lesser extent) when retrieving A in CB**A** trials (see Mayr & Keele, 2000).

Indeed, the n-2 repetition cost seems to be a better index of inhibitory control than the n-1 shift cost (i.e., switch cost) discussed in the previous section. This is because the linguistic n-1 shift cost might not originate from language inhibition, but rather from persistant language activation of one language having these carry-over effects on the subsequent production of the other language. In fact, the asymmetries of the switch costs can also be explained as an after-effect of language activation in the previous trial, which is larger when passing from L2 to L1 than the reverse because the weaker language (L2) needs to be overactivated in order to be correctly pronounced (for a review, refer to Koch et al., 2010). In this respect, the n-2 repetition cost does seem to be a more appropriate effect to explore the role of inhibitory processes since it cannot be captured by the account presented above.

Phillip et al. (2007) asked participants to name digits in three different languages according to a language cue. As expected, the n-2 repetition cost was present for each of the three languages. Importantly, there was an asymmetrical n-2 repetition cost that was larger for the dominant rather than for the two non-dominant languages. This larger cost for the dominant language is consistent with the ICM. However, if inhibitory processes were responsible for this asymmetry, one would have expected a difference between the two non-dominant languages in the magnitude of the n-2 repetition cost, with the cost being larger for the more dominant of the two. This was not the case, but rather the contrary: the n-2 repetition cost was larger for the less dominant language, a result that it is clearly at odds with the inhibitory control assumption.

The pattern of n-2 repetition costs for language seems to be also somewhat shaky. This is because successive studies have either failed to detect any modulation of the n-2 repetition cost associated with dominance (Guo, Ma, & Liu, 2013; Philipp & Koch, 2009) or have failed to detect n-2 repetition costs at all (Guo et al., 2013). Hence, at present, evidence of the n-2 repetition cost suggesting support for the differential involvement of inhibitory processes associated with proficiency level (or dominance) in bilingual language control is at best weak.

### 22.2.3 Switching between blocked languages

As we have just reviewed, the evidence coming from language switching studies involving the continuous use of two (or more) languages is somewhat inconsistent. More recently, however, researchers have made use of a different instantiation of the language switching task, one in which the language of the response is blocked for a certain number of trials, and then the language is switched for another set of blocked trials. For example, participants are asked to name a set of pictures in language A, and afterwards they are asked to name a set (the same or not) of pictures in language B. This instantiation allows an assessment of the after-effects of naming in language A on naming in language B. In the context of the ICM, the logic of some of these studies is straightforward: if naming in language A involves the inhibition of language B, then naming in language B after naming in language A should be harder than naming in language B without the previous use of language A. These studies usually involve comparisons across groups of participants. For example, a group of participants start the experiment naming in the dominant language and then proceed naming the pictures in the non-dominant language, while the other group of participants perform the task in the opposite order. A comparison of the naming latencies for the dominant language between groups serves as an index of how easy (or difficult) the task becomes when the dominant language is used after having performed the naming task in the non-dominant language.

The current evidence reveals differential order effects according to language dominance. Naming in the dominant language (L1) is usually hampered by having previously named a set of items in the non-dominant language (L2). However, this effect is not present for the non-dominant language, but rather the after-effect of having named in the dominant language appears to be beneficial (at least when the task involves the same items; Branzi et al., 2014; Misra et al., 2012). Note that as in the case of the asymmetrical switch costs, the detrimental effect in the L1 appears to find a ready explanation both in terms of inhibitory or persistent activation processes. However, as we discuss in depth in the section concerning the scope of the bLC, these results are modulated, to some extent, by whether the same or different pictures are used in the two language blocks.

The after-effects of using one language on the subsequent performance in the other language have also been addressed using paradigms borrowed from memory research. Levy and colleagues (2007) aimed at exploring the presence of inhibitory processes in bLC by means of the Retrieval-Induced forgetting (RIF) effect (for a review, see Anderson & Levy, 2007). In their study, participants were asked to memorize a set of pictures in their dominant language. Subsequently they were asked to name the same set of pictures in the non-dominant language, either 1, 5, or 10 times. Finally, in the critical test (the retrieval phase), participants were asked to come up with the L1 labels of the pictures presented in the initial phase, upon the presentation of a rhyming cue for each picture's name. Interestingly, the more times a given picture was named in the non-dominant language, the worse the retrieval of the corresponding label in the dominant language in the retrieval phase. That is, naming the pictures in the non-dominant language hampered subsequent retrieval of the corresponding translation names in the dominant language. This result is certainly in accordance with the involvement of inhibitory processes. However, caution needs to be exercised when interpreting these results, since in a larger-scale study, the RIF effect across languages has proved to be very elusive (see Runnqvist & Costa, 2012).

One of the problems interpreting the results coming from this blocked paradigm refers to whether the different studies make use of repeated or novel stimuli across languages. Importantly, this property also affords the testing of other important aspects of the bLC, such as whether it involves local vs. global control. The section on the scope of bLC is devoted to this issue.

### 22.2.4 Interim summary

In this section we have reviewed the experimental evidence on bLC, which has focused primarily on determining whether bilingual lexical selection is ensured by means of inhibitory mechanisms (Green, 1998). However, up to now the results obtained from the different paradigms, whether involving constant switches between languages or keeping the languages blocked, have not allowed researchers to argue in favor of or against the inhibitory processes during bilingual speech production (for a review on the language switching paradigm, see Bobb & Wodniecka, 2013). Then, the question of whether bLC is ensured by inhibition or by any other mechanism remains still an open issue. Alternative accounts of bLC have challenged the idea that bilingual lexical selection needs to be solved by inhibition. The *language selectivity account* (Costa & Caramazza, 1999; Costa et al., 1999) for instance, assumes that bilinguals have the ability to focus their attention on the intended language and this suffices to create an imbalance between the two languages. That is, lexical competition is then restricted to the target language. Within this framework, the symmetrical switch cost observed for highly proficient bilinguals can be easily explained. However, other results such as the after-effects of one language on the subsequent production of the other (e.g., Branzi et al., 2014) seem to be more problematic for the selectivity account. Finally, as we already mentioned, more recent proposals consider bLC to rely on language activation rather than on inhibition (Philipp et al., 2007; Finkbeiner et al., 2006; Runnqvist et al., 2012). Besides differences between these proposals, all of them agree that speaking in one language suffices to increase the level of activation of those words belonging to the target language. However, as we described, the fact that inhibition and activation accounts can explain the same phenomenon makes it difficult to determine whether language inhibition or activation are the key feature of bLC.

In the following section, we review the evidence on the scope of bLC, which has tried to answer whether bLC mechanisms, inhibition or activation, applied to specific representations of the language or to the whole language and whether the bLC system flexibly adapts to the linguistic context in which bilinguals can participate.

## 22.3 The scope of bLC

### 22.3.1 Global versus local language control

One of the critical issues that models of bLC need to tackle refers to the extent to which control mechanisms (e.g., inhibition or over-activation) are applied. For example, whether the language control mechanisms operate exclusively over those lexical representations previously activated or rather over all linguistic representations of the language. These two views are often referred to as local vs. global control (de Groot & Christoffels, 2006). For example, consider an Italian–English bilingual naming a picture of a "chair" in English. According to the local control view, only the word corresponding to chair in Italian (*sedia*) would be affected. In contrast, according to the global control view, the intention to name the picture in English would suffice to exert control over the entire language, whether inhibition on all the lexical representations of the non-target language or activation of all the lexical representations in the weak language.

The most obvious way to explore these two potential mechanisms is to address whether any after-effect of language use affects repeated and non-repeated items alike. To put it simply and following the example above, will naming the picture of chair in English hamper subsequent naming in Italian of any picture (global control) or will it hamper specifically the translation word *sedia* (local control)?

To our knowledge there are only few studies that have addressed this issue more or less directly. The first one is the already reviewed study by Finkbeiner et al. (2006). Recall that in that study, participants had to name digits in their two languages (according to a cue) and to name interspersed pictures only in the dominant language. Interestingly, a language switch cost was observed for digit naming but not for picture naming. Although in an indirect way, this result suggests that naming digits in the non-dominant language hampers naming the same digits in the dominant language. The fact that this inhibitory effect is not found for representations that are not being produced in the non-dominant language (pictures) suggests that the inhibitory control is of a local nature.

Branzi et al. (2014) tested this question explicitly by comparing two groups of bilingual speakers in a blocked naming task. One group of participants had the following block sequence: dominant to the non-dominant language, and the other group named in the reverse order. Crucially, some of the pictures in the second block were the same as used in the first block while others were new pictures. Hence, some of the pictures to be named in the second block had already been named in the other language while other pictures had not been. The critical comparison was across groups, since naming latencies for the same language when used in the first and second blocks have to be compared. For the non-dominant language, naming latencies in the second block were faster than in the first block but only for repeated items. This result likely reveals the benefit of perceptual/conceptual priming. Hence, there are no obvious signs of inhibitory control applied when naming first in the dominant language. The results for the dominant language are more interesting: naming latencies in the second block as compared to the first block were the same for repeated items. Hence, the perceptual/conceptual priming was not detectable. The authors argued that this priming effect was not detectable because naming in the non-dominant language negatively affected subsequent naming in the dominant language, canceling out the conceptual/perceptual priming. Consistent with this interpretation, for new items, responses were slower in the second block. Thus, according to these authors, naming in the dominant language is hindered (both for repeated and new items) by previously naming in the non-dominant language. This result clearly supports the notion of global control.[5]

Van Assche, Duyck, and Gollan (2013) also addressed the issue of local vs. global control by means of a letter fluency task. In this task, the authors used a blocked design (one group L1/L2 and the other L2/L1) but rather than asking participants to name pictures, they asked them to come up with as many words as possible starting with a given letter in the target language (i.e., produce as many words as possible in English beginning with the letter A). Critically, some of the letters used to elicit the responses were the same for the two languages while other letters were different. Comparing performance across languages in the first set allows for assessing local effects, and comparing performance in the second affords exploring global effects. Performance in the dominant language was poorer in the second block (after having performed the task in the non-dominant language). However, this poorer performance was restricted to those letters that were used for the two languages, but not for those that were use uniquely for the dominant language (and had not been used before in the non-dominant language). The presence of detrimental effects for the repeated letters suggests local control, and similarly, the absence of any detrimental effect for those letters used only in one language suggests the absence of global control. Furthermore, this detrimental effect was only observed for the dominant language (Van Assche et al., 2013). Note, however, that in a subsequent experiment with a different group of bilinguals, these authors found evidence of both local and global control.

The studies described above have approached the issue of global and local control by addressing the after-effects of naming in one language over the other language for repeated and new stimuli. We believe this is the right way to approach this issue and further research needs to be conducted with this in mind to assess the reliability of the phenomena reported. However, there is still some confusion in the interpretation of the results as indexing local and global control mechanisms. For instance, using a blocked naming task (similar to the ones reported above), Misra et al. (2012) concluded that their results revealed global control over the non-response language, when in fact these results were consistent with a local control given that they only used repeated pictures. Hence, interesting as these results are, they remain unable to shed light on the global or local nature of the control processes.

There are other studies that have claimed to address global and local control but that, we think, conflate other processing demands that make it difficult to tackle the scope of the control processes. Perhaps this conflation stems from the misuse of the terms "global" and "local," since the control processes described in these studies might be better described in

---

[5] See Experiment 2 of Philipp & Koch (2009) in which the results of the language switching task demonstrated that inhibition is not restricted to a specific stimulus/response set, supporting the global inhibition account.

terms of sustained control as indexed by mixing cost (see below). Consider, for example, the study conducted by Guo et al. (2011), in which participants performed two different naming tasks. In the blocked naming task, participants were asked to name the pictures in their two languages in a blocked fashion, with the order of the languages counterbalanced across participants. After this task, participants were asked to perform the trial-by-trial language switching task. Importantly, the pictures presented in all these conditions were the same, hence compromising the ability to separate local and global control effects. The authors compared the brain activations (measured with functional magnetic resonance imaging, fMRI) elicited in the blocked and mixed conditions and argued that this comparison allowed them to detect the control mechanisms involved in keeping the two languages active but controlled during speech production. That is, since language switching requires the constant activation and deactivation of the two language systems, and blocked naming does not, by comparing these two tasks one can have an index of this constant (or sustained) control activity. This sounds logical, but surprisingly the authors refer to this contrast as revealing "local control effects." We think that this is a bit confusing, and that it is better to refer to it as mixing cost effects or sustained control (see next and last sections for a more detailed description of this effect).

Be this as it may, what is interesting from Guo et al.'s (2011) study is that the neural network responsible for this mixing cost (or sustained control) appears to be different than that involved in the after-effects during blocked naming. Unfortunately, however, the fact that only repeated items were used in the blocked conditions does not allow the neural correlates of this control to be attributed to local or global processes.

In general terms, the reviewed studies suggest two general conclusions, with the first one being that language control is likely applied globally. Meaning that when producing words in a given language, a certain control on the other language is applied not only to those items previously activated in the other language, but to the whole language set. The second is that only the dominant language (L1) seems to be affected by the previous use of the other language (L2). This asymmetry, that resembles results from trial-by-trial language switching tasks, might be influenced by language proficiency (but see Branzi et al., 2014 that revealed asymmetries in highly proficient bilinguals). Future research will have to establish whether or not this is the case and also whether proficiency might influence local and global process differently.

### 22.3.2 A flexible bilingual language control adaptable to context: the mixing cost

We have reviewed different evidence that can be very informative regarding the functioning of the bLC. Importantly, those studies have also considered the different real-world interaction contexts in which the two languages of a bilingual might be involved (Green & Abutalebi, 2013). There are contexts in which the two languages are constantly mixed (in which the n-1 shift cost and the n-2 repetition cost are found) and contexts in which they are blocked. For the sake of parsimony, researchers try to find a common system supporting both situations. However, it is possible that the bLC mechanism adapts to the different naming contexts (Green & Abutalebi, 2013). Indeed, it is reasonable to assume that the bLC system may work differently depending on whether the speaker is constantly changing languages (as in the case of bilingual conversations) or is in a situation in which only one language is being used (for a comment on the importance of considering the bilingual context, see Wu & Thierry, 2010).

This issue has been addressed by comparing the two experimental situations in which bilinguals are required to use their two languages, namely, the trial-by-trial language switching task and the blocked naming task. The difference between switching and blocked language conditions is referred to as the mixing cost. This cost is calculated by comparing responses to repeat trials (in the trial-by-trial language switching tasks) with responses in blocked naming contexts.[6] The logic behind this comparison is that any difference between these two experimental situations can be only attributed to the fact that in the mixed context, bilinguals have to deal with the constant competition between their two languages (for a review on the non-linguistic domain, see Rubin & Meiran, 2005).

One of the first studies that explored these two processes was conducted by Christoffels et al. (2007; but see, Gollan & Ferreira, 2009; Philipp & Koch, 2007; Prior & Gollan, 2011), which reports a rather surprising result. While behavioral responses in the dominant language (L1) were affected by mixing costs, responses in the non-dominant language (L2) were not. These conclusions were further consistent with the ERP results.

Not surprisingly, it has been shown that contexts involving constant switching between languages are more demanding than blocked contexts. This is revealed by the extra participation of executive control areas (left inferior frontal cortex and the bilateral dorsolateral prefrontal cortex) in the switching context (Hernandez, Martinez, & Kohnert, 2000; Hernandez et al., 2001). However, Hernandez et al. (2001) considered all the trials in the language switching task rather than only those repeat trials as in Christoffels et al. (2007), making it more difficult to make direct comparisons regarding the mixing costs. In a successive study, Wang et al. (2009) obtained similar results (bilateral activation of dorsolateral prefrontal cortex) in late and low-proficient Chinese–English bilinguals using a single-digit-naming task in mixed and blocked naming conditions. Also,

---

[6] Mixing costs can be calculated as the difference between blocked and mixed conditions (Koch, Prinz, & Allport, 2005; Los, 1996) or as the difference between blocked and repeat trials of mixed conditions (Kray & Lindenberger, 2000; Meiran, 2000; Rubin & Meiran, 2005). When calculated in the latter way, mixing costs can be separated from switch costs.

authors have found an additional activation in the SMA (see Guo et al., 2011, for similar results in low-proficient bilinguals) and a more extensive recruitment of areas involved in executive processes such as the ACC, the posterior superior and middle temporal gyrus or the caudate nucleus (Abutalebi et al., 2008).

Despite being scarce, the evidence regarding the bilingual contextual effects seem to concur on bLC mechanisms working differently depending on the context in which bilinguals are engaged: whether it requires switching constantly between languages or to use just one language. As indicated by Wu and Thierry (2011), future studies should take into consideration the influence of the bilingual context when exploring bLC.

### 22.3.3 On control demands and representational issues

In the previous sections we have presented the evidence related to the scope of bLC (local and global control) and that related to the different linguistic contexts in which bLC mechanisms might operate (switch and mixing costs). We presented this evidence separately because we believe that it reflects two relatively independent aspects of bLC: those related to the representational scope of bLC ("local" and "global" control) and those related to the timing of such control (i.e., transient and sustained control, Christoffels et al., 2007). However, in our view there is some confusion in the literature about the boundaries between these two dimensions of bLC, since quite often the very same terms are used to define these different and relatively independent aspects of bLC. This last section is devoted to clarifying the relationship between the aspects related to the representational scope of bLC and those related to the timing of bLC (i.e., Christoffels et al., 2007).

As explained previously, "global" control refers to the inhibition or activation of complete languages systems whereas "local" control involves specifically those task-relevant lexical representations (e.g., de Groot & Christoffels, 2006). In other words, what distinguishes "local" from "global" control would be only the type of lexical representation that needs to be controlled. Based on this distinction, the only way of testing local vs global control processes is by comparing different types of lexical items: those that have to be repeated in both languages (local control) and those that are not repeated from one language to the other (global control). We believe that at the present only three studies have properly addressed this issue (i.e., Branzi et al., 2014; Finkbeiner, 2006; Van Assche et al., 2013) and that the rest of the available evidence is confounded by other aspects of the bLC more related to the timing of bLC (i.e., Christoffels et al., 2007), such as "transient control" and "sustained control." "Transient control" refers to trial-by-trial intentional control applied during the continuous switching between languages (or tasks) and is generally measured through the so called "switch costs." Thus, the evidence on transient control comes from experimental paradigms such as language switching task (e.g., Meuter & Allport, 1999; Phillip et al., 2007), and the bilingual version of the cumulative semantic interference (CSIE) (Runnqvist et al., 2012). Conversely, "sustained control" refers to a more automatic control influenced by the control demands imposed by the context in which a given language has to be produced. This type of control is necessary for maintaining language (or task set) at a relatively high level of activation and it is measured through the so-called "mixing cost" (Christoffels et al., 2007) (see Braver et al., 2003, for the same distinction in domain-general cognitive control). Then, only the blocked naming and the mixing cost allow exploring of sustained control.

Both components of control, "sustained" and "transient" appear to be differently involved in the control of L1 and L2 production (e.g., Christoffels et al., 2007; Jackson et al., 2001). However, important and interesting as they are, these results have been interpreted as reflecting not only differences tied to the temporal aspects of bLC, but also to the representational aspects. For example, some studies explored some aspects related to the timing of bLC, i.e., "sustained" and "transient" control but they referred to them as "global" and "local" control, respectively. As suggested, to the extent that the same lexical representations (repeated items) are involved in the task, we will only have a measure of "local" control. In this context, "transient" control, measured through switch costs, will be taken as a form of "local" control. However, the same correspondence does not hold when considering the measure of "sustained" control and "global" control: whenever the very same lexical items are involved in the conditions to be compared (mixed versus blocked conditions), sustained control might be considered a measure of "local" rather than a global control. For example, while using the exact same paradigm, a blocked naming task, Misra et al. (2012) measured sustained and local control,[7] since repeated items were used, while Branzi et al. (2014) measured both sustained local and global control as both repeated and non-repeated items were employed.

All in all, this last section is intended as a sort of clarification about what differentiates some important aspects of bLC and to persuade future researchers to orthogonally investigate the effects of global and local control and those of sustained and transient control.

## 22.4 Conclusion

In this chapter we have critically reviewed the main literature on bLC, which has been mainly devoted to understanding how bilinguals select

---

[7] Interestingly, these authors demonstrated that sustained and local control were long-lasting since the detrimental L1 effects remained across the two blocks.

words in their desired language while avoiding intrusions from the unintended one, and, specifically whether inhibitory mechanisms are in charge of controlling the two languages. Thus, most of the experimental evidence, be it from different behavioral, neurophysiological, or neuroimaging paradigms, has focused on the role of inhibition during bilingual speech production. However, as we have noted, after more than two decades of exploring inhibition by means of different instantiations of the language switching task, it seems that we have not sufficiently advanced our understanding of what exactly the asymmetrical/symmetrical switch costs mean. Future studies need to reconsider what exactly the switch cost pattern means regarding inhibition, whether the language switching paradigm should be considered a direct test of the inhibitory mechanisms proposed by ICM or whether the language switching paradigm involves inhibition at all. Finally, another important aspect of future research would be to take into account other variables that might influence the nature of the mechanisms involved in bLC besides proficiency. For example, it has been suggested that also the "frequency of language switching" in daily life might influence the mechanisms involved in the control of the two languages (see Prior & Gollan, 2011; for symmetrical patterns of switch costs; see also Christoffels et al., 2007). We believe that all these issues need to be considered seriously when designing new language switching paradigms.

To explore the scope of bLC, comparing local vs. global control or investigating how the bLC system works in different bilingual contexts seem to be promising research areas. However, in order to shed light on the scope of these control processes, it is necessary that future studies accurately describe how given patterns of results relate to bLC models.

# 23

# Behavioral measures of language control

Production and comprehension

Julia Festman and John W. Schwieter

## 23.1 The early use of the term *language control*

In the domain of foreign language instruction, two types of language control have commonly been distinguished (see Palmer, 1979). One is "compartmentalized control" and is mainly restricted to the acquisition and mastery of instructed content, since it is defined as "the language user's control of language elements or mastery of a particular set of teaching points" (p. 170). According to this definition, language control is relatively unrelated to the learner's general ability to communicate. The other type of language control is the so-called "integrated control," whereby both the speaker's mastery of certain language elements acquired through instruction and his/her general communicative abilities are assumed to be highly correlated.

In studies of English as a foreign language, "language control tests" usually measure the participant's ability to produce correct English, including phonology, lexico-semantics, and grammatical structures (for a review, see Davies, 1978a, 1978b). The goal of such tests is to assess language production in the target language. In an early study by Upshur and Palmer (1974), for instance, grammatical structures and vocabulary items were elicited directly by means of translation equivalents in Thai. Participants were asked to produce the correct English words and structures, and this language control test was predominantly used as a tool for assessing foreign language learning.

Thus, in the frame of foreign language instruction, the use of the term *language control* has been restricted to the classroom, linked to academic achievement, and measured by tests requiring the students to rely on knowledge acquired in a classroom setting. With the teachers' focus on the correct use of the target language in terms of grammar, lexicon, and pronunciation, language control has been used as an indicator of learners' foreign language proficiency.

## 23.2 "Language control" in experimental bilingualism

Green's (1986, 1998) influential model of activation, inhibition, and control drew attention to the processes involved in using either one of a bilingual's languages. Hence, within this frame, language control principally describes two cognitive processes used by bilingual speakers: the first cognitive process refers to the language control that is necessary for a bilingual to maintain the use of only one of his/her two languages (i.e., when speech must be confined to one language only, even though two languages are principally available). At the same time, the bilingual mind has to prevent interference from the non-target language; that is, the bilingual has to block out any unintentional, unplanned, and inappropriate intrusions of the other available language.[1] The second cognitive process involves language control that is employed in changes of the target language. For instance, a bilingual meets person A (a monolingual of language A) in the street and they talk for 5 minutes in language A. Then person A leaves the scene and the bilingual immediately meets person B (a monolingual of language B) and talks, of course, in language B for the next 5 minutes. This language switch from language A to language B is necessary if the bilingual wants to be a language-appropriate interlocutor. Since the language knowledge of the monolingual interlocutor determines the selection of the language to be used in these conversations, any use of the other language would thus be considered inappropriate in this conversational context. The bilingual speaker therefore has to make a language switch from language A to language B as soon as the conversational partners change. This is made possible by the cognitive process of language control, executing a voluntary choice of language use.

## 23.3 Behavioral measures in language control research

Different from the earlier use of language control measures in the classroom, where tests assessed language comprehension and production in a non-native secondary language (L2) only, language control in bilingual experimental studies examines language abilities in both languages of a speaker: the L1 and the L2. Two types of processing costs are commonly used as indicators of language control, namely time and accuracy. More specifically, two different time measures can be distinguished: language switch costs; and language mixing costs. In addition, the accuracy of the performance can be considered in terms of content and target language.

---

[1] It has also been suggested that bilinguals can be in monolingual or bilingual mode (Grosjean, 1982) and that while in bilingual mode, both languages are activated, involving a certain degree of competition/interference. More about this will be discussed later in the chapter.

Perhaps the first highly influential study on processing costs for bilingual language processing was conducted by Meuter and Allport (1999), with much theoretical underpinning nourished from task-switching theories (Allport & Wylie, 1999; Rogers & Monsell, 1995). An experimental task might involve color or shape naming, in/animate picture categorization, parity or number magnitude classification, etc.

In order to assess switch costs, most task-switching studies include two types of experimental blocks, namely single-task blocks and mixed-task blocks. As such, participants' performance on one task (e.g., a single-task block) can be contrasted with performance on switching between two tasks (a mixed-task block). The mixed-task block is commonly presented either with a regular task-switch sequence (i.e., switching between task A and B on every trial, such as in ABAB) or with the alternating-runs paradigm (i.e., switching on every second trial between task A and B, such as AABBAABB; Rogers & Monsell, 1995). Following this approach from the task-switching literature, some language switching studies compare both types of blocks (e.g., Cherkasova et al., 2002) while others only measure switching performance within one mixed block (e.g., Schwieter & Sunderman, 2008). We will argue in this chapter that both types of blocks should be included in future studies on bilingual and trilingual language control. Performance on single-language blocks allows for a measure of language maintenance, the first language control ability as mentioned above, namely the use of only language A or language B.[2] Speed and accuracy for each language are valid indicators of language proficiency, even if a task simply involves production of bare nouns (e.g., a picture-naming task). The mixed-language blocks provide a measure of language switching, the second language control ability described earlier, indicating how quickly and correctly a speaker can switch into a predetermined language for a given task.

A general finding in the switching literature is that mixed-language blocks are more difficult than single-language blocks, an observation that is found for task-switching studies as well as for language switching studies (Weissberger et al., 2012). In principle, this is due to high working memory demands imposed by having to perform two tasks and switch between them (Rogers & Monsell, 1995). Regarding language switching studies, there is ample evidence for parallel language activation (Calabria et al., 2012), but the degree of involvement of the other language is different between a single and a mixed block. In a single block, the participant can focus on the current target language, which remains the same throughout a block, presumably by inhibiting the non-target language. In a mixed block, the target language changes frequently, and

---

[2] This does not imply, however, that maintaining one language is a separable control function from language switching. Language maintenance involves language activation and control implies that the other language must be inhibited or deactivated. We will continue to discuss this throughout the chapter.

global inhibition of one of the languages is not an effective strategy to perform this task.[3] Thus, language control has to be more flexibly executed in this condition to meet the frequent switching requirement of this task. Participants can be prepared to some extent for the upcoming target language if it is known in advance, for example, if there is a language cue or a regular language switching pattern.

Processing costs involved in switching between two languages have attracted much attention in the bilingualism literature. It is apparent that further elaboration is merited to explore the interest in and significance of understanding the mechanisms underlying processing costs in bilingual language use. In what follows, we describe them in more detail, while considering studies from both language production and language comprehension.

### 23.3.1 Task switching and language switch cost

A "switch cost" or "local switch cost" is reflected in terms of longer reaction times (RTs) when there is a switch (switch trials) than when there is no switch (typically referred to as non-switch, repetition, or stay trials; e.g., Meiran, 1996; Monsell, 2003). In a mixed block, where there are both switch and non-switch trials, the switch cost is calculated as the difference in mean RT between non-switch and switch trials. It is generally understood as reflecting transient adjustments between task configurations from trial to trial (Rogers & Monsell, 1995). In other words, the difficulty of switching between tasks and the control processes involved is the selection of the appropriate task. In addition, when a participant receives information about the upcoming switch (i.e., a preparatory cue) the switch can be anticipated and the switch cost may be diminished but cannot be eliminated entirely (for a review, see Monsell, 2003).

### 23.3.2 The "asymmetrical" switch cost

This phenomenon has been observed in studies investigating switching between languages as well as between tasks. When two tasks are of equal difficulty, the switch cost into either direction is symmetrical. In other words, it takes the same time to switch from task 1 to task 2 as it does to switch from task 2 to task 1. If, however, one of the tasks is more difficult, it takes longer to switch to the easier task (asymmetrical switch cost; for a review, see Koch et al., 2010). Inhibition plays a crucial role in explaining this asymmetry (Allport, Styles, & Hsieh, 1994). Easy tasks have to be more strongly inhibited than difficult ones. Thus, more time is needed to switch

---

[3] As interpreted in terms of language mode (Grosjean, 1982), in the mixed blocks, bilinguals are in bilingual mode in which both languages need to be activated whereas in the single blocks bilinguals may find themselves in monolingual mode.

from a difficult task back to an easy task, because the strong inhibition applied to the easy task has to be overcome and the easy task has to be made available. With regard to bilingualism, the same asymmetrical switch cost was observed by Meuter and Allport (1999) for 16 unbalanced bilinguals (English as L1 or L2) in one of the first experimental studies on switching language for naming digits (1 to 9) on more than 2,000 trials. Therefore, larger switch costs are usually observed when switching into a more dominant language (usually the L1) as opposed to switching into a weaker language (usually the L2). Theoretically, this suggests that the more dominant language requires greater inhibition, which must be overcome when switching from a less dominant to more dominant, thereby leading to greater RTs.

For highly proficient (balanced) bilinguals, symmetrical switch costs were found in two separate experiments conducted by Costa and Santesteban (2004a). In a picture-naming task (Experiment 2), 10 different items were presented in 950 trials (30 percent switch trials and 70 percent non-switch trials), with half of the latter requiring responses in the L1 (475 trials) and the other half requiring responses in the L2 (475 trials). Thus, each picture was presented 95 times during the entire experiment. In Experiment 3 of the same study, the diversity of pictures was increased from 10 to 40 and repetition of the same picture was reduced to 23–24 times. The results of both experiments (each with twelve highly proficient balanced Spanish–Catalan bilinguals) revealed that "when L2 proficiency is almost as high as that of L1, the asymmetrical switch cost disappears" (p. 499). Although the analysis focused on the switch cost, it remained unclear as to why both groups showed an advantage in the non-switch trials of their L2 (in Experiment 2 latencies were 12 ms faster in L2 than in L1, and in Experiment 3 this difference was about 100 ms).

These results demonstrate clearly that proficiency and task difficulty can influence RTs on non-switch trials and modulate the symmetry of switch costs: for same language proficiency and task difficulty, symmetric switch costs may be observed. In contrast, asymmetric switch costs can be found for differences in language proficiency and task difficulty, with a dominant language and an easier task being more difficult to switch into than a non-dominant language or a more difficult task.

### 23.3.3  Task mixing and language mixing costs

In the task-switching literature, a "mixing cost" (for a review, see Los, 1996) is found when two types of stimuli are mixed in a trial block. It is revealed in terms of slower responses to each stimulus type than when those stimuli were presented on their own in a single block. The mixing cost is calculated as the difference in mean RTs between trials in single-task blocks and non-switch trials in mixed-task blocks.

Several explanations have been put forward to account for mixing costs. Participants show an inability to prepare effectively for a certain stimulus. They must keep in mind two types of strategies in mixed blocks and the switching between the different strategies in order to deal with different types of stimuli is effortful. In contrast, in single blocks, participants are confident about which type of stimulus will be presented and need to deal with one strategy only. Thus, the processing load of a single block is much smaller than that of a mixed block. The same is true for language switching studies which have been largely inspired by the task-switching paradigm. In a single block, the participant is informed about the use of one language only and thus adopts a "monolingual mode" (Grosjean, 1982). Language mode is defined as the state of activation of a bilingual's languages and language processing mechanisms at a given point in time. In a monolingual mode, bilinguals deactivate one language (but never totally), whereas in a bilingual mode, they choose a base language and activate the other language for cross-language switching (Grosjean, 2001; Myers-Scotton, 1993). In processing terms, the participant can make use of the monolingual mode in a single block, whereby the target language of the current block functions as the "selected" language, while the non-target language is activated to a lesser degree (Green, 1986). In a mixed block, however, a bilingual is required to adopt a "bilingual mode" of speech such that both languages are readily available, enabling the participant to switch quickly between the two languages.[4]

The mixing cost seems to reflect a more sustained control process affecting all the trials in a mixed block (Los, 1996). Namely, the participant has to maintain two competing tasks and monitor the task cue. For bivalent stimuli, stimuli which are associated with at least two tasks in a mixed block, additional control mechanisms are required to resolve stimulus-driven conflict and to sustain performance (e.g., inhibition of the competing task). Such mechanisms would then operate in a sustained fashion, as a result of the detection of heightened levels of conflict, and affect switch and non-switch trials in mixed blocks.

If the two types of stimuli are of different difficulty, easier stimuli are associated with a mixing cost while more difficult stimuli reveal a mixing benefit (Lupker, Brown, & Colombo, 1997). Specifically, there is a greater cost for the condition that yields shorter latencies in single blocks than for the condition that yields longer latencies in single blocks. For instance, Monsell et al. (1992) reported that high-frequency irregular words were named more quickly when they were presented in a single-language block

---

[4] The reader should note, however, that there is a difference between cued/forced switching as in a picture-naming task and voluntary switching as in a conversation. For a further discussion on how voluntary-switching costs may differ from cued language switching, see Gollan and Ferreira (2009).

versus when they were mixed with nonwords. The researchers argued that this effect emerged due to a reduction of the emphasis of an assembly route in the single-language block.

Because the single block and the mixed block conditions rely on different processing modes, we argue here that it is not recommended to replace the information obtained from performance on a single block with information obtained from non-switch trials in a mixed block. Additionally, Marí-Beffa, Cooper, and Houghton (2011) suggest that throughout a mixed block participants adopt an "antirepetition bias," resulting in readiness for a switch trial rather than for a non-switch trial. Consequently, repeat trials reveal a cost because, if participants always inhibit the stimulus–response mapping of the previous trial, they have to overcome such an inhibition in cases of trial repetition. Therefore, it is highly recommended to include single-language blocks to provide a reliable baseline for performance ability in each language separately without task/language uncertainty, reduced processing load, effortless task/language repetition, and possible anti-repetition biases that can be found in the performance on non-switch trials on mixed blocks.

In a study on trilinguals, Costa and Santesteban (2004a, Experiment 4) focused on switching between the dominant (L1) and less-dominant language (L3). Twelve highly proficient trilinguals performed on 10 pictures in a mixed-language condition only. Surprisingly, the RTs on non-switch trials were higher for speakers' L1 than for their L3 (703 ms vs. 664 ms, respectively). Such a result can only be understood following Lupker et al. (1997) as mentioned above: The dominant L1 suffers from the mixing cost while the clearly non-dominant L3 gains from the mixing benefit. However, as no single blocks were included in this study these data only allow an indirect indication of the effect of language proficiency on switch costs. Therefore, as mentioned above, future studies should include a single-language block for each language under investigation to provide the option for calculating a solid baseline of performance and language dominance/proficiency. Then, a comparison of single and mixed blocks would be possible and the calculation of switch costs in the mixed block might be more convincing.

The study by Linck, Schwieter, and Sunderman (2012) also used a limited set of stimuli, i.e., 10 black-and-white line drawings, to be named only in a mixed-language condition. However, the study included a large participant group, i.e., 56 native English (L1) speakers learning French (L2) and Spanish (L3). Speakers' mean RTs in non-switch trials in the mixed-language block indicate more convincingly the level of language proficiency in each language, which decreased from L1 to L3: latencies on non-switch trials were on average 788 ms in L1, 916 ms in L2, and 934 ms in L3 (see also Schwieter, 2013). However, performance on a single-language condition was not included in the study and thus, the researchers were not able to establish a baseline for performance in each of the three languages.

In another study by Festman (2009) on picture naming (96 black-and-white line drawings), 17 German (L1) language learners of English (L2) and French (L3) were tested on single- and mixed-language blocks in each of their languages. Performance on single blocks was faster for each of the three languages than that of each language in the mixed condition on non-switch trials (808 ms vs. 973 ms for L1; 1322 ms vs. 1426 ms for L2; and 1442 ms vs. 1647 ms for L3). The study also found that in mixed-language blocks, cross-language interference effects were relative to the strength of the interfering language: L2-interference errors were observed in the next strongest language (L1) but not vice versa; L3 was not strong enough for interference errors to occur in either the L1 or the L2; and when the L3 was the target language, both the L1 and L2 triggered cross-language interference effects.

### 23.3.4 Accuracy of content and target language

Switch trials typically elicit more errors than non-switch trials. This finding is explained in terms of working memory load and effortful switching, reasons also found responsible for larger RTs in switch trials compared to non-switch trials. However, the analysis of error data has not attracted much attention. Few studies have sought to analyze error data with regard to target language and content accuracy. While treating accuracy and speed separately has not been a practiced norm in the literature, there have been some rather interesting results which deserve discussion here.

Festman, Rodriguez-Fornells, and Münte (2008) used a bilingual picture-naming task with an "alternating-runs paradigm" (Russian-RussianGermanGerman …) in which 240 different black-and-white line drawings were presented to a group of 29 Russian–German balanced bilinguals. Three major error categories were observed: no responses ("don't know"), when the participant did not provide any answer; within-language substitutions, when the target word was substituted by a word from the target language; and errors of cross-language interference, when a response was given in the non-target language (a translation equivalent or a word similar to the target meaning). Cross-language interference, defined as the involuntary use of the non-target language during target language production, was considered as inaccurate performance due to failures of control with regard to the target language, whereas substitution errors reflected inaccurate performance with regard to the content.

Similarly, in Festman (2009), errors yielded in a trilingual picture-naming task were divided into three different error categories comprising retrieval difficulties (e.g., tip-of-the-tongue states), substitution errors (superordinates, coordinates, or associates from the target language), and interlingual production errors ("cross-language interference" or lexical inventions). The study reported that more errors per category and language were found on switch compared to non-switch trials and that more errors were produced in the weaker languages compared to the dominant L1.

These two studies present examples of error distinction based on accuracy of content versus accuracy of target language. While substitution errors might reflect lack of sufficient processing time or reduced processing resources, errors of cross-language interference represent failure of language control. In fact, cross-language interference has been used as an indicator of language control in a line of studies by Festman and colleagues (Festman, 2009, 2012; Festman et al., 2008, 2010). These authors categorized errors as "cross-language interference" errors when there were violations of the use of the target language despite the existence of language cues and regardless of the participant's awareness of the language knowledge of his/her interlocutor.

In Festman (2012), Russian–German balanced bilinguals were tested on a verbal fluency task. Participants were required to produce as many words as possible belonging to a certain semantic category (*semantic fluency*; FOOD, CLOTHING, ANIMALS, PLANTS & FLOWERS) or starting with a particular letter (*phonemic fluency*; S, H, P and R) within a given time period (e.g., one minute). For each language, two categories and two letters were used as stimuli, and languages were alternated after every test to increase the likelihood of cross-language interference errors due to frequent switching. Responses belonging to any of the following categories were classified as errors due to pre-established rule violation: cross-language interference; repetition of the same word; fragment; lexical invention; proper name; not a category member/does not start with target letter; word starting with same root; and slang. The analysis of errors that emerge due to cross-language interference can reveal cognitive control in multilingual production as the errors represent involuntary and accidental deviation from the intended language of production (Green, 1986).

In addition, a bilingual interview was conducted with the same group of bilinguals with three predefined topics per language. Two native speakers acted as interviewers and were told to use only their native language when asking questions. The interviewers' task was to elicit spontaneous verbal speech from the interviewee. In order to keep the interviewees talking about the same topic for five minutes, the interviewers were instructed to use predefined questions (about eight per topic). Interviewers alternated during the interview task after every topic. The interviewees' task was to answer the questions according to the language used by the interviewer, resulting in a change of the response language every five minutes. Due to these clearly defined language time-frames, any use of the current non-target language was considered cross-language interference.

Thus far we have presented two views of the term "language control," one which has been used in foreign language teaching and testing and one which has been employed in the experimental bilingualism literature, referring to a bilingual's ability to restrict language use to the target language only and to switch on command between two languages. A number of possible measures of language control, such as switch costs, mixing costs, accuracy of content, and target language were discussed along with a few illustrative examples following a more methodological approach.

Future studies should reveal the conditions under which mixing costs and mixing benefits occur and how naming latencies and response accuracy are influenced by task demands – in particular, the effect of parameters such as frequency of stimulus repetition; number of trials and number of languages involved; as well as the time lag between presentation of a language cue and a stimulus. Furthermore, the inclusion of single-language blocks provides not only an objective online measure of language proficiency for each language used in a given task, but also allows for calculation of mixing costs and benefits.

The following section highlights bilingual studies that have investigated language control. The presentation of these studies is organized according to language domain (production followed by comprehension) and the tasks employed to provide a better understanding of the current state of knowledge on language control.

## 23.4  Experimental studies

### 23.4.1  Production

#### 23.4.1.1  Picture naming

Perhaps the first picture-naming task presenting data on bilinguals' performance on single- and mixed-language blocks is the behavioral part of an fMRI study conducted by Hernandez, Martinez, and Kohnert (2000). Six Spanish–English early bilinguals (mean age 23.5) took part in the study. The Boston Naming Test that was administered to the participants to assess their language proficiency showed better performance in English than in Spanish. Experimental materials consisted of 180 different pictures which had to be named in single- and mixed-language blocks. The results revealed a main effect of language dominance with English RTs being faster than Spanish RTs across both the mixed- and single-language conditions. The results of accuracy rate of performance in single-language blocks confirmed participants' unbalanced level of proficiency (for English, 93% vs. for Spanish 80%). There was also a main effect of mixing cost with the single-language block condition revealing faster RTs than the mixed-language block condition (for English, 1,010 ms vs. 1,276 ms and for Spanish, 1,148 ms vs. 1,298 ms). Furthermore, performance in the mixed blocks was slower than that of single blocks for both languages.

In another fMRI study, Hernandez et al. (2001) investigated activation similarities and differences across languages in a single-language and mixed-language switching task. Six early English–Spanish bilinguals (mean age 21.7) scored higher on the Boston Naming Test in English than in Spanish. Participants' behavioral performance was measured with a mixed-language condition in which 72 pictures of concrete nouns were presented (e.g., the book, the cake) and two block types were used (single and mixed block). Results revealed a main effect of language dominance in accuracy and reaction time, with faster and more accurate performance in English than in Spanish: for English single-language block 805 ms vs. 907 ms for the mixed-language block; for Spanish single-language block 1012 ms vs. 996 ms for the mixed-language block. The authors concluded that the effect of mixed vs. single-language condition did not reach significance but was in the expected direction. As we argued earlier in this chapter, faster RTs in the L2 than in the L1 in mixed-language blocks might reflect a mixing benefit for the less-dominant L2 (see Lupker et al., 1997 for a similar view).

In the behavioral part of their fMRI study, Abutalebi et al. (2008) administered a picture-naming task to twelve advanced German–French students of translation studies (average age of acquisition of 11.6 years). Participants performed on a total of 175 black-and-white drawings of familiar objects in two single-language blocks, called "single naming context": in one block, participants were required to name objects in their L1, and in the other block, to generate verbs in the L1. A mixed-language block followed, called "language selection context," for object naming in the participants' L1 or L2. The lexical frequency of the target words (middle to high lexical frequency) was comparable across languages and the pictures in the three blocks did not differ in visual complexity.

Abutalebi et al. (2008) reported mixing effects in terms of slower responses in the mixed-language block compared to the single-language block (note that this was only reported for the L1, since there was no single-language block for L2, as it was out of the scope of the study), while accuracy scores were similar for both conditions in the L1. Comparing participants' performance across languages in the mixed-language condition, RTs to L1 object naming did not differ from those to L2 naming, but responses were significantly more accurate in L1 than in L2. When considering task measures of time and accuracy, clearly language dominance cannot be determined with certainty. Moreover, at the time of testing, participants' overall actual exposure for daily activities was higher in L2 than in L1. As argued earlier, naming performance in a mixed-language condition is not the ideal indicator of language proficiency, since mixing effects can play a role. The translation test administered to this small group of late bilinguals demonstrated high proficiency in the L2. This finding fits well with the group's daily training (i.e., translation). The authors considered this group as having a weaker L2, despite the fact that participants scored highly on the translation task, responded as quickly in the L2 as in the L1, and had more daily exposure to the L2 than to the L1. Hence, reduced accuracy in the L2 appears to be the indicator which the researchers used to interpret that the L2 was less dominant than the L1.

In Festman (2012), 29 late Russian–German bilinguals (mean age of 24.6 years), with balanced proficiency in the two languages performed a picture-naming task in which an alternating-runs paradigm was employed. Prior to stimulus presentation, a cue informed participants as to the language to be used for naming the upcoming picture using a bare noun. Overall, 240 black-and-white line drawings were used, with two trials for each target language: two trials in Russian, two in German, two in Russian, and so on. Critically, based on the errors of interference that were yielded during the picture-naming task, reflecting language control differences among the speakers, participants were classified into *switchers* (those who were more inclined to switch unintentionally) and *non-switchers* (those who did not switch unintentionally). Results showed that both groups performed with similar accuracy in Russian (about 79% correct) and German (only the switchers were less correct than the non-switchers with 71% and 79%, respectively). On non-switch trials, the two groups of participants demonstrated similar performance: in German 1,164 ms for the switchers and 1,093 ms for the non-switchers; in Russian 1,174 ms for the switchers and 1,081 ms for the non-switchers. As expected, following the switch cost effect, performance on switch trials was slower than performance on non-switch trials for both languages and both groups. The main significant difference between the two groups was the frequency of occurrence of cross-language interference. While the switchers produced on average five errors of cross-language interference in all conditions, the non-switchers produced only one on average. Although measures of speed and accuracy did not allow distinguishing between the two groups in the mixed block condition, a more subtle error analysis did. The study suggested that the robust difference in language control, as indicated by frequency of cross-language interference despite speakers' balanced proficiency, was related to more domain-general cognitive control differences between the two groups, which was revealed in a number of neuropsychological tests operationalizing executive functions (Festman et al., 2010).

Voluntary language switching (as opposed to predetermined language switching) was used by unbalanced bilinguals who were free to choose in which language to name pictures (Gollan & Ferreira, 2009). Interestingly, frequent words were named in the weaker L2, whereas infrequent words were produced in participants' stronger L1. Asymmetric switch costs were not observed, a finding that was explained in the following way: if L2 words were only accessed and produced when their activation level was high (i.e., when they were easy to retrieve), L1 did not need to be strongly inhibited. When words were less frequent, participants would always refer to their stronger L1. This was taken as evidence for reduced or absent switch costs, when lexical switching was under the control of the speaker and not predetermined by the experimenter. This is in line with the common observation that bilinguals switch with no apparent effort between their languages during conversations.

University students in Catalonia were asked to switch between Spanish and Catalan while naming eight different pictures, half of which were cognates (Calabria et al., 2012). The participants' L1 was Catalan and they had learned Spanish before the age of six. Self-ratings were used as the only indication of language proficiency. Following 80 practice trials, 320 trials were presented. That is, each picture was already named 5 times in each language during practice. Symmetrical switch costs were reported for switching between L1 and L2 (i.e., a non-significant trial type x language interaction), despite numerically faster naming in L1 than in L2. The accuracy data revealed that both languages as well as both trial types were equally easy to perform. Similar findings were reported for switching between L1 and L3 (Experiment 2). RTs for L3 were even faster than for L1 on non-switch trials (804 vs. 824 ms). According to our suggestion put forward earlier, this pattern of results could be explained in terms of a mixing benefit for the non-dominant language. Again, no difference in accuracy between switch and repeat trials was observed. This might indicate that the highly frequent use of a very limited set of stimulus pictures can neutralize existing differences when speakers process languages of different proficiency status. If the L3 was indeed the weaker language according to participants' self-ratings (and the participants were categorized as "low-proficient"), it is interesting that the participants were faster in naming the same eight pictures in their L3 compared to their L1 on non-switch trials and that there were no differences in accuracy, not even for switch trials (92.6 percent accuracy for the L1; 92.2 percent accuracy for the L3). According to RTs for non-switch trials and percentage of accuracy for switch and non-switch trials, it is clear from this study that picture naming in L1 or L3 was equally easy.

The picture-naming studies we have described so far differ in size of participant group, often dictated by the experimental approach adopted (behavioral vs. fMRI), and the number of stimuli repetition. Balanced bilinguals perform similarly in both their languages in terms of response latencies and accuracy, and usually do not show mixing benefits for a certain language. Moreover, a mixing cost is commonly expected in both languages (e.g., Calabria et al., 2012). Although the role of mixing benefit for a non-dominant language has been overlooked to date, it could be used in the future to explain findings such as those presented by Hernandez et al. (2000, 2001), and Calabria et al. (2012), whereby the dominant language shows larger mixing costs than the non-dominant language. It should be stressed that whenever performance on mixed blocks only is used to determine participants' language proficiency, mixing effects (mixing costs and benefits) come into play and act as confounding factor. We argue that it is recommended to use single-language blocks as a better online indicator of language proficiency related to production of bare nouns and the speed and accuracy of lexical retrieval. If language control is the focus of a study, a closer look at error categories might be advantageous given that the occurrence of cross-language interference is a robust indicator of language control failure.

### 23.4.1.2 Digit naming

Compared to picture naming, digit naming (1–9) is less demanding since digits have lower visual complexity than line drawings, are more frequently used than words; many of them are monosyllabic; and are often cognates depending on the language combination.

Wang et al. (2009) tested 15 native Chinese speakers (mean age 20.5 years) with L2 English (AoA 12.06) with low proficiency self-ratings (mean speaking ability 2.93 on a five-point scale), despite 7 to 11 years of L2 learning and 2.8 hours of daily exposure to L2 English. Participants were asked to name digits from 1 to 9 in Chinese or English depending on a visual language cue in a behavioral task following an fMRI scanning session. Both single- and mixed-language blocks were administered. Naming digits in the pure language block was faster in Chinese than in English (L1: 523 ms; L2: 595 ms). Response latencies increased for both languages in the mixed-language block (L1: 580 ms; L2: 640 ms) and revealed significant mixing costs (main effect of language and block type). Repeat trials were 50 ms faster in the L1 (590 ms) than in the L2 (645 ms), and the L1 showed a larger switch effect than the L2 (L1: 625 ms; L2: 650 ms; main effect of language and trial type). The fMRI results additionally demonstrated that sustained and transient language control modulated lateral activation patterns and as a result, the behavioral costs associated during language switching and control.

Prior and Gollan (2011) provided a good example for a clear distinction and transparent presentation of mixing and switch costs in a study involving digit naming (1–9) in two early bilingual groups (Spanish–English and Mandarin–English, each N > 40) with English as their dominant language. Both groups performed according to language dominance (see Table 23.1). In single-language blocks, responses were significantly faster, but no more accurate, in the dominant language than in the non-dominant language. The results revealed also a standard mixing cost effect of significantly faster naming latencies and higher accuracy in single-language blocks than in mixed-language blocks. Additionally, performance in the dominant language showed larger mixing costs than performance in the non-dominant language, but did not differ in terms of accuracy. With regard to language switching, bilinguals were

**Table 23.1** Mean reaction times, standard deviations, accuracy rates, and costs in the language switching task, by language dominance and by group (adapted from Prior & Gollan, 2011)

|  | Spanish–English | | | | | | Mandarin–English | | | | | |
|---|---|---|---|---|---|---|---|---|---|---|---|---|
|  | Dominant | | | Non-dominant | | | Dominant | | | Non-dominant | | |
|  | M | SD | ACC | M | SD | ACC | M | SD | ACC | M | SD | ACC |
| Trial type |  |  |  |  |  |  |  |  |  |  |  |  |
| Single | 491 | 52 | .99 | 504 | 52 | .99 | 488 | 50 | .99 | 516 | 73 | .99 |
| Repeat | 599 | 84 | .98 | 596 | 93 | .99 | 578 | 77 | .99 | 593 | 96 | .98 |
| Switch | 628 | 92 | .93 | 632 | 95 | .94 | 640 | 107 | .96 | 650 | 127 | .95 |
| Switch cost | 29 | 33 | .05 | 37 | 34 | .05 | 62 | 49 | .03 | 57 | 50 | .03 |
| Mixing cost | 108 | 69 | .01 | 92 | 75 | .005 | 91 | 57 | .004 | 77 | 52 | .01 |

significantly slower and less accurate on switch trials than on repeat trials in mixed-language blocks, in line with common switch cost predictions. However, there was no influence of language dominance; both groups performed equally fast in both their languages, so that switching into the dominant language was no slower than switching into the non-dominant language. The authors argued that the task was highly repetitive and as such, not challenging. They also claimed that it might be "easier in some respects to maintain separation and control over two very different languages such as Mandarin and English, than the more similar Spanish and English" (p. 689). This point of language typology/distance has recently attracted some attention (see Guo et al., 2011; Hoshino & Kroll, 2008) and should prompt researchers to carefully check the linguistic characteristics of their materials, such as syllable length, cross-language similarity (e.g., cognates, homophones), and so on that might explain some of the reported result patterns. Additionally, one could also argue that the task (digit naming vs. picture naming) might be manipulating the amount of errors produced particularly in the weaker language. If possible, future studies should include both task types to provide a solid picture for processing single digits and bare nouns.

For studies involving participants with a clearly non-dominant language (Wang et al., 2009), the switch and mixing cost–benefit distinction could be observed as well in a digit-naming task, whereas the early bilingual groups with a dominant L2 in Prior and Gollan's (2011) study did not show all the expected patterns. In the latter study, the results revealed language dominance in single-language blocks with regard to speed and the expected mixing cost effect for both languages (slower in the mixed than in the single condition, and larger mixing costs for RTs in the dominant language). As mentioned above, the mixed-language condition in Prior and Gollan's study did not demonstrate an effect of language dominance for switch directions. Thus, the question that begs an answer is whether the lack of impact of language dominance for the switch direction was due to participants' early bilingualism. Concerning the digit-naming task, a more systematic investigation is needed into the effects of early vs. late bilingualism, language proficiency, and language typology. Finally, measures of speed and accuracy should be obtained for all task conditions (single and mixed).

### 23.4.1.3 Verbal fluency

Gollan, Sandoval, and Salmon (2011) used the verbal fluency task in two groups of Spanish–English bilinguals to examine cross-language intrusion as an indicator of language control failure. Eighteen older (mean age 77 years) and eighteen younger (mean age 19.7 years) bilinguals were matched for age of acquisition and degree of daily reported use of each of their languages. However, the older bilinguals had a lower educational level and their self-ratings of language proficiency were lower than those of the younger bilinguals. Participants were given 60 seconds to produce members of semantic categories (e.g., animals, musical instruments, adjectives, supermarket items, colors, sports, country names, occupations, nouns, fruits, and vegetables) or letter categories (e.g., words that start with S, F, A, and L for English, and P, M, R, and D for Spanish). First, five semantic and four letter subtests were administered in English and then both subtests were administered in Spanish in order to minimize language switching. Rather than only reporting the total number of errors, Gollan et al. categorized errors into different types, such as within-language errors (e.g., perseverations, malapropisms, and instruction violations). Unfortunately, verbal responses for the semantic categories were not reported in the results section, thus it remains unclear as to whether the same responses were given for certain categories such as "supermarket" and "fruits and vegetables." Also, adjective–noun categories are not usually categorized as a semantic category, but rather as a linguistically functional category. Gollan et al. reported 1 percent cross-language intrusions for the older bilinguals and 0.4 percent of cross-language intrusions for the younger bilinguals. Hence even for the older group this error type did not occur all too often. In a future study, it would be interesting to replicate this finding using the same materials and similar participant groups, but manipulating the order of target language. That is, rather than blocking English and Spanish categories in their entirety, participants could be asked to switch language after each category. This might increase the frequency of cross-language intrusions.

### 23.4.1.4 Production of phrases

An entirely different and innovative study enlarged the scope from mere focus on lexical access to production of phrases upon predefined response language switching (Tarlowski, Wodniecka, & Marzecova, 2013). The study involved fourteen native speakers of Polish with different levels of proficiency in L2 (English). Proficiency level was operationalized through a language questionnaire of self-assessment which included a seven-point scale of several aspects of language abilities (reading, writing, speaking, and listening). Although 192 trials were presented in total (51 percent of trials involving switch trials), only 6 different actions were used. The participants were asked to switch between their L1 and L2 while describing pictures of ongoing and completed actions with simple subject–verb progressive and perfective phrases. The surprising finding was that fewer errors were committed in the L2 than in the L1 for the progressive nonswitch condition. In addition, mean RTs for non-switch trials in the progressive condition were more than 100 ms shorter for the L2 than for the L1. Considering these findings, a number of relevant questions can be generated: What impact does high repetition rate have on performance, especially in the easier L1 condition? Does the frequency of occurrence of structures such as progressive and perfective correlate with the amount of errors made in the task, particularly in the L1? These questions are fruitful to probe in future work.

The main conclusion that can be drawn from this brief review of studies on bilingual (and trilingual) language production is that language proficiency appears to be the main factor influencing speed and accuracy of naming in production. Despite a significant amount of research conducted in this area so far, a more systematic investigation is clearly lacking. Most likely this is due to the missing "first condition," the single-language blocks, from a number of studies, which would be a hallmark of information regarding language proficiency and processing. Consequently, language switching and mixing costs and benefits could be calculated more accurately and aspects of language control could be examined and understood more thoroughly.

Additionally, the necessity to determine in much greater detail bilinguals' language proficiency, exposure to each of their two languages, and daily active language use should not be replaced by self-ratings of language proficiency. If proficiency plays the key role in language control, that is, modulating language processing speed and accuracy with regard to switching, more care needs to be taken to understand this construct. Next, we discuss a few examples of language control from the language comprehension literature, a domain that has attracted less interest in the effects of switching and mixing costs but is beginning to draw the interest of researchers.

## 23.4.2 Comprehension

### 23.4.2.1 Reading aloud

Gullifer, Kroll, and Dussias (2013) investigated inter-sentential switch costs (i.e., processing costs of switching across languages after having read a sentence in one language and then another one in another language). Spanish–English bilinguals were asked to read sentences word by word printed in black, and to name the red target word aloud (either a cross-language cognate or a control word) for which naming latencies were recorded. Gullifer et al. used two conditions: language switching every two sentences (Experiment 1), and single-language presentation (Experiment 2). Drawing on previous lexical switching studies, the authors predicted that naming on a switch trial in Experiment 1 should be slower than naming on a repeat-language trial. Furthermore, they hypothesized that results should reveal a language mixing effect when comparing naming latencies from Experiment 1 and Experiment 2. However, the authors found no apparent switch costs. In Experiment 1, for control words, participants performed as accurately and as quickly in English as in Spanish, regardless of having switched language at the start of the sentence or not. Cognates were named significantly faster than control words, a finding that was explained by parallel language activation resulting in facilitation of lexical access and naming speed. In Experiment 2, a different participant group similar to that of the first experiment performed faster in L2 than in L1 (only significant in the item analysis), and significantly faster on cognate targets than on control words. When comparing Experiments 1 and 2, faster performance on the single than the mixed-language condition can be identified in the mean raw scores, but this difference was not significant. Cognates were named significantly faster on both conditions than control words. The authors interpreted their results by claiming that context does not influence word recognition or naming latencies in reading a target word aloud.

However, a question arising from Gullifer et al.'s (2013) study remains to be clarified: why was a later position of the target word (i.e., how far into the sentence) preferred over an early position? Perhaps switch costs were detected only shortly after a switch. This can be argued on the basis of the non-adjacent position of the language switch and the target word that had to be named. Although a language switch had to take place at the beginning of every second sentence and preparation was possible due to the alternating-runs paradigm, naming latencies were recorded for the target word that appeared somewhere in the middle of the sentence (between the fifth and the twelfth position in a sentence).

In a study investigating the multiple levels of bilingual language control in reading aloud, Gollan et al. (2014) induced cross-language intrusion errors in Spanish–English balanced bilinguals in both single-language (either Spanish or English) or mixed-language contexts. Interestingly, the participants nearly exclusively produced language intrusions (e.g., saying *él* instead of *he*) in mixed-language readings and most frequently when producing dominant-language targets (although accent-only errors exhibited reversed language-dominance effects).[5] The study also analyzed eye movements and revealed that fixation on words in the nontarget language increased errors only for function words. In all, Gollan et al.'s study provides support for a more complex picture of language control than was originally anticipated, one which entails multiple mechanisms of language control. Furthermore, the researchers argue that there is: "(a) inhibition of the dominant language at both lexical and sub-lexical processing levels; (b) special retrieval mechanisms for function words in mixed-language utterances; and (c) attentional monitoring of the target word for its match with the intended language" (p. 585).

### 23.4.2.2 Self-paced reading

Ibáñez, Macizo, and Bajo (2010) examined switch costs in a self-paced reading experiment with Spanish–English bilinguals and translators. Sentences were presented word by word in pseudo-random order in one or the other language. The first word of a sentence which was presented on a computer screen was a language-specific article such as the definite article *la* (the) or indefinite article *una* (a). Reading time for the first word was used to determine switch costs. In Experiment 1, both groups of participants yielded faster reading times on non-switch trials for their dominant language compared to their non-dominant language, in line with their self-rated proficiency. Ibáñez et al. argued that the asymmetrical switch costs were linked to the participant experience in professional translation: while the bilinguals showed asymmetrical switch costs (i.e., slower reading when switching to their dominant L1 compared to reading on a non-switch trial), no switch costs were observed for the L2 between switch and non-switch trials. For the translators, it did not matter whether they read sentences on switch or non-switch trials: L1 was read faster in both conditions than the L2. In Experiment 2, an additional group of participants performed the same task without repeating the sentences. Participants did not exhibit any difference in reading time between their L1 and L2, nor between switch and non-switch trials. The difference in reading time between Experiment 1 and Experiment 2 was explained in terms of manipulation of task demands which were higher for Experiment 1 due to reading and maintaining information in working memory until the sentence was repeated. Unfortunately, no specific mean reading times for the first word were included in that study. However, the authors reported mean reading times for the first five or ten words and overall reading times, which were faster for the L1 than for the L2. Yet no information was provided either on trial types, switch plus non-switch, or on non-switch trials only. Based on the fact that the first word of each sentence was language specific, the authors claimed that translators were better able to prepare for a switch than the bilinguals in Experiment 1.

---

[5] For more information on reverse switch-cost asymmetries, see Monsell, Yeung, and Azuma (2000).

When task demands were reduced, reading for comprehension only (and not for repetition) was easier for all participant groups and allowed for fast reading times in all languages and in all conditions.

### 23.4.2.3 Categorization of animacy

Macizo, Bajo, and Paolieri (2012) conducted a word reading task (Experiment 1) with twenty Spanish–English bilingual students and found the standard asymmetric switch cost effect (larger switch costs for L2 to L1 than for L1 to L2). Participants were asked to read aloud 144 experimental words (presented four times) with half of the trials being switch trials per language. No single-language block was included. Performance showed clear language dominance for L1 (faster and better performance on non-switch trials) and a larger switch cost from L2 to L1. Although bilinguals were classified as "highly proficient in L2…," L1 was clearly participants' dominant language. The authors concluded that "it might be possible that the relative balance of L1–L2 proficiency modulates the asymmetrical switch cost in language production tasks" (Macizo et al., 2012: 138).

Experiments 2 and 3 in Macizo et al. (2012) were categorization tasks (classification of a presented word as animate or inanimate entity) with pseudo-randomized language switching. A group of highly proficient bilinguals was compared to a group of low proficient bilinguals. For the high proficiency group, the usual switch cost was observed, with slower performance and more errors on switch than on non-switch trials. However, switch costs were not affected by switch direction, supporting the view of symmetric switch costs for highly proficient bilinguals. Experiment 3 revealed that when proficiency in L2 was low, performance on the categorization task revealed an effect of language dominance, with slower RTs for L2 than L1 on non-switch trials. As for switch costs, these were slightly larger for L2 than for L1, but this difference was not significant. In the discussion of the results of Experiment 3, the authors point to the striking difference in overall RTs between the high and low proficiency groups with the average performance of low proficient L2 speakers taking about half the time to perform the task compared to the highly proficient L2 speakers (858 ms and 1,682 ms, respectively). As an explanation for this highly unexpected between-group difference, the authors suggested the "larger within-group variability in the case of high proficient bilinguals relative to that of low proficient bilinguals" (p. 143). One has to remember that this is performance on a mixed-language block, and unfortunately the authors did not include a single-language block which as we have repeatedly suggested here would function as a more reliable indicator of language dominance. It would have been interesting to see if the large within-group variability also influenced the speed of categorization in a single-language condition.

The studies we have presented in this last section of the chapter are first steps for shedding light on language control in language comprehension. Perhaps their conclusions should be treated with caution as the tasks used in these studies are of a more exploratory nature compared to the rather established paradigms of language production studies. Thus, some of the tasks might need more fine-tuning. Additionally, the role of language proficiency is rather questionable, since predictions derived from the production literature are not easily replicated in language comprehension studies and do not fall into the same line of argumentation.

## 23.5 Conclusion

In this chapter, we have reviewed various methodologies (e.g., picture naming, digit naming, the verbal fluency measure, phrasal production, reading aloud, self-paced reading, and categorization of animacy) that measure language control in language production and comprehension among multilinguals. We began by introducing the term *language control* as a notion that has been around for more than four decades primarily in foreign language teaching and assessment and transitioned to its more recent application to experimental work in multilingualism. We focused on production and comprehension processing costs as indicators of language control by analyzing both language switch and mixing costs. In our discussion, we have identified proficiency as a potential modulating factor of speed and accuracy of language production. However, we argue that future studies would benefit by incorporating both mixed-language and single-language blocks to establish a baseline for proficiency and performance abilities. Indeed, inconsistent findings regarding the apparent observation of larger mixing costs for the dominant language compared to the less-dominant language perhaps can be clarified by avoiding the confounding repercussions of methods that limit themselves to mixed-language blocks instead of including both mixed- and single-language blocks.

Furthermore, because various types of switching tasks (e.g., numeral naming vs. picture naming) appear to modulate accuracy in less-dominant languages, it may be beneficial for future studies to include a combination of several measures. Research may also benefit from rich analyses of categorical errors produced during these language switching tasks. Finally, future research should consider the conditions that lead to mixing costs and benefits and should begin to tease apart the relationship between task demands and methodological specificities (e.g., frequency of stimulus repetition, number of trials, and the time interval between the presentation of a language cue and the stimulus) and their modulation of accuracy and RTs. In sum, we call for the conceptualization of innovative methodologies that thoroughly explore behavioral aspects of the control of multiple languages in one mind.

# 24

# Neural perspectives of language control

Arturo Hernandez

## 24.1 Introduction

The nature of cognitive control and its implications for bilingualism have gained a great deal of notoriety in recent years. Results from work in the past decade suggest that bilinguals may benefit from the use of two languages with an improved ability to resist interference in non-verbal cognitive control tasks (Bialystok et al., 2004, 2005; Bialystok, Craik, & Ryan, 2006; Garbin et al., 2010). Furthermore, there is evidence that differences in brain activity when comparing monolinguals and bilinguals have been found in areas that are associated with cognitive control. The finding that cognitive control may benefit from bilingualism, however, has overshadowed a longer more profound set of issues that arises. Specifically, what is the extent of this advantage and what can the brain tell us about this. I will start with a discussion of the neural bases of control in the non-verbal domain. Then I will transition to a discussion of how areas associated with cognitive control may play a role in bilingualism. Finally, I will end with some points that require additional consideration when considering the neural bases of control in bilinguals.

## 24.2 On the neural bases of cognitive control

The neural bases of cognitive control have received considerable interest in the field. These studies suggest that control plays a role in task switching (Dreher et al., 2002; Jimura & Braver, 2011; Madden et al., 2010; Mecklinger et al., 1999), control of emotion (Banich et al., 2009; Ochsner & Gross, 2005; Ochsner, Silvers, & Buhle, 2012), and in memory (Badre & Wagner, 2007; Depue, Banich, & Curran, 2006; Mecklinger, 2010; Richter & Yeung, 2012). This field is too broad to summarize in this chapter alone. Hence, rather than taking a broad view of this field I will provide a more thematic focused review in which I take a developmental view of control.

For many, Jean Piaget is associated with many things aside from cognitive control (Piaget, 1954, 1970). He is well known for suggesting that infants come to the world with just a few reflexes. In his view, learning involves a process of adaptation in which two opposing processes are used for learning. On the one hand, a child could use assimilation in order to make a particular environmental object fit into an existing schema. Opposing this was the process of change in which a child would accommodate an existing schema in order to fit an environmental stimulus. For example, a child might take the sucking reflex that is initially used to breastfeed in order to suck on objects. Whereas breastfeeding involves assimilation for the most part, learning to suck on different objects would involve accommodation of an existing schema.

Piaget was criticized for his model of cognitive development, mostly because of his adherence to developmental stages and for his view that newborns were born with a few basic reflexes. There is now ample evidence that newborns already show a bias toward the sounds of their native language (Dehaene-Lambertz, Dehaene, & Hertz-Pannier, 2002; Eimas et al., 1971; Kovács & Mehler, 2009; Vouloumanos & Werker, 2004; Werker & Curtin, 2005) and that newborns will follow a face figure minutes after birth (Goren, Sarty, & Wu, 1975; Morton & Johnson, 1991). The presence of these very early biases is in conflict with Piaget's assertion that newborns come equipped with only a few basic reflexes in terms of cognitive processes.

Despite the intense criticism of Piaget, there are some ways in which his work still resonates today. According to Piaget, the ability to know something exists without seeing it is one of the hallmarks of development. Piaget first established this by observing whether infants would search for an object that was in plain sight (Piaget, 1954). Then he would cover the object to see if infants would still search for it. What he found was that until about eight months of age, infants would not search for an object that was covered up. It was as if the object was out of sight and out of mind. Around 10 months of age, children began to search for an object even when it was hidden. Subsequent research has suggested that object permanence appears much earlier in infancy (Baillargeon, 2004). Despite the debate about when infants are able to represent objects in the world with their minds, researchers agree that changes in early life involve an improving ability to keep objects in mind even when they are not present in the world.

At the time that Piaget carried out his research, he did not couch his framework for cognitive development within a theory of brain development. However, more recent research has begun to consider the link between object permanence and the neural changes occurring during early life. Yuko Munakata is one of a handful of researchers who have started to rethink what Piaget's stages mean in terms of brain development (Shinskey & Munakata, 2003). Along with Jane Shinskey, she sought to uncover the root of this effect. They started by replicating an experiment that dates back to the days of Piaget. To do this they placed 6.5-month-old infants in front of toys that were covered by a cloth or not. They found that infants were more likely to reach for a toy if it was in plain sight than if it was covered by a cloth. Next they placed a toy in front of the child and then gradually dimmed the room to complete darkness. What they found was that infants would reach for an object that was covered in darkness to a greater extent than when the object was covered by a blanket in plain sight. What these results show is that the difficulty with finding a hidden object was due at least in part to the fact that the infant was distracted by the real world. Hence, the ability to see an object that is covered depends on keeping two things in mind, what they see and what they do not see. When the lights are off, infants cannot see anything at all. So their performance actually improved because the mind can create an image without the real world getting in the way.

The results of research show that infants initially relegated to a sensorimotor world of fleeting images and simple movement during the first few months of life quickly transition to a concrete world by the end of the first year. By the end of the second year children move past this sensorimotor stage and emerge with the ability to use and understand symbols (Bates et al., 1979; Piaget 1954). Even before speaking, infants can associate hand gestures with the real world. It is well known that most 10-month-olds can learn simple signs to communicate (Bates, 1976; Bates et al., 1979).

The most profound use of symbols in humans appears around a child's first birthday when they begin to use language. Although object permanence and language may not seem to have much in common, according to Piaget there is a very strong connection. Specifically, both of these activities involve forming an internal representation of an object. Symbols are a way of describing the world without directly referencing its physical characteristics. Language allows us to communicate without playing charades.

From the first birthday on, normally developing children go through a dizzying array of changes. These changes spread beyond language as a child begins to develop a sense of self. Elizabeth Bates did her early work with children, looking at how symbols emerge at this young age (Bates et al., 1979). She realized that children were very good at forming alternative representations of the world in their third year of life. For example, she would ask them to play a game in which they would use the conditional. Children could imagine all sorts of things. They were happy to imagine that the moon was made out of chocolate. They could even imagine that they were an animal or someone else. Then came the clincher. She would say to them, "Imagine that you were you." This left some kids in tears. "Of course I am me. Who else would I be?" So, symbolic representation only goes so far, at least at age 3 or so (Bates, 1974).

Bates' early work points to another remarkable milestone in human development. Children begin to understand that their view is different from that of others. Piaget termed the inability to do this "egocentrism." He thought it was impossible for young children to understand that what they saw in the world was different from what another person saw. Piaget tested this using a three-mountain problem, in which an experimenter and a child would sit on opposite sides of a display. The experimenter would then ask the child which display matched his or her view. Inevitably, the child at first would choose his or her own view as the one that matched the experimenter's view even up to the age of 5. By age 7, most children would begin to choose the experimenter's view. Researchers extended Piaget's original finding to consider whether children can reason about what other people see compared with what they see. In these false-belief tasks, children are asked to observe a scene (Wimmer & Perner, 1983). In the first scene, a toy is placed in one drawer while a small puppet named Tommy is viewing it. The experimenter then lets the child know that "little Tommy" has left the room. The experimenter then moves the toy to a different place in the room such as under the bed. When little Tommy comes back the child is asked to indicate where he will look for the toy. The key to this task is that the child has to understand that little Tommy thinks the toy is in the drawer not under the bed. However, young children will indicate that Tommy will look under the bed. That is, they are unable to distinguish between what someone else knows and what they know. Only by age 4 or so will they begin to realize that Tommy will look in the drawer (Wimmer & Perner, 1983). In short, only by age 4 are children able to realize that others think differently than they do.

The ability to overcome "egocentrism" continues into adolescence. As puberty approaches, humans begin to understand that others see the world differently than they do. Furthermore, they begin to create thoughts that are more and more divorced from physical reality. Abstract thought is a reflection of a child's ability to think beyond the physical world that exists. In fact, at the end of childhood the advent of abstract thought appears as discussions in classrooms turn to topics such as truth, honesty, or liberty. These concepts are not directly based on the physical attributes of the world.

Based on all his work with children, Piaget suggested that across development humans become less and less bound by the physical world. Specifically, adolescent thought is marked by a distinct ability to imagine what is not true. It is unlikely that an adolescent would end up in tears when asked what if they were themselves. The dissociation of ourselves is perhaps the greatest skill we possess and definitely relies on the expanded power of our prefrontal cortex (Uddin et al., 2007).

## 24.3 Cognitive control across development

The progress from sensorimotor to more complex forms of thinking during development also lines up nicely with brain development. Areas of the brain involved in sensory and motor activities are the first to develop. Subsequent maturation adds to the function of these basic areas as a child grows older. As this happens, areas that integrate different sensory and motor systems begin to mature. The final cog in the cerebral wheel comes with the development of the prefrontal cortex, which lies directly in front of the basic motor areas of our brain. The prefrontal cortex, which is thought to be crucial for delayed gratification and higher level reasoning, does not develop fully until age 18. This late developing area is also thought to be important in reasoning about the real (concrete) and abstract (formal) world. The progression from sensorimotor to abstract thinking observed by Piaget shows an interesting parallel with brain development (Gogtay et al., 2004).

Neuronal changes that occur across development were first investigated by observing the anatomy of neurons in the brains of a few individuals under a microscope (Huttenlocher, 1990, 1994; Huttenlocher & Dabholkar, 1997; Huttenlocher & de Courten, 1987; Huttenlocher et al., 1982a, 1982b). Differential development of areas under the microscope revealed changes in two different processes: the production of synapses and synaptic pruning. The third process involves myelination, the addition of a fatty sheath surrounding the axon of each nerve cell. Production of synapses is strongest in the occipital lobe (i.e., visual regions) of the cortex between 4 and 8 months of age (Huttenlocher & de Courten, 1987). In the frontal lobe, synapse production reaches its peak at 15 months of age (Huttenlocher & Dabholkar, 1997). The lag in the frontal lobe's overproduction of synapses is also observed in the reduction of synapses via pruning (Huttenlocher, 1994). So, not only does the frontal lobe produce synapses later than other areas of the brain, it also shows a later reduction in these synapses via pruning.

In a groundbreaking study, Elizabeth Sowell and colleagues examined gray matter density using high resolution structural MRI scans in a group of individuals who ranged between 7 and 87 years of age (Sowell et al., 2003). Results revealed a number of changes in density of gray matter, the part of the cortex composed of neural cell bodies that carry out neural computations. Across ages most areas showed a linear decrease in gray matter density. The authors speculate that changes in gray matter density may be due to increased myelination, which leads to increased white matter. For example, regions in the frontal lobe showed decreases in gray matter density from ages 7 and beyond. The authors attribute some of this to an increase in myelination up until age 40 with a decrease in neural density ensuing into older adulthood. Hence, the prefrontal cortex shows a later pattern of development much as was seen in studies that used histological methods mentioned earlier.

## 24.4 Flexibility

As I outlined previously, work in the developmental literature has begun to form a link between executive function, which is mediated by the prefrontal cortex, and the ability to form internal representations. Interestingly, a parallel line of research has developed with regard to cognitive flexibility. Control and flexibility can be seen in driving. A driver might notice that the car in front of her is speeding up and speed up to match her speed. At the same time, she may notice that the car coming by her is about to change lanes. As she is switching between what is in front of her and what is behind her she might hear her favorite song on the radio and turn up the volume. The ability to switch between these different tasks is what researchers have come to term cognitive flexibility (Scott, 1962). A person with little flexibility would have trouble switching between driving and adjusting the radio. Hence, cognitive flexibility is reflected in the ability to use cognitive control to switch between different tasks.

The nature of switching has been the topic of extensive study in the literature with college-age adults. Like many discoveries in psychology, the presence of switching effects was first noted over 80 years ago (Jersild, 1927). To do this Arthur Jersild presented stimuli in a pure condition that required only one task or in a mixed condition that involved having to perform a different task on every other trial. Interestingly, mixing tasks did not always lead to a slowing of responses. For example, when participants had to see a two-digit number and a word (i.e., 64 bad) and were instructed to subtract 6 from the number and produce the opposite word, they were actually faster than when just viewing words or numbers. Notice that in this task each stimulus (i.e., the word or number) can only yield one operation. You cannot subtract 6 from the word "bad." However, when asked to alternate between adding 6 and subtracting 6 for separately presented two-digit numbers there is a substantially larger cost than when having to perform only one of these tasks. The key to this effect is that the two-digit number triggers both tasks (you can subtract or add). The participant has to choose one of these tasks and then switch on each subsequent trial.

For many years, Jersild's seminal findings stood untested until Spector and Biedermann (1976) sought to use more modern experimental designs to address some of the potential limitations of the original studies. For example, they presented each stimulus independently rather than using a list of items on a single sheet of paper. Since then a number of studies have replicated the costs of switching between tasks relative to performing a single task (Allport, 1989; Allport, Styles, & Hsieh, 1994; Hsieh & Allport, 1994; Jersild, 1927; Spector & Biederman, 1976). Although switch costs appear for both errors and response latencies, the majority of studies index costs in terms of latency.

## 24.5 Task switching and development

The notion of task switching and cognitive control shows an interesting parallel in both the developmental and the cognitive psychology literature. Earlier we discussed examples of how having to find a hidden toy or imagine that someone sees something different from what you see involve having to attend to an internal stimulus and ignore an external one. In a similar fashion, task switching involves having to attend to a certain aspect of one stimulus and ignore another. If one has to switch between adding and subtracting then there is always a cost on trials where one switches to another task. For example, subtracting the number 6 from 25 on one trial requires ignoring the instruction to add both numbers on the previous trial. Subsequent switch trials would require doing the reverse.

In the 2000s, researchers began to use the same switching tasks that were revived in the 1970s and 1980s to look at changes across development. One of the most comprehensive studies in this respect was conducted by Davidson along with Adele Diamond (2006), a researcher with a long-standing interest in the developmental changes that allow individuals to perform better and better on cognitive control and switching tasks. To explore this, the researchers gave participants three different versions of classic cognitive control tasks. These three tasks involved presenting either circles, pictures, or arrows. In each case, the stimuli would signal a response either on the left or right side of the screen. For example, in the dots test a filled dot would signal a left button response and a striped dot would signal a right button response. In addition, the filled or the striped dot can be placed on the same side as the response or on the opposite side of the response. That is, a filled dot on the right side of the computer screen would be incompatible, whereas the same dot on the left side is compatible. Results from many studies find that individuals slow down when the stimulus signals a button press on the opposite side of its physical location on the computer screen. Finally, Davidson and colleagues also presented the stimuli in a mixed format, which involved having items switch from congruent to incongruent and vice versa.

The results revealed considerable changes across age. First, younger children tended to show a larger incompatibility effect. They really slowed down and made many more errors when the dot signaled a response on the opposite side. Furthermore, slower responses and more errors were observed when children had to switch across a task (i.e., make compatible and incompatible decisions) versus when they did not have to switch (i.e., make only compatible or incompatible decisions in one series of stimuli). The cost of switching diminished as children got older and was reduced the most in adults in their twenties.

Given that task switching shows a reduction across development and that the frontal lobes are also known to show an increase in myelination from childhood to adulthood, it is natural to think that both of these facts might be directly related. To test this, Crone et al. (2006) asked groups of children, adolescents, and young adults to perform tasks in which a switch was required or was not required while being scanned with fMRI. Furthermore, they made the tasks have single mappings or double mappings, much as Jersild did with words (single) or numbers (double). What the authors found was that the possibility of two rules applying to a single stimulus was particularly difficult for children, less difficult for adolescents, and much less difficult for adults.

The results are consistent with the brain development principles that I discussed earlier. Specifically, not all brain areas showed the same pattern of neural activity across ages. Areas in the parietal cortex, a posterior, an area which develops earlier in life, showed no real difference in neural activity between children, adolescents, and adults. The supplementary motor area, which is involved in simpler forms of cognitive control, differed in children relative to both adolescents and adults. It was only the prefrontal cortex that revealed a difference between children, adolescents, and adults. Specifically, this area showed a relative reduction across each age group. The results from these studies with task switching confirm that the prefrontal cortex is a late developing area. They also establish that the frontal cortex is involved to a great extent when individuals perform switching tasks. The natural question that arises is whether this is also true in bilinguals who switch between languages.

## 24.6 The language switch

The need to control which language is active at a particular point in time has been the subject of considerable attention in the psychological literature. Researchers wondered how bilinguals could keep information in one language from constantly interfering with processing of the other language. The potential for interference is (at least in theory) massive, particularly in view of the overlap in neural tissue. Interestingly, the notion of a switch mechanism was originally proposed by Wilder Penfield, who felt that there must be an interface which helps to mediate between motor and sensory systems in the brain (Penfield, 1950). Penfield then extended this idea by proposing a language switch in order to account for the lack of interference in bilinguals (Penfield & Roberts, 1959).

As the 1960s approached, more and more researchers sought to identify language switch costs. However, results from a series of studies found mixed evidence for effects of language switching on behavioral performance in healthy young adult bilinguals. Some found no evidence of language switching effects (Dalrymple-Alford & Aamiry, 1969; Kolers,

1966) while others found significant effects of language switching particularly in terms of processing speed (Macnamara, Krauthammer, and Bolgar 1968; MacNamara & Kushnir, 1971; Soares & Grosjean, 1984).

A second wave of interest in language switching came during the late 1980s through the early 2000s using computer-controlled experiments. In a classic study, Grainger and Beauvillain asked participants to make word decisions to a set of French and English words. The catch was that the words could be all in French, all in English, or they could be in either language (Grainger & Beauvillain, 1988). Bilinguals were slower to make word decisions when the language was mixed relative to the single language conditions. In other words, having to read words in both languages made bilinguals slow down.

Von Studnitz and Green expanded on these results by asking participants to make two different types of word decisions for stimuli in paired alternation between German and English (von Studnitz & Green, 1997). This paired alternation (GGEEGGEEGGEE) allowed the investigators to look at the difference between a switch trial (GG**E**E) and a no switch trial (GGE**E**). In Experiment 1, participants saw words in either a green or red color font and were asked to decide if the word was a real word or not. The color indicated the language of their word decisions. If the word was in red, they would decide if it was an English word or not. If it was in green, they would decide if it was a German word or not. Half of the subjects paired English with red and half of them paired German with red. Experiment 2 allowed participants to make word decisions without having to attend to any particular language.

The results revealed slower responses when participants had to make a word decision in only one language. This is not surprising, since this required bilinguals to focus on one language while ignoring the other. The additional control needed to focus on only one language for each word would naturally lead to slower responses. The interesting result was that both experiments showed slower responses for the switch condition (GG**E**E) relative to the no switch condition (GGE**E**). Hence, it appears that having to go from one language to the other slows people down even if it has no role in the response that they are making.

The nature of language switching was also the topic of initial work in my laboratory (Hernandez, Bates, & Avila, 1996). In this experiment, bilingual participants were asked to listen to a spoken paragraph that had gaps in it. In these gaps, written words were presented on a computer screen either in the same language or in another language. It was an experimental twist on a task made famous by David Swinney and Donald Foss (Foss & Speer, 1983; Swinney, 1979). The idea was to manipulate the predictability of the language of the word in that particular paragraph. In the mixed language condition, the visually presented words that filled gaps in a spoken passage could appear in either language. In the blocked condition, the word would appear either in the same language or in the other language during a particular passage. Hence, subjects in the mixed condition were not sure of the language in which the visual word would appear. When the language of the auditory paragraph and word matched, subjects processed the meaning of the word in both the blocked and mixed condition. When the language was completely predictable the meaning affected reading speed. Interestingly, studies with EEG suggest that a sentence that ends with a word in the other language leads to an elongated N400, a negative wave that is sensitive to how easily a word can be read (Moreno, Federmeier, & Kutas, 2002). Hence, it appears that changing languages involves having to read a word in a more effortful manner.

The most interesting effect appeared when participants were not sure of the language in which the visual words would appear. In this unpredictable mixed language condition, participants were able to read the words as fast as in the predictable condition. They were also just as accurate. We could see a clear priming effect in the same language condition regardless of language predictability. However, cross-language priming only appeared under predictable conditions. In the unpredictable mixed condition, there was no cross-language priming. So bilinguals seemed to be trading off the processing of meaning in order to complete the task successfully which required them to read words on a computer screen.

The nature of switching has also been explored in verbal production tasks. In a classic study, Meuter and Allport asked participants to say the names of single digits (1–9) out loud (Meuter & Allport, 1999). Participants were presented with single numbers in either yellow or blue. Each person was trained to name the single digit in one language or the other depending on the color of the font. The results revealed that participants were faster for no switch (GGEE) conditions relative to switch conditions (GGEE). Furthermore, there was an effect of mixing such that naming digits in a single language was faster than having to switch between languages. These results confirmed that switching slows people down even when saying digits out loud. Since digits are easily named in both languages, the results suggest that bilinguals are slowed by the act of switching and not by a lack of knowledge in either language. Finally, both Meuter and Allport (1999) and Jackson (2001) have found that switching is asymmetric such that it is harder to suppress the more proficient language. This suggests that added control is present in switching and particularly needed when having to access the more proficient language and not the least proficient one.

The results we have discussed so far fit in with the view that bilinguals slow their responses during switching due to the need to control which language will be accessed. Switching tasks are most likely reliant on frontal lobe function. This carries two implications. First, there should be brain activity in areas of the frontal lobe when looking at conditions of switching relative to conditions with only one language. Second, there should be changes in the size of this switching effect depending on the age of the subjects tested. Specifically, children and older adults should show larger switching effects relative to young adults' age-related differences in frontal lobe function.

Work in collaboration with Kathryn Kohnert and Elizabeth Bates sought to look at the nature of language switching across development. The results from 100 child bilinguals and 30 older adult bilinguals showed a clear developmental pattern (Hernandez & Kohnert, 1999; Kohnert, Bates, & Hernandez, 1999). Children were much slower when switching between languages compared to naming pictures in one language. The size of this switching effect was reduced in adulthood and stood stable through bilinguals' thirties and forties. However, for older adults who were 60 and above the size of the switching effect grew considerably larger, reaching half a second relative to the one-tenth of a second in college-age adults. Our results were eerily similar to those discussed earlier across development in non-linguistic domains. This naturally leads to the question of whether language switching would also be revealed in the amount of brain activity seen in the prefrontal areas of the brain.

## 24.7 The brain bases of language switching

The interest in language switching had also extended to the possible neural locus of this effect. At the neuroanatomical level, researchers had found mixed evidence for one area that was exclusively involved in language switching. Classic cases in aphasia presented by Potzl and Kauders suggested that the language switch was localized in the supramarginal gyrus, which is in the parietal lobe (Herschmann & Potzl, 1983; Potzl, 1983). However, others had found evidence of patients with lesions in the supramarginal gyrus area, the posterior part of the Sylvian fissure, and adjoining areas of the parietal lobe in whom there was no switching difficulty (Gloning & Gloning, 1983; Minkowski, 1983; Stengel & Zelmanowicz, 1933). One of the cases presented by Stengel and Zelmanowicz is of particular interest, given that it was one of the few cases in which language mixing appears both in spontaneous conversation and in picture naming for a person with a motor aphasia that was thought to be due to a frontal lesion. Hence, there was very little consistency in the areas that when damaged were leading to difficulties with language switching. In short, work in the neuropsychology literature up until that point had not found any clear evidence for a single neural center involved in language switching. Rather there was evidence of lesions to frontal, temporal, and parietal areas that led to impairment in language mixing. Given these findings there appeared to be no specific area of the brain that was dedicated exclusively to language switching.

The brain areas involved in language switching have also been explored in a series of studies using modern neuroimaging techniques. The first of these studies was published by Price et al. (1999). These researchers looked at the nature of translation and language switching in a group of German–English bilinguals. Participants were asked to read a word on a computer screen and mouth the word or its translation while being scanned with positron emission tomography, an indirect measure of blood flow in the brain. Translation relative to reading led to increases in subcortical areas involved in motor control such as the putamen and the caudate nucleus as well as other areas involved in control such as the anterior insula, cerebellum, and the anterior cingulate gyrus. In addition, Price and colleagues asked participants either to respond in one language or to alternate between languages when responding in a particular block. When comparing switching to processing of a single language, there was increased activity in the supramarginal gyrus and inferior frontal gyrus for switching relative to the single language condition.

The neural correlates of language switching that were explored both with older adults and children were also the topic of the two neuroimaging studies conducted (Hernandez, Dapretto, & Bookheimer, 2000; Hernandez & Kohnert, 2000). In these studies, a group of Spanish–English bilinguals were asked to imagine saying the names of a set of pictures covertly. This covert naming task was used extensively at the time to avoid the head motion that accompanies talking thereby increasing motion artefacts. The results revealed more activity in the dorsolateral prefrontal cortex when bilinguals had to switch between languages compared to when they had to simply covertly name in only one language. A second study conducted with Susan Bookheimer, Mirella Dapretto, and John Mazziotta at UCLA replicated the switching effect discussed above. Specifically, there was more neural activity in the right dorsolateral prefrontal cortex in the mixed language condition relative to the single language condition. Interestingly, the reverse comparison revealed increased activity in Broca's area (which is part of the ventrolateral prefrontal cortex) on the left. Taken together these results suggest that having to switch between languages involves activity in brain areas that show increased activity for cognitive control tasks.

The importance of the dorsolateral prefrontal cortex (DLPFC) in language switching has also been observed in a series of studies that have investigated the effects of transcranial magnetic stimulation, or TMS. TMS is performed by radiating a magnetic pulse to a specific neuronal cluster via a coil applied over a small portion of the surface of the scalp. This pulse penetrates the surface of the cortex and can temporarily alter firing of neurons. In one study, Holtzheimer and colleagues (Holtzheimer, Fawaz, Wilson, & Avery, 2005) applied a TMS pulse over the left DLPFC to an English–German and an English–Spanish bilingual who were being treated for major depressive disorders. Both patients reported thinking in their second language to a greater extent after the treatment. The fact that stimulation of the prefrontal cortex leads to a language invading a patient's thoughts to a greater extent provides an indirect link between the dorsolateral prefrontal cortex and control of a language.

Since the original studies, a number of additional studies have looked at the nature of language switching. These studies have identified a much larger set of structures that are involved in the control of language. For example, Crinion and colleagues asked participants to look at pairs of words that were related or not and that matched across languages or did not (Crinion et al., 2006). Results showed a decrease in neural activity in the anterior portions of the temporal lobe when participants read words that were related to each other. In addition, activity in the caudate nucleus differed depending on whether the language matched or did not. The caudate nucleus is known to play a role in the learning of new tasks with rules that can be stated verbally and is highly linked with activity in language areas of the temporal and parietal cortices along with the dorsolateral portion of the prefrontal cortex (Ashby & Crossley, 2012). Friederici (2006) has proposed that the caudate nucleus plays a role in language control and may play a particularly crucial role for bilinguals, who must maintain control of each language. Finally, the importance of the caudate nucleus in control has also been documented in the neuropsychological literature. In a case study, Abutalebi and colleagues tested a trilingual patient with damage to the caudate nucleus (Vitali et al., 2010). The patient had no difficulty in naming pictures but showed involuntary switching during language production during regular speech. Thus the caudate nucleus seems to play a role in the control of language as part of a frontal-subcortical loop that is dedicated to the use of declarative memory and cognitive control. Finally, Gabriele Garbin, Albert Costa, and colleagues have found that the caudate nucleus plays a role in switching to the dominant language in highly proficient bilinguals (Garbin et al., 2011). Thus the caudate nucleus is important in overcoming interference for bilinguals.

Language switching has also received considerable attention in the literature (Hervais-Adelman, Moser-Mercer, & Golestani, 2011). These studies have begun to converge on a network of brain areas; the dorsolateral prefrontal cortex, the caudate nucleus, the anterior cingulate gyrus, and the supramarginal gyrus in the parietal lobe play important roles in cognitive control tasks for monolinguals.

To make sense of these data, Jubin Abutalebi and David Green have looked at how each component of the network plays a role in language switching and more generally in control (Abutalebi, 2008; Abutalebi et al., 2009; Abutalebi & Green, 2007; Green & Abutalebi, 2008). They postulate that more anterior areas, such as the dorsolateral prefrontal cortex and the anterior cingulate gyrus, are involved in selecting the appropriate language for response and correcting for any possible errors in this process. The caudate nucleus, which is part of the basal ganglia, plays a role in control and is thought to be involved in supervising the correct selection. Finally, the supramarginal gyrus, in the parietal lobe, is involved in providing a bias toward the correct language and away from the incorrect language. Interestingly, Abutalebi and Green (2007) also argue that this network is used when a second language is spoken with lower proficiency. The idea is that expertise in a language involves having to do things well. When speakers are less proficient, it requires more effort to obtain the same result. Naturally, cognitive control areas should become involved in any new activity that is taken on.

Work has also confirmed this in a cued picture-naming experiment on a group of late Spanish–English bilinguals (Hernandez & Meschyan, 2006). The results from this study using functional magnetic resonance imaging (fMRI) revealed increased activity in four separate areas: the dorsolateral prefrontal cortex, the anterior cingulate gyrus, the anterior insula, and the fusiform gyrus. The dorsolateral prefrontal cortex and anterior cingulate gyrus, as noted earlier, are involved in selecting the correct language. The anterior insula is known to play a role in the articulation of physical movements necessary for producing words. Finally, the fusiform gyrus is present since the task involves having to identify the labels associated with an object.

The results from the fMRI study conducted in my lab provide an interesting extension of Abutalebi and Green's model. They suggest that control areas do not operate in a vacuum. At least in our study, we found that frontal control areas were used to activate both the object representations and the motor programs associated with those objects. In short, speaking in a late learned second language requires bilinguals to cycle between what an object is and its corresponding label. These results suggest that even when a second language learner is immersed in that language, inhibition is needed in order to overcome interference from their more proficient first language.

Based on the data discussed so far we should be able to observe similar control networks in a group of bilinguals performing a non-verbal switch task. Surprisingly, early research did not uncover brain areas involved in non-verbal control (Hernandez et al., 2001). The lack of a within-language switching effect had two possible causes. One possibility is that there was very little sensitivity to detect this difference. That is, there was an effect but we missed it. The second more interesting possibility is that bilinguals are not as sensitive to these task manipulations as monolinguals are. That is, no within-language switching effect because bilinguals are very good switchers. At the time Ellen Bialystok had begun to discuss the issue of attentional flexibility in bilingual children (Bialystok, 1988; Bialystok & Harris, 1992). Interestingly, this idea would influence the field many years later.

## 24.8 The bilingual advantage

Ellen Bialystok began to suggest in the late 1990s that bilingual flexibility might actually enhance thinking in nonlanguage functions (Bialystok,

1999). In two separate studies, Bialystok asked children to do a dimensional card sort task in which children are given a set of cards with colored shapes ( □ red • green ○ red ■ green). At first, children are asked to sort the cards by color (□ red ○ / ■ green • green). Once they have finished creating different piles for each color, they are asked to sort these again by shape (□red ■ green /○ red • green). This task resembles an executive task. Hence, what is difficult for children is that on the second step they need to ignore the color and attend only to the shape. Bialystok found that bilingual children outperformed monolingual children on this task.

There are a few possible reasons that monolingual or bilingual children might differ on these tasks. Bilinguals may differ from monolinguals in their ability to conceptualize what color and shape are, in their ability to change their motor responses for each task, or in their ability to shift from one rule to another. To test this, Bialystok and Martin (2004) asked children to perform a series of tasks that probed the concepts, the motor response, or the act of switching independently. What they found was that bilingual and monolingual children did not differ in their ability to represent each rule. They were also equally good at switching their motor responses. The main difference was in their ability to switch between different concepts. In short, bilingual children were better at ignoring one dimension and attending to a different one.

Follow-up work by Yoshida and Tran has found not only that these advantages appear early in life but also a possible cause for the advantage in bilinguals. In a first study, Yoshida and Tran asked a group of young children to play the Hungry Fish game, a cognitive control task designed for children (Yoshida et al., 2011). In adult tasks, like the ones discussed earlier, the usual instructions are to ask the person to indicate some aspect of the stimulus. For example, they might ask which way the middle arrow is facing in the following set of stimuli (→ → → → →). To look at cognitive control, experimenters create a congruent condition (→ → → → → or ← ← ← ← ←) or an incongruent condition (→ → ← → → or ← ← → ← ←). The task is simply to indicate which way the middle arrow is facing. To make finding the middle arrow a bit easier a small asterisk is flashed above the location where the middle arrow will be immediately before presenting it.

Although this task seems a bit complicated, most adults are able to learn to do it quite quickly. However, children find this task too difficult. In order to simplify this, Rueda et al. (2004) designed a variant of this task called the hungry fish game. In this task, children are shown a row of fish and asked to feed the middle fish that is hungry by pointing to its mouth. Children are then given feedback with a "woohoo!" if they are correct or a "huh?" if they are wrong. The results from this task show that children improve in their ability to attend to the fish and perform the task in both accuracy and speed even after the age of 10. Hence, this is a good task for measuring the development of cognitive control.

Yoshida et al. (2011) were interested in testing even younger children. So they presented a simplified version of the hungry fish task to make it friendly for young children. The results yielded an interesting pattern of results. In the hungry fish game, bilingual children were faster and more accurate than monolinguals. Interestingly, this advantage appeared at age 2.5 years but then became smaller between the ages of 3 and 4. Bilingual children showed a short-lived advantage in their ability to attend to the relevant information (the middle fish) and ignore the irrelevant information (the distracting fish around the hungry fish). This is evidence of a bilingual advantage early in life that fits in nicely with other findings by Bialystok and colleagues.

## 24.9 The bilingual disadvantage

The fact that bilingual children are better at ignoring certain concepts and attending to others is interesting in light of other findings. Work on language switching had found that both children and older adults show larger language switching effects than young adults. In addition, the brain activity in young adults in this condition shows increased activity in the dorsolateral prefrontal cortex. Work in the bilingual literature has found some evidence of a bilingual disadvantage in the domain of word production. For example, bilinguals are slower to say the names of pictures in either language relative to monolinguals (Ivanova & Costa, 2008). Work by Tamar Gollan, at University of California, San Diego, has confirmed this (Gollan, Montoya, & Bonanni, 2005; Gollan et al., 2008). She has sought to uncover the factors that influence how bilinguals recognize and produce the names of pictures by comparing the response times to those of monolinguals. When bilinguals were asked to classify the objects as either human made or natural, bilinguals and monolinguals showed no differences. However, when asked to produce the names of these pictures bilinguals were slower than monolinguals. After naming the pictures, bilinguals were asked which of these words they could translate. Then Gollan checked to see if the words that could be translated were produced faster or slower than those that were not. Interestingly, it turns out that bilinguals were faster to name a picture in English when they knew the translation of the word in Spanish. This effect did not appear in monolinguals indicating that there was no difference in the pictures themselves.

To account for these effects, Gollan suggests that bilinguals suffer from greater difficulties coming up with a specific label because of the increased number of words across both languages. The increased number of words leads to weaker links between each word and a particular concept. These effects are not specific to bilinguals. In monolinguals, weaker links are observed in words that occur less frequently. For example, a group of monolinguals will be able to say the word "window" faster when looking at a picture of it than they will be able to say the name of a picture of a squirrel. Now imagine a German–English bilingual who has two concepts but now has four words to express them. "Window" and "*Fenster*" have roughly half the strength that they would in a monolingual. Because these words are encountered frequently you might not really notice the effect so much. However, "squirrel" and "*Eichhörnchen*" will take a much bigger hit because of the fact that these links are weak to begin with in a single language. The effect is particularly striking in a language spoken with lower proficiency. Gollan suggests that a weaker language behaves similarly to weaker words in one language. Hence, the increased difficulty in coming up with a specific word has the same underlying principle in bilinguals and monolinguals.

The work by Gollan brings up an interesting possibility. On the one hand, the fact that bilinguals must deal with multiple labels for everyday objects seems to slow them down. On the other hand, there is the possibility that this increased effort could lead to a benefit. Similar benefits exist for other cognitive phenomena. For example, it is now well documented that increased effort when learning material can lead to better recall later which has led to coining the term *desirable difficulties* (Bjork & Bjork, 2011). Similarly, one of the classic treatments for cognitive decline in aging is to give people brain exercise. If, in fact, having to keep more than one label in mind occurs frequently for bilinguals, then it is possible that the extra effort required to do this could create a benefit in older age. Ellen Bialystok and Fergus Craik began to explore the possibility of enhanced cognition in a series of studies with older adults. Specifically, they wondered whether older adult bilinguals might have an advantage in tasks requiring controlled attention (Bialystok et al., 2004). Could bilingualism actually reduce costs associated with aging?

The results from Bialystok and Craik's study were very revealing. Bilinguals were given the Simon task, in which they had to attend to the color of an object and press a button on the right or left. This is a classic cognitive control task, since the color is mapped to the side of response. For example, seeing a red diamond on the right (---♦) would require a right-button response. However, the same shape on the left (♦---) would still require a right-button response. In this condition there is a mismatch between color and side of response, which leads to slower reaction times. This condition ♦---) leads to slower responses than when the color and side match (---♦). Bilinguals in their forties were half a second faster than monolinguals when ignoring the side and attending to the shape. By the time bilinguals reach their sixties this effect morphed into a 1,500-ms advantage over their monolingual peers. In short, a small advantage in middle age results in an increased advantage in the elderly.

Bialystok and Craik carried it even further. Together they wondered if bilingualism might protect against the biggest contributor to the decline in mental abilities in older adults (Bialystok, Craik, & Freedman, 2007),

Alzheimer's disease. Autopsies of the cognitively unimpaired population finds that the rate of AD-like pathology without symptoms can be as high as 30 percent (Valenzuela & Sachdev, 2006a, 2006b). Recent work in the Alzheimer's literature has begun to consider the notion of *cognitive reserve*. That is, people who otherwise would show symptoms of Alzheimer's dementia may be relatively unsymptomatic (Driscoll & Troncoso, 2011a, 2011b). The natural question is whether the use of two languages might have a similar type of effect. To determine this, the authors looked through 184 case studies. Of those studied, 51 percent were bilingual and 49 percent were monolingual. They also found that bilinguals showed symptoms four years later than monolinguals.

One possible factor that has been considered is whether the bilingual advantage may really be an immigrant advantage in disguise. To control for this factor, Bialystok and Craik conducted a second study in which they looked at the effects of immigration status on the bilingual advantage (Craik, Bialystok, & Freedman, 2010). A second group of bilingual older adults diagnosed with probable Alzheimer's disease was tested. In this case, additional language history information was gathered. Results from this study found that bilinguals were diagnosed with Alzheimer's four years later than monolinguals and showed significant cognitive decline five years later. The effect of immigration status did not in any way alter this effect. In short, the bilingual advantage, at least in older adults, cannot be explained as an immigration effect in disguise.

## 24.10 Beyond the bilingual advantage

Despite the widespread interest in the bilingual advantage, there are studies that have begun to qualify the circumstances under which the effect is and is not observed. There are a couple of issues that need to be considered in this respect. One interesting factor is whether the advantage for bilinguals with two spoken languages also appears in those who use a spoken and a signed language. An initial study by Karen Emmorey, Ellen Bialystok, and colleagues (Emmorey et al., 2008) compared a group of monolinguals with two groups of bilinguals who either spoke two auditory languages or spoke one auditory language and a sign language. Participants were asked to perform a flanker task in which the head of an arrow (e.g., < or >) was surrounded by a group of Xs (X X X X < X X X X) on either side as well as a set of additional arrows (< < < < < or < < < > < < <), similar to an adult version of the hungry fish task. Participants were asked to indicate where the arrow was pointing when surrounded by Xs or to withhold the response when surrounded by other arrows. Bilinguals showed a much smaller processing cost relative to monolinguals. However, there was no advantage for bimodal bilinguals.

The absence of an advantage is not unique to bimodal bilinguals. For example, recent work by Shanna Kousaie, Natalie Phillips, and colleagues has found similar results with adult French–English bilinguals (Kousaie & Phillips, 2012a). In this study, a group of bilingual and monolingual subjects from the Montreal area were asked to perform three separate executive function tasks while being monitored with EEG equipment. Results from this study showed no difference between monolinguals and bilinguals in reaction times and percentage correct. Results from the EEG experiment found very subtle differences between monolinguals and bilinguals on the three different ERP components: the N200, an early negative going wave that indicates conflict monitoring, the P300, and the error-related negativity that appears when monitoring for errors. However, these three EEG wave differences did not appear across all tasks. This suggests subtle differences between the groups but no clear advantage for bilinguals over monolinguals.

Taken together these results leave one wondering why some studies find a difference and others do not. Part of the answer may have to do with the type of bilingual tested. For example, Emmorey, Bialystok, and colleagues claim that bimodal bilinguals, who are bilingual in a spoken and signed language, do not show the same advantage on tasks of cognitive control due to the way in which both languages are used. Bilinguals in two spoken languages in general tend to have a conflict with regard to which language comes in and out of a single mouth. Because both languages share the same input and output motor and sensory systems there is a conflict between them. Hence, speaking two auditory languages requires control in order to avoid interference between them.

The reason that bimodal bilinguals do not show the same type of interference as that seen in unimodal bilinguals is because of the way in which both languages are used. Because one language uses hands and the other uses a speaker's mouth, bimodal bilinguals end up mouthing the words as they sign. This code-blending is much less conflictive than the type of conflict seen in unimodal bilingualism.

So what about the bilinguals in Kousaie and Phillips' (2012a) study? Interestingly, these participants are from Montreal, a place where there is frequent use of both languages in daily life. It is possible that this particular context yields less conflict than that seen in an immigrant context, where each language is associated with very specific home and environmental situations. As noted above, work by Bialystok and Craik suggests that the bilingual advantage in older adults is not just applicable in immigrant populations. Future work is needed to investigate this further.

Finally, I want to end by considering a couple of studies that have questioned the nature of the bilingual effect. In a meta-analysis that pooled results across many studies, Hilchey and Klein (2011) found considerably more studies that failed to show a bilingual advantage than studies that did find an advantage. Furthermore, they argued that the advantage was present in an overall improvement in reaction time rather than a tendency toward a smaller interference effect. The lack of replication across studies brings up the question of whether there might be underlying differences that are driving this effect. One such difference is socioeconomic status, as researchers found that the bilinguals and monolinguals no longer differ when this factor is controlled (Morton & Harper, 2007). Finally, studies by Julia Festman, Antoni Rodriguez-Fornells, and Tomas Munte (Festman & Munte, 2012; Festman, Rodriguez-Fornells, & Munte, 2010; Rodriguez-Fornells et al., 2011) have found that bilinguals vary in the amount of control that they can use. This research team has documented in a series of papers that bilinguals vary in their ability to produce the name of a picture out loud in the correct language when switching between languages. This difference is related to the ability to perform non-verbal control tasks such as the Simon task described earlier, in which participants had to press a button on the right side if the item was red. This task creates greater interference when the side and color do not match (♦---) than when the color and the side match (---♦). The interesting part is that bilinguals also vary in how well they can perform this task. Those who show more interference are more prone to inadvertently blurting out the name of a picture in the wrong language during language switching tasks. Those who show better performance on cognitive control tasks are also better at controlling which language they should produce. These results suggest that individual differences in cognitive control do exist. However, these may not be due to bilingualism per se but may be due to differences in control across any particular group of subjects. Future studies are needed to uncover the conditions under which the bilingual advantage in tasks of cognitive control is or is not observed.

## 24.11 Final observations

In this chapter, we considered some issues with regard to the neural bases of control in the context of bilingualism. Rather than providing an exhaustive review of the literature, this review focused on two specific topics. First, it considered the nature of control across development. In this sense, newer interpretations suggest that childhood and adolescent development is a period during which there is considerable improvement in the ability to utilize cognitive control and executive function. Second, the nature of task switching as a particular instance of control and particularly as a way to investigate the nature of flexibility was discussed. This discussion included a focused review on studies that have investigated the neural bases of language switching in bilinguals. This work suggests a link between intense switching and control needed during bilingual language processing and a potential for advantage for bilinguals.

Finally, there is one area that could use more attention in the field. The presence of an advantage in bilinguals relative to monolinguals seems to have gained considerable traction in the popular press and to a great extent in the scientific literature. The majority of these studies have sought to compare monolinguals and bilinguals and matched them on other relevant variables. However, to date few studies have sought to explore the influence of each variable on executive function. In this sense, executive function involves a series of variables both internal (i.e., genotype) as well as external (socioeconomic status, schooling, parental interaction) that influence the phenotypic expression which is reflected in measures of executive function. In addition, executive control develops over time even in speakers of a single language. The majority of research has taken a rather static view of the process in which monolinguals and bilinguals are compared at particular moments and time. The question that has yet to be answered is to what extent different factors such as language experience, socioeconomic status, and genetic predispositions contribute to the development of cognitive control. A second related question is the role that each factor plays during development. Once this is established we can begin to ask what patterns of brain activity are observed as result of differences in these factors. Furthermore, researchers could investigate how each of these factors is reflected in brain activity at different ages. This would certainly be an ambitious proposal that would require a considerable number of resources. However, such a database would allow us to understand how large these effects are relatively speaking and to place the neural correlates of cognitive control within a framework that takes into account the dynamic nature of development and change.[1]

---

[1] A more fleshed-out version of this final point can be found in Hernandez (2013).

# Part VII

Consequences of bilingualism

# 25

# Cognitive consequences of bilingualism

Executive control and cognitive reserve

Ellen Bialystok and Fergus Craik

## 25.1 Introduction

It is now well known that some environmental factors act to maintain cognitive functioning in healthy aging and postpone the onset of symptoms in those suffering from dementia. These factors, called "cognitive reserve" or "brain reserve" (Stern, 2002, 2009), include education, occupational status, socioeconomic class, and involvement in physical, intellectual, and social activities (Bennett et al., 2003, 2006). Postponing symptoms of dementia and enabling people to function independently for a longer time has immediate social benefit; the ability to function in spite of disease adds quality of life to the patient and time during which health care resources are not required. An emerging body of research now suggests that bilingualism is a potent source of this cognitive reserve. Across the lifespan, bilinguals have been shown to outperform monolinguals in the set of abilities involved in controlling attention, inhibiting distraction, and shifting between goals, collectively known as executive control (EC). These effects have been found for infants (Kovács & Mehler, 2009), children (Carlson & Meltzoff, 2008), and younger (Costa, Hernandez, & Sebastián-Gallés, 2008) and older adults (Salvatierra & Rosselli, 2010). This bilingual advantage in EC is generally attributed to the ongoing need to manage two jointly activated language systems (for a review, see Bialystok et al., 2009). In conjunction with these bilingual advantages, however, studies assessing verbal proficiency have consistently shown that bilingual children (Bialystok et al., 2010) and adults (Bialystok & Luk, 2012) who are fluent speakers of English and another language control a smaller receptive vocabulary in English than do comparable monolingual English speakers, even if English is their first language. As most psychological research is conducted in English, it is not always clear whether or how these initial linguistic differences influence results. In other words, it is not clear if performance differences between monolinguals and bilinguals are the result of cognitive processes or are influenced by different levels of verbal ability in the language of testing. Therefore, the interaction between the language proficiency of individuals and the linguistic demands of tasks is a central issue in bilingual research.

## 25.2 Bilingualism, aging, and cognitive processing

The interpretation of the bilingual advantage in EC is based on substantial evidence that both languages are always active to some extent in bilingual minds; there is no "language switch" (for a review, see Kroll et al., 2012). Therefore, bilinguals recruit the general EC system to select the target language, inhibit the unwanted language, and monitor the environment for cues to switch between languages. The accumulation of experience and practice in using EC for these language-specific purposes has the broad effect of strengthening that system, making it more efficient for other purposes as well. This general effect of better inhibitory control in bilinguals has been shown in such tasks as the Simon task (Simon & Wolf, 1963), in which participants see one of two color patches and respond as rapidly as possible to its color. The response keys are situated laterally under the monitor, and the color patches appear either directly above their relevant response key (congruent condition) or under the other key (incongruent condition). Reaction times (RTs) are typically faster in the congruent condition, and the difference in RTs between congruent and incongruent conditions is taken to be a measure of EC ("the Simon effect"). Studies comparing performance of younger and older monolingual and bilingual adults on the Simon task (Bialystok et al., 2004; Salvatierra & Rosselli, 2010), Stroop task (Bialystok, Craik & Luk, 2008a), and switching task (Gold et al., 2013) report significantly better performance for bilinguals in the older group with mixed results for the younger group. It is important to note, however, that these bilingual advantages are not always found: Kousaie and Phillips (2012b) for example reported overall speed advantages for bilinguals performing a Simon task with no language group differences for older adults. The reasons behind age differences are still unclear; the difference may be attributable to the longer duration of bilingualism in older individuals, or possibly because the bilingual advantage is more apparent in more effortful combinations of tasks and participants.

The first study to demonstrate these effects in adults and older adults was reported by Bialystok et al. (2004). They conducted three experiments in which bilingual effects on EC were assessed by means of the Simon task. Two experiments were conducted; the first involved 40 younger and older participants and the second 94 participants aged between 30 and 80 years. Half of the participants in each study were bilingual and half were monolingual, matched on age, education, and social class. Both studies found that the Simon effect was smaller in the bilingual samples, leading to the conclusion that bilingualism is associated with enhanced cognitive control. Additionally, executive control declines with age so there is typically a larger Simon effect in older adults than younger ones, but this decline was less severe in the older bilingual groups. This last result suggests that bilingualism may therefore be one factor that mitigates the negative effects of aging on cognitive processing and executive control.

Another study examining different participants was reported by Bialystok and colleagues (2008a). Again younger and older adult monolinguals and bilinguals were tested on various measures of EC, using the Simon arrows task (in which the stimuli are directional arrows instead of color patches) and the Stroop color–word task. In the Simon arrows task participants were instructed to press a key indicating the direction of an arrow presented on a computer monitor, regardless of the arrow's position on the screen. As in the previously described study, conflict was manipulated by having the arrow appear either on the side of the screen indicated by the arrow (congruent) or on the opposite side (incongruent). In this experiment the Simon effect was not significantly different between the younger adult monolinguals and bilinguals, but in the older participants the Simon effect was significantly smaller in the bilingual group.

A second experiment used the Stroop paradigm in which participants named the font color of verbal stimuli as rapidly as possible. The three crucial conditions were first a set of Xs (neutral – no word present), second a facilitation condition in which a color word (e.g., GREEN) was printed in its own color, and third an interference condition in which a color word was printed in a different color (e.g., GREEN typed in red font). In all cases the participant's task was to name the font color. Facilitation was measured as the RT benefit associated with the facilitation condition relative to the neutral condition and cost was measured as the difference between neutral and interference conditions. The results for the four groups are shown in Figure 25.1. The older bilinguals showed greater facilitation and less cost than their monolingual counterparts; both results indicated greater amounts of EC. In the younger groups there was no significant language effect for facilitation, and a small but significant bilingual advantage in the measure of cost. In summary, the experiments reported by Bialystok et al. (2008a) confirmed the conclusion that bilingualism is associated with greater degrees of EC, and that this bilingual advantage may be greater in older adults.

The same basic result was reported by Gold et al. (2013) using a different measure of EC, namely the ability to switch flexibly from one basis of decision-making to another. In one condition of their paradigm, participants decided whether a visually presented figure was a circle or a square; in a second condition the same stimuli were presented but now participants decided whether the figure was red or blue in color. On all trials in

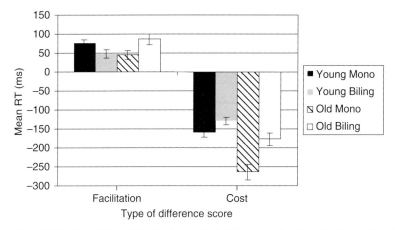

**Figure 25.1** Mean RT and standard error for facilitation and cost in the Stroop task. The values are mean differences from baseline (0 ms) calculated as the average time to name colors from neutral stimuli (Xs) (Adapted from Bialystok, Craik, & Luk, 2008)

these conditions the figure was preceded by the appropriate instruction for responding (i.e., SHAPE or COLOR). In a third condition, both shape and color decisions occurred in the same test block, signaled unpredictably by the appropriate instruction. RTs in this switch block were longer than in either of the single-task conditions. This difference, called "mixing cost," is used as a measure of cognitive control. The results in two experiments showed that older adult bilinguals had smaller mixing costs than their monolingual counterparts. The second experiment showed additionally that this bilingual advantage was found in the older adults but not in the younger group. Importantly, Gold and colleagues demonstrated that the language group differences in task switching could not be attributed to other demographic or cognitive variables. Specifically, there were no language group differences in education levels, socioeconomic status (SES), intelligence or working memory as indicated by digit span performance.

## 25.3 Bilingualism and memory

Although it is clear that EC is central to cognitive functioning and that there are substantial declines of EC with aging (see Craik & Bialystok, 2006), the primary complaint of cognitive aging is not failure of EC but rather loss of memory. The course of such decline with normal aging is well documented (for reviews, see Kester et al., 2002; Park & Reuter-Lorenz, 2009; Zacks, Hasher, & Li, 2000), but there is little research on memory decline in bilinguals. The general pattern is that age-related losses are greater for some memory functions than others, with free recall, paired-associate learning, and working memory being particularly age-sensitive, and recall from primary memory, recognition memory and implicit memory being relatively spared (Kester et al., 2002; Zacks et al., 2000).

When analyzing retrieval effects in recognition memory, a number of authors (e.g., Jacoby, 1991; Yonelinas, 2002) have distinguished between two components called familiarity (F) and conscious recollection (R). The difference is in the representational detail required for each judgment: for F, one might find a face to be familiar but be unable to recall where and when the person was encountered, but for R, one must recall details of one or more previous meetings. When overall recognition scores are broken down into these F and R components, differences between young and older adults are negligible in the former but substantial in the latter (Jennings & Jacoby, 1993). One interpretation of this pattern is that age-related memory deficits are minimal when the task or memory judgment can be accomplished on the basis of habit information but substantial when consciously controlled self-initiated activities must be deployed (Craik, 1983) and contextual details of the original event retrieved. Examples of memory tasks that require such control processes are working memory (WM), retrieval with no cues (free recall) and the recollection component in recognition. As EC is involved in these specific aspects of memory, any bilingual advantage in memory performance is likely to be found in tasks that involve these control processes.

In two experiments from our group, Wodniecka et al. (2010) measured recognition memory for both verbal and non-verbal materials and decomposed the overall scores into estimates of F and R. There was no significant difference between language groups for younger adults, but for older adults, the bilingual participants outperformed monolinguals in R scores on the non-verbal task in Experiment 1 and on both verbal and non-verbal task in Experiment 2. This pattern is consistent with previous findings that the bilingual advantage appears more readily in older participants. The absence of a bilingual advantage with verbal material in Experiment 1 is also consistent with findings of a bilingual disadvantage in verbal processing, presumably because of the lower vocabulary levels described above (Bialystok et al., 2010; Bialystok & Luk, 2012) and benefits to bilinguals in performing tasks involving control processes, presumably because of higher EC ability.

There is also some evidence that bilinguals perform better on working memory tasks than monolinguals, but only on non-verbal versions of such tasks. Luo et al. (2013) demonstrated that bilinguals outperformed monolinguals on a WM span task that was based on non-verbal spatial information but not on a comparable task based on verbal stimuli. Similarly, Bialystok et al. (2004) administered a non-verbal task in which the target stimulus appeared in the center of the screen and participants needed to hold in mind either 2 rules or 4 rules to respond as rapidly as possible to the color of the stimulus. Older participants were slower than their younger counterparts and all participants produced longer RTs in the 4-rule condition, but this increased RT cost was significantly larger for monolinguals, especially in the older adult group. Thus, bilingualism attenuated the negative effect of aging on WM costs.

Few studies have examined the effects of bilingualism on episodic memory and again these studies often use verbal materials and so disadvantage bilinguals. A study by Fernandes et al. (2007) found that bilinguals recalled fewer words than comparable monolinguals in a free recall task, but when vocabulary scores were partialed out, the negative effect of bilingualism disappeared.

Clearer results are reported in two studies by Kormi-Nouri and colleagues (Kormi-Nouri, Moniri, & Nilsson 2003; Kormi-Nouri et al., 2008) who do provide evidence for a bilingual advantage in episodic memory performance. Both studies were conducted with children ranging in age from 7 to 17 years, and both explored language differences in episodic and semantic memory. One study (Kormi-Nouri et al., 2003) was conducted in Sweden on children from the same state schools in central Stockholm. Half of the participants were monolinguals who spoke Swedish at home and at school; the other half were Iranian-Swedish children who spoke Persian at home and Swedish at school. The children in the two language groups were well matched on socioeconomic status and other demographic variables; they were also equivalent on a test of Swedish vocabulary. The tasks involved memory for simple command phrases such as "give me the spoon," and "hug the doll." These commands were either acted out by the children ('subject-performed tasks' or SPTs) using real objects, acted out using imagined objects, or were simply learned as verbal phrases. The results showed a small bilingual advantage in subsequent free recall of the nouns in each phrase, and also a bilingual advantage when memory was tested using the sentence frame as a cue ("give me the _?" "hug the _?"), but only in the condition using real objects. A bilingual advantage in semantic memory was also found when children were asked to generate words beginning with a specified letter, although the effect was small – 15.4 words on average for the bilingual children compared with 13.8 words for monolinguals. This result may reflect superior frontal lobe functioning in the bilinguals as the word generation task ("phonemic fluency") is used by neuropsychologists as a test of frontal efficiency (Baldo et al., 2006). Previous research with monolingual and bilingual adults who are matched on vocabulary scores also demonstrates that bilinguals generate more words in this task than monolinguals (Bialystok, Luk, & Craik, 2008b; Luo et al., 2010).

A further study using similar methods was conducted in Iran by Kormi-Nouri and colleagues (2008). Children aged 9–17 years were tested for episodic and semantic memory abilities using either lists of words or phrases as in the previous study. Three groups of children were tested; monolingual Iranians who spoke Persian at home and at school; Turkish-Iranians who spoke Turkish exclusively at home and in the street but Persian at school; and Kurdish-Iranians who spoke Kurdish at home but

Persian at school. All the families lived in their home cities, so none of the participants were immigrants; they were also well matched on education and socioeconomic status. In all, 488 children were tested. The results showed that there was a bilingual advantage in both episodic and semantic memory, and that this advantage was more pronounced in the older children. This last result was interpreted as demonstrating that the longer two languages are used in everyday life, the greater the benefit from bilingualism. There was also some tendency for a larger bilingual advantage in the Turkish-Persian group than in the Kurdish-Persian group. Kurdish and Persian are related to each other in phonology, morphology and syntax whereas the Turkish and Persian languages are completely different. The authors suggest that this difference induces greater flexibility in the need to deal with two languages and that this greater flexibility in mental operations generalizes to other cognitive abilities including memory.

Taken together, these studies suggest that a bilingual advantage in memory performance is most likely to be observed using non-verbal materials and under conditions requiring EC. There is also some suggestion that effects are stronger in children and older adults than in young adults. These factors were acknowledged in a study by Schroeder and Marian (2012). Monolingual and bilingual adults ranging in age from 73–88 years, matched on non-verbal intelligence and vocabulary level, recalled complex visual scenes. The bilinguals recalled significantly more scenes than monolinguals, and within the bilingual group those who had more years of speaking two languages showed better recall. Participants in this study also completed the Simon task. The results showed that bilinguals had a significantly smaller Simon effect, indicating better EC, and there was suggestive evidence that better EC was associated with higher levels of performance on the scene recall test. The authors concluded that extensive practice managing two languages may lead to improved attentional control and that this in turn is related to enhanced retrieval in this non-verbal episodic memory task.

## 25.4 Cognitive decline and the onset of dementia

Most of the research on adult age differences in the bilingual advantage has been conducted with older adults who were experiencing healthy cognitive aging. The majority of the evidence has shown enhanced ability of older bilinguals to perform tasks requiring EC than is found in their monolingual counterparts. Similarly, in the few studies aimed at examining memory in older age, bilingual advantages are largely confined to tasks that are based on EC, such as free recall and the recollection component of recognition, consistent with the claim that it is EC ability that distinguishes monolingual from bilingual cognition. What is not known at this point is whether these preserved cognitive functions in bilinguals extend to situations in which there is dementia. From one perspective, it would be surprising if bilingualism provided protection against dementia: dementia is primarily indicated by memory failure, for which there are relatively few cognitive advantages, and Alzheimer's disease (AD) in particular is characterized by deterioration in the medial temporal lobe, a region not directly involved in EC functioning. However, it may be that the protection to EC and frontal brain regions attributed to bilingualism has broader effects.

In the first study to investigate the possibility that bilingualism is associated with a delay in the onset of dementia, we studied the clinic records of 184 patients diagnosed with dementia, of whom 93 reported being lifelong bilinguals and the remainder were monolingual (Bialystok, Craik, & Freedman, 2007). Patients who could not reliably be classified as either monolingual or bilingual were excluded from the analyses. The criterion for bilingualism was that the patient (or their family member or caregiver) reported to the neurologist in the initial clinical interview that they spoke at least two languages fluently and had used at least two languages regularly, preferably daily, since the age of 20 years. Given the age of these individuals at the time of the interview, this criterion resulted in a minimum of fifty years of bilingual experience. The patients in the final sample were equivalent in occupational status and in cognitive level as assessed by the Mini-Mental State Examination (MMSE) (Folstein, Folstein, & McHugh, 1975). All patients had been diagnosed with dementia, the primary type (72 percent) being probable AD. The other diagnoses included possible AD, dementias due to other degenerative disorders and cerebrovascular disease. The crucial comparison was the estimated age at which these patients first demonstrated symptoms of dementia. For the monolinguals, the mean age was 71.4 years, with an average age of 75.4 years at the time of diagnosis; for the bilinguals, the mean age of symptom onset was 75.5 years, with an average age of 78.6 years at the time of diagnosis. This language group difference is highly significant and shows as well no difference in the length of time between the first evidence of symptoms and the time of their diagnosis. That is, bilingual patients and their families did not simply wait longer to seek treatment for symptoms but rather the symptoms themselves appeared at a later time.

To confirm these results, a second study examined the records of 109 monolingual and 102 bilingual patients (Craik, Bialystok, & Freedman, 2010). In this study, all the patients had been diagnosed with probable AD and again the samples were equivalent on cognitive level (MMSE), duration of illness and occupational status. As in the first study, there was a delay in symptom onset for the bilinguals of 5.1 years. In this case, the monolingual patients were 72.6 years old when symptoms first appeared and 76.5 years old at their first clinical appointment; the bilingual patients were 77.7 years old when symptoms appeared and 80.8 years old at their first visit to the clinic. In both studies, the monolinguals had received more education than the bilinguals, a factor associated with delayed onset of AD, so the bilingual delay is even more impressive. Also, the bilinguals and monolinguals in both studies represented substantial cultural diversity, minimizing the possibility that the effect was associated with a specific group. Finally, both studies contained immigrants in both language groups, but this factor did not affect age of onset. Our conclusion is that bilingualism is associated with a delay in the onset of symptoms of AD of between 3–5 years. Similarly, Chertkow and colleagues (Chertkow et al., 2010) reported that multilinguals were diagnosed with AD later than comparable monolinguals with a nonsignificant trend in that direction for bilinguals, and Gollan et al. (2011) showed that a higher degree of bilingualism in Spanish–English bilinguals was associated with later ages of onset of probable AD.

These studies provide evidence that bilingualism provides some protection in delaying the initial symptoms of probable AD. Two questions, however, follow from these results. The first is that AD is often preceded by a pre-clinical stage in which there is cognitive impairment but normal MMSE scores, making the detection of disease difficult. The second is that bilingual advantages have typically been reported in EC but AD is essentially a disease of memory, so the relation between EC and memory for patients with AD is not clear. Both issues were investigated in a study of patients diagnosed with mild cognitive impairment (MCI) (Ossher et al., 2013).

MCI consists of several diagnostic subcategories that are associated with different types of cognitive impairment. The main distinction is between amnestic MCI (aMCI) and varieties that do not include memory loss. Within aMCI, there is a further distinction between single-domain aMCI, in which only memory impairment is evident, and multiple-domain aMCI, which includes impairment in an additional domain, usually EC. Amnestic MCI has a high rate of conversion to AD and is sometimes considered to be pre-clinical AD. The exact rates of conversion from single- and multiple-domain aMCI are controversial, but there is evidence that patients with multiple-domain aMCI are further along in the progression toward dementia and may be at greater risk of conversion to AD. Ossher and colleagues (2013) examined patients diagnosed with aMCI, including 68 with single-domain aMCI and 43 with multiple-domain aMCI. In the multiple-domain group, there was a non-significant difference in age of diagnosis between the two language groups in which (atypically) monolinguals (75.2) were older than bilinguals (72.6), but in the single-domain group the difference for monolinguals (74.9) and bilinguals (79.4) was significant, with the bilinguals being older at diagnosis as in the previous studies. There were no significant group differences in duration of symptoms, education, MMSE, or neuropsychological test scores. Importantly, multiple-domain aMCI is characterized by greater frontal lobe pathology than found in single-domain aMCI (Bell-McGinty et al., 2005). Our interpretation of these results is that the bilingual patients with multiple-domain aMCI may have lost a frontally based compensatory mechanism through impairment in the location that would normally afford cognitive support. Without the benefit of an enhanced EC system, the bilingual multiple-domain aMCI patients showed no postponement of symptoms relative to their monolingual counterparts.

Finally, the studies of AD and MCI were combined in a recent investigation of monolingual and bilingual patients that included more detailed cognitive assessment and a longitudinal component (Bialystok et al., 2014). The participants included 38 monolingual and 36 bilingual patients diagnosed with MCI (although no distinction was made among subcategories of MCI) and 35 monolingual and 40 bilingual patients diagnosed with AD. There were three purposes for this study. The first was to confirm the earlier results showing a delay in the onset of symptoms of AD and MCI for bilinguals. To this end, there was a significant delay in the onset of symptoms for bilinguals in both diagnostic categories. The second purpose was to obtain more detailed assessments of cognitive function so that the difference in onset age could be interpreted within a more exact cognitive profile. Therefore, we administered tests from the Delis-Kaplan Executive Function System (D-KEFS; Delis, Kaplan, & Kramer, 2001) battery to all patients participating in the study. Although patients with MCI consistently obtained higher scores than did patients with AD, there were few reliable differences between patients in the two language groups within each diagnostic category. Therefore, on detailed assessments of cognitive level, the monolingual and bilingual patients performed at an equivalent level. The third purpose was to determine whether these initial differences in age of onset, in spite of similar cognitive level at the time of diagnosis, were associated with different rates of cognitive decline. Therefore, patients were visited up to three times over a period of about 1.5 years and the tests from the D-KEFS battery were administered. Although there was considerable attrition over the three testing sessions, the results showed a similar rate of decline for monolingual and bilingual patients. Thus, in spite of being diagnosed at an older age, the rate of cognitive decline for bilinguals was similar to that found for monolinguals, although some caution is required in interpreting this result because the number of cases is relatively small.

The general conclusion that follows from this last result, namely, that cognitive reserve delays the onset of symptoms but has no effect on the subsequent rate of cognitive decline, is controversial at the present time. Some studies have reported that higher levels of brain reserve continue to slow the rate of cognitive decline in older individuals (Valenzuela & Sachdev, 2006b), but other studies have shown that whereas high levels of cognitive or brain reserve delay the onset of symptoms of dementia, once the symptoms are evident, the subsequent rate of cognitive decline is faster for those with higher levels of reserve (Hall et al., 2007, 2009; Scarmeas et al., 2006).

## 25.5 Structural and functional brain differences in bilingualism

The evidence discussed to this point has been based on behavioral research in which various cognitive abilities are compared for monolinguals and bilinguals in both healthy and abnormal cognitive aging. In addition, a number of studies have also investigated differences in brain structure and function between monolinguals and bilinguals. Given our argument that the bilingual advantage observed in behavioral experiments is attributable to enhanced executive control, we would expect to find a parallel enhancement in brain areas associated with such functions. It is well established that the neural correlates of executive control are located primarily in frontal regions of the brain (Stuss & Knight, 2012), so our expectation is that bilingualism is to be associated with better developed and more effective frontal lobe functions.

Fabbro (2001) surveyed studies that reported neural correlates of bilingualism and noted that several such studies found activations in the left inferior frontal cortex and in the dorsolateral frontal cortex while participants performed a variety of word processing tasks. For example, an fMRI experiment by Hernandez and colleagues (Hernandez, Martinez, & Kohnert, 2000) found increased activation in dorsolateral frontal areas when bilingual participants performed a language switching task relative to single language processing. In our own laboratory, we carried out a study using magneto-encephalography (MEG; Bialystok et al., 2005) in which two groups of young adult bilinguals (French–English and Cantonese–English) and a monolingual group performed the Simon task. Brain–behavior correlations between activated regions and reaction times (RTs) showed that faster RTs for the monolinguals were associated with activation in middle frontal regions; faster RTs for bilinguals, in contrast, were associated with greater activity in superior and middle temporal, cingulate, and superior and inferior frontal regions, largely in the left hemisphere. These regions are part of the general EC system. The interpretation was that management of two language systems resulted in systematic changes in the organization of frontal EC networks, despite large differences in the specific languages involved. Similar results were reported by Luk et al. (2010) in an fMRI study in which young adult monolinguals and bilinguals activated different networks of regions in frontal, temporal and subcortical areas while performing aspects of a flanker task, a common non-verbal measure of EC.

Consistent with the notion that bilingualism enhances frontal functions and their connections with other brain regions, Luk et al. (2011) found better maintained white matter in healthy older bilinguals than in comparable monolinguals, specifically in the anterior corpus callosum, extending posteriorly to the bilateral superior longitudinal fasciculus and anteriorly to the right inferior frontal-occipital fasciculus and uncinate fasciculus. When different types of diffusivity were assessed there were no group differences in axial diffusivity, but monolinguals showed higher values of radial diffusivity (indicating a decline in myelin integrity) in the corpus callosum. Therefore, bilinguals had better connectivity across frontal brain regions than monolinguals. A similar result was reported for bilingual children (Mohades et al., 2012). The study by Luk et al. (2011) also found evidence for enhanced resting state connectivity between frontal and occipito-parietal gray matter regions adjacent to the white matter changes, suggesting that the structural changes associated with bilingualism have some functional effect. We take this as further evidence that the lifelong necessity to manage attention to two active languages leads to the enhancement of frontal networks and to more effective control functions.

Finally, two fMRI studies have reported evidence supporting the interpretation that bilinguals have better neural efficiency than monolinguals, particularly in the frontal regions responsible for EC. First, Abutalebi et al. (2012) administered the flanker task as a non-verbal EC task to young adults and found that the bilinguals responded more rapidly than monolinguals; also the faster responses in bilinguals were associated with less activation and higher gray matter density in the relevant brain region, namely, the anterior cingulate cortex (ACC). The ACC is a central part of the general EC network and is also involved in language control, specifically switching between languages. Thus, Abutalebi and colleagues concluded that the effect of bilingualism on EC is mediated directly through enhancement of the ACC that comes from managing attention to two languages.

Second, Gold et al. (2013) reported that older bilingual adults performed significantly faster than their monolingual peers in an EC switching task and showed less frontal activation in the EC network than did the monolinguals. Again, there was a significant correlation between RT and frontal activation for both language groups, with faster RT associated with less activation. In both studies, therefore, bilinguals achieved faster performance on an EC task while requiring less activation of the frontal EC regions, supporting the notion of greater neural efficiency in EC networks for healthy bilingual adults.

One final matter concerns the apparent discrepancy between studies that found an association between bilingualism and *reduced* neural activation, suggesting greater processing efficiency (e.g., Abutalebi et al., 2012; Gold et al., 2013) and other studies that found increased neural activation in bilinguals (e.g., Bialystok et al., 2005; Hernandez et al., 2000). One possibility is that the increases in activation reflect more active control mechanisms, whereas reductions in activation reflect more effective task-related processing, but this speculation awaits further developments in our understanding of brain–behavior relations.

## 25.6 Cognitive reserve and the bilingual brain

Our interpretation of the cognitive and memory advantages found for bilinguals in both healthy aging and dementia is that bilingualism contributes to cognitive reserve, thereby preserving these functions in older age. Cognitive reserve is still a somewhat nebulous concept, but has been defined recently as "differences in cognitive processes as a function of lifetime intellectual activities and other environmental factors that explain differential susceptibility to functional impairment in the presence of pathology or other neurological insult" (Barulli & Stern, 2013). In the case of bilingualism, our suggestion is that by recruiting executive control in routine language processing, bilinguals develop more efficient control of that system (e.g., Gold et al., 2013) and more robust brain networks that subserve those functions (e.g., Luk et al., 2011). Thus, cognitive and memory processes that rely on EC also benefit from that enhancement.

The precise mechanism by which cognitive reserve functions to preserve cognitive performance is controversial. Essentially there are two options: direct protection of relevant brain regions or a compensatory mechanism. According to the direct account, cognitive activity fortifies brain health making the brain more resilient and less vulnerable to effects of aging. Thus, cognitive reserve enables the brain to resist the development of neuropathological changes associated with Alzheimer's disease (e.g., β-amyloid), slows the age-related atrophy of medial-temporal areas associated with memory loss, or otherwise renders the brain less likely to express the disease. This direct mechanism is often referred to as brain reserve. In contrast, the indirect account is based on the use of preserved circuits or functions to compensate for the decline in other cognitive domains or brain regions. By this account, a more active and engaged cognitive and social lifestyle does not slow the accumulation of neuropathology, but rather develops specific aspects of brain structure and function that then compensate for the impaired functions and permit the person to cope with the pathology. This is the approach more generally described as cognitive reserve.

Evidence for the direct approach has been presented by Landau et al. (2012) and Valenzuela et al. (2008). Landau and colleagues studied sixty-five older individuals who had reported their degree of lifetime involvement in demanding cognitive and physical activities. The investigators found that greater participation in such activities, especially during early and middle years of life, was associated with reduced uptake of Pittsburgh compound

B (PiB) in a brain scan. This reduced uptake indicates reduced levels of amyloid deposits in the cerebral cortex, and this in turn is typically a marker for reduced risk of suffering from Alzheimer's disease. In a study with a similar conclusion, Valenzuela and colleagues (2008) reported an association between levels of lifespan cognitive activity and reduced rates of atrophy in hippocampal regions. However, in a later study based on histological analysis of brain tissue recovered from autopsy, Valenzuela and colleagues (Valenzuela et al., 2012) found no relation between level of cognitive activity and hippocampal neural density, but did find a positive relation between cognitive activity and neural density in the prefrontal cortex. Their interpretation was that in this case at least, the effect of stimulating activity was through a compensatory pathway involving frontal brain regions. Their conclusion was that there may well be multiple mechanisms involved in cognitive reserve including both direct and compensatory systems.

Evidence for the compensation position is in line with observations of 'asymptomatic Alzheimer's disease' involving patients with Aβ pathology but no signs of dementia (e.g., Bennett et al., 2006). The implication is that some other part of the brain may be better developed or better preserved and thus acts to compensate for the negative effects of brain pathology. Our own research to date which investigates the effect of bilingualism as a demanding cognitive activity has supported the compensation approach and endorses the view that enhancement of the frontal networks controlling EC is the most likely mechanism for cognitive reserve. First, in a study by Schweizer et al. (2012), 20 monolingual and 20 bilingual patients who were diagnosed with AD were matched on age and performance on a battery of cognitive tests. Thus, all patients presented themselves to the neurologist with similar symptoms and similar levels of impairment. Nonetheless, CT scans showed that the bilinguals had significantly *more* medial-temporal (MTL) atrophy than monolinguals (Schweizer et al., 2012) with no other significant differences in brain volume or brain atrophy. Thus, for the same cognitive level, bilinguals had more neurodegeneration and therefore more advanced disease even though they were able to function at the same cognitive level as the monolinguals who had less advanced disease. Similarly, Kidron et al. (1997) reported that for individuals functioning at the same cognitive level, those with more education showed more ventricular enlargement in parietal regions, indicating more atrophy than for individuals with less education. Our interpretation is that preserved functioning for the bilinguals and more highly educated individuals was achieved through compensation from the enhanced EC network. These EC networks are primarily located in frontal regions (Raz, 2000; Stuss & Benson, 1986), but also include medial areas, such as the anterior cingulate cortex (ACC), and subcortical regions, such as the caudate nucleus (Abutalebi & Green, 2007). These areas appear to be better preserved in bilinguals than in monolinguals (Luk et al., 2011).

One interpretive problem with cognitive reserve is the direction of causation: do factors such as education increase cognitive reserve or are people with 'better brains' more likely to be involved in intellectual pursuits and resist dementia? Bilingualism is less vulnerable to this difficulty than are other forms of cognitive reserve: people do not typically become bilingual as a consequence of education or choice but rather because of personal (e.g., immigration) or social (e.g., bilingual community) factors that require them to learn a second language. The first language continues to be their home language, so their children are also usually bilingual. Thus, bilingualism becomes a necessary life experience rather than a chosen pursuit.

## 25.7 Conclusion

There is increasing interest in the possibility that stimulating activities and other lifestyle factors can protect cognitive function, not only from the declines associated with normal aging but also from the more dramatic changes indicative of dementia and other forms of cognitive dysfunction. The search for a pharmaceutical intervention for dementia has shown little success: there are currently several drugs prescribed for AD but their effectiveness is limited (for a review, see Zhu et al., 2013). A more promising approach from a public health perspective, therefore, is to encourage the sort of lifestyle that has been shown to contribute to cognitive reserve. Many of these factors are difficult to incorporate into one's life, are too time consuming to be effective, or are simply unavailable to some people because of required levels of resources, mobility, or expense. Bilingualism is more democratic: for those whose life has already provided them with another language, the main message would be to keep that language as a part of one's life; for young people whose lives do not give them easy access to other languages, education policy should guarantee the availability of high quality foreign language courses along with incentives to take them. In contrast to many other activities that contribute to cognitive reserve, such as musical performance, physical exercise, or reading, bilingualism expands to fill almost all of an individual's waking life, creating a situation of massive practice that far exceeds any other activity. Because the basis of the effect of bilingualism is in the joint activation of both languages, the cognitive benefit of bilingualism is enhanced every time an individual engages in a verbal exchange. The personal and social benefits of bilingualism are self-evident, and the specific cognitive benefits to EC have been reported in much research over the past decade. However, the possibility that this experience also has the potential to protect cognitive function even in the presence of neurodegenerative disease is an exciting prospect and will undoubtedly be the basis for much further research.

# 26

# Does bilingual exercise enhance cognitive fitness in traditional non-linguistic executive processing tasks?

Matthew O. Hilchey, Jean Saint-Aubin, and Raymond M. Klein

## 26.1 On the origins of non-linguistic bilingual processing advantages

It is conventional wisdom that through the pressures of Darwinian natural selection human beings are biologically prepared to learn a language. Children will normally acquire the human languages to which they are appropriately exposed. Although there are no proper figures on the worldwide incidence of people who have mastered more than one language, it is often said that over half the world's population is at least bilingual (Grosjean, 2010). Although we might infer from this that humans are similarly biologically prepared to be bilingual or multilingual, it is just as likely that the capacity for multilingualism is, like the mastery of written language, something that recent cultural forces have made available to humankind rather than something that was pressured to evolve through many generations of natural selection.

Whether we are biologically prepared to master more than one language, a question that has been of great interest for many generations is: are there extra-linguistic cognitive costs and/or benefits of multilingual mastery? This question is the focus of our chapter. By confining our question to "cognitive" costs and benefits we are purposely excluding consideration of the possible economic, social, and cultural costs and benefits; though we think it is important to note that in the vast majority of cases for which families make a choice about whether to encourage their children to be monolingual versus bilingual the benefits of bilingualism on these dimensions far outweigh the costs. And, recognizing that linguistic processes are "cognitive," by referring to "extra-linguistic" we are excluding consideration of potential linguistic benefits (e.g., metalinguistic awareness) and costs (e.g., vocabulary) of multilingualism which are relatively well documented (for a review, see Bialystok, 2009a).

In the earliest empirical studies addressed to this question, the relatively undifferentiated construct of "intelligence," using standardized IQ tests, was the target measure of "cognition." Some of the earliest studies (Saer, 1923; Smith, 1923) found higher IQ scores in monolinguals. While it was later suggested that this bilingual disadvantage was confined to verbal IQ (Seidl, 1937) with bilinguals even showing an advantage on non-verbal measures, that interesting asymmetry was not replicated by Jones and Stewart (1951) who found bilingual disadvantages on both verbal and non-verbal measures of intelligence. All of these studies were critically evaluated in a review paper by Darcy (1953) and by Peal and Lambert (1962) in their empirical investigation comparing the intellectual performance of monolingual and bilingual francophone children in Montreal. The Peal and Lambert study stands out for its use of several tests of mental functioning (in addition to standardized IQ tests), for its methodological improvements over the earlier studies (though its methods, too, have been critiqued, e.g., see MacNamara, 1966), and especially for its finding of bilingual advantages on most tests.

Peal and Lambert's description of these bilingual advantages foreshadows some recent thinking and the caveats they introduce remain relevant to any discussion of possible differences in cognition between monolinguals and bilinguals:

> The picture that emerges of the French–English bilingual in Montreal is that of a youngster whose wider experiences in two cultures have given him advantages which a monolingual does not enjoy. Intellectually his experience with two language systems seems to have left him with a mental flexibility, a superiority in concept formation, and a more diversified set of mental abilities, in the sense that the patterns of abilities developed by bilinguals were more heterogeneous. It is not possible to state from the present study whether the more intelligent child became bilingual or whether bilingualism aided his intellectual development, but there is no question about the fact that he is superior intellectually. (Peal & Lambert, 1962: 20)

Let's begin with the caveats. First, Peal and Lambert were careful to restrict their description to the francophone bilingual child in Montreal. Second, it is not simply bilingualism but also "experiences in two cultures" that is thought to contribute to the bilingual advantages. Finally, and very importantly for the question addressed in the title of this chapter, it is acknowledged that the finding that bilinguals were more intelligent ("intellectually superior") does not imply a causal direction: bilingualism may have aided intellectual development but also more intelligent children may have been more likely to meet the selection criteria for "bilingual."

Following publication of this paper, Peal and Lambert's claim that these particular bilinguals benefited from "a more diversified set of mental abilities" fell by the wayside while "mental flexibility" became a catch phrase for describing the nature of the cognitive advantage that bilinguals may enjoy over monolinguals. Mental flexibility is certainly, and usefully, more specific than the broader "intelligence," but it is primarily descriptive and doesn't tell us much about what cognitive representations and/or processes might underlie the better scores on particular tests. Indeed, despite scores of papers on this topic in the next few decades, Cummins (1979, 1984) was impelled to advise the field that what was needed was "A theoretical framework for relating language proficiency to academic achievement among bilingual students" (1984).

Because the "cognitive revolution" was still in its infancy when Peal and Lambert wrote their paper it is not surprising that their description of the advantage was somewhat lacking in mechanism(s). Broadbent (1958) had only recently proposed an information processing theory of attention; the field of psycholinguistics that was launched by Chomsky's classic (Chomsky, 1965) did not exist; the powerful methods of mental chronometry (Posner, 1978, Sternberg, 1969) were yet to be recognized; and Luria's now classic description of higher cortical functions in man (Luria, 1966), which provided a foundation for modern ideas about the networks of attention (Posner & Peterson, 1990) and the executive functions (Norman & Shallice, 1980) of the frontal network (Shallice, 1988), did not appear in English until 1966. That revolution and advances in neuroscience have provided scholars with tools (conceptual, mathematical, and technological) that enable computationally explicit theories of human mental behavior of a complexity that do justice to the complexity of the behavior and, amazingly, to generate data that can be used to localize a theory's hypothesized mental representations and processes to specific parts of the central nervous system (Cabeza & Kingstone, 2001; Posner & Raichle, 1994). Not surprisingly, advances in our understanding of bilingualism's potential impacts on cognition have been enabled by these tools.

As we see it, the next advance in thinking about the possible extralinguistic benefits of bilingualism was made by Bialystok (2001) who, in her book, *Bilingualism in Development: Language, Literacy, and Cognition*, began to develop the kind of theoretical framework that Cummins (1984) had admonished his colleagues was needed. Of course, a considerable amount of research had been conducted since Peal and Lambert's exploration of "the relation of bilingualism to intelligence." Bialystok's review of this literature led her to the following description which places a considerable emphasis on the concept of selective attention achieved through the inhibition of task-irrelevant information: "Tasks that showed a bilingual advantage had in common a misleading context and moderate conceptual demands ... what bilingual children are able to do is to inhibit attention to misleading information of greater salience or complexity than monolingual children can" (pp. 213–214). Then, after identifying the source of this inhibition in the prefrontal cortex and noting that research on bilinguals shows that both languages remain active during language processing, she develops a theory to explain how this bilingual advantage might come about:

> But if both languages are active, then how do speakers (or listeners, or readers) manage to maintain performance in only one of the languages without suffering from massive intrusions from the other? According to some researchers, the explanation is that there is a constant inhibition of the nonrelevant languages, allowing the desired system to carry out the processing (Green, 1998; Kroll & de Groot, 1997). This inhibition is undoubtedly achieved by means of processes carried out in the frontal lobe. If this model is correct, then bilingual children experience extensive practice of these functions in the first few years of life, at least once both languages are known to a sufficient level of proficiency to offer viable processing systems. It would appear that this practice in inhibiting linguistic processing carries over to processing in highly disparate domains. (Bialystok, 2001: 216)

As noted by Kroll and Bialystok (2013), "The past decade has seen an explosion in the amount of research addressing the language and cognitive processing of bilinguals" (p. 498). We believe that this very clear and exciting proposal from Bialystok's important book provided a key stimulus for this explosion of interest. Adding fuel to the fire, were the positive results from the very first study to explore whether these extra-linguistic cognitive benefits carry over into adulthood (Bialystok et al., 2004).

## 26.2 Contemporary bilingual research on non-linguistic executive processing tasks

Much of the contemporary literature exploring the relationship between bilingualism and putative enhancements in domain-general cognitive function has indeed been predicated on lynchpin findings from Bialystok, Craik, Klein and Viswanathan's (2004) non-linguistic executive processing tasks. At the outset of Bialystok et al.'s investigation, the researchers considered Green's (1998) IC model for bilingual language selection which postulated a centralized inhibitory control network that selected between competitively interactive lexicons (see Chapter 27 in this handbook) by reactively inhibiting the context-irrelevant language. Bialystok et al. extended this framework beyond psycholinguistics by evaluating whether bilinguals and monolinguals would differ in performance in experiments involving non-linguistic conflict resolution. Bialystok et al. thus proposed the more complete kind of theoretical framework for which Cummins, years earlier, had been looking. The rationale was as follows: if (1) the selection mechanisms involved in resolving conflict between simultaneously active language representations are also involved in non-linguistic conflict resolution, and if (2) bilingual language selection mechanisms are fine-tuned owing to a massive amount of experience inhibiting irrelevant lexical representations, then (3) bilinguals should outperform monolinguals on tasks involving non-linguistic conflict. Bialystok et al.'s (2004) theory clearly predicted domain-general inhibitory control advantages in bilinguals as compared to monolinguals. Nevertheless, previous findings in young children using non-linguistic executive processing tasks (Martin & Bialystok, 2003; Bialystok, Martin & Viswanathan, 2005) aroused some suspicion concerning the validity of the inhibitory control account. In one early study (Martin & Bialystok, 2003), bilingual children did not simply outperform monolingual children in conditions involving non-linguistic conflict resolution; rather bilingual children were privileged as compared to monolinguals even in conditions involving no apparent conflict. These findings raised the possibility of a bilingual advantage that was not necessarily related to superior domain-general inhibitory control but rather to the bilinguals' abilities to "manage their attention to a complex set of rapidly changing task demands" (Bialystok et al., 2004: 292; cf. Bialystok, 2006; Costa et al., 2009; Hernandez, Costa, & Humphreys, 2012; Hernandez, et al., 2013), a theme that has long permeated Bialystok's research. Nevertheless, insofar as Bialystok has long considered that efficient attentional selection in complex tasks necessitates ignoring – or inhibiting – irrelevant input (Bialystok, 1988, 1999), inhibition has remained an important feature of her theoretical framework (for a review, see Bialystok, 2007; Kroll & Bialystok, 2013).[1]

[1] Martin-Rhee and Bialystok (2008; see also Bialystok, Craik & Luk, 2008a) make a distinction between two forms of inhibition: one form is referred to as response inhibition and the other as interference suppression (see also Kroll & Bialystok, 2013). Response inhibition is thought to occur when two response options occur for the same stimulus feature. This form of inhibition is thought to occur in univalent displays as when a subject must overcome the natural tendency to make a saccadic eye-movement response to a transient flash of light in favor of an arbitrary, unnatural, stimulus–response mapping (i.e., the anti-saccade paradigm; Bialystok, Craik, & Ryan, 2006). Another example of a univalent task is the Stroop picture-naming task. In one blocked condition, the participant is required to name a picture as quickly as possible (i.e., 'night' for a picture of night). In another blocked condition, the participant is required to provide the opposite name (i.e., 'day' for a picture of night). Conflict may occur because of the natural tendency to provide a name corresponding with the picture in the opposite name condition (though it should be noted that there was no statistical evidence for conflict in Martin-Rhee & Bialystok, 2008). In these cases, there are competing responses to a single feature. The argument (see below) is that bilinguals are not advantaged in conditions requiring response inhibition. Interference suppression is thought to occur when a potential conflict arises between features presented at the same time. For example, in the Simon task (see the paragraph below in the main text), the task-irrelevant location (feature 1) of the response can interfere with the task-relevant identity (feature 2) on which the response must be based. Although, historically, bilingual advantages are found in tasks involving interference suppression (Hilchey & Klein, 2011) leading to claims like "bilingual advantages were found for some types of inhibition but not others; specifically, bilinguals outperformed monolinguals on tasks that required inhibition of interfering cues but not on tasks that required inhibition of executing a salient response" (Kroll & Bialystok, 2013: 500), it is important to remain mindful that bilinguals outperformed monolinguals commensurately on conflict and non-conflict trials. Thus, precisely whether "inhibition" related to "interference suppression" is responsible for the observed bilingual advantages remains highly speculative, if not completely undermined by the extant data.

The three experiments that Bialystok et al. (2004) conducted compared performance between old (M = ~ 70 y/o) and middle-aged (M = ~ 40 y/o) bilinguals and monolinguals across several variations of a non-linguistic Simon task (see Mordkoff & Hazeltine, 2011). In their conventional two-alternative forced choice implementation of this task, a to-be-discriminated stimulus appears randomly in the left or right visual field relative to a central fixation stimulus. When participants see a brown square, they press (with their right index finger) the right shift key. When participants see a blue square, they press (with their left index finger) the left shift key. The robust finding in this task is that responding is fastest and most accurate when there is spatial correspondence between the location of the response and target (e.g., superior performance is observed when a brown square appears to the right of a central reference point as compared to the left). Conventionally, the Simon effect materializes because of a natural tendency of the most proximal effector to respond to the source of stimulation (Hilchey et al., 2011). A cost arises when there is incompatibility between the location of the correct response and the location of the target because the two activated response tendencies are in conflict; a conflict that might be resolved via inhibition. Simon's eponymous effect – the difference in response time (RT) and accuracy between conflict and non-conflict conditions – is more generally referred to as an interference or conflict effect.

Bialystok et al. (2004) in older adults, contrary to Martin and Bialystok (2003) in young children, obtained evidence in favor of a bilingual advantage on inhibitory control in the form of smaller Simon effect in bilinguals relative to monolinguals. This advantage was driven principally by disproportionately superior bilingual performance on conflict as compared to non-conflict trials which is consistent with the prediction of the IC model. However, there were several aspects of the seminal Bialystok et al. (2004) findings that were not easily accounted for by the IC model: (1) the bilingual advantage was not constrained to conditions in which there were conflicting inputs; rather, bilinguals outperformed monolinguals in conditions in which there was no apparent conflict (i.e., when the location of the response and target were compatible); (2) bilinguals unexpectedly outperformed monolinguals in a control condition in which all targets were presented at a central reference frame (i.e., there was no possibility for conflicting spatial inputs) but only if there were four stimulus–response mappings (e.g., respond with the left index finger to a pink or green square but with the right index finger to a blue or yellow square), not two (e.g., respond with the left or right index fingers to blue or brown squares, respectively); and (3) the bilingual advantage on inhibitory control only appeared sporadically across 10 blocks of trials (Experiment 3; see also Bialystok, Craik, & Luk, 2012).

The Bialystok et al. (2004) investigation has rightfully garnered a lot of attention. The investigation was important for a number of reasons but several, in particular, stand out. First and foremost and as already noted, the study marked a seminal effort in this field to explore whether the unique skills and mechanisms (Abutalebi & Green, 2007) involved in bilingual language management would translate into objectively measured performance differences between bilingual and monolingual language groups in decisively non-linguistic processing tasks (see also Bialystok & Majumder, 1998, for earlier efforts). Second, the report ushered in an era of research using well-studied non-linguistic executive processing tasks to discern the neurocognitive mechanisms putatively underlying the bilingual performance advantages. Third, on balance, the findings indicated that the processing advantages from dual-language proficiency extended far beyond an inhibitory control model. Findings like these invited the exciting question: Just how profound and widespread is the bilingual advantage on cognitive functioning (Adesope et al., 2010)?

The question is addressed in considerable detail by Bialystok and Craik in this handbook (Chapter 25). Contrary to previous assertions and evidence (see Bialystok, 2009a; Bialystok, Craik, & Luk, 2008a; Engel de Abreu, 2011), bilingual advantages have recently been observed in non-verbal working memory (Luo et al., 2013, but not generally in verbal working memory which may account for some divergent findings – because of the difficulty of finding non-verbal working memory tasks to which verbal working memory cannot contribute) and episodic memory (Shroeder & Marian, 2012). Some consideration has been given to whether these memory advantages are directly attributable to the effect of bilingualism on bolstering memory networks or whether bilingualism improves memory and protects against memory loss indirectly by enhancing domain-general executive processing (Ossher et al., 2013), perhaps for example by maintaining white-matter connectivity and increasing diffusivity of resting-state functional connectivity in frontal brain regions commonly associated with higher level cognitive processing or executive functioning (Luk et al., 2011). These alternative, but not mutually exclusive, hypotheses are discussed succinctly and in detail by Bialystok and Craik in this handbook (Chapter 25). The first hypothesis – associated with "brain reserve" – predicts differences between language groups on memory-related tasks and, specifically, in brain regions directly associated with memory, especially during both normal and aberrant age-related neurocognitive degeneration. The second hypothesis – associated with "cognitive reserve" – predicts neurocognitive and behavioral differences between language groups on executive functioning and in networks over which executive processes preside, including the memory networks. Convincing verification of the latter hypothesis necessitates that bilinguals reliably and in a consistent way differ from monolinguals on assays of executive functioning.

In an effort to answer whether bilinguals outperform monolinguals on executive functioning, Hilchey and Klein (2011) conducted a comprehensive review of non-linguistic assays of executive function in the bilingual literature. The focus of the review was on spatial Stroop[2] (Bialystok, 2006), Simon (Bialystok et al., 2004), and flanker tasks (Costa, Hernandez, & Sebastián-Gallés, 2008) primarily because these tasks appeared least likely to recruit language processing networks while each entails the necessity to ignore irrelevant and potentially conflicting information. Although some consideration was given to the now-popular perceptual task-switching paradigm (e.g., see Prior & MacWhinney, 2010 for a bilingual advantage on task-switching; but see Hernandez et al., 2013; Paap & Greenberg, 2013 for failures to replicate), and Stroop task (see Bialystok et al., 2008 for a bilingual advantage on the Stroop interference effect but see Koussaie & Phillips, 2012a; Coderre, van Heuven, & Conklin, 2013, for failures to replicate), caution seemed advisable given the high potential for linguistic mediation. The data from Hilchey and Klein's review of non-linguistic executive processing tasks indicated that the bilingual inhibitory control advantage (BICA) (i.e., interference effect) was at best sporadic and at worst spurious. However, a second conclusion from Hilchey and Klein's review was that the magnitude of the bilingual advantage on both conflict and non-conflict trials in non-linguistic executive processing tasks was relatively robust throughout the lifespan. Hilchey and Klein referred to this as a bilingual executive processing advantage (BEPA) (i.e., global effect) and, to ensure its measurement is not confounded by interference effects, we will follow their lead and measure global effects by comparing group performance on only congruent trials. To be sure, a purer measure (unconfounded by the possibility of facilitation on congruent trials) would use some sort of neutral trial. Aside from the difficulty of defining "neutral," a practical consideration is that all Simon and flanker studies have congruent trials whereas very few studies collected data from trials that might be considered neutral. The elusiveness of a bilingual advantage on inhibitory control (see Chapter 24 in this handbook) despite widespread global performance advantages lent credence to a movement in the field away from inhibitory control models toward more "holistic" interpretations (Bialystok, 2011: 232; Kroll & Bialystok, 2013). These interpretations are typically consonant with a non-traditional form of conflict monitoring theory (Abutalebi & Green, 2007, 2008; Costa et al., 2009; Hilchey & Klein, 2011), and modern models of bilingual language representation that minimize the role of inhibitory processes in lexical selection (e.g., van Heuven et al., 2008; see Dijkstra & van Heuven, 2002 for the BIA+ model). In short, these theories are better able to account for BEPAs in the absence of BICAs.

---

[2] The spatial Stroop (or Simon arrows) task is essentially a Simon task in which the stimuli calling for spatial (e.g., left and right) responses are directional arrows whose task-irrelevant locations are congruent or incongruent with the locations of the correct responses.

## 26.3 Nature of the empirical review

No paradigms have been as influential in recent years in advancing this literature, nor have any paradigms been more commonly administered, than what we will refer to as "traditional non-linguistic executive processing tasks" (e.g., the Simon and flanker tasks). Indeed, a recent surge in research on bilingualism and non-linguistic executive processing tasks has occurred in the years since our last review (Hilchey & Klein, 2011). This renewed popularity allows us to take stock of the evidence anew (the new studies covered in this chapter are listed in Table 26.1, pages 595–596). If bilinguals consistently outperform monolinguals then, ceteris paribus, there is likely to be a BICA, a BEPA, or both. To be clear, BICA will be expressed behaviorally in the form of reduced interference effects (due to better performance on incongruent trials) in bilinguals relative to monolinguals; BEPA will be expressed behaviorally in the form of global advantages (e.g., similar advantages on congruent and incongruent trials). Consistency among studies in showing BEPAs, BICAs or both would support the notion of a bilingual advantage and call for neuroscientific investigations and modeling efforts dedicated to identifying the underlying neural mechanisms (e.g., Abutalebi et al., 2012; Gold et al., 2013; Luk et al., 2010).

Although we focus principally on the relationship of bilingualism to performance on frequently administered non-linguistic executive processing tasks, it is important to acknowledge that a variety of innovative tasks, ostensibly targeting high-level attentional control or executive function, have been aimed at the question before us (e.g., Kharkhurin, 2008; Kovács & Mehler, 2009). These are excluded from the present review simply because their uniqueness precludes the possibility of detecting a consistent pattern of results across several studies.

## 26.4 Performance of bilingual and monolingual children on traditional non-linguistic executive processing tasks

Hilchey and Klein's (2011) review revealed that bilingual children never significantly outperformed monolingual children on inhibitory control or synonymously interference suppression (Martin-Rhee & Bialystok, 2008) in non-linguistic executive processing tasks (Bialystok, Martin, & Viswanathan, 2005; Carlson & Melztoff, 2008; Martin-Rhee & Bialystok, 2008; Morton & Harper, 2007). This is to say quite simply that the difference score between conflict and non-conflict trials was comparable between language groups (no BICA). Bilingual children did however typically outperform monolinguals in non-linguistic executive processing tasks in the form of commensurately large advantages on both conflict

Table 26.1 Summary of the recent literature on bilingualism and non-linguistic executive function

| Study | Age | N | Task | Number of expt'l trials |
|---|---|---|---|---|
| | | **Children** | | |
| Bialystok et al. (2010) | 3.5 | 84 | Flanker (Child ANT) | 80 |
| Yang, Yang, & Lust (2011) both monolinguals combined | 4.7 | 58 | Flanker (Child ANT) | 144 |
| Morales, Calvo, & Bialystok (2013) | 5.5 | 56 | Simon (2-AFC) | 48 |
| Morales, Calvo, & Bialystok (2013) | 5.5 | 56 | Simon (4-AFC) | 48 |
| Poarch & van Hell (2012) | 7 | 38 | Simon (2-AFC) | 126 |
| Engel de Abreu et al. (2012) | 6.2 | 80 | Flanker (Child ANT) | 40 |
| Gathercole et al. (2014) | 8 | 64 | Simon (2-AFC) | 48 |
| Gathercole et al. (2014) | 15 | 114 | Simon (2-AFC) | 48 |
| Anton et al. (2014) | 9.5 | 360 | Flanker (Child ANT) | 288 |
| Kapa & Colombo (2013) Earlier L2 acquisition | 9.5 | 43 | Flanker (Child ANT) | 144 |
| Kapa & Colombo (2013) Later L2 acquisition | 9.8 | 58 | Flanker (Child ANT) | 144 |
| | | **Young adults** | | |
| Salvatierra & Rosselli (2011) | 26.3 | 133 | Simon (2-AFC) | 48 |
| Salvatierra & Rosselli (2011) | 26.3 | 133 | Simon (4-AFC) | 48 |
| Kousaie & Philipps (2012a) | 24.2 | 51 | Flanker | 620 |
| Kousaie & Philipps (2012b) | 24.2 | 51 | Simon (2-AFC) | 720 |
| Paap & Greenberg (2013) | Undergraduates | 79 | Simon (2-AFC) | 100 |
| Paap & Greenberg (2013) | Undergraduates | 86 | Simon (2-AFC) | 40 or 80 |
| Paap & Greenberg (2013) | Undergraduates | 106 | Simon (2-AFC) | <100 |
| Paap & Greenberg (2013) | Undergraduates | 104 | Flanker (ANT) | 208 |
| Tao et al. (2011) Earlier L2 acquisition | 19.6 | 70 | Flanker (LANT) | 288 |
| Tao et al. (2011) Later L2 acquisition | 20.6 | 64 | Flanker (LANT) | 288 |
| Yudes, Macizo, & Bajo (2011) | 23.7 | 32 | Simon (2-AFC) | 126 |
| Marzecova et al. (2013) | 21.8 | 35 | Flanker (LANT) | 576 |
| Pelham & Abrams (2014) | 20.5 | 90 | Flanker (ANT) | 144 |
| Gathercole et al. (2014) | 25.5 | 85 | Simon (2-AFC) | 48 |
| Abutalebi et al. (2012) | 25.2 | 31 | Flanker | 96 |
| Abutalebi et al. (2012) | 25.2 | 31 | Flanker | 96 |

**Table 26.1** Continued

| Study | Age | N | Task | Number of expt'l trials |
|---|---|---|---|---|
| Luk, de Sa, & Bialystok (2011) – early AOA | 21.2 | 80 | Flanker | 96 |
| Luk, de Sa, & Bialystok (2011) – late AOA | 21.1 | 81 | Flanker | 96 |
| **Older adults** | | | | |
| Billig & Scholl (2011) | 49 | 41 | Spatial Stroop | 48 |
| Billig & Scholl (2011) | 65.3 | 42 | Spatial Stroop | 48 |
| Salvatierra & Rosselli (2011) | 64.2 | 100 | Simon (2-AFC) | 48 |
| Salvatierra & Rosselli (2011) | 64.2 | 100 | Simon (4-AFC) | 48 |
| Gathercole et al. (2014) | 67 | 84 | Simon (2-AFC) | 48 |
| Kirk, Scott-Browne, & Kempe (2013) | 70.1 | 32 | Simon (2-AFC) | 28 |
| Shroeder & Marian (2012) | 80.8 | 36 | Simon (2-AFC) | 48 |

Note: Although 288 trials were collected, one-half of the trials, those with a spatially uninformative warning cue, were excluded from analysis.

and non-conflict trials (BEPA). One study, however, failed to support BEPA. This study was conducted by Morton and Harper (2007) who modeled their task on Bialystok et al. (2004) while controlling for socioeconomic status (SES) by creating a composite score factoring in parent education and family income. According to these authors, SES which is well known to predict superior executive function (e.g., Mezzacappa, 2004; Noble, Norman, & Farah, 2005), had not been sufficiently controlled in previous studies.

Before examining the studies that have been conducted since Hilchey and Klein's (2011) review, we will first discuss the results from a study that was overlooked in that review. Bialystok et al. (2010) examined language group differences in children on a standard flanker interference task embedded in the child version of the attentional network test. They compared linguistically diverse samples of Canadian bilingual children (mean ages were 3.5 and 4.6 years in the "young" and "old" groups, respectively) against age-matched English-speaking monolinguals from Canada and French-speaking monolinguals from France on a battery of cognitive assessment tests targeting various components of executive functioning. The critical finding for the present review (see Figure 26.1) was that language groups did not differ significantly on the flanker task (neither in the flanker effect, where there was a non-significant monolingual advantage of about 70 ms, nor in congruent RT, our measure of global processing efficiency). Of further theoretical interest was the unusual finding that the bilingual children exhibited superior response inhibition, as indexed by superior accuracy as compared to monolingual children on a reverse imitation task (Luria's tapping task; e.g., if the experimenter taps a dowel once, the child must tap twice). Recall that bilingual children do not typically outperform monolingual children on measures putatively targeting response inhibition (see note 7; Martin-Rhee & Bialystok, 2008; Bialystok & Viswanathan, 2009).[3]

---

[3] There are several possible reasons for the discrepancy: (1) it is possible, as noted by Bialystok et al. (2010), that there is a bilingual advantage on response inhibition early in child development (mean age < 5) whereas the advantage shifts to attentional selection later in development (mean age > 5) and then, even later in life (mean age > 25), the advantage is on attentional selection and response inhibition (Bialystok, Craik, & Ryan, 2006). Nevertheless, it is worth noting that that Martin-Rhee and Bialystok (2008; Experiment 2) found no bilingual advantages on response inhibition in children who were on average 4.6 years old using the Stroop picture-naming task (see also Yang, Yang, & Lust, 2011) and that any bilingual advantage on attentional selection in the elderly is unlikely (see section 26.5). (2) Although the Stroop picture-naming task, Luria's tapping task and a component of the "Faces task" (Bialystok et al., 2006) allegedly measure response inhibition, the neurocognitive mechanisms underlying performance in these tasks may be dissociable such that childhood bilingualism affects performance in Luria's tapping task (Bialystok et al., 2010) but not the response inhibition component of the "Faces task" (Bialystok & Viswanathan, 2009) or Stroop picture-naming task (Martin-Rhee & Bialystok, 2008). In this case, ascribing to each of these tasks a common neural substrate related to response inhibition would be a misattribution error. (3) It remains a possibility that uncontrolled factors associated with bilingualism were more directly responsible for the performance differences (see Hilchey & Klein, 2011) and that bilingualism merely acts as a mediating variable. By the same token, it remains possible that bilingualism is directly responsible for certain processing advantages but that these advantages are sometimes obscured by unique monolingual experiences that also afford cognitive processing advantages.

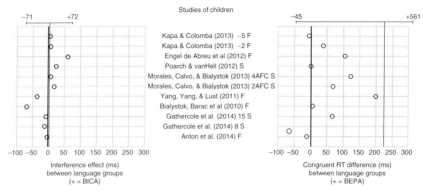

**Figure 26.1** Group differences in inhibitory control and executive processing in children. Positive values, in both cases, are indicative of an advantage for bilinguals. In both panels the vertical lines that terminate in horizontal arrows represent the unweighted mean of the effect reported from studies of children in Hilchey & Klein (2011, Figure 7) and the numbers above these lines represent the range of scores reported previously. Notes: F = data from a flanker task; S = data from a Simon task. For the Kapa and Colombo entries, the numbers (5 and 2) represent the average age of L2 acquisition in their two groups of bilinguals who were compared to a single group of monolinguals. For the Gathercole et al. entries, their three groups of bilinguals were combined because there were few effects of bilingual subgroup and no effects that were consistent (this applies to the remaining figures). The numbers (8 and 15) for these entries represent the age of participants. Morales, Calvo, & Bialystok (2013) tested the same participants on both 2- and 4-alternative forced choice tasks from which Simon effects could be derived. Yang et al. compared a single group of American bilingual children to two separate groups of American monolingual children (Korean and English) whose data have been combined in this graph because they did not differ substantially; a third group of Korean monolinguals from the Republic of Korea was not considered here as our focus remains on language group, not cross-cultural and language group, differences. Bialystok, Barac et al.'s study included two monolingual groups whose data have been combined.

Since 2011, to our knowledge, seven studies have been published exploring the effect of bilingualism on child (age 3–15 years old) performance in non-linguistic executive processing tasks (Antón et al., 2014; Engel de Abreu et al., 2012; Kapa & Colombo, 2013; Morales et al., 2013; Poarch & van Hell, 2012; Yang, Yang, & Lust, 2011). The results from these seven studies[4] as well as from Bialystok, Barac et al. (2010) are illustrated, along with the mean effects across the studies reviewed by Hilchey and Klein (2011), in Figure 26.1. Three studies administered a flanker interference task in the context of the child attentional network test (i.e., Antón et al., 2014; Kapa & Colombo, 2013; Rueda et al., 2004; Yang, Yang & Lust, 2011). One study administered a standard flanker interference task (Engel de Abreu et al., 2012). Three studies administered Simon tasks (Morales et al., 2013; Gathercole et al., 2014; Poarch & van Hell, 2012).

---

[4] Not shown in Figure 26.1 are the data from 3-, 4-, and 5-year-olds collected by Gathercole et al. (2014). Because they used a unique, touch-screen Simon task with only sixteen trials, we were reluctant to plot these data along with the rest of the studies. That noted, for children in this age group, it was the monolinguals who showed large advantages on congruent trials and on interference.

Although contrary to previous research, two of these studies (Engel de Abreu et al., 2012; Poarch & van Hell, 2012) revealed a significant bilingual advantage on inhibitory control, the pattern across all the new studies is very similar to the overall null finding reported in Hilchey and Klein's review. With regard to the global advantage, although none of the new studies reported a bilingual advantage as large as the mean value reported by Hilchey and Klein (2011), the general trend is in the direction of a bilingual advantage. An interesting result was reported by Kapa and Colombo (2013) who found no BEPA in 10-year-old children whose mean age of acquisition of a second language (L2) was ~ 5 years old whereas bilingual children were advantaged on executive processing when they had acquired L2 much earlier, at a mean age of ~ 2 years old. This finding reinforces the longstanding notion that lifelong bilingualism may be a critical factor for generating processing advantages (see Bialystok & Barac, 2012, for converging evidence, from a multiple regression approach, revealing that degree of bilingualism and time in a bilingual education environment predict reduced interference effects in a flanker task;[5] see also Luk, de Sa, & Bialystok, 2011; Soveri, Rodriguez-Fornells, & Laine, 2011).

This comprehensive review of the literature with children reveals the following diverse set of findings: (1) the absence of any bilingual advantages in a traditional non-linguistic executive processing task (e.g., Anton et al., 2014; Bialystok et al., 2010; Gathercole et al., 2014; Morton & Harper, 2007, 8-year-olds); (2) the presence of BICAs in the absence of BEPAs (Poarch & van Hell, 2012); (3) the presence of BEPAs in the absence of BICAs (e.g., Bialystok, Martin, & Viswanathan, 2005; Gathercole et al., 2014; Kapa & Colombo, 2013; Martin-Rhee & Bialystok, 2008; Morales et al., 2013;[6] Yang, Yang, & Lust, 2011, 15-year-olds); (4) the concomitance of BICAs and BEPAs (Engel de Abreu et al., 2012); and (5) the presence of a bilingual advantage on response inhibition in some tasks (Bialystok et al., 2010) but not others (Bialystok, & Viswanathan, 2009; Martin-Rhee, & Bialystok, 2008). Collectively, the findings do not paint the most coherent picture of how or whether bilingualism, specifically, improves cognitive functioning in childhood. It is still noteworthy that the balance of evidence in studies of children leans in favor of BEPAs. Granted, the variability in

---

[5] This result can just as easily be taken as support for the proposition that among children who are exposed to a bilingual environment those with better executive control are more likely to turn out more balanced (and proficient in L2). If degree of bilingualism turns out to be consistently associated with better inhibitory control or executive processing (in group or correlational studies) additional methodologies (e.g., retrospective study of twins raised apart or longitudinal design) will be needed to disambiguate the direction of causality.

[6] Bilingual children were more accurate than monolingual children on incongruent trials in the two – but not four – alternative forced choice version of the Simon task despite no significant differences between groups on the temporal measure of the Simon effect. Nevertheless, a bilingual advantage on incongruent trials on accuracy instead of response time is ultimately consistent with a BICA. Thus, one might argue that – at least in this experiment – the two-alternative forced choice task data denote BICAs and BEPAs whereas the four-alternative forced choice data denote only BEPAs (see also Yang, Yang, & Lust, 2011, for differences between bilinguals and monolinguals on accuracy in a flanker task).

findings leaves much to be desired. Given the results from Kapa and Colombo, some of the variability may be related to unreported differences in the age of L2 acquisition. Another possibility is that some of the findings are type 1 or type 2 errors. A third possibility is that hidden factors, correlated with language group membership, have been overlooked.

Generally, given the findings that (1) BEPAs can occur in the absence of BICAs, (2) BICAs can occur in the absence of BEPAs, and (3) BICAs and BEPAs can occur in tandem, it seems reasonably clear that the mechanisms driving these performance outcomes must be dissociable. The presence of one behavioral outcome in no way appears to predict/necessitate the presence of the other. Considerable confusion arises, however, when one considers that – in all cases – 'bilingualism' is the common denominator. How can 'bilingualism' affect performance in fundamentally different ways? One possible answer, as has been noted by Luk and Bialystok (2013), is that bilingualism is not a unitary phenomenon. This solution invites the possibility that some forms of bilingualism may result in inhibitory control advantages, others in executive processing advantages and others still may result in no advantages at all. For example, the frequency of language switching on a daily basis (Prior & Gollan, 2011), the balance between languages (Goral, Campanelli, & Sprio, 2015), and the length of time spent in immersion programs (Bialystok, & Barac, 2012) are some of the psycholinguistic variables that have been related to executive functioning. In many ways, these considerations are reminiscent of earlier threshold models (e.g., Cummins, 1979; Diaz, 1985; Ricciardelli, 1992) positing bilingual advantages on domain-general cognition only when a certain level of proficiency is achieved in both languages. Nevertheless, at the core of these proposals is the idea that all performance differences can be attributed to the various ways in which bilingualism uniquely configures the central nervous system (see Chapter 27 in this handbook). Historically, this viewpoint relates closely to cognitive bilingualism (Hakuta, Ferdman, & Diaz, 1987) which stresses a direct, neuropsychological relationship between dual-language management and domain-general cognitive functioning (see also Kroll & Bialystok, 2013). In contrast to cognitive bilingualism is the possibility that uncontrolled sociological factors unrelated to the cognitive processing demands of bilingualism but correlated with the bilingual experience are responsible for the divergent findings. This perspective, more consistent with what has historically been referred to as bilingual social psychology (Hakuta et al. 1987), maintains that bilingualism indirectly improves cognitive function by, for example, increasing socioeconomic status, nurturing a sense of belonging with the community, or broadening cultural horizons. It is doubtlessly true that both perspectives have more than a modicum of truth. Nevertheless, consideration of the bilingual social psychology perspective raises the question: how do researchers, who are exploring whether bilingual executive or inhibitory processing advantages exist, select their language groups when examining measures of executive control in children?

In studies for which language group is treated as a factor it is common practice to equate between language groups on age and, in many cases, the bilinguals had been exposed to two languages from a very young age. Sometimes the groups are equated on various cognitive measures like fluid intelligence (Morales et al., 2013) or short-term memory (Kapa & Colombo, 2013; Martin-Rhee & Bialystok, 2008) whereas in other studies differences between language groups on abstract reasoning and memory are assessed (Engel de Abreu et al., 2012) or simply not considered (Poarch & van Hell, 2012; Yang, Yang, & Lust, 2011). Bilingual proficiency and balance is typically measured via parental or subjective appraisals although more objective measures would be preferred (Gollan et al., 2011) and designs and analyses more sensitive to the degree of proficiency and balance advisable (Bialystok & Barac, 2012). One factor on which the language groups are sometimes equated is socioeconomic status (e.g., Cummins, 1976; Cummins & Gulutson, 1974; Peal & Lambert, 1962). Control over this factor is particularly critical given its established relationship to executive control (Mezzacappa, 2004; Noble et al., 2005) and the presumed role it played (Lee, 1996) in accounting for the bilingual disadvantages in cognitive function in studies prior to Peal and Lambert (1962).

Only four of the group-factorial studies exploring language differences among children in these non-linguistic executive processing tasks have attempted to measure socioeconomic status and equate between language groups on this measure. Two of these studies have used parent education levels as a proxy for socioeconomic status between language groups (Kapa & Colombo, 2013; Poarch & van Hell, 2012). Despite their common attention to socioeconomic status, Kapa and Colombo identify a bilingual advantage on BEPA, not BICA, whereas Poarch and van Hell identify a bilingual advantage on BICA, not BEPA. Another study, Morton and Harper (2007), controlled for both parent education and family income and found no language group differences at all. In our view, the study that best controlled for socioeconomic status was conducted by Engel de Abreu et al. (2012); furthermore, this is the only group study of children reporting statistically significant BICAs and BEPAs. Their measure of socioeconomic status considered disposable household income, household possessions and size, stimulation in the home, caregiver education, caregiver occupation, and nutritional status of the child. These factors were aggregated into an International Socioeconomic Index (Ganzeboom, 2010) on which the language groups were matched. This study is also unique for this age group insofar as it controlled for years of education, which may modulate bilingual processing advantages in older populations (Gollan et al., 2011). Nevertheless, despite these strengths, it is worth noting that the bilingual children in Engel de Abreu et al.'s investigation resided in

Luxembourg whereas the monolingual children resided in Portugal. Thus, despite Engel de Abreu et al.'s careful control over other potentially relevant factors like ethnicity and classroom size, this difference allows for the possibility that unaccounted-for social experiences unique to each country were responsible for the unusual finding of a bilingual advantages on inhibitory control and executive processing in this age group.

Although very few studies have formally controlled for socioeconomic status, the practice of not directly measuring socioeconomic status has been justified by some researchers. The following passage from Bialystok et al. (2010) is representative of a tack that is commonly taken:

> All the children living in Canada came from the same middle-class neighborhoods and attended the same day care centers. Although we did not formally measure socioeconomic status (SES), there is no evidence for a systematic bias in SES that could be correlated with language experience. The schools were private day care centers in which parents paid fees; there were no subsidies available. The large sample size also attenuates the possibility of bias. Moreover, the wide range of bilinguals in the sample precludes the possibility that bilingualism is confounded with language, ethnicity, or culture. Although some have argued that monolingual and bilingual children in Canada cannot be compared because of differences in SES (Morton & Harper, 2007), our carefully matched groups of children in targeted neighborhoods provide a reliable control over extraneous factors and isolate home bilingualism as the relevant factor that distinguishes between the groups. (Bialystok, 2009b)

We agree that sampling from children residing in the same middle-class neighborhoods and attending the same daycare might reduce the contribution of socioeconomic status and the unique social opportunities that come with it. But we see little reason to assume that this group selection procedure guarantees equivalence between language groups on socioeconomic status, ethnicity or cultural experience. Furthermore, we see little reason to assume that a large sample size or wide range of bilinguals precludes the possibility of a relationship between language, culture, ethnicity, or socioeconomic status. Although, practically, we understand that a rigorous approach to measuring socioeconomic status like that taken by Engel de Abreu et al. (2012) is laborious, such a rigorous and consistent approach to measuring socioeconomic status seems warranted given the strong influence that socioeconomic status can have on high level cognitive function. We remain, as were Hilchey and Klein in 2011, concerned by the general disregard of sociological factors that could covary with bilingualism in certain samples and influence performance. Immigration status, for example, was only controlled in one study (Poarch & van Hell, 2012; however, for some consideration of this issue, see Martin-Rhee & Bialystok, 2008). This is somewhat problematic given recent findings suggesting that bilingualism protects against the onset of symptoms associated with Alzheimer's disease when comparing between immigrant populations but not when comparing between native-English speakers and native-English bilinguals (Chertkow et al., 2010; but see Alladi et al., 2013; Sanders et al., 2012). Consider further that Poarch and van Hell (2012), the lone study controlling for immigration status, is also the only study in this age group showing a bilingual advantage on inhibitory control but not executive processing.

In point of fact, the sociological factor that receives the most attention is socioeconomic status. As we have noted, however, control of socioeconomic status is somewhat derisory given its importance. Although we recognize that dual-language learning necessitates exposure to a unique set of social factors – likely so broad and diverse in nature that it would be impossible to take stock of the entire set – we caution strongly against ignoring or downplaying the bilingual social psychology perspective. For example, and sensitive to the social psychological perspective, Barac and Bialystok (2012) showed consistent childhood (mean age = ~ 6 years old) bilingual advantages in a perceptual task-switching paradigm comparing Chinese–English, Spanish–English and French–English samples against one another (among which there were no differences) and an English-speaking monolingual sample from a large multicultural city. The groups had different cultural background, education and language history. Yet, in all cases, the bilingual advantage was expressed in the same way (lower global switch costs but no language group differences on local switch costs) – a finding that at least partly undermines sociological factors and bolsters the cognitive bilingualism perspective. At this juncture, we tentatively conclude – in the tradition of the cognitive bilingualism perspective – that childhood bilingualism may enhance executive processing (BEPA) but not inhibitory control (no BICA), in flanker and Simon tasks. However, because social factors, potentially co-varying with bilingualism in different samples, have been insufficiently considered, these executive processing differences cannot be confidently attributed to bilingualism.

## 26.5 Performance of bilingual and monolingual young adults on traditional non-linguistic executive processing tasks

Hilchey and Klein's (2011) review of studies that compared bilingual and monolingual young adults revealed two consistent patterns: There was no evidence in favor of BICA and there was a robust BEPA. As can be seen in Figure 26.2, which illustrates results from studies conducted since Hilchey and Klein's review, the BICA picture remains unchanged with most of the data hovering around the "no difference" zone (much as before). In striking contrast, the last two years of research have dramatically challenged their observation that evidence for a BEPA is robust in young adults. In point of fact, many experiments since that review have failed to

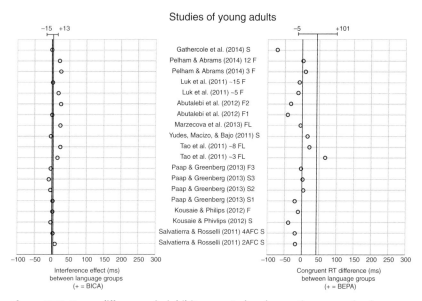

**Figure 26.2** Group differences in inhibitory control and executive processing in young adults. Positive values, in both cases, are indicative of an advantage for bilinguals. In both panels the vertical lines that terminate in horizontal arrows represent the unweighted mean of the effect reported from studies of young adults in Hilchey & Klein (2011, Figure 6a, from conventional interference tasks) and the numbers above these lines represent the range of scores reported previously. Notes: S = data from a Simon task; F = data from a Flanker task; FL = data from the Flanker component of the Lateralized Attention Network Test. Salvatierra & Rosselli tested the same participants on both 2- and 4-alternative forced choice tasks from which Simon effects could be derived. The numbers (1–3) in the Paap & Greenberg entries correspond to "study" number. The numbers (1,2) in the entries for Abutalebi et al. represent whether the data are from block 1 or block 2. In each of the entries for Tao et al. (3 and 8), Luk et al. (5 and 15) and Pelham & Abrams (3 and 12) the numbers represent the average age of L2 acquisition in two groups of bilinguals who were compared to a single group of monolinguals.

detect BEPAs in young adults (e.g., Abutalebi et al., 2012; Gathercole et al., 2014; Humphrey & Valian, 2012; Koussaie & Phillips, 2012b; Luk, de Sa, & Bialystok, 2011; Marzecova, et al., 2013; Paap & Greenberg, 2013; Pelham & Abrams, 2014; Salvatierra & Rosselli, 2011; Yudes, Macizo, & Bajo, 2011). We are uncertain why most available data in 2011 strongly tended toward this form of a bilingual advantage whereas most current data clearly contest these findings.[7] Perhaps bilingual advantages in young adulthood

---

[7] An expert reviewer suspected that data in the years preceding 2011 might have tended strongly toward bilingual processing advantages because of either publication or outcome reporting biases (see Dwan et al., 2008, for a general treatment of this issue and see Paap, 2014, for a treatment focused on the literature covered in this chapter). The reviewer speculated that widespread popularity for the bilingual advantage (e.g., Adesope et al., 2010) might have discouraged other researchers from attempting to publish null effects. Since Hilchey and Klein's (2011) review, the integrity of the bilingual advantage has been challenged (e.g., Paap & Greenberg, 2013) which may in turn be facilitating the proliferation of additional null results. We agree that publication biases may account for the divergence between the pre- and post-2011 research reports and consider that the proposal warrants a more formal mathematical and complete treatment that is beyond the scope of this book chapter.

occur only when processing demands are highest, as in when many rules or response-mappings must be represented simultaneously (e.g., Hernandez et al., 2013). Still, there is very little indication that the variations on the non-linguistic executive processing tasks that emerged after Hilchey and Klein's (2011) review were any less complex than those that had been used to establish the bilingual advantage.

Regardless of the reason, even early on in this literature there was an indication that bilingual advantages in young adults could be elusive. For example, upon evaluating the effect of bilingualism on performance in non-linguistic executive processing tasks across the lifespan, Bialystok, Martin, and Viswanathan (2005: 117) remarked:

> As clear as the bilingual advantage was for children and older adults, there was no trace of a processing difference for young adults who were university undergraduates. Our explanation is that the subtle advantage in inhibitory control that comes from bilingualism is irrelevant for individuals who are already in control of efficient processing ... Instead, the effect of bilingualism can be seen only when these processes are developing in childhood, giving bilinguals a developmental boost, or when they are beginning to wane in adulthood, protecting bilinguals from a steep decline.

Despite the elusiveness of evidence for BICA in young adults, when a significant bilingual advantage is obtained (even if it takes some looking to find it), the authors reporting such an advantage are often so impressed by it that they seem unaware of its uniqueness or the possibility that it is simply the result of normal variation. And there is no lack of imagination for explaining why the advantage was only obtained in some situations. Unfortunately there is often a lack of consideration of similar studies with different results. Consider, for example, the recent neuroimaging study by Abutalebi et al. (2012). They administered two blocks of the attention network test (ANT, from Fan et al., 2002) to participants in an fMRI study. The ANT is essentially a flanker task with different types of cue preceding the target. As shown in Figure 26.2, Abutalebi et al. found no evidence for BICA in the first block of 96 trials but there was a significant bilingual advantage in the second block. Their explanation for this pattern was as follows: "Bilinguals, but not monolinguals, revealed a marked decrease in the conflict effect in the second session of the flanker task suggesting that they are better able to adjust to conflict, hence, to adapt to conflicting situations" (p. 2085). It is a simple and satisfying story until you consider Costa, Hernandez, and Sebastián-Gallés (2008). They administered 3 blocks of the same flanker task (albeit with shorter and more regular intervals between trials as these were lengthened and jittered in the fMRI study) and found a strikingly different pattern of results. The change in interference scores as a function of block are shown for the two experiments in Figure 26.3. There are two remarkable differences here: (1) In the 2012 study BICA emerged with practice while in 2008 BICA disappeared with

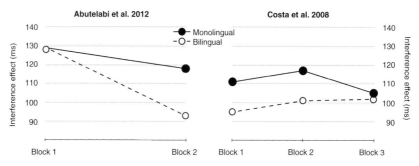

**Figure 26.3** Discrepancy in interference effects as a function practice.

practice; and (2) interference scores in the bilingual group decreased with practice in 2012 while they increased in 2008. Costa et al. offered, without endorsing, the following explanation for their pattern of results. It is, necessarily, different from that of Abutalebi et al: "the advantage of bilinguals over monolinguals is more likely to be observed in conditions requiring high attentional control demands ... when the task is overpracticed, it recruits fewer attentional demands, and as a consequence the effects of bilingualism are reduced" (Costa et al., 2008: 79). To us, it seems more likely, particularly in light of the results illustrated in the left panel of Figure 26.2, that both patterns were the result of normal variation than that both of the explanations offered for them are true.

## 26.6. Performance of bilingual and monolingual older adults on traditional non-linguistic executive processing tasks.

Hilchey and Klein (2011) concluded that the balance of evidence indicated that there were likely BEPAs throughout the lifespan in traditional non-linguistic executive processing tasks (e.g., Martin-Rhee & Bialystok, 2008, for children; e.g., Costa et al., 2009, for young adults; e.g., Emmorey et al., 2008, for middle-aged adults; e.g., Bialystok et al., 2004, for older adults). Nevertheless, Hilchey and Klein were concerned about replicability, especially in older cohorts given the discrepancies between the few studies that had been conducted on these populations (Bialystok et al., 2004; see also Bialystok, Martin, & Viswanathan, 2005; Bialystok, Craik, & Luk, 2008; Emmorey et al., 2008). Bialystok et al. (2004), generally, identified co-occurring bilingual advantages on executive processing and inhibitory control in middle-aged (ranging from 30–54 years) and old-aged (ranging from 60–88 years) samples using variations on the Simon task. Contrasting with Bialystok et al. (2004), Emmorey et al. (2008) identified a BEPA but not

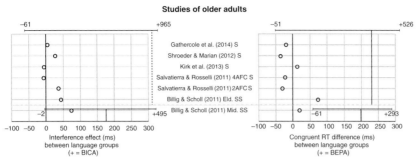

**Figure 26.4** Group differences in inhibitory control and executive processing in older adults. The dotted horizontal line separates studies of middle-age participants (below the line, average age ~50) from studies of elderly adults (above the line, average age ~70). Positive values, in both cases, are indicative of an advantage for bilinguals. In both panels the vertical lines that terminate in horizontal arrows represent the unweighted mean of the effect reported from studies of older adults in Hilchey & Klein (2011, Figures 4 and 5) and the numbers above these lines represent the range of scores reported previously. The dashed line in the left panel is plotted off the graph because the mean magnitude (~500 ms) for this group could not be represented given the scale we are using. Notes: S = data from a Simon task; SS = data from a spatial Stroop task. Salvatierra & Rosselli tested the same participants on both 2- and 4-alternative forced choice tasks from which Simon effects could be derived. Billig & Scholl tested two different age groups on the same task.

a BICA in middle-aged (mean age was 47.76 years) samples using a flanker interference task. Also contrasting with Bialystok et al. (2004), Bialystok et al. (2008) identified a BICA but not a BEPA in old-aged (mean age was 68 years) samples using the spatial Stroop task. Perhaps most troubling for a BICA attribution, the bilingual "advantage" shown by Bialystok et al. (2008) was actually due to a monolingual advantage on non-conflict trials. That is to say that monolinguals were generally faster than bilinguals on non-conflict trials whereas there was no difference between language groups on conflict trials. In order to develop a sense of which pattern best represents bilingual and monolingual language groups, we now review recent performance data comparing older bilingual and monolingual adults on traditional non-linguistic executive processing tasks.

Several investigations have compared older bilingual and monolingual language groups on traditional non-linguistic executive processing tasks since Hilchey and Klein's (2011) review (Billig & Scholl, 2011; Gathercole et al., 2014; Kirk, Scott-Brown, & Kempe, 2013; Salvatierra & Rosselli, 2011; Schroeder & Marian, 2012). Two of these investigations (Salvatierra & Rosselli, 2011; Schroeder & Marian, 2012) replicated the findings from Bialystok, Craik, and Luk (2008a) while using a two-alternative forced choice Simon task: they found reduced interference effects in bilinguals as compared to monolinguals, which in both cases were due to a monolingual advantage on non-conflict trials. In the group of studies illustrated in Figure 26.4, there were no significant BEPAs and the clustering of congruent difference scores around zero departs substantially from what Hilchey and Klein had reported. Kirk, Scott-Brown, and Kempe found no statistically significant language group differences on the Simon task; neither were any of the data trending toward the possibility of a bilingual 'advantage.'

Although Billig and Scholl (2011) reported no statistically significant language group differences on the Simon and spatial Stroop task in middle-aged (mean age was ~ 49 years) and old-aged (mean age was ~ 65 years) samples, because there were relatively substantial numerical differences between their language groups on mean overall response times and interference effects we will inspect these patterns a bit more closely to determine whether the data parallel any other findings. In their spatial Stroop task (which is illustrated in Figure 26.4), the middle-aged and old-aged bilinguals were numerically 20 ms and 70 ms faster on congruent trials, respectively. These numerical RT differences, however, are more likely reflections of speed–accuracy tradeoffs than genuine processing advantages, because while responding somewhat more slowly on congruent trials, the monolinguals were considerably more accurate than the bilinguals (4.2 percent and 8.4 percent, for the middle-aged and old-aged groups, respectively). Because Billig and Scholl did not present data from congruent and incongruent trials in the Simon task separately, we cannot comment on any patterns there. Note simply that middle- and old-aged monolinguals were on average 70 and 40 ms faster overall as compared to their age-matched bilingual groups, respectively.

Because Salvatierra and Rosselli (2011) modeled their Simon tasks on those used by Bialystok et al. (2004, Experiment 2) we have an opportunity to compare the results from two similar studies. In both studies the Simon effects from each of the simple and complex tasks (administered in a counterbalanced order) were based on a relatively small (48) number of total trials. In the simple (2AFC) task, squares of two possible colors could appear on the left or right side of the display. One color called for a left and the other a right keypress response. In the complex (4AFC) task, squares of four different colors could be presented, with two colors calling for left keypress responses and the other two colors calling for right keypress responses.

In their elderly sample (average age = ~ 70) of 15 monolinguals and 15 bilinguals, Bialystok et al. found evidence for both BEPA and BICA. Importantly, the BICA was substantially larger in the 4-AFC task (see the left panel of Figure 26.5) with its greater working memory load and it was suggested: "that the bilingual advantage appears in situations with high processing demands (e.g., four colors vs. two colors)." In Salvatierra and Rosselli's elderly sample (average age of ~ 64) of 42 monolinguals and 58 bilinguals they found no evidence of BEPA (indeed, mathematically, their participants were showing a monolingual advantage on congruent trials, MEPA!, see Figure 26.4). Importantly, in striking disagreement with

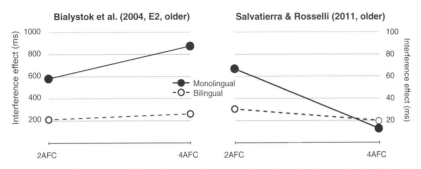

**Figure 26.5** Discrepancy in interference effects as a function of task complexity. Note the scale difference for the data from the two studies

Bialystok et al., and illustrated in the right panel of Figure 26.5, the BICA was only present in the two-alternative forced choice task.

Naturally aware of the discrepancy in how the BICA had been affected by task complexity (memory load) Salvatierra and Rosselli considered sample size, age and type of bilingualism. While it is true that the sample sizes were different (favoring Salvatierra and Rosselli) this seems an unlikely place to look for such a discrepancy. In the elderly data we have chosen to illustrate here, age also seems an unlikely source as the difference in age is not that large (70 vs 64). Salvatierra and Rosselli correctly note that different types of bilinguals were tested in the two studies: Theirs were Spanish–English bilinguals while most of Bialystok et al.'s were Tamil–English and Cantonese–English. Because Spanish and English are more similar than the pairings used by Bialystok et al., it might be that the executive networks of Bialystok's participants had experienced more difficulty and hence more effective dual-language management exercise. Relatedly, the frequencies with which bilinguals switch between languages on a daily basis has been demonstrated to modulate performance on executive control tasks (Prior & Gollan, 2011). Because neither investigation formally accounted for the daily frequency of language switching, it could be argued that the discrepancy might be accounted for by this factor. It was also noted that the age of L2 acquisition was earlier in the Bialystok et al. study. Examination of the pattern of results in Figure 26.5, however, suggests that the discrepancy cannot be explained by any of these differences between the bilingual participants in the two studies because it is the monolinguals from the two studies who are behaving so differently as a function of task complexity: Bialystok's monolinguals show an increase in Simon effects with increasing task complexity while Salvatierra and Rosselli's monolinguals show a decrease.

So far, we have focused attention on the different natures of the effect of task complexity on the BICA in these two studies. The dramatic difference in the magnitude of the Simon effects (note that the scales in the two panels of Figure 26.5 differ by a factor of 10) cries out for an explanation. We do not have a confident answer to the question. What could possibly have made the Simon effects in Bialystok et al.'s (2004) investigation approximately ten times larger than is typical for this literature? One factor worth considering is the large difference in levels of accuracy between the studies: whereas Salvatierra and Rosselli's (2011) elderly participants were making approximately 10 percent errors, Bialystok et al.'s participants were making only about 1 percent errors. The magnitude of the difference, however, was somewhat unprecedented: Salvatierra and Rosselli's elderly participants were about 700 ms faster than Bialystok et al.'s. Nevertheless, how might a more conservative attitude toward errors translate into much higher interference scores and much larger BICAs? The ogival shape of the speed–accuracy trade-off function might help explain this: at high levels of accuracy small differences in accuracy can trade for large differences in reaction time which might serve to magnify interference effects measured in reaction time for participant groups that are especially accurate (e.g., see D'Aloisio & Klein, 1990: 456).

Generally speaking, the most common finding in this age group is a bilingual advantage on the interference effect. The most frequent expression of it, however, is comparable performance between language groups on conflict trials and slower bilingual responding on non-conflict trials (Bialystok, Craik, & Luk, 2008; Schroeder, & Marian, 2012; see Salvatierra & Rosselli, 2011, for some discussion of this finding). It is thus noteworthy that, overall, the monolinguals tend to outperform bilinguals in the Simon and spatial-Stroop tasks. While we could speculate on why the bilinguals are slower on non-conflict trials – perhaps, for example, because they are primed for conflict in conditions where none exists owing to frequent cross-language competition and, by extension, tonic upregulation of the domain-general conflict monitoring system[8] – we believe that this particular pattern (which can hardly be called a bilingual advantage) requires additional replications better controlling for potentially relevant sociolinguistic factors. The only sociological variable on which the groups were objectively and consistently balanced was years of education. Bialystok, Craik, and Luk (2008) reported that many of their bilinguals were immigrants but no such data was made available for the monolingual samples. Only when the groups are more carefully matched on a wide range of sociolinguistic factors and the pattern of results more stable does it seem reasonable to endorse any notion that bilingualism conduces directly to improved non-linguistic cognitive functioning in this age group (or any age group for that matter).

---

[8] See note 7.

## 26.7 Conclusions

Research on the effect of bilingualism on cognitive functioning has a long and storied history. The earliest empirical forays into bilingualism and cognitive functioning in the 1920s tended in favor of bilingual disadvantages on, by today's standards, relatively crude metrics of intelligence. The pendulum swung when Peal and Lambert (1962) published their landmark study demonstrating bilingual advantages across a broad range of tests of mental function, while taking into account various sociological constructs. Controversy abounded in the years following Peal and Lambert's report as some researchers struggled to develop a coherent theoretical framework for explaining why dual-language management might confer processing advantages while others vehemently and adamantly contested claims endorsing bilingual processing advantages. At the dawn of the cognitive revolution, research methods, and theory development improved and so too did our understanding of the bilingual mind. Bialystok (2001), enabled by this conceptual revolution, provided one of the first clear theoretical frameworks aimed at accounting for why bilingualism might enhance domain-general cognitive processing. By advancing a domain-general inhibitory control model of dual-language management, Bialystok's work in this field launched twenty-first-century investigative efforts aimed squarely at exploring language group differences in performance on well-studied non-linguistic assays of executive functioning, on which the present review shines the spotlight.

Ellen Bialystok and Fergus Craik, a world-class expert in his own right on memory and aging, are the driving forces behind much of the twenty-first-century research on bilingualism and domain-general cognitive functioning. These two trailblazers dazzle our imaginations with compelling new ideas and theories rooted in contemporary neuropsychological principles and methods. In Chapter 25 of this handbook, Bialystok and Craik (see also Bialystok et al., 2014) team up again to marshal studies on bilingualism and cognitive functioning that favor the idea that dual-language management provides a kind of cognitive exercise that not only generates a domain-general bilingual advantage in "the set of abilities involved in controlling attention, inhibiting distraction, and shifting between goals, collectively known as executive control (EC)" but also contributes to "cognitive reserve" which, in effect, delays the appearance of the clinical symptoms associated with age-related memory-based neuropathologies. At the core of their proposal is the idea that when fronto-parietal brain networks, associated with executive function, are spared from age-related degeneration these networks are available in the bilingual to provide strategies that can compensate for age-related decline or pathologies in brain regions to which the executive network projects.

In our chapter, we have reviewed the corpus of behavioral evidence on bilingualism and executive functioning throughout the lifespan, as commonly assessed by traditional non-linguistic assays of executive functioning, and could find little in the way of substantive evidence consistent with the notion that dual-language management, specifically, advantages bilingual performance on these tasks. That is not to say that bilingualism does not uniquely configure the central nervous system or that the executive network, specifically, is not affected by bilingualism. Indeed, neuroimaging data tend to reveal unique neurocognitive landscapes between language groups (e.g., Bialystok et al., 2005; Garbin et al., 2010; Luk et al., 2010).

If, however, the argument is that bilingualism conduces to a superior form of cognitive functioning – not just a different form – throughout the lifespan, the research must demonstrate that bilinguals, in a consistent way, outperform monolinguals on assays of high level cognition. That is to say that a different neurocognitive architecture should only be considered cognitively advantageous if it translates into objectively measurable performance gains on measures of cognitive functioning. Moreover, if the argument is that bilingualism, specifically and directly, leads to improved cognitive functioning, the research must rigorously demonstrate that bilingual performance advantages are unmitigated by sociological factors potentially related to bilingualism.

In young children, there may indeed be BEPAs but our enthusiasm for such a conclusion is dampened considerably by a general disregard of, or only derisory attention to, what we refer to as the bilingual social psychological perspective. Indeed, and contrary to claims made by others (e.g., Bialystok, 2009b), if researchers are assiduously ensuring that bilingual and monolingual samples are carefully selected – matched on a variety of sociological factors – precisely how, objectively, this careful selection is occurring is often not clear from the research reports. Moreover, we attributed at least some of the variation among studies to possibly untoward group selection protocols.

In young adults, the data since 2011 – at this juncture – are reasonably clear. The overall pattern is in line with Hilchey and Klein's conclusion that there was no evidence for a BICA in this group. On the other hand, the influx of data strongly repudiates Hilchey and Klein's conclusion that bilingualism leads to BEPAs in this group. Although a few of the new findings tend weakly toward BICAs, it is not clear to what extent these findings are driven by normal variations in the data, hidden sociological factors, or more generally, differences in the group selection protocols. The variation in these data may also have something to do with the idea that bilingualism is not a unitary construct (e.g., the age of acquisition of a second language, proficiency, or balance) despite the fact that, oftentimes, it is treated as such. Even if it turns out that there are consistent, positive relationships between bilingual proficiency or balance and executive function, as foreshadowed by Peal and Lambert (1962), determining the direction of causality is difficult: is bilingualism enhancing executive function or vice versa. Nevertheless, we are optimistic that when appropriate designs (e.g., longitudinal for inferring causality) and optimal statistical methods (e.g., regression, for determining the relative contributions of the multiple characteristics of bilingualism and cultural contexts) are used in conjunction with carefully selected measures of executive function, this difficulty can be overcome.

In the elderly, the performance data on traditional non-linguistic executive processing tasks simply do not support, in any compelling way, the notion of a bilingual processing advantage. Across studies in this age group, the monolinguals either outperform the bilinguals in these tasks or there is perhaps no difference at all. Bilingualism may protect against memory decline into old age (but see Zahodne et al., 2013), as reviewed by Bialystok and Craik in this handbook (Chapter 25) and maybe the unique effect of bilingualism on increasing efficiency in the fronto-parietal networks plays a direct and critical role. Certainly it is possible that a "bilingual" neural architecture might protect, through cognitive compensation, against the effects of age-related neuropathologies; nevertheless, we are obliged to acknowledge that the veracity of any theory postulating a form of cognitive compensation arising from bilingual-fortified executive processing networks remains largely unknown and controversial.

In sum, we have reviewed the recent literature exploring differences across the lifespan between bilinguals and monolinguals on selected tasks targeting high level cognition and we have integrated these recent findings with those reported in the comprehensive review of Hilchey and Klein (2011). The picture that emerges is a veritable potpourri of findings from research reports using otherwise similar and common tasks aimed at assessing executive control. This diversity provides little support for the popular beliefs that bilingualism is not only associated with superior cognitive abilities but may even be responsible for them. On the contrary, the patterns of results across the lifespan are simply too variable and vulnerable to non-replication to confidently ascribe a central role of bilingualism, in and of itself, to superior executive functioning and by extension improved cognitive fitness. As such, only when a host of overlooked sociolinguistic factors are better accounted for will the association between greater executive function and bilingualism be satisfactorily determined.

# 27

# Neural consequences of bilingualism for cortical and subcortical function

Jennifer Krizman and Viorica Marian

> We are what we repeatedly do.
> Excellence, then, is not an act, but a habit.
>
> (Aristotle)

## 27.1 Introduction

Experience is a prime catalyst for change in the human brain and this capacity for change enables us to optimally engage with our environment. Just as continued practice swinging a tennis racket can lead to increased muscle strength in the racket-swinging hand (Lucki & Nicolay, 2007), the nervous system dynamically adapts to meet task demands. Underlying this experience-dependent plasticity are structural and functional changes in brain regions engaged by these experiences. For example, learning to play golf results in plasticity of the sensorimotor cortex (Bezzola et al., 2011), learning to juggle induces plasticity in neural centers devoted to complex visual processing (Draganski et al., 2004), and practicing a musical instrument drives plasticity in auditory areas (Kraus & Chandrasekaran, 2010; Schlaug, 2001; Schlaug, Norton, Overy, & Winner, 2005). While active engagement in skill-based training reshapes training-related neural circuits, native language acquisition, a fundamental aspect of normal human development, plays a key role in shaping neural circuitry throughout the brain (reviewed in Huttenlocher, 2009). This pervasive wiring of cognitive and sensory circuits for language facilitates expertise in a given language and in doing so language exerts a stronghold on sensory abilities such that

<sub>The authors would like to thank Anthony Shook, Scott Schroeder, James Bartollotti, Sarah Chabal, and Dr. Tuan Lam for helpful comments on earlier drafts of this manuscript. Preparation of this chapter was supported in part by grant NICHD 1R01HD059858 to Viorica Marian.</sub>

seeing an object is sufficient to activate its linguistic label (Chabal & Marian, 2015).

Acquisition of more than one language offers a distinct way to tune cognitive and sensory circuits to wire the brain with the ability to communicate in a multilingual environment (e.g., Abutalebi et al., 2011; Luk et al., 2011; Mechelli et al., 2004). For example, by learning more than one language, bilinguals necessarily have to make a variety of sound-to-meaning connections that they must subsequently compartmentalize into their two language systems (Shook & Marian, 2013). Moreover, whereas language input leads to activation of the single language system in a monolingual, in a bilingual both languages are automatically activated (Kuipers & Thierry, 2010; Marian & Spivey, 2003a; Shook & Marian, 2012; Spivey & Marian, 1999) and so one language must be inhibited for communication to proceed (Kroll et al., 2008; van Heuven et al., 2008). This process of cross-linguistic co-activation and the need to inhibit the irrelevant language necessitates increased activation of the executive system during communication for a bilingual relative to a monolingual. The heightened need to actively engage inhibitory and attentional processes – functions of the executive system – during communication leads to an enhancement in some executive abilities. For example, bilinguals show cognitive control advantages on tasks requiring attentional focus, conflict resolution, switching, and flexibility (Bialystok, 2005, 2009c, 2011; Bialystok & Craik, 2010; Bialystok & Majumder, 1998; Bialystok & Martin, 2004; Bialystok, Martin, & Viswanathan, 2005; Bialystok & Viswanathan, 2009; Carlson & Meltzoff, 2008; Krizman et al., 2012; Martin-Rhee & Bialystok, 2008). Moreover, because bilinguals may utilize the components of the executive network differently as a result of their experience managing multiple languages (Abutalebi et al., 2011) this may result in differences in how they interact with their auditory environment relative to monolinguals (Blumenfeld & Marian, 2011). Given this unique auditory–executive link resulting from experience with more than one language, in this chapter we explore the neural consequences of multilingualism on cognitive and sensory function through the lens of the auditory and executive systems.

## 27.2 Anatomy of the auditory and executive systems

### 27.2.1 Overview of the executive system

The executive system exerts top-down control on cognitive and sensory processing. Brain areas that are implicated in cognitive control include the prefrontal cortex, the anterior cingulate cortex, and the basal ganglia, including the caudate and putamen of the striatum (see Figure 27.1) (MacDonald et al., 2000; Redgrave, Prescott, & Gurney, 1999; Zou et al.,

2012). The left dorsolateral prefrontal cortex is involved in the implementation of control and in representing and maintaining the attentional demands of the task (MacDonald et al., 2000). The dorsolateral prefrontal cortex is activated when tasks require maintenance and manipulation of information in working memory. The anterior cingulate cortex is involved in performance monitoring (MacDonald et al., 2000) and is called upon in tasks that require divided attention, novel or open-ended responses, or overcoming an automatic or primed response (Abutalebi et al., 2008; Abutalebi & Green, 2007). It tracks errors and is involved in response conflict by providing feedback to lower level processing centers (MacDonald et al., 2000). The basal ganglia are composed of the substantia nigra, globus pallidus, nucleus accumbens, subthalamic nuclei, and the striate, which include the caudate and putamen. In the striate, the caudate is involved in learning and memory as well as feedback processing (reviewed in Packard & Knowlton, 2002). It is also involved in sentence comprehension and language switching (Zou et al., 2012).

### 27.2.2 Overview of the auditory system

The auditory system encodes sounds, including language, and consists of a series of neural relays extending from the cochlea to the cortex (see Figure 27.1). At the cochlea, the sound wave is translated into electricity, the currency of the nervous system, and from there is conducted along the ascending auditory pathway. These ascending fibers, or "bottom-up" pathway, carry all auditory-based sensory signals to the brain: there is not a unique ascending pathway for speech relative to non-speech sounds. However, the auditory midbrain and primary auditory cortex do show specialized responses to meaningful vocalizations (De Lucia, Clarke, & Murray, 2010; Woolley et al., 2005; Woolley, Gill, & Theunissen, 2006; Woolley, Hauber, & Theunissen, 2010). What mediates this differential neural response for conspecific vocalizations relative to other auditory stimuli is signaling from the "top-down" or descending auditory system, which extends from the cortex to the cochlea. These descending fibers carry regulatory or feedback information from higher to lower processing centers with the effect of modifying the ascending signal along the auditory pathway. This pathway can function to enhance sensory encoding of relevant signals and inhibit or minimize encoding of irrelevant ones, suggesting an intimate link between auditory and executive systems. Structural support for this link is seen in the projections between executive and auditory centers of the cortex, such as the link between the superior temporal gyrus (i.e., auditory cortex, see Figure 27.1) and the anterior cingulate cortex (Jürgens, 1983), as well as connections between the inferior colliculus

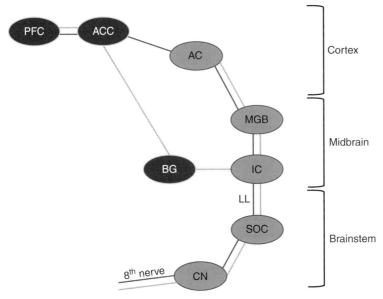

**Figure 27.1** Schematic of the nuclei of the auditory and executive systems. Note: Auditory processing begins at the cochlea, where sound waves are translated into electricity, the currency of the nervous system. This electrical signal is carried from the cochlea to the cochlear nuclei (CN) via the cochlear division of the vestibulocochlear nerve (i.e., 8th nerve) and it subsequently ascends to the superior olivary complex (SOC) of the brainstem. From the brainstem, the signal travels to the inferior colliculus (IC) of the midbrain by way of the lateral lemniscus (LL). The inferior colliculus projects auditory information to the medial geniculate body (MGB) of the thalamus in the midbrain, which subsequently sends auditory information to the primary and secondary auditory cortex (AC) in the left and right superior temporal gyri located on the temporal lobes. At each neural relay, innervation from the ascending system is tonotopically maintained, meaning that the frequency information from the sensory signal is conserved in a spatial arrangement throughout the auditory system. Brain areas that are implicated in cognitive control include the prefrontal cortex, the anterior cingulate cortex, and the basal ganglia, including the caudate and putamen of the striatum. Gray lines indicate top-down (efferent) connections, black lines indicate bottom-up (afferent) projections. Gray ovals are nuclei of the auditory system and black ovals are relays of the executive system.

(i.e., auditory midbrain, see Figure 27.1)[1] and basal ganglia (Casseday et al., 2002; Moriizumi & Hattori, 1991). Additionally, encoding of auditory information in both the midbrain and cortical structures are sensitive to attention (Hairston, Letowski, & McDowell, 2013; Jäncke, Mirzazade, & Joni Shah, 1999; Mesgarani & Chang, 2012; Rinne et al., 2008; Woldorff et al., 1993). These connections between neural regions devoted to auditory processing and executive function likely exist to enhance encoding of acoustic stimuli that carry a learned behavioral significance, such as

---

[1] The inferior colliculus is located in the midbrain. It is an auditory nucleus that integrates across many ascending auditory fibers and is innervated by efferent fibers from cortical structures. The inferior colliculus plays a key role in sound localization, integration of sensory information across different sensory systems (e.g., audio and visual), and potentially filtering of relevant from irrelevant auditory signals (the inferior colliculus is discussed in great detail in Casseday, Fremouw, & Covey, 2002; Huffman & Henson, 1990).

language, and may underlie the specialized neural responses to speech that are evident in these auditory cortical and midbrain structures.

## 27.3 Auditory and executive systems develop under the influence of language experience

### 27.3.1 A monolingual perspective on language development

From infancy, the brain is sculpted by experience and experience provides a strong influence on our subsequent interactions with the world. Through experience, our nervous system becomes capable of dynamically responding to the world in a behaviorally appropriate manner. Within the context of language learning, experience-dependent plasticity in the auditory and executive systems is a natural developmental process that selectively strengthens communication abilities for one's native language. Indeed, while infants are able to discriminate phonetic contrasts across many languages for a short period after birth (Eimas et al., 1971; Trehub, 1976; Werker & Tees, 1984), with continued exposure to a native language, discrimination abilities are selectively honed for that native language (Kuhl et al., 2006). As this process occurs, the infant transitions from being a universal speech perceiver to a language-specific speech perceiver by 6 to 12 months of age (Cheour et al., 1998; Kuhl et al., 1992, 2006). These enhancements of within-language phoneme discrimination provide the building blocks on which sound-to-meaning mappings for that language can be made. However, expertise in the native language comes at the expense of perception of non-native languages: as fluency in the native language increases from phoneme discrimination to knowledge of words and phrases and the acquisition of syntax, the individual becomes relatively insensitive to non-native contrasts (Krishnan et al., 2005; Miyawaki et al., 1975). Accompanying this change in behavior is a change in the underlying neural architecture.

During normal development of a single language, exposure to native phonemic contrasts sculpts the neural architecture to selectively enhance the recognition of these contrasts while diminishing discrimination of non-native contrasts (Cheour et al., 1998; Kuhl et al., 2006). The neural changes underlying language development appear to rely on the same mechanisms that are known to underlie development generally (Nixdorf-Bergweiler et al., 1995). Normal development is characterized by excessive proliferation of synapses early in life, which can be indexed as changes in gray matter[2] density or gray matter volume (Craik & Bialystok, 2006; Gilmore et al., 2007). Across the brain, this heightened synaptic density[3]

---

[2] Gray matter is the collective of neuronal cell bodies, dendrites, unmyelinated axons, glial cells (i.e., supporting cells), and blood vessels (i.e., capillaries).
[3] Synaptic density refers to the number of synapses per unit area on a given neuron.

persists through early childhood but synapses are subsequently pruned through late childhood into early adulthood to include those that are necessary for function, such as the connections enabling communication in one's native tongue[4] (Chechik, Meilijson, & Ruppin, 1999; Craik & Bialystok, 2006; Paolicelli et al., 2011). This synaptic pruning is experience dependent (Zuo et al., 2005), is a neural correlate of learning (Craik & Bialystok, 2006), and is competitively driven by Hebbian mechanisms (Hebb, 1949), where neurons activated in response to an experience can strengthen one another and their strengthened activation can lead to the elimination of quiescent synapses (Chechik et al., 1999; Glazewski & Fox, 1996). Ultimately, synaptic pruning increases synaptic efficiency (Balice-Gordon & Lichtman, 1994; Kerschensteiner et al., 2009; Mimura, Kimoto, & Okada, 2003). The outcome of this synaptic pruning is the formation of an expert system that is optimally primed to respond to the environment in a way that has been behaviorally meaningful in prior experiences (e.g., a native English speaker becomes expertly capable of communicating in English).

Additionally, during this period of early language development, changes are occurring in white matter, which is primarily made up of myelinated[5] axons. Although changes in myelination may be largely genetically pre-programmed (Craik & Bialystok, 2006; Tsuneishi & Casaer, 2000), experience does appear to play some role in myelination as it has been shown that increased electrical activity in axons can drive increases in myelination, while a lack of electrical activity can lead to reductions in myelination of those silent axons (Demerens et al., 1996). Given this relationship between myelination and neural activity, it is possible that white matter density may increase with second language experience (e.g., Mohades et al., 2012).

### 27.3.2 A sensitive period for language learning

Optimal native-language learning occurs within a sensitive period (Werker & Tees, 2005).[6] Though the term critical period and sensitive period have sometimes been used interchangeably (e.g., Bruer, 2001; Ruben, 1997), they refer to two distinct ideas. A *critical period* is defined as a developmental time point in which an experience must occur for a skill (such as language) to be acquired (Lenneberg, 1967). A *sensitive (i.e., optimal) period*, however, is defined as a time when an experience can have the

---

[4] These changes in synaptic density are not uniform throughout the brain. Maturation of brain structures occurs in a caudal-to-rostral direction (Rakic, Bourgeois, & Goldman-Rakic, 1994) with synaptic density peaking in the auditory system at 3 months (Huttenlocher & Dabholkar, 1997), followed by experience-based pruning, a timescale that supports a relationship between changes in synaptic connectivity in auditory structures and language development.

[5] Myelination is the accumulation of a fatty layer around a nerve cell, normally around the axon of the nerve cell, to improve transduction of the electrical signal that is carried by the nerve.

[6] To avoid confusion, Werker and Tees refer to this period as an "optimal period." This is because until recently 'critical period' and 'sensitive period' were used interchangeably when describing language acquisition.

greatest influence on acquiring a particular skill (Bornstein, 1989; Knudsen, 2004). Early childhood is a developmental period when neural resources are in abundance and the nervous system is highly malleable (Chechik, Meilijson, & Ruppin, 1998), two necessary ingredients of a sensitive period (Greenough, Black, & Wallace, 1987; Jolles & Crone, 2012; Knudsen, 2004) and so early childhood has been suggested as being a sensitive (i.e., optimal) period. It is within a sensitive period that the greatest changes in synaptic density, and subsequently gray matter volume, occur (i.e., experience-dependent pruning of the overabundance of existing synaptic connections; Knudsen, 2004). Native language experience within this sensitive window of development facilitates expertise in the language while failure to be exposed to language within this optimal period results in difficulty acquiring native-like language abilities (as evidenced by children raised in isolation, Curtiss, 1977, 1989). Auditory-based language input during the sensitive period appears to be a major factor in language outcomes as evidenced by the relationship between age of cochlear implantation and eventual language abilities (McConkey Robbins et al., 2004) and the inability of a young bird to learn its song in the absence of a tutor early in life (Doupe & Kuhl, 1999; Mooney, 1999). Moreover, evidence from deaf children implanted with cochlear implants at various ages within this optimal developmental window also suggests that auditory-based language experience provides the scaffolding upon which some executive abilities develop (Cleary, Pisoni, & Geers, 2001; Conway, Pisoni, & Kronenberger, 2009).

### 27.3.3 Neural consequences of second language learning

In regard to second language learning, there is a strong relationship between the age at which a second language is acquired and the subsequent proficiency in that language (e.g., see Hakuta, Bialystok, & Wiley, 2003), where a later age of acquisition often relates to lower proficiency. Given that some level of second language proficiency is seen throughout life, this has been taken as evidence against the 'critical period hypothesis' (Birdsong & Molis, 2001; Flege, 1999; Hakuta et al., 2003), which posits that the nervous system is only capable of language acquisition within a finite developmental period extending from infancy to puberty (e.g., see Lenneberg, 1967). In addition to second language learning, evidence of late-in-life learning and subsequent neuroplasticity for other skills has further debunked the hypothesis that acquisition of a skill must occur before the door to the critical period closes (Boyke et al., 2008; Draganski et al., 2004).

Although the greatest neural and behavioral changes tend to occur early in childhood, in contrast to the critical period hypothesis, experience-based neuroplasticity persists throughout life, suggesting that the door for learning never fully closes. That ultimate attainment wanes with increasing age of acquisition would however support the proposed 'sensitive period' (Johnson & Newport, 1989; Krashen, Long, & Scarcella, 1979). Indeed, it would be expected that a sensitive period – especially one that slowly declines but never fully closes – would result in a negative relationship between age of acquisition and proficiency, with the trend that earlier acquisition relates to higher proficiency and later acquisition relates to lower proficiency. Alternatively, the relationship between age of acquisition and proficiency has been interpreted as resulting from greater interference by the more developed native language system with increasing age of second language acquisition (e.g., see Flege, Yeni-Komshian, & Liu, 1999). Whether the relationship between proficiency and age of acquisition results from maturational (i.e., optimal period) changes or interference from prior learning, it is likely that neural encoding of the second language is influenced by proficiency and acquisition age. In support of a relationship between brain structure and behavior, these metrics (i.e., proficiency and age of acquisition) have been shown to track with differences in neural encoding of the second language: poorer neural responses to second language utterances, as indexed by evoked response potentials, are seen with increasing age of second language acquisition (e.g., Peltola et al., 2012; Weber-Fox & Neville, 1996) and decreased proficiency (Peltola et al., 2003).

These changes in the evoked neural response to second language utterances likely reflect differences in the neural architecture underlying the second language abilities, with more robust evoked responses relating to enhancements in the neural structures. Support for this link between auditory evoked potentials and neural structure comes from work in congenitally deaf cats fitted with cochlear implants which find that evoked activity increases as gray matter density increases (i.e., with increased synaptic density; Kral & Sharma, 2012; Kral et al., 2005). Therefore, increases in evoked response potential in individuals who acquired their second language early in life suggest that linguistic experience increases gray matter density, potentially through increases in synaptic connectivity, and that differences in age of second language acquisition are linked to differences in the underlying neural architecture (e.g., Grogan et al., 2012). Moreover, if the auditory and executive systems are involved in second language acquisition and language acquisition is heightened during the sensitive period, then areas devoted to auditory and executive processing should show greater gray matter density in multilinguals relative to monolinguals and this change in gray matter density should be dependent on age of acquisition, with larger increases in gray matter density being seen in bilinguals who learned both languages earlier in life (e.g., see Mechelli et al., 2004). Furthermore, if plasticity in the auditory and executive systems are dependent on language experience, then the degree of plasticity observed in these regions should be dependent upon the number of languages the

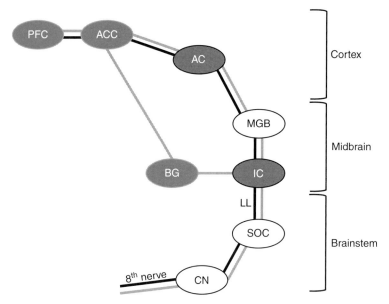

**Figure 27.2** Schematic of the nuclei of the auditory and executive systems. Note: The darker-colored structures are neural relays known to be sensitive to multilingualism. Abbreviations are: CN: cochlear nucleus; SOC: superior olivary complex; IC: inferior colliculus; MGB: medial geniculate body; AC: auditory cortex; BG: basal ganglia; ACC: anterior cingulate cortex; PFC: prefrontal cortex

individual knows (e.g., trilinguals would show greater plasticity than bilinguals).

Indeed, evidence for language-dependent plasticity resulting in enhancements in neural structure for bilinguals relative to monolinguals is seen in both auditory-related and executive systems. Bilinguals who learned both languages within the presumed sensitive period for language (Johnson & Newport, 1989; Ruben, 1997) demonstrate structural differences from monolinguals in Heschl's gyrus (Ressel et al., 2012), an area of the brain that comprises the primary auditory cortex (Figure 27.2). Ressel and colleagues found that early Spanish–Catalan bilinguals had larger Heschl's gyrus volume than Spanish monolinguals. This volume difference was driven by greater volume of both white and gray matter in Heschl's gyrus. Moreover, enhanced gray matter density in the inferior colliculus (i.e., auditory midbrain, Figure 27.2) has been found for simultaneous interpreters (Green, Crinion, & Price, 2006), lending further support to the involvement of auditory areas in multilingual language acquisition and use.

These structural enhancements in the auditory system are not limited to those who learned to speak multiple languages earlier in life. Longitudinal studies assessing second language learning in adults have found structural enhancements following second language learning in areas known to subserve language and auditory function, including increases in gray matter volume in the left inferior frontal gyrus (Osterhout et al., 2008; Stein et al., 2012), and increased cortical thickness in the superior temporal gyrus (which contains the primary auditory cortex, see Figure 27.2; Mårtensson et al., 2012). Additionally, although unable to disentangle pre-existing differences in neural structure from language training induced plasticity, two recent studies have shown that for monolinguals learning a foreign speech contrast, those who learned the foreign contrasts had a larger Heschl's gyrus volume than those who struggled to learn the contrast (Golestani et al., 2007; Wong et al., 2008). Taken together, these results show that cortical and subcortical areas involved in auditory processing are sensitive to language experience and that these structures are likely involved in language acquisition and use for both monolinguals and bilinguals. Through their role in language learning, these auditory regions show higher gray matter density with increasing proficiency in the second language, suggesting a heightened involvement of these regions during multilingual communication.

Additionally, observations have been made for structural plasticity in areas that integrate auditory signals with information from other systems involved in language processing; and these studies have found that the amount of plasticity in these regions is related to age of second language acquisition. For example, Mechelli and colleagues found higher gray matter density in the left inferior parietal cortex for bilinguals relative to monolinguals (Mechelli et al., 2004). The left inferior parietal region includes the angular gyrus and supramarginal gyrus. It lies roughly superior and posterior to the primary auditory cortex and it may provide an important connection between the auditory perception of a speech sound and its motor production (Hickok & Poeppel, 2000) as it is known to project to Broca's area (Aboitiz & García, 1997). Not only are these auditory-related areas sensitive to age of acquisition of the second language, but they also demonstrate increased plasticity with increased number of languages. For example, Grogan and colleagues (2012) examined structural plasticity in bilinguals and multilinguals and found that multilinguals who spoke two or more non-native languages had higher gray matter density in the right posterior supramarginal gyrus compared to bilinguals who only spoke one non-native language. Moreover, in bilinguals, gray matter density in the left pars opercularis (i.e., part of the left inferior frontal gyrus that comprises Broca's area) was positively related to lexical efficiency in their second language. Other recent work has shown that in L1-German speakers, increases in gray matter volume in the supramarginal gyrus and Broca's area relate to better imitation of words and sentences in their second language (i.e., English) as well as a foreign language (i.e., Hindi) (Reiterer et al., 2011). Though for a long time Broca's area was thought to be involved exclusively in language production, there is evidence that this area is also involved in language comprehension, including the processing of complex sentences (D'Ausilio, Craighero, & Fadiga, 2012;

Rogalsky & Hickok, 2011) and understanding of auditorily presented instructions (Schäffler et al., 1993). Thus, not only is the neural architecture of the auditory midbrain (i.e., inferior colliculus) and auditory cortex (i.e., superior temporal gyrus) shaped by language experience, but the cortical areas that these structures send auditory information to, such as the angular gyrus and supramarginal gyrus, are also sculpted by experience with multiple languages. This plasticity suggests that brain regions that interact with auditory structures are also highly involved in multilingual communication.

It is not only auditory areas or auditory-associated areas of the brain that show plasticity with the acquisition of a second language. Studies have also shown that following acquisition of novel phonological-to-orthographic mappings, larger evoked responses to the learned orthography are seen in the visual word-form area, which has been taken as evidence for experience-dependent plasticity (Song et al., 2010). Moreover, while future research should investigate the structural changes associated with improved production in a second language, behavioral measures of learning a difficult-to-perceive phonetic contrast in a second language (e.g., /r/–/l/ distinctions for Japanese speakers) appear to support the idea that changes in performance are driven by Hebbian-based plasticity (McCandliss et al., 2002).

Moreover, the brain areas implicated in cognitive control (i.e., the prefrontal cortex, the anterior cingulate cortex, the caudate and putamen of the striatum, the inferior parietal lobe and the supplementary motor area) (Abutalebi et al., 2011; Zou et al., 2012) also show plasticity that is related to language experience (Figure 27.2). For example, it has been shown that bimodal[7] bilinguals have greater gray matter density than monolinguals in the head of the left caudate nucleus (Zou et al., 2012). This neural structure is called upon when bilinguals switch between languages (Abutalebi et al., 2008) or when bilinguals encounter response competition (Abutalebi et al., 2008). It is likely, then, that the continued use of the caudate by bilinguals during daily communication leads to experience-based enhancements in the synaptic density of this structure. Furthermore, differences have been found between monolinguals and bilinguals in the anterior cingulate cortex. Though differences were not seen in overall gray matter density in this region, only in bilinguals was there a positive relationship between gray matter density in the anterior cingulate cortex and a measure of conflict resolution (Abutalebi et al., 2011). These results suggest that the neural infrastructure of the bilingual anterior cingulate cortex is optimally wired for resolving conflict and that the executive system is enhanced through experience with more than one language. Additional research should address the roles of age of acquisition and effects of knowing

---

[7] Bimodal bilinguals are individuals who know two languages that differ in modality (e.g., oral and signed language), while a unimodal bilingual is an individual whose two languages are in the same modality (e.g., two spoken languages).

three or more languages on the structural plasticity of networks within this system.

Language is a multifaceted ability that relies on the integration of information across systems and so in addition to greater neural connectivity *within* the neural structures involved in auditory and executive processing, it is likely that the connections *between* these structures would be heightened in multilinguals as well. Indeed, in children aged 8–11 years, using fractional anisotropy[8] as an index of white matter organization and structure, white matter along the left inferior occipitofrontal fasciculus was found to be higher in simultaneous bilinguals as compared to monolinguals, while sequential bilinguals had levels that were intermediate relative to the two other language groups (Mohades et al., 2012). This inferior occipitofrontal fasciculus is thought to be involved in semantic processing (Mandonnet et al., 2007) and is a tract that connects the venterolateral and dorsolateral prefrontal cortex with the posterior temporal lobe and the occipital lobe (Maheshwari, Klein, & Ulmer, 2012). Similarly, in older adults, white matter integrity in the corpus callosum is maintained in bilinguals, whereas monolinguals show age-related declines in white matter (Luk et al., 2011). The corpus callosum is the largest white matter structure in the brain and runs along the base of the cortex. It consists of a bundle of myelinated neural fibers that connect the two cerebral hemispheres. The differences in white matter integrity that are observed between older adult bilinguals and monolinguals were evidenced by higher fractional anisotropy values in the bilingual group that extended from the bilateral superior longitudinal fasciculi[9] to the right inferior occipitofrontal fasciculus and uncinate fasciculus[10] (Luk et al., 2011). Enhancement of these neural tracts in bilinguals suggests that multi-language experience leads to a pervasive rewiring in the neural architecture, likely to meet the need for enhanced and efficient communication between the multitude of systems (e.g., auditory, visual, motor, executive) that are involved in language processing, a need that is presumed to increase with the addition of more than one language. Finally, young adults participating in intensive classroom instruction of Chinese demonstrated pervasive increases in white matter throughout the brain, which the authors interpreted as likely reflecting increased myelination; and, these increases positively correlated with class performance (Schlegel & Rudelson, 2012). The observed changes in white matter during language

---

[8] Fractional anisotropy is a measure of the directionality of diffusion of water molecules in the brain, whereby molecules located within a tract are restricted to diffuse in a specific (i.e., anisotropic) direction while water molecules outside of a tract have less restrictions on their movement. Fractional anisotropy is often used in diffusion imaging as an index of fiber density, myelination, or axon diameter (discussed in Hasan & Narayana, 2003).

[9] The bilateral superior longitudinal fasciculi are a pair of bidirectional bundles of neurons that connect the fronterior to the posterior of the cortex. This tract lies superior to the corpus callosum.

[10] The uncinate fasciculus is a white matter tract that connects structures of the limbic system located in the temporal lobe with limbic structures in the frontal lobe.

learning provide additional evidence for the role of language in driving neural enhancements.

### 27.3.4 Potential mechanisms underlying differences in neural infrastructure

Two possible mechanisms may underlie differences in neural structure between monolinguals and multilinguals: increased synaptic pruning in monolinguals (de Bot, 2006) and structural plasticity in multilinguals (Mechelli et al., 2004). The close of the sensitive period is marked by stabilization of neural circuitry and a significant reduction in experience-dependent synaptic pruning (Jolles & Crone, 2012; Knudsen, 2004). It is possible that monolingual language abilities are optimal in a system that has fewer synaptic connections than are needed to facilitate multilingual communication. Experience with a single language within this sensitive window would therefore lead to greater synaptic pruning in the monolingual brain (de Bot, 2006). This honed system would afford the monolingual expertise in the native language but may come at the expense of easily acquiring new languages. A relationship between language experience and amount of synaptic pruning would suggest that acquisition of more than one language inside the sensitive period would result in a greater number of synaptic connections being retained in multilinguals. Moreover, it is possible that the number of connections that are maintained are also dependent on age of acquisition (e.g., Mechelli et al., 2004) in addition to the number of languages acquired within this window (one language vs. two languages, e.g., Mohades et al., 2012).

It is also likely that differences in the neural architecture of monolinguals and multilinguals result from experience-induced plasticity and growth of additional neural connections in the multilingual brain. The differences in gray matter density and volume observed between multilinguals and monolinguals could come from experience-induced increases in synaptic connectivity in areas that subserve multilingual language abilities. Experience with more than one language, then, may serve as one form of environmental enrichment in humans that bolsters gray matter changes in the brain. Through animal work on environmental enrichment, it is known that the mechanisms underlying gray matter increases include dendritic arborization (i.e., an increase in the proliferation of dendrites) which leads to greater dendritic density (Ip et al., 2002), sprouting of new axon terminals (Knudsen, 2004), the formation of new blood vessels (i.e., angiogenesis, Black, Sirevaag, & Greenough, 1987), and increased proliferation of both supporting cells (i.e., gliogenesis; Soffié et al., 1999) and nerve cells (i.e., neurogenesis; Kempermann, Kuhn, & Gage, 1997; Nilsson et al., 1999) in the neural region undergoing experience-dependent changes.

Through the enriched environment of multiple languages, multilinguals also demonstrate white matter plasticity. Increased myelination, through myelination of previously unmyelinated axons, or thickening of the myelin sheath of myelinated axons (Juraska & Kopcik, 1988; Markham et al., 2009; Sanchez et al., 1998) underlie the experience-dependent changes in white matter. These changes in myelination may improve conduction velocity, or improve the connection between separate areas of the brain that are simultaneously engaged during the plasticity-inducing experience (e.g., multilingual communication).

## 27.4 Connectivity between auditory and executive systems

Interestingly, the processes that are involved in auditory comprehension of language are presumed to provide the scaffolding for the development of domain-general executive functions (Conway et al., 2009; Pisoni & Cleary, 2004), suggesting that there is a strong link between development of cognitive skills and phonetic discrimination abilities (Kuhl & Rivera-Gaxiola, 2008). Indeed, the auditory and executive systems appear to be highly intertwined, with connections between auditory and executive systems evident both cortically and subcortically (Figure 27.2). These connections have been structurally observed between the anterior cingulate cortex and the auditory cortex (Jürgens, 1983) and between the basal ganglia and the inferior colliculus (Casseday et al., 2002). There have been functional connections observed between the frontal cortex and inferior colliculus (Raizada & Poldrack, 2007) as well as frontal cortex and auditory cortex (Wu et al., 2007). These structural and functional links between the auditory and executive system suggest a privileged role of auditory-based stimuli in facilitating interaction with the environment in a behaviorally relevant manner.

At any given moment, the various sensory systems will receive and subsequently bombard the brain with more information than the brain is capable of processing (e.g., see Marois & Ivanoff, 2005). The ability to perform higher-level actions, such as those involved in communication, requires the cognitive system to not be solely influenced by the incoming stimulus but to also incorporate prior experience (e.g., whether that signal was behaviorally meaningful in the past) in influencing how the stimulus is encoded and responded to. Activation of the executive system influences sensory encoding to focus the brain's processing capacity on the encoding of sensory stimuli necessary for achieving behaviorally relevant goals as opposed to responding to sensory stimuli in a reflex-like manner (Koechlin & Summerfield, 2007).

The auditory system is sensitive to the effects of the executive system on neural processing. For example, attention to stimuli in another modality decreases neural encoding of auditory stimuli in the inferior colliculus (i.e., auditory midbrain) and auditory cortex (Hairston et al., 2013; Oatman, 1976). On the other hand, attentional focus to auditory stimuli selectively enhances important features of the auditory signal in both the auditory midbrain and cortex (Galbraith & Arroyo, 1993; Galbraith et al., 1998; Jäncke et al., 1999). Although the afferent, bottom-up auditory signal begins as a faithful encoding of the incoming stimulus, through descending projections, the executive system configures neural processing in auditory midbrain and cortical structures to meet the current task demands. Physiological studies demonstrate that the top-down (i.e., efferent) pathway can affect many aspects of subcortical processing, including filtering, sharpness of tuning, and response plasticity (Gao & Suga, 1998, 2000; Hairston et al., 2013; Rinne et al., 2008; Sakai & Suga, 2001; Suga, 2008). Top-down feedback will tune the ascending auditory signal at midbrain and cortical nuclei to selectively encode stimulus features deemed behaviorally important based on experience and prior-knowledge (Gao & Suga, 1998, 2000).

The top-down feedback signal will preferentially reinforce patterns of neural firing that represent the behaviorally relevant features of incoming signals. Preferentially selecting the same behaviorally relevant features of a signal can lead to greater synchrony in the stimulus-evoked response across a population of neurons, thereby increasing the consistency of the neural response to that signal (i.e., better neural synchrony) and decreasing the neural encoding of irrelevant cues (e.g., noise, Faisal et al., 2008). This heightened neural synchrony across a population of neurons can enhance the saliency of neural responses (Engel & Singer, 2001). Exerting this experience-dependent influence (i.e., enhancing synchrony of response to behaviorally relevant features) earlier in the signaling pathway (e.g., auditory midbrain relative to cortex) is preferable for optimal sound transmission and decoding (Faisal et al., 2008). This is because the synchronous neural response is projected to additional structures along the ascending pathway and at these subsequent structures the synchronous firing can exert a greater influence than neural firings that are temporally disorganized (Engel & Singer, 2001).

This auditory–executive link functions to encode a consistent and precise representation of sound for everyone (e.g., Hornickel & Kraus, 2013). The relationship between executive function and auditory processing likely aids both monolinguals and multilinguals in managing the within-language competition that occurs during communication. However, because multilinguals also must manage cross-linguistic co-activation when communicating, their auditory–executive link may be strengthened (i.e., greater top-down influence, resulting in greater consistency in the representation of the incoming auditory signal) and plasticity of these systems may result from experience with multiple languages (e.g., Krizman et al., 2014).

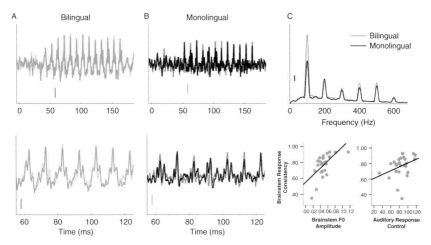

**Figure 27.3** Bilinguals demonstrate unique relationships between auditory and executive systems. Note: Bilinguals have more consistent brainstem responses to auditory stimuli as evidenced by greater similarity between responses from the first half (A-lighter lines, B-darker lines) and second half (A-lighter lines, B-darker lines) of a recording session. In A and B, the top panel is the entire response to the speech syllable (0–180 ms) and the bottom panel is the response to the vowel portion of the speech syllable (60–180 ms) to better illustrate the amount of overlap between the first half and last half responses for bilinguals (A) and monolinguals (B) (adapted from Krizman et al., 2014). In bilinguals, consistency of the neural response relates to enhancement of the response to the fundamental frequency ($F_0$, $r = 0.68$, $p < 0.0005$), a cue that may be behaviorally relevant for a bilingual (C and D, adapted from Krizman et al., 2012). Bilingual response consistency is also linked to auditory attentional focus ($r = 0.42$, $p < 0.05$), an ability that requires inhibitory control (D). Vertical lines indicate 0.1 $\mu V$ scale

## 27.4.1 Heightened integration of auditory and executive systems in multilinguals: a proposal

While the auditory–executive link necessarily must develop in everyone to allow us to navigate complex sensory environments and is a normal process that occurs throughout maturation, we propose that this connection may be particularly strong for speakers of more than one language due to the additional demands of cross-linguistic co-activation during communication, resulting in synergistic activation of both the auditory and executive systems. As described above, it has been shown that both the auditory and executive systems are structurally enhanced in multilinguals relative to monolinguals (Ressel et al., 2012; Stein et al., 2012; Zou et al., 2012). Furthermore, it has been shown that this executive-auditory network functions more efficiently during auditory comprehension for multilinguals relative to monolinguals (Blumenfeld & Marian, 2011). Moreover, we have seen relationships between attentional control and auditory processing that are unique to speakers of more than one language (Figure 27.3; Blumenfeld & Marian, 2011; Krizman et al., 2012, 2014); and, importantly, we have seen these relationships at subcortical levels of auditory processing, which may boost signal transmission and processing at a greater number of ascending auditory nuclei in a multilingual (Faisal et al., 2008).

From this relationship between attentional control and subcortical auditory function, we propose that, in multilinguals, the executive system biases the neural response of auditory cues important to early and accurate selection of the appropriate language. One potential cue[11] may be the fundamental frequency ($F_0$), a speech feature that may be subtly manipulated by a bilingual speaker (see Figure 27.3; Altenberg & Ferrand, 2006; Krizman et al., 2012). Through the experience of juggling two languages, the neural pathway encoding these cues (e.g., $F_0$) is continuously selected via top-down feedback from higher order processing centers (Miller & Cohen, 2001), resulting in these pathways being strengthened through Hebbian plasticity mechanisms (Hebb, 1949). We suggest that the bilingual's unique experience of cross-linguistic co-activation (Marian & Spivey, 2003b; Spivey & Marian, 1999) leads to a rewiring of neural circuitry so that over time the neural architecture of the bilingual brain reflects the experience of using two languages and the heightened need for executive and auditory circuits to interact to manage language co-activation during communication.

This strengthened interaction between auditory and executive systems may facilitate enhancements in bilingual foreign language learning (Bartolotti & Marian, 2012; Marian & Kaushanskaya, 2009) in that bilinguals are able to focus their encoding on the relevant acoustic features (Bartolotti et al., 2011). These enhancements in novel language learning suggest that bilinguals have learned how to actively engage the executive system when the sensory signal is ascending the bottom-up pathway so that the behaviorally relevant features of the signal are emphasized.

## 27.5 Conclusions

In conclusion, both auditory and executive systems are sculpted by language experience. Learning and using more than one language leads to structural enhancements in auditory and executive systems at both cortical and subcortical processing centers. The degree of plasticity observed in these systems appears to be dependent on both age of acquisition and the number of languages acquired. Through normal development, the relationship between executive and auditory relays is established to facilitate efficient and meaningful interactions with the auditory world. Given the unique relationships seen in multilinguals between auditory and executive functions, we propose that the connection between these two systems is strengthened by experience with more than one language. The strengthened network leads to fundamental differences in how multilinguals and monolinguals process sounds.

---

[11] Future work should determine whether there are additional cues that are important for bilingual communication.

# 28

# How bilingualism shapes the mental lexicon

Gary Libben and Mira Goral

## 28.1 Introduction

The title of this chapter, "how bilingualism shapes the mental lexicon" can be interpreted in two ways. One interpretation treats the terms "bilingualism" and "mental lexicon" as fields of inquiry and asks the question: how has the study of bilingualism shaped our conceptualization of the human mental lexicon? As we discuss below, the mental lexicon as a theoretical construct was initially articulated in the context of monolingualism as the default. Indeed, the term "lexicon" itself was coined as the cognitive equivalent of a paper dictionary, co-indexing form and meaning within a single language. However, advances in the field of bilingualism and the acknowledgment that bilingualism (or even multilingualism) is the norm rather than the exception, have necessitated the re-evaluation of accepted notions of the mental lexicon.

The other interpretation of the chapter's title treats the terms "bilingualism" and "mental lexicon" as properties of an individual and asks the question: how do learning, using, and losing additional languages shape the manner in which words are represented and processed in an individual's brain? Research studies have consistently demonstrated that bilinguals differ from monolinguals when performing tasks, such as word-list generation, picture naming, and word association, demonstrating the influences of bilingual experience on lexical processing.

In the sections below, we review theories of lexical processing and their adaptation to the bilingual context and explore how we can best conceptualize the manner in which bilingualism changes the mental lexicon from a monolingual to a bilingual functional configuration. A key focus of our discussion – one that has not been at the center of the bilingual lexicon research published to date – will be the consequences that morphological differences between the languages of a bilingual have for the organization of the mental lexicon. We conclude that the conceptualization of the mental lexicon as a construct needs to be adjusted to accommodate bilingualism as the default adult state.

## 28.2 The lexicon as process

The notion of a mental lexicon has turned out to be one of the most compelling constructs in psycholinguistics. Over the years, it has served as a meeting ground for theoreticians, experimentalists, and clinicians, and has provided a domain in which fundamental properties of human cognition could be explored and debated. At the same time, the notion of a mental lexicon has served as a modeling space in which proposals concerning the nature of lexical knowledge and processing could be concretized and contrasted.

A substantial portion of the studies of the mental lexicon has focused on the recognition and production of single words, often single nouns. Such studies have, for instance, sought evidence for connections among semantically related words (e.g., Forster, 2004; Holcomb & Anderson, 1993; Neely, Keefe, & Ross, 1989), and for the roles of variables, such as word frequency and orthographic and phonological neighborhood density on the speed of lexical processing (e.g., Ferrand & Grainger, 1992; Forster & Taft, 1994; Westbury & Hollis, 2007; Ziegler, Muneaux, & Grainger, 2003). Models that use notions such as spreading activation, competitor inhibition, and lexical selection have been introduced to explain processes of lexical access (e.g., Collins & Loftus, 1975; Dell & O'seaghdha, 1992; Levelt, 2001). Another subset of studies has focused on morphologically complex words. Here, for example, purely decompositional models of the mental lexicon such as the one attributed to Taft and Forster as a result of their work in the mid 1970s carry with them the claim that the fundamental unit of representation is the morpheme. Thus in this framework, multimorphemic words must be decomposed into their constituent morphemes during the processes of lexical comprehension and recomposed during production.

Models of the mental lexicon can be generally grouped into two main types: list-based and connectionist-based models. List-based models are typically linked to lexical access algorithms that are serial in nature. Connectionist models are typically linked to threshold-based parallel access algorithms, in which the metaphor of 'search' has little relevance. In addition, an important recent trend in the modeling of the mental lexicon has involved the dominance of models that are computationally implemented. In computationally implemented models, the box-and-arrow notation that characterized a good deal of earlier modeling has given way to reports of the behavior of a model given a particular input. These computationally implemented models are distinguished by their assumptions concerning, for example, the fundamental units of representation, distributed knowledge within the network, the links among elements, and the manner in which lexical access can be said to have occurred.

As the discussion above suggests, the conceptual and metaphoric concreteness of the mental lexicon as "a dictionary in the mind" has enabled a great deal of scientific progress. However, this static image has also generated disadvantages.

In many very important ways, the human mental lexicon is not a static store. Indeed, perhaps more than any other component of the human language system, it is characterized by change. To a large extent, both phonological and syntactic systems are fixed relatively early on in life for one's native language(s). An individual's vocabulary store, in contrast, changes throughout adulthood. People are always learning new words and may lose command over words that they have not encountered very often or very recently. Throughout their lives, people create new connections among words through the multidimensional associations that are enabled by the lexical system. We address the nature of these changes and their relevance to the bilingual lexicon under the heading of fluidity below.

There are three other aspects of the dictionary metaphor that have substantial consequences. The first pertains to the lexical entries themselves. There is a tendency, particularly in research on English, to assume that the prototypical lexical entry is a simple monomorphemic word. In fact, however, most words of English – and of many other languages – are multimorphemic (Libben, 2007). Thus, most of the building blocks within the mental lexicon are themselves composed of meaningful subunits.

The second consequence of the concrete dictionary metaphor concerns the "individualness" of lexical entries. Dictionaries are characterized by an orderly arrangement of individual entries. The human mental lexicon is characterized by extensive multidimensional connectedness among words and among their morphological components.

Finally, the third consequence of the metaphor concerns the extent to which the dictionary of a language is coextensive with the mental dictionary of a person. As we will discuss under the heading of homogeneity below, there is good reason to believe that this is not the case. Most people in the world speak more than one language and, thus, monolingualism is the minority linguistic state. Under the assumption of homogeneity that we discuss below, an individual possesses a single lexical processing system. This system changes to accommodate the acquisition of new vocabulary items and also entirely new vocabulary systems (as is the case in the acquisition of a new language). Thus our mental lexicons do not belong to individual languages – they belong to individual people.

## 28.3 The bilingual mental lexicon as an extension of the monolingual lexicon

The current conceptualization of the bilingual mental lexicon is on the verge of a major paradigm shift: Rather than adapting models of the (monolingual) mental lexicon to accommodate the lexicons of speakers of more than one language, a growing body of literature supports the idea of treating the mental lexicon as a process capable of handling more than one language. We briefly review past models of the bilingual mental lexicon and summarize the argumentation for postulating a lexicon that comprises multiple languages as the default state.

### 28.3.1 Previous models of the bilingual lexicon and their assumptions

Early models of the bilingual lexicon reflect in their architecture the relationship between the two languages, positing that it is determined by the time (and manner) of becoming bilingual. For example, in Weinreich's model – considered the first formal model of the bilingual lexicon (Weinreich, 1954) – a shared lexical representation is assumed for individuals who acquire both languages from birth (termed *compound bilinguals*), whereas two separate lexicons are assumed for individuals who learned their second language following the acquisition of their first (termed *coordinate bilinguals*). Interdependency between the two lexicons is assumed for people who are in the process of learning their second language via their first (termed *subordinate bilinguals*) (Ervin & Osgood, 1954; Weinreich, 1954).

A distinction between a conceptual or semantic level and a lexical level within the mental lexicon underlines these early models; this distinction is shared by later models of the bilingual lexicon, along with the assumption that bilinguals have a single "store" for semantic knowledge but separate – albeit connected – stores for lexical-level, language-specific word knowledge. Such later models, among them the hierarchical model (Kroll & Stewart, 1994; Potter et al., 1984), have focused on the nature and strength of connections between these separate lexical stores, hypothesizing a fundamental asymmetry in the connection between the lexicon of L1 vs. L2 and the (single) semantic storage. The box-and-arrow depictions of these stores gave way to a connectionist approach, in models such as the distributed features model (e.g., Kroll & de Groot, 1997), in which interactive activation between elements in the lexical structure is influenced by shared semantic, phonemic, and orthographic features within and across languages, but the fundamental assumption about two lexicons has been maintained.

Nevertheless, models such as the bilingual activation model (BIA, e.g., Dijkstra & van Heuven 1998, 2002; Dijkstra, van Heuven, & Grainger, 1998) shift from a discussion of the bilingual mental lexicon as "stores" to a bilingual lexical processing system, and thus allow for a dynamic, interactive account of word processing.

Indeed, recent studies of the bilingual lexicon have extended the scope of questions asked and have concentrated on affirming whether words from both languages are active during processing or whether processing in bilinguals can be language selective (e.g., Kroll et al., 2008; Libben & Titone, 2009). Evidence suggests that, at least at the lexical level and in experimental settings, words from both languages are always active. For example, words from both languages compete for selection during picture-naming tasks (e.g., Colomé, 2001; Hermans et al., 1998; Kroll, Bobb, & Wodniekca, 2006) and during lexical recognition required for lexical-decision tasks (e.g., Dijkstra et al., 2005; Ko, Wang, & Kim, 2011; van Heuven, Dijkstra, & Grainger, 1998). A recent debate in the literature has focused on the stage of lexical processing at which the non-target language may be inhibited (e.g., Costa, Caramazza, & Sebastián-Gallés, 2000; Finkbeiner, Gollan, & Caramazza, 2006). Many researchers would now endorse a notion of a unified bilingual lexicon, at least as far as simultaneous processing of words from both languages is concerned (e.g., Kroll, Bobb, & Wodniecka, 2006; Misra, Guo, Bobb, & Kroll, 2012). In summary, models of the bilingual lexicon put forward to date seem to assume some separation of the lexical store of each of the bilingual's languages, and a shared semantic store with varying connections to the lexical stores.

Recently, attention has been paid to possible changes in the semantic and conceptual representation (associated with L1) that may result from the experience of learning and using a second language (Ameel et al., 2009; Bylund & Jarvis, 2011; Grainger, Midgley, & Holcomb, 2010). These changes fit within the growing literature on the mutual influences of L1 on L2 (e.g., Selinker, 1972; van Hell & Tanner, 2012) and of L2 on L1 (e.g., Cook, 2003; Schmid, 2010). We will address some of these findings next.

### 28.3.2 Bilingualism is more common than monolingualism

Bilinguals comprise more than half of the world's population (Grosjean, 2010) and individuals who use more than one language on a regular basis are the norm, not the exception, in many communities. Therefore, any model that attempts to elucidate human communication abilities must accommodate the ability to communicate in more than one language. Furthermore, following Grosjean's assertion that bilinguals are not two monolinguals in one person (Grosjean, 1989), it has been demonstrated repeatedly that bilinguals' performance in each of their languages could not be assumed to be identical to that of a monolingual speaker of either language (e.g., Gollan & Goldrick, 2012; Gollan et al., 2005; Ivanova & Costa, 2008; Kohnert, Hernandez, & Bates, 1998). Consequently, we maintain that there is no compelling reason to start off with a monolingual model and adjust it to accommodate more than one language; rather, following Grosjean's holistic view of bilingualism (e.g., Grosjean, 2008), we argue for models that allow – from the outset – for the representation and processing of more than one language. In our attempt to lay the groundwork for such models we put forward two assumptions as described next.

## 28.4 The bilingual mental lexicon as a homogeneous and fluid process

In what follows, we propose an alternative approach to conceptualizing the mental lexicon by promoting two assumptions, namely, the (1) homogeneity and (2) fluidity of the (bilingual) mental lexicon.

### 28.4.1 Homogeneity

The homogeneity hypothesis (Libben, 2000) claims that although the mental lexicon of an individual can be functionally partitioned to accommodate different languages, dialects, and even situational social restrictions on vocabulary selection, it is nevertheless a single integrated cognitive system. Indeed, if we consider the mental lexicon from a dynamic rather than static perspective, conceptualizing it as a process (rather than a static entity), we would have to think of the mental lexicon as the instantiation of the human capacity for lexical action.

The homogeneity hypothesis is concerned with the consequences of hypothesizing a single integrated cognitive system for our modeling of bilingual lexical representation and processing. This follows from the suggestions first put forward by Paradis (1987) as the Subset Hypothesis, a claim that the individual languages of a bilingual form a de facto subset of a larger lexical store that emerges from patterns of language use.

At the simplest level, thinking about the mental lexicon in terms of homogeneity suggests that bilingualism brings with it organizational pressures on the mental lexicon. A person who maintains native speaker ability in a first language and then develops a high level of ability in a new language will have learned many new words as a result. Under the assumption that new words are incorporated into a single cognitive lexical system, there are many new opportunities for lexical associations. The individual will know many more near synonyms (which is a way to conceive of translation equivalent words) and, as a result, there is great opportunity for inappropriate lexical activation. This must be managed so that the bilingual holds the advantages of the larger lexical set, while maintaining the ability to speak using only the words of one language under conditions in which that is required (see Green, 1998).

Within the framework of recent studies of bilingual lexical processing, evidence supporting simultaneous activation of words from both languages of a bilingual, even when the task apparently requires the use of only one language, is consistent with the notion of the shared nature of the bilingual lexicon not only for cognate words – which have long been conceptualized as shared between two languages (e.g., Peeters, Dijkstra, & Grainger, 2013) – but for all words (e.g., Dijkstra & van Heuven, 2002). Consistently, neuroimaging studies of bilinguals have demonstrated largely overlapping areas of activation during processing of words from both or all languages of speakers of more than one language (Abutalebi & Green, 2007; Green & Abutalebi, 2008; Indefrey, 2006; Sebastián, Laird, & Kiran, 2011).

We may consider the issues outlined above as all dealing with the *organizational level* of the mental lexicon. For the most part, the early discourse associated with contrasting theories of the bilingual mental lexicon has been at this organizational level. But even with the recent shift from the organizational level to the processes that may allow a bilingual to appropriately select lexical items that are relevant to the target language in the relevant context, research on the bilingual mental lexicon continues to employ single, monomorphemic nouns as the default case. In our view, the morphological level requires greater scrutiny if we are to understand the full implications of a homogeneous lexical system for both monolinguals and multilinguals.

### 28.4.1.1 Homogeneity and the morphological level

As we have noted above, most words of a language are not simple. Rather, they are composed of more than one morpheme (e.g., Sandra, 1994). Even in Chinese, a language famous for the simplicity of its morphological system, the number of multimorphemic words is equal to the number of monomorphemic words. The morphological structure of words plays a very large role in how a language creates new words and how words are related to one another both grammatically and semantically (e.g., Bauer, 2001). However, languages differ in their specific morphological processes and their productivity. For example, English and Hebrew both have prefixed, suffixed and compound words, yet the manner in which the morphological systems of the languages are organized differs quite markedly.

Consider verb derivation in English and Hebrew. English verbs may be derived from nouns, as in *to chair; to impart*; others are derived from adjectives, as in *to enlarge*. In English, many noun-related verbs do not differ in form from their corresponding nouns (*chair–to chair*). Adjective-related verbs are often constructed by an addition of a prefix, as in *en-* (*large– to enlarge*) or a suffix as in *-en* (*white– to whiten*). However, many verbs in English do not immediately semantically relate to any noun or any other lexical item, as in *to lean*. Word families – words that may be hypothesized to be linked in the lexical architecture – may be constructed by linking noun-related verbs to their corresponding nouns and adjectives.

Root-based verbal systems, such as Hebrew, are characterized by high internal semantic and morphological relatedness among verbs and between verbs and nouns. Many verbs in Hebrew can be clustered together with a large number of additional verbs, as well as nouns and adjectives that share core semantic features as well as portions of their form, in a rather systematic fashion, with the use of derivational morphemes. For example, ללבוש *to wear*, להלביש *to dress*, להתלבש *to get dressed*, and לבוש *clothing* all share the root לבש LVŠ; and ללמוד *to learn*, ללמד *to teach*, להתלמד *to become educated*, and תלמיד *student* all share the root LMD (למד). Verbal groups (binyanim) in Hebrew contribute to the meaning of a verb and its argument structure, for example whether the verb is reflexive and whether it is transitive or intransitive. This complex and productive morphological system has led researchers to suggest that words in the mental lexicon of Hebrew speakers are organized around or processed via shared roots (Bick, Goleman, & Frost, 2011; Feldman, Frost, & Pnini 1995; Frost, Deutsch, & Forster, 2000), not unlike the satellite organization suggested by Lukatela and colleagues (1980) for other morphologically rich languages.

Another difference between root-based morphology and non-root-based morphological systems concerns the process of stringing the morphemes together. In languages such as English, the primary morphological tool is affixation, adding prefixes directly before another morpheme (e.g., re + learn = relearn) or affixes at the end of morphemes (e.g., rapid + ly = rapidly). Hebrew morphology uses prefixes (בבית ba 'in'+ bayit 'house' = babayit 'in the house') and suffixes חתולה (xatul 'cat[m]' + a + xatula 'cat[f]') as well as infixes, when roots combine with verbal and nominal morphological patterns in a non-linear fashion (e.g., LMD + the verbal pattern C+a+C+a+C as in למד *lamad* 'learned' or the nominal pattern C + ə + C + i + C + a = למידה *lemida* 'learning'). For a complete description of such processes see, for example, Deutsch, Frost, and Forster (1998) and Shimron (2003). This non-linear concatenation is part of the underlying knowledge of a Hebrew speaker about morphological relationships among words, but not of that of an English speaker. It is possible then that connections within the mental lexicon that are typical of lexical items in Hebrew elude English speakers who are learning Hebrew as a second language, at least at early stages of second language learning.

What are the consequences of such differences for the mental lexicon? If indeed, the mental lexicon is constrained such that it can only possess a homogeneous functional architecture, then we would expect that language tagging mechanisms could handle differences at the morphological level. Another possibility is that the acquisition of a new language brings with it a change at the morphological level so that, if high levels of ability are developed across languages, these are supported by an expanded morphological system that differs from that of monolingual native speakers, but encompasses features of both. Moreover, features of one language now in the extended system will influence the processing of the other language.

Thus, for example, we may speculate on stronger connections among verbs that share root-like aspects in English in the mental lexicon of Hebrew–English bilinguals than in that of English monolingual speakers. This would predict that Hebrew–English bilinguals make use of shared morphemes in borrowed words in English (*mazal tov – shlimazal*) in a way that is less obvious to monolinguals. Similarly, English–Hebrew bilinguals may make connections between words of shared origin that are no longer transparent in English (two-between), or ascribe a great role to obviously related words, such as *large* and *to enlarge* and *part* and *impart*.

Another realm of morphology that presents similar potentials is lexical gender. It is likely that in languages that denote lexical gender morphologically, such as Spanish, Italian, and Hebrew, gender is encoded as part of the word representation in the mental lexicon. Studies that examined the processing of translation equivalents that are marked for different gender in each language have revealed evidence for competition between the masculine and feminine attributes associated with the same word in two different languages (e.g., Lemhöfer, Spalek, & Schriefers, 2008; Sato, Gygax, & Gabriel, 2013). How can we conceptualize the mental representation of such translation equivalents within the homogeneity approach? And what may happen to words from languages that do not mark lexical gender (e.g., English) when the speaker becomes bilingual and now marks those lexical items for gender? It is possible that the word *house* becomes masculine also in English in the mind of the Hebrew-English bilingual because of its masculine translation equivalent in Hebrew and feminine in the mind of the Spanish–English bilingual because of it being a feminine noun in Spanish. Lexical gender has consequences beyond the core lexical representation. Adjectives may be linked differently to a noun they modify in languages with noun and adjective gender morphology and, similarly, sentences with multiple nouns and adjectives may be interpreted based on agreement. Would the co-indexation between nouns and adjectives in English become stronger in an English–Hebrew bilingual than in a monolingual speaker of English?

It is also possible then that, within a single system, the existence of translation equivalents that are similar in their meaning but differ in their morphology lead to a less specified system. In addition to translation equivalents that are feminine in one language and masculine in another (e.g., *moon* in German and French), there are translation equivalents that are single words in one language and compounds in another (e.g., Hebrew רקע *reka* for the English *background*); translation equivalents that are count noun in one language and mass noun in another (e.g., *people* in English and Italian); and translation equivalents that are singular in one language and plural in another (e.g., *mayim* מים in Hebrew, *water*, in English water). Thus, *water* in the mind of an English–Hebrew bilingual may include the possibility of being plural or singular, masculine or not.

Research findings demonstrate differences in judgments between bilinguals and monolinguals and between bilinguals who use both their languages and those who use mostly one language that corroborate this uncertainty. Such differences have been shown for compound processing in Hebrew–English bilinguals (Goral et al., 2008) and for mass and count nouns (Barner, Inagaki, & Li, 2009). Similar arguments can be made for points of interface between the mental lexicon and other aspects of language. One example is the study of Schmiedtova, von Stutterheim, and Carroll (2011), who examined the inclusion of endpoints in event description and its relation to the existence of grammatical aspect in the speakers' languages. The authors found differences between monolinguals and bilinguals and among bilingual speakers of various languages in the frequency with which they included endpoints of events (versus verb tenses that reflect ongoing events). A detailed survey of such differences in additional domains is beyond the scope of this chapter.

The examples above illustrate the manner in which issues of homogeneity at the morphological level can have substantial consequences for theories of lexical representation in the mind and for our models of associations within the mental lexicon. In addition, homogeneity at this level will affect the manner in which morphological parsing can take place. Morphological parsing has been an essential component of mental lexicon research because of the manner in which it interacts with models of lexical access and thus core organization. In early approaches to English, for example, it was assumed that multimorphemic words are processed serially from beginning to end and that lexical access followed the obligatory stripping of prefixes from stems. Within such models, this prefix stripping was required so that, for example, the word "retype" could be looked up in the mental lexicon under its stem form "type." In contrast, the last two decades of research on lexical processing among typologically diverse languages has shown that lexical parsing systems seem to adapt to the particular properties of individual languages, and exploit morphological markers both in speech and in writing, where possible (e.g., Frost & Grainger, 2000).

Accommodating the notions of homogeneity and uncertainty with such language-specific organizational principles presents both difficult and exciting challenges for theories of the bilingual mental lexicon. An additional characteristic of the lexicon that becomes notable for models that assume a bilingual state as their default state is the fluid nature of the mental lexicon. We turn to the notion of this fluidity next.

### 28.4.2 Fluidity

The process of lexical acquisition has occupied a great deal of the language acquisition literature, with a focus on documenting the process and progression of word learning and theories of lexical learning (e.g., Benedict, 1979; Clark, 1993; Diesendruck, 2007; Hansen & Markman, 2009). Clark (2010), for example, concludes that children's learning of new words can only be understood in the context in which these words are introduced (see also Baayen (2010) and McDonald and Shillcock (2001) for related perspectives). Strategies such as linking the meaning of new words to known words, and using syntactic frames (e.g., word final, contrastive stress) to emphasize the new word being introduced are evident in child-directed language. Variation in strategies appears related to the child's age and the word class of the new lexical item (Clark, 2010). Several principles of lexical learning have been promoted in the literature to account for the impressive rate with which children identify and learn new lexical items. These include the whole object assumption (e.g., Markman & Wachtel, 1988; Soja, Carey, & Spelke, 1991) according to which children assume that a new term they hear refers to the whole object of the potential referent rather than to one of its parts or its attributes. Another is the mutual exclusivity assumption (Markman & Wachtel, 1988), according to which children assume that each object has only one name. So, if they hear a new term referring to an object for which they already have a label, they assume the new term refers to one of the object's parts, attributes, etc. In later ages, the process of lexical learning has been clearly linked to reading and literacy, and to morphological learning (e.g., Jarmulowicz, & Taran, 2013; Nir-Sagiv, Bar-Ilan, & Berman, 2008). Speakers' vocabularies continue to grow as they encounter new terms and lexical nuances. Even in older age, evidence suggests that vocabulary knowledge has an upward trajectory (Botwinick, & Stordandt, 1974; Goral et al., 2007).

The widely accepted observation that older people have trouble "remembering" names of people, places, and objects has been supported by extensive experimental findings demonstrating that some older adults experience increased instances of "tip-of-the-tongue" states (i.e., the feeling that you know the name of an item, have partial phonological information but fail to retrieve the complete form) (Burke et al., 1991; Gollan & Brown, 2006), name fewer items correctly on confrontation naming tests (e.g., Au et al., 1995; Connor et al., 2004), and may retrieve words of lower frequency or relevance in discourse production (e.g., Kavé & Nussbaum, 2012). However, it has been hypothesized that it is the retrieval process that becomes less efficient due to slowing or decreased executive functioning, that the search is more demanding with increasing vocabulary size, or both (e.g., Kavé, Knafo, & Gilboa, 2010; Wingfield & Stine-Morrow, 2000). Burke and colleagues proposed that the strength of connections among lexical and semantic representations within the architecture of the mental lexicon deteriorates with increased age and with decreased frequency of use (e.g., the Transmission Deficit Hypothesis, Burke et al., 1991) but evidence supporting the exact nature of such changes is elusive.

Returning to the notion of process, it is possible to speculate that what changes with lexical learning, on the one hand, and with aging and attrition, on the other hand, is the efficiency and ease of information flow and the integrity of inter-connections among words.

These processes of change assume a greater magnitude in bilinguals. Childhood bilinguals learn multiple words, including two different labels for the same object or action. Speakers of one language who learn a second language in early childhood or in adulthood have been demonstrated to apply the semantic scope of a word from one language to its translation equivalent in the other language. Such processes of transfer are found in the morphological domain as well and extend in both directions, that is, from the first language to the second (Davies, Criper, & Howatt, 1984; Selinker, 1972) and also from the second language to the first (Cook, 2003).

Perhaps the clearest example of lexical fluidity is embodied in a process termed lexical attrition. Here, the influence of the second language on the first over time results in changes in the processing of the first language that may appear less transient. Studies of L1 attrition have demonstrated that bilinguals who are immersed in their L2 differ in their lexical processing from monolinguals and from bilinguals who use their L2 only sporadically and may experience lexical retrieval difficulties that are evident in tasks such as picture naming and in conversation (Datta, 2010; Goral et al., 2008; Schmid et al., 2004; Seliger & Vago, 1991). There is also evidence that suggests change in morphological parsing along the lines described above (Goral et al., 2008; Gürel 2004).

It is evident, then, that the bilingual lexicon can be conceived as more fluid than the monolingual lexicon. The bilingual lexicon is inherently larger – whereas the number of words in each language is typically smaller than each lexicon of a monolingual – together the total number of words that a bilingual speaker commands is larger than that of a monolingual. Indeed, is has been hypothesized that the larger vocabulary size of bilinguals is the reason for their less efficient retrieval (Gollan et al., 2005, 2008). One can argue that the larger one's vocabulary, the less often each lexical item is retrieved. As well, the larger the vocabulary, the more potential competitors may be activated and may need to be inhibited at any given time. Such considerations may affect vocabulary growth in childhood, difficulty with word retrieval in older age, and the need for constant reorganization throughout the lifespan.

## 28.5 A new view of the mental lexicon

In the sections above, we have presented an overview of the manner in which bilingualism has changed, and can further change, conceptions of the mental lexicon. We began by noting the centrality of the mental lexicon for issues of language processing. In many ways, the mental lexicon can be seen as the backbone of language processing. Yet, paradoxically, the mental lexicon is characterized by change.

Our review has underscored the fact that recent decades of research on lexical representation and processing have both broadened and deepened our understanding of the manner in which words are represented and processed in the mind/brain. We are now in a position to build upon these advances by re-evaluating the following default assumptions:

1. The default lexical representation is a monomorphemic word.
2. The default mental lexicon is that of an adult educated monolingual.
3. A successful multilingual will build and maintain a mental lexicon for each language.
4. The mental lexicon is a static knowledge store.

Assumption (1) fails to take into consideration the fact that most words, even of a morphologically impoverished language such as English, are multimorphemic. In our view, considering multimorphemic words as the default is not only a matter of more accurately reflecting the nature of the linguistic landscape, it also places us in a position to better appreciate the role of morphology in the mental lexicon. Morphology is much more than the structure of words. It captures the capacity of a language user to create and understand new words. This may turn out to be the true center of lexical knowledge.

Under assumption (2), the monolingual lexicon is seen as the 'normal' condition. An acknowledgment that it is in fact the bilingual (or multilingual) lexicon that is the norm leads us to a much more desirable state of research – one in which we move away from using terms such as the (monolingual) mental lexicon and bilingual mental lexicon to describe separate research domains. The state that we are moving toward is one in which there is a unified domain of inquiry that has been able to incorporate insights and tools from both of its predecessor domains. If we do so, it becomes impossible to ignore encoding of gender, morphological structure, and other cross-language variations in our modeling of the lexicon. Moreover, we cannot assume that the lexicons of all speakers have the same shape. The study of multilinguals reminds us that the lexicon is shaped by experience of the individual speaker; the assumption that the structure of the mental lexicon is shared among speakers thus must be wrong. The role of experience in shaping concepts and connections in the mental lexicon is fertile ground for future research.

We have claimed that although assumption (3) may describe a functional ability (i.e., the ability to keep languages separate), the mental lexicon can be most profitably viewed as functionally and structurally homogeneous. As a consequence, the lexical dynamics of a bilingual are considerably more complex that those of a monolingual.

Finally, we have noted that assumption (4) suggests the mental lexicon is an inert knowledge store. Recent research has shown that this is not the case. Lexical ability, particularly among bilinguals, is fluid and variable. It seems reasonable to assume that its development is experience based. Thus there may turn out to be very substantial differences in the functional architecture of the mental lexicon that are related to the specific languages maintained, patterns of use, patterns of education, and patterns of change over the lifespan. Investigations of how such factors may interact in online lexical processing across situations opens up, in our view, very promising lines of investigation.

If the points above are correct, they demonstrate the extent to which the consideration of bilingualism as a phenomenon has had a profound effect on our core notions of how words are represented and processed in the mind. In turn, this revised, much more dynamic, view of the construct of a mental lexicon has helped us to better understand the nature of lexical representation and processing in bilingualism. Models of the mental lexicon that are able to accommodate these key properties of lexical processing in bilingualism will have moved very far beyond the original conception of a mental lexicon as a list of exceptions with a functional architecture equivalent to that of a paper dictionary.

# 29

# Losing a first language to a second language

Eve Higby and Loraine Obler

> When you're a teenager you have so many other concerns,
> and, [my first language] just sort of slipped away
> and I didn't realize what I had lost until it was gone.
> (Greta, who immigrated to Canada from the Netherlands as a child)
> (Kouritzin, 1999: 171)

## 29.1 Introduction

The loss of one's native language seems more distressing than the loss of a later learned language. The native language is inextricably linked to one's history and sense of self. Even more than that, it is most often tied to associations with family, tradition, culture, and heritage, making it an integral part of one's identity. Indeed, the shift in language dominance to a later learned language has sometimes been described by people who have undergone it as a shift in personality or self-identification (e.g., Kouritzin, 1999). Sometimes the suppression of the native language is intentional, as in the case of immigrants who want to assimilate as quickly as possible into the new society (e.g., Isurin, 2005) or in the case of strong societal pressures against speaking one's native language (Schmid, 2002). Other cases of first language loss are unintentional. Children adopted from abroad often join a community in which there are no other speakers who share their native language (Isurin, 2005; Nicoladis & Grabois, 2002). Even those who grow up in a family environment where the native language continues to be spoken may feel that the maintenance of the language is automatic, only to find later in adulthood that, without continuous exposure, much of their prior ability in that language has been lost (Kouritzin, 1999).

Research on first language attrition has seen a rapid increase in the past twenty years, investigating a wide range of situations in which attrition can occur. Nevertheless, some of the fundamental questions pertaining to first language loss continue to elude clear answers. For instance, when one experiences native language attrition, does the effect represent a true loss of the knowledge, of the speaker's linguistic competence, or does the knowledge simply become inaccessible? Studies of re-immersion in a childhood language suggest that elements of a "forgotten" language can become somewhat reactivated, implying that the language was not completely lost (e.g., Au et al., 2008). However, few vestiges of language without re-exposure do not seem to be detected in behavioral or neuroimaging measures (Pallier et al., 2003; Singh et al. 2011).

This chapter focuses on cases of native language attrition that occur after a complete or near-complete cessation of input from that language. While the term 'attrition' is sometimes used to refer only to language change or language decline after acquisition has been completed (typically adulthood), we would argue that the L1 is never 'completely' acquired, or that there is no point in time at which one can claim it is, and thus we use the term 'attrition' to refer to any decline in language abilities that were previously demonstrated by an individual. The newly learned language (the L2) is usually acquired to the same degree as for native speakers of that language who had input from birth, although this is not always the case. Several studies have explored what kind of vestiges of memory for the first language remain in individuals who can no longer speak it, while others have looked at whether such individuals demonstrate any sort of relearning advantage due to a re-activation of long-buried memory traces. While the findings are not so clear with regard to what sort of influences are important for first language loss or maintenance in these cases, the data hint at factors such as the age at which L1 input ceased, social pressures, and attitudinal factors, and possibly the density of one's social network. Finally, several theories of language attrition are considered in light of the data presented on instances of complete or near-complete first language (L1) loss.

## 29.2 Dramatic first language loss

Some of the most dramatic examples of native language loss have been found among international adoptees. Children in this circumstance are often brought to a new country at a very young age and enter an environment where they no longer have any exposure to their native language. Given this abrupt shift in the linguistic environment, the child begins to acquire the new language, often with great rapidity (Gauthier, Genesee, & Kasparian, 2012; Isurin, 2005; Nicoladis & Grabois, 2002). When adoption occurred at early ages, especially at less than one year old, adoptees have been shown to perform in their new language just like their non-adopted peers by the time they reach two to three years of age (Glennen & Masters,

2002; Krakow & Roberts, 2003; Tan & Yang, 2005). Nevertheless, some effects of the later age of second language acquisition of the adoptees compared to non-adoptees can be detected using sensitive measures of language production and comprehension. Hyltenstam et al. (2009) found that as young adults, only one out of the four international adoptees they studied performed like native Swedish speakers across a battery of ten linguistic tests; the age of adoption of that individual was one year old. Despite the fact that the others were adopted at 2 years, 4 years, and 9 years old, they all showed some deviance from native-like patterns of performance when tested between the ages of 28 and 33.

Subtle differences between adoptees and native-born controls have also been reported in terms of hemispheric lateralization of the dominant language (Rajagopal et al., 2013). While the control participants showed clear left-hemisphere dominance for English, the adoptees demonstrated more bilateral activation. These children had been adopted between the ages of 9 months and 3 years old and were 6–10 years of age at testing. While differences in hemispheric lateralization for language do not necessarily imply that differences in language behavior or ultimate language attainment exist – and for these pre-teen participants we are not given data on proficiency relative to their monolingual peers – they do suggest that an abrupt switch in language input at a young age may have effects on how language is processed by the brain. This intriguing area warrants additional investigation to understand how the brain responds to these changes during early language development. Overall, international adoptees are successful in acquiring their new language to a level that is considered native-like or near-native-like with greater success associated with earlier ages of adoption.

Does the success with which adoptees gain proficiency in their second language necessitate native language loss? According to Pallier (2007), the stabilization of brain networks involved in processing the native language makes it more difficult to acquire a second language. Thus, rather than maturational constraints on neural plasticity, it is the developmental stabilization of the native language that interferes with second language acquisition. If international adoptees are able to "erase" the first language from their minds, this presumably frees up the language learning mechanism to acquire the second language without first language interference. In fact, these learners are sometimes called "sequential monolinguals" (e.g., Schmid, 2012), which implies that their language development is distinct from that of early bilinguals.

One way of testing this hypothesis is by comparing second language acquisition success in individuals who began acquiring the second language at the same age but who differ in whether or not they experienced a complete stop in first language use. A situation similar to this was tested by Schmid (2012). Her corpus contained interviews from adults who had left Germany during the Holocaust between the ages of 11 and 15 and moved to English-speaking countries. Some of them emigrated with their families while others were part of a child-rescue program called Kindertransport, which placed children in the homes of English-speaking families. The latter group has many similarities with the international adoptees from other studies in that the use of the native language was abruptly halted due to both the lack of access to German speakers and the political situation at that time, which was hostile toward German speakers. Crucially, however, these adoptees were much older than typical international adoptees. Schmid found no significant differences between the two groups of older adults in their English production, measured for complexity, fluency, and accuracy of syntax, morphology, and lexical semantics. This finding contradicts the prediction made by Pallier (2007) that the abrupt stop and subsequent forgetting of the native language facilitate second-language acquisition. However, it must be noted that even the children who migrated with their families stopped using German in public, with many families switching to the use of English even at home. Thus, the length of time that the native language continued to be used was not much greater for the family migrants than for the Kindertransport migrants. There are other crucial differences between the participants in Schmid (2012) and the international adoptees, including age at migration and attitudes toward both languages. Therefore, it is crucial that additional research investigate the role of first language loss and maintenance in second language acquisition before strong conclusions can be drawn.

What happens with the first learned language in the case of international adoption? Pallier et al. (2003) tested adults who had been adopted from Korea and grew up in France. In their twenties and thirties they were tested on their ability to identify Korean speech from other unknown languages such as Japanese, Polish, Swedish, and Wolof. They were also asked to identify which of two Korean words was the translation of a given French word. The eight Korean adoptees all considered themselves monolingual French speakers and had not studied Korean or used it since they were adopted, which ranged from 3 to 8 years of age. The participants were no better at identifying Korean sentences among sentences including other unknown languages than a group of French-speaking controls, nor were they any better than controls at identifying any of the other languages. In fact, both Korean and Japanese sentences were rated just as likely to be Korean by both groups of participants. The participants were then tested in an fMRI scanner to determine whether listening to Korean sentences produced different patterns of brain activation in the adoptees and non-adoptees. Comparing activation patterns for French and Korean sentences revealed no significant differences between the two groups. In fact, listening to Korean sentences produced the same activation as listening to Polish sentences in the group of adoptees. This study reveals important findings about the nature of language maintenance for early-learned languages in individuals who experience an abrupt loss of input and use.

Both behaviorally and neurologically, there appeared to be no trace of the first language becoming reactivated with re-exposure. However, other researchers (e.g., Hyltenstam et al., 2009) have challenged these findings, pointing out that the method used by Pallier et al. to test residual L1 knowledge may not have been sensitive enough to detect memory traces of the first language. They support their argument with the observations that no differences were detected between the adoptees and native French controls nor were any effects of age of L2 acquisition found in the group of adoptees, factors which Hyltenstam et al. argue should have been present in the data obtained by Pallier et al. based on other research finding robust effects of these factors.

Another study of Korean adoptees in France tested phonological discrimination of Korean voiceless consonant contrasts that are difficult for French speakers to perceive (Ventureyra, Pallier, & Yoo, 2004). Eighteen Korean adoptees discriminated the Korean phonological contrasts no better than French controls and far below the performance of Korean controls. These two studies suggest that the abrupt halt in the acquisition of one's native language at an early age (in this case, up to 9 years) results in the complete inability to discriminate phonological contrasts in that language or even recognize when one is hearing that language. Additionally, neural resources recruited for processing the dominant language in adulthood can appear to be the same regardless of whether it was the first learned language or the second in adoptees like these.

Not all studies of international adoptees show total native language loss, however. Pierce et al. (2014) tested 9–17-year-old French monolingual early adoptees from China (with no post-adoption exposure to Chinese). They processed Chinese lexical tone in left brain regions just like Chinese heritage speakers growing up with their families in France. By contrast, monolingual native French speakers employed right temporal brain regions, suggesting that they did not treat the stimuli as linguistic. Montrul (2011) reported on a woman of Guatemalan descent who was adopted at the age of 9 by a family in the USA and received no input in Spanish for her first five years in the new country. Her level of Spanish at the time of the study was marked by a fair degree of fluency, but frequent errors on object marking and verbal morphology. Since the participant had taken Spanish classes in high school and college and made attempts to speak Spanish at her workplace, it is not clear that her Spanish was actually retained and not relearned. The later age of adoption of this participant may also be an important factor – though recall that one of the participants in the Ventureyra et al. study was 9 at the time of adoption. As mentioned previously, the Kindertransport migrants discussed in Schmid (2012) had a background similar to other international adoptees, but they were older at migration (11–15 years old). Despite the fact that their German input stopped abruptly when they emigrated, many of them retained enough of the language to give the interview in German in late adulthood (65–92 years old). In fact, seven out of the nine Kindertransport migrants chose to speak in German for their interview compared to nine out of 16 interviewees who had migrated with their families. When asked to rate the relative ease with which they could currently speak German, three rated their German use as "effortless," four chose "with some effort," and only one reported speaking German "with great difficulty." This, in fact, was about the same distribution of self-perceived proficiencies found in the family migrants. However, even in this study, the interviewees could have reactivated their native language in adulthood.

The better retention of these migrants' native language skills compared to the other international adoptees could have two possible explanations. As in the case of the Guatemalan adoptee described in Montrul (2011), the German migrants were older at the time of adoption than the Korean adoptees tested by Pallier et al. (2003). The German migrants were 11–15 years of age at the time of emigration while the Koreans were 3–8 years old when adopted. The conflicting results seen between these two studies are consistent with predictions made by the Critical Period Hypothesis, which proposes that a decrease in the brain's neural plasticity around the time of puberty results in decreased ability to acquire language skills with native-like proficiency. The stabilization of neural networks at this age would also presumably lead to less language attrition if input ceased after this stabilization point. Another possible explanation, however, could be the role of continued L1 input or re-exposure to the language. While Pallier et al. (2003) specifically excluded Korean participants who had had exposure to Korean since their adoption, Schmid (2012) does not provide information regarding the extent to which interviewees were exposed to German since their emigration or used it in their adult lives, and Montrul's (2011) participant reported having had re-exposure through high school and college Spanish classes. Thus, it is just as plausible that re-exposure to the native language in adulthood helped these participants recover certain language elements that had attrited after input ceased.

## 29.3 Relearning advantages for a "lost" language

If international adoptees have been reported to show an advantage in relearning their native language compared to learners with no previous exposure to the language, then we must conclude that the language had not been altogether lost. This long-dormant residual knowledge may not be easy to tap into, however. Recall and recognition tests may not be able to access buried fragments of memory. Nelson (1978) argued that a 'savings' paradigm should be able to reveal the presence of less accessible stored memories by identifying relearning advantages of previously learned items over new items. In fact, de Bot and Stoessel (2000) employed this paradigm to investigate L2 retention and found evidence for residual vocabulary knowledge in two individuals who had not had exposure to a language learned in childhood for more than thirty years. Other studies of savings in relearning L2 vocabulary after input has ceased have shown similar findings in terms of a relearning advantage for previously known words, though this effect appears to depend on the length of time without input (up to forty-five years in some cases), the age at which input in that language ceased, and the proficiency that was previously attained in the language (de Bot, Martens, & Stoessel, 2004; Hansen, Umeda, & McKinney, 2002; Ioup, 2001; Tomiyama, 2001; van der Hoeven & de Bot, 2012). While these studies looked at savings in L2 knowledge rather than the native language, the application of the savings method for the retrieval of long-unused language knowledge may prove useful for probing L1 residual memory.

When the re-exposure to one's native language occurs in childhood, the findings point to a rapid reacquisition of the language. Three case studies of young children who spent up to fifteen months abroad demonstrate the rapidity with which children at this age become dominant in the L2 and then again in the L1 when re-exposed to it. The first case (Berman, 1979) chronicles the transition of a native Hebrew-speaking child with some passive comprehension in English starting at the age of 2;11. During the year she spent living in the USA with her family, she spoke only the L2, English. Upon returning to Israel at age 3;11, the child began recovering her use of the native language within a month and was considered an L1-dominant bilingual by about four months after returning to the home country. The second case illustrates a more dramatic example of a switch in language dominance. Slobin et al. (1993) describe a native English-speaking child who, at the age of 2;6, moved to Turkey with his family for a stay of five months. While the child maintained comprehension of English during his stay in Turkey, he spoke only Turkish. The reacquisition of his English skills upon returning to the USA was dramatic; within two months he could no longer communicate in Turkish and was considered to be, once again, an English monolingual. Finally, Dahl et al. (2010) document the case of a child who was a balanced Norwegian–English bilingual at the age of 2;11 when he moved to the USA for fifteen months, during which time he rarely heard Norwegian. Upon returning to Norway, the child communicated for the first two months mainly by code-switching and code-mixing English and Norwegian, speaking more Norwegian with his peers at preschool and using more code-mixing patterns with the adults at the preschool, who understood both languages, but in either case he rarely produced utterances only in Norwegian. At week 8, there was a sudden shift in the child's communication patterns to mostly Norwegian utterances and by week 11, the child no longer code-switched.

It is possible that the reacquisition process is less rapid in older children who are re-immersed in their native language after a time away from it. One such report is of an adolescent who spoke three languages quite fluently until the age of 6 and then spent six years abroad between the ages of 6 and 12 during which time he only communicated in his newly learned language, English (Faingold, 2004). At age 12, he was re-immersed in two of his native languages (Hebrew and Spanish) through classes at school and is reported to have become proficient in them again quite quickly, which the author attributes to positive attitudes toward the languages, which were tied to the student's cultural heritage. Unfortunately, no quantitative data is available for this participant to ascertain to what extent and at what rate he was able to recover proficiency in the two native languages. However, another study involving three adolescent siblings does provide data assessing language skills before emigration, after a period of two years nine months in the new country, and again seven months after returning to the native language environment (Hubbell-Weinhold, 2005). The three children were aged 11;5, 10;2, and 8;7 at the time of their emigration from the United States to Switzerland. When tested almost three years after immigrating, all three children showed large declines in both receptive and expressive language. Four months later, they returned to the USA, at which point German input almost entirely ceased. When tested in English seven months later, their English skills in all areas tested had recovered but only by 20–45 percent of their original language scores. These case studies demonstrate that reacquisition of a native language is typically quite rapid when it occurs in early childhood, though from the limited set of data we are able to examine, it appears that either the age of immigration and re-immersion or the duration of the time without L1 input may affect the speed with which one is able to regain attrited language skills, though they may both play important roles.

Residual memory of a native language from childhood is less apparent when individuals are tested as adults, though many of the studies of adults investigated either the presence of retained language abilities without relearning or abilities manifested in very early stages of relearning, mostly in terms of phonetic discrimination. As mentioned previously, Ventureyra et al. (2004) found that Korean adoptees in France performed far below 50 percent accuracy in discriminating among Korean consonants that were not distinguishable to their French-speaking peers, and those with re-exposure to Korean performed better than those with no re-exposure. However, a very similar study of Korean adoptees to the USA showed a clear advantage by Korean adoptees on two of the three consonant types (plain and aspirated, but not tense) over novice Korean learners after only two weeks of college-level beginner Korean classes (Oh, Au, & Jun, 2010). Unlike the previous studies of adoptees, all but one of the adoptees in the Oh et al. study were adopted by the age of 1.

Oh et al.'s (2010) findings are supported by other studies showing that early language exposure without continued use may confer some long-lasting benefits in speech sound discrimination. Tees and Werker (1984) found that English monolingual adults who had been exposed to Hindi in early childhood (until 1–2 years of age) showed significantly better performance distinguishing a Hindi dental/retroflex contrast compared to adults without early Hindi experience when they were tested as young adults only seven to ten days after the start of a Hindi college class for beginners. In fact, their scores were similar to those of a group of English–Hindi bilinguals with more than five years' experience studying Hindi and still much better than the scores obtained a year later by the Hindi learners without early exposure.

In another college-level first-year Korean language class (Oh et al., 2003), participants were tested who had been exposed to Korean in early childhood, but experienced a rapid decline in Korean input before the age of 7. Based on their language background questionnaires, they were divided into those who overheard Korean as youngsters but rarely spoke it and those who spoke Korean regularly for at least three years. On the phoneme perception task, which included the same trio of stop consonant contrasts as the previous Korean studies, childhood speakers and hearers performed similarly to native speakers, outperforming novice learners. By contrast, only the childhood Korean speakers and native speakers reliably distinguished between all three consonants in their speech production, while childhood Korean hearers and novice learners did not differentiate them in speech. Overall accent ratings for childhood speakers were higher than for childhood hearers and novice learners, though they were still lower than native speakers. This benefit for accent is also reported for English-dominant childhood Spanish speakers in a Spanish language learning setting as adults, in which both childhood Spanish speakers and hearers spoke Spanish with a better accent than novice learners (Au et al., 2008). The childhood speakers showed better performance than hearers and novice learners on grammatical measures. By contrast, Au et al. (2002) found that adult Spanish childhood hearers performed better on measures of Spanish phonetic production and overall accent, but no better than novice learners on measures of morphosyntax.

These studies suggest that a slight relearning advantage may exist for adults who had childhood exposure to the language, but most tested these adults at the very early stages of re-immersion. Does continued learning show even greater facilitation effects for these learners? Bowers, Mattys, and Gage (2009) suggest that this might be the case. They asked English-dominant speakers who had been exposed to Hindi or Zulu as children to perform a same-different task on a set of Hindi and Zulu phonemic contrasts that are difficult for English speakers to perceive. Compared to a group of controls, the "relearners" showed significantly better performance on these contrasts, but only for the participants who were under age 40 at time of testing. In addition, evidence of improved learning only became apparent after fifteen to twenty sessions of training. Thus, studies testing participants with no re-exposure or at very early stages of relearning may fail to find any advantage (e.g., Pallier et al., 2003).

One study importantly suggests there are individual differences among individuals who have lost their L1. Hyltenstam et al. (2009) compared the performance of two groups of college-level students studying Korean: one group consisted of Korean adoptees to Sweden and the other included native Swedish speakers. The participants were tested on a phonological discrimination task of Korean phonemes differing in VOT length and a grammaticality judgment task testing case morphology, verb morphology, and adverb placement. The native Swedish speakers scored significantly higher than the adoptees on the grammaticality judgment task. Considering the fact that the Swedish natives had spent more years studying Korean than the adoptees and more time living in Korea, this result was not particularly surprising. Despite the differences between groups in length of time learning, both groups scored similarly on the phonological discrimination task. The authors note, however, that the range of scores by the Korean adoptees was quite a bit greater than that seen for the native Swedes and that about one-third of the Korean adoptee participants demonstrated scores on this task that were higher than any of the native Swedish speakers. In fact, the two highest performers were the two participants with the oldest age of adoption (10 and 9 years), lending support to the idea that re-learning of this phonological distinction could have been facilitated in the group of Korean adoptees, particularly for those with a greater number of years of exposure to Korean before adoption in Sweden. Nevertheless, the advantage is slight and could only be seen on the phonological perception task. In addition to the high-scoring adoptees, another one-third of the Korean adoptees performed below any of the native Swedes on this task. These were not necessarily those who were youngest at age of adoption, however, so it remains a curious finding. Moreover, without appropriate pre-tests before re-immersion in the native language, we cannot adequately distinguish what has been retained from what has been relearned, as is the case for several of the other studies.

Most of the studies investigating re-immersion in a native language involve participants who were children when they immigrated, but a single case study of an adult with a long period of no L1 exposure investigated recovery of first language skills through re-exposure during a series of interviews over four years. Stolberg and Münch (2010) report on a German immigrant who had moved to the USA at the age of 28 and had been living there for almost fifty years. The researchers gathered conversational data from the informant fifteen times over the course of four years. Throughout this time, there was a noticeable increase in fluency as well as a decrease in the number of lexical–semantic, syntactic, and morphological errors. The lexical–semantic errors made up a greater proportion of errors at the beginning and also showed the greatest improvement over time. Syntactic errors appeared to fluctuate quite a bit from session to session with a slight overall tendency to decrease. Morphological errors, by contrast, were quite stable overall, showing a barely decreasing tendency.

Since this participant was not taking German language classes in order to brush up her language skills, but rather was engaged in increased communicative exposure through the interview sessions, this seems to provide clear evidence of a certain "reawakening" of long-forgotten native language skills. In the end, there was not what the authors would consider a complete recovery of native language functions. Thus, it remains to be seen whether those aspects are forever lost or if continued exposure would also bring those back.

## 29.4  Recovering a lost language through hypnosis

The contradictory findings in the literature on relearning advantages might have to do with the presence or absence of re-exposure to the native language, as we have suggested above. In the case of Pallier et al. (2003) and Ventureyra et al. (2004), most of the participants were not enrolled in second language classes, while in the rest of the cases they were, even if only for two weeks. The one participant reported in Ventureyra et al. (2004) who had taken Korean language classes for a few months prior to the testing showed better performance on the phonological contrast than the rest of the adoptee group. Could it be that a long-forgotten language from childhood simply needs to be "turned on" again with a little stimulation? If this were the case, then other forms of "reactivation" should be able to stimulate the memories of a long-unused language as well. One technique that has been tried is hypnosis. Only a few researchers have published case studies on this technique. As (1962) reported on a native Swedish speaker who moved to the USA with his family at the age of 5 and began to speak English exclusively by the age of 7. Under age-regression hypnosis, the participant was able to answer more questions in Swedish correctly. In a more dramatic case, a Japanese-American man who claimed to not be able to speak Japanese was suddenly able to speak it rapidly during the psychiatric session with the author when under age-regression hypnosis that brought him back to 3 years of age (Fromm, 1970).

A third study comes not from the recovery of a forgotten native language, but rather a second language learned early in childhood. Footnick (2007) reports on a native French speaker who spent 3.5 years in Togo at an early age (2.5–6 years old) and spoke fluent Mina (a dialect of the region). Upon returning to France, the participant was told not to use Mina anymore so as not to hinder his development in French, and thus the participant had not used the language in fifteen years and could only produce about thirty isolated words at the time of the study, but could not participate in conversations. While the first four hypnosis sessions resulted in only limited responses by the participant in Mina, in the fifth session he responded in Mina 72 percent of the time and spoke in complete, grammatical sentences. Upon listening to the recordings after the hypnosis session, the participant was astonished to hear himself speaking fluently in Mina, and when asked to translate what he said to French, was unable to do so. Interestingly, by the sixth session, the participant was able to comprehend many more questions in Mina out of hypnosis than previously, though still less than what was observed during hypnosis. The author suggests that there is a distinction between a "hidden language" which is not lost but rather, inaccessible, and a "forgotten language" which is no longer able to be recovered by any means. She proposes that in a situation in which a language is "actively" forgotten, i.e., actively suppressed, hypnosis may help by removing the conflict associated with that memory and allowing the mind to access it. However, in a case where the language is truly "forgotten," hypnosis would have no effect and the language would not be recoverable.

The studies on hypnosis bring us back to the central question posed in the introduction: can a language learned in early life be completely lost or does it just become inaccessible? Bjork and Bjork (2006) offer a distinction between storage strength and retrieval strength. They posit that information that becomes entrenched in long-term memory storage remains there and does not decay, and that it is the retrieval strength that decays over time due to non-use. This theory would predict that storage strength would increase as opportunities to practice increase, which should be directly related to amount of input and number of years of exposure before that exposure is broken. Thus, age of acquisition would predict the level of entrenchment of the first language. Second, the theory would predict that re-immersion would increase the language's retrieval strength, though it is not clear whether the process is item-specific or generalizable.

## 29.5 Factors in first language loss and maintenance

The rate at which native language proficiency declines has often been observed to be quite rapid in children. Several longitudinal studies of immigrant children give us a glimpse into the rapid transition from being dominant in one language to becoming highly fluent and dominant in a new language. Nicoladis and Grabois (2002) followed the language development of a Chinese child adopted into an English-speaking Canadian home at the age of 17 months. Between the ages of 1;6 and 1;9, the child was observed ten times, five times during English-speaking playtime and five times during Cantonese-speaking playtime with a native-speaking play partner in each language. At the first session, conducted four weeks after the child's arrival, the girl produced three utterances in Chinese and only one in English. In subsequent sessions, the child only demonstrated comprehension in Chinese but did not attempt to produce it, and even evidence of comprehension ceased by the fourth session. In contrast, starting with the second session, the child began producing a number of utterances in English and also showed an increase in comprehension abilities and imitations. Thus, less than six weeks after arrival, the child had stopped producing utterances in the native language and by three months, she no longer showed evidence of comprehension.

Kaufman and Aronoff (1991) describe a similarly rapid switch in language dominance, though a period of bilingual code-mixing seems to lengthen the process somewhat. In this study, a Hebrew-speaking child, who immigrated with her family to an English-speaking environment at the age of 2;6, went through several stages in the process of switching language dominance. Unlike the case study just described, this child remained within a Hebrew-speaking family environment but began attending an English-speaking nursery school soon after arriving. The first stage of Hebrew attrition began just three months after immigrating and was characterized by lexical borrowings from English which were inflected with Hebrew morphosyntactic elements. This stage lasted for about four months, after which there was a very brief stage of balanced bilingualism (only two months), in which the child exhibited a high level of fluency in both languages in the appropriate environments. Starting at age 3;2, the Hebrew production of the child began to show signs of noticeable decline at home, although her parents continued to speak only Hebrew with her. This was coupled with a change in attitude toward her native language and a refusal to speak Hebrew at times. In the final stage of language change observed in this study (from 3;5–4;6), about a year after her immersion in English, the child used a simplified version of Hebrew morphosyntax in which all verbal paradigms had been reduced to a single idiosyncratic verbal template. Decline in L1 use, then, may be more or less abrupt depending on the circumstances and environment and, likely, on individual differences as well.

In particular, we might consider the young age of some of the participants described in this section to accelerate their shift in language dominance. Given the reduced input of the native language at such an early stage in language development (which was more severe in the case of the Cantonese-speaking child than the Hebrew-speaking child), there might be fewer opportunities for these children to gather evidence, both positive and negative, that would allow them to continue to develop native language capacities. However, this suggestion predicts only a stagnation of development – as Merino (1983) reported for first language comprehension – not a reversal. As was seen in several of the case studies described earlier (e.g., Berman, 1979; Hubbell-Weinhold, 2005; Slobin et al., 1993), a reduction of L1 input results in a decline in L1 language skills rather than simply a lack of development. Indeed, this was even seen in older children (Isurin, 2000, 2005; Ventureyra et al., 2004), whose L1 can be said to have been quite developed by the time their exposure to the language stopped.

Another important factor in language maintenance may be attitudinal changes. A number of studies involving children note the participants' reluctance or unwillingness to continue speaking the native language, even when the opportunity to interact in this language still exists (e.g., Isurin, 2005; Kaufman & Aronoff, 1991; Leopold, 1939–1949). This may be due to social pressures or the desire to fit in with a new social environment. Schmid (2012), for example, mentions that her interviewees noticed some loss of their first language "within a few months" of arriving in their new country. Her participants were German speakers immigrating to England or North America just before the start of the Second World War, so their motivation for not using or appearing German was strong. Thus, it seems that the attentional resources toward second language acquisition and the implicit social pressures to learn a new language may be key contributing factors in language loss. Indeed, quite rapid language loss has also been observed in older children. For instance, Isurin (2000, 2005) observed changes in lexical retrieval efficiency and word order patterns within the first year after adoption by a Russian girl who was adopted at the age of 9 by an American family. When tested two years after her adoption, she was able to successfully retrieve less than 40 percent of the Russian words she was tested on. The participants in Schmid (2012) were between the ages of 11 and 15, though the rate of decline in their native language skills is only anecdotal.

On the other hand, there do seem to be important effects of age of immigration on native language retention. As mentioned previously, the case study described by Stolberg and Münch (2010), a woman who immigrated at the age of 28, showed that even after fifty years of nearly complete disuse, the participant's speech was relatively fluent, though prone to self-interruptions and a variety of deviations from the norm. Nevertheless, a similar situation in younger children appears to have a much greater impact on native language retention. The relationship between age of immigration and native language maintenance is not exactly straightforward, however. While some studies show a small degree of native language maintenance or relearning advantage in individuals whose input had ceased by just one or two years of age (Oh et al., 2010; Tees & Werker, 1984), others show no retention even for those who spoke the native language exclusively until the age of 8 or 9 (Pallier et al., 2003; Ventureyra et al., 2004). Köpke and Schmid (2004) suggest that stabilization of the native language linguistic system – which occurs around puberty – is necessary to prevent dramatic language loss. However, this proposal does not account for the retention of certain native language features in individuals with early cessation of language exposure. Additionally, some individuals who emigrated before puberty are able to retain enough language skills to be interviewed in the language as young adults (Flores, 2012), though what may be termed errors (since they were surely mastered prior to emigration) are relatively frequent.

Continued exposure to a language seems to have a positive effect on language retention, as can be seen in the general better language outcome of heritage language speakers compared to international adoptees (e.g., Kenji & D'Andrea, 1992; Mikulski, 2010; Oh et al., 2003; Tran, 2010). Nevertheless, it is interesting to note that rapid declines in native language processing were found both in cases of adoption, where children often had no one to converse with in their native language, as well as in cases of familial migration, where children still had opportunities to speak their native language, if only with other family members (e.g., Hubbell-Weinhold, 2005; Kaufman & Aronoff, 1991; Slobin et al., 1993).

For example, Schmid (2012) found almost no significant differences between Kindertransport migrants and family migrants when they produced German later in life, nor were there significantly fewer participants in the Kindertransport group who chose to speak German for the interview. Oh et al. (2010) and Ventureyra et al. (2004) also found no significant differences between those who had had exposure after immigration and those who had not. What may be most important for preventing first language loss is a certain minimal level of continued exposure. The question of just how much is yet to be explored.

As well, the density of one's social network has been reported to be an important factor in the degree of adult first language attrition (Hulsen et al., 2000; Schmid, 2012) as well as in the amount of first language development in heritage language speakers (Tran, 2010), and it may also be an important factor in first language loss or maintenance in children who immigrate to a place where there are no first language connections outside the home. Additionally, age of second language acquisition and amount of language input are often confounded, making it difficult to determine what role each of these factors plays in both second language acquisition and first language attrition. For instance, Jia and Aaronson (1999) provide evidence that younger immigrants were more likely to become dominant in the second language than adolescent immigrants. However, younger participants also received more years of second language input (and, presumably, less native language input) than older immigrants. These issues need to be separately examined in order to understand their contributions to first language loss.

Some researchers argue that certain aspects of language are more vulnerable than others to language attrition. Since few of the studies described in this paper looked at language loss longitudinally, it is not clear whether the loss of L1 skills occurs at different rates for different aspects of language. Most studies that were longitudinal in nature constrained their analysis to only specific areas of language (morphosyntax in Kaufman & Aronoff, 1991, lexical retrieval in Isurin, 2000, and word order in Isurin, 2005) or only described general language use preferences (Berman, 1979; Faingold, 2004; Slobin et al., 1993). Hubbell-Weinhold (2005), however, included tests of both semantics and syntax, as well as including both receptive and expressive language measures, and found that semantics showed a greater decline than syntax, while expressive and receptive language skills showed a similar degree of decline. On the other hand, Isurin (2000) notes that her participant became reluctant to participate in storytelling and picture description tasks at later testing sessions but continued to perform the lexical retrieval tasks, implying that she felt more comfortable with lexical retrieval than with syntax. Within syntax, Flores (2012) found that overt pronoun realization was more vulnerable to attrition than word order constraints. An interesting observation has been made noting that similar errors are seen in the production of heritage language speakers and in second-language acquirers and that these errors may indicate certain aspects of grammar that are both harder to acquire in second language acquisition and easier to lose in first language attrition (Montrul, 2005). Such parallels are intriguing and warrant further study.

A hypothesis presented by Sorace (2005) proposes that aspects of "pure" syntax are not vulnerable to attrition once acquired since they are proceduralized, but that syntactic constructions that incorporate discourse, lexical, or pragmatic information (so-called "interface" phenomena) are more likely to undergo attrition. The consolidation of purely syntactic components is thought to occur around the age of puberty, predicting that the cessation of L1 input before and after puberty will result in qualitatively different patterns of language loss, a prediction that has received some support (Flores, 2010, 2012). It is not so clear how this applies to early cases of first language attrition, and the question of which facets of language tend to be lost first in situations of total cessation of input is yet to be explored.

Age of immigration, then, social reasons to lose the L1, and possibly the number of social contacts in the L1 appear to enter into whether the L1 attrites and into the rate at which it does. Syntactic complexity and whether or not certain structures extend beyond 'pure' syntax may determine which structures are 'lost' first. Other factors, like interference into L1 from L2 (see Higby, Kim, & Obler, 2013) have not been explored in much detail in the literature on dramatic first language loss, though Isurin (2000) notes that the retention of L1 words shows a strong relationship with the acquisition of their L2 translation equivalents in that the L2 words that were learned last are the translation equivalents of the L1 words that were retained the longest. Given that L2 interference has been found to play an important role in the general research on L1 attrition (e.g., Cook, 2003), this relationship should be explored in more depth in cases of early first language loss to discover in what ways language attrition in younger and older individuals may differ.

## 29.6 Theoretical and neurological explanations of language loss

A number of theories have been proposed to account for the patterns seen in research on first language attrition. For the most part, these models were developed to account for changes in L1 language patterns or processing in bilinguals rather than to explain such dramatic L1 loss as has been reviewed in this chapter. Nevertheless, we consider how they might handle the set of findings we have described.

One set of these theories assigns the process of second language acquisition as the driving force of attrition seen in the first language. For instance, the Speech Learning Model (Flege, 1995, 2002) proposes that the first and second languages exist in the same "phonological space" and therefore mutually influence each other, and that language-specific speech categorization mechanisms remain intact throughout the lifespan after the first year. Language input and language dominance, then, can influence speech perception and production in the native language by adapting these to second language categories. There is limited evidence for this theory in the data described in this chapter, however. While some individuals showed a 'savings' advantage when relearning certain phonological contrasts in their native language (Oh et al., 2003, 2010; Tees & Werker, 1984), others, some of whom had had exposure to the native language for much longer than one year did not (Bowers et al., 2009; Hyltenstam et al., 2009; Pallier et al., 2003).

A second proposal, mentioned earlier in the chapter, is the Language Replacement Hypothesis (Pallier et al., 2003). This hypothesis states that the first language serves as a barrier to successful acquisition of the second language, and therefore the extinction of the native language allows the second language to be fully acquired and to replace the first as the person's 'native' language. Related to this is Footnick's (2007) proposal that the process of 'active forgetting' of the native language is key in first language loss and may occur due to environmental pressures or the suppression of negative associated memories. Recently, the role of active inhibition has been implicated in short-term losses in first language abilities and associated second language gains (Linck, Kroll, & Sunderman, 2009). After native English speakers spent three months studying in a Spanish-speaking country, they produced significantly more responses on a Spanish semantic verbal fluency task than a comparable group of Spanish learners who stayed in their home country. The immersion in the second language seemed to have made the first language less accessible, however, as the immersion students produced significantly fewer responses in the native language than their counterparts did.

Given that many adult balanced bilinguals exist, Pallier's proposal thus appears to be too strong to account for data showing successful second language acquisition in the face of first language maintenance. However, the idea that active suppression of the native language may be involved in the cases described in this chapter is not implausible. If children find that their native language is no longer useful and experience social pressures to acquire the new language quickly, inhibition of the native language may be a useful strategy. Evidence for this comes from Isurin's (2000) finding that response times for native language lexical retrieval increased across the testing sessions (which may indicate the inhibition of these items) and that high frequency L1 items and cognate words were more likely to evidence difficulty for retrieval than low frequency, non-cognate words.

Another set of proposals places a stronger emphasis on L1 language use for language maintenance. The Weaker Links Hypothesis (Gollan et al., 2005; 2008) proposes that reduced use of a given language leads to weaker links between the semantics and phonology of its lexical system. A similar account is the Activation Threshold Hypothesis (Paradis, 2007). 'Activation threshold' refers to the resting-state activation level of language items that determines how much effort is needed in order to activate them for language use. Items with a higher threshold require more processing resources in order to activate them, and activation thresholds change over time according to language-use patterns. The hypothesis predicts that native language disuse will lead to higher activation thresholds and that highly frequent items in the second language will replace their counterparts in the native language with time. The Dynamic Model of Multilingualism (de Bot, Lowie, & Verspoor, 2007; Herdina & Jessner, 2002) suggests that language is a dynamic system, in which limited resources must be applied to the maintenance of all languages. Thus, increased use of the second language leads to natural decay of the first language because of the increased effort required to maintain it. Each of these theories is potentially applicable to the studies of complete and near-complete first language loss if extended to their extremes. For instance, if the links between semantics and phonology weaken, do they eventually weaken to the point where they are "broken," making access to the phonological shapes of words impossible? Studies of savings in relearning previously known words imply that weakened connections can be restrengthened with training. This presumably applies to the first language as well. The Dynamic Model of Multilingualism may be able to account for the particular vulnerability of younger children to rapid first-language decline if we assume that the resources needed to maintain languages in an active state are even more limited for younger children than for adolescents and adults.

Another aspect of a dynamic systems perspective on language attrition involves the primary role of social adaptation. In their description of language as a complex adaptive system, Beckner et al. (2009) place the central force driving language acquisition and language change on social interactions. In this view, adaptation of the linguistic system to environmental factors such as input and social interactions continues throughout one's lifetime. Language input factors, such as form frequency and the continuous co-occurrence of form, meaning, and usage patterns of a particular construction, are essential for both language acquisition and language maintenance (de Bot et al., 2007; Ellis & Larsen-Freeman, 2009). Indeed, social interactions and attitudes toward languages appear to play an important role in language maintenance especially for children and adolescents (Kaufman & Aronoff, 1991; Kouritzin, 1999; Slobin et al., 1993).

How these theories might incorporate those aspects of neurology that must be called upon to explain L1 loss and attrition has not yet been postulated beyond speculation. Certain of the terms in the theories mentioned above imply neurological notions, though they could, in principle, be strictly psychological constructs: the Language Replacement Hypothesis of Pallier and colleagues is consistent with cortical and subcortical regions structured for language learning and maintenance being called upon for L2 learning in ways that displace networks and/or reduce synaptic strengths associated with the L1. Footnick's notion of active forgetting and that of Linck et al. of active inhibition might bring about similar neurological consequences whereby networks and pathways used in L1 are taken over by L2. Paradis' (2007) activation thresholds must also involve neural substrates. The notion of L1 having achieved a certain degree of stability in order to resist attrition must reflect underlying neural pathways, perhaps including myelination and chemical processes as well. Plasticity would interact with any and all of these neurological changes, in dynamic ways (as the model of de Bot and colleagues suggests) as one language dominates and then another one does, and daily frequency of input and output appear to enter as well.

## 29.7 Conclusion

What is perhaps most surprising about first language attrition is the range of findings that have been reported. In some adults, there is no evidence of an L1 that was learned up until adoption as late as age 9; in other children who immigrate to another country with another language as young as 1–2 years of age, the ability to still discriminate some of their native-language sound contrasts remain accessible even if only implicitly. It is not surprising that age of immigration enters into determining the relative end-state achieved for L1 in such situations, since relatively less input of L1 to a young brain will understandably result in less well-consolidated mastery of it. Moreover, aspects of the language that had not been learned at the time when a sharp increase in L2 exposure occurs may never be acquired, or, if they were only partially learned but not fully mastered, may attrite in the child. What remains unclear are what role attitude toward the L1 (and L2) plays in determining the amount of attrition or loss, and the extent to which a 'lost' language might be stored, hidden but inaccessible. Virtually unstudied at this time are individual differences in language-learning abilities, or cognitive abilities that underlie them, that may determine how two individuals in very similar situations of L1 and L2 exposure may show more or less L1 attrition, as we know two individuals in very similar

L2-learning or acquiring situations may show different degrees of success in L2 acquisition (e.g., Novoa, Fein, & Obler, 1988). From the number of serious theories proposed to account for subsets of the language attrition data, it appears this field is well into its early adolescence. With more neurological studies to follow, greater precision of our understanding of the biological and psychological aspects of first language loss should evolve.

# 30

# Moving beyond two languages

The effects of multilingualism on language processing and language learning

Jared Linck, Erica Michael, Ewa Golonka, Alina Twist, and John W. Schwieter

## 30.1 Introduction

A growing body of psycholinguistic research has been devoted to the study of bilingual language processing and second language (L2) acquisition. Although these terms are often used in the scientific literature to refer to processing or learning any language other than one's native tongue (L1), relatively little research has focused on issues that are specific to processing or learning[1] a third language (L3) or beyond. Yet the study of multilinguals provides unique opportunities to advance our understanding of the complex interactions between language and cognition. In this chapter, we review existing research on the psycholinguistic and cognitive factors that may affect the use and learning of languages beyond the L2. Before we begin, it is important to note precisely how we are using certain terms:

**L1:** one's native language or mother tongue; the language learned from birth; individuals who are raised in multilingual environments may consider themselves to have multiple L1s.

**L2:** a language that is learned sometime after the L1; it may be learned as a child or as an adult, in a formal setting such as a classroom or an informal setting such as a grandparent's home.

**L3:** any language beyond the second (sometimes also referred to as L*n*); for example, if a native English speaker studies Spanish in high school, German in college, and Arabic on the job, both German and Arabic would be considered L3s.

---

[1] Although we recognize that some scholars draw a distinction between acquiring a language (usually implicitly) and learning a language (usually explicitly), we use the terms interchangeably.

**Bilingual:** having some degree of proficiency (not necessarily native-like) in two languages, regardless of age of acquisition; balanced bilinguals have near equal proficiency in the two languages, whereas unbalanced bilinguals exhibit dominance of one language over the other.

**Multilingual:** having some degree of proficiency in *more than* two languages.

We begin this chapter with a brief description of various psycholinguistic theories, models, principles, and findings from the large literatures on bilingualism and second language acquisition that are particularly relevant to the discussion of L3 issues. In particular, we summarize key research on multilingual language processing in individuals who have already attained some degree of proficiency in an L3, focusing on evidence for multilingual transfer. In the following section, we describe a number of factors that appear to modulate multilingual transfer. We then review the literature on multilingual learning, focusing on some of the ways in which previous language-learning experience may facilitate or interfere with L3 learning, before turning to a discussion of how L3 instruction might be informed by the research described in the earlier sections. A main goal of this chapter is to better understand how multiple languages interact in the human mind in the hope that such research will help shed light on some of the cognitive constraints and other factors that may have consequences for learning and using an L3.

## 30.2 Cognitive models of bilingualism and multilingual extensions

Theoretical models of the bilingual mind (including models of the lexicon, language processing, or learning) provide an understanding of how L2 words are learned and processed, which can inform language pedagogy. Considering how these models can accommodate the multilingual mind can further inform our understanding of multilingualism. As will be discussed below, some existing models can accommodate the multilingual case without the need for modifications. However, for some other models, modifications to the model's assumptions or mechanisms are required to appropriately address phenomena that arise when a third language is involved. These potential modifications lead to testable predictions that do not emerge from considering only the bilingual case, and provide an opportunity for new insights about multilingual language processing and multilingual learning.

Most models of the multilingual mind have been developed with a specific focus on individuals who know two languages. In contrast, the Dynamic Model of Multilingualism (e.g., Herdina & Jessner, 2002) was developed specifically to consider how a linguistic system changes in the presence of three or more languages. This model espouses the assumptions of chaos theory, claiming that the linguistic system is forever in an unpredictable state of change (language gain, sustainment, or attrition) that is influenced by changes to any of the languages in the system. Although this model provides an important and appropriate acknowledgement of the complexities of the multilingual mind, it unfortunately fails to provide a theoretical framework from which hypotheses and testable predictions can be generated regarding the nature of multilingual language processing.

In a few instances, theorists have considered how to extend existing models of bilingualism to the multilingual case. For example, Dijkstra (2003) discussed the ability of the Bilingual Interactive Activation (BIA+) model to include a third language and concluded that such extensions can easily be accommodated within the BIA+'s existing mechanisms. In the current BIA+ model, language membership is represented via language nodes, or "tags" that are attached to the orthographic representations of words. Words from an L3 could be represented by linking an L3 language node to the L3 orthographic representations. As in the bilingual case, trilingual word identification would proceed by virtue of the facilitatory and inhibitory connections across and within the sub-lexical and lexical levels of the model. Dijkstra reported results of simulations suggesting that the system does not experience catastrophic interference when a third language is introduced, but rather the three languages can coexist by virtue of the mechanisms already in place within the BIA+. Therefore, according to Dijkstra, considering multilinguals does not require any explicit changes to the model's architecture or mechanisms, nor does the multilingual BIA+ make any predictions not already established in the bilingual case.

As with the BIA+, some models of bilingual language processing may be able to accommodate multiple languages, whereas in other cases it may be necessary to make certain adjustments to the existing architecture or processing mechanisms. As a demonstration, below we consider two prominent bilingual models: the Revised Hierarchical Model (RHM; Kroll & Stewart, 1994), which describes the structure of the bilingual lexicon; and the Inhibitory Control (IC) model (Green, 1998), which posits mechanisms for language control particularly during speech production. Considering multilingual extensions of existing models may lead to unique predictions and further insights into the fundamental mechanisms underlying multilingualism. We focus on the RHM and the IC Model because these two examples provide an interesting contrast in the necessity to modify the model to accommodate multilingual phenomena. Specifically, the fundamental assumptions of the RHM appear to successfully account for the phenomena documented in the relevant trilingual language processing studies reviewed below, whereas results from trilingual language switching studies suggest that the mechanisms of the IC Model may require further specification regarding the precise nature of inhibition. We return to this point below. Although numerous models could be considered in this fashion, a systematic review and expansion of existing models is beyond the scope of this chapter.

### 30.2.1 The Revised Hierarchical Model

The RHM (Kroll & Stewart, 1994) addresses the nature of the connections among a bilingual's L1 lexical representations, L2 lexical representations, and conceptual representations. The model posits separate lexicons for the two languages, both of which access a common conceptual store. The model is developmental in that the relative strengths of various connections are believed to change as a bilingual gains proficiency in the L2. At early stages of L2 acquisition, the learner develops direct lexical connections between new L2 words and their L1 counterparts, but L2 words typically are not strongly linked to concepts. With increasing proficiency, the bilingual develops stronger lexico-semantic connections between the L2 lexical items and their corresponding conceptual representations.

The RHM could be extended to the multilingual case by simply adding a language-specific lexicon for the L3, along with the corresponding interlingual lexical connections (e.g., between L2–L3 translation pairs) and lexico-semantic connections. There is already empirical evidence to support such an extension. Abunuwara (1992) compared picture naming and word naming in trilinguals. Similar to proficiency-related, between-subjects differences found with bilinguals in other studies (e.g., Talamas, Kroll, & Dufour, 1999), Abunuwara found that the more dominant non-native language demonstrated greater conceptual mediation, whereas the less dominant non-native language showed more lexical mediation. De Groot and Hoeks (1995) examined forward translation (from the L1) and translation recognition in trilinguals. The materials included a concreteness manipulation, which has been shown to affect semantic processing (i.e., participants are faster to recognize or translate concrete words relative to abstract words). In translation production, clear concreteness effects were found during L1–L2 translation but not during L1–L3 translation; less robust effects were found in translation recognition, but the same general pattern was found. The results suggest that the relative proficiency of the non-native language impacts the extent to which lexical access is lexically or conceptually mediated, as evidenced within the same participants by studying trilinguals with differing proficiency in L2 and L3. Taken together, these results indicate that the developmental predictions of the RHM hold with multilinguals and suggest that the architecture can easily be expanded to accommodate multiple languages. Because it models the development of lexical representations in the bilingual/multilingual mind, the RHM provides an important framework for understanding the process of vocabulary learning and can inform methods for enhancing vocabulary knowledge.

## 30.2.2 The Inhibitory Control (IC) Model

Whereas the RHM describes the connections between words and concepts in a bilingual's two languages, the IC Model (Green, 1998) is concerned with the mechanisms that support a bilingual's access to and use of two languages. The IC Model posits that all language tasks require a bilingual to inhibit the language that is not needed in order to function in the other language. For example, naming pictures in L2 would require inhibition of the L1 lexicon so as not to inadvertently produce words in the non-target language. The model further proposes that the amount of effort required to inhibit a language is dependent in part on the individual's level of proficiency in that language; thus for an unbalanced bilingual, it would be much more difficult to inhibit the L1 than to inhibit the relatively weaker L2.

Although Green (1998) originally hypothesized that inhibition occurs at the level of the lemma, subsequent research has attempted to test this hypothesis and more precisely pinpoint what aspects of the bilingual language system might be subject to inhibition. A common approach to addressing this question has been to conduct experiments involving language switching during cognitive tasks. To examine the nature of inhibition during language switching, Philipp and Koch (2009) manipulated the repetition of cues (Experiment 1) and of specific response sets (e.g., L1 colors, L1 digits; Experiment 2) to examine whether inhibition during language switching operates at the level of specific language cues, specific stimulus–response sets, or more globally across the entire language. They found that evidence of inhibition (namely, n-2 repetition costs; for details, see section 30.4.1.2) were not dependent on the repetition of a language cue or a specific stimulus–response set (see Finkbeiner et al., 2006). These results were interpreted to suggest that inhibition during language switching operates across the entire inhibited language.

In the context of experiments on trilingual language switching, Linck, Schwieter, and Sunderman (2012) discussed how Green's (1998) Inhibitory Control model could be extended to the trilingual case. One possibility is a language-specific inhibitory model, by which task schemas inhibit each language separately. For example, when naming in the L3, the L3 naming schema would induce inhibition of the L1 and the L2, and would likely require greater inhibition of the L1. In contrast, a more general account would posit that the inhibition is applied across any representation not associated with the current target language, without any distinction between the non-target languages. So when naming in the L3, inhibition would be applied to any L1 or L2 representation. If we assume that the task schema can be activated to different levels, then we might expect to see greater differences in inhibition applied to L1 representations in the former case vs. the latter case, as the language-specific inhibition account could allow the system to be biased toward inhibiting the more dominant

L1 to support speaking in the non-dominant languages. The results from Linck et al.'s trilingual switching study supported the language-specific inhibition account: they found that better inhibitors showed reduced language switch costs, but only when switching into or out of the L1.

It will be important for future research to design experiments to contrast these different theoretical positions with multilingual participants in order to further elucidate how and when inhibitory control supports multilingual speech production. This line of research could inform the design of particular pedagogical approaches that encourage inhibitory processing during L3 learning or that leverage learners' inhibitory control abilities to enhance the learning process.

## 30.3 Evidence of multilingual transfer

A critical observation in the literature on multilingualism is that individuals can experience both facilitation (i.e., positive transfer) and interference (i.e., negative transfer) from one language to another across a range of tasks and contexts. In this section, we review available evidence of such facilitation and interference during multilingual language processing. In the next section, we then consider some of the factors that might influence when transfer does or does not occur, as these factors may inform pedagogical approaches to multilingual instruction.

Cross-language facilitation has been frequently observed in the processing of cognates, words that overlap across languages in their written form, sounds, and meaning (e.g., *piano*, Spanish for piano). Lemhöfer, Dijkstra, and Michel (2004) asked Dutch–English–German trilinguals to perform a lexical-decision task in which they were instructed to indicate whether the letter string formed a word specifically in the L3, which was German. To assess the degree of cross-language activation during this task, the word list included two types of cognates: double cognates, in which word forms and sounds were shared between the L1 and L3, but not the L2 (e.g., *kunst*, Dutch and German for *art*), and triple cognates, in which word forms and sounds overlapped across all three languages (e.g., *echo*). Lemhöfer et al. found cognate facilitation for both types of cognates, with greater facilitation for the triple cognates than the double cognates, suggesting that the greater amount of overlapping information across all three languages offered even more benefits to processing. Van Hell and Dijkstra (2002) found trilingual cognate facilitation even when participants performed the lexical decision in their dominant L1. Participants included Dutch–English–French trilinguals who all had relatively high proficiency in the L2 but varied in their L3 proficiency (either low or medium). For L1–L2 cognates, clear cognate facilitation effects were found for both proficiency groups. For L1–L3 cognates, however, cognate facilitation effects were only found for the participants with higher L3 proficiency, suggesting that a minimum degree of proficiency in the L3 was required for the cognates to be activated sufficiently (or rapidly enough) to impact participants' judgments of the words in the dominant L1. Multilingual cognate facilitation has also been found during L3–L1 translation by Russian–English–Swedish trilinguals in a study including L1–L3, L2–L3, and L1–L2–L3 cognates (Tkachenko, 2001).

These results show that lexical decision tasks provide a sensitive measure of word retrieval and can demonstrate (sometimes subtle) effects of various factors that may impact word learning and fluent L3 use. As such, the information from lexical decision tasks can inform multilingual pedagogy by making instructors and students aware of the types of factors that may impact learning. For example, the studies above demonstrating L1 and L2 cognate effects on L3 lexical processing lend empirical support to the long-held pedagogical technique of focusing on cognates at early stages of learning, as learners can rely on their more established L1 and L2 knowledge to bootstrap into the L3. Therefore, the results of studies employing the lexical decision task might inform the development of vocabulary lists at various stages of L3 learning.

These facilitative effects are not simply restricted to highly overlapping word forms such as cognates. In fact, there is evidence that cross-language interactions in multilinguals can lead to facilitation from an entirely task-irrelevant language (i.e., a language not being accessed at the moment). Using a variation of the semantic masked priming paradigm,[2] Duyck et al. (2008) examined numerical distance effects as a measure of semantic processing during L1–L3 translation. They presented Dutch-English-French trilinguals with numerical words (i.e., the numbers one through nine) in either the L1 or L3, with masked primes of the L2 numerical words that varied in their numerical distance from the target number. Previous studies have found that primes that are numerically close to the target word (e.g., prime = four, target = five) lead to larger priming effects than primes that are numerically further from the target (e.g., prime = three, target = five). This effect, termed the *numerical distance effect*, has been interpreted to suggest that the participants are accessing the semantic meaning of both the primes and the targets. Duyck et al. found that the trilinguals showed numerical distance effects in both directions of translation, indicating that activation of the non-target, task-irrelevant L2 (the masked prime) impacted processing at the semantic level when producing in both the less dominant L3 and the dominant L1. Note that the task was designed to never require L2 access (i.e., naming and translation only involved the L1 and L3), demonstrating further that multilingual effects can emerge even when in a purely "bilingual" context or mode. These

---

[2] In a masked priming paradigm, a meaningless visual stimulus (e.g., ####) precedes the prime, which is presented only briefly (e.g., 25 ms). This protocol prevents a visual trace of the prime. Although the participant is typically not consciously aware of the form or meaning of such masked primes, the primes have still been shown to impact processing of a subsequently presented target word.

results indicate that the L1 and L2 will always be active to some degree within the multilingual classroom, suggesting that efforts to completely ignore the L1 and L2 may be futile. Rather than avoiding the L1 or L2, it may be more beneficial to openly employ these languages where they can be useful in order to encourage positive transfer during L3 instruction.

Cross-language interactions can also lead to interference that has deleterious effects on performance in the target language. These negative transfer effects have been documented in trilinguals in several studies using cross-language Stroop (1935) paradigms (e.g., Abunuwara, 1992; Marian et al., 2013). In Abunuwara's study, trilinguals showed interlingual Stroop effects in all combinations of response and distractor language pairings – that is, when naming the font color in one language, a Stroop effect was found even when the color word was presented in a different language. However, L1 interference effects were stronger when naming in the less dominant L3 than when naming in the more proficient L2, and L1 naming was impacted more by L2 distractors than by L3 distractors. These asymmetries in the magnitude of the Stroop effects highlight the importance of the relative dominance of languages in multilingual processing, a point to which we will return below when discussing factors that impact cross-language effects. These results suggest that even when naming in the dominant L1, a multilingual's other languages may interfere with speech production. With respect to multilingual instruction, these results further highlight the importance of considering how both positive and negative transfer among all known languages can impact learning and language use within the multilingual instructional setting.

To examine cross-language transfer in the use of function words (specifically, conjunctions, determiners, prepositions, or pronouns) during multilingual written production, De Angelis (2005) asked multilingual learners of Italian whose previously known languages included English, Spanish, and/or French to first read a passage in their L1, then write a summary of the passage in their L3. The results indicated that learners transferred function words from L1 or L2 during L3 written production, even though the L2 had never been read during the experiment. However, interesting differences were found based on the combination of known languages, such that greater transfer of L2 than L1 function words was found among learners for whom L2 was more typologically similar to the L3; that is, greater L2–L3 similarity was related to greater L2 transfer. The transfer effects were sometimes positive and sometimes negative, depending, in part, on the featural overlap between the languages in question. These findings suggest that one cannot make an across-the-board prediction regarding the nature of transfer without also taking into consideration the specific languages and features known by the multilingual learner.

In a study examining processing of adjective placement by trilinguals, Rothman (2011) asked participants who knew English in addition to two

Romance languages to complete two sentence processing tasks. In the Semantic Interpretation task, participants first read a short sentence containing an adjective phrase, and then indicated which of two descriptions properly captured the meaning of the sentence. In the context-based collocation task, participants read a short story that contained a number of nouns that were both preceded and followed by a blank line. Participants were instructed to fill in the appropriate blank with the adjective that followed in parentheses (e.g., "Magda es una ____ amiga ____ (viejo)."). This design took advantage of the fact that in some languages the placement of an adjective either before or after a noun alters the nuances of interpretation of the noun phrase, whereas this variation does not exist in English. Participants were at near-native proficiency in their L2 and intermediate proficiency in the L3. No differences in response accuracy were found between the trilingual groups and a monolingual control group, which Rothman concluded provided evidence that L3 transfer had occurred. That is, the trilingual participants had completed the tasks with native-like grammar for this specific adjective placement property, suggesting that positive transfer had benefited their L3 knowledge. However, it is worth noting that the author's conclusions were based on a pair of null results (main effect of group, and group by condition interaction) obtained with a research design involving only five observations per participant in each condition, leaving the strength of the inferences somewhat in question. Given these weaknesses, further replication is needed with independent samples before any conclusive inferences are drawn from these results.

As demonstrated by the findings described above, a multilingual's L1 and L2 knowledge can impact L3 learning and processing, and this transfer can either benefit the learner (i.e., positive transfer) or interfere with learning or using the L3 (i.e., negative transfer). There is some suggestion that the specific languages in consideration can limit or affect the types of transfer effects – a point that we consider below (see section 30.4.3). These results suggest that any pedagogical techniques that can increase positive transfer and reduce negative transfer will benefit the multilingual learner.

## 30.4 Factors that affect cross-language interactions

To understand more fully the nature of cross-linguistic interaction, it is important to examine not only what types of transfer effects occur, but also under what circumstances. In this section we review the literature on a number of factors that appear to constrain or inform when cross-linguistic interactions will impact language processing or learning.

### 30.4.1 Relative proficiency

One of the strongest factors affecting cross-language transfer appears to be the relative proficiency in all known languages – not just the L3. That is, it is not simply the degree of proficiency in the L3 that matters, nor in the L2; rather, all languages contribute to the linguistic profile of the language user and have the potential to impact performance or learning. Rah (2010) also points out that classification of learned languages as L2 vs. L3 is not necessarily straightforward; the earlier learned language is not always more proficient than the later learned language, and transfer effects can be modulated by both relative order of learning and relative proficiency. Evidence of the impact of relative proficiency comes from a range of tasks demonstrating a breadth of both facilitation (positive transfer) and interference (negative transfer) effects. We turn now to a review of this evidence.

#### 30.4.1.1 Cognate facilitation

In the van Hell and Dijkstra (2002) study mentioned above, L1 lexical decisions were facilitated by L3 cognates, but only for the more proficient participants. In Tkachenko's (2001) study involving L3–L1 translation, participants were trilinguals who had a high level of proficiency in their L2 but varied in their L3 proficiency. Although the sample size in each group was fairly small (10 beginner, 10 intermediate, and 6 advanced L3 learners), the results suggest that cognate facilitation was smallest for the most proficient L3 learners. Although the findings from these two studies may seem contradictory, it is important to note that in van Hell and Dijkstra, participants were completing the lexical-decision task entirely in their L1, and we would not expect processing in a strong L1 to be significantly affected by a relatively weak L3. In the study by Tkachenko, on the other hand, the translation task required processing of the L3, and thus individuals with lower L3 proficiency benefited more from overlap with their other, stronger languages.

#### 30.4.1.2 Switch costs

Linck et al. (2012) examined the performance of a language switching task with English–French–Spanish trilinguals who were L1 dominant and were more proficient in their L2 than in their L3. Participants were presented a series of pictures and were instructed to name each picture in the L1, L2, or L3, as cued by the colored background of the picture. On some trials, the language of naming was repeated from the previous trial (a *non-switch trial*), whereas on other trials the language of naming was different from the previous trial (a *switch trial*). Previous studies have found that bilingual participants are slower to name pictures on switch trials relative to non-switch trials (termed "switch costs") and, counterintuitively, that switch costs are larger when switching into one's dominant L1 than when switching into the less dominant L2 (e.g., Meuter & Allport, 1999). Linck et al. (2012) also found that switch costs differed as a function of proficiency, with the greatest costs being for switches into the L1 and the smallest costs being for switches into the L3. Using a similar sample of English–French–Spanish trilinguals, Schwieter and Sunderman (2011) examined the relationship between language switching performance and individual differences in lexical robustness (i.e., vocabulary size). Greater L2 lexical robustness was associated with faster picture naming in both the L2 *and* the L3, suggesting that learners who are able to develop a deeper vocabulary in the first non-native language are perhaps better at accessing their L2 and L3 lexicons, and therefore are faster overall on a mixed language task. Interestingly, larger L3 lexical robustness was only related to smaller switch costs into the L3 – suggesting a more constrained impact of the L3 lexicon on the L2 when switching between languages.

Costa and colleagues (e.g., Costa & Santesteban, 2004a; Costa, Santesteban, & Ivanova, 2006) have hypothesized that one key component of the proficiency factor is whether individuals have achieved "balanced" bilingualism in at least two languages (i.e., they have attained high-level proficiency in at least one non-native language). Once such a state has been achieved, Costa and colleagues have argued that these multilinguals have developed the ability to control cognitive attention such that lexical items can be selected via a "language-specific" mechanism: lexical candidates in the non-target language become activated along with the target language, but they do not compete for selection. In other words, the claim is that, for balanced bilinguals, words in the non-target language do not influence the process of lexical access. By this account, Costa and colleagues argued for a qualitative shift in how cross-linguistic activation is managed by the multilingual mind once a certain level of proficiency is attained in a non-L1. It is important to note that the results reported by Costa and colleagues come from studies involving childhood bilinguals living in a largely bilingual environment. Nonetheless, it is plausible that their claims regarding the shift away from the need to rely on inhibitory control could also be found with adult learners who achieve high-level proficiency in an L2. As Schwieter and Ferreira (2013) point out, this area is ripe for future research, as the results have implications for theories of bilingual control (and its development) as well as for our understanding of whether age of acquisition constrains when or how general cognitive control mechanisms support multilingual processing. Furthermore, findings from such research could inform pedagogy by determining the optimal time within the learning trajectory to implement language training methods aimed at encouraging inhibitory processing or leveraging an individual's inhibitory control abilities.

The results of bilingual/multilingual language switching studies have been interpreted most frequently in the context of the discussion of the potential role of inhibition in multilingual speech production. Although switch costs per se may not provide the most conclusive inferences regarding the role of inhibition during speech production (see Bobb & Wodniecka, 2013; Kroll, Bobb, & Wodniecka, 2006), studies by Philipp and colleagues demonstrate how examining language switching with multilinguals provides opportunities to test hypotheses regarding the underlying (inhibitory) mechanisms in ways that are unavailable in studies of bilingual participants. For example, Philipp, Gade, and Koch (2007) designed a language switching task similar to the picture-naming task employed by Linck et al. (2012), but with the additional sequential manipulation that the language used on trial $n$ and trial n-2 either repeated or did not repeat, and the intervening trial (n-1) involved a third language. They found that language repetitions were associated with slower responses than language non-repetitions (so-called n-2 repetition costs), indicating that inhibition of the previously abandoned language persisted to trial $n$. This repetition cost was largest for the dominant L1, indicating that relative proficiency modulated the inhibitory effects. Curiously, the repetition effect was larger in the least dominant L3 than in the L2, a finding that does not completely fit with the dominance-based predictions of the IC Model. Additional mixed results were uncovered when Guo et al. (2013) conducted a similar trilingual switching study in which they compared the magnitude of the n-2 repetition costs for each of the three languages. They found that the n-2 repetition costs for the L1 and L2 were larger than the n-2 repetition costs for the L3 but, interestingly, the n-2 repetition costs for the L2 were also larger than the n-2 repetition costs for the L1. The researchers explained that because of the very high L2 proficiency level (i.e., participants had been living in an L2-speaking environment for several years), it might not be surprising that the n-2 repetition costs were largest for the L2. This finding is not contrary to the IC Model because it demonstrated that the magnitude of inhibition of non-target languages during multilingual language production increases with higher levels of language proficiency. Jointly examining switch costs and n-2 repetition costs offers opportunities to further explore the nature of control mechanisms during language switching. Further replication of Philipp et al.'s and Guo et al.'s results with other samples – and with other language sets – is needed to provide additional evidence of the contributions of inhibitory control to multilingual language switching. We consider potential implications of this line of research for multilingual pedagogy below (see section 30.6.2) in the context of the broader literature on cognitive control and executive functions.

### 30.4.1.3 Stroop effects

As mentioned above, cross-language interference has been demonstrated in the Stroop task. However, the patterns of interference depend in part on the relative proficiency of the multilinguals' languages. For example,

Abunuwara (1992) found interlingual Stroop effects in all three languages of Arabic–Hebrew–English trilinguals, with differing patterns across the three languages. The L1 interference effects were larger when naming in the L3 than when naming in the L2, which is congruent with dominance accounts of cross-language interference (e.g., the IC Model) that predict a less dominant L3 will suffer more L1 interference than a more dominant L2 because of the greater asymmetry in language dominance. However, during L1 naming, interference was greater from L2 words than from L3 words, indicating that the more proficient L2 was interfering more with lexical access of the dominant L1, a finding that is also congruent with dominance accounts of cross-language interference. Interestingly, the L2 and L3 interfered little with each other. This finding goes counter to the predictions of the "L2 status" factor or "foreign language effect" (e.g., Bardel & Falk, 2007), which suggests that during L3 learning, the L2 is more likely than the L1 to transfer to the L3 due to its status of being a foreign language. Arguments based on the L2 status factor would posit that L3 naming should show greater interference from the (non-native) L2 than from the L1. Indeed, as will be discussed further in section 30.4.3, the currently available evidence does not seem to support this claim.

### 30.4.1.4 Phonological and grammatical processing

As noted above, when considering the L3 in particular, there is some evidence that the amount of cross-language interaction changes as a function of the degree of proficiency in the L3. Focusing on phonological processing, there is some evidence that a less proficient L3 tends to be affected by the L2 substantially, whereas this L2-on-L3 influence attenuates as the L3 becomes more proficient. Hammarberg and Hammarberg (1993, 2005) examined the L3 Swedish speech of an English/German speaker at two points in time, focusing on the articulation of a number of different segments (e.g., the relative positioning of the tongue during the articulation of /l/) to determine whether the L3 speech was more heavily influenced by L1 or L2. They concluded that in early learning, the speaker used her L2 articulatory settings in order to suppress L1 influence. In later learning, the L2 effects attenuated, thereby allowing the L1 to influence L3 speech. For grammatical processing, Peyer, Kaiser, and Berthele (2010) showed that as L3 proficiency increases, the relative asymmetry in proficiency with other languages seems to matter less, presumably because the L3 is developing stronger lexical representations and more direct access to the grammar. Evaluating the reading comprehension performance of French/English and Spanish/English speaking students of German, they found that students with high German proficiency performed equally well regardless of their reading comprehension in their other languages. Learners with low L3 proficiency, however, performed better if their proficiency in other languages was also high, suggesting that competency in one or more foreign languages enhances performance in an L3. Taken together with the results reviewed above, these studies indicate that relative proficiency affects cross-language interactions across many levels, from lexical access to semantic and syntactic processing to articulation of the phonology.

The patterns of results reviewed here indicate that the relative proficiency of all of one's known languages will impact language processing and language learning in a new L3. This suggests that a learner's language profile provides important information that can inform decisions about how to leverage other known languages in L3 instruction.

### 30.4.2 Cognitive control/executive functions

Another important factor affecting the presence or absence of transfer effects is the individual learner's cognitive control abilities, otherwise known as 'executive functions' or 'executive control.' There is growing evidence that executive functions are called upon to support L2 use (e.g., Abutalebi & Green, 2008; Hernandez & Meschyan, 2006), in part to help negotiate the potential cross-language interference from the L1. This evidence suggests that executive control may be especially important in multilingual language processing because there are more opportunities for negative transfer to occur between languages. Indeed, although the empirical data are currently sparse, there is encouraging evidence of the impact of executive functions on multilingual processing. We review the few extant studies below, then consider implications for multilingual instruction.

Linck et al. (2012) found not only that trilingual switch costs varied according to the relative proficiency of the three languages, but also that the magnitude of the switch costs was related to individual differences in domain-general inhibitory control abilities, with better inhibitors showing reduced switch costs when switching into or out of the dominant L1. By this account, better inhibitors may be capable of more efficiently applying inhibition to non-target representations in the L1 when naming targets in the other languages, such that less inhibition is required to successfully speak in the L2 or L3. That is, the spike in activation of the non-target L1 can be attenuated sooner (i.e., at lower levels of activation), and thus a smaller amount of inhibition is required to prevent the L1 from intruding on the target language. The fact that the inhibitory control effects were restricted to conditions involving the L1 indicates that relative proficiency also plays a role, which suggests that individual differences in inhibitory control – and perhaps executive functions more generally – also contribute to the complicated situation of multilinguals managing cross-language interactions.

A related line of research has found that bilingualism appears to incur more general cognitive benefits to one's ability to manage interference from conflicting information (for reviews, see Bialystok, 2010; Bialystok & Craik in this handbook, Chapter 25; Bialystok et al., 2009; Hilchey, Saint-Aubin, & Klein in this handbook, Chapter 26; Krizman & Marian in this handbook, Chapter 27). That is, a lifetime of experience managing and successfully using two languages may enhance a bilingual's executive control abilities. Both behavioral and neuroimaging studies suggest that bilingualism enhances one's *cognitive reserve* – i.e., the maintenance of cognitive functioning in the face of age-related declines (e.g., Bialystok & Craik in this handbook, Chapter 25; Schweizer et al., 2012). This line of research raises the question of whether these cognitive consequences are further enhanced as the number of mastered languages increases. There is some evidence suggesting this may be the case. Kavé et al. (2008) tested aging adults in their eighties with two standardized tests of attention and memory (e.g., Mini Mental State Exam) and retested them into their nineties to examine how linguistic experiences were related to age-related cognitive decline. They found that multilingualism was related to enhanced cognitive reserve as evidenced by superior cognitive functioning in multilinguals relative to monolinguals; moreover, an examination of the multilinguals suggests that as the number of mastered languages increased, so too did the extent of the enhancements to cognitive reserve. These results suggest that attaining proficiency in additional languages beyond an L2 may provide opportunities to further strengthen one's cognitive control mechanisms that support multilingual language use. However, additional research is needed to elucidate the precise relationship between quantitative and qualitative characteristics of the multilingual experience and enhanced cognitive control.

### 30.4.3 (Psycho)typological similarity

Research from the fields of linguistics and applied psycholinguistics indicates that language pairs with greater typological similarity tend to demonstrate more cross-language interactions than do more dissimilar pairs, resulting in both positive and negative transfer. The body of research from the field of linguistics has generated discussions on one of the most widely recognized constraints on transfer: the degree of congruence among all involved languages. These discussions have led to the concepts of "cross-linguistic similarity" and "cross-linguistic difference." These two concepts have been often further divided into objective and subjective similarities (or differences). In the relevant literature, objective similarity (or difference) refers to the actual degree of congruence that exists between the languages on measurable features, whereas subjective similarity (or difference) refers to the degree of congruence that the learner either perceives or assumes to exist (Jarvis & Pavlenko, 2008). In general, the subjective similarities (or differences) appear essential to the occurrence of transfer because it is the learner's awareness of those similarities that determines which features of one language are transferable to the other (Kellerman, 1978, 1983). Both *perceived* subjective similarities and *assumed* subjective similarities have been described in the literature, and they are not always mutually exclusive (Jarvis, 1998; Ringbom, 2007). A perceived similarity is a learner's judgment, either conscious or unconscious, that a given feature of the languages is similar, whereas an assumed similarity refers to a learner's hypothesis that a given feature of one language exists in the other language. These distinctions might be helpful in explaining instances of positive and negative transfer, because, as Jarvis and Pavlenko (2008) argued, "positive transfer occurs when assumed similarities are compatible with objective similarities, whereas negative transfer occurs when assumed similarities conflict with objective differences" (p. 182). These results suggest that multilingual instruction could benefit from efforts to explicitly draw the learner's attention to any potential conflicts between observed and perceived language similarities in order to reduce negative transfer and increase positive transfer. We return to this point in section 30.6.

The body of research from the field of applied psycholinguistics has motivated the development of three somewhat contradictory accounts of transfer. According to the Cumulative Enhancement Model (e.g., Flynn, Foley, & Vinnitskaya, 2004), all previously learned languages can be drawn upon in subsequent language learning. In contrast, other researchers have claimed that the "L2 status" is the most critical factor, such that transfer is more likely to come from the L2 than the native L1 (e.g., Bardel & Falk, 2007). However, Rothman (2010) argued that neither of these accounts is fully able to capture the extant results. Instead, Rothman claimed that psychotypological similarity (i.e., perceived similarity) trumps the L2 status factor when they are pitted against one another. In his study of adjective placement, Rothman examined two groups of trilinguals: English–Portuguese–Spanish speakers, whose L1 lacked the adjective placement flexibility manipulated in the materials, and Italian–English–Spanish speakers, whose L1 allowed such flexibility in adjective placement. Rothman reasoned that if L2 status is the key factor, then we would expect to see transfer on the adjective processing task for the native English speakers but not the Spanish–English–Portuguese trilinguals; if instead psychotypological similarity drives transfer, then both groups should show transfer effects. Indeed, both groups were indistinguishable from monolinguals, suggesting that psychotypological similarity similarly trumped L2 status (but see comments above regarding the methodological and inferential limitations of this study).

For phonological processing, Llama, Cardoso, and Collins (2010) argued that L2 status has more influence on transfer than does typological similarity, but that ultimately, L3 phonological output is likely a function of combined cross-language interference (De Angelis, 2007). In a study of English–French and French–English bilinguals learning Spanish, they found that both groups of learners behaved similarly in their production of Spanish stops with respect to voice onset time (VOT). If typological similarity were the bigger influence on L3 pronunciation, native French speakers should have had an advantage in producing native-like Spanish aspiration, which is almost identical to French aspiration. Instead, the native French speakers in the study seem to have resorted to VOTs more similar to their non-native English values. However, the authors concede that they relied on averages from the literature to estimate native VOT values for both groups, as well as expected target ranges for Spanish. Because VOT can be highly variable across speaker populations, and the range of averages for French, English, and Spanish all overlap, it is difficult to confidently conclude that L2 status really trumps psychotypological similarity.

### 30.4.4 Age of acquisition/exposure

There is a rich literature examining age of acquisition effects in L2 learning (for a brief overview and additional references, see DeKeyser, 2013). The general pattern suggests that childhood learning tends to result in a higher likelihood of attaining substantial proficiency in the L2, whereas adult learning tends to be much less successful. For this chapter, we largely focus on adult learners of an L3, although we do consider the impact of age of acquisition on some specific factors below (e.g., inhibitory control). Nonetheless, when considering factors that influence multilingual learning, one must take into account the learner's linguistic profile and prior learning experiences. Indeed, aside from age of acquisition per se, a number of other factors impacting L3 learning indicate that the learner's previous experience with language has a strong effect on L3 learning. We turn to those factors in section 30.5.

It is worth noting that heritage speakers represent a unique type of bilingual (e.g., Montrul, 2010), facing specific issues by virtue of not necessarily having a formalized understanding of the grammar of their L1, and, in some cases, lacking literacy entirely. This situation raises a number of questions regarding when and how L1 transfer will interact with L2 transfer to affect L3 learning. Further work focusing on heritage learners of an L3 is needed to better understand whether the factors identified above apply to their learning situation as well.

### 30.4.5 Type of task

In light of the number of factors shown to influence language transfer in L3 learning, it is important to consider that a research design itself may inadvertently favor some types of interference. For instance, Hammarberg and Hammarberg's (1993) case study of an English–German learner of Swedish clearly showed that language influence is task dependent. Their learner evidenced more interference from L1 phonology in a read-on-your-own task and more L2 transfer in a picture-narration task and a read-after-me task, in which the speaker shadowed the pronunciation of a native Swedish speaker. The authors note that the speaker explicitly expressed a desire to suppress any English accent on her Swedish speech. When faced with speaking freely or reading without a model, she was able to rely more on her L2 phonological knowledge to fill in the gaps in her Swedish pronunciation. When mimicking native speech, however, she was not as successful at suppressing her L1 influence. These results further complicate the research landscape by suggesting that learners may be able to consciously control some of the effects of language transfer, at least in some situations or when performing certain tasks. More research is needed to further elucidate how the type of task impacts positive and negative transfer. This line of research could inform the selection of learning tasks that are well suited to facilitating positive transfer and reducing negative transfer in L3 learning situations.

## 30.5 Multilingual learning

In addition to examining factors that influence multilingual language processing, it is important to consider how these (and other) factors might influence language learning. A small number of studies have explicitly examined vocabulary learning by multilinguals. Below, we review the extant studies on vocabulary learning within the multilingual context. We then consider the importance of metalinguistic awareness for the multilingual learning process and discuss relevant literature where available.

### 30.5.1 Vocabulary learning

There is a growing literature examining bilingual advantages in L3 learning, with many of the studies focusing on vocabulary learning. For example, Kaushanskaya and Marian (2009) compared monolingual English speakers to a group of bilinguals whose two languages share the same script (early English–Spanish bilinguals) and a group of bilinguals whose two languages use different writing systems (early English–Mandarin bilinguals). Participants came into the lab to perform a novel word-learning task involving an artificial phonological system. In the initial learning phase, participants were taught forty-eight disyllabic novel foreign language words; participants first heard each word over headphones while its English translation was presented on the computer screen, after which they were instructed to produce the word and its translation aloud. To assess learning, participants completed tests of recognition and recall both immediately and after a one-week delay. Results for the immediate recall test indicated that both bilingual groups correctly recalled nearly half of the new words, whereas the monolinguals recalled only about 25 percent. The bilingual groups also outperformed the monolinguals on the delayed recall test and on both immediate and delayed recognition tests, with no differences between same-script and different-script bilinguals in their overall performance.

Similar patterns of bilingual advantages have been found with native Italian speakers learning Russian as an L3 (Papagno & Vallar, 1995) and native Dutch speakers learning Spanish (van Hell & Mahn, 1997). However, an important point to note is that these studies all employed a research design in which the language of instruction for the novel words was always the L1. Given that both the L1 and L2 can transfer during L3 learning, it is possible that learning would be further enhanced by instruction in the L2. To examine whether learning would be affected by the language of instruction, Bogulski (2009) designed an experiment in which Dutch words were learned via their English translations. She compared the performance of two bilingual groups: English–Spanish bilinguals (instruction in L1), and Mandarin–English bilinguals (instruction in L2). On an immediate test of translation recognition, the English–Spanish bilinguals were both faster and more accurate than the Chinese–English bilinguals (78.1 percent vs. 70.7 percent accuracy, respectively), indicating that learning via the L1 enhanced performance. However, a different picture emerged on a delayed post-training lexical decision task, on which both bilingual groups performed similarly and outperformed a group of monolingual English speakers, indicating a bilingual advantage on retention of the newly learned vocabulary, regardless of the language of instruction. One possible explanation of these differences relates to the languages involved in the tasks. The translation recognition task materials involved Dutch–English word pairs, such that the Chinese–English bilinguals were performing the task in their L2 and L3 whereas the English–Spanish bilinguals were performing it in their L1 and L3. This involvement of the less automatized L2 for the Chinese–English bilinguals may have impaired their performance on the translation recognition task, leading to lower accuracy relative to the English–Spanish bilinguals. In contrast, the lexical decision task simply involved making judgments of whether a word string was a word in Dutch without any explicit requirement to use English. By eliminating the need to use the L2, this task may have allowed the Chinese–English bilinguals to perform at a higher level. Taken together, these results suggest that bilinguals may bring language learning skills to the experience of learning a new L3, which can enhance the learning process.

The results of laboratory studies on novel vocabulary learning indicate that prior L2 experience benefits the learning of vocabulary in a new language. Although the study by Bogulski (2009) suggests a short-lived effect of the language of instruction (i.e., learning via the L1 vs. the L2) on L3 word learning, the question remains of whether (perceived) similarities between existing languages and the novel language might modulate this effect. In her study, the participants who learned via the L2 were also native speakers of a language that did not share script with the L2 or L3. A ripe area for future research will be to examine the interactions between script overlap and other features of a bilingual's known languages with the language of instruction to optimize L3 word learning.

### 30.5.2 Metalinguistic awareness

One intuitively apparent benefit for bilinguals over monolinguals is the very experience of having learned a foreign language; as such, bilingual advantages in L3 learning are often attributed to enhanced metalinguistic awareness (e.g., Gibson & Hufeisen, 2003, 2006; Jessner, 2003; Klein, 1995; Thomas, 1988). However, relatively few authors include precise operational definitions of metalinguistic awareness, discussing concepts ranging from an understanding of language as a system to an awareness of learning strategies that have worked well in past language learning contexts.

Measures purported to assess metalinguistic awareness are also sparse and inconsistent throughout the literature. For example, Gibson and Hufeisen (2006) defined metalinguistic awareness as including "heightened abilities to differentiate, keep track of and manipulate ... form vs. meaning" (p. 141). Based on a finding that multilingual learners of English performed well on a task requiring judgment of grammatical errors in the presence of semantic anomalies, they concluded that multilingualism may indeed confer advantages in metalinguistic awareness (although it is important to note that the study did not include any monolingual controls). Kemp (2007) focused on strategy use, examining grammar learning strategies in participants who knew between two and twelve languages each. The study did not test actual L3 learning or performance. However, questionnaire results revealed that individuals who knew more languages reported using more strategies, although it is important to note that there is no known relationship between number of strategies and language learning or performance. Bono and Stratilaki (2009) argued that an important factor that may be driving some of these multilingual advantages is a motivational one – individuals' perceptions regarding their multilingualism; in other words, it is important for learners to view their multilingualism as a strategic asset in learning additional languages.

Although studies of metalinguistic awareness and related constructs hold promise for better understanding of how past language learning experience can be leveraged in L3 learning contexts, it will be important for researchers to develop precise operational definitions and include validated measures to allow for a more direct evaluation of the benefits to learning that multilingualism is claimed to confer.

## 30.6 Multilingual pedagogy

In spite of the growing body of literature on multilingualism and L3 acquisition, there is still a lack of a systematic investigation of L3 instruction. Relevant literature offers general policy-related recommendations for designing L3 programs in countries where learning three languages in primary and secondary education is a common experience (Cenoz, Hufeisen, & Jessner, 2001; Cummins, 2001; Hufeisen, 1995; Jessner, 2008; Jessner & Cenoz, 2007; Ytsma, 2001). For the most part, these recommendations call for establishing links between languages, creating a common curriculum for all languages involved, and making teachers and learners aware of linguistic features of languages. Likewise, other publications concerning L3 instruction generally suggest maximizing attempts to leverage students' previous language knowledge and learning experience in the process of learning a consecutive language (Hufeisen & Neuner, 2004; Jessner, 1999). However, how exactly this can be done has not been investigated or documented. What techniques are most effective in L3 instruction? Should they differ from techniques used in any other foreign language classroom? If L3 acquisition is distinguished from L2 acquisition, should this difference be reflected in the instruction? Although the available literature does not provide explicit answers to these questions, there is some evidence that may at least indirectly inform the issues.[3]

As in the case of any foreign language course, the starting point in the design of an L3 course is to systematically collect and analyze information about students' backgrounds, their previous linguistic experience, and their language learning goals. This information can be gathered through a process called needs analysis that should happen during the course-design stage (e.g., Brown, 2009). A needs analysis can be completed through a triangulation of qualitative data (e.g., surveys, interviews) collected from learners, other individuals who are currently using the foreign language for its intended purpose and who hence are aware of learning and usage problems (the so called *in situ* needs analysis), and job supervisors (Long, 2005). Curriculum developers and instructors familiar with their students' linguistic backgrounds, needs, and goals will be more knowledgeable and consequently better off when it comes to designing L3 courses and developing materials for these courses. Equipped with this knowledge and these materials, instructors and curriculum developers can help the learners to establish links between objective features of the languages and learners' perceived similarities among languages, which should benefit learning by increasing positive transfer and attenuating negative transfer.

---

[3] One exception is the work conducted under the EuroCom project (McCann, Klein, & Stegmann, 2003), that provides specific techniques for learners of Romance languages to show them that they already know a lot of a given language just because they know a similar language. While these techniques seem to be useful, their effectiveness has not been evaluated or documented.

Below we propose some ways in which implications for adult L3 language instruction can be derived from available empirical evidence on language factors such as objective and perceived proximities among languages as well as learner factors such as individual differences in executive control. It is important to note that the link between available evidence and implications for instruction is, for the most part, solely our interpretation of how this evidence can be extended into L3 instruction. Moreover, we focus our discussion on factors relevant to L3 instruction in particular, not language acquisition in general.

### 30.6.1 Language factors

#### 30.6.1.1 Objective features of languages

The relationship among all languages in the multilingual mind is crucial for L3 instruction, especially when it comes to their proximity, because this information can facilitate student selection for L3 learning as well as the development of effective instructional techniques and materials. However, proximity among multiple languages cannot be easily measured or quantified on a large scale because of the large number of possibilities that need to be investigated, which can prove rather impractical. That is, developing relatedness measures among possible L1–L2–L3 triads would require consideration of a large number of possibilities; even if one language (e.g., English) is singled out as the starting point, there are still thousands of possible combinations. Despite the emergence of some promising approaches for estimating the relative distance among languages based on computational measures of entropy between parallel corpora (Nakhleh, Ringe, & Warnow, 2005), these methods have not been used to test learnability. Although large-scale analyses of language proximity involving multiple languages are difficult to perform, identifying structural features of two languages can be successfully accomplished using available linguistic tools. One excellent and widely available tool that can be very useful in identifying and comparing structural features of languages is the World Atlas of Linguistic Structures (WALS; Dryer & Haspelmath, 2011), which encompasses a large database of phonological, grammatical, and lexical properties of hundreds of languages, with chapters describing given properties, comparison tables, and maps, allowing the user to compare selected properties for specific language combinations.

More traditional methods of language comparison have drawn on the works of comparative or contrastive linguistics, from which contrastive and error analyses developed. The two latter methods have received more criticism than praise in the last few decades for their inability to support their claims that they can either predict or explain a learner's errors based on their knowledge of the learner's L1 and L2. Although this criticism is justified and contrastive analysis has been shown to be ineffective when applied to foreign language learning (e.g., Klein, 1986; Tarone, 1979;

Whitman & Jackson, 1972), its tools can be used for the purposes of describing linguistic systems in question.

It seems very relevant to use methods from descriptive and comparative linguistics as well as available tools, such as WALS, to describe a learner's L1, L2, and L3. The outcomes of these comparisons can be used later to make learners aware of objective features of languages (both similarities and differences) so that the objective similarities can become perceived similarities, which should lead to positive transfer. Because language instructors do not always have extensive background in linguistics, they will benefit from having linguistic tools for language description, which may give them means to acquire the background linguistic knowledge they can use to help their students to facilitate positive transfer and mitigate negative transfer. However, empirical studies are needed to evaluate the effectiveness for language pedagogy.

### 30.6.1.2 Perceived features of languages

For positive transfer to occur, learners must perceive similarities among languages (Jarvis, 2000; Kellerman, 1995; Odlin, 2003; Ringbom, 2001). Indeed, one implication of Kellerman's seminal (1983) work discussed earlier is that learners themselves need to realize – or be made to realize – the similarities. Ringbom (2007) argued that what is important to the language learner is language proximity (i.e., similarities) and not language distance (i.e., differences). Teachers can facilitate this process by providing materials that explicitly point out similarities between a learner's languages, for example, with reference to lexical items, or information on sound and case systems. Consequently, the more similar the features, the more time savings are possible because less attention may be required during L3 instruction (Gribble, 1987; Kulman & Tetrault, 1992). In L3 instruction, similarities should be identified and pointed out to students to facilitate positive transfer; differences, on the other hand, should also be identified and then explicitly taught in order to mitigate negative transfer. For example, Gribble stated that the notion of aspect in his Bulgarian course for learners with background in Russian does not receive much attention because the concept of aspect is essentially the same in both languages. Similarly, in *Pois Não: Brazilian Portuguese Course for Spanish Speakers*, Simões (2008) focuses early on the sounds of Brazilian Portuguese that are not part of the inventory of Spanish sounds as well as morphosyntactic differences between the two languages. The entire content of Ulsh's (2011) *From Spanish to Portuguese* manual contains explicit comparisons between the two languages, including their sound systems, morphology, syntax, and lexicons. These approaches should benefit multilingual learners by making them more aware of similarities and differences, which can increase positive transfer and mitigate negative transfer. It is important to note that awareness of similarities and differences is most facilitative when they are fully perceived by learners. For example, Zobl (1982) notes that in L2 acquisition, zero relations between languages are sometimes facilitative, whereas close, but not exact, likeness results in a delay (i.e., negative transfer).

There is some empirical evidence that L3 learners can learn a new language in a shorter amount of time than L2 learners, especially when learning an L3 that is closely related to the L1 or L2 (e.g., shares linguistic features, contains many cognates; see review in Rivers & Golonka, 2009). Generally, this evidence shows that adult L3 courses that are shorter than regular L2 courses can produce similar results (Corin, 1994; Rivers, 1996). Such "conversion courses" are conceptualized based on an idea of the high degree of mutual intelligibility between language pairs, such as Spanish and Portuguese (Holton, 1954; Jensen, 1989; Jordan, 1991), Russian and Czech (Townsend, 1995), and Czech and Serbian/Croatian (Corin, 1994). Corin provided some data supporting a claim that in a conversion course, learning can happen much faster than in a regular L2 course. At the end of a three-month conversion course involving forty Czech linguists, the median oral proficiency on the Interagency Language Roundtable (ILR) scale[4] was 2 and the mode was 1+. Simões (2008) argued that his book teaches the equivalent of one year of college Portuguese in one semester; however it should be noted that the effectiveness of the course has not been empirically evaluated.

In sum, multilingual learners who perceive the similarity of linguistic features among their languages are more likely to experience positive transfer, suggesting that multilingual pedagogy should leverage these similarities by explicitly making students aware of them in order to enhance L3 learning. In contrast, awareness of differences in linguistic features may reduce the extent of negative transfer between a multilingual's languages, and therefore multilingual instruction should explicitly teach differences among specific language groupings to facilitate the learner's perception of these differences. That is, multilingual instruction should benefit from the implementation of methods aimed at increasing student awareness of similarities and differences.

### 30.6.2 Learner factors

Other types of potential methods for enhancing L3 instructional techniques come from studies investigating how multiple languages interact from a cognitive perspective. In this section, we speculate (because more research is needed) on a few ways in which the research reviewed in the first half of this chapter might be applied to the L3 instructional context.

The robust cross-language interactions involving cognates support the current practice in L3 pedagogy of drawing the learner's explicit attention to the existence of cognates (e.g., Simões, 2008). Similarly, transfer effects

---

[4] Visit www.govtilr.org for the history of the development of the ILR scale and details of the level descriptions.

involving grammatical processing also suggest that instructors should make explicit any and all cases of direct overlap in syntactic features between the L3 and the L1 or L2. As discussed above in section 30.4.3, making learners aware of any assumed and/or previously unnoticed between-language similarities should increase the likelihood of positive transfer, thereby facilitating learning. However, when overlap is not beneficial – such as situations in which assumed or perceived similarities do not represent true overlap and are in fact misleading – the instructor should explicitly point out this false overlap in order to mitigate any potential for negative transfer to lead to difficulties in L3 learning and/or use. For example, false cognates are words that overlap in form and sound but do not share the same meaning (e.g., *room* in Dutch, meaning *cream*). By making students aware of the presence of such false cognates and explicitly teaching those words, learners should be better prepared to reduce the effects of negative transfer.

The explicit discussion of these shared and similar features among known languages may also provide opportunities for learners to develop or be encouraged to use metalinguistic strategies to facilitate L3 learning and use. For example, if the L3 contains many cognates and few false cognates, learners may shift their focus to more explicitly take advantage of any overlap with the L1 and/or L2. In contrast, in situations in which the L3 has fewer cognates but a higher proportion of false cognates, learners may want to try to ignore or suppress the L1 or L2 – or at least attempt to minimize any tendency to rely on the other languages to access the meaning of an L3 word. In terms of methods for novel vocabulary learning, some preliminary evidence on L3 word learning suggests that, at least in the context of explicit learning, paired associates task, learning L3 words via existing L1 words – rather than through L2 words – may facilitate learning (Bogulski, 2009). This finding suggests that during initial stages of learning, relying on the L1 (as the learner) and drawing attention to the L1 (as the instructor) may help learners to bootstrap into the L3 to begin establishing L3 lexical representations. It is possible that the established automaticity of lexical retrieval in the L1 allows the learner to focus attentional resources on making the association with the new L3 vocabulary word, suggesting that explicit learning situations (such as Bogulski's paired associates task) might be more beneficial when they involve more automatized languages. Taking this hypothesis one step further, it might suggest that as multilingual learners develop automaticity in a number of languages, they may show a greater benefit from explicit learning techniques by virtue of the faster, more automatic lexical processing of the previously learned languages.

The structure of the multilingual lexicon according to the RHM would suggest that learning L3 words via existing L1 words would benefit learners due to their ability to rely on direct lexical links between the well-established L1 and the to-be-established L3, thereby facilitating access to the semantics of the associated words. By providing opportunities to more rapidly access the semantics, a stronger association between the novel L3 word and its underlying conceptual meaning could begin forming earlier in the learning process. As overall L3 proficiency increases and the L3 representations are strengthened, learners should be able to shift away from reliance on the L1 to access the semantics more directly via L3 lexical–conceptual links. Further research is needed to corroborate these preliminary results with other language pairs with differing extents of feature overlap, as well as with other types of word-learning tasks. It will also be important to extend the learning paradigm beyond rote learning and recall and recognition outcome measures to investigate productive and receptive language use.

The findings on cognitive control that were reviewed earlier indicate that executive functions are relevant to understanding L3 learning and processing. This line of research suggests that learners and instructors should take advantage of these individual differences in any way possible. One such method could be to employ aptitude–treatment interaction (ATI) approaches, whereby instruction is tailored to characteristics of the individual learner to leverage strengths and mitigate weaknesses (for a recent review of ATI studies in L2 learning, see Vatz et al., 2013). For example, as discussed above, inhibitory control abilities have been implicated in studies of L3 processing. Perhaps speakers with greater inhibitory control abilities could be selected for positions requiring L3 learning. The integration of L3-specific factors as well as other factors known to affect SLA more generally could provide a powerful ATI pedagogical approach to enhance L3 learning. The systematic application of ATI methods to L3 instruction is a vital area of research for exploration that would allow the extant theoretical and empirical developments in psycholinguistic and SLA research on multilingualism to directly enhance L3 pedagogy, while also informing the broader SLA literature with respect to learning principles and the application of ATI methods.

Another approach could involve the use of training regimens to enhance cognitive abilities. Previous research suggests that focused cognitive training of the working memory (WM) system can lead to measureable benefits not only to memory processes but also to L2 processing, for instance the resolution of an ambiguous sentence (e.g., Novick et al., 2014; for a recent review of the implications of cognitive training for language processing, see Hussey & Novick, 2012; for contrasting views on the efficacy of cognitive training methods, see, e.g., Shipstead, Redick, & Engle, 2012). There is a broad research base on L2 processing and learning that indicates that better WM is related to enhanced L2 outcomes (for a recent meta-analysis, see Linck et al., 2014). This evidence suggests that cognitive training focusing on either enhancing WM abilities or developing learner strategies to better use WM may benefit L3 learning and L3 use. There remain many unanswered questions regarding the impact of individual differences in cognitive processes on L3 learning, and this exciting area of research has only recently begun to expand beyond bilinguals to examine multilinguals in a systematic way (e.g., see the trilingual switching studies of Linck et al., 2012, and Philipp & Koch, 2009, that may have implications for the potential benefit of cognitive training for L3 learning).

A related potential direction is motivated by the claims that language switching relies on domain-general inhibitory control (e.g., Green, 1998), and that individual differences in inhibitory control abilities account for a learner's ability to control interference from the L1 when speaking in the L3 (Linck et al., 2012). One potential implication of this body of research is that engaging in systematic multilingual language switching may provide a method to train or enhance one's inhibitory control abilities while simultaneously gaining additional practice with the L3. Various manipulations of the type of linguistic materials included in the switching task (e.g., cognates, semantic categories, culturally specific content) could provide practice managing cross-language interactions with task- or job-relevant material that is tailored to the learner's needs. This exciting possibility for future research merits exploration in future empirical studies with multilingual learners and highly proficient multilinguals alike.

## 30.7 Conclusion

Our discussion of three prominent models of bilingual language representation and processing suggests that models such as the BIA+ and RHM can easily be adapted to multilingual contexts in which they could prove very useful for generating testable hypotheses about the nature of interaction among three or more languages. Once the IC Model is further specified to describe the nature of inhibitory mechanisms across multiple languages and is then tested empirically, such an effort could shed light on the types of cognitive control required for successful multilingualism.

Although considerable evidence has now been amassed to show both facilitation (e.g., cognate effects) and interference (e.g., Stroop effects) among languages, further research is needed to disentangle the many factors that contribute to and/or moderate the occurrence of these kinds of transfer, such as relative proficiency, age of acquisition, individual differences in cognitive control, objective and perceived similarities among languages, and task-specific variables.

Numerous studies have also shown that bilinguals have advantages over monolinguals in learning a new language, perhaps due to factors such as metalinguistic awareness and familiarity with multiple language learning strategies. More precise operational definitions and validated measures are required both to better understand the mechanisms underlying the bilingual advantage in subsequent language learning and to develop specific recommendations for leveraging that advantage in the L3 classroom.

In Table 30.1 we have attempted to synthesize the findings reviewed in this chapter to develop some preliminary suggestions for incorporating

Table 30.1 Summary of implications for L3 course design and instruction

| Goal | Proposed strategies | Method | Implementation steps |
|---|---|---|---|
| Design a relevant L3 course | Perform needs analysis | Prior to the beginning of the course, collect information either on individual students' language learning history, needs, and goals, or on a group of students' needs and goals through survey of learners, interviews/focus groups with job supervisors, etc. | Triangulation among survey of learners, in situ needs analysis, interviews/focus groups with job supervisors. (Long, 2005) |
| Improve student selection for L3 courses | Identify optimal language pairings for L3 learning | Use available tools such as WALS | Select languages that share most features |
|  | Select students with demonstrated proficiency in a particular L2 |  | Select students with highest L2 proficiency in the selected languages |
| Maximize leveraging of students' previous linguistic and metalinguistic knowledge | Develop resources that draw upon comparative descriptions of languages | Use objective descriptions of languages to identify similarities and differences | Explicitly discuss shared and similar features among languages |
|  | Encourage learners to use strategies for metalinguistic awareness to facilitate learning | Identify relevant strategies | Train students in explicit strategies |
| Facilitate positive transfer | Establish links between objective and perceived features of languages by capitalizing on similarities and differences among L1, L2, and L3 | Develop materials based on objective features of languages and use instructional techniques to facilitate students' awareness of the features | Identify or develop instructional techniques relevant to the current L3 learning scenario |
| Reduce possibilities of negative transfer | Encourage learners to evaluate their assumed language similarities and formulate perceived similarities, as appropriate | Change objective differences into perceived differences | Expose learners to a large amount of relevant input in which they will encounter corresponding features of the languages |
|  |  | Identify and correct student errors that are based on assumed similarities | Use implicit (recasts) and explicit (prompts, overt corrections, metalinguistic explanations) negative feedback, as appropriate |
| Facilitate vocabulary learning | Take advantage of the facilitative effects of cognates | Present cognates early on in instruction | If applicable, teach TL alphabet using cognates |
|  |  | Identify and teach triple cognates | Identify triple cognates using IBM's Rich Lexical Explorer Tool |

| | | |
|---|---|---|
| Leverage learner's strengths and mitigate weaknesses | Employ ATI approaches | Tailor instruction to individual learners Assess language aptitude, then provide more implicit learning tasks to better implicit learners (Jackson et al., 2012). For a summary of findings and methods of implementing ATI with L2 learning, see Vatz et al. (2013) |
| Enhance learning-relevant cognitive abilities | Use cognitive training regimes | Complete working memory training to enhance cognitive control (e.g., Novick et al., 2014) Have students complete working memory training immediately prior to instruction Engage in systematic multilingual language switching to enhance inhibitory control abilities Have students name pictures, alternating among languages (see Linck et al., 2012, for a non-training version of a language switching task) |

evidence from psycholinguistic research into L3 course design and pedagogy. Given the previously mentioned lack of systematic investigation of L3 instruction, it is critical to bring rigorous scientific inquiry to bear on these questions. A multi-pronged approach including careful classroom studies and laboratory studies with an instructional focus is needed to inform and improve L3 teaching and learning.

# References

Aboitiz, F., & García, R. (1997). The evolutionary origin of the language areas in the human brain. A neuroanatomical perspective. *Brain Research Reviews*, 25(3), 381–396.

Abreu, A., Macaluso, E., Azevedo, R., Cesari, P., Urgesi, C., & Aglioti, S. (2012). Action anticipation beyond the action observation network: A functional magnetic resonance imaging study in expert basketball players. *European Journal of Neuroscience*, 35(10), 1646–1654.

Abunuwara, E. (1992). The structure of the trilingual lexicon. *European Journal of Cognitive Psychology*, 4, 311–322.

Abutalebi, J. (2008). Neural aspects of second language representation and language control. *Acta Psychologica*, 128(3), 466–478.

Abutalebi, J., Annoni, J., Zimine, et al. (2008). Language control and lexical competition in bilinguals: An event-related fMRI Study. *Cerebral Cortex*, 18, 1496–1505.

Abutalebi, J., Brambati, S., Annoni, J., Moro, A., Cappa, S., & Perani, D. (2007). The neural cost of the auditory perception of language switches: An event-related functional magnetic resonance imaging study in bilinguals. *Journal of Neuroscience*, 27, 13762–13769.

Abutalebi, J., Cappa, S., & Perani, D. (2005). What can functional neuroimaging tell us about the bilingual brain? In J. Kroll & A. de Groot (eds.), *Handbook of bilingualism: Psycholinguistic approaches* (pp. 497–515). New York: Oxford University Press.

Abutalebi, J., Della Rosa, P., Green, D., et al. (2012). Bilingualism tunes the anterior cingulate cortex for conflict monitoring. *Cerebral Cortex*, 22(9), 2076–2086.

Abutalebi, J., Della Rosa, P., Tettamanti, M., Green, D., & Cappa, S. (2009). Bilingual aphasia and language control: A follow-up fMRI and intrinsic connectivity study. *Brain and Language*, 109(2-3), 141–156.

Abutalebi, J., & Green, D. (2007). Bilingual language production: The neurocognition of language representation and control. *Journal of Neurolinguistics*, 20(3), 242–275.

(2008). Control mechanisms in bilingual language production: Neural evidence from language switching studies. *Language and Cognitive Processes*, 23(4), 557–582.

Acha, J., & Perea, M. (2008). The effect of neighborhood frequency in reading: Evidence with transposed-letter neighbors. *Cognition*, 108, 290–300.

Ackerman, P. (2003). Aptitude complexes and trait complexes. *Educational Psychologist*, 38, 85–93.

Adamic, L. (2002). Zipf, Power-laws, and Pareto: A ranking tutorial. Accessed from: www.hpl.hp.com/research/idl/papers/ranking/ranking.html.

Adamic, L., & Huberman, B. (2002). Zipf's law and the Internet. *Glottometrics*, 3, 143–150.

Addyman, C., & French, R. (2012). Computational modeling in cognitive science: A manifesto for change. *Topics in Cognitive Science*, 4(3), 332–341.

Adesope, O., Lavin, T., Thompson, T., & Ungerleider, C. (2010). A systematic review and meta-analysis of the cognitive correlates of bilingualism. *Review of Educational Research*, 80(2), 207–245.

Adrover-Roig, D., Galparsoro-Izagirre, N., Marcotte, K., Ferré, P., Wilson, M., & Inés Ansaldo, A. (2011). Impaired L1 and executive control after left basal ganglia damage in a bilingual Basque-Spanish person with aphasia. *Clinical Linguistics & Phonetics*, 25, 480–498.

Albareda-Castellot, B., Pons, F., & Sebastián-Gallés, N. (2011). The acquisition of phonetic categories in bilingual infants: New data from an anticipatory eye movement paradigm. *Developmental Science*, 14(2), 395–401.

Albert, M., & Obler, L. (1978). *The bilingual brain: Neurophysiological and neurolinguistic aspects of bilingualism*. New York: Academic Press.

Alexiadou, A., & Anagnostopoulou, E. (1998). Parametrizing AGR: Word order, V-movement and EPP-checking. *Natural Language & Linguistic Theory*, 16, 491–539.

Alladi, S., Bak, T., Duggirala, V., et al. (2013). Bilingualism delays age at onset of dementia, independent of education and immigration status. *Neurology*, 81, 1938–1944.

Allan, L. (1980). A note on measurement of contingency between two binary variables in judgment tasks. *Bulletin of the Psychonomic Society*, 15, 147–149.

Allen, D., & Conklin, K. (2013). Cross-linguistic similarity and task demands in Japanese–English bilingual processing. *PLoS ONE*, 8, e72631.

Allen, L. (2000). Form–meaning connections and the French causative: An experiment in processing instruction. *Studies in Second Language Acquisition*, 22, 69–84.

Allopenna, P., Magnuson, J., & Tanenhaus, M. (1998). Tracking the time course of spoken word recognition using eye movements: Evidence for continuous mapping models. *Journal of Memory and Language*, 38, 419–439.

Allport, A. (1989). Visual attention. In M. Posner (ed.), *The foundations of cognitive science* (pp. 631–682). Cambridge, MA: MIT Press.

Allport, A., Styles, E., & Hsieh, S. (1994). Shifting intentional set: Exploring the dynamic control of tasks. In C. Umilta & M. Moscovitch (eds.), *Attention and performance XV: Conscious and nonconscious information processing* (pp. 421–452). Hillsdale, NJ: Erlbaum.

Allport, D., & Wylie, G. (1999). Task-switching: Positive and negative priming of task-set. In G. Humphreys, J. Duncan, & A. Treisman (eds.), *Attention, space and action: Studies in cognitive neuroscience* (pp. 273–296). Oxford, UK: Oxford University Press.

Altarriba, J. (1992). The representation of translation equivalents in bilingual memory. In R. Harris (ed.), *Cognitive processing in bilinguals* (pp. 157–174). Oxford, UK: Oxford University Press.

(2003). Does *cariño* equal "liking?" A theoretical approach to conceptual nonequivalence between languages. *International Journal of Bilingualism*, 7, 305–322.

(2006). Cognitive approaches to the study of emotion-laden and emotion words in monolingual and bilingual memory. *Bilingual Education and Bilingualism*, 56, 232–256.

(2008). Expressions of emotion as mediated by context. *Bilingualism: Language and Cognition*, 11, 165–167.

(2012). Emotion and mood: Over 120 years of contemplation and exploration. *American Journal of Psychology*, 125, 409–422.

Altarriba, J., & Basnight-Brown, D. (2011). The representation of emotion vs. emotion-laden words in English and Spanish in the Affective Simon Task. *International Journal of Bilingualism*, 15(3), 310–328.

(2012). The acquisition of concrete, abstract, and emotion words in a second language. *International Journal of Bilingualism*, 16, 446–452.

Altarriba, J., & Bauer, L. (2004). The distinctiveness of emotion concepts: A comparison between emotion, abstract, and concrete words. *American Journal of Psychology*, 117(3), 389–410.

Altarriba, J., Bauer, L., & Benvenuto, C. (1999). Concreteness, context availability, and imageability ratings and word associations for abstract, concrete, and emotion words. *Behavior Research Methods, Instruments, & Computers*, 31(4), 578–602.

Altarriba, J., & Canary, T. (2004). The influence of emotional arousal on affective priming in monolingual and bilingual speakers. *Journal of Multilingual and Multicultural Development*, 25, 248–265.

Altarriba, J., & Mathis, K. (1997). Conceptual and lexical development in second language acquisition. *Journal of Memory and Language*, 36, 550–568.

Altarriba, J., & Santiago-Rivera, A. (1994). Current perspectives on using linguistic and cultural factors in counseling the Hispanic client. *Professional Psychology: Research and Practice*, 25, 388–397.

Altarriba, J., & Soltano, E. (1996). Repetition blindness and bilingual memory: Token individuation for translation equivalents. *Memory & Cognition*, 24(6), 700–711.

Altarriba, J., Kroll, J., Sholl, A., & Rayner, K. (1996). The influence of lexical and conceptual constraints on reading mixed-language sentences: Evidence from eye fixations and naming times. *Memory & Cognition*, 24, 477–92.

Altenberg, E., & Cairns, H. (1983). The effects of phonotactic constraints on lexical processing in bilingual and monolingual subjects. *Journal of Verbal Learning and Verbal Behavior*, 22, 174–188.

Altenberg, E., & Ferrand, C. (2006). Fundamental frequency in monolingual English, bilingual English/Russian, and bilingual English/Cantonese young adult women. *Journal of Voice*, 20(1), 89–96.

Altmann, G. (1998). Ambiguity in sentence processing. *Trends in Cognitive Sciences*, 2(4), 146–152.

Altmann, G., Garnham, A., & Dennis, Y. (1992). Avoiding the garden path: Eye movements in context. *Journal of Memory and Language*, 31(5), 685–712.

Altmann, G., & Mirković, J. (2009). Incrementality and prediction in human sentence processing. *Cognitive Science*, 33(4), 583–609.

Alvarez, R., Holcomb, P., & Grainger, J. (2003). Accessing word meaning in two languages: An event-related brain potential study of beginning bilinguals. *Brain and Language*, 87, 290–304.

Ameel, E., Malt, B., Storms, G., & Van Assche, F. (2009). Semantic convergence in the bilingual lexicon. *Journal of Memory and Language*, 60, 270–290.

Ameel, E., Storms, G., Malt, B., & Sloman, S. (2005). How bilinguals solve the naming problem. *Journal of Memory and Language*, 53, 60–80.

Amrhein, P., & Sanchez, R. (1997). The time it takes bilinguals and monolinguals to draw pictures and write words. *Journal of Experimental Psychology: Learning, Memory, and Cognition*, 23, 1439.

Amuzu, E. (2011). Ewe contact database. (Unpublished corpus), University of Ghana, Legon.

Anderson, J. (1983). A spreading activation theory of memory. *Journal of Verbal Learning & Verbal Behavior*, 22(3), 261–295.

Anderson, J., Morgan, J., & White, K. (2003). A statistical basis for speech sound discrimination. *Language and Speech*, 46, 155–182.

Anderson, M., Brumbaugh, J., & Şuben, A. (2010). Investigating functional cooperation in the human brain using simple graph-theoretic methods. *Computational Neuroscience* (pp. 31–42). New York: Springer.

Anderson, M., & Levy, B. (2007). Theoretical issues in inhibition: Insights from research on human memory. In D. Gorfein & C. MacLeod (eds.),

*Inhibition in cognition* (pp. 81–102). Washington, DC: American Psychological Association.

Andrews, S. (1989). Frequency and neighborhood effects on lexical access: Activation or search? *Journal of Experimental Psychology: Learning, Memory, and Cognition*, 15, 802–814.

(1996). Lexical retrieval and selection processes: Effects of transposed-letter confusability. *Journal of Memory and Language*, 35, 775–800.

(1997). The effect of orthographic similarity on lexical retrieval: Resolving neighborhood conflicts. *Psychonomic Bulletin & Review*, 4, 439–461.

Androulaki, A., Gômez-Pestaña, N., Mitsakis, C., Jover, J., Coventry, K., & Davies, I. (2006). Basic colour terms in Modern Greek: Twelve terms including two blues. *Journal of Greek Linguistics*, 7, 3–45.

Anooshian, L., & Hertel, P. (1994). Emotionality in free recall: Language specificity in bilingual memory. *Cognition and Emotion*, 8, 503–514.

Antón, E., Duñabeitia, J., Estévez, A., Hernández, J., Castillo, A., Fuentes, L., Davidson, D., & Carreiras, M. (2014). Is there a bilingual advantage in the ANT task? Evidence from children. *Frontiers in Psychology*, 5.

Aparicio, X., Midgley, K.J., Holcomb, P.J., Pu, H., Lavaur, J.-M., & Grainger, J. (2012). Language effects in trilinguals: An ERP study. *Frontiers in Psychology*, 3(402), 1–9.

Appelbaum, L. G., Liotti, M., Perez, R., Fox, S. P., & Woldorff, M. G. (2009). The temporal dynamics of implicit processing of non-letter, letter, and word-forms in the human visual cortex. *Frontiers in Human Neuroscience*, 3, 1–11.

Ardal, S., Donald, M. W., Meuter, R., Muldrew, S., & Luce, M. (1990). Brain responses to semantic incongruity in bilinguals. *Brain and Language*, 39, 187–205.

Arêas da Luz Fontes, A., & Schwartz, A. (2010). On a different plane: Cross-language effects on the conceptual representations of within-language homonyms. *Language and Cognitive Processes*, 25(4), 508–532.

(2011). Working memory influences on cross-language activation during bilingual lexical disambiguation. *Bilingualism: Language and Cognition*, 14(3), 360–370.

Arêas da Luz Fontes, A., Yeh, L., & Schwartz, A. (2010). Bilingual lexical disambiguation: The nature of cross-language activation effects. *Letronica*, 3(1), 107–128.

Arias-Trejo, N., & Plunkett, K. (2009). Lexical-semantic priming effects during infancy. *Philosophical Transactions of the Royal Society B: Biological Sciences*, 364(1536), 3633–3647.

Arnedt, C., & Gentile, R. (1986). A test of dual coding theory for bilingual memory. *Canadian Journal of Psychology*, 40, 290–299.

As, A. (1962). The recovery of forgotten language knowledge through hypnotic age regression: A case report. *American Journal of Clinical Hypnosis*, 5, 24–29.

Ashby, F., & Crossley, M. (2012). Automaticity and multiple memory systems. *Wiley Interdisciplinary Reviews: Cognitive Science*, 3(3), 363–376.

Athanasopoulos, P. (2006). Effects of the grammatical representation of number on cognition in bilinguals. *Bilingualism: Language and Cognition*, 9, 89–96.

(2009). Cognitive representation of color in bilinguals: The case of Greek blues. *Bilingualism: Language and Cognition*, 12, 83–95.

Athanasopoulos, P., & Bylund, E. (2013). Does grammatical aspect affect motion event cognition? A cross-linguistic comparison of English and Swedish speakers. *Cognitive Science*, 37, 286–309.

Athanasopoulos, P., Dering, B., Wiggett, A., Kuipers, J., & Thierry, G. (2010). Perceptual shift in bilingualism: Brain potentials reveal plasticity in pre-attentive colour perception. *Cognition*, 116, 437–443.

Athanasopoulos, P., & Kasai, C. (2008). Language and thought in bilinguals: The case of grammatical number and non-verbal classification preferences. *Applied Psycholinguistics*, 29(3), 105–123.

Atkinson, R., & Raugh, M. (1975). An application of the mnemonic keyword method to the acquisition of a Russian vocabulary. *Journal of Experimental Psychology: Human Learning and Memory*, 104, 126–133.

Au, R., Joung, P., Nicholas, M., Obler, L., Kass, R., & Albert, M. (1995). Naming ability across the adult life span. *Aging and Cognition*, 2(4), 300–311.

Au, T., & Glusman, M. (1990). The principle of mutual exclusivity in word learning: To honor or not to honor? *Child Development*, 61, 1474–1490.

Au, T., Knightly, L., Jun, S.-A., & Oh, J. (2002). Overhearing a language during childhood. *Psychological Science*, 13(3), 238–243.

Au, T., Oh, J., Knightly, L., Jun, S., & Romo, L. (2008). Salvaging a childhood language. *Journal of Memory and Language*, 58(4), 998–1011.

Auer, P. (ed.). (1998). *Code-switching in conversation*. London: Routledge.

Ayçiçeği-Dinn, A., & Caldwell-Harris, C. (2009). Emotion memory effects in bilingual speakers: A levels-of-processing approach. *Bilingualism: Language and Cognition*, 12, 291–303.

Ayçiçeği, A., & Harris, C. (2004). Bilinguals' recall and recognition of emotion words. *Cognition & Emotion*, 18, 977–987.

Baayen, R. (2010). Demythologizing the word frequency effect: A discriminative learning perspective. *Mental Lexicon*, 5, 436–461.

Baayen, R., Wurm, L., & Aycock, J. (2007). Lexical dynamics for low-frequency complex words: A regression study across tasks and modalities. *Mental Lexicon*, 2(3), 419–463.

Babcock, L., Stowe, J., Maloof, C., Brovetto, C., & Ullman, M. (2012). The storage and composition of inflected forms in adult-learned second language: A study of the influence of length of residence, age of arrival, sex, and other factors. *Bilingualism: Language and Cognition*, 15(4), 820–840.

Backus, A. (1992). *Patterns of language mixing, a study of Turkish–Dutch bilingualism*. Wiesbaden, Germany: Otto Harrassowitz.

(1996). *Two in one: Bilingual speech of Turkish immigrants in the Netherlands.* Tilburg, the Netherlands: Tilburg University Press.

Baddeley, A. (1986). *Working memory.* Oxford, UK: Oxford University Press.

(1996). Exploring the central executive. *Quarterly Journal of Experimental Psychology*, 49A, 5–28.

(2000). The episodic buffer: a new component of working memory? *Trends in Cognitive Sciences*, 4, 417–423.

(2003). Working memory: looking back and looking forward. *Nature Reviews Neuroscience*, 4, 829–839.

Baddeley, A., & Hitch, G. (1974). Working memory. In G. Bower (ed.), *The psychology of learning and motivation* (pp. 47–90). New York: Academic Press.

Baddeley, A., & Logie, R. (1999). Working memory: The multiple component model. In A. Miyake & P. Shah (eds.), *Models of working memory: Mechanisms of active maintenance and executive control* (pp. 28–61). Cambridge, UK: Cambridge University Press.

Badre, D., & Wagner, A. (2007). Left ventrolateral prefrontal cortex and the cognitive control of memory. *Neuropsychologia*, 45(13), 2883–2901.

Bahrick, H., & Phelps, E. (1987). Retention of Spanish vocabulary over 8 years. *Journal of Experimental Psychology: Learning, Memory, and Cognition*, 13, 344–349.

Bahrick, H., Bahrick, L., Bahrick, A., & Bahrick, P. (1993). Maintenance of foreign language vocabulary and the spacing effect. *Psychological Science*, 4, 316–321.

Bai, J., Shi, J., Jiang, T., He., S., & Weng, X. (2011). Chinese and Korean characters engage the same visual word form area in proficient early Chinese-Korean bilinguals. *PLoS ONE*, 6, e22765.

Baillargeon, R. (2004). Infants' reasoning about hidden objects: Evidence for event-general and event-specific expectations. *Developmental Science*, 7(4), 391–424.

Bak, P. (1996). *How nature works: The science of self-organized criticality.* New York: Copernicus.

Baker, S., & MacIntyre, P. (2000). The role of gender and immersion in communication and second language orientations. *Language Learning*, 50, 311–341.

Balass, M., Nelson, J., & Perfetti, C. (2010). Word learning: An ERP investigation of word experience effects on recognition and word processing. *Contemporary Educational Psychology*, 35, 126–140.

Baldo, J., Schwartz, S., Wilkins, D., & Dronkers, N. (2006). Role of frontal versus temporal cortex in verbal fluency as revealed by voxel-based lesion symptom mapping. *Journal of the International Neuropsychological Society*, 12, 896–900.

Balice-Gordon, R., & Lichtman, J. (1994). Long-term synapse loss induced by focal blockade of postsynaptic receptors. *Nature*, 372(6506), 519.

Balling, L. (2013). Reading authentic texts: What counts as a cognate? *Bilingualism: Language & Cognition*, 16(3), 637–653.

Banich, M., Mackiewicz, K., Depue, B., Whitmer, A., Miller, G., & Heller, W. (2009). Cognitive control mechanisms, emotion and memory: a neural perspective with implications for psychopathology. *Neuroscience & Biobehavioral Reviews*, 33(5), 613–630.

Barac R., & Bialystok, E. (2012). Bilingual effects on cognitive and linguistic development: Role of language, cultural background, and education. *Child Development*, 83(2) 413–422.

Barcelo, F. (2003). The Madrid card sorting test (MCST): A task switching paradigm to study executive attention with event-related potentials. *Brain Research Protocols*, 11(1), 27–37.

Barcroft, J. (2002). Semantic and structural elaboration in L2 lexical acquisition. *Language Learning*, 52, 323–363.

Barcroft, J., & Sommers, M. (2005). Effects of acoustic variability on second language vocabulary learning. *Studies of Second Language Acquisition*, 27, 387–414.

Barcroft, J., Sommers, M., & Sunderman, G. (2011). Some costs of fooling Mother Nature: A priming study on the keyword method and the quality of developing L2 lexical representations. In P. Trofimovic & K. McDonough (eds.), *Applying priming research to L2 learning and teaching: Insights from psycholinguistics* (pp. 49–72). Amsterdam/Philadelphia, PA: John Benjamins Publishing.

Bard, E., Robertson, D., & Sorace, A. (1996). Magnitude estimation of linguistic acceptability. *Language*, 72, 32–68.

Bardel, C., & Falk, Y. (2007). The role of the second language in third language acquisition: The case of Germanic syntax. *Second Language Research*, 23, 459–484.

Bar-Kochva, I. (2011). Does processing a shallow and a deep orthography produce different brain activity patterns? An ERP study conducted in Hebrew. *Developmental Neuropsychology*, 36, 933–938.

Barner, D., Inagaki, S., & Li, P. (2009). Language, thought, and real nouns. *Cognition*, 111(3), 329–344.

Barron-Hauwaert, S. (2004). *Language strategies for bilingual families: The one-parent-one-language approach*. Clevedon, UK: Multilingual Matters.

Bartolotti, J., & Marian, V. (2012). Language learning and control in monolinguals and bilinguals. *Cognitive Science*, 36(6), 1129–1147.

Bartolotti, J., Marian, V., Schroeder, S., & Shook, A. (2011). Bilingualism and inhibitory control influence statistical learning of novel word forms. *Frontiers in Psychology*, 2(324).

Barulli, D., & Stern, Y. (2013). Efficiency, capacity, compensation, maintenance, plasticity: emerging concepts in cognitive reserve. *Trends in Cognitive Sciences*, 17, 502–509.

Basnight-Brown, D., & Altarriba, J. (2007). Differences in semantic and translation priming across languages: The role of language direction and language dominance. *Memory & Cognition*, 35, 953–965.

Basnight-Brown, D., Chen, L., Hua, S., Kostic, A., & Feldman, L. (2007). Monolingual and bilingual recognition of regular and irregular English verbs: Sensitivity to form similarity varies with first language experience. *Journal of Memory and Language*, 57(1), 65–80.

Baten, K., Hofman, F., & Loeys, T. (2011). Cross-linguistic activation in bilingual sentence processing: The role of word class meaning. *Bilingualism: Language and Cognition*, 14(3), 351–359.

Bates, E. (1974) The acquisition of conditional verbs by Italian children. *Proceedings from the 10th Regional Meetings of the Chicago Linguistic Society* (pp. 27–36). Chicago, IL: University of Chicago Press.

(1976). *Language and context: The acquisition of pragmatics*. New York: Academic Press.

Bates, E., Benigni, L., Bretherton, I., Camaioni, L., & Volterra, V. (1979). *The emergence of symbols: Cognition and communication in infancy*. New York: Academic Press.

Bates, E., Devescovi, A., Hernandez, A., & Pizzamiglio, L. (1996). Gender priming in Italian. *Perception & Psychophysics*, 58(7), 992–1004.

Bauer, L. (2001). *Morphological productivity*. Cambridge, UK: Cambridge University Press.

Bauer, L., & Altarriba, J. (2008). An investigation of sex differences in word ratings across concrete, abstract, and emotion words. *Psychological Record*, 58, 465–474.

Bauer, L., Olheiser, E., Altarriba, J., & Landi, N. (2009). Word type effects in false recall: Concrete, abstract, and emotion word critical lures. *American Journal of Psychology*, 122, 469–481.

Baum, S., & Titone, D. (2014). Moving towards a neuroplasticity view of bilingualism, executive control, and aging. *Applied Psycholinguistics*, 35 (5), 857–894.

Baus, C., Costa, A., & Carreiras, M. (2013). On the effects of second language immersion on first language production. *Acta Psychologica*, 142, 402–409.

Beauvillain, C., & Grainger, J. (1987). Accessing interlexical homographs: Some limitations of a language-selective access. *Journal of Memory & Language*, 26(6), 658–672.

Beck, I., McKeown, M., & Kucan, L. (2002). *Bringing words to life: Robust vocabulary instruction*. New York: The Guilford Press.

Beckner, C., Blythe, R., Bybee, J., et al. (2009). Language is a complex adaptive system: Position paper. *Language Learning*, 59, 1–26.

Bedore, L., & Peña, E. (2008). Assessment of bilingual children for identification of language impairment: Current findings and implications for practice. *International Journal of Bilingual Education and Bilingualism*, 11(1), 1–29.

Behrens, H. (2009). First language acquisition from a usage-based perspective. In K. de Bot & R. Schrauf (eds.), *Language development over the life span* (pp. 19–39). New York: Routledge.

Bell-McGinty, S., Lopez, O., Cidis Meltzer, C., et al. (2005). Differential cortical atrophy in subgroups of mild cognitive impairment. *Archives of Neurology*, 62, 1393–1397.

Benati, A. (2001). A comparative study of the effects of processing instruction and output-based instruction on the acquisition of the Italian future tense. *Language Teaching Research*, 5, 95–127.

(2005). The effects of processing instruction, traditional instruction, and meaning-output instruction on the acquisition of the English past simple tense. *Language Teaching Research*, 9, 67–93.

(forthcoming). The effects of re-exposure to instruction and the use of discourse-level interpretation tasks on processing instruction and the Japanese passive. *International Review of Applied Linguistics in Language Teaching*.

Benati, A., & Lee, J. (2008). *Grammar acquisition and processing instruction: Secondary and cumulative effects*. Bristol, UK: Multilingual Matters.

Benati, A., & Lee, J. (eds.) (2010). *Processing instruction and discourse level input*. London: Continuum Press.

Benedict, H. (1979). Early lexical development: comprehension and production. *Journal of Child Language*, 6(2), 183–200.

Benjamin, A. & Tullis, J. (2010). What makes distributed practice effective? *Cognitive Psychology*, 61, 228–247.

Bennett, D., Schneider, J., Tang, Y., Arnold, S., & Wilson, R. (2006). The effect of social network on the relation between Alzheimer's disease pathology and level of cognitive function in old people: a longitudinal cohort study. *Lancet Neurology*, 5, 406–412.

Bennett, D., Wilson, R., Schneider, J., et al. (2003). Education modifies the relation of AD pathology to level of cognitive function in older persons. *Neurology*, 60, 1909–1915.

Bentahila, A., & Davies, E. (1983). The syntax of Arabic–French code-switching. *Lingua*, 59, 301–330.

(1992). Code-switching and language dominance. In R. Harris (ed.), *Cognitive processing in bilinguals* (pp. 443–458). Amsterdam: Elsevier.

Bentin, S., Allison, T., Puce, A., Perez, E., & McCarthy, G. (1996). Electrophysiological studies of face perception in humans. *Journal of Cognitive Neuroscience*, 8, 551–565.

Bentin, S., Mouchetant-Rostaing, Y., Giard, M., Echallier, J., & Pernier, J. (1999). ERP manifestations of processing printed words at different psycholinguistic levels: Time course and scalp distribution. *Journal of Cognitive Neuroscience*, 11, 235–260.

Ben-Zeev, S. (1977). The influence of bilingualism on cognitive development and cognitive strategy. *Child Development*, 48, 1009–1018.

Bergelson, E., & Swingley, D. (2012). At 6–9 months, human infants know the meanings of many common nouns. *Proceedings of the National Academy of Sciences*, 109(9), 3253–3258.

Bergelson, E., & Swingley, D. (2013). The acquisition of abstract words by young infants. *Cognition*, 127(3), 391–397.

Berman, R. (1979). The re-emergence of a bilingual: A case study of a Hebrew–English speaking child. *Working Papers on Bilingualism*, 19, 157–177.

Berman, R., & Slobin, D. (eds.). (1994). *Relating events in narrative: A Crosslinguistic developmental study*. Hillsdale, NJ: Lawrence Erlbaum.

Bernolet, S., Hartsuiker, R., & Pickering, M. (2007). Shared syntactic representations in bilinguals: Evidence for the role of word-order repetition. *Journal of Experimental Psychology: Learning, Memory, and Cognition*, 33, 931–949.

Bertsch, S., Pesta, B., Wiscott, R., & McDaniel, M. (2007). The generation effect: A meta-analytic review. *Memory & Cognition*, 35, 201–210.

Best, C. (1995). A direct realist view of cross-language speech perception. In W. Strange (ed.), *Speech perception and linguistic experience* (pp. 171–206). Baltimore, MD: York Press.

Best, C., & Tyler, M. (2007). Nonnative and second-language speech perception: Commonalities and complementarities. In O. Bohn & M. Munro (eds.), *Language experience in second language speech learning: In honor of James Emil Flege* (pp. 13–34). Amsterdam/Philadelphia, PA: John Benjamins Publishing.

Bialystok, E. (1988). Levels of bilingualism and levels of linguistic awareness. *Developmental Psychology*, 24(4) 560–567.

(1999). Cognitive complexity and attentional control in the bilingual mind. *Child Development*, 70(3), 636–644.

(2001). *Bilingualism in development: Language, literacy, and cognition*. Cambridge, UK: Cambridge University Press.

(2005). Consequences of bilingualism for cognitive development. In J. Kroll & A. de Groot, *Handbook of bilingualism: Psycholinguistic approaches* (pp. 417–432). Oxford, UK: Oxford University Press.

(2006). Effect of bilingualism and computer video game experience on the simon task. *Canadian Journal of Experimental Psychology*, 60(1), 68–79.

(2007). Language acquisition and bilingualism: consequences for a multilingual society. *Applied Psycholinguistics*, 28(3), 393–397.

(2009a). Claiming evidence from non-evidence: A reply to Morton and Harper. *Developmental Science*, 14, 499–503.

(2009b). Bilingualism: the good, the bad, and the indifferent. *Bilingualism: Language and Cognition*, 12(1) 3–11.

(2009c). Effects of bilingualism on cognitive and linguistic performance across the lifespan. *Streitfall Zweisprachigkeit: The bilingualism controversy*, 53–67. Wiesbaden, Germany: Springer Fachmedien Wiesbaden GmbH.

(2010). Bilingualism. *Wiley Interdisciplinary Reviews: Cognitive Science*, 1(4), 559–572.

(2011). Reshaping the mind: The benefits of bilingualism. *Canadian Journal of Experimental Psychology*, 65(4), 229–235.

Bialystok, E., & Barac, R. (2012). Emerging bilingualism: Dissociating advantages for metalinguistic awareness and executive control. *Cognition*, 122(1) 67–73.

Bialystok, E., Barac, R., Blaye, A., & Poulin-Dubois, D. (2010). Word mapping and executive functioning in young monolingual and bilingual children. *Journal of Cognition and Development*, 11(4) 485–508.

Bialystok, E., & Craik, F. (2010). On structure and process in lifespan cognitive development. In W. Overton (ed.), *Cognition, biology, and methods across the lifespan* (pp. 195–225). Hoboken, NJ: Wiley.

(2010). Cognitive and linguistic processing in the bilingual mind. *Current Directions in Psychological Science*, 19(1), 19–23.

Bialystok, E., Craik, F., Binns, M., Ossher, L., & Freedman, M. (2014). Effects of bilingualism on the age of onset and progression of MCI and AD: Evidence from executive function tests. *Neuropsychology*, 28(2), 290–304.

Bialystok, E., Craik, F., & Freedman, M. (2007). Bilingualism as a protection against the onset of symptoms of dementia. *Neuropsychologia*, 45(2), 459–464.

Bialystok, E., Craik, F., Klein, R., & Viswanathan, M. (2004). Bilingualism, aging, and cognitive control: Evidence from the Simon task. *Psychology of Aging*, 19, 290–303.

Bialystok, E., Craik, F., Grady, C., et al. (2005). Effect of bilingualism on cognitive control in the Simon task: Evidence from MEG. *Neuroimage*, 24(1), 40–49.

Bialystok, E., Craik, F., Green, D., & Gollan, T. (2009). Bilingual minds. *Psychological Science in the Public Interest*, 10, 89–129.

Bialystok, E., Craik, F., & Luk, G. (2008a). Cognitive control and lexical access in younger and older bilinguals. *Journal of Experimental Psychology: Learning, Memory, and Cognition*, 34, 859–873.

(2008b). Lexical access in bilinguals: Effects of vocabulary size and executive control. *Journal of Neurolinguistics*, 21, 522–538.

(2012). Bilingualism: Consequences for mind and brain. *Trends in Cognitive Sciences*, 16(4) 240–250.

Bialystok, E., Craik, F., & Ryan, J. (2006). Executive control in a modified antisaccade task: Effects of aging and bilingualism. *Journal of Experimental Psychology: Learning, Memory, and Cognition*, 32(6), 1341–1354.

Bialystok, E., & Harris, R. (1992). Selective attention in cognitive processing: The bilingual edge. In R. Harris (ed.), *Cognitive processing in bilinguals* (pp. 501–513). Oxford, UK: North-Holland.

Bialystok, E., & Luk, G. (2012). Receptive vocabulary differences in monolingual and bilingual adults. *Bilingualism: Language and Cognition*, 15, 397–401.

Bialystok, E., Luk, G., Peets, K., & Yang, S. (2010). Receptive vocabulary differences in monolingual and bilingual children. *Bilingualism: Language and Cognition*, 13, 525–531.

Bialystok, E., & Majumder, S. (1998). The relationship between bilingualism and the development of cognitive processes in problem solving. *Applied Psycholinguistics*, 19(1) 69–85.

Bialystok, E., Majumder, S., & Martin, M. (2003). Developing phonological awareness: Is there a bilingual advantage? *Applied Psycholinguistics*, 24(1), 27–44.

Bialystok, E., & Martin, M. (2004). Attention and inhibition in bilingual children: Evidence from the dimensional change card sort task. *Developmental Science*, 7(3), 325–339.

Bialystok, E., Martin, M., & Viswanathan, M. (2005). Bilingualism across the lifespan: The rise and fall of inhibitory control. *International Journal of Bilingualism*, 9(1), 103–119.

Bialystok, E., & Viswanathan, M. (2009). Components of executive control with advantages for bilingual children in two cultures. *Cognition*, 112(3), 494–500.

Biberauer, T., & Roberts, I. (2010). Subjects, tense, and verb-movement. In T. Birberauer, A. Holmberg, I. Roberts, & M. Sheehan (eds.), *Parametric variation: Null subjects in Minimalist theory* (pp. 263–302). Cambridge, UK: Cambridge University Press.

Bick, A. S., Goleman, G., & Frost, R. (2011). Hebrew brain vs. English brain: Language modulates the way it is processed. *Journal of Cognitive Neuroscience*, 23, 2280–2290.

Bijeljac-Babic, R., Biardeau, A., & Grainger, J. (1997). Masked orthographic priming in bilingual word recognition. *Memory & Cognition*, 25, 447–457.

Bijeljac-Babic, R., Nassurally, K., Havy, M., & Nazzi, T. (2009). Infants can rapidly learn words in a foreign language. *Infant Behavior and Development*, 32, 1–5.

Bijeljac-Babic, R., Serres, J., Höhle, B., & Nazzi, T. (2012). Effect of bilingualism on lexical stress pattern discrimination in French-learning infants. *PLoS ONE*, 7(2), e30843.

Billig, J., & Scholl, A. (2011). The impact of bilingualism and aging on inhibitory control and working memory. *Organon*, 26(51), 39–52.

Binder, J. R., Frost, J. A., Hammeke, T. A., Cox, R. W., Rao, S., & Prieto, T. (1997). Human brain language areas identified by functional magnetic resonance imaging. *Journal of Neuroscience*, 17, 353–362.

Binder, K., & Rayner, K. (1998). Contextual strength does not modulate the subordinate bias effect: Evidence from eye fixations and self-paced reading. *Psychonomic Bulletin and Review*, 5, 271–276.

Birdsong, D., & Molis, M. (2001). On the evidence for maturational constraints in second-language acquisition. *Journal of Memory and Language*, 44(2), 235–249.

Bjork, R., & Bjork, E. (2006). Optimizing treatment and instruction: Implications of a new theory of disuse. In L.-G. Nilsson & N. Ohta (eds.), *Memory and society: Psychological perspectives* (pp. 109–133). New York, NY: Psychology Press.

   (2011). Making things hard on yourself, but in a good way: Creating desirable difficulties to enhance learning. In M. Gernsbacher, R. Pew, L. Hough, & J. Pomerantz (eds.), *Psychology and the real world: Essays illustrating fundamental contributions to society* (pp. 56–64). New York, NY: Worth Publishers.

Black, J., Sirevaag, A., & Greenough, W. (1987). Complex experience promotes capillary formation in young rat visual cortex. *Neuroscience Letters*, 83(3), 351–355.

Blakemore, D. (2002). *Relevance and linguistic meaning, the semantics and pragmatics of discourse markers*. Cambridge, UK: Cambridge University Press.

Blazquez-Domingo, R. (1998). *Spanish–English code switching corpus*. University of South Carolina, Columbia, SC.

Bleasdale, F. (1987). Concreteness-dependent associative priming: Separate lexical organization for concrete and abstract words. *Journal of Experimental Psychology: Learning, Memory, and Cognition*, 13(4), 582–594.

Blom, E., & Unsworth, S. (2010). *Experimental methods in language acquisition research*. Amsterdam/Philadelphia, PA: John Benjamins Publishing.

Blumenfeld, H., & Marian, V. (2007). Constraints on parallel activation in bilingual spoken language processing: Examining proficiency and lexical status using eye-tracking. *Language and Cognitive Processes*, 22(5), 633–660.

   (2011). Bilingualism influences inhibitory control in auditory comprehension. *Cognition*, 118(2), 245–257.

BNC. (2007). BNC XML Edition. Accessed from www.natcorp.ox.ac.uk/corpus.

Boada, R., Sánchez-Casas, R., Gavilán, J., García-Albea, J., & Tokowicz, N. (2013). Effect of multiple translations and cognate status on translation recognition performance of balanced bilinguals. *Bilingualism: Language and Cognition*, 16, 183–197

Bobaljik, J. 2002. Realizing Germanic inflection: Why morphology does not drive syntax. *Journal of Comparative German Linguistics*, 6, 129–167.

Bobb, S., & Wodniecka, Z. (2013). Language switching in picture naming: What asymmetric switch costs (do not) tell us about inhibition in bilingual speech planning. *Journal of Cognitive Psychology*, 25, 568–585.

Bock, K., & Levelt, W. (1994). Language production: grammatical encoding. In M. Gernsbacher (ed.), *Handbook of Psycholinguistics*. New York: Academic Press, pp. 945–984.

Bock, K., & Miller, C. (1991). Broken agreement. *Cognitive psychology*, 23(1), 45–93.

Boehm, S. G., Dering, B., & Thierry, G. (2011). Category-sensitivity in the N170 range: A question of topography and inversion, not one of amplitude. *Neuropsychologia*, 49, 2082–2089.

Bogulski, C. (2009). Learning words in a new language: The effect of language experience on vocabulary acquisition and inhibitory control. (Unpublished master's thesis), Pennsylvania State University, University Park, PA.

Bogulski, C., & Kroll, J. F. (in preparation). A bilingual advantage in vocabulary acquisition depends on learning via the dominant language.

Bolger, D. J., Perfetti, C. A., & Schneider, W. (2005). Cross-cultural effect on the brain revisited: Universal structures plus writing system variation. *Human Brain Mapping*, 25, 92–104.

Bond, M., & Lai, T. (1986). Embarrassment and code-switching into a second language. *Journal of Social Psychology*, 126, 179–186.

Bono, M., & Stratilaki, S. (2009). The M-factor, a bilingual asset for plurilinguals? Learners' representations, discourse strategies and third language acquisition in institutional contexts. *International Journal of Multilingualism*, 6, 207–227.

Bornstein, M. (1989). Sensitive periods in development: structural characteristics and causal interpretations. *Psychological Bulletin*, 105(2), 179.

Boroditsky, L., Schmidt, L., & Phillips, W. (2003). Sex, syntax, and semantics. In D. Gentner & S. Goldin-Meadow (eds.), *Language in mind: Advances in the study of language and thought* (pp. 61–79). Cambridge, UK: Cambridge University Press.

Bosch, L., Costa, A., & Sebastián-Gallés, N. (2000). First and second language vowel perception in early bilinguals. *European Journal of Cognitive Psychology*, 12, 189–222.

Bosch, L., Figueras, M., Teixidó, M., & Ramon-Casas, M. (2013). Rapid gains in segmenting fluent speech when words match the rhythmic unit: Evidence from infants acquiring syllable-timed languages. *Frontiers in Psychology*, 4(106), 1–12.

Bosch, L., & Ramon-Casas, M. (2011). Variability in vowel production by bilingual speakers: Can input properties hinder the early stabilization of contrastive categories? *Journal of Phonetics*, 39, 514–526.

Bosch, L., & Sebastián-Gallés, N. (1997). Native-language recognition abilities in 4-month-old infants from monolingual and bilingual environments. *Cognition*, 65, 33–69.

(2001). Evidence of early language discrimination abilities in infants from bilingual environments. *Infancy*, 2(1), 29–49.

(2003). Simultaneous bilingualism and the perception of a language-specific vowel contrast in the first year of life. *Language and Speech*, 46, 217–243.

Botvinick, M., Braver, T., Barch, D., Carter, C., & Cohen, J. (2001). Conflict monitoring and cognitive control. *Psychological Review*, 108(3) 624–652.

Botwinick, J., & Stordandt, M. (1974). Vocabulary ability later in life. *Journal of Genetic Psychology*, 125, 303–308.

Boutonnet, B., Athanasopoulos, P., & Thierry, G. (2012). Unconscious effects of grammatical gender during object categorisation. *Brain Research*, 1479, 72–79.

Bowden, H., Gelfand, M., Sanz, C., & Ullman, M. (2010). Verbal inflectional morphology in L1 and L2 Spanish: A frequency effects study examining storage versus composition. *Language Learning*, 60(1), 44–87.

Bowers, J. (2002). Challenging the widespread assumption that connectionism and distributed representations go hand-in-hand. *Cognitive Psychology*, 45(3), 413–445.

Bowers, J., Davis, C., & Hanley, D. (2005). Interfering neighbours: The impact of novel word learning on the identification of visually similar words. *Cognition*, 97, B45–B54.

Bowers, J., Mattys, S., & Gage, S. H. (2009). Preserved implicit knowledge of a forgotten childhood language. *Psychological Science*, 20(9), 1064–1069.

Bowers, J., Mimouni, Z., & Arguin, M. (2000). Orthography plays a critical role in cognate priming: Evidence from French/English and Arabic/French cognates. *Memory & Cognition*, 28, 1289–1296.

Boyke, J., Driemeyer, J., Gaser, C., Büchel, C., & May, A. (2008). Training-induced brain structure changes in the elderly. *Journal of Neuroscience*, 28(28), 7031–7035.

Bozic, M., Tyler, L., Ives, D., Randall, B., & Marslen-Wilson, W. (2010). Bihemispheric foundations for human speech comprehension. *Proceedings of the National (USA) Academy of Sciences*, 107(40), 17439–17444.

Braet, W., Wagemans, J., & Op de Beeck, H. P. (2011). The visual word form area is organized according to orthography. *NeuroImage*, 59, 2751–2759.

Branzi, F., Martin, C., Abutalebi, J., & Costa, A. (2014). The after-effects of bilingual language production. *Neuropsychologia*, 52, 102–116.

Braver, T., Reynolds, J., & Donaldson, D. (2003). Neural mechanisms of transient and sustained cognitive control during task switching. *Neuron*, 39, 713–726.

Brito, N., & Barr, R. (2012). Influence of bilingualism on memory generalization during infancy. *Developmental Science*, 15, 812–816.

Broadbent, D. (1958). *Perception and Communication*. London: Pergamon.

Broersma, M. (2009). Triggered codeswitching between cognate languages. *Bilingualism: Language and Cognition*, 12, 447–462.

Broersma, M. (2011). Triggered code-switching: Evidence from picture naming experiments. In M. Schmid & W. Lowie (eds.), *Modeling bilingualism from structure to chaos: In honor of Kees de Bot* (pp. 37–57). Amsterdam/Philadelphia, PA: John Benjamins Publishing.

(2012). Increased lexical activation and reduced competition in second-language listening. *Language and Cognitive Processes*, 27, 1205–1224.

Broersma, M., & Cutler, A. (2008). Phantom word activation in L2. *System*, 36, 22–34.

Broersma, M., & de Bot, K. (2006). Triggered codeswitching: A corpus-based evaluation of the original triggering hypothesis and a new alternative. *Bilingualism Language and Cognition*, 9, 1–13.

Broersma, M., Isurin, L., Bultena, S., & de Bot, K. (2009). Triggered code-switching: Evidence from Dutch–English and Russian–English bilinguals. In L. Isurin, D. Winford, & K. de Bot (eds.), *Multidisciplinary approaches to code switching* (pp. 85–102). Amsterdam/Philadelphia, PA: John Benjamins Publishing.

Brown, A., & Gullberg, M. (2008). Bidirectional crosslinguistic influence in L1–L2 encoding of manner in speech and gesture: A study of Japanese speakers of English. *Studies in Second Language Acquisition*, 30, 225–251.

(2010). Changes in encoding of PATH of motion in a first language during acquisition of a second language. *Cognitive Linguistics*, 21, 263–286.

Brown, J. D. (2009). Foreign and second language needs analysis. In M. Long & C. Doughty (eds.), *The handbook of language teaching* (pp. 269–293). Oxford, UK: Blackwell.

Bruer, J. (2001). A critical and sensitive period primer. In D. Bailey, J. Bruer, & J. McDonnell, *Critical thinking about critical periods* (pp. 3–26). Baltimore, MD: Brookes Publishing.

Brysbaert, M., & Duyck, W. (2010). Is it time to leave behind the Revised Hierarchical Model of bilingual language processing after fifteen years of service? *Bilingualism: Language and Cognition*, 13, 359–371.

Brysbaert, M., Van Dyck, G., & Van de Poel, M. (1999). Visual word recognition in bilinguals: Evidence from masked phonological priming. *Journal of Experimental Psychology: Human Perception and Performance*, 25, 137–148.

Bullock, B., & Toribio, A. (2009). *The Cambridge handbook of linguistic code-switching*. New York: Cambridge University Press.

Bultena, S., Dijkstra, T., & van Hell, J. (2014). Cognate facilitation effects in sentence context depend on word class, L2 proficiency and task. *Quarterly Journal of Experimental Psychology*, 67(6):1214–1241.

(forthcoming). Language switch costs in comprehension depend on language dominance: Evidence from self-paced reading. *Bilingualism: Language and Cognition*.

(2015). Switch cost modulations in bilingual sentence processing: Evidence from shadowing. *Language, Cognition, and Neuroscience,* 30, 586–605

Burgess, C., & Lund, K. (1997). Modeling parsing constraints with high-dimensional context space. *Language and Cognitive Processes*, 12, 177–210.

Burke, D., MacKay, D., Worthley, J., & Wade, E. (1991). On the tip of the tongue: What causes word finding failure in young and older adults? *Journal of Memory and Language*, 30, 542–579.

Burns, T., Yoshida, K., Hill, K., & Werker, J. (2007). The development of phonetic representation in bilingual and monolingual infants. *Applied Psycholinguistics*, 28, 455–474.

Butler, Y., & Hakuta, K. (2004). Bilingualism and second language acquisition. In T. Bhatia & W. Ritchie (eds.), *The handbook of bilingualism* (pp. 114–144). Malden, MA: Blackwell.

Bybee, J. (2001). *Phonology and language use.* Cambridge, UK: Cambridge University Press.
  (2002). Word frequency and context of use in the lexical diffusion of phonetically conditioned sound change. *Language Variation and Change*, 14(3), 261–290.
  (2010). *Language, usage, and cognition.* Cambridge, UK: Cambridge University Press.
Bybee, J., & Hopper, P. (eds.). (2001). *Frequency and the emergence of linguistic structure.* Amsterdam/Philadelphia, PA: John Benjamins Publishing.
Byers-Heinlein, K. (2013). Parental language mixing: Its measurement and the relation of mixed input to young bilingual children's vocabulary size. *Bilingualism: Language and Cognition*, 16(1), 32–48.
Byers-Heinlein, K., Burns, T., & Werker, J. (2010). The roots of bilingualism in newborns. *Psychological Science*, 21, 343–348.
Byers-Heinlein, K., & Fennell, C. (2014). Perceptual narrowing in the context of increased variation: Insights from bilingual infants. *Developmental Psychobiology*. 56(2), 274–291.
Byers-Heinlein, K., Fennell, C., & Werker, J. (2013). The development of associative word learning in monolingual and bilingual infants. *Bilingualism: Language and Cognition*, 16, 198–205.
Byers-Heinlein, K., & Werker, J. F. (2009). Monolingual, bilingual, trilingual: Infants' language experience influences the development of a word-learning heuristic. *Developmental Science*, 12(5), 815–823.
  (2013). Lexicon structure and the disambiguation of novel words: Evidence from bilingual infants. *Cognition*, 128(3), 407–416.
Bylund, E. (2009). Effects of age of L2 acquisition on L1 event conceptualization patterns. *Bilingualism: Language and Cognition*, 12, 305–322.
Bylund, E., & Athanasopoulos, P. (2014). Language and thought in a multilingual context: The case of isiXhosa. *Bilingualism: Language and Cognition*, 17(2), 431–441
Bylund, E., & Jarvis, S. (2011). L2 effects on L1 event conceptualization. Bilingualism: *Language and Cognition*, 14(1), 47–59.
Cabeza R., & Kingstone, A. (eds.). (2001). *Handbook of functional neuroimaging of cognition.* Cambridge, MA: MIT Press.
Cadierno, T. (1995). Formal instruction from a processing perspective: an investigation into the Spanish past tense. *Modern Language Journal*, 79, 179-93.
  (2008). Learning to talk about motion in a foreign language. In P. Robinson & N. Ellis (eds.), *Handbook of cognitive linguistics and second language acquisition* (pp. 239–275). London: Routledge.
Calabria, M., Hernández, M., Branzi, F., & Costa, A. (2012). Qualitative differences between bilingual language control and executive control: Evidence from task-switching. *Frontiers in Psychology*, 2(399), 9–18.

Caldwell-Harris, C., Tong, J., Lung, W., & Poo, S. (2011). Physiological reactivity to emotional phrases in Mandarin–English bilinguals. *International Journal of Bilingualism*, 15, 329–352.

Calvo, M., & Eysenck, M. (1996). Phonological working memory and reading test anxiety. *Memory*, 4, 289–305.

Campbell, J. (2005). Asymmetrical language switch costs in Chinese–English bilinguals' number naming and simple arithmetic. *Bilingualism: Language and Cognition*, 8, 85–91.

Cao, F., Tao, R., Liu, L., Perfetti, C. A., & Booth, J. (2013). High proficiency in a second language is characterized by greater involvement of the first language network: Evidence from Chinese learners of English. *Journal of Cognitive Neuroscience*, 1–15.

Caramazza, A. (1997). How many levels of processing are there in lexical access? *Cognitive Neuropsychology*, 14(1), 177–208.

Caramazza, A., & Brones, I. (1979). Lexical access in bilinguals. *Bulletin of the Psychonomic Society*, 13, 212–214.

 (1980). Semantic classification by bilinguals. *Canadian Journal of Psychology/Revue Canadienne de Psychologie*, 34, 77–81.

Caramazza, A., Yeni-Komshian, G., & Zurif, E. (1974). Bilingual switching: The phonological level. *Canadian Journal of Psychology/Revue canadienne de psychologie*, 28, 310–318.

Carlson S., & Meltzoff, A. (2008). Bilingual experience and executive functioning in young children. *Developmental Science*, 11, 282–298.

Carminati, M. (2002). The processing of Italian subject pronouns. (Unpublished doctoral dissertation), University of Massachusetts, Amherst.

Carpenter, S., & DeLosh, E. (2006). Impoverished cue support enhances subsequent retention: Support for the elaborative retrieval explanation of the testing effect. *Memory & Cognition*, 34, 268–276.

Carpenter, S., & Olson, K. (2012). Are pictures good for learning new vocabulary in a foreign language? Only if you think they are not. *Journal of Experimental Psychology: Learning, Memory, and Cognition*, 38, 92–101.

Carreiras, M., & Clifton, C. (1993). Relative clause interpretation preferences in Spanish and English. *Language and Speech*, 36(4), 353–372.

Carreiras, M., Perea, M., & Grainger, J. (1997). Effects of orthographic neighborhood in visual word recognition: Cross-task comparisons. *Journal of Experimental Psychology: Learning, Memory, & Cognition*, 23, 857–871.

Carroll, J. (1981). Twenty-five years of research on foreign language aptitude. In K. Diller (ed.), *Individual differences and universals in language learning aptitude* (pp. 119–154). Rowley, MA: Newbury House.

Carroll, J., & Sapon, S. (1959). *The modern language aptitude test*. San Antonio, TX: Psychological Corporation.

Carroll, S. (2001). *Input and evidence: The raw material of second language acquisition*. Amsterdam/Philadelphia, PA: John Benjamins Publishing.

Caspi, T. (2010). A dynamic perspective on second language development. (Unpublished doctoral dissertation), University of Groningen, the Netherlands.

Caspi, T., & Lowie, W. (2013). The dynamics of L2 vocabulary development: A case study of receptive and productive knowledge. *Revista Brasiliera de Linguistica*, 13(2), 45–106.

Casseday, J., Fremouw, T., & Covey, E. (2002). The inferior colliculus: a hub for the central auditory system Integrative functions in the mammalian auditory pathway. In D. Oertel, R. Fay, & A. Popper (eds.), *Integrative functions in the mammalian auditory pathway* (238–318). New York: Springer.

Cattell, J. (1887). Experiments on the association of ideas. *Mind*, 12, 68–74.

CDI Advisory Board. (n.d.). CDIs in Other Languages. Retrieved from www.sci.sdsu.edu/cdi/adaptations_ol.htm.

Cenoz, J., Hufeisen, B., & Jessner, U. (2001). Towards trilingual education. *International Journal of Bilingual Education and Bilingualism*, 4(1), 1–10.

Cepeda, N., Vul, E., Rohrer, D., Wixted, J., & Pashler, H. (2008). Spacing effects in learning: A temporal ridgeline of optimal retention. *Psychological Science*, 19, 1095–1102.

Chabal, S., & Marian, V. (2015). Automatic language activation during visual processing. *Journal of Experimental Psychology: General*, 144(3),

Chambers, C., & Cooke, H. (2009). Lexical competition during second-language listening: sentence context, but not proficiency, constrains interference from the native lexicon. *Journal of Experimental Psychology: Learning, Memory, and Cognition*, 35, 1029–1040.

Chambers, S. M. (1979). Letter and order information in lexical access. *Journal of Verbal Learning and Verbal Behavior*, 18, 225–241.

Chan, B. (2009). Code-switching between typologically distinct languages. In B. Bullock & A. Toribio (eds.), *The Cambridge handbook of linguistic code-switching* (pp. 182–198). Cambridge, UK: Cambridge University Press.

Chan, H. (2014). A dynamic approach to the development of lexicon and syntax in a second language. (Unpublished doctoral dissertation), University of Groningen, the Netherlands.

Chan, H., Lowie, W., & de Bot, K. (forthcoming). Input outside the classroom and vocabulary development: A dynamic perspective. In J. Robinson and M. Reif (eds.), *Culture and cognition in bilingualism*. Berlin: Mouton de Gruyter.

Chan, M.-C., Chau, H., & Hoosain, R. (1983). Input/output switch in bilingual code switching. *Journal of Psycholinguistic Research*, 12, 407–416.

Chauncey, K., Grainger, J., & Holcomb, P. (2008). Code-switching effects in bilingual word recognition: A masked priming study with event-related potentials. *Brain and Language*, 105, 161–174.

Chauncey, K., Holcomb, P., & Grainger, J. (2009). Primed picture naming within and across languages: An ERP investigation. *Cognitive, Affective, & Behavioral Neuroscience*, 9, 286–303.

Chechik, G., Meilijson, I., & Ruppin, E. (1998). Synaptic pruning in development: A computational account. *Neural Computation*, 10(7), 1759–1777.

Chechik, G., Meilijson, I., & Ruppin, E. (1999). Neuronal regulation: A mechanism for synaptic pruning during brain maturation. *Neural Computation*, 11(8), 2061–2080.

Chee, M. W., Hon, N., Lee, H. L., & Soon, C. S. (2001). Relative language proficiency modulates BOLD signal change when bilinguals perform semantic judgments. *NeuroImage*, 13, 1155–1163.

Chen, H.-C. (1990). Lexical processing in a non-native language: Effects of language proficiency and learning strategy. *Memory & Cognition*, 18, 279–288.

Chen, H.-C., Cheung, H., & Lau, S. (1997). Examining and reexamining the structure of Chinese-English bilingual memory. *Psychological Research*, 60, 270–283.

Chen, H.-C., & Ho, C. (1986). Development of Stroop interference in Chinese-English bilinguals. *Journal of Experimental Psychology: Learning, Memory, and Cognition*, 12, 397–401.

Chen, H.-C., & Leung, Y. (1989). Patterns of lexical processing in a non-native language. *Journal of Experimental Psychology: Learning, Memory, and Cognition*, 15, 316–325.

Chen, H.-C., & Ng, M.-L. (1989). Semantic facilitation and translation priming effects in Chinese-English bilinguals. *Memory & Cognition*, 17, 454–462.

Chen, L., Shu, H., Liu, Y., Zhao, J., & Li, P. (2007). ERP signatures of subject-verb agreement in L2 learning. *Bilingualism: Language and Cognition*, 10(2), 161–174.

Cheng, Y., Horwitz, E., & Schallert, D. (1999). Language writing anxiety: Differentiating writing and speaking components. *Language Learning*, 49, 417–446.

Cheour, M., Ceponiene, R., Lehtokoski, A., et al. (1998). Development of language-specific phoneme representations in the infant brain. *Nature Neuroscience*, 1(5), 351–353.

Cheour, M., Imada, T., Taulu, S., Ahonen, A., Salonen, J., & Kuhl, P. (2004). Magnetoencephalography is feasible for infant assessment of auditory discrimination. *Experimental Neurology*, 190, 44–51.

Cherkasova, M., Manoach, D., Intriligator, J., & Barton, J. (2002). Antisaccades and task-switching: Interactions in controlled processing. *Experimental Brain Research*, 144, 528–537.

Chertkow H., Whitehead V., Phillips, N., Wolfson, C., Atherton, J., & Bergman, H. (2010). Multilingualism (but not always bilingualism) delays the onset of Alzheimer disease: Evidence from a bilingual community. *Alzheimer Disease & Associated Disorders*, 24, 118–125.

Chomsky, N. (1965). *Aspects of the theory of syntax*. Cambridge, MA: MIT Press.

Christiansen, M., & Chater, N. (2001a). Connectionist psycholinguistics: Capturing the empirical data. *Trends in Cognitive Sciences*, 5, 82–88.

(eds.). (2001b). *Connectionist psycholinguistics*. Westport, CO: Ablex.

Christoffels, I., de Groot, A., & Kroll, J. F. (2006). Memory and language skills in simultaneous interpreters: The role of expertise and language proficiency. *Journal of Memory and Language*, 54, 324–345.

Christoffels, I., Firk, C., & Schiller, N. (2007). Bilingual language control: An event-related brain potential study. *Brain Research*, 1147, 192–208.

Clahsen, H., Balkhair, L., Schutter, J. S., & Cunnings, I. (2013). The time course of morphological processing in a second language. *Second Language Research*, 29(1), 7–31.

Clahsen, H., & Felser, C. (2006). Grammatical processing in language learners. *Applied Psycholinguistics*, 27(1), 3–42.

Clahsen, H., Felser, C., Neubauer, K., Sato, M., & Silva, R. (2010). Morphological structure in native and nonnative language processing. *Language Learning*, 60(1), 21–43.

Clark, E. (1978). Discovering what words can do. In D. Farkas, W. Jacobsen, & K. Todrys (eds.), *Papers from the parasession on the lexicon, Chicago Linguistics Society April 14–15* (pp. 34–57). Chicago, IL: Chicago Linguistics Society.

(1993) *The lexicon in acquisition*. Cambridge, UK: Cambridge University Press.

(2010). Adult offer, word-class, and child uptake in early lexical acquisition. *First Language*, 30(3–4), 250–269.

Clauset, A., Newman, M., & Moore, C. (2004). Finding community structure in very large networks. *Physical Review E*, 70, 066111.

Cleary, M., Pisoni, D., & Geers, A. (2001). Some measures of verbal and spatial working memory in eight- and nine-year-old hearing-impaired children with cochlear implants. *Ear and Hearing*, 22(5), 395–411.

Clifton, C., Jr., & Frazier, L. (1989). Comprehending sentences with long-distance dependencies. In G. Carlson & M. Tanenhaus (eds.), *Linguistic structure in language processing* (pp. 273–317). Dordrecht: Kluwer.

Clyne, M. (1967). *Transference and triggering*. The Hague: Nijhoff.

(2003). *Dynamics of language contact*. Cambridge, UK: Cambridge University Press.

Coderre, E. L. (2012). Exploring the cognitive effects of bilingualism: Neuroimaging investigations of lexical processing, executive control, and the bilingual advantage. (Unpublished doctoral thesis), University of Nottingham, UK.

Coderre, E. L., Filippi, C. G., Newhouse, P. A., & Dumas, J. A. (2008). The Stroop effect in kana and kanji scripts in native Japanese speakers: An fMRI study. *Brain and Language*, 107, 124–132.

Coderre E. L., van Heuven W. J. B., & Conklin, K. (2013). The timing and magnitude of Stroop interference and facilitation in monolinguals and bilinguals. *Bilingualism: Language Cognition*, 16, 420–441.

Cohen, L., Dehaene, S., Naccache, L., et al. (2000). The visual word form area: Spatial and temporal characterization of an initial stage of reading in normal subjects and posterior split-brain patients. *Brain*, 123, 291–307.

Cohen, J., Dunbar, K., & McClelland, J. (1990). On the control of automatic processes: A parallel-distributed processing account of the Stroop effect. *Psychological Review*, 97, 332–361

Colé, P., & Segui, J. (1994). Grammatical incongruency and vocabulary types. *Memory & Cognition*, 22(4), 387–394.

*Collins English Dictionary: Complete & Unabridged* (10th edn, n.d.). Access from http://dictionary.reference.com/browse/bilingual.

Collins, A., & Loftus, E. (1975). A spreading-activation theory of semantic processing. *Psychological Review*, 82, 407–426.

Collins, L., & Ellis, N. (2009). Input and second language construction learning: frequency, form, and function. *Modern Language Journal*, 93(2).

Colombo, J., & Mitchell, D. W. (2009). Infant visual habituation. *Neurobiology of Learning and Memory*, 92(2), 225–234.

Colomé, A. (2001). Lexical activation in bilinguals' speech production: Language-specific or language-independent? *Journal of Memory and Language*, 45, 721–736.

Colomé, A., & Miozzo, M. (2010). Which words are activated during bilingual word production? *Journal of Experimental Psychology: Learning, Memory, and Cognition*, 36, 96–109.

Coltheart, M., Rastle, K., Perry, C., Langdon, R., & Ziegler, J. (2001). DRC: A dual route cascaded model of visual word recognition and reading. *Psychological Review*, 108, 204–256.

Comer, W. & deBenedette, L. (2010). Processing instruction and Russian: Issues, materials, and preliminary experimental results. *Slavic and East European Journal*, 54, 118–146.

Conboy, B., & Kuhl, P. (2011). Impact of second-language experience in infancy: brain measures of first- and second-language speech perception. *Developmental Science*, 14(2), 242–248.

Conboy, B., & Mills, D. (2006). Two languages, one developing brain: Event-related potentials to words in bilingual toddlers. *Developmental Science*, 9(1), F1–F12.

Conboy, B., & Thal, D. (2006). Ties between the lexicon and grammar: Cross-sectional and longitudinal studies of bilingual toddlers. *Child Development*, 77(3), 712–735.

Connor, L., Spiro, A., Obler, L., & Albert, M. (2004). Change in object naming during adulthood. *Journal of Gerontology: Psychological Sciences*, 59(5), 203–209.

Conway, C., Pisoni, D., & Kronenberger, W. (2009). The importance of sound for cognitive sequencing abilities. *Current Directions in Psychological Science*, 18(5), 275–279.

Cook, S. (2012). Phonological form in L2 lexical access: Friend or foe? (Unpublished doctoral dissertation), University of Maryland, College Park.

Cook, V. (ed.). (2003). *Effects of the second language on the first*. Clevedon, UK: Multilingual Matters.

Cook, V., & Bassetti, B. (2005). An introduction to researching second language writing systems. In V. Cook and B. Bassetti (eds.), *Second language writing systems* (pp. 1–67). Clevedon, UK: Multilingual Matters.

Cook, V., Bassetti, B., Kasai, C., Sasaki, M., & Takahashi, J. (2006). Do bilinguals have different concepts? The case of shape and material in Japanese L2 users of English. *International Journal of Bilingualism*, 10, 137–152.

Corbett, G. (2005). Number of genders. In M. Haspelmath, M. Dryer, D. Gil, & B. Comrie (eds.), *World atlas of language structures* (pp. 126–129). Oxford, UK: Oxford University Press.

Core, C., Hoff, E., Rumiche, R., & Señor, M. (2013). Total and conceptual vocabulary in Spanish–English bilinguals from 22 to 30 months: Implications for assessment. *Journal of Speech, Language and Hearing Research*, 56, 1637–1649.

Corin, A. (1994). Teaching for proficiency: The conversion principle. A Czech to Serbo-Croatian conversion course at the Defense Language Institute. *ACTR Letter: Newsletter of the American Council of Teachers of Russian*, 20(1), 1–5.

Corrigan, R. (2012). Using the CHILDES database. In E. Hoff (ed.), *Research methods in child language: A practical guide* (pp. 271–284). Malden, MA: Wiley-Blackwell.

Costa, A. (2005). Lexical access in bilingual production. In J. Kroll & A. de Groot (eds.), *Handbook of bilingualism: Psycholinguistic approaches* (pp. 308–325). New York: Oxford University Press.

Costa, A., Albareda, B., & Santesteban, M. (2008). Assessing the presence of lexical competition across languages: Evidence from the Stroop task. *Bilingualism Language and Cognition*, 11, 121.

Costa, A., & Caramazza, A. (1999). Is lexical selection in bilingual speech production language-specific?: Further evidence from Spanish–English and English–Spanish bilinguals. *Bilingualism: Language and Cognition*, 2(3), 231–244.

Costa, A., Caramazza, A., & Sebastián-Gallés, N. (2000). The cognate facilitation effect: Implications for models of lexical access. *Journal of Experimental Psychology: Learning, Memory, and Cognition*, 26, 1283–1296.

Costa, A., Colomé, A., Gómez, O., & Sebastián-Gallés, N. (2003). Another look at cross-language competition in bilingual speech production: Lexical and phonological factors. *Bilingualism: Language and Cognition*, 6, 167–179.

Costa, A., Hernandez, M., Costa-Faidella, J., & Sebastián-Gallés, N. (2009). On the bilingual advantage in conflict processing: Now you see it, now you don't. *Cognition*, 113(2) 135–149.

Costa, A., Hernandez, M., & Sebastián-Gallés, N. (2008). Bilingualism aids conflict resolution: Evidence from the ANT task. *Cognition*, 106, 59–86.

Costa, A., Miozzo, M., & Caramazza, A. (1999). Lexical selection in bilinguals: Do words in the bilingual's two lexicons compete for selection? *Journal of Memory and Language*, 41, 365–397.

Costa, A., & Santesteban, M. (2004a). Lexical access in bilingual speech production: Evidence from language switching in highly proficient bilinguals and L2 learners. *Journal of Memory and Language*, 50(4), 491–511.

Costa, A., & Santesteban, M. (2004b). Bilingual word perception and production: Two sides of the same coin? *Trends in Cognitive Science*, 8, 253.

Costa, A., Santesteban, M., & Ivanova, I. (2006). How do highly-proficient bilinguals control their lexicalization process? Inhibitory and language-specific selection mechanisms are both functional. *Journal of Experimental Psychology: Learning, Memory, and Cognition*, 32, 1057–1074.

Costa, P., & McCrae, R. (1992). *NEO-PI-R. Professional manual.* Odessa, FL: Psychological Assessment Resources.

Coulson, S., King, J., & Kutas, M. (1998). Expect the unexpected: Event-related brain response to morphosyntactic violations. *Language and Cognitive Processes*, 13, 21–58.

Cowan, N. (1995). *Attention and memory.* Oxford, UK: Oxford University Press.

Craik, F. (1983). On the transfer of information from temporary to permanent memory. *Philosophical Transactions of the Royal Society of London, Series B*, 302, 341–359.

Craik, F., & Bialystok, E. (2006). Cognition through the lifespan: Mechanisms of change. *Trends in Cognitive Sciences*, 10(3), 131–138.

Craik, F., Bialystok, E., & Freedman, M. (2010). Delaying the onset of Alzheimer disease: bilingualism as a form of cognitive reserve. *Neurology*, 75(19), 1726–1729.

Craik, F., & Tulving, E. (1975). Depth of processing and the retention of words in episodic memory. *Journal of Experimental Psychology: General*, 104, 268–294

Crepaldi, D., Rastle, K., Coltheart, M., & Nickels, L. (2010). 'Fell' primes 'fall,' but does 'bell' prime 'ball'? Masked priming with irregularly-inflected primes. *Journal of Memory and Language*, 63(1), 83–99.

Crinion, J., Turner, R., Grogan, A., et al. (2006). Language control in the bilingual brain. *Science*, 312(5779), 1537–1540.

Cristoffanini, P., Kirsner, K., & Milech, D. (1986). Bilingual lexical representation: The status of Spanish-English cognates. *Quarterly Journal of Experimental Psychology*, 38, 367–393.

Croft, W. (2001). *Radical construction grammar: Syntactic theory in typological perspective.* Oxford, UK: Oxford University Press.

Croft, W., & Cruise, A. (2004). *Cognitive linguistics.* Cambridge, UK: Cambridge University Press.

Crone, E., Donohue, S., Honomichl, R., Wendelken, C., & Bunge, S. (2006). Brain regions mediating flexible rule use during development. *Journal of Neuroscience*, 26(43), 11239–11247.

Cross, E., & Burke, D. (2004). Do alternative names block young and older adults' retrieval of proper names? *Brain and Language*, 89, 174–181.

Csizér, K., Kormos, J., & Sarkadi, Á. (2010). The dynamics of language learning attitudes and motivation: lessons from an interview study with dyslexic language learners. *Modern Language Journal*, 97, 470–487.

Cummins, J. (1976). Cognitive basis of uznadze illusion. *International Journal of Psychology*, 11(2) 89–100.

(1978). Bilingualism and the development of metalinguistic awareness. *Journal of Cross-Cultural Psychology*, 9, 131–149.

(1979). Linguistic interdependence and the educational development of bilingual children. *Review of Educational Research*, 49(2) 222–251.

(1984). Wanted: A theoretical framework for relating language proficiency to academic achievement among bilingual students. In C. Rivera (ed.), *Language proficiency and academic achievement* (pp. 2–19). Clevedon, UK: Multilingual Matters.

(2001). Instructional conditions for trilingual development. *International Journal of Bilingual Education and Bilingualism*, 4(1), 61–75.

Cummins, J., & Gulutsan, M. (1974). Bilingual education and cognition. *Alberta Journal of Educational Research*, 20(3) 259–269.

Cuppini, C., Magosso, E., & Ursino, M. (2013). Learning the lexical aspects of a second language at different proficiencies: A neural computational study. *Bilingualism: Language and Cognition*, 16(2), 266.

Curtin, S., Byers-Heinlein, K., & Werker, J. (2011). Bilingual beginnings as a lens for theory development: PRIMIR in focus. *Journal of Phonetics*, 39(4), 492–504.

Curtiss, S. (1977). *Genie: A psycholinguistic study of a modern-day "wild child."* New York: Academic Press.

(1989). The case of Chelsea: A new test case of the critical period for language acquisition. (Unpublished master's thesis), University of California, LA.

Cutler, A., & Weber, A. (2006). First-language phonotactics in second-language listening. *Journal of the Acoustical Society of America*, 19(1), 597–607.

Cutler, A., Weber, A., & Otake, T. (2006). Asymmetric mapping from phonetic to lexical representations in second-language listening. *Journal of Phonetics*, 34, 269–284.

Cutler, A., Weber, A., Smits, R., & Cooper. (2004). Patterns of English phoneme confusions by native and non-native listeners. *Journal of the Acoustical Society of America*, 116(6), 3668–3678.

D'Ausilio, A., Craighero, L., & Fadiga, L. (2012). The contribution of the frontal lobe to the perception of speech. *Journal of Neurolinguistics*, 25(5), 328–335.

D'Aloisio, A., & Klein, R. (1990). Aging and the deployment of visual attention. In J. Enns (ed.), *The development of attention: Research and theory* (pp. 447–466). Amsterdam: Elsevier.

Dahan, D., Swingley, D., Tanenhaus, M., & Magnuson, J. (2000). Linguistic gender and spoken-word recognition in French. *Journal of Memory and Language*, 42(4), 465–480.

Dahl, T., Rice, C., Steffensen, M., & Amundsen, L. (2010). Is it language relearning or language reacquisition? Hints from a young boy's code-switching during his journey back to his native language. *International Journal of Bilingualism*, 14(4), 490–510.

Dale, P., & Fenson, L. (1996). Lexical development norms for young children. *Behavior Research Methods, Instruments, & Computers*, 28, 125–127.

Dale, R., & Spivey, M. (2005). From apples and oranges to symbolic dynamics: a framework for conciliating notions of cognitive representation. *Journal of Experimental & Theoretical Artificial Intelligence*, 17(4), 317–342.

(2006). Unraveling the dyad: Using recurrence analysis to explore patterns of syntactic coordination between children and caregivers in conversation. *Language Learning*, 56(3), 391–430.

Dallas, A. (2008). Influences of verbal properties on second language filler-gap resolution: A cross-methodological study. (Unpublished doctoral dissertation), University of Florida, Gainesville.

Dalrymple-Alford, E. (1968). Interlingual interference in a color naming task. *Psychonomic Science*, 10, 215–216.

(1985). Language switching during bilingual reading. *British Journal of Psychology*, 76, 111–122.

Dalrymple-Alford, E., & Aamiry, A. (1969). Language and category clustering in bilingual free recall. *Journal of Verbal Learning and Verbal Behavior*, 8, 762–768.

(1970). Word associations of bilinguals. *Psychonomic Science*, 21, 319–320.

Dalrymple-Alford, E., & Budayr, B. (1966). Examination of some aspects of the Stroop color–word test. *Perceptual and motor skills*, 23, 1211–1214.

Daneman, M. (1991). Working memory as a predictor of verbal fluency. *Journal of Psycholinguistic Research*, 20, 445–464.

Daniels, P. T., & Bright, W. (1996). *The world's writing systems*. New York: Oxford University Press.

Danon, G. (2011). Agreement and DP-internal feature distribution. *Syntax*, 14(4), 297–317.

Danon, L., Díaz-Guilera, A., Duch, J., & Arenas, A. (2005). Comparing community structure identification methods. *Journal of Statistical Mechanics*, 29, P09008.

Darcy, I., Dekydspotter, L., Sprouse, R., et al. (2012). Direct mapping of acoustics to phonology: On the lexical encoding of front rounded vowels in L1 English–L2 French acquisition. *Second Language Research*, 28(1), 5–40.

Darcy, N. (1953). A review of the literature on the effects of bilingualism upon the measurement of intelligence. *Journal of Genetic Psychology*, 82, 21–57.

Das, T., Padakannaya, P., Pugh, K. R., & Singh, N. C. (2011). Neuroimaging reveals dual routes to reading in simultaneous proficient readers of two orthographies. *NeuroImage*, 54, 1476–1487.

Datta, H. (2010). Brain bases for first language lexical attrition in Bengali-English speakers. (Unpublished doctoral dissertation), The City University of New York, New York City.

David, A., & Wei, L. (2008). Individual differences in the lexical development of French-English bilingual children. *International Journal of Bilingual Education and Bilingualism*, 11(5), 598–618.

Davidson, D., & Tell, D. (2005). Monolingual and bilingual children's use of mutual exclusivity in the naming of whole objects. *Journal of experimental child psychology*, 92, 25–45.

Davidson, M., Amso, D., Anderson, L., & Diamond, A. (2006). Development of cognitive control and executive functions from 4 to 13 years: Evidence from manipulations of memory, inhibition, and task switching. *Neuropsychologia*, 44(11), 2037–2078.

Davies, A. (1978a). Language testing: Part I. *Language Teaching*, 11(3), 145–159.

(1978b). Language testing: Part II. *Language Teaching*, 11(4), 215–231.

Davies, A., Criper, C., & Howatt, A. (eds.). (1984). *Interlanguage*. Edinburgh: Edinburgh University Press.

Davis, C., Sánchez-Casas, R., García-Aibea, J., Guasch, M., Molero, M., & Ferré, P. (2010). Masked translation priming: Varying language experience and word type with Spanish–English bilinguals. *Bilingualism: Language and Cognition*, 13, 137–155.

De Angelis, G. (2005). Multilingualism and non-native lexical transfer: An identification problem. *International Journal of Multilingualism*, 2, 1–25.

(2007). *Third or additional language acquisition*. Clevedon, UK: Multilingual Matters.

De Bot, K. (1992). A bilingual production model: Levelt's "speaking" model adapted. *Applied Linguistics*, 13(1), 1–24.

(2006). The plastic bilingual brain: Synaptic pruning or growth?: Commentary on Green et al. *Language Learning*, 56(s1), 127–132.

(2008). The imaging of what in the multilingual mind? *Second Language Research*, 24(1), 111–133.

(2010). Cognitive processing in bilinguals: From static to dynamic models. In R. Kaplan (ed.), *Oxford handbook of applied linguistics* (pp. 335–348). Oxford, UK: Oxford University Press.

(2012). Time scales in second language development. *Dutch Journal of Applied Linguistics*, 1(1), 144–150.

De Bot, K., Broersma, M., & Isurin, L. (2009). Sources of triggering in code switching. In K. de Bot (ed.), *Cross-disciplinary approaches to code switching* (pp. 103–120). Amsterdam/Philadelphia, PA: John Benjamins Publishing.

De Bot, K., & Lowie, W. (2010). On the stability of representations in the multilingual lexicon. In M. Pütz & L. Sicola (eds.), *Cognitive processing in second language acquisition* (pp. 117–134). Amsterdam/Philadelphia, PA: John Benjamins Publishing.

De Bot, K., Lowie, W., & Verspoor, M. (2007). A dynamic systems theory approach to second language acquisition. *Bilingualism: Language and Cognition*, 10(1), 7–21.

De Bot, K., Martens, V., & Stoessel, S. (2004). Finding residual lexical knowledge: The "Savings" approach to testing vocabulary. *International Journal of Bilingualism*, 8(3), 373–382.

De Bot, K., & Stoessel, S. (2000). In search of yesterday's words: Reactivating a long-forgotten language. *Applied Linguistics*, 21(3), 333–353.

de Diego Balaguer, R., Rodríguez-Fornells, A., Rotte, M., Bahlmann, J., Heinze, H.-J., & Münte, T. (2006). Neural circuits subserving the retrieval of stems and grammatical features in regular and irregular verbs. *Human Brain Mapping*, 27, 874–888.

De Groot, A. (1992a). Bilingual lexical representation: A closer look at conceptual representations. In R. Frost & L. Katz (eds.), *Orthography, phonology, morphology, meaning* (pp. 389–412). Amsterdam: Elsevier.

(1992b). Determinants of word translation. *Journal of Experimental Psychology: Learning, Memory, and Cognition*, 18, 1001–1018.

(1993). Word-type effects in bilingual processing tasks: Support for a mixed-representational system. In R. Schreuder & B. Weltens (eds.), *The bilingual lexicon* (pp. 27–51). Amsterdam/Philadelphia, PA: John Benjamins Publishing.

(2000). On the source and nature of semantic and conceptual knowledge. *Bilingualism: Language and Cognition*, 3(1), 7–9.

(2006). Effects of stimulus characteristics and background music on foreign language vocabulary learning and forgetting. *Language Learning*, 56(3), 463–506.

(2011). *Language and cognition in bilinguals and multilinguals: An introduction*. New York: Psychology Press.

(2012). Vocabulary learning in bilingual first-language acquisition and late second-language learning. In M. Faust (ed.), *The handbook of the neuropsychology of language* (pp. 472–493). Malden, MA: Blackwell.

De Groot, A., & Christoffels, I. (2006). Language control in bilinguals: Monolingual tasks and simultaneous interpreting. *Bilingualism: Language and Cognition*, 9(2), 189–201.

De Groot, A., & Comijs, H. (1995). Translation recognition and translation production: Comparing a new and an old tool in the study of bilingualism. *Language Learning*, 45(3), 467–509.

De Groot, A., Dannenburg, L., & van Hell, J. (1994). Forward and backward word translation by bilinguals. *Journal of Memory and Language*, 33, 600–629.

De Groot, A., Delmaar, P., & Lupker, S. (2000). The processing of interlexical homographs in translation recognition and lexical decision: Support for non-selective access to bilingual memory. *The Quarterly Journal of Experimental Psychology: Section A*, 53(2), 397–428.

De Groot, A., & Hoeks, J. (1995). The development of bilingual memory: Evidence from word translation by trilinguals. *Language Learning*, 45(4), 683–724.

De Groot, A., & Keijzer, R. (2000). What is hard to learn is easy to forget: The roles of word concreteness, cognate status, and word frequency in foreign language vocabulary learning and forgetting. *Language Learning*, 50, 1–56.

De Groot, A., & Kroll, J. F. (eds.) (1997). *Tutorials in bilingualism: Psycholinguistic perspectives*. Mahwah, NJ: Lawrence Erlbaum Associates.

De Groot, A., & Nas, G. (1991). Lexical representation of cognates and noncognates in compound bilinguals. *Journal of Memory and Language*, 30(1), 90–123.

De Groot, A., & Poot, R. (1997). Word translation at three levels of proficiency in a second language: The ubiquitous involvement of conceptual memory. *Language Learning*, 47, 215–264.

De Groot, A., Starreveld, P., & Geambaçu, A. (in preparation). Lexical activation in unbalanced bilinguals' word production as measured in a phoneme-monitoring task: Effects of language dominance and sentence context.

De Groot, A., & van den Brink, R. (2010). Foreign language vocabulary learning: Word-type effects during the labeling stage. In M. Kail & M. Hickmann (eds.), *Language acquisition across linguistic and cognitive systems* (pp. 285–297). Amsterdam/Philadelphia, PA: John Benjamins Publishing.

De Groot, A., & van Hell, J. (2005). The learning of foreign language vocabulary. In J. Kroll & A. de Groot (eds.), *Handbook of bilingualism: Psycholinguistic approaches* (pp. 9–29). New York: Oxford University Press.

De Houwer, A. (1990). *The acquisition of two languages from birth*. Cambridge, UK: Cambridge University Press.

(1995). Bilingual language acquisition. In P. Fletcher & B. MacWhinney (eds.), *Handbook of child Language* (pp. 219–250). Oxford, UK: Blackwell.

(1998). By way of introduction: Methods in studies of bilingual first language acquisition. *International Journal of Bilingualism*, 2(3), 249–263.

(2007). Parental language input patterns and children's bilingual use. *Applied Psycholinguistics*, 28(3), 411–424.

De Houwer, A., & Bornstein, M. (2003). Balancing on the tightrope: Language use patterns in bilingual families with young children. Paper presented at the 4th International Symposium on Bilingualism, Tempe, AZ.

De Houwer, A., Bornstein, M., & De Coster, S. (2006). Early understanding of two words for the same thing: A CDI study of lexical comprehension in infant bilinguals. *International Journal of Bilingualism*, 10(3), 331–347.

De Houwer, A., Bornstein, M., & Putnick, D. (2013). A bilingual–monolingual comparison of young children's vocabulary size: Evidence from comprehension and production. *Applied Psycholinguistics*, 1–23.

De Houwer, J., & Eelen, P. (1998). An affective variant of the Simon paradigm. *Cognition & Emotion*, 12, 45–61.

De Lucia, M., Clarke, S., & Murray, M. (2010). A temporal hierarchy for conspecific vocalization discrimination in humans. *Journal of Neuroscience*, 30(33), 11210–11221.

de Nooy, W., Mrvar, A., & Batagelj, V. (2010). *Exploratory social network analysis with Pajek*. Cambridge, UK: Cambridge University Press.

Declerck, M., Koch, I., & Philipp, A. (2012). Digits vs. pictures: The influence of stimulus type on language switching. *Bilingualism: Language and Cognition*, 15, 896–904.

DeFrancis, J. (1989). *Visual speech: The diverse oneness of writing systems*. Honolulu, HI: University of Hawai'i Press.

Degani, T., Prior, A., & Tokowicz, N. (2011). Bidirectional transfer: The effect of sharing a translation. *Journal of Cognitive Psychology*, 23, 18–28.

Degani, T., & Tokowicz, N. (2010a). Ambiguous words are harder to learn. *Bilingualism: Language and Cognition*, 13, 299–314.

(2010b). Semantic ambiguity within and across languages: An integrative review. *Quarterly Journal of Experimental Psychology*, 63(7), 1266–1303.

(2013). Cross-language influences: Translation status affects intra-word sense relatedness. *Memory & Cognition*, 41, 1046–1064.

Degani, T., Tseng, A., & Tokowicz, N. (2014). Together or apart? Learning of ambiguous words. *Bilingualism: Language and Cognition*, 17, 749–765.

Degner, J., Doycheva, C., & Wentura, D. (2012). It matters how much you talk: On the automaticity of affective connotations of first and second language words. *Bilingualism: Language and Cognition*, 15(1), 181–189.

Dehaene, S., & Cohen, L. (2011). The unique role of the visual word form area in reading. *Trends in Cognitive Sciences*, 15, 254–262.

Dehaene, S., Cohen, L., Sigman, M., & Vinckier, F. (2005). The neural code for written words: a proposal. *Trends in Cognitive Sciences*, 9, 335–341.

Dehaene-Lambertz, G., Dehaene, S., & Hertz-Pannier, L. (2002). Functional neuroimaging of speech perception in infants. *Science*, 298(5600), 2013–2015.

DeKeyser, R. (2013). Age effects in second language learning: Stepping stones toward better understanding. *Language Learning*, 63, 52–67.

DeKeyser, R., & Sokalski, K. (1996). The differential role of comprehension and production practice. *Language Learning*, 46, 613–642.

Delis, D., Kaplan, E., & Kramer, J. (2001). *Delis Kaplan Executive Function System*. San Antonio, TX: The Psychological Corporation.

Dell, G. (1986). A spreading activation theory of retrieval in language production. *Psychological Review*, 93, 283–321.

Dell, G., & O'Seaghdha, P. (1992). Stages of lexical access in language production. *Cognition*, 42(1–3), 287–314.

Demerens, C., Stankoff, B., Logak, M., et al. (1996). Induction of myelination in the central nervous system by electrical activity. *Proceedings of the National Academy of Sciences*, 93(18), 9887–9892.

Depue, B., Banich, M., & Curran, T. (2006). Suppression of emotional and nonemotional content in memory: effects of repetition on cognitive control. *Psychological Science*, 17(5), 441–447.

Desmet, T., & Declercq, M. (2006). Cross-linguistic priming of syntactic hierarchical configuration information. *Journal of Memory and Language*, 54(4), 610–632.

Desrochers, A., & Petrusic, W. (1983). Comprehension effects in comparative judgments. In J. Yuille (ed.), *Imagery, memory and cognition* (pp. 131–159). Hillsdale, NJ: Erlbaum.

Deutsch, A., Frost, R., & Forster, K. (1998). Verbs and nouns are organized and accessed differently in the mental lexicon: Evidence from Hebrew. *Journal of Experimental Psychology: Learning Memory, and Cognition*, 24, 1238–1255.

Dewaele, J.-M. (2004). The emotional force of swear words and taboo words in the speech of multilinguals. *Journal of Multicultural and Multilingual Development*, 25, 204–222.

(2008). The emotional weight of *I love you* in multilinguals' languages. *Journal of Pragmatics*, 40, 1753–1780.

(2010). *Emotions in multiple languages*. Basingstoke, UK: Palgrave MacMillan.

(2012). Psychological factors in second language acquisition. In J. Herschensohn & M. Young-Scholten (eds.), *The Cambridge handbook of second language acquisition* (pp. 159–179). Cambridge, UK: Cambridge University Press.

Dewaele, J.-M. & Costa, B. (2013) Multilingual clients' experience of psychotherapy. *Language and Psychoanalysis*, 2(2), 31–50.

Dewaele, J.-M., & Pavlenko, A. (2002). Emotion vocabulary in interlanguage. *Language Learning*, 52, 263–322.

Díaz, B., Mitterer, H., Broersma, M., & Sebastián-Gallés, N. (2012). Individual differences in late bilinguals' L2 phonological processes: From acoustic–phonetic analysis to lexical access. *Learning and Individual Differences*, 22, 680–689.

Diaz, F. (1985). Extracranial-intracranial bypasses. *Journal of Vascular Surgery*, 2(1) 234–236.

Diependaele, K., Duñabeitia, J., Morris, J., & Keuleers, E. (2011). Fast morphological effects in first and second language word recognition. *Journal of Memory and Language*, 64, 344–358.

Diependaele, K., Lemhöfer, K., & Brysbaert, M. (2013). The word frequency effect in first- and second-language word recognition: A lexical entrenchment account. *Quarterly Journal of Experimental Psychology*, 66(5), 843–863.

Diesendruck, G. (2007). Mechanisms of word learning. In E. Hoff & M. Shatz (eds.), *Handbook of language development* (pp. 257–276). New York: Blackwell.

Dietrich, A. (2014). The role of probabilistic cues in L2 processing: Verb bias in Spanish and English. (Unpublished doctoral dissertation), Pennsylvania State University, University Park.

Dietrich, R., Klein, W., & Noyau, C. (eds.). (1995). *The acquisition of temporality in a second language*. Amsterdam/Philadelphia, PA: John Benjamins Publishing.

Dijkstra, T. (2003). Lexical processing in bilinguals and multilinguals: The word selection problem. In J. Cenoz, B. Hufeisen, & U. Jessner (eds.), *The multilingual lexicon* (pp. 11–26). Dordrecht, the Netherlands: Springer.

(2005). Bilingual visual word recognition and lexical access. In J. Kroll & A. de Groot (eds.), *Handbook of bilingualism: Psycholinguistic approaches*, (pp. 179–201). New York: Oxford University Press.

Dijkstra, T., De Bruijn, E., Schriefers, H., & Brinke, S. (2000). More on interlingual homograph recognition: Language intermixing versus explicitness of instruction. *Bilingualism: Language and Cognition*, 3(1), 69–78.

Dijkstra, T., Grainger, J., & van Heuven, W. J. B. (1999). Recognition of cognates and interlingual homographs: The neglected role of phonology. *Journal of Memory and Language*, 41, 496–518.

Dijkstra, T., Miwa, K., Brummelhuis, B., Sappelli, M., & Baayen, H. (2010). How cross-language similarity and task demands affect cognate recognition. *Journal of Memory and Language*, 62(3), 284–301.

Dijkstra, T., Moscoso del Prado Martín, F., Schulpen, B., Schreuder, R., & Baayen, H. (2005). A roommate in cream: Morphological family size effects on interlingual homograph recognition. *Language and Cognitive Processes*, 20(1–2), 7–41.

Dijkstra, T., Timmermans, M., & Schriefers, H. (2000). On being blinded by your other language: Effects of task demands on interlingual homograph recognition. *Journal of Memory and Language*, 42(4), 445–464.

Dijkstra, T., & van Hell, J. (2003). Testing the language mode hypothesis using trilinguals. *International Journal of Bilingual Education and Bilingualism*, 6(1), 2–16.

Dijkstra, T., & van Heuven, W. J. B. (1998). The BIA model and bilingual word recognition. In J. Grainger & A. Jacobs (eds.), *Localist connectionist approaches to human cognition* (pp. 189–225). Hillsdale, NJ: Erlbaum.

(2002). The architecture of the bilingual word recognition system: From identification to decision. *Bilingualism: Language and Cognition*, 5(3), 175–197.

Dijkstra, T., van Heuven, W. J. B., & Grainger, J. (1998). Simulating cross-language competition with the bilingual interactive activation model. *Psychologica Belgica*, 38, 177–196.

Dijkstra, T., Van Jaarsveld, H., & Ten Brinke, S. (1998). Interlingual homograph recognition: effects of task demands and language intermixing. *Bilingualism: Language and Cognition*, 1, 51–66.

Dillon, B., Dunbar, E., & Idsardi, W. (2013). A single-stage approach to learning phonological categories: Insights from Inuktitut. *Cognitive Science*, 37, 344–377.

Diniz, A., Wijnants, M., Torre, K., et al. (2011). Contemporary theories of 1/f noise in motor control. *Human Movement Science*, 30(5), 889–905.

Doerksen, S., & Shimamura, A. P. (2001). Source memory enhancement for emotional words. *Emotion*, 1, 5–11.

Dong, Y., Gui, S., & MacWhinney, B. (2005). Shared and separate meanings in the bilingual lexical memory. *Bilingualism: Language and Cognition*, 8, 221–238.

Döpke, S. (1998). Can the principle of one person-one language be disregarded as unrealistically elitist? *Australian Review of Applied Linguistics*, 21(1), 41–56.

Dörnyei, Z. (2003). Attitudes, orientations, and motivations in language learning: Advances in theory, research, and applications. In Z. Dörnyei (ed.), *Attitudes, orientations and motivations in language learning* (pp. 3–32). Oxford, UK: Blackwell.

(2010). The relationship between language aptitude and language learning motivation. In E. Macaro (ed.), *Continuum companion to second language acquisition* (pp. 247–267). London: Continuum.

(2013). Researching complex dynamic systems: 'Retrodictive qualitative modelling' in the language classroom. *Language Teaching*, 47(1), 80–91.

Dörnyei, Z., & Kormos, J. (2000). The role of individual and social variables in oral task performance. *Language Teaching Research*, 4, 275–300.

Dörnyei, Z., & Tseng, W-T. (2009). Motivational processing in interactional tasks. In A. Mackey and C. Polio (eds.), *Multiple perspectives on interaction. Second language research in honor of Susan M. Gass* (pp. 117–134). London: Routledge.

Doupe, A., & Kuhl, P. (1999). Birdsong and human speech: common themes and mechanisms. *Annual Review of Neuroscience*, 22(1), 567–631.

Draganski, B., Gaser, C., Busch, V., Schuierer, G., Bogdahn, U., & May, A. (2004). Neuroplasticity: Changes in grey matter induced by training. *Nature*, 427(6972), 311–312.

Dreher, J., Koechlin, E., Ali, S., & Grafman, J. (2002). The roles of timing and task order during task switching. *Neuroimage*, 17(1), 95–109.

Driscoll, I., & Troncoso, J. (2011a). Asymptomatic Alzheimer's disease: a prodrome or a state of resilience? *Current Alzheimer Research*, 8(4), 330–335.

Dryer, M., & Haspelmath, M. (eds.). (2011). *The world atlas of language structures online*. Munich: Max Planck Digital Library. Retrieved from: http://wals.info.

Duffy, S., Henderson, J., & Morris, R. (1989). Semantic facilitation of lexical access during sentence processing. *Journal of Experimental Psychology: Learning, Memory, and Cognition*, 15(5), 791–801.

Duffy, S., Kambe, G., & Rayner, K. (2001). The effect of prior disambiguating context on the comprehension of ambiguous words: Evidence from eye movements. In D. Gorfein (ed.), *On the consequences of meaning selection: Perspectives on resolving lexical ambiguity: Decade of behavior* (pp. 27–43). Washington, DC: American Psychological Association.

Duffy, S., Morris, R., & Rayner, K. (1988). Lexical ambiguity and fixation times in reading. *Journal of Memory and Language*, 27(4), 429–46.

Dufour, R., & Kroll, J. F. (1995). Matching words to concepts in two languages: A test of the concept mediation model of bilingual representation. *Memory and Cognition*, 23, 166–180.

Dumay, N., & Gaskell, M. (2007). Sleep-associated changes in the mental representation of spoken words. *Psychological Science*, 18, 35–39.

Duñabeitia, J., Dimitropoulou, M., Morris, J., & Diependaele, K. (2013). The role of form in morphological priming: Evidence from bilinguals. *Language and Cognitive Processes*, 28(7), 969–987.

Duñabeitia, J., Perea, M., & Carreiras, M. (2010). Masked translation priming effects with highly proficient simultaneous bilinguals. *Experimental Psychology*, 57, 98–107.

Dunlosky, J., Rawson, K., Marsh, E., Nathan, M., & Willingham, D. (2013). Improving students' learning with effective learning techniques: Promising directions from cognitive and educational psychology. *Psychological Science in the Public Interest*, 14, 4–58.

Dussias, P. (2001). Sentence parsing in fluent Spanish–English bilinguals. In J. Nicol (ed.), *One mind, two languages: bilingual language processing* (pp. 159–176). Malden, MA: Blackwell.

Dussias, P. (2003). Syntactic ambiguity resolution in second language learners: Some effects of bilinguality on L1 and L2 processing strategies. *Studies in Second Language Acquisition*, 25(4), 529–557.

Dussias, P., & Cramer, T. R. (2006). The role of L1 verb bias on L2 sentence parsing. In D. Bamman, T. Magnitskaia, & C. Zaller (eds.), *Proceedings of the 30th annual Boston University conference on language development*, vol. 1 (pp. 166–177). Somerville, MA: Cascadilla Press.

Dussias, P., & Cramer Scaltz, T. (2008). Spanish–English L2 speakers' use of subcategorization bias information in the resolution of temporary ambiguity during second language reading. *Acta Psychologica*, 128(3), 501–513.

Dussias, P., Marful, A., Gerfen, C., & Bajo, M. (2010). Usage frequencies of complement-taking verbs in Spanish and English: Data from Spanish monolinguals and Spanish–English bilinguals. *Behavior Research Methods*, 42(4), 1004–1011.

Dussias, P., Perrotti, L., & Brown, M. (2013). Re-learning to parse a first language: The role of experience in sentence comprehension. Poster presented at the International Workshop on Bilingualism and Cognitive Control. Krakow, Poland.

Dussias, P., & Piñar, P. (2010). Effects of reading span and plausibility in the reanalysis of wh-gaps by Chinese–English second language speakers. *Second Language Research*, 26(4), 443–472.

Dussias, P., & Sagarra, N. (2007). The effect of exposure on syntactic parsing in Spanish–English bilinguals. *Bilingualism: Language and Cognition*, 10 (1), 101–116.

Dussias, P., Valdés Kroff, J., Guzzardo Tamargo, R., & Gerfen, C. (2013). When gender and looking go hand in hand. *Studies in Second Language Acquisition*, 35(2), 353–387.

Duyck, W. (2005). Translation and associative priming with cross-lingual pseudohomophones: Evidence for nonselective phonological activation in bilinguals. *Journal of Experimental Psychology: Learning, Memory, and Cognition*, 31, 1340–1359.

Duyck, W., & Brysbaert, M. (2004). Forward and backward number translation requires conceptual mediation in both balanced and unbalanced bilinguals. *Journal of Experimental Psychology: Human Perception and Performance*, 30, 889–906.

Duyck, W., Depestel, I., Fias, W., & Reynvoet (2008). Cross-lingual numerical distance priming with second-language number words in native to third-language number word translation. *Quarterly Journal of Experimental Psychology*, 61, 1281–1290.

Duyck, W., & Warlop, N. (2009). Translation priming between the native language and a second language: New evidence from Dutch–French bilinguals. *Experimental Psychology*, 56, 173–179.

Duyck, W., Van Assche, E., Drieghe, D., & Hartsuiker, R. (2007). Visual word recognition by bilinguals in a sentence context: Evidence for nonselective lexical access. *Journal of Experimental Psychology: Learning, Memory, and Cognition*, 33, 663–679.

Duyck, W., Vanderelst, D., Desmet, T., & Hartsuiker, R. (2008). The frequency effect in second-language visual word recognition. *Psychonomic Bulletin & Review*, 15(4), 850–855.

Dwan, K., Altman, D., Arnaiz, J., et al. (2008). Systematic review of the empirical evidence of study publication bias and outcome reporting. *Plos one*, 1–31.

Dyer, E. (1971). Color-naming interference in monolinguals and bilinguals. *Journal of Verbal Learning and Verbal Behavior*, 10, 297–302.

Eberhard, K. (1999). The accessibility of conceptual number to the processes of subject–verb agreement in English. *Journal of Memory and Language*, 41(4), 560–578.

Eddington, C., & Tokowicz, N. (2013). Examining English–German translation ambiguity using primed translation recognition. *Bilingualism: Language and Cognition*, 16, 442–457.

Eddington, C., Martin, K., & Tokowicz, N. (2012). How meaning-based strategies and the generation effect influence German vocabulary learning. Paper presented at the University of Illinois at Chicago BilForum.

Eddington, D. (2002). Spanish gender assignment in an analogical framework. *Journal of Quantitative Linguistics*, 9(1), 49–75.

Ehri, L., & Ryan, E. (1980). Performance of bilinguals in a picture-word interference task. *Journal of Psycholinguistic Research*, 9(3), 285–302.

Eickhoff, S., Laird, A., Grefkes, C., Wang, L., Zilles, K., & Fox, P. (2009). Coordinate-based activation likelihood estimation meta-analysis of neuroimaging data: A random-effects approach based on empirical estimates of spatial uncertainty. *Human Brain Mapping*, 30, 2907–2926.

Eid, M. (1992). Directionality in Arabic–English code-switching. In A. Rouchdy (ed.), *The Arabic language in America* (pp. 50–70). Detroit, MI: Wayne State University Press.

Eilola T., & Havelka, J. (2011). Behavioural and physiological responses to the emotional and taboo Stroop tasks in native and non-native speakers of English. *International Journal of Bilingualism*, 15, 353–369.

Eilola, T., Havelka, J., & Sharma, D. (2007). Emotional activation in the first and second language. *Cognition and Emotion*, 21, 1064–1076.

Eimas, P., Siqueland, E., Jusczyk, P., & Vigorito, J. (1971). Speech perception in infants. *Science*, 171(3968), 303–306.

Ellis, N. (1998). Emergentism, connectionism and language learning. *Language Learning*, 48(4), 631–664.

(2002). Frequency effects in language processing: A review with implications for theories of implicit and explicit language acquisition. *Studies in Second Language Acquisition*, 24(2), 143–188.

(2003). Constructions, chunking, and connectionism: The emergence of second language structure. In C. Doughty & M. Long (eds.), *Handbook of second language acquisition* (pp. 33–68). Oxford, UK: Blackwell.

(2006a). Language acquisition as rational contingency learning. *Applied Linguistics*, 27(1), 1–24.

(2006b). Selective attention and transfer phenomena in SLA: Contingency, cue competition, salience, interference, overshadowing, blocking, and perceptual learning. *Applied Linguistics*, 27(2), 1–31.

(2007). Learned attention in language acquisition: Blocking, salience, and cue competition. Paper presented at the EuroCogSci07, the Second European Cognitive Science Conference, Delphi, Greece.

Ellis, N., & Cadierno, T. (2009). Constructing a second language. *Annual Review of Cognitive Linguistics*, 7(special section), 111–290.

Ellis, N., & Ferreira-Junior, F. (2009a). Construction learning as a function of frequency, frequency distribution, and function. *Modern Language Journal*, 93, 370–386.

(2009b). Constructions and their acquisition: Islands and the distinctiveness of their occupancy. *Annual Review of Cognitive Linguistics*, 7, 111–139.

Ellis, N., & Larsen-Freeman, D. (2009). Constructing a second language: Analyses and computational simulations of the emergence of linguistic constructions from usage. *Language Learning*, 59(supplement 1), 93–128.

Ellis, N., & O'Donnell, M. (2011). Robust language acquisition: An emergent consequence of language as a complex adaptive system. In L. Carlson, C. Hölscher, & T. Shipley (eds.), *Proceedings of the 33rd Annual Conference of the Cognitive Science Society* (pp. 3512–3517). Austin, TX: Cognitive Science Society.

  (2012). Statistical construction learning: Does a Zipfian problem space ensure robust language learning? In J. Rebuschat, & J. Williams (eds.), *Statistical learning and language acquisition*. Berlin: Mouton de Gruyter.

Ellis, N., O'Donnell, M., & Römer, U. (2014a). The processing of verb-argument constructions is sensitive to form, function, frequency, contingency, and prototypicality. *Cognitive Linguistics*, 25(1), 55–98.

Ellis, N., O'Donnel, M., &. Römer, U. (2014b). Second language verb–argument constructions are sensitive to form, function, frequency, contingency, and prototypicality. *Linguistics Approaches to Bilingualism*, 4(4), 405–431.

Ellis, N., & Sagarra, N. (2011). Learned attention in adult language acquisition: A replication and generalization study and meta-analysis. *Studies in Second Language Acquisition*, 33(4), 589–624.

Elman, J. (1990). Finding structure in time. *Cognitive Science*, 14, 179–211.

  (1993). Learning and development in neural networks: The importance of starting small. *Cognition*, 48(1), 71–99.

Elman, J., Bates, E., Johnson, M., Karmiloff-Smith, A., Parisi, D., & Plunkett, K. (1996). *Rethinking innateness: A connectionist perspective on development*. Cambridge, MA: MIT Press.

Elston-Güttler, K., Gunter, T., & Kotz, S. (2005). Zooming into L2: Global language context and adjustment affect processing of interlingual homographs in sentences. *Cognitive Brain Research*, 25(1), 57–70.

Elston-Güttler, K., Paulmann, S., & Kotz, S. (2005). Who's in control?: Proficiency and L1 influence on L2 processing. *Journal of Cognitive Neuroscience*, 17(10), 1593–1610.

Emmorey, K., Borinstein, H., Thompson, R., & Gollan, T. (2008). Bimodal bilingualism. *Bilingualism: Language and Cognition*, 11, 43–61.

Emmorey, K., Luk, G., Pyers, J., & Bialystok, E. (2008). The source of enhanced cognitive control in bilinguals: Evidence from bimodal bilinguals. *Psychological Science*, 19, 1201–1206.

Engel, A., & Singer, W. (2001). Temporal binding and the neural correlates of sensory awareness. *Trends in Cognitive Sciences*, 5(1), 16–25.

Engle, R., Kane, M., & Tuholski, S. (1999). Individual differences in working memory capacity and what they tell us about controlled attention, general fluid intelligence, and functions of the prefrontal cortex. In A. Miyake & P. Shah (eds.), *Models of working memory* (pp. 102–134). Cambridge, UK: Cambridge University Press.

Engel de Abreu, P. (2011). Working memory in multilingual children: Is there a bilingual effect? *Memory*, 19, 529–537.

Engel de Abreu, P., Cruz-Santos, A., Tourinho, C., Martin, R., & Bialystok, E. (2012). Bilingualism enriches the poor: enhanced cognitive control in low-income minority children. *Psychological Science*, 23(11), 1364–71.

Erlam, R. (2003). Evaluating the effectiveness of structured input and output-based instruction in foreign language learning. *Studies in Second Language Acquisition*, 25, 559–582.

Ervin, S. (1961). Learning and recall in bilinguals. *The American Journal of Psychology*, 74, 446–451.

Ervin, S. M., & Osgood, C. E. (1954). Second language learning and bilingualism. In C. E. Osgood & F. Sebeok (eds.), *Psycholinguistics: A survey of theory and research problems* (pp. 139–146). Baltimore: Waverly Press.

Ervin-Tripp, S. (1974). Is second language learning like the first? *TESOL Quarterly*, 8, 111–127.

Escudero, P. (2005). Linguistic perception and second language acquisition: explaining the attainment of optimal phonological categorization. (Unpublished doctoral dissertation), Utrecht University, the Netherlands.

Escudero, P., Hayes-Harb, R., & Mitterer, H. (2008). Novel second-language words and asymmetric lexical access. *Journal of Phonetics*, 36, 345–360.

Escudero, P., & Wanrooij, K. (2010). The effect of L1 orthography on non-native vowel perception. *Language and Speech*, 53, 343–365.

Eulitz, C., & Lahiri, A. (2004). Neurobiological evidence for abstract phonological representations in the mental lexicon during speech recognition. *Journal of Cognitive Neuroscience*, 16(4), 577–583.

Evans, J., Workman, L., Mayer, P., & Crowley, K. (2002). Differential bilingual laterality: Mythical monster found in Wales. *Brain and Language*, 83, 291–299.

Eysenck, M. (1992). *Anxiety: The cognitive perspective*. Hove, UK: Erlbaum.

Eysenck, M., & Calvo, M. (1992). Anxiety and performance: The processing efficiency theory. *Cognition and Emotion*, 6, 409–434.

Eysenck, M., Derekshan, N., Santos, R., & Calvo, M. (2007). Anxiety and performance: Attentional control theory. *Emotion*, 7, 336–353.

Fabbro, F. (2001). The bilingual brain: Cerebral representation of languages. *Brain and Language*, 79, 211–222.

Fabbro, F., Peru, A., & Skrap, M. (1997). Language disorders in bilingual patients after thalamic lesions. *Journal of Neurolinguistics*, 10, 347–367.

Faingold, E. (2004). *Multilingualism from infancy to adolescence: Noam's experience*. Charlotte, NC: Information Age Publishing.

Faisal, A., Selen, L., & Wolpert, D. (2008). Noise in the nervous system. *Nature Reviews Neuroscience*, 9(4), 292–303.

Fan, J., McCandliss, B., Sommer, T., Raz, A., & Posner, M. (2002). Testing the efficiency and independence of attentional networks. *Journal of Cognitive Neuroscience*, 14(3), 340–347.

Farley, A. (2005). *Structured input*. New York: McGraw-Hill.

Federal Interagency Forum on Child and Family Statistics. (2002). *American's children: Key national indicators of well-being*. Washington, DC: US Government Printing Office.

Feldman, L., Frost, R., & Pnini, T. (1995). Decomposing words into their constituent morphemes: Evidence from English and Hebrew. *Journal of Experimental Psychology: Learning, Memory and Cognition*, 21, 947–960.

Feldman, L., Kostić, A., Basnight-Brown, D., Filipović Đurđević, D., & Pastizzo, M. (2010). Morphological facilitation for regular and irregular verb formations in native and non-native speakers: Little evidence for two distinct mechanisms. *Bilingualism: Language and Cognition*, 13(2), 119–135.

Felser, C., Roberts, L., Marinis, T., & Gross, R. (2003). The processing of ambiguous sentences by first and second language learners of English. *Applied Psycholinguistics*, 24(3), 453–489.

Fennell, C. (2012). Habituation procedures. In E. Hoff (ed.), *Research methods in child language: A practical guide* (pp. 3–16). Malden, MA: Wiley-Blackwell.

Fennell, C., & Byers-Heinlein, K. (2014). You sound like Mommy: Bilingual and monolingual infants learn words best from speakers typical of their language environments. *International Journal of Behavioral Development*, 38(4), 309–316.

Fennell, C., Byers-Heinlein, K., & Werker, J. F. (2007) Using speech sounds to guide word learning: The case of bilingual infants. *Child Development*, 78(5), 1510–1525.

Fennell, C., & Werker, J. (2003). Early word learners' ability to access phonetic detail in well-known words. *Language & Speech*, 46(2), 245–264.

Fenson, L., Dale, P., Steven Reznick, J., Thal, D., Bates, E., & Hartung, J. (1993). *MacArthur Communicative Development Inventories* (1st edn). Baltimore, MD: Brookes.

Fenson, L., Marchman, V., Thal, D., Dale, P., Steven Reznick, J., & Bates, E. (2007). *MacArthur-Bates Communicative Development Inventories* (2nd edn). Baltimore, MD: Brookes.

Fernald, A. (1985). Four-month-old infants prefer to listen to motherese. *Infant Behavior and Development*, 8(2), 181–195.

Fernandes, M., Craik, F., Bialystok, E., & Kreuger, S. (2007). Effects of bilingualism, aging, and semantic relatedness on memory under divided attention. *Canadian Journal of Experimental Psychology*, 61, 128–141.

Fernández, C. (2008). Reexamining the role of explicit information in processing instruction. *Studies in Second Language Acquisition*, 30, 277–305.

Fernández, E. (2003). *Bilingual sentence processing: Relative clause attachment in English and Spanish*. Amsterdam/Philadelphia, PA: John Benjamins Publishing.

Ferrand, L., & Grainger, J. (1992). Phonology and orthography in visual word recognition: Evidence from masked nonword priming. *Quarterly Journal of Experimental Psychology*, 45A, 353–372.

Ferré, P., García, T., Fraga, I., Sánchez-Casas, R., & Molero, M. (2010). Memory for emotional words in bilinguals: Do words have the same emotional intensity in the first and in the second language? *Cognition and Emotion*, 24(5), 760–785.

Ferreira, V., & Pashler, H. (2002). Central bottleneck influences on the processing stages of word production. *Journal of Experimental Psychology: Learning, Memory, and Cognition*, 28, 1187–1199.

Ferstl, E., Neumann, J., Bogler, C., & Von Cramon, D. Y. (2008). The extended language network: A meta-analysis of neuroimaging studies on text comprehension. *Human Brain Mapping*, 29, 581–593.

Festman, J. (2009). *Three languages in mind*. Saarbrücken: VMD.

  (2012). Language control abilities of late bilinguals. *Bilingualism: Language and Cognition*, 15(3), 580–593.

Festman, J., & Munte, T. (2012). Cognitive control in Russian–German bilinguals. *Frontiers in Psychology*, 3, 115.

Festman, J., Rodríguez-Fornells, A., & Münte, T. (2010). Individual differences in control of language interference in late bilinguals are mainly related to general executive abilities. *Behavioral and Brain Functions*, 6(5).

Filippi, R., Karaminis, T., & Thomas, M. (2014). Language switching in bilingual production: Empirical data and computational modelling. *Bilingualism: Language and Cognition*, 17(2), 294–315.

Fillmore, C. (1979). On fluency. In D. Kempler & W. Wang (eds.), *Individual differences in language ability and language behavior* (pp. 85–102). New York: Academic Press.

Finkbeiner, M., Almeida, J., Janssen, N., & Caramazza, A. (2006). Lexical selection in bilingual speech does not involve language suppression. *Journal of Experimental Psychology: Learning, Memory, and Cognition*, 32, 1075–1089.

Finkbeiner, M., Forster, K., Nicol, J., & Nakamura, K. (2004). The role of polysemy in masked semantic and translation priming. *Journal of Memory and Language*, 51, 1–22.

Finkbeiner, M., Gollan, T., & Caramazza, A. (2006). Lexical access in bilingual speakers: What's the (hard) problem? *Bilingualism: Language and Cognition*, 9, 153–166.

Finkbeiner, M., & Nicol, J. (2003). Semantic category effects in second language word learning. *Applied Psycholinguistics*, 24, 369–383.

Flege, J. (1987). The production of "new" and "similar" phones in a foreign language: Evidence for the effect of equivalence classification. *Journal of Phonetics*, 15(1), 47–65.

  (1995). Second language speech learning: Theory, findings, and problems. In W. Strange (ed.), *Speech perception and linguistic experience: Issues in cross-language research* (pp. 233–277). Timonium, MD: York Press.

  (1999). Age of learning and second-language speech. In D. Birdsong (ed.), *Second language acquisition and the Critical Period Hypothesis* (pp. 101–131). Mahwah, NJ: Erlbaum.

(2002). Interactions between the native and second-language phonetic systems. In P. Burmeister, T. Piske, & A. Rohde (eds.), *An integrated view of language development: Papers in honor of Henning Wode* (pp. 217–224). Trier, Germany: Wissenschaftlicher Verlag.

Flege, J., & Eefting, W. (1987). Cross-language switching in stop consonant perception and production by Dutch speakers of English. *Speech Communication*, 6(3), 185–202.

Flege, J., Yeni-Komshian, G., & Liu, S. (1999). Age constraints on second-language acquisition. *Journal of Memory and Language*, 41(1), 78–104.

Flores, C. (2010). The effect of age on language attrition: Evidence from bilingual returnees. *Bilingualism: Language and Cognition*, 13(4), 533–546.

(2012). Differential effects of language attrition in the domains of verb placement and object expression. *Bilingualism: Language and Cognition*, 15, 550–567.

Flynn, S., Foley, C., & Vinnitskaya, I. (2004). The Cumulative-Enhancement Model for language acquisition: Comparing adults' and children's patterns of development in first, second and third language acquisition of relative clauses. *International Journal of Multilingualism*, 1, 3–16.

Folse, K. (2004). *Vocabulary myths: Applying second language research to classroom teaching*. Ann Arbor, MI: University of Michigan Press.

Folstein, M., Folstein, S., & McHugh, P. (1975). Mini-mental state: A practical method for grading the cognitive state of patients for the clinician. *Journal of Psychiatric Research*, 12(3), 189–198.

Footnick, R. (2007). A hidden language: Recovery of a 'lost' language is triggered by hypnosis. In B. Kopke, M. Schmid, M. Keijzer, & S. Dostert (eds.), *Language attrition: Theoretical perspectives* (pp. 169–187). Amsterdam/Philadelphia, PA: John Benjamins Publishing.

Forster, K. (2004). Category size effects revisited: Frequency and masked priming effects in semantic categorization. *Brain and Language*, 90, 276–286.

Forster, K., & Davis, C. (1984). Repetition priming and frequency attenuation in lexical access. *Journal of Experimental Psychology: Learning, Memory, and Cognition*, 10, 680–698.

Forster, K., & Taft, M. (1994). Bodies, antibodies, and neighborhood density effects in masked form-priming. *Journal of Experimental Psychology: Learning, Memory, and Cognition*, 20, 844–863.

Fortkamp, M. (1999). Working memory capacity and elements of L2 speech production. *Communication and Cognition*, 32, 259–295.

Foss, D., & Speer, S. (1983). Global and local context effects in sentence processing. In R. Palermo (ed.), *Cognition and the symbolic processes: Applied ecological perspectives* (pp. 115–139). Hillsdale, NJ: Lawrence Erlbaum Associates.

Foucart, A., & Frenck-Mestre, C. (2011). Grammatical gender processing in L2: Electrophysiological evidence from ERPs of the effect of

L1–L2 syntactic similarity. *Bilingualism: Language and Cognition*, 14, 379–399.

(2012). Can late L2 learners acquire new grammatical features? Evidence from ERPs and eye-tracking. *Journal of Memory and Language*, 66(1), 226–248.

Francis, G., Hunston, S., & Manning, E. (eds.). (1996). *Grammar patterns 1: Verbs. The COBUILD series*. London: Harper Collins.

Francis, W., Corral, N., Jones, M., & Sáenz, S. (2008). Decomposition of repetition priming components in picture naming. *Journal of Experimental Psychology*, 137(3), 566–590.

Francis, W., & Gallard, S. (2005). Concept mediation in trilingual translation: Evidence from response time and repetition priming patterns. *Psychonomic Bulletin & Review*, 12, 1082–1088.

Francis, W., & Sáenz, S. (2007). Repetition priming endurance in picture naming and translation: Contributions of component processes. *Memory & Cognition*, 35, 481–493.

Francis, W., Augustini, B., & Sáenz, S. (2003). Repetition priming in picture naming and translation depends on shared processes and their difficulty: Evidence from Spanish–English bilinguals. *Journal of Experimental Psychology: Learning, Memory, and Cognition*, 29, 1283–1297.

Frazier, L. (1979). On comprehending sentences: Syntactic parsing strategies. (Unpublished doctoral dissertation), University of Connecticut, Storrs.

Frazier, L. (1987). Sentence processing. In M. Coltheart (ed.), *Attention and performance XII* (pp. 559–586). Hillsdale, NJ: Erlbaum.

(1990). Exploring the architecture of the language processing system. In G. Altmann (ed.), *Cognitive models of speech processing* (pp. 409–433). Cambridge, MA: MIT Press.

Frazier, L., & Clifton Jr., C. (1996). *Construal*. Cambridge, MA: MIT Press.

Frazier, L., & Rayner, K. (1982). Making and correcting errors during sentence comprehension: Eye movements in the analysis of structurally ambiguous sentences. *Cognitive Psychology*, 14(2), 178–210.

French, R. (1998). A simple recurrent network model of bilingual memory. In M. A. Gernsbacher & S. Derry (eds.), *Proceedings of the 20th Annual Conference of the Cognitive Science Society* (pp. 368–373). Mahwah, NJ: Erlbaum.

Frenck, C., & Pynte, J. (1987). Semantic representation and surface forms: A look at cross-language priming in bilinguals. *Journal of Psycholinguistic Research*, 16, 383–396.

Frenck-Mestre, C. (1999). Examining second language reading: an on-line look. In A. Sorace, C. Heycock, & R. Shillcock (eds.), *Language acquisition: Knowledge representation and processing* (pp. 474–478). Amsterdam: North-Holland.

(2002). An on-line look at sentence processing in the second language. In R. Heredia & J. Altarriba (eds.), *Bilingual sentence processing* (pp. 217–236). Amsterdam: Elsevier.

Frenck-Mestre, C., Foucart, A., Carrasco-Ortiz, H., & Herschensohn, J. (2009). Processing of grammatical gender in French as a first and second language: Evidence from ERPs. In L. Roberts, G. Véronique, A. Nilsson, & M. Tellier (eds.), *Eurosla yearbook 9* (pp. 76–106). Amsterdam/Philadelphia, PA: John Benjamins Publishing.

Frenck-Mestre, C., & Pynte, J. (1997). Syntactic ambiguity resolution while reading in second and native languages. *Quarterly Journal of Experimental Psychology*, 50A(1), 119–148.

Friederici, A. (1995). The time course of syntactic activation during language processing: a model based on neuropsychological and neurophysiological data. *Brain and Language*, 50, 259–281.

(2006). What's in control of language? *Nature Neuroscience*, 9(8), 991–992.

Friederici, A., & Jacobsen, T. (1999). Processing grammatical gender during language comprehension. *Journal of Psycholinguistic Research*, 28(5), 467–484.

Fromm, E. (1970). Age regression with unexpected reappearance of a repressed childhood language. *International Journal of Clinical and Experimental Hypnosis*, 18, 79–88.

Frost, R. (2012). Towards a universal model of reading. *Behavioral and Brain Sciences*, 35, 263–279.

Frost, R., Deutsch, A., & Forster, K. (2000). Decomposing morphologically complex words in a nonlinear morphology. *Journal of Experimental Psychology Learning Memory, and Cognition*, 26, 751–765.

Frost, R., & Grainger, J. (2000). Cross-linguistic perspectives on morphological processing. *Language and Cognitive Processes*, 15, 321–328.

Gahl, S., & Garnsey, S. (2004). Knowledge of grammar, knowledge of usage: Syntactic probabilities affect pronunciation variation. *Language*, 80(4), 748–775.

Gais, S., Lucas, B., & Born, J. (2006). Sleep after learning aids memory recall. *Learning & Memory*, 13, 259–262.

Galbraith, G., & Arroyo, C. (1993). Selective attention and brainstem frequency-following responses. *Biological Psychology*, 37(1), 3–22.

Galbraith, G., Bhuta, S., Choate, A., Kitahara, J., & Mullen Jr., T. (1998). Brain stem frequency – following response to dichotic vowels during attention. *Neuroreport*, 9(8), 1889–1893.

Ganzeboom, H. (2010). A new international socio-economic index (ISEI) of occupational status for the International Standard Classification of Occupations 2008 (ISCO-08) constructed with data from the ISSP 2002–2007. Paper presented at the Annual Meeting of the International Social Survey Programme, Lisbon, Portugal.

Gao, E., & Suga, N. (1998). Experience-dependent corticofugal adjustment of midbrain frequency map in bat auditory system. *Proceedings of the National Academy of Sciences of the United States of America*, 95(21), 12663–12670.

(2000). Experience-dependent plasticity in the auditory cortex and the inferior colliculus of bats: role of the corticofugal system. *Proceedings of the National Academy of Sciences of the United States of America*, 97(14), 8081–8086.

Garbin, G., Costa, A., Sanjuan, A., et al. (2011). Neural bases of language switching in high and early proficient bilinguals. *Brain and Language*, 119(3), 129–135.

Garbin, G., Sanjuan, A., Forn, C., et al. (2010). Bridging language and attention: Brain basis of the impact of bilingualism on cognitive control. *Neuroimage*, 53(4), 1272–1278.

García, N., Chelminski, P., & Hernández, E. (2013). The effects of language on attitudes towards advertisements and brands trust in Mexico. *Journal of Current Issues & Research in Advertising*, 34, 77–92.

García-Orza, J., Perea, M., & Munoz, S. (2010). Are transposition effects specific to letters? *The Quarterly Journal of Experimental Psychology*, 63, 1603–1618.

Garcia-Sierra, A., Rivera-Gaxiola, M., Percaccio, C., Conboy, B., Romo, H., & Klarman, L. (2011). Bilingual language learning: An ERP study relating early brain responses to speech, language input, and later word production. *Journal of Phonetics*, 39(4), 546–557.

Gardner, D. (2007). Validating the construct of *word* in applied corpus-based vocabulary search: A critical survey. *Applied Linguistics*, 28(2), 241–265.

Gardner, H. (1987). *The mind's new science: A history of the cognitive revolution*. New York: Basic books.

Gardner, R. (1985). *Social psychology and second language learning: The role of attitudes and motivation*. London: Edward Arnold.

Gardner, R., & MacIntyre, P. (1993). On the measurement of affective variables in second language learning. *Language Learning*, 43, 157–194.

Gardner-Chloros, P. (2009). *Code-switching*. Cambridge, UK: Cambridge University Press.

Garnsey, S., Pearlmutter, N., Myers, E., & Lotocky, M. (1997). The contributions of verb bias and plausibility to the comprehension of temporarily ambiguous sentences. *Journal of Memory and Language*, 37(1), 58–93.

Gaskell, G., & Dumay, N. (2003). Lexical competition and the acquisition of novel words. *Cognition*, 89, 105–132.

Gass, S. (1987). The resolution of conflicts among competing systems: A bidirectional perspective. *Applied Psycholinguistics*, 8(4), 329–350.

Gass, S., & Selinker, L. (eds.). (1983). *Language transfer in language learning*. Rowley, MA: Newbury House.

Gathercole, S. (1999). Cognitive approaches to the development of short-term memory. *Trends in Cognitive Sciences*, 3, 410–419.

Gathercole, V., Thomas, E., Kennedy, I., Prys, C., Young, N., Viñas Guasch, N., et al. (2014). Does language dominance affect cognitive performance in bilinguals? Lifespan evidence from preschoolers through older adults on card sorting, Simon, and metalinguistic tasks. *Frontiers in Psychology*, 5(11).

Gauthier, K., Genesee, F., & Kasparian, K. (2012). Acquisition of complement clitics and tense morphology in internationally adopted children acquiring French. *Bilingualism: Language and Cognition*, 15(2), 304–319.

Gehrke, B. (2008). *Ps in motion: On the semantics and syntax of P elements and motion events*. Utrecht, the Netherlands: LOT Publications.

Genesee, F., Hamers, J., Lambert, W., Mononen, L., Seitz, M., & Starck, R. (1978). Language processing in bilinguals. *Brain and language*, 5(1), 1–12.

Gennari, S., & MacDonald, M. (2009). Linking production and comprehension processes: The case of relative clauses. *Cognition*, 111(1), 1–23.

Gentner, D., & Toupin, C. (1986). Systematicity and surface similarity in the development of analogy. *Cognitive science*, 10(3), 277–300.

Gerard, L., & Scarborough, D. (1989). Language-specific lexical access of homographs by bilinguals. *Journal of Experimental Psychology: Learning, Memory, and Cognition*, 15(2), 305–315.

Gernsbacher, M., & Faust, M. (1991). The mechanism of suppression: A component of general comprehension skill. *Journal of Experimental Psychology: Learning, Memory, and Cognition*, 17(2), 245–262.

(1995). Skilled suppression. In F. Dempster (ed.), *Interference and inhibition in cognition* (pp. 295–327). San Diego, CA: Academic Press.

Gernsbacher, M., & St. John, M. (2001). Modeling suppression in lexical access. In D. Gorfein (ed.), *On the consequences of meaning selection: Perspectives on resolving lexical ambiguity* (pp. 47–65). Washington, DC: American Psychological Association.

Gervain, J., Mehler, J., Werker, J., Nelson, C., Csibra, G., & Lloyd-Fox, S. (2011). Near-infrared spectroscopy: A report from the McDonnell infant methodology consortium. *Accident Analysis and Prevention*, 1(1), 22–46.

Gibson, E. (1998). Linguistic complexity: Locality of syntactic dependencies. *Cognition*, 69, 1–76.

Gibson, E., Pearlmutter, N., Canseco-Gonzalez, E., & Hickok, G. (1996). Recency preference in the human sentence processing mechanism. *Cognition*, 59(1), 23–59.

Gibson, E., & Warren, T. (2004). Reading time evidence for intermediate linguistic structure in long distance dependencies. *Syntax*, 7(1), 55–78.

Gibson, M., & Hufeisen, B. (2003). Investigating the role of prior foreign language knowledge. In J. Cenoz, B. Hufeisen, & U. Jessner (eds.), *The multilingual lexicon* (pp. 87–102). Dordrecht, the Netherlands: Springer Netherlands.

(2006). Metalinguistic processing control mechanisms in multilingual learners of English. *International Journal of Multilingualism*, 3, 139–153.

Gilabert, R., & Muñoz, C. (2010). Differences in attainment and performance in a foreign language: The role of working memory capacity. *International Journal of English Studies*, 10(1), 19–42.

Gillon-Dowens, M., Guo, T., Guo, J., Barber, H., & Carreiras, M. (2011). Gender and number processing in Chinese learners of Spanish: Evidence from Event Related Potentials. *Neuropsychologia*, 49(7), 1651–1659.

Gillon-Dowens, M., Vergara, M., Barber, H., & Carreiras, M. (2010). Morphosyntactic processing in late second-language learners. *Journal of Cognitive Neuroscience*, 22(8), 1870–1887.

Gilmore, J., Lin, W., Prastawa, M., Looney, C., Vetsa, Y., Knickmeyer, R., & Lieberman, J. (2007). Regional gray matter growth, sexual dimorphism, and cerebral asymmetry in the neonatal brain. *Journal of Neuroscience*, 27(6), 1255–1260.

Gitelman, D. R., Nobre, A. C., Sonty, S., Parrish, T. B., & Mesulam, M.-M. (2005). Language network specializations: An analysis with parallel task designs and functional magnetic resonance imaging. *NeuroImage*, 26, 975–985.

Glanzer, M., & Duarte, A. (1971). Repetition between and within languages in free recall. *Journal of Verbal Learning and Verbal Behavior*, 10, 625–630.

Glazewski, S., & Fox, K. (1996). Time course of experience-dependent synaptic potentiation and depression in barrel cortex of adolescent rats. *Journal of Neurophysiology*, 75(4), 1714–1729.

Glennen, S., & Masters, M. (2002). Typical and atypical language development in infants and toddlers adopted from eastern Europe. *American Journal of Speech Language Pathology*, 11, 417–433.

Gloning, I., & Gloning, K. (1983). Aphasia in polyglots' contribution to the dynamics of language disintegration as well as to the question of the localization of these impairments. In M. Paradis (ed.), *Readings on aphasia in bilinguals and polyglots* (pp. 681–716). Montreal: Marcel Didier.

Gogtay, N., Giedd, J., Lusk, L., et al. (2004). Dynamic mapping of human cortical development during childhood through early adulthood. *Proceedings of the National Academy of Sciences of the United States of America*, 101(21), 8174–8179.

Gold, B., Kim, C., Johnson, N., Kryscio, R., & Smith, C. (2013). Lifelong bilingualism maintains neural efficiency for cognitive control in aging. *Journal of Neuroscience*, 33(2), 387–396.

Goldberg, A. (1995). *Constructions: A construction grammar approach to argument structure*. Chicago, IL: University of Chicago Press.

Goldberg, A., Casenhiser, D., & Sethuraman, N. (2004). Learning argument structure generalizations. *Cognitive Linguistics*, 15, 289–316.

Goldinger, S. (1998). Echoes of echoes?: An episodic theory of lexical access. *Psychological Review*, 105, 251–279.

Goleman, D. (1995). *Emotional intelligence*. New York: Bantam Books.

Golestani, N., Molko, N., Dehaene, S., LeBihan, D., & Pallier, C. (2007). Brain structure predicts the learning of foreign speech sounds. *Cerebral Cortex*, 17(3), 575–582.

Golinkoff, R., Hirsh-Pasek, K., Cauley, K., & Gordon, L. (1987). The eyes have it: Lexical and syntactic comprehension in a new paradigm. *Journal of Child Language*, 14(1), 23–45.

Golinkoff, R., Ma, W., Song, L., & Hirsh-Pasek, K. (2013). Twenty-five years using the intermodal preferential looking paradigm to study language acquisition: What have we learned? *Perspectives on Psychological Science*, 8 (3), 316–339.

Gollan, T., & Brown, A. (2006). From tip-of-the-tongue (TOT) data to theoretical implications in two steps: When more TOTs means better retrieval. *Journal of Experimental Psychology: General*, 135, 462–483.

Gollan, T., & Ferreira, V. (2009). Should I stay or should I switch? A cost–benefit analysis of voluntary language switching in young and aging bilinguals. *Journal of Experimental Psychology: Learning, Memory, and Cognition*, 35, 640–665.

Gollan, T., Forster, K., & Frost, R. (1997). Translation priming with different scripts: Masked priming with cognates and noncognates in Hebrew-English bilinguals. *Journal of Experimental Psychology: Learning, Memory, and Cognition*, 23, 1122–1139.

Gollan, T., & Goldrick, M. (2012). Does bilingualism twist your tongue? *Cognition*, 125, 491–497.

Gollan, T., Montoya, R., & Bonanni, M. (2005). Proper names get stuck on bilingual and monolingual speakers' tip of the tongue equally often. *Neuropsychology*, 19(3), 278–287.

Gollan, T., Montoya, R., Cera, C., & Sandoval, T. (2008). More use almost always means a smaller frequency effect: Aging, bilingualism, and the weaker links hypothesis. *Journal of Memory and Language*, 58(3), 787–814.

Gollan, T., Montoya, R., & Werner, G. (2002). Semantic and letter fluency in Spanish–English bilinguals. *Neuropsychology*, 16(4), 562.

Gollan, T., Salmon, D., Montoya, R., & Galasko, D. (2011). Degree of bilingualism predicts age of diagnosis of Alzheimer's disease in low-education but not in highly educated Hispanics. *Neuropsychologia*, 49 (14), 3826–3830.

Gollan, T., Sandoval, T., & Salmon, D. (2011). Cross-language intrusion errors in aging. *Psychological Science*, 22(9), 1155–1164

Gollan, T., Schotter, E., Gomez, J., Murillo, M., & Rayner, K. (2014). Multiple levels of bilingual language control: Evidence from language intrusions in reading aloud. *Psychological Science*, 25(2) 585–595.

Gollub, D., & Healy, A. (1987). Word recall as a function of sentence generation and sentence context. *Bulletin of the Psychonomic Society*, 25, 359–360.

Goodman, G., Haith, M., Guttentag, R., & Rao, S. (1985). Automatic processing of word meaning: intralingual and interlingual interference. *Child Development*, 56, 103–118.

Goodz, N. (1989). Parental language mixing in bilingual families. *Infant Mental Health Journal*, 10(1), 1–21.

Gor, K. (2010). Beyond the obvious: Do second language learners process inflectional morphology? *Language Learning*, 60(1), 1–20.

Gor, K., & Cook, S. (2010). Non-native processing of verbal morphology: In search of regularity. *Language Learning*, 60(1), 88–126.

Gor, K., & Jackson, S. (2013). Morphological decomposition and lexical access in a native and second language: A nesting doll effect. *Language and Cognitive Processes*, 28(7), 1065–1091.

Gor, K., & Lukyanchenko, A. (2013). Inflectional paradigm in native and nonnative processing of nouns: What mediates decomposition? Poster presented at 8th Morphological Processing Conference, Cambridge University.

Gor, K., Cook, S., & Jackson, S. (2010). Lexical access in highly proficient late L2 learners: Evidence from semantic and phonological auditory priming. Paper presented at the Second Language Research Forum, University of Maryland.

Goral, M. (2004). First-language decline in healthy aging: Implications for attrition in bilingualism. *Journal of Neurolinguistics*, 17, 31–52.

Goral, M., Campanelli, L., & Spiro, A. (2015). Language dominance and inhibition abilities in bilingual older adults. *Bilingualism: Language and Cognition*, 18(1), 79–89.

Goral, M., Libben, G., Obler, L., Jarema, G., & Ohayon, K. (2008). Lexical attrition in younger and older bilingual adults. *Clinical Linguistics and Phonetics*, 22, 509–522.

Goral, M., Spiro, A., Albert, M., Obler, L., & Connor, L. (2007). Change in lexical-retrieval skills in adulthood. *Mental Lexicon*, 2(2), 215–238.

Gordon, P., Hendrick, R., & Johnson, M. (2004). Effects of noun phrase type on sentence complexity. *Journal of Memory and Language*, 51(1), 97–114.

Goren, C., Sarty, M., & Wu, P. (1975). Visual following and pattern discrimination of face-like stimuli by newborn infants. *Pediatrics*, 9, 415–421.

Gottlob, L., Goldinger, S., Stone, G., & Van Orden, G. (1999). Reading homographs: Orthographic, phonologic, and semantic dynamics. *Journal of Experimental Psychology: Human Perception and Performance*, 25(2), 561–574.

Goyvaerts, D., & Zembele, T. (1992). Codeswitching in Bukavu. *Journal of Multilingual and Multicultural Development*, 13, 71–82.

Grainger, J. (1987). L'accès au lexique bilingue: Vers une nouvelle orientation de recherche. *L'Année Psychologique*, 87, 553–566.

(1990). Word frequency and neighborhood frequency effects in lexical decision and naming. *Journal of Memory and Language*, 29, 228–244.

(1992). Orthographic neighborhoods and visual word recognition. In R. Frost & L. Katz (eds.), *Orthography, phonology, morphology, and meaning* (pp. 131–146). Elsevier: Amsterdam.

(1993). Visual word recognition in bilinguals. In R. Schreuder & B. Weltens (eds.), *The bilingual lexicon* (pp. 11–25). Amsterdam/Philadelphia, PA: John Benjamins.

(2008). Cracking the orthographic code. *Language and Cognitive Processes*, 23, 1–35.

Grainger, J., & Beauvillain, C. (1987). Language blocking and lexical access in bilinguals. *Quarterly Journal of Experimental Psychology: Human Experimental Psychology*, 39(2), 295–319.

(1988). Associative priming in bilinguals: Some limits of interlingual facilitation effects. *Canadian Journal of Psychology/Revue canadienne de psychologie*, 42, 261–273.

Grainger, J., & Dijkstra, T. (1992). On the representation and use of language information in bilinguals. In R. J. Harris (ed.), *Cognitive processing in bilinguals* (pp. 207–220). Amsterdam: Elsevier Science Publishers.

Grainger, J., & Frenck-Mestre, C. (1998). Masked Priming by Translation equivalents in proficient bilinguals. *Language and Cognitive Process*, 13, 601–623.

Grainger, J., Granier, J.-P., Farioli, F., van Assche, E., & van Heuven, W. J. B. (2006). Letter position information and printed word perception: The relative-position priming constraint. *Journal of Experimental Psychology: Human Perception and Performance*, 32, 865–884.

Grainger, J., & Holcomb, P. (2009). Watching the word go by: On the time-course of component processes in visual word recognition. *Language and Linguistic Compass*, 3, 128–156.

Grainger, J., & Jacobs, A. (1996). Orthographic processing in visual word recognition: A multiple read-out model. *Psychological Review*, 103, 518–565.

Grainger, J., Midgley, K., & Holcomb, P. (2010). Re-thinking the bilingual interactive-activation model from a developmental perspective (BIA-d). In M. Kail & M. Hickman (eds.), *Language Acquisition across linguistic and cognitive systems* (pp. 267–284). Amsterdam/Philadelphia, PA: John Benjamins Publishing.

Grainger, J., Rey, A., & Dufau, S. (2008). Letter perception: from pixels to pandemonium. *Trends in Cognitive Sciences*, 12, 381–387.

Grainger, J., & Segui, J. (1990). Neighborhood frequency effects in visual word recognition: A comparison of lexical decision and masked identification latencies. *Perception & Psychophysics*, 47(2), 191–198.

Grainger, J., & van Heuven, W. J. B. (2003). Modelling letter position coding in printed word perception. In P. Bonin (ed.), *Mental lexicon: "Some words to talk about words"* (pp. 1–23). New York: Nova Science Publishers.

Grainger, J., & Ziegler, J. (2011). A dual-route approach to orthographic processing. *Frontiers in Psychology*, 2, 1–13.

Green, D. W. (1986). Control, activation, and resource: A framework and a model for the control of speech in bilinguals. *Brain and Language*, 27, 210–223.

(1998). Mental control of the bilingual lexico-semantic system. *Bilingualism: Language and Cognition*, 1, 67–81.

(2003). The neural basis of the lexicon and the grammar in L2 acquisition. In R. van Hout (ed.), *The lexicon–syntax interface in second language acquisition* (pp. 197–218). Amsterdam/Philadelphia, PA: John Benjamins Publishing.

Green, D. W., & Abutalebi, J. (2008). Understanding the link between bilingual aphasia and language control. *Journal of Neurolinguistics*, 21 (6), 558–576.

(2013) Language control in bilinguals: The adaptive control hypothesis. *Journal of Cognitive Psychology*, 25, 515–530.

Green, D. W., Crinion, J., & Price, C. (2006). Convergence, degeneracy, and control. *Language Learning*, 56(s1), 99–125.

Greenough, W., Black, J., & Wallace, C. (1987). Experience and brain development. *Child Development*, 58(3), 539–559.

Gribble, C. (1987). *Reading Bulgarian through Russian*. Columbus, OH: Slavica.

Gries, S., & Stefanowitsch, A. (2004). Extending collostructional analysis: A corpus-based perspective on 'alternations.' *International Journal of Corpus Linguistics*, 9, 97–129.

Gries, S., & Wulff, S. (2005). Do foreign language learners also have constructions? Evidence from priming, sorting, and corpora. *Annual Review of Cognitive Linguistics*, 3, 182–200.

(2009). Psycholinguistic and corpus linguistic evidence for L2 constructions. *Annual Review of Cognitive Linguistics*, 7, 164–187.

Grogan, A., Jones, P., Ali, N., et al. (2012). Structural correlates for lexical efficiency and number of languages in non-native speakers of English. *Neuropsychologia*, 50(7), 1347–1352.

Grosjean, F. (1982) *Life with two languages: An introduction to bilingualism*. Cambridge, MA: Harvard University Press.

(1989). Neurologists, beware! The bilingual is not two monolinguals in one person. *Brain and Language*, 36, 3–15.

(1997). Processing mixed language: issues, findings, and models. In A. de Groot & J. Kroll (eds.), *Tutorials in bilingualism* (pp. 225–254). Mahwah, NJ: Lawrence Erlbaum.

(1998). Studying bilinguals: Methodological and conceptual issues. *Bilingualism: Language and Cognition*, 1, 131–149.

(2008). *Studying bilinguals*. Oxford, UK: Oxford University Press.

(2010). *Bilingual: Life and reality*. Cambridge, MA: Harvard University Press.

Grosjean, F., Kroll, J. F., Meisel, J., & Muysken, P. (founding eds.) (1998). *Bilingualism: Language and Cognition Journal*. Cambridge, UK: Cambridge University Press.

Grosjean, F., & Li, P. (2013). *The psycholinguistics of bilingualism*. New York: John Wiley & Sons.

Grossi, G., Savill, N., Thomas, E., & Thierry, G. (2010). Posterior N1 asymmetry to English and Welsh words in early and late English–Welsh bilinguals. *Biological Psychology*, 85, 124–133.

(2012). Electrophysiological cross-language neighborhood density effects in late and early English-Welsh bilinguals. *Frontiers in Psychology*, 3, 408.

Grüter, T., Lew-Williams, C., & Fernald, A. (2012). Grammatical gender in L2: A production or a real-time processing problem? *Second Language Research*, 28(2), 191–215.

Guillelmon, D., & Grosjean, F. (2001). The gender marking effect in spoken word recognition: The case of bilinguals. *Memory & Cognition*, 29(3), 503–511.

Gullberg, M. (2011). Thinking, speaking, and gesturing about motion in more than one language. In A. Pavlenko (ed.), *Thinking and speaking in two languages* (pp. 143–169). Bristol, UK: Multilingual Matters.

Gullberg, M., Indefrey, P., & Muysken, P. (2009). Research techniques for the study of code-switching. In B. Bullock, & A. Toribio (eds.), *The Cambridge handbook of linguistic code-switching* (pp. 21–39). Cambridge, UK: Cambridge University Press.

Gullifer, J. W., Kroll, J. F., & Dussias, P. (2013). When language switching has no apparent cost: Lexical access in sentence context. *Frontiers in Psychology*, 4, 278.

Gumperz, J. (1982). Conversational code switching. In J. Gumperz, *Discourse strategies* (pp. 55–99). Cambridge, UK: Cambridge University Press.

Guo, J., Guo, T., Yan, Y., Jiang, N., & Peng, D. (2009). ERP evidence for different strategies employed by native speakers and L2 learners in sentence processing. *Journal of Neurolinguistics*, 22(2), 123–134.

Guo, T., Liu, H., Misra, M., & Kroll, J. F. (2011). Local and global inhibition in bilingual word production: fMRI evidence from Chinese–English bilinguals. *NeuroImage*, 56, 2300–2309.

Guo, T., Ma, F., & Liu, F. (2013). An ERP study of inhibition of non-target languages in trilingual word production. *Brain and Language*, 127(1), 12–20.

Gürel, A. (2004). Selectivity in L2-induced L1 attrition: A psycholinguistic account. *Journal of Neurolinguistics*, 17(1), 53–78.

Guttentag, R., Haith, M., Goodman, G., & Hauch, J. (1984). Semantic processing of unattended words by bilinguals: A test of the input switch mechanism. *Journal of Verbal Learning and Verbal Behavior*, 23, 178–188.

Guzzardo Tamargo, R. (2012). Linking comprehension costs to production patterns during the processing of mixed language. (Unpublished doctoral dissertation), Pennsylvania State University, University Park.

Guzzardo Tamargo, R., & Dussias, P. (2013). Processing of Spanish–English code-switches by late bilinguals. *BUCLD 37 Proceedings*. Somerville, MA: Cascadilla Press.

Hahne, A. (2001). What's different in second-language processing? Evidence from event-related brain potentials. *Journal of Psycholinguistic Research*, 30(3), 251–266.

Hahne, A., & Friederici, A. (2001). Processing a second language: Late learners' comprehension mechanisms as revealed by event-related brain potentials. *Bilingualism: Language and Cognition*, 4(2), 123–141.

Hairston, W., Letowski, T., & McDowell, K. (2013). Task-Related Suppression of the brainstem frequency following response. *PLoS ONE*, 8(2), e55215.

Hakuta, K., Bialystok, E., & Wiley, E. (2003). Critical evidence: A test of the critical-period hypothesis for second-language acquisition. *Psychological Science*, 14(1), 31–38.

Hakuta, K., Ferdman, B., & Diaz, R. (1987). Bilingualism and cognitive development: Three perspectives. *Advances in Applied Psycholinguistics*, 2, 284–319.

Halberda, J. (2003). The development of a word-learning strategy. *Cognition*, 87(1), B23–B34.

Hall, C., Derby, C., LeValley, A., Katz, M., Verghese, J., & Lipton, R. (2007). Education delays accelerated decline on a memory test in persons who develop dementia. *Neurology*, 69, 1657–1664.

Hall, C., Lipton, R., Sliwinski, M., Katz, M., Derby, C., & Verghese, J. (2009). Cognitive activities delay onset of memory decline in persons who develop dementia. *Neurology*, 73, 356–361.

Hamann, S., & Canli, T. (2004). Individual differences in emotion processing. *Current Opinion in Neurobiology*, 14, 233–238.

Hamers, J., & Lambert, W. (1972). Bilingual interdependencies in auditory perception. *Journal of Verbal Learning and Verbal Behavior*, 11, 303–310.

Hammarberg, B., & Hammarberg, B. (1993). Articulatory re-setting in the acquisition of new languages. *PHONUM*, 2, 61–67.

  (2005). Re-setting the basis of articulation in the acquisition of new languages: A third-language case study. In B. Hammarberg (ed.), *Introductory readings in L3* (pp. 74–85). Edinburgh: University of Edinburgh Press.

Han, Z.-H., & Peverly, S. (2007). Input processing: A study of ab initio learners with multilingual backgrounds. *International Journal of Multilingualism*, 4, 17–37.

Hansen, L., Umeda, Y., & McKinney, M. (2002). Savings in the relearning of second language vocabulary: The effects of time and proficiency. *Language Learning*, 52(4), 653–678.

Hansen, M., & Markman, E. (2009). Children's use of mutual exclusivity to learn labels for parts of objects. *Developmental Psychology*, 45(2), 592–596.

Hanulová, J., Davidson, D., & Indefrey, P. (2011). Where does the delay in L2 picture naming come from? Psycholinguistic and neurocognitive evidence on second language word production. *Language and Cognitive Processes*, 26, 902–934.

Harm, M. W., & Seidenberg, M. S. (1999). Phonology, reading acquisition, and dyslexia: Insights from connectionist models. *Psychological Review*, 106, 491–528.

Harrington, M. (1987). Processing transfer: Language-specific processing strategies as a source of interlanguage variation. *Applied Psycholinguistics*, 8(4), 351–377.

Harris, C. (2004). Bilingual speakers in the lab: Psychophysiological measures of emotional reactivity. *Journal of Multilingual and Multicultural Development*, 25, 223–247.

Harris, C., Ayçiçeği, A., & Gleason, J. (2003). Taboo words and reprimands elicit greater autonomic reactivity in a first than in a second language. *Applied Psycholinguistics*, 4, 561–578.

Harris, C., Gleason, J., & Ayçiçeği, A. (2005). When is a first language more emotional? Psychophysiological evidence from bilingual speakers. In A. Pavlenko (ed.), *Bilingual minds: Emotional experience, expression, and representation* (pp. 257–283). Clevedon, UK: Multilingual Matters.

Harris, R. (ed.). (1992). *Cognitive processing in bilinguals*. Amsterdam: North Holland.

Hartsuiker, R., & Pickering, M. J. (2008). Language integration in bilingual sentence production. *Acta Psychologica*, 128, 479–489.

Hartsuiker, R., Pickering, M., & Veltkamp, E. (2004). Is syntax separate or shared between languages? Cross-linguistic syntactic priming in Spanish–English bilinguals. *Psychological Science*, 15, 409–414.

Hasan, K., & Narayana, P. (2003). Computation of the fractional anisotropy and mean diffusivity maps without tensor decoding and diagonalization: Theoretical analysis and validation. *Magnetic Resonance in Medicine*, 50, 589–598.

Hasegawa, M., Carpenter, P. A., & Just, M. A. (2002). An fMRI study of bilingual sentence comprehension and workload. *NeuroImage*, 15, 647–660.

Hasselgren, A. (1994). Lexical teddy bears and advanced learners: A study into the ways Norwegian students cope with English vocabulary. *International Journal of Applied Linguistics*, 4, 237–260.

Hatzidaki, A., Branigan, H., & Pickering, J. (2011). Co-activation of syntax in bilingual language production. *Cognitive Psychology*, 62, 123–150.

Hauk, O., & Pulvermüller, F. (2004). Effects of word length and frequency on the human event-related potential. *Clinical Neurophysiology*, 115, 1090–1103.

Hauk, O., Pulvermüller, F., Ford, M., Marslen-Wilson, W. D., & Davis, M. H. (2009). Can I have a quick word? Early electrophysiological manifestations of psycholinguistic processes revealed by event-related regression analysis of the EEG. *Biological Psychology*, 80, 64–74.

Hayes-Harb, R., Nicol, J., & Barker, J. (2010). Learning the phonological forms of new words: Effects of orthographic and auditory input. *Language and Speech*, 53(3), 367–381.

Haykin, S. (1999). *Neural networks: A comprehensive foundation* (2nd edn). Upper Saddle River, NJ: Prentice Hall.

Hebb, D. (1949). *The organization of behavior: A neuropsychological theory*. New York: Wiley.

Heilenman, L., & McDonald, J. (1993). Processing strategies in L2 learners of French: The role of transfer. *Language Learning*, 43(4), 507–557.

Henderson, B. (2006). Multiple agreement and inversion in Bantu. *Syntax*, 9, 275–289.

Henry, N., Culman, H., & VanPatten, B. (2009). More on the effects of explicit information in processing instruction: A partial replication and response to Fernández (2008). *Studies in Second Language Acquisition*, 31, 359–375.

Herdina, P., & Jessner, U. (2002). *A dynamic model of multilingualism: Perspectives of change in psycholinguistics*. Clevedon, UK: Multilingual Matters.

Heredia, R., & Altarriba, J. (2001). Bilingual language mixing: Why do bilinguals code-switch? *Current Directions in Psychological Science*, 10, 164–168.

Hermans, D., Bongaerts, T., de Bot, K., & Schreuder, R. (1998). Producing words in a foreign language: Can speakers prevent interference from their first language? *Bilingualism: Language and Cognition*, 1, 213–229.

Hermans, D., Ormel, E., Van Besselaar, R., & van Hell, J. (2011). Lexical activation in bilinguals' speech production is dynamic: How language ambiguous words can affect cross-language activation. *Language and Cognitive Processes*, 26, 1687–1709.

Hernandez, A. (2013). *The bilingual brain*. Oxford, UK: Oxford University Press.

Hernandez, A., Bates, E., & Avila, L. (1994). On-line sentence interpretation in Spanish–English bilinguals: What does it mean to be "in between?" *Applied Psycholinguistics*, 15(4), 417–446.

(1996). Processing across the language boundary: A cross modal priming study of Spanish–English bilinguals. *Journal of Experimental Psychology: Learning, Memory, & Cognition*, 22, 846–864.

Hernandez, A., Dapretto, M., Mazziotta, J., & Bookheimer, S. (2001). Language switching and language representation in Spanish–English bilinguals: An fMRI study. *Neuroimage*, 14(2), 510–520.

Hernandez, A., & Kohnert, K. (1999). Aging and language switching in bilinguals. *Aging, Neuropsychology and Cognition*, 6, 69–83.

(2000). In search of the language switch: An fMRI Study of picture naming in Spanish–English bilinguals. *Brain and Language*, 73, 421–431.

Hernandez, A., Li, P., & MacWhinney, B. (2005). The emergence of competing modules in bilingualism. *Trends in Cognitive Sciences*, 9(5), 220–225.

Hernandez, M., Costa, A., & Humphreys, G. (2012). Escaping capture: Bilingualism modulates distraction from working memory. *Cognition*, 122, 37–50.

Hernandez, A., Martinez, A., & Kohnert, K. (2000). In search of the language switch: An fMRI study of picture naming in Spanish–English bilinguals. *Brain and Language*, 73, 421–431.

Hernandez, A., & Meschyan, G. (2006). Executive function is necessary to enhance lexical processing in a less proficient L2: Evidence from fMRI during picture naming. *Bilingualism: Language and Cognition*, 9, 177–188.

Hernandez, M., Martin, C., Barcelo, F., & Costa, A. (2013). Where is the bilingual advantage in task-switching? *Journal of Memory and Language*, 69(3) 257–276.

Hernandez, M., Martin, C., Sebastián-Gallés, N., & Costa, A. (2013). Bilingualism beyond language: On the impact of bilingualism on executive control. In B. Cedric & K. Kleanthes (eds.), *The Cambridge handbook of neurolinguistics* (pp. 160–178). Cambridge, UK: Cambridge University Press.

Herschmann, H., & Potzl, O. (1983). Observations on aphasia in polyglots. In M. Paradis (ed.), *Readings on aphasia in bilinguals and polyglots* (pp. 148–154). Montreal: Marcel Didier.

Hervais-Adelman, A., Moser-Mercer, B., & Golestani, N. (2011). Executive control of language in the bilingual brain: Integrating the evidence from neuroimaging to neuropsychology. *Frontiers in Psychology*, 2, 234.

Hickok, G., & Poeppel, D. (2000). Towards a functional neuroanatomy of speech perception. *Trends in cognitive sciences*, 4(4), 131–138.

Higby, E., Kim, J., & Obler, L. (2013). Multilingualism and the brain. *Annual Review of Applied Linguistics*, 33, 68–101.

Hilchey, M., Ivanoff, J., Taylor, T., & Klein, R. (2011). Visualizing the temporal dynamics of spatial information processing for the Simon effect and its amplification by inhibition of return. *Acta Psychologica*, 136, 235–244.

Hilchey, M., & Klein, R. (2011). Are there bilingual advantages on nonlinguistic interference tasks? Implications for the plasticity of executive control processes. *Psychonomics Bulletin & Review*, 18, 625–658.

Hinton, G., & Sejnowski, T. (1999). *Unsupervised learning: Foundations of neural computation*. Cambridge, MA: MIT Press.

Hlavac, J. (2011). Hesitation and monitoring phenomena in bilingual speech: A consequence of code-switching or a strategy to facilitate its incorporation? *Journal of Pragmatics*, 43, 3793–3806.

Hoff, E. (ed.). (2012). *Research methods in child language: A practical guide*. Malden, MA: Wiley-Blackwell.

Hoff, E., & Luz Rumiche, R. (2012). Studying children in bilingual environments. In E. Hoff (ed.), *Research methods in child language: A practical guide* (pp. 300–316). Oxford, UK: Wiley-Blackwell.

Holcomb, P. J., & Grainger, J. (2006). On the time course of visual word recognition: An event-related potential investigation using masked repetition priming. *Journal of Cognitive Neuroscience*, 18, 1631–1643.

Holcomb, P. J., Grainger, J., & O'Rourke, T. (2002). An electrophysiological study of the effects of orthographic neighborhood size on printed word perception. *Journal of Cognitive Neuroscience*, 15, 938–950.

Holden, J. (2002). Fractal characteristics of response time variability. *Ecological Psychology*, 14(1–2), 53–86.

Holton, J. (1954). Portuguese for Spanish Speakers. *Hispania*, 37, 446–452.

Holtzheimer, P., Fawaz, W., Wilson, C., & Avery, D. (2005). Repetitive transcranial magnetic stimulation may induce language switching in bilingual patients. *Brain and Language*, 94(3), 274–277.

Hong, E.-L., & Yelland, G. W. (1997). The generality of lexical neighbourhood effects. In H.-C. Chen (ed.), *Cognitive processing of Chinese and related Asian languages* (pp. 187–203). Hong Kong: Chinese University Press.

Hoover, M., & Dwivedi, V. (1998). Syntactic processing by skilled bilinguals. *Language Learning*, 48(1), 1–29.

Hopp, H. (2006). Syntactic features and reanalysis in near-native processing. *Second Language Research*, 22(3), 369–397.

(2010). Ultimate attainment in L2 inflection: Performance similarities between non-native and native speakers. *Lingua*, 120, 901–931.

(2012). The on-line integration of inflection in L2 processing: Predictive processing of German gender. In A. Biller, E. Chung, & A. Kimball (eds.), *Proceedings of the 36th Annual Boston University Conference on Language Development* (pp. 226–241). Somerville, MA: Cascadilla Press.

(2013). Grammatical gender in adult L2 acquisition: Relations between lexical and syntactic variability. *Second Language Research*, 29(1), 33–56.

Hopper, P. (1998). Emergent grammar. In M. Tomasello (ed.), *The new psychology of language: Cognitive and functional approaches to language structure* (pp. 155–176). Mahwah: Erlbaum.

Hornickel, J., & Kraus, N. Unstable representation of sound: A biological marker of dyslexia. *Journal of Neuroscience*, 33(8), 3500–3504.

Horton, W., & Keysar, B. (1996). When do speakers take into account common ground? *Cognition*, 59, 91–117.

Horwitz, E. (2000). It ain't over 'til it's over: On foreign language anxiety, first language deficits, and the confounding of variables. *Modern Language Journal*, 84, 256–259.

Horwitz, E., Horwitz, M., & Cope, J. (1986). Foreign language classroom anxiety. *Modern Language Journal*, 70, 25–132.

Hoshino, N., & Kroll, J. F. (2008) Cognate effects in picture naming: Does cross-linguistic activation survive a change of script? *Cognition*, 106, 501–511.

Hoshino, N., & Thierry, G. (2011). Language selection in bilingual word production: Electrophysiological evidence for cross-language competition, *Brain Research*, 1371, 100–109.

Houston-Price, C., Caloghiris, Z., & Raviglione, E. (2010). Language experience shapes the development of the mutual exclusivity bias. *Infancy*, 15(2), 125–150.

Hsieh, S., & Allport, A. (1994). Shifting attention in a rapid visual search paradigm. *Perceptual & Motor Skills*, 79(1, pt 1), 315–335.

Huang, H.-W., Lee, C.-Y., Tsai, J.-L., Lee, C.-L., Hung, D., & Tzeng, O. G.-L. (2006). Orthographic neighborhood effects in reading Chinese two-character words. *NeuroReport*, 17, 1061–1065.

Hubbell-Weinhold, J. (2005). L1 attrition and recovery: A case study. In J. Cohen, K. T. McAlister, K. Rolstad, & J. MacSwan (eds.), *Proceedings of the 4th International Symposium on Bilingualism* (pp. 1045–1052). Somerville, MA: Cascadilla Press.

Hudon, T., Fennell, C., & Hoftyzer, M. (2013). Quality not quantity of television viewing is associated with bilingual toddlers' vocabulary scores. *Infant Behavior and Development*, 36(2), 245–254.

Hufeisen, B. (1995). Multilingual language acquisition in Canada and Germany. *Language, Culture and Curriculum*, 8, 175–181.

Hufeisen, B., & Neuner, G. (2004). *The plurilingualism project: Tertiary language learning – German after English*. Strasbourg, France: Council of Europe.

Huffman, R., & Henson, O. (1990). The descending auditory pathway and acousticomotor systems: connections with the inferior colliculus. *Brain Research Reviews*, 15(3), 295–323.

Hulsen, M., de Bot, K., & Weltens, B. (2002). Between two worlds. Social networks, language shift, and language processing in three generations of Dutch migrants in New Zealand. *International Journal of the Sociology of Language*, 153, 27–52.

Humphrey, A., & Valian, V. (2012). Multilingualism and cognitive control: Simon and flanker task performance in monolingual and multilingual young adults. Paper presented at the *53rd Annual meeting of the Psychonomic Society*, Minneapolis, MN.

Hunt, R., & Ellis, H. (1994). *Fundamentals of cognitive psychology*. Boston, MA: McGraw Hill.

Hunter, M., & Ames, E. (1988). A multifactor model of infant preferences for novel and familiar stimuli. *Advances in Infancy Research*, 5, 69–95.

Hurtado, N., Gruter, T., Marchman, V., & Fernald, A. (2014). Relative language exposure, processing efficiency and vocabulary in Spanish–English bilingual toddlers. *Bilingualism: Language and Cognition*, 17(1), 189–202.

Hussey, E., & Novick, J. (2012). The benefits of executive control training and the implications for language processing. *Frontiers in Psychology*, 3, 158.

Huttenlocher, P. (1990). Morphometric study of human cerebral cortex development. *Neuropsychologia*, 28(6), 517–527.

(1994). Synaptogenesis in the human cerebral cortex. In G. Dawson & K. Fischer (eds.), *Human behavior and the developing brain* (pp. 137–152). New York: Guilford Press.

(2009). *Neural plasticity: The effects of environment on the development of the cerebral cortex*. Cambridge, MA: Harvard University Press.

Huttenlocher, P., & de Courten, C. (1987). The development of synapses in striate cortex of man. *Human Neurobiology*, 6(1), 1–9.

Huttenlocher, P., de Courten, C., Garey, L., & Van der Loos, H. (1982a). Synaptic development in human cerebral cortex. *International Journal of Neurology*, 16–17, 144–154.

(1982b). Synaptogenesis in human visual cortex: Evidence for synapse elimination during normal development. *Neuroscience Letters*, 33(3), 247–252.

Hyltenstam, K., Bylund, E., Abrahamsson, N., & Park, H.-S. (2009). Dominant language replacement: The case of international adoptees. *Bilingualism: Language and Cognition*, 12(2), 121–140.

Ibáñez, A., Macizo, P., & Bajo, M. (2010). Language access and language selection in professional translators. *Acta Psychologica*, 135, 257–266.

Ihlen, E., & Vereijken, B. (2010). Interaction-dominant dynamics in human cognition: Beyond 1/f(alpha) fluctuation. *Journal of Experimental Psychology: General*, 139(3), 436–463.

Imai, M., & Gentner, D. (1997). A crosslinguistic study of early word meaning: Universal ontology and linguistic influence. *Cognition*, 62, 169–200.

Imai, M., & Mazuka, R. (2003). Re-evaluating linguistic relativity: Language-specific categories and the role of universal ontological knowledge in the construal of individuation. In D. Gentner & S. Goldin-Meadow (eds.), *Language in mind: Advances in the study of language and thought* (pp. 429–464). Cambridge, MA: MIT Press.

Indefrey, P. (2006). A meta-analysis of hemodynamic studies on first and second language processing: Which suggested differences can we trust and what do they mean? *Language Learning*, 56, 279–304.

Ioup, G. (2001). Exploring age and loss using the savings paradigm. Paper presented at the American Association for Applied Linguistics, Missouri, USA.

Ip, E., Giza, C., Griesbach, G., & Hovda, D. (2002). Effects of enriched environment and fluid percussion injury on dendritic arborization within the cerebral cortex of the developing rat. *Journal of Neurotrauma*, 19(5), 573–585.

Isurin, L. (2000). Deserted island or a child's first language forgetting. *Bilingualism: Language and Cognition*, 3(2), 151–166.

(2005). Cross linguistic transfer in word order: Evidence from L1 forgetting and L2 acquisition. In J. Cohen, K. McAlister, K. Rolstad, & J. MacSwan (eds.), *Proceedings of the 4th International Symposium on Bilingualism* (pp. 1115–1130). Somerville, MA: Cascadilla Press.

Isurin, L., Winford, D., & de Bot, K. (eds.) (2009). *Multidisciplinary approaches to code switching*. Amsterdam/Philadelphia, PA: John Benjamins Publishing.

Itier, R. J., Latinus, M., & Taylor, M. J. (2006). Face, eye and object early processing: What is the face specificity? *NeuroImage*, 29, 667–676.

Ivanova, I., & Costa, A. (2008). Does bilingualism hamper lexical access in speech production? *Acta Psychologica*, 127(2), 277–288.

Jackson, C. (2008). Proficiency level and the interaction of lexical and morphosyntactic information during L2 sentence processing. *Language Learning*, 58(4), 875–909.

Jackson, C., & Dussias, P. (2009). Cross-linguistic differences and their impact on L2 sentence processing. *Bilingualism: Language and Cognition*, 12(1), 65–82.

Jackson, C., Dussias, P., & Hristova, A. (2012). Using eye-tracking to study the on-line processing of case-marking information among intermediate L2 learners of German. *IRAL: International Review of Applied Linguistics in Language Teaching*, 50(2), 101–133.

Jackson, G., Swainson, R., Cunnington, R., & Jackson, S. (2001). ERP correlates of executive control during repeated language switching. *Bilingualism: Language and Cognition*, 4(2), 169–178.

Jackson, G., Swainson, R., Mullin, A., Cunnington, R, & Jackson, S. (2004). ERP correlates of a receptive language-switching task. *Quarterly Journal of Experimental Psychology*, 57A, 223–240.

Jackson, S., Berens, M., Benson, S., et al. (2012). *Unit language development: 2012 annual report (TTO82106)*. College Park, MD: University of Maryland Center for Advanced Study of Language.

Jacoby, L. (1991). A process dissociation framework: Separating automatic from intentional uses of memory. *Journal of Memory and Language*, 30(5), 513–541.

Jacquet, M., & French, R. (2002). The BIA++: Extending the BIA+ to a dynamical distributed connectionist framework. *Bilingualism: Language and Cognition*, 5(3), 202–205.

Jake, J. (2001). Chaupi Lengua: Imbabura Quichua-Spanish convergence in written folktales. Paper presented at the International Workshop in the Study of Stable Mixed languages, University of Manchester, UK.

Jake, J., & Myers-Scotton, C. (2009). Which language? Participation potentials across lexical categories in codeswitching. In L. Isurin, D. Winford, & K. de Bot (eds.), *Multidisciplinary approaches to code switching* (pp. 307–342). Amsterdam/Philadelphia, PA: John Benjamins Publishing.

Jake, J., Myers-Scotton, C., & Gross, S. (2002). Making a minimalist approach to codeswitching work: Adding the Matrix Language. *Bilingualism: Language and Cognition*, 5(1), 69–91.

Jakobovits, L., & Lambert, W. (1961). Semantic satiation among bilinguals. *Journal of Experimental Psychology*, 62, 576–582.

James, C. (1980). *Contrastive analysis*. London: Longman.

Jäncke, L., Mirzazade, S., & Joni Shah, N. (1999). Attention modulates activity in the primary and the secondary auditory cortex: a functional magnetic resonance imaging study in human subjects. *Neuroscience Letters*, 266(2), 125–128.

Jared, D. (2002). Spelling-sound consistency and regularity effects in word naming. *Journal of Memory and Language*, 46(4), 723–750.

Jared, D., & Kroll, J. F. (2001). Do bilinguals activate phonological representations in one or both of their languages when naming words? *Journal of Memory and Language*, 44(1), 2–31.

Jared, D., Pei Yun Poh, R., & Paivio, A. (2013). L1 and L2 picture naming in Mandarin-English bilinguals: A test of Bilingual Dual Coding Theory. *Bilingualism: Language and Cognition*, 16, 383–396.

Jared, D., & Szucs, C. (2002). Phonological activation in bilinguals: Evidence from interlingual homograph naming. *Bilingualism: Language and Cognition*, 5(3), 225–239.

Jarmulowicz, L., & Taran, V. (2013). Lexical morphology: Structure, process, and development. *Topics in Language Disorders*, 33(1), 57–72.

Jarvis, S. (1998). *Conceptual transfer in the interlingual lexicon*. Bloomington, IN: Indiana University Linguistics Club Publications.

  (2000). Methodological rigor in the study of transfer: Identifying L1 influence in the interlanguage lexicon. *Language Learning*, 50, 245–309.

Jarvis, S., & Pavlenko, A. (2008). *Crosslinguistic influence in language and cognition*. New York: Routledge.

Jennings, J., & Jacoby, L. (1993). Automatic versus intentional uses of memory: Aging, attention, and control. *Psychology and Aging*, 8(2), 283–293.

Jensen, J. (1989). On the mutual intelligibility of Spanish and Portuguese. *Hispania*, 72, 848–852.

Jersild, A. (1927). Mental set and shift. *Archives of Psychology*, 14(89), 81.

Jessner, U. (1999). Metalinguistic awareness in multilinguals: Cognitive aspects of third language learning. *Language Awareness*, 8, 201–209.

  (2003). The nature of cross-linguistic interaction in the multilingual system. In J. Cenoz, B. Hufeisen, & U. Jessner (eds.), *The multilingual lexicon* (pp. 45–56). New York: Springer.

Jessner, U., & Cenoz, J. (2007). Teaching English as a third language. In J. Cummins & C. Davison (eds.), *International handbook of English language teaching* (pp. 155–167). New York: Springer.

Jia, G., & Aaronson, D. (1999). Age differences in second language acquisition: The dominant language switch and maintenance hypothesis. In A. Greenhill, H. Littlefield, & C. Tano (eds.), *Proceedings of the 23rd Annual Boston University Conference on Language Development* (pp. 301–312). Somerville, MA: Cascadilla Press.

Jiang, N. (1999). Testing processing explanations for the asymmetry in masked cross-language priming. *Bilingualism: Language and Cognition*, 2, 59–75.

  (2004). Morphological insensitivity in second language processing. *Applied Psycholinguistics*, 25(4), 603–634.

(2007). Selective integration of linguistic knowledge in adult second language learning. *Language Learning*, 57(1), 1–33.

Jiang, N., & Forster, K. I. (2001). Cross-Language priming asymmetries in lexical decision and episodic recognition. *Journal of Memory and Language*, 44, 32–51.

Jimura, K., & Braver, T. (2011). Age-related shifts in brain activity dynamics during task switching. *Cerebral Cortex*, 20(6), 1420–1431.

Jin, Y.-S. (1990). Effects of concreteness on cross-language priming in lexical decisions. *Perceptual and Motor Skills*, 70, 1139–1154.

Johnson Jr., G. (1953). Bilingualism as measured by a reaction-time technique and the relationship between a language and a non-language intelligence quotient. *Pedagogical Seminary and Journal of Genetic Psychology*, 82, 3–9.

Johnson, J., & Newport, E. (1989). Critical period effects in second language learning: The influence of maturational state on the acquisition of English as a second language. *Cognitive Psychology*, 21(1), 60–99.

Jolles, D., & Crone, E. (2012). Training the developing brain: A neurocognitive perspective. *Frontiers in Human Neuroscience*, 6(76), 1–13.

Jones, M., & Mewhort, D. (2007). Representing word meaning and order information in a composite holographic lexicon. *Psychological Review*, 114, 1–37.

Jones, W., & Stewart, W. (1951). Bilingualism and verbal intelligence. *British Journal of Psychology*, 4, 3–8.

Jordan, I. (1991). Portuguese for Spanish speakers: A case for contrastive analysis. *Hispania*, 74, 788–792.

Jouravlev, O. & Jared, D. (2014). Reading Russian–English homographs in sentence contexts: Evidence from ERPs. *Bilingualism: Language and Cognition*, 17(1), 153–168.

Ju, M., & Luce, P. (2004). Falling on sensitive ears: Constraints on bilingual lexical activation. *Psychological Science*, 15(5), 314–318.

Juffs, A. (2005). The influence of first language on the processing of wh-movement in English as a second language. *Second Language Research*, 21(2), 121–151.

(2009). Second language acquisition of the lexicon. In W. Ritchie & T. Bhatia (eds.), *The new handbook of second language acquisition* (pp. 181–209). Bingley, UK: Emerald Group Publishers.

Juffs, A., & Harrington, M. (1995). Parsing effects in second language sentence processing. *Studies in Second Language Acquisition*, 17(4), 483–516.

(1996). Garden path sentences and error data in second language sentence processing. *Language Learning*, 46(2), 283–323.

(2011). Aspects of working memory in L2 learning. *Language Teaching: Reviews and Studies*, 42, 137–166.

Junker, D., & Stockman, I. (2002). Expressive vocabulary of German-English bilingual toddlers. *American Journal of Speech-Language Pathology*, 11(4), 381–394.

Jurafsky, D. (1996). A probabilistic model of lexical and syntactic access and disambiguation. *Cognitive Science*, 20(2), 137–194.

Jurafsky, D., Bell, A., Gregory, M., & Raymond, W. (2001). Probabilistic relations between words: Evidence from reduction in lexical production. In J. Bybee & P. Hopper (eds.), *Frequency and the emergence of linguistic structure* (pp. 229–254). Amsterdam/Philadelphia, PA: John Benjamins Publishing.

Juraska, J., & Kopcik, J. (1988). Sex and environmental influences on the size and ultrastructure of the rat corpus callosum. *Brain Research*, 450(1), 1–8.

Jürgens, U. (1983). Afferent fibers to the cingular vocalization region in the squirrel monkey. *Experimental Neurology*, 80(2), 395–409.

Jusczyk, P. (1985). The high-amplitude sucking technique as a methodological tool in speech perception research. In G. Gottlieb & N. Krasnegor (eds.), *Measurement of audition and vision in the first year of postnatal life: A methodological overview* (pp. 195–222). Westport, CT: Ablex Publishing.

Just, M., Carpenter, P., & Woolley, J. (1982). Paradigms and processes in reading comprehension. *Journal of Experimental Psychology: General*, 111, 228–38.

Kaan, E. (2014). Predictive sentence processing in L2 and L1: What is different? *Linguistic Approaches to Bilingualism* 4(2), 257–282.

Kaan, E., Dallas, A. C., & Wijnen, F. (2010). Syntactic predictions in second-language sentence processing. In J.-W. Zwart & M. de Vries (eds.), *Structure preserved: Studies in syntax for Jan Koster* (pp. 208–213). Amsterdam/Philadelphia, PA: John Benjamins Publishing.

Kaan, E., Harris, A., Gibson, E., & Holcomb, P. (2000). The P600 as an index of syntactic integration difficulty. *Language and Cognitive Processes*, 15, 159–201.

Kamwangamalu, N. (1994). English codeswitching: The matrix language principle and linguistic constraints. *South African Journal of Linguistics*, 17, 256–274.

Kang, S., Gollan, T., & Pashler, H. (2013). Don't just repeat after me: Retrieval practice is better than imitation in foreign vocabulary learning. *Psychonomic Bulletin & Review*, 20(6):1259–65.

Kantola, L., & van Gompel, R. (2011). Between-and within-language priming is the same: Evidence for shared bilingual syntactic representations. *Memory & Cognition*, 39, 276–290.

Kapa, L., & Colombo, J. (2013). Attentional control in early and later bilingual children. *Cognitive Development*, 28, 233–246.

Karpicke, J., & Roediger, H. III (2008). The critical role of retrieval for learning. *Science*, 319, 966–968.

Karpicke, J., Butler, A., & Roediger, H. III (2009). Metacognitive strategies in student learning: Do students practice retrieval when they study on their own? *Memory*, 17, 471–479.

Katz, L., & Frost, R. (1992). The reading process is different for different orthographies: The orthographic depth hypothesis. In R. Frost & L. Katz (eds.), *Orthography, phonology, morphology, and meaning*. Amsterdam: North Holland.

Kaufman, D., & Aronoff, M. (1991). Morphological disintegration and reconstruction in first language attrition. In H. Seliger & R. Vago (eds.), *First language attrition* (pp. 175–188). Cambridge, UK: Cambridge University Press.

Kaushanskaya, M. (2012). Cognitive mechanisms of word learning in bilingual and monolingual adults: The role of phonological memory. *Bilingualism: Language and Cognition*, 15, 470–489.

Kaushanskaya, M. & Marian, V. (2007). Bilingual language processing and interference in bilinguals: Evidence from eye tracking and picture naming. *Language Learning*, 57, 119–163.

(2009a). Bilingualism reduced native-language interference during novel word learning. *Journal of Experimental Psychology: Learning, Memory, and Cognition*, 35, 829–835.

(2009b). The bilingual advantage in novel word learning. *Psychonomic Bulletin & Review*, 16, 705–710.

Kaushanskaya, M., & Rechtzigel, K. (2012). Concreteness effects in bilingual and monolingual word learning. *Psychonomic Bulletin & Review*, 19, 935-941.

Kaushanskaya, M., & Yoo, J. (2011). Rehearsal effects in adult word learning. *Language and Cognitive Processes*, 26, 121–148.

Kaushanskaya, M., Yoo, J., & Van Hecke, S. (2013). Word learning in adults with second-language experience: Effects of phonological and referent familiarity. *Journal of Speech, Language, and Hearing Research*, 56, 667–678.

Kavé, G., Eyal, N., Shorek, A., & Cohen-Mansfield, J. (2008). Multilingualism and cognitive state in the oldest. *Psychology of Aging*, 23, 70–78.

Kavé, G., Knafo, A., & Gilboa, A. (2010). The rise and fall of word retrieval across the lifespan. *Psychology and Aging*, 25(3), 719–724.

Kavé, G., & Nussbaum, S. (2012). Characteristics of noun retrieval in picture descriptions across the adult lifespan. *Aphasiology*, 26(10), 1238–1249.

Kawabata Duncan, K. J., Twomey, T., Parker Jones, O., et al. (2014). Inter- and intrahemispheric connectivity differences when reading Japanese Kanji and Hiragana. *Cerebral Cortex*, 24(6), 1601–1608.

Keating, G., VanPatten, B., & Jegerski, J. (2011.) Who was walking on the beach? Anaphora resolution in Spanish heritage speakers and adult second language learners. *Studies in Second Language Acquisition*, 33, 193–221.

Keatley, C. (1992). History of bilingualism research in cognitive psychology. In R. Harris (ed.), *Cognitive processing in bilinguals* (pp. 15–49). Amsterdam: Elsevier.

Keatley, C., & De Gelder, B. (1992). The bilingual primed lexical decision task: Cross-language priming disappears with speeded responses. *European Journal of Cognitive Psychology*, 4, 273-292.

Keatley, C., Spinks, J., & De Gelder, B. (1994). Asymmetrical cross-language priming effects. *Memory and Cognition*, 22(1), 70-84.

Kellerman, E. (1978). Giving learners a break: Native language intuitions as a source of predictions about transferability. *Working Papers in Bilingualism*, 15, 59-92.

   (1983). Now you see it, now you don't. In S. Gass & L. Selinker (eds.), *Language transfer and language learning* (pp. 112-134). Rowley, MA: Newbury House.

   (1995). Crosslinguistic influence: Transfer to nowhere. *Annual Review of Applied Linguistics*, 15, 125-150.

Kello, C. (2013). Critical branching neural networks. *Psychological review*, 120(1), 230.

Kello, C., Anderson, G., Holden, J., & Van Orden, G. (2008). The pervasiveness of 1/f scaling in speech reflects the metastable basis of cognition. *Cognitive Science*, 32(7), 1217-1231.

Kello, C., Beltz, B., Holden, J., & Van Orden, G. (2007). The emergent coordination of cognitive function. *Journal of Experimental Psychology: General*, 136(4), 551-568.

Kelly, D., Quinn, P., Slater, A., Lee, K., Ge, L., & Pascalis, O. (2007). The other-race effect develops during infancy: Evidence of perceptual narrowing. *Psychological Science*, 18, 1084-1089.

Kemler Nelson, D., Jusczyk, P., Myers, J., Turk, A., & Gerken, L. (1995). The head-turn preference procedure for testing auditory perception. *Infant Behavior and Development*, 18(1), 111-116.

Kemp, C. (2007). Strategic processing in grammar learning: Do multilinguals use more strategies? *International Journal of Multilingualism*, 4, 241-261.

Kemper, S. (1986). Imitation of complex syntactic constructions by elderly adults. *Applied Psycholinguistics*, 7(3), 277-287.

Kempermann, G., Kuhn, H., & Gage, F. (1997). More hippocampal neurons in adult mice living in an enriched environment. *Nature*, 386(6624), 493-495.

Kenji, H., & D'Andrea, D. (1992). Some properties of bilingual maintenance and loss in Mexican background high-school students. *Applied Linguistics*, 13(1), 72-99.

Kensinger, E., & Corkin, S. (2003). Memory enhancement for emotional words: Are emotional words more vividly remembered than neutral words? *Memory and Cognition*, 31(8), 1169-1180.

Kerkhofs, R., Dijkstra, T., Chwilla, J. D., & de Bruijn, E. R. A. (2006). Testing a model for bilingual semantic priming with interlingual homographs: RT and N400 effects. *Brain Research*, 1068, 170-183.

Kerschensteiner, D., Morgan, J., Parker, E., Lewis, R., & Wong, R. (2009). Neurotransmission selectively regulates synapse formation in parallel circuits in vivo. *Nature*, 460(7258), 1016–1020.

Kersten, A., Meissner, C., Lechuga, J., Schwartz, B., Albrechtsen, J., & Iglesias, A. (2010). English speakers attend more strongly than Spanish speakers to manner of motion when classifying novel objects and events. *Journal of Experimental Psychology: General*, 139, 638–653.

Kester, J., Benjamin, A., Castel, A., & Craik, F. (2002). Memory in the elderly. In A. Baddeley, B. Wilson, & M. Kopelman (eds.), *Handbook of memory disorders* (2nd edn) (pp. 543–567). Chichester, UK: Wiley.

Keysar, B., Hayakawa, S., & An, S. (2012). The foreign language effect: Thinking in a foreign language reduces decision biases. *Psychological Science*, 23(6), 661–668.

Kharkhurin, A. (2008). The effect of linguistic proficiency, age of second language acquisition, and length of exposure to a new cultural environment on bilinguals' divergent thinking. *Bilingualism: Language and Cognition*, 11, 225–243.

Kidd, E., & Bavin, E. (2002). English-speaking children's comprehension of relative clauses: Evidence for general-cognitive and language-specific constraints on development. *Journal of Psycholinguistic Research*, 31(6), 599–617.

Kidron, D., Black, S., Stanchev, P., Buck, B., Szalai, J., & Parker, J. (1997). Quantitative MR volumetry in Alzheimer's disease. *Neurology*, 49, 1504–1512.

Kiefer, M., & Pulvermüller, F. (2012). Conceptual representations in mind and brain: Theoretical developments, current evidence and future directions. *Cortex*, 48(7), 805–825.

Kiesel, A., Steinhauser, M., Wendt, M., et al. (2010). Control and interference in task switching: A review. *Psychological Bulletin*, 136, 849–874.

Kim, J., & Davis, C. (2003). Task effects in masked cross-script translation and phonological priming. *Journal of Memory and Language*, 49, 484–499.

Kim, K., Relkin, N., Lee, K., & Hirsch, J. (1997). Distinct cortical areas associated with native and second languages. *Nature*, 388(6638), 171–174.

Kim, S., & Starks, D. (2008). The role of emotions in L1 attrition: The case of Korean-English late bilinguals in New Zealand. *International Journal of Bilingualism*, 12, 303–319.

Kim, Y., & Tracy-Ventura, N. (2011). Task complexity, language anxiety, and the development of simple past. In P. Robinson (ed.), *Second language task complexity: Researching the Cognition Hypothesis of language learning and performance* (pp. 287–306). Amsterdam/Philadelphia, PA: John Benjamins Publishing.

Kimball, J. (1973). Seven principles of surface structure parsing in natural language. *Cognition*, 2(1), 15–47.

Kinoshita, S., & Lupker, S.J. (2003). *Masked priming: State of the art*. Psychology Press: New York.

Kintsch, W. (1970). Recognition memory in bilingual subjects. *Journal of Verbal Learning and Verbal Behavior*, 9(4), 405–409.

Kiran, S., Graesman, U., Sandberg, C., & Miikkulainen, R. (2013). A computational account of bilingual aphasia rehabilitation. *Bilingualism: Language and Cognition*, 16(2), 325.

Kirk, N., Scott-Brown, K., & Kempe, V. (2013). Do older Gaelic-English bilinguals show an advantage in inhibitory control? *Proceedings of the Annual Meeting of the Cognitive Science Journal*, 782–787.

Kirkici, B., & Clahsen, H. (2013). Inflection and derivation in native and non-native language processing: Masked priming experiments on Turkish. *Bilingualism: Language and Cognition*, 16(4), 776–791.

Kirsner, K., Brown, H., Abrol, S., Chadha, N., & Sharma, N. (1980). Bilingualism and lexical representation. *The Quarterly Journal of Experimental Psychology*, 32, 585–594.

Kirsner, K., Smith, M., Lockhart, R., King, M., & Jain, M. (1984). The bilingual lexicon: Language specific units in an integrated network. *Journal of Verbal Learning and Verbal Behavior*, 23, 519–539.

Kiyak, H. (1982). Interlingual interference in naming color words. *Journal of Cross-Cultural Psychology*, 13, 125–135.

Klavans, J. (1985). The syntax of code-switching: Spanish and English. In L. King & C. Maley (eds.), *Proceedings of the Linguistic Colloquium on Romance Linguistics* (pp. 213–231). Amsterdam/Philadelphia, PA: John Benjamins Publishing.

Klein, E. (1995). Second versus third language acquisition: Is there a difference? *Language Learning*, 45, 419–465.

Klein, W. (1986). *Second language acquisition*. Cambridge, UK: Cambridge University Press.

Knickerbocker, H., & Altarriba, J. (2013). Differential repetition blindness with emotion and emotion-laden word types. *Visual Cognition*, 21, 599–627.

Knudsen, E. (2004). Sensitive periods in the development of the brain and behavior. *Journal of Cognitive Neuroscience*, 16(8), 1412–1425.

Ko, I., Wang, M., & Kim, S. (2011). Bilingual reading of compound words. *Journal of Psycholinguistic Research*, 40, 49–73.

Koch, I., Prinz, W., & Allport, A. (2005). Involuntary retrieval in alphabet-arithmetic tasks: Task-mixing and task-switch costs. *Psychological Research*, 69(4), 252–261.

Koechlin, E., & Summerfield, C. (2007). An information theoretical approach to prefrontal executive function. *Trends in Cognitive Sciences*, 11(6), 229–235.

Kohnert, K. (2010). Bilingual children with primary language impairment: Issues, evidence and implications for clinical actions. *Journal of Communication Disorders*, 43(6), 456–473.

Kohnert, K., Bates, E., & Hernandez, A. (1999). Balancing bilinguals: Lexical-semantic production and cognitive processing in children learning Spanish and English. *Journal of Speech, Language and Hearing Research*, 42, 1400–1413.

Kohnert, K., Hernandez, A., & Bates, E. (1998). Bilingual performance on the Boston Naming Test: Preliminary norms in Spanish and English. *Brain and Language*, 65, 422–440.

Kohonen, T. (2001). *Self-organizing maps* (3rd edn). Berlin: Springer.

Kolers, P. (1963). Interlingual word associations. *Journal of Verbal Learning and Verbal Behavior*, 2, 291–300.

(1965). Bilingualism and bicodalism. *Language and Speech*, 8, 122–126.

(1966a). Interlingual facilitation of short-term memory. *Journal of Verbal Learning and Verbal Behavior*, 5, 314–319.

(1966b). Reading and talking bilingually. *American Journal of Psychology*, 79, 357–376.

Kolk, H., & Chwilla, D. (2007). Late positivities in unusual situations. *Brain and Language*, 100, 257–261.

Kootstra, G. (2012). Code-switching in monologue and dialogue: Activation and alignment in bilingual language production. (Unpublished doctoral dissertation), Radboud University Nijmegen, the Netherlands.

Kootstra, G., van Hell, J., & Dijkstra, T. (2010). Syntactic alignment and shared word order in code-switched sentence production: Evidence from bilingual monologue and dialogue. *Journal of Memory and Language*, 63, 210–231.

(2012). Priming of code-switches in sentences: The role of lexical repetition, cognates, and language proficiency. *Bilingualism: Language and Cognition*, 15(4), 797–819.

(in revision). Interactive alignment drives lexical triggering of code-switching in bilingual dialogue.

Köpke, B., & Schmid, M. (2004). Language attrition: The next phase. In M. Schmid, B. Köpke, M. Keijzer, & L. Weilemar (eds.), *First language attrition: Interdisciplinary perspectives on methodological issues* (pp. 1–43). Amsterdam/Philadelphia, PA: John Benjamins Publishing.

Kormi-Nouri, R., Moniri, S., & Nilsson, L.-G. (2003). Episodic and semantic memory in bilingual and monolingual children. *Scandinavian Journal of Psychology*, 44, 47–54.

Kormi-Nouri, R., Shojaei, R., Moniri, S., Gholami, A., Moradi, A., Akbari-Zardkhaneh, S., & Nilsson, L. (2008). The effect of childhood bilingualism on episodic and semantic memory tasks. *Scandinavian Journal of Psychology*, 49(2), 93–109.

Kormos, J. (1999). Monitoring and self-repair in L2. *Language Learning*, 49, 303–342.

(2006). *Speech production and second language acquisition*. Mahwah, NJ: Lawrence Erlbaum.

(2011). Speech production and the Cognition Hypothesis. In P. Robinson (ed.), *Second language task complexity: Researching the Cognition Hypothesis of language learning and performance* (pp. 39–60). Amsterdam/Philadelphia, PA: John Benjamins Publishing.

Kormos, J., & Dörnyei, Z. (2004). The interaction of linguistic and motivational variables in second language task performance. *Zeitschrift für Interkulturellen Fremdsprachenunterricht* [online], 9(2), 19.

Kormos, J., & Sáfár, A. (2008). Phonological short term-memory, working memory and foreign language performance in intensive language learning. *Bilingualism: Language and Cognition*, 11, 261–271.

Kormos, J., & Trebits, A. (2012). The role of task complexity, modality and aptitude in narrative task performance. *Language Learning*, 61, 439–472.

Kotz, S. (2009). A critical review of ERP and fMRI evidence on L2 syntactic processing. *Brain and Language*, 109(2), 68–74.

Kouritzin, S. (1999). *Face[t]s of first language loss*. Mahwah, NJ: Lawrence Erlbaum Associates.

Kousaie S., & Phillips, N. (2012a). Conflict monitoring and resolution: Are two languages better than one? Evidence from reaction time and event-related brain potentials. *Brain Research*, 1446, 71–90.

(2012b). Aging and bilingualism: Absence of a "bilingual advantage" in Stroop interference in a nonimmigrant sample. *Quarterly Journal of Experimental Psychology*, 65, 356–369.

Kousta, S., Vigliocco, G., Vinson, D., Andrews, M., & Del Campo, E. (2011). The representation of abstract words: Why emotion matters. *Journal of Experimental Psychology: General*, 140, 14–34.

Kousta, S., Vinson, D., & Vigliocco, G. (2009). Emotion words, regardless of polarity, have a processing advantage over neutral words. *Cognition*, 112(3), 473–481.

Kovács, Á., & Mehler, J. (2009a). Cognitive gains in 7-month-old bilingual infants. *Proceedings of the National Academy of Sciences of the United States of America*, 106, 6556–6560.

(2009b). Flexible learning of multiple speech structures in bilingual infants. *Science*, 325(5940), 611–612.

Krakow, R., & Roberts, J. (2003). Acquisition of English vocabulary by young Chinese adoptees. *Journal of Multilingual Communication Disorders*, 1(3), 169–176.

Kral, A., & Sharma, A. (2012). Developmental neuroplasticity after cochlear implantation. *Trends in Neurosciences*, 35(2), 111–122.

Kral, A., Tillein, J., Heid, S., Hartmann, R., & Klinke, R. (2005). Postnatal cortical development in congenital auditory deprivation. *Cerebral Cortex*, 15(5), 552–562.

Krashen, S., Long, M., & Scarcella, R. (1979). Age, rate and eventual attainment in second language acquisition. *Tesol Quarterly*, 13(4), 573–582.

Kraus, N., & Chandrasekaran, B. (2010). Music training for the development of auditory skills. *Nature Reviews Neuroscience*, 11(8), 599–605.

Kray, J., & Lindenberger, U. (2000). Adult age differences in task switching. *Psychology and Aging*, 15(1), 126–147.

Krishnan, A., Xu, Y., Gandour, J., & Cariani, P. (2005). Encoding of pitch in the human brainstem is sensitive to language experience. *Cognitive Brain Research*, 25(1), 161–168.

Krizman, J., Marian, V., Shook, A., Skoe, E., & Kraus, N. (2012). Subcortical encoding of sound is enhanced in bilinguals and relates to executive function advantages. *Proceedings of the National Academy of Sciences*, 109 (20), 7877–7881.

Krizman J., Skoe E., Marian V., & Kraus, N. (2014). Bilingualism increases neural response consistency and attentional control: Evidence for sensory and cognitive coupling. *Brain and Language*, 128, 34–40.

Kroll, J. F., & Bialystok, E. (2013). Understanding the consequences of bilingualism for language processing and cognition. *Journal of Cognitive Psychology*, 25(5), 497–514.

Kroll, J. F., Bobb, S., Misra, M., & Guo, T. (2008). Language selection in bilingual speech: Evidence for inhibitory processes. *Acta Psychologica*, 128, 416–430.

Kroll, J. F., Bobb, S., & Wodniecka, Z. (2006). Language selectivity is the exception, not the rule: Arguments against a fixed locus of language selection in bilingual speech. *Bilingualism: Language and Cognition*, 9, 119 – 135.

Kroll, J. F., & Curley, J. (1988). Lexical memory in novice bilinguals: The role of concepts in retrieving second language words. In M. Grunebel, P. Morris, & R. Sykes (eds.), *Practical aspects of memory* (pp. 389–395). London: Wiley.

Kroll J. F., & de Groot, A. (1997). Lexical and conceptual memory in the bilingual: Mapping form to meaning in two languages. In A. de Groot & J. Kroll (eds.), *Tutorials in bilingualism* (pp. 169–199). Mahwah NJ: Lawrence Erlbaum.

Kroll, J. F., & de Groot, A. (eds.). (2005). *Handbook of bilingualism: Psycholinguistic approaches*. New York: Oxford University Press.

Kroll, J. F., Dijkstra, T., Janssen, N., & Schriefers, H. (2000). Selecting the language in which to speak: Experiments on lexical access in bilingual production. Paper presented at the 41st Annual Meeting of the Psychonomic Society, New Orleans, LA.

Kroll, J. F., & Gollan, T. (2014). Speech planning in two languages: What bilinguals tell us about language production. In V. Ferreira, M. Goldrick, & M. Miozzo (eds.). *The Oxford handbook of language production* (pp. 165–181). Oxford, UK: Oxford University Press.

Kroll, J. F., Michael, E., & Sankaranarayanan, A. (1998). A model of bilingual representation and its implications for second language acquisition. In A. Healy & L. Bourne Jr. (eds.), *Foreign language learning: Psycholinguistic studies on training and retention* (pp. 365–395). Mahwah, NJ: Lawrence Erlbaum Associates, Inc.

Kroll, J. F., & Potter, M. (1984). Recognizing words, pictures, and concepts: A comparison of lexical, object, and reality decisions. *Journal of Verbal Learning & Verbal Behavior*, 23, 39–66.

Kroll, J. F., & Stewart, E. (1994). Category interference in translation and picture naming: Evidence for asymmetric connections between bilingual memory representations. *Journal of Memory and Language*, 33, 149–174.

Kroll, J. F., Sumutka, B., & Schwartz, A. (2005). A cognitive view of the bilingual lexicon: Reading and speaking words in two languages. *International Journal of Bilingualism*, 9, 27–48.

Kroll, J. F., & Tokowicz, N. (2005). Models of bilingual representation and processing. In J. Kroll & A. de Groot (eds.), *Handbook of bilingualism: Psycholinguistic approaches* (pp. 531–553). Oxford, UK: Oxford University Press.

Kroll, J. F., van Hell J., Tokowicz, N., & Green, D. (2010). The Revised Hierarchical Model: A critical review and assessment. *Bilingualism: Language and Cognition*, 13, 373–381.

Kuhl, P. (2009). Early language acquisition: Neural substrates and theoretical models. In M. Gazzaniga (ed.), *The Cognitive Neurosciences* (4th edn) (pp. 837–854). Cambridge, MA: MIT Press.

  (2010). Brain mechanisms in early language acquisition. *Neuron*, 67, 713–727.

Kuhl, P., Conboy, B., Padden, D., Nelson, T., & Pruitt, J. (2005). Early speech perception and later language development: Implications for the "critical period." *Language Learning and Development*, 1, 237–264.

Kuhl, P., & Iverson, P. (1995). Linguistic experience and the "Perceptual Magnet Effect." In W. Strange (ed.), *Speech perception and linguistic experience: Issues in cross-language research* (pp. 121–154). Timonium, MD: York Press.

Kuhl, P., & Rivera-Gaxiola, M. (2008). Neural substrates of language acquisition. *Annual Review of Neuroscience*, 31, 511–534.

Kuhl, P., Stevens, E., Hayashi, A., Deguchi, T., Kiritani, S., & Iverson, P. (2006). Infants show a facilitation effect for native language phonetic perception between 6 and 12 months. *Developmental Science*, 9(2), F13–F21.

Kuhl, P., Tsao, F.-M., & Liu, H.-M. (2003). Foreign-language experience in infancy: Effects of short-term exposure and social interaction on phonetic learning. *Proceedings of the National Academy of Sciences*, 100(15), 9096–9101.

Kuhl, P., Williams, K., Lacerda, F., Stevens, K., & Lindblom, B. (1992). Linguistic experience alters phonetic perception in infants by 6 months of age. *Science*, 255(5044), 606–608.

Kuhlen, A., Allefeld, C., & Haynes, J. (2012). Content-specific coordination of listeners' to speakers' EEG during communication. *Frontiers in Human Neuroscience*, 6, article 266.

Kuipers, J., & Thierry, G. (2010). Event-related brain potentials reveal the time-course of language change detection in early bilinguals. *NeuroImage*, 50(4), 1633–1638.

(2013). ERP-pupil size correlations reveal how bilingualism enhances cognitive flexibility. *Cortex*, 49(10), 2853–2860.

Kulman, A., & Tetrault, E. (1992). Language cross-training: Alternatives and permutations. *Cryptologic Quarterly*, 11, 145–153.

Kurinski, E., & Sera, M. (2011). Does learning Spanish grammatical gender change English-speaking adults' categorization of inanimate objects? *Bilingualism: Language and Cognition*, 14, 203–220.

Kutas, M., & Federmeier, K. (2000). Electrophysiology reveals semantic memory use in language comprehension. *Trends in Cognitive Neuroscience*, 4, 463–470.

Kutas, M., & Hillyard, S. (1980). Reading senseless sentences: Brain potentials reflect semantic incongruity. *Science*, 207(4427), 203–205.

La Heij, W. (2005). Selection processes in monolingual and bilingual lexical access. In J. Kroll & A. de Groot (eds.), *Handbook of bilingualism: Psycholinguistic approaches* (pp. 289–307). New York: Oxford University Press.

La Heij, W., Hooglander, A., Kerling, R., & Van Der Velden, E. (1996). Non-verbal context effects in forward and backward word translation: Evidence for concept mediation. *Journal of Memory and Language*, 35, 648–665.

La Heij, W., & van den Hof, E. (1995). Picture-word interference increases with target-set size. *Psychological Research*, 58(2), 119–133.

Labov, W. (1963). The social motivation of a sound change. *Word*, 19, 273–309.

(1966). *The social stratification of English in New York City*. Washington, DC: Center for Applied Linguistics.

(1972). *Sociolinguistic patterns*. Philadelphea, PA: University of Pennsylvania Press.

Lado, R. (1957). *Linguistics across cultures: Applied linguistics for language teachers*. Ann Arbor, MI: University of Michigan Press.

Lado, R. (1964). *Language teaching: A scientific approach*. New York: McGraw-Hill.

Lagrou, E., Hartsuiker, R., & Duyck, W. (2011). Knowledge of a second language influences auditory word recognition in the native language. *Journal of Experimental Psychology: Learning, Memory, and Cognition*, 37, 952–965.

Lallier, M., Carreiras, M., Tainturier, M.-J., Savill, N., & Thierry, G. (2013). Orthographic transparency modulates the grain size of orthographic processing: Behavioral and ERP evidence from bilingualism. *Brain Research*, 10, 47–60.

Lambert, W. (1955). Measurement of the linguistic dominance of bilinguals. *Journal of abnormal psychology*, 50, 197–200.

(1981). Bilingualism and language acquisition. *Annals of the New York Academy of Sciences*, 379(1), 9–22.

Lambert, W., Havelka, J., & Crosby, C. (1958). The influence of language-acquisition contexts on bilingualism. *Journal of Abnormal and Social Psychology*, 56, 239–244.

Lambert, W., Havelka, J., & Gardner, R. (1959). Linguistic manifestations of bilingualism. *American Journal of Psychology*, 72, 77–82.

Lambert, W., & Moore, N. (1966). Word-association responses: Comparisons of American and French monolinguals with Canadian monolinguals and bilinguals. *Journal of Personality and Social Psychology*, 3, 313.

Lambert, W., & Rawlings, C. (1969). Bilingual processing of mixed-language associative networks. *Journal of Verbal Learning and Verbal Behavior*, 8, 604–609.

Landau, S., Mintun, M., Joshi, A., et al. (2012). Amyloid deposition, hypometabolism, and longitudinal cognitive decline. *Annals of Neurology*, 72, 578–586.

Landauer, T., & Dumais, S. (1997). A solution to Plato's problem: The latent semantic analysis theory of the acquisition, induction, and representation of knowledge. *Psychological Review*, 104, 211–211–240.

Langacker, R. (1987). *Foundations of cognitive grammar: Vol. 1. Theoretical prerequisites*. Stanford, CA: Stanford University Press.

(1999). *Grammar and conceptualization*. Amsterdam: Walter De Gruyter.

(2000). A dynamic usage-based model. In M. Barlow & S. Kemmer (eds.), *Usage-based models of language* (pp. 1–63). Stanford, CA: CSLI Publications.

Larsen, R., Mercer, K., & Balota, D. (2006). Lexical characteristics of words used in emotion Stroop studies. *Emotion*, 6, 62–72.

Larsen, R., Mercer, K., Balota, D., & Strube, M. (2008). Not all negative words slow down lexical decision and naming speed: Importance of word arousal. *Emotion*, 8(4), 445–452.

Larsen-Freeman, D. (1985). State of the art on input in second language acquisition. In S. Gass & C. Madden (eds.), *Input in second language acquisition* (pp. 89–114). Rowley, MA: Newbury House.

(1997). Chaos/complexity science and second language acquisition. *Applied Linguistics*, 18(2), 140–165.

Larsen-Freeman, D., & Cameron, L. (2008). *Complex systems and applied linguistics*. Oxford, UK: Oxford University Press.

Laufer, B. (1989). A factor of difficulty in vocabulary learning: Deceptive transparency. *AILA Review*, 6, 10–20.

Laxén, J., & Lavaur, J.-M. (2010). The role of semantics in translation recognition: Effects of number of translations, dominance of translations and semantic relatedness of multiple translations. *Bilingualism: Language and Cognition*, 13, 157–183.

Lee, E., Lu, D., & Garnsey, S. (2013). L1 word order and sensitivity to verb bias in L2 processing. *Bilingualism: Language and Cognition*, 16(4), 761–775.

Lee, H., & Taft, M. (2011). Subsyllabic structure reflected in letter confusability effects in Korean word recognition. *Psychonomic Bulletin & Review*, 18, 129–134.

Lee, J., & Benati, A. (2013). *Individual differences and processing instruction*. London: Equinox.

Lee, J., & VanPatten, B. (1995). *Making communicative language teaching happen* (1st edn). New York: McGraw-Hill.

  (2003). *Making communicative language teaching happen* (2nd edn). New York: McGraw-Hill.

Lee, M., & Williams, J. (2001). Lexical access in spoken word production by bilinguals: Evidence from the semantic competitor priming paradigm. *Bilingualism: Language and Cognition*, 4, 233–248.

Lee, P. (1996). Cognitive development in bilingual children: A case for bilingual instruction in early childhood education. *Bilingual Research Journal*, 20(3–4), 499–522.

Lehtonen, M., Hultén, A., Rodríguez-Fornells, A., Cunillera, T., Tuomainen, J., & Laine, M. (2012). Differences in word recognition between early bilinguals and monolinguals: Behavioral and ERP evidence. *Neuropsychologia*, 50, 1362–1371.

Lemhöfer, K., & Dijkstra, T. (2004). Recognizing cognates and interlingual homographs: Effects of code similarity in language-specific and generalized lexical decision. *Memory & Cognition*, 32(4), 533–550.

Lemhöfer, K., Dijkstra, T., & Michel, M. (2004). Three languages, one ECHO: Cognate effects in trilingual word recognition. *Language and Cognitive Processes*, 19, 585–611.

Lemhöfer, K., Spalek, K., & Schriefers, H. (2008). Cross-language effects of grammatical gender in bilingual word recognition and production. *Journal of Memory and Language*, 59(3), 312–330.

Leminen, A., Leminen, M., Lehtonen, M., Nevalainen, P., Ylinen, S., Kimppa, L., et al. (2011). Spatiotemporal dynamics of the processing of spoken inflected and derived words: A combined EEG and MEG study. *Frontiers in Human Neuroscience*, 5, 66.

Lenneberg, E. (1967). *Biological foundations of language*. New York: Wiley.

Leopold, W. (1939–1949). *Speech development of a bilingual child* (4 vols.). Evanston, IL.: Northwestern University Press.

Lev-Ari, S., & Peperkamp, S. (2013). Low inhibitory skill leads to non-native perception and production in bilinguals' native language. *Journal of Phonetics*, 41, 320–331.

Levelt, W. (1983). Monitoring and self-repair in speech. *Cognition*, 33, 41–103.

  (1989). *Speaking, from intention to articulation*. Cambridge, MA: MIT Press.

  (1999). Language production: A blueprint of the speaker. In C. Brown & P. Hagoort (eds.), *Neurocognition of language* (pp. 83–122). Oxford, UK: Oxford University Press.

Levelt, W. (2001). Spoken word production: A theory of lexical access. *Proceedings of the National Academy of Sciences*, 98(23), 13464–13471.

Levelt, W., Praamsma, P., Meyer, A., Helenius, P., & Salmelin, R. (1998). An MEG study of picture naming. *Journal of Cognitive Neuroscience*, 10, 553–557.

Levelt, W., Roelofs, A., & Meyer, A. (1999). A theory of lexical access in speech production. *Behavioral and Brain Sciences*, 22(1), 1–38.

Levinson, S. (1996). Relativity in spatial conception and description. In J. Gumperz & S. Levinson (eds.), *Rethinking linguistic relativity* (pp. 177–202). Cambridge, UK: Cambridge University Press.

(2001). Yélî Dnye and the theory of basic color terms. *Journal of Linguistic Anthropology*, 10, 3–55.

Levy, B., McVeigh, N., Marful, A., & Anderson, M. (2007). Inhibiting your native language: The role of retrieval-induced forgetting during second language acquisition. *Psychological Science*, 18, 29–34.

Levy, E. (2009). Language experience and consonantal context effects on perceptual assimilation of French vowels by American-English learners of French. *Journal of the Acoustical Society of America*, 125, 1138–52.

Lew-Williams, C., & Fernald, A. (2007). Young children learning Spanish made rapid use of the grammatical gender in spoken word recognition. *Psychological Science*, 18(3), 193–198.

(2010). Real-time processing of gender-marked articles by native and non-native Spanish speakers. *Journal of Memory and Language*, 63(4), 447–464.

Lewy, N., & Grosjean, F. (2008). The Lewy and Grosjean BIMOLA model. In F. Grosjean (ed.), *Studying bilinguals* (pp. 201–210). Oxford, UK: Oxford University Press.

Li, L., Mo, L., Wang, R., Luo, X., & Chen, Z. (2009). Evidence for long-term cross-language repetition priming in low fluency Chinese-English bilinguals. *Bilingualism: Language and Cognition*, 12, 13–21.

Li, P. (2009). Lexical organization and competition in first and second languages: Computational and neural mechanisms. *Cognitive Science*, 33, 629–664.

(ed.). (2013). Computational modelling of bilingualism: How can models tell us more about the bilingual mind? *Bilingualism: Language and Cognition*, 16(2), 241–245.

(2015). Bilingualism as a dynamic process. In B. MacWhinney & W. O'Grady (eds.), *Handbook of language emergence* (pp. 511–536). New York: Wiley.

Li, P., & Farkas, I. (2002). A self-organizing connectionist model of bilingual processing. *Advances in Psychology*, 134, 59–85.

Li, P., Farkas, I., Li, P., Zhao, X., & MacWhinney, B. (2007). Dynamic self-organization and early lexical development in children. *Cognitive Science: A Multidisciplinary Journal*, 31, 581–612.

Li, P., Farkas, I., & MacWhinney, B. (2004). Early lexical development in a self-organizing neural network. *Neural Networks*, 17, 1345–1362.

Li, P., & MacWhinney, B. (1996). Cryptotype, overgeneralization and competition: A connectionist model of the learning of English reversive prefixes. *Connection Science*, 8(1), 3–30.
  (2002). PatPho: A phonological pattern generator for neural networks. *Behavior Research Methods, Instruments & Computers*, 34(3), 408–415.
Li, P., & Zhao, X. (2012). Connectionism. In M. Aronoff (ed.), *Oxford bibliographies online: Linguistics*. New York, NY: Oxford University Press.
Li, Q.-L., Bi, H.-Y., Wei, T.-Q., & Chen, B.-G. (2011). Orthographic neighborhood size effect in Chinese character naming: Orthographic and phonological activations. *Acta Psychologica*, 136, 35–41.
Libben, G. (2000). Representation and processing in the second language lexicon: The homogeneity hypothesis. In J. Archibald (ed.), *Second language grammars* (pp. 228–248). New York: Blackwell.
  (2007). Reading complex morphological structures. In S. Andrews (ed.), *From inkmarks to ideas: Current issues in lexical processing* (pp. 192–215). Hove, UK: Psychology Press,
Libben, M., & Titone, D. (2009). Bilingual lexical access in context: Evidence from eye movement recordings during reading. *Journal of Experimental Psychology: Learning, Memory, and Cognition*, 35, 381–390.
Liepmann, D., & Saegert, J. (1974). Language tagging in bilingual free recall. *Journal of Experimental Psychology*, 103, 1137–41.
Lin, S., Chen, H., Zhao, J., Li, S., He, S., & Weng, X. C. (2011). Left-lateralized N170 response to unpronounceable pseudo but not false Chinese characters – the key role of orthography. *Neuroscience*, 190, 200–206.
Linck, J., Hughes, M., Campbell, S., et al. (2013). Hi-LAB: A new measure of aptitude for high-level language proficiency. *Language Learning*, 63, 530–566.
Linck, J., Kroll, J. F., & Sunderman, G. (2009). Losing access to the native language while immersed in a second language: Evidence for the role of inhibition in second-language learning. *Psychological Science*, 20(12), 1507–1515.
Linck, J., Osthus, P., Koeth, J., & Bunting, M. (2014). Working memory and second language comprehension and production: A meta-analysis. *Psychonomic Bulletin & Review*, 21(4), 861–883.
Linck, J., Schwieter, J. W., & Sunderman, G. (2012). Inhibitory control predicts language switching performance in trilingual speech production. *Bilingualism: Language and Cognition*, 15(3), 651–662.
Lindsay, S., & Gaskell, M. (2013). Lexical integration of novel words without sleep. *Journal of Experimental Psychology: Learning, Memory, and Cognition*, 39, 608–622.
Lipski, J. (2005). Code-switching or borrowing? No sé *so* no puedo decir, you know. In L. Sayahi & M. Westmoreland (eds.), *Selected Proceedings of the Second Workshop on Spanish Sociolinguistics* (pp. 1–15). Somerville, MA: Cascadilla Proceedings project.

Litcofsky, K. (2013). Sentential code-switching and lexical triggering: A neurocognitive study. (Unpublished master's thesis), Pennsylvania State University.

Litcofsky, K., & van Hell, J. (in revision). Sentential code-switching in Spanish–English bilinguals: Behavioral and electrophysiological evidence.

Litcofsky, K., Midgley, K., Holcomb, P., & Grainger, J. (2009). Exploring language switching with lexical decision and event related potentials. Poster presented at the Annual Meeting of the Cognitive Neuroscience Society, San Francisco, CA, March 19–24.

Liu, C., Zhang, W.-T., Tang, Y.-Y., et al. (2008). The visual word form area: Evidence from an fMRI study of implicit processing of Chinese characters. *NeuroImage*, 40, 1350–1361.

Liu, H., Bates, E., & Li, P. (1992). Sentence interpretation in bilingual speakers of English and Chinese. *Applied Psycholinguistics*, 13(4), 451–484.

Liu, L., & Kager, R. (2013). How bilingualism alters non-tone-learning infants' perception in the first year of life. Paper presented at the 37th Annual Boston University Conference on Child Language Development.

Liu, Y., & Perfetti, C. A. (2003). The time course of brain activity in reading English and Chinese: An ERP study of Chinese bilinguals. *Human Brain Mapping*, 18(3), 167–175.

Liu, Y., Perfetti, C. A., & Wang, M. (2006). Visual analysis and lexical access of Chinese characters by Chinese as second language readers. *Language and Linguistics*, 7, 637–657.

Llama, R., Cardoso, W., & Collins, L. (2010). The influence of language distance and language status on the acquisition of L3 phonology. *International Journal of Multilingualism* 7(1), 39–57.

Llamas, C. (2011). Sociolinguistics. In J. Simpson (ed.), *Routledge handbook of applied linguistics* (pp. 501–514). London: Routledge.

Lloyd-Fox, S., Blasi, A., & Elwell, C. (2010). Illuminating the developing brain: The past, present and future of functional near infrared spectroscopy. *Neuroscience & Biobehavioral Reviews*, 34(3), 269–284.

Loebell, H., & Bock, K. (2003). Structural priming across languages. *Linguistics*, 41, 791–824.

Long, M. (1990). The least a second language acquisition theory needs to explain. *TESOL Quarterly*, 24, 649–666.

(2005). Methodological issues in learner needs analysis. In M. Long (ed.), *Second language needs analysis* (pp. 19–76). Cambridge, UK: Cambridge University Press.

Lopez, M., & Young, R. K. (1974). The linguistic interdependence of bilinguals. *Journal of Experimental Psychology*, 102, 981–983.

Lorenzen, B., & Murray, L. L. (2008). Bilingual aphasia: A theoretical and clinical review. *American Journal of Speech-Language Pathology*, 17, 299–317.

Los, S. (1996). On the origin of mixing costs: Exploring information processing in pure and mixed blocks of trials. *ActaPsychologica*, 94(2), 145–188.

Lotto, L., & de Groot, A. (1998). Effects of learning method and word type on acquiring vocabulary in an unfamiliar language. *Language Learning*, 48(1), 31–69.

Love, T., & Swinney, D. (1996). Coreference processing and levels of analysis in object-relative constructions; demonstration of antecedent reactivation with the cross-modal priming paradigm. *Journal of Psycholinguistic Research*, 25(1), 5–24.

Lowie, W. (2012). Dynamic systems theory approaches to second language acquisition. In C. Chapel (ed.), *The encyclopedia of applied linguistics* (pp. 1806–1813). London: Wiley-Blackwell.

Lowie, W. (under review). L2 phonological development: A plea for a dynamic, process-based methodology.

Lowie, W., Caspi, T., Van Geert, P., & Steenbeek, H. (2011). Modeling development and change. In M. Verspoor, K. de Bot, & W. Lowie (eds.), *A dynamic approach to second language development: Methods and techniques* (pp. 22–122). Amsterdam/Philadelphia, PA: John Benjamins Publishing.

Lowie, W., Plat, R., & de Bot, K. (2014). Pink noise in language production: A nonlinear approach to the multilingual lexicon. *Ecological Psychology*, 26(3), 216–228.

Lowie, W., & Verspoor, M. (2015). Variability and variation in second language acquisition olders: A dynamic re-evaluation. *Language Learning*: 65(1), 63–88.

Luck, S., Heinze, H., Mangun, G., & Hillyard, S. (1990). Visual event-related potentials index focused attention within bilateral stimulus arrays. II. Functional dissociation of P1 and N1 components. *Electroencephalography and Clinical Neurophysiology*, 75(6), 528–542.

Lucki, N., & Nicolay, C. (2007). Phenotypic plasticity and functional asymmetry in response to grip forces exerted by intercollegiate tennis players. *American Journal of Human Biology*, 19(4), 566–677.

Lucy, J. (1992). *Grammatical categories and cognition. A case study of the linguistic relativity hypothesis*. Cambridge, UK: Cambridge University Press.

(1997). Linguistic relativity. *Annual Review of Anthropology*, 26, 291–312.

Luk, G., Anderson, J., Craik, F., Grady, C., & Bialystok, E. (2010). Distinct neural correlates for two types of inhibition in bilinguals: Response inhibition and interference suppression. *Brain and Cognition*, 74, 347–357.

Luk, G., & Bialystok, E. (2013). Bilingualism is not a categorical variable: Interaction between language proficiency and usage. *Journal of Cognitive Psychology*, 25(5), 605–621.

Luk, G., Bialystok, E., Craik, F., & Grady, C. (2011). Lifelong bilingualism maintains white matter integrity in older adults. *Journal of Neuroscience*, 31(46), 16808–16813.

Luk, G., DeSa, E., & Bialystok, E. (2011). Is there a relation between onset age of bilingualism and enhancement of cognitive control? *Bilingualism: Language and Cognition*, 14(4) 588–595.

Luk, G., Green, D., Abutalebi, J., & Grady, C. (2012). Cognitive control for language switching in bilinguals: A quantitative meta-analysis of functional neuroimaging studies. *Language and Cognitive Processes*, 27(10), 1479–1488.

Lukatela, G., Gligorijević, B., Kostić, A., & Turvey, M. (1980). Representation of inflected nouns in the internal lexicon. *Memory and Cognition*, 8, 415–423.

Lukyanchenko, A., & Gor, K. (2011). Perceptual correlates of phonological representations in heritage speakers and L2 learners. *Proceedings of the 35th Annual Boston University Conference on Language Development*. Somerville, MA: Cascadilla Press.

Luo, L., Craik, F., Moreno, S., & Bialystok, E. (2013). Bilingualism interacts with domain in a working memory task: Evidence from aging. *Psychology and Aging*, 28(1), 28–34.

Luo, L., Luk, G., & Bialystok, E. (2010). Effect of language proficiency and executive control on verbal fluency performance in bilinguals. *Cognition*, 114, 29–41.

Lupker, S., Brown, P., & Colombo, L. (1997). Strategic control in a naming task: Changing routes or changing deadlines? *Journal of Experimental Psychology: Learning, Memory, and Cognition*, 23, 570–590.

Luria, A. (1966). *Higher cortical functions*. New York: Basic Book.

McCallum, W., Farmer, S., & Pocock, P. (1984). The effects of physical and semantic incongruities on auditory event-related potentials. *Electroencephalography and Clinical Neurophysiology*, 59, 447–488.

McCandliss, B. D., Cohen, L., & Dehaene, S. (2003). The visual word form area: Expertise for reading in the fusiform gyrus. *Trends in Cognitive Sciences*, 7, 293–299.

McCandliss, B. D., Fiez, J., Protopapas, A., Conway, M., & McClelland, J. (2002). Success and failure in teaching the [r]-[l] contrast to Japanese adults: Tests of a Hebbian model of plasticity and stabilization in spoken language perception. *Cognitive, Affective, & Behavioral Neuroscience*, 2(2), 89–108.

McCann, W., Klein, H., & Stegmann, T. (2003). *EuroComRom: The seven sieves: How to read all the Romance languages right away* (2nd rev. edn). Aachen, Germany: Shaker Verlag.

McClelland, J. L. (2009). The place of modeling in cognitive science. *Topics in Cognitive Science*, 1, 11–28.

(2014). Explorations in parallel distributed processing: A handbook of models, programs, and exercises. Accessed from http://www.stanford.edu/group/pdplab/pdphandbook.

McClelland, J. L., & Rumelhart, D. E. (1981). An interactive activation model of context effects in letter perception: I. An account of basic findings. *Psychological Review*, 88, 375–407.

McConkey Robbins, A., Koch, D., Osberger, M., Zimmerman-Phillips, S., & Kishon-Rabin, L. (2004). Effect of age at cochlear implantation on auditory skill development in infants and toddlers. *Archives of Otolaryngology-Head & Neck Surgery*, 130(5), 570.

McCormack, P. (1977). Bilingual linguistic memory: The independence-interdependence issue revisited. In P. Hornby (ed.), *Bilingualism: Psychological, social, educational implications* (pp. 57–66). New York: Academic Press.

McCormack, P., Brown, C., & Ginis, B. (1979). Free recall from mixed-language lists by Greek-English and French-English bilinguals. *Bulletin of the Psychonomic Society*, 14, 447–448.

McCormack, P., & Novell, J. (1975). Free recall from unilingual and trilingual lists. *Bulletin of the Psychonomic Society*, 6, 173–174.

MacDonald, A., Cohen, J., Stenger, V., & Carter, C. (2000). Dissociating the role of the dorsolateral prefrontal and anterior cingulate cortex in cognitive control. *Science*, 288(5472), 1835–1838.

McDonald, J. (1987). Sentence interpretation in bilingual speakers of English and Dutch. *Applied Psycholinguistics*, 8(4), 379–413.

  (2006). Beyond the critical period: Processing-based explanations for poor grammaticality judgment performance by late second language learners. *Journal of Memory and Language*, 55(3), 381–401.

McDonald, J., & Heilenman, L. (1991). Determinants of cue strength in adult first and second language speakers of French. *Applied Psycholinguistics*, 12(3), 313–348.

MacDonald, M. (1994). Probabilistic constraints and syntactic ambiguity resolution. *Language and Cognitive Processes*, 9(2), 157–201.

  (2013). How language production shapes language form and comprehension. *Frontiers in Psychology*, 4, 1–16.

MacDonald, M., & Seidenberg, M. (2006). Constraint satisfaction accounts of lexical and sentence comprehension. In M. Traxler & M. Gernsbacher (eds.), *Handbook of psycholinguistics* (2nd edn) (pp. 581–611). London: Elsevier.

MacDonald, M., & Thornton, R. (2009). When language comprehension reflects production constraints: Resolving ambiguities with the help of past experience. *Memory & Cognition*, 37(8), 1177–1186.

McDonald, S., & Shillock, R. (2001). Rethinking the word frequency effect: The neglected role of distributional information in lexical processing. *Language and Speech*, 44(3), 295–322.

McDonough, K., & De Vleeschauwer, J. (2012). Prompt type frequency, auditory pattern discrimination, and EFL learners' production of wh-questions. *Studies in Second Language Acquisition*, 34(3), 355–377.

McElree, B., & Griffith, T. (1995). Syntactic and thematic processing in sentence comprehension: Evidence for a temporal dissociation. *Journal of Experimental Psychology: Learning, Memory, and Cognition*, 21(1), 134.–157.

MacIntyre, P. (1995). How does anxiety affect second language learning? A reply to Sparks and Ganschow. *Modern Language Journal*, 79, 90–99.

  (2007). Willingness to communicate in a second language: Understanding the decision to speak as a volitional process. *Modern Language Journal*, 91, 564–576.

MacIntyre, P., Baker, S., Clément, R., & Donovan, L. (2003). Talking in order to learn: Willingness to communicate and intensive language programs. *Canadian Modern Language Review*, 59, 589-607.

MacIntyre, P., Dörnyei, Z., Clément, R., & Noels, K. (1998). Conceptualizing willingness to communicate in a L2: A situational model of L2 confidence and affiliation. *Modern Language Journal*, 82, 545-562.

MacIntyre, P., & Gardner, R. (1994). The subtle effects of language anxiety on cognitive processing in the second language. *Language Learning*, 44, 283-305.

MacIntyre, P., & Legatto, J. (2011). A dynamic systems approach to willingness to communicate: Developing an idiodynamic approach to capture rapidly changing affect. *Applied Linguistics*, 32, 149-171.

Macizo, P., Bajo, M., & Martín, M. (2010). Inhibitory processes in bilingual language comprehension: Evidence from Spanish-English interlexical homographs. *Journal of Memory and Language*, 63, 232-244.

Macizo, P., Bajo, M., & Paolieri, D. (2012). Language switching and language competition. *Second Language Research*, 28(2), 131-149.

McKenna, F. (1986). Effects of unattended emotional stimuli on color-naming performance. *Current Psychological Research and Reviews*, 5(1), 445-452.

McKenna, F., & Sharma, D. (2004). Reversing the emotional Stroop effect reveals that it is not what it seems: The role of fast and slow components. *Journal of Experimental Psychology: Learning, Memory, and Cognition*, 30(2), 382-382.

Mackey, A., & Sachs, R. (2012). Older learners in SLA research: A first look at working memory, feedback, and L2 development. *Language Learning*, 61, 704-740.

Mackey, A., Philp, J., Egi, T., Fujii, A., & Tatsumi, T. (2002). Individual differences in working memory, noticing of interactional feedback, and L2 development. In P. Robinson (ed.), *Individual differences and instructed language learning* (pp.181-209). Amsterdam/Philadelphia, PA: John Benjamins Publishing.

McLaughlin, B., & Heredia, R. (1996). Information processing approaches to the study of second language acquisition. In W. Ritchie & T. Bhatia (eds.), *Handbook of second language acquisition* (pp. 213-228). New York: Academic Press.

MacLeod, C. (1976). Bilingual episodic memory: Acquisition and forgetting. *Journal of Verbal Learning and Verbal Behavior*, 15, 347-364.

(1991). Half a century of research on the Stroop effect: An integrative review. *Psychological Bulletin*, 109, 163-203.

McMurray, B., & Aslin, R. (2004). Anticipatory eye movements reveal infants' auditory and visual categories. *Infancy*, 6(2), 203-229.

Macnamara, J. (1966). *Bilingualism and primary education: A study of Irish experience*. Edinburgh: Edinburgh University Press.

(1967a). The bilingual's linguistic performance-a psychological overview. *Journal of Social Issues*, 23(2), 58–77.

(1967b). The linguistic independence of bilinguals. *Journal of Verbal Learning and Verbal Behavior*, 6, 729–736.

Macnamara, J., Krauthammer, M., & Bolgar, M. (1968). Language switching in bilinguals as a function of stimulus and response uncertainty. *Journal of Experimental Psychology*, 78, 208–215.

MacNamara, J., & Kushnir, S. L. (1971). Linguistic independence of bilinguals: The input switch. *Journal of Verbal Learning and Verbal Behavior*, 10 (5), 480–487.

McQueen, J., Cutler, A., & Norris, D. (2006). Phonological abstraction in the mental lexicon. *Cognitive Science*, 30, 1113–1126.

McRae, K., Cree, G., Seidenberg, M., & McNorgan, C. (2005). Semantic feature production norms for a large set of living and nonliving things. *Behavior Research Methods*, 37(4), 547–559.

MacSwan, J. (2000). The architecture of the bilingual language faculty: Evidence from intrasentential code switching. *Bilingualism, Language and Cognition* 3, 37–74.

MacWhinney, B. (1987a). Applying the competition model to bilingualism. *Applied Psycholinguistics*, 8(4), 315–327.

(1987b). The Competition Model. In B. MacWhinney (ed.), *Mechanisms of language acquisition* (pp. 249–308). Hillsdale, NJ: Erlbaum.

(2000). *The CHILDES Project: The database* (3rd edn). Mahwah, NJ: Lawrence Erlbaum.

(2001). Emergentist approaches to language. In J. Bybee & P. Hopper (eds.), *Frequency and the emergence of linguistic structure* (pp. 449–470). Amsterdam/Philadelphia, PA: John Benjamins Publishing.

(2005). A unified model of language acquisition. In J. Kroll & A. de Groot (eds.), *Handbook of bilingualism: Psycholinguistic approaches* (pp. 49–67). Oxford University Press.

(2010). Computational models of child language learning: An introduction. *Journal of Child language*, 37(3), 477.

(n.d.) Bilingual Corpora: Biling. Accessed from http://childes.psy.cmu.edu/manuals/04biling.pdf.

MacWhinney, B., & Bates, E. (1989). *The cross-linguistic study of sentence processing*. New York: Cambridge University Press.

MacWhinney, B., Bates, E., & Reinhold, K. (1984). Cue validity and sentence interpretation in English, German, and Italian. *Journal of Verbal Learning & Verbal Behavior*, 23(2), 127–150.

Madden, D., Costello, M., Dennis, N., et al. (2010). Adult age differences in functional connectivity during executive control. *Neuroimage*, 52(2), 643–657.

Mägiste, E. (1979). The competing language systems of the multilingual: A developmental study of decoding and encoding processes. *Journal of Verbal Learning and Verbal Behavior*, 18, 79–89.

(1984). Stroop tasks and dichotic translation: The development of interference patterns in bilinguals. *Journal of Experimental Psychology: Learning, Memory, and Cognition*, 10, 304–315.

(1985). Development of intra-and interlingual interference in bilinguals. *Journal of Psycholinguistic Research*, 14, 137–154.

Magnuson, J., Tanenhaus, M., Aslin, R., & Dahan, D. (1999). Spoken word recognition in the visual world paradigm reflects the structure of the entire lexicon. In *Proceedings of the Twenty First Annual Conference of the Cognitive Science Society* (pp. 331–336). Hillsdale, NJ: Lawrence Erlbaum.

Maheshwari, M., Klein, A., & Ulmer, J. (2012). *White matter: Functional anatomy of key tracts of functional neuroradiology*. New York: Springer.

Malt, B., & Sloman, S. (2003). Linguistic diversity and object naming by non-native speakers of English. *Bilingualism: Language and Cognition*, 6, 47–68.

Mandonnet, E., Nouet, A., Gatignol, P., Capelle, L., & Duffau, H. (2007). Does the left inferior longitudinal fasciculus play a role in language? *A brain stimulation study. Brain*, 130(3), 623–629.

Mangun, G., Buonocore, M. H., Girelli, M., & Jha, A. P. (1998). ERP and fMRI measures of visual spatial selective attention. *Human Brain Mapping*, 6, 383–389.

Mani, I., & Pustejovski, J. (2012). *Interpreting motion: Grounded representations for spatial language*. Oxford, UK: Oxford University Press.

Marantz, A. (2013). No escape from morphemes in morphological processing. *Language and Cognitive Processes*, 28(7), 905–916.

Marchman, V., & Martinez-Sussmann, C. (2002). Concurrent validity of caregiver/parent report measures of language for children who are learning both English and Spanish. *Journal of Speech, Language and Hearing Research*, 45(5), 983.

Marchman, V., Martinez-Sussmann, C., & Dale, P. (2004). The language-specific nature of grammatical development: Evidence from bilingual language learners. *Developmental Science*, 7(2), 212–224.

Marian, V., Blumenfeld, H., & Kaushanskaya, M. (2007). The Language Experience and Proficiency Questionnaire (LEAP-Q): Assessing language profiles in bilinguals and multilinguals. *Journal of Speech, Language and Hearing Research*, 50(4), 940.

Marian, V., Blumenfeld, H., Mizrahi, E., Kania, U., & Corder, A.-K. (2013). *International Journal of Multilingualism*, 10, 82–104.

Marian, V., & Kaushanskaya, M. (2004). Self-construal and emotion in bicultural bilinguals. *Journal of Memory and Language*, 51, 190–201.

(2009). The bilingual advantage in novel word learning. *Psychonomic Review Bulletin*, 16(4), 705–710.

Marian, V., & Neisser, U. (2000). Language-dependent recall of autobiographical memories. *Journal of Experimental Psychology: General*, 129(3), 361.

Marian, V., & Spivey, M. (2003a). Bilingual and monolingual processing of competing lexical items. *Applied Psycholinguistics*, 24(2), 173–193.

(2003b). Competing activation in bilingual language processing: Within- and between-language competition. *Bilingualism: Language and Cognition*, 6(2), 97–115.

Marian, V., Spivey, M., & Hirsch, J. (2003). Shared and separate systems in bilingual language processing: Converging evidence from eyetracking and brain imaging. *Brain and language*, 86(1), 70–82.

Marí-Beffa, P., Cooper, S., & Houghton, G. (2011). Unmixing the Mixing Cost: Contributions from dimensional relevance and stimulus-response suppression. *Journal of Experimental Psychology: Human Perception and Performance*, 38(2), 478–488.

Mariën, P., Abutalebi, J., Engelborghs, S., & De Deyn, P. (2005). Pathophysiology of language switching and mixing in an early bilingual child with subcortical aphasia. *Neurocase*, 11, 385–398.

Marinis, T. (2010). Using on-line processing methods in language acquisition research. *Experimental Methods in Language Acquisition Research*, 27, 139.

Marinis, T., Roberts, L., Felser, C., & Clahsen, H. (2005). Gaps in second language sentence processing. *Studies in Second Language Acquisition*, 27(1), 53–78.

Markham, J., Herting, M., Luszpak, A., Juraska, J., & Greenough, W. (2009). Myelination of the corpus callosum in male and female rats following complex environment housing during adulthood. *Brain Research*, 1288, 9–17.

Markham, J., & Wachtel, G. F. (1988). Children's use of mutual exclusivity to constrain the meanings of words. *Cognitive Psychology*, 20(2), 121–157.

Marois, R., & Ivanoff, J. (2005). Capacity limits of information processing in the brain. *Trends in cognitive sciences*, 9(6), 296–305.

Mårtensson, J., Eriksson, J., Bodammer, N., et al. (2012). Growth of language-related brain areas after foreign language learning. *NeuroImage*, 63,(1), 240–244.

Martin, C., Barcelo, F., Hernandez, M., & Costa, A. (2011). The time course of the asymmetrical "local" switch cost: Evidence from event-related potentials. *Biological Psychology*, 86(3), 210–218.

Martin, C., Dering, B., Thomas, M., & Thierry, G. (2009). Brain potentials reveal semantic priming in both the 'active' and the 'non-attended' language in early bilinguals. *NeuroImage*, 47, 326–333.

Martin, C., Strijkers, K., Santesteban, M., Escera, C., Hartsuiker, R., & Costa, A. (2013). The impact of early bilingualism on controlling a language learned late: An ERP study. *Frontiers*, 4, 815.

Martin, C., Thierry, G., Kuipers, J., Boutonnet, B., Foucart, A., & Costa, A. (2013). Bilinguals reading in their second language do not predict upcoming words as native readers do. *Journal of Memory and Language*, 69(4), 74–588.

Martin, K., & Ellis, N. (2012). The roles of phonological short-term memory and working memory in L2 grammar and vocabulary learning. *Studies in Second Language Acquisition*, 34, 379–413.

Martin, M., & Bialystok, E. (2003). The development of two kinds of inhibition in monolingual and bilingual children: Simon vs. Stroop. Poster presented at Meeting of the Cognitive Development Society, Park City, Utah.

Martín, M., Bajo, M., & Kroll, J. F. (2013). When bilinguals chose the words they speak: Evidence for multiple control mechanisms. Poster presented at 54th Annual Meeting of the Psychonomic Society, Toronto, Canada.

Martín, M., Macizo, P., & Bajo, M. (2010). Time course of inhibitory processes in bilingual language processing. *British Journal of Psychology*, 101, 679–693.

Martín, M., Macizo, P., Bajo, M., & Kroll, J. F. (under review). Two contexts for bilingualism: How language immersion and expertise in translation influence language control.

Martinovic, I., & Altarriba, J. (2012). Bilingualism and emotion: Implications for mental health. In T. Bhatia & W. Ritchie (eds.), *The handbook of bilingualism and multilingualism* (2nd edn) (pp. 292–320). Oxford, UK: Blackwell.

Martin-Rhee, M., & Bialystok, E. (2008). The development of two types of inhibitory control in monolingual and bilingual children. *Bilingualism: Language and Cognition*, 11(1) 81–93.

Martohardjono, G., Otheguy, R., Gabriele, A., et al. (2005). The role of syntax in reading comprehension: A study of bilingual readers. *Proceedings of the 4th International Symposium on Bilingualism* (pp. 1522–1544). Somerville, MA: Cascadilla Press.

Marzecová, A., Asanowicz, D., Krivá, L., & Wodniecka, Z. (2013). The effects of bilingualism on efficiency and lateralization of attentional networks. *Bilingualism: Language and Cognition*, 16, 608–623

Massol, S., Dunabeitia, J. A., Carreiras, M., & Grainger, J. (2013). Evidence for letter-specific position coding mechanisms. *PLoS ONE*, 8, e68460.

Matsumoto, D., Anguas-Wong, A., & Martinez, E. (2008). Priming effects of language on emotion judgments in Spanish–English bilinguals. *Journal of Cross-Cultural Psychology*, 39(3), 335–342.

Mattock, K., Polka, L., Rvachew, S., & Krehm, M. (2010). The first steps in word learning are easier when the shoes fit: Comparing monolingual and bilingual infants. *Developmental Science*, 13(1), 229–243.

Maurer, U., Brem, S., Bucher, K., & Brandeis, D. (2005). Emerging neurophysiological specialization for letter strings. *Journal of Cognitive Neuroscience*, 17, 1532–1552.

Maurer, U., Rossion, B., & McCandliss, B. D. (2008). Category specificity in early perception: Face and word n170 responses differ in both lateralization and habituation properties. *Frontiers in Human Neuroscience*, 2, 1–7.

Maurer, U., Zevin, D. J., & McCandliss, B. D. (2008). Left-lateralized N170 effects of visual expertise in reading: Evidence from Japanese syllabic and logographic scripts. *Journal of Cognitive Neuroscience*, 20, 1878–1891.

Mayor, J., & Plunkett, K. (2010). A neurocomputational account of taxonomic responding and fast mapping in early word learning. *Psychological Review*, 117(1), 1–31.

Mayr, R., & Escudero, P. (2010). Explaining individual variation in L2 perception: Rounded vowels in English learners of German. *Bilingualism: Language and Cognition*, 13(3), 279–297.

Mayr, U., & Keele, S. (2000). Changing internal constraints on action: The role of backward inhibition. *Journal of Experimental Psychology: General*, 129(1), 4–26.

Mechelli, A., Crinion, J., Noppeney, U., & Price, C. (2004). Neurolinguistics: Structural plasticity in the bilingual brain. *Nature*, 431(7010), 757–757.

Mecklinger, A. (2010). The control of long-term memory: brain systems and cognitive processes. *Neuroscience and Biobehavioral Review*, 34(7), 1055–1065.

Mecklinger, A., von Cramon, D., Springer, A., & Matthes-von Cramon, G. (1999). Executive control functions in task switching: Evidence from brain injured patients. *Journal of Clinical & Experimental Neuropsychology*, 21(5), 606–619.

Mehler, J., Jusczyk, P., Lambertz, G., Halsted, N., Bertoncini, J., & Amiel-Tison, C. (1988). A precursor of language acquisition in young infants. *Cognition*, 29, 143–178.

Meijer, P., & Fox Tree, J. (2003). Building syntactic structures in speaking: A bilingual exploration. *Experimental Psychology*, 50, 184–195.

Meiran, N. (1996). Reconfiguration of processing mode prior to task performance. *Journal of Experimental Psychology: Learning, Memory, and Cognition*, 22(6), 1423–1442.

Meiran, N. (2000). Modeling cognitive control in task-switching. *Psychological Research*, 63(3–4), 234–249.

Merino, B. (1983). Language loss in bilingual Chicano children. *Journal of Applied Developmental Psychology*, 4(3), 277–294.

Meschyan, G., & Hernandez, A. (2006). Impact of language proficiency and orthographic transparency on bilingual word reading: An fMRI investigation. *NeuroImage*, 29, 1135–1140.

Mesgarani, N., & Chang, E. (2012). Selective cortical representation of attended speaker in multi-talker speech perception. *Nature*, 485 (7397), 233–236.

Meuter, R., & Allport, A. (1999). Bilingual language switching in naming: Asymmetrical costs of language selection. *Journal of Memory and Language*, 40(1), 25–40.

Meyer, D., & Ruddy, M. (1974). Bilingual word recognition: Organization and retrieval of alternative lexical codes. Paper presented at Annual Meeting of the Eastern Psychological Association, Philadelphia.

Meyer, L. (2000). Barriers to meaningful instruction for English learners. *Theory into practice*, 39(4), 228–236.

Mezzacappa, E. (2004). Alerting, orienting, and executive attention: Developmental properties and sociodemographic correlates in an epidemiological sample of young, urban children. *Child Development*, 75, 1373–1386.

Miccio, A., Scheffuer Hammer, C., & Rodriguez, B. (2009). Code-switching and language disorders in bilingual children. In B. Bullock & A. Toribio (eds.), *The Cambridge handbook of linguistic code-switching* (pp. 241–252). Cambridge, UK: Cambridge University Press.

Midgley, K., Holcomb, P., & Grainger, J. (2011). Effects of cognate status on word comprehension in second language learners: An ERP investigation. *Journal of Cognitive Neuroscience*, 23, 1634–1647.

Midgley, K., Holcomb, P., van Heuven, W. J. B., & Grainger, J. (2008). An electrophysiological investigation of cross-language effects of orthographic neighborhood. *Brain Research*, 1246, 123–135.

Miikkulainen, R. (1997). Dyslexic and category-specific aphasic impairments in a self-organizing feature map model of the lexicon. *Brain and Language*, 59, 334–366.

Miikkulainen, R., & Kiran, S. (2009). Modeling the bilingual lexicon of an individual subject. In *Lecture notes in Computer Science 5629: Proceedings of the Workshop on Self-Organizing Maps (WSOM'09, St. Augustine, FL)*. Berlin: Springer.

Mikulski, A. (2010). Age of onset of bilingualism, language use, and the volitional subjunctive in heritage learners of Spanish. *Heritage Language Journal*, 7(1), 28–46.

Milian, S. (1995). Spanish–English codeswitching. (Unpublished corpus.)

Milin, P., Filipović Đurđević, D., & Moscoso del Prado Martín, F. (2009). The simultaneous effects of inflectional paradigms and classes on lexical recognition: Evidence from Serbian. *Journal of Memory and Language*, 60, 50–64.

Miller, E., & Cohen, J. (2001). An integrative theory of prefrontal cortex function. *Neuroscience*, 24(1), 167.

Miller, G. (1990). WordNet: An on-line lexical database. *International Journal of Lexicography*, 3, 235–312.

(2009). WordNet-About us. Accessed from http://wordnet.princeton.edu.

Mimura, K., Kimoto, T., & Okada, M. (2003). Synapse efficiency diverges due to synaptic pruning following overgrowth. *Physical Review E*, 68(3), 031910.

Minkowski, M. (1983). A clinical contribution to the study of polyglot aphasia especially with respect to Swiss-German. In M. Paradis (ed.), *Readings on aphasia in bilinguals and polyglots* (pp. 205–232). Montreal: Marcel Didier.

Misra, M., Guo, T., Bobb, S., & Kroll, J. F. (2012). When bilinguals choose a single word to speak: Electrophysiological evidence for inhibition of the native language. *Journal of Memory and Language*, 67, 224–237.

Miyake, A., Friedman, N., Emerson, M., Witzki, A., Howerter, A., & Wager, T. (2000). The unity and diversity of executive functions and their contributions to complex "frontal lobe" tasks: A latent variable analysis. *Cognitive Psychology*, 41, 49–100.

Miyawaki, K., Jenkins, J., Strange, W., Liberman, A., Verbrugge, R., & Fujimura, O. (1975). An effect of linguistic experience: The discrimination of [r] and [l] by native speakers of Japanese and English. *Perception & Psychophysics*, 18(5), 331–340.

Mizera, G. (2006). Working memory and L2 oral fluency. (Unpublished doctoral dissertation), University of Pittsburgh, PA.

Mohades, S., Struys, E., Van Schuerbeek, P., Mondt, K., Van De Craen, P., & Luypaert, R. (2012). DTI reveals structural differences in white matter tracts between bilingual and monolingual children. *Brain Research*, 1435, 72–80.

Monner, D., Vatz, K., Morini, G., Hwang, S., & DeKeyser, R. (2013). A neural network model of the effects of entrenchment and memory development on grammatical gender learning. *Bilingualism: Language and Cognition*, 16(2), 246.

Monsell, S. (1996). Control of mental processes. In V. Bruce (ed.), *Unsolved mysteries of the mind: Tutorial essays in cognition* (pp. 93–148). Mahwah. NJ: Lawrence Erlbaum.

Monsell, S. (2003). Task switching. *Trends in Cognitive Sciences*, 7(3), 134–140.

Monsell, S., Patterson, K., Graham, A., Hughes, C., & Milroy, R. (1992). Lexical and sub-lexical translation of spelling to sound: Strategic anticipation of lexical status. *Journal of Experimental Psychology Learning Memory and Cognition*, 18(3), 452–467

Monsell, S., Yeung, N., & Azuma, R. (2000). Reconfiguration of task-set: Is it easier to switch to the weaker task? *Psychological Research*, 63, 250–264.

Montalbetti, M. (1984). After binding: On the interpretation of pronouns. (Unpublished doctoral dissertation), Massachusetts Institute of Technology, Cambridge, MA.

Montrul, S. (2005). Second language acquisition and first language loss in adult early bilinguals: Exploring some differences and similarities. *Second Language Research*, 21(3), 199–249.

(2010). Current issues in heritage language acquisition. *Annual Review of Applied Linguistics*, 30, 3–23.

(2011). First language retention and attrition in an adult Guatemalan adoptee. *Interaction and Acquisition*, 2(2), 276–311.

Moon, C., Cooper, R., & Fifer, W. (1993). Two-day-olds prefer their native language. *Infant Behavior and Development*, 16, 495–500.

Moon, C., & Jiang, N. (2012). Nonselective lexical access in different-script bilinguals. *Bilingualism: Language and Cognition*, 15, 173–180.

Mooney, R. (1999). Sensitive periods and circuits for learned birdsong. *Current Opinion in Neurobiology*, 9(1), 121–127.

Morales, J., Calvo, A., & Bialystok, E. (2013). Working memory development in monolingual and bilingual children. *Journal of Experimental Child Psychology*, 114(2) 187–202.

Morales, L., Paolieri, D., Dussias, P., Valdés Kroff, J., Gerfen, C., & Bajo, M. (forthcoming). The gender congruency effect during bilingual spoken-word recognition. *Bilingualism: Language and Cognition.*

Mordkoff, J., & Hazeltine, E. (eds.). (2011). Responding to the Source of Stimulation: J. Richard Simon and the Simon Effect [Special Issue]. *Acta Psychologica*, 136(2).

Moreno, E., Federmeier, K., & Kutas, M. (2002). Switching languages, switching palabras (words): An electrophysiological study of code switching. *Brain and Language*, 80(2), 188–207.

Morford, J., Wilkinson, E., Villwock, A., Piñar, P., & Kroll, J. (2011). When deaf signers read English: Do written words activate their sign translations? *Cognition*, 118, 286–292.

Morgan Short, K., Sanz, C., Steinhauer, K., & Ullman, M. (2010). Second language acquisition of gender agreement in explicit and implicit training conditions: An event-related potential study. *Language Learning*, 60(1), 154–193.

Moriizumi, T., & Hattori, T. (1991). Pallidotectal projection to the inferior colliculus of the rat. *Experimental Brain Research*, 87(1), 223–226.

Morris, J., Frank, T., Grainger, J., & Holcomb, P. J. (2007). Semantic transparency and masked morphological priming: An ERP investigation. *Psychophysiology*, 44, 506–521.

Morris, N., & Jones, D. (1990). Memory updating in working memory: The role of the central executive. *British Journal of Psychology*, 81, 111–121.

Morton, J., & Harper, S. (2007). What did Simon say? Revisiting the bilingual advantage. *Developmental Science*, 10, 719–726.

　(2009). Bilinguals show an advantage in cognitive control: The question is why. *Developmental Science*, 12(4), 502–503.

Morton, J., & Johnson, M. (1991). Conspec and conlern: A two process theory of infant face recognition. *Psychological Review*, 98, 164–181.

Mota, M. (1995). Working memory capacity and L2 fluent speech production. (Unpublished MA dissertation), Universidade Federal de Santa Catarina, Florianopolis, Brazil.

Muysken, P. (1997). Media Lengua. In S. Thompson (ed.), *Contact languages: A wider perspective* (pp. 356–426). Amsterdam/Philadelphia, PA: John Benjamins Publishing.

Myers-Scotton, C. (1988). Swahili-English Nairobi CS corpus.

　(1993a, [1997]). *Duelling languages, grammatical structure in codeswitching*. Oxford, UK: Oxford University Press.

　(1993b). *Social motivations for codeswitching: Evidence from Africa*. Oxford, UK: Oxford University Press.

　(2002a). *Contact linguistics, bilingual encounters and grammatical outcomes*. Oxford, UK: Oxford University Press.

　(2002b). Frequency and intentionality in (un)marked choices in codeswitching: 'This is a 24-hour country.' *International Journal of Bilingualism*, 6, 205–219.

(2004). Xhosa-English bilingual corpus. (Unpublished manuscript), University of South Carolina.

(2005a). Embedded language elements in Acholi/English codeswitching: What's going on? *Language Matters*, 36, 3–18.

(2005b). Supporting a differential access hypothesis: Code switching and other contact data. In J. Kroll & A. de Groot (eds.), *Handbook of bilingualism, psycholinguistic approaches* (pp. 326–358). New York: Oxford University Press.

(2013). Swahili-English Nairobi CS corpus. (Unpublished corpus), Michigan State University, MI.

Myers-Scotton, C. & Jake, J. (1995). Matching lemmas in a bilingual competence and performance model: Evidence from intrasentential code switching. *Linguistics*, 33, 981–1024.

Myers-Scotton, C., & Jake, J. (2000a). Four types of morpheme: Evidence from intrasentential codeswitching. *Linguistics*, 38(6), 1053–1100.

Myers-Scotton, C., & Jake, J. (eds.) (2000b). Testing a model of morpheme classification with language contact data. Special issue: *International Journal of Bilingualism*, 4(1), 1–8.

(2001). Explaining aspects of code-switching and implications. In J. Nichol (ed.), *One mind, two languages: Bilingual language processing* (pp. 84–116). Oxford, MA: Blackwell.

(2009). A universal model of code-switching and bilingual language processing and production. In B. Bullock & A. Toribio (eds.) *The Cambridge handbook of linguistic code-switching* (pp. 336–357). Cambridge, UK: Cambridge University Press.

(2014). Nonfinite verbs and negotiating bilingualism in codeswitching: Implications for a language production model. *Bilingualism: Language and Cognition*, 17(3), 511–525.

Myers-Scotton, C., Jake, J., & Okasha, M. (1996). Arabic and constraints on codeswitching. In M. Eid & D. Parkinson (eds.), *Perspectives on Arabic Linguistics IX: Papers from the Ninth Annual Symposium on Arabic Linguistics* (pp. 9–43). Amsterdam/Philadelphia, PA: John Benjamins Publishing.

Naigles, L. (2012). Not sampling, getting it all. In E. Hoff (ed.), *Research methods in child language: A practical guide* (pp. 240–253). Malden, MA: Wiley-Blackwell.

Nakhleh, L., Ringe, D., & Warnow, T. (2005). Perfect phylogenetic networks: A new methodology for reconstructing the evolutionary history of natural languages. *Language*, 81, 382–420.

Nas, G. (1983). Visual word recognition in bilinguals: Evidence for a cooperation between visual and sound based codes during access to a common lexical store. *Journal of Verbal Learning and Verbal Behavior*, 22, 526–534.

Nazzi, T., Bertoncini, J., & Mehler, J. (1998). Language discrimination by newborns: Toward an understanding of the role of rhythm. *Journal of Experimental Psychology, Human Perception and Performance*, 24, 756–766.

Nazzi, T., Jusczyk, P., & Johnson, E. (2000). Language discrimination by English-learning 5-month-olds: Effects of rhythm and familiarity. *Journal of Memory and Language*, 43, 1–19.

Neely, J., Keefe, D., & Ross, K. (1989). Semantic priming in the lexical decision task: Roles of prospective prime-generated expectancies and retrospective semantic matching. *Journal of Experimental Psychology: Learning, Memory, & Cognition*, 15(6), 1003–1019.

Neisser, U. (1998). Interpreting Harry Bahrick's discovery: What confers immunity against forgetting? *Journal of Experimental Psychology: General*, 113, 32–35.

Nelson, J. R., Balass, M., & Perfetti, C. A. (2005). Differences between written and spoken input in learning new words. *Written Language & Literacy*, 8, 25–44.

Nelson, J. R., Liu, Y., Fiez, J., & Perfetti, C. A. (2009). Assimilation and accommodation patterns in ventral occipitotemporal cortex in learning a second writing system. *Human Brain Mapping*, 30, 810–820.

Nelson, T. (1978). Detecting small amounts of information in memory: Savings for non-recognized items. *Journal of Experimental Psychology: Human Learning and Memory*, 4(5), 453–468.

Neubauer, K., & Clahsen. H. (2009). Decomposition of inflected words in a second language. *Studies in Second Language Acquisition*, 31, 403–435.

Neufeld, G. (1976). The bilingual's lexical store. *ITL Review of Applied Linguistics*, 14, 15–35.

Newmeyer, F. (2006). On Gahl and Garnsey on grammar and usage. *Language*, 82(2), 399–404.

Nicol, J., & Greth, D. (2003). Production of subject–verb agreement in Spanish as a second language. *Experimental Psychology*, 50(3), 196–203.

Nicoladis, E., & Grabois, H. (2002). Learning English and losing Chinese: A case study of a child adopted from China. *International Journal of Bilingualism*, 6, 441–454.

Nilsson, M., Perfilieva, E., Johansson, U., Orwar, O., & Eriksson, P. (1999). Enriched environment increases neurogenesis in the adult rat dentate gyrus and improves spatial memory. *Journal of Neurobiology*, 39(4), 569–578.

Ninio, A. (1999). Pathbreaking verbs in syntactic development and the question of prototypical transitivity. *Journal of Child Language*, 26, 619–653.

Nir-Sagiv, B., Bar-Ilan, L., & Berman, R. (2008). Vocabulary development across adolescence: Text-based analyses. In A. Stavans, & I. Kupferberg (eds.), *Studies in language and language education: Essays in honor of Elite Olshtain* (pp 47–74). Jerusalem: Magnes Press.

Niwa, Y. (2000). Reasoning demands of L2 tasks and L2 narrative production: Effects of individual differences in working memory, intelligence, and aptitude. (Unpublished master's dissertation), Aoyama Gakuin University, Tokyo.

Nixdorf-Bergweiler, B., Wallhäusser-Franke, E., & DeVoogd, T. (1995). Regressive development in neuronal structure during song learning in birds. *Journal of Neurobiology*, 27(2), 204–215.

Noble, K., Norman, M., & Farah, M. (2005). Neurocognitive correlates of socioeconomic status in kindergarten children. *Developmental Science*, 8(1) 74–87.

Norman, D., & Shallice, T. (1980). Attention to action: Willed and automatic control of behavior. Center for Human Information Processing (Technical report No. 99). Reprinted (in revised form) in R. Davidson, G. Schartz, & D. Shapiro (eds.), *Consciousness and self-regulation, advances in research* (pp. 1–18). New York/London: Plenum Press.

Norris, D. (2013). Models of visual word recognition. *Trends in Cognitive Sciences*, 17, 517–524.

Norris, D., McQueen, J., & Cutler, A. (2000). Merging information in speech recognition: Feedback is never necessary. *Behavioral and Brain Sciences*, 23, 299–325.

Nott, C., & Lambert, W. (1968). Free recall of bilinguals. *Journal of Verbal Learning and Verbal Behavior*, 7, 1065–1071.

Novick, J., Hussey, E., Teubner-Rhodes, S., Harbison, J., & Bunting, J. (2014). Clearing the garden-path: Improving sentence processing through cognitive control training. *Language and Cognitive Processes*, 29(2), 186–217.

Novoa, L., Fein, D., & Obler, L. (1988). Talent in foreign languages: A case study. In L. Obler & D. Fein (eds.), *The exceptional brain: Neuropsychology of talent and special abilities* (pp. 294–303). New York: Guilford.

Oatman, L. (1976). Effects of visual attention on the intensity of auditory evoked potentials. *Experimental Neurology*, 51(1), 41–53.

O'Brien, I., Segalowitz, N., Collentine, J., & Freed, B. (2006). Phonological memory and lexical narrative, and grammatical skills in second language oral production by adult learners. *Applied Psycholinguistics*, 27, 377–402.

Ochsner, K., & Gross, J. (2005). The cognitive control of emotion. *Trends in Cognitive Sciences*, 9(5), 242–249.

Ochsner, K., Silvers, J., & Buhle, J. (2012). Functional imaging studies of emotion regulation: A synthetic review and evolving model of the cognitive control of emotion. *Annals of the New York Academy of Sciences*, 1251, E1–24.

Odlin, T. (1989). *Language transfer*. New York: Cambridge University Press.
  (2003). Cross-linguistic influence. In C. Doughty & M. Long (eds.), *The handbook of second language acquisition* (pp. 436–486). Oxford, UK: Blackwell.
  (2008). Conceptual transfer and meaning extensions. In P. Robinson & N. C. Ellis (eds.), *Handbook of cognitive linguistics and second language acquisition* (pp. 306–340). London: Routledge.

Oh, J., Au, T., & Jun, S. (2010). Early childhood language memory in the speech perception of international adoptees. *Journal of Child Language*, 37, 1123–1132.

Oh, J., Jun, S.-A., Knightly, L., & Au, T. (2003). Holding on to childhood language memory. *Cognition*, 86(3), B53–B64.

Okano, K., Grainger, J., & Holcomb, P. J. (2013). An ERP investigation of visual word recognition in syllabary scripts. *Cognitive, Affective, & Behavioral Neuroscience*, 13, 390–404.

Okasha, M. (1998). Arabic–English data. (Unpublished corpus.)
  (1999). Structural constraints on Arabic–English codeswitching: Two generations. (Unpublished doctoral dissertation), University of South Carolina, Columbia.
Onifer, W., & Swinney, D. (1981). Accessing lexical ambiguities during sentence comprehension: Effects of frequency of meaning and contextual bias. *Memory and Cognition*, 9(3), 225–236.
Orfanidou, E., & Sumner, P. (2005). Language switching and the effects of orthographic specificity and response repetition. *Memory & Cognition*, 33, 355–369.
Osgood, C. (1952). The nature and measurement of meaning. *Psychological Bulletin*, 49, 197–237.
Ossher, L., Bialystok, E., Craik, F., Murphy, K., Troyer, A. (2013). The effect of bilingualism on amnestic mild cognitive impairment. *Journals of Gerontology Series B: Psychological Sciences and Social Sciences*, 68, 8–12.
Osterhout, L., & Holcomb, P. (1992). Event-related brain potentials elicited by syntactic anomaly. *Journal of Memory and Language*, 31(6), 785–806.
Osterhout, L., Poliakov, A., Inoue, K., McLaughlin, J., Valentine, G., Pitkanen, I., & Hirschensohn, J. (2008). Second-language learning and changes in the brain. *Journal of Neurolinguistics*, 21(6), 509–521.
Ota, M., Hartsuiker, R., & Haywood, S. (2009). The key to the rock: Near-homophony in nonnative visual word recognition. *Cognition*, 111, 263–269.
Otheguy, R., & Lapidus, N. (2003). An adaptive approach to noun gender in New York contact Spanish. In R. Nuñez-Cedeño & L. López (eds.), *A Romance perspective on language knowledge and use* (pp. 209–229). Amsterdam/Philadelphia, PA: John Benjamins Publishing.
Paap, K. (2014). The role of componential analysis, categorical hypothesising, replicability and confirmation bias in testing for bilingual advantages in executive functioning. *Journal of Cognitive Psychology*, 26(3), 242–255.
Paap, K., & Greenberg, Z. (2013). There is no coherent evidence for a bilingual advantage in executive processing. *Cognitive psychology*, 66, 232–258.
Packard, M., & Knowlton, B. (2002). Learning and memory functions of the basal ganglia. *Annual Review of Neuroscience*, 25(1), 563–593.
Pagani, M., Lombardi, F., Guzzetti, S., et al. (1986). Power spectral analysis of heart rate and arterial pressure variabilities as a marker of sympatho-vagal interaction in man and conscious dog. *Circulation Research*, 59, 178–193.
Paivio, A. (1971). *Imagery and verbal processes*. New York: Holt, Rinehart, & Winston.
Paivio, A., Clark, J., & Lambert, W. (1988). Bilingual dual-coding theory and semantic repetition effects on recall. *Journal of Experimental Psychology: Learning, Memory, and Cognition*, 14, 163–172.

Paivio, A., & Desrochers, A. (1980). A dual-coding approach to bilingual memory. *Canadian Journal of Psychology*, 34, 388–399.

Paivio, A., & Lambert, W. (1981). Dual coding and bilingual memory. *Journal of Verbal Learning and Verbal Behavior*, 20, 532–539.

Pallier, C. (2007). Critical periods in language acquisition and language attrition. In B. Köpke, M. Schmid, M. Keijzer, & S. Dostert (eds.), *Language attrition: Theoretical perspectives* (pp. 99–120). Amsterdam/Philadelphia, PA: John Benjamins Publishing.

Pallier, C., Bosch, L., & Sebastián-Gallés, N. (1997). A limit on behavioral plasticity in speech perception. *Cognition*, 64, B9–B17.

Pallier, C., Colomé, A., & Sebastián-Gallés, N. (2001). The influence of native-language phonology on lexical access: Exemplar-based versus abstract lexical entries. *Psychological Science*, 12, 445–449.

Pallier, C., Dehaene, S., Poline, J.-B., et al. (2003). Brain imaging of language plasticity in adopted adults: Can a second language replace the first? *Cerebral Cortex*, 13(2), 155–161.

Palmer, A. (1979). Compartmentalized and integrated control: An assessment of some evidence for two kinds of competence and implications for the classroom. *Language Learning*, 29(1), 169–180.

Panayiotou, A. (2004). Switching codes, switching code: Bilinguals' emotional responses in English and Greek. *Journal of Multilingual and Multicultural Development*, 25, 124–139.

Paolicelli, R., Bolasco, G., Pagani, F., et al. (2011). Synaptic pruning by microglia is necessary for normal brain development. *Science*, 333 (6048), 1456–1458.

Papadopoulou, D., & Clahsen, H. (2003). Parsing strategies in L1 and L2 sentence processing. *Studies in Second Language Acquisition*, 25(4), 501–528.

Papagno, C., & Vallar, G. (1995). Verbal short-term memory and vocabulary learning in polyglots. *The Quarterly Journal of Experimental Psychology*, 48, 98–107.

Paradis, J., Genesee, F., & Crago, M. (2010). *Dual language development and disorders: A handbook on bilingualism and second language learning*. Baltimore: Brookes.

Paradis, M. (1978). The stratification of bilingualism. In M. Paradis (ed.), *Aspects of bilingualism* (pp. 165–176). Columbia, SC: Hornbeam Press.

(1987). Neurolinguistic perspectives on bilingualism. In M. Paradis & G. Libben (eds.), *The assessment of bilingual aphasia* (pp. 1–17). Hillsdale, NJ: Lawrence Erlbaum.

(1997). The cognitive neuropsychology of bilingualism. In A. de Groot & J. Kroll (eds.), *Tutorials in bilingualism. Psycholinguistic perspectives* (pp. 331–354). Mahwah, NJ: Lawrence Erlbaum.

(2002). The bilingual Loch Ness Monster raises its non-asymmetric head again – or, why bother with such cumbersome notions as validity and reliability? Comments on Evans et al. (2002). *Brain and Language*, 87, 441–448.

(2007). L1 attrition features predicted by a neurolinguistic theory of bilingualism. In B. Köpke, M. Schmid, M. Keijzer, & S. Dostert (eds.), *Language attrition: Theoretical perspectives* (pp. 121–133). Amsterdam/Philadelphia, PA: John Benjamins Publishing.

Paradis, M., & Libben, G. (1987). *The assessment of bilingual aphasia*. Hillsdale, NJ: Lawrence Erlbaum Associates.

Park, D., & Reuter-Lorenz, P. (2009). The adaptive brain: Aging and neurocognitive scaffolding. *Annual Review of Psychology*, 60, 173–196.

Parker Jones, O., Green, D., Grogan, A., et al. (2012). Where, when and why brain activation differs for bilinguals and monolinguals during picture naming and reading aloud. *Cerebral Cortex*, 22, 892–902.

Pashler, H., Bain, P., Bottge, B., Graesser, A., Koedinger, K., McDaniel, M., & Metcalfe, J. (2007). *Organizing instruction and study to improve student learning (NCER 2007-2004)*. Washington, DC: National Center for Education Research, Institute of Education Sciences, U.S. Department of Education.

Patel, A. (1998). Syntactic processing in language and music: different cognitive operations, similar neural resources? *Music Perception*, 16(1), 27–42.

Patterson, J. (2000). Observed and reported expressive vocabulary and word combinations in bilingual toddlers. *Journal of Speech, Language and Hearing Research*, 43, 121–1288.

(2004). Comparing bilingual and monolingual toddlers' expressive vocabulary size: Revisiting Rescorla & Achenbach (2002). *Journal of Speech, Language and Hearing Research*, 47(5), 1213–1215.

Paulesu, E., McCrory, E., Fazio, F., Menoncello, L., Brunswick, N., Cappa, S. F., & Frith, U. (2000). A cultural effect on brain function. *Nature Neuroscience*, 3, 91–96.

Pavlenko, A. (1999). New approaches to concepts in bilingual memory. *Bilingualism: Language and Cognition*, 2, 209–230.

Pavlenko, A. (2005a). Bilingualism and thought. In J. Kroll & A. de Groot (eds.), *Handbook of bilingualism: Psycholinguistic approaches* (pp. 433–453). Oxford, UK: Oxford University Press.

(2005b). *Emotions and multilingualism*. New York: Cambridge University Press.

(2008). Emotion and emotion-laden words in the bilingual lexicon. *Bilingualism: Language and Cognition*, 11, 147–164.

(2009). Conceptual representation in the bilingual lexicon and second language vocabulary learning. In A. Pavlenko (ed.), *The bilingual mental lexicon: Interdisciplinary approaches* (pp. 125–160). Clevedon, UK: Multilingual Matters.

(2012). Affective processing in bilingual speakers: Disembodied cognition? *International Journal of Psychology*, 47, 405–428.

Pavlenko, A., & Driagina, A. (2007). Russian emotion vocabulary in American learners' narratives. *Modern Language Journal*, 91, 213–234.

Pavlenko, A., & Malt, B. (2011). Kitchen Russian: Crosslinguistic differences and first language object naming by Russian-English bilinguals. *Bilingualism: Language and Cognition*, 14, 19-45.

Pavlik, P., & Anderson, J. (2005). Practice and forgetting effects on vocabulary memory. *Cognitive Science*, 29, 559-586.

Peal, E., & Lambert, W. (1962). The relation of bilingualism to intelligence. *Psychological Monographs: General and Applied*, 76, 1-23.

Pearlmutter, N., & Gibson, E. (2001). Recency in verb phrase attachment. *Journal of Experimental Psychology: Learning, Memory, and Cognition*, 27(2), 574-590.

Pearson, B. (1998). Assessing lexical development in bilingual babies and toddlers. *International Journal of Bilingualism*, 2(3), 347-372.

(2008). *Raising a bilingual child*. New York, NY: Random House.

Pearson, B., Fernández, S., & Oller, D. (1993). Lexical development in bilingual infants and toddlers: Comparison to monolingual norms. *Language Learning*, 43(1), 93-120.

(1995). Cross-language synonyms in the lexicons of bilingual infants: One language or two? *Journal of Child Language*, 22(2), 345-368.

Peeters, D., Dijkstra, T., & Grainger, J. (2013). The representation and processing of identical cognates by late bilinguals: RT and ERP effects. *Journal of Memory and Language*, 68(4), 315-332.

Pelham, S., & Abrams, L. (2014). Cognitive advantages and disadvantages in early and late bilinguals. *Journal of Experimental Psychology: Learning, Memory and Cognition*, 40, 313-325.

Peltola, M., Kujala, T., Tuomainen, J., Ek, M., Aaltonen, O., & Näätänen, R. (2003). Native and foreign vowel discrimination as indexed by the mismatch negativity (MMN) response. *Neuroscience Letters*, 352(1), 25-28.

Peltola, M., Tamminen, H., Toivonen, H., Kujala, T., & Näätänen, R. (2012). Different kinds of bilinguals - Different kinds of brains: The neural organisation of two languages in one brain. *Brain and Language*, 121(3), 261-266.

Penfield, W. (1950). *The physical basis of mind*. Oxford, UK: Basil Blackwell.

Penfield, W., & Roberts, L. (1959). *Speech and brain mechanisms*. Princeton, NJ: Princeton University Press.

Peng, C., Havlin, S., Hausdorff, J., Mietus, J., Stanley, H., & Goldberger, A. (1995). Fractal mechanisms and heart rate dynamics: Long-range correlations and their breakdown with disease. *Journal of Electrocardiology*, 28, 59-65.

Perdue, C. (ed.). (1993). *Adult language acquisition: Crosslinguistic perspectives*. Cambridge, UK: Cambridge University Press.

Perea, M., & Lupker, S. J. (2003). Transposed-letter confusability effects in masked form priming. In S. Kinoshita & S. Lupker (eds.), *Masked priming: State of the art* (pp. 97-120). Hove, UK: Psychology Press.

Perea, M., & Pollatsek, A. (1998). The effects of neighborhood frequency in reading and lexical decision. *Journal of Experimental Psychology: Human Perception and Performance*, 24, 767-779.

Perea, M., & Rosa, E. (2000). The effects of orthographic neighborhood in reading and laboratory word identification tasks: A review. *Psicológica*, 21, 327–340.

Perea, M., Duñabeitia, J., & Carreiras, M. (2008). Masked associative/semantic priming effects across languages with highly proficient bilinguals. *Journal of Memory and Language*, 58, 916–930.

Perea, M., Nakatani, C., & van Leeuwen, C. (2011). Transposition effects in reading Japanese Kana: Are they orthographic in nature? *Memory & Cognition*, 39, 700–707.

Pérez-Leroux, A., & Glass, W. (1999). Null anaphora in Spanish second language acquisition: Probabilistic versus generative approaches. *Second Language Research*, 15, 220–249.

Perfetti, C. A. (2007). Reading ability: Lexical quality to comprehension. *Scientific Studies of Reading*, 11(4), 357–383.

Perfetti, C. A., Liu, Y., Fiez, J., Nelson, J., Bolger, D. J., & Tan, L. M. (2007). Reading in two writing systems: Accommodation and assimilation of the brain's reading network. *Bilingualism: Language and Cognition*, 10, 131–146.

Perfetti, C. A., Liu, Y., & Tan, L. H. (2005). The lexical constituency model: Some implications of research on Chinese for general theories of reading. *Psychological Review*, 112, 43–59.

Perziosa-Di Quinzio, I. (1992). *Teoreticamente la firma la indietro: Frammisitione di Italiano e Schwyzertötsch nella convesazione di figli di emigrati*. Universitá di Zurigo, Facoltá di Lettere e di Filosofia: Vavoro di licenza in linguistica italiana.

Petersen, J. (1988). Word-internal code-switching constraints in a bilingual child's grammar. *Linguistics*, 26(3), 479–494.

Petit, J.-P., Midgley, K., Holcomb, P. J., & Grainger, J. (2006). On the time course of letter perception: A masked priming ERP investigation. *Psychonomic Bulletin & Review*, 13, 674–681.

Petitto, L., Berens, M., Kovelman, I., Dubins, M., Jasinska, K., & Shalinsky, M. (2011). The "Perceptual Wedge Hypothesis" as the basis for bilingual babies' phonetic processing advantage: New insights from fNIRS brain imaging. *Brain and Language*, 121(2), 1–14.

Pexman, P., & Lupker, S. (1999). Ambiguity and visual word recognition: Can feedback explain both homophone and polysemy effects? *Canadian Journal of Experimental Psychology*, 53(4), 323–334.

Peyer, E., Kaiser, I., & Berthele, R. (2010). The multilingual reader: Advantages in understanding and decoding German sentence structure when reading German as an L3. *International Journal of Multilingualism*, 7, 225–239.

Pfaff, C. (1979). Constraints on language mixing: Intrasentential code-switching and borrowing in Spanish/English. *Language*, 55(2), 291–318.

Philipp, A., Gade, M., & Koch, I. (2007). Inhibitory processes in language switching: Evidence from switching language-defined response sets. *European Journal of Cognitive Psychology*, 19, 395–416.

Philipp, A., & Koch, I. (2006). Task inhibition and task repetition in task switching. *European Journal of Cognitive Psychology*, 18(4), 624–639.

(2009). Inhibition in language switching: What is inhibited when switching between languages in naming tasks? *Journal of Experimental Psychology: Learning, Memory, and Cognition*, 35, 1187–1195.

Phillips, E. (1992). The effects of language anxiety on students' oral test performance and attitudes. *Modern Language Journal*, 76, 14–26.

Piaget, J. (1954). *The construction of reality in the child* (M. Cook, trans.). New York: Basic Books.

(1970). *Genetic epistemology* (E. Duckworth, trans.). New York: Columbia University Press.

Pickering, M., & Branigan, H. (1998). The representation of verbs: Evidence from syntactic priming in language production. *Journal of Memory and Language*, 39(4), 633–651.

Pierce, L., Klien, D., Chen, J.-K., Delcenscrie, A., & Geuessee, F. (2014). Mapping the unconscious maintenance of a lost first language. *Proceedings of the National Academy of Sciences*, 111(48), 17314–17319.

Pierrehumbert, J. (2001). Exemplar dynamics: Word frequency, lenition and contrast. In J. Bybee & P. Hopper (eds.), *Frequency and the emergence of linguistic structure* (pp. 137–157). Amsterdam/Philadelphia, PA: John Benjamins Publishing.

Pinker, S. (1989). *Learnability and cognition: The acquisition of argument structure*. Cambridge, MA: Bradford Books.

Pisoni, D., & Cleary, M. (2004). Learning, memory, and cognitive processes in deaf children following cochlear implantation. In F. Zeng, A. Popper, & R. Fay (eds.), *Springer Handbook of Auditory Research* (pp. 377–426). New York: Springer.

Pivneva, I., Mercier, J., & Titone, D. (2014). Executive control modulates cross-language lexical activation during L2 reading: Evidence from eye movements. *Journal of Experimental Psychology: Learning, Memory and Cognition*, 40(3), 787–796.

Place, S., & Hoff, E. (2010). Properties of dual language exposure that influence two-year-olds' bilingual proficiency. *Child Development*, 82(6), 1834–1849.

Plat, R., Lowie, W., & de Bot, K. (under review). L2 word naming and semantic processing: A Dynamic Systems Approach.

Plaut, D. C. (1997). Structure and function in the lexical system: Insights from distributed models of word reading and lexical decision. *Language and Cognitive Processes*, 12, 767–808.

Plaut, D. C., McClelland, J. L., Seidenberg, M. S., & Patterson, K. (1996). Understanding normal and impaired word reading: Computational principles in quasi-regular domains. *Psychological Review*, 103, 56–115.

Pliatsikas, C., & Marinis, T. (2013). Processing empty categories in a second language: When naturalistic exposure fills the (intermediate) gap. *Bilingualism: Language and Cognition*, 16(1), 167–182.

Plunkett, K., & Elman, J. (1997). *Exercises in rethinking innateness: A handbook for connectionist simulations.* Cambridge, MA: MIT Press.

Poarch, G., & van Hell, J. (2012). Cross-language activation in children's speech production: Evidence from second language learners, bilinguals, and trilinguals. *Journal of Experimental Child Psychology*, 111, 419–438.

Poeppel, D., Idsardi, W., & van Wassenhove, V. (2008). Speech perception at the interface of neurobiology and linguistics. *Philosophical Transactions of the Royal Society*, 363, 1071–1086.

Polivanov, E. (1931). La perception des sons d'une langue étrangère (The perception of the sounds of a foreign language). *Travaux du Cercle Linguistique de Prague*, 4, 79–96.

Popiel, S. (1987). Bilingual comparative judgments: Evidence against the switch hypothesis. *Journal of Psycholinguistic Research*, 16, 563–576.

Poplack, S. (1980). Sometimes I'll start a sentence in Spanish y termino en español: Toward a typology of code-switching. *Linguistics*, 18(7), 581–618.

Poplack, S., & Meechan, M. (eds.). (1998). How languages fit together in codemixing. *International Journal of Bilingualism*, 2, 127–138.

Port, R., & van Gelder, T. (1995). *Mind as motion: Exploration in the dynamics of cognition.* Cambridge, MA: Bradford.

Portin, M., Lehtonen, M., Harrer, G., Wande, E., Niemi, J., & Laine, M. (2008). L1 effects on the processing of inflected nouns in L2. *Acta Psychologica*, 128(3), 452–465.

Portin, M., Lehtonen, M., & Laine, M. (2007). Processing of inflected nouns in late bilinguals. *Applied Psycholinguistics*, 28(1), 135–56.

Posner, M. (1978). *Chronometric explorations of mind.* New York: Oxford University Press.

Posner, M., & Keele, S. (1970). Retention of abstract ideas. *Journal of Experimental Psychology*, 83, 304–308.

Posner, M., & Petersen, S. (1990). The attention system of the human brain. *Annual Review of Neuroscience*, 13, 25–42.

Posner, M., & Raichle, M. (1994). *Images of mind.* New York: Scientific American Library/Scientific American Books.

Postman, W. (2004). Processing of complex sentences in a case of aphasia in Indonesian: Thematic vs. linear strategies. *Journal of Neurolinguistics*, 17(6), 455–489.

Potts, R., & Shanks, D. (2012). Can testing immunize memories against interference? *Journal of Experimental Psychology: Learning, Memory, and Cognition*, 38, 1780–1785.

Potzl, O. (1983). Aphasia and multilingualism. In M. Paradis (ed.), *Readings on aphasia in bilinguals and polyglots* (pp. 301–316). Montreal: Marcel Didier.

Poulin-Dubois, D., Bialystok, E., Blaye, A., Polonia, A., & Yott, J. (2012). Lexical access and vocabulary development in very young bilinguals. *International Journal of Bilingualism*, 17(1), 1–15.

Poulin-Dubois, D., Blaye, A., Coutya, J., & Bialystok, E. (2011). The effects of bilingualism on toddlers' executive functioning. *Journal of Experimental Child Psychology*, 108(3), 567–579.

Poulisse, N., & Bongaerts, T. (1994). First language use in second language production. *Applied Linguistics*, 15(1), 36–57.

Preston, D. (1996). Variationist perspectives on second language acquisition. In R. Bayley & D. Preston (eds.), *Second language acquisition and linguistic variation* (pp. 1–45). Amsterdam/Philadelphia, PA: John Benjamins Publishing.

  (2002). A variationist perspective on second language acquisition. In R. Kaplan (ed.), *The Oxford handbook of applied linguistics* (pp. 141–159). Oxford, UK: Oxford University Press.

Preston, M., & Lambert, W. (1969). Interlingual interference in a bilingual version of the Stroop color-word task. *Journal of Verbal Learning and Verbal Behavior*, 8, 295–301.

Price, C., Green, D., & Von Studnitz, R. (1999). A functional imaging study of translation and language switching. *Brain*, 122, 2221–2235.

Price, M. (1991). The subjective experience of foreign language anxiety: Interviews with highly anxious students. In D. Young & E. Horwitz (eds.), *Language anxiety: From theory and research to classroom implications* (pp. 101–108). Englewood Cliffs, NJ: Prentice Hall.

Prior, A., & Gollan, T. (2011). Good language-switchers are good task-switchers: Evidence from Spanish-English and Mandarin-English bilinguals. *Journal of the International Neuropsychological Society*, 17(4), 682–691.

Prior, A., Kroll, J. F., & MacWhinney, B. (2013). Translation ambiguity but not word class predicts translation performance. *Bilingualism: Language and Cognition*, 16, 458–474.

Prior, A., & MacWhinney, B. (2010). A bilingual advantage in task switching. *Bilingualism: Language and Cognition*, 13, 253–262.

Prior, A., MacWhinney, B., & Kroll, J. F. (2007). Translation norms for English and Spanish: The role of lexical variables, word class, and L2 proficiency in negotiating translation ambiguity. *Behavior Research Methods*, 39, 1029–1038.

Pritchett, B. (1992). *Grammatical competence and parsing performance*. Chicago, IL: University of Chicago Press.

Proverbio, A. A., Adorni, R., & Zani, A. (2009). Inferring native language from early bio-electrical activity. *Biological Psychology*, 80, 52–63.

Proverbio, A. A., Čok, B., & Zani, A. (2002). Electrophysiological measures of language processing in bilinguals. *Journal of Cognitive Neuroscience*, 14, 994–1017.

Proverbio, A. A., Leoni, G., & Zani, A. (2004). Language switching mechanisms in simultaneous interpreters: An ERP study. *Neuropsychologia*, 42(12), 1636–1656.

Pulido, D. (2003). Modeling the role of second language proficiency and topic familiarity in second language incidental vocabulary acquisition through reading. *Language Learning*, 53, 233–284.

Pulvermüller, F. (2003). *The neuroscience of language: On brain circuits of words and serial order*. Cambridge, MA: Cambridge University Press.

(2005). Brain mechanisms linking language and action. *Nature Reviews Neuroscience*, 6, 576–582.

Pulvermüller, F., & Fadiga, L. (2010). Active perception: Sensorimotor circuits as a cortical basis for language. *Nature Reviews Neuroscience*, 11, 351–360.

Puntoni, S., de Langhe, B., & van Osselaer, S. (2009). Bilingualism and the emotional intensity of advertising language. *Journal of Consumer Research*, 35, 1012–1025.

Qin, J. (2008). The effect of processing instruction and dictogloss tasks on acquisition of the English passive voice. *Language Teaching Research*, 12, 61–82.

Quay, S. (2001). Managing linguistic boundaries in early trilingual development. In J. Cenoz & F. Genesee (eds.), *Trends in bilingual acquisition* (pp. 149–199). Amsterdam/Philadelphia, PA: John Benjamins Publishing.

Rah, A. (2010). Transfer in L3 sentence processing: Evidence from relative clause attachment ambiguities. *International Journal of Multilingualism*, 7, 147–161.

Raizada, R., & Poldrack, R. (2007). Challenge-driven attention: interacting frontal and brainstem systems. *Frontiers in Human Neuroscience*, 1(3), 1–8.

Rajagopal, M., Holland, S., Walz, N., Staat, M., Altaye, M., & Wade, S. (2013). A functional magnetic resonance imaging study of language function in international adoptees. *Journal of Pediatrics*, 163(5), 1458–1464.

Rakic, P., Bourgeois, J.-P., & Goldman-Rakic, P. (1994). Synaptic development of the cerebral cortex: implications for learning, memory, and mental illness. *Progress in Brain Research*, 102, 227–243.

Ramon-Casas, M., & Bosch, L. (2010). Are non-cognate words phonologically better specified than cognates in the early lexicon of bilingual children? *Selected Proceedings of the 4th Conference on Laboratory Approaches to Spanish Phonology*, 31–36.

Ramon-Casas, M., Swingley, D., Sebastián-Gallés, N., & Bosch, L. (2009). Vowel categorization during word recognition in bilingual toddlers. *Cognitive Psychology*, 59, 96–121.

Ramus, F., Hauser, M., Miller, C., Morris, D., & Mehler, J. (2000). Language discrimination by human newborns and by cotton-top tamarin monkeys. *Science*, 288, 349–351.

Ransdell, S., & Fischler, I. (1987). Memory in a monolingual mode: When are bilinguals at a disadvantage? *Journal of Memory and Language*, 26(4), 392–405.

Rastle, K., & Davis, M. (2008). Morphological decomposition based on the analysis of orthography. *Language and Cognitive Processes*, 23, 942–971.

Rayner, K. (1997). Understanding eye movements in reading. *Scientific Studies of Reading*, 1(4), 317–339.

  (1998). Eye movements in reading and information processing: 20 years of research. *Psychological Bulletin*, 124(3), 372.

Rayner, K., & Duffy, S. (1986). Lexical complexity and fixation times in reading: Effects of word frequency, verb complexity, and lexical ambiguity. *Memory & Cognition*, 14, 191–201.

Rayner, K., Pacht, J., & Duffy, S. (1994). Effects of prior encounter and global discourse bias on the processing of lexically ambiguous words. *Journal of Memory and Language*, 33, 527–544.

Raz, N. (2000). Aging of the brain and its impact on cognitive performance: Integration of structural and functional findings. In F. Craik & T. Salthouse (eds.), *The handbook of aging and cognition* (2nd edn) (pp. 1–90). Mahwah, NJ: Erlbaum.

Rebuschat, P., & Williams, J. (eds.). (2012). *Statistical learning and language acquisition*. Berlin: Mouton de Gruyter.

Redgrave, P., Prescott, T., & Gurney, K. (1999). The basal ganglia: A vertebrate solution to the selection problem? *Neuroscience*, 89(4), 1009–1023.

Redouane, R. (2005). Linguistic constraints on codeswitching and codemixing of bilingual Moroccan Arabic–French speakers in Canada. In J. Cohen, K. McAlister, K. Rolsted, & J. MacSwan (eds.), *Proceedings of the 4th International Symposium on Bilingualism* (pp. 1921–1933). Somerville, MA: Cascadilla Press.

Regan, V. (2013). Variation. In J. Herschensohn & M. Young-Scholten (eds.), *The Cambridge handbook of second language acquisition* (pp. 272–291). Cambridge, UK: Cambridge University Press.

Reitan, R. (1958). Validity of the Trail Making Test as an indicator of organic brain damage. *Perceptual and Motor Skills*, 8, 271–276.

Reiterer, S., Hu, X., Erb, M., Rota, G., Nardo, D., Grodd, W., & Ackermann, H. (2011). Individual differences in audio-vocal speech imitation aptitude in late bilinguals: Functional neuro-imaging and brain morphology. *Frontiers in Psychology*, 2, 271.

Rescorla, R., & Wagner, A. (1972). A theory of Pavlovian conditioning: Variations in the effectiveness of reinforcement and nonreinforcement. In A. Black & W. Prokasy (eds.), *Classical conditioning II: Current theory and research* (pp. 64–99). New York: Appleton-Century-Crofts.

Ressel, V., Pallier, C., Ventura-Campos, N., et al. (2012). An effect of bilingualism on the auditory cortex. *Journal of Neuroscience*, 32(47), 16597–16601.

Rey, A., Dufau, S., Massol, S., & Grainger, J. (2009). Testing computational models of letter perception with item-level event-related potentials. *Cognitive Neuropsychology*, 26, 7–22.

Rhodes, T., & Turvey, M. (2007). Human memory retrieval as Lévy foraging. *Physica A: Statistical Mechanics and its Applications*, 385(1), 255–260.

Ricciardelli, L. (1992). Bilingualism and cognitive development in relation to threshold theory. *Journal of Psycholinguistic Research*, 21, 301–16.

Richardson, D., & Dale, R. (2005). Looking to understand: The coupling between speakers' and listeners' eye movements and its relationship to discourse comprehension. *Cognitive Science*, 29(6), 1045–1060.

Richardson, D., Dale, R., & Kirkham, N. (2007). The art of conversation is coordination common ground and the coupling of eye movements during dialogue. *Psychological Science*, 18(5), 407–413.

Richardson, D., Dale, R., & Spivey, M. (2007). Eye movements in language and cognition: A brief introduction. In M. Gonzalez-Marquez, S. Coulson, I. Mittelberg, & M. Spivey (eds.), *Methods in cognitive linguistics* (pp. 323–344). Amsterdam/Philadelphia, PA: John Benjamins Publishing.

Richardson, F. M., Seghier, M. L., Leff, A. P., Thomas, M. S. C., & Price, C. J. (2011). Multiple routes from occipital to temporal cortices during reading. *Journal of Neuroscience*, 31, 8239–8247.

Richter, F., & Yeung, N. (2012). Memory and cognitive control in task switching. *Psychological Science*, 23(10), 1256–1263.

Ringbom, H. (2001). Lexical transfer in L3 production. In J. Cenoz, B. Hufeisen, & U. Jessner (eds.), *Cross-linguistic influence in third language acquisition: Psycholinguistic perspective* (pp. 59–68). Clevedon, UK: Multilingual Matters.

(2007). *Cross-linguistic similarity in foreign language learning*. Clevedon, UK: Multilingual Matters.

Rinne, T., Balk, M., Koistinen, S., Autti, T., Alho, K., & Sams, M. (2008). Auditory selective attention modulates activation of human inferior colliculus. *Journal of Neurophysiology*, 100(6), 3323–3327.

Ritter, H., & Kohonen, T. (1989). Self-organizing semantic maps. *Biological Cybernetics*, 61, 241–254.

Rivers, W. (1996). Self-directed language learning and third language learner. Retrieved from: http://eric.ed.gov/?id=ED411679.

Rivers, W., & Golonka, E. (2009). Third language acquisition theory and practice. In M. Long & C. Doughty (eds.), *The handbook of language teaching* (pp. 250–266). Oxford, UK: Blackwell.

Roberson, D., Davies I., & Davidoff, J. (2000). Colour categories are not universal: Replications and new evidence from a Stone-Age culture. *Journal of Experimental Psychology: General*, 129, 369–398.

Robinson, P. (2001). Individual differences: Cognitive abilities, aptitude complexes and learning conditions in second language acquisition. *Second Language Research*, 17, 368–392.

(2005). Aptitude and second language acquisition. *Annual Review of Applied Linguistics*, 25, 45–73.

(2007). Task complexity, theory of mind, and intentional reasoning: Effects on L2 speech production, interaction, uptake and perceptions of task difficulty. *International Review of Applied Linguistics*, 45, 237–257.

Robinson, P., & Ellis, N. (2008b). Conclusion: Cognitive linguistics, second language acquisition and L2 instruction – Issues for research. In P. Robinson & N. Ellis (eds.), *Handbook of cognitive linguistics and second language acquisition* (pp. 489–546). London: Routledge.

Robinson, P., & Ellis, N. (eds.) (2008a). *A handbook of cognitive linguistics and second language acquisition*. London: Routledge.

Rodd, J., Gaskell, G., & Marslen Wilson, W. (2002). Making sense of semantic ambiguity: Semantic competition in lexical access. *Journal of Memory and Language*, 46(2), 245–266.

Rodríguez Festman, J., Rodríguez-Fornells, A., & Münte, T. (2008). Performance accuracy affected by control over bilingual language production: A study of balanced L2 users. In S. Van Daele, A. Housen, F. Kuiken, et al. (eds.), *Complexity, accuracy and fluency in second language use, learning & teaching* (pp. 65–76). Amsterdam/Philadelphia, PA: John Benjamins Publishing.

Rodríguez-Fornells, A., Kramer, U., Lorenzo-Seva, U., Festman, J., & Munte, T. (2011). Self-assessment of individual differences in language switching. *Frontiers in Psychology*, 2, 388.

Rodríguez-Fornells, A., Rotte, M., Heinze, H. J., Nösselt, T., & Münte, T. F. (2002). Brain potential and functional MRI evidence for how to handle two languages with one brain. *Nature*, 415, 1026–1029.

Rodríguez-Fornells, A., Van der Lugt, A., Rotte, M., Britti, B., Heinze, H.-J., & Münte, T. (2005). Second language interferes with word production in fluent bilinguals: Brain potential and functional imaging evidence. *Journal of Cognitive Neuroscience*, 17, 422–433.

Roediger, H., & Butler, A. (2011). The critical role of retrieval practice in long-term retention. *Trends in Cognitive Sciences*, 15, 20–27.

Roelofs, A. (1992). A spreading-activation theory of lemma retrieval in speaking. *Cognition*, 42, 107–142.

Roelofs, A. (2010). Attention and facilitation: Converging information versus inadvertent reading in Stroop task performance. *Journal of Experimental Psychology: Learning, Memory, and Cognition*, 36, 411–422.

Rogalsky, C., & Hickok, G. (2011). The role of Broca's area in sentence comprehension. *Journal of Cognitive Neuroscience*, 23(7), 1664–1680.

Rogers, R., & Monsell, S. (1995). Costs of a predictable switch between simple cognitive tasks. *Journal of Experimental Psychology: Learning, Memory, and Cognition*, 31, 1477–1491.

Römer, U., O'Donnell, M., & Ellis, N. (2013). Using COBUILD grammar patterns for a large-scale analysis of verb–argument constructions: Exploring corpus data and speaker knowledge. In M. Charles, N. Groom, & S. John (eds.), *Corpora, grammar, text and discourse: In*

*Honour of Susan Hunston.* Amsterdam/Philadelphia, PA: John Benjamins Publishing.

(2014). Second language learner knowledge of verb–argument constructions: Effects of language transfer and typology. *Modern Language Journal*, 98(4), 952–975.

Ronjat, J. (1913). *Le développement du langage observé chez un enfant bilingue*. Paris: Champion.

Rosch, E., & Mervis, C. (1975a). Family resemblances: Studies in the internal structure of categories. *Cognitive Psychology*, 7(4), 573–605.

(1975b). Cognitive representations of semantic categories. *Journal of Experimental Psychology: General*, 104, 192–233.

Rosch, E., Mervis, C., Gray, W., Johnson, D., & Boyes-Braem, P. (1976). Basic objects in natural categories. *Cognitive Psychology*, 8, 382–439.

Rose, R., & Carroll, J. (1974). Free recall of mixed language list. *Bulletin of the Psychonomic Society*, 3, 267–268.

Rossell, S., & Nobre, A. (2004). Semantic priming of different affective categories. *Emotion*, 4(4), 354–363.

Rossion, B., Joyce, C. A., Cottrell, G. W., & Tarr, M. J. (2003). Early lateralization and orientation tuning for face, word, and object processing in the visual cortex. *NeuroImage*, 20, 1609–1624.

Rothman, J. (2010). On the typological economy of syntactic transfer: Word order and relative clause high/low attachment preference in L3 Brazilian Portuguese. *IRAL*, 48, 245–273.

(2011). L3 syntactic transfer selectivity and typological determinacy: The typological primacy model. *Second Language Research*, 27, 107–127.

Rousselet, G., Macé, M. J. M., & Fabre-Thorpe, M. (2004). Animal and human faces in natural scenes: How specific to human faces is the N170 ERP component? *Journal of Vision*, 4, 13–21.

Ruben, R. (1997). A time frame of critical/sensitive periods of language development. *Acta Oto-Laryngologica*, 117(2), 202–205.

Rubin, O., & Meiran, N. (2005). On the origins of the task mixing cost in the cuing task-switching paradigm. *Journal of Experimental Psychology: Learning, Memory, and Cognition*, 31(6), 1477–1491.

Rueda, M., Fan, J., McCandliss, B., et al. (2004). Development of attentional networks in childhood. *Neuropsychologia*, 42(8), 1029–1040.

Ruh, N., & Westermann, G. (2009a). Simulating German verb inflection with a constructivist neural network. In J. Mayor, N. Ruh, & K. Plunkett (eds.), *Connectionist models of behavior and cognition* (pp. 313–324). London: World Scientific.

(2009b). OXlearn: A new MATLAB-based simulation tool for connectionist models. *Behavior Research Methods, Instruments & Computers*, 41, 1138–1143.

Rumelhart, D. (1989). The architecture of mind: A connectionist approach. In M. Posner (ed.), *Foundations of cognitive science* (pp. 133–154). Cambridge, MA: MIT Press.

Rumelhart, D., Hinton, G., & Williams, R. (1986). Learning internal representations by error propagation. In D. Rumelhart, J. McClelland, & the PDP Research Group (eds.), *Parallel distributed processing: explorations in the microstructures of cognition* (pp. 318–362). Cambridge, MA: MIT Press.

Rumelhart, D., McClelland, J., & the PDP Research Group (eds.). (1986). *Parallel distributed processing: Explorations in the microstructure of cognition.* Vol. 1, *foundations*. Cambridge, MA: MIT Press.

Runnqvist, E., & Costa, A. (2012). Is retrieval-induced forgetting behind the bilingual disadvantage in word production? *Bilingualism: Language and Cognition*, 15(2), 365–377.

Runnqvist, E., Gollan, T., Costa, A., Ferreira, V. (2013). A disadvantage in bilingual sentence production modulated by syntactic frequency and similarity across languages. *Cognition*, 129, 256–63.

Rüschemeyer, S.-A., Zysset, S., & Friederici, A. D. (2006). Native and non-native reading of sentences: An fMRI experiment. *NeuroImage*, 31, 354–365.

Ruz, M., & Nobre, A. C. (2008). Attention modulates initial stages of visual word processing. *Journal of Cognitive Neuroscience*, 20, 1727–1736.

Sabourin, L., & Stowe, L. (2008). Second language processing: When are first and second languages processed similarly? *Second Language Research*, 24(3), 397–430.

Saegert, J., Kazarian, S., & Young, R. (1973). Part/whole transfer with bilinguals. *The American Journal of Psychology*, 86, 537–546.

Saegert, J., Obermeyer, J., & Kazarian, S. (1973). Organizational factors in free recall of bilingually mixed lists. *Journal of Experimental Psychology*, 97, 397–399.

Saer, D. (1923). The effects of bilingualism on intelligence. *British Journal of Psychology*, 14, 25–38.

Sakai, M., & Suga, N. (2001). Plasticity of the cochleotopic (frequency) map in specialized and nonspecialized auditory cortices. *Proceedings of the National Academy of Science*, 98(6), 3507–3512.

Sakurai, Y., Momose, T., Iwata, M., Sudo, Y., Ohtomo, K., & Kanazawa, I. (2000). Different cortical activity in reading of Kanji words, Kana words and Kana nonwords. *Cognitive Brain Research*, 9, 111–115.

Salaberry, M. (1997). The role of input and output practice in second language acquisition. *Canadian Modern Language Review*, 53, 422–451.

Salamoura, A., & Williams, J. (2007). Processing verb argument structure across languages: Evidence for shared representations in the bilingual lexicon. *Applied Psycholinguistics*, 28, 627.

Salvatierra, J., & Rosselli, M. (2011). The effect of bilingualism and age on inhibitory control. *International Journal of Bilingualism*, 15, 26–37.

Sanchez, M., Hearn, E., Do, D., Rilling, J., & Herndon, J. (1998). Differential rearing affects corpus callosum size and cognitive function of rhesus monkeys. *Brain Research*, 812(1), 38–49.

Sánchez-Casas, R., Davis, C., & García-Albea, J. (1992). Bilingual lexical processing: Exploring the cognate/non-cognate distinction. *European Journal of Cognitive Psychology*, 4, 293–310.

Sánchez-Casas, R., & García-Albea, J. (2005). The representation of cognate and noncognate words in bilingual memory: Can cognate status be characterized as a special kind of morphological relation? In J. Kroll & A. de Groot (eds.), *Handbook of bilingualism: Psycholinguistic approaches* (pp. 226–250). New York: Oxford University Press.

Sanders, A., Hall, C., Katz, M., & Lipton, R. (2012). Non-native language use and risk of incident dementia. *Journal of Alzheimer's Disease*, 29(1), 99–108.

Sandoval, T., Gollan, T., Ferreira, V., & Salmon, D. (2010). What causes the bilingual disadvantage in verbal fluency? The dual-task analogy. *Bilingualism: Language and Cognition*, 13(2), 231–252.

Sandra, D. (1994). The morphology of the mental lexicon: Internal word structure viewed from a psycholinguistic perspective. In D. Sandra & M. Taft (eds.), *Morphological structure, lexical representation and lexical access*. Hove, UK: Lawrence Erlbaum Associates.

Santiago-Rivera, A., & Altarriba, J. (2002). The role of language in therapy with the Spanish–English bilingual client. *Professional Psychology: Research and Practice*, 33, 30–38.

Santiago-Rivera, A., Altarriba, J., Poll, N., Gonzalez-Miller, N., & Cragun, C. (2009). Therapists' views on working with bilingual Spanish–English speaking clients: A qualitative investigation. *Professional Psychology: Research and Practice*, 40, 436–443.

Sanz, C., & Morgan-Short, K. (2004). Positive evidence vs. explicit rule presentation and explicit negative feedback: A computer assisted study. *Language Learning*, 54, 35–78.

Sasaki, Y. (1994). Paths of processing strategy transfers in learning Japanese and English as foreign languages. *Studies in Second Language Acquisition*, 16(1), 43–72.

Sato, S., Gygax, P., & Gabriel, U. (2013). Gender inferences: Grammatical features and their impact on the representation of gender in bilinguals. *Bilingualism: Language and Cognition*, 16(4), 792–807.

Scarborough, D., Gerard, L., & Cortese, C. (1984). Independence of lexical access in bilingual word recognition. *Journal of Verbal Learning & Verbal Behavior*, 23, 84–99.

Scarmeas, N., Albert, S., Manly, J., & Stern, Y. (2006). Education and rates of cognitive decline in incident Alzheimer's disease. *Journal of Neurology, Neurosurgery, and Psychiatry*, 77, 308–316.

Schacht, A., & Sommer, W. (2009). Time course and task dependence of emotion effects in word processing. *Cognitive, Affective, and Behavioral Neuroscience*, 9(1), 28–43.

Schäffler, L., Lüders, H., Dinner, D., Lesser, R., & Chelune, G. (1993). Comprehension deficits elicited by electrical stimulation of Broca's area. *Brain*, 116(3), 695–715.

Scheepers, C. (2003). Syntactic priming of relative clause attachments: Persistence of structural configuration in sentence production. *Cognition*, 89(3), 179–205.

Schlaug, G. (2001). The brain of musicians. A model for functional and structural adaptation. *Annals of the New York Academy of Sciences*, 930, 281–299.

Schlaug, G., Norton, A., Overy, K., & Winner, E. (2005). Effects of music training on the child's brain and cognitive development. *Annals of the New York Academy of Sciences*, 1060, 219–230.

Schlegel, A., & Rudelson, J. (2012). White matter structure changes as adults learn a second language. *Journal of Cognitive Neuroscience*, 24(8), 1664–1670.

Schmid, M. (2002). *First language attrition, use and maintenance: The case of German Jews in Anglophone countries*. Amsterdam/Philadelphia, PA: John Benjamins Publishing.

  (2010). Languages at play: The relevance of L1 attrition to the study of bilingualism. *Bilingualism: Language and Cognition*, 13, 1–7.

  (2012). The impact of age and exposure on bilingual development in international adoptees and family migrants: A perspective from Holocaust survivors. *Linguistic Approaches to Bilingualism*, 2(2), 177–208.

Schmid, M., Köpke, B., Keijzer, M., & Weilemar, L. (eds.) (2004). *First language attrition: Interdisciplinary perspectives on methodological issues*. Amsterdam/Philadelphia, PA: John Benjamins Publishing.

Schmid, S. (2005). Code-switching and Italian abroad: Reflections on language contact and bilingual mixture. *Italian Journal of Linguistics*, 17, 113–155.

Schmidt, R. (1990). The role of consciousness in second language learning. *Applied Linguistics*, 11, 129–158.

  (2001). Attention. In P. Robinson (ed.), *Cognition and second language instruction* (pp. 3–32). Cambridge, UK: Cambridge University Press.

Schmidt, R., & Bjork, R. (1992). New conceptualizations of practice: Common principles in three paradigms suggest new concepts for training. *Psychological Science*, 3, 207–217.

Schmiedtová, B., von Stutterheim, C., & Carroll, M. (2011). Language-specific patterns in event construal of advanced second language speakers. In A. Pavlenko (ed.), *Thinking and speaking in two languages* (pp. 66–107). Bristol, UK: Multilingual Matters.

Schneider, D., & Anderson, J. (2010). Asymmetric switch costs as sequential difficulty effects. *The Quarterly Journal of Experimental Psychology*, 63(10), 1873–1894.

Schoonbaert, S., Duyck, W., Brysbaert, M., & Hartsuiker, R. J. (2009). Semantic and translation priming from a first language to a second and back: Making sense of the findings. *Memory & Cognition*, 37(5), 569–586.

Schoonbaert, S., Hartsuiker, R., & Pickering, M. (2007). The representation of lexical and syntactic information in bilinguals: Evidence from syntactic priming. *Journal of Memory and Language*, 56, 153–171.

Schoonbaert, S., Holcomb, P. J., Grainger, J., & Hartsuiker, R. (2011). Testing asymmetries in noncognate translation priming: Evidence from RTs and ERPs. *Psychophysiology*, 48, 74–81.

Schreuder, R., & Weltens, B. (1993). *The bilingual lexicon*. Amsterdam/Philadelphia, PA: John Benjamins Publishing.

Schriefers, H., Meyer, A., & Levelt, W. (1990). Exploring the time course of lexical access in language production: Picture-word interference studies. *Journal of Memory and Language*, 29, 86–102.

Schroeder, S., & Marian, V. (2012). A bilingual advantage for episodic memory in older adults. *Journal of Cognitive Psychology*, 24(5), 591–601.

Schwanenflugel, P., & Rey, M. (1986). Interlingual semantic facilitation: Evidence for a common representational system in the bilingual lexicon. *Journal of Memory and Language*, 25, 605–618.

Schwartz, A., & Arêas da Luz Fontes, A. (2008). Cross-language mediated priming: Effects of context and lexical relationship. *Bilingualism: Language and Cognition*, 11, 95–110.

Schwartz, A., & Kroll, J. F. (2006). Bilingual lexical activation in sentence context. *Journal of Memory and Language*, 55, 197–212.

Schwartz, A., Kroll, J. F., & Diaz, M. (2007). Reading words in Spanish and English: Mapping orthography to phonology in two languages. *Language & Cognitive Processes*, 22(1), 106–129.

Schwartz, A., Yeh, L., & Shaw, M. (2008). Lexical representation of second language words: Implications for second language vocabulary and use. *The Mental Lexicon*, 3(3), 309–324.

Schwartz, B. (2010). The effects of emotion on tip-of-the-tongue states. *Psychonomic Bulletin & Review*, 17, 82–87.

Schweinberger, M. (2011). The discourse marker LIKE in Irish English. In B. Migge & M. Chiosáin (eds.), *New perspectives on Irish English* (pp. 179–202). Amsterdam/Philadelphia, PA: John Benjamins Publishing.

Schweizer, T., Ware, J., Fischer, C., Craik, F., & Bialystok, E. (2012). Bilingualism as a contributor to cognitive reserve: Evidence from brain atrophy in Alzheimer's disease. *Cortex*, 48, 991–996.

Schwieter, J. W. (2013). Lexical inhibition in trilingual speakers. In J. Tirkkonen & E. Anttikoski (eds.), *Proceedings of the 24th Conference of Scandinavian Linguistics. Publications of the University of Eastern Finland: Reports and Studies in Education, Humanities, and Theology* (pp. 249–260). Joensuu, Finland: University of Eastern Finland Press.

Schwieter, J. W. (founding series ed.) (2014). *Bilingual Processing and Acquisition*. Amsterdam/Philadelphia, PA: John Benjamins Publishing.

Schwieter, J. W., & Ferreira, A. (2013). Language selection, control, and conceptual-lexical development in bilinguals and multilinguals. In J. W. Schwieter (ed.), *Innovative research and practices in second language acquisition and bilingualism* (pp. 241–266). Amsterdam/Philadelphia, PA: John Benjamins Publishing.

Schwieter, J. W., & Sunderman, G. (2008). Language switching in bilingual speech production: In search of the language-specific selection mechanism. *Mental Lexicon*, 3(2), 214–238.

(2009). Concept selection and developmental effects in bilingual speech production. *Language Learning*, 59(4), 897–927.

(2011). Inhibitory control processes and lexical access in trilingual speech production. *Linguistic Approaches to Bilingualism*, 1, 391–412.

Scott, W. (1962). Cognitive complexity and cognitive flexibility. *Sociometry*, 25(4), 405–414.

Sebastián, R., Laird, A., & Kiran, S. (2011). Meta-analysis of the neural representation of first language and second language. *Applied Psycholinguistics*, 32(4), 799–819.

Sebastián-Gallés, N. (2013). Eyes wide shut: Linking brain and pupil in bilingual and monolingual toddlers. *Trends in Cognitive Sciences*, 17(5), 197–198.

Sebastián-Gallés, N., Albareda-Castellot, B., Weikum, W., & Werker, J. (2012). A bilingual advantage in visual language discrimination in infancy. *Psychological Science*, 23(9), 994–999.

Sebastián-Gallés, N., & Bosch, L. (2002). Building phonotactic knowledge in bilinguals: Role of early exposure. *Journal of Experimental Psychology: Human Perception and Performance*, 28(4), 974–989.

(2009). Developmental shift in the discrimination of vowel contrasts in bilingual infants: Is the distributional account all there is to it? *Developmental Science*, 12(6), 874–887.

Sebastián-Gallés, N., Bosch, L., & Pons, F. (2008). Early bilingualism. In M. Haith & J. Benson (eds.), *Encyclopedia of infant and early childhood development* (pp.172–182). San Diego: Elsevier.

Sebastián-Gallés, N., & Díaz, B. (2012). First and second language speech perception: Graded learning. *Language Learning*, 62, 131–147.

Sebastián-Gallés, N., Echeverría, S., & Bosch, L. (2005). The influence of initial exposure on lexical representation: Comparing early and simultaneous bilinguals. *Journal of Memory and Language*, 52, 240–255.

Sebastián-Gallés, N., Rodríguez-Fornells, A., de Diego Balaguer, R., & Díaz, B. (2006). First- and second-language phonological representations in the mental lexicon. *Journal of Cognitive Neuroscience*, 18(8), 1277–1291.

Sebastián-Gallés, N., & Soto-Faraco, S. (1999). Online processing of native and non-native phonemic contrasts in early bilinguals. *Cognition*, 72, 111–123.

Segalowitz, N. J. (2010). *Cognitive bases of second language fluency*. Oxon, NY: Routledge.

Segalowitz, N. J., Watson, V., & Segalowitz, S. (1995). Vocabulary skill: Single-case assessment of automaticity of word recognition in a timed lexical decision task. *Second Language Research*, 11(2), 121–136.

Segalowitz, S. J., & Zheng, X. (2009). An ERP study of category priming: Evidence of early lexical semantic access. *Biological Psychology*, 80, 122–129.

Seidenberg, M., & McClelland, J. (1989). A distributed developmental model of word recognition and naming. *Psychological Review*, 96, 523–568.

Seidl, J. (1937). The effect of bilingualism on the measurement of intelligence. (Unpublished doctoral dissertation), Fordham University, New York City.

Seliger, H., & Vago, R. (1991). *First language attrition*. New York: Cambridge University Press.

Selinker, L. (1972). Interlanguage. *International Review of Applied Linguistics*, 10, 209–230.

Sereno, S. C., O'Donnell, P., & Rayner, K. (2006). Eye movements and lexical ambiguity resolution: Investigating the subordinate-bias effect. *Journal of Experimental Psychology: Human Perception and Performance*, 32(2), 335–350.

Sereno, S. C., Rayner, K., & Posner, M. I. (1998). Establishing a time-line of word recognition: Evidence from eye movements and event-related potentials. *Neuroreport*, 9, 2195–2200.

Servan-Schreiber, D., Cleeremans, A., & McClelland, J. (1991). Graded state machines: The representation of temporal contingencies in simple recurrent networks. *Machine Learning*, 7, 161–193.

Shafer, V., Yu, Y., & Datta, H. (2011). The development of English vowel perception in monolingual and bilingual infants: Neurophysiological correlates. *Journal of Phonetics*, 39(4), 527–545.

Shafer, V., Yu, Y., & Garrido-Nag, K. (2012). Neural mismatch indices of vowel discrimination in monolingually and bilingually exposed infants: Does attention matter? *Neuroscience Letters*, 526(1), 10–14.

Shallice, T. (1982). Specific impairments of planning. *Philosophical Transactions of the Royal Society London B*, 298, 199–209.

 (1988). *From neuropsychology to mental structure*. Cambridge, UK: Cambridge University Press.

Shanks, D. (1995). *The psychology of associative learning*. New York: Cambridge University Press.

Shea, C., & Curtin, S. (2010). Discovering the relationship between context and allophones in a second language: Evidence for distribution-based learning. *Studies in Second Language Acquisition*, 32, 581–606.

Sheen, Y. (2008). Recasts, language anxiety, modified output and L2 learning. *Language Learning*, 58, 835–874.

Sheng, L., Lu, Y., & Kan, P. (2011). Lexical development in Mandarin-English bilingual children. *Bilingualism: Language and Cognition*, 14(4), 579–587.

Shimron, J. (2003). Semitic languages: Are they really root-based? In J. Shimron (ed.), *Language processing and acquisition in languages of*

*Semitic, root-based, morphology* (pp. 1-28). Amsterdam/Philadelphia, PA: John Benjamins Publishing.

Shin, J., & Christianson, K. (2009). Syntactic processing in Korean-English bilingual production: Evidence from cross-linguistic structural priming. *Cognition*, 112, 175-180.

Shin, N., & Cairns, H. (2009). Subject pronouns in child Spanish and continuity of reference. In J. Collentine, M. García, B. Lafford, & F. Marín (eds.), *Selected proceedings of the 11th Hispanic Linguistics Symposium* (pp. 155-164). Somerville, MA: Cascadilla Press.

Shinskey, J., & Munakata, Y. (2003). Are infants in the dark about hidden objects? *Developmental Science*, 6(3), 273-282.

Shipstead, Z., Redick, T., & Engle, R. (2012). Is working memory training effective? *Psychological Bulletin*, 138, 628-654.

Shockley, K., Santana, M., & Fowler, C. (2003). Mutual interpersonal postural constraints are involved in cooperative conversation. *Journal of Experimental Psychology: Human Perception and Performance*, 29(2), 326-332.

Sholl, A., Sankaranarayanan, A., & Kroll, J. F. (1995). Transfer between picture naming and translation: A test of asymmetries in bilingual memory. *Psychological Science*, 6, 45-49.

Shook, A., & Marian, V. (2012). Bimodal bilinguals co-activate both languages during spoken comprehension. *Cognition*, 124(3), 314-324.

(2013). The bilingual language interaction network for comprehension of speech. *Bilingualism: Language and Cognition*, 16(2), 304-324.

Showalter, C., & Hayes-Harb, R. (2013). Unfamiliar orthographic information and second language word learning: A novel lexicon study. *Second Language Research*, 29, 185-200.

Shultz, T. (2003). *Computational developmental psychology*. Cambridge, MA: MIT Press.

Silva, R., & Clahsen, H. (2008). Morphologically complex words in L1 and L2 processing: Evidence from masked priming experiments in English. *Bilingualism: Language and Cognition*, 11, 245-260.

Silverberg, S., & Samuel, A. (2004). The effect of age of second language acquisition on the representation and processing of second language words. *Journal of Memory and Language*, 51, 381-398.

Simango, R. (1995). Chichewa-English dataset. (Unpublished.)

Simcox, T., Pilotti, M., Mahamane, S., & Romero, E. (2012). Does the language in which aversive stimuli are presented affect their processing? *International Journal of Bilingualism*, 16, 419-427.

Simões, A. (2008). *Pois não: Brazilian Portuguese course for Spanish speakers, with basic reference grammar*. Austin, TX: University of Texas Press.

Simon, G., Bernard, C., Lalonde, R., & Rebaï, M. (2006). Orthographic transparency and grapheme–phoneme conversion: An ERP study in Arabic and French readers. *Brain Research*, 1104, 141-152.

Simon, G., Bernard, C., Largy, P., Lalonde, R., & Rebaï, M. (2004). Chronometry of visual word recognition during passive and lexical decision tasks: An ERP investigation. *International Journal of Neuroscience*, 114, 1401–1432.

Simon, G., Petit, L., Bernard, C., & Rebaï, M. (2007). N170 ERPs could represent a logographic processing strategy in visual word recognition. *Behavioral and Brain Functions*, 3, 1–11.

Simon, J., & Wolf, J. (1963). Choice reaction time as a function of angular stimulus–response correspondence and age. *Ergonomics*, 6(1), 99–105.

Singh, L. (2014). One world, two languages: Cross-language semantic priming in bilingual toddlers. *Child Development*, 85(2), 755–766.

Singh, L., & Foong, J. (2012). Influences of lexical tone and pitch on word recognition in bilingual infants. *Cognition*, 124(2), 128–142.

Singh, L., Liederman, J., Mierzejewski, R., & Barnes, J. (2011). Rapid acquisition of native phoneme contrasts after disuse: You do not always lose what you do not use. *Developmental Science*, 14(5), 949–959.

Singleton, D. (2005). The critical period hypothesis: A coat of many colours. *IRAL*, 43, 269–285.

Siok, W., Kay, P., Wange, W., Chana, A., Chen, L., Luke, K.-K., & Tan, L. (2009). Language regions of brain are operative in color perception. *Proceedings of the National Academy of Sciences*, 106, 8140–8145.

Siok, W. T., Spinks, J. A., Jin, Z., & Tan, L. M. (2009). Developmental dyslexia is characterized by the co-existence of visuospatial and phonological disorders in Chinese children. *Current Biology*, 19, 890–892.

Skehan, P. (1986). Cluster analysis and the identification of learner types. In V. Cook (ed.), *Experimental approaches to second language acquisition* (pp. 81–94). Oxford, UK: Pergamon.

Skehan, P. (2009). Modelling second language performance: Integrating complexity, accuracy, fluency and lexis. *Applied Linguistics*, 30, 510–532.

Skehan, P., & Foster, P. (2001). Cognition and tasks. In P. Robinson (ed.), *Cognition and second language instruction* (pp. 183–205). Cambridge, UK: Cambridge University Press.

Slabakova, R. (2013). The effect of construction frequency and native transfer on second language knowledge of the syntax-discourse interface. *Applied Psycholinguistics*, 1–29.

Slamecka, N., & Graf, P. (1978). The generation effect: Delineation of a phenomenon. *Journal of Experimental Psychology: Human Learning and Memory*, 4, 592–604.

Slobin, D. (1993). Adult language acquisition: A view from child language study. In C. Perdue (ed.), *Adult language acquisition: cross-linguistic perspectives* (pp. 239–252). Cambridge, UK: Cambridge University Press.

  (1996). From "thought and language" to "thinking for speaking." In J. Gumperz & S. Levinson (eds.), *Rethinking linguistic relativity* (pp. 70–96). Cambridge, UK: Cambridge University Press.

(2003). Language and thought online: Cognitive consequences of linguistic relativity. In D. Gentner & S. Goldin-Meadow (eds.), *Language in mind: Advances in the study of language and thought* (pp. 157–192). Cambridge, MA: MIT Press.

(2003). Language and thought online: Cognitive consequences of linguistic relativity. In D. Gentner & S. Goldin-Meadow (eds.), *Language in Mind: Advances in the study of language and thought* (pp. 157–192). Cambridge, MA: MIT Press.

Slobin, D., Dasinger, L., Küntay, A., & Toupin, C. (1993). Native language reacquisition in early childhood. In E. Clark (ed.), *The Proceedings of the Twenty-Fourth Annual Child Language Research Forum* (pp. 179–196). Stanford, CA: Center for the Study of Language and Information.

Smith, F. (1923). Bilingualism and mental development. *British Journal of Psychology*, 13, 270–282.

Smith, M., & Kirsner, K. (1982). Language and orthography as irrelevant features in colour-word and picture-word Stroop interference. *Quarterly Journal of Experimental Psychology: Human Experimental Psychology*, 34, 153–170.

Snedeker, J., & Yuan, S. (2008). Effects of prosodic and lexical constraints on parsing in young children (and adults). *Journal of Memory and Language*, 58(2), 574–608.

Snodgrass, J. (1984). Concepts and their surface representations. *Journal of Verbal Learning & Verbal Behavior*, 23, 3–22.

Soares, C., & Grosjean, F. (1984). Bilinguals in a monolingual and a bilingual speech mode: The effect on lexical access. *Memory & Cognition*, 12 (4), 380–386.

Soffié, M., Hahn, K., Terao, E., & Eclancher, F. (1999). Behavioural and glial changes in old rats following environmental enrichment. *Behavioural Brain Research*, 101(1), 37–49.

Soja, N., Carey, S., & Spelke, E. (1991). Ontological categories guide young children's inductions of word meaning: Object terms and substance terms. *Cognition*, 38, 179–211.

Sommers, M., & Barcroft, J. (2007). An integrated account of the effects of acoustic variability in first language and second language: Evidence from amplitude, fundamental frequency, and speaking rate variability. *Applied Psycholinguistics*, 28, 231–249.

(2013). Effects of referent token variability on L2 vocabulary learning. *Language Learning*, 63, 186–210.

Song, Y., Bu, Y., Hu, S., Luo, Y., & Liu, J. (2010). Short-term language experience shapes the plasticity of the visual word form area. *Brain Research*, 1316, 83–91.

Sorace, A. (2005). Selective optionality in language development. In L. Cornips & K. P. Corrigan (eds.), *Syntax and variation: Reconciling the biological and the social* (pp. 55–80). Amsterdam/Philadelphia, PA: John Benjamins Publishing.

Soveri, A, Rodríguez., Rodriguez-Fornells, A., & Laine, M. (2011). Is there a relationship between language switching and executive functions in bilingualism? Introducing a within-group analysis approach. *Frontiers in Psychology*, 2, 1–8.

Sowell, E., Peterson, B., Thompson, P., Welcome, S., Henkenius, A., & Toga, A. (2003). Mapping cortical change across the human life span. *Nature Neuroscience*, 6, 309–315.

Sparks, R., & Ganschow, L. (1991). Foreign language learning differences: Affective or native language aptitude. *Modern Language Journal*, 75, 2–16.

Spector, A., & Biederman, I. (1976). Mental set and mental shift revisited. *American Journal of Psychology*, 89(4), 669–679.

Spielberger, C. (1983). *Manual for the state-trait anxiety inventory*. Palo Alto, CA: Consulting Psychologists Press.

Spier, L., Hallowell, A., & Newman, S. (1941). Language, culture, and personality: Essays in memory of Edward Sapir. Menasha, WI: Sapir Memorial Publication Fund.

Spivey, M. (2007). *The continuity of mind*. New York: Oxford University Press.

Spivey, M., Grosjean, M., & Knoblich, G. (2005). Continuous attraction toward phonological competitors. *Proceedings of the National Academy of Sciences of the United States of America*, 102(29), 10393–10398.

Spivey, M., & Marian, V. (1999). Cross talk between native and second languages: Partial activation of an irrelevant lexicon. *Psychological Science*, 10, 281–284.

Spivey, M., Tanenhaus, M., Eberhard, K., & Sedivy, J. (2002). Eye movements and spoken language comprehension: Effects of visual context on syntactic ambiguity resolution. *Cognitive Psychology*, 45(4), 447–481.

Spivey-Knowlton, M., & Sedivy, J. (1995). Resolving attachment ambiguities with multiple constraints. *Cognition*, 55(3), 227–267.

Spoelman, M., & Verspoor, M. (2010). Dynamic patterns in the development of accuracy and complexity: A longitudinal case study on the acquisition of Finnish. *Applied Linguistics*, 31(4), 532–553.

Stager, C., & Werker, J. (1997). Infants listen for more phonetic detail in speech perception than in word-learning tasks. *Nature*, 388(6640), 381–382.

Starreveld, P. A. (2000). On the interpretation of onsets of auditory contexts in word production. *Journal of Memory and Language*, 42, 497–525.

Starreveld, P. A., de Groot, A., Rossmark, B., & van Hell, J. G. (2014). Parallel language activation during word processing in bilinguals: Evidence from word production in sentence context. *Bilingualism: Language and Cognition*, 17(2), 258–276.

Starreveld, P. A., & La Heij, W. (1995). Semantic interference, orthographic facilitation, and their interaction in naming tasks. *Journal of Experimental Psychology: Learning, Memory, and Cognition*, 21, 686–698.

(1996). Time-course analysis of semantic and orthographic context effects in picture naming. *Journal of Experimental Psychology: Learning, Memory, and Cognition*, 22, 896–918.

Stefanowitsch, A., & Gries, S. (2003). Collostructions: Investigating the interaction between words and constructions. *International Journal of Corpus Linguistics*, 8, 209–243.

Stein, M., Federspiel, A., Koenig, et al. (2012). Structural plasticity in the language system related to increased second language proficiency. *Cortex*, 48(4), 458–465.

Stengel, E., & Zelmanowicz, J. (1933). On polyglot motor aphasia. In M. Paradis (ed.), *Readings on aphasia in bilinguals and polyglots* (pp. 356–375). Montreal: Marcel Didier.

Stern, Y. (2002). What is cognitive reserve? Theory and research application of the reserve concept. *Journal of the International Neuropsychological Society*, 8, 448–460.

(2009). Cognitive reserve. *Neuropsychologia*, 47, 2015–2028.

Sternberg, S. (1969). The discovery of processing stages: Extensions of Donder's method. *Acta Psychologica*, 30, 276–315.

Stolberg, D., & Münch, A. (2010). "Die Muttersprache vergisst man nicht" – or do you? A case study in L1 attrition and its (partial) reversal. *Bilingualism: Language and Cognition*, 13(1), 19–31.

Stowe, L. A., & Sabourin, L. (2006). Imaging the processing of a second language: Effects of maturation and proficiency on the neural processes involved. *International Review of Applied Linguistics*, 43, 329–353.

Strijkers, K., Costa, A., & Thierry, G. (2010). Tracking lexical access in speech production: Electrophysiological correlates of word frequency and cognate effects. *Cerebral Cortex*, 20, 912–928.

Stroop, J. (1935). Studies of interference in serial verbal reactions. *Journal of Experimental Psychology*, 18, 643–662.

Stuss, D., & Benson, D. (1986). *The frontal lobes*. New York: Raven Press.

Stuss, D., & Knight, R. (eds.) (2012). *Principles of Frontal Lobe Function* (2nd edn). New York: Oxford University Press.

Styles, S., & Plunkett, K. (2009). How do infants build a semantic system? *Language and Cognition*, 1(1), 1–24.

Su, I. (2001). Transfer of sentence processing strategies: A comparison of L2 learners of Chinese and English. *Applied Psycholinguistics*, 22(1), 83–112.

Su, I.-F., Mak, S.-C. C., Cheung, L.-Y. M., & Law, S.-P. (2012). Taking a radical position: Evidence for position-specific radical representations in Chinese character recognition using masked priming ERP. *Frontiers in Psychology*, 3, 333.

Suga, N. (2008). The neural circuit for tone-specific plasticity in the auditory system elicited by conditioning. *Learning & Memory*, 15(4), 198–201.

Sundara, M., Polka, L., & Molnar, M. (2008). Development of coronal stop perception: Bilingual infants keep pace with their monolingual peers. *Cognition*, 108(1), 232–242.

Sundara, M., & Scutellaro, A. (2011). Rhythmic distance between languages affects the development of speech perception in bilingual infants. *Journal of Phonetics*, 39(4) 505–513.

Sunderman, G., & Kroll, J. F. (2006). First language activation during second language lexical processing: An investigation of lexical form, meaning, and grammatical class. *Studies in Second Language Acquisition*, 28, 387–422.

Sutton, T., & Altarriba, J. (2011). The automatic activation and perception of emotion in word processing: Evidence from a modified dot probe paradigm. *Journal of Cognitive Psychology*, 23, 736–747.

Sutton, T., Altarriba, J., Gianico, J., & Basnight-Brown, D. (2007). Emotional Stroop effects in monolingual and bilingual speakers. *Cognition and Emotion*, 21, 1077–1090.

Svirsky, M., Teoh, S.-W., & Neuburger, H. (2004). Development of language and speech perception in congenitally, profoundly deaf children as a function of age at cochlear implantation. *Audiology and Neurotology*, 9 (4), 224–233.

Swain, M. (1993). The output hypothesis: Just speaking and writing aren't enough. *Canadian Modern Language Review*, 50, 158–164.

(1995). Three functions of output in second language learning. In G. Cook & B. Seidlhofer (eds.), *Principle and practice in applied linguistics: Studies in honour of H. G. Widdowson*. Oxford, UK: Oxford University Press.

Swinney, D. (1979). Lexical access during sentence comprehension: (Re)consideration of context effects. *Journal of Verbal Learning and Verbal Behavior*, 18(6), 645–659.

Tabossi, P. (1988). Accessing lexical ambiguity in different types of sentential contexts. *Journal of Memory and Language*, 27(3), 324–340.

Tabossi, P., & Johnson-Laird, P. (1980). Linguistic context and the priming of semantic information. *Quarterly Journal of Experimental Psychology*, 32 (4), 595–603.

Tabossi, P., & Zardon, F. (1993). Processing ambiguous words in context. *Journal of Memory and Language*, 32, 359–372.

Tabossi, P., Colombo, L., & Job, R. (1987). Accessing lexical ambiguity: Effects of context and dominance. *Psychological Research*, 49(2–3), 161–167.

Taft, M., & Zhu, X. (1997). Submorphemic processing in reading Chinese. *Journal of Experimental Psychology: Learning, Memory, and Cognition*, 23, 761–775.

Taft. M. (2004). Morphological decomposition and the reverse base frequency effect. *The Quarterly Journal of Experimental Psychology*, 57(4), 745–765.

Talamas, A., Kroll, J. F., & Dufour, R. (1999). From form to meaning: Stages in the acquisition of second-language vocabulary. *Bilingualism: Language and Cognition*, 2, 45–58.

Talmy, L. (1985). Lexicalization patterns: Semantic structure in lexical form. In T. Shopen (ed.), *Language typology and syntactic description: Grammatical categories and the lexicon* (pp. 57–149). Cambridge, UK: Cambridge University Press.

Talmy, L. (2000). *Toward a cognitive semantics: Typology and process in concept structuring*. Cambridge MA: MIT Press.

Tan, L. H., Laird, A. R., Li, K. T., & Fox, P. (2005). Neuroanatomical correlates of phonological processing of Chinese characters and alphabetic words: A meta-analysis. *Human Brain Mapping*, 25, 83–91.

Tan, L. H., Liu, H. L., Perfetti, C. A., Spinks, J. A., Fox, P. T., & Gao, J. M. (2001). The neural system underlying Chinese logograph reading. *NeuroImage*, 13, 836–846.

Tan, L. M., Spinks, J. A., Eden, G. F., Perfetti, C. A., & Siok, W. T. (2005). Reading depends on writing, in Chinese. *Proceedings of the National Academy of Sciences*, 102, 8781–8785.

Tan, T. X., & Yang, Y. (2005). Language development of Chinese adoptees 18–35 months old. *Early Childhood Research Quarterly*, 20(1), 57–68.

Tanaka, J. W., & Curran, T. (2001). A neural basis for expert object recognition. *Psychological Science*, 12, 43–47.

Tanenhaus, M., Spivey-Knowlton, M., Eberhard, K., & Sedivy, J. (1995). Integration of visual and linguistic information in spoken language comprehension. *Science*, 268(5217), 1632–1634.

Tanenhaus, M., & Trueswell, J. C. (1995). Sentence comprehension. In J. L. Miller & P. D. Eimas (eds.), *Speech, language, and communication: Handbook of perception and cognition* (pp. 217–262). San Diego, CA: Academic Press.

Tao, L., Marzecova, A., Taft, M., Asanowicz, D., & Wodniecka, Z. (2011). The efficiency of attentional networks in early and late bilinguals: The role of age of acquisition. *Frontiers in Psychology*, 2, 1–19.

Tarlowski, A., Wodniecka, Z., & Marzecova, A. (2013). Language switching in the production of phrases. *Journal of Psycholinguistic Research*, 42(2), 103–118.

Tarone, E. (1979). Interlanguage as chameleon. *Language Learning*, 29, 181–191.
  (1988). *Variation in interlanguage*. London: Edward Arnold.
  (2007). Sociolinguistic approaches to second language acquisition research – 1997–2007. *Modern Language Journal*, 91, 837–848.

Taylor, I. (1971). How are words from two languages organized in bilinguals' memory? *Canadian Journal of Psychology/Revue canadienne de psychologie*, 25, 228–240.
  (1976). Similarity between French and English words: A factor to be considered in bilingual language behavior? *Journal of Psycholinguistic Research*, 5, 85–94.

Taylor, J. (2002). *Cognitive grammar*. Oxford, UK: Oxford University Press.

Tees, R., & Werker, J. (1984). Perceptual flexibility: Maintenance or recovery of the ability to discriminate non-native speech sounds. *Canadian Journal of Psychology*, 38(4), 579–590.

Teinonen, T., Fellman, V., Näätänen, R., Alku, P., & Huotilainen, M. (2009). Statistical language learning in neonates revealed by event-related brain potentials. *BMC Neuroscience*, 10(1), 21.

Thierry, G., & Wu, Y. J. (2007). Brain potentials reveal unconscious translation during foreign-language comprehension. *Proceedings of the National Academy of Sciences*, 104, 12530–12535.

Thierry, G., Athanasopoulos, P., Wiggett, A., Dering, B., & Kuipers, J. (2009). Unconscious effects of language-specific terminology on pre-attentive colour perception. *Proceedings of the National Academy of Sciences*, 106, 4567–4570.

Thomas, J (1988). The role played by metalinguistic awareness in second and third language learning. *Journal of Multilingual and Multicultural Development*, 9, 235–247.

Thomas, M. S. C. (1997). Connectionist networks and knowledge representation: The case of bilingual lexical processing. (Unpublished doctoral dissertation), Oxford University, UK.

Thomas, M. S. C., & Allport, A. (2000). Language switching costs in bilingual visual word recognition. *Journal of Memory and Language*, 43, 44–66.

Thomas, M. S. C., & van Heuven, W. J. B. (2005). Computational models of bilingual comprehension. In J. Kroll & A. de Groot (eds.), *Handbook of bilingualism: Psycholinguistic approaches* (pp. 202–225). New York: Oxford University Press.

Thordardottir, E. (2011). The relationship between bilingual exposure and vocabulary development. *International Journal of Bilingualism*, 15, 426–445.

Tight, D. (2012). The first-noun principle and ambitransitive verbs. *Hispania*, 95(1), 103–115.

Timm, L. (1983). Does code switching take time? A comparison of results in experimental and natural settings, with some implications for bilingual language processing. *Hispanic Journal of Behavioral Sciences*, 5, 401–416.

Tinkham, T. (1993). The effect of semantic clustering on the learning of second language vocabulary. *System*, 21, 371–380.

  (1997). The effects of semantic and thematic clustering on the learning of second language vocabulary. *Second Language Research*, 13, 138–163.

Titone, D., Libben, M., Mercier, J., Whitford, V., & Pivneva, I. (2011). Bilingual lexical access during L1 sentence reading: The effects of L2 knowledge, semantic constraint, and L1–L2 intermixing. *Journal of Experimental Psychology: Learning, Memory, and Cognition*, 37, 1412–1431.

Tkachenko, N. (2001). The relative influence of English (L2) vs. Russian (L1) on the translation from Swedish (L3) into Russian depending on proficiency in L3. (Unpublished master's thesis), Lund University, Sweden.

Tobias, S. (1986). Anxiety and cognitive processing of instruction. In R. Schwarzer (ed.), *Self-related cognition in anxiety and motivation* (pp. 35–54). Hillsdale, NJ: Erlbaum.

Tokowicz, N. (2014). Translation ambiguity affects language processing, learning, and representation. In R. Miller, K. Martin, C. Eddington, et al. (eds.), *Selected Proceedings of the 2012 Second Language Research Forum: Building Bridges Between Disciplines* (pp. 170–180). Somerville, MA: Cascadilla Press.

Tokowicz, N., & Degani, T. (2010). Translation ambiguity: Consequences for learning and processing. In B. VanPatten & J. Jegerski (eds.), *Research on second language processing and parsing* (pp. 281-293). Amsterdam/Philadelphia, PA: John Benjamins Publishing.

Tokowicz, N., & Jarbo, K. (2009). The generation effect applied to second language vocabulary learning. Poster presented at *The Fiftieth Annual Meeting of the Psychonomic Society*, Boston, MA.

Tokowicz, N., & Jarbo, K. (under review). Generation improves second language vocabulary learning.

Tokowicz, N., & Kroll, J. F. (2007). Number of meanings and concreteness: Consequences of ambiguity within and across languages. *Language and Cognitive Processes*, 22, 727-779.

Tokowicz, N., Kroll, J. F., de Groot, A., & van Hell, J. (2002). Number-of-translation norms for Dutch-English translation pairs: A new tool for examining language production. *Behavior Research Methods, Instruments, & Computers*, 34, 435-451.

Tomiyama, M. (2001). Detecting a savings effect in longitudinal L2 attrition data. Paper presented at AAAL Symposium, Reactivating a Forgotten Language: The savings-paradigm applied, Missouri, USA.

Toribio, A. (2000), Setting parametric limits on dialectal variation in Spanish. *Lingua*, 10, 315-341.

Toro, J., Trobalon, J., & Sebastián-Gallés, N. (2003). The use of prosodic cues in language discrimination tasks by rats. *Animal Cognition*, 6, 131-136.

Towell, R., & Hawkins, R. (1994). *Approaches to second language acquisition*. Clevedon: Multilingual Matters.

Townsend, C. (1995). *Teaching the Czech language through Russian: Преподавание ческого языка посредством русского (Prepodavanije čéškogo jazyka posredstvom russkogo)*. Columbus, OH: Slavica.

Tran, V. (2010). English gain vs. Spanish loss? Language assimilation among second-generation Latinos in young adulthood. *Social Forces*, 89(1), 257-284.

Trehub, S. (1976). The discrimination of foreign speech contrasts by infants and adults. *Child Development*, 47(2), 466-472.

Treiman, R., Clifton, C., Meyer, A., & Wurm, L. (2003). Language comprehension and production. In A. Healy, & R. Proctor (eds.), *Comprehensive handbook of psychology* (pp. 527-548). New York: John Wiley & Sons, Inc.

Trousdale, G., & Hoffmann, T. (eds.). (2013). *The Oxford handbook of construction grammar*. Oxford, UK: Oxford University Press.

Trueswell, J., & Kim, A. (1998). How to prune a garden path by nipping it in the bud: Fast priming of verb argument structure. *Journal of Memory and Language*, 39(1), 102-123.

Trueswell, J., & Tanenhaus, M. (1994). Toward a lexicalist framework of syntactic ambiguity resolution. In C. Clifton, L. Frazier, & K. Rayner (eds.), *Perspectives on sentence processing* (pp. 155-180). Hillsdale, NJ: Erlbaum.

Trueswell, J., Tanenhaus, M., & Kello, C. (1993). Verb-specific constraints in sentence processing: Separating effects of lexical preference from garden-paths. *Journal of Experimental Psychology: Learning, Memory, and Cognition*, 19(3), 528–553.

Truscott, J. (1998). Noticing in a second language: A critical review. *Second Language Research*, 14, 103–135.

Truscott, J., & Sharwood Smith, M. (2004). Acquisition by processing: A modular perspective on language development. *Bilingualism: Language and Cognition*, 7, 1–20.

(2011) Input, intake, and consciousness: The quest for a theoretical foundation. *Studies in Second Language Acquisition*, 33(4), 497–528.

Tsai, J.-L., Lee, C.-Y., Lin, Y.-C., Tzeng, O. J. L., & Hung, S. L. (2006). Neighborhood size effects of Chinese words in lexical decision and reading. *Language and Linguistics*, 7, 659–675.

Tsao, F., Liu, H., & Kuhl, P. (2004). Speech perception in infancy predicts language development in the second year of life: A longitudinal study. *Child Development*, 75, 1067–1084.

Tse, C., & Pu, X. (2012). The effectiveness of test-enhanced learning depends on trait test anxiety and working-memory capacity. *Journal of Experimental Psychology: Applied*, 18, 253–264.

Tse, C.-S., & Altarriba, J. (2009). The word concreteness effect occurs for positive, but not negative, emotion words in immediate serial recall. *British Journal of Psychology*, 100, 91–109.

Tseng, A. M., Chang, L.-Y., & Tokowicz, N. (2014). Translation ambiguity between English and Mandarin Chinese: The roles of proficiency and word characteristics. In J. W. Schwieter & A. Ferreira (eds.), *The development of translation competence: Theories and methodologies from psycholinguistics and cognitive science* (pp. 107–165). Newcastle, UK: Cambridge Scholars Publishing.

Tseng, A. M., Doppelt, M., & Tokowicz, N. (under review). *Lexical and semantic interconnections aid adult second language vocabulary learning*.

Tsuneishi, S., & Casaer, P. (2000). Effects of preterm extrauterine visual experience on the development of the human visual system: A flash VEP study. *Developmental Medicine & Child Neurology*, 42(10), 663–668.

Tulving, E., & Colotla, V. (1970). Free recall of trilingual lists. *Cognitive Psychology*, 1, 86–98.

Turkeltaub, P., Eden, G., Jones, K., & Zeffiro, T. (2002). Meta-analysis of the functional neuroanatomy of single-word reading: method and validation. *Neuroimage*, 16, 765–780.

Türker, E. (2005). Resisting the grammatical change: Nominal groups in Turkish-Norwegian codeswitching. *International Journal of Bilingualism*, 9, 453–476.

Uddin, L., Iacoboni, M., Lange, C., & Keenan, J. (2007). The self and social cognition: The role of cortical midline structures and mirror neurons. *Trends in Cognitive Sciences*, 11(4), 153–157.

Ullman, M. (2001). The neural basis of lexicon and grammar in first and second language: The declarative/procedural model. *Bilingualism: Language and Cognition*, 4, 105–22.

(2012). The declarative/procedural model. In P. Robinson (ed.), *Routledge encyclopedia of second language acquisition* (pp. 160–164). New York & London: Routledge.

Ulsh, J. (2011). *From Spanish to Portuguese*. Madison, CT: Audio-Forum, Jeffrey Norton Publishers, Inc.

Uludag, O., & VanPatten, B. (2012). The comparative effects of processing instruction and dictogloss on the acquisition of the English passive by speakers of Turkish. *International Review of Applied Linguistics*, 50, 187–210.

Umbel, V., Pearson, B., Fernández, M., & Oller, D. (1992). Measuring bilingual children's receptive vocabularies. *Child Development*, 63(4), 1012–1020.

Unsworth, N., & Spillers, G. (2010). Working memory capacity: Attention, memory, or both? A direct test of the dual-component model. *Journal of Memory and Language*, 62, 392–406.

Unsworth, S. (2013). Assessing the role of current and cumulative exposure in simultaneous bilingual acquisition: The case of Dutch gender. *Bilingualism: Language and Cognition*, 16(1), 86–110.

Uriagareka, J. (1995). Aspects of the syntax of clitic placement in Western Romance. *Linguistic Inquiry*, 26, 79–123.

Upshur, J., & Palmer, A. (1974). Measures of accuracy, communicatively, and social judgment for two classes of foreign language speakers. *Selected papers from the third international congress of applied linguistics*, Vol. 2 (pp. 201–221). Heidelberg: Julius Gross Verlag.

Vaid, J. (1988). Bilingual memory representation: A further test of dual coding theory. *Canadian Journal of Psychology*, 42, 84–90.

Vaid, J., & Frenck-Mestre, C. (2002). Do orthographic cues aid language recognition? A laterality study with French–English bilinguals. *Brain and Language*, 82, 47–53.

Vaid, J., & Genesee, F. (1980). Neuropsychological approaches to bilingualism: A critical review. *Canadian Journal of Psychology*, 34, 417–445.

Vainio, S., Pajunen, A., & Huönä, J. (2013). L1 and L2 word recognition in Finnish: Examining L1 effects on L2 processing of morphological complexity and morphophonological transparency. *Studies in Second Language Acquisition*, 36, 133–162.

Valdés Kroff, J. (2012). Using eye-tracking to study auditory comprehension in codeswitching: Evidence for the link between comprehension and production. (Unpublished doctoral dissertation), Pennsylvania State University, University Park, PA.

Valenzuela, M., Matthews, F., Brayne, et al. (2012). Multiple biological pathways link cognitive lifestyle to protection from dementia. *Biological Psychiatry*, 71, 783–791.

Valenzuela, M., & Sachdev, P. (2006a). Brain reserve and cognitive decline: A non-parametric systematic review. *Psychological Medicine*, 36(8), 1065–1073.

(2006b). Brain reserve and dementia: A systematic review. *Psychological Medicine*, 36(4), 441–454.

Valenzuela, M., Sachdev, P., Wen, W., Chen, X., & Brodaty, H. (2008). Lifespan mental activity predicts diminished rate of hippocampal atrophy. *PLoS ONE*, 3, e2598.

Van Assche, E., Drieghe, D., Duyck, W., Welvaert, M., & Hartsuiker, R. (2011). The influence of semantic constraints on bilingual word recognition during sentence reading. *Journal of Memory and Language*, 64(1), 88–107.

Van Assche, E., Duyck, W., & Brysbaert, M. (2013). Verb processing by bilinguals in sentence context. *Studies in Second Language Acquisition*, 35, 237–259.

Van Assche, E., Duyck, W., & Gollan, T. (2013). Whole-language and item-specific control in bilingual language production. *Journal of Experimental Psychology: Learning, Memory and Cognition*, 39(6), 1781–1792.

Van Assche, E., Duyck, W., Hartsuiker, R., & Diependaele, K. (2009). Does bilingualism change native-language reading? Cognate effects in a sentence context. *Psychological Science*, 20(8), 923–927.

Van Berkum, J. (1996). The psycholinguistics of grammatical gender: Studies in language comprehension and production. (Unpublished doctoral dissertation), Max Planck Institute for Psycholinguistics, the Netherlands.

Van den Noort, M., Bosch, M., & Hugdahl, K. (2006). Foreign language proficiency and working memory capacity. *European Psychologist*, 11, 289–296.

Van der Hoeven, N., & de Bot, K. (2012). Relearning in the elderly: Age-related effects on the size of savings. *Language Learning*, 62(1), 42–67.

Van der Meij, M., Cuetos, F., Carreiras, M., & Barber, H. (2011). Electrophysiological correlates of language switching in second language learners. *Psychophysiology*, 48, 44–54.

Van Dijk, M. (2003). Child language cuts capers: Variability and ambiguity in early child development. (Unpublished doctoral dissertation), University of Groningen, the Netherlands.

Van Dijk, M., & van Geert, P. (2002). Focus on variability: New tools to study intra-individual variability in developmental data. *Infant Behavior and Development*, 25(4), 340–375.

(2007). Wobbles, humps and sudden jumps: A case study of continuity, discontinuity and variability in early language development. *Infant and Child Development*, 16(1), 7–33.

Van Dyke, J., & McElree, B. (2006). Retrieval interference in sentence comprehension. *Journal of Memory and Language*, 55(2), 157–166.

Van Geert, P. (2008). The dynamic systems approach in the study of L1 and L2 acquisition: An introduction. *Modern Language Journal*, 92, 179–199.

(2011). The contribution of complex dynamic systems to development. *Child Development Perspectives*, 5(4), 273–278.

Van Hell, J., & Candia Mahn, A. (1997). Keyword mnemonics versus rote rehearsal in learning concrete and abstract foreign words by experienced and inexperienced foreign language learners. *Language Learning*, 47, 507–546.

Van Hell, J., & de Groot, A. (1998a). Conceptual representation in bilingual memory: Effects of concreteness and cognate status in word association. *Bilingualism: Language and Cognition*, 1, 193–211.

(1998b). Disentangling context availability and concreteness in lexical decision and word translation. *Quarterly Journal of Experimental Psychology, Section A: Human Experimental Psychology*, 51(1), 41–63.

(2008). Sentence context modulates visual word recognition and translation in bilinguals. *Acta Psychologica*, 128(3), 431–451.

Van Hell, J., & Dijkstra, T. (2002). Foreign language knowledge can influence native language performance in exclusively native contexts. *Psychonomic Bulletin and Review*, 9(4), 780–789.

Van Hell, J., & Mahn, A. (1997). Keyword mnemonics versus rote rehearsal: Learning concrete and abstract foreign words by experienced and inexperienced learners. *Language Learning*, 47, 507–546.

Van Hell, J., Sánchez-Casas, R., & Ting, C. (in preparation). Enrique Iglesias tops the charts with newly released canción!: How socio-contextual information facilitates code-switching.

Van Hell, J., & Tanner, D. (2012). Second language proficiency and cross-language lexical activation. *Language Learning*, 62, 148–171.

Van Hell, J., & Witteman, M. (2009). The neurocognition of switching between languages: A review of electrophysiological studies. In L. Isurin, D. Winford, & K. de Bot (eds.), *Multidisciplinary approaches to code-switching* (pp. 53–84). Amsterdam/Philadelphia, PA: John Benjamins Publishing.

Van Heuven, W. J. B. (2005). Bilingual interactive activation models of word recognition in a second language. In V. Cook & B. Bassetti (eds.), *Second language writing systems* (pp. 260–288). Clevedon, UK: Multilingual Matters.

Van Heuven, W. J. B., Conklin, K., Coderre, E. L., Guo, T., & Dijkstra, T. (2011). The influence of cross-language similarity on within- and between-language Stroop effects in trilinguals. *Frontiers in Psychology*, 2, 1–15.

Van Heuven, W. J. B., & Dijkstra, A. (2001). The semantic, orthographic, and phonological interactive activation model. Poster presented at 12th Conference of the European Society for Cognitive Psychology, Edinburgh, Scotland.

Van Heuven, W. J. B., & Dijkstra, T. (2003). Modeling bilingual visual word recognition: The SOPHIA model. Paper presented at 13th Meeting of the European Society for Cognitive Psychology. Granada, Spain.

(2010). Language comprehension in the bilingual brain: fMRI and ERP support for psycholinguistic models. *Brain Research Reviews*, 64, 104–122.

Van Heuven, W. J. B., Dijkstra, T., & Grainger, J. (1998). Orthographic neighborhood effects in bilingual word recognition. *Journal of Memory and Language*, 39(3), 458–483.

Van Heuven, W. J. B., Dijkstra, T., Grainger, J., & Schriefers, H. (2001). Shared neighborhood effects in masked orthographic priming. *Psychonomic Bulletin and Review*, 8(1), 96–101.

Van Heuven, W. J. B., Schriefers, H., Dijkstra, T., & Hagoort, P. (2008). Language conflict in the bilingual brain. *Cerebral Cortex*, 18(11), 2706–2716.

Van Kesteren, R., Dijkstra, T., & de Smedt, K. (2012). Markedness effects in Norwegian–English bilinguals: Task-dependent use of language-specific letters and bigrams. *Quarterly Journal of Experimental Psychology*, 65, 2129–2154.

Van Leerdam, M., Bosman, A., & de Groot, A. (2009). When MOOD rhymes with ROAD: Dynamics of phonological coding in bilingual visual word perception. *Mental Lexicon*, 4, 303–335.

Van Orden, G., Holden, J., & Turvey, M. (2003). Self-organization of cognitive performance. *Journal of Experimental Psychology: General*, 132(3), 331–350.

Vanderwart, M. (1984). Priming by pictures in lexical decision. *Journal of Verbal Learning & Verbal Behavior*, 23, 67–83.

VanPatten, B. (1984). Learners' comprehension of clitic object pronouns: More evidence for a word order strategy. *Hispanic Linguistics*, 1, 57–67.

(2004). Input processing in second language acquisition. In B. VanPatten (ed.), *Processing instruction: Theory, research, and commentary* (pp. 5–31). Mahwah, NJ: Lawrence Erlbaum & Associates.

(2007). Input processing in adult second language acquisition. In B. VanPatten & J. Williams (eds.), *Theories in second language acquisition* (pp. 115–136). Mahwah, NJ: Erlbaum.

(2009). Processing matters. In T. Piske & M. Young-Scholten (eds.), *Input matters* (pp. 47–61). Clevedon, UK: Multilingual Matters.

(2013). Mental representation and skill in instructed SLA. In J. W. Schwieter (ed.), *Innovative research and practices in second language acquisition and bilingualism* (pp. 3–22). Amsterdam/Philadelphia, PA: John Benjamins Publishing.

(2014). Input processing in adult SLA. In B. VanPatten & J. Williams (eds.), *Theories in second language acquisition* (2nd edn). New York: Routledge.

VanPatten, B., Borst, S., Collopy, E., Qualin, A., & Price, J. (2013). Explicit information, grammatical sensitivity, and the first-noun Principle: A cross-linguistic study in processing instruction. *Modern Language Journal*, 97, 504–525.

VanPatten, B., & Cadierno, T. (1993). Explicit instruction and input processing. *Studies in Second Language Acquisition*, 15, 225–243.

VanPatten, B., Farmer, J., & Clardy, C. (2009). Processing instruction and meaning-based output instruction: A response to Keating & Farley (2008). *Hispania*, 92, 116–126.

VanPatten, B., & Fernández, C. (2004.) The long-term effects of processing instruction. In B. VanPatten (ed.), *Processing instruction: theory, research, and commentary* (pp. 273–289). Mahwah, NJ: Lawrence Erlbaum Associates.

VanPatten, B., & Inclezan, D., Salazar, H., & Farley, A. (2009). Processing instruction and dictogloss: A study on object pronouns and word order in Spanish. *Foreign Language Annals*, 42, 557–575.

VanPatten, B., Keating, G., & Leeser, M. (2012). Missing verbal inflections as a representational issue: Evidence from on-line methodology. *Linguistic Approaches to Bilingualism*, 2, 109–140.

VanPatten, B., & Oikkenon, S. (1996). Explanation versus structured input in processing instruction. *Studies in Second Language Acquisition*, 18, 495–510.

VanPatten, B., & Rothman, J. (2014). Against "rules." In A. Benati, C. Laval, & M. J. Arche (eds.), *The grammar dimension in instructed second language acquisition: Theory, research, and practice* (pp. 15–35). London: Bloomsbury.

VanPatten, B., & Sanz, C. (1995). From input to output: Processing instruction and communicative tasks. In F. Eckman, D. Highland, P. Lee, J. Milcham, & R. Ruthkowski Weber (eds.), *Second language acquisition theory and pedagogy* (pp.169–85). Mahwah, NJ: Lawrence Erlbaum Associates.

VanPatten, B., & Uludag, O. (2011). Transfer of training and processing instruction: from input to output. *System*, 39, 44–53.

Vatz, K., Tare, M., Jackson, S., & Doughty, C. (2013). Aptitude–treatment interaction studies in second language acquisition: Findings and methodology. In G. Granena & M. Long (eds.), *Sensitive periods, language aptitude, and ultimate L2 attainment* (pp. 273–292). Amsterdam/Philadelphia, PA: John Benjamins Publishing.

Veivo, O., & Järvikivi, J. (2013). Proficiency modulates early orthographic and phonological processing in L2 spoken word recognition. *Bilingualism: Language and Cognition*, 16(4), 864–883.

Ventureyra, V., Pallier, C., & Yoo, H.-Y. (2004). The loss of first language phonetic perception in adopted Koreans. *Journal of Neurolinguistics*, 17(1), 79–91.

Vergara-Martínez, M., & Swaab, T. Y. (2012). Orthographic neighborhood effects as a function of word frequency: An event-related potential study. *Psychophysiology*, 49, 1277–1289.

Verhoef, K., Roelofs, A., & Chwilla, D. (2009). Role of inhibition in language switching: Evidence from event-related brain potentials in overt picture naming. *Cognition*, 110(1), 84–99.

(2010). Electrophysiological evidence for endogenous control of attention in switching between languages in overt picture naming. *Journal of Cognitive Neuroscience*, 22(8), 1832–1843.

Verspoor, M., Lowie, W., & de Bot, K. (eds.). (2010). *A dynamic approach to second language development: Methods and techniques*. Amsterdam/Philadelphia, PA: John Benjamins Publishing.

Verspoor, M., Lowie, W., & van Dijk, M. (2008). Variability in second language development from a dynamic systems perspective. *Modern Language Journal*, 92(2), 214-231.

Vigliocco, G., Antonini, T., & Garrett, M. (1997). Grammatical gender is on the tip of Italian tongues. *Psychological science*, 8(4), 314–317.

Vigliocco, G., Kousta, S., Della Rosa, et al. (2013). The neural representation of abstract words: The role of emotion. *Cerebral Cortex*, 24(7), 1767–1777.

Vihman, M., Thierry, G., Lum, J., Keren-Portnoy, T., & Martin, P. (2007). Onset of word form recognition in English, Welsh, and English–Welsh bilingual infants. *Applied Psycholinguistics*, 28(3), 475–493.

Vincente, A., & Ziamari, K. (2008). L'arabe morocain au contact du français de l'espagnol. In S. Procházka & V. Ritt-Benmimoun (eds.), *Between the Atlantic and Indian Oceans: Studies in contemporary Arabic dialects*. Proceedings of the 7th AIDA Conference (2006), *Neue Beihefte zur Wiener Zeitschrift für die Kunde des Morgenlandes*, 4, 457–469.

Vingerhoets, G., Van Borsel, J., Tesink, C., et al. (2003). Multilingualism: An fMRI study. *NeuroImage*, 20, 2181–2196.

Vitali, P., Tettamanti, M., Abutalebi, J., et al. (2010). Generalization of the effects of phonological training for anomia using structural equation modelling: A multiple single-case study. *Neurocase*, 16(2), 93–105.

Voga, M., & Grainger J. (2007). Cognate status and cross-script translation priming. *Memory & Cognition*, 35, 938–952.

Vogel, A. C., Church, J. A., Power, J. D., Miezin, F. M., Petersen, S. E., & Schlaggar, B. I. (2013). Functional network architecture of reading-related regions across development. *Brain and Language*, 125, 231-243.

Von Holzen, K., & Mani, N. (2012). Language nonselective lexical access in bilingual toddlers. *Journal of Experimental Child Psychology*, 113, 569-586.

Von Studnitz, R., & Green, D. (1997). Lexical decision and language switching. *International Journal of Bilingualism*, 1, 3–24.

(2002a). Interlingual homograph interference in German-English bilinguals: Its modulation and locus of control. *Bilingualism: Language and Cognition*, 5(1), 1–23.

(2002b). The cost of switching language in a semantic categorization task. *Bilingualism: Language and Cognition*, 5, 241–251.

Vouloumanos, A., & Werker, J. (2004). Tuned to the signal: The privileged status of speech for young infants. *Developmental Science*, 7(3), 270–276.

Vu, H., Kellas, G., & Paul, S. (1998). Sources of sentence constraint on lexical ambiguity resolution. *Memory & Cognition*, 26(5), 979–1001.

Vu, H., Kellas, G., Metcalf, K., & Herman, R. (2000). The influence of global discourse on lexical ambiguity resolution. *Memory & Cognition*, 28(2), 236–252.

Wagenmakers, E. (2013). Real-time processing: The dynamics of productive and perceptive vocabulary knowledge in L1 and L2. (Unpublished master's thesis), University of Amsterdam, the Netherlands.

Wagenmakers, E., Farrell, S., & Ratcliff, R. (2005). Human cognition and a pile of sand: A discussion on serial correlations and self-organized criticality. *Journal of Experimental Psychology: General*, 134(1), 108–116.

Wakefield, J., Bradley, P., Yom, B., & Doughtie, E. (1975). Language switching and constituent structure. *Language and Speech*, 18, 14–19.

Wang, X., & Forster, K. (2010). Masked translation priming with semantic categorization: Testing the Sense Model. *Bilingualism: Language and Cognition*, 13, 327–340.

Wang, Y., Kuhl, P., Chen, C., & Dong, Q. (2009). Sustained and transient language control in the bilingual brain. *NeuroImage*, 47, 414–422.

Wang, Y., Xue, G., Chen, C., Xue, F., & Dong, Q. (2007). Neural bases of asymmetric language switching in second-language learners: An ER-fMRI study. *NeuroImage*, 35, 862–870.

Waninge, F., Dörnyei, Z., & de Bot, K. (2014). Motivational dynamics in language learning: Change, stability and context. *Modern Language Journal*, 98(3), 704–723.

Waring, R. (1997). The negative effects of learning words in semantic sets: A replication. *System*, 25, 261–274.

Warren, T., & Gibson, E. (2002). The influence of referential processing on sentence complexity. *Cognition*, 85(1), 79–112.

Wartenburger, I., Heekeren, H., Abutalebi, J., Cappa, S. F., Villringer, A., & Perani, D. (2003). Early setting of grammatical processing in the bilingual brain. *Neuron*, 37, 159–170.

Weber, A., & Cutler, A. (2004). Lexical-competition in non-native spoken-word recognition. *Journal of Memory and Language*, 50, 1–25.

Weber, A., & Paris, G. (2004). The origin of the linguistic gender effect in spoken-word recognition: Evidence from non-native listening. In K. Forbus, D. Gentner, & T. Regier (eds.), *Proceedings of the twenty-sixth annual meeting of the Cognitive Science Society* (pp. 1446–1451). Mahwah, NJ: Lawrence Erlbaum.

Weber-Fox, C., & Neville, H. (1996). Maturational constraints on functional specializations for language processing: ERP and behavioral evidence in bilingual speakers. *Journal of Cognitive Neuroscience*, 8(3), 231–256.

Wei, L. (2000). Types of morphemes and their implications for second language acquisition. *International Journal of Bilingualism* 4, 29–43.

Wei, L., & Moyer, M. (eds.). (2008). *Blackwell guide to research methods in bilingualism and multilingualism*. Malden, MA: Blackwell.

Weikum, W., Oberlander, T., Hensch, T., & Werker, J. (2012). Prenatal exposure to antidepressants and depressed maternal mood alter trajectory of infant speech perception. *Proceedings of the National Academy of Sciences of the United States of America*, 109(2), 17221–17227.

Weikum, W., Vouloumanos, A., Navarra, J., Soto-Faraco, S., Sebastián-Gallés, N., & Werker, J. (2007). Visual language discrimination in infancy. *Science*, 316 (5828), 1159–1159.

Weinrich, M., Boser, K., & McCall, D. (1999). Representation of linguistic rules in the brain: Evidence from training an aphasic patient to produce past tense verb morphology. *Brain and Language*, 70(1), 144–158.

Weinreich, U. (1953). *Languages in contact: Findings and problems*. The Hague: Mouton.

Weisleder, A., & Fernald, A. (2011). Variation in early language experience influences processing and language growth. Paper presented at 24th Annual CUNY Conference on Human Sentence Processing, Stanford University, CA.

(2013). Talking to children matters: Early language experience strengthens processing and builds vocabulary. *Psychological Science*, 1–22.

Weissberger, G., Wierenga, C., Bondi, M., & Gollan, T. (2012). Partially overlapping mechanisms of language and task control in young and older bilinguals. *Psychology and Aging*, 27(4), 959–974.

Werker, J., & Gervain, J. (2013). Language acquisition: Perceptual foundations in infancy. In P. Zelazo (ed.), *The Oxford handbook of developmental psychology* (pp. 909–925). Oxford, UK: Oxford University Press.

Werker, J. (2012). Perceptual foundations of bilingual acquisition in infancy. *Annals of the New York Academy of Sciences*, 1251(1), 50–61.

Werker, J., & Byers-Heinlein, K. (2008). Bilingualism in infancy: First steps in perception and comprehension. *Trends in Cognitive Sciences*, 12(4), 144–151.

Werker, J., Byers-Heinlein, K., & Fennell, C. (2009). Bilingual beginnings to learning words. *Philosophical Transactions of the Royal Society of London. Series B, Biological Sciences*, 364(1536), 3649–3663.

Werker, J., Cohen, L., Lloyd, V., Casasola, M., & Stager, C. (1998). Acquisition of word-object associations by 14-month-old infants. *Developmental Psychology*, 34(6), 1289–1309.

Werker, J., & Curtin, S. (2005). PRIMIR: A developmental framework of infant speech processing. *Language Learning and Development*, 1(2), 197–234.

Werker, J., Gilbert, J., Humphrey, K., & Tees, R. (1981). Developmental aspects of cross-language speech perception. *Child Development*, 52, 349–355.

Werker, J., & Tees, R. (1984). Cross-language speech perception: Evidence for perceptual reorganization during the first year of life. *Infant behavior and development*, 7(1), 49–63.

(2005). Speech perception as a window for understanding plasticity and commitment in language systems of the brain. *Developmental Psychobiology*, 46(3), 233–251.

West, R., & Stanovich, K. (1982). Source of inhibition in experiments on the effect of sentence context on word recognition. *Journal of Experimental Psychology: Learning, Memory, and Cognition*, 8(5), 385.

Westbury, C., & Hollis, G. (2007). Putting Humpty together again: Synthetic approached to nonlinear variable effects underlying lexical access. In G. Jarema & G. Libben (eds.) *The mental lexicon: Core perspectives*. Amsterdam: Elsevier.

White, J. (forthcoming). The effect of input-based instruction type on the acquisition of Spanish accusative clitics. *Hispania*.

White, J., & DeMil, A. (2013a). Transfer of training in PI: The role of FREI. *Studies in Second Language Acquisition*, 35, 519–544.

(2013b). Primary and secondary effects of PI: A replication of Leeser & DeMil (2013). *International Journal of Language Studies*, 7, 59–88.

Whitman, R., & Jackson, K. (1972). The unpredictability of contrastive analysis. *Language Learning*, 22, 29–41.

Whorf, B. (1956). *Language, thought, and reality: Selected writings of Benjamin Lee Whorf* (J. B. Carroll, ed.). Cambridge, MA: MIT Press.

Williams, J. (1994). The relationship between word meanings in the first and second language: Evidence for a common, but restricted, semantic code. *European Journal of Cognitive Psychology*, 6, 195–220.

(1996). Is automatic priming semantic? *European Journal of Cognitive Psychology*, 8, 113–161.

(2006). Incremental interpretation in second language sentence processing. *Bilingualism: Language and Cognition*, 9(1), 71–88.

Williams, J., Möbius, P., & Kim, C. (2001). Native and non-native processing of English wh-questions: Parsing strategies and plausibility constraints. *Applied Psycholinguistics*, 22(4), 509–540.

Wilson, D., & Sperber, D. (1993). Linguistic form and relevance. *Lingua*, 90, 1–25.

(2012). *Meaning and relevance*. Cambridge, UK: Cambridge University Press.

Wilson, M., & Garnsey, S. (2009). Making simple sentences hard: Verb bias effects in simple direct object sentences. *Journal of Memory and Language*, 60(3), 368–392.

Wimmer, H., & Perner, J. (1983). Beliefs about beliefs: Representation and constraining function of wrong beliefs in young children's understanding of deception. *Cognition*, 13(1), 103–128.

Wingfield, A., & Stine-Morrow, E. (2000). Language and speech. In F. Craik & T. Salthouse (eds.), *The handbook of aging and cognition* (2nd edn) (pp. 359–416). Mahwah, NJ: Erlbaum.

Winograd, E., Cohen, C., & Barresi, J. (1976). Memory for concrete and abstract words in bilingual speakers. *Memory & Cognition*, 4, 323–329.

Winskel, H. (2013). The emotional Stroop task and emotionality rating of negative and neutral words in late Thai–English bilinguals. *International Journal of Psychology*, 48(6), 1090–1098.

Witteman, M., & van Hell, J. (2008). Code switching in bilinguals: An electrophysiological and behavioral study of lexical and discourse triggering. *Abstracts of the Psychonomic Society, 49th Annual Meeting*, 13, 119.

Witzel, J., Witzel, N., & Nicol, J. (2012). Deeper than shallow: Evidence for structure-based parsing biases in second-language sentence processing. *Applied Psycholinguistics*, 33(2), 419–456.

Witzel, N., & Forster, K. (2012). How L2 words are stored: The episodic L2 hypothesis. *Journal of Experimental Psychology: Learning, Memory, and Cognition*, 38, 1608–1021.

Wodniecka, Z., Craik, F., Luo, L., & Bialystok, E. (2010). Does bilingualism help memory? Competing effects of verbal ability and executive control. *International Journal of Bilingual Education and Bilingualism*, 13, 575–595.

Woldorff, M., Gallen, C., Hampson., et al. (1993). Modulation of early sensory processing in human auditory cortex during auditory selective attention. *Proceedings of the National Academy of Sciences*, 90(18), 8722–8726.

Wong, A. C. N., Gauthier, I., Woroch, B., DeBuse, C., & Curran, T. (2005). An early electrophysiological response associated with expertise in letter perception. *Cognitive, Affective, & Behavioral Neuroscience*, 5, 306–318.

Wong, P., Warrier, C., Penhune, V, et al. (2008). Volume of left Heschl's Gyrus and linguistic pitch learning. *Cerebral Cortex*, 18(4), 828–836.

Wong, W. (2004). The nature of processing instruction. In B. VanPatten (ed.), *Processing instruction: Theory, research, and commentary* (pp. 33–63). Mahwah, NJ: Lawrence Erlbaum Associates.

(2005). *Input enhancement: From theory and research to classroom practice*. New York: McGraw-Hill.

(2010). The effects of discourse level SI activities on the French Causative. In A. Benati & J. Lee (eds), *Processing instruction and discourse* (pp. 198–216). London: Continuum Press.

Woodrow, L. (2006). Anxiety and speaking in English as a second language. *RELC Journal*, 37, 308–328.

Woolley, S., Fremouw, T., Hsu, A., & Theunissen, F. (2005). Tuning for spectro-temporal modulations as a mechanism for auditory discrimination of natural sounds. *Nature Neuroscience*, 8(10), 1371–1379.

Woolley, S., Gill, P., & Theunissen, F. (2006). Stimulus-dependent auditory tuning results in synchronous population coding of vocalizations in the songbird midbrain. *Journal of Neuroscience*, 26(9), 2499–2512.

Woolley, S., Hauber, M., & Theunissen, F. (2010). Developmental experience alters information coding in auditory midbrain and forebrain neurons. *Developmental neurobiology*, 70(4), 235–252.

Workman, L., Brookman, F., Mayer, P., Rees, V., & Bellin, W. (2000). Language laterality in English/Welsh bilinguals: Language-acquisitional and language-specific factors in the development of lateralisation. *Laterality*, 5, 289–313.

Wu, C., Weissman, D., Roberts, K., & Woldorff, M. (2007). The neural circuitry underlying the executive control of auditory spatial attention. *Brain Research*, 1134(1), 187.

Wu, C.-Y., Ho, M.-H. R., & Chen, S.-H. A. (2012). A meta-analysis of fMRI studies on Chinese orthographic, phonological, and semantic processing. *NeuroImage*, 63, 381–391.

Wu, Y., & Thierry, G. (2010). Investigating bilingual processing: The neglected role of language processing contexts. *Frontiers in Psychology*, 1(178), 1–6.

(2012). How reading in a second language protects your heart. *Journal of Neuroscience*, 32, 6485–6489.

(2013). Fast modulation of executive function by language context in bilinguals. *Journal of Neuroscience*, 33, 13533–13537.

Wulfeck, B., Juarez, L., Bates, E., & Kilborn, K. (1986). Sentence interpretation strategies in healthy and aphasic bilingual adults. In J. Vaid (ed.), *Language processing in bilinguals: Psycholinguistic and neuropsychological perspectives* (pp. 199–220). Hillsdale, NJ: Lawrence Erlbaum Associates.

Yang, C., & Roeper, T. (2011). Minimalism and language acquisition. In C. Boeckx (ed.), *The Oxford handbook of linguistic minimalism* (pp. 551–573). Oxford, UK: Oxford University Press.

Yang, J., McCandliss, B. D., Shu, H., & Zevin, J. (2009). Simulating language-specific and language-general effects in a statistical learning model of Chinese reading. *Journal of Memory and Language*, 61, 238–257.

Yang, J., Shu, H., McCandliss, B. D., & Zevin, J. (2013). Orthographic influences on division of labor in learning to read Chinese and English: Insights from computational modeling. *Bilingualism: Language and Cognition*, 16, 354–366.

Yang, S., Yang, H., & Lust, B. (2011). Early childhood bilingualism leads to advances in executive attention: Dissociating culture and language. *Bilingualism: Language and Cognition*, 14, 412–422.

Yarkoni, T., Balota, D., & Yap, M. (2008). Moving beyond Coltheart's N: A new measure of orthographic similarity. *Psychonomic Bulletin & Review*, 15, 971–979.

Yashima, T., Zenuk-Nishide, L., & Shimizu, K. (2004). The influence of attitudes and affect on willingness to communicate and second language communication. *Language Learning*, 54, 119–152.

Yermolayeva, Y., & Rakison, D. (2013). Connectionist modeling of developmental changes in infancy: Approaches, challenges, and contributions. *Psychological Bulletin*, 140(1), 224–255.

Yonelinas, A. (2002). The nature of recollection and familiarity: A review of 30 years of research. *Journal of Memory and Language*, 46(3), 441–517.

Yoshida, H., Tran, D., Benitez, V., & Kuwabara, M. (2011). Inhibition and adjective learning in bilingual and monolingual children. *Frontiers in Psychology*, 2, 210.

Young, R., & Navar, M. (1968). Retroactive inhibition with bilinguals. *Journal of experimental psychology*, 77, 109–115.

Ytsma, J. (2001). Towards a typology of trilingual primary education. *International Journal of Bilingual Education and Bilingualism*, 4(1), 11–22.

Yudes, C., Macizo, P., & Bajo, M. (2011). The influence of expertise in simultaneous interpreting on non-verbal executive processes. *Frontiers in Psychology*, 2, 1–9.

Yum, Y. N., Holcomb, P. J., & Grainger, J. (2011). Words and pictures: An electrophysiological investigation of domain specific processing in native Chinese and English speakers. *Neuropsychologia*, 49, 1910–1922.

Zacks, R., Hasher, L., & Li, K. (2000). Human memory. In F. Craik & T. Salthouse (eds.), *The handbook of aging and cognition* (pp. 293–357). Mahwah, NJ: Erlbaum.

Zahodne, L., Schofield, P., Farrell, M., Stern, Y., & Manly, J. (2013). Bilingualism does not alter cognitive decline or dementia risk among Spanish-speaking immigrants. *Neuropsychology*, 28(2), 238–246.

Zeelenberg, R., & Pecher, D. (2003). Evidence for long-term cross-language repetition priming in conceptual implicit memory tasks. *Journal of Memory and Language*, 49, 80–94.

Zhang, S., Morris, M., Cheng, C.-Y., & Yap, A. (2013). Heritage-culture images disrupt immigrants' second language processing, fostering first-language intrusion. *Proceedings of the National Academy of Sciences*, 110, 11272–11277.

Zhang, T., van Heuven, W. J. B., & Conklin, K. (2011). Fast automatic translation and morphological decomposition in Chinese–English bilinguals. *Psychological Science*, 22, 1237–1242.

Zhao, J., Li, Q.-L., & Bi, H.-Y. (2012). The characteristics of Chinese orthographic neighborhood size effect for developing readers. *PLoS ONE*, 7, e46922.

Zhao, X., & Li, P. (2009). An online database of phonological representations for Mandarin Chinese. *Behavior Research Methods*, 41, 575–583.

  (2010). Bilingual lexical interactions in an unsupervised neural network model. *International Journal of Bilingual Education and Bilingualism*. 13, 505–524.

Zhao, X., Doyle-Smith, N., & Li, P. (2011). A comparative study of semantic representations across three languages. Paper presented at 41st Annual Meeting of the Society for Computers in Psychology, Seattle, WA.

Zhao, X., Li, P., & Kohonen, T. (2011). Contextual self-organizing map: Software for constructing semantic representation. *Behavior Research Methods*, 43, 77–88.

Zhou, H., Chen, B., Yang, M., & Dunlap, S. (2010). Language nonselective access to phonological representations: Evidence from Chinese-English bilinguals. *Quarterly Journal of Experimental Psychology*, 63, 2051–2066.

Zhu, C., Livote E., Scarmeas, N., et al. (2013). Long-term associations between cholinesterase inhibitors and memantine use and health outcomes among patients with Alzheimer's disease. *Alzheimer's and Dementia*, 9(6), 733–740.

Ziamari, K. (2007). Development and linguistic change in Moroccan Arabic-French code switching. In C. Miller, D. Caubert, J. Watson, & A. Wer (eds.), *Arabic in the city* (pp. 275–290). London: Routledge.

(2008). *Le code switching arabe marocain/français au Maroc: L'arab marocain au contact du français*. Paris: L'Harmattan.

Ziegler, J., & Goswami, U. (2005). Reading acquisition, developmental dyslexia, and skilled reading across languages: A psycholinguistic grain size theory. *Psychological Bulletin*, 131, 3–29.

Ziegler, J., Muneaux, M., & Grainger, J. (2003). Neighborhood effects in auditory word recognition: Phonological competition and orthographic facilitation. *Journal of Memory & Language*, 48, 779–793.

Zipf, G. (1935). *The psycho-biology of language: An introduction to dynamic philology*. Cambridge, MA: MIT Press.

Zobl, H. (1982). A direction for contrastive analysis: The comparative study of developmental sequences. *TESOL Quarterly*, 16(2), 169–183.

Zou, L., Ding, G., Abutalebi, J., Shu, H., & Peng, D. (2012). Structural plasticity of the left caudate in bimodal bilinguals. *Cortex*, 48(9), 1197–1206.

Zuo, Y., Yang, G., Kwon, E., & Gan, W.-B. (2005). Long-term sensory deprivation prevents dendritic spine loss in primary somatosensory cortex. *Nature*, 436(7048), 261–265.

# Index

4-M model, xi, 420, 422, 423, 425, 427, 436, 445, 448, 450
abstract concepts, 225, 229, 293
Abstract Level model, 423, 425, 427, 435, 436, 437, 444
abstract words, 12, 35, 50, 51, 53, 59, 66, 223, 225, 227, 287, 295, 296, 297, 668, 705, 708, 763, 821, 824
abstractionist–episodic model, 9, 177
accommodation strategy, 319
Acholi, 431, 432, 784
acquisition by processing, 208, 215
Activation Likelihood Estimation (ALE) method, 480
Activation Threshold Hypothesis, 662
act-out task, 113
Adaptive Control Hypothesis, 493, 506
adjacency, 86
adolescent, 20, 301, 305, 551, 567, 651, 659, 741
adoption. *See* international adoption
adult bilingualism, vii, 5, 108, 153
adverbial subordinators, 444, 445, 457
affective factors, 15, 369, 380, 387
affective structured input activities, 211
affixes, 191, 428, 429, 431, 433, 434, 453, 638
age of acquisition (AoA), x, 12, 26, 44, 85, 97, 99, 103, 104, 105, 106, 110, 137, 174, 279, 290, 292, 300, 306, 307, 319, 344, 345, 350, 537, 540, 542, 579, 580, 596, 599, 612, 620, 621, 623, 624, 626, 630, 656, 666, 675, 681, 691, 706
age of arrival, 283, 700
agent, 209, 422, 426
age-related memory deficits, 575, 611
agglutinative language, 191
aging, 22, 564, 571, 572, 573, 574, 576, 577, 581, 583, 585, 611, 642, 679, 703, 706, 707, 734, 741, 742, 743, 824, 827
agreement errors, 113
allomorphy, 173, 194, 195, 197, 199
allophone, 160, 167, 174, 188
allophonic variation, 9, 178, 181, 184
alphabetic, 92, 308, 311, 314, 315, 316, 317, 318, 319, 321, 322, 323, 325, 812
alternating-runs paradigm, 529, 534, 538, 544
Alzheimer's disease, 565, 578, 583, 584, 704, 728, 760, 801, 803, 828
ambiguity, 10, 204, 205, 216, 219, 226, 227, 353, 361, 433, 488, 491, 492, 499, 725, 729, 730, 738, 740, 774, 794, 796, 798, 805, 809, 811, 813, 814, 815, 817, 822
amnestic mild cognitive impairment (aMCI), 579, 580
anterior cingulate cortex (ACC), 478, 479, 480, 497, 502, 514, 515, 524, 582, 584, 615, 616, 617, 622, 624, 627, 695, 774
anticipatory eye movements, 133, 149
anxiety, 14, 15, 369, 370, 378, 380, 381, 382, 383, 384, 385, 386, 387, 713, 715, 751, 760, 774, 775, 792, 805, 809, 813, 815
aphasia, 7, 101, 423, 477, 480, 497, 558, 695, 696, 741, 745, 750, 761, 771, 778, 781, 789, 793, 810
aptitude, 212, 256, 369, 375, 378, 388, 690, 693, 713, 728, 763, 770, 785, 796, 797, 809, 820
Arabic, 66, 193, 218, 219, 220, 308, 313, 314, 375, 418, 419, 427, 430, 431, 446, 447, 448, 449, 450, 451, 452, 453, 455, 457, 472, 665, 677, 710, 731, 784, 787, 796, 806, 821, 828
articulation, 43, 184, 272, 370, 371, 374, 387, 394, 561, 677, 747, 768
artificial language, 91, 127, 227, 231, 356
assimilation, 173, 184, 319, 326, 549, 769, 791, 814
attention network test (ANT), xi, 595, 604, 605, 606, 719
attention(al) control, 14, 15, 130, 369, 370, 371, 372, 373, 374, 377, 380, 382, 386, 463, 564, 577, 594, 606, 629, 630, 705, 732, 733, 757, 764
attentional resources, 169, 371, 373, 376, 378, 380, 382, 387, 658, 689
attitudes, 25, 256, 304, 384, 385, 387, 432, 433, 452, 610, 648, 652, 657, 662, 663, 720, 739, 792, 826
attractor states, 11, 263, 264
attrition, 5, 12, 24, 25, 145, 278, 284, 286, 289, 580, 631, 642, 645, 646, 650, 657, 659, 660, 661, 662, 663, 667, 722, 736, 743, 746, 752, 758, 760, 762, 782, 788, 789, 802, 805, 810, 814
auditory lexical decision task, 490
auditory stimulus type, 149
auditory system, 24, 614, 616, 617, 619, 622, 627, 714, 738, 810
autobiographical memory, 114, 299, 302, 303
auxiliary, 208, 363, 364

backpropagation, 92, 97
balanced homonym, 335
Bantu, 431, 437, 450, 749

Basque, xviii, 64, 65, 142, 171, 190, 477, 696
behaviorally relevant features, 628, 630
best matching unit (BMU), 92, 93, 95
between-script repetition, 314
bigrams, 321, 322, 324, 819
bilateral activation, 316, 523, 647
bilingual advantage, xi, 5, 7, 21, 22, 23, 24, 130, 229, 230, 563, 565, 566, 571, 572, 573, 574, 575, 576, 577, 581, 589, 590, 591, 592, 593, 594, 597, 598, 599, 601, 603, 604, 605, 607, 608, 610, 611, 683, 691, 707, 709, 716, 718, 750, 758, 763, 777, 787, 794, 803, 804
Bilingual Aphasia Test (BAT), 477
bilingual behavior, 101, 109, 351
bilingual disadvantage, 130, 563, 575, 587, 800, 801
Bilingual Executive Processing Advantage (BEPA), 593, 594, 597, 599, 600, 601, 603, 604, 606, 607, 608, 612
bilingual exercise, viii, 23, 586
bilingual first language acquisition, 137, 724
bilingual inhibitory control advantage (BICA), 593, 594, 599, 601, 603, 605, 607, 608, 609, 612
Bilingual Interactive Activation (BIA) Model, xi, 6, 25, 96, 322, 323, 331, 332, 667
Bilingual Interactive Activation Plus (BIA+) Model, xi, 6, 25, 57, 58, 96, 100, 323, 324, 331, 332, 333, 334, 337, 342, 343, 344, 347, 391, 488, 491, 499, 593, 667, 691, 754
Bilingual Language Interaction Network for Comprehension of Speech (BLINCS) Model, 13, 100, 101, 324
bilingual lexicon. *See* mental lexicon
bilingual memory, 12, 32, 34, 50, 277, 286, 287, 289, 292, 302, 697, 698, 699, 715, 723, 724, 737, 765, 788, 789, 801, 806, 818
Bilingual Model of Lexical Access (BIMOLA) Model, 100, 769
Bilingual Re-Ordered Activation (B-RAM) Model, 14, 334, 335, 341, 342, 343, 344, 347
bilingual representation, vii, 6, 29, 30, 32, 40, 50, 52, 59, 60, 66, 83, 84, 105, 255, 275, 729, 764, 765
Bilingual Simple Recurrent Network (BSRN) Model, 6, 91, 97, 98
Bilingual Single Network (BSN) Model, 6, 91, 97, 98
bimodal, 21, 220, 489, 498, 565, 566, 624, 732, 828
blocking, 81, 296, 542, 731, 744
Boston naming task, 130, 469
Boston Naming Test, 536, 537, 762
bottom-up, 57, 71, 96, 174, 188, 327, 331, 337, 395, 397, 467, 488, 494, 495, 497, 499, 616, 617, 628, 630
brain reserve. *See* cognitive reserve
brain-based methods, 7, 133, 134, 145, 152
brain-style computation, 87
British National Corpus, x, xi, 235, 238, 239, 240, 241, 242, 243, 244, 245, 246, 247, 250, 708
Broca's area, 117, 478, 559, 623, 798, 801
Bukavu, 430, 743

Cantonese, 581, 609, 656, 657, 698
cascade-correction network, 94
cascading activation, 499

Catalan, 72, 77, 148, 149, 150, 160, 162, 164, 167, 168, 171, 178, 179, 375, 398, 402, 403, 500, 508, 531, 539, 622
category interference effect, 55, 56
central executive, 257, 372, 377, 382, 783
central nodes, 241
Chichewa, 428, 449, 806
Child Language Data Exchange System (CHILDES) Database, 103, 125, 718
Chinese, 13, 35, 45, 47, 57, 60, 64, 74, 91, 98, 103, 105, 116, 123, 141, 191, 194, 201, 249, 301, 308, 309, 310, 311, 313, 316, 318, 319, 320, 321, 322, 324, 325, 326, 351, 352, 357, 488, 489, 501, 502, 515, 523, 540, 603, 625, 637, 656, 683, 701, 713, 715, 730, 741, 746, 751, 752, 763, 769, 770, 771, 785, 791, 807, 810, 811, 812, 815, 826, 827, 828
clausal connectors, 416, 423
clitics, 210, 211, 213, 214, 440, 816, 819
cluster analysis, 96, 807
co-activation, 100, 118, 121, 229, 329, 335, 342, 391, 393, 402, 467, 485, 487, 488, 491, 492, 493, 494, 506, 615, 628, 629, 630
code-mixing, 651, 657, 793, 796
code-switching (CS), viii, 5, 15, 16, 17, 45, 126, 268, 349, 351, 361, 362, 363, 364, 416, 417, 418, 419, 420, 421, 422, 423, 424, 426, 427, 428, 429, 430, 431, 432, 433, 434, 435, 438, 440, 442, 443, 444, 445, 446, 447, 448, 449, 450, 451, 452, 453, 454, 455, 456, 457, 458, 459, 460, 462, 464, 465, 466, 467, 468, 469, 470, 471, 473, 474, 476, 480, 481, 482, 493, 651, 709, 710, 711, 714, 721, 731, 746, 750, 754, 757, 761, 762, 771, 781, 783, 784, 787, 791, 793, 796, 815, 816, 818
cognate effect, 16, 75, 318, 324, 389, 391, 393, 398, 399, 400, 401, 406, 407, 408, 411, 412, 413, 414, 493
cognate facilitation, 75, 100, 116, 126, 330, 336, 337, 338, 339, 344, 345, 346, 347, 499, 670, 674, 718
cognate output node, 412, 413
cognate overlap, 231
Cognition Hypothesis, 383, 760, 763
cognitive control, 5, 20, 21, 26, 117, 131, 459, 461, 479, 480, 486, 505, 510, 525, 535, 538, 548, 549, 553, 554, 555, 559, 560, 561, 562, 564, 566, 567, 568, 573, 574, 615, 617, 624, 675, 676, 678, 679, 690, 691, 693, 701, 706, 709, 710, 722, 726, 732, 733, 739, 741, 752, 772, 774, 780, 783, 786, 797
cognitive decline, 564, 565, 577, 580, 679, 767, 801, 817, 827
cognitive development, 20, 168, 170, 262, 263, 548, 549, 704, 705, 706, 747, 802
cognitive fitness, viii, 23, 586, 613
cognitive flexibility, 130, 131, 553, 766, 804
cognitive interference theory, 381
cognitive reserve, 571, 580, 583, 592, 817
cognitive revolution, 327, 588, 611, 739
co-index, 202, 418, 421, 424, 429, 431, 434, 437, 440, 458, 631
Collins Birmingham University International Language Dictionary (COBUILD) corpus-based project, 238, 737, 798
Communicative Development Inventories (CDI), 103, 141, 142, 165, 714, 724, 734
compartmentalized control, 527

competition, 18, 29, 55, 57, 101, 105, 106, 119, 120, 122, 127, 128, 131, 174, 186, 187, 198, 220, 232, 265, 267, 328, 335, 336, 342, 343, 417, 434, 436, 466, 485, 486, 488, 495, 496, 499, 504, 505, 506, 509, 510, 515, 519, 523, 528, 610, 624, 628, 639, 695, 710, 714, 718, 727, 731, 739, 751, 769, 770, 775, 776, 778, 798, 822, 828
Competition Model, 349, 776
competitors, 75, 328, 395, 490, 494, 497, 508, 642
complementizers, 417, 418, 421, 423, 444, 447, 448, 449, 450, 453, 455
complexity theory. *See* Dynamic System Theory (DST)
compound bilingual, 36, 37, 43, 285, 634, 724
compound system, 32
computationally implemented models, 85, 632
concept mediation. *See* conceptual mediation
concept mediation hypothesis, 43
conceptual access, 286, 495
conceptual attrition, 278, 284, 289
conceptual change, viii, xii, 4, 12, 275, 278, 286, 287, 288, 289, 290, 292
conceptual coexistence, 279, 289
conceptual convergence, 278, 280, 282
conceptual internalization, 280, 281
conceptual level (of mental representation), 32, 37, 40, 45, 51, 53, 55, 84, 275, 292, 416, 419, 421, 424, 425, 427, 433, 434, 440, 444, 446, 448, 449, 451, 453, 454, 456, 457, 499, 509
conceptual mediation, 42, 43, 45, 52, 56, 668, 729, 730, 737, 766
conceptual non-equivalence, 275, 277
conceptual representation, viii, 12, 32, 36, 53, 54, 69, 100, 112, 275, 276, 277, 278, 279, 280, 281, 282, 285, 286, 287, 289, 290, 291, 292, 395, 635, 668, 699, 723, 789, 818
conceptual restructuring, 278, 284
conceptual shift, 278, 282
conceptual store, 275, 285, 289
conceptual transfer, 12, 275, 278, 279, 280, 285, 286, 287, 289, 291, 755, 786
conceptualizer, 58
concrete concepts, 227, 229, 277, 281
concrete words, 50, 51, 53, 66, 225, 227, 287, 296, 668, 697
concreteness effect, 50, 56, 668, 758, 815
confrontation naming tests, 641
congruence checking, 421, 425, 426, 427, 428, 434, 442, 453, 456, 679
conjunctions, 16, 416, 418, 423, 444, 450, 451, 452, 453, 454, 456, 457, 672
connectionism, 86, 87, 710, 731, 770
connectionist models, 6, 85, 86, 88, 89, 96, 97, 99, 101, 105, 107, 632, 748, 799
construction grammar theories, 234, 252, 719, 741, 814
constructivist neural network, 94, 799
content morphemes, 419, 421, 422, 425, 426, 427, 436, 445, 446, 450, 451, 452, 453, 454, 457, 458
contingency, 11, 147, 234, 235, 236, 237, 239, 241, 242, 243, 245, 246, 253, 696, 731, 732
continuity of exposure, 136, 139, 204, 806, 817
Contrastive Analysis Hypothesis, 248

control mechanisms, 18, 19, 373, 386, 486, 487, 493, 494, 495, 503, 504, 505, 512, 516, 518, 519, 521, 522, 526, 532, 583, 676, 691, 696, 702, 740, 779
convergence hypothesis, 100
coordinate bilingual, 37, 285, 286, 634
coordinate system, 32
corpus linguistics, 234, 237, 745
corpus-based approaches, 90, 91, 154, 459, 460, 710, 739, 745
critical period, 7, 99, 103, 105, 619, 620, 621, 622, 626, 650, 709, 711, 720, 735, 756, 761, 765, 774, 782, 788, 799, 807, 820
Croatian, 472, 506, 688, 718
cross-cultural methods, 275, 276, 277, 292
cross-cultural variation, 275, 277, 292
cross-language/linguistic activation, 333, 338, 339, 340, 341, 342, 343, 344, 345, 346, 347, 467, 485, 488, 494, 495, 496, 499, 504, 670, 675, 699, 703, 749, 751, 793
cross-language/linguistic competition, 496, 497, 505, 510, 610, 718, 727, 751
cross-language/linguistic effects, 54, 62, 70, 71, 318, 323, 392, 490, 492, 672, 699, 768, 781
cross-language/linguistic interactions, 100, 317, 320, 322, 324, 325, 349, 350, 360, 495, 671, 673, 678, 679, 688, 691
cross-language/linguistic priming, 29, 41, 42, 44, 51, 52, 54, 56, 59, 60, 61, 62, 63, 66, 68, 69, 70, 81, 83, 107, 121, 127, 151, 557, 737, 755, 756, 759
cross-language/linguistic research, 175, 248, 765
cross-language/linguistic script differences, 498
cross-language/linguistic variation, 485, 489, 643
cross-modal priming, 177, 186, 192, 194, 195, 198, 772
cultural specificity, 275, 290
cumulative semantic interference effect (CSIE), 512, 525
Cyrillic, 308
Czech, x, xi, xii, 234, 235, 244, 245, 246, 247, 249, 250, 251, 252, 253, 688, 718, 814

declarative/procedural model, 191, 193, 816
decomposition, 173, 189, 190, 191, 192, 193, 194, 195, 196, 197, 199, 743, 796, 811, 827
default lexicon, 24, 631, 643
definiteness, 419, 435, 437, 438, 439, 440, 442, 443, 457
degree centrality, 240
degree of bilingualism, 6, 31, 32, 41, 579, 599, 742
delayed naming task, 116
dementia, 22, 565, 571, 577, 578, 579, 580, 583, 584, 585, 696, 706, 747, 801, 816, 817, 827
derivation, 173, 188, 189, 190, 191, 194, 199, 422, 429, 637, 638, 761
determiner phrases (DPs), 16, 416, 418, 423, 434, 435, 436, 437, 438, 439, 440, 441, 442, 443, 444, 447, 457, 721
Developmental lexicon (DevLex) model, 94, 98, 99
Developmental lexicon II (DevLex-II) model, x, 93, 99, 102, 103, 105, 107
Differential Access Hypothesis, 422, 424, 435, 436, 437, 442, 444, 784

different-script bilinguals, 308, 309, 317, 318, 320, 321, 324, 489, 683, 782
digit span tasks, 227, 229, 347, 376, 377, 574
directed vocabulary instruction, 216, 232
discourse, 107, 125, 203, 204, 205, 213, 248, 262, 303, 353, 354, 392, 415, 416, 422, 431, 445, 447, 449, 451, 452, 454, 456, 459, 460, 462, 473, 476, 481, 487, 491, 492, 637, 641, 660, 704, 708, 709, 796, 797, 803, 807, 822, 825
distinctive features, 172, 183, 184
Distributed Conceptual Feature Model (DFM), 52, 53, 287
Distributed Lexical/Conceptual Feature Model (DLCF), 54, 634
domain-general cognitive function and control, 494, 504, 510, 525, 538, 589, 600, 611
dominance, xii, 31, 32, 33, 35, 41, 47, 101, 106, 110, 340, 345, 347, 406, 452, 458, 500, 503, 516, 517, 518, 533, 536, 537, 540, 541, 545, 546, 632, 645, 647, 651, 657, 661, 666, 672, 676, 677, 702, 704, 711, 724, 743, 766, 767, 811
dual-coding theory, 50, 51, 787, 788
Dutch, 49, 60, 62, 64, 65, 66, 69, 71, 72, 75, 96, 113, 116, 119, 120, 126, 128, 167, 171, 177, 179, 182, 183, 185, 186, 190, 221, 222, 223, 226, 228, 266, 280, 283, 311, 317, 321, 337, 338, 344, 346, 355, 390, 396, 398, 399, 400, 403, 404, 406, 414, 424, 428, 471, 472, 473, 474, 475, 476, 477, 487, 490, 492, 500, 502, 670, 671, 683, 689, 700, 711, 722, 730, 736, 752, 774, 814, 816
Dynamic Model of Multilingualism, 662, 666
Dynamic System Theory (DST), 8, 11, 255, 256, 257, 258, 261, 262, 263, 271, 272
dyslexia, 308, 324, 325, 748, 807, 828

early bilingual(ism), 31, 34, 133, 134, 135, 137, 154, 159, 160, 165, 171, 172, 192, 228, 279, 282, 283, 299, 317, 319, 404, 536, 540, 541, 542, 647, 709, 766, 768, 778, 782, 804
early left anterior negativity (ELAN), 359
early system morphemes, 421, 422, 423, 425, 436, 437
ecological validity, 108, 109, 111, 115, 118, 132
education level, 21, 259, 542, 574, 601
EEG. See electroencephalography (EEG)
egocentrism, 551
electroencephalography (EEG), 115, 116, 117, 125, 189, 192, 311, 314, 320, 557, 566, 748, 766
electrophysiological techniques, 14, 23, 163, 169, 308, 350, 355, 359, 476, 509, 513, 514, 614, 704, 736, 748, 751, 771, 781, 783, 794, 810, 817, 818, 821, 825
embedded language (EL), xii, 418, 420, 421, 422, 424, 425, 426, 427, 428, 429, 430, 431, 432, 433, 434, 435, 438, 439, 440, 441, 442, 443, 444, 445, 447, 448, 449, 450, 452, 453, 456, 457, 458, 784
embedded subsystems, 258, 263
emergentism, 6, 88, 270, 731
emerging bilingual, 297
emerging bilingualism, 706
emotion memory, 303, 307, 700
emotion Stroop tasks, 299
emotion word processing, viii, 12, 13, 293, 294, 299, 305

emotion words, 4, 12, 293, 295, 296, 297, 299, 302, 303, 697, 700, 703, 763, 815
emotional component, 293, 297
emotional language, 293, 294, 301, 307
emotional Stroop effects, 295, 299, 306, 811
emotion-laden words, 293, 297, 298, 299, 697, 789
endogenous attentional control, 463, 503, 821
English, ii, x, xi, xii, xiv, 11, 13, 17, 35, 37, 42, 45, 47, 48, 49, 50, 51, 55, 57, 60, 61, 62, 64, 66, 68, 69, 71, 72, 73, 74, 75, 79, 83, 91, 96, 98, 101, 103, 104, 105, 112, 113, 114, 116, 119, 120, 121, 122, 123, 126, 127, 128, 130, 134, 139, 141, 142, 143, 144, 145, 146, 151, 160, 162, 163, 166, 167, 168, 169, 172, 173, 174, 179, 180, 182, 183, 184, 185, 186, 188, 189, 190, 192, 193, 194, 195, 201, 202, 203, 204, 206, 209, 211, 217, 218, 219, 220, 221, 222, 223, 224, 226, 228, 229, 230, 232, 234, 235, 236, 238, 241, 243, 244, 245, 246, 247, 249, 250, 253, 254, 266, 269, 276, 278, 279, 280, 281, 282, 283, 284, 287, 289, 291, 297, 298, 299, 300, 301, 302, 303, 305, 306, 307, 308, 309, 311, 314, 315, 316, 317, 318, 319, 320, 321, 324, 325, 326, 328, 329, 335, 336, 337, 338, 339, 340, 341, 342, 344, 345, 346, 347, 351, 352, 353, 354, 355, 357, 358, 360, 361, 362, 363, 364, 374, 375, 376, 377, 383, 390, 391, 392, 396, 398, 399, 400, 403, 404, 406, 418, 419, 426, 428, 429, 430, 431, 432, 434, 435, 436, 437, 438, 439, 440, 442, 443, 444, 445, 446, 447, 448, 449, 450, 451, 452, 455, 457, 461, 462, 464, 465, 466, 467, 468, 469, 472, 473, 474, 475, 477, 487, 488, 489, 490, 492, 495, 496, 500, 501, 502, 505, 506, 510, 515, 519, 520, 521, 523, 527, 531, 533, 534, 536, 537, 540, 541, 542, 543, 544, 545, 546, 556, 559, 561, 563, 564, 566, 571, 579, 581, 587, 588, 597, 598, 603, 609, 619, 623, 633, 637, 638, 639, 640, 643, 647, 648, 651, 652, 653, 655, 656, 657, 661, 665, 670, 671, 672, 674, 677, 680, 681, 682, 683, 684, 686, 696, 697, 698, 700, 703, 704, 705, 707, 710, 711, 713, 715, 717, 718, 719, 720, 721, 722, 727, 729, 730, 731, 734, 736, 737, 740, 741, 742, 745, 746, 748, 749, 752, 755, 756, 757, 760, 761, 762, 763, 766, 769, 770, 771, 774, 775, 776, 777, 779, 780, 781, 782, 783, 784, 785, 787, 788, 790, 794, 795, 801, 803, 805, 806, 810, 812, 813, 814, 815, 816, 819, 821, 824, 825, 826, 827, 828
entrenchment, 7, 99, 105, 181, 184, 186, 198, 243, 656, 726, 782
episodic buffer, 372, 701
episodic L2 hypothesis, 67, 825
episodic memory, 576, 577, 592, 719, 775, 803
episodic model, 177
episodic recognition, 67, 756
equivalence constraint hypothesis, 481
ERP. See event-related potential (ERP)
European Science Foundation (ESF) corpus, 236
event-related potential (ERP), 7, 30, 115, 116, 133, 145, 152, 163, 280, 292, 299, 301, 307, 311, 312, 313, 314, 318, 320, 323, 325, 340, 341, 344, 345, 354, 355, 393, 405, 461, 462, 465, 467, 468, 469, 470, 471, 475, 491, 500, 501, 513, 514, 515, 523, 566, 699, 701, 702,

704, 714, 715, 737, 738, 739, 746, 754, 756, 763, 766, 768, 772, 773, 777, 778, 781, 783, 786, 790, 791, 794, 796, 799, 803, 805, 806, 807, 810, 819, 822
executive control, viii, 5, 20, 21, 22, 24, 116, 338, 345, 347, 468, 470, 477, 478, 479, 515, 523, 548, 568, 571, 573, 581, 583, 599, 601, 609, 611, 613, 614, 678, 679, 686, 696, 701, 703, 706, 707, 712, 716, 742, 750, 752, 754, 773, 776, 780, 792, 825, 826
executive function(s). *See* executive functioning
executive functioning, xi, 21, 23, 229, 372, 373, 477, 479, 493, 538, 553, 566, 567, 568, 586, 588, 592, 593, 594, 597, 600, 606, 609, 611, 612, 613, 617, 627, 628, 630, 641, 676, 678, 690, 706, 713, 722, 761, 764, 781, 794, 809, 826
executive network, 609, 611, 612, 615
executive system, xi, 23, 614, 615, 616, 617, 618, 621, 622, 624, 627, 629, 630
exogenous attentional control, 463
expertise, xvii, 129, 228, 285, 312, 373, 486, 561, 614, 618, 620, 626, 716, 773, 779, 825, 827
Extended Projection Principle (EPP), 201, 202, 203, 205, 696
eye fixations, 333, 393, 698, 707
eye movements, 7, 71, 73, 75, 120, 125, 126, 148, 149, 230, 272, 339, 362, 364, 392, 464, 496, 545, 590, 696, 697, 729, 770, 775, 792, 797, 805
eye-tracking, 7, 69, 123, 129, 151, 179, 182, 231, 333, 336, 337, 338, 339, 344, 345, 346, 417, 464, 491, 708, 737, 754, 758, 816

facilitation, xi, 37, 68, 126, 179, 184, 186, 187, 190, 191, 194, 195, 198, 295, 330, 337, 338, 339, 343, 344, 346, 394, 395, 472, 488, 491, 499, 501, 544, 573, 574, 593, 653, 670, 671, 674, 691, 715, 716, 718, 728, 734, 762, 765, 798, 803, 809, 828
familiarity, 10, 47, 145, 148, 181, 184, 198, 216, 220, 225, 306, 575, 691, 758, 785, 795, 826
feedback processing, 616
Filipino, 144, 145
Finnish, 189, 194, 299, 816
Finno-Ugric, 249
First Fixation Duration (FFD), 126, 333, 337, 339
first language attrition. *See* attrition
First-noun principle (FNP), 209, 210, 211
flanker task, xi, 565, 581, 582, 593, 597, 598, 599, 605, 606, 607, 752
flexibility, 19, 85, 101, 106, 287, 290, 322, 423, 444, 459, 509, 553, 561, 567, 577, 586, 587, 588, 615, 680, 812
fluidity, 633, 636, 640, 642
fMRI. *See* functional magnetic resonance imaging (fMRI)
forced switching, 501, 532
foreign vocabulary, 217, 218, 220, 224, 225, 227, 757
forgetting, 217, 518, 648, 661, 663, 723, 724, 753, 769, 775, 785, 790, 800
form overlap, 10, 62, 66, 195, 216, 329, 336, 338, 340, 489
form-related, 61, 62, 219, 225, 229, 232, 488, 499
formulator, 17, 416, 419, 421, 422, 423, 424, 426, 433, 434, 436, 438, 439, 440, 442, 443, 444, 446, 447, 448, 449, 450, 453, 454, 456, 457, 458
framing satellite, 248
framing verb, 248

free association, 241, 242, 244
French, x, 7, 37, 42, 45, 47, 49, 51, 55, 60, 61, 62, 64, 66, 68, 73, 74, 79, 89, 90, 97, 99, 107, 116, 119, 139, 141, 142, 143, 146, 162, 166, 168, 169, 172, 180, 184, 228, 280, 283, 308, 309, 311, 313, 314, 317, 321, 345, 346, 347, 352, 354, 355, 390, 427, 430, 431, 432, 452, 461, 462, 478, 533, 534, 537, 556, 566, 581, 587, 597, 603, 639, 648, 649, 652, 655, 670, 671, 672, 674, 677, 680, 696, 707, 710, 721, 722, 730, 737, 738, 740, 749, 754, 767, 769, 774, 796, 806, 812, 816, 825, 828
frequency, x, xi, 9, 11, 35, 49, 51, 57, 72, 83, 106, 119, 123, 126, 153, 161, 176, 181, 184, 185, 186, 187, 188, 189, 193, 194, 195, 196, 197, 199, 234, 235, 236, 237, 238, 239, 241, 242, 243, 244, 245, 246, 247, 252, 253, 267, 292, 296, 297, 306, 321, 328, 330, 334, 335, 336, 342, 343, 346, 347, 360, 363, 364, 374, 379, 391, 416, 426, 427, 454, 468, 488, 499, 526, 532, 536, 537, 538, 542, 543, 547, 600, 609, 617, 629, 630, 632, 640, 641, 662, 663, 696, 698, 700, 710, 712, 717, 724, 726, 730, 731, 732, 736, 738, 742, 743, 744, 747, 748, 774, 787, 790, 792, 796, 800, 807, 808, 810, 811, 820
frontal, 117, 118, 315, 316, 317, 355, 468, 477, 478, 479, 480, 502, 523, 552, 555, 557, 558, 559, 560, 561, 576, 578, 579, 581, 582, 584, 588, 589, 592, 623, 625, 627, 701, 720, 782, 795, 810
functional magnetic resonance imaging (fMRI), 7, 30, 115, 116, 117, 128, 131, 152, 189, 192, 199, 311, 314, 317, 405, 478, 480, 500, 502, 522, 536, 537, 539, 540, 555, 561, 581, 582, 605, 648, 695, 716, 746, 748, 749, 763, 771, 777, 780, 800, 819, 821, 822, 826
functional near-infrared spectroscopy (fNIRS), 133, 152, 153, 791
functional projection, 214

gap processing, 350, 352, 357
gaze duration (GD), 333, 337, 339, 344, 347
gender, 99, 112, 142, 259, 280, 281, 350, 354, 355, 356, 357, 358, 359, 361, 362, 436, 437, 438, 439, 442, 447, 457, 639, 643, 701, 709, 721, 730, 731, 736, 738, 746, 751, 766, 768, 769, 782, 783, 787, 801, 816, 821, 822
generation effect, 222, 223, 705, 731, 807, 814
German, x, xi, xii, 48, 79, 112, 116, 122, 152, 171, 185, 191, 192, 209, 210, 228, 232, 234, 235, 243, 244, 245, 246, 247, 249, 250, 251, 252, 253, 280, 308, 321, 341, 344, 345, 355, 356, 357, 405, 435, 440, 441, 442, 443, 444, 457, 461, 462, 467, 471, 475, 534, 535, 537, 538, 556, 559, 564, 623, 639, 648, 649, 650, 652, 654, 658, 659, 665, 670, 677, 681, 708, 730, 731, 735, 751, 752, 754, 756, 776, 780, 791, 799, 802, 821
gestures, 141, 175, 270, 280, 550
go/no-go semantic categorization task, 313, 462
grammatical processing, 677, 689, 716, 822
grammaticality judgment task, 7, 111, 112, 119, 352, 654, 774
grapheme, 182, 183, 313, 324, 806
gray matter, 552, 582, 618, 620, 621, 622, 623, 624, 626, 728, 741
Greek, 64, 79, 123, 276, 277, 282, 284, 289, 304, 308, 357, 699, 700, 774, 788

grouping, 10, 140, 216, 217, 218, 219, 225, 233, 245, 247, 277, 332, 408, 409, 688

habituation, 7, 133, 144, 145, 146, 147, 148, 149, 150, 162, 167, 717, 779
Hanzi, 308
Hebbian learning, 94, 98, 100, 102, 103, 243, 619, 624, 630, 773
Hebrew, 60, 61, 64, 130, 224, 308, 313, 391, 637, 638, 639, 640, 651, 652, 657, 677, 702, 705, 707, 726, 734, 742
hemispheric lateralization, 647
hesitations, 374, 417, 506
hidden layer, 92, 95
hierarchical models, 25, 32, 37, 40, 41, 52, 54, 178, 181, 216, 286, 290, 312, 324, 356, 371, 634, 667, 668, 711, 765
high amplitude sucking, 133, 144, 145
Hindi, 42, 319, 623, 652, 653
Hinton diagram, 96
homogeneity, 633, 636, 637, 639, 640, 770
homophones, 66, 179, 187, 329, 472, 490, 491, 495, 541
Hungarian, 171, 194, 375, 377, 471
hungry fish game, 562, 563, 565
hypnosis, 25, 645, 655, 656, 736

ideographic processing, 315, 319, 320
ideographic script, 191
imageability effect, 56
immersion, 354, 358, 360, 361, 498, 503, 600, 646, 653, 654, 657, 661, 701, 703, 779
immigrant, 159, 281, 565, 566, 603, 654, 656
immigration, 25, 565, 585, 603, 652, 658, 659, 660, 663, 696
individual differences, viii, 14, 15, 16, 25, 26, 50, 176, 185, 186, 212, 255, 276, 297, 327, 328, 338, 345, 346, 347, 348, 359, 369, 370, 373, 380, 386, 387, 503, 504, 567, 654, 657, 663, 675, 678, 686, 690, 691, 713, 722, 732, 735, 747, 768, 775, 780, 785, 796, 797, 798
individual variation. See individual differences
infinitive, 195, 339, 428, 429, 430, 431, 432, 433
inflection, 173, 188, 190, 191, 192, 194, 196, 197, 199, 708, 751, 799
inflectional morphology, 192, 194, 710, 743
inflectional paradigm, 192, 196, 199, 743
inhibitory control, 19, 52, 58, 78, 149, 169, 463, 464, 471, 481, 494, 496, 501, 502, 503, 510, 511, 512, 513, 516, 517, 520, 572, 586, 589, 591, 592, 593, 594, 599, 600, 602, 603, 605, 606, 611, 629, 670, 675, 676, 678, 681, 690, 691, 693, 702, 707, 708, 709, 761, 779, 800
Inhibitory Control (IC) Model, 19, 26, 463, 500, 508, 509, 510, 589, 591, 669
inhibitory effect, 62, 345, 347, 496, 505, 520, 676
inhibitory mechanisms. See control mechanisms
inhibitory process, 19, 495, 497, 500, 504, 507, 509, 510, 512, 513, 514, 516, 517, 518, 519, 593, 764, 779
initial conditions, 256, 257
input, 6, 9, 10, 25, 39, 68, 69, 70, 71, 87, 88, 89, 90, 91, 92, 93, 94, 95, 97, 98, 101, 102, 103, 106, 109, 114, 115, 118, 119, 120, 123, 126, 127, 135, 136, 138, 159, 160, 162, 165, 169, 170, 173, 174, 177, 178, 183, 184, 186, 188, 193, 197, 200, 202, 204, 205, 206, 207, 208, 209, 210, 211, 213, 214, 215, 216, 217, 222, 225, 234, 235, 236, 237, 253, 257, 258, 263, 309, 323, 324, 343, 357, 358, 365, 371, 379, 381, 408, 409, 410, 411, 412, 471, 488, 490, 505, 566, 590, 615, 620, 632, 645, 646, 647, 648, 649, 650, 651, 652, 653, 656, 657, 658, 659, 660, 661, 662, 663, 692, 704, 709, 712, 724, 733, 739, 746, 749, 767, 776, 785, 800, 820, 824
input flood, 211, 212, 215
input layer, 92, 408
input processing, 200, 207, 208, 210, 212, 215
integrated control, 527, 788
intelligence, 369, 574, 577, 587, 588, 601, 611, 721, 732, 741, 756, 785, 790, 800, 805
Interactive Activation (IA) Model, 96
interhemispheric connectivity, 316
interlexical homographs. See interlingual homographs
interlexical neighbors, 390, 391
interlingual homographs, 14, 49, 74, 76, 119, 317, 321, 323, 329, 330, 335, 336, 337, 339, 340, 341, 343, 344, 345, 347, 390, 391, 393, 487, 495, 505, 703, 723, 727, 755, 759, 768, 775
intermediate hypothesis, 43, 44
intermodal preferential looking procedure, 7, 150
internalization, 12, 278, 281, 282, 286, 288, 291
international adoption, 25, 645, 646, 647, 648, 649, 650, 659, 753, 786, 795, 802
interpersonal variation, 255
inter-sentential code-switching, 460
inter-sentential switch costs, 543
intervention, 10, 22, 50, 200, 201, 207, 208, 211, 212, 213, 215, 585
interventions, 8, 9, 200, 201, 207, 211, 212, 213, 214, 215
intonation, 147, 157, 445
intralexical neighbors, 390
intralingual interference, 47
intra-sentential code-switching, viii, 459, 460, 464, 465, 466, 467, 468, 469, 470, 471, 480, 481, 482
IQ, 587
IsiXhosa, 284, 712
Italian, xii, xiii, xiv, xv, 101, 167, 172, 309, 314, 315, 435, 440, 441, 442, 443, 444, 457, 461, 466, 472, 478, 479, 519, 520, 639, 672, 680, 683, 703, 704, 713, 776, 802, 821

Japanese, 160, 172, 180, 182, 183, 203, 204, 217, 249, 276, 278, 279, 281, 282, 283, 291, 308, 311, 314, 316, 318, 351, 357, 383, 624, 648, 655, 696, 704, 711, 716, 718, 758, 773, 779, 782, 791, 801

keyword mnemonic, 10, 216, 222, 232, 818
Korean, 64, 72, 83, 303, 308, 311, 320, 353, 598, 648, 649, 650, 652, 653, 654, 655, 701, 760, 768, 806
Kurdish, 576, 577

language change, 259, 262, 504, 646, 657, 662, 766
language comparison methods, 686
language control, 19, 405, 508, 509, 510, 511, 513, 514, 515, 516, 517, 518, 519, 522, 523, 524, 525, 526, 544, 712, 742
language decision, 58, 70, 321
Language Dependent Memory Hypothesis, 303

language development, 11, 33, 142, 170, 171, 255, 256, 257, 258, 261, 265, 267, 270, 271, 272, 618, 619, 647, 656, 657, 659, 714, 722, 726, 729, 736, 741, 751, 754, 755, 765, 771, 772, 773, 788, 799, 808, 815, 817, 821
language experience, 101, 110, 135, 228, 276, 282, 312, 365, 504, 505, 506, 565, 568, 602, 603, 614, 618, 619, 620, 621, 623, 624, 625, 626, 630, 685, 703, 705, 709, 712, 717, 722, 758, 764, 765, 782, 808, 823
language history. *See* language experience
language loss, 645, 646, 647, 648, 649, 656, 658, 659, 660, 661, 662, 664, 763, 780, 782
language maintenance, 349, 351, 529, 645, 646, 648, 656, 657, 658, 659, 661, 662, 663
language mixing costs, 20, 527, 528, 531
language mode, 334, 493, 530, 532, 727
language non-selectivity, 327, 329, 330, 332, 336, 337, 338, 340, 341, 343, 345, 346, 414, 495
language processing system, 26, 115, 737
Language Replacement Hypothesis, 661, 663
language retention, 658, 782
language selectivity, 29, 30, 41, 45, 48, 49, 51, 63, 69, 74, 81, 83, 329, 489, 519, 764
language specificity, viii, xii, 4, 12, 275, 288, 290, 699
language switch costs, 17, 20, 29, 38, 45, 79, 101, 461, 462, 463, 466, 513, 516, 520, 528, 530, 555, 670, 713
language switching task, xii, 19, 509, 511, 514, 517, 521, 522, 523, 525, 526, 537, 541, 581, 674, 676, 693
language system, 6, 8, 12, 14, 16, 31, 39, 50, 108, 114, 123, 157, 158, 159, 170, 255, 256, 257, 261, 318, 319, 349, 351, 360, 365, 383, 390, 410, 414, 522, 571, 581, 587, 615, 621, 633, 669, 776, 810, 824
language use, 29, 32, 59, 62, 76, 108, 109, 114, 117, 122, 125, 134, 252, 255, 256, 257, 261, 272, 286, 292, 303, 369, 387, 471, 485, 487, 488, 492, 503, 520, 528, 530, 536, 543, 636, 647, 659, 662, 672, 679, 690, 712, 781, 798, 801
language(s) of exposure, 136, 140, 202
language-specific script differences, 313
late bilingual, 117, 128, 283, 284, 319, 326, 404, 537, 542, 735
Late Positive Complex, 462, 465, 466, 467, 468, 469, 470
late sequential bilingual(ism), 14, 278, 287, 349, 350, 625
late system morphemes, 422, 423, 426, 433, 436, 444, 446, 448, 450, 453, 454, 456, 458
learner factors, 10, 216, 230, 686
left inferior frontal gyrus (LIFG), 315
left-hemisphere dominance, 647
left-lateralization, 313
lemma access, 173, 199
lemma level (of mental representation), 54, 59, 189, 197, 442, 472
lemmas, 54, 58, 84, 195, 236, 241, 419, 422, 436, 463, 472, 510, 784
less-is-more hypothesis, 99
letter position coding, 308, 310, 311, 744
level of processing hypothesis, 219
lexical access, viii, 4, 13, 41, 48, 49, 53, 57, 58, 68, 69, 70, 73, 74, 78, 83, 105, 121, 130, 173, 174, 175, 176, 177, 178, 181, 182, 186, 188, 189, 190, 191, 193, 195, 196, 197, 198, 199, 322, 327, 328, 330, 331, 332, 333, 334, 335, 336, 337, 338, 339, 345, 346, 350, 465, 469, 477, 491, 492, 494, 495, 542, 544, 632, 640, 668, 675, 677, 678, 695, 699, 706, 713, 714, 718, 719, 725, 727, 728, 730, 733, 735, 736, 740, 741, 743, 744, 754, 764, 768, 769, 770, 771, 782, 788, 793, 798, 801, 803, 804, 808, 810, 811, 813, 821, 824
lexical activation, 16, 100, 120, 126, 186, 327, 335, 337, 341, 389, 394, 409, 636, 710, 717, 724, 749, 756, 792, 803, 818
lexical decision task (LDT), 29, 35, 36, 42, 45, 48, 49, 58, 59, 61, 62, 63, 64, 66, 67, 68, 69, 70, 71, 72, 73, 74, 75, 76, 78, 79, 119, 120, 121, 127, 130, 177, 178, 179, 180, 181, 185, 191, 192, 196, 197, 295, 296, 309, 310, 313, 317, 318, 321, 325, 329, 333, 336, 337, 338, 341, 344, 462, 469, 490, 491, 492, 493, 670, 671, 683, 723, 743, 744, 756, 759, 767, 768, 790, 792, 804, 807, 815, 818, 819
lexical encoding, 179, 180, 181, 182, 721
lexical item, 19, 89, 173, 177, 179, 180, 181, 185, 193, 204, 206, 207, 208, 211, 236, 249, 286, 418, 471, 481, 509, 510, 524, 525, 633, 637, 638, 639, 641, 642, 668, 675, 687, 777
lexical level (of mental representation), 41, 43, 45, 51, 54, 65, 67, 83, 107, 162, 323, 327, 399, 465, 507, 508, 509, 634, 635, 667
lexical mediation, 668
lexical node, 396, 398, 399, 400, 401, 408, 412, 413
lexical organization, 6, 31, 33, 34, 35, 36, 38, 39, 40, 41, 63, 308, 317, 708
lexical overlap, 327, 338
Lexical Preference Principle, 209, 211
lexical priming, 126, 277
lexical processing, vii, 4, 8, 9, 24, 37, 44, 112, 131, 173, 174, 189, 193, 269, 309, 314, 327, 329, 344, 346, 347, 472, 478, 479, 487, 504, 545, 631, 632, 633, 635, 637, 640, 642, 644, 671, 689, 698, 715, 716, 727, 770, 774, 813
lexical representations, 9, 29, 52, 54, 81, 98, 100, 101, 103, 119, 120, 121, 122, 126, 131, 173, 175, 177, 178, 179, 180, 181, 182, 183, 184, 185, 186, 187, 188, 195, 198, 270, 309, 323, 327, 331, 344, 359, 395, 396, 398, 508, 510, 514, 519, 520, 524, 525, 590, 634, 636, 639, 640, 643, 644, 668, 677, 689, 702, 719, 720, 723, 761, 801, 804
lexical retrieval, 130, 173, 199, 540, 642, 658, 659, 662, 689, 699
lexical robustness, 675
lexical selection, 371, 395, 495, 509, 518, 593, 632, 718, 719, 735
lexical–conceptual structure, 423, 434, 436, 437, 438, 439, 444
lexicalization, 283, 287, 508, 510
lexicon. *See* mental lexicon
lexis, 236, 243, 253, 258, 807
Linguistic Coding Differences Hypothesis, 381
linguistic competence, 83, 84, 111, 130, 182, 214, 258, 276, 307, 587, 646, 682, 684, 687, 691, 692, 706, 720, 756, 813
linguistic experience. *See* language experience
linguistic formulation, 371, 385
linguistic knowledge. *See* linguistic competence
linguistic meaning, 275, 708

linguistic performance, 70, 111, 185, 414, 705, 776
linguistic relativity, 112, 753, 769, 772, 807, 808
listening span task, 227
literacy, 123, 308, 641, 681, 705
local control, 519, 520, 521, 524, 525
local processing, 209, 211
localist representation, x, 89, 90, 91
localization, 108, 116, 189, 311, 617, 741
logographic, 47, 308, 310, 315, 316, 319, 321, 779, 807
long-forgotten language, 655, 723
longitudinal studies, 257, 265, 266, 387, 580, 582, 599, 613, 625, 656, 659, 704, 717, 767, 777, 809, 814, 815
long-term memory, 277, 372, 373, 656, 780

magnetic resonance imaging (MRI), 477, 552
magneto-encephalography (MEG), 115, 117, 189, 192, 581, 706, 769
Malay, 321
Mandarin, 116, 151, 182, 228, 278, 301, 540, 682, 683, 713, 755, 794, 805, 815, 827
manner of motion, 249, 252, 279, 283, 760
masked priming, 59, 60, 65, 189, 190, 191, 192, 309, 311, 312, 318, 671, 714, 719, 742, 744, 761, 791, 806, 810
masked priming effect, 62, 64, 190, 195, 325, 736
Matrix Language (ML), 418, 419, 420, 421, 422, 423, 424, 426, 427, 428, 429, 431, 432, 433, 434, 435, 438, 440, 441, 442, 443, 444, 445, 447, 448, 449, 450, 451, 452, 453, 454, 455, 456, 457, 458
Matrix Language Frame (MLF) Model, 418, 420, 421, 422, 424, 425, 434, 435, 436, 441, 448, 457
Matthew Effect, 228
medial-temporal (MTL) atrophy, 583, 584
memory capacity, 10, 14, 15, 216, 227, 231, 345, 347, 369, 370, 373, 374, 375, 376, 377, 378, 379, 380, 386, 732, 736, 741, 783, 815, 816, 817
memory load, 534, 608, 609
memory organization, 33, 35, 40, 50
memory recall task, 296, 299
mental flexibility. See flexibility
mental lexicon, ix, 5, 22, 24, 25, 41, 57, 107, 173, 174, 177, 183, 188, 198, 285, 287, 309, 317, 327, 331, 337, 340, 342, 347, 348, 382, 390, 393, 394, 395, 407, 423, 438, 442, 631, 632, 633, 634, 635, 636, 637, 638, 639, 640, 641, 642, 643, 644, 665, 667, 698, 726, 733, 761, 765, 776, 781, 789, 800, 803, 804
metalinguistic awareness. See linguistic competence
middle frontal gyrus (MFG), 315
mild cognitive impairment (MCI), 579, 580, 704, 787
Mini-Mental State Examination (MMSE), 578, 579, 736
mixed-language processing, 349, 351, 362, 745
mixing costs. See language mixing costs
Modified Hierarchical Model (MHM), 288, 290, 291, 292
monitoring, 69, 72, 337, 371, 372, 373, 374, 378, 382, 385, 387, 389, 401, 402, 403, 405, 406, 407, 468, 470, 506, 545, 566, 593, 610, 616, 695, 709, 724, 750, 763, 768
monolingualism, 10, 216, 228, 631, 633, 635

monomorphemic word, 24, 173, 189, 194, 631, 633, 637, 643
morphological decomposition. See decomposition
morphological realization patterns, 423, 424, 426, 436, 444
morphology, ii, vii, 4, 9, 89, 113, 118, 157, 173, 188, 189, 190, 194, 198, 203, 204, 205, 338, 355, 383, 422, 446, 455, 577, 638, 639, 643, 648, 649, 654, 687, 708, 723, 738, 740, 743, 744, 755, 758, 796, 801, 806, 823
morphosyntax, 107, 189, 236, 435, 653, 657, 659
motion event, 248, 249, 279, 282, 283, 284, 287, 700, 740
motion verbs, 249, 252
motivation, 44, 136, 137, 211, 213, 231, 256, 267, 369, 370, 382, 384, 385, 386, 387, 432, 658, 684, 701, 720, 728, 739, 763, 766, 783, 813
moving window paradigm, 122, 333, 475
multilingual transfer, 666, 670
multilingualism, ix, xiv, 108, 231, 276, 547, 586, 615, 622, 631, 662, 665, 666, 667, 670, 679, 684, 685, 690, 691, 709, 715, 722, 733, 736, 740, 747, 750, 752, 758, 759, 771, 777, 779, 789, 795, 821, 822
multi-modal, 275, 276, 277, 280, 291, 292
multimorphemic words, 632, 633, 637, 640, 643
myelination, 552, 555, 619, 625, 627, 663, 725, 778

naïve learners, 8, 10, 175, 222, 223, 230, 231
naming performance, 339, 360, 537, 775
naming time, 39, 119, 297, 400, 401
Native Language Magnet (NLM), 174, 175
natural (language) context, 90, 234, 236, 254, 278, 361, 492, 792
negative transfer, 670, 672, 673, 674, 678, 679, 682, 685, 687, 688, 689, 692
neighborhood, 71, 93, 95, 183, 187, 310, 313, 322, 323, 602
neighborhood density (effect), 71, 313, 317, 632, 736, 746
neural activity, 87, 115, 555, 559, 560, 619
neural architecture, 21, 23, 108, 613, 614, 618, 621, 624, 625, 626, 630
neural infrastructure. See neural architecture
neural mechanisms, 132, 460, 464, 465, 477, 480, 594, 769
neural networks, 86, 87, 88, 103, 107, 264, 315, 324, 396, 486, 503, 504, 522, 650, 732, 759, 770, 782, 827
neural resources, 620, 649, 789
neuroimaging methods, 7, 19, 23, 85, 100, 106, 108, 115, 118, 123, 128, 145, 152, 315, 323, 465, 476, 477, 478, 479, 480, 509, 514, 515, 526, 558, 559, 605, 612, 614, 637, 646, 679, 695, 712, 716, 722, 725, 731, 735, 750, 773
neuroplasticity, 620, 703, 728, 763
neuroscience, 100, 108, 118, 275, 287, 588, 697, 756, 795
Nilotic, 431
non-cognate output node, 410, 412, 413
nonfinite verbs, 16, 416, 422, 428, 430, 431, 432, 433, 434, 456, 458, 784
non-linguistic conflict resolution, 589, 590
non-linguistic executive processing tasks, viii, 23, 586, 589, 592, 593, 594, 597, 598, 601, 603, 605, 606, 607, 613

non-selective access hypothesis. *See* language non-selectivity
non-selective activation. *See* language non-selectivity
non-switch trials, 76, 77, 81, 462, 530, 531, 532, 533, 534, 535, 538, 539, 543, 545, 546, 674
nonword repetition tasks, 227, 229, 375, 377, 378, 379
Norwegian, 321, 426, 427, 651, 815, 819
noticing, 10, 167, 211, 212, 213, 214, 215, 404, 775
null subject, 172, 202, 203, 204, 205, 437
numerical distance effects, 671

occipital, 117, 468, 552, 582, 625, 797
occupational status, 571, 578, 738
one-person-one-language, 140
ongoing learners, 10, 216, 230, 231, 233
optimal period. *See* critical period
orthographic coding, 182, 316, 492
orthographic depth, 309, 315, 319, 758
orthographic overlap, 66, 190, 312, 338
orthographic processing, viii, 12, 13, 308, 309, 311, 312, 314, 316, 320, 322, 323, 324, 325, 326, 468, 744, 766
orthographic representations, 13, 58, 219, 225, 324, 325, 336, 391, 667
orthographic similarities, 4, 13
orthographic units, 309, 343
orthography, 9, 46, 47, 54, 66, 97, 119, 121, 122, 181, 182, 183, 220, 225, 230, 308, 309, 314, 316, 319, 325, 329, 338, 339, 340, 467, 474, 476, 487, 489, 494, 495, 624, 702, 710, 723, 733, 734, 744, 758, 770, 796, 803, 808
output, 31, 39, 52, 68, 81, 92, 93, 94, 95, 97, 102, 103, 115, 123, 124, 178, 213, 217, 257, 258, 324, 369, 370, 371, 372, 374, 375, 376, 377, 378, 379, 381, 382, 383, 385, 408, 409, 410, 411, 412, 413, 414, 466, 487, 503, 505, 566, 663, 680, 704, 714, 733, 800, 805, 811, 820
Output Hypothesis, 379
output layer, 92, 97
Overt Pronoun Constraint (OPC), 201, 202, 205, 206
overt subject, 202, 203, 205

paired-associate learning, 574
parallel activation, viii, 5, 16, 18, 57, 128, 131, 169, 172, 317, 327, 328, 333, 336, 389, 391, 392, 393, 396, 398, 401, 402, 405, 406, 407, 472, 485, 487, 493, 494, 496, 497, 507, 508, 529, 544, 637, 708, 809
parallel distributed processing (PDP), 6, 86, 87, 89, 97, 107, 773, 800
parallel processing, 87, 371
parameters, 85, 92, 94, 95, 96, 106, 194, 198, 202, 203, 205, 214, 401, 409, 412, 413, 536
parietal, 117, 316, 477, 478, 479, 502, 514, 555, 558, 560, 582, 584, 611, 613, 623, 624
parsing, 123, 157, 175, 204, 352, 353, 356, 357, 360, 361, 363, 365, 640, 642, 711, 730, 794, 808, 814, 825
participle, 192, 364, 432
passives, 209, 248, 651, 704, 795, 807, 816
pauses, 208, 374, 417, 506
pedagogical intervention. *See* intervention
Perceptual Assimilation Model (PAM), 175
perceptually difficult, 173, 187, 198

perceptually salient, 181
Persian, 576
phi-features, 437, 438, 439, 440, 442, 443, 444, 447, 448, 449, 450, 457
phoneme perception, x, 161, 162, 163, 164, 653
phoneme-monitoring task, 403
phonetic categorization, 9, 173, 174, 175, 176, 178, 180, 184, 185, 186, 198
phonetic contrasts, 9, 618
phonetic cues, 178, 180, 184, 188
phonetic encoding, 394
phonological coding/encoding, 173, 178, 186, 187, 188, 198, 207, 228, 316, 370, 372, 374, 394, 395, 405, 819
phonological contrast, 173, 175, 176, 178, 179, 180, 183, 184, 185, 186, 649, 655, 661
phonological discrimination, 179, 649, 654
phonological form, 173, 177, 188, 189, 198, 219, 220, 330, 373, 749
phonological loop, 372, 373, 382
phonological processing, 174, 176, 206, 479, 677, 680, 812, 820
phonological properties, 100, 172, 177, 198, 313, 495
phonological representations, 9, 90, 91, 98, 162, 174, 177, 178, 181, 183, 185, 186, 187, 188, 229, 329, 391, 394, 395, 397, 398, 733, 755, 773, 804, 827, 828
phonological short-term memory, 227, 229, 230, 369, 373, 375, 376, 377, 379, 778
phonological-translation distracter, 396, 397
phonology, ii, vii, 4, 9, 89, 91, 102, 118, 122, 157, 165, 171, 173, 174, 175, 176, 178, 180, 181, 182, 185, 188, 198, 220, 222, 225, 230, 231, 236, 258, 266, 313, 315, 316, 319, 320, 324, 325, 329, 330, 360, 392, 467, 472, 474, 476, 487, 488, 489, 491, 495, 499, 506, 527, 577, 662, 678, 682, 712, 721, 723, 727, 734, 744, 748, 758, 771, 788, 803
phonology–lexicon interface, 173, 174, 198
phonotactic information, 48, 51, 147, 164, 698, 804
phrase structure, 201, 354, 356
picture naming, xi, 16, 20, 29, 33, 43, 44, 47, 51, 55, 58, 68, 69, 70, 76, 77, 80, 81, 130, 180, 221, 269, 318, 324, 389, 394, 395, 396, 399, 401, 402, 403, 405, 406, 407, 409, 410, 411, 412, 413, 414, 462, 467, 474, 500, 502, 513, 520, 529, 531, 532, 534, 536, 537, 538, 539, 540, 541, 547, 558, 561, 590, 597, 631, 642, 668, 675, 676, 708, 710, 715, 737, 747, 749, 751, 755, 758, 765, 769, 789, 806, 809, 820, 821
picture repetition, 389, 406, 407, 408, 412, 413
picture training, 221, 225, 232
picture–word interference task, 51, 120, 389, 394, 396, 397, 402, 404, 731, 766, 803
pitch, 172, 764, 807, 825
plasticity, 5, 21, 22, 23, 105, 106, 349, 351, 614, 618, 621, 622, 623, 624, 626, 627, 628, 630, 647, 650, 663, 700, 702, 739, 753, 773, 780, 788, 800, 808, 810, 824, 828
Polish, 192, 542, 648
polymorphemic word, 173, 194
Portuguese, xiii, xiv, xv, 45, 172, 374, 461, 680, 687, 688, 751, 755, 756, 799, 806, 816
positive transfer, 670, 672, 673, 674, 680, 682, 685, 687, 688, 689, 692

positron emission tomography (PET), 192, 480, 559
postural sway, 125
practice testing, 10, 216, 223, 224, 225, 233
pragmatics, ii, 203, 436, 438, 703, 708, 726, 750
predicate–argument structure, 423, 426, 427, 434, 436, 438, 440, 444, 456
predictive sentence processing, 359
Preference for Meaning and Non-redundancy Principle, 209
preference procedures, 144, 146, 147, 148, 759
preselective search hypothesis, 80
Primacy of Content Words Principle, 208
prime-target relation, 45, 46, 59, 60, 61, 62, 65, 152, 312, 313, 339, 462
priming direction, 60, 61, 63, 64, 66, 67, 68, 69, 105
priming experiments, 42, 187, 192, 194, 243, 301, 473, 474
principal component analysis (PCA), 96, 97
print-to-sound mapping, 315
problem-solving skills, 130
processing advantage, 358, 613, 763, 791
processing costs, 19, 196, 197, 456, 460, 466, 527, 528, 529, 530, 543, 547, 565
Processing Efficiency Theory, 382, 733
processing instruction, 10, 200, 201, 210, 211, 214, 215, 696, 704, 717, 734, 749, 768, 795, 816, 819, 820, 825
processing oriented pedagogical intervention. *See* intervention
pro-drop, 172, 437, 440
production costs, 16, 433, 444, 452, 457
production of synapses, 552
Production–Distribution–Comprehension model, 365
productivity, 173, 189, 195, 197, 199, 637, 703
proficiency, 9, 12, 14, 16, 20, 22, 26, 29, 33, 43, 47, 54, 55, 56, 57, 74, 85, 97, 98, 99, 101, 106, 109, 111, 113, 134, 174, 181, 185, 186, 187, 190, 191, 192, 193, 194, 195, 197, 198, 199, 231, 258, 279, 283, 286, 289, 290, 291, 292, 299, 300, 301, 306, 313, 316, 319, 320, 325, 327, 335, 336, 338, 341, 345, 346, 347, 350, 351, 353, 355, 357, 361, 365, 371, 372, 374, 375, 376, 377, 379, 381, 389, 393, 397, 399, 400, 404, 405, 407, 408, 410, 411, 412, 413, 462, 465, 468, 469, 470, 471, 475, 486, 498, 500, 502, 503, 504, 512, 513, 516, 517, 522, 526, 527, 529, 531, 533, 536, 537, 538, 539, 540, 542, 543, 545, 546, 547, 561, 564, 571, 588, 589, 592, 600, 601, 612, 620, 621, 623, 647, 650, 651, 652, 656, 666, 668, 669, 670, 673, 674, 675, 676, 677, 678, 679, 681, 688, 690, 691, 692, 708, 711, 713, 714, 715, 716, 718, 720, 724, 747, 754, 762, 770, 772, 773, 777, 780, 792, 794, 795, 810, 813, 815, 817, 818, 820
pronouns, 202, 203, 204, 205, 210, 213, 214, 422, 437, 440, 443, 447, 482, 672, 713, 782, 806, 819, 820
pronunciation, 71, 73, 91, 146, 172, 224, 302, 309, 317, 527, 681, 682, 738
prosodic cues, 172, 814
prosody, 147, 207, 208, 359, 445
prototype, 174, 237, 243, 282
prototypicality, 11, 234, 235, 236, 241, 243, 246, 253, 732

pseudowords, 312, 313, 315, 320, 321
psycholinguistics, i, xv, xvi, xviii, 29, 52, 108, 113, 124, 260, 275, 417, 588, 589, 632, 679, 680, 700, 702, 703, 705, 707, 708, 711, 716, 724, 733, 734, 735, 739, 746, 747, 748, 749, 755, 759, 771, 774, 776, 777, 786, 793, 800, 804, 807, 808, 810, 815, 817, 821, 824, 825

Quechua, 418, 423, 424, 453, 455
Quichua, 444, 452, 453, 454, 455, 456, 457, 754

rapid serial visual presentation task, 122, 333
reaction time (RT) methods, 7, 29, 33, 101, 118, 133, 192, 193, 231, 255, 286, 295, 310, 341, 345, 537, 567, 610, 763, 807
reactivation, 511, 646, 655
reading aloud, 20, 38, 46, 119, 322, 374, 544, 547, 742, 789
reading time, 76, 122, 126, 333, 337, 339, 347, 357, 492, 545
real world, 132, 277, 281, 358, 359, 426, 445, 456, 523, 550, 708
real-time cognitive processes, 108
recall task, 34, 51, 114, 232, 296, 576
recognition test, 302, 376, 377, 379
recomposition, 197, 199
recurrence quantification analysis (RQA), 125
re-exposure, 25, 645, 646, 649, 650, 651, 653, 654, 655, 704
referential context, 359
relative clauses, 83, 113, 123, 353, 356, 357, 358, 361, 376, 736, 740, 760, 795, 799, 802
relearning advantages, 650, 655
Re-Ordered Access Model, 14, 334
reorganization, 23, 614, 642, 823
repellors, 11, 263
repetition blindness (RB), 298, 299, 698, 761
restructuring, 12, 283, 287, 288, 289, 290, 456, 468, 470
retention, 217, 219, 223, 224, 225, 232, 233, 372, 650, 658, 660, 683, 713, 714, 719, 765, 798
Retrieval-Induced Forgetting (RIF) Effect, 518, 769, 800
reverse transfer, 278, 283, 285, 289, 290
Revised Hierarchical Model (RHM), 25, 54, 56, 63, 67, 216, 286, 287, 288, 289, 291, 292, 324, 667, 668, 669, 689, 691, 711, 765
rhyming decision task, 313
Roman script, 309, 313
Romance languages, xv, 161, 171, 172, 214, 249, 355, 673, 685, 761, 787, 816
rote learning, 221, 222, 690
rule learning, 207, 211, 213
Russian, 71, 114, 120, 127, 184, 187, 193, 194, 195, 196, 209, 210, 222, 277, 283, 340, 357, 392, 472, 534, 535, 538, 658, 671, 683, 687, 688, 698, 700, 711, 717, 718, 735, 745, 756, 789, 790, 813, 814

saliency, 93, 162, 163, 184, 186, 238, 249, 281, 291, 311, 379, 416, 421, 423, 425, 426, 435, 436, 437, 438, 439, 443, 444, 453, 454, 456, 590, 628
same-script bilinguals, 308, 309, 317, 318, 320, 321, 683
satellite-framed, 234, 235, 248, 249, 251, 254
schooling, 568

Second Language Linguistic Perception Model (L2LP), 175, 176, 185
selection mechanisms, 485, 494, 504, 509, 512, 590, 719, 804
selective access, 48, 49, 57, 70, 72, 73, 74, 328, 334, 336, 491, 703
self-confidence, 258, 369, 384, 385
self-organization, 124, 258, 263, 268, 769, 819
self-organized criticality (SOC), 267, 268, 269, 617, 622, 701, 822
self-organizing map (SOM), 6, 13, 93, 94, 95, 96, 98, 100, 101, 102, 762, 781
self-organizing model of bilingual processing (SOMBIP), 98, 100, 101, 103, 105
self-paced reading task, 122, 123
self-rated proficiency, 469, 539, 540, 542, 543
semantic bias, 328, 346
semantic constraint, 75, 327, 337, 338, 813
semantic features, 53, 89, 95, 103, 218, 225, 275, 341, 638
semantic groupings. *See* grouping
semantic interpretation task, 673
semantic memory, 243, 576, 762, 766
semantic network, x, 234, 235, 240, 241, 243, 244, 246, 395
semantic overlap, 62, 68, 218, 339, 340, 341, 343
semantic processing, 190, 232, 271, 315, 316, 322, 329, 465, 625, 668, 671, 717, 792, 826
semantic prototypicality, 234, 241, 243
semantic relationship, 34, 61, 62, 280, 341
semantic representations, x, 90, 91, 94, 97, 98, 100, 102, 103, 104, 105, 112, 276, 323, 329, 398, 641, 827
semantic structure, 234, 235, 481
semantic transparency, 173, 190, 191, 197, 199, 312
semantic verification task, 339
Semantic, Orthographic, and Phonological Interactive Activation (SOPHIA) Model, 323, 391, 818
semantic-interference effect, 394, 395
Semitic languages, 249, 805
sensitive period. *See* critical period
sentence completion tasks, 112, 113
sentence comprehension, viii, 4, 10, 13, 113, 211, 327, 333, 336, 337, 339, 346, 348, 351, 358, 362, 364, 365, 460, 616, 729, 737, 748, 774, 787, 798, 811, 817
sentence processing, viii, 12, 14, 112, 122, 123, 213, 328, 349, 351, 352, 354, 356, 358, 360, 361, 365, 673, 698, 703, 711, 728, 734, 736, 737, 740, 746, 754, 756, 757, 776, 786, 788, 795, 810, 814, 815, 824, 825
sentential complementizers, 444, 448, 450
separate hypothesis, 34
separate-lexicon model, 131
sequential bilinguals, 14, 137, 351
sequential monolinguals, 647
Serbian, 194, 195, 196, 688, 781
Shallow Structure Hypothesis, 356, 357, 359
Shared Distributed Asymmetrical Model (SAM), 289
shared hypothesis, 34, 35
shared representation, 275, 279, 280, 287, 290, 291, 800
short-term memory, 227, 229, 372, 373, 375, 377, 379, 382, 601, 739, 762, 788
sign language, 142, 489, 565

Simon effect, xi, 298, 572, 573, 577, 591, 599, 609, 750, 783
Simon task, 117, 298, 299, 486, 598, 603, 608, 697
Simple Recurrent Network (SRN), 91, 92, 97, 107
simultaneous activation. *See* parallel activation
simultaneous bilinguals, 137, 139, 283, 285, 325, 326, 625, 729, 804, 816
skin conductance, 13, 299, 300
Slavic, 196, 249, 717
social class, 259, 573
sociocultural selection device, 261
socioeconomic status, 21, 23, 135, 567, 568, 574, 576, 577, 597, 600, 601, 602, 603, 786
sociolinguistic variation, 255, 272
Spanish, i, x, xi, xii, xiii, xiv, xv, 17, 42, 44, 48, 49, 55, 64, 65, 68, 72, 73, 75, 77, 99, 101, 112, 113, 116, 121, 126, 128, 138, 139, 148, 149, 150, 160, 162, 163, 164, 167, 168, 169, 171, 178, 179, 184, 190, 193, 199, 201, 203, 204, 205, 206, 208, 209, 210, 211, 213, 214, 220, 222, 225, 228, 229, 234, 235, 244, 245, 246, 247, 249, 250, 251, 252, 253, 279, 280, 281, 282, 287, 297, 298, 299, 302, 305, 307, 311, 329, 335, 336, 339, 341, 342, 345, 351, 352, 353, 354, 356, 358, 360, 361, 362, 363, 364, 375, 376, 398, 402, 403, 405, 418, 419, 423, 424, 431, 432, 434, 435, 436, 437, 438, 439, 440, 442, 443, 444, 445, 446, 447, 448, 449, 450, 451, 452, 453, 454, 455, 456, 457, 461, 462, 464, 465, 468, 469, 472, 475, 477, 490, 491, 492, 495, 500, 508, 510, 531, 533, 536, 537, 539, 540, 542, 544, 545, 546, 559, 561, 563, 579, 603, 609, 622, 639, 649, 650, 652, 653, 661, 665, 670, 672, 674, 677, 680, 682, 683, 687, 688, 696, 697, 701, 710, 712, 713, 718, 719, 722, 727, 730, 731, 734, 737, 741, 742, 746, 748, 749, 751, 752, 754, 755, 756, 758, 760, 761, 762, 766, 769, 770, 771, 775, 777, 779, 781, 785, 787, 791, 793, 794, 801, 803, 806, 814, 816, 820, 824, 827
Speech Learning Model (SLM), 175, 661
spelling, 42, 56, 182, 183, 236, 309, 314, 317, 319, 324, 330, 782
spelling-to-sound mappings, 309, 319, 324
spoken performance, 369, 370, 374, 375, 376, 377, 379, 381, 382, 385
stimulus factors, 10, 216, 225, 227
stress, 147, 184, 419, 641, 707
Stroop effect, 30, 39, 40, 46, 47, 56, 70, 122, 321, 593, 672, 676, 677, 691, 715, 716, 717, 763, 775, 808, 818
Stroop task, xi, 39, 121, 299, 302, 321, 572, 574, 593, 607, 608, 676, 718, 798, 825
structurally assigned, 419, 422, 425, 436, 438, 439, 444
sub-lexical, 220, 228, 309, 311, 312, 321, 330, 343, 398, 399, 400, 401, 413, 545, 667, 782
subordinate bilinguals, 285, 634
subordinators, 16, 416, 418, 423, 444, 445, 446, 447, 448, 449, 450, 452, 453, 454, 455, 456, 457, 458
Subset Hypothesis, 636
substitution neighbors, 310, 313, 317
supervised learning, 92, 93, 98
supervisory attentional system (SAS), 58, 59
supplementary motor area (SMA), 315, 480, 502, 555, 624

suppression, 58, 78, 79, 80, 81, 83, 321, 505, 590, 594, 645, 661, 735, 740, 778
sustained control, 522, 524, 525, 532
Swahili, 221, 223, 224, 418, 419, 429, 430, 783, 784
Swedish, 174, 193, 194, 284, 576, 647, 648, 654, 655, 671, 677, 681, 700, 813
switch costs. *See* language switch costs
switch direction, 461, 478, 542, 546
switch trials, 76, 77, 78, 80, 81, 101, 460, 462, 500, 511, 513, 514, 516, 530, 531, 533, 534, 538, 539, 541, 543, 544, 545, 546, 554, 556, 674
switching tasks. *See* language switching task
syllabic, 308, 316, 779
synaptic density, 618, 619, 620, 621, 624
synonyms, 37, 143, 212, 231, 276, 508, 636, 790
syntactic ambiguity, 353, 729
syntactic priming, 83, 113, 748, 792, 803
syntactic processing, 5, 189, 349, 350, 351, 352, 358, 359, 360, 478, 678, 763
syntactic structures, 111, 119, 248, 349, 351, 361, 363, 373, 379, 382, 420, 422, 423, 436, 438, 471, 475, 780
System Morpheme Principle, 421, 423, 436, 448, 456

Tagalog, 145, 167
Tamil, 249, 609
task-switching, 461, 514, 529, 532, 593, 603, 712, 715, 750, 780, 799
temporal dynamics, 108, 111, 123, 131, 323, 699, 750
temporal lobe, 315, 560, 578, 625
tense phrase, 214
Tense–Mood–Aspect (TMA), 428, 429, 431, 432, 434
text enhancement, 211, 212, 213, 215
Thai, 300, 527, 825
thematic groupings. *See* grouping
thematic roles, 356, 421, 422, 426, 427, 445, 446, 448, 453, 456
theta roles, 425, 427
third language (L3), 56, 64, 77, 139, 320, 330, 512, 533, 534, 539, 665, 666, 667, 668, 669, 670, 671, 672, 673, 674, 675, 676, 677, 678, 680, 681, 682, 683, 684, 685, 686, 687, 688, 689, 690, 691, 692, 694, 702, 709, 736, 747, 755, 761, 771, 791, 795, 797, 799, 813
Three-Factor Framework, 14, 333, 334, 335, 337, 343, 347
tip-of-the-tongue (TOT) states, 296, 534, 641, 742, 803
top-down, 57, 58, 96, 174, 188, 327, 332, 337, 395, 397, 492, 498, 499, 615, 616, 617, 628, 630
topic shift, 205
total conceptual vocabulary, 143
Trail Making Task (TMT), 477
Transcranial Magnetic Stimulation (TMS), 559, 751
transfer, vii, 4, 8, 10, 12, 14, 25, 26, 68, 212, 234, 235, 247, 248, 250, 254, 280, 282, 288, 316, 349, 351, 352, 353, 354, 355, 356, 360, 642, 665, 666, 670, 672, 673, 674, 677, 678, 679, 680, 681, 683, 687, 688, 691, 719, 722, 725, 731, 739, 748, 749, 753, 755, 759, 786, 795, 797, 799, 800, 806, 807, 810, 820, 824
transient control, 524, 525
transitivity, 238, 240, 785
translation ambiguity. *See* ambiguity
translation pair, 31, 53, 55, 222, 390
translation priming, 56, 60, 61, 62, 63, 64, 65, 66, 67, 69, 83, 312, 318, 325, 702, 715, 722, 729, 735, 802, 803, 821, 822
translation production, 220, 226, 668, 723
translation recognition task, 29, 53, 55, 70, 121, 226, 329, 491, 668, 683, 708, 723, 730, 767
transliteration, 219, 220, 225
Transmission Deficit Hypothesis, 641
transposition neighbors, 310, 322
triggering hypothesis, 17, 471, 472, 473, 481, 710
trilingualism, 35, 56, 68, 79, 139, 151, 320, 321, 325, 529, 533, 534, 543, 560, 622, 667, 668, 669, 670, 671, 672, 673, 674, 675, 676, 677, 678, 680, 691, 695, 699, 712, 714, 720, 724, 727, 737, 746, 768, 770, 774, 793, 795, 803, 804, 815, 818, 827
Turkish, 47, 191, 204, 301, 424, 426, 427, 428, 433, 576, 651, 700, 701, 761, 815, 816
Type of Processing-Resource Allocation (TOPRA) Model, 219
type-token frequency distribution, 234, 235, 236, 238, 239, 241, 266
typological similarity, 162, 167, 171, 172, 191, 192, 194, 234, 235, 249, 254, 424, 431, 444, 447, 453, 457, 472, 498, 640, 672, 679, 680, 681, 714, 719, 799

Uighur, 321
U-matrix, 96
Uniform Structure Principle (USP), 421, 434, 435, 448, 458
unimodal, 161, 220, 487, 493, 566, 624
Universal Grammar (UG), 200, 201, 202, 204, 206, 214, 261
Universal Structure Principle, 421, 424, 435
unmasked priming, 59, 65, 310
unrelated prime, 62, 67, 151, 310, 462
unsupervised learning, 92, 93, 94, 98, 101
Urdu, 116
usage-based approaches, vii, 4, 10, 234, 236, 243, 252, 253, 703, 767

valence, 12, 80, 295, 296, 297, 298, 301, 302
verb bias, 353, 359, 727, 729, 739, 768
verbal fluency task, 20, 123, 130, 241, 535, 542, 547, 661
verbal inflections, 203, 206, 209, 211, 418, 433, 710, 820
verbal IQ. *See* IQ
verb–argument constructions (VACs), x, xi, 8, 10, 11, 234, 235, 236, 237, 238, 239, 240, 241, 242, 243, 244, 245, 246, 247, 248, 249, 250, 251, 252, 253, 732
verb-framed language, 234, 235, 248, 249, 252, 254
Vietnamese, 472
visual word form area (VWFA), 315, 316, 319, 624, 701, 710, 725, 771, 773
visual word recognition, 58, 69, 97, 100, 194, 308, 309, 310, 312, 314, 323, 391, 404, 489, 492, 713, 717, 727, 730, 734, 744, 750, 786, 787, 791, 800, 807, 818, 819
visuo-spatial sketchpad, 372
vocabulary learning, 4, 8, 9, 10, 165, 174, 188, 198, 216, 219, 223, 225, 228, 230, 231, 233,

668, 682, 683, 689, 692, 702, 723, 724, 731, 767, 778, 788, 789, 808, 814, 815
voice onset time (VOT), 73, 490, 681

Welsh, 315, 317, 320, 321, 746, 821, 826
Wernicke's area, 117
white matter, 552, 582, 619, 625, 627, 772, 777, 782
wh-movement, 351, 352, 357, 360, 756
whole-word access, 192, 197, 309
whole-word representations, 189, 192, 194, 197, 311, 324
whole-word storage, 192, 193, 195, 199
Whorfian hypothesis, 112, 276
wh-processing, 350
willingness to communicate (WTC), 14, 15, 370, 384, 386, 387, 774, 775, 826
Wolof, 648
word association, 29, 34, 35, 40, 41, 42, 43, 44, 50, 52, 54, 114, 631, 818
word class, 189, 337, 491, 641, 703, 711, 794
word comprehension, 16, 100, 103, 157, 781
word-naming task, 33, 61, 70, 73, 119, 270, 329, 330, 333, 336, 375, 668, 755, 792
word order, 83, 107, 147, 172, 209, 210, 355, 475, 658, 659, 696, 753, 762, 768, 799, 819, 820
word production, viii, 5, 16, 69, 72, 103, 389, 393, 394, 395, 396, 397, 398, 400, 401, 402, 406, 407, 415, 508, 563, 717, 724, 735, 739, 746, 748, 751, 768, 769, 798, 800, 809
word rating, 296, 297, 703

word recognition, 33, 43, 57, 58, 69, 70, 71, 72, 73, 74, 80, 96, 100, 120, 133, 166, 196, 199, 309, 310, 311, 315, 317, 322, 323, 324, 327, 328, 389, 390, 391, 392, 393, 396, 397, 399, 405, 406, 407, 465, 488, 489, 490, 491, 492, 493, 494, 495, 496, 499, 544, 697, 707, 711, 713, 714, 721, 726, 727, 730, 744, 746, 766, 768, 769, 777, 780, 783, 795, 804, 805, 807, 816, 817, 818, 819, 820, 822, 824, 828
word translation, 232, 329, 375, 723, 724, 730, 766, 818
word type effect, 53, 703
WordNet, x, 103, 240, 781
word-production, 395, 396, 400, 415
working memory (WM), 14, 15, 99, 227, 284, 327, 338, 345, 346, 347, 348, 369, 370, 372, 373, 374, 375, 376, 377, 378, 379, 380, 382, 383, 386, 403, 479, 529, 534, 545, 574, 575, 592, 608, 616, 690, 693, 699, 701, 707, 713, 716, 721, 732, 736, 741, 750, 756, 763, 770, 773, 775, 778, 782, 783, 785, 806, 816, 817
writing systems, 308, 309, 311, 313, 314, 315, 316, 319, 320, 321, 325, 682, 709, 718, 721, 725, 785, 791, 818

Xhosa, 426, 429, 445, 784

young adults, xi, 555, 558, 563, 577, 581, 582, 603, 604, 605, 606, 612, 625, 647, 653, 658, 698, 752

Zipfian profile, 236, 239, 241, 253, 732